Thomas W. Alford's Shawnee Translation of the Gospels

With Normalized Orthography and Glossary

Original Shawnee Translation by Thomas W. Alford

Normalized Shawnee and Glossary by Carl Schaefer

Petoskey, Michigan

Mundart Press

2023

A publication of the Recovering Voices Program of the Smithsonian Institution, supported in part by a gift from the Shoniya Fund.

Publisher's Cataloging-in-Publication Data

Names: Bible. Gospels. Shawnee. | Alford, Thomas Wildcat, 1860-1938, translator. | Schaefer, Carl, 1945- editor, compiler.

Title: Thomas W. Alford's Shawnee translation of the Gospels : in normalized orthography and with glossary / original Shawnee translation by Thomas W. Alford ; normalized Shawnee and glossary by Carl Schaefer.

Other titles: Shawnee translation of the Gospels.

Description: Petoskey Michigan : Mundart Press, 2023. | Includes bibliographical references. | "A publication of the Recovering Voices Program of the Smithsonian Institution, supported in part by a gift from the Shoniya Fund"--Title page verso.

Identifiers: ISBN: 979-8-9865450-2-8 | LCCN: 2022922082

Subjects: LCSH: Shawnee language--Texts. | Shawnee language--Glossaries, vocabularies, etc. | Algonquian languages--Texts. | Algonquian languages--Glossaries, vocabularies, etc. | Shawnee Indians--Language--Glossaries, vocabularies, etc. | Absentee-Shawnee Tribe of Indians of Oklahoma--Language--Glossaries, vocabularies, etc. | Eastern Shawnee Tribe of Oklahoma--Language--Glossaries, vocabularies, etc.

Classification: LCC: BS345.S47 A44 2023 | DDC: 226.0497317--dc23

PREFACE

As stated in his autobiography (Alford 1936), Thomas W. Alford (Shawnee name Keenwaapyehsika) was born a member of the Absentee Shawnee in 1860 and spoke only Shawnee until he began school at the age of twelve. In 1879 he enrolled in Hampton Institute, and it was during his time at Hampton that he converted to Christianity. His translation of the Gospels, *The Four Gospels of Our Lord Jesus Christ Translated in Shawnee Language,* was published in 1929. While he did not include the English verses in his book, the title page states that his translation was based on the English Revised Version (ERV) of 1881. Though ingenious in many respects, Alford's Shawnee orthography is forbidding at first glance and some of his conventions obscure the precise phonological representation of words. Schaefer (2019) discusses issues with this orthography in detail. The absence of a glossary or a verse-by-verse English parallel version increases the challenge for someone who does not know Shawnee to engage with his translation.

This version of Alford's Gospels normalizes Alford's spelling to that adopted by the Shawnee Tribe for their current language revitalization program, with one exception: the Shawnee Tribe spelling uses the apostrophe to represent the glottal stop, while this normalization follows Alford in using *h* for both glottal stop (which never occurs before a vowel or *w*) and the glottal spirant (which occurs only before a vowel or *w*). The ERV verses are given in parallel with the Shawnee, and a glossary with morphological annotations is provided.

The mapping of Alford's original orthography to the normalized orthography is summarized in the following table:

Original	Normalized		Original	Normalized
l	l		i	i, y
m	m		e	ii
n	n		u	o
b, p	p		o	oo
d, t	t		a	e, ee
g, k	k		v	a
j, c	c [č]		r	aa
f	f [θ]		w	w
s	s		y	y
q	kw		h	h
x	ks			

With respect to the stop consonants, Alford's choice of *b/p*, *d/t*, *g/k*, and *j/c* was mostly determined by phonetic context: if the stop is followed by a long vowel, then he wrote *b, d, g, j*; in other phonetic contexts he wrote *p, t, k, c*. But his handling of the short syllable *ki* (in normalized spelling) was complex: if the *ki* is an inflectional prefix or suffix, he overwhelming preferred the spelling *ki*; elsewhere he preferred the spelling *gi*. The vowel represented by Alford's *a* is ambiguous except after a stop consonant. When following a non-stop like *l, m, n, f, s,* Alford's *a* could be normalized as short *e* or as long *ee*. To disambiguate Alford's *a*, this normalization draws on paradigmatic information (for example, the 3rd proximate plural independent form for animate intransitive verbs always has a long vowel before the final *-ki*), on other sources, e.g., Voegelin (1938-1940), Voegelin (n.d.), Selstad (1970), and on usage by current Shawnee speakers.

Several other spelling conventions merit mention. Alford omitted the predictable word-initial, pre-vocalic spirant *h*, which is explicit in the normalization. Thus Alford wrote simply *u* for the 3rd-person prefix, which is here normalized to *ho*. Alford's sequence *wh* is normalized to *hw* to reflect actual pronunciation; for example, Alford's *gi nvtunawhv* "you seek (animate object)" is normalized to *kinatonehwa*. Most likely, Alford wrote *wh* in imitation of the variant pronunciation of word-initial English *wh* as /hw/, as in English *where*. For front glide plus vowel (V) following stem-initial /p/, /k/, /m/ or /n/, Alford typically wrote simply *yV* or *iV*. Thus he wrote *biawv* "(animate) comes", *gircfagi* "(inanimate) is secret", *myawi* "path", *nyawana* "four times". Based on the practice in Voegelin (1938-1940), Voegelin (n.d.) and Selstad (1998), these sequences are here normalized to *iyV*, thus *piyeewa, kiyaacfeki, miyeewi, niyeewene*. Finally, Alford sometimes introduced short vowels, most frequently *i*, to break consonant clusters that might be difficult for an English speaker to pronounce. Based on comparisons with other sources, these orthographic epentheses are removed in the normalization. Thus Alford's *gitikv* "field" is normalized to *ktika*. See Schaefer (2016) for additional details on interpreting Alford's orthography.

Alford's notion of a written word – a space-separated piece of a written text – was highly analytical and apparently influenced by English written style. While he always attached inflectional suffixes directly to a word, he separated personal prefixes (*ni, ki, ho*) from the following noun, verb, or preverb to which it is phonologically bound. In addition, he always space-separated a preverb from following preverbs and generally separated a preverb from the verb itself, though in some instances he separated the rightmost preverb from the verb with a hyphen. This normalization always attaches a personal prefix directly to the following word, but always space-separates a preverb from following preverbs and from the preverb itself. This has the beneficial consequence of reducing to 9,600 the number of word-forms that need to be included in the glossary. Applied as a general rule, this also accommodates another peculiarity of Alford's original. Most likely under the influence of English syntax in the ERV, Alford constructed complexes in which the leftmost preverb is separated from the verb not only by other preverbs but also by plain adverbials, pronouns, and occasionally nouns. Furthermore, in a small number of cases, he created a verb phrase embedded within a matrix verb phrase. For example, in Mark:14;35 the matrix phrase is *wahsi ... hini yaatefaki menawahke pemhfaalekoci*, the embedded phrase *kwehkwi katawi hinike*:

wahsi kwehkwi katawi hinike hini yaatefaki menawahke pemhfaalekoci
"that, if it were possible, the hour might pass away from him"

This normalization uses only lowercase and omits all of Alford's punctuation. Some of Alford's hyphens have been retained in compound words, for example the possessed noun *hopeemi-hoci-lenaweewiiwe,* which translates "his living" (literally "that from which he lives").

Glossary

The glossary lists every word form used in the Gospels. Words related as inflectional or phonological variants are grouped under an abstract headword. Transitive verb headwords are given without their independent-mode theme sign. The following tables explain the abbreviations used in word-class and inflectional designations:

Word Class Abbreviations	
NI	inanimate noun
NA	animate noun
PR	pronoun
CNJ	conjunction
PP	postposition
PM	pre-modifier
PV	preverb
MDL	modal
TA	transitive animate verb (i.e., animate object)
TI	transitive inanimate verb (i.e., inanimate object); subclasses are TI_1 (*-aa* independent-mode theme sign), TI_2 (*-oo*), TI_3 (*-i/e*), and TI-O ("objectless" or unspecified object)
AI	animate intransitive verb (i.e., animate actor)
II	inanimate intransitive verb (i.e., inanimate actor)

Inflectional Abbreviations	
ind	independent mode
conj	conjunct mode
imp	imperative mode
part	participial mode
subj	subjunctive mode
1	1st person
2	2nd person
3	3rd animate proximate
4	3rd animate obviative
0	inanimate

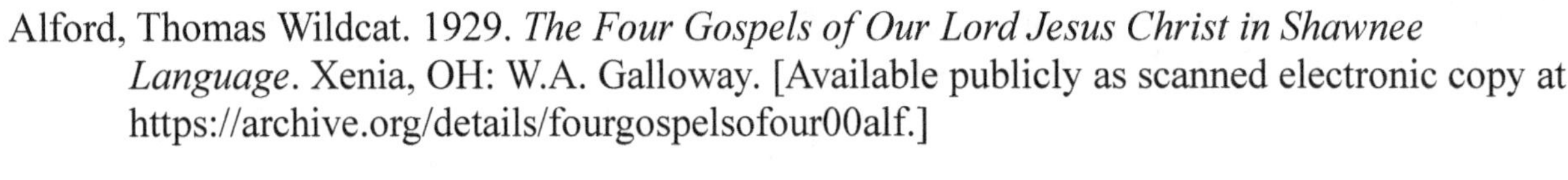

s	singular
p	plural
1i	1st person inclusive
1x	1st exclusive
/LOC	noun inflected for locative
/POSS	noun inflected for possession
/IC	initial change

References

Alford, Thomas Wildcat. 1929. *The Four Gospels of Our Lord Jesus Christ in Shawnee Language*. Xenia, OH: W.A. Galloway. [Available publicly as scanned electronic copy at https://archive.org/details/fourgospelsofour00alf.]

________. 1936. *Civilization*. Norman: University of Oklahoma Press.

Schaefer, Carl. 2019. Alford's Shawnee Translation of the Gospels. *Papers of the Forty-Eighth Algonquian Conference*, ed. by M. Macaulay and M. Noodin, pp. 221-238. Michigan State University Press.

Selstad, Leif. 1998. *English-Shawnee Shawnee-English Dictionary*. Unpublished manuscript.

Voegelin, Carl F. 1938-1940. Shawnee Stems and the Jacob P. Dunn Miami Dictionary, Parts I-V. *Indiana Historical Society Prehistory Research Series*, vol 1, pp. 63-108, 135-167, 289-323, 345-406, 409-478. Indianapolis.

________. n.d. *Shawnee texts*. Unpublished manuscripts in the Library of the American Philosophical Society, Philadelphia.

MATTHEW

Matthew:1

1. yooma hini heewikaateeki hotananhkawi nhhalweeletiiwe ciisisii klaistii nili hokwihfali teepitii nili hokwihfali heplehemii

The book of the generation of Jesus Christ, the son of David, the son of Abraham.

2. heplehemii honiicaaninaali haisikiili chiine haisiki honiicaaninaali ceekapiili chiine ceekapii honiicaaninaali cootali mecimi hoceeninahi

Abraham begat Isaac; and Isaac begat Jacob; and Jacob begat Judah and his brethren;

3. chiine coota honiicaaninaali peeliyeesiili mecimi seleli teemaali hoci chiine peeliyeesii honiicaaninaali heslaniili chiine heslanii honiicaaninaali lemiili

and Judah begat Perez and Zerah of Tamar; and Perez begat Hezron; and Hezron begat Ram;

4. chiine lemii honiicaaninaali heminitepiili chiine heminitepii honiicaaninaali naasoniili chiine naasonii honiicaaninaali selmaniili

and Ram begat Amminadab; and Amminadab begat Nahshon; and Nahshon begat Salmon;

5. chiine selmanii honiicaaninaali pooesiili lehapiili hoci chiine pooesii honiicaaninaali hoopitiili loofiili hoci chiine hoopitii honiicaaninaali cesiili

and Salmon begat Boaz of Rahab; and Boaz begat Obed of Ruth; and Obed begat Jesse;

6. chiine cesii honiicaaninaali teepitiili nili hokimaali chiine teepitii honiicaaninaali salamaniili nili hoci yehki wiiwali holaaya

and Jesse begat David the king. And David begat Solomon of her that had been the wife of Uriah;

7. chiine salamanii honiicaaninaali lihoopoemiili chiine lihoopoemii honiicaaninaali hapaicali chiine hapaica honiicaaninaali hesiili

and Solomon begat Rehoboam; and Rehoboam begat Abijah; and Abijah begat Asa;

8. chiine hesii honiicaaninaali cihoosifetiili chiine cihoosifetii honiicaaninaali coolemiili chiine coolemii honiicaaninaali hosaayali

and Asa begat Jehoshaphat; and Jehoshaphat begat Joram; and Joram begat Uzziah;

9. chiine hosaaya honiicaaninaali coofemiili chiine coofemii honiicaaninaali hehesiili chiine hehesii honiicaaninaali hesikaayali

and Uzziah begat Jotham; and Jotham begat Ahaz; and Ahaz begat Hezekiah;

10. chiine hesikaaya honiicaaninaali menesali chiine menesa honiicaaninaali hemaniili chiine hemanii honiicaaninaali coosayali

and Hezekiah begat Manasseh; and Manasseh begat Amon; and Amon begat Josiah;

11. chiine coosaya honiicaaninaali cikonaayali mecimi hoceeninahi hine laakwa hine pepelooni siweletiiwe

and Josiah begat Jechoniah and his brethren, at the time of the carrying away to Babylon.

12. chiine hine pepelooni siweletiiwe hahkowihi cikonaaya honiicaaninaali selhtiyeeli chiine selhtiye honiicaaninaali solopeepaliili

And after the carrying away to Babylon, Jechoniah begat Shealtiel; and Shealtiel begat Zerubbabel;

13. chiine solopeepalii honiicaaninaali hepaitiili chiine hepaitii honiicaaninaali hilaikamiili chiine hilaikamii honiicaaninaali hesooli

and Zerubbabel begat Abiud; and Abiud begat Eliakim; and Eliakim begat Azor;

14. chiine heso honiicaaninaali setakali chiine setaka honiicaaninaali hekimiili chiine hekimii honiicaaninaali hiliatiili

and Azor begat Sadoc; and Sadoc begat Achim; and Achim begat Eliud;

15. chiine hiliatii honiicaaninaali hiliyeesali chiine hiliyeesa honiicaaninaali metfeniili chiine metfenii honiicaaninaali ceekapiili

and Eliud begat Eleazar; and Eleazar begat Matthan; and Matthan begat Jacob;

16. chiine ceekapii honiicaaninaali coosiili nili wehsici melii hina neniikinaata ciisisiili klaistii yaaloofolici

and Jacob begat Joseph the husband of Mary, of whom was born Jesus, who is called Christ.

17. weecikeenahi caayahki nili hanhkawi skwiiwena heplehemii hoci paalohi teepitii hkwi metahfwi-kite-niyeewi skwiiwena chiine teepitii hoci paalohi hine pepelooni siweletiiwe hkwi metahfwi-kite-niyeewi hanhkawi skwiiwena

So all the generations from Abraham unto David are fourteen generations; and from David unto the carrying away to Babylon fourteen generations; and from the carrying away to Babylon unto the Christ fourteen generations.

18. howe hini hoskilenaweewiiwe ciisisii klaistii halayooma yeeki nili hokeeli meliili yeh mehci hohsihoofolici coosiili payeekwa wihsi pwaa nihki hotfetiwaaci mhkoofo hina hotapelohfemi hina hofepi hocacaalahkwa honiicaanali

Now the birth of Jesus Christ was on this wise: When his mother Mary had been betrothed to Joseph, before they came together she was found with child of the Holy Ghost.

19. chiine coosii wehsici melii teewahi tepasawi-leni mecimi homeelawaaci hpenalaali nili wahsi tepiskwi waakomekofilici memekinitehe wahsi kiimi pikeewhaaci

And Joseph her husband, being a righteous man, and not willing to make her a public example, was minded to put her away privily.

20. payeekwa ye hine memekineeletaki yooloma wiyehi waapamehko hotfekooli hahpoweeweneki hina teepeelemiweeta hotenhcaliimali coosii kiila hokwihfali teepitii teki kwtano wahsi mamaci kiiwa melii ksake hina nili peepiimotaakoci hina hofepi hocacaalahkwa hociwi hina

But when he thought on these things, behold, an angel of the Lord appeared unto him in a dream, saying, Joseph, thou son of David, fear not to take unto thee Mary thy wife: for that which is conceived in her is of the Holy Ghost.

21. mecimi hina weh niikinaali hokwihfimaali chiine kiila ciisisii keh sita howiifoowe ksake yoona homaciisilawiiwenilici we hoci waapaneshahi hotelenaweemhhi hina hiwali

And she shall bring forth a son; and thou shalt call his name JESUS; for it is he that shall save his people from their sins.

22. howe caayahki yooma hini piyeemikatwi wahsi menawah hini hokwaawfeki mayehci kalawici hina teepeelemiweeta saapwi nili maamoosikiiskwelici

Now all this is come to pass, that it might be fulfilled which was spoken by the Lord through the prophet, saying,

23. waapamehko hina seskihkwe we hotapelohfemi mecimi weh niikinaali hokwihfimaali chiine himenoel weh sitaanaawa nihki hina howiifoowe maneto wiici kiilawe hiyoowe hini yeelaapaatotooteeki

Behold, the virgin shall be with child, and shall bring forth a son, And they shall call his name Immanuel; which is, being interpreted, God with us.

24. mecimi coosii honhska honepaawe hoci chiine yeesi tepimekoci nili silawi hina teepeelemiweeta hotenhcaliimali mecimi homamaali wiiwali

And Joseph arose from his sleep, and did as the angel of the Lord commanded him, and took unto him his wife;

25. chiine mata howaakomaali nili paalohi hina homehci piyeelaali hokwihfimaali mecimi ciisisii hotesinaali

and knew her not till she had brought forth a son: and he called his name JESUS.

Matthew:2

1. howe hine hoskiniiki ciisisii peflihemi tasi piici taamhkwe cotiye hine kakiisekanemi heletii hina hokima waapamehko lepwaawileniiki hini weetahkofaki hoci colooseelemii si piyeeki

Now when Jesus was born in Bethlehem of Judaea in the days of Herod the king, behold, wise men from the east came to Jerusalem,

2. taanawe hina weski niikita hokimaamwaali coosaki ksake hini weetahkofaki niteh neewaape hotalaakomali mecimi nipiyaape wahsi hosasilawehakici hiwaki

saying, Where is he that is born King of the Jews? for we saw his star in the east, and are come to worship him.

3. chiine hine heletii hina hokima yeh nootaki hini petfakitehe mecimi caayahki colooseelemii howiiciimeko

And when Herod the king heard it, he was troubled, and all Jerusalem with him.

4. chiine hotepetwi maawatonahi caayahki nihi hokimaawi mhkateewkolayeemwahi mecimi hoteewikeemwahi nihki lenaweeki honatohtawahi nihi tasi wah ta hoski niikici klaistii

And gathering together all the chief priests and scribes of the people, he inquired of them where the Christ should be born.

5. mecimi nihki peflihemi tasi piici taamhkwe cotiye hotelaawaali ksake hini yeelawikeeki saapwi hina maamoosikiiskweeta

And they said unto him, In Bethlehem of Judaea: for thus it is written by the prophet,

6. chiine kiila peflihemi hotasiskiimi coota mata wiyehisi kitesi kcimaaciloofi heelekiina hokimaawoosaakanhhi coota ksake kiiyaaki we hoci lohfe yeelaapameta wah kiikeenaata nitelenaweemhi hiswiilahi

And thou Bethlehem, land of Judah, Art in no wise least among the princes of Judah: For out of thee shall come forth a governor, Which shall be shepherd of my people Israel.

7. hine howe heletii hokiimi hotahpimahi nihi lepwaawelenihi mecimi nihi hoci waakotefi hini mayaawi laakwa hina halaakwa teepinaakofici

Then Herod privily called the wise men, and learned of them carefully what time the star appeared.

8. mecimi peflihemiki hoteleskawahi nihi nhhaakone mecimi mayaawi natonehikeeko hina mayaani hapelohfa si chiine mehci mhkaweekwe hina nohki piyeetawiko kalawiiwe wahsi nehfaapi menawahi piyaaya mecimi hosasilawehaki hotelahi

And he sent them to Bethlehem, and said, Go and search out carefully concerning the young child; and when ye have found him, bring me word, that I also may come and worship him.

9. mecimi nihki yeesi mehci nootawaawaaci nili hokimaali weepfeeki yehaawaaci chiine scih hina halaakwa nihki hini weetahkofaki yeeneewaawaaci yeelahfamiilici nihi si weepfe paalohi hini piyeewa mecimi hapiwa tepila spemeki ta hapici hina mayaani hapelohfa

And they, having heard the king, went their way; and lo, the star, which they saw in the east, went before them, till it came and stood over where the young child was.

10. chiine yeh neewaawaaci nili halaakwali nihki hosasilepwaaki hanhhiweewi mhsi hosasilepwaawe

And when they saw the star, they rejoiced with exceeding great joy.

11. chiine piicfeeki hini wiikiwa mecimi honeewaawaali nili mayaani hapelohfali wiici melii

And they came into the house and saw the young child with Mary his mother;

hina hokeeli chiine nihki sahkiki sfeeki
hosasilawehaawaali nili mecimi hotawenaanaawa
hopawaawenwa hopakfenamawaawaali teephetiiwena
hofaawimoni chiine pootefamaacikani sekwa chiine
maa

and they fell down and worshipped him;
and opening their treasures they offered
unto him gifts, gold and frankincense
and myrrh.

12. chiine teewahi hotalenekowaali manetooli
hahpoweeweneki wahsi teki peteki haawaaci heletiili
payakila wayeeci si weepfeeki nihki nehalwaaka
hotaamhkomwaaki heeki

And being warned of God in a dream
that they should not return to Herod,
they departed into their own country
another way.

13. howe hine yeh saaweewaaci nihki waapamehko
coosiili hotfaali hahpoweeweneki hina teepeelemiweeta
hotenhcaliimali honhskaalo chiine mami hina mayaani
hapelohfa mecimi hokeeli chiine hiceptii lesimolo
mecimi nitasi hapilo paalohi wiitamoola ksake heletii
weh natonehwaali nili mayaani hapelohfali wahsi
nhfaaci hotelaali

Now when they were departed, behold,
an angel of the Lord appeareth to Joseph
in a dream, saying, Arise and take the
young child and his mother, and flee
into Egypt, and be thou there until I tell
thee: for Herod will seek the young
child to destroy him.

14. mecimi honhska hina chiine homamaali nili
mayaani hapelohfali mecimi hokeeli hina chiine
hiceptii si saawe tepehki

And he arose and took the young child
and his mother by night, and departed
into Egypt;

15. mecimi nitasi hapiwa paalohi hini honepoowe
heletii wahsi menawah hini hokwaawfeki keekalawici
hina teepeelemiweeta saapwi nili maamoosikiiskwelici
hiceptii ninatoma nikwihfa hiwa

and was there until the death of Herod:
that it might be fulfilled which was
spoken by the Lord through the prophet,
saying, Out of Egypt did I call my son.

16. hine howe heletii yeh neemeki yeesi hina
waapalaacihekoci nihi lepwaawilenihi hanhhiweewi
wiyakowe mecimi waawiinhke chiine honhfahi
caayahki nihi skilawehfiwi hapelofhi yeepilici
peflihemiki mecimi caayahki hini skwaaya tasi hine
niiswi kkatoowilici mecimi hotahpi hini laakwa si
hakinaye nihi lepwaawilenihi mayehci hoci mayaawi
waakotefici

Then Herod, when he saw that he was
mocked of the wise men, was exceeding
wroth, and sent forth, and slew all the
male children that were in Bethlehem,
and in all the borders thereof, from two
years old and under, according to the
time which he had carefully learned of
the wise men.

17. hine howe hokwaawfenwi hini keekalawiki saapwi
celemaaya hina maamoosikiiskweeta

Then was fulfilled that which was
spoken by Jeremiah the prophet, saying,

18. kalaweewihsimoowe nootaakwatwi laa lema peemi
wihfakweeki mecimi maweeki lecali peemi mawimaaci
hotapelohfemhhi mecimi hina haalwi
menwiteheeskoofo ksake matalaakwa nihi hiwa

A voice was heard in Ramah, Weeping
and great mourning, Rachel weeping for
her children; And she would not be
comforted, because they are not.

19. payeekwa hine yeh nepeki heletii waapamehko hina
teepeelemiweeta hotenhcaliimali hotfaali
hahpoweeweneki coosiili hiceptiiki

But when Herod was dead, behold, an
angel of the Lord appeareth in a dream
to Joseph in Egypt,

20. honhskaalo chiine mami hina mayaani hapelohfa
mecimi hokeeli chiine hini hiswiila hotasiskiimi haalo
ksake nihki nepooki neetonehakki hini
hotelenaweewiiwe hina mayaani hapelohfa hotelaali

saying, Arise and take the young child
and his mother, and go into the land of
Israel: for they are dead that sought the
young child's life.

21. mecimi hina honhska chiine homamaali nili mayaani hapelohfali mecimi hokeeli chiine hini hiswiila hotasiskiimi si piyeewa

And he arose and took the young child and his mother, and came into the land of Israel.

22. payeekwa yeh nootaakeeci yeesi hekeeleasi hasowe peemi hokimaawtaki cotiye yehki ta hapilici hohfali heletiili hokwta wahsi hini haaci chiine teewahi hotalenekooli manetooli hahpoweeweneki hini laa keelelii si saawe

But when he heard that Archelaus was reigning over Judaea in the room of his father Herod, he was afraid to go thither; and being warned of God in a dream, he withdrew into the parts of Galilee,

23. mecimi piyeewa chiine hoteeweneki teewa naaselefi sitoote wahsi menawah hini hokwaawfeki keekalawiki saapwi nihki maamoosikiiskwecki wahsi hina naaseliini sinoofoci

and came and dwelt in a city called Nazareth: that it might be fulfilled which was spoken by the prophets, that he should be called a Nazarene.

Matthew:3

1. chiine yooloone kaasekiki piyeewa caanii hina fafahkwiholelhiwena pemi nanahimiwe hini piileski cotiye

And in those days cometh John the Baptist, preaching in the wilderness of Judaea,

2. mataiini siteheeko kiilawa ksake hini weefepahkamikiki hokimaawitaamhkwe howe maalaakwahi pemi hiwa

saying, Repent ye; for the kingdom of heaven is at hand.

3. yoona yaama ksake yaacimeta saapwi hina haisaya maamoosikiiskweeta hini hokalawihsimoowe wiyeefa peemi talahootaki hini piileski mecfetooko hini homiyeewi hina teepeelemiweeta tepilahi stooko homiyeeweneefa hiwa

For this is he that was spoken of by Isaiah the prophet, saying, The voice of one crying in the wilderness, Make ye ready the way of the Lord, Make his paths straight.

4. howe caanii keemaliiwi wihfaya hopiitenikani chiine meskwahteeki kitapifoowe kaawaci hosehkiki mecimi pakwaci hemoowimelaasi howihfeniiweni

Now John himself had his raiment of camel's hair, and a leathern girdle about his loins; and his food was locusts and wild honey.

5. hine howe lohfaleti colooseelemii nili heewa mecimi caayahki cotiye chiine hini caayahki kaayaawkitaamhkwe hini caatenii

Then went out unto him Jerusalem, and all Judaea, and all the region round about Jordan;

6. mecimi nihki hofafahkwi holelhekowaali nili hini caateniiwi fiipiiki pemi tepaacimooki homaciisilawiiwenwa

and they were baptized of him in the river Jordan, confessing their sins.

7. payeekwa hine hina yeh neewaaci meci nihi pelesihi chiine setosihi peemi piyeelotamaakoci hofafahkwiholelhiweewe neefawe kitalenekowa kiilawa leewaaki hotoosaakanaki wahsi hositameekwe hini hahkwikiteewe waasa piyeeyaaki hotelaali

But when he saw many of the Pharisees and Sadducees coming to his baptism, he said unto them, Ye offspring of vipers, who warned you to flee from the wrath to come?

8. piyeetooko weecikeenahi mawifoowe nahiika mataiini siteheewe yeyhkweelemekoki

Bring forth therefore fruit worthy of repentance:

9. chiine teki siteheeko piitike kiiyaawa wahsi nipoonaape heplehemii niyohfipe hiyoyeekwe ksake kitelepwa niila yeesi hina maneto teepiilefici wahsi

and think not to say within yourselves, We have Abraham to our father: for I say unto you, that God is able of these

yohoma siikonhhi hoci honhskaanamawaaci
heplehemiili hapelofhi

stones to raise up children unto
Abraham.

10. chiine teetepila hini howe tekhaaka sekfenwi ta hini
hoceepkahkatowiki nili mhteko caaki mhtekwi
weecikeenahi weeci pwaa niikiki howesi mawifoowe
kawhoote mecimi hini skoteeki hipakitoote

And even now is the axe laid unto the
root of the trees: every tree therefore
that bringeth not forth good fruit is hewn
down, and cast into the fire.

11. sapkahi niila kifafahkwi holelhelepwa nepiki
mataiini siteheeweneki si weeka hina hahkowi
peepiyaata niila halika mhsiilefi noota niila hina
homahkifena ninootkwiilefi wahsi pah niimeya niila
hina keh fafahkwi holelhekowa nili hofepi
hocacaalahkwali mecimi skoteeki

I indeed baptize you with water unto
repentance: but he that cometh after me
is mightier than I, whose shoes I am not
worthy to bear: he shall baptize you with
the Holy Ghost and with fire:

12. howeewefhoowe hina holeciki hahteewi mecimi
hina weh tateekakwi fafayaakilota hopawaskwhaawi
tepakofenoowe chiine hina weh si maawatona
hokawaskomi hini hokawaskwikaaneki weeka nili
wihsiikwaya yaalwi-ahtehooteeki skote weh si
caakatefaana hina

whose fan is in his hand, and he will
throughly cleanse his threshing-floor;
and he will gather his wheat into the
garner, but the chaff he will burn up
with unquenchable fire.

13. hine howe ciisisii keelelii homwa caateniiki caaniili
si piyeewa wahsi fafahkwi holelhekoci nili

Then cometh Jesus from Galilee to the
Jordan unto John, to be baptized of him.

14. payeekwa caanii wih mehci nakinaali weekhi
nitakaawaafi wahsi kiila fafahkwi holelhiyani mecimi
kiila ha kipiyeelotawi hisiwe

But John would have hindered him,
saying, I have need to be baptized of
thee, and comest thou to me?

15. payeekwa haapafse ciisisii wiilaani leeletano hini
hinoki ksake halayini kitelefipe kiilawe wahsi
hokwaawfetooyakwe caayahki tepasawiilefiiwe
hotelaali hine howe hina wiilaani hoteleelemaali nili

But Jesus answering said unto him,
Suffer it now: for thus it becometh us to
fulfill all righteousness. Then he
suffereth him.

16. mecimi ciisisii hine yeh fafahkwi holelhoofoci
weelena hini nepiki hoci moskwife chiine scih nili
menhkwato tawenamaakwi hina mecimi hina
honeewaali nili hocacaalahkomali maneto peemi
laasiyofelici paasi miyaasipawiifa mecimi hoskici
wiiya si piyeeli

And Jesus, when he was baptized, went
up straightway from the water: and lo,
the heavens were opened unto him, and
he saw the Spirit of God descending as a
dove, and coming upon him;

17. chiine scih nili menhkwato hoci nootaakwatwi
kalawihsimoowe halayaama yeeahkweelemaka
nikwihfa wiiyaaki nimenwilepwa hiyooya

and lo, a voice out of the heavens,
saying, This is my beloved Son, in
whom I am well pleased.

Matthew:4

1. hine howe ciisisii nili hocacaalahkwali hini piileski
hotesiwelekooli wahsi koci maci-ashekoci nili
macimanetooli

Then was Jesus led up of the Spirit into
the wilderness to be tempted of the
devil.

2. chiine hine yeh mehci fafahkwi hocikeeci
niyeewaapitaki tfoko kite niyeewaapitaki tepokwe hina
hahkowihi skwaalawe

And when he had fasted forty days and
forty nights, he afterward hungered.

3. mecimi hina kocilehfi piyeewa chiine kwehkwi kiiyaawiyane nili hokwihfali maneto tepikeemolo wahsi yohkoma siikonaki takhwaaniwiwaaci hotekooli

And the tempter came and said unto him, If thou art the Son of God, command that these stones become bread.

4. payeekwa hina haapafse mecimi yeelawikeeki hini mata takhwa pehi we hoci lenaweewi hileni weeka caaki kalawiiwe hini hotooni maneto weemooyaaki hotelaali

But he answered and said, It is written, Man shall not live by bread alone, but by every word that proceedeth out of the mouth of God.

5. hine howe hina macimaneto hini hofepi hoteeweneki hotesiwelaali nili mecimi hina hini hanahkwaski hini mamaatomeewikamikwi hoteh lemataphaali nili

Then the devil taketh him into the holy city; and he set him on the pinnacle of the temple,

6. chiine kwehkwi kiiyaawiyane nili hokwihfali maneto sahkiki hipakitano kiiya ksake yeelawikeeki hini weh miilahi hina hotenhcaliimhhi tepimetiiwe kiila si chiine holeciwaaki nihki keh pah niimekooki piilepe ke pkitehfeto kifici siikoneki hotelaali

and saith unto him, If thou art the Son of God, cast thyself down: for it is written, He shall give his angels charge concerning thee: And on their hands they shall bear thee up, Lest haply thou dash thy foot against a stone.

7. teki ke hosto kiila hokotahkowaafoowe hina teepeelemiweeta kimanetooma lawikeepi hini nohki hotelaali ciisisii

Jesus said unto him, Again it is written, Thou shalt not tempt the Lord thy God.

8. nohki hina macimaneto hanhhiweewi sehpateki waciwahki hotesiwelaali nili mecimi howaapatelaali caayahki nili hokimaawitaamhkweewali hini yeelekokwahkamikiki mecimi nili hoci wahfaacimekofiiwe

Again, the devil taketh him unto an exceeding high mountain, and sheweth him all the kingdoms of the world, and the glory of them;

9. chiine caayahki yooloma wiyehi keh miilele niila sahkiki sfaayane mecimi hosasilawehiyane hotelaali

and he said unto him, All these things will I give thee, if thou wilt fall down and worship me.

10. hine howe ciisisii halika haale setenii ksake ke hosasilaweha kiila hina teepeelemiweeta kimanetooma mecimi hina pehi keh memekinilotawa lawikeepi hini hotelaali

Then saith Jesus unto him, Get thee hence, Satan: for it is written, Thou shalt worship the Lord thy God, and him only shalt thou serve.

11. hine howe hina macimaneto honakalaali nili mecimi waapamehko henhcaliiki piyeeki mecimi homiisamawaawaali nili

Then the devil leaveth him; and behold, angels came and ministered unto him.

12. howe hine hina yeh nootaakeeci yeesi caaniili mesenoofolici keeleliiki si saawe

Now when he heard that John was delivered up, he withdrew into Galilee;

13. chiine honakata naaselefi keepaaniamii si piyeewa mecimi nitasi teewa yehteeki skwaapiyeeki hini mhsinepi piicitaamhkwe skwaaya hini sipolani chiine niftelii

and leaving Nazareth, he came and dwelt in Capernaum, which is by the sea, in the borders of Zebulun and Naphtali:

14. wahsi menawah hini hokwaawfeki keekalawiki saapwi haisaya hina maamoosikiiskweeta

that it might be fulfilled which was spoken by Isaiah the prophet, saying,

15. hini sipolaniiwi hasiski chiine hini nifteliiwi hasiski hini mhsinepi wayeeci halika hini caatenii hokeeleliimwa nihki nanahkawileniiki

The land of Zebulun and the land of Naphtali, Toward the sea, beyond Jordan, Galilee of the Gentiles,

16. nihki lenaweeki lematapicki laa pepekica honeemenaawa mehsaaki wayahfeeyaaki chiine nihki lematapicki hini laawitaamhkwe mecimi nepoowi heewikaki nihki si mohkeeska wayahfeeyaaki hiwapi

The people which sat in darkness Saw a great light, And to them which sat in the region and shadow of death, To them did light spring up.

17. hine laakwa hoci ciisisii halemi nanahimiwe mecimi mataiini siteheeko kiilawa ksake hini weefepahkamikiki hokimaawitaamhkwe howe maalaakwahi hisiwe

From that time began Jesus to preach, and to say, Repent ye; for the kingdom of heaven is at hand.

18. chiine paamhfe pakaci hini keeleliiwi mhsinepi hina honeewahi niiswi weeceeninaatihi saiman' piita yaaloofota mecimi hoceeninaali heenhtlooli peemi hini mhsinepiki hipakitamelici haakwaskwhaaka ksake naanamefkeecki nihki

And walking by the sea of Galilee, he saw two brethren, Simon who is called Peter, and Andrew his brother, casting a net into the sea; for they were fishers.

19. chiine piyaako naawaloskawiko kiilawa mecimi hilenihi neenamefkaalaacki ke shelepwa hotelahi nihi

And he saith unto them, Come ye after me, and I will make you fishers of men.

20. chiine nihki weelena honakataanaawa nili haakwaskwhaakana mecimi honeekalaawaali nihi

And they straightway left the nets, and followed him.

21. chiine yooci halika heewa honeewahi niiswi kotakhi weeceeninaatihi ceemhsii nili hokwihfali sepetii mecimi hoceeninaali caaniili wiici hofwaali sepetiili hini holakeeleki peemi cahtokwenamowaaci hotaakwskwhaakanwa mecimi hoteh wihkomahi nihi

And going on from thence he saw other two brethren, James the son of Zebedee, and John his brother, in the boat with Zebedee their father, mending their nets; and he called them.

22. chiine nihki weelena honakataanaawa hini holakeesi mecimi hohfwaali chiine honeekalaawaali nili

And they straightway left the boat and their father, and followed him.

23. chiine mefhiike laa keelelii paamhfe ciisisii kakehkimiwe piitike homhsikamikomwaaki chiine nanahimiwe hini hokimaawitaamhkwe hoci howesi piyeetaacimoowe chiine kiikehiwe caayahki yeeki katoneewe mecimi caayahki yeeki hahkwilokeewe heelekiina nihi lenawehi

And Jesus went about in all Galilee, teaching in their synagogues, and preaching the gospel of the kingdom, and healing all manner of disease and all manner of sickness among the people.

24. mecimi hini hotelaacimekofiiwe weepfeeya mefhiike laa siliye heeya mecimi nihki hopiyeetawaawaali caayahki yeeahkwilokeelici fayookinekocki kwakwetaki si katoneewena mecimi hahkwilokeewena lekoskaakocki waninehfihi chiine maamaatakoskaacki chiine nenekificki mecimi hokiikehahi nihi

And the report of him went forth into all Syria: and they brought unto him all that were sick, holden with divers diseases and torments, possessed with devils, and epileptic, and palsied; and he healed them.

25. chiine nitasi honeekalaawaali nili mehsi mehseelekki keelelii hoci chiine tikeepolasi chiine colooseelemii chiine cotiye mecimi halika hini caatenii hoci

And there followed him great multitudes from Galilee and Decapolis and Jerusalem and Judaea and from beyond Jordan.

Matthew:5

1. chiine yeesi neewaaci nihi mehseelelici hina weepfe hini meekwahkiki si kkwicsinwa chiine hine hina yeh mehtahkeepici hokakehkimaafhi hotfekohi

And seeing the multitudes, he went up into the mountain: and when he had sat down, his disciples came unto him:

2. chiine hotawena hotooni mecimi hokakehkimahi nihi

and he opened his mouth and taught them, saying,

3. kisaateelemekofiiki nihki keetemaasilepwaskaacki ksake wiilawa hini weefepahkamikiki hokimaawitaamhkwe

Blessed are the poor in spirit: for theirs is the kingdom of heaven.

4. kisaateelemekofiiki nihki meemaweecki ksake weh menwiteheeskoofooki nihki

Blessed are they that mourn: for they shall be comforted.

5. kisaateelemekofiiki nihki nanahpaacilefaki ksake weh laapi howiilaamiiki hini yeelekokwahkamikiki

Blessed are the meek: for they shall inherit the earth.

6. kisaateelemekofiiki nihki meemameteelemocki mecimi kahkalaamocki hini tepasawiilefiiwe ksake weh teepeelemooki nihki

Blessed are they that hunger and thirst after righteousness: for they shall be filled.

7. kisaateelemekofiiki nihki keeteminaakweelemeficki ksake weh katawihkaanaawa kiteminaakweelemefiiwe

Blessed are the merciful: for they shall obtain mercy.

8. kisaateelemekofiiki nihki feefayaakiteheecki ksake weh neewaawaali manetooli nihki

Blessed are the pure in heart: for they shall see God.

9. kisaateelemekofiiki nihki kaamaaniilefiiwe weeostoocki ksake maneto hokwifhi we haaloofooki nihki

Blessed are the peacemakers: for they shall be called sons of God.

10. kisaateelemekofiiki nihki mayehci naanohkaachoofocki ksake tepasawiilefiiwe hoci wiilawa ksake hini weefepahkamikiki hokimaawitaamhkwe

Blessed are they that have been persecuted for righteousness' sake: for theirs is the kingdom of heaven.

11. kikisaateelemekofipwa kiilawa hine hileniiki hahtelelwaakwe chiine naanohkaachelwaakwe mecimi caayahki yeeki mecaafiki si naanhhaacimelwaakwe niila hoci

Blessed are ye when men shall reproach you, and persecute you, and say all manner of evil against you falsely, for my sake.

12. hosasilepwaako mecimi hanhhiweewi howesilepwaako ksake mhsaawi hini kitephofiiwenwa piitike weefepahkamikiki yooni ksake yeesi nihki naanohkaachaawaaci nihi maamoosikiiskwelici yeepilici wihsi pwaa kiilawa hapiyeekwe

Rejoice, and be exceeding glad: for great is your reward in heaven: for so persecuted they the prophets which were before you.

13. hini hasiskitaamhkwe si nepipemi hini kiiyaawa payeekwa kwehkwi mehci wanhtoote yeepokwaki hini nepipemi taaniwe we hoci pskipete hini hini matawiyeefekisi hine hoci weeka wahsi lohfe pakitooteeki hinwi mecimi kakeelhkooteeki laameki hoficiwa hileniiki

Ye are the salt of the earth: but if the salt have lost its savour, wherewith shall it be salted? it is thenceforth good for nothing, but to be cast out and trodden under foot of men.

14. kiiyaawa hini wayahfeeyaaki hini yeelekokwahkamikiki si hoteewe wehseteki meekwahkiifiki hahteewi mata yah katawi kikitoote

Ye are the light of the world. A city set on a hill cannot be hid.

15. mata nohki hileniiki hofaafakfwaawaali niitawaakanali mecimi laameki hini posiliiki hotaasi poonaawaali nili weeka hoskici yaatah niipawilici mecimi honiitawaalekowaali nili caayahki hini wiikiwaapeki yeepicki

Neither do men light a lamp, and put it under the bushel, but on the stand; and it shineth unto all that are in the house.

16. teetepilahi yooni si wiilaani kiwahfeeyaamwa niitaweyeekwe yeelahfamiiwaaci hileniiki wahsi menawahi nihki neemowaaci koowesi pekatefiiwenwa mecimi wahfaacimekofiheekwe kohfwa weefepahkamikiki yeepita

Even so let your light shine before men, that they may see your good works, and glorify your Father which is in heaven.

17. yeesi piyaaya niila wahsi macilotama hini kwteletiiwe weelaa nihki maamoosikiiskwecki teki siteheeko mata wahsi macilawiiya nooci piyaa wahsi hokwaawilawiiya weeka

Think not that I came to destroy the law or the prophets: I came not to destroy, but to fulfill.

18. ksake tepilo kitelepwa niila paalohi menhkwatwi mecimi hasiskitaamhkwe we haseno mata nekoti kcimaalecihi weelaa nekoti pekwe we hini kwteletiiweneki hoci wiyehisi hasenwi paalohi caayahki wiyehi weh mehcilotoote

For verily I say unto you, Till heaven and earth pass away, one jot or one tittle shall in no wise pass away from the law, till all things be accomplished.

19. weecikeenahi kookwe-neefa-kaaci weh poskona nekoti yooloma kcimeckwaafiki tepikeemoowena mecimi yooni weh si kakehkimaaci hilenihi kcimaaciloofi we haaloofo piitike hini weefepahkamikiki hokimaawitaamhkwe weeka kookwe-neefa-kaaci weh silawi mecimi weh kakehkimiwe nili hina mehsiilefi we haaloofo piitike hini weefepahkamikiki hokimaawitaamhkwe

Whosoever therefore shall break one of these least commandments, and shall teach men so, shall be called least in the kingdom of heaven: but whosoever shall do and teach them, he shall be called great in the kingdom of heaven.

20. ksake kitelepwa niila weeciwephi hanhtaweekwe kitepasawiilefiiwenwa yeenwilici hini hotepasawiilefiiwenwa nihki yaayawikeecki mecimi pelesiiki mata kiilawa keh wiyehisi piicfaapwa hini weefepahkamikiki hokimaawitaamhkwe

For I say unto you, that except your righteousness shall exceed the righteousness of the scribes and Pharisees, ye shall in no wise enter into the kingdom of heaven.

21. kimehci nootaakeepwa kiilawa yeesi hini hiloofowaaci nihki sehkamika teki ke nhsiwe mecimi kookwe-neefa-kaaci we nhsiwe we hoci nanaskaci hilefi hini mehtahkowaafoowe

Ye have heard that it was said to them of old time, Thou shalt not kill; and whosoever shall kill shall be in danger of the judgment:

22. weeka kitelepwa niila caakiwiyeefa weewiyakowehtawaata hoceeninaali weh nanaskaci hilefi hini mehtahkowaafoowe chiine kookwe-neefa-kaaci meyale we hilaali hoceeninaali weh nanaskaci hilefi hini tepoweewe chiine kookwe-neefa-kaaci

but I say unto you, that every one who is angry with his brother shall be in danger of the judgment; and whosoever shall say to his brother, Raca, shall be in danger of the council; and whosoever

wanihsaka kiila we hiwa weh nanaskaci hilefi hini hahkwinamoowi skote

23. kwehkwi kiila weecikeenahi pakfenikeeyane kiteephetiiwe hini pootefamaacikaneki mecimi nitasi mhkaweeletamane yeesi kiceenina piimeelemehki

24. nitasi nakatano kiteephetiiwe yeelahfamiiyaaki hini pootefamaacika mecimi nhhaale howelaakoomi nhhihta kiceenina howe hine chiine piyaalo chiine pakfenikeelo kiteephetiiwe

25. howelaacimoomi kimateeletiiwena weeweetepi yeheeyehi kiila wiiciimaci hini wayeeci piilepe hina mateeletiiwena nili teepasawahkoniweeli keh si poonekwa mecimi hina teepasawahkoniwe nili wiyehsimekofiiwenali keh si poonekwa mecimi kiphotiiweneki ke hpakilekoopi

26. tepilo kitele niila mata keh wiyehisi hini hoci lohfa kiila paalohi hini ceeyehkwi mhskwakkwe keh mehci tephike

27. kimehci nootaakeepwa kiilawa yeesi hini hiyoki teki keh macilawi waapasiphikeewe

28. weeka kitelepwa niila yeesi caakiwiyeefa yeelaapamaata hkweeli wahsi weepeelemaaci neyehka macilawihtawaaci nili waapasiphikeewe hotehiki

29. chiine kwehkwi kimayaaoskiisekwi wahsi hotakikahsinani hpenalekoyane kwakwatenano hini mecimi kiiya hoci halika hikwakitano hini ksake hini mhkahfooweni kiila si wahsi nekotweelena kiiya hkwi hilefiiyaaki mecimi mata melhske kiiya hipakitoote hahkwi namooweneki

30. chiine kwehkwi kimayaawiinhki wahsi hotakikahsinani hpenalekoyane kwakwkotano hini mecimi kiiya hoci halika hipakitano hini ksake hini mhkahfooweni kiila si wahsi nekotweelena kiiya hkwi hilefiiyaaki mecimi mata melhske kiiya nhheeya hahkwi namooweneki

31. nehfaapi hini hiyopi kookwe-neefa-kaaci weh payakila si poonaali wiiwali weh miilaali wiilaani pkehotiiwi heewikaateeki

32. weeka kitelepwa niila yeesi caakiwiyeefa peepayakila si poonaata wiiwali weeciwep hini weepeeletiiwe hoci waapasiphikeewiikweli shaaci nili mecimi kookwe-neefa-kaaci weh wiiwinaali nili hine nili payakila si poonoofooli macilawi waapasiphikeewe

shall say, Thou fool, shall be in danger of the hell of fire.

If therefore thou art offering thy gift at the altar, and there rememberest that thy brother hath aught against thee,

leave there thy gift before the altar, and go thy way, first be reconciled to thy brother, and then come and offer thy gift.

Agree with thine adversary quickly, whiles thou art with him in the way; lest haply the adversary deliver thee to the judge, and the judge deliver thee to the officer, and thou be cast into prison.

Verily I say unto thee, Thou shalt by no means come out thence, till thou have paid the last farthing.

Ye have heard that it was said, Thou shalt not commit adultery:

but I say unto you, that every one that looketh on a woman to lust after her hath committed adultery with her already in his heart.

And if thy right eye causeth thee to stumble, pluck it out, and cast it from thee: for it is profitable for thee that one of thy members should perish, and not thy whole body be cast into hell.

And if thy right hand causeth thee to stumble, cut it off, and cast it from thee: for it is profitable for thee that one of thy members should perish, and not thy whole body go into hell.

It was said also, Whosoever shall put away his wife, let him give her a writing of divorcement:

but I say unto you, that every one that putteth away his wife, saving for the cause of fornication, maketh her an adulteress: and whosoever shall marry her when she is put away committeth adultery.

33. nohki kimehci nootaakeepwa kiilawa yeesi hini hiloofowaaci nihki sehkamika teki keh naanhhaaci ciikinhkemota kiiya weeka keh pekatenamawa kiila hina teepeelemiweeta kiciiikinhkemoowena

Again, ye have heard that it was said to them of old time, Thou shalt not forswear thyself, but shalt perform unto the Lord thine oaths:

34. weeka kitelepwa niila teki ciikinhkemoko teki nohki hini weefepahkamikiki hoci ksake hini hokimaawi hotpapiiwe maneto

but I say unto you, Swear not at all; neither by the heaven, for it is the throne of God;

35. weelaa teki hini hasiskitaamhkwe hoci ksake hini hpalhkiiwenili hofitali weelaa teki colooseelemii wayeeci ksake hini hototeewe hina mhsi-okima

nor by the earth, for it is the footstool of his feet; nor by Jerusalem, for it is the city of the great King.

36. teki nohki keh ciikinhkemo kiisi hoci mata kiila kitah katawi waapito weelaa mhkateewto nekoti wiilehfi

Neither shalt thou swear by thy head, for thou canst not make one hair white or black.

37. weeka wiilaani hanhka hanhka mata mata hike kikalawiiwenwa mecimi kookwe-nehi-kaaci halika tfenwi yooloma hina maci wiyeefa hociwi hini

But let your speech be, Yea, yea; Nay, nay: and whatsoever is more than these is of the evil one.

38. kimehci nootaakeepwa kiilawa yeesi hini hiyoki hoskiisekwi hasowe hoskiisekwi chiine wiipici hasowe wiipici

Ye have heard that it was said, An eye for an eye, and a tooth for a tooth:

39. weeka kitelepwa niila teki ppehtenehko hina meciilefita weeka kookwe-neefa-kaaci kipkitehokwa kimayaawi-nowaaki kokiikwehtawi hina hini kotaki nehfaapi

but I say unto you, Resist not him that is evil: but whosoever smiteth thee on thy right cheek, turn to him the other also.

40. chiine kwehkwi hileni wiyeefa kwteletiiweneki wi heewa wiici kiila mecimi kimamaakwa kikootiimi wiilaani miili kipihtawipiitenika nehfaapi

And if any man would go to law with thee, and take away thy coat, let him have thy cloke also.

41. chiine kookwe-neefa-kaaci keh mamiiloowihekwa wahsi nekoti maiili haayani wiiteemi niiswi

And whosoever shall compel thee to go one mile, go with him twain.

42. miili hina neetotamawehka mecimi teki kiila hina wahataamehka hoci payakila si kotekwiilo

Give to him that asketh thee, and from him that would borrow of thee turn not thou away.

43. kimehci nootaakeepwa kiilawa yeesi hini hiyoki ke hahkweelema kiila kimaapiyeecikaaletiima mecimi siikeelemi kimateeletiiwena

Ye have heard that it was said, Thou shalt love thy neighbour, and hate thine enemy:

44. weeka kitelepwa niila hahkweelemehko kimateeletiiwenwaaki mecimi mamaatomawehko nihki neenaanohkaachelwaakwe

but I say unto you, Love your enemies, and pray for them that persecute you;

45. wahsi menawah hokwihfinelwaakwe kohfwa weefepahkamikiki yeepita ksake hina hoteshaali hokiisekikiisfoomali wahsi piyeetahkofamawaaci nili meciilefilici mecimi nili weeowesiilefilici chiine hotesfatawaali keemowaaki nili teepasawefilici mecimi nili pwaayaatepasawefilici

that ye may be sons of your Father which is in heaven: for he maketh his sun to rise on the evil and the good, and sendeth rain on the just and the unjust.

46. ksake kwehkwi hahkweelemeekwe nihki yeeahkweelemelwaakwe nehiwesi tephofiiwe kipoonaanaawa ha teetepila hini yaska silawiiki nihki teeksiiwi-maawatonikehfiiki

For if ye love them that love you, what reward have ye? do not even the publicans the same?

47. chiine kwehkwi kiilawa hosilawaaleekwe kiceeninaawaaki pehi nehiwe kooci halika hpenalaawaaki noota kotakaki ha mata teetepila hini yaska silawiiki nihki nanahkawiyeeniiki

And if ye salute your brethren only, what do ye more than others? do not even the Gentiles the same?

48. keh mefefipwa weecikeenahi kiilawa yeesi hina mefefici weefepefita kohfwa

Ye therefore shall be perfect, as your heavenly Father is perfect.

Matthew:6

1. kcitawaafiiko wahsi pwaa pekilotameekwe kitepasawiilefiiwenwa yeelahfamiiwaaci hileniiki wahsi nihki noolwaakwe piilepe kiilawa mata kipoonaanaawa tephofiiwe kohfwaaki yeepita weefepahkamikiki

Take heed that ye do not your righteousness before men, to be seen of them: else ye have no reward with your Father which is in heaven.

2. hine weecikeenahi kiila kisaacikeewe silawiiyane teki holwehtoolo pepikwa yeelahfamiiyani paasi nihki nayeelohcilawiicki yaasilawiiwaaci piitike nili mhsikamiko mecimi nili laa hoteewenimiyeewali wahsi nihki menawahi poonamowaaci howahfaacimekofiiwenwa hileniiki tepilo kitelepwa niila neyehka nihki hotfekonaawa hotephofiiwenwa

When therefore thou doest alms, sound not a trumpet before thee, as the hypocrites do in the synagogues and in the streets, that they may have glory of men. Verily I say unto you, They have received their reward.

3. weeka kiila hine kisaacikeewe silawiiyane teki wiilaani kinamaciinhki waakotefiiyaake yeesilawiiyaaki kimayaawiinhki

But when thou doest alms, let not thy left hand know what thy right hand doeth:

4. wahsi kiila kikisaacikeewe menawahi kiyaacfeki mecimi kohfa keekiyaaci si tepinaka keh petekfetaakwa kiila

that thine alms may be in secret: and thy Father which seeth in secret shall recompense thee.

5. chiine hine kiilawa mamaatomeeyeekwe teki paasi nihki nayeelohcilawiicki ke hilefipwa ksake nihki hotahkweeletaanaawa wahsi niipawiwaaci mecimi mamaatomaawaaci piitike nili mhsikamiko chiine nili tah piipooceeyaaki nili hoteewenimiyeewali wahsi menawahi nihki nookowaaci hilenihi tepilo kitelepwa niila neyehka nihki hotfekonaawa hotephofiiwenwa

And when ye pray, ye shall not be as the hypocrites: for they love to stand and pray in the synagogues and in the corners of the streets, that they may be seen of men. Verily I say unto you, They have received their reward.

6. weeka kiila hine mamaatomeeyane hottano pihtawi piitike yeetaayani mecimi mehci kiphamane kiskwaateemi mamaatomi kohfa keekiyaacsika mecimi kohfa keekiyaaci si tepinaka keh petekfetaakwa kiila

But thou, when thou prayest, enter into thine inner chamber, and having shut thy door, pray to thy Father which is in secret, and thy Father which seeth in secret shall recompense thee.

7. chiine mamaatomeeyane teki nelohci pihtoweewena hawelo paasi nihki nanahkawileniiki yaasilawiiwaaci

And in praying use not vain repetitions, as the Gentiles do: for they think that

ksake nihki wahsi nootamawoofowaaci homaali pekikalawiiwenwa siteheeki nihki

they shall be heard for their much speaking.

8. teki weecikeenahi paasi nihki hilefiko ksake kohfwa howaakota wiyehi yeekaawaatameekwe kiilawa wihsi pwaa natotamaweekwe

Be not therefore like unto them: for your Father knoweth what things ye have need of, before ye ask him.

9. weecikeenahi naawalwi yooma yeeki si mamaatomeeko nohfena yeepiyani weefepahkamikiki hahpeelemekwanwi kiwiifoowe

After this manner therefore pray ye: Our Father which art in heaven, Hallowed be thy name.

10. kookimaawiiwe piyeeya kitesiteheewe wih silawiipi paasi piitike weefepahkamikiki yooni yaska hoskitaamhkwe

Thy kingdom come. Thy will be done, as in heaven, so on earth.

11. miilinaake tfene waapaki nitakhwaanena hinoki kaasekiki

Give us this day our daily bread.

12. mecimi pakfeeletamawinaake nimoosinehikanena yeesi nehfaapi mehci pakfeeletamawakici meemoosinehwiyamekicki

And forgive us our debts, as we also have forgiven our debtors.

13. chiine teki miyaasi-ashetiiweneki si piyeesinaake weeka hina hoci hotweninaake maci wiyeefa

And bring us not into temptation, but deliver us from the evil one.

14. ksake kwehkwi pakfeeletamaweekwe hileniiki hotalhfwaacilawiiwenwa kiilawa koofepi kohfwa nehfaapi keh pakfeeletamaakowa kiilawa

For if ye forgive men their trespasses, your heavenly Father will also forgive you.

15. weeka kiilawa pwaa pakfeeletamaweekwe hotalhfwaacilawiiwenwa hileniiki mata nohki kohfwa keh pakfeeletamaakowa kiilawa kitalhfwaacilawiiwenwa

But if ye forgive not men their trespasses, neither will your Father forgive your trespasses.

16. chiine nohki hine fafahkwi hocikeeyeekwe kiilawa teki hilefiiki paasi nayeelohcilawiicki macilepwaapeskaaki ksake nihki howiyakaacitoonaawa hotelaapeewenwa wahsi menawah hilenihi nookowaaci yeesi fafahkwi hocikeewaaci tepilo kitelepwa niila neyehka nihki hotfekonaawa hotephofiiwenwa

Moreover when ye fast, be not, as the hypocrites, of a sad countenance: for they disfigure their faces, that they may be seen of men to fast. Verily I say unto you, They have received their reward.

17. weeka kiila hine fafahkwi hocikeeyane lomhkwiilo mecimi kifiikwaalo

But thou, when thou fastest, anoint thy head, and wash thy face;

18. wahsi pwaa kiila neewohki hileniiki yeesi fafahkwi hocikeeyani kohfa weeka keekiyaacsika mecimi kohfa keekiyaaci si tepinaka keh petekfetaakwa kiila

that thou be not seen of men to fast, but of thy Father which is in secret: and thy Father, which seeth in secret, shall recompense thee.

19. teki kiiyaawa si nhhawaaci poonahfatamoko paweewe hini hoskici taamhkwe yaatah mookwatekwa mecimi yeekwaakwalhki caakilotaki mecimi yaatah kaakimootekiki saapwiiwaaci mecimi kimootowaaci

Lay not up for yourselves treasures upon the earth, where moth and rust doth consume, and where thieves break through and steal:

20. weeka nhhawaaci si poonahfatamoko kiiyaawa paweewe piitike weefepahkamikiki yaatah mookwatekwa mecimi yeekwaakwalhki pwaa

but lay up for yourselves treasures in heaven, where neither moth nor rust doth consume, and where thieves do not break through nor steal:

caakilotaki mecimi yaatah kaakimootekiki pwaa
saapwiiwaaci mecimi pwaa kimootowaaci

21. ksake ta hahteeki kipaweewe nehfaapi nitasi we
hahteewi kitehi

for where thy treasure is, there will thy
heart be also.

22. hina wiiyaana honiitawaakani hini hoskiisekwi
kwehkwi weecikeena hini kiskiisekwi nayehfaawike
melhske kiiyaana we hokwaawefi wayahfeeyaaki

The lamp of the body is the eye: if
therefore thine eye be single, thy whole
body shall be full of light.

23. weeka kwehkwi kiskiisekwi macaafike melhske
kiiyaana we hokwaawefi peepekicaaki kwehkwi
weecikeena hini wayahfeeyaaki yehteeki kiiyaaki
pepekicaake mhsaawi ce hini peepekicaaki

But if thine eye be evil, thy whole body
shall be full of darkness. If therefore the
light that is in thee be darkness, how
great is the darkness!

24. mata hileni hokatawi memekinilotawahi niiswi
mestelehi ksake naanekoti nili weh siikeelemaali
mecimi nili kotakali hotahkweelemaali weelaake we
haayitatenaali nekoti mecimi holasiikaateelemaali nili
kotakali mata kitah katawi memekinilotawaawa maneto
mecimi pawaawilehfi

No man can serve two masters: for
either he will hate the one, and love the
other; or else he will hold to one, and
despise the other. Ye cannot serve God
and mammon.

25. weecikeenahi kitelepwa niila teki si
wiisaaciteheeko kitelenaweewiiwenwa wiyehi wah
miiciyeekwe weelaa wah meneyeekwe weelaa teki
nohki kiiyaanwa wiyehi wah piitenameekwe ha mata
hini lenaweewiiwe halika hinwi noota hini wihfeniiwe
mecimi hina wiiyaana noota hini piitenika

Therefore I say unto you, Be not
anxious for your life, what ye shall eat,
or what ye shall drink; nor yet for your
body, what ye shall put on. Is not the life
more than the food, and the body than
the raiment?

26. waapamehko nihki wiskilohfaki hini laa
menhkwatwi yeesi pwaa nihki hahcikeewaaci nohki
pwaa kawaskwhaawaaci nihki pwaa nohki
kawaskwikaana si mawatonikeewaaci mecimi hofepi
kohfwa hotsamahi nihi ha mata kiilawa mhsi halika
kiteleelemekofipwa noota nihki

Behold the birds of the heaven, that they
sow not, neither do they reap, nor gather
into barns; and your heavenly Father
feedeth them. Are not ye of much more
value than they?

27. chiine taanawe hina kiilawa yeewiisaaciteheeci hoci
katawi kooloto nekoti kiopit hini hotelenaweewiiwe si
tepacikaneki

And which of you by being anxious can
add one cubit unto his stature?

28. chiine koociwe piitenika kitesi wiisaafiipwa
memekineeletamoko nili wiisiwalakeemi hini yeele
lhskahki yeesi nili skwiniikiki mata paapekatefiiya nili
nohki mata paapiyeeminakweya

And why are ye anxious concerning
raiment? Consider the lilies of the field,
how they grow; they toil not, neither do
they spin:

29. payeekwa kitelepwa niila yeesi wiikinaakwi
salamanii hocaayahki wahfaacimekofiiweneki pwaa
laseci paasi nekoti yooloma

yet I say unto you, that even Solomon in
all his glory was not arrayed like one of
these.

30. weeka kwehkwi maneto yooni lasehtoote nili
mhskotehkwalo hini yeele lhskahki yeeki nili hinoki
kaasekiki mecimi waapake hini kisifikaneki hipakitoote
ha mata mecilekhi si halika ke hina lasekhokowa o
kiilawa caki teepwehseefaki

But if God doth so clothe the grass of
the field, which today is, and tomorrow
is cast into the oven, shall he not much
more clothe you, O ye of little faith?

31. teki weecikeenahi wiisaafiiko nehiwe keh miicipe hiyoko weelaa nehiwe keh menepe weelaa taaniwe ke hoci piitenikeepe

Be not therefore anxious, saying, What shall we eat? or, What shall drink? or, Wherewithal shall we be clothed?

32. ksake caayahki yooloma wiyehi nihki nanahkawileniiki honatonehaanaawa ksake hofepi kohfwa howaakota yeesi hekaawaatameekwe caayahki yooloma wiyehi

For after all these things do the Gentiles seek; for your heavenly Father knoweth that ye have need of all these things.

33. payeekwa kiilawa nhhihta natonehamoko hokimaawihotaamhkomi mecimi hotepasawiilefiiwe mecimi caayahki yooloma wiyehi keh koolotaakoopwa kiilawa

But seek ye first his kingdom, and his righteousness; and all these things shall be added unto you.

34. teki weecikeena hini wayaapaki si wiisaafiiko ksake hini wayaapaki weh pesikwi wiisaafiiya teepfeke hini kaasekiki hini tasi hahteewi mecaafiki

Be not therefore anxious for the morrow: for the morrow will be anxious for itself. Sufficient unto the day is the evil thereof.

Matthew:7

1. teki wiyehi lahkowaasiweeko wahsi pwaa kiilawa wiyehi lahkowaafoyeekwe

Judge not, that ye be not judged.

2. ksake wiyehi lahkowaasiweewe weeci wiyehi lahkowaasiweeyeekwe ke hotahkowaafopwa kiilawa mecimi hini tepacika teepacikeeyeekwe hini keh tepalekoopwa kiilawa

For with what judgment ye judge, ye shall be judged: and with what measure ye mete, it shall be measured unto you.

3. chiine koociwe kitelaapata hini pefenoowe kiceenina yehteelici hoskiisekoki weeka mata kimemekineeleta hini peemakofeki nehalwaaka kiskiisekoki yehteeki

And why beholdest thou the mote that is in thy brother's eye, but considerest not the beam that is in thine own eye?

4. weelaa nehiwe keh si hila kiceenina ceh keh lohfe pakitamoole hini pefenoowe kiskiisekwi hoci mecimi scih hini peemakofeki hahteewi nehalwaaka kiskiisekoki

Or how wilt thou say to thy brother, Let me cast out the mote out of thine eye; and lo, the beam is in thine own eye?

5. kiila nelohcilawiwehfi nhhihta lohfe pakitano hini peemakofeki nehalwaaka kiskiisekoki hoci hine chiine keh tepinaakwi neeme kiila wahsi lohfe pakitamani hini pefenoowe kiceenina hoskiisekwi hoci

Thou hypocrite, cast out first the beam out of thine own eye; and then shalt thou see clearly to cast out the mote out of thy brother's eye.

6. miilehko teki hini weefepiyaaki nihki wihsiiki teki nohki yeelahfamiiwaaci nihki koskooki pakilehko kimiikehfemwaaki piilepe nihki hokakeelhkawaawahi nihi laameki hofitwa mecimi kokiiki chiine kilelhkamekowaaki kiilawa

Give not that which is holy unto the dogs, neither cast your pearls before the swine, lest haply they trample them under their feet, and turn and rend you.

7. natotamaakeeko mecimi hini keh miilekoopwa natonehikeeko mecimi ke mhkahfopwa towathikeeko mecimi hini keh tawenamaakoopwa

Ask, and it shall be given you; seek, and ye shall find; knock, and it shall be opened unto you:

8. ksake caakiwiyeefa neetotamaakeeta hotefi mecimi hina neetonehikeeta mhkahfo chiine hina teetowathikeeta weh tawenamaakwi hini

for every one that asketh receiveth; and he that seeketh findeth; and to him that knocketh it shall be opened.

9. weelaa neefawe hileni hapiwa nitasi kiilawa hina kwehkwi hokwihfali weh natotamaakooli weepskweeteeki ha siikonali weh miilaali nili

Or what man is there of you, who, if his son shall ask him for a loaf, will give him a stone;

10. weelaa kwehkwi hina namehfali weh natomaali ha manetooli weh miilaali nili

or if he shall ask for a fish, will give him a serpent?

11. kwehkwi weecikeenahi weekhi kimaciilefipwa waakotameekwe wahsi miileekwe howesi wiyehi kitapelohfemwaaki taaniwe si halika kohfwa weefepahkamikiki yeepita weh si miilahi howesi wiyehi nihi neenatotamaakoci

If ye then, being evil, know how to give good gifts unto your children, how much more shall your Father which is in heaven give good things to them that ask him?

12. caayahki wiyehi weecikeenahi kookwe-nehi-kaaci skata nih silawihtaakonaaki hileniiki yeesiteheeyeekwe teetepilahi yooni silawihtawehko nehfaapi kiilawa ksake yooma hini kwteletiiwe chiine nihki maamoosikiiskwecki

All things therefore whatsoever ye would that men should do unto you, even so do ye also unto them: for this is the law and the prophets.

13. hoci piicfaako kiilawa hini meckwaalakatoofiki skwaate ksake mhfaalakatwi hini skwaate mecimi mhfaapiyeeya hini miyeewi yeesfeki hkwinamooweneki chiine meci nihki nitasi weeci piicfaacki

Enter ye in by the narrow gate: for wide is the gate, and broad is the way, that leadeth to destruction, and many be they that enter in thereby.

14. ksake maackwaalakatoofi hini skwaate mecimi wiiseya hini miyeewi yeesfeki lenaweewiiweneki chiine laakofwihi nihki meemhkakki hini

For narrow is the gate, and straitened the way, that leadeth unto life, and few be they that find it.

15. mahkeeni miyaasi maamoosikiiskwecki peepiyeelotoolwaakwe meekiifiwi piitenikaneki payeekwa pkameewi mhhweewaki laameki nihki

Beware of false prophets, which come to you in sheep's clothing, but inwardly are ravening wolves.

16. homawifoowenwa ke hoci kiilawa waakomaawaaki nihki ha hileniiki kaawiisehi hotatenaanaawa mhfaloomi weelaa kicimi hahfawikaanaskohi

By their fruits ye shall know them. Do men gather grapes of thorns, or figs of thistles?

17. teetepilahi yooni caaki howesi mhtekwi hoci niikinwi howesi mawifoowe weeka hini waskalhki mhtekwi hoci niikinwi macaafi mawifoowe

Even so every good tree bringeth forth good fruit; but the corrupt tree bringeth forth evil fruit.

18. howesi mhtekwi hoci haalwi niikinwi mecaafiki mawifoowe mata nohki waskalhki mhtekwi hoci katawi niikinwi howesi mawifoowe

A good tree cannot bring forth evil fruit, neither can a corrupt tree bring forth good fruit.

19. caaki mhtekwi pwaayaa hoci niikiki howesi mawifoowe kawhoote mecimi hini skoteeki hipakitoote

Every tree that bringeth not forth good fruit is hewn down, and cast into the fire.

20. weecikeenahi homawifoowenwa ke hoci kiilawa waakomaawaaki nihki

Therefore by their fruits ye shall know them.

21. mata caakiwiyeefa teepeelemiweeta teepeelemiweeta yeesita weh piicfe hini weefepahkamikiki hokimaawitaamhkwe hina weeka yeesilawiita hini hotesiteheewe nohfa yeepita weefepahkamikiki

Not every one that saith unto me, Lord, Lord, shall enter into the kingdom of heaven; but he that doeth the will of my Father which is in heaven.

22. meci teepeelemiweeta teepeelemiweeta ha mata kiwiifoowe hoci nimoosikiiskwaacimope chiine kiwiifoowe hoci nilohfe pakilaape waninehfiiki mecimi kiwiifoowe nooci lawiipe meci makiici pekatefiiwena ne hikooki hine kaasekiki

Many will say to me in that day, Lord, Lord, did we not prophesy by thy name, and by thy name cast out devils, and by thy name do many mighty works?

23. mecimi hine howe mata kiwaakomelepwa kiilama niila hoci saaweko kiilawa peekatenakki wanaatefiiwe neh si tepaacimohtawaaki nihki

And then will I profess unto them, I never knew you: depart from me, ye that work iniquity.

24. caakiwiyeefa weecikeenahi neenootaka yooloma nikalawiiwena niila mecimi hotesilawihtaana nili weh si takweelemekofi lepwaawi hileni mayectoota yeetaaci wiikiwa hoskici nili siikonali

Every one therefore which heareth these words of mine, and doeth them, shall be likened unto a wise man, which built his house upon the rock:

25. chiine hini keemowaaki laasiwehfenwi chiine nili yaamikamiki piyeeya chiine nili mehsikkaki pootaacikeeya mecimi pkitehfeno hini wiikiwaapeki mecimi hini mata haakicifeeya ksake hini hoskici nili siikonali lahkehfenwi

and the rain descended, and the floods came, and the winds blew, and beat upon that house; and it fell not: for it was founded upon the rock.

26. chiine caakiwiyeefa neenootaka yooloma nikalawiiwena niila mecimi mata nili silawi weh si takweelemekofi wanihsaka hileni mayectoota yeetaaci wiikiwa hoskici hini leekawi

And every one that heareth these words of mine, and doeth them not, shall be likened unto a foolish man, which built his house upon the sand:

27. chiine hini keemowaaki laasiwehfenwi chiine nili yaamikamiki piyeeya chiine nili mehsikkaki pootaacikeeya mecimi pkitehfeno hini wiikiwaapeki mecimi haakicfeeya hini mecimi mhsaawi hini haakicfaawe nitasi

and the rain descended, and the floods came, and the winds blew, and smote upon that house; and it fell: and great was the fall thereof.

28. chiine hini piyeemikatwi hine ciisisii yeh mehcilotaki yooloma kalawiiwena nihki mehseelekki hokwakwehtaaneeletaanaawa hokakehkimiweewe

And it came to pass, when Jesus ended these words, the multitudes were astonished at his teaching:

29. ksake hina hotesi kakehkimahi nihi paasi nekoti peemi poonaka wiyehsimekofiiwe chiine mata paasi hoteewikeemwahi

for he taught them as one having authority, and not as their scribes.

Matthew:8

1. chiine hine ye hoci piyeci paalacsiki hini meekwahkiki meci mehseelekki honeekalaawaali

And when he was come down from the mountain, great multitudes followed him.

2. chiine waapamehko nitasi hopiyeelotaakooli weeskilhakeemekilici mecimi hosasilawehekooli teepeelemiweeta kwehkwi siteheeyane keh katawi fafayaakhi kiila hiwali

And behold, there came to him a leper and worshipped him, saying, Lord, if thou wilt, thou canst make me clean.

3. chiine maa si ciikinhkeelwa holeci mecimi hoteh pehsenaali hiini yeesiteheeya fafayaakhoofolo hiwa mecimi weelena hini hoskilhakeemekiiwe fafayaakitooteeli

And he stretched forth his hand, and touched him, saying, I will; be thou made clean. And straightway his leprosy was cleansed.

4. mecimi waapatano teki wiitamawi hileni weeka nhhaale waapatesi kiiya hina mhkateewkolaye mecimi pakfenano hini miiliweewe teepikeemoci moosisii wahsi hoci teepweeweniwaaci nihki hotelaali ciisisii

And Jesus saith unto him, See thou tell no man; but go thy way, shew thyself to the priest, and offer the gift that Moses commanded, for a testimony unto them.

5. chiine hine ye hottaki keepaaniamii nitasi hopiyeelotaakooli kaptiinali honanahpaacimekooli

And when he was entered into Capernaum, there came unto him a centurion, beseeching him,

6. teepeelemiweeta nitaloolaaka seksinwa hini wiikiwaapeki hahkwiloke hini nenekifiiwe mamiyeenaani hahkwinamwa hotekooli

and saying, Lord, my servant lieth in the house sick of the palsy, grievously tormented.

7. mecimi neh piya chiine neh kiikeha hotelaali

And he saith unto him, I will come and heal him.

8. chiine hina kaptiina haapafse mecimi teepeelemiweeta mata niteepiilefi wahsi kiila piicfaayani siipaaci nitapahkweewe weeka hini kalawiiwe pe hiyolo mecimi nitaloolaaka weh kiikehoofo

And the centurion answered and said, Lord, I am not worthy that thou shouldest come under my roof: but only say the word, and my servant shall be healed.

9. ksake nehfaapi niila wiiwasi hileni simekofiiwe nipoonaaki samaakanaki chiine nhhaale nitela yaama nekoti mecimi hina nhheewa chiine kotaka piyaalo mecimi hina piyeewa chiine nitaloolaaka yooma silawiilo mecimi hina hini silawi hisiwe

For I also am a man under authority, having under myself soldiers: and I say to this one, Go, and he goeth; and to another, Come, and he cometh; and to my servant, Do this, and he doeth it.

10. chiine ciisisii yeh nootaki hini mayacitehe mecimi tepilo kitelepwa niila mata nimeemhka yooni si mehsaaki teepwehseewe mata matalaakwa laa hiswiila hotelahi nihi neeneekalekoci

And when Jesus heard it, he marveled, and said to them that followed, Verily I say unto you, I have not found so great faith, no, not in Israel.

11. chiine kitelepwa niila meci hini weetahkofaki we hoci piyeeki mecimi hini yeepaksimoki chiine weh wiitapiimaawaali heplehemiili chiine haisikiili chiine ceekapiili piitike hini weefepahkamikiki hokimaawitaamhkwe

And I say unto you, that many shall come from the east and the west, and shall sit down with Abraham, and Isaac, and Jacob, in the kingdom of heaven:

12. weeka nihki hini hokimaawitaamhkwe hoci hokwihfimaaki weh si lohfe pakiloofooki hini faakici peepekicaaki nitasi we hahteewi hini wihfakweewe mecimi hini yeetalweki wiipitali

but the sons of the kingdom shall be cast forth into the outer darkness: there shall be the weeping and gnashing of teeth.

13. mecimi nhhaale yehaayani yeesi mehci teepwehseeyani yooni hini hpenaloofolo hotelaali nili kaptiinali ciisisii mecimi hina haloolaaka kiikehoofo hini yaatefaki

And Jesus said unto the centurion, Go thy way; as thou hast believed, so be it done unto thee. And the servant was healed in that hour.

14. chiine hine yeetaalici piitali wiikiwa piitike yeepiyaaci ciisisii honeewaali piita wiiwali hokeeli peemi seksinelici hahkwilokeeli weepikisifoowe

And when Jesus was come into Peter's house, he saw his wife's mother lying sick of a fever.

15. mecimi hoteh pehsileceenaali mecimi hina honakaleko hini weepikisifoowe chiine honhska mecimi homiisamawaali nili

And he touched her hand, and the fever left her; and she arose, and ministered unto him.

16. chiine hine weelaakwiifiki yeepiyeeyaaki nihki hopiyeetawaawaali meci lekoskaakocki waninehfihi mecimi hina kalawiiwe hoci lohfe pakilahi nihi hilefiiwenhhi mecimi hokiikehahi caayahki yeeahkwilokeelici

And when even was come, they brought unto him many possessed with devils: and he cast out the spirits with a word, and healed all that were sick:

17. wahsi menawah hini hokwaawfeki keekalawiki saapwi haisaya hina maamoosikiiskweeta wiila homamena kikatoneewenena mecimi wiiwasi kitesilokeewenena hiyopi

that it might be fulfilled which was spoken by Isaiah the prophet, saying, Himself took our infirmities, and bare our diseases.

18. howe hine ciisisii yeh neewaaci meci mehseelelici kaayaawka wiila miiliwe tepikeemoowe wahsi hini hasowe kaameki haaki

Now when Jesus saw great multitudes about him, he gave commandment to depart unto the other side.

19. chiine nitasi piyeewa yaayawikeeta mecimi keekehkimiwe keh neekalele kookwe-laakwa-kaaci yehaayani hotekooli

And there came a scribe, and said unto him, Master, I will follow thee whithersoever thou goest.

20. mecimi ciisisii nihki waakocehfiiki hopoonaanaawa waasaalako chiine nihki hini menhkwatwi hoci wiskilohfaki hopoonaanaawa hofihfana weeka hina hokwihfali hileni mata hopoona wah tah sekfetooci wiisi hotelaali

And Jesus saith unto him, The foxes have holes, and the birds of the heaven have nests; but the Son of man hath not where to lay his head.

21. chiine kotaka nohki nihki hoci kakehkimaafaki teepeelemiweeta wiilaani leelemilo wahsi nhhihta nhhaaya mecimi lekonaki nohfa hotelaali

And another of the disciples said unto him, Lord, suffer me first to go and bury my father.

22. payeekwa ciisisii neekasilo mecimi nakasi nihki neepekiki wahsi lekonaawaaci nehalwaaka honepoowenwaali hotelaali nili

But Jesus saith unto him, Follow me; and leave the dead to bury their own dead.

23. chiine hine holakeeleki ye lhkaki kakehkimaafhi honeekalekohi

And when he was entered into a boat, his disciples followed him.

24. mecimi waapatamoko nitasi pafekwiiya mhsaawi mehsikkaki hini mhsinepiki weecikeena hini holakeesi petakhooya nili peepookaki payeekwa hina nepeewa

And behold, there arose a great tempest in the sea, insomuch that the boat was covered with the waves: but he was asleep.

25. chiine nihki hopiyeelotawaawaali mecimi hotamacihaawaali nili waapaneshiweelo teepeelemiweeta nitkwiilefipe hiwaki

And they came to him, and awoke him, saying, Save, Lord; we perish.

26. mecimi koociwe kiwiisaalepwaapwa o caki teepwehseefaki kiilawa hotelahi hine howe honhska mecimi hokilhamaata hini mehsikkaki chiine hini mhsinepi mecimi nitasi mhsi kaamehkawanwi

And he saith unto them, Why are ye fearful, O ye of little faith? Then he arose, and rebuked the winds and the sea; and there was a great calm.

27. mecimi nihki hileniiki mayaciteheeki nehiwesi hileni yaama yeesi wiikinaakwi nili mehsikkaki mecimi hini mhsinepi pefetaakoci hiwaki

And the men marveled, saying, What manner of man is this, that even the winds and the sea obey him?

28. chiine hine hini hasowe kaameki yeh si piyaaci piictaamhkwe hini hotasiskiimwa nihki keeteliinaki honakskaakohi nitasi niiswi lekoskaakocki waninehfihi

And when he was come to the other side into the country of the Gadarenes, there met him two possessed with devils,

nili nepoowaalako hoci piyeci lohfehi hanhhiweewi wiyakowehi weecikeenahi mata hini wayeeci si katawi pemhfe hileni

coming forth out of the tombs, exceeding fierce, so that no man could pass by that way.

29. mecimi waapamehko wiyakahootamooki nihki nehiwe nipoonaape wa hpenalelaake kiila hokwihfali maneto ha hotahfa kita wahsi mamiyeenaanhhiyaake wihsi pwaa hini piyeelaakwaamhki hiwaki

And behold, they cried out, saying, What have we to do with thee, thou Son of God? art thou come hither to torment us before the time?

30. howe nitasi pelowihi nihi hoci hapiwa meci nekotweeleka kosko peemi wihfenici

Now there was afar off from them a herd of many swine feeding.

31. chiine hokcihkawaawaali nili nihki waninehfiiki kwehkwi kiila lohfe pakisiyaake hina nekotweeleka kosko leskawinaake hiwaki

And the devils besought him, saying, If thou cast us out, send us away into the herd of swine.

32. mecimi hina nhhaakone hotelahi nihi mecimi nihki piyeci lohfeeki chiine nihi koskohi si piicfeeki mecimi waapamehko hina melhske nekotweeleka kosko hini sehpaamehkiki si paalacipto lekowhaske hini mhsinepiki mecimi hkwinamwa hini nepiki

And he said unto them, Go. And they came out, and went into the swine: and behold, the whole herd rushed down the steep into the sea, and perished in the waters.

33. chiine nihki yeesamaacki nihi hosimooki mecimi weepfeeki hini hoteeweneki heeki mecimi haacimooki caakiwiyehi chiine hini yeesinamelici nihi lekoskaakolici waninehfihi

And they that fed them fled, and went away into the city, and told everything, and what was befallen to them that were possessed with devils.

34. mecimi waapamehko caayahki hina hoteewe piyeci lohfe honakskaakooli ciisisii mecimi hine nihki yeh neewaawaaci nili hokcihkawaawaali wahsi yeeikwihsinowaaci hoci saawelici

And behold, all the city came out to meet Jesus: and when they saw him, they besought him that he would depart from their borders.

Matthew:9

1. mecimi hina holakeeleki lhkamwa chiine kaameki heewa nehalwaaka hototeeweneki si piyeewa

And he entered into a boat, and crossed over, and came into his own city.

2. mecimi waapamehko hopiyeetawaawaali nihki hileniili hahkwilokeeli hini nenekifiiwe seksinooli tfaneki mecimi honeemawahi hoteepwehseewenilici hokwihfima howesilepwaalo kimaciilefiiwena pakfeeletoote hotelaali ciisisii nili yee-hahkwilokeelici hini nenekifiiwe

And behold, they brought to him a man sick of the palsy, lying on a bed: and Jesus seeing their faith said unto the sick of the palsy, Son, be of good cheer; thy sins are forgiven.

3. chiine waapamehko naanekoti nihki yaayawikeecki pahtaamo yaama hileni hiwaki wiiyaawaaki

And behold, certain of the scribes said within themselves, This man blasphemeth.

4. mecimi ciisisii howaakotamawahi hotesiteheewenilici koociwe mecaafiki kitesiteheepwa hiwa

And Jesus knowing their thoughts said, Wherefore think ye evil in your hearts?

5. ksake taaniwe hini halika weecihi wahsi kimaciilefiiwena pakfeeletoote weelaa toke honhskaalo mecimi pemhfeelo hiyoki

For whether is easier, to say, Thy sins are forgiven; or to say, Arise, and walk?

6. weeka wahsi kiilawa menawahi waakotameekwe yeesi hina hokwihfali hileni poonaki simekofiiwe hoskitaamhkwe wahsi pakfeeletaki maciilefiiwena hine howe nili yeekwilokeelici hini nenekifiiwe honhskaalo mecimi mamelo kitfani chiine nhhaale wiikiwa yeetaayani hotelaali nili

But that ye may know that the Son of man hath power on earth to forgive sins (then saith he to the sick of the palsy), Arise, and take up thy bed, and go unto thy house.

7. chiine hina honhska mecimi weepfe yeetaaci wiikiwa heewa

And he arose, and departed to his house.

8. payeekwa nihki mehseelekki yeh neemowaaci hini kaawilaweeki mecimi howahfaacimekohwaawaali manetooli mayehci miilaata simekofiiwe hilenihi

But when the multitudes saw it, they were afraid, and glorified God, which had given such power unto men.

9. chiine yeesi hini hoci pemhfeeci ciisisii honeewaali hileniili mefiyoo yaaloofooli peemahkeepilici yaatah maawatonooteeki tephikeewe mecimi neekasilo hotelaali mecimi hina pafekwi chiine honeekalaali

And as Jesus passed by from thence, he saw a man, called Matthew, sitting at the place of toll: and he saith unto him, Follow me. And he arose, and followed him.

10. chiine hini piyeeya wahsi pemhfeeyaaki yeesi lematapici tah wihfeniki piitike hini wiikiwa waapamehko meci maawatonikehfiiki chiine meciileficki piyeeki chiine howiitapiimaawaali ciisisiili mecimi hokakehkimaafhi

And it came to pass, as he sat at meat in the house, behold, many publicans and sinners came and sat down with Jesus and his disciples.

11. chiine yeh nihki pelesiiki neemowaaci hini koociwe howihpomahi kikakehkimiwemwa nihi maawatonikehfihi chiine meciilefilici hotelaawahi hokakehkimaafhi

And when the Pharisees saw it, they said unto his disciples, Why eateth your Master with the publicans and sinners?

12. payeekwa yeh nootaki hini nihki waasikatowicki mata hotakaawaalaawaali naanatawhcikeelici nihki weeka yeekwilokeecki hiwa

But when he heard it, he said, They that are whole have no need of a physician, but they that are sick.

13. payeekwa nhhaakone mecimi waakotefiko yeeyooyaaki yooma skata niteleeleta kiteminaakweeletiiwe mecimi mata hapenaweewe ksake mata nipiya wahsi natomaki nihki meeyaawiileficki meciileficki weeka

But go ye and learn what this meaneth, I desire mercy, and not sacrifice: for I came not to call the righteous, but sinners.

14. hine howe hotfaawaali nihki caanii hokakehkimaafhi koociwe kitawilahi niilawe chiine nihki pelesiiki nifafahkwi-hocikeepe weeka kikakehkimaafaki mata hocikeeki hiwaki

Then come to him the disciples of John, saying, Why do we and the Pharisees fast oft, but thy disciples fast not?

15. chiine ciisisii ha wih katawi nihki hini hoci hokwihfimaaki mayakinhhaakaneykweewika maweeki laakwasi yeepiimekowaaci nili mayakinhhaakanali payeekwa nili kaasekiki weh piyeeya hine nili mayakinhhaakanali weh mamaakwiiki mecimi hine howe weh fafahkwi hocikeeki hotelahi nihi

And Jesus said unto them, Can the sons of the bride-chamber mourn, as long as the bridegroom is with them? but the days will come, when the bridegroom shall be taken away from them, and then will they fast.

16. chiine mata hileni hotaasi poona maalekhi hoskimota kehta piitenikaneki ksake wa hini si

And no man putteth a piece of undressed cloth upon an old garment; for that

hohkwihfeki mamaakeeya hini piitenika hoci mecimi halika si lelhkehkaaki mectoote

which should fill it up taketh from the garment, and a worse rent is made.

17. mata nohki hileniiki hotaasi poonaanaawa mayaki waiini kehta waiiniiwi pootaalaawahi piilepe nihki wiyehsiwaaki pohkiceskaaki mecimi hini waiini fiikehka chiine nihki wiyehsiwaaki miyaalefiiki weeka hotaasi poonaanaawa nihki mayaki waiini weskilici waiiniiwi pootaalaawahi mecimi neyiiswi kifoskaatiiya

Neither do men put new wine into old wineskins: else the skins burst, and the wine is spilled, and the skins perish: but they put new wine into fresh wineskins, and both are preserved.

18. yeheeyehi kaloolaaci nihi yooma wiyehi waapamehko piyeewa nitasi yeelaapameta mecimi hosasilawehaali nili nitaanehfa teetepilahi howe hkwiilefi payeekwa piyaalo chiine hoskici hina keh si poona kileci mecimi hina weh lenaweewi hisiwe

While he spake these things unto them, behold, there came a ruler, and worshipped him, saying, My daughter is even now dead: but come and lay thy hand upon her, and she shall live.

19. chiine pafekwi ciisisii chiine honeekalaali nili mecimi hokakehkimaafhi kileki

And Jesus arose, and followed him, and so did his disciples.

20. chiine waapamehko hkweewa peepoonaka mhskowilokeewe metahfwi kkato kiteniiswi piyeewa hotaanaaki nili chiine hoteh pehsenamawaali hini ta nhpenikwaateeki hopiitenikanilici

And behold, a woman, who had an issue of blood twelve years, came behind him, and touched the border of his garment:

21. ksake hiwa piitike wiiya mohci kateski pehsenamawake hopiitenika neh mefefihekoopi

for she said within herself, If I do but touch his garment, I shall be made whole.

22. payeekwa ciisisii pemi kokiiwa mecimi hopemi neewaali nili hotanhfima howesilepwaalo kiteepwehseewe neyehka kimefefiheko hotelaali mecimi hina hkweewa mefefihoofo hine hoci yaatefaki

But Jesus turning and seeing her said, Daughter, be of good cheer; thy faith hath made thee whole. And the woman was made whole from that hour.

23. chiine yeh piyaaci ciisisii piitike hini wiikiwa yeetaaci yeelaapamoofota mecimi honeewahi nihi peepikwelici chiine nihi yeefoskaalici pemi tatawaanhkehi

And when Jesus came into the ruler's house, and saw the flute-players, and the crowd making a tumult,

24. miiliweeko teetawaaki ksake mata yo nepwa hina hkweefa nepeewa weeka hisiwe mecimi howaapaleelemaawaali nihki

he said, Give place: for the damsel is not dead, but sleepeth. And they laughed him to scorn.

25. payeekwa nihki yeefoskaacki yeh lohfelhkoofowaaci piicfe chiine hoteh fakileceenaali nili mecimi hina hkweefa honhska

But when the crowd was put forth, he entered in, and took her by the hand; and the damsel arose.

26. chiine yooma waawiinekofiiwe hotasi hoci weepfeeya mefhiike hini hasiskiiki heeya

And the fame hereof went forth into all that land.

27. chiine yeesi hini hoci pemhfeeci ciisisii niiswi kakeepiikweewi lenihi honeekalekohi pemi wiyakahootamohi poonamawinaake kiteminaakweeletiiwe kiila hokwihfali teepitii lahootamohi

And as Jesus passed by from thence, two blind men followed him, crying out, and saying, Have mercy on us, thou son of David.

28. chiine piitike hini wiikiwa yeh piyaaci hotfekohi nihi keekeepiikweewi lenihi mecimi ciisisii ha

And when he was come into the house, the blind men came to him: and Jesus

kiteepwehseepwa kiilawa yeesi teepiilefiya wahsi yooma silawiiya hotelahi hanhka teepeelemiweeta hotelaawaali nihki

saith unto them, Believe ye that I am able to do this? They say unto him, Yea, Lord.

29. hine howe hoteh pehsenamawahi hoskiisekowilici yeesfeki kiteepwehseewenwa hini hpenaloofoko hotelahi

Then touched he their eyes, saying, According to your faith be it done unto you.

30. mecimi tawenooteeli hoskiisekowa chiine hotepinalekwimahi ciisisii waapatamoko wahsi teki hileni waakotaki hini hiwa

And their eyes were opened. And Jesus strictly charged them, saying, See that no man know it.

31. payeekwa nihki weepfeeki mecimi holhfwaatotaanaawa howaawiinekofiiwe mefhiike hini hasiskiiki

But they went forth, and spread abroad his fame in all that land.

32. chiine yeesi weepfeewaaci nihki waapamehko nitasi piyeetaakwi keekeepileniili lekoskaakota waninehfiili

And as they went forth, behold, there was brought to him a dumb man possessed with a devil.

33. chiine yeh lohfe pakiloofolici nili waninehfiili kalawi hina keekeepileni mecimi nihki mehseelekki kwakwehtaaniteheeki matalaakwa hini yooni si neemoote laa hiswiila hiwaki

And when the devil was cast out, the dumb man spake: and the multitudes marveled, saying, It was never so seen in Israel.

34. payeekwa nihki pelesiiki nili hokimaawoosaakanwaali nihki waninehfiiki hoci katawi lohfe pakilahi waninehfihi hiwaki

But the Pharisees said, By the prince of the devils casteth he out devils.

35. chiine mefhiike nili hoteewena mecimi nili hoteeweneefa paamhfe ciisisii pemi kakehkimiwe homhsikamikomwaaki chiine pemi nanahimiwe hini howesi piyeetaacimoowe hini hokimaawitaamhkwe hoci mecimi pemi kiikehiwe caayahki si katoneewe mecimi caayahki si hahkwilokeewe

And Jesus went about all the cities and the villages, teaching in their synagogues, and preaching the gospel of the kingdom, and healing all manner of disease and all manner of sickness.

36. payeekwa yeh neewaaci nihi mehseelelici hokiteminaakweelemahi nihi ksake kwiilahsiteheeki nihki chiine lhfweskaaki paasi meekiifaki pwaa pemi poonaacki kehcitawahekowaaci

But when he saw the multitudes, he was moved with compassion for them, because they were distressed and scattered, as sheep not having a shepherd.

37. hine howe hotelahi hokakehkimaafhi hini kawaskwhaawe sapkahi maaletwi payeekwa nihki peekateficki maatfwihi

Then saith he unto his disciples, The harvest truly is plenteous, but the labourers are few.

38. mamaatomehko weecikeenahi hina teepeeletaka hini kawaskwhaawe wahsi hini leskawaaci paapekatefilici hokawaskwhaaweneki

Pray ye therefore the Lord of the harvest, that he send forth labourers into his harvest.

Matthew:10

1. chiine hoteh wihkomahi hokakehkimaafhi metahfwi-kite-niiswi mecimi homiilahi nihi haliwi simekofiiwe noota wiyakilehfihi wahsi lohfe pakilaawaaci nihi

And he called unto him his twelve disciples, and gave them authority over unclean spirits, to cast them out, and to

mecimi wahsi kiikehiweewaaci caayahki si katoneewe chiine caayahki si hahkwilokeewe

heal all manner of disease and all manner of sickness.

2. howe nili howiifoowenwa nihki metahfwi-kite-niiswi hepastaliiki halayooloma hina nhhihta saimanii piita yaaloofota mecimi hoceeninaali heenhtlooli ceemhsii nili hokwihfali sepetii mecimi hoceeninaali caaniili

Now the names of the twelve apostles are these: The first, Simon, who is called Peter, and Andrew his brother; James the son of Zebedee, and John his brother;

3. filapii chiine pafalamiyo taamosii chiine mefiyoo hina maawatonikehfi ceemhsii nili hokwihfali helhfiasi chiine fatiyasii

Philip, and Bartholomew; Thomas, and Matthew the publican; James the son of Alphaeus, and Thaddaeus;

4. saimanii hina keenaniiwileni chiine cootas' hiskeeletii niliini memestaawimekoci nehfaapi

Simon the Cananaean, and Judas Iscariot, who also betrayed him.

5. yohooni metahfwi-kite-niiswi ciisisii howaawiinahi mecimi hotepinalekwimahi nihi teki nihki nanahkawileniiki wayeeci haako mecimi teki hottamawehko wiyehsi hototeewenwa semeliaki

These twelve Jesus sent forth, and charged them, saying, Go not into any way of the Gentiles, and enter not into any city of the Samaritans:

6. weeka nhhaakone kaaciika nihki waaniiwi meekiifaki hini hiswiila yeetfwikeeci hoci hisiwe

but go rather to the lost sheep of the house of Israel.

7. mecimi yeele haayeekwe nanahimiweeko hini weefepahkamikiki hokimaawitaamhkwe howe maalaakwahi hisiweeko

And as ye go, preach, saying, The kingdom of heaven is at hand.

8. kiikehehko nihki yeekwilokeecki honhskaanehko nihki neepekiki fafayaakhehko nihki weeskilhakeemekicki lohfe pakilehko waninehfiiki kikisaachekoopwa kiilawa kisaaci miiliweeko

Heal the sick, raise the dead, cleanse the lepers, cast out devils: freely ye received, freely give.

9. teki mameko hofaawimoni weelaa teki waapimoni weelaa teki hofaawakokwa kimonipiitaakanwaaki

Get you no gold, nor silver, nor brass in your purses;

10. mata hale piitaakaniko yeelaamiiyeekwe mata nohki niiswi kootiiwali weelaa mhkifena weelaa haapathoowe ksake hina peekatefita nahiika hikweelemekofi howihfeniiwe

no wallet for your journey, neither two coats, nor shoes, nor staff: for the labourer is worthy of his food.

11. chiine kookwe-nehi-si hoteewe weelaa hoteewenehi kiilawa ke hottaanaawa natonehohko neefawe hini piitike teepi leelemekofi mecimi nitasi hapiko paalohi kiilawa weepfeeyeekwe

And into whatsoever city or village ye shall enter, search out who in it is worthy; and there abide till ye go forth.

12. chiine yeesi piicfaayeekwe hini wiikiwa hosilawaatamoko hini

And as ye enter into the house, salute it.

13. chiine hini wiikiwa teepi leelemekofiiyaake wiilaani kikaamaaniilefiiwenwa hoskici weh si piyeeya hini weeka hini pwaa teepi leelemekofiiyaake wiilaani peteki kiilawa wi heeya kikaamaaniilefiiwenwa

And if the house be worthy, let your peace come upon it: but if it be not worthy, let your peace return to you.

14. chiine kookwe-neefa-kaaci mata ke hotahpenekowa weelaa mata hopefetaana kikalawiiwenwa yeesi lohfaayeekwe hini wiikiwa weelaa hini hoteewe kifitwaaki hoci pawatenamoko hini pekwi

And whosoever shall not receive you, nor hear your words, as ye go forth out of that house or that city, shake off the dust of your feet.

15. tepilo kitelepwa niila hini we haliwi kaakilweewefiiya hini saatamiiwi hasiski mecimi hini komaalawi hasiski hini tah ceeyehkwahkoweewi kiisekiki noota yooma hoteewe

Verily I say unto you, It shall be more tolerable for the land of Sodom and Gomorrah in the day of judgment, than for that city.

16. waapatamoko nikiteleskoolepwa paasi meekiifaki hini heele mhhweewhi lepwaawefiko weecikeenahi paasi manetooki mecimi nanahpaaciilefiko paasi miyaasipawiifaki

Behold, I send you forth as sheep in the midst of wolves: be ye therefore wise as serpents, and harmless as doves.

17. payeekwa mahkeeni hileniiki ksake nihki tepoweewena keh si pakfenekowaaki chiine homhsikamikomwaaki keh lihfiiwanhhokowaaki nihki

But beware of men: for they will deliver you up to councils, and in their synagogues they will scourge you;

18. hanhka mecimi yeelahfamiiwaaci kapenaliiki chiine hokimaaki keh si piyeelekoopwa ksake niila hoci wahsi ksake nihki teepweewenhkaawaaci chiine nihki nanahkawileniiki

yea and before governors and kings shall ye be brought for my sake, for a testimony to them and to the Gentiles.

19. payeekwa hine nihki mesenelwaakwe teki wiisaafiiko wah saiyeekwe weelaa wah kalawiyeekwe ksake hini keh miilekoopwa hine yaatefaki wah kalawiyeekwe

But when they deliver you up, be not anxious how or what ye shall speak: for it shall be given you in that hour what ye shall speak.

20. ksake mata hini kiilawa kikalawipwa weeka nili hocacaalahkwali kohfwa kalawiili kiiyaawaaki

For it is not ye that speak, but the Spirit of your Father that speaketh in you.

21. chiine hoceeninaana weh si pakfenaali hoceeninaanali hkwinamooweneki mecimi hina hohfima hotapelohfemali chiine hapelohfaki weh pafekwicfatawaawahi kehkiyaamhi mecimi hotpenalaawahi wahsi hkwinamooweneki si poonoofolici

And brother shall deliver up brother to death, and the father his child: and children shall rise up against parents, and cause them to be put to death.

22. chiine keh siikeelemekofiimekowaaki caayahki hileniiki ksake niwiifoowe hoci payeekwa hina nahiika yehkwi wiisikiteheeta hiina weh waapaneshoofo

And ye shall be hated of all men for my name's sake: but he that endureth to the end, the same shall be saved.

23. payeekwa nihki hofaamhelwaakwe yooma hoteeweneki lesimoko hini maalaakwahi kotaki ksake kitelepwa niila mata kitah mehci saapwiipwa nili hototeewena hiswiila paalohi hina piyeewa hokwihfali hileni

But when they persecute you in this city, flee into the next: for verily I say unto you, Ye shall not have gone through the cities of Israel, till the Son of man be come.

24. kakehkimaafa mata haliwi hilefi keekehkimekoci weelaa mata haloolaaka haliwi teepeelemekoci

A disciple is not above his master, nor a servant above his lord.

25. teepi hini wahsi hina kakehkimaafa hilefici paasi keekehkimekoci mecimi hina haloolaaka paasi teepeelemekoci kwehkwi nihki piyeelhsipalii mehci sinaawaate nili hini hoci wiikiwa mesteleli taaniwe si halika nihi yeetaalici hoci

It is enough for the disciple that he be as his master, and the servant as his lord. If they have called the master of the house Beelzebub, how much more shall they call them of his household!

26. teki kwfehko weecikeenahi ksake mata hahteewi wiyehi petakhoote yah pwaa hini pahkaseenoote mecimi kikitoote yah pwaa hini waakotoote

Fear them not therefore: for there is nothing covered, that shall not be revealed; and hid, that shall not be known.

27. kiilawa weewiitamoolako hini laa pepekica kalawiko hini laa wayahfeeyaaki mecimi neenootameekwe hini hotawakaaki kiilawa lhfwaatotamoko hoskici nili wiikiwaapi hakocikami

What I tell you in the darkness, speak ye in the light: and what ye hear in the ear, proclaim upon the housetops.

28. chiine teki kwfehko nihki naanhfaacki nili wiyawfiwiiyaanali payeekwa haalwi katawefiiki wahsi nhfaawaaci nili mayaawiwiiyaanali weeka kwfehko kaaciika hina teeteepi hilefita wahsi macilotawaaci neyiiswi mayaawiwiiyaanali mecimi wiyawfiwiiyaanali hahkwinamooweneki

And be not afraid of them which kill the body, but are not able to kill the soul: but rather fear him which is able to destroy both soul and body in hell.

29. ha mata nekoti mhskwakokwe si miyeekipi niiswi hoteeweniwiskilohfaki mecimi mata nekoti nihki hini hoskitaamhkwe weh si penhsinwa faakici kohfwa

Are not two sparrows sold for a farthing? and not one of them shall fall on the ground without your Father:

30. weeka tepilo nili kiilehfwa caayahki kikinootakite

but the very hairs of your head are all numbered.

31. teki kwsiweeko weecikeenahi haliwi kiteleelemekofipwa kiilawa noota meci hoteeweniwiskilohfaki

Fear not therefore; ye are of more value than many sparrows.

32. caakiwiyeefa weecikeenahi neh mohkaaci tepaaci haacimekwa yeelahfamiiwaaci hileniiki nehfaapi niila hina neh mohkaaci tepaaci haacima yeelahfamiici nohfa weefepahkamikiki yeepita

Every one therefore who shall confess me before men, him will I also confess before my Father which is in heaven.

33. weeka kookwe-neefa-kaaci neh kiyaacimekwa yeelahfamiiwaaci hileniiki nehfaapi neh kiyaacima hina yeelahfamiici nohfa weefepahkamikiki yeepita

But whosoever shall deny me before men, him will I also deny before my Father which is in heaven.

34. teki siteheeko yeesi piyaaya wahsi hini hoskitaamhkwe sfatooya kaamaaniilefiiwe mata nipiya wahsi piyeci fatooya kaamaaniilefiiwe kiskhika weeka

Think not that I came to send peace on the earth: I came not to send peace, but a sword.

35. ksake nipiya wahsi hileni pakicihkaatiimaaci hohfali lahkeephaki chiine hina hotaanhfima nili hokeeli mecimi hina hohfemima nili weesilemaaci hkweeli

For I came to set a man at variance against his father, and the daughter against her mother, and the daughter in law against her mother in law:

36. mecimi hileni homateeletiiwenhhi we hilefihi nehalwaaka yeetaaci hoci

and a man's foes shall be they of his own household.

37. hina yeeahkweelemaata hofimaali weelaa hokeeli haliwi noota niila nootkweelemekofi niiya mecimi hina yeeahkweelemaata hokwihfimaali weelaa hotaanhfimaali haliwi noota niila nootkweelemekofi niiya

He that loveth father or mother more than me is not worthy of me; and he that loveth son or daughter more than me is not worthy of me.

38. chiine hina peepwaa mameka hotaasitehfekiimi mecimi ninaawalwi neekalekwa nootkweelemekofi niiya

And he that doth not take his cross and follow after me, is not worthy of me.

39. hina meemhkaka hotelenaweewiiwe weh wanhto hini mecimi hina weewanhtoota hotelenaweewiiwe niila hoci we mhka hini

He that findeth his life shall lose it; and he that loseth his life for my sake shall find it.

40. hina kiilawa we hotahpenelwaakwe nootahpenekwa niila mecimi hina we hotahpenita niila hotahpenaali nili weewaawiinilici

He that receiveth you receiveth me, and he that receiveth me receiveth him that sent me.

41. hina we hotahpenaata maamoosikiiskwelici hini howiifooweneki maamoosikiiskweeta we hotfeko maamoosikiiskweeta hotephofiiwe mecimi hina we hotahpenaata tepasawi-leniili hini howiifooweneki tepasawi-leni we hotfeko tepasawi-leni hotephofiiwe

He that receiveth a prophet in the name of a prophet shall receive a prophet's reward; and he that receiveth a righteous man in the name of a righteous man shall receive a righteous man's reward.

42. chiine kookwe-neefa-kaaci weh miilaali wahsi menelici nekoti yohoma meciloofilici nekoti tephika pehi tehkaki nepi hini howiifooweneki kakehkimaafa tepilo kitelepwa niila mata we hina wiyehisi wanhto hotephofiiwe

And whosoever shall give to drink unto one of these little ones a cup of cold water only, in the name of a disciple, verily I say unto you, he shall in no wise lose his reward.

Matthew:11

1. chiine hini piyeemikatwi hine ciisisii homehci tepikeemahi metahfwi-kite-niiswi hokakehkimaafhi hini hoci weepfe wahsi kakehkimiweeci mecimi nanahimiweeci hoteewenwaaki

And it came to pass, when Jesus had made an end of commanding his twelve disciples, he departed thence to teach and preach in their cities.

2. howe hine caanii yeh nootaakeeci hini kiphotiiweneki nili hopekatefiiwena hina klaistii hoteh mecicimahi hokakehkimaafhi

Now when John heard in the prison the works of the Christ, he sent by his disciples,

3. mecimi ha kiiya hina peepiyaata weelaa toke nih natawaapamaape kotaka hotelaali

and said unto him, Art thou he that cometh, or look we for another?

4. mecimi ciisisii haapafse chiine nhhaakone mecimi wiitamawehko caanii nili wiyehi kiilawa neenootameekwe chiine neeneemeyeekwe

And Jesus answered and said unto them, Go your way and tell John the things which ye do hear and see:

5. nihki keekeepiikweecki hotfekonaawa tepinamoowe chiine nihki meemiyaalakatowikaateecki pemooteeki nihki weeskilhakeemekicki fafayaakhoofooki chiine nihki keekeepseeki nootaakeeki chiine nihki neepekiki honhskaanoofooki chiine nihki kitemaafaki hopoonaanaawa howesi piyeetaacimoowe nanahimoofooki

the blind receive their sight, and the lame walk, the lepers are cleansed, and the deaf hear, and the dead are raised up, and the poor have good tidings preached to them.

6. chiine kisaateelemekofi hina kookwe-neefa-kaaci mata we mhka wa hoci hotakikahsineki niiyaaki hotelaali nihi

And blessed is he, whosoever shall find none occasion of stumbling in me.

7. chiine yeesi yohkoma haawaaci yehaawaaci ciisisii hotalemi hilahi nihi mehseelelici caaniili hisi nehiwe kiilawa kimah waapataanaawa weeci hini piileski si lohfaayeekwe ha mhfaskwalwi naanoomilohanwi

And as these went their way, Jesus began to say unto the multitudes concerning John, What went ye out into the wilderness to behold? a reed shaken with the wind?

8. weeka nehiwe kimah waapataanaawa weeci lohfaayeekwe ha hileni piitenike skanoofi piitenika waapamehko nihki paapiitenakki skanoofi piitenika hapiiki piitike hokimaawikaana

But what went ye out for to see? a man clothed in soft raiment? Behold, they that wear soft raiment are in kings' houses.

9. payeekwa koociwe kiilawa kilohfaapwa ha wahsi neeweekwe maamoosikiiskweeta haanhka kitelepwa niila mecimi mecilekhi si halika maamoosikiiskweeta

But wherefore went ye out? to see a prophet? Yea, I say unto you, and much more than a prophet.

10. hina yaama weeci hini mehtawikeeki waapami niteleskawa nimiisamaakeema yeelahfamiiyani hina weh nanahihfeto kimiyeewi yeelahfamiiyani kiila

This is he, of whom it is written, Behold, I send my messenger before thy face, Who shall prepare thy way before thee.

11. tepilo kitelepwa niila heelekiina nihki hkwehi neeniikinekocki mata meh pafekwi nitasi halika yeelefita caaniili hina fafahkwiholelhiweewena payeekwa hina meciloofita piitike hini weefepahkamikiki hokimaawitaamhkwe halika hilefi noota hina

Verily I say unto you, Among them that are born of women there hath not arisen a greater than John the Baptist: yet he that is but little in the kingdom of heaven is greater than he.

12. chiine hine hokakiisekanema caanii fafahkwiholelhiweewena hoci paalohinoki hini weefepahkamikiki hokimaawitaamhkwe hahkwimawinahkaate mecimi mawinahkeewi leniiki homamiiloowilotaanaawa hini

And from the days of John the Baptist until now the kingdom of heaven suffereth violence, and men of violence take it by force.

13. ksake caayahki nihki maamoosikiiskwecki mecimi hini kwteletiiwe moosikiiskwaacimooki paalohi caaniili

For all the prophets and the law prophesied until John.

14. chiine kwehkwi kiilawa wahsi hotahpenameekwe siteheeyeekwe hilaica yaama hina waasa piyaata

And if ye are willing to receive it, this is Elijah, which is to come.

15. hina peepoonaka hotawakaawali wahsi nootaakeeci wiilaani nootaakeete hina

He that hath ears to hear, let him hear.

16. payeekwa taaniwe niila neh si hilawaatota yooma hinoki skwiiwe paasi hini hilefiiki hapelohfaki peemi lematapicki nili yaatah wiiwiitkiiki nihki howaawihkomaawahi howiicikwakwileniimwahi

But whereunto shall I liken this generation? It is like unto children sitting in the marketplaces, which call unto their fellows,

17. mecimi kipepikwehtoolepe mecimi mata kimenyeelepwa nimaweewahootaape mecimi mata kimawepwa yaawaki

and say, We piped unto you, and ye did not dance; we wailed, and ye did not mourn.

18. ksake caanii piyeewa mata pemi wihfeni nohki mata pemi menwa mecimi hopoonaali waninehfiili hiwaki nihki

For John came neither eating nor drinking, and they say, He hath a devil.

19. hina hokwihfali hileni piyeewa pemi wihfeni mecimi pemi menwa mecimi nihki waapamehko pkamefiwi-leni chiine maci weenefo wihkaanwaali teeksiiwi-maawatonikehfiiki chiine meciileficki hiwaki mecimi lepwaawe hotepasawhekona hopekatefiiwena

The Son of man came eating and drinking, and they say, Behold, a gluttonous man, and a winebibber, a friend of publicans and sinners! And wisdom is justified by her works.

20. hine howe hotalemi lhskitaana nili hoteewena ta halika tfeki hopekatefiiwena mayehci lawiiki ksake nihki mata mataiini siteheeki

Then began he to upbraid the cities wherein most of his mighty works were done, because they repented not.

21. macilepwaawe cehi kiila si kolesinii macilepwaawe cehi kiila si pefseite ksake kwehkwi neyehka nili makiici pekatefiiwena mehci lawiike taayaaki chiine saataniiki mayehci lawiiki kiiyaaki neyehka nihki sehkamika wih mehci mataiini siteheeki piitaakanimotaaki mecimi pekoki

Woe unto thee, Chorazin! woe unto thee, Bethsaida! for if the mighty works had been done in Tyre and Sidon which were done in you, they would have repented long ago in sackcloth and ashes.

22. payeekwa kitelepwa niila we hini haliwi kaakilweewefiiya taayaa chiine saatenii hini hine ceeyehkwahkoweewi kaasekiki noota kiilawa

Howbeit I say unto you, it shall be more tolerable for Tyre and Sidon in the day of judgment, than for you.

23. chiine kiila keepaaniamii ha weefepahkamikiki keh si moospeelemekofihekoopi sahkiki kiila ke ha hahkwinamooweneki ksake kwehkwi neyehka mehci lawiike nili makiici pekatefiiwena saatamiiki mayehci lawiiki kiiyaaki yaska hini we hahteewi paalohinoki kaasekiki

And thou, Capernaum, shalt thou be exalted unto heaven? thou shalt go down unto Hades: for if the mighty works had been done in Sodom which were done in thee, it would have remained until this day.

24. payeekwa kitelepwa niila we hini haliwi kaakilweewefiiya hini saatamiiwi hasiski hini hine ceeyehkwahkoweewi kaasekiki noota kiila

Howbeit I say unto you, that it shall be more tolerable for the land of Sodom in the day of judgment, than for thee.

25. hine laakwa ciisisii haapafse mecimi hiwa niyaawe kiila hohfima teepeeletaka weefepahkamikiki mecimi hasiskitaamhkwe yeesi kiila sapkahi kkitawaci yooloma wiyehi lepwaawefita mecimi nenohseewefita chiine sapkahi kipahkinamawaaki nili hapelohfeefaki

At that season Jesus answered and said, I thank thee, O Father, Lord of heaven and earth, that thou didst hide these things from the wise and understanding, and didst reveal them unto babes:

26. hanhka hohfima ksake yooni yeesi hini menwilaasamamooweniki kitelaapiiweneki hiwa

yea, Father, for so it was well-pleasing in thy sight.

27. caayahki wiyehi neyehka nimehci piyeci pakfenamaakwa nohfa mecimi mata nekoti howaakomaali nili hokwihfimaali weeciwephi hina hohfima mata nohki sapkahi wiyeefa howaakomaali nili hohfimaali weeciwephi hina hokwihfima mecimi hina kookwe-neefali-kaaci hina hokwihfima sitehe wahsi pahkinamawaaci nili

All things have been delivered unto me of my Father: and no one knoweth the Son, save the Father; neither doth any know the Father, save the Son, and he to whomsoever the Son willeth to reveal him.

28. piyeelotawiko caayahki kiilawa paapekateficki kweekofekolaakwicki chiine keh miilelepwa halwaakahsiiwe

Come unto me, all ye that labour and are heavy laden, and I will give you rest.

29. mameko nifakikwehoowe mecimi waakotefiko niila ksake ninanahpaaciilefi mecimi ninanahpaaciteheeweni chiine ke mhkaanaawa kiilawa halwaakahsiiwe mayaawikiiyaanwaaki

Take my yoke upon you, and learn of me; for I am meek and lowly in heart: and ye shall find rest unto your souls.

30. ksake nifakikwehoowe weecihiwatwi chiine niwiiwasiiwe laakanoofi

For my yoke is easy, and my burden is light.

Matthew:12

1. hine laakwa ciisisii weepfe hini ta halwaakahsi kiisekiki hale saapwi nili kawaskwiktikaana chiine hokakehkimaafhi skwaalawehi mecimi nihki hotalemi kiskikwenaanaawa hini wahsi miiciwaaci

At that season Jesus went on the sabbath day through the cornfields; and his disciples were an hungred, and began to pluck ears of corn, and to eat.

2. payeekwa nihki pelesiiki yeh neemowaaci hini waapami kikakehkimaafaki yeesilawiiwaaci hini pwaayaa mayaawhki kwteletiiweneki wahsi lawiiki ta halwaakahsi kiisekiki hotekohi

But the Pharisees, when they saw it, said unto him, Behold, thy disciples do that which it is not lawful to do upon the sabbath.

3. payeekwa ha mata kimeh laapaatotaanaawa yeesilawiici teepitii yeh skwaalaweeci chiine nihi weewiitfemekoci

But he said unto them, Have ye not read what David did, when he was an hungred, and they that were with him;

4. yeesi piicfaaci hini howiikiwaapimi maneto chiine homiici hini hofepi takhwa pwaayaa hini mayaawhki kwteletiiweneki wahsi wiila miicici mata nohki nihi weewiitfemekoci weeka nihki mhkateewkolayeeki pehi hotelahi

how be entered into the house of God, and did eat the shewbread, which it was not lawful for him to eat, neither for them that were with him, but only for the priests?

5. weelaa ha mata kimeh laapaatotaanaawa hini kwteletiiweneki yeesi nihki mhkateewkolayeeki miyaastoowaaci hini halwaakahsi kaasekiki piitike hini mamaatomeewikamikwi ta halwaakahsi kiisekiki mecimi mata macilawiiki

Or have ye not read in the law, how that on the sabbath day the priests in the temple profane the sabbath, and are guiltless?

6. payeekwa kitelepwa niila yeesi nekoti halika hilefi noota hini mamaatomeewikamikwi hotasi hapici

But I say unto you, that one greater than the temple is here.

7. weeka neyehka waakotameekwe yeeyooyaaki yooma skata niteleeleta kiteminaakweeletiiwe mecimi mata hapenaweewe mata kitah meh pakitaamaawaaki pwaayaa macilawiicki

But if ye had known what this meaneth, I desire mercy, and not sacrifice, ye would not have condemned the guiltless.

8. ksake hina hokwihfali hileni teepeeletaka hini halwaakahsi kaasekiki

For the Son of man is lord of the sabbath.

9. chiine hini hoci weepfe mecimi homhsikamikomwaaki si piicfe

And he departed thence, and went into their synagogue:

10. chiine waapamehko hileni hopoona hahkapwileceewe mecimi nihki honatohtawaawaali nili ha mayaawatwi hini kwteletiiweneki wahsi kiikehiweeki ta hini halwaakahsi kiisekiki hiwaki wahsi menawahi mestaawimaawaaci nihki

and behold, a man having a withered hand. And they asked him, saying, Is it lawful to heal on the sabbath day? that they might accuse him.

11. mecimi hina neefawe hileni nitasi hapiwa kiilawa weh poonaali nekoti meekiifali chiine kwehkwi yooloma waasaalakoki si penhsinooli ta hini halwaakahsi kiisekiki ha mata hina hotah si fookinaali mecimi hokokwitapilaali nili hotelahi

And he said unto them, What man shall there be of you, that shall have one sheep, and if this fall into a pit on the sabbath day, will he not lay hold on it, and lift it out?

12. taaniwe lekhi si haliwi weecikeena hileni leelemekofi noota meekiifa yooni hoci hini

How much then is a man of more value than a sheep! Wherefore it is lawful to do good on the sabbath day.

mayaawatwi kwteletiiweneki wahsi weeowesaaki
silawiiki ta hini halwaakahsi kiisekiki

13. hine howe hina ciikileceskaalo hotelaali nili
hileniili chiine hina maa si ciikileceska mecimi hini
peteki meftooteeli paasi hini hasowe kotaki

Then saith he to the man, Stretch forth
thy hand. And he stretched it forth; and
it was restored whole, as the other.

14. payeekwa nihki pelesiiki lohfeeki mecimi
hotepowaalaawaali nili wahsi nihki menawahi
macilotawaawaaci nili

But the Pharisees went out, and took
counsel against him, how they might
destroy him.

15. chiine ciisisii homooleeleta hini mecimi hini hoci
saawe mecimi meci honeekalaawaali nili mecimi hina
hokiikehahi caayahki nihi

And Jesus perceiving it withdrew from
thence: and many followed him; and he
healed them all,

16. chiine hotepinalekwimahi nihi wahsi pwaa nihki
waakomekofihaawaaci nili

and charged them that they should not
make him known:

17. wahsi hini menawahi hokwaawfeki keekalawiki
saapwi haisaya hina maamoosikiiskweeta

that it might be fulfilled which was
spoken by Isaiah the prophet, saying,

18. waapamehko nitaloolaaka mayehci mamaka
nitahkweeletiima niliini mayaawiniiyaana
menweelemaaci hoskici hina neh si poona
nicacaalahkwa chiine weh mohkaatotamawahi
mehtahkoweewe nihi nanahkawilenihi

Behold, my servant whom I have
chosen; My beloved in whom my soul is
well pleased: I will put my Spirit upon
him, And he shall declare judgment to
the Gentiles.

19. mata weh mawinahke weelaa holaamahootamwa
mata nohki wiyeefa weh nootamawaali
hotesihsimoowe laa nili hoteewenimiyeewena

He shall not strive, nor cry aloud;
Neither shall any one hear his voice in
the streets.

20. sesekwafkooteeki mhfaskwalwi mata weh poska
mecimi mafaanali peemi liiwafikeelici mata we
hahtehwaali paalohi hina kolepkaaweeweneki sfatoote
mehtahkoweewe

A bruised reed shall he not break, And
smoking flax shall he not quench, Till he
send forth judgment unto victory.

21. mecimi howiifoowenilici weh si nihki
nanahkawileniiki nanaaciteheeki hiyopi

And in his name shall the Gentiles hope.

22. hine howe piyeetaakwi nekoti holekoskaakooli
waninehfiili kakeepiikwe mecimi kipitonwa mecimi
hina hokiikehaali nili teepi lekhi wahsi hina
kipitoneewileni kalawici mecimi tepinaki

Then was brought unto him one
possessed with a devil, blind and dumb:
and he healed him, insomuch that the
dumb man spake and saw.

23. mecimi caayahki nihki mehseelekki
kwakwehtaaniteheeki chiine kanhha yaama nili
hokwihfali teepitii hiwaki

And all the multitudes were amazed, and
said, Is this the son of David?

24. payeekwa hine nihki pelesiiki yeh nootamowaaci
hini mata yaama hileni holohfe pakilahi waninehfihi
piyeelhsipaliili hoci weeka nili
hokimaawoosaakanwaali nihki waninehfiiki hiwaki

But when the Pharisees heard it, they
said, This man doth not cast out devils,
but by Beelzebub the prince of the
devils.

25. mecimi hina howaakota yeesiteheewenilici caakisi
hokimaawiiwe pahfehkaatiiya liikatahkamikifiiweneki
si piyeetoote chiine caaki hoteewe weelaa wiikiwa
pahfehkaatiiya mata yah niipawiiya hotelahi

And knowing their thoughts he said unto
them, Every kingdom divided against
itself is brought to desolation; and every
city or house divided against itself shall
not stand:

26. chiine kwehkwi setenii lohfe pakilaate seteniili pahfehkaati hina nehiwe howe weh si niipawiiyaali hookimaawiiwe

and if Satan casteth out Satan, he is divided against himself; how then shall his kingdom stand?

27. chiine kwehkwi niila piyeelhsipalii hoci katawi lohfe pakilake waninehfiiki neefaliwe kikwihfwaaki hoci katawi lohfe pakilaawahi nihi weecikeenahi nihki ke hotepasawahkowemipwa

And if I by Beelzebub cast out devils, by whom do your sons cast them out? therefore shall they be your judges.

28. weeka kwehkwi niila nili maneto hocacaalahkwali hoci katawi lohfe pakilake waninehfiiki howe keela hini hookimaawiiwe maneto kimatalekonaawa

But if I by the Spirit of God cast out devils, then is the kingdom of God come upon you.

29. weelaa nehiwe wih si katawi piicfe wiyeefa hini yeetaalici wiikiwa nili wiisikileniili mecimi macilotamawaali howiyehiimilici weeciwephi hina nhhihta kciipilaate nili wiisikileniili mecimi hine chiine weh macilotamawaali yeetaalici wiikiwa

Or how can one enter into the house of the strong man, and spoil his goods, except he first bind the strong man? and then he will spoil his house.

30. hina peepwaa wiiciimita nippehtenekwa chiine hina peepwaa wiici maawatonikeemita lhfwenike

He that is not with me is against me; and he that gathereth not with me scattereth.

31. weecikeenahi kitelepwa niila caakisi maciisilawiiwe mecimi pahtaamoowe weh pakfeeletamaakwiiki hileniiki weeka hini hopahtaamoofoowe hina hocacaalahkwa mata yah pakfeeletoote

Therefore I say unto you, Every sin and blasphemy shall be forgiven unto men; but the blasphemy against the Spirit shall not be forgiven.

32. chiine kookwe-neefa-kaaci we ppehcimaali kalawiiwe nili hokwihfali hileni hini weh pakfeeletamaakwi hina weeka kookwe-neefa-kaaci we ppehcimaali nili hofepi hocacaalahkwali mata hini yah pakfeeletamaakwi hina neyiisweelena mata hotasi yeelekokwahkamikiki mecimi hini piitike waasa piyeeyaaki

And whosoever shall speak a word against the Son of man, it shall be forgiven him; but whosoever shall speak against the Holy Spirit, it shall not be forgiven him, neither in this world, nor in that which is to come.

33. weelaa howestooko hini mhtekwi mecimi hini mawifoowe howesa weelaa miyaastooko hini mhtekwi mecimi hini mawifoowe miyaaletwi ksake hini mhtekwi hini mawifoowe hoci waakotoote

Either make the tree good, and its fruit good; or make the tree corrupt, and its fruit corrupt: for the tree is known by its fruit.

34. kiilawa leewaki hotoosaakanaki nehiwe kih si katawi kiilawa meciilefiyeekwe kalawipwa howesi wiyehi ksake hini hotehi si maalefiiwe hoci kalawiiya hini hotooni

Ye offspring of vipers, how can ye, being evil, speak good things? for out of the abundance of the heart the mouth speaketh.

35. hina howesi hileni howesi hopaweeweneki hoci piyeeto howesi wiyehi chiine hina meciilefita hileni homaci paweeweneki hoci piyeeto macaafi wiyehi

The good man out of his good treasure bringeth forth good things: and the evil man out of his evil treasure bringeth forth evil things.

36. chiine kitelepwa niila caakisi nelohci kalawiiwe keekalawiwaaci hileniiki weh miiliweeki tepasawaacimoowe nitasi hine ceeyehkwahkoweewi kaasekiki

And I say unto you, that every idle word that men shall speak, they shall give account thereof in the day of judgment.

37. ksake kikalawiiwena kiila ke hoci tepasawhekoopi mecimi kikalawiiwena ke hoci matahkowaalekoopi

For by thy words thou shalt be justified, and by thy words thou shalt be condemned.

38. hine howe naanekoti nihki yaayawikeecki chiine pelesiiki hotaapaftawaawaali nili keekehkimiwe nih neemepe kikinooloowe kiila hoci hisiweeki

Then certain of the scribes and Pharisees answered him, saying, Master, we would see a sign from thee.

39. payeekwa hina haapafse mecimi maciilefi chiine waapasiphikeewefi skwiiwena honatoneha kikinooloowe mecimi mata weh miilaawa kikinooloowe weeka hini coona hokikinooloowe hina maamoosikiiskweeta hotelahi nihi

But he answered and said unto them, An evil and adulterous generation seeketh after a sign; and there shall no sign be given to it but the sign of Jonah the prophet:

40. ksake yeesi coona nhfwi kiiskwe mecimi nhfwi tepokwe hapici hopehkwataaki hina mhsi namehfilehfi yooni weh si hina hokwihfali hileni hapici nhfwi kiiskwe mecimi nhfwi tepokwe hini hotehiki hina hasiskitaamhkwe

for as Jonah was three days and three nights in the belly of the whale; so shall the Son of man be three days and three nights in the heart of the earth.

41. nihki nenifa hoci leniiki weh niipawiiki hine ceeyehkwahkoweeweneki wiici yooloma skwiiwenali mecimi weh mataamaawaali ksake nihki mataiini siteheeki ta hini honanahimiweewilici coonali mecimi waapamehko haliwi yeelefita noota coona hotasi hapiwa

The men of Nineveh shall stand up in the judgment with this generation, and shall condemn it: for they repented at the preaching of Jonah; and behold, a greater than Jonah is here.

42. hina hini yeelaawahkweeki hoci hokimaawiyhkwe weh pafekwi hine ceeyehkwahkoweeweneki wiici yooloma skwiiwenali mecimi weh mataamaali ksake hina hini yeeikwihkwihfeki hini hasiskitaamhkwe hoci piyeewa wahsi nootaki hini holepwaawe salamanii mecimi waapamehko haliwi yeelefita noota salamanii hotasi hapiwa

The queen of the south shall rise up in the judgment with this generation, and shall condemn it: for she came from the ends of the earth to hear the wisdom of Solomon; and behold, a greater than Solomon is here.

43. weeka hina wiyakilehfi hine nili hileniili ye hoci lohfaaci pemi saapwi pemhfe tah pwaa-laakwasi hahteeki nepi hopemi natoneha halwaakahsiiwe mecimi hini hokwiila

But the unclean spirit, when he is gone out of the man, passeth through waterless places, seeking rest, and findeth it not.

44. hine howe peteki ne ha yeetaaya wiikiwa weeci piyeci lohfaaya hiwa mecimi hine yeh piyaaci homhka hini sesipaaya ciikathoote mecimi waawesihkate

Then he saith, I will return into my house whence I came out; and when he is come, he findeth it empty, swept, and garnished.

45. hine howe nhheewa mecimi hokilekina wiiya niiswahfwi kotakhi lehfihi haliwi si maciilefihi noota wiila chiine nihki piicfeeki mecimi nitasi teeki mecimi hini ceeyehkwi hotelefiiwe hina hileni haliwi si macaafi noota hini weski teetepilahi yooni nehfaapi we hisi namoci yaama maci skwiiwena

Then goeth he, and taketh with himself seven other spirits more evil than himself, and they enter in and dwell there: and the last state of that man becometh worse than the first. Even so shall it be also unto this evil generation.

46. yeheeyehi keewaki kaloolaaci nihi mehseelelici waapamehko hokeeli mecimi hoceeninahi faakici niipawihi peemi natonehamelici wahsi kaloolekoci

While he was yet speaking to the multitudes, behold, his mother and his brethren stood without, seeking to speak to him.

47. mecimi wiyeefali waapami kikiya chiine kiceeninaaki faakici niipawiiki peemi natonehamowaaci wahsi kaloolehki hotekooli

And one said unto him, Behold, thy mother and thy brethren stand without, seeking to speak to thee.

48. payeekwa haapafse mecimi neefawe nikiya mecimi neefakiwe niceeninaaki hotelaali nili weewiitamaakoci

But he answered and said unto him that told him, Who is my mother? and who are my brethren?

49. mecimi maa si ciikinhkeeska hokakehkimaafhi wayeeci chiine waapamehko nikiya chiine niceeninaaki

And he stretched forth his hand towards his disciples, and said, Behold, my mother and my brethren!

50. ksake kookwe-neefa-kaaci we hini silawi hotesiteheewe nohfa yeepita weefepahkamikiki hina niceenina chiine nitikweema mecimi nikiya hiwa

For whosoever shall do the will of my Father which is in heaven, he is my brother, and sister, and mother.

Matthew:13

1. hine hini kaasekiki hini wiikiwaapeki hoci lohfe ciisisii mecimi pakaci hini mhsinepi lematapiwa

On that day went Jesus out of the house, and sat by the sea side.

2. mecimi nitasi meci mehseelelici homaawatoskaamekohi weecikeena holakeeleki lhkamwa mecimi lematapiwa mecimi caayahki hina mehseeleka hini skwaapiyeeki niipawi

And there were gathered unto him great multitudes, so that he entered into a boat, and sat; and all the multitude stood on the beach.

3. chiine hokaloolahi nihi meci wiyehi pemaatoweeweneki waapamehko hisiwe hina yeeahcikeeta weepfe wahsi hahcikeeci

And he spake to them many things in parables, saying, Behold, the sower went forth to sow;

4. mecimi yeesi hina hahcikeeci naaleta miinhkaana hini pakacikana si penhfeno mecimi nihki wiskilohfaki piyeeki chiine hocaakataanaawa nili

and as he sowed, some seeds fell by the way side, and the birds came and devoured them:

5. chiine kotakali hini tah siikonahkiki si penhfeno tah pwaa weeyahka hahteeki hasiski mecimi weelena nili faakino ksake mata weeyahka spihfenwi hasiski

and others fell upon the rocky places, where they had not much earth: and straightway they sprang up, because they had no deepness of earth:

6. mecimi hine hina kiisekikiisfwa yeh piyeetahkofaki sahte nili chiine ksake mata hoceepkahkatowi nepote nili

and when the sun was risen, they were scorched; and because they had no root, they withered away.

7. chiine kotakali laa nihi kaawiisehi si penhfeno mecimi nihki kaawiiseki skwiniikiiki chiine honepwaskwehtoonaawa nili

And others fell upon the thorns; and the thorns grew up, and choked them:

8. chiine kotakali hini howesi hasiskiiki si penhfeno mecimi niikinwi mawifoowe naaleta tepeewe tfweekfenwi naaleta nekotwaasi naaleta nhfwaapitaki

and others fell upon the good ground, and yielded fruit, some a hundredfold, some sixty, some thirty.

9. hina peepoonaka hotawakaawali wiilaani nootaakeete

He that hath ears, let him hear.

10. chiine nihki kakehkimaafaki piyeeki mecimi koociwe kiila kikaloolaaki nihki pemaatoweewena hotelaawaali

And the disciples came, and said unto him, Why speakest thou unto them in parables?

11. chiine hina haapafse mecimi kiilawa si miiliweepi hini wahsi waakotameekwe nili hini weefepahkamikiki hokimaawitaamhkwe hoci meeyatki weeka nihki mata si miiliweepi hini

And he answered and said unto them, Unto you it is given to know the mysteries of the kingdom of heaven, but to them it is not given.

12. ksake kookwe-neefa-kaaci hopoona hina weh si miiliweepi mecimi hina weh poona maalefiiwe weeka kookwe-neefa-kaaci mata hopoona weh mamaakwi mohci hini peepoonaki hina

For whosoever hath, to him shall be given, and he shall have abundance: but whosoever hath not, from him shall be taken away even that which he hath.

13. weecikeenahi niila pemaatoweewena nikaloolaaki nihki ksake neekeeki mata tepinamooki nihki chiine nootaakeeki mata tepehseeki nihki mata nohki nenohseeki nihki

Therefore speak I to them in parables; because seeing they see not, and hearing they hear not, neither do they understand.

14. mecimi nihki si hokwihfetoote hini homoosikiiskweewe haisaya yeeyooyaaki nootaakeewe ke hoci nootaakeepwa kiilawa mecimi mata keh wiyehisi nenohseepwa chiine nekeewe ke hoci neekeepwa kiilawa mecimi mata keh wiyehisi neewiweepwa

And unto them is fulfilled the prophecy of Isaiah, which saith, By hearing ye shall hear, and shall in no wise understand; And seeing ye shall see, and shall in no wise perceive:

15. ksake yaama lenawe hotehi halalika si kofekwanwi mecimi hotawakaawa nootaakeewe si sekwano chiine hoskiisekowa neyehka pefakokwiinooki nihki piilepe nihki hoskiisekowa wi hoci neewiweeki mecimi hoci nootaakeeki hotawakaawa mecimi hoci nenohseeki hotehiwa chiine wi kotekwiiki nohki mecimi nih kiikehaaki nihki

For this people's heart is waxed gross, And their ears are dull of hearing, And their eyes they have closed; Lest haply they should perceive with their eyes, And hear with their ears, And understand with their heart, And should turn again, And I should heal them.

16. payeekwa kiilawa kisaateelemekwato kiskiisekowa ksake nili tepinamooya mecimi kitawakaawa ksake nili nootaakeeya

But blessed are your eyes, for they see; and your ears, for they hear.

17. ksake tepilo kitelepwa niila yeesi meci maamoosikiiskwecki mecimi tepasawi-leniiki maatawi neemowaaci nili wiyehi kiilawa neeneemeyeekwe mecimi mata honeemenaawa nili

For verily I say unto you, that many prophets and righteous men desired to see the things which ye see, and saw them not; and to hear the things which ye hear, and heard them not.

18. nootamoko kiilawa weecikeena hini hopemaatowaafoowe hina yeeahcikeeta

Hear then ye the parable of the sower.

19. hine wiyeefa yeh nootaki hini hoci kalawiiwe hini hokimaawitaamhkwe mecimi mata nenohse hini hine hina howe piyeewa maciwiyeefa mecimi hokwakwatenamaakooli hini mayehci hahtooteelici hotehiki hina yaama yeeahcikeeki hini pakacikana

When any one heareth the word of the kingdom, and understandeth it not, then cometh the evil one, and snatcheth away that which hath been sown in his heart. This is he that was sown by the way side.

20. chiine hina yeeahcikeeki tah nili siikonakiki hina yaama neenootaka hini kalawiiwe mecimi weelena howesilepwaawi hotahpena hini

And he that was sown upon the rocky places, this is he that heareth the word, and straightway with joy receiveth it;

21. keewaki mata hopoona hoceepkahkatwi wiiyaaki payeekwa wiisikifi maalaakwasihi mecimi kiisenaacinamoowe weelaa naanohkaachetiiwe yeh pafekwiiyaalici ksake hini kalawiiwe hoci weelena hotakikahsinwa hina

yet hath he not root in himself, but endureth for a while; and when tribulation or persecution ariseth because of the word, straightway he stumbleth.

22. chiine hina yeeahcikeeki heelekiina nihi kaawiisehi hina yaama neenootaka hini kalawiiwe mecimi hini hotamefiiwe hini yeelekokwahkamikiki hoci chiine hini pawaawena hoci wanimefiiwe nepwaskweyaali hini kalawiiwe mecimi mata mawifooewe niwi hina

And he that was sown among the thorns, this is he that heareth the word; and the care of the world, and the deceitfulness of riches, choke the word, and he becometh unfruitful.

23. chiine hina yeeahcikeeki hini howesi hasiskiiki hina yaama neenootaka hini kalawiiwe mecimi nenohse hini yoona tepilo honiikto mawifooewe mecimi hopiyeeto naaleta tepeewe tfweekfenwi naaleta nekotwaasi naaleta nhfwaapitaki

And he that was sown upon the good ground, this is he that heareth the word, and understandeth it; who verily beareth fruit, and bringeth forth, some a hundredfold, some sixty, some thirty.

24. kotaki nohki pemaatoweewe hoteh pakfenamawahi yeelahfamiilici nihi hini weefepahkamikiki hokimaawitaamhkwe paasi hileni yeetoota howesi miinhka hoktikaaneki si takweelemekwatwi

Another parable set he before them, saying, The kingdom of heaven is likened unto a man that sowed good seed in his field:

25. payeekwa yeheeyehi nepaalici hilenihi homateeletiiwenali piyeeli hotitaakooli nehfaapi miyaasiwasko heelekiina hini kawaskwi chiine weepfeeli

but while men slept, his enemy came and sowed tares also among the wheat, and went away.

26. payeekwa yeh faakipakiki hini mecimi niipeki hine howe nookwato nili miyaasiwasko nehfaapi

But when the blade sprang up, and brought forth fruit, then appeared the tares also.

27. chiine nihi hotaloolaakanhhi piyehi hina teepeeletaka wiikiwa yeeleniwiyani ha mata howesi miinhka kitito kiktikaaneki howe taaniwe hocifeya nili miyaasiwasko hotekohi

And the servants of the householder came and said unto him, Sir, didst thou not sow good seed in thy field? whence then hath it tares?

28. mecimi mateeletiiwena yeesilawiici yooma hotelahi chiine ha nine haape howe wahsi mecimi maawatonamaake nili hotekohi nihi haloolaakanhhi

And he said unto them, An enemy hath done this. And the servants say unto him, Wilt thou then that we go and gather them up?

29. payeekwa mata hotelahi piilepe keh wiici pohkwahkeenanaawa hini kawaskwi yeesi maawatonameekwe nili miyaasiwasko

But he saith, Nay; lest haply while ye gather up the tares, ye root up the wheat with them.

30. wiilaani neyiiswi wi skwiniikino nekotwesi paalohi hini kawaskwhaaweke mecimi hini laakwaanike hini kawaskwhaawe maawatonamoko nhhihta nili miyaasiwasko mecimi hafipitooko nili wahsi fakfameekwe weeka hini kawaskwi

Let both grow together until the harvest: and in the time of the harvest I will say to the reapers, Gather up first the tares, and bind them in bundles to burn them: but gather the wheat into my barn.

nikawaskwikaaneki si maawatonamoko ne hilaaki nihki keekawaskwhaawecki hotelahi

31. nohki kotaki pemaatoweewe hoteh pakfenamawahi yeelahfamiilici nihi hini weefepahkamikiki hokimaawitaamhkwe paasi nekoti pekwe mastatiiwi miinhka hinwi meemameki hileni mecimi hotito hoktikaaneki

Another parable set he before them, saying, The kingdom of heaven is like unto a grain of mustard seed, which a man took, and sowed in his field:

32. hiini sapkahi kci hotahpi lekokwa caayahki miinhkaana payeekwa yeh katemooyaaki hini haliwi hinwi noota nili memekinasko mecimi mhtekoniwi weecikeenahi nihki wiskilohfaki hini menhkwatwi hoci piyeeki mecimi nili si lwahsinooki peepkeeyakoki hiwa

which indeed is less than all seeds; but when it is grown, it is greater than the herbs, and becometh a tree, so that the birds of the heaven come and lodge in the branches thereof.

33. nohki kotaki pemaatoweewe hokaloolahi nihi hini weefepahkamikiki hokimaawitaamhkwe paasi hini honalescika meemameki hkweewa hinwi mecimi hokkito nhfwi tepacikaneki lokhaana paalohi hini caayahki honete hiwa

Another parable spake he unto them; The kingdom of heaven is like unto leaven, which a woman took, and hid in three measures of meal, till it was all leavened.

34. caayahki yooloma wiyehi ciisisii hokaloolahi pemaatoweeweneki nihi mehseelelici mecimi faakici pemaatoweewe mata wiyehi hokaloolahi nihi

All these things spake Jesus in parables unto the multitudes; and without a parable spake he nothing unto them:

35. wahsi menawah hini hokwihfeki yeeyoki saapwi hina maamoosikiiskweeta pemaatoweewena neh si tawena nitooni ne haatota wiyehi kikifooya hine hoskahkehfenwi hini yeelekokwahkamikiki hoci

that it might be fulfilled which was spoken by the prophet, saying, I will open my mouth in parables; I will utter things hidden from the foundation of the world.

36. hine howe honakalahi nihi mehseelelici mecimi hini wiikiwa si piicfe chiine hokakehkimaafhi hotfekohi mecimi tepinaakwi wiitamawinaake hini pemaatoweewe nili si hini laa ktika miyaasiwasko hotekohi

Then he left the multitudes, and went into the house: and his disciples came unto him, saying, Explain unto us the parable of the tares of the field.

37. mecimi haapafse chiine hina yehahtoota hini howesi miinhka hokwihfali hileni hina

And he answered and said, He that soweth the good seed is the Son of man;

38. chiine hini ktika yeelekokwahkamikiki hini chiine hini howesi miinhka yohkooni nihki hini hokimaawitaamhkwe hoci hokwihfimaaki chiine nili miyaasiwasko nihiini hokwifhi hina maciwiyeefa

and the field is the world; and the good seed, these are the sons of the kingdom; and the tares are the sons of the evil one;

39. chiine hina mateeletiiwena yeeahtoota nili macimaneto hina chiine hini kawaskwhaawe hini yeekwaaki hini yeelekokwahkamikiki chiine nihki keekawaskwhaawecki henhcaliiki nihki hiwa

and the enemy that sowed them is the devil: and the harvest is the end of the world; and the reapers are angels.

40. yeesi weecikeenahi maawatonooteeki nili miyaasiwasko mecimi fakfooteeki skoteeki yooni we hiki hine ceeyehkwahkamikike

As therefore the tares are gathered up and burned with fire; so shall it be in the end of the world.

41. hina hokwihfali hileni weh waawiinahi hotenhcaliimhhi mecimi nihki hini

The Son of man shall send forth his angels, and they shall gather out of his

hokimaawitaamhkwemi we hoci maawatwi lohfenaanaawa caayahki wiyehi weeci pemi hotakikahsineki mecimi nihi mecaafiki yeesilawiilici

kingdom all things that cause stumbling, and them that do iniquity,

42. chiine hini weh si piicfe pakilaawahi nihi keesiteeki skote nitasi weh pemi wihfakweeweni mecimi hini weh talweewehfeno wiipitali

and shall cast them into the furnace of fire: there shall be the weeping and gnashing of teeth.

43. hine howe nihki meeyaawiileficki weh wahfefamooki paasi hina kiisekikiisfwa piitike hini hokimaawiiwenilici hofwaali hina peepoonaka hotawakaawali wiilaani nootaakeete

Then shall the righteous shine forth as the sun in the kingdom of their Father. He that hath ears, let him hear.

44. hini weefepahkamikiki hokimaawitaamhkwe paasi pawaawe hinwi kikitoote hini ktikaaneki meemhkaki hileni mecimi hokkito chiine weepfe hale howesilepwaaweni mecimi hina homiyeeke caayahki peepoonaki mecimi hotepena hini ktika

The kingdom of heaven is like unto a treasure hidden in the field; which a man found, and hid; and in his joy he goeth and selleth all that he hath, and buyeth that field.

45. nohki hini weefepahkamikiki hokimaawitaamhkwe paasi hileni hinwi waatkiita hopemi natonehwahi howesi miikeefhi

Again, the kingdom of heaven is like unto a man that is a merchant seeking goodly pearls:

46. mecimi homehci mhkawaali nekoti miikeefali keesoweelemekofilici weepfe hina mecimi homiyeeke caayahki peepoonaki mecimi hotepenaali nili

and having found one pearl of great price, he went and sold all that he had, and bought it.

47. nohki hini weefepahkamikiki hokimaawitaamhkwe paasi haakwaskwhaaka hinwi ye hipakitooteeki hini mhsinepiki mecimi maawatonikeeya caaki yehteelici

Again, the kingdom of heaven is like unto a net, that was cast into the sea, and gathered of every kind:

48. hini ye hokwihfeki nihki hotahpenaanaawa skwaapiyeekiisi mecimi nihki lematapiiki chiine hoteh maawatonaawahi nihi weelefilici nili poonahfocikana weeka nihi metefiifilici hotpakilaawahi

which, when it was filled, they drew up on the beach; and they sat down, and gathered the good into vessels, but the bad they cast away.

49. yooni we hiki hini hine ceeyehkwahkamikike nihki henhcaliiki weh piyeeki mecimi weh pkinaawahi nihi meciilefilici heelekiina hoci nihi meeyaawiilefilici

So shall it be in the end of the world: the angels shall come forth, and sever the wicked from among the righteous,

50. chiine ni weh si piicfe pakilaawahi nihi keesiteeki skote nitasi weh pemi wihfakweeweni mecimi hini weh talweewehfeno wiipitali

and shall cast them into the furnace of fire: there shall be the weeping and gnashing of teeth.

51. ha kinenohseepwa kiilawa caayahki yooloma wiyehi hanhka hotelaawaali nihki

Have ye understood all these things? They say unto him, Yea.

52. chiine weecikeenahi caaki yaayawikeeta mayehci kakehkimaafihoofota hini weefepahkamikiki hokimaawitaamhkwe hisi paasi hileni hilefi teepeeletaka wiikiwa hina hopiyeci lohfato hopawaawe hoci wiyehi hoskinwi mecimi kehta hotelahi nihi

And he said unto them, Therefore every scribe who hath been made a disciple to the kingdom of heaven is like unto a man that is a householder, which bringeth forth out of his treasure things new and old.

53. chiine hini piyeemikatwi yeh mehcilotaki ciisisii yooloma pemaatoweewena nhhoci weepfe

And it came to pass, when Jesus had finished these parables, he departed thence.

54. chiine wiila hotasiskiimeki si pemi piyeewa hokakehkimahi nihi piitike homhsikamikomwaaki weecikeenahi nihki cihsiteheeki chiine taaniwe hoci poona yaama hileni yooma lepwaawe mecimi yooloma makiici pekatefiiwena hiwaki

And coming into his own country he taught them in their synagogue, insomuch that they were astonished, and said, Whence hath this man this wisdom, and these mighty works?

55. ha mata yaama hina hotkwipekatefiiwileni hokwihfali ha mata hokeeli melii yaaloofooli chiine hoceeninahi ceemhsiili chiine coosiili chiine saimaniili chiine cootasiili

Is not this the carpenter's son? is not his mother called Mary? and his brethren, James, and Joseph, and Simon, and Judas?

56. mecimi hotikwemhhi ha mata caayahki nihki wiici kiilawe taaniwe howe hoci poonaana yaama hileni caayahki yooloma wiyehi

And his sisters, are they not all with us? Whence then hath this man all these things?

57. mecimi hokisfekowaali nili payeekwa ciisisii maamoosikiiskweeta mata pwaa hahteeli hotakeelemekofiiwe weeciwephi nehalwaaka hotasiskiimeki mecimi yeetaaci wiikiwa hotelahi

And they were offended in him. But Jesus said unto them, A prophet is not without honour, save in his own country, and in his own house.

58. chiine sapkahi mata meci silawi makiici pekatefiiwena nitasi ksake mata teepwehseewenihi

And he did not many mighty works there because of their unbelief.

Matthew:14

1. hine laakwa heletii hina nekotehfepati-hokima nootaake hini yeelaacimoofolici ciisisiili

At that season Herod the tetrarch heard the report concerning Jesus,

2. mecimi caanii yaama hina fafahkwiholelhiwena honhska hina nili nepelici hoci mecimi hini weeci yooloma waasikaki pekatefiiyaalici wiiyaaki hotelahi nihi hotaloolaakanhhi

and said unto his servants, This is John the Baptist; he is risen from the dead; and therefore do these powers work in him.

3. ksake heletii homehci mesenaali caaniili mecimi hokiciipilaali chiine kiphotiiweneki hoteh poonaali ksake nili helootiasiili hocihaali wiiwali filapii hoceeninaali heletii

For Herod had laid hold on John, and bound him, and put him in prison for the sake of Herodias, his brother Philip's wife.

4. ksake mata hini mayaawatwi kwteletiiweneki wahsi kiila poonaci hina hotekooli caaniili

For John said unto him, It is not lawful for thee to have her.

5. chiine yeh wiisa neyehka nhfaaci nili hokwfahi nihi mehseelelici ksake nihki maamoosikiiskweeta hotelakimaawaali nili

And when he would have put him to death, he feared the multitude, because they counted him as a prophet.

6. payeekwa yeh piyeeyaaki heletii honiikiiwi kaasekiki nili hotaanehfali helootiasii menyeelooli hini heelekhi mecimi homenwi lepwahekooli heletii

But when Herod's birthday came, the daughter of Herodias danced in the midst, and pleased Herod.

7. hiini hoci mehcimiwe kileki ciikinhkemoowe wahsi miilaaci nili kookwe-nehi-kaaci hina wih natota

Whereupon he promised with an oath to give her whatsoever she should ask.

8. chiine hina hopemi niinhkaakooli hokeeli miiliko hotasi mhsi seswilaakaneki hini wiisi caanii hina fafahkwiholelhiwena hisiwe

And she, being put forward by her mother, saith, Give me here in a charger the head of John the Baptist.

9. chiine macilepwa hina hokima payeekwa ksake nili hociikinhkemoowena chiine nihi weewiitapiimekoci tah wihfeniki hoci tepikeemo wahsi hini miiliweeki

And the king was grieved; but for the sake of his oaths, and of them which sat at meat with him, he commanded it to be given;

10. mecimi waawiinhke chiine hokiskikwethwaali caaniili hini kiphotiiweneki

and he sent, and beheaded John in the prison.

11. chiine wiisi hina piyeetoote mhsi seswilaakaneki mecimi miiloofo hina hkweefa mecimi hina hopiyeetawaali hini hokeeli

And his head was brought in a charger, and given to the damsel: and she brought it to her mother.

12. chiine hina hokakehkimaafhi piyehi chiine nihki homamaawaali nili wiiyaanali mecimi holekonaawaali chiine weepfeeki nihki mecimi howiitamawaawaali ciisisiili

And his disciples came, and took up the corpse, and buried him; and they went and told Jesus.

13. howe yeh nootaki hini ciisisii nhhoci saawe holakeelho tah papskwahkiki heewa naanhsihka chiine nihki mehseelekki yeh nootaakeewaaci yooma honeekalaawaali nili hoteewena hoci ktohfeeki

Now when Jesus heard it, he withdrew from thence in a boat, to a desert place apart: and when the multitudes heard thereof, they followed him on foot from the cities.

14. chiine piyeci weepfe hina mecimi honeewahi meci mehseelelici chiine hokiteminaakweelemahi chiine hokiikehtawahi hotahkwilokeemilici

And he came forth, and saw a great multitude, and he had compassion on them, and healed their sick.

15. chiine ye holaakwiifiki nihki kakehkimaafaki hotfaawaali ceh papskwahki hotasi chiine hini kaasekiki neyehka pemhfeeya haameskawi nihki mehseelekki wahsi menawah haawaaci nili hoteeweneefa mecimi tepenamowaaci wihfeniiwe pesikwi wiilawa hotelaawaali

And when even was come, the disciples came to him, saying, The place is desert, and the time is already past; send the multitudes away, that they may go into the villages, and buy themselves food.

16. payeekwa ciisisii nelohci nihki wih weepfeeki miilehko wah miiciwaaci hotelahi

But Jesus said unto them, They have no need to go away; give ye them to eat.

17. chiine nihki nipoonaape hotasi niyaalanwi payeekwa weepskweeteewali chiine niiswi namehfaki hotelaawaali

And they say unto him, We have here but five loaves, and two fishes.

18. chiine piyeetawiko nili maatasi hisiwe

And he said, Bring them hither to me.

19. mecimi hotepimahi nihi mehseelelici wahsi lematapilici sahkiki hoskici nili mhskotehkwalo chiine hoteh mamena nili niyaalanwi weepskweeteewali mecimi nihi niiswi namefhi chiine spemeki pemi laapi menhkwatoki kisaatefi chiine hoposkonaana mecimi hoteh miilahi nihi kakehkimaafhi nili weepskweeteewali chiine nihki kakehkimaafaki hoci nihi mehseelelici

And he commanded the multitudes to sit down on the grass; and he took the five loaves, and the two fishes, and looking up to heaven, he blessed, and brake and gave the loaves to the disciples, and the disciples to the multitudes.

20. chiine wihfeniiki caayahki mecimi teephoolooki chiine nihki homaawatonaanaawa seskwatooteeki nili peekskehkaaki hoci metahfwi-kite-niiswi soosooniwali hokwihfeno

And they did all eat, and were filled: and they took up that which remained over of the broken pieces, twelve baskets full.

21. mecimi nihki weewihfenicki nawito niyaalane metahfene tepeewe hileniiki tepaane hkweeki chiine hapelohfaki

And they that did eat were about five thousand men, beside women an children.

22. chiine weelena howihkwihkawahi nihi kakehkimaafhi wahsi hini holakeeleki lhkamelici chiine wahsi hini hasowe kaameki si niikaaniilici paalohi wi haameskawahi nihi mehseelelici

And straightway he constrained the disciples to enter into the boat, and to go before him unto the other side, till he should send the multitudes away.

23. mecimi yeh mehci haameskawaaci nihi mehseelelici hini meekwahkiki si kkwicsinwa naanhsihka wahsi mamaatomeeci chiine naanhsihka nitasi hapiwa ye holaakwiifiki

And after he had sent the multitudes away, he went up into the mountain apart to pray: and when even was come, he was there alone.

24. weeka hini holakeesi howe hini laawtekwe hini mhsinepi piyeethanwi hokwiilahsilepwahekonaawa nili peepookaki ksake honakskaanaawa hini mehsikkaki

But the boat was now in the midst of the sea, distressed by the waves; for the wind was contrary.

25. chiine hini mawi-niyeewene kcitawaafiiwe hini tepehki hotfahi pemi ktohfe hoskitepiye hini mhsinepi

And in the fourth watch of the night he came unto them, walking upon the sea.

26. mecimi nihki kakehkimaafaki yeh neewaawaaci pemi ktohfeeli hoskitepiye hini mhsinepi petfakiteheeki nihki hina ciipa hiwaki mecimi wiyakahootamooki ksake kaawilaweeki

And when the disciples saw him walking on the sea, they were troubled, saying, It is an apparition; and they cried out for fear.

27. payeekwa weelena ciisisii hotelahi howesilepwaako niila hina teki kih kaawilawepwa hisiwe

But straightway Jesus spake unto them, saying, Be of good cheer; it is I; be not afraid.

28. mecimi piita hotaapaftawaali teepeelemiweeta kiilaawiyane hina piyaalo hisilo wahsi piyeelotoola hoskitepiye hini nepiki hisiwe

And Peter answered him and said, Lord, if it be thou, bid me come unto thee upon the waters.

29. mecimi hina piyaalo hotelaali chiine piita laasiwe hini holakeeleki hoci mecimi hini hoskitepiye nepiki pemhfe mecimi hopiyeelotawaali ciisisiili

And he said, Come. And Peter went down from the boat, and walked upon the waters, to come to Jesus.

30. payeekwa yeh neemeki hini mehsikkaki kaawilawe mecimi halemi kooki wiyakahootamwa teepeelemiweeta waapaneshilo hisiwe

But when he saw the wind, he was afraid; and beginning to sink, he cried out, saying, Lord, save me.

31. mecimi weelena ciisisii maa si ciikileceska hoteh fookinaali chiine o kiila caki teepwehseefa nehiwe kooci haanwehse hotelaali

And immediately Jesus stretched forth his hand, and took hold of him, and saith unto him, O thou of little faith, wherefore didst thou doubt?

32. chiine nihki spemeki hini holakeeleki ye haawaaci nakeeska hini mehsikkaki

And when they were gone up into the boat, the wind ceased.

33. chiine nihki holakeeleki yeepicki hosasilawehaawaali nili teepweewe hina hokwihfali maneto kiila hisiweeki

And they that were in the boat worshipped him, saying, Of a truth thou art the Son of God.

34. chiine yeh mehci kapaawaaci nihki hini hasiskiiki si piyeeki kinesoletiiwi taamhkwe

And when they had crossed over, they came to the land, unto Gennesaret.

35. chiine nihki nitasi hoci hileniiki yeh waakomaawaaci nili mefhiike si waawiinhkeeki hini

And when the men of that place knew him, they sent into all that region round

kaayaawkitaamhkwe chiine hopiyeetawaawaali caayahki yeekwilokeelici

about, and brought unto him all that were sick;

36. mecimi hokatowamaaawaali wahsi menawahke kateski pehsenamawaawaaci hini ta nhpenikwaateelici hopiitenika chiine yeetfwi pehsenamowaaci mefefihoofooki

and they besought him that they might only touch the border of his garment: and as many as touched were made whole.

Matthew:15

1. hine howe nitasi hotfaawaali ciisisiili colooseelemii hoci pelesiiki chiine yaayawikeecki

Then there come to Jesus from Jerusalem Pharisees and scribes, saying,

2. koociwe kikakehkimaafaki holaalhfwaacilotaanaawa hini hokehtaacimoowenwa nihki kikileniiki ksake mata kaakifilecaaki yeh miiciwaaci takhwa hisiweeki

Why do thy disciples transgress the tradition of the elders? for they wash not their hands when they eat bread.

3. mecimi hotaapaftawahi chiine koociwe kiilawa nehfaapi kilaalhfwaacilotaanaawa hini hotepikeemoowe maneto ksake kikehtaacimoowenwa hoci hotelahi

And he answered and said unto them, Why do ye also transgress the commandment of God because of your tradition?

4. ksake maneto hotakeelemi kohfa chiine kikiya mecimi hina meemacikaloolaata hofimaali weelaa hokeeli wiilaani hina nepeke hini nepoowe hiwa

For God said, Honour thy father and thy mother: and, He that speaketh evil of father or mother, let him die the death.

5. weeka kiilawa kookwe-neefa-kaaci we hilaali hohfali weelaa hokeeli hini mayehci menawahke neyehka hotwaafiiyani niila hoci hini miiloofo maneto

But ye say, Whosoever shall say to his father or his mother, That wherewith thou mightest have been profited by me is given to God;

6. teki hina we hotakeelemaali hohfali kitaayopwa mecimi kimatawiyeefekisihtoonaawa hini hokalawiiwe maneto ksake kikehtaacimoowenwa hoci

he shall not honour his father. And ye have made void the word of God because of your tradition.

7. kiilawa nelohcilawiwehfiiki koowesi moosikiiskwaacimekowa haisaya yeeyoci

Ye hypocrites, well did Isaiah prophesy of you, saying,

8. yaama lenawe nootakeelemekwa hoskisaawa hoci weeka hotehiwa pelowaamatwi niiya hoci

This people honoureth me with their lips; But their heart is far from me.

9. payeekwa nelohci niwaaosasilawehekooki pemi kakehkimiweeki kikeemohkaaki nili hileniiki hokikeemoowenwa

But in vain do they worship me, Teaching as their doctrines the precepts of men.

10. chiine hoteh wihkomahi nihi mehseelelici nootaakeeko mecimi nenohseeko

And he called to him the multitude, and said unto them, Hear, and understand:

11. mata hini hotooneki yeesfaaki homaamiyaasheko hileni hini hotooneki weecifaaki weeka yooma hina hileni homaamiyaasheko hotelahi

Not that which entereth into the mouth defileth the man; but that which proceedeth out of the mouth, this defileth the man.

12. hine howe piyeeki nihki kakehkimaafaki mecimi ha kiwaakota yeesi nihki pelesiiki kisfoofowaaci yeh nootamowaaci yooma hiyoowe hotelaawaali

Then came the disciples, and said unto him, Knowest thou that the Pharisees were offended, when they heard this saying?

13. payeekwa haapafse caakisi hahcika pwaayaa hahtooci weefepahkamikiki nohfa weepokwahkiceephoote

But he answered and said, Every plant which my heavenly Father planted not, shall be rooted up.

14. wiilaani nihki nihkiini kakeepiikweewi naakaaniicki mecimi hina keekeepiikweeta niikaaniwelaate nili keekeepiikweelici neyiiswi waasaalakoki weh si penhsinooki hiwa

Let them alone: they are blind guides. And if the blind guide the blind, both shall fall into a pit.

15. chiine piita haapafse tepiwiitamawinaake hini pemaatoweewe hotelaali

And Peter answered and said unto him, Declare unto us the parable.

16. halah nehfaapi wiikinaakwi kiilawa mata keewaki kinootkofipwa nenohseewe

And he said, Are ye also even yet without understanding?

17. ha mata kinenaanaawa yeesi kookwe-nehi-kaaci hini hotooniki heeyaaki hini hopehkwataaki si pemhfeeya mecimi hini si lohfeska wahoci lohfeskaaki

Perceive ye not, that whatsoever goeth into the mouth passeth into the belly, and is cast out into the draught?

18. weeka nili wiyehi hini hotooni weemooyaaki hini hotehiki hoci piyeci lohfeya mecimi niliini homiyaashekona hina hileni

But the things which proceed out of the mouth come forth out of the heart; and they defile the man.

19. ksake hini hotehiki hoci piyeci lohfeya maci memekiniteheewena nhfetiiwena waapasiphikeewena weepeeletiiwena kimootoowena naanhhaaci ciikinhkemoowena lhskimetiiwena

For out of the heart come forth evil thoughts, murders, adulteries, fornications, thefts, false witness, railings:

20. yoolooni nili wiyehi maamiyaashekoci hina hileni weeka wahsi wihfenici pwaa kifilecaate mata homiyaasheko hina hileni hiwa

these are the things which defile the man: but to eat with unwashen hands defileth not the man.

21. chiine nhhoci lohfe ciisisii hini maalaakwahi taayaa chiine saatanii si saawe

And Jesus went out thence, and withdrew into the parts of Tyre and Sidon.

22. mecimi waapamehko keenaniiwiikweewa piyeci lohfe nele skwaaya hoci chiine poonamawilo kiteminaakweeletiiwe o teepeelemiweeta kiila hokwihfali teepitii nitaanehfa hotahkwi petfakhekooli waninehfiili lahootamwa

And behold, a Canaanitish woman came out from those borders, and cried, saying, Have mercy on me, O Lord, thou son of David; my daughter is grievously vexed with a devil.

23. payeekwa mata nekoti kalawiiwe hotehaapafatawaali chiine hokakehkimaafhi piyehi mecimi hokocimekohi haameskawi hina hkweewa ksake kitahkomekona hotekohi

But he answered her not a word. And his disciples came and besought him, saying, Send her away; for she crieth after us.

24. payeekwa haapafse mata niteh waawiinekoopi weeka nihki waaniiwi meekiifaki hini hiswiila hoci kamiki hisiwe

But he answered and said, I was not sent but unto the lost sheep of the house of Israel.

25. payeekwa piyeeli nili hkweeli mecimi hosasilawehekooli teepeelemiweeta naatamawilo hotekooli

But she came and worshipped him, saying, Lord, help me.

26. chiine haapafse mata hini howesfenwi wahsi mameya hini hotakhwaanemwa hapelohfaki mecimi nihki wihsiiki ni hipakitamawaaki hini hisiwe

And he answered and said, It is not meet to take the children's bread and cast it to the dogs.

27. payeekwa hiwa hina hkweewa hanhka
teepeelemiweeta ksake wiikinaakwi nihki wihsiiki
homiicinaawa nili peekitehtooteeki weeci penhfeki hini
tah wihfenilici homestelemwahi

But she said, Yea, Lord: for even the
dogs eat of the crumbs which fall from
their masters' table.

28. hine howe ciisisii haapafse mecimi o hkweewa
mhsaawi cehi kiteepwehseeewe hiini hpenaloofolo
teetepilahi yeesiteheeyani hotelaali mecimi nili
hotaanehfali hina kiikehoofooli hini yaatefaki

Then Jesus answered and said unto her,
O woman, great is thy faith: be it done
unto thee even as thou wilt. And her
daughter was healed from that hour.

29. chiine ciisisii nhhoci weepfe mecimi maalaakwahi
hini keeleliiwi mhsinepi si piyeewa chiine hini
meekwahkiki si kkwicsinwa mecimi nitasi lematapi

And Jesus departed thence, and came
nigh unto the sea of Galilee; and he
went up into the mountain, and sat there.

30. chiine nitasi hotfaawaali meci mehseelekki hopemi
kilekinaawahi nihi meemiyaalakikaateelici
keekeepiikweelici paapwaa kalawilici
meemiyaalakatowilici chiine meci kotakhi chiine nihki
hoteh pakfenaawahi nihi maalaakwahi hofitali hina
mecimi hina hokiikehahi nihi

And there came unto him great
multitudes, having with them the lame,
blind, dumb, maimed, and many others,
and they cast them down at his feet; and
he healed them:

31. weecikeenahi nihki mehseelekki
kwakwehtaaniteheeki yeh neewaawaaci nihi paapwaa
kalawilici pemi kalawihi nihi meemiyaalakatowilici
mefefihi chiine nihi meemiyaalakikaateelici pemhfehi
chiine nihi keekeepiikweelici tepinamohi mecimi nihki
howahfaacimekohwaawaali nili homanetoomali
hiswiila

insomuch that the multitude wondered,
when they saw the dumb speaking, the
maimed whole, and the lame walking,
and the blind seeing: and they glorified
the God of Israel.

32. chiine ciisisii hoteh wihkomahi hokakehkimaafhi
mecimi ceh nikiteminaakweelemaaki nihki
mehseelekki ksake howe nhfoko hoci nimoosatawi
wiici hapiimekooki mecimi mata wiyehi
hopoonaanaawa wah miiciwaaci chiine mata halika
niisa leskawaaki pemi skwaalaweewaate piilepeeke
nihki hini laakwa wi hale mekihkofiiki hiwa

And Jesus called unto him his disciples,
and said, I have compassion on the
multitude, because they continue with
me now three days and have nothing to
eat: and I would not send them away
fasting, lest haply they faint in the way.

33. chiine taaniwe kooci poonaape yooni si meci
weepskweeteewali tah papskwahkiki wahsi
teephoolakwe yooni si meci mehseelekki hotelaawaali

And the disciples say unto him, Whence
should we have so many loaves in a
desert place, as to fill so great a
multitude?

34. mecimi kehfwi kipoonaanaawa weepskweeteewali
kiilawa hotelahi ciisisii niiswahfwi chiine
laakofwiimehi caki namehfiifaki hotelaawaali

And Jesus saith unto them, How many
loaves have ye? And they said, Seven,
and a few small fishes.

35. chiine hotepimahi nihi mehseelelici wahsi
lematapilici hini sahkiki

And he commanded the multitude to sit
down on the ground;

36. chiine hoteh mamena nili niiswahfwi
weepskweeteewali mecimi nihi namefhi chiine miiliwe
niyaawe mecimi hoposkonaana chiine hoteh miilahi
nihi kakehkimaafhi mecimi nihki kakehkimaafaki nihi
mehseelelici

and he took the seven loaves and the
fishes; and he gave thanks and brake,
and gave to the disciples, and the
disciples to the multitudes.

37. chiine caayahki wihfeniiki mecimi teephoolooki
chiine homaawatonaanaawa nihki seskwatooteeki nili
peekskehkaaki niiswahfwi soosooniwali hokwihfeno

And they did all eat, and were filled: and
they took up that which remained over
of the broken pieces, seven baskets full.

38. chiine nihki weewihfenicki niyeewene metahfene
tepeewe hileniiki tepaane hkweeki chiine hapelohfaki

And they that did eat were four thousand
men, beside women and children.

39. chiine hotaameskawahi nihi mehseelelici mecimi
hini holakeeleki lhkamwa chiine hini skwaaya
mekeeteni si piyeewa

And he sent away the multitudes, and
entered into the boat, and came into the
borders of Magadan.

Matthew:16

1. chiine nihki pelesiiki chiine setosiiki piyeeki mecimi
hopemi wiisa kotahkowaalaawaali hokocimaawaali
wahsi waapatelekowaaci kikinooloowe
weefepahkamikiki hoci

And the Pharisees and Sadducees came,
and tempting him asked him to shew
them a sign from heaven.

2. payeekwa hotaapaftawahi mecimi hini ye
holaakwiifiki we howesi kiiseki hinoki ksake hini
mhskwaawi menhkwatwi kitaayopwa hotelahi

But he answered and said unto them,
When it is evening, ye say, It will be fair
weather: for the heaven is red.

3. chiine hini yeh kolahwaapaki weh macikiiseki hinoki
ksake hini mhskwaawi menhkwatwi mecimi
kipakokwatwi kiwaakotaanaawa kiilawa wahsi
nenofiyeekwe yeelaapeeyaaki menhkwatwi payeekwa
kitaalwi katawi nenofipwa nili kikinooloowena hini
peemi laakwahkamikiki

And in the morning, It will be foul
weather today: for the heaven is red and
lowring. Ye know how to discern the
face of the heaven; but ye cannot discern
the signs of the times.

4. matefiifi mecimi waapasiphikeewefi skwiiwena
honatoneha kikinooloowe mecimi weh miilaawa mata
kikinooloowe weeka hini coona hokikinooloowe hisiwe
chiine honakalahi mecimi nhhoci weepfe

An evil and adulterous generation
seeketh after a sign; and there shall no
sign be given unto it, but the sign of
Jonah. And he left them, and departed.

5. chiine nihki kakehkimaafaki piyeeki hini hasowe
wiyeetahkwe mecimi howanihkaataanaawa wahsi
mamowaaci takhwa

And the disciples came to the other side
and forgot to take bread.

6. chiine ciisisii kcitawaafiiko mecimi mahkeeni hini
honalescikanwa nihki pelesiiki chiine setosiiki hotelahi

And Jesus said unto them, Take heed
and beware of the leaven of the
Pharisees and Sadducees.

7. chiine nihki memekiniteheeki heelekiina wiilawa
mata kimamepe takhwa hiwaki

And they reasoned among themselves,
saying, We took no bread.

8. mecimi ciisisii hopemi mooleeletamawahi hini o
caki teepwehseefaki kiilawa koociwe
kimemekiniteheepwa heelekiina kiilawa ksake mata
kipoonaanaawa takhwa hotelahi

And Jesus perceiving it said, O ye of
little faith, why reason ye among
yourselves, because ye have no bread?

9. ha keewaki kiilawa mata kimoositeheepwa weelaa
mata kimhkaweeletaanaawa nili niyaalanwi
howeepskweteemwa nihki niyaalane metahfene
tepeewe mecimi kehfwi soosooniwali kimamenaawa

Do ye not yet perceive, neither
remember the five loaves of the five
thousand, and how many baskets ye
took up?

10. ha mata nohki nili niiswahfwi howeepskweteemwa nihki niyeewene metahfene tepeewe mecimi kehfwi soosooniwali kimamenaawa

Neither the seven loaves of the four thousand, and how many baskets ye took up?

11. nehiwe hini kitesi pwaa kiilawa mooleeletaanaawa yeesi pwaa haatotamoolako takhwa payeekwa mahkeeni hini honalescikanwa nihki pelesiiki chiine setosiiki

How is it that ye do not perceive that I spake not to you concerning bread? But beware of the leaven of the Pharisees and Sadducees.

12. hine howe nihki nenohseeki yeesi pwaa hina mahkeeni hilaaci hini takhwaani honalescika weeka hini hokakehkimiweewenwa nihki pelesiiki chiine setosiiki

Then understood they how that he bade them not beware of the leaven of bread, but of the teaching of the Pharisees and Sadducees.

13. howe hini sisaliye filipaayi yeh si piyaaci ciisisii honatohtawahi hokakehkimaafhi neefaliwe hina hiwaki hileniiki nili hokwihfali hileni hotelahi

Now when Jesus came into the parts of Caesarea Philippi, he asked his disciples, saying, Who do men say that the Son of man is?

14. chiine nihki naaleta caanii na fafahkwiholelhiwena hiwaki naaleta hilaica chiine kotakaki celimaaya weelaa nekoti nihki maamoosikiiskwecki hiwaki hotelaawaali

And they said, Some say John the Baptist; some, Elijah: and others, Jeremiah, or one of the prophets.

15. weeka neefawe niila kiteyopwa kiilawa hotelahi

He saith unto them, But who say ye that I am?

16. mecimi saiman' piita haapafse hina klaistii kiila nili hokwihfali hina yeepita maneto hotelaali

And Simon Peter answered and said, Thou art the Christ, the Son of the living God.

17. chiine ciisisii haapafse kikisaatefi kiila saiman' paacoona ksake mata wiyawfi mecimi mhskwi kimehci pahkinamaako hini nohfa weeka yeepita weefepahkamikiki

And Jesus answered and said unto him, Blessed art thou, Simon Bar-Jonah: for flesh and blood hath not revealed it unto thee, but my Father which is in heaven.

18. mecimi niila nehfaapi kitele yeesi piitawiyani kiila chiine hoskici yaama siikona ne hopatena nimamaatomeewika mecimi mata nili hahkwinamoowi skwaateewali we hoci katawahkonoote hini

And I also say unto thee, that thou art Peter, and upon this rock I will build my church; and the gates of Hades shall not prevail against it.

19. keh miilele nili tawenehikana hini weefepahkamikiki hokimaawitaamhkwe hoci mecimi kookwe-nehi-kaaci ke kciipile hoskitaamhkwe we kciipite piitike weefepahkamikiki chiine kookwe-nehi-kaaci keh pelha hoskitaamhkwe weh pelhoote piitike weefepahkamikiki hotelaali

I will give unto thee the keys of the kingdom of heaven: and whatsoever thou shalt bind on earth shall be bound in heaven: and whatsoever thou shalt loose on earth shall be loosed in heaven.

20. hine howe hotepinalekwimahi nihi kakehkimaafhi wahsi pwaa nihki wiitamawaawaaci hileniili yeesi hinawici nili klaistiili

Then charged he the disciples that they should tell no man that he was the Christ.

21. hine laakwa hoci hotalemi waapatelahi ciisisii hokakehkimaafhi wahsi kwiilahi colooseelemii haaci mecimi hahkwinaki meci wiyehi nihi hoci kikilenihi chiine hokimaawi mhkateewkolayehi chiine

From that time began Jesus to shew unto his disciples, how that he must go unto Jerusalem, and suffer many things of the yaayawikeelici mecimi wahsi nhfekwici chiine hini nhfwi kaasekiki honhskaanoofoci

elders and chief priests and scribes, and be killed, and the third day be raised up.

22. chiine hoteh fookinaali piita mecimi hotalemi kilhamawaali pelowaamatwi cehi hini kiiya hoci teepeelemiweeta mata yooma we hinwi kiiyaaki hisiwe

And Peter took him, and began to rebuke him, saying, Be it far from thee, Lord: this shall never be unto thee.

23. payeekwa maa si kokiiwa hina mecimi hotaanaaki niila haalo setenii pemi hotakikahsinoowe kiila niiyaaki ksake mata kimemekineeletaana nili howiyehiima maneto nili weeka howiyehiimwa hileniiki hotelaali piitali

But he turned, and said unto Peter, Get thee behind me, Satan: thou art a stumbling-block unto me: for thou mindest not the things of God, but the things of men.

24. hine howe ciisisii hotelahi hokakehkimaafhi kwehkwi wiyeefa hileni nih wiisa neekalekwa wiilaani hina kiyaateeletake wiiya chiine homame hotaasitehfekiimi mecimi nineekalekwa

Then said Jesus unto his disciples, If any man would come after me, let him deny himself, and take up his cross, and follow me.

25. ksake kookwe-neefa-kaaci wih wiisa waapanesto hotelenaweewiiwe we wanhto hini chiine kookwe-neefa-kaaci we wanhto hotelenaweewiiwe ksake niila hoci we mhka hini

For whosoever would save his life shall lose it: and whosoever shall lose his life for my sake shall find it.

26. nehiwe ksake we mhkahfo hileni kwehkwi katawihkake melhske hini yeelekokwahkamikiki mecimi pakiteenake hotelenaweewiiwe weelaa nehiwe weh miiliwe hileni haasoonake hotelenaweewiiwe

For what shall a man be profited, if he shall gain the whole world, and forfeit his life? or what shall a man give in exchange for his life?

27. ksake hina hokwihfali hileni weh piyeewa hini howahfaacimekofiiwenilici hohfali kileki hotenhcaliimhhi mecimi hine howe weh tepasawi miilaali caakisi hileniili yeesilawiiwenilici

For the Son of man shall come in the glory of his Father with his angels; and then shall he render unto every man according to his deeds.

28. tepilo kitelepwa niila hapiiki nihki naaleta neniipawicki hotasi nihkiini mata weh wiyehi si kotataanaawa nepoowe paalohi nihki weh neewaawaali nili hokwihfali hileni pemi piyeewa hini hokimaawiiweneki

Verily I say unto you, There be some of them that stand here, which shall in no wise taste of death, till they see the Son of man coming in his kingdom.

Matthew:17

1. chiine nekotwahfokonakiki hahkowihi ciisisii hotaamwelahi piitali chiine ceemhsiili mecimi hoceeninaali caaniili chiine hotekkwiciwelahi moospatenwi meekwahkiki naanhsihka

And after six days Jesus taketh with him Peter, and James, and John his brother, and bringeth them up into a high mountain apart:

2. mecimi yeelahfamiilici hale kotaki hitwa yeelekokwaapeeci wahfefamooya paasi hina kiisekikiisfwa chiine hopiitenika wahkanakiya paasi hini wayahfeeyaaki

and he was transfigured before them: and his face did shine as the sun, and his garments became white as the light.

3. chiine waapamehko nitasi hotepinaakwi hotfekohi moosisiili chiine hilaicali peemi kaloolekoci hina

And behold, there appeared unto them Moses and Elijah talking with him.

4. chiine piita haapafse mecimi teepeelemiweeta howesa hini wahsi kiilawe hotasi hapiyakwe

And Peter answered, and said unto Jesus, Lord, it is good for us to be here:

siteheeyane ne hostoona hotasi nhfwi haaciiwikamiko nekoti kiila chiine nekoti moosisii chiine nekoti hilaica hotelaali ciisisiili

if thou wilt, I will make here three tabernacles; one for thee, and one for Moses, and one for Elijah.

5. yeheeyehi keewaki pemi kalawici waapatamoko wahfete paafkwahki hotawikanhskaakonaawa mecimi sci kalaweewihsimoowe hini paafkwahki hocifeya yaama hina yeeahkweelemaka nikwihfa wiiyaaki hina nimenwitehe nootawehko kiilawa hiyooya

While he was yet speaking, behold, a bright cloud overshadowed them: and behold, a voice out of the cloud, saying, This is my beloved Son, in whom I am well pleased; hear ye him.

6. mecimi nihki kakehkimaafaki yeh nootamowaaci hini maa si holemhkwi piikwehsinooki chiine lakokwe wiisaalepwaaki

And when the disciples heard it, they fell on their face, and were sore afraid.

7. mecimi ciisisii piyeewa mecimi hoteh pehsenahi chiine pafekwiiko teki wiisaalepwaako hotelahi

And Jesus came and touched them and said, Arise, and be not afraid.

8. chiine maa pemi laapiiki mata wiyeefali honeewaawaali nihki weeciwephi ciisisiili pehi

And lifting up their eyes, they saw no one, save Jesus only.

9. chiine yeesi pemi piyeci paalacsinowaaci hini meekwahkiki hoci ciisisii hotepimahi nihi teki hini sinamoowe wiitamawehko hileni paalohi hina hokwihfali hileni nili nepelici hoci honhskaate hotelahi

And as they were coming down from the mountain, Jesus commanded them, saying, Tell the vision to no man, until the Son of man be risen from the dead.

10. chiine hokakehkimaafhi honatohtaakohi koociwe chiine nihki yaayawikeecki yaawaki wahsi hilaica kwiilahi nhhihta piyaaci hotekohi

And his disciples asked him, saying, Why then say the scribes that Elijah must first come?

11. mecimi haapafse chiine sapkahi hilaica piyeewa chiine weh petekfeto caayahki wiyehi

And he answered and said, Elijah indeed cometh, and shall restore all things:

12. payeekwa kitelepwa niila yeesi neyehka piyaaci hilaica mecimi nihki mata howaakomaawaali nili weeka kookwe-nehi-kaaci yeesiteheewaaci hotpenalaawaali teetepilahi yooni nehfaapi weh si hahkwinaki nihiini hoci hina hokwihfali hileni hotelahi

but I say unto you, that Elijah is come already, and they knew him not, but did unto him whatsoever they listed. Even so shall the Son of man also suffer of them.

13. hine howe nenohseeki nihki kakehkimaafaki yeesi haatotamaakowaaci caaniili hina fafahkwiholelhiwena

Then understood the disciples that he spake unto them of John the Baptist.

14. chiine nihi mehseelelici yeh si piyaawaaci nitasi hotfekooli hileniili pemi piyeci hociikwanahkeepiili mecimi

And when they were come to the multitude, there came to him a man, kneeling to him, and saying,

15. teepeelemiweeta poonamawi kiteminaakweeletiiwe nikwihfa ksake hina maamaatakoska mecimi mamiyeenaani hahkwinamwa moosaki laakwa ksake hini skoteeki yaasfe chiine moosaki hini nepiki

Lord, have mercy on my son: for he is epileptic, and suffereth grievously: for oft-times he falleth into the fire, and oft-times into the water.

16. chiine nipiyeetawaaki kikakehkimaafaki mecimi hotaalwi kiikehaawaali nihki hotekooli

And I brought him to thy disciples, and they could not cure him.

17. chiine ciisisii haapafse o pwaayaa teepwehseeweni mecimi weenaatefita skwiiwena taaniwe laakwasi keh wiici hapiimelepwa taaniwe laakwasi keh kihfehwaacihkoolepwa piyeetawilo hina niila hisiwe

And Jesus answered and said, O faithless and perverse generation, how long shall I be with you? how long shall I bear with you? bring him hither to me.

18. chiine ciisisii hokwtelaali nili mecimi hina waninehfi nili hoci lohfe chiine kiikehoofo hina skilawehfiifa hini yaatefaki

And Jesus rebuked him; and the devil went out from him: and the boy was cured from that hour.

19. hine howe hotfaawaali ciisisiili nihki kakehkimaafaki naanhsihka koociwe niilawe nitaalwi lohfe pakilaape hina hotelaawaali

Then came the disciples to Jesus apart, and said, Why could not we cast it out?

20. ksake maackwaafi kiteepwehseewenwa tepilo kitelepwa niila ksake poonameekwe kiilawa teepwehseewe paasi nekoti pekwe mastatiiwi miinhka yooci halayine haale hitameyeekwe yooma meekwahkiki mecimi hini we heeya

And he saith unto them, Because of your little faith: for verily I say unto you, If ye have faith as a grain of mustard seed, ye shall say unto this mountain, Remove hence to yonder place; and it shall remove;

21. chiine mata wiyehi weh matayeeciwatwi kiiyaawaaki hotelahi

and nothing shall be impossible unto you.

22. chiine ciisisii hina hokwihfali hileni nili holeciwa hileniiki weh si pakfenoofo

And while they abode in Galilee, Jesus said unto them, The Son of man shall be delivered up into the hands of men;

23. mecimi nihki we nhfaawaali nili chiine hini meewinhfokonakiki we honhskaanoofo hotelahi nihi chiine nihki hanhhiweewi macilepwaaki

and they shall kill him, and the third day he shall be raised up. And they were exceeding sorry.

24. chiine keepaaniamii yeh si piyaawaaci nihki wa hotahpenakki hini pahfisekali moni hotfaawaali piitali chiine ha mata taatephike kikakehkimaamwa hini pahfisekali hotelaawaali nili

And when they were come to Capernaum, they that received the half-shekel came to Peter, and said, Doth not your master pay the half-shekel?

25. hanhka hiwa hina chiine nili wiikiwaapeki yeh piyaalici ciisisii nhhihta hokaloolaali nehiwe kitesitehe saiman' nihki hini hoskitaamhkwe hoci hokimaaki neefhiwe howahoci hotfekonaawa hini tephikeewe weelaa teekshotiiwe ha hokwihfwahi weelaa toke kookweeneefhi hotelaali

He saith, Yea. And when he came into the house, Jesus spake first to him, saying, What thinkest thou, Simon? the kings of the earth, from whom do they receive toll or tribute? from their sons, or from strangers?

26. mecimi ciisisii nihi kookweeneefhi hoci yeeyolici nili weecikeenahi nihki hokwihfimaaki tepeeletamefiiki

And when he said, From strangers, Jesus said unto him, Therefore the sons are free.

27. payeekwa piilepeeke wahsi hotakikahsinowaaci ki hpenalaape nihki nhhaale hini mhsinepiki chiine nhpakitano kokaati mecimi mami hina namehfa nhhihta memoskifaata chiine hine mehci taawalonate ke mhka nekoti sekali mamelo hini chiine miili nihki niila mecimi kiila hoci hotelaali

But, lest we cause them to stumble, go thou to the sea, and cast a hook, and take up the fish that first cometh up; and when thou hast opened his mouth, thou shalt find a shekel: that take, and give unto them for me and thee.

Matthew:18

1. hine hini yaatefaki hotfaawaali ciisisiili nihki kakehkimaafaki neefawe chiine haliwi mhsiilefi piitike hini weefepahkamikiki hokimaawitaamhkwe hisiweeki

In that hour came the disciples unto Jesus, saying, Who then is greatest in the kingdom of heaven?

2. chiine hina hoteh wihkomaali hapelohfeefali mecimi holemataphaali hini heelekhi nihi

And he called to him a little child, and set him in the midst of them,

3. chiine tepilo kitelepwa niila weeciwephi kiilawa kotekwiiyeekwe mecimi hilefiyeekwe paasi hapelohfeefaki mata kiilawa keh wiyehisi piicfaapwa hini weefepahkamikiki hokimaawitaamhkwe hisiwe hina

and said, Verily I say unto you, Except ye turn, and become as little children, ye shall in no wise enter into the kingdom of heaven.

4. kookwe-neefa-kaaci weecikeenahi weh nanahpaacilotaa wiiya paasi yaama hapelohfeefa yoona hina haliwi mhsiilefi piitike hini weefepahkamikiki hokimaawitaamhkwe

Whosoever therefore shall humble himself as this little child, the same is the greatest in the kingdom of heaven.

5. chiine kookweeneefa we hotahpenaali yooniisi hapelohfeefali niwiifooweneki nootahpenekwa niila

And whoso shall receive one such little child in my name receiveth me:

6. weeka kookweeneefa wahsi hotakikahsinelici we hpenalaali nekoti yohoma meciloofilici teeteepwehseelici niiya mhkafooweni hina wahsi mhsi poothaakani siikonali laapicimoofolici hokwekakaneki mecimi hina hini wih si kookinoofo hini yeespitemiki hini mhsinepi

But whoso shall cause one of these little ones which believe on me to stumble, it is profitable for him that a great millstone should be hanged about his neck, and that he should be sunk in the depth of the sea.

7. macilepwaaweni cehi hini yeelekokwahkamikiki ksake wayahoci pemi hotakikahsineki hoci ksake kwiilahi hini yeeki wahsi nili piyeeyaaki payeekwa macilepwaaweni cehi hina hileni wehoci saapwi piyeeyaaki hini

Woe unto the world because of occasions of stumbling! for it must needs be that the occasions come; but woe to that man through whom the occasion cometh!

8. chiine kwehkwi kileci weelaa kifici hpenalekoyane wahsi hotakikahsinani kwakwkotano hini mecimi kiiya hoci hini halika hipakitano howesa hini kiila piicfaayane hini lenaweewiiwe mamiyaalakatowiyane weelaa kihkiicsinane noota kaaciika pemi niiswi poonamane holeciwali weelaa niiswi hofitali hini wa hipakitooteeki kookwelaakwasi skoteeki

And if thy hand or thy foot causeth thee to stumble, cut it off, and cast it from thee: it is good for thee to enter into life maimed or halt, rather than having two hands or two feet to be cast into the eternal fire.

9. chiine kwehkwi hini kiskiisekwi hpenalekoyane wahsi hotakikahsinani kwakwatenano hini chiine kiiya hoci hini halika hipakitano howesa hini kiila piicfaayane hini lenaweewiiwe kileki nekoti hoskiisekwi noota kaaciika niiswi pemi poonamane hoskiiseko hini wa hipakitooteeki hahkwinamoowi skoteeki

And if thine eye causeth thee to stumble, pluck it out, and cast it from thee: it is good for thee to enter into life with one eye, rather than having two eyes to be cast into the hell of fire.

10. waapatamoko wahsi pwaa kiilawa siikeelemeekwe nekoti yohkoma mecilooficki ksake kitelepwa niila nihki hotenhcaliimwahi piitike weefepahkamikiki sapkahi moosatawi hotelaapatamaakohi hotelaapeewe nohfa yeepita weefepahkamikiki

See that ye despise not one of these little ones; for I say unto you, that in heaven their angels do always behold the face of my Father which is in heaven.

12. nehiwe kitesiteheepwa kiilawa kwehkwi wiyeefa hileni poonaate tepeewe meekiifhi mecimi nekoti nihi

How think ye? if any man have a hundred sheep, and one of them be gone

pikeeli ha mata hotah nakalahi nihi caakakitecaakatfwi chiine nili meekwahkiki heewa mecimi honatonehwaali nili peepikeelici

astray, doth he not leave the ninety and nine, and go unto the mountains, and seek that which goeth astray?

13. chiine kwehkwike hinwi hina mhkawaali nili tepilo kitelepwa niila halika hosasilepwa nili hoci noota nihi caakakitecaakatfwi pwaayaa mehci pikeelici

And if so be that he find it, verily I say unto you, he rejoiceth over it more than over the ninety and nine which have not gone astray.

14. yooni teetepilahi mata hini hotesiteheewe kohfwa yeepita weefepahkamikiki wahsi nekoti yohoma meciloofilici haselelici

Even so it is not the will of your Father which is in heaven, that one of these little ones should perish.

15. chiine kwehkwi kiceenina macipenalehke nhhaale waapatesi hopiimilawiiwe naanhsihka kiilawa pehi hahkawehtawehke kimehci katawihkawa keela kiceenina

And if thy brother sin against thee, go, shew him his fault between thee and him alone: if he hear thee, thou hast gained thy brother.

16. weeka pwaa hahkawehtawehke haamwesi nekoti weelaa niiswi keewaki wahsi menawa haayicfeki caaki kalawiiwe nili hoci hotoonwa niiswi weelaa nhfwi teepweewenaki

But if he hear thee not, take with thee one or two more, that at the mouth of two witnesses or three every word may be established.

17. chiine haalawinake wahsi hahkawehtawaaci nihi haatotano hini mamaatomeewimaawatweloooweneki chiine nehfaapi haalawinake wahsi hahkawehtaki hini mamaatomeewimaawatweloowe wiilaani keh laakooma kiila paasi hina nanahkawileni chiine hina maawatonikehfi

And if he refuse to hear them, tell it unto the church: and if he refuse to hear the church also, let him be unto thee as the Gentile and the publican.

18. tepilo kitelepwa niila kookwe-neh-si wiyehi kiilawa ke kciipilenaawa hoskitaamhkwe we kciipite piitike weefepahkamikiki mecimi kookwe-neh-si wiyehi keh pelhaanaawa hoskitaamhkwe we pelhoote piitike weefepahkamikiki

Verily I say unto you, What things soever ye shall bind on earth shall be bound in heaven: and what things soever ye shall loose on earth shall be loosed in heaven.

19. kitelepwa nohki kwehkwi niiswi kiilawa weh takwaacimooki hoskitaamhkwe wiyehi wah natotamowaaci hini we hpenatawaaci nohfa yeepita weefepahkamikiki

Again I say unto you, that if two of you shall agree on earth as touching anything that they shall ask, it shall be done for them of my Father which is in heaven.

20. ksake laakwa tasi niiswi weelaa nhfwi maawatweelooki niwiifooweneki nitasi niila heelekhi nihki

For where two or three are gathered together in my name, there am I in the midst of them.

21. hine howe piyeewa piita mecimi teepeelemiweeta taaniwe tfene neh macipenaleekwe niceenina chiine nih pakfeeletamawa ha paalohi niiswahfene hotelaali nili

Then came Peter, and said to him, Lord, how oft shall my brother sin against me, and I forgive him? until seven times?

22. mata paalohi niiswahfene kitele weeka paalohi niiswaasiitfene niiswahfene hotelaali ciisisii

Jesus saith unto him, I say not unto thee, Until seven times; but, Until seventy times seven.

23. weecikeenahi hini weefepahkamikiki hokimaawitaamhkwe paasi naanekoti hokima si takweelemekwatwi hina wih pemi hakitahfoomahi hotaloolaakanhhi

Therefore is the kingdom of heaven likened unto a certain king, which would make a reckoning with his servants.

24. chiine yeh mehci halemi hakitahfoci nekoti piyeetaakwi meemoosinehokoci metahfene metahfene tepeewe telenht-moni

And when he had begun to reckon, one was brought unto him, which owed him ten thousand talents.

25. payeekwa hina mata hini tfwi hopoona wa hoci tephikeeci tepikeemooli teepeelemekoci wahsi miyeekinoofoci mecimi wiiwali chiine hapelofhi chiine caayahki hina peepoonaki mecimi tephikeewe wahsi mectooteeki

But forasmuch as he had not wherewith to pay, his lord commanded him to be sold, and his wife, and children, and all that he had, and payment to be made.

26. hina haloolaakaafa weecikeenahi sahkiki sfe chiine hosasilawehaali nili teepeelemiweeta poonamawilo piisiteheewe mecimi keh tephole caayahki hisiwe

The servant therefore fell down and worshipped him, saying, Lord, have patience with me, and I will pay thee all.

27. mecimi nili teepeelemekoci peemi kiteminaakweelemekoci hopakfenekooli hina haloolaakaafa chiine hopakfeeletamaakooli hini moosinehika

And the lord of that servant, being moved with compassion, released him, and forgave him the debt.

28. payeekwa hina haloolaakaafa lohfe homhkawaali nekoti howiici-aloolaakaafhi meemoosinehokoci tepeewe seleni chiine homawinachaali mecimi hokihkitonenaali nili tephikeelo memoosinehikeeyani hotelaali

But that servant went out, and found one of his fellow-servants, which owed him a hundred pence: and he laid hold on him, and took him by the throat, saying, Pay what thou owest.

29. weecikeenahi sahkiki sfeeli nili howiici-aloolaakaafali mecimi honanahpaacimekooli poonamawilo piisiteheewe mecimi keh tephole hotekooli

So his fellow-servant fell down and besought him, saying, Have patience with me, and I will pay thee.

30. chiine mata sitehe paameci weepfe chiine hopiicfe pakilaali kiphotiiweneki paalohi tephamelite hini moosinehika

And he would not: but went and cast him into prison, till he should pay that which was due.

31. weecikeenahi howiici-aloolaakaafhi yeh neemelici yeesilawiiki hanhhiweewi macilepwahi chiine nihki piyeeki mecimi howiitamawaawaali teepeelemekowaaci caayahki yeesilawiiki

So when his fellow-servants saw what was done, they were exceeding sorry, and came and told unto their lord all that was done.

32. hine howe hina teepeelemekoci hotahpimekooli mecimi kiila weenaatefita haloolaaka kipakfeeletamoole kiila caayahki hini moosinehika ksake kinanahpaacimi

Then his lord called him unto him, and saith to him, Thou wicked servant, I forgave thee all that debt, because thou besoughtest me:

33. ha mata nehfaapi kiila neyehka kih poonamawa kiteminaakweeletiiwe kiwiici-aloolaaka teetepilahi yeesi neyehka poonamoola kiteminaakweeletiiwe kiila hotelaali

shouldest not thou also have had mercy on thy fellow-servant, even as I had mercy on thee?

34. mecimi wiyakoweeli teepeelemekoci chiine hoteh pakfenekooli nihi maamamiyeenaanhhiweelici paalohi wih tepha hini caayahki moosinehika

And his lord was wroth, and delivered him to the tormentors, till he should pay all that was due.

35. yooni nehfaapi we hpenalelwaakwe kiilawa weefepahkamikiki nohfa pwaa pakfeeletamaweekwe caakiwiyeefa hoceeninaali kitehiwaaki hoci

So shall also my heavenly Father do unto you, if ye forgive not every one his brother from your hearts.

Matthew:19

1. chiine hini piyeemikatwi hine ciisisii yeh mehcilotaki yooloma kalawiiwena keelelii hoci weepfe mecimi skwaaya cotiye si piyeewa halika hini caatenii

And it came to pass when Jesus had finished these words, he departed from Galilee, and came into the borders of Judaea beyond Jordan;

2. chiine meci mehseelelici honeekalekohi mecimi hokiikehahi nitasi

and great multitudes followed him; and he healed them there.

3. chiine nitasi hotfekohi pelesihi hopemi kotahkowaalekohi ha hini mayaawatwi kwteletiiweneki wahsi hileni pkehwaaci wiiwali caakiwiyehi hoci hotekohi

And there came unto him Pharisees, tempting him, and saying, Is it lawful for a man to put away his wife for every cause?

4. chiine haapafse mecimi ha mata kiilawa kimeh laapaatotaanaawa yeesi hina memechaata nihi hine halemahkamikatwi hoci hileni chiine hkweewa hoteshahi nihi

And he answered and said, Have ye not read, that he which made them from the beginning made them male and female,

5. mecimi ksake yooma hoci hileni weh nakalaali hohfali mecimi hokeeli chiine we haayiteelemaali wiiwali mecimi nihki weh nekotiifenili wiyawfi hiwa hisiwe

and said, For this cause shall a man leave his father and mother, and shall cleave to his wife; and the twain shall become one flesh?

6. weecikeenahi wahsi pwaa kiteeni nihki niiswiwaaci weeka nekotiimehi wiyawfi wiyehi weecikeenahi maneto mayehci takwinaki teki wiilaani hileni wi pikina hotelahi

So that they are no more twain, but one flesh. What therefore God hath joined together, let not man put asunder.

7. koociwe chiine moosisii tepikeemo wahsi miiliweeki pkehotiiwi heewikaateeki chiine wahsi pkehoofoci hina hotekohi

They say unto him, Why then did Moses command to give a bill of divorcement, and to put her away?

8. moosisii ksake siipefiiya kitehiwa wiilaani kiteleelemekowa wahsi pkeewheekwe kiiwaaki weeka hine halemahkamikatwi hoci mata hini piyeci hinwi

He saith unto them, Moses for your hardness of heart suffered you to put away your wives: but from the beginning it hath not been so.

9. mecimi kitelepwa niila kookwe-neefa-kaaci we pkehwaali wiiwali weeciwephi weepeeletiiwe hoci mecimi kotakali weh wiiwinaali macilawi waapasiphikeewe mecimi hina weewiiwinaata nili yeh pkehoofolici macilawi waapasiphikeewe hotelahi

And I say unto you, Whosoever shall put away his wife, except for fornication, and shall marry another, committeth adultery: and he that marrieth her when she is put away committeth adultery.

10. kwehkwi yooni lefiimaate hileni wiiwali mata howesfenwi fapa wahsi wiichetiki hotekohi nihi kakehkimaafhi

The disciples say unto him, If the case of the man is so with his wife, it is not expedient to marry.

11. payeekwa mata caayahki hileniiki hotah katawi hotahpenaanaawa yooma hiyoowe nihki weeka hini meemiiloofocki hotelahi

But he said unto them, All men cannot receive this saying, but they to whom it is given.

12. ksake hapiiki naapehfemooki weecita yooni yeesi niikicki hokiwahi holaamataakanilici hoci chiine hapiiki naapehfemooki nenaapehfemhaawaaci hileniiki chiine hapiiki naapehfemooki pesikwi nenaapehfemhtoocki wiiyaawa ksake hini weefepahkamikiki hokimaawitaamhkwe hoci hina wiyeefa keekatawi hilefita wahsi hotahpenaki hini wiilaani hina hotahpenake hini

For there are eunuchs, which were so born from their mother's womb: and there are eunuchs, which were made eunuchs by men: and there are eunuchs, which made themselves eunuchs for the kingdom of heaven's sake. He that is able to receive it, let him receive it.

13. hine howe nitasi piyeetaakwi hapelohfeefhi wi hoskici nihi si poonaki holeciwali mecimi mamaatomeeci chiine nihki kakehkimaafaki hokwtelaawahi nihi

Then were there brought unto him little children, that he should lay his hands on them, and pray: and the disciples rebuked them.

14. payeekwa ciisisii wiilaani leelemehko nihki hapelohfeefaki mecimi teki kwtelehko nihki wahsi piyeelotawiwaaci ksake yohkooni wiilawa hini weefepahkamikiki hokimaawitaamhkwe hisiwe

But Jesus said, Suffer the little children, and forbid them not, to come unto me: for of such is the kingdom of heaven.

15. chiine hoskici nihi hopoonaana holeciwali chiine hini hoci weepfe

And he laid his hands on them, and departed thence.

16. chiine waapamehko nekoti wiyeefali hotfekooli mecimi keekehkimiweeta nehiwe weeowesaaki wiyehi neh silawi wahsi menawahi poonama kookwelaakwasi lenaweewiiwe hotekooli

And behold, one came to him and said, Master, what good thing shall I do, that I may have eternal life?

17. chiine koociwe niila kinatohtawi hini weeowesaaki nekotihi hapiwa hina weelefita payeekwa wiisa piicfaayane hini lenaweewiiwe kciitawefilo nili tepikeemoowena hotelaali nili

And he said unto him, Why askest thou me concerning that which is good? One there is who is good: but if thou wouldest enter into life, keep the commandments.

18. taaniliwe hotelaali hina mecimi ciisisii teki kiila ke nhsiwe teki kiila keh macilawi waapasiphikeewe teki kiila keh kimoote teki kiila keh naanhhaacimoowi ciikinhkemo

He saith unto him, Which? And Jesus said, Thou shalt not kill, Thou shalt not commit adultery, Thou shalt not steal, Thou shalt not bear false witness,

19. hotakeelemi kohfa mecimi kikiya chiine hahkweelemi kiila maapayeecikaalehka paasi nehalwaaka kiiya hotelaali nili

Honour thy father and thy mother: and, Thou shalt love thy neighbour as thyself.

20. caayahki yooloma neyehka nikciitawefi nehiwe keewaki ninootkofi hotekooli ciisisii nili mayaanileniili

The young man saith unto him, All these things have I observed: what lack I yet?

21. wiisa mefefiyane nhhaale miyeekilo peepoonamani mecimi miili hina kitemaafa chiine keh poona pawaawe piitike weefepahkamikiki mecimi piyaalo neekasilo hotelaali ciisisii

Jesus said unto him, If thou wouldest be perfect, go, sell that thou hast, and give to the poor, and thou shalt have treasure in heaven: and come, follow me.

22. payeekwa hina mayaanileni yeh nootaki hini hiyoowe weepfe macilepwa ksake hina nekoti mehsi poonaka pawaawena

But when the young man heard the saying, he went away sorrowful: for he was one that had great possessions.

23. chiine tepilo kitelepwa niila kiisenaatetwi hini wahsi piicfaaci paweewi hileni hini weefepahkamikiki hokimaawitaamhkwe hotelahi ciisisii hokakehkimaafhi

And Jesus said unto his disciples, Verily I say unto you, It is hard for a rich man to enter into the kingdom of heaven.

24. chiine kitelepwa nohki halika weecihi hini weh si saapwiici keemali ta hoskiisekowiki saaponika noota paweewi hileni wahsi piicfaaci hini hokimaawitaamhkomi maneto

And again I say unto you, It is easier for a camel to go through a needle's eye, than for a rich man to enter into the kingdom of God.

25. mecimi nihki kakehkimaafaki yeh nootamowaaci hini hanhhiweewi cihsiteheeki neefawe howe wih katawi waapaneshoofo hiwaki

And when the disciples heard it, they were astonished exceedingly, saying, Who then can be saved?

26. chiine ciisisii hoteh waapamahi wiilawa hileniiki matayeeciwatwi yooma weeka maneto caayahki wiyehi katawatwi hotelahi nihi

And Jesus looking upon them said to them, With men this is impossible; but with God all things are possible.

27. hine piita haapafse mecimi ci ninakataape niilawa caayahki chiine kineekalelepe nehiwe howe neh poonaape hotelaali

Then answered Peter and said unto him, Lo, we have left all, and followed thee; what then shall we have?

28. mecimi ciisisii tepilo kitelepwa niila kiilawa neyehka neeneekasiyeekwe hini laapilenaweewiiweneki hine hina hokwihfali hileni we hpapi hini howahfaacimekofiiwe hoci hokimaawi hpapiiwe nehfaapi kiilawa ke hpapinaawa metahfwi-kite-niiswi hokimaawi hpapiiwena pemahkowaalaawaaki nihki metahfwi-kite-niiswi hotfweeloowenhhi hiswiila hotelahi

And Jesus said unto them, Verily I say unto you, that ye which have followed me, in the regeneration when the Son of man shall sit on the throne of his glory, ye also shall sit upon twelve thrones, judging the twelve tribes of Israel.

29. chiine caakiwiyeefa mayehci nakataka wiikiwaapali weelaa hoceeninaanahi weelaa hotikwemimahi weelaa hofimaali weelaa hokeeli weelaa hapelofhi weelaa hasiskiwali ksake niwiifoowe hoci we hotfeko tepeewe tfweekfenwi mecimi weh laapsinwa kookwelaakwasi lenaweewiiwe

And every one that hath left houses, or brethren, or sisters, or father, or mother, or children, or lands, for my name's sake, shall receive a hundredfold, and shall inherit eternal life.

30. payeekwa meci we kci hotaanaakifiiki nenhhihtaawicki mecimi nenhhihtaawicki we kci hotaanaakifiiki

But many shall be last that are first; and first that are last.

Matthew:20

1. ksake hini weefepahkamikiki hokimaawitaamhkwe paasi hileni hinwi teepeeletaka wiikiwa hina lohfe hini kwelahwaapaki hopa haloolahi wah pekatefilici homhfaloomiktikaaneki

For the kingdom of heaven is like unto a man that is a householder, which went out early in the morning to hire labourers into his vineyard.

2. chiine yeh mehtaacimoomaaci nihi paapekatefilici nekoti seleni nekoti kiiskwe hoteleskawahi homhfaloomiktikaaneki

And when he had agreed with the labourers for a penny a day, he sent them into his vineyard.

3. chiine lohfe nawito hini mawi-nhfene yaatefaki mecimi honeewahi kotakhi pah niipawihi hini yaatah wiitkiiki mata wiyehi silawihi

And he went out about the third hour, and saw others standing in the marketplace idle;

4. chiine nhhaakone nehfaapi kiilawa hini mhfaloomiktikaaneki kookwe-nehi-kaaci mayaawatwi keh miilelepwa hotelahi nihi mecimi nihki nhheeki

and to them he said, Go ye also into the vineyard, and whatsoever is right I will give you. And they went their way.

5. nohki hina lohfe hini mawi-nekotwahfwi mecimi hini mawi-caakatfwi yaatefaki mecimi yaska hini yeesilawiici

Again he went out about the sixth and the ninth hour, and did likewise.

6. chiine nawito hini metahfwi-kite-nekoti yaatefaki hina lohfe mecimi homhkawahi kotakhi pah niipawihi chiine koociwe hotasi kiilawa kiniipawipwa nehkiiskwe mata wiyehi kitesilawiipwa hotelahi

And about the eleventh hour he went out, and found others standing; and he saith unto them, Why stand ye here all the day idle?

7. ksake mata nime haloolekona hileni hotekohi nihi nhhaakone nehfaapi kiilawa hini mhfaloomiktikaaneki hotelahi

They say unto him, Because no man hath hired us. He saith unto them, Go ye also into the vineyard.

8. chiine weelaakwiifiki yeh piyeeyaaki hina teepeeletaka hini mhfaloomiktika wihkomi nihki peekateficki mecimi tepwhi hotephotiiwenwa nihki ceeyehkwi hoci halemi lawiilo paalohi nihki nhhihta hotelaali honoosaacikanali

And when even was come, the lord of the vineyard saith unto his steward, Call the labourers, and pay them their hire, beginning from the last unto the first.

9. chiine yeh piyaawaaci nihki yeelooloofocki hini nawito metahfwi-kite-nekoti yaatefaki hotfekonaawa nihki caaki hileni nekoti seleni

And when they came that were hired about the eleventh hour, they received every man a penny.

10. chiine nihki nhhihta hine yeh piyaawaaci halika lekhi ne hotfekope siteheeki nihki mecimi nehfaapi hotfekonaawa caaki hileni nekoti seleni

And when the first came, they supposed that they would receive more; and they likewise received every man a penny.

11. chiine yeh mamowaaci hini hopekihkawaawaali nihki nili teepeeletamelici wiikiwa

And when they received it, they murmured against the householder,

12. yohkoma ceeyehkwiifaki nekotiimehi yaatefaki pekatefiiki mecimi kiila kiceeceshaaki niilawe hini yeetalatelaakwiyaake hini nehkiiskwe mecimi hini yeetalatefoyaake hini keesiteeki hisiweeki

saying, These last have spent but one hour, and thou hast made them equal unto us, which have borne the burden of the day and the scorching heat.

13. payeekwa hina haapafse mecimi wihkaanima mata kipiimilotoole ha mata nekoti seleni kitesi mehtaacimoomi

But he answered and said to one of them, Friend, I do thee no wrong: didst not thou agree with me for a penny?

14. mamelo hini weewiilaamiyani mecimi nhhaale hini yeesiteheeya niila wahsi miilaki yaama hotaanaakiifa teetepilahi paasi kiila

Take up that which is thine, and go thy way; it is my will to give unto this last, even as unto thee.

15. ha mata hini mayaawatwi kwteletiiweneki yeesiteheeya hpenatooya nehalwaaka niwiyehiimi weelaa toke kiskiisekwi macaafi ksake niila noowesiilefi hotelaali nekoti nihi

Is it not lawful for me to do what I will with mine own? or is thine eye evil, because I am good?

16. weecikeenahi hina hotaanaakiifa we nhhihtaawi mecimi hina nhhihtaafa we hotaanaakiwi

So the last shall be first, and the first last.

17. chiine yeesi wiisa colooseelemii si kkwicsinowaaci homamahi nihi metahfwi-kite-niiswi kakehkimaafhi tepaane chiine hini yeele haawaaci

And as Jesus was going up to Jerusalem, he took the twelve disciples apart, and in the way he said unto them,

18. waapatamoko colooseelemii kite kkwicsinepe chiine hina hokwihfali hileni nihi hokimaawi mhkateewkolayehi chiine yaayawikeelici weh si pakfenoofo mecimi nihki nepooweneki weh si poonaawaali

Behold, we go up to Jerusalem; and the Son of man shall be delivered unto the chief priests and scribes; and they shall condemn him to death,

19. chiine weh si pakfenaawaali nihi nanahkawilenihi wahsi waapalaachaawaaci chiine wahsi lihfiiwanhhwaawaaci mecimi wahsi haasitefhwaawaaci nili chiine hini mawi-nhfokonakike hina we honhskaanoofo hotelahi

and shall deliver him unto the Gentiles to mock, and to scourge, and to crucify: and the third day he shall be raised up.

20. hine howe hotfekooli nili hokiwaali nihki sepetii hokwifhi kileki hina hokwifhi hosasilawehekooli mecimi honatotamaakooli naanekoti wiyehi

Then came to him the mother of the sons of Zebedee with her sons, worshipping him, and asking a certain thing of him.

21. chiine nehiwe skata kiila hotelaali tepikeemolo wahsi yohkoma niiswi nikwihfaki menawahi lematapiwaaci nekoti kimayaawiinhkiki chiine nekoti kinamaciinhkiki kookimaawiiweneki hotekooli

And he said unto her, What wouldest thou? She saith unto him, Command that these my two sons may sit, one on thy right hand, and one on thy left hand, in thy kingdom.

22. payeekwa ciisisii haapafse mecimi mata kiwaakotaanaawa neetotameekwe ha kiteepiilefipwa kiilawa wahsi meneyeekwe hina tephika waasa nawito howe meneya hisiwe niteepiilefipe hotekohi

But Jesus answered and said, Ye know not what ye ask. Are ye able to drink the cup that I am about to drink? They say unto him, We are able.

23. sapkahi keh menepwa nitephika payeekwa wahsi lematapiyeekwe nimayaawiinhkiki chiine ninamaciinhkiki mata niila hini wahsi miiliweeya weeka nihkiini wiilawa hini nihi neyehka mayehci nanasfetawaaci nohfa hotelahi

He saith unto them, My cup indeed ye shall drink: but to sit on my right hand, and on my left hand, is not mine to give, but it is for them for whom it hath been prepared of my Father.

24. chiine nihki metahfwi yeh nootamowaaci hini maaciteheeki kisfetiiwe nihisi niiswi hoceeninaanahi

And when the ten heard it, they were moved with indignation concerning the two brethren.

25. payeekwa ciisisii hoteh wihkomahi nihi mecimi kiwaakotaanaawa yeesi hini nihi teepeeletamhpenalekowaaci nihki nanahkawileniiki yeelaapamaawaaci mecimi wiilawa homhsikiloomwahi mhsi mekofihtaakowaaci hotelahi

But Jesus called them unto him, and said, Ye know that the rulers of the Gentiles lord it over them, and their great ones exercise authority over them.

26. mata yooni we hinwi hini heelekiina kiilawa weeka kookwe-neefa-kaaci wi mhsiilefiwi heelekiina kiilawa ke homiisamaakeemipwa

Not so shall it be among you: but whosoever would become great among you shall be your minister;

27. mecimi kookwe-neefa-kaaci wi nhhihtaawefi heelekiina kiilawa ke hotaloolaakanipwa

and whosoever would be first among you shall be your servant:

28. teetepilahi paasi hina hokwihfali hileni piyeewa
mata wahsi miisamaweci wahsi miisamaakeeci weeka
mecimi wahsi miiliweeci hotelenaweewiiwe wahsi
hotwenikanici meci

even as the Son of man came not to be
ministered unto, but to minister, and to
give his life a ransom for many.

29. chiine yeesi nihki lohfaawaaci celekoo hoci meci
mehseelelici honeekalekohi

And as they went out from Jericho, a
great multitude followed him.

30. chiine waapamehko niiswi kakeepiikweewi lenihi
peemi lematapilici hini pakacikana yeh nootaakeewaaci
nihki yeesi pemi pemhfeelici ciisisiili
wiyakahootamooki teepeelemiweeta poonamawinaake
kiteminaakweeletiiwe kiila hokwihfali teepitii
hisiweeki

And behold, two blind men sitting by
the way side, when they heard that Jesus
was passing by, cried out, saying, Lord,
have mercy on us, thou son of David.

31. chiine nihki mehseelekki hokilhamawaawahi wahsi
nihki tfwahootamowaaci payeekwa nihki paameci hini
halika lahootamooki teepeelemiweeta
poonamawanaake kiteminaakweeletiiwe kiila
hokwihfali teepitii hisiweeki

And the multitude rebuked them, that
they should hold their peace: but they
cried out the more, saying, Lord, have
mercy on us, thou son of David.

32. chiine ciisisii noole niipawi mecimi hoteh
wihkomahi nehiwe kitesiteheepwa wa hpenalelako
hotelahi

And Jesus stood still, and called them,
and said, What will ye that I should do
unto you?

33. teepeelemiweeta wahsi menawahi tawenooteeki
niskiisekona hotekohi

They say unto him, Lord, that our eyes
may be opened.

34. chiine ciisisii peemi kiteminaakweelemaaci hoteh
pehsenamawahi hoskiisekowilici mecimi weelena nihki
hotfekonaawa hotepinamoowenwa chiine
honeekalekohi

And Jesus, being moved with
compassion, touched their eyes: and
straightway they received their sight,
and followed him.

Matthew:21

1. chiine maalaakwahi colooseelemii ye
halemhfeewaaci mecimi pefeci si piyeeki hini halifiwi
meekwahkiki hine howe ciisisii hoteh waawiinahi
niiswi kakehkimaafhi

And when they drew nigh unto
Jerusalem, and came unto Bethphage,
unto the mount of Olives, then Jesus
sent two disciples,

2. nhhaakone hini hoteewenehi yehteeki
yeelahfamiiyeekwe mecimi weelena ke mhkawaawa
ceekiifa kciipifo chiine mahkootelefa wiici nili
pelhhohko nihki mecimi piyeetawiko

saying unto them, Go into the village
that is over against you, and straightway
ye shall find an ass tied, and a colt with
her: loose them, and bring them unto
me.

3. chiine kwehkwi wiyeefa wiyehi hilelwaakwe hina
teepeelemiweeta skata hoteleelemahi ke hilaawa
mecimi weelena hotahfa we sfahahi nihi hotelahi nihi

And if any one say aught unto you, ye
shall say, The Lord hath need of them;
and straightway he will send them.

4. howe yooma piyeemikatwi wahsi hini menawah
hokwaawfeki yeeyoki saapwi hina
maamoosikiiskweeta

Now this is come to pass, that it might
be fulfilled which was spoken by the
prophet, saying,

5. wiitamawehko kiilawa nili hotaanehfali saayani
waapami kookimaama kootfekwa nanahpaaciilefi

Tell ye the daughter of Zion, Behold, thy
King cometh unto thee, Meek, and

chiine hopemi nayekooli ceekiifali mecimi hoskici mahkootelefali honiicaanali ceekiifa hiyopi

riding upon an ass, And upon a colt the foal of an ass.

6. chiine nihki kakehkimaafaki weepfeeki mecimi teetepilahi silawiiki yeesimekowaaci ciisisiili

And the disciples went, and did even as Jesus appointed them,

7. chiine hopiyeelaawaali nili ceekiifali mecimi nili mahkootelefali chiine hotapkawhaawahi nihi hopiitenikanwa mecimi hina honayekohi

and brought the ass, and the colt, and put on them their garments; and he sat thereon.

8. chiine nihki haliwi tfwi mehseelekki hosekatenaanaawa hopiitenikanwa yeele miyeewiki chiine kotakaki hokiskipiyeethaanaawa nili mhteko mecimi hosekatenaanaawa nili hini yeele miyeewiki

And the most part of the multitude spread their garments in the way; and others cut branches from the trees, and spread them in the way.

9. chiine nihki mehseelekki yeele niikaaniilici mecimi hotaanaaki weemelici hoosena cehi hina hokwihfali teepitii kisaateelemekofi ce hina peepiyaata hini howiifooweneki hina teepeelemiweeta hoosena cehi wihkoci lhspi lahootamooki

And the multitudes that went before him, and that followed, cried, saying, Hosanna to the son of David: Blessed is he that cometh in the name of the Lord; Hosanna in the highest.

10. chiine colooseelemii yeh si piyaaci caayahki hini hoteewe tatawaanwi neefawe yaama hiyopi

And when he was come into Jerusalem, all the city was stirred, saying, Who is this?

11. chiine nihki mehseelekki hiina yaama maamoosikiiskweeta ciisisii naaselefi keeleliiwi taamhkwe hoci hiwaki

And the multitudes said, This is the prophet, Jesus, from Nazareth of Galilee.

12. chiine hini homamaatomeewikamikwi maneto si piicfe ciisisii mecimi holohfe pakilahi nihi caayahki weewiitkiilici mecimi teepenikeelici piitike hini mamaatomeewikamikwi chiine hokolepi-pakitamawahi nili hoteepaliimwa nihki moni haasoonikehfiiki mecimi nili hotpapiiwenwa nihki maamiyeekinaacki nihi miyaasipawiifhi

And Jesus entered into the temple of God, and cast out all them that sold and bought in the temple, and overthrew the tables of the money-changers, and the seats of them that sold the doves;

13. mecimi mehtawikeepi hini hotelahi niwiikiwaapimi mamaatomeewika weh sitoote weeka kiilawa ciikoniwehfiiki howaasaalakomwa kitestoonaawa hini hotelahi nihi

and he saith unto them, It is written, My house shall be called a house of prayer: but ye make it a den of robbers.

14. chiine nihi keekakeepiikweelici chiine nihi meemiyaalakikaateelici hotfekohi piitike hini mamaatomeewikamikwi mecimi hokiikehahi

And the blind and the lame came to him in the temple: and he healed them.

15. payeekwa nihki hokimaawi mhkateewkolayeeki chiine nihki yaayawikeecki yeh neemowaaci nili lakokwehtaani wiyehi yeesilawiilici nili mecimi nihi hapelofhi hoosena cehi hina hokwihfali teepitii peemi lahootamelici piitike hini mamaatomeewikamikwi kisfetiiwe maaciteheeki nihki

But when the chief priests and the scribes saw the wonderful things that he did, and the children that were crying in the temple and saying, Hosanna to the son of David; they were moved with indignation,

16. mecimi ha kinootawaaki yohkoma yeeyowaaci hotekohi mecimi ciisisii hanhka ha matalaakwa kiilawa kilaapaatotaanaawa nili hotoonwa hapelohfeefaki

and said unto him, Hearest thou what these are saying? And Jesus saith unto them, Yea: did ye never read, Out of the

chiine neenoonooficki kooci poona kiila meftoote wiyawaacimetiiwe hotelahi

17. chiine honakalahi nihi mecimi hale weepfe lohfe hini hoteewe pefene heewa chiine nitasi kkehsi

18. howe hini kwelahwaapaki yeesi peteki hini hoteeweneki haaci skwaalawe

19. mecimi maa hoteh neeme kicimiisi hini pakackana hini si piyeewa chiine mata wiyehi homhka nitasi weeka mhsiske pehi mecimi wiilaani matalaakwa mawifoowe ya hteewi kiila hoci yooci kookwelaakwasi hoteta hini chiine weelena hini kicimiisi nepote

20. mecimi yeh neemowaaci hini nihki kakehkimaafaki kwakwehtaaniteheeki nehiwesi weelena nepote hini kicimiisi hiwaki

21. chiine haapafse ciisisii mecimi tepilo kitelepwa niila kwehkwi poonameekwe teepwehseewe mecimi teki haanwehseeko mata hini kicimiisi yehpenatooteeki pehi keh silawiipwa weeka wiikinaakwi kwehkwi yooma meekwahkiki mamoofolo mecimi hini mhsinepiki hipakiloofolo ke hitaanaawa hini we hpenatoote

22. mecimi caayahki wiyehi kookwe-nehi-kaaci kiilawa keh natotaanaawa mamaatomeeweneki pemi teepwehseeyeekwe ke hotfekonaawa kiilawa hotelahi

23. chiine yeh piyaaci piitike hini mamaatomeewikamikwi hotfekohi nihi hokimaawi mhkateewkolayehi chiine nihi hokikileniimwahi nihki lenaweeki yeesi pemi kakehkimiweeci mecimi taaniwe hoci mekofiiwe kooci yooloma wiyehi silawi chiine neefawe kimiilekwa yooma simekofiiwe hotekohi

24. chiine haapafse ciisisii mecimi nehfaapi niila keh natohtoolepwa nekotweelena natohtwaatiiwe hini kwehkwi kiilawa wiitamawiyeekwe nehfaapi niila keh wiitamoolepwa hini simekofiiwe wahoci yooloma wiyehi silawiiya hotelahi

25. hini hofafahkwiholelhiweewe caanii taaniwe hoci hini ha weefepahkamikiki hoci weelaa toke hileniiki hoci hotelahi mecimi nihki memekiniteheeki pesikwi wiilawa kwehkwi weefepahkamikiki hoci ke hiyope koociwe chiine mata kiteepwehtawaawa ke hikona

26. weeka kwehkwi hileniiki hoci ke hiyope kikwfaape nihki mehseelekki ksake maamoosikiiskweeta hotelakimaawaali caaniili hiwaki

mouth of babes and sucklings thou hast perfected praise?

And he left them, and went forth out of the city to Bethany, and lodged there.

Now in the morning as he returned to the city, he hungered.

And seeing a fig tree by the way side, he came to it, and found nothing thereon, but leaves only; and he saith unto it, Let there be no fruit from thee henceforward for ever. And immediately the fig tree withered away.

And when the disciples saw it, they marveled, saying, How did the fig tree immediately wither away?

And Jesus answered and said unto them, Verily I say unto you, If ye have faith, and doubt not, ye shall not only do what is done to the fig tree, but even if ye shall say unto this mountain, Be thou taken up and cast into the sea, it shall be done.

And all things, whatsoever ye shall ask in prayer, believing, ye shall receive.

And when he was come into the temple, the chief priests and the elders of the people came unto him as he was teaching, and said, By what authority doest thou these things? and who gave thee this authority?

And Jesus answered and said unto them, I also will ask you one question, which if ye tell me, I likewise will tell you by what authority I do these things.

The baptism of John, whence was it? from heaven or from men? And they reasoned with themselves, saying, If we shall say, From heaven; he will say unto us, Why then did ye not believe him?

But if we shall say, From men; we fear the multitude; for all hold John as a prophet.

27. chiine hotaapaftawaawaali ciisisiili mecimi mata niwaakotaape hotelaawaali nehfaapi mata nohki niila kitah wiitamoolepwa hini simekofiiwe wahoci yooloma wiyehi silawiiya hotelahi

And they answered Jesus, and said, We know not. He also said unto them, Neither tell I you by what authority I do these things.

28. payeekwa nehiwe kitesiteheepwa kiilawa nekoti hileni hopoonahi niiswi hokwifhi chiine nhheewa nili nhhihta hokwihfima nhhaale pekatefilo hinoki kaasekiki hini mhfaloomiktikaaneki hotelaali

But what think ye? A man had two sons; and he came to the first, and said, Son, go work today in the vineyard.

29. chiine hina haapafse mata hiwa payeekwa mayohkwaaci hina mataiini sitehe wiila mecimi nhheewa

And he answered and said, I will not: but afterward he repented himself, and went.

30. chiine nili mawi-niiswi heewa mecimi yaska hini yeeyoci chiine hina haapafse mecimi nine ha yeeleniwiyani hotekooli mecimi mata nhheewa

And he came to the second, and said likewise. And he answered and said, I go, sir: and went not.

31. taanawe nihki niiswi yeesiteheelici hohfali silawi hotelahi hina nhhihta hiwaki nihki tepilo kitelepwa niila yeesi nihki teeksiiwi-maawatonikehfiiki mecimi nihki naakahoowiikweki piicfaawaaci hini maneto hokimaawitaamhkomi yeelahfamiiyeekwe kiilawa

Whether of the twain did the will of his father? They say, The first. Jesus saith unto them, Verily I say unto you, that the publicans and the harlots go into the kingdom of God before you.

32. ksake caanii kootfekowa piyeci metemiye hini mayaawiilefiiwe mecimi kiilawa mata kiteepwehtawaawa hina weeka nihki teeksiiwi-maawatonikehfiiki chiine nihki naakahoowiikweki hoteepwehtawaawaali nili chiine kiilawa yeh neemeyeekwe hini mata mohci mayohkwaaci mataiini kitesiteheepwa kiiyaawa wahsi menawahke teepwehtaweekwe hina hotelahi ciisisii

For John came unto you in the way of righteousness, and ye believed him not: but the publicans and the harlots believed him: and ye, when ye saw it, did not even repent yourselves afterward, that ye might believe him.

33. nootamoko nohki kotaki pemaatoweewe hapiwa hileni peepoonaka yeetaaci wiikiwa hotito maloomikitika mecimi howakha kaayaawka hini chiine waalhke waiiniiwi fiikiceepicika piitike hini chiine hopatena taweteewika mecimi ktikeewilenihi hotawhhahi hini chiine payakila hasiski si haaci

Hear another parable: There was a man that was a householder, which planted a vineyard, and set a hedge about it, and digged a winepress in it, and built a tower, and let it out to husbandmen, and went into another country.

34. chiine hine naanemi hini laakwa ta hatiteeki hini mawifoowe hoteleskamawahi nihi ktikeewilenihi hotaloolaakanhhi wahsi hotahpenaki homawifoowe

And when the season of the fruits drew near, he sent his servants to the husbandmen, to receive his fruits.

35. chiine nihki ktikeewileniiki homesenaawahi hotaloolaakanhhi mecimi hopkitehwaawaali nekoti chiine honhfaawaali nekoti mecimi hosiikonhhwaawaali nohki nekoti

And the husbandmen took his servants, and beat one, and killed another, and stoned another.

36. nohki hoteleskawahi kotakhi hotaloolaakanhhi halika tfwi noota hini weski mecimi nihki hini yaska yehpenalaawaaci nihi

Again, he sent other servants more than the first: and they did unto them in like manner.

37. payeekwa mayohkwaaci hoteleskamawahi hokwihfali we hotakeelemaawaali keela nikwihfali nihki hiwapi

But afterward he sent unto them his son, saying, They will reverence my son.

38. payeekwa nihki ktikeewileniiki yeh neewaawaaci nili hokwihfimaali halayaama hina layaapitepeeletaka piyaako nhfaataako mecimi mametaako hini laapi howiyehiimi hitiiki heelekiina wiilawa

But the husbandmen, when they saw the son, said among themselves, This is the heir; come, let us kill him, and take his inheritance.

39. mecimi homesenaawaali nili chiine hini mhfaloomiktika hoci lohfe pakilaawaali mecimi honhfaawaali

And they took him, and cast him forth out of the vineyard, and killed him.

40. hine weecikeenahi hina teepeeletaka hini mhfaloomiktika weh piyeewa nehiwe we hpenalahi hina yohoma ktikeewilenihi hotelahi

When therefore the lord of the vineyard shall come, what will he do unto those husbandmen?

41. weh mamiyeetaakwi nhfahi hina yohoma mamiyeetahkweyi lenihi mecimi we hawhhahi kotakhi ktikeewilenihi hini mhfaloomiktika nihi wah miilekoci nili mawifoowena laakwa ta hatiteeki hotekohi

They say unto him, He will miserably destroy those miserable men, and will let out the vineyard unto other husbandmen, which shall render him the fruits in their seasons.

42. ha matalaakwa kilaapaatotaanaawa nili tepilo heewikaateewali nili siikonali yeelawinawaawaaci nihki waakkaacki hina yaska mechoofo howiisiwi hini poocaaki yaama hina teepeelemiweeta hociwi mecimi hina hanhhiweewi naakofi kiskiisekonaaki hotelahi ciisisii

Jesus saith unto them, Did ye never read in the scriptures, The stone which the builders rejected, The same was made the head of the corner: This was from the Lord, And it is marvelous in our eyes?

43. weecikeenahi kitelepwa niila hini hokimaawiiwe maneto keh mamaakoopwa mecimi weh miiloofo kotaki si lenawe hini weeci pemi piyeetoota hini mawifoowe

Therefore say I unto you, The kingdom of God shall be taken away from you, and shall be given to a nation bringing forth the fruits thereof.

44. chiine hina hoskici yooloma siikonali yeesi penhsika weh pohposkwihsinwa weeka kookwe-neefali-kaaci hina weh si penhsinwa weh lhfweskawaali nili paasi pekwi

And he that falleth on this stone shall be broken to pieces: but on whomsoever it shall fall, it will scatter him as dust.

45. chiine hine nihki hokimaawi mhkateewkolayeeki chiine pelesiiki yeh nootamawaawaaci hopemaatoweewe moositeheeki nihki yeesi nihi hina haacimaaci

And when the chief priests and the Pharisees heard his parables, they perceived that he spake of them.

46. mecimi yeh wiisa nihki mesenaawaaci nili hokwfaawahi nihi mehseelelici ksake nihki maamoosikiiskweeta hoteleelemaawaali nili

And when they sought to lay hold on him, they feared the multitudes, because they took him for a prophet.

Matthew:22

1. chiine ciisisii haapafse mecimi hokaloolahi nohki pemaatoweewena

And Jesus answered and spake again in parables unto them, saying,

2. hini weefepahkamikiki hokimaawitaamhkwe naanekoti hokima si takweelemekwatwi mayecfetawaata hokwihfali wiichetiiwi wihfenhcikeewe

The kingdom of heaven is likened unto a certain king, which made a marriage feast for his son,

3. chiine howaawiinahi hotaloolaakanhhi wahsi hotahpimaawaaci nihi yeesi halanoofolici hini wiichetiiwi wihfenhcikeewe mecimi mata wiisa piyehi nihi

and sent forth his servants to call them that were bidden to the marriage feast: and they would not come.

4. nohki howaawiinahi kotakhi haloolaakanhhi waapatamoko nimecfeto nitenaliiwe nitaaksiniimaki mecimi niweelakwiimaki nhfekwiiki chiine caayahki wiyehi mecfenwi piyaako hini wiichetiiwi wihfenhcikeeweneki hilehko nihki yeelanoofocki hisiwe

Again he sent forth other servants, saying, Tell them that are bidden, Behold, I have made ready my dinner: my oxen and my fatlings are killed, and all things are ready: come to the marriage feast.

5. payeekwa nihki holaakeeletawtoonaawa hini mecimi weepfeeki yehaawaaci nekoti nehalwaaka hoktikaaneki heewa nohki nekoti howiitkiiweneki

But they made light of it, and went their ways, one to his own farm, another to his merchandise:

6. chiine nihki maisi naaleta homawinactaakohi hotaloolaakanhhi chiine hotekweewpenalaawahi mecimi honhfaawahi nihi

and the rest laid hold on his servants, and entreated them shamefully, and killed them.

7. payeekwa hina hokima wiyakowe chiine hoteleskawahi hosamaakanemhhi chiine honhfahi yohoma naanhsiweelici mecimi hofakfamawahi hoteewenilici

But the king was wroth; and he sent his armies, and destroyed those murderers, and burned their city.

8. hine howe mecfenwi hini wiichetiiwe payeekwa nihki yeelanoofocki nootkweelemekofiiki

Then saith he to his servants, The wedding is ready, but they that were bidden were not worthy.

9. nhhaakone kiilawa weecikeenahi nili tah piipkeeweniki nili miyeewali mecimi kookwe tfwi ke mhkawaawaaki hini wiichetiiwi wihfenhcikeewe si halanehko hotelahi hotaloolaakaafhi

Go ye therefore unto the partings of the highways, and as many as ye shall find, bid to the marriage feast.

10. mecimi yohkoma haloolaakaafaki nili si lohfeeki mecimi homaawatonaawahi caayahki yeetfwi mhkawaawaaci neyiisweelena weenaatefilici chiine weeowesiilefilici mecimi hini wiichetiiwe hokwihfetoote yeelanoofocki

And those servants went out into the highways, and gathered together all as many as they found, both bad and good: and the wedding was filled with guests.

11. payeekwa hina hokima yeh piyeci piicfaaci wahsi neewaaci nihi yeelanoofolici honeewaali nitasi peepwaa piitenikeelici wiichetiiwi piitenika

But when the king came in to behold the guests, he saw there a man which had not on a wedding-garment:

12. wihkaanima nehiwe kitesi hotahfa si piicfa mata kipoona wiichetiiwipiitenika hotelaali mecimi hina haalwi kalawi

and he saith unto him, Friend, how camest thou in hither not having a wedding-garment? And he was speechless.

13. hine howe hina hokima kciipilehko holeci mecimi hofici mecimi hini faakici si lohfe pakilehko laa

Then the king said to the servants, Bind him hand and foot, and cast him out into

pepekica nitasi we hahteewi hini wihfakweewe mecimi hini yeetalweewehfeki wiipitali hotelahi nihi haloolaakaafhi

the outer darkness; there shall be the weeping and gnashing of teeth.

14. ksake meci wihkomoofooki payeekwa maatwiimehi mamoofooki

For many are called, but few chosen.

15. hine howe nihki pelesiiki weepfeeki mecimi tepoweeki wahsi menawah pethanaawaaci nili hokalawiiweneki

Then went the Pharisees, and took counsel how they might ensnare him in his talk.

16. chiine nihki hoteleskamawaawaali hokakehkimaafemwahi wiici nihi heletiifhi keekehkimiwe niwaakotaape yeesi kiila mayaawi hilefiyani chiine kakehkimiweeyani hini homiyeewi maneto teepweeweneki mecimi pwaa makofeelemaci wiyeefa ksake mata wiyehi kiteleeletaana howeeyaanwa hileniiki

And they send to him their disciples, with the Herodians, saying, Master, we know that thou art true, and teachest the way of God in truth, and carest not for any one: for thou regardest not the person of men.

17. wiitamawinaake weecikeenahi nehiwe kitesitehe ha mayaawatwi kwteletiiweneki wahsi miiloofoci teeksiiwi moni siisa weelaa toke mata hiwaki

Tell us therefore, What thinkest thou? Is it lawful to give tribute unto Caesar, or not?

18. payeekwa homooleeletamawahi ciisisii howanaatefiiwenilici mecimi koociwe kikotahkowaasipwa kiilawa nelohcilawiwehfiiki

But Jesus perceived their wickedness, and said, Why tempt ye me, ye hypocrites?

19. waapatesiko hini teeksiiwi moni hisiwe mecimi hopiyeetawaawaali nekoti teneliyas

Shew me the tribute money. And they brought unto him a penny.

20. chiine neefawe hokiishoowe yooma mecimi holhspawikaafoowe hotelahi

And he saith unto them, Whose is this image and superscription?

21. siisa wiila hotekohi hine howe hina peteki miilehko weecikeenahi siisa nili wiyehi siisa weewiilaamici mecimi maneto nili wiyehi maneto weewiilaamici hotelahi

They say unto him, Caesar's. Then saith he unto them, Render therefore unto Caesar the things that are Caesar's; and unto God the things that are God's.

22. chiine hine nihki yeh nootamowaaci hini cihfefiiki mecimi honakalaawaali nili chiine weepfeeki

And when they heard it, they marveled, and left him, and went their way.

23. hine kaasekiki nitasi hotfekohi setosihi yeesi pwaa hahteeki haapefiiwi-honhskaawe yaawaki nihki mecimi honatohtaakohi

On that day there came to him Sadducees, which say that there is no resurrection: and they asked him,

24. keekehkimiwe kwehkwi hileni nepeke pwaa pemi poonaate hapelofhi hoceeninaali weh wiiwili wiiwali chiine hina we honhskaanamawaali homiinhkaanilici hoceeninaali hiwa moosisii

saying, Master, Moses said, If a man die, having no children, his brother shall marry his wife, and raise up seed unto his brother.

25. howe nitasi hapiiki wiici niilawe niiswahfwi hoceeninaaki mecimi hina nhhihta hosiletamwa chiine hasenwa mecimi mata hopemi poona miinhka honakatamawaali hoceeninaali wiiwali

Now there were with us seven brethren: and the first married and deceased, and having no seed left his wife unto his brother;

26. nehfaapi hina mawi-niiswi hini yaska chiine hina mawi-nhfwi paalohi hina mawi-niiswahfwi

in like manner the second also, and the third, unto the seventh.

27. chiine mayohkwaaci nihi caayahki hina hkweewa nepwa

And after them all the woman died.

28. hini haapefiiweneki weecikeenahi neefawe we howiiwi nili nihki niiswahfwi ksake caayahki homehci poonaawaali nili hotekohi

In the resurrection therefore whose wife shall she be of the seven? for they all had her.

29. payeekwa ciisisii haapafse mecimi kipaapiimi lawiipwa kiilawa mata kipemi waakotaanaawa nili tepilo heewikaateewali nohki mata hini howiisikatowiiwe maneto

But Jesus answered and said unto them, Ye do err, not knowing the scriptures, nor the power of God.

30. ksake hini haapefiiweneki mata nihki waawiichetiiki mata nohki wiichetiiweneki yaasi miiletipi weeka hilefiiki paasi henhcaliiki piitike weefepahkamikiki

For in the resurrection they neither marry, nor are given in marriage, but are as angels in heaven.

31. payeekwa yeeki hini hotaapefiiwe hina nepeka ha mata kimeh laapaatotaanaawa yeelelwaakwe maneto

But as touching the resurrection of the dead, have ye not read that which was spoken unto you by God, saying,

32. niiya hina homanetoomali heplehem' chiine hina homanetoomali haisik' chiine hina homanetoomali ceekap' hiwa manetooli mata niliini homanetoomali hina nepeka hina lenaweewita weeka hotelahi nihi

I am the God of Abraham, and the God of Isaac, and the God of Jacob? God is not the God of the dead, but of the living.

33. chiine hini yeh nootamowaaci nihki mehseelekki hocihfeeletamawaawaali hokakehkimiweewe

And when the multitudes heard it, they were astonished at his teaching.

34. payeekwa nihki pelesiiki yeh nootaakeewaaci yeesi hina mehci teepimaaci nihi setosihi maawaskaaki

But the Pharisees, when they heard that he had put the Sadducees to silence, gathered themselves together.

35. chiine nekoti nihki laya honatohtawaali natohtwaatiiwe hopemi kotahkowaalaali

And one of them, a lawyer, asked him a question, tempting him,

36. keekehkimiwe taaniwe mhsaawi tepikeemoowe hini kwteletiiweneki hotelaali

Master, which is the great commandment in the law?

37. mecimi hina hahkweelemi kiila hina teepeelemiweeta kimanetooma kileki caayahki kitehi mecimi kileki caayahki mayaawikiiya mecimi kileki caayahki kimemekinitehaaka

And he said unto him, Thou shalt love the Lord thy God with all thy heart, and with all thy soul, and with all thy mind.

38. yooma hini mhsaawi mecimi nhhihtawatwi tepikeemoowe

This is the great and first commandment.

39. chiine mawi-niiswi paasi hini yeeki halayooma hahkweelemi kiila maapayeecikaalehka paasi kiiya

And a second like unto it is this, Thou shalt love thy neighbour as thyself.

40. yoolooni niiswi tepikeemoowena tah laapiteki melhske hini kwteletiiwe chiine nihki maamoosikiiskwecki hotelaali nili

On these two commandments hangeth the whole law, and the prophets.

41. howe yeheeyehi maawaskaawaaci nihki pelesiiki ciisisii honatohtawahi nihi natohtwaatiiwe

Now while the Pharisees were gathered together, Jesus asked them a question,

42. nehiwe kiilawa kiteleelemaawa hina klaistii neefawe hokwihfali nili hotelahi teepitii hokwihfali nili hotelaawaali nihki

saying, What think ye of the Christ? whose son is he? They say unto him, The son of David.

43. koociwe chiine teepitii teepeelemiweeta hotesinaali hini hocacaalahkoki

He saith unto them, How then doth David in the Spirit call him Lord, saying,

44. hina teepeelemiweeta hotelaali niteepeelemiweemali lematapilo kiila nimayaawiinhkiki paalohi niila laameki kifitali si poonake kimateeletiiwenaki hiwa

The Lord said unto my Lord, Sit thou on my right hand, Till I put thine enemies underneath thy feet?

45. kwekkwi teepitii hine teepeelemiweeta sinaate nili nehiwe hotesi hokwihfinaali hotelahi

If David then calleth him Lord, how is he his son?

46. mecimi mata nekoti wiyeefa katawiilefi wahsi haapaftawaaci nekoti kalawiiwe mata nohki kiteeni hileni hine kaasekiki hoci natohtawaali natohtwaatiiwe

And no one was able to answer him a word, neither durst any man from that day forth ask him any more questions.

Matthew:23

1. hine howe hokaloolahi ciisisii nihi mehseelelici mecimi hokakehkimaafhi

Then spake Jesus to the multitudes and to his disciples,

2. nihki yaayawikeecki chiine nihki pelesiiki lematapiiki hoskici moosisii hotpapiiwe

saying, The scribes and the Pharisees sit on Moses' seat:

3. caayahki wiyehi weecikeenahi kookwe-nehi-kaaci nihki yeelelwaakwe yoolooni silawiiko mecimi kcitawaapiko payeekwa teki kikinamoko hopekatefiiwenwa ksake kalawiiki nihki chiine mata wiyehi silawiiki

all things therefore whatsoever they bid you, these do and observe: but do not ye after their works; for they say, and do not.

4. hanhka hokaakciipilenaawa kofekwi wiiwasiiwena mecimi mamiyeetaawato wahsi nawooteeki chiine hoskici hoteliwa hileniiki hotaasi poonaanaawa nili payeekwa mata nihki wiilawa hotah maatenaanaawa nili nekoti holeciwaali hoci

Yea, they bind heavy burdens and grievous to be borne, and lay them on men's shoulders; but they themselves will not move them with their finger.

5. weeka caayahki hopekatefiiwenwa yaasilawiiwaaci nihki wahsi hilenihi nookowaaci hoci ksake homaamhfaapiyehtoonaawa hokikinoocipiitenikanwa mecimi homaamhsihtoonaawa ta nipenikwaateeki hopiitenikanwa

But all their works they do for to be seen of men: for they make broad their phylacteries, and enlarge the borders of their garments,

6. chiine homenwiiletaanaawa hini haliwi yeeki tah wiiwihfenhcikeeki chiine nili haliwi yeeki hpapiiwena piitike nili mhsikamiko

and love the chief place at feasts, and the chief seats in the synagogues,

7. chiine nili hosilawaatiiwena tah wiiwiitkiiki mecimi lepaayii wi hikowaaci hilenihi

and the salutations in the marketplaces, and to be called of men, Rabbi.

8. payeekwa kiilawa teki lepaayii ki hikoopwa ksake nekotihi kikakehkimiwemwa chiine caayahki kiilawa hoceeninaaki

But be not ye called Rabbi: for one is your teacher, and all ye are brethren.

9. chiine teki hileni kohfwa ki hilaawa hini hoskitaamhkwe ksake nekotihi kohfwa tepilahi hina piitike yeepita weefepahkamikiki

And call no man your father on the earth: for one is your Father, which is in heaven.

10. teki nohki kiilawa mesteleki ki hikoopwa ksake nekotihi kimestelemwa klaistii hina

Neither be ye called masters: for one is your master, even the Christ.

11. weeka hina kci haliwi yeelefita heelekiina kiilawa ke hotaloolaakanipwa

But he that is greatest among you shall be your servant.

12. chiine kookwe-neefa-kaaci weh moospeelemekofihto wiiya weh nanahpaachoofo mecimi kookwe-neefa-kaaci weh nanahpaacto wiiya weh moospeelemehoofo

And whosoever shall exalt himself shall be humbled; and whosoever shall humble himself shall be exalted.

13. payeekwa kimacilepwaawenipwa cehi kiilawa yaayawikeecki chiine pelesiiki nelohcilawiwehfiiki ksake kiilawa kikiphamawaawaaki hileniiki hini weefepahkamikiki hokimaawi taamhkwe mhfehkaaci mata kipiicfaapwa kiilawa mata nohki wiilaani kiteleelemaawaaki nihki peemi hottakki wahsi piicfaawaaci

But woe unto you, scribes and Pharisees, hypocrites! because ye shut the kingdom of heaven against men: for ye enter not in yourselves, neither suffer ye them that are entering in to enter.

15. kimacilepwaawenipwa cehi kiilawa yaayawikeecki chiine pelesiiki nelohcilawiwehfiiki ksake kipaapemesitoonaawa kaawaci mhsinepi chiine hasiski wahsi hosheekwe nekoti kwelepkoofota chiine hina yooni yeh lefici pihtawiniisene si halika hahkwinamoowi hokwihfima kitaashaawa hina noota kiilawa

Woe unto you, scribes and Pharisees, hypocrites! for ye compass sea and land to make one proselyte; and when he is become so, ye make him twofold more a son of hell than yourselves.

16. kimacilepwaawenipwa cehi kiilawa kakeepiikweewi naakaaniicki kookwe-neefa-kaaci we hatooci ciikinhkemo hini mamaatomeewikamikwi mata wiyehi hini weeka kookwe-neefa-kaaci we hatooci ciikinhkemo hini mamaatomeewikamikwi hoci kooli memoosinehikeeta hina yaayocki

Woe unto you, ye blind guides, which say, Whosoever shall swear by the temple, it is nothing; but whosoever shall swear by the gold of the temple, he is a debtor.

17. kiilawa wanihsakaaki mecimi keekeepiikweecki ksake taaniwe halika hinwi ha hini kooli weelaa toke hini mamaatomeewikamikwi weeci hofepiyaaki hini kooli

Ye fools and blind: for whether is greater, the gold, or the temple that hath sanctified the gold?

18. chiine kookwe-neefa-kaaci we hatooci ciikinhkemo hini pootefamaacika mata wiyehi hini weeka kookwe-neefa-kaaci we hatooci ciikinhkemo hini pakfenikeewe hoskici hini yehteeki memoosinehikeeta hina

And, Whosoever shall swear by the altar, it is nothing; but whosoever shall swear by the gift that is upon it, he is a debtor.

19. kiilawa kakeepiikwaki ksake taaniwe halika hinwi ha hini pakfenikeewe weelaa toke nipootefamaacika weeci hofepiyaaki hini pakfenikeewe

Ye blind: for whether is greater, the gift, or the altar that sanctifieth the gift?

20. hina weecikeenahi yeeatooci ciikinhkemota hini pootefamaacika hatooci ciikinhkemo hini mecimi caayahki wiyehi nitasi yehteeki hoskici

He therefore that sweareth by the altar, sweareth by it, and by all things thereon.

21. chiine hina yeeatooci ciikinhkemota hini mamaatomeewikamikwi hatooci ciikinhkemo hini mecimi nili nitasi piitike yeetaalici

And he that sweareth by the temple, sweareth by it, and by him that dwelleth therein.

22. chiine hina yeeatooci ciikinhkemota hini
weefepahkamikiki hatooci ciikinhkemo hini hokimaawi
hotpapiiwe maneto mecimi nili nitasi lematapilici

And he that sweareth by the heaven, sweareth by the throne of God, and by him that sitteth thereon.

23. kimacilepwaawenipwa cehi kiilawa yaayawikeecki
chiine pelesiiki nelohcilawiwehfiiki ksake
kitaateekshaanaawa mhseeweewaskwi mecimi
tiliwaskwi mecimi kaminiwaskwi chiine
kinakataanaawa mata mehcilotoote nili haliwi
kwefekwaki wiyehi hini kwteletiiwe hoci
tepasawhpenaletiiwe chiine kiteminaakweeletiiwe
chiine teepwehseewe weeka kiilawa yoolooni yo
neyehka kih mehci lawiipwa mecimi mata yo kita hini
kotaki pwaa neyehka mehci lawiipwa

Woe unto you, scribes and Pharisees, hypocrites! for ye tithe mint and anise and cummin, and have left undone the weightier matters of the law, judgment, and mercy, and faith: but these ye ought to have done, and not to have left the other undone.

24. kiilawa kakeepiikweewi naakaaniicki
faafihkaanaacki nili paapaakehfiifali mecimi
kwaakonaacki nili keemaliili

Ye blind guides, which strain out the gnat, and swallow the camel.

25. kimacilepwaawenipwa cehi kiilawa yaayawikeecki
chiine pelesiiki nelohcilawiwehfiiki ksake
kifaafafayaakhaawa hina tephika faakici wayeetahkwe
mecimi hini seswilaaka payeekwa piitike nihki
hokwihfenwi siikwitoowefiiwe mamiiloowilawiiwe
chiine hofaamilawiiwe

Woe unto you, scribes and Pharisees, hypocrites! for ye cleanse the outside of the cup and of the platter, but within they are full from extortion and excess.

26. kiila kakeepiikweewi pelesi fafayaakhi nhhihta hini
piitike wayeetahkwe hina tephika mecimi hini
seswilaaka wahsi hini faakici wayeetahkwe menawahi
fafayaakiyaaki nehfaapi

Thou blind Pharisee, cleanse first the inside of the cup and of the platter, that the outside thereof may become clean also.

27. kimacilepwaawenipwa cehi kiilawa yaayawikeecki
chiine pelesiiki nelohcilawiwehfiiki ksake
weewaaptooteeki nepoowena yeesi naakofiyeekwe
howesinaakwato nili faakici hoci payeekwa laameki
hokwihfeno nepoowi hileniiki hokanemwa mecimi
caayahki weyakaacaaki

Woe unto you, scribes and Pharisees, hypocrites! for ye are like unto whited sepulchres, which outwardly appear beautiful, but inwardly are full of dead men's bones, and of all uncleanness.

28. teetepilahi yooni kiilawa nehfaapi faakici hoci
kimayaawiilefiiwi naakowaaki hileniiki payeekwa
laameki kiilawa hokwihfeno nelohcilawiiwe mecimi
wanaatefiiwe

Even so ye also outwardly appear righteous unto men, but inwardly ye are full of hypocrisy and iniquity.

29. kimacilepwaawenipwa cehi kiilawa yaayawikeecki
chiine pelesiiki nelohcilawiwehfiiki ksake kiilawa
koopatenamawaawaaki nili honepoowenwa nihki
maamoosikiiskwecki mecimi kinaaswihtawaawaaki
honepoowaalakomwa nihki meeyaawiileficki

Woe unto you, scribes and Pharisees, hypocrites! for ye build the sepulchres of the prophets, and garnish the tombs of the righteous,

30. chiine ni hapipe hine tah kakiisekanemiwaaci
nohfenaaki mata niilawe mayehci wihpomaacki nihi
hini homhskomwa nihki maamoosikiiskwecki ni
hilefipe kiteyopwa

and say, If we had been in the days of our fathers, we should not have been partakers with them in the blood of the prophets.

31. hiini hoci pesikwi kiilawa kicahtawaacimopwa kiiyaawa yeesi kiilawa hokwihfinelwaakwe nihki nenhfaacki nihi maamoosikiiskwelici

Wherefore ye witness to yourselves, that ye are sons of them that slew the prophets.

32. hokwihfetooko weecikeenahi hini hotepacikanwa kohfwaaki

Fill ye up then the measure of your fathers.

33. kiilawa manetooki leewaaki hotoosaakanaki kiilawa nehiwe keh si katawesitaanaawa hini hahkwinamoowe hoci mehtahkowaaletiiwe

Ye serpents, ye offspring of vipers, how shall ye escape the judgment of hell?

34. weecikeenahi waapamehko kiteleskamoolepwa maamoosikiiskwecki chiine lepwaawileniiki chiine yaayawikeecki naaleta nihki ke nhfaawaaki mecimi ke haasitefhwaawaaki chiine naaleta nihki keh lihfiiwanhhwaawaaki piitike kimhsikamikomwaaki mecimi keh naanohkaachaawaaki hoteeweneki hoci hoteeweneki si

Therefore, behold, I send unto you prophets, and wise men, and scribes: some of them shall ye kill and crucify; and some of them shall ye scourge in your synagogues, and persecute from city to city:

35. wahsi kiilawa menawahi staki caayahki hini mayaawiilefiiwi mhskwi fefiikhooteeki hini hoskitaamhkwe hini homhskomi hepalii hoci hina meeyaawiilefita paalohi hina homhskomi sekalaaya hokwihfali peelekaaya nenhfeekwe lalakwi hini hofepikamikwi chiine hini pootefamaacika

that upon you may come all the righteous blood shed on the earth, from the blood of Abel the righteous unto the blood of Zachariah son of Barachiah, whom ye slew between the sanctuary and the altar.

36. tepilo kitelepwa niila caayahki yooloma wiyehi we hotfeko yaama hinoki skwiiwena

Verily I say unto you, All these things shall come upon this generation.

37. o colooseelem' colooseelem' naanhfaata nihi maamoosikiiskwelici mecimi saasiikonhhwaata nihi peepiyeelhkamaweci taaniwe tfene nimehci maawatonaaki kitapelohfemaki teetepilahi paasi peleewa yaasi maawatonaaci hopelefemhhi laameki holekwana mecimi mata kitesiteheepwa

O Jerusalem, Jerusalem, which killeth the prophets, and stoneth them that are sent unto her! how often would I have gathered thy children together, even as a hen gathereth her chickens under her wings, and ye would not!

38. waapatano yeetaayeekwe wiikiwa kinakatamaakoopwa liikatahkamikatwi

Behold, your house is left unto you desolate.

39. ksake kitelepwa niila mata kiteeni yooci hinoki kitah neewipwa paalohi kiilawa kisaateelemekofi cehi hina peepiyaata hini howiifooweneki teepeelemiweeta ke hiyopwa

For I say unto you, Ye shall not see me henceforth, till ye shall say, Blessed is he that cometh in the name of the Lord.

Matthew:24

1. chiine lohfe ciisisii hini mamaatomeewikamikwi hoci mecimi yehaaci heewa chiine hokakehkimaafhi hotfekohi wahsi waapatelekoci nili wiikiwaapali hini mamaatomeewikamikwi hoci

And Jesus went out from the temple, and was going on his way; and his disciples came to him to shew him the buildings of the temple.

2. payeekwa haapafse mecimi ha mata kineemenaawa halayooma caayahki wiyehi tepilo kitelepwa niila mata hotasi we skonoofo nekoti hapiwa siikona hoskici kotakali wah pwaa penenoofota hotelahi nihi

But he answered and said unto them, See ye not all these things? verily I say unto you, There shall not be left here one stone upon another, that shall not be thrown down.

3. chiine yeesi lematapici wehseteki hini halifiwi meekwahkiki hokiimi hotfekohi nihi kakehkmaafhi wiitamawinaake taaniwe laakwa hine we hateewa yooloma wiyehi chiine nehiwe weh si kikinoolooweniwi kipiyaawe mecimi hini ceeyehkwaake hini yeelekokwahkamikiki hotekohi

And as he sat on the mount of Olives, the disciples came unto him privately, saying, Tell us, when shall these things be? and what shall be the sign of thy coming, and of the end of the world?

4. chiine haapafse ciisisii mecimi kcitawaafiiko wahsi pwaa hileni piimiwelelwaakwe

And Jesus answered and said unto them, Take heed that no man lead you astray.

5. ksake meci weh piyeeki niwiifooweneki niiya hina klaistii we hiwaki mecimi meci weh piimiwelaawahi

For many shall come in my name, saying, I am the Christ; and shall lead many astray.

6. chiine kiilawa keh nootaakeepwa noochetiiwena mecimi yeelaatotooteeki noochetiiwena kcitawaapiko wahsi pwaa kiilawa petfakifiyeekwe ksake yooloma wiyehi kwiilahi paapiyeeci weh piyeemikato payeekwa hini ceeyehkwiiwe mata keewaki

And ye shall hear of wars and rumours of wars: see that ye be not troubled: for these things must needs come to pass; but the end is not yet.

7. ksake nekotweelena si lenawe weh pafekwicfatawaali nekotweelena si lenaweeli mecimi hokimaawiiwe hoppehtena hokimaawiiwe chiine nitasi we hateewa seeskwaalaweeweniki mecimi hasiskinoomeskaawena caceepi tasi

For nation shall rise against nation, and kingdom against kingdom: and there shall be famines and earthquakes in divers places.

8. payeekwa yooloma wiyehi niliini weeci halemahkamikiki hahkwilaasamamoowe

But all these things are the beginning of travail.

9. hine howe kiisenaacinamooweneki keh si pakfenekowaaki nihki mecimi keh nhfekowaaki chiine keh siikeelemekofiimekowaaki nihki caayahki tfweelena si lenaweeki ksake niwiifoowe hoci

Then shall they deliver you up unto tribulation, and shall kill you: and ye shall be hated of all the nations for my name's sake.

10. mecimi hine howe meci we hotakikahsinooki chiine pesikwi weh mestaawhetiiki mecimi weh siikeeletiiki

And then shall many stumble, and shall deliver up one another, and shall hate one another.

11. chiine meci miyaasi maamoosikiiskwecki weh pafekwiiki mecimi weh piimiwelaawahi meci

And many false prophets shall arise, and shall lead many astray.

12. chiine ksake wanaatefiiwe we skwiiya hini hotahkweeletiiwenwa meci we tikiniikinili

And because iniquity shall be multiplied, the love of the many shall wax cold.

13. payeekwa hina nahiika hini yehkwi wiisikifita hiina hina weh waapaneshoofo

But he that endureth to the end, the same shall be saved.

14. chiine yooma howesi piyeetaacimoowe hini hokimaawitaamhkwe hoci weh nanahimiweepi hini melhske yeelekokwahkamikiki wahsi hoteepweeweniwaaci nihki caayahki tfweelena si lenaweeki chiine hine howe weh piyeeya hini ceeyehkwiiwe

And this gospel of the kingdom shall be preached in the whole world for a testimony unto all the nations; and then shall the end come.

15. hine weecikeenahi kiilawa neemeyeekwe hini lasiikaaciwefiiwe hoci siikwahkamikifiiwe yaatotooteeki saapwi teenial' hina maamoosikiiskweeta pah niipawi hini weefepiyaaki tasi wiilaani hina leelaapaatotaka nenohseete

When therefore ye see the abomination of desolation, which was spoken of by Daniel the prophet, standing in the holy place (let him that readeth understand),

16. hine howe wiilaani nihki cotiyeeki yeepicki nili meekwahkiki lesimowaate

then let them that are in Judaea flee unto the mountains:

17. wiilaani hina hini hakocikami yeepita pwaa laasiweete wahsi lohfatooci nili wiyehi piitike yehteeki yeetaaci wiikiwa

let him that is on the housetop not go down to take out the things that are in his house:

18. mecimi wiilaani hina hini laa ktika yeepita pwaa peteki si naateke hokootiimi

and let him that is in the field not return back to take his cloke.

19. weeka macilepwaaweniiki cehi nihki leelaamotaakocki hapelohfali mecimi nihki neenoonhhiweecki nele kaasekiki

But woe unto them that are with child and to them that give suck in those days!

20. chiine mamaatomaako kiilawa wahsi pwaa hateeki koosimoowenwa kwena hini pepooki weelaa kwena halwaakahsi kiisekiki

And pray ye that your flight be not in the winter, neither on a sabbath:

21. ksake hine howe hateewi mehsaaki kiisenaacinamoowe hini yeeki matalaakwa me hateewi hine halemahkamikatwi hini yeelekokwahkamikiki hoci paalohinoki mata nohki mata kiteeni we hateewi

for then shall be great tribulation, such as hath not been from the beginning of the world until now, no, nor ever shall be.

22. chiine weeciwephi nele kaasekiki mehci neyehka hoceekinooteeke mata wiyawfi yehki yah mehci waapanestoote payeekwa ksake hina memoofota hoci nele kaasekiki we hoceekinoote

And except those days had been shortened, no flesh would have been saved: but for the elect's sake those days shall be shortened.

23. hine howe kwehkwi wiyeefa hileni ce halayaama hina klaistii weelaa hotasi hilelwaakwe teki teepwehtamoko hini

Then if any man shall say unto you, Lo, here is the Christ, or, Here; believe it not.

24. ksake nitasi weh pafekwiiki miyaasi klaistiiki chiine miyaasi maamoosikiiskwecki mecimi weh waapatesiweeki maki kikinooloowena mecimi kweekwehtaaniki wahsi piimiwesiweewaaci katawi-ike wiikinaakwi nili memoofolici

For there shall arise false Christs, and false prophets, and shall shew great signs and wonders; so as to lead astray, if possible, even the elect.

25. waapatamoko kimehci wiitamoolepwa kaasa

Behold, I have told you beforehand.

26. kwehkwi weecikeenahi nihki waapamehko hina hini piileski hapiwa ke hikowaaki teki nhhaako waapamehko hina nili piicikaana hapiwa teki hini teepwehtamoko

If therefore they shall say unto you, Behold, he is in the wilderness; go not forth: Behold, he is in the inner chambers; believe it not.

27. ksake yeesi hini peepaki hini weetahkofaki homooyaaki mecimi si neemooteeki wiikinaakwi hini yeepaksimoki yooni we hiki hini hopiyaawe hina hokwihfali hileni

For as the lightning cometh forth from the east, and is seen even unto the west; so shall be the coming of the Son of man.

28. kookwe-tasi-kaaci hina nepeka hapiwa nitasi weh maawatoskaaki nihki teetahkwaki

Wheresoever the carcase is, there will the eagles be gathered together.

29. payeekwa weelena hahkowihi hini kiisenaacinamoowe nele kaasekiki hoci hina kiisekikiisfwa weh pepekichoofo mecimi hina tepehkikiisfwa mata weh miiliwe howahfaayaami chiine nihki halaakwaki menhkwatoki we hoci penhsinooki mecimi nili waasikaki nili menhkwato hoci weh noomenoote

But immediately, after the tribulation of those days, the sun shall be darkened, and the moon shall not give her light, and the stars shall fall from heaven, and the powers of the heavens shall be shaken:

30. chiine hine howe menhkwatoki weh tepinaakwatwi hini hokikinooloowe hina hokwihfali hileni chiine howe hine caayahki lenawe hotfweeloowena hini hoskitaamhkwe hoci weh mawe mecimi nihki weh neewaawaali nili hokwihfali hileni pemi piyeeli hoskici nili menhkwatwi paafkwahki kileki waasikaki chiine mehsaaki wahfaacimekofiiwe

and then shall appear the sign of the Son of man in heaven: and then shall all the tribes of the earth mourn, and they shall see the Son of man coming on the clouds of heaven with power and great glory.

31. chiine hina weh waawiinahi hotenhcaliimhhi wiici mehsi lweki pepikwa chiine nihki nili niyeewi mehsikkaki we hoci maawatonaawahi homamaawenhhi nekotweelena yeekwihfeki menhkwatwi hoci paalohi hini kotaki

And he shall send forth his angels with a great sound of a trumpet, and they shall gather together his elect from the four winds, from one end of heaven to the other.

32. howe hoci waakotefiko hina kicimiisa hopemaatoweewe hine hopkeeyahkofiiwe kokoskwaafi mecimi paskahkweeya homhsiskeema kiwaakotaanaawa kiilawa yeesi hini peelaawiki maalaakwahiki

Now from the fig tree learn her parable: when her branch is now become tender, and putteth forth its leaves, ye know that the summer is nigh;

33. teetepilahi yooni nehfaapi kiilawa hine neemeyeekwe caayahki yooloma wiyehi waakotamoko yeesi hina maalaakwahiwici teetepilahi nahiika nili skwaateewali

even so ye also, when ye see all these things, know ye that he is nigh, even at the doors.

34. tepilo kitelepwa niila yaama hinoki skwiiwena mata we hasenwa paalohi caayahki yooloma wiyehi weh mehcilotoote

Verily I say unto you, This generation shall not pass away, till all these things be accomplished.

35. menhkwatwi mecimi hasiski we haseno weeka nikalawiiwena mata we haseno

Heaven and earth shall pass away, but my words shall not pass away.

36. payeekwa hine si kaasekiki mecimi yaatefaki mata wiyeefa howaakota mata wiikinaakwi nihki henhcaliiki weefepahkamikiki hoci mata nohki hina hokwihfima hina weeka hohfima pehi

But of that day and hour knoweth no one, not even the angels of heaven, neither the Son, but the Father only.

37. chiine paasi nili hokiisekanema nowa yeeki yooni we hiki hini hopiyaawe hina hokwihfali hileni

And as were the days of Noah, so shall be the coming of the Son of man.

38. ksake paasi hine nele kaasekiki yeeki wihsi pwaa hini hateeki lekhokwiiwe nihki pemi wihfeniiki mecimi pemi menooki pemi wiichetiiki mecimi wiichetiiweneki si pemi miiletipi paalohi hini kaasekiki wah ta hini mhsi-olakeeleki lhkaki nowa

For as in those days which were before the flood they were eating and drinking, marrying and giving in marriage, until the day that Noah entered into the ark,

39. chiine nihki mata howaakotaanaawa paalohi hini lekhokwiiwe piyeeya mecimi hotaamwelekonaawa nihki caayahki yooni we hiki hini hopiyaawe hina hokwihfali hileni

and they knew not until the flood came, and took them all away; so shall be the coming of the Son of man.

40. hine howe niiswi hileniiki we hapiiki hini ktikaaneki nekoti mamoofo mecimi nekoti ckonoofo

Then shall two men be in the field; one is taken, and one is left:

41. niiswi hkweeki weh pemi takwhikeeki hini poothaakaneki nekoti mamoofo mecimi nekoti ckonoofo

two women shall be grinding at the mill; one is taken, and one is left.

42. kcitawaapiko weecikeenahi ksake mata kiwaakotaanaawa si kaasekiki tah piyaaci teepeelemelwaakwe

Watch therefore: for ye know not on what day your Lord cometh.

43. payeekwa waakotamoko halayooma kwehkwi hina hini wiikiwa hoci mestele neyehka waakotake laakwa waasa piyaaci hina kaakimooteka neyehka hina wi kcitawaapi mecimi mata neyehka wiilaani wih leeleta yeetaaci wiikiwa wahsi saapwi pokhooteelici

But know this, that if the master of the house had known in what watch the thief was coming, he would have watched, and would not have suffered his house to be broken through.

44. weecikeenahi nehfaapi kiilawa mehciilefiko ksake pwaayaa siteheeyeekwe yaatefaki hina hokwihfali hileni piyeewa

Therefore be ye also ready: for in an hour that ye think not the Son of man cometh.

45. neefawe chiine hina tepasawefi mecimi lepwaawefi haloolaaka mayehci talwahfekota teepeelemekoci yeetaalici wiyehi wahsi miilaaci nihi howihfeniiwenilici kwenaani laakwa

Who then is the faithful and wise servant, whom his lord hath set over his household, to give them their food in due season?

46. kisaateelemekofi cehi hina haloolaaka hina hine piyaalite teepeelemekoci we mhkaakooli peemi yooni silawiici

Blessed is that servant, whom his lord when he cometh shall find so doing.

47. tepilo kitelepwa niila nili weh talwahfwaali hina caayahki peepoonaki

Verily I say unto you, that he will set him over all that he hath.

48. weeka kwehkwi hina maci haloolaakaafa ceh naakaafi teepeelemita we hiwa hotehiki

But if that evil servant shall say in his heart, My lord tarrieth;

49. mecimi we halemi ppaktehwahi howiici-aloolaakanhhi chiine weh wihpomahi mecimi wiitaapoweemahi nihi weenefolici

and shall begin to beat his fellow-servants, and shall eat and drink with the drunken;

50. weh piyeeli hina haloolaaka nili teepeelemekoci hine kaasekiki mata hopiyeeteeleta mecimi hine yaatefaki mata howaakota

the lord of that servant shall come in a day when he expecteth not, and in an hour when he knoweth not,

51. chiine weh kiskhokooli nili mecimi weh si takwinamaakooli hini wiila nihi nelohcilawiwehfihi nitasi weh pemi wihfakweeweni mecimi hini weh talweewehfeno wiipitali

and shall cut him asunder, and appoint his portion with the hypocrites: there shall be the weeping and gnashing of teeth.

Matthew:25

1. hine howe hini weefepahkamikiki hokimaawitaamhkwe paasi metahfwi seskiikweefaki

Then shall the kingdom of heaven be likened unto ten virgins, which took

weh si takweelemekwatwi meemaacki honiitawaakanwahi mecimi weepfeeki hopah nakskawaawaali nili mayakinhhaakanali

their lamps, and went forth to meet the bridegroom.

2. chiine niyaalanwi nihki wanihsakaawefiiki mecimi niyaalanwi lepwaawefiiki

And five of them were foolish, and five were wise.

3. ksake nihki wanihsakaaki mata kileki hotaamwetoonaawa pemi yeh mamaawaaci honiitawaakanwahi

For the foolish, when they took their lamps, took no oil with them:

4. weeka nihki lepwaacki hotaamwetoonaawa pemi hopoonahfowakokonwaaki kileki honiitawaakanwahi

but the wise took oil in their vessels with their lamps.

5. howe yeheeyehi naakaafiilici nili mayakinhhaakanali nihki caayahki katokwaamooki mecimi nepeeki

Now while the bridegroom tarried, they all slumbered and slept.

6. payeekwa tah laawi tepehkiki nitasimopi waapamehko hina mayakinhhaakana piyaako kiilawa pah nakskawehko hiyopi

But at midnight there is a cry, Behold, the bridegroom! Come ye forth to meet him.

7. hine howe nehke caayahki seskiikweefaki honhskaaki mecimi honhhekolaawahi honiitawaakanwahi

Then all those virgins arose, and trimmed their lamps.

8. chiine nihki wanihsakaaki miilinaake kipemimwa ksake niniitawaakanenaaki wiisa hahfooki hotelaawahi nihi lepwaalici

And the foolish said unto the wise, Give us of your oil; for our lamps are going out.

9. payeekwa nihki lepwaacki haapafseeki poofi menawahi mata kikamooci yah teepatwi niilawe chiine kiilawa nhhaakone kaaciika nihki maa miyeekicki mecimi tepenamoko pesikwi kiilawa hisiweeki

But the wise answered, saying, Peradventure there will not be enough for us and you: go ye rather to them that sell, and buy for yourselves.

10. chiine yeheeye weepfeewaaci nihki wahsi tepenikeewaaci hina mayakinhhaakana piyeewa mecimi nihki mayehci nanahiicki hoteh wiiteemaawaali nili hini wiichetiiwi wihfenhcikeeweneki mecimi hini skwaate kiphoote

And while they went away to buy, the bridegroom came; and they that were ready went in with him to the marriage feast: and the door was shut.

11. mayohkwaaci piyeeki nehfaapi nihki naaleta seskiikweefaki teepeelemiweeta teepeelemiweeta tawenamawinaake hisiweeki

Afterward come also the other virgins, saying, Lord, Lord, open to us.

12. payeekwa hina haapafse mecimi tepilo kitelepwa niila mata kiwaakomelepwa hotelahi

But he answered and said, Verily I say unto you, I know you not.

13. kcitawaapiko weecikeenahi ksake mata kiwaakotaanaawa hini kaasekiki kiilawa nohki hini yaatefaki mata

Watch therefore, for ye know not the day nor the hour.

14. ksake paasi keela hinwi hileni kotaki hasiskiiki yeewiisa haaci howihkomahi nehalwaaka hotaloolaakaafhi mecimi hoteh pakfenamawahi nihi howiyehiimi

For it is as when a man, going into another country, called his own servants, and delivered unto them his goods.

15. chiine nekoti niyaalanwi teleniwali homiilaali kotakali nekoti niiswi nohki kotakali nekoti moosa tfwi

And unto one he gave five talents, to another two, to another one; to each

nekoti yeetfweelenawakiki hokatawiilefiiwena chiine hina weepfe yeelaamiici

according to his several ability; and he went on his journey.

16. weelena weepfe hina weetahpenaka nili niyaalanwi teleniwali mecimi haasoonike nili mecimi kotakali homectoona niyaalanwi teleniwali

Straightway he that received the five talents went and traded with them, and made other five talents.

17. hina hini yaska nehfaapi weetahpenaka nili niiswi hokatawihkaana kotakali niiswi

In like manner he also that received the two gained other two.

18. weeka hina weetahpenaka hini nekoti weepfe chiine waalhke hini hasiskiiki hokkito homonemilici teepeelemekoci

But he that received the one went away and digged in the earth, and hid his lord's money.

19. howe mayohkwaaci keelo laakwa hina teepeelemaata nehe haloolaakaafhi piyeewa chiine hopemi hakitahfoomahi nihi

Now after a long time the lord of those servants cometh, and maketh a reckoning with them.

20. chiine hina weetahpenaka nili niyaalanwi teleniwali piyeewa mecimi hopiyeetoona kotakali niyaalanwi teleniwali teepeelemiweeta kipakfenamawi niyaalanwi teleniwali sci neyehka nikatawihkaana niyaalanwi kotakali teleniwali hisiwe

And he that received the five talents came and brought other five talents, saying, Lord, thou deliveredst unto me five talents: lo, I have gained other five talents.

21. koowesilawi cehi howesi mecimi tepasawi haloolaakaafa kimehci tepasawefi laakofwiimehi wiyehi meci wiyehi keh talwahfele niila piicfaalo kiila hini howesilepwaaweneki teepeelemehka hotekooli teepeelemekoci

His lord said unto him, Well done, good and faithful servant: thou hast been faithful over a few things, I will set thee over many things: enter thou into the joy of thy lord.

22. chiine nehfaapi hina weetahpenaka nili niiswi teleniwali piyeewa teepeelemiweeta kipakfenamawi niiswi teleniwali sci neyehka nikatawihkaana niiswi kotakali teleniwali hisiwe

And he also that received the two talents came and said, Lord, thou deliveredst unto me two talents: lo, I have gained other two talents.

23. koowesilawi cehi howesi mecimi tepasawi haloolaakaafa kimehci tepasawefi laakofwiimehi wiyehi meci wiyehi keh talwahfele niila piicfaalo kiila hini howesilepwaaweneki teepeelemehka hotekooli teepeelemekoci

His lord said unto him, Well done, good and faithful servant; thou hast been faithful over a few things, I will set thee over many things: enter thou into the joy of thy lord.

24. chiine hina nehfaapi weetahpenaka hini nekoti teleni piyeewa teepeelemiweeta kiwaakomele kiila yeesi kiisenaacileniwiyani kipemi kawaskwhaawe tah pwaa kiila hahcikeeyani mecimi kipemi maawatonike tah pwaa kiila lhfwepakitaaweyani

And he also that had received the one talent came and said, Lord, I knew thee that thou art a hard man, reaping where thou didst not sow, and gathering where thou didst not scatter:

25. chiine nikwpene mecimi niweepfe chiine nikkito hasiskiiki kitelenimi sci kipoona hini nehalwaaka kiila hisiwe

and I was afraid, and went away and hid thy talent in the earth: lo, thou hast thine own.

26. payeekwa haapafseeli teepeelemekoci mecimi kiila weenaatefi mecimi mayeelawaatefi haloolaaka kiwaakota yaasi kawaskwhaaweya tah pwaa niila hahcikeeya mecimi maawatonnikeeya tah pwaa niila lhfwepakitaaweya

But his lord answered and said unto him, Thou wicked and slothful servant, thou knewest that I reap where I sowed not, and gather where I did not scatter;

27. weecikeenahi neyehka yo nihki monikaafaki kih si poona nimonemi mecimi tah piyaaya neyehka ni hotahpena peteki nehalwaaka niila kileki hini tah skwiiyaaki hotelaali nili

thou oughtest therefore to have put my money to the bankers, and at my coming I should have received back mine own with interest.

28. mamawehko weecikeenahi hini teleni mecimi miilehko hini hina metahfwi peepoonaka

Take ye away therefore the talent from him, and give it unto him that hath the ten talents.

29. ksake caakiwiyeefa peepoonaka weh miiloofo mecimi hina weh poona maalefiiwe weeka hina pwaayaa poonaka wiikinaakwi hini peepoonaki we hoci mamaakwi

For unto every one that hath shall be given, and he shall have abundance: but from him that hath not, even that which he hath shall be taken away.

30. mecimi kiilawa hini faakici si lohfe pakilehko hina haloolaaka pwaayaa mhkahfoowefita laa pepekica mecimi nitasi weh pemi wihfakweeweni chiine hini weh talweewehfeno wiipitali hisiwe

And cast ye out the unprofitable servant into the outer darkness: there shall be the weeping and gnashing of teeth.

31. payeekwa hine hina hokwihfali hileni weh piyeewa howahfaacimekofiiweneki chiine caayahki nihki henhcaliiki wiici nili hine howe we hpapi hini hokimaawi hpapiiwe howahfaacimekofiiwe hoci

But when the Son of man shall come in his glory, and all the angels with him, then shall he sit on the throne of his glory:

32. mecimi yeelahfamiilici nili weh maawatoska caayahki nili hotfweeloowena lenawe chiine hina weh nohpiyeenahi nekoti hoci nekoti yaasi hina kehcitawahaata nohpiyeenaaci nihi meekiifhi nihi miyaasimeekiifhi hoci

and before him shall be gathered all the nations: and he shall separate them one from another, as the shepherd separateth the sheep from the goats:

33. mecimi nihi meekiifhi homayaawiinhkiki weh si lemataphahi weeka nihi miyaasimeekiifhi hini namaciinhkiki

and he shall set the sheep on his right hand, but the goats on the left.

34. hine howe hina hokima we hilahi nihi homayaawiinhkiki piyaako kiilawa keekisaateelemaaci nohfa laapi howiilaamiko hini hokimaawitaamhkwe mayecfetoofoyeekwe hine mehtahkehfenwi hini yeelekokwahkamikiki hoci

Then shall the King say unto them on his right hand, Come, ye blessed of my Father, inherit the kingdom prepared for you from the foundation of the world:

35. ksake niskwaalawe mecimi kiilawa kimiilipwa wah miiciya nikahkalaamo mecimi kiilawa kimiilipwa menoowe nikookweeneefiwi mecimi kiilawa kipiitikeenipwa

for I was an hungred, and ye gave me meat: I was thirsty, and ye gave me drink: I was a stranger, and ye took me in;

36. nisahsaakitwi mecimi kiilawa kipiitenikehipwa nitahkwiloke mecimi kiilawa kinawhhipwa kiphotiiweneki nitapi mecimi kiilawa kipiyeelotawipwa we hilahi

naked, and ye clothed me: I was sick, and ye visited me: I was in prison, and ye came unto me.

37. hine howe nihki meeyaawiileficki we haapaftawaawaali teepeelemiweeta taaniwe laakwa kinoolepe kiskwaalawe mecimi kitsamelepe weelaa kikahkalaamo mecimi kimiilelepe menoowe

Then shall the righteous answer him, saying, Lord, when saw we thee an hungred, and fed thee? or athirst, and gave thee drink?

38. chiine taaniwe laakwa kinoolepe kikookweeneefiwi mecimi kipiitikeenelepe weelaa kisahsaakitwi mecimi kipiitenikehelepe

And when saw we thee a stranger, and took thee in? or naked, and clothed thee?

39. chiine taaniwe laakwa kinoolepe kitahkwiloke weelaa kikipho mecimi kinawhhelepe we hisiweeki

And when saw we thee sick, or in prison, and came unto thee?

40. mecimi hina hokima we haapafse chiine tepilo kitelepwa niila ksake yeesi hini hpenaleekwe nekoti yohkoma niceeninaaki wiikinaakwi yohkoma kehcimecilooficki niila hini kitpenasipwa we hilahi

And the King shall answer and say unto them, Verily I say unto you, Inasmuch as ye did it unto one of these my brethren, even these least, ye did it unto me.

41. hine howe nehfaapi we hilahi nihi hini honamaciinhkiki niila hoci saaweko kiilawa pahtahkaafaki hini haako kookwelaakwasi skote mayecfetoofoci hina macimaneto mecimi hotenhcaliimhhi

Then shall he say also unto them on the left hand, Depart from me, ye cursed, into the eternal fire which is prepared for the devil and his angels:

42. ksake niskwaalawe mecimi kiilawa mata kimiilipwa wah miiciya nikahkalaamo mecimi kiilawa mata kimiilipwa menoowe

for I was an hungred, and ye gave me no meat: I was thirsty, and ye gave me no drink:

43. nikookweeneefiwi mecimi kiilawa mata kipiitikeenipwa nisahsaakitwi mecimi kiilawa mata kipiitenikehipwa nitahkwiloke chiine nikipho mecimi kiilawa mata kinawhhipwa we hilahi

I was a stranger, and ye took me not in; naked, and ye clothed me not; sick, and in prison, and ye visited me not.

44. hine nehfaapi nihki we haapafseeki teepeelemiweeta taaniwe laakwa kinoolepe kiskwaalawe weelaa kikahkalaamo weelaa kikookweeneefiwi weelaa kisahsaakitwi weelaa kitahkwiloke weelaa kikipho mecimi mata kikisaacipenalelepe we hisiweeki

Then shall they also answer, saying, Lord, when saw we thee an hungred, or athirst, or a stranger, or naked, or sick, or in prison, and did not minister unto thee?

45. hine hina we haapaftawahi nihi tepilo kitelepwa niila ksake yeesi pwaa kiilawa hini hpenaleekwe nekoti yohkoma kcimecilooficki mata hini kitpenasipwa niila we hilahi

Then shall he answer them, saying, Verily I say unto you, Inasmuch as ye did it not unto one of these least, ye did it not unto me.

46. chiine yohkoma kookwelaakwasi halotaafiiweneki we heeki weeka nihki meeyaawiileficki kookwelaakwasi lenaweewiiweneki we heeki

And these shall go away into eternal punishment: but the righteous into eternal life.

Matthew:26

1. chiine hini piyeemikatwi yeh mehcilotaki ciisisii yooloma kalawiiwena

And it came to pass, when Jesus had finished all these words, he said unto his disciples,

2. kiwaakotaanaawa mehci niisokonakike hini pemhfaasiweewe piyeeya mecimi hina hokwihfali hileni howe wahsi haasitefhoofoci si pakfenoofo hotelahi hokakehkimaafhi

Ye know that after two days the passover cometh, and the Son of man is delivered up to be crucified.

3. hine nihki hokimaawi mhkateewkolayeeki chiine nihi hokikileniimwahi nihki lenaweeki maawaskaaki

Then were gathered together the chief priests, and the elders of the people,

hini yaatah tepoweci hina moospimekofiiwi mhkateewkolaye keeyeefesii yaaloofo

unto the court of the high priest, who was called Caiaphas;

4. chiine nihki tepetwi tepoweeki wahsi menawahke mesenaawaaci ciisisiili kiiminhhefiiwe hoci mecimi nhfaawaaci

and they took counsel together that they might take Jesus by subtilty, and kill him.

5. payeekwa teki hini laakwasi weewihfenhcikeeki piilepe tatawaanhkeewe weh pafekwiiya heelekiina nihki lenaweeki hiwaki

But they said, Not during the feast, lest a tumult arise among the people.

6. howe ciisisii pefeneki ye hapici hini yeetaaci saimanii hina weeskilhakeemekita

Now when Jesus was in Bethany, in the house of Simon the leper,

7. nitasi hotfekooli hkweeli hopah niimeli helepeestawakokoofeki hanhhiweewe kisoweelemekwatwi lomhkoowe mecimi nili wiileki hoteh fiikinamaakooli hini yeesi lematapici tah wihfeniki

there came unto him a woman having an alabaster cruse of exceeding precious ointment, and she poured it upon his head, as he sat at meat.

8. payeekwa nihki kakehkimaafaki yeh neemowaaci hini hopoonaanaawa kisfekwiiwe taaniwe si waleskhotoote yooma

But when the disciples saw it, they had indignation, saying, To what purpose is this waste?

9. ksake yooma lomhkoowe neyehka menawahi wih mehci kisowi miyeekipi mecimi si miiliweepi hina kitemaafa hiwaki

For this ointment might have been sold for much, and given to the poor.

10. payeekwa ciisisii hopemi mooleeleta hini koociwe kiilawa kipetfakhaawa hina hkweewa ksake yo nimehci pekatenamaakwa howesi pekatefiiwe niiyaaki hotelahi nihi

But Jesus perceiving it said unto them, Why trouble ye the woman? for she hath wrought a good work upon me.

11. ksake moosatawi kipoonaawa wiici kiilawa hina kitemaafa weeka niila mata moosatawi kipoonipwa

For ye have the poor always with you; but me ye have not always.

12. ksake hini hina hoteh fiikina yooma lomhkoowe niiyaaki hina hini silawi wahsi nanahilotamawici nilekonoofoowe

For in that she poured this ointment upon my body, she did it to prepare me for burial.

13. tepilo kitelepwa niila kookwe-tasi-kaaci yooma howesi piyeetaacimoowe weh nanahimiweepi hini melhske yeelekokwahkamikiki hini nehfaapi yaama hkweewa mayehci silawiici we haatotoote wahsi maamhkaweelemoofoci hina

Verily I say unto you, Wheresoever this gospel shall be preached in the whole world, that also which this woman hath done shall be spoken of for a memorial of her.

14. hine howe nekoti nihki metahfwi-kite-niiswi hina cootas' hiskeeletii yaaloofota nhheewa nihi hokimaawi mhkateewkolayehi

Then one of the twelve, who was called Judas Iscariot, went unto the chief priests,

15. mecimi nehiwe keh si menwi miilipwa chiine keh pakfemoolepwa hina hotelahi mecimi hokotakoocitawaawaali nihki nhfwaapitaki peekskahki waapimoni

and said, What are ye willing to give me, and I will deliver him unto you? And they weighed unto him thirty pieces of silver.

16. mecimi hine laakwa hoci hina honatoneha tawaafiiwe wahsi nili pakfenamawaaci nihi

And from that time he sought opportunity to deliver him unto them.

17. howe hini weski kaasekiki pwaayaa honeteeki takhwa hoci nihki kakehkimaafaki hotfaawaali ciisisiili taaniwe tasi kitesitehe wahsi hosfetoolaake kiila wahsi miiciyani hini pemhfaasiweewe hotelaawaali

Now on the first day of unleavened bread the disciples came to Jesus, saying, Where wilt thou that we make ready for thee to eat the passover?

18. mecimi hina nhhaakone hini hoteeweneki hina yooniisi hileni chiine hina keekehkimiwe hiwa nitelaakwaamefiiwe howe nahiika nikciitawefi hini pemhfaasiweewe yeetaayani wiikiwaapeki kileki nikakehkimaafaki ke hilaawa hotelahi

And he said, Go into the city to such a man, and say unto him, The Master saith, My time is at hand; I keep the passover at thy house with my disciples.

19. mecimi nihki kakehkimaafaki yeesfetaakowaaci ciisisiili silawiiki chiine hosfetoonaawa hini pemhfaasiweewe

And the disciples did as Jesus appointed them; and they made ready the passover.

20. howe ye holaakwiifiki lematapiwa tah wihfeniki wiici nihi metahfwi-kite-niiswi kakehkimaafhi

21. mecimi yeesi nihki pemi wihfeniwaaci tepilo kitelepwa niila nekoti kiilawa neh mestaawhekwa hisiwe

Now when even was come, he was sitting at meat with the twelve disciples; and as they were eating, he said, Verily I say unto you, that one of you shall betray me.

22. chiine nihki hanhhiweewi macilepwaaki mecimi teepeelemiweeta ha niila hotalemi hilaawaali caayaki

And they were exceeding sorrowful, and began to say unto him every one, Is it I, Lord?

23. chiine hina haapafse mecimi hina weewiici pemhkaamita holeci hini holaakaneki hiina hina neh mestaawhekwa hotelahi

And he answered and said, He that dipped his hand with me in the dish, the same shall betray me.

24. hina hokwihfali hileni nhheewa teetepilahi hini yeesi mehtawikeeki payeekwa macilepwaaweni cehi hina hileni weeci saapoci mestaawhoofoci hina hokwihfali hileni howesaali hini yehki hina hileni pwaa mehci lenaweewite hiwa

The Son of man goeth, even as it is written of him: but woe unto that man through whom the Son of man is betrayed! good were it for that man if he had not been born.

25. chiine cootasii hina mayestaawhaata haapafse lepaayii ha niila hisiwe kimehtowe hiloofo

And Judas, which betrayed him, answered and said, Is it I, Rabbi? He saith unto him, Thou hast said.

26. chiine yeesi wihfeniwaaci ciisisii homame takhwa mecimi kisaacike chiine hoposkona hini mecimi hoteh miilahi nihi kakehkimaafhi mecimi mameko miiciko halayooma niiya hisiwe

And as they were eating, Jesus took bread, and blessed, and brake it; and he gave to the disciples, and said, Take, eat; this is my body.

27. chiine hoteh mamaali tephikanali mecimi miiliwe niyaawe chiine hoteh miilahi nihi meneko kiilawa caayahki hini

And he took a cup, and gave thanks, and gave to them, saying, Drink ye all of it;

28. ksake halayooma nimhskomi hini mehtaacimoowe hoci feefiikinamawoofoci meci wahsi maciilefiiwena hoci pakfefiiweniki

for this is my blood of the covenant, which is shed for many unto remission of sins.

29. payeekwa kitelepwa niila mata neh mene yooci hinoki yooma hini tetepahtekwi hoci mawifoowe paalohi halaane kaasekiki hine hini nih mene hoski wiici kiilawa piitike hokimaawitaamhkomi nohfa

But I say unto you, I will not drink henceforth of this fruit of the vine, until that day when I drink it new with you in my Father's kingdom.

30. chiine nihki yeh mehtekamowaaci hofepekamoowe lohfeeki hini halifiwi meekwahkiki heeki

And when they had sung a hymn, they went out unto the mount of Olives.

31. hine hotelahi ciisisii caayahki kiilawa keh kisfelepwa niiyaaki hinoki tepehkike ksake hini mehtawikeepi neh kicithwa hina kehcitawahaata meekiifhi mecimi hina nekotweelena meekiifa mefhiike weh si lhfwelhkoofo

Then saith Jesus unto them, All ye shall be offended in me this night: for it is written, I will smite the shepherd, and the sheep of the flock shall be scattered abroad.

32. payeekwa mehci niila honhskaanoofoya keeleliiki ne ha mayohkwaaci kiilawa hotelahi

But after I am raised up, I will go before you into Galilee.

33. payeekwa piita hotaapaftawaali mecimi kwehkwi caayahki keh kisfaaki kiila mata niila nitah kisfekoopi hotelaali

But Peter answered and said unto him, If all shall be offended in thee, I will never be offended.

34. tepilo kitele niila yeesi hinoki tepehkiki wihsi pwaa hina naapeeya kalhootaki nhfene kiila keh kiyaacimi hotelaali ciisisii

Jesus said unto him, Verily I say unto thee, that this night, before the cock crow, thou shalt deny me thrice.

35. wiikinaakwi kwehkwi kwiilahi keh wiici nepoomele kiila keewaki mata kitah kiyaacimele hotelaali piita hiini yaska nehfaapi yeelaawaaci nihki caayahki kakehkimaafaki

Peter saith unto him, Even if I must die with thee, yet will I not deny thee. Likewise also said all the disciples.

36. hine howe nitasi piyeewa ciisisii keefsemeni sitoote kileki nihi chiine lematapiko kiilawa hotasi laakwasi halaane haaya mecimi mamaatomeeya hotelahi hokakehkimaafhi

Then cometh Jesus with them unto a place called Gethsemane, and saith unto his disciples, Sit ye here, while I go yonder and pray.

37. mecimi piitali hotaamwelaali chiine nihi niiswi hokwifhi sepetii mecimi halemi hokwaawefi macilepwaawe chiine hahkwi petfakifi

And he took with him Peter and the two sons of Zebedee, and began to be sorrowful and sore troubled.

38. hine howe nimayaawiniiya hanhhiweewi hokwaawefi macilepwaawe teetepilahi nepoowefi hotasi kiilawa hapiko mecimi wiici kcitawaafiimiko hotelahi nihi

Then saith he unto them, My soul is exceeding sorrowful, even unto death: abide ye here, and watch with me.

39. chiine halika si weepfe tekawihi mecimi maa si holemhkwi paksinwa weetaapeeci chiine mamaatome nohfehi kwehkwi katawi hinike wiilaani yaama tephika pemhfeete niiyaaki hoci payeekwa mata yeesiteheeya niila weeka kiila yeesiteheeyani hiwa

And he went forward a little, and fell on his face, and prayed, saying, O my Father, if it be possible, let this cup pass away from me: nevertheless, not as I will, but as thou wilt.

40. chiine nihi kakehkimaafhi si piyeewa mecimi homhkawahi nihi peemi nepaalici chiine piitali nehiwe ha mata kikatawi kcitawaafiimipwa nekoti yaatefaki hotelaali

And he cometh unto the disciples, and findeth them sleeping, and saith unto Peter, What, could ye not watch with me one hour?

41. kcitawaapiko mecimi mamaatomeeko wahsi pwaa kiilawa hottameekwe hini miyaasi-ashetiiwe sapkahi hini hilefiiwe hiini siteheeya payeekwa hini wiyawfi mekihkofiiya

Watch and pray, that ye enter not into temptation: the spirit indeed is willing, but the flesh is weak.

42. nohki mawi-niisene weepfe chiine mamaatome nohfehi kwehkwi yooma pwaa katawi pemhfeeyaake

Again a second time he went away, and prayed, saying, O my Father, if this

weeciwephi niila meneya kitesiteheewe we hisilawiipi hiwa

cannot pass away, except I drink it, thy will be done.

43. chiine nohki piyeewa mecimi homhkawahi nihi peemi nepaalici ksake kofekwanili hoskiisekowa

And he came again and found them sleeping, for their eyes were heavy.

44. chiine honakalahi nohki mecimi hale weepfe chiine mamaatome mawi-nhfene laakwa nohki niliini yaska kalawiiwena pemi hiwa

And he left them again, and went away, and prayed a third time, saying again the same words.

45. hine howe hotfahi nihi kakehkimaafhi chiine howe yaska nepaako mecimi mameko kitalwaakahsiiwenwa waapatamoko hini yaatefaki howe maalaakwahi mecimi hina hokwihfali hileni howe nili holeciwaaki meciileficki si mestaawhoofo

Then cometh he to the disciples, and saith unto them, Sleep on now, and take your rest: behold, the hour is at hand, and the Son of man is betrayed into the hands of sinners.

46. honhskaako weepfeetaako howe maalaakwahi hina mayehtaawhita hotelahi

Arise, let us be going: behold, he is at hand that betrayeth me.

47. chiine yeheeyehi keewaki kalawilici ceh yaama cootasii piyeewa nekoti nihki metahfwi-kite-niiswi chiine wiici nili meci mehseelekki hokiskhikaniiki chiine cifhikana nihki hoci hokimaawi mhkateewkolayeeki chiine lenaweeki hokikileniimwahi

And while he yet spake, lo, Judas, one of the twelve, came, and with him a great multitude with swords and staves, from the chief priests and elders of the people.

48. howe hina memestaawhaata nili homiilahi nihi kikinooloowe kookwe-neefa-kaaci neh pacikama hiina hina mesenehko hisiwe

Now he that betrayed him gave them a sign, saying, Whomsoever I shall kiss, that is he: take him.

49. mecimi weelena hina ciisisiili si piyeewa chiine hei lepaayii hisiwe mecimi hopacikamaali nili

And straightway he came to Jesus, and said, Hail, Rabbi; and kissed him.

50. chiine ciisisii wihkaanima hini silawiilo weeci kiila piyaayani hotelaali hine howe nihki piyeeki mecimi homawinachaawaali nili chiine hotaamwelaawaali

And Jesus said unto him, Friend, do that for which thou art come. Then they came and laid hands on Jesus, and took him.

51. chiine waapamehko nekoti nihki peepah wiitfeemaata ciisisiili maa si leceska mecimi holohfena hokiskhika chiine hokiskehsethwaali nili hotaloolaakanali hina moospimekofiiwi mhkateewkolaye

And behold, one of them that were with Jesus stretched out his hand, and drew his sword, and smote the servant of the high priest, and struck off his ear.

52. hine ciisisii yaata hateeki nohki si poonano kikiskhika ksake caayahki nihki meemamekki hini kiskhika we hocineeki hini kiskhika

Then saith Jesus unto him, Put up again thy sword into its place: for all they that take the sword shall perish with the sword.

53. weelaa toke kitesitehe yeesi niila haalwi katawi nanahpaacimaki nohfa chiine hina wiikinaakwi hinoki hotahfa neh leskamaakwa henhcalihi halika tfwi hini metahfwi-kite-niiswi tfweelena mehseeleka

Or thinkest thou that I cannot beseech my Father, and he shall even now send me more than twelve legions of angels?

54. nehiwe howe wih si hokwaawfetoote nili tepilo heewikaateewali wahsi yooni si kwiila hiki hini hotelaali nili

How then should the scriptures be fulfilled, that thus it must be?

55. hine yaatefaki ciisisii hotelahi nihi mehseelelici ha kiilawa kipiyeci lohfaapwa paasi kimawinehwaawa ciikoniwehfi kikiskhikanipwa chiine cifhikana wahsi meseniyeekwe tfene waapaki niila nilematapi piitike hini mamaatomeewikamikwi nipemi kakehkimiwe mecimi mata kimesenipwa

In that hour said Jesus to the multitudes, Are ye come out as against a robber with swords and staves to seize me? I sat daily in the temple teaching, and ye took me not.

56. payeekwa caayahki yooma howe piyeemikatwi wahsi nili tepilo hoteewikaateemwa nihki maamoosikiiskwecki menawahi hokwihfeki hotelahi hine howe caayahki nihki kakehkimaafaki honakalaawaali mecimi hosimooki

But all this is come to pass, that the scriptures of the prophets might be fulfilled. Then all the disciples left him, and fled.

57. chiine nihki mayehci mesenaacki ciisisiili hotesiwelaawaali hini wiikiwa yeetaaci keeyeefesii hina moospimekofiiwi mhkateewkolaye tah maawaskaawaaci nihki yaayawikeecki chiine nihki kikileniiki

And they that had taken Jesus led him away to the house of Caiaphas the high priest, where the scribes and the elders were gathered together.

58. piita weeka pelowi hoteh neekalaali nili paalohi hini yaatah tepoweci hina moospimekofiiwi mhkateewkolaye mecimi piicfe chiine lematapi wiici nihi wiyehisimekofiiwenhhi wahsi hini ceeyehkwi neekeeci

But Peter followed him afar off, unto the court of the high priest, and entered in, and sat with the officers, to see the end.

59. howe nihki hokimaawi mhkateewkolayeeki mecimi caayahki hina teepoweeta honatonehaanaawa miyaasi teepweewe wa hoci nalaawaaci ciisisiili wahsi menawahke nepooweneki si poonaawaaci nili

Now the chief priests and the whole council sought false witness against Jesus, that they might put him to death;

60. mecimi nihki mata homhkaanaawa hini weekhi meci miyaasi teepweewenaki piyeeki payeekwa mayohkwaaci piyeeki niiswi

and they found it not, though many false witnesses came. But afterward came two,

61. mecimi yaama hileni niteepiilefi wahsi liikatenama hini homamaatomeewikamikwi maneto mecimi hopatenama hini nhfoko hiwa hisiweeki

and said, This man said, I am able to destroy the temple of God, and to build it in three days.

62. chiine hina moospimekofiiwi mhkateewkolaye pafekwi mecimi ha mata wiyehi kitaapafta nehiwe hini yohkoma ceecahtawaacimehki hotelaali

And the high priest stood up, and said unto him, Answerest thou nothing? what is it which these witness against thee?

63. payeekwa ciisisii nooleewi chiine hina moospimekofiiwi mhkateewkolaye kimayaawi hahtoocimele hina lenaweewita maneto wahsi kiila wiitamawiyaake kwehkwi toke kiiya hina klaistii nili hokwihfali maneto hotelaali

But Jesus held his peace. And the high priest said unto him, I adjure thee by the living God, that thou tell us whether thou be the Christ, the Son of God.

64. kimehtowe hotelaali ciisisii payeekwa kitelepwa niila yooci hinoki keh neewaawa kiilawa hina hokwihfali hileni pemi lematapi ta hini mayaawiinhkiki waasikaki mecimi pemi piyeewa hoskici nili menhkwatwi hoci paafkwaki hotelaali nili

Jesus saith unto him, Thou hast said: nevertheless I say unto you, Henceforth ye shall see the Son of man sitting at the right hand of power, and coming on the clouds of heaven.

65. hine howe hina moospimekofiiwi mhkateewkolaye holiilelhkinaana hopiitenikana pahtaamoowe mehtowe hina nehiwe keewaki kooci skata leelemaape teepweewenaki waapatamoko howe kimehci nootaanaawa hini pahtaamoowe kiilawa

Then the high priest rent his garments, saying, He hath spoken blasphemy: what further need have we of witnesses? behold, now ye have heard the blasphemy:

66. nehiwe kitesiteheepwa hotelahi haapafseeki nihki mecimi nahiika hikofi nepoowe hiwaki

what think ye? They answered and said, He is worthy of death.

67. hine howe hofiifekwaalaawaali yeelaapeelici mecimi hopiipokwilecwhaawaali chiine naaleta hotapakileceewi pkitewhaawaali

Then did they spit in his face and buffet him: and some smote him with the palms of their hands,

68. moosikiiskwaacimohtawinaake kiila klaistii neefawe hina peepkitehohka hiwaki

saying, Prophesy unto us, thou Christ: who is he that struck thee?

69. howe piita faakici lematapiwa piitike hini tah tepoweeki chiine hkweefali hotfekooli kiila nehfaapi kiwiiciwi ciisisii hina keeleliiwileni hotekooli

Now Peter was sitting without in the court: and a maid came unto him, saying, Thou also wast with Jesus the Galilaean.

70. payeekwa kiyaacimo yeelahfamiilici caayahki nihi mata niwaakota yeeyoyani kiila hisiwe

But he denied before them all, saying, I know not what thou sayest.

71. chiine yeh si lohfaaci hini hawikanefoowikaaneki kotakali nohki hkweefali honookooli mecimi hina halayaama hileni nehfaapi wiiciwi ciisisiili naaselefi hoci hotelahi nihi nitasi yeepilici

And when he was gone out into the porch, another maid saw him, and saith unto them that were there, This man also was with Jesus the Nazarene.

72. mecimi nohki kiyaacimo kileki macikalawiiwe mata niwaakoma hina hileni hisiwe

And again he denied with an oath, I know not the man.

73. chiine mayohkwaaci peloocih laakwa nihki maalaakwahi neniipawicki piyeeki mecimi teepweewe nehfaapi nekoti kiila nihki ksake hini kikalawiiwe kiwaakomekofiheko hotelaawaali piitali

And after a little while they that stood by came and said to Peter, Of a truth thou also art one of them; for thy speech bewrayeth thee.

74. hine howe hina halemi pahtaamo chiine macikalawi mata niwaakoma hina hileni hiwa mecimi weelena hina naapeeya kalhootamwa

Then began he to curse and to swear, I know not the man. And straightway the cock crew.

75. chiine homhkaweeleta piita hini kalawiiwe mayehci hikoci ciisisiili wihsi pwaa kalhootaki hina naapeeya nhfene keh kiyaacimi mecimi lohfe chiine wihfakwe mamiyeenenila

And Peter remembered the word which Jesus had said, Before the cock crow, thou shalt deny me thrice. And he went out, and wept bitterly.

Matthew:27

1. howe yeh waapaki caayahki nihi hokimaawi mhkateewkolayehi chiine nihi hokikileniimwahi nihki lenaweeki hotepowaalekohi ciisisii wahsi nepooweneki si poonekoci

Now when morning was come, all the chief priests and the elders of the people took counsel against Jesus to put him to death:

2. chiine hokciipilekohi mecimi hotaamwelekohi chiine hoteh pakfenekohi paalatiili hina kapenali

and they bound him, and led him away, and delivered him up to Pilate the governor.

3. hine howe cootasii hina mayestaawhaata nili yeh neemeki yeesi miyaalahkowaafolici mataiini sitehe wiiya mecimi peteki hotesiwetawahi nihi hokimaawi mhkateewkolayehi chiine kikilenihi nili nhfwaapitaki peekskahki waapimoni

Then Judas, which betrayed him, when he saw that he was condemned, repented himself, and brought back the thirty pieces of silver to the chief priests and elders,

4. nimacilawi yeesi mehci mestaawtooya fafayaaki mhskwi hisiwe payeekwa nihki nehiwe hini niilawe si kiila hini memekinaapatano hotekohi

saying, I have sinned in that I betrayed innocent blood. But they said, What is that to us? see thou to it.

5. mecimi sahkiki hini hofepikamikwi hoteh piicfe pakitaana nili peekskahki waapimoni chiine hini hoci saawe mecimi weepfe chiine holaapicito wiiya

And he cast down the pieces of silver into the sanctuary, and departed; and he went away and hanged himself.

6. chiine nihki hokimaawi mhkateewkolayeeki homamenaawa nili peekskahki waapimoni chiine mata mayaawatwi kwteletiiweneki wahsi hini monikaaneki si poonooteeki nili ksake hini mhskwi yeeleelemekoki nili hiwaki

And the chief priests took the pieces of silver, and said, It is not lawful to put them into the treasury, since it is the price of blood.

7. chiine tepoweeki mecimi nili hoci tepenaanaawa hini yeesiskiwakkonhkeeta hoktika wah tah lekonaawaaci kookweeneefhi

And they took counsel, and bought with them the potter's field, to bury strangers in.

8. yooni hoci hini ktika hini mhskwi si ktika sitoote yaska hinoki kaasekiki

Wherefore that field was called, The field of blood, unto this day.

9. hine howe hokwaawfetoote hini yeesi kalawiki saapwi celemaaya hina maamoosikiiskweeta mecimi homamenaawa nili nhfwaapitaki peekskahki waapimoni hini yeeleelemekofici hina hini yeelakimoofota nili yeelakimaawaaci nihki naanekoti hotapelohfemhhi hiswiila

Then was fulfilled that which was spoken by Jeremiah the prophet, saying, And they took the thirty pieces of silver, the price of him that was priced, whom certain of the children of Israel did price;

10. mecimi nihki miiliweeki nili hasowe hini yeesiskiwakkonhkeeta hoktika yeesfetawaaci hina teepeelemiweeta hiyopi

and they gave them for the potter's field, as the Lord appointed me.

11. howe niipawi ciisisii yeelahfamiilici nili kapenaliili chiine hina kapenali honatohtawaali ha nihki coosaki hokimaamwaali kiila hotelaali kiteyo kiila hotelaali ciisisii

Now Jesus stood before the governor: and the governor asked him, saying, Art thou the King of the Jews? And Jesus said unto him, Thou sayest.

12. chiine yeh cahtawaacimekoci nihi hokimaawi mhkateewkolayehi chiine kikilenihi mata wiyehi haapafse

And when he was accused by the chief priests and elders, he answered nothing.

13. hine paalatii ha mata kinoota kiila yeesi meci wiyehi nihki cahtawaacimehki hotelaali

Then saith Pilate unto him, Hearest thou not how many things they witness against thee?

14. mecimi mata homiilaali hotaapafseewe mata mohci nekoti kalawiiwe weecikeenahi hina kapenali holaami mayacitehe

And he gave him no answer, not even to one word: insomuch that the governor marveled greatly.

15. howe hini tah wihfenhcikeeki hina kapenali hopaapakfenamawahi nihi mehseelelici nekoti kiikeenikaafali yoona yeesiteheewaaci nihki

Now at the feast the governor was wont to release unto the multitude one prisoner, whom they would.

16. chiine hopoonaawaali hine kikinooteelemekofiili kiikeenikaafali palepasii yaaloofooli

And they had then a notable prisoner, called Barabbas.

17. hine weecikeenahi yeh maawatoskaalici paalatii taanawe yoona kitesiteheepwa wah pakfenamoolako ha palepasii weelaa toke ciisisii hina klaistii yaaloofota hotelahi

When therefore they were gathered together, Pilate said unto them, Whom will ye that I release unto you? Barabbas, or Jesus which is called Christ?

18. ksake howaakota yeesi hahpeeletiiwe hoci nihi piyeetaakoci nili

For he knew that for envy they had delivered him up.

19. chiine yeheeyehi hini tepoweewiyahpapiiweneki lematapici wiiwali piyeci waawiinhkeeli teki wiyehi poonano wa hpenalaci hina tepasawi-leni ksake nimehci hahkwina meci wiyehi hahpoweeweneki hinoki kaasekiki hotekooli

And while he was sitting on the judgment-seat, his wife sent unto him, saying, Have thou nothing to do with that righteous man: for I have suffered many things this day in a dream because of him.

20. howe nihki hokimaawi mhkateewkolayeeki chiine nihki kikileniiki hokolepkaamaawahi nihi mehseelelici wahsi nihki natomaawaaci palepasiili mecimi macilotawaawaaci ciisisiili

Now the chief priests and the elders persuaded the multitudes that they should ask for Barabbas, and destroy Jesus.

21. payeekwa hina kapenali haapafse mecimi taanawe hina nihki niiswi yoona kitesiteheepwa wah pakfenamoolako hotelahi mecimi palepasii hiwaki nihki

But the governor answered and said unto them, Whether of the twain will ye that I release unto you? And they said, Barabbas.

22. nehiwe howe ne hpenala ciisisii hina klaistii yaaloofota hotelahi paalatii wiilaani wi haasitefhoofo hiwaki caayahki nihki

Pilate saith unto them, What then shall I do unto Jesus which is called Christ? They all say, Let him be crucified.

23. mecimi koociwe nehiwe mecaafiki si mehci lawi hina hisiwe payeekwa nihki hanhhiweewahootamooki wiilaani wi haasitefhoofo lahootamooki

And he said, Why, what evil hath he done? But they cried out exceedingly, saying, Let him be crucified.

24. weecikeenahi yeh neemeki paalatii yeesi paameci kaaciika tatawaanhkeewe pemi pafekwiiyaalici hoteh mame nepi mecimi kifileca yeelahfamiilici nihi mehseelelici nifafayaakifi hini homhskomi yaama tepasawi-leni kiilawa memekinaapatamoko hisiwe

So when Pilate saw that he prevailed nothing, but rather that a tumult was arising, he took water, and washed his hands before the multitude, saying, I am innocent of the blood of this righteous man: see ye to it.

25. chiine nihki caayahki lenaweeki haapafseeki wiilaani hoskici niiyaana wi hateewi homhskomi mecimi nitapelohfemenaaki hiwaki

And all the people answered and said, His blood be on us, and on our children.

26. hine howe nihi hopakfenamawahi palepasiili weeka ciisisiili holihfiiwanhhwaali mecimi pakfenamaake wahsi haasitefhifolici

Then released he unto them Barabbas: but Jesus he scourged and delivered to be crucified.

27. hine howe nihki hosamaakanemhhi hina kapenali piitike hini pletooliam' hotesiwelaawaali ciisisiili mecimi caayahki nihki nekotweelena samaakanaki homaawaskotawaawaali

Then the soldiers of the governor took Jesus into the palace, and gathered unto him the whole band.

28. chiine hosahsaakitoonaawaali mecimi hopiitenikehaawaali mhskwaawi makootakooti

And they stripped him, and put on him a scarlet robe.

29. chiine nihki hotapkeenaanaawa hokimaawipetakhoowe kaawihi mecimi wiileki hoteh poonamawaawaali hini chiine mhfaskwalwi homayaawiinhkiki chiine hociikwanahkeepiiki yeelahfamiilici mecimi howaapalaacimaawaali hei hokimaamwaali coosaki hiwaki

And they plaited a crown of thorns and put it upon his head, and a reed in his right hand; and they kneeled down before him, and mocked him, saying, Hail, King of the Jews!

30. mecimi hofiifekwaalaawaali chiine homamenaawa hini mhfaskwalwi mecimi hocacinalaawaali wiileki

And they spat upon him, and took the reed and smote him on the head.

31. chiine yeh mehci waapalaachaawaaci nihki holiikinaawaali hini makootakooti chiine hopiitenikehaawaali wiila hopiitenikana mecimi hotaamwelaawaali wahsi haasitefhwaawaaci

And when they had mocked him, they took off from him the robe, and put on him his garments, and led him away to crucify him.

32. chiine yeesi piyeci lohfaawaaci nihki homhkawaawaali hileniili saiman' sifooli saailiinii hoci niliini nihki homamiiloowihkawaawaali wahsi wiiteemekowaaci wahsi menawah hina haamwetawaaci nili hotaasitehfekiimilici

And as they came out, they found a man of Cyrene, Simon by name: him they compelled to go with them, that he might bear his cross.

33. chiine nihki yeh piyaawaaci nitasi kalhkoofe sitoote hini hokanaatepiki yeeyoki hini

And when they were come unto a place called Golgotha, that is to say, The place of a skull,

34. homiilaawaali waiini wahsi menelici kilekfenwi wiifwi chiine yeh mehci kotataki hina mata wiisa menwa

they gave him wine to drink mingled with gall: and when he had tasted it, he would not drink.

35. chiine yeh mehci nihki haasitefhwaawaaci nili papahfenamaatiiki hopiitenikanilici pemi kiskinikanitalwaatiiki

And when they had crucified him, they parted his garments among them, casting lots:

36. chiine nitasi lematapiiki hokcitawaapamaawaali

and they sat and watched him there.

37. chiine hoteh poonaanaawa nihki spemefeki wiileki hoci hina hocahtawaacimoofoowe mehtawikaate halayaama hina ciisisii nili hokimaamwaali nihki coosaki lawikaate

And they set up over his head his accusation written, THIS IS JESUS THE KING OF THE JEWS.

38. hine nitasi hapiiki wiici haasitefhoofooki nili niiswi ciikoniwehfiiki nekoti hini mayaawiinhkiki chiine nekoti hini namaciinhkiki

Then are there crucified with him two robbers, one on the right hand, and one on the left.

39. chiine nihki pemhfeecki hopekiskimaawaali hopemi papawkwehtawaawaali

And they that passed by railed on him, wagging their heads,

40. mecimi kiila wah liikatenaka hini mamaatomeewikamikwi mecimi hini wa hopatenaka

and saying, Thou that destroyest the temple, and buildest it in three days,

nhfoko waapanestoolo kiiya hiinawiyane hokwihfali maneto hini yaasitehfeki hoci kwasfaalo hotelaawaali

save thyself: if thou art the Son of God, come down from the cross.

41. hiini yaska nehfaapi nihki hokimaawi mhkateewkolayeeki hopemi waapalaacimaawaali nili kileki nihki yaayawikeecki chiine kikileniiki

In like manner also the chief priests mocking him, with the scribes and elders, said,

42. howaapaneshahi kotakhi wiiya hotaalwi waapanesto hiina yo nili hokimaamali hiswiila wiilaani howe hini yaasitehfeki hoci kwasfaate mecimi keh teepwehtawaape wiiya

He saved others; himself he cannot save. He is the King of Israel; let him now come down from the cross, and we will believe on him.

43. homhfeelemaali yo manetooli wiilaani howe nili pakfenekote skata leelemaate nili ksake niiya hina hokwihfali maneto hiwa yo hotekohi

He trusteth on God; let him deliver him now, if he desireth him: for he said, I am the Son of God.

44. chiine nihki ciikoniwehfiiki weewiici haasitefhoofocki nili nehfaapi hotpakitamawaawaali hini yaska si mataametiiwe

And the robbers also that were crucified with him cast upon him the same reproach.

45. howe hini mawi-nekotwahfene yaatefaki hoci nitasi hahteewi peepekicaaki petakwfenwi melhske hini hasiskiiki paalohi hini mawi-caakatfene yaatefaki

Now from the sixth hour there was darkness over all the land until the ninth hour.

46. chiine nawito hini mawi-caakatfene yaatefaki holaamahootamwa ciisisii hilai hilai laama sepakfenai nimanetooma nimanetooma koociwe kipakiteelemi hiwa keela hini

And about the ninth hour Jesus cried with a loud voice, saying, Eli, Eli, lama sabachthani? that is, My God, my God, why hast thou forsaken me?

47. chiine naaleta nihki nitasi neniipawicki yeh nootamowaaci hini yaama hileni honatomaali hilaicali hiwaki

And some of them that stood there, when they heard it, said, This man calleth Elijah.

48. mecimi weelena nekoti nihki memekwi chiine homamaali kcikamiiwatowali mecimi hokwikamhaali nili pskipaapo chiine mhfaskwaloki hoteh poonaali nili mecimi hoteh miilaali ciisisiili wahsi menelici

And straightway one of them ran, and took a sponge, and filled it with vinegar, and put it on a reed, and gave him to drink.

49. chiine nihki maisi naaleta wiilaani waapamaataako kwehkwi hilaica weh piyeewa wahsi waapaneshaaci hiwaki

And the rest said, Let be; let us see whether Elijah cometh to save him.

50. chiine nohki holaamahootamwa ciisisii mecimi hopakfenaali hocacaalahkwali

And Jesus cried again with a loud voice, and yielded up his spirit.

51. mecimi waapatamoko hini laapicimota hini mamaatomeewikamikwi hoci niisweelena si pahfehka hini spemeki hoci paalohi hini sahkiki chiine hini hasiski noomeska chiine nihki siikonaki papahfehkaaki

And behold, the veil of the temple was rent in twain from the top to the bottom; and the earth did quake; and the rocks were rent;

52. mecimi nili nepoowaalako tawenoote chiine meci howiiyaanwahi nihki weefepeficki mayehci haakicfaacki nepaawe honhskaanoofohi

and the tombs were opened; and many bodies of the saints that had fallen asleep were raised;

53. mecimi pemi piyeci lohfehi nili nepoowaalako hoci yeesi mehci haapefiiwi-honhskaawenici nihki hottaanaawa hini hofepi hoteewe mecimi hotepinaakofihtawaawahi meci

and coming forth out of the tombs after his resurrection they entered into the holy city and appeared unto many.

54. howe hina kaptiina chiine nihki wiici nili peemi kcitawaapamaacki ciisisiili yeh neemowaaci hini hasiskinoomeskaawe mecimi nili wiyehi yehpenatooteeki hanhhiweewi kwpeneeki teepweewe yaama niliini hokwihfali maneto hiwaki

Now the centurion, and they that were with him watching Jesus, when they saw the earthquake, and the things that were done, feared exceedingly, saying, Truly this was the Son of God.

55. chiine meci hkweeki nitasi pelowihi hoci pemi hilaapamaawaali nihi mayehci keelelii hoci neekalekoci ciisisii hopemi miisamaakohi

And many women were there beholding from afar, which had followed Jesus from Galilee, ministering unto him:

56. heelekiina nihi melii mekiteliina chiine nili hokiwaali hokwifhi sepetii

among whom was Mary Magdalene, and Mary the mother of James and Joses, and the mother of the sons of Zebedee.

57. chiine ye holaakwiifiki nitasi piyeewa paweewi hileni haalimefiye hoci coosii sinoofo niliini nehfaapi ciisisii hokakehkimaafali

And when even was come, there came a rich man from Arimathaea, named Joseph, who also himself was Jesus' disciple:

58. yaama hileni paalatiili heewa mecimi natotamaake nili howiiyaanali ciisisii hine howe paalatii tepikeemo nili wahsi miiliweeki

this man went to Pilate, and asked for the body of Jesus. Then Pilate commanded it to be given up.

59. chiine coosii homamaali nili wiiyaanali mecimi hote hofepatenaali fafayaaki mafaanimotaaki

And Joseph took the body, and wrapped it in a clean linen cloth,

60. mecimi hoteh seksimaali nili piitike hoskinwi nehalwaaka wiila nepoowaalakwi mayehci hini siikoneki hotaalakhaki chiine hoteh tetepenaali mhsi siikonali skwaateeki hini nepoowaalakwi mecimi hini hoci saawe

and laid it in his own new tomb, which he had hewn out in the rock: and he rolled a great stone to the door of the tomb, and departed.

61. chiine melii mekiteliina nitasi hapiwa mecimi hina kotaka melii pemapiiki hasowe wayeetahkwe hini nepoowe

And Mary Magdalene was there, and the other Mary, sitting over against the sepulchre.

62. howe hini wayaapaki holaakosi hini nanahiiwe si kaasekiki nihki hokimaawi mhkateewkolayeeki chiine nihki pelesiiki paalatiili si maawaskaaki

Now on the morrow, which is the day after the Preparation, the chief priests and the Pharisees were gathered together unto Pilate,

63. yeeleniwiyani nimhkaweeletaape yeesi hina weenikeemo yeheeyehi keewaki lenaweewici mehci nhfokonakike ne honhska nohki hiyoci

saying, Sir, we remember that that deceiver said, while he was yet alive, After three days I rise again.

64. tepikeemolo weecikeenahi wahsi haayici kcitawaafiiki paalohi hini mawi-nhfokonakike wahsi pwaa kikamooci hokakehkimaafhi piyaalici chiine kiimiwelaawaaci nili mecimi honhska hina nili nepelici hoci hilaawaaci lenawehi chiine hini ceeyehkwi piimilawiiwe halika we hinwi noota hini nhhihta hisiweeki

Command therefore that the sepulchre be made sure until the third day, lest haply his disciples come and steal him away, and say unto the people, He is risen from the dead: and the last error will be worse than the first.

65. howe paalatii kipoonaawa kiilawa kaakcitawahtoota nhhaakone hini si haayicitooko yeesi kiilawa katawiilefiyeekwe hotelahi nihi

Pilate said unto them, Ye have a guard: go your way, make it as sure as ye can.

66. weecikeenahi nhheeki nihki mecimi hotaayiicifetoonaawa hini nepoowe hotaayicsimaawaali nili siikonali hina kehcitawahtoota pemi wiici nihi

So they went, and made the sepulchre sure, sealing the stone, the guard being with them.

Matthew:28

1. howe keelo hini halwaakahsi kaasekiki yeesi hini halemi waapaki wayeeci hini weski kaasekiki hini peeleko menetoowikiisekiki piyeewa melii mekiteliina chiine hina kotaka melii wahsi neemowaaci hini nepoowe

Now late on the sabbath day, as it began to dawn toward the first day of the week, came Mary Magdalene and the other Mary to see the sepulchre.

2. chiine waapatamoko nitasi mhsi noomeska hasiski ksake hina teepeelemiweeta hotenhcaliimali laasiyofeeli menhkwatoki hoci chiine piyeewa mecimi halika hoteh kolepenaali nili siikonali chiine hoskici nili lematapiwa

And behold, there was a great earthquake; for an angel of the Lord descended from heaven, and came and rolled away the stone, and sat upon it.

3. hotesinaakofiiwe paasi peepaki mecimi hopiitenika wahkanakiya paasi koona

His appearance was as lightning, and his raiment white as snow:

4. chiine ksake hokwfaawaali nili nihki kehcitawaapicki sapkahi papaeskaaki mecimi paasi keela neepekiki hileniiki hilefiiki

and for fear of him the watchers did quake, and became as dead men.

5. chiine hina henhcali haapafse teki kaawilaweko ksake niwaakota yeesi ciisisii natonehweekwe hina mayehci haasitefhoofota

And the angel answered and said unto the women, Fear not ye: for I know that ye seek Jesus, which hath been crucified.

6. matalaakwa hina hotasi ksake honhska hina teetepilahi yeeyoci piyaako waapatamoko hini tah seksiki hina teepeelemiweeta

He is not here; for he is risen, even as he said. Come, see the place where the Lord lay.

7. chiine nhhaakone weeweetepi chiine wiitamawehko hokakehkimaafhi honhska hina nili nepelici hoci chiine sci keeleliiki si niikaani kiilawa nitasi keh neewaawa sci neyehka kiwiitamoolepwa hotelahi nihi hkwehi

And go quickly, and tell his disciples, He is risen from the dead; and lo, he goeth before you into Galilee; there shall ye see him: lo, I have told you.

8. chiine nihki weeweetepi hini nepoowaalakoki hoci weepfeeki kileki kaawilaweeki chiine mhsi howesilepwaaki mecimi memekwiiki wahsi piyeetawaawaaci kalawiiwe hokakehkimaafhi hina

And they departed quickly from the tomb with fear and great joy, and ran to bring his disciples word.

9. chiine waapamehko ciisisii honakskawahi nihi howesilaasamamoowe caayahki cehi hisiwe chiine piyeeki nihki mecimi hoteh fookinamaakohi hofitali chiine hosasilawehekohi

And behold, Jesus met them, saying, All hail. And they came and took hold of his feet, and worshipped him.

10. howe ciisisii teki kaawilaweko nhhaakone wiitamawehko niceeninaaki wahsi nihki keeleliiki haawaaci mecimi nitasi neh nookooki hotelahi nihi

Then saith Jesus unto them, Fear not: go tell my brethren that they depart into Galilee, and there shall they see me.

11. howe yeheeyehi nihki nhhaawaaci waapamehko naaleta nihki kehcitawahtoocki piyeeki hini hoteeweneki mecimi howiitamawaawahi nihi

Now while they were going, behold, some of the guard came into the city,

hokimaawi mhkateewkolayehi caayahki nili wiyehi peepiyeemikaki

and told unto the chief priests all the things that were come to pass.

12. chiine nihki yeh meh-tapiimaawaaci nihi kikilenihi mecimi mehci tepoweeki homiilaawahi nihki nihi samaakanhhi mecilekhi moni

And when they were assembled with the elders, and had taken counsel, they gave large money unto the soldiers,

13. hokakehkimaafhi piyehi tepehki mecimi hokiimiwelaawaali nili yeheeyehi nepaayaake niilawe hiyoko

saying, Say ye, His disciples came by night, and stole him away while we slept.

14. mecimi kwehkwi yooma hotawakaaki piyeeyaalite hina kapenali niilawe neh kolepkaamaape hina keh pakfenelepe petfakiteheewe hisiweeki

And if this come to the governor's ears, we will persuade him, and rid you of care.

15. weecikeenahi nihki hotahpenaanaawa hini moni mecimi nihki yeesi kakehkimoofowaaci silawiiki chiine yooma hiyoowe lhfwenoote melhske heelekiina nihki coosaki mecimi yaska hini yeelhfeeyaaki paalohinoki kaasekiki

So they took the money, and did as they were taught: and this saying was spread abroad among the Jews, and continueth until this day.

16. weeka nihki metahfwi-kite-nekoti kakehkimaafaki keeleliiki heeki hini meekwahkiki tasi yeewiitamawaaci ciisisii

But the eleven disciples went into Galilee, unto the mountain where Jesus had appointed them.

17. mecimi yeh neewaawaaci nihki hosasilawehaawaali nili payeekwa naaleta nanawaciteheeki

And when they saw him, they worshipped him: but some doubted.

18. chiine ciisisii hotfahi nihi mecimi hokaloolahi caayahki simekofiiwe nimehci miilekoopi piitike weefepahkamikiki mecimi hoskitaamhkwe

And Jesus came to them and spake unto them, saying, All authority hath been given unto me in heaven and on earth.

19. nhhaakone kiilawa weecikeenahi mecimi hina hoci hoshehko kakehkimaafaki caayahki hina hotfweeloowena lenawe pemi fafahkwi holelhehko hini howiifooweneki hina hohfima chiine hina hokwihfima chiine hofepi hocacaalahkwa

Go ye therefore, and make disciples of all the nations, baptizing them into the name of the Father and of the Son and of the Holy Ghost:

20. pemi kakehkimehko nihki wahsi kikinamowaaci caayahki wiyehi kookwe-nehi-kaaci kitepimelepwa mecimi sci niila wiici kiilawa moosatawi wiikinaakwi paalohi hini ceeyekwahkamikike hini yeelekokwahkamikiki

teaching them to observe all things whatsoever I commanded you: and lo, I am with you alway, even unto the end of the world.

MARK

Mark:1

1. weeci halemiki hini howesi hopiyeetaacimoowe ciisisii klaistii nili hokwihfali maneto

The beginning of the gospel of Jesus Christ, the Son of God.

2. teetepilahi yeesi mehtawikeeci hini haisaya hina maamoosikiiskweeta waapami niteleskawa nimiisamaakeema yeelahfamiikweeyani hiina weh nanahihfeto kimiyeewi

Even as it is written in Isaiah the prophet, Behold, I send my messenger before thy face, Who shall prepare thy way;

3. hini hokalaweewihsimoowe wiyeefa pemi talahootamwa hini piileski mecfetooko hini homiyeewi hina teepeelemiweeta tepilahi stooko homiyeeweneefa

The voice of one crying in the wilderness, Make ye ready the way of the Lord, Make his paths straight;

4. caanii piyeewa hina fafahkwi holelhiwe hini piileski mecimi nanahimiwe hini matayinisiteheewe hoci fafahkwiholelhiweewe wahsi haalhofiiweniki maciilefiiwena

John came, who baptized in the wilderness and preached the baptism of repentance unto remission of sins.

5. chiine nitasi hoci lohfeeki caayahki hini cotiyeewi taamhkwe hotfaawaali nili chiine nihki caayahki colooseelemii hoci mecimi hofafahkwi holelhekowaali nili hini caateniiwi fiipiiki pemi tepaacimooki homaciilefiiwenwa

And there went out unto him all the country of Judaea, and all they of Jerusalem; and they were baptized of him in the river Jordan, confessing their sins.

6. chiine caanii keemaliiwi wihfaya piitenike chiine meskwahteeki kitapifoowe kitapifo mecimi waakeefhi hotamwahi chiine pakwaci hemoowimelaasi homiici

And John was clothed with camel's hair, and had a leathern girdle about his loins, and did eat locusts and wild honey.

7. chiine si nanahimiwe nitasi piyeewa mayohkwaaci niila hiina halika mhsiilefi noota niila hini menihfepi hina homahkifena hoci mata nitkwiilefi wahsi sahkiki si waakiiya mecimi pelhama

And he preached, saying, There cometh after me he that is mightier than I, the latchet of whose shoes I am not worthy to stoop down and unloose.

8. niila nepiki kiteh fafahkwi holelhelepwa weeka hina nili hofepi hocacaalahkwali keh si fafahkwi holelhekowa hisiwe

I baptized you with water; but he shall baptize you with the Holy Ghost.

9. chiine hini piyeemikatwi hine nele kaasekiki yeesi ciisisii piyaaci naaselefi hoci piici taamhkwe keelelii mecimi hofafahkwi holelhekooli caaniili hini caateniiki

And it came to pass in those days, that Jesus came from Nazareth of Galilee, and was baptized of John in the Jordan.

10. mecimi weelena pemi moskofe hini nepiki hoci honeemena nili menhkwato pahfehka chiine hina hocacaalahkwa paasi miyaasipawiifa pemi si laasiwehsinooli hoskici wiiya

And straightway coming up out of the water, he saw the heavens rent asunder, and the Spirit as a dove descending upon him:

11. chiine kalaweewihsimoowe nili menhkwato homooya kiila hina yeeahkweelemaka nikwihfa kiiyaaki nimenwitehe

And a voice came out of the heavens, Thou art my beloved Son, in thee I am well pleased.

12. chiine weelena nili hocacaalahkwali hoteleskaakooli hini piileski

And straightway the Spirit driveth him forth into the wilderness.

13. mecimi nitasi hapiwa niyeewaapitaki tfoko hokwakwecihkaakooli seteniili mecimi howiici hapiimahi nihi pakwaci mekinhhwehi chiine nihki henhcaliiki homiisamawaawaali nili

And he was in the wilderness forty days tempted of Satan; and he was with the wild beasts; and the angels ministered unto him.

14. howe caaniili yeh mehci mesenoofolici ciisisii keeleliiki si piyeewa pemi nanahimiwe hini howesi hopiyeetaacimoowe maneto

Now after that John was delivered up, Jesus came into Galilee, preaching the gospel of God,

15. chiine hini laakwaamefiiwe howe hokwihfetoote chiine hini hokimaawiiwe maneto howe nahiika mata hini siteheeko kiilawa chiine teepwehtamoko hini howesi piyeetaacimoowe hisiwe

and saying, The time is fulfilled, and the kingdom of God is at hand: repent ye, and believe in the gospel.

16. chiine heele skwaapiyeeki hini keeleliiwi mhsinepi pemi pemhfe honeewaali saimaniili mecimi heenhtlooli nili hoceeninaali saimanii peemi hipakitamelici haakwaskwhaaka hini mhsinepiki ksake naanamefkeecki nihki

And passing along by the sea of Galilee, he saw Simon and Andrew the brother of Simon casting a net in the sea: for they were fishers.

17. mecimi ciisisii piyaako kiilawa hahkowiko chiine naanamefkaalaacki hilenihi ke shelepwa hotelahi nihi

And Jesus said unto them, Come ye after me, and I will make you to become fishers of men.

18. chiine weelena nihki honakataanaawa nili haakwaskwhaakana mecimi honeekalaawaali

And straightway they left the nets, and followed him.

19. chiine halikaamehi heewa honeewaali ceemhsiili nili hokwihfali sepetii chiine caaniili hoceeninaali nehfaapi holakeeleki hapiiki hocahtokwaataanaawa nili haakwaskwhaakana

And going on a little further, he saw James the son of Zebedee, and John his brother, who also were in the boat mending the nets.

20. chiine weelena howihkomahi nihi mecimi nihki honakalaawaali hohfwaali sepetiili hini holakeeleki wiici nihi haloolaakaafhi chiine homawi nalaawaali

And straightway he called them: and they left their father Zebedee in the boat with the hired servants, and went after him.

21. chiine nihki keepaaniamii heeki mecimi kweeyehkwi piicfe hini mhsikamikwi hini halwaakahsi kaasekiki chiine kakehkimiwe

And they go into Capernaum; and straightway on the sabbath day he entered into the synagogue and taught.

22. mecimi nihki hocihfeeletamaawaawaali hokakehkimiweewe ksake hotesi kakehkimahi paasi hopoona wiyehsimekofiiwe mata paasi nihki yaayawikeecki

And they were astonished at his teaching: for he taught them as having authority, and not as the scribes.

23. chiine kweeyehkwi nitasi homhsikamikomwaaki hapiwa hileni wiiciwi wiyakilehfiili mecimi hina wiyakahootamwa

And straightway there was in their synagogue a man with an unclean spirit; and he cried out,

24. nehiwe nipoonaape wa hpenalelaake kiila ciisisii naaselefileni ha kipiya wahsi macilotawiyaake kiwaakomele kiila weeciwiyani hina hofepi wiyeefa maneto hoci hisiwe

saying, What have we to do with thee, thou Jesus of Nazareth? art thou come to destroy us? I know thee who thou art, the Holy One of God.

25. mecimi ciisisii hokwtelaali nili nooleewilo chiine hina hoci lohfaalo hotelaali

And Jesus rebuked him, saying, Hold thy peace, and come out of him.

26. chiine hina wiyakilehfi hopemi maatakoskahaali nili mecimi wiyakahootamwa piyeci lohfe nili hoci

And the unclean spirit, tearing him and crying with a loud voice, came out of him.

27. chiine caayahki nihki kwakwehtaaniteheeki weecikeenahi niinatohtwaatiiki heelekiina wiilawa nehiwe yooma mayaki kakehkimiweewe simekofiiwe hoci tepimahi wiikinaakwi nihi wiyakilehfihi mecimi hopefetaakohi nihi hiwaki

And they were all amazed, insomuch that they questioned among themselves, saying, What is this? a new teaching! with authority he commandeth even the unclean spirits, and they obey him.

28. chiine hotelaacimekofiiwe weepfeeyaali weelena mefhiike hini laa keeleliiwi taamhkwe kaayaawka heeya

And the report of him went out straightway everywhere into all the region of Galilee round about.

29. chiine weelena yeh piyeci lohfaawaaci hini mhsikamikwi hoci hini si piyeeki yeetaawaaci wiikiwa saimanii chiine heenhtlo kileki ceemhsii chiine caanii

And straightway, when they were come out of the synagogue, they came into the house of Simon and Andrew, with James and John.

30. howe saimanii wiiwali hokeeli seksinooli hahkwilokeeli kisifoowe mecimi weelena nihi howiitamaakohi nili

Now Simon's wife's mother lay sick of a fever; and straightway they tell him of her:

31. chiine piyeewa chiine hoteh fakileceenaali nili mecimi honhskaanaali chiine hina hini kisifoowe honakaleko mecimi homiisamawaali hina

and he came and took her by the hand, and raised her up; and the fever left her, and she ministered unto them.

32. chiine weelaakwiifiki yeh paksimoci hina kiisekikiisfwa hopiyeetawaawaali nihki nihi caayahki yeekwilokeelici chiine nihi lekoskaakolici waninehfihi

And at even, when the sun did set, they brought unto him all that were sick, and them that were possessed with devils.

33. mecimi caayahki nihi hoteeweneki hoci maawatoskahi hini skwaateeki

And all the city was gathered together at the door.

34. chiine meci yeekwilokeelici hokiikehahi kwakwetaki silokeewena mecimi holohfe pakilahi meci waninehfihi chiine mata wiilaani hoteleelemahi nihi waninehfihi wahsi kalawilici ksake nihki howaakomaawaali nili

And he healed many that were sick with divers diseases, and cast out many devils; and he suffered not the devils to speak, because they knew him.

35. chiine hini kwelahwaapaki mhsi kookwelaakwa wihsi pwaa waapaki honhska mecimi lohfe chiine tah papskwahkiki heewa mecimi nitasi mamaatome

And in the morning, a great while before day, he rose up and went out, and departed into a desert place, and there prayed.

36. chiine saimanii mecimi nihki peepah wiitfeemaacki honeekalaawaali

And Simon and they that were with him followed after him;

37. mecimi nihki homhkawaawaali chiine caayahki kipemi natonehokooki hotelaawaali

and they found him, and say unto him, All are seeking thee.

38. payakila haataako nili hanhka hoteeweneefa wahsi menawahi nitasi nehfaapi nanahimiweeya ksake yooma yo hini weeci piyaaya hotelahi nihi

And he saith unto them, Let us go elsewhere into the next towns, that I may preach there also; for to this end came I forth.

39. chiine mefhiike keelelii si saapwi homhsikamikomwaaki heewa pemi nanahimiwe mecimi hopemi lohfe pakilahi waninehfihi

And he went into their synagogues throughout all Galilee, preaching and casting out devils.

40. chiine nitasi hotfekooli weeskilhakeemekilici hopemi nanahpaacimekooli mecimi hopemi hociikwanah-keeptaakooli chiine siteheeyane keh katawi fafayaakhi hotekooli

And there cometh to him a leper, beseeching him, and kneeling down to him, and saying unto him, If thou wilt, thou canst make me clean.

41. chiine pemi maacitehe kiteminaakweeletiiwe maa si ciikinhkeelwa chiine hopehsenaali chiine hiini yeesiteheeya fafayaakhoofolo hotelaali

And being moved with compassion, he stretched forth his hand, and touched him, and saith unto him, I will; be thou made clean.

42. mecimi weelena hini hoskilhaki-mekiiwe nili hoci saaweya mecimi hina fafayaakhoofo

And straightway the leprosy departed from him, and he was made clean.

43. chiine homayaawimaali nili mecimi weelena faakici hoteleskawaali

And he strictly charged him, and straightway sent him out,

44. chiine waapatano teki wiyehi hisi hileni kiila weeka nhhaale waapatesi kiiya hina mhkateewkolaye chiine pakfenikeelo yeesi fafayaakhoofoyani nili wiyehi teepikeemoci moosisii wahsi hoteepweeweniwaaci nihki hotelaali nili

and saith unto him, See thou say nothing to any man: but go thy way, shew thyself to the priest, and offer for thy cleansing the things which Moses commanded, for a testimony unto them.

45. payeekwa hina lohfe mecimi hotalemi lhfwaatota hini holaami mecimi holhfwena mefhiike hini wiyehi weecikeenahi ciisisii haalwi kiteeni tawaaci piicfe hoteewe weeka faakici hapiwa tah laa papskwahki chiine nihi hopiyeelotaakohi caaki wayeeci hoci

But he went out, and began to publish it much, and to spread abroad the matter, insomuch that Jesus could no more openly enter into a city, but was without in desert places: and they came to him from every quarter.

Mark:2

1. chiine keepaaniamii ye hottaki nohki laakofoko hisi mayohkwaaci hini talaacimopi yeesi hini yeetaaci hapici wiikiwa

And when he entered again into Capernaum after some days, it was noised that he was in the house.

2. chiine meci maawatweelooki weecikeenahi matalaakwa kiteeni teewaaki mata mata wiikinaakwi hini skwaateeki chiine hokaloolahi hini kalawiiwe

And many were gathered together, so that there was no longer room for them, no, not even about the door: and he spake the word unto them.

3. chiine piyeeki nihki hopiyeetawaawaali hileniili hahkwilokeeli nenekifiiwe niyeewi honiimaawaali

And they come, bringing unto him a man sick of the palsy, borne of four.

4. chiine ye haalwi nihki maalaakwahi piyaawaaci nili ksake nihki yeefoskaacki hoci hopahkinaanaawa hini hapahkwehfecika ta hapici hina chiine yeh mehci

And when they could not come nigh unto him for the crowd, they uncovered the roof where he was: and

pokhamowaaci hini hoteh laasiwenaanaawa hini tfani ta hapici hina yeekwilokeeta hini nenekifiiwe

when they had broken it up, they let down the bed whereon the sick of the palsy lay.

5. chiine ciisisii honeemawahi hoteepwehseewenwa nihki hokwihfima kimaciilefiiwena pakfeeletoote hotelaali nili yeekwilokeelici hini nenekifiiwe

And Jesus seeing their faith saith unto the sick of the palsy, Son, thy sins are forgiven.

6. payeekwa nitasi lematapiiki naanekoti nihki yaayawikeecki mecimi pemi memekiniteheeki

But there were certain of the scribes sitting there, and reasoning in their hearts,

7. koociwe yaama hileni halayini si kalawi pahtaamo hina neefawe hokatawi pakfeeletaana maciilefiiwena nekoti payeekwa maneto hina siteheeki

Why doth this man thus speak? he blasphemeth: who can forgive sins but one, even God?

8. mecimi weelena ciisisii pemi moositehe hocacaalahkoki yeesi nihi yooni si memekiniteheelici laameki wiiyaawa koociwe kimemekineeletaanaawa yooma wiyehi kitehiwaaki hotelahi

And straightway Jesus, perceiving in his spirit that they so reasoned within themselves, saith unto them, Why reason ye these things in your hearts?

9. taaniwe haliwi weecihi ha kimaciilefiiwena pakfeeletoote weelaa toke honhskaalo chiine mamelo kitfani mecimi pemhfeelo wahsi hiloofoci hina yeekwilokeeta hini nenekifiiwe

Whether is easier, to say to the sick of the palsy, Thy sins are forgiven; or to say, Arise, and take up thy bed, and walk?

10. payeekwa wahsi kiilawa menawahi waakotameekwe yeesi hina hokwihfali hileni poonaki simekofiiwe hoskitaamhkwe wahsi pakfeeletaki maciilefiiwena hoteh kaloolaali nili yeekwilokeelici hini nenekifiiwe

But that ye may know that the Son of man hath power on earth to forgive sins (he saith to the sick of the palsy),

11. kitele niila honhskaalo mamelo kitfani mecimi nhhaale yeetaayani wiikiwa hotelaali

I say unto thee, Arise, take up thy bed, and go unto thy house.

12. mecimi hina honhska chiine weelena homame hini tfani chiine hale weepfe yeelahfamiiwaaci nihki caayahki weecikeenahi caayahki kwakwehtaaniteheeki mecimi howahfaacimekowhaawaali manetooli matalaakwa kineemepe hini yeeki yooma hiwaki

And he arose, and straightway took up the bed, and went forth before them all; insomuch that they were all amazed, and glorified God, saying, We never saw it on this fashion.

13. chiine nohki hini skwaapiyeeki mhsinepi heewa chiine caayahki nihki mehseelekki homaamawaapamaawaali mecimi hokakehkimaafhi

And he went forth again by the sea side; and all the multitude resorted unto him, and he taught them.

14. chiine yeesi maalaakwahi pemhfeeci honeewaali liifaayiili nili hokwihfali halhfiyas peemi lematapilici yaata hini teekshiweeki mecimi neekasilo hotelaali chiine hina pafekwi mecimi honeekalaali

And as he passed by, he saw Levi the son of Alphaeus sitting at the place of toll, and he saith unto him, Follow me. And he arose and followed him.

15. chiine hini piyeemikatwi yeesi lematapici tah wihfeniki piitike yeetaaci wiikiwa chiine meci teeksiiwi-maawatonikehfiiki chiine meciileficki howiitapiimaawaali ciisisiili mecimi hokakehkimaafhi ksake meci nitasi chiine nihki honeekalaawaali

And it came to pass, that he was sitting at meat in his house, and many publicans and sinners sat down with Jesus and his disciples: for there were many, and they followed him.

16. chiine nihki yaayawikeecki pelesiiki hoci yeh neemowaaci yeesi pemi wihpomekoci nihi meciilefilici

And the scribes of the Pharisees, when they saw that he was eating with the chiine teeksiiwi-maawatonikehfihi nehiwe hini yeesi hina wihpomaaci mecimi wiitaapowemaaci nihi teeksiiwi-maawatonikehfihi chiine meciilefilici hotelaawahi hina hokakehkimaafhi

sinners and publicans, said unto his disciples, He eateth and drinketh with publicans and sinners.

17. chiine hini yeh nootaki ciisisii nihki weewiisikatowicki mata skata hoteleelemaawaali naanatawhcikeelici nihki yeekwilokeecki weeka mata nipiya wahsi hotahpimaki nihki meeyaawiileficki meciileficki weeka hotelahi nihi

And when Jesus heard it, he saith unto them, They that are whole have no need of a physician, but they that are sick: I came not to call the righteous, but sinners.

18. chiine caanii hokakehkimaafhi chiine nihki pelesiiki pemi fafahkwi hocikeeki chiine piyeeki nihki mecimi koociwe caanii hokakehkimaafhi chiine nihki pelesiiki fafahkwi hocikeeki weeka mata fafahkwi hocikeeki kikakehkimaafaki hotekohi

And John's disciples and the Pharisees were fasting: and they come and say unto him, Why do John's disciples and the disciples of the Pharisees fast, but thy disciples fast not?

19. mecimi ha wih katawi fafahkwi hocikeeki nihki hini hoci hokwihfimaaki mayakinhhaakanehkweewikaaneki yeheeyehi nili mayakinhhaakanali wiici hapiimekowaaci laakwasi peepoonaawaaci nili mayakinhhaakanali howiici hapiimekowaali nili mata yah katawi fafahkwi hocikeeki hotelahi ciisisii

And Jesus said unto them, Can the sons of the bride-chamber fast, while the bridegroom is with them? as long as they have the bridegroom with them, they cannot fast.

20. payeekwa nili kaasekiki weh piyeeya hine nili mayakinhhaakanali weh mamaakwiiki hine chiine weh fafahkwi hocikeeki hine kaasekiki

But the days will come, when the bridegroom shall be taken away from them, and then will they fast in that day.

21. mata hileni hotah si kipokwaata maalekhi hoskimota kehta piitenikaneki piilepe hini ceecahtokweki hini hoci mamawiweya hini mayaki hini kehta hoci mecimi hini haliwi yeesi lelhkehkaaki mectoote

No man seweth a piece of undressed cloth on an old garment: else that which should fill it up taketh from it, the new from the old, and a worse rent is made.

22. chiine mata hileni hotah si poona mayaki waiini kehta waiiniiwi pootaalaawahi piilepe hini waiini weh pohkiceskaakonaawa nihki pootaalaawaaki mecimi hini waiini miyaalefiiya chiine nihki pootaalaawaaki weeka mayaki waiini hoski waiiniiwi pootaalaawahi hotaasi poonaanaawa nihki

And no man putteth new wine into old wineskins: else the wine will burst the skins, and the wine perisheth, and the skins: but they put new wine into fresh wineskins.

23. chiine hini piyeemikatwi yeesi pemi saapwi haaci nili kawaskwikitikaana ta halwaakahsi kiisekiki mecimi hokakehkimaafhi yeele lhfeelici halemi kiskikwenamehi hini kawaskwi

And it came to pass, that he was going on the sabbath day through the cornfields; and his disciples began, as they went, to pluck the ears of corn.

24. mecimi nihki pelesiiki waapatano koociwe yeesilawiiwaaci nihki hini pwaayaa mayaawhki kwteletiiweneki halwaakahsi kiisekiki hotekohi

And the Pharisees said unto him, Behold, why do they on the sabbath day that which is not lawful?

25. mecimi ha matalaakwa kiilawa kilaapaatotaanaawa yeesilawiici teepitii ye hakaawaafiici chiine skwaalawe hina mecimi nihi peepah wiitfeemekoci

And he said unto them, Did ye never read what David did, when he had

need, and was an hungred, he, and
they that were with him?

26. yeesi hottaki piitike hini wiikiwe yeetaaci maneto
hine yeh moospimekofiiwi mhkateewkolayeewici
heepayeefa chiine homiici hini peepoonooteeki takhwa
pwaayaa hini mayaawhki kwteletiiweneki wahsi miiciki
weeciwephi nihki mhkateewkolayeeki mecimi nehfaapi
homiilahi nihi peepah wiitfeemekoci hotelahi

How he entered into the house of God
when Abiathar was high priest, and
did eat the shewbread, which it is not
lawful to eat save for the priests, and
gave also to them that were with him?

27. chiine hini halwaakahsi kaasekiki hostaakwi hileni
mata hileniili hostaakwi hina halwaakahsi kaasekiki

And he said unto them, The sabbath
was made for man, and not man for
the sabbath:

28. weecikeenahi hina hokwihfali hileni teepeeletaka
wiikinaakwi hini halwaakahsi kaasekiki

so that the Son of man is lord even of
the sabbath.

Mark:3

1. chiine hotta nohki hini mhsikamikwi chiine nitasi
hapiwa hileni peepoonaka hahkapwileceewe

And he entered again into the
synagogue; and there was a man there
which had his hand withered.

2. chiine nihki hokcitawaapamaawaali kwehkwi hina wih
kiikehaali nili ta halwaakahsi kiisekiki wahsi menawahke
mestaawimaawaaci nihki

And they watched him, whether he
would heal him on the sabbath day;
that they might accuse him.

3. mecimi hini heelekhi si pafekwiilo hotelaali nili
hileniili peepoonamelici hini hahkapwileceewe

And he saith unto the man that had his
hand withered, Stand forth.

4. chiine hoteh kaloolahi nihi ha mayaawatwi hini
halwaakahsi kiisekiki wahsi weeowesaaki silawiiki
weelaa wahsi macilawiiki wahsi waapanestooteeki
lenaweewiiwe weelaa wahsi nhsiweeki payeekwa
matalaakwa tasimooki nihki

And he saith unto them, Is it lawful on
the sabbath day to do good, or to do
harm? to save a life, or to kill? But
they held their peace.

5. chiine yeh mehci kaayaawka si kisfi waapamaaci nihi
teewahi homacilepwaskaako hini peemi siipenilici
hotehiwa maa si ciikileceskaalo hotelaali nili hileniili
mecimi hina maa si ciikileceska hini mecimi peteki
stooteeli holeci

And when he had looked round about
on them with anger, being grieved at
the hardening of their heart, he saith
unto the man, Stretch forth thy hand.
And he stretched it forth: and his hand
was restored.

6. chiine nihki pelesiiki lohfeeki mecimi weelena wiici
nihki heletiifaki hotepowaalaawaali wahsi menawahi
macilotawaawaaci

And the Pharisees went out, and
straightway with the Herodians took
counsel against him, how they might
destroy him.

7. mecimi ciisisii kileki hokakehkimaafhi hini mhsinepiki
si saawe chiine meci mehseelekki keelelii hoci
neekasiweeki chiine cotiye hoci

And Jesus with his disciples withdrew
to the sea: and a great multitude from
Galilee followed: and from Judaea,

8. chiine colooseelemii hoci chiine haitoomiye hoci
chiine halika hini caatenii chiine kaayaawka taayaa
mecimi saatanii meci mehseelekki pemi nootaakeeki
caayahki hini wiyehi yeesilawiilici hopiyeelotawaawaali

and from Jerusalem, and from
Idumaea, and beyond Jordan, and
about Tyre and Sidon, a great

multitude, hearing what great things he did, came unto him.

9. chiine hoteh kaloolahi hokakehkimaafhi wahsi caki holakeesihi hahkawaapamekoci ksake nihi yeefoskaalici hoci kikamooci wih kiposkaakohi nihi

And he spake to his disciples, that a little boat should wait on him because of the crowd, lest they should throng him:

10. ksake meci homehci kiikehahi weecikeenahi yeetfwilici peepoonamelici hahkwi hpeneewena hofakkehkaakohi wahsi menawahke nihi pehsekoci

for he had healed many; insomuch that as many as had plagues pressed upon him that they might touch him.

11. chiine nihi wiyakilehfihi kookwe-kaaci-laakwa honookohi haakicfehi yeelahfamiici chiine wiyakahootamohi kiila hina nili hokwihfali maneto hiwaki nihki

And the unclean spirits, whensoever they beheld him, fell down before him, and cried, saying, Thou art the Son of God.

12. mecimi holaami homayaawimahi wahsi pwaa waakomekofihekoci

And he charged them much that they should not make him known.

13. chiine hini meekwahkiki si kkwicsinwa chiine hotahpimaali wiyeefali hina yeeleelemaaci wiila mecimi nihiini hotfekohi

And he goeth up into the mountain, and calleth unto him whom he himself would: and they went unto him.

14. chiine homamahi metahfwi-kite-niiswi wahsi nihi menawahke wiiciimekoci chiine wahsi menawahke waawiineskawaaci wahsi nanahimiweelici

And he appointed twelve, that they might be with him, and that he might send them forth to preach,

15. mecimi poonamelici simekofiiwe wahsi lohfe pakilaawaaci waninehfihi

and to have authority to cast out devils:

16. chiine saimaniili piita hote hanhkawi wiinaali

and Simon he surnamed Peter;

17. chiine ceemhsiili nili hokwihfali sepetii chiine caaniili nili hoceeninaali ceemhsii mecimi nihi pooenaciis hote hanhkawi wiinahi nenemhki hokwifhi keela hini

and James the son of Zebedee, and John the brother of James; and them he surnamed Boanerges, which is, Sons of thunder:

18. chiine heenhtlo chiine filapii chiine pafalamiyo chiine mefiyoo chiine taamosii chiine ceemhsii nili hokwihfali halhfiyas chiine fatiyasii chiine saimanii hina keenaniiwileni

and Andrew, and Philip, and Bartholomew, and Matthew, and Thomas, and James the son of Alphaeus, and Thaddaeus, and Simon the Cananaean,

19. chiine cootas' hiskeeletii niliini memestaawhekoci nehfaapi chiine wiikiwaapeki si piyeewa

and Judas Iscariot, which also betrayed him. And he cometh into a house.

20. chiine nihki mehseelekki maawatwi piyeeki nohki weecikeenahi nihki hotaalwi katawi miicinaawa mohci takhwa

And the multitude cometh together again, so that they could not so much as eat bread.

21. chiine wihkaanhhi yeh nootaakeelici hini lohfehi homawi fookinekohi ksake mata howaakota yeesilawiici hiwaki nihki

And when his friends heard it, they went out to lay hold on him: for they said, He is beside himself.

22. chiine nihki yaayawikeecki colooseelemii weeci piyeci paalacsikiki hopoonaali piyeelhsipaliili mecimi

And the scribes which came down from Jerusalem said, He hath

nili hokimaawoosaakanwaali nihki waninehfiiki hoci katawi lohfe pakilahi nihi waninehfihi hiwaki nihki

Beelzebub, and, By the prince of the devils casteth he out the devils.

23. chiine hote hotahpimahi nihi mecimi nehiwe wih si katawi setenii lohfe pakilaali seteniili hotelahi pemaatoweewena

And he called them unto him, and said unto them in parables, How can Satan cast out Satan?

24. chiine kwehkwi hokimaawiiwe pahfenetiiyaake hini hokimaawiiwe haalwi niipawiiya

And if a kingdom be divided against itself, that kingdom cannot stand.

25. chiine kwehkwi wiikiwa pahfenetiiyaake we haalwi hilefiiya hini wiikiwa wahsi niipawiiyaaki

And if a house be divided against itself, that house will not be able to stand.

26. chiine kwehkwi setenii mehci pafekwicfatake wiiya mecimi pahfehka mata yah katawi niipawi weeka ceeyehkofiiwe hopoona

And if Satan hath risen up against himself, and is divided, he cannot stand, but hath an end.

27. payeekwa mata wiyeefa yah katawi piicfe hini wiikiwa yeetaalici waasikatowilici hileniili mecimi macilotawaaci howiyehiimilici weeciwephi nhhihta hina kciipilaate nili waasikatowilici hileniili hine chiine hina weh katawi macilotamawaali yeetaalici wiikiwa

But no one can enter into the house of the strong man, and spoil his goods, except he first bind the strong man; and then he will spoil his house.

28. tepilo kitelepwa niila caayahki homaciisilawiiwenwa weh pakfeeletamaakwihi nihi hokwihfwahi hileniiki mecimi hopahtaamoowenwa kookwe-nehi-kaaci nihki weh si pahtaamooki

Verily I say unto you, All their sins shall be forgiven unto the sons of men, and their blasphemies wherewith soever they shall blaspheme:

29. weeka kookwe-neefa-kaaci weh pahtaamaali nili hofepi hocacaalahkwali hopoona matalaakwasi pakfeeletamawoofoowe weeka macilawi kookwelaakwasi mecaafiki

but whosoever shall blaspheme against the Holy Spirit hath never forgiveness, but is guilty of an eternal sin:

30. ksake nihki hopoonaali wiyakilehfiili hiwaki

because they said, He hath an unclean spirit.

31. chiine nitasi piyeeli hokeeli mecimi hoceeninahi chiine pemi niipawiiki faakici nihki nili si waawiinhkeeki hotahpimaawaali

And there come his mother and his brethren; and, standing without, they sent unto him, calling him.

32. chiine mehseelekki kaayaawka lematapiiki nili chiine waapami kikiya chiine kiceeninaaki faakici kinatonehokooki hotelaawaali nihki

And a multitude was sitting about him; and they say unto him, Behold, thy mother and thy brethren without seek for thee.

33. chiine hotaapaftawahi neefawe nikiya chiine niceeninaaki

And he answereth them, and saith, Who is my mother and my brethren?

34. mecimi kaayaawka hoteh waapamahi nihi lematapilici kaayaawka wiila waapamehko nikiya chiine niceeninaaki

And looking round on them which sat round about him, he saith, Behold, my mother and my brethren!

35. ksake kookwe-neefa-kaaci weh silawi hini hotesiteheewe maneto hiina hina niceenina chiine nitikweema chiine nikiya hiwa

For whosoever shall do the will of God, the same is my brother, and sister, and mother.

Mark:4

1. chiine nohki halemi kakehkimiwe hini skwaapiyeeki mhsinepi chiine nitasi homaawatweelotaakohi lakokwe meci mehseelelici weecikeenahi holakeeleki lhkamwa mecimi hini mhsinepiki lematapi chiine caayahki nihki mehseelekki hini skwaapiyeeki mhsinepi hapiiki pakwatahki

2. chiine meci wiyehi hokakehkimahi nihi pemaatoweeweneki mecimi hotelahi hopemikakehkimiweeweneki

3. hahkawehseeko waapamehko hina yeeahcikeeta hale weepfe wahsi hacikeeci

4. chiine hini piyeemikatwi yeesi hacikeeci naaleta miinhka hini pakacikana si penhfenwi chiine nihki wiskilohfaki piyeeki mecimi hocaakataanaawa hini

5. chiine naaleta hini tah siikonahkiki hasiski si penhfenwi tah pwaa hini weeyahka hahteeki hasiski mecimi weelena hini faakinwi ksake hini mata weeyahka spihfenwi hasiski

6. chiine hina kiisekikiisfwi yeh piyeetahkofaki sahte hini chiine ksake mata hoceepkahkatowi nepote hini

7. chiine naaleta heelekiina nihi kaawiisehi si penhfenwi mecimi nihki kaawiiseki skwiniikiiki chiine honepwaskwehtoonaawa hini mecimi mata mawifoowe niikinwi

8. chiine naaleta hini howesi hasiskiiki si penhfenwi mecimi niikinwi mawifoowe pemi skwiniikinwi chiine skwiiya mecimi hini homooya nhfwaapitaki tfweekfenwi chiine nekotwaasi tfweekfenwi chiine tepeewe tfweekfenwi

9. chiine peepoonaka hotawakaawali wahsi nootaakeeci wiilaani hina nootaakeete hiwa

10. chiine yeh naanhsihka hapici nihi yeepilici kaayaawka wiila kileki nihi metahfwi-kite-niiswi honatohtaakohi nili pemaatoweewena

11. chiine hotelahi kiilawa si miiletipi hini meemayatki hini hokimaawiiweneki maneto hoci weeka nihki yeepicki faakici caayahki wiyehi pemaatoweeweneki hpenatoote

12. wahsi nihki neekeewaate menawahi neemowaaci mecimi pwaa moositeheewaaci chiine nootaakeewaate nihki menawahi nootaakeewaaci mecimi pwaa nenohseewaaci piilepeeke nihki wih kokiiki nohki mecimi hini wih pakfeeletamawoofooki

And again he began to teach by the sea side. And there is gathered unto him a very great multitude, so that he entered into a boat, and sat in the sea; and all the multitude were by the sea on the land.

And he taught them many things in parables, and said unto them in his teaching,

Hearken: Behold, the sower went forth to sow:

and it came to pass, as he sowed, some seed fell by the way side, and the birds came and devoured it.

And other fell on the rocky ground, where it had not much earth; and straightway it sprang up, because it had no deepness of earth:

and when the sun was risen, it was scorched; and because it had no root, it withered away.

And other fell among the thorns, and the thorns grew up, and choked it, and it yielded no fruit.

And others fell into the good ground, and yielded fruit, growing up and increasing; and brought forth, thirtyfold, and sixtyfold, and a hundredfold.

And he said, Who hath ears to hear, let him hear.

And when he was alone, they that were about him with the twelve asked of him the parables.

And he said unto them, Unto you is given the mystery of the kingdom of God: but unto them that are without, all things are done in parables:

that seeing they may see, and not perceive; and hearing they may hear, and not understand; lest haply they should turn again, and it should be forgiven them.

13. chiine ha kiilawa mata kiwaakotaanaawa yooma pemaatoweewe mecimi nehiwe keh si waakotaanaawa caayahki nili pemaatoweewena hotelahi

And he saith unto them, Know ye not this parable? and how shall ye know all the parables?

14. hina yeeahcikeeta hototo hini kalawiiwe

The sower soweth the word.

15. chiine yohkoma nihki hini pakacikana yeepicki ta hatooteeki hini kalawiiwe chiine yeh mehci nootaakeewaaci nihki weelena setenii piyeewa mecimi homame hini kalawiiwe mayehci hatooteeki wiiyaawaaki nihki

And these are they by the way side, where the word is sown; and when they have heard, straightway cometh Satan, and taketh away the word which hath been sown in them.

16. chiine yohkoma nehfaapi nihki yeetoofocki hini tah siikonahkiki yohkooni yeh mehci nootamowaaci hini kalawiiwe weelena hotahpenaanaawa hini wiici howesilepwaawe

And these in like manner are they that are sown upon the rocky places, who, when they have heard the word, straightway receive it with joy;

17. chiine mata hopoonaanaawa wiiyaawaaki hoceepkahkatwi weeka maalaakwasi wiisikifiiki howe hine kiisenaacinamoowe weelaa naanohkaachetiiwe yeh pafekwiiyaalici ksake hini kalawiiwe hoci weelena nihki hotakikahsinooki

and they have no root in themselves, but endure for a while; then, when tribulation or persecution ariseth because of the word, straightway they stumble.

18. chiine nihki naaleta yeetoofocki hini heelekiina nihi kaawiisehi yohkoma nihki mayehci nootakki hini kalawiiwe

And others are they that are sown among the thorns; these are they that have heard the word,

19. chiine nili hotamefiiwena hini yeelekokwahkamikiki chiine paweewi wanimefiiwe mecimi hini maciskata siteheewe kotaki wiyehi piicfeeya hoci nepwaskwehtoote hini kalawiiwe mecimi hini mata mawifooweniwi

and the cares of the world, and the deceitfulness of riches, and the lusts of other things entering in, choke the word, and it becometh unfruitful.

20. chiine nehke nihki yeetoofocki hini howesi hasiskiiki nihkiini honootaanaawa hini kalawiiwe mecimi homamenaawa hini chiine honiiktoonaawa mawifoowe nhfwaapitaki tfweekfenwi chiine nekotwaasi tfweekfenwi chiine tepeewe tfweekfenwi hotelahi

And those are they that were sown upon the good ground; such as hear the word, and accept it, and bear fruit, thirtyfold, and sixtyfold, and a hundredfold.

21. hina niitawaaka ha piyeeloofo wahsi laameki poonoofoci hini posiliiki weelaa laamitahfa hini tfaneki ha mata wahsi hini hoskici yaatah niipawici si poonoofoci hotelahi

And he said unto them, Is the lamp brought to be put under the bushel, or under the bed, and not to be put on the stand?

22. ksake mata wiyehi hahteewi kikitoote wahsi hini weeciwephi tepinawkofetooteeki mata nohki wiyehi hahteewi kiyaacitoote kateski wahsi hini wayahfeeyaaki si piyeeyaaki

For there is nothing hid, save that it should be manifested; neither was anything made secret, but that it should come to light.

23. wiyeefa hileni poonake hotawakaawali wahsi nootaakeeci wiilaani hina nootaakeete

If any man hath ears to hear, let him hear.

24. chiine kcitawaafiiko hini neenootameekwe wiyehsi tepacika teepacikeeyeekwe kiilawa hini keh tepacikaalekoopwa kiilawa mecimi haliwi keh si miilekoopwa kiilawa hotelahi

And he said unto them, Take heed what ye hear: with what measure ye mete it shall be measured unto you: and more shall be given unto you.

25. ksake hina peepoonaka hina weh miilekwi chiine hina pwaayaa poonaka hina we hoci mamoote hini wiikinaakwi peepoonaki

For he that hath, to him shall be given: and he that hath not, from him shall be taken away even that which he hath.

26. chiine hiwa yooni yeeki hini hokimaawiiwe maneto paasi hileni wi hipakita miinhka hini hoskitaamhkwe

And he said, So is the kingdom of God, as if a man should cast seed upon the earth;

27. mecimi wih nepeewa chiine wi honhska tepehki kite kiiseki mecimi hini miinhka wih faakinwi mecimi skwiniikinwi mata howaakota weeci hiniki

and should sleep and rise night and day, and the seed should spring up and grow, he knoweth not how.

28. hina hasiskitaamhkwe honiikito mawifoowe pesikwi wiila hoci nhhihta hini mhsiski howe hini mefahkwimi howe hini yeetteeki hini mefahkwimiki

The earth beareth fruit of herself; first the blade, then the ear, then the full corn in the ear.

29. payeekwa ye hatteelici weelena hociikina kiskathika ksake hini kawaskwhaawe howe piyeeya

But when the fruit is ripe, straightway he putteth forth the sickle, because the harvest is come.

30. chiine hiwa taaniwe keh si takweeletaape hini hokimaawiiwe maneto weelaa nehiwesi pemaatoweeweneki lahkehfetoope hini

And he said, How shall we liken the kingdom of God? or in what parable shall we set it forth?

31. hini hinwi paasi hini nekoti pekwe mastatiiwi miinhka hine yeetooteeki hini hini hoskitaamhkwe weekhi hini hotahpi hinwi nili caayahki miinhkaana yehteeki hini hoskitaamhkwe

It is like a grain of mustard seed, which, when it is sown upon the earth, though it be less than all the seeds that are upon the earth,

32. payeekwa hine hatoote hini skwiniikinwi mecimi halika hinwi noota caayahki nili memekinasko chiine makamaki pkeeyahkwatwi weecikeenahi nihki wiskilohfaki hini spemeki hoci katawi lwahsinooki siipaaci hini yeewikaki nitasi

yet when it is sown, groweth up, and becometh greater than all the herbs, and putteth out great branches; so that the birds of the heaven can lodge under the shadow thereof.

33. chiine meci niliini yeeki pemaatoweewena hokileki kaloolahi hini kalawiiwe nihi yeesi nihki katawiilefiwaaci wahsi nootamowaaci hini

And with many such parables spake he the word unto them, as they were able to hear it:

34. mecimi faakici pemaatoweewe mata hokaloolahi nihi weeka nehalwaaka hokakehkimaafhi hotepaani tepiwiitamawahi caayahki wiyehi

and without a parable spake he not unto them: but privately to his own disciples he expounded all things.

35. chiine hini kaasekiki ye holaakwiifiki hini hasowe kaameki haataako hotelahi nihi

And on that day, when even was come, he saith unto them, Let us go over unto the other side.

36. mecimi honakalaawahi nihi mehseelelici hotaamwelekohi nihi yaska yeesi hapici hini holakeeleki chiine kotakali holakeelali howiiteemekona

And leaving the multitude, they take him with them, even as he was, in the boat. And other boats were with him.

37. chiine nitasi pafekwiiya mhsaawi mehsikkaki mecimi nili peepookaki hini si piicfehfeno holakeeleki weecikeenahi hini holakeesi howe pemi hokwikami

And there ariseth a great storm of wind, and the waves beat into the boat, insomuch that the boat was now filling.

38. chiine hina wiila hini hotaanaaki hapiwa nepeewa hoskici nili hanahkanali chiine nihki hotamachaawaali

And he himself was in the stern, asleep on the cushion: and they awake mecimi keekehkimiwe ha mata kimakofeeleta wahsi hkwinamooyakwe hotelaawaali

him, and say unto him, Master, carest thou not that we perish?

39. chiine hina hamamo mecimi hokoteta hini mehsikkaki chiine kaamehkawefiiwe cehi nooleewilo hoteta hini mhsinepi mecimi hini mehsikkaki nakeeska chiine nitasi hahteewi mehsi kaamehkawaki

And he awoke, and rebuked the wind, and said unto the sea, Peace, be still. And the wind ceased, and there was a great calm.

40. chiine koociwe kiwiisaalepwaapwa ha mata keewaki kimeh poonaanaawa teepwehseewe hotelahi nihi

And he said unto them, Why are ye fearful? have ye not yet faith?

41. chiine hanhhiweewi wiisaalepwaaki nihki mecimi neefawe howe yaama yeesi wiikinaakwi hini mehsikkaki chiine hini mhsinepi pefetaakoci hitiiki

And they feared exceedingly, and said one to another, Who then is this, that even the wind and the sea obey him?

Mark:5

1. chiine kaameki hini mhsinepi si piyeeki nihki piitike hini hotasiskiimwaaki nihki kiyaalesiinaki

And they came to the other side of the sea, into the country of the Gerasenes.

2. chiine hini holakeeleki ye hoci piyeci lohfaaci weelena nitasi honakskaakooli hileniili nili nepoowaalako homooli wiiciwefi wiyakilehfiili

And when he was come out of the boat, straightway there met him out of the tombs a man with an unclean spirit,

3. hina hopoona yeetaaci nili laa nepoowaalako mecimi mata hileni kiteeni hokatawi kciipilaali nili mata mata wiikinaakwi hokwaanhhi

who had his dwelling in the tombs: and no man could any more bind him, no, not with a chain;

4. ksake hina neyehka mehci moosaki kciipifo fakikaapifoowena chiine hokwaanhhi mecimi hina neyehka homehci pkinahi nihi hokwaanhhi chiine nili fakikaapifoowena hopekskinaana chiine mata hileni hopoona wiisikatowiiwe wahsi weecamehaaci nili

because that he had been often bound with fetters and chains, and the chains had been rent asunder by him, and the fetters broken in pieces: and no man had strength to tame him.

5. chiine moosatawi tepehki chiine kiiseki nili laa nepoowaalako mecimi nili laa mamakwahkiki hina pah talahootamwa chiine hopemi kakiskotaa wiiya siikonhhi

And always, night and day, in the tombs and in the mountains, he was crying out, and cutting himself with stones.

6. chiine hina yeh neewaaci ciisisiili maalaakwa hoci memekwi mecimi hosasilawehaali nili

And when he saw Jesus from afar, he ran and worshipped him;

7. chiine wiyakahootamwa kalaweewihsimoowe nehiwe nipoona wah hpenalela kiila ciisisii hokwihfali hina kci moospi maneto kite hahtoocimele maneto teki mamiyeenaanhhilo hisiwe

and crying out with a loud voice, he saith, What have I to do with thee, Jesus, thou Son of the Most High God? I adjure thee by God, torment me not.

8. ksake piyeci lohfaalo kiila wiyakilehfi hina hileni hoci hotelaali nili

For he said unto him, Come forth, thou unclean spirit, out of the man.

9. chiine honatohtawaali nehiwe kitesifo mehseeleka nitesifo ksake meci niilawe hotekooli

And he asked him, What is thy name? And he saith unto him, My name is Legion; for we are many.

10. chiine holaami honanahpaacimekooli wih pwaa hini hoci taamhkwe lohfelhkawaaci nihi

And he besought him much that he would not send them away out of the country.

11. howe nitasi hapiiki yeepfateki hini meekwahkiki mhseelooki koskooki peemi wihfeniwaaci

Now there was there on the mountain side a great herd of swine feeding.

12. nihki leskawinaake koskooki wahsi niilawe menawahi piicfaamakici nihki hotesi nanahpaacimekohi nihi

And they besought him, saying, Send us into the swine, that we may enter into them.

13. mecimi homiilahi wiilaani nihi chiine nihki wiyakilehfiiwi piyeci lohfeeki mecimi hotfaawahi nihi koskohi chiine hina nekotweeleka kosko paalacipto hini keekiskaapkahki hini mhsinepiki si lekowhaske yeetfwici nawito niisene metahfene tepeewe mecimi nihki nephokwiiki hini mhsinepiki

And he gave them leave. And the unclean spirits came out, and entered into the swine: and the herd rushed down the steep into the sea, in number about two thousand; and they were choked in the sea.

14. chiine nihki yeesamaacki hosimooki mecimi hini haacimooki hini hoteeweneki chiine hini piileski taamhkwe chiine nihki piyeeki homawaapataanaawa hini mayehci piyeemikaki

And they that fed them fled, and told it in the city, and in the country. And they came to see what it was that had come to pass.

15. mecimi ciisisiili si piyeeki nihki chiine hotelaapamaawaali nili lekoskaakota waninehfihi peemi lematapilici piitenikeeli chiine mayaawi kiiskweeli hina mayehci poonaata nili mayehseelelici chiine kaawilaweeki nihki

And they come to Jesus, and behold him that was possessed with devils sitting, clothed and in his right mind, even him that had the legion: and they were afraid.

16. chiine nihki neeneemekki hini hotaacimohtawaawahi nihi yeesinaki hina lekoskaakota waninehfihi chiine nihi koskohi

And they that saw it declared unto them how it befell him that was possessed with devils, and concerning the swine.

17. chiine nihki hotalemi kcihkawaawaali wahsi hoskwaayaamwaaki hoci saawelici nili

And they began to beseech him to depart from their borders.

18. chiine yeesi hini holakeeleki pemi lhkaki hina mayehci lekoskaakota waninehfihi honanahpaacimaali wahsi menawahke wiici hapiimaaci

And as he was entering into the boat, he that had been possessed with devils besought him that he might be with him.

19. chiine mata wiilaani hoteleelemaali weeka nhhaale yeetaayani wiikiwa kihkaanaki mecimi wiitamawi yeesi mhsaaki wiyehi hina teepeelemiweeta mayehci hpenalehki chiine yeesi poonamoolehki kiteminaakweeletiiwe hotelaali nili

And he suffered him not, but saith unto him, Go to thy house unto thy friends, and tell them how great things the Lord hath done for thee, and how he had mercy on thee.

20. chiine hina weepfe yehaaci mecimi hotalemi lhfwaatota tiikeepolasiiki yeesi mhsaaki wiyehi mayehci hpenalekoci ciisisiili mecimi mayaciteheeki caayahki hileniiki

And he went his way, and began to publish in Decapolis how great things Jesus had done for him: and all men did marvel.

21. chiine yeh mehci ciisisii kapaaci nohki hini holakeeleki hasowe wayeetahkwe meci mehseelelici

And when Jesus had crossed over again in the boat unto the other side, a

homaawatweelotaakooli mecimi maalaakwahi hini mhsinepi hapiwa

22. chiine nitasi hotfekooli nekoti nihki teepeelecikeecki hini mhsikamikwi hoci ceealasii sifo chiine teewa honookooli nahiika hofitali si haakicfeeli nili

23. mecimi honanahpaacimekooli nitaanehfefa howe naanemi hasenwa kimamaatomele wahsi kiila piyaayani chiine kileciwali hoskici hina si poonamani wahsi hina menawahi mefefihoofoci mecimi lenaweewici hotekooli

24. chiine howiiteemaali nili mecimi meci mehseelelici honeekalekohi chiine hofakkehkaakohi

25. chiine hkweewa peepoonaka mhskowilokeewe metahfwi-kite-niiswi kkato

26. mecimi mehci hahkwinamwa meci wiyehi meci naanatawhcikeelici hoci chiine homehci pakita caayahki peepoonaki hina chiine mata wiyehi si weyahkaawi weeka paameci haliwi hilefi

27. neyehka pemi nootaake hini wiyehi ciisisiili si piyeewa hini nekotoskaaweneki hotaanaaki chiine hoteh pehsenamaawaali nili hopiitenikanilici

28. ksake kwehkwi kateski pehsenamawake hopiitenikana neh mefefihekoopi hiwapi

29. mecimi weelena hini weectaki homhskomi kahkiteeli mecimi homoosto wiiyaaki yeesi kiikehoofoci hotahkwilokeewe

30. chiine weelena ciisisii hopemi moosto wiiyaaki yeesi hini waasikaki wiiyaaki hoci neyehka weepfeeyaaki hokotekoneko hini hini nekotwelooweneki mecimi neefawe nipehsenamaakwa nipiitenikana hisiwe

31. chiine hokakehkimaafhi kineewaaki nihki mehseelekki kipemi fakkehkaakooki mecimi neefawe nipehsenekwa kiteyo hotekohi

32. mecimi natawaapi kaayaawka wahsi neewaaci nili mayehci silawiilici yooma wiyehi

33. payeekwa hina hkweewa pemi kaawilawe mecimi papaweska hopemi waakota hini mayehci hpenaloofoci piyeewa chiine yeelahfamiilici nili si haakicife mecimi howiitamawaali caayahki hini teepweewe

34. chiine hotaanhfima kiteepwehseewe kimehci mefefiheko kaamaani weepfeelo mecimi kiikeelo kithahkwilokeewe hotelaali

great multitude was gathered unto him: and he was by the sea.

And there cometh one of the rulers of the synagogue, Jairus by name; and seeing him, he falleth at his feet,

and beseecheth him much, saying, My little daughter is at the point of death: I pray thee, that thou come and lay thy hands on her, that she may be made whole, and live.

And he went with him; and a great multitude followed him, and they thronged him.

And a woman, which had an issue of blood twelve years,

and had suffered many things of many physicians, and had spent all that she had, and was nothing bettered, but rather grew worse,

having heard the things concerning Jesus, came in the crowd behind, and touched his garment.

For she said, If I touch but his garments, I shall be made whole.

And straightway the fountain of her blood was dried up; and she felt in her body that she was healed of her plague.

And straightway Jesus, perceiving in himself that the power proceeding from him had gone forth, turned him about in the crowd, and said, Who touched my garments?

And his disciples said unto him, Thou seest the multitude thronging thee, and sayest thou, Who touched me?

And he looked round about to see her that had done this thing.

But the woman fearing and trembling, knowing what had been done to her, came and fell down before him, and told him all the truth.

And he said unto her, Daughter, thy faith hath made thee whole; go in peace, and be whole of thy plague.

35. yeheeyehi keewaki kalawici nihki hoci piyeeki hina yeetaaci wiikiwa teepeelecikeeta hini mhsikamikwi kitaanehfa nepwa koociwe nelohci halika kitesi petfakha hini keekehkimiwe hisiweeki

While he yet spake, they come from the ruler of the synagogue's house, saying, Thy daughter is dead: why troublest thou the Master any further?

36. payeekwa ciisisii mata makofeeletamwa hini kalawiiwe yeeyoki teki wiisaalepwaalo teepwehseelo pehi hotelaali nili teepeelecikeelici hini mhsikamikwi

But Jesus, not heeding the word spoken, saith unto the ruler of the synagogue, Fear not, only believe.

37. chiine mata hileniili wiilaani hoteleelemaali wahsi neekalekoci weeciwephi piitali chiine ceemhsiili chiine caaniili nili hoceeninaali ceemhsii

And he suffered no man to follow with him, save Peter, and James, and John the brother of James.

38. chiine nihki piyeeki hini wiikiwaapeki yeetaaci hina teepeelecikeeta hini mhsikamikwi chiine honeeme tatawaanhkeewe mecimi meci pemi wihfakweeki mamiyaatweewahootamooki holaami

And they come to the house of the ruler of the synagogue; and he beholdeth a tumult, and many weeping and wailing greatly.

39. chiine yeh piicfaaci koociwe kitatawaanhkeepwa mecimi kiwihfakweepwa hina hapelohfa mata nepwa nepeewa weeka hotelahi nihi

And when he was entered in, he saith unto them, Why make ye a tumult, and weep? the child is not dead, but sleepeth.

40. mecimi howaapaleelemaawaali nihki payeekwa hina hopemi neyehka halika leskawahi caayahki nihi hotaamwelaali nili hohfali hina hapelohfa mecimi hokeeli chiine nihi peepah wiitfeemekoci chiine nhheeki ta hapilici nili hapelohfali

And they laughed him to scorn. But he, having put them all forth, taketh the father of the child and her mother and them that were with him, and goeth in where the child was.

41. chiine hoteh fakileceenaali nili hapelohfali talife komai hotelaali yeh laapaacimoki hkweefa kitele honhskaalo yeeyoki hini

And taking the child by the hand, he saith unto her, Talitha cumi; which is, being interpreted, Damsel, I say unto thee, Arise.

42. mecimi weelena hina hkweefa honhska chiine paamhfe ksake metahfwi-kite-niiswi tfwi kkatoowi hina chiine nihki kwakwehtaaniteheeki weelena mhsi kwakwehtaaniteheewe

And straightway the damsel rose up, and walked; for she was twelve years old. And they were amazed straightway with a great amazement.

43. chiine holaami hotepimahi nihi wahsi pwaa hileni waakotaki yooma mecimi tepikeemo wahsi nehcipeh wiyehi miiloofolici nili hkweefali wah miicilici

And he charged them much that no man should know this: and he commanded that something should be given her to eat.

Mark:6

1. chiine hini hoci lohfe mecimi nehalwaaka hotasiskiiki si piyeewa chiine hokakehkimaafhi honeekalekohi

And he went out from thence; and he cometh into his own country; and his disciples follow him.

2. chiine yeh piyeeyaaki hini halwaakahsi kaasekiki halemi kakehkimiwe piitike hini mhsikamikwi chiine meci honootawaawaali cihfefiiki taaniwe hoci poonanaana yaama hileni yooloma wiyehi chiine nehiwesi hini lepwaawe meemiiloofoci yaama hileni

And when the sabbath was come, he began to teach in the synagogue: and many hearing him were astonished, saying, Whence hath this man these things? and, What is the wisdom that

mecimi nehiwe hiyooya halayini yeeki makiici
pekatefiiwena holeciwali hoci pekatenaana

is given unto this man, and what mean such mighty works wrought by his hands?

3. ha mata hina yaama hotkwipekatefiiwileni nili hokwihfali melii chiine hoceeninaali ceemhsii chiine coosisi chiine saimanii mecimi ha mata hotikwemhhi wiici hotasi kiilawe hiwaki mecimi hokisfekowaali nihki

Is not this the carpenter, the son of Mary, and brother of James, and Joses, and Judas, and Simon? and are not his sisters here with us? And they were offended in him.

4. chiine ciisisii maamoosikiiskweeta mata pwaa hateeli hotakeelemekofiiwe weeciwephi nehalwaaka hotasiskiiki chiine heelekiina nehalweelemaaci mecimi nehalwaaka yeetaaci wiikiwaapeki hotelahi nihi

And Jesus said unto them, A prophet is not without honour, save in his own country, and among his own kin, and in his own house.

5. chiine haalwi nitasi lawi makiici pekatefiiwe weeciwephi wahsi holeciwali hoskici si poonamawaaci laakofwi yeekwilokeelici lenawehi mecimi hokiikehahi nihi

And he could there do no mighty work, save that he laid his hands upon a few sick folk, and healed them.

6. chiine hokwakwehtaaneeletamawahi hopwaateepwehseewenilici chiine kaayaawka nili hoteeweneefa paamhfe pemi kakehkimiwe

And he marveled because of their unbelief. And he went round about the villages teaching.

7. chiine hotahpimahi nihi metahfwi-kite-niiswi chiine hotalemi waawiineskawahi nihi maasa niiswi mecimi homiilahi wahsi mekofihtawaawaaci nihi wiyakilehfihi

And he called unto him the twelve, and began to send them forth by two and two; and he gave them authority over the unclean spirits;

8. mecimi homayaawimahi wahsi pwaa wiyehi haamwetoolici yeelaamiilici weeciwe haapathoowe pehi mata takhwa mata piitaaka mata moni homoni-piitaakanwaaki

and he charged them that they should take nothing for their journey, save a staff only; no bread, no wallet, no money in their purse;

9. weeka wahsi nhhaalici pfekhohi mefikwahfoowena chiine teki niiswi kootiiwali kih piitenikeepwa hisiwe

but to go shod with sandals: and, said he, put not on two coats.

10. chiine kookwe-laakwa-kaaci tasi piicfaayeekwe wiikiwa nitasi hapiko paalohi hini hoci weepfeeko hotelahi

And he said unto them, Wheresoever ye enter into a house, there abide till ye depart thence.

11. chiine kookwe-kaaci-tasi mata ke hotahpenekoopwa mecimi mata nihki ke hahkawehtaakowaaki yeesi hini hoci weepfeeyeekwe papawatenamoko hini pekwi ye teeki siipaaci kifitwaaki wahsi hoteepweeweniwaaci nihki

And whatsoever place shall not receive you, and they hear you not, as ye go forth thence, shake off the dust that is under your feet for a testimony unto them.

12. chiine nihki lohfeeki mecimi nanahimiweeki wahsi hileniiki mataiini siteheeweniwaaci

And they went out, and preached that men should repent.

13. chiine holohfe pakilaawahi meci waninehfihi chiine meci holomhkoonaawahi pemi yeekwilokeelici mecimi hokiikehaawahi

And they cast out many devils, and anointed with oil many that were sick, and healed them.

14. chiine hokima heletii nootaake hini ksake howiifoowe neyehka waakotoote chiine caanii hina fafahkwiholelhiwena howe honhska nili nepelici hoci

And king Herod heard thereof; for his name had become known: and he said, John the Baptist is risen from the dead,

mecimi weecikeenhhi yooloma waasikaki pekatefiiyaali wiiyaaki hiwapi

and therefore do these powers work in him.

15. payeekwa kotakaki hilaica hina hiwaki chiine naaleta maamoosikiiskweeta hina neeyoole naanekoti nihki maamoosikiiskwecki hiwaki

But others said, It is Elijah. And others said, It is a prophet, even as one of the prophets.

16. payeekwa heletii yeh nootaakeeci hini caanii hina keekiskikwethwaka howe honhska hina hiwa

But Herod, when he heard thereof, said, John, whom I beheaded, he is risen.

17. ksake heletii mehci wiila waawiinhke chiine homesenaali caaniili mecimi hokciipilaali kiphotiiweneki nili helootiasiili hoci wiiwali filapii wiila hoceeninaali ksake homehci wiiwinaali nili

For Herod himself had sent forth and laid hold upon John, and bound him in prison for the sake of Herodias, his brother Philip's wife: for he had married her.

18. ksake caanii mata mayaawatwi kwteletiiweneki wahsi poonaci kiceenina wiiwali hotelaali heletiili

For John said unto Herod, It is not lawful for thee to have thy brother's wife.

19. mecimi helootiasii homateelemaali nili chiine maatawi tehe wahsi nhfaaci mecimi haalwi katawiilefi

And Herodias set herself against him, and desired to kill him; and she could not;

20. ksake heletii hokwfaali caaniili waakotamwa yeesi nili mayaawiilefilici chiine hofepi hileniili mecimi hokcitawahaali mecimi yeh nootawaaci holaami wanhfoneewefi chiine homenwi nootawaali

for Herod feared John, knowing that he was a righteous man and a holy, and kept him safe. And when he heard him, he was much perplexed; and he heard him gladly.

21. chiine yeh tawaawi kiisekiki heletii hooskiniikiiwi kaasekiki homectawahi sapa hoteepeelecikeemhhi chiine nihi moospimekofiiwi kaptiinhhi chiine nihi hokimaawi lenihi keeleliiki hoci

And when a convenient day was come, that Herod on his birthday made a supper to his lords, and the high captains, and the chief men of Galilee;

22. chiine hine nili hotaanehfali helootiasii wiici piyeci piicfeeli mecimi menyeelooli homenwi lepwaskawaali hiiletiili hina chiine nihi weewiitapiimekoci mecimi hina hokima natotamawilo kookwe-nehi-kaaci yeesiteheeyani mecimi hini keh miilele hotelaali nili hkweefali

and when the daughter of Herodias herself came in and danced, she pleased Herod and them that sat at meat with him; and the king said unto the damsel, Ask of me whatsoever thou wilt, and I will give it thee.

23. mecimi hociikinhkemoomaali kookwe-nehi-kaaci keh natotamawi keh miilele hini paalohi hini pahfi nookimaawiiwe

And he sware unto her, Whatsoever thou shalt ask of me, I will give it thee, unto the half of my kingdom.

24. chiine hina lohfe mecimi nehiwe neh natota hotelaali hokeeli ce hini wiisi caanii hina fafahkwiholelhiwena hiwa hina

And she went out, and said unto her mother, What shall I ask? And she said, The head of John the Baptist.

25. mecimi weelena hina piyeci piicfe weeweetepi nili hokimaali heewa chiine natohse wahsi miiliyani kweeyehkwi hoskici mhsi seswilaakaneki hini wiisi caanii hina fafahkwiholelhiwena nitesitehe hisiwe

And she came in straightway with haste unto the king, and asked, saying, I will that thou forthwith give me in a charger the head of John the Baptist.

26. chiine hina hokima hanhhiweewi macilepwa payeekwa ksake nili hociikinhkemoowena chiine nihi lematapilici tah wihfeniki hoci meelawaaci pwaa nhkomaali

And the king was exceeding sorry; but for the sake of his oaths, and of them that sat at meat, he would not reject her.

27. chiine weelena hina hokima howaawiineskawaali samaakanali kehcitawahekoci hoci mecimi tepikeemo wahsi piyeetooteeki howiisi chiine hina nhheewa mecimi hokiskikwethwaali nili hini kiphotiiweneki

And straightway the king sent forth a soldier of his guard, and commanded to bring his head: and he went and beheaded him in the prison,

28. chiine hopiyeeto howiisiwilici hoskici mhsi seswilaaka mecimi hini homiilaali nili hkweefali chiine hina hkweefa hini homiilaali hokeeli

and brought his head in a charger, and gave it to the damsel; and the damsel gave it to her mother.

29. chiine hina hokakehkimaafhi yeh nootaakeewaaci nihki piyeeki mecimi homamaawaali howiiyaanali chiine hofepsimaawaali nili nepoowaalakoki

And when his disciples heard thereof, they came and took up his corpse, and laid it in a tomb.

30. chiine nihki heepastaliiki homaawaskaamaawaali ciisisiili mecimi howiitamawaawaali caayahki wiyehi kookwe-nehi-kaaci mayehci silawiiwaaci nihki mecimi kookwe-nehi-kaaci mayehci kiikehkimiweewaaci

And the apostles gather themselves together unto Jesus; and they told him all things, whatsoever they had done, and whatsoever they had taught.

31. mecimi kiilawa naanhsihka piyaako laa papskwahki tasi chiine halwaakahsiko maalaakwasi hotelahi nihi ksake meci nitasi peemi piyaawaaci mecimi peemi weepfeewaaci chiine nihki mata hopoonaanaawa tawaawiinamiiwe mohci wahsi wihfeniwaaci

And he saith unto them, Come ye yourselves apart into a desert place, and rest a while. For there were many coming and going, and they had no leisure so much as to eat.

32. chiine nihki weepfeeki hini holakeeleki naanhsihka laa papskwahki tasi heeki

And they went away in the boat to a desert place apart.

33. chiine nihki lenaweeki honeewaawahi weepfehi chiine meci howaakomaawahi mecimi nihki maawatwi hinisi kciptooki caayahki nili hoteewena hoci mecimi honawafwaawahi nihi

And the people saw them going, and many knew them, and they ran there together on foot from all the cities, and outwent them.

34. chiine piyeci weepfe wiila mecimi honeewahi meci mehseelelici chiine hokiteminaakweelemahi ksake nihki paasi meekiifaki pwaayaa poonaacki kehcitawahekowaaci hilefiiki mecimi hotalemi kakehkimahi meci wiyehi

And he came forth and saw a great multitude, and he had compassion on them, because they were as sheep not having a shepherd: and he began to teach them many things.

35. chiine hini kaasekiki howe ye holaakwiifiki hokakehkimaafhi hotfekohi chiine ceh papskwahki hotasi chiine howe hini kaasekiki holaakwiifi

And when the day was now far spent, his disciples came unto him, and said, The place is desert, and the day is now far spent:

36. halika leskawi nihki wahsi menawahi hini piileski haawaaci chiine hoteeweneefa kaayaawka mecimi tepenamowaaci pesikwi wiilawa tekawihi wah miiciwaaci hiwaki nihki

send them away, that they may go into the country and villages round about, and buy themselves somewhat to eat.

37. payeekwa haapafse mecimi miilehko kiilawa wah miiciwaaci hotelahi mecimi ha nine haape mecimi neh

But he answered and said unto them, Give ye them to eat. And they say unto him, Shall we go and buy two hundred

tepenaape niisene tepeewe seleni yeeleelemekoki takhwa chiine ha neh miilaape nihki wahsi miiciwaaci hotekohi

pennyworth of bread, and give them to eat?

38. kehfwi kipoonaanaawa kiilawa weepskweeteewali nhhaakone chiine waapatamoko hotelahi chiine yeh waakotamowaaci nihki niyaalanwi chiine niiswi namehfaki hisiweeki

And he saith unto them, How many loaves have ye? go and see. And when they knew, they say, Five, and two fishes.

39. chiine hotepimahi nihi caayahki wih lematapilici maasa ceetfwi sahkiki laa skipakskahki

And he commanded them that all should sit down by companies upon the green grass.

40. mecimi nihki lematapiiki yeetiitfweelenawakifiwaaci maasa tepeewe chiine maasa niyaalanwaapitaki

And they sat down in ranks, by hundreds, and by fifties.

41. chiine hoteh mamena nili niyaalanwi weepskweeteewali chiine nihi niiswi namefhi chiine pemi spemeki menhkwatoki laapi kisaacilawi chiine hoposkonaana nili weepskweeteewali chiine homiilahi nihi kakehkimaafhi wahsi yeelahfamiilici nihi si poonamelici mecimi nihi niiswi namefhi hopahfenamawahi heelekiina nihi caayahki

And he took the five loaves and the two fishes, and looking up to heaven, he blessed, and brake the loaves; and he gave to the disciples to set before them; and the two fishes divided he among them all.

42. chiine caayahki nihki wihfeniiki mecimi teephoolooki

And they did all eat, and were filled.

43. chiine homekinaanaawa nihki peekskahki maayaalekhi metahfwi-kite-niiswi soosoona hokwihfeno mecimi nehfaapi nihi namefhi hoci

And they took up broken pieces, twelve basketfuls, and also of the fishes.

44. chiine nihki meemiicicki nili weepskweeteewali niyaalane metahfene tepeewe hileniiki

And they that ate the loaves were five thousand men.

45. chiine weelena homamiiloowihkawahi hokakehkimaafhi wahsi hini holakeeleki lhkamelici mecimi wahsi pefseite si niikaaniilici hini hasowe wayeetahkwe yeheeyehi wiila haameskawaaci nihi mehseelelici

And straightway he constrained his disciples to enter into the boat, and to go before him unto the other side to Bethsaida, while he himself sendeth the multitude away.

46. chiine yeh mehci nakalekoci weepfe hini meekwahkiki heewa mawi mamaatome

And after he had taken leave of them, he departed into the mountain to pray.

47. chiine ye holaakwiifiki hini holakeesi howe laawtekwe hini mhsinepiki piyeethanwi chiine wiila pehi hini pakwatahki

And when even was come, the boat was in the midst of the sea, and he alone on the land.

48. mecimi hopemi neewahi kwiilahsitehehi yeesi coomeelici ksake hini mehsikkaki honakskaanaawa nihki nawito niyeewene ta kcitawahtooteeki hini tepehki laakwa hotfahi pemi pemhfe hoskici hini mhsinepiki mecimi wih pemhfaalahi

And seeing them distressed in rowing, for the wind was contrary unto them, about the fourth watch of the night he cometh unto them, walking on the sea; and he would have passed by them:

49. payeekwa nihki yeh neewaawaaci pemi pemhfeeli hoskici hini mhsinepiki ciipa hina siteheeki mecimi wiyakahootamooki

but they, when they saw him walking on the sea, supposed that it was an apparition, and cried out:

50. ksake caayahki nihki honeewaawaali mecimi petfakiteheeki payeekwa weelena hokalooletiimahi

for they all saw him, and were troubled. But he straightway spake mecimi howesilepwaafiiko niila hina teki kwpeneko hotelahi

with them, and saith unto them, Be of good cheer: it is I; be not afraid.

51. chiine spemeki heewa nihi piitike hini holakeesi mecimi hini mehsikkaki nakeeska chiine nihki holaami kwakwehtaaniteheeki

And he went up unto them into the boat; and the wind ceased: and they were sore amazed in themselves;

52. ksake mata nili si nenohseeki weepskweeteewali weeka hotehiwa siipfenwili

for they understood not concerning the loaves, but their heart was hardened.

53. chiine yeh mehci kaameki haawaaci hini si piyeeki kinesoletiiwi hasiskiiki mecimi hini skwaapiyeeki hotahpicikeeki

And when they had crossed over, they came to the land unto Gennesaret, and moored to the shore.

54. chiine hini holakeesi ye hoci piyeci lohfaawaaci weelena nihki lenaweeki howaakomaawaali nili

And when they were come out of the boat, straightway the people knew him,

55. mecimi mefhiike hini kaayaawkwi taamhkwe si kwakwiiki chiine hotalemi paamwelaawahi hotfanemwaaki yohoma yeekwilokeelici yeesi nootaakeewaaci ta hapilici nili

and ran round about that whole region, and began to carry about on their beds those that were sick, where they heard he was.

56. mecimi kookwe-kaaci-tasi si piicfe hoteeweneefa weelaa hoteewena weelaa piileski nihki hoseksimaawahi nihi yeekwilokeelici hini yaatah wiiwiitkiiki mecimi honanahpaacimaawaali wahsi menawahke pehsenamaakoci kwehkwike hini ta nipenikwaateeki hopiitenika chiine yeetfwi pehsenamaakoci mefefihoofooki nihki

And wheresoever he entered, into villages, or into cities, or into the country, they laid the sick in the marketplaces, and besought him that they might touch if it were but the border of his garment: and as many as touched him were made whole.

Mark:7

1. chiine nitasi homaawatweelotawaawaali nihki pelesiiki chiine naanekoti nihki yaayawikeecki colooseelemii hoci mehci piyeeki

And there are gathered together unto him the Pharisees, and certain of the scribes, which had come from Jerusalem,

2. mecimi mehci neekeeki yeesi naaleta hokakehkimaafhi miyaasi miicilici hotakhwaanemwa mata kifilecaaki keela

and had seen that some of his disciples ate their bread with defiled, that is, unwashen, hands.

3. ksake nihki pelesiiki chiine caayahki nihki coosaki mata waawihfeniiki weeciwephi howesi kifilecaawaate chiine hopemi fookinaanaawa hini hokehtaacimoowenwa nihki kikileniiki

For the Pharisees, and all the Jews, except they wash their hands diligently, eat not, holding the tradition of the elders:

4. chiine hini tah wiitkiiki ye homowaaci nihki mata waawihfeniiki weeciwephi holelwiiwaate mecimi meci kotaki wiyehi mayehci hotfekowaaci wahsi fookinamowaaci pemi kifinikeewena tephikanaki hoci chiine hokaaciwakokooki mecimi hofaawakokooki

and when they come from the marketplace, except they wash themselves, they eat not: and many other things there be, which they have received to hold, washings of cups, and pots, and brasen vessels.

5. chiine nihi pelesihi mecimi nihi yaayawikeelici honatohtaakohi koociwe mata hini yaalhfeeki

And the Pharisees and the scribes ask him, Why walk not thy disciples

kikakehkimaafaki yeesfeki hokehtaacimoowenwa nihki kikileniiki weeka homiicinaawa hotakhwaanemwa wiyakileceeki hotekohi

according to the tradition of the elders, but eat their bread with defiled hands?

6. mecimi koowesi moosikiiskwaacimekowa haisaya kiilawa nelohcilawiwehfiiki yeelawikeeki hini hotelahi yaama lenawe notakeelemekwa hoskisaawa hoci weeka hotehiwa pelowaamatwi niiya hoci

And he said unto them, Well did Isaiah prophesy of you hypocrites, as it is written, This people honoureth me with their lips, But their heart is far from me.

7. payeekwa nelohci niwaaosasilawehekooki pemi kakehkimiweeki kikeemohkaaki nili hileniiki hokikeemoowenwa

But in vain do they worship me, Teaching as their doctrines the precepts of men.

8. kinakataanaawa kiilawa hini hotepikeemoowe maneto mecimi kitaayiitatenaanaawa hini hokehtaacimoowenwa hileniiki

Ye leave the commandment of God, and hold fast the tradition of men.

9. chiine koowesi hokwaawi si halawinaanaawa hini hotepikeemoowe maneto wahsi kiilawa menawahi kciitonameekwe kikehtaacimoowenwa hotelahi

And he said unto them, Full well do ye reject the commandment of God, that ye may keep your tradition.

10. ksake moosisii hotakeelemi kohfa mecimi kikiya chiine hina meemataamaata hohfali weelaa hokeeli wiilaani hina nepeke hini nepoowe hiwa

For Moses said, Honour thy father and thy mother; and, He that speaketh evil of father or mother, let him die the death:

11. weeka kiilawa kiteyopwa kwehkwi hileni hilaate hohfali weelaa hokeeli hini mayehci menawahke neyehka hotwaafiiyani niila hoci kaapeni hini miiloofo maneto yeeyoki hini

but ye say, If a man shall say to his father or his mother, That wherewith thou mightest have been profited by me is Corban, that is to say, Given to God;

12. mata kiteeni wiilaani kiteleelemaawa hina wahsi wiyehi silawihtawaaci hohfali weelaa hokeeli

ye no longer suffer him to do aught for his father or his mother;

13. kipemi matawiyeefekisihtoonaawa hini hokalawiiwe maneto kikehtaacimoowenwa hoci hini mayehci pakfenameekwe mecimi meci hini yeeki wiyehi kitesilawiipwa hotelahi

making void the word of God by your tradition, which ye have delivered: and many such like things ye do.

14. chiine hoteh wihkomahi nohki nihi mehseelelici chiine nootawiko caayahki kiilawa mecimi nenohseeko hotelahi

And he called to him the multitude again, and said unto them, Hear me all of you, and understand:

15. matalaakwa wiyehi faakici hoci hina hileni peemi wiiyaaki heeyaalici hotah katawi miyaasheko hina weeka nili wiyehi hina hileni weemooyaaki yoolooni homaamiyaashekona hina hileni

there is nothing from without the man, that going into him can defile him: but the things which proceed out of the man are those that defile the man.

17. chiine nihi mehseelelici ye hoci piicfaaci hini wiikiwa hokakehkimaafhi honatohtaakohi hini pemaatoweewe

And when he was entered into the house from the multitude, his disciples asked of him the parable.

18. mecimi ha nehfaapi kiilawa yooni yeesi pwaa nenohsaakaniyeekwe hotelahi nihi ha mata kinenaanaawa

And he saith unto them, Are ye so without understanding also? Perceive ye not, that whatsoever from without

yeesi kookwe-nehi-kaaci faakici weeci hina hileni
heeyaaki mata hini hotah katawi miyaasheko hina

goeth into the man, it cannot defile
him;

19. ksake mata hotehiki heeyaali hini hopehkwataaki
weeka mecimi hini si lohfeya faakici yooma hiwa
hopemi fafayaakto caayahki wiyawfi

because it goeth not into his heart, but
into his belly, and goeth out into the
draught? This he said, making all
meats clean.

20. chiine hiwa hina weemooyaaki hileni hini
homaamiyaasheko hina hileni

And he said, That which proceedeth
out of the man, that defileth the man.

21. ksake laameki hoci nili hotehiwa hileniiki hoci
lohfeya maci memekiniteheewena weepeeletiiwena
kimootoowena nhfetiiwena waapasiphikeewena

For from within, out of the heart of
men, evil thoughts proceed,
fornications, thefts, murders,
adulteries,

22. hahpeeletiiwena maciilefiiwena wanimetiiwe
naakahoowefiiwe maciliikweewe lhskimetiiwe mhsi
siteheewe wanihsakaawiiwe

covetings, wickednesses, deceit,
lasciviousness, an evil eye, railing,
pride, foolishness:

23. caayahki yooloma mecaafiki wiyehi laameki
homooya mecimi homiyaashekona hina hileni

all these evil things proceed from
within, and defile the man.

24. chiine hini hoci pafekwi chiine weepfe hini skwaaya
taayaa chiine saatanii heewa chiine hotta wiikiwa mecimi
mata sitehe hileniili wih waakotamelici hini mecimi
haalwi yo kkifo

And from thence he arose, and went
away into the borders of Tyre and
Sidon. And he entered into a house,
and would have no man know it: and
he could not be hid.

25. weeka weelena hkweewa caki hotaanehfefali
hopoonameli wiyakilehfiili piyeewa pemi nootaake nili
mecimi sahkiki si haakicfe yeelahfamefiteelici

But straightway a woman, whose little
daughter had an unclean spirit, having
heard of him, came and fell down at
his feet.

26. howe kwiikiiwiikwe hina siliyeewifeniisiyeewi
lenawe chiine hina honanahpaacimaali nili wahsi nili
hotaanehfali hoci lohfe pakilaaci hina nili wiyakilehfiili

Now the woman was a Greek, a
Syrophoenician by race. And she
besought him that he would cast forth
the devil out of her daughter.

27. mecimi wiilaani nihki hapelohfaki nhhihta wih
teephoolooki ksake mata hini howesfenwi wahsi
mamooteeki hini hotakhwaanemwa hapelohfaki mecimi
wahsi hini wihsiiki hipakitamaweci hotelaali nili

And he said unto her, Let the children
first be filled: for it is not meet to take
the children's bread and cast it to the
dogs.

28. payeekwa hina haapafse mecimi hanhka
teepeelemiweeta wiikinaakwi nihki wihsiiki laamitahfa
yaatah wihfeniki homiicinaawa nili peekitehtamowaaci
nihki hapelohfaki hotekooli

But she answered and saith unto him,
Yea, Lord: even the dogs under the
table eat of the children's crumbs.

29. mecimi ksake yooma hiyoowe hoci nhhaale
yehaayani hina waninehfi kitaanehfali hoci lohfe
hotelaali

And he said unto her, For this saying
go thy way; the devil is gone out of
thy daughter.

30. chiine hina weepfe yeetaaci wiikiwa heewa mecimi
homhkawaali nili hapelohfali seksinooli tfaneki chiine
hina waninehfi matalaakwa

And she went away unto her house,
and found the child laid upon the bed,
and the devil gone out.

31. chiine nohki hini hoci lohfe skwaaya taayaa chiine piyeci saapwi saatanii hini keeleliiwi mhsinepiki heewa saapwi hini heelekiina hini skwaaya tikeepolasi

And again he went out from the borders of Tyre, and came through Sidon unto the sea of Galilee, through the midst of the borders of Decapolis.

32. chiine nihki hopiyeetawaawaali nekoti keekeepehseelici mecimi peepoonaka weetamhekoci hokalawiiweneki chiine honanahpaacimekohi nihi wahsi hoskici nili si poonaki holeci

And they bring unto him one that was deaf, and had an impediment in his speech; and they beseech him to lay his hand upon him.

33. chiine nihi mehseelelici hoci tepaane siwelaali naanhsihka chiine holecehi hopiitaalakehseenaali mecimi fekwiwa chiine hopehsenaamawaali howiilanilici

And he took him aside from the multitude privately, and put his fingers into his ears, and he spat, and touched his tongue;

34. mecimi spemeki menhkwatoki pemi laapi chiine mhsi lehfe iffafa hotelaali tawenoofolo yeeyoki hini

and looking up to heaven, he sighed, and saith unto him, Ephphatha, that is, Be opened.

35. mecimi hina hotawakaawali tawenooteeli chiine hini yeeyicfeki howiilani pelhskohkaali mecimi tepinaakwi kalawi

And his ears were opened, and the bond of his tongue was loosed, and he spake plain.

36. chiine hotepinalekwimahi nihi wahsi pwaa nihki wiitamawaawaaci hileniili payeekwa yeesi hini halika si tepinalekwimaaci paameci yooni si halika lhfwaatotamowaaci hini nihki

And he charged them that they should tell no man: but the more he charged them, so much the more a great deal they published it.

37. chiine hanhhiweewi si cihsiteheeki nihki howesi hina mehcilota caayahki wiyehi wahsi tepehseelici hoteshahi wiikinaakwi nihi keekeepseelici chiine nihi keekeepitonelici wahsi kalawilici hiwaki

And they were beyond measure astonished, saying, He hath done all things well: he maketh even the deaf to hear, and the dumb to speak.

Mark:8

1. hine nele kaasekiki nohki ye hapiwaaci meci mehseelekki mecimi mata wiyehi hopoonaanaawa nihki wah miiciwaaci hoteh wihkomahi hokakehkimaafhi mecimi

In those days, when there was again a great multitude, and they had nothing to eat, he called unto him his disciples, and saith unto them,

2. ceh nipoonamawaaki kiteminaakweeletiiwe nihki mehseelekki ksake moosatawi niwiiciimekooki howe nhfwi kiiskwe mecimi mata wiyehi hopoonaanaawa wah miiciwaaci

I have compassion on the multitude, because they continue with me now three days, and have nothing to eat:

3. chiine kwehkwi halika leskawake yeetaawaaci skwaalaweewaate laakwa we hale mekihkofiiki mecimi naaleta pelowi hoci piyeeki hotelahi

and if I send them away fasting to their home, they will faint in the way; and some of them are come from far.

4. chiine hotaapaftaakohi hokakehkimaafhi taaniwe wiyeefa we hoci teepiilefi wahsi teephoolaaci takhwa yohoma hilenihi hotasi laa papskwahki hotekohi

And his disciples answered him, Whence shall one be able to fill these men with bread here in a desert place?

5. mecimi honatohtawahi kehfwi kipoonaanaawa weepskweeteewali hotelahi niiswahfwi hiwaki nihki

And he asked them, How many loaves have ye? And they said, Seven.

6. mecimi hotepimahi nihi mehseelelici wahsi lematapilici sahkiki hini hasiskiiki chiine homamena nili niiswahfwi weepskweeteewali mecimi pemi mehci miiliwe niyaawe hoposkonaana chiine homiilahi hokakehkimaafhi wahsi yeelahfamiilici nihi si pakfenamelici mecimi nihki hoteh pakfenaanaawa nili yeelahfamiilici nihi mehseelelici

And he commandeth the multitude to sit down on the ground: and he took the seven loaves, and having given thanks, he brake, and gave to his disciples, to set before them; and they set them before the multitude.

7. chiine laakofwiimehi hopoonaawahi maaciloofihi namefhi chiine homehci pemi kisaacilotawahi nihi tepikeemo wahsi nehfaapi yohoma pakfenoofolici yeelahfamiilici nihi

And they had a few small fishes: and having blessed them, he commanded to set these also before them.

8. chiine wihfeniiki nihki mecimi teephoolooki chiine nihki homekinaanaawa peekskinooteeki hoci maayaalecihi seskwatooteeki niiswahfwi soosoone

And they did eat, and were filled: and they took up, of broken pieces that remained over, seven baskets.

9. chiine nihki nawito niyeewene metahfene tepeewe cisiiki mecimi hotaameskawahi nihi

And they were about four thousand: and he sent them away.

10. chiine weelena hini holakeeleki lhkamwa kileki hokakehkimaafhi chiine hini skwaaya talmanoofa si piyeeki

And straightway he entered into the boat with his disciples, and came into the parts of Dalmanutha.

11. chiine nihki pelesiiki piyeeki mecimi hotalemi natohtawaawaali hopemi natonehamawaawaali weefepahkamikiki hoci kikinooloowe hopemi kotahkowaalaawaali

And the Pharisees came forth, and began to question with him, seeking of him a sign from heaven, tempting him.

12. chiine macilepwa holaami hotesiteheeweneki mecimi koociwe yaama skwiilenawe honatoneha kikinooloowe tepilo kitelepwa niila mata kikinooloowe weh miiloofo yaama skwiilenawe hisiwe

And he sighed deeply in his spirit, and saith, Why doth this generation seek a sign? verily I say unto you, There shall no sign be given unto this generation.

13. mecimi honakalahi chiine nohki hini holakeeleki lhkamwa weepfe hini hasowe wiyeetahkwe heewa

And he left them, and again entering into the boat departed to the other side.

14. chiine howanihkaataanaawa wahsi mamowaaci takhwa chiine mata hopoonaanaawa hini holakeeleki halika tfwi nekoti weepskweeteeki

And they forgot to take bread; and they had not in the boat with them more than one loaf.

15. chiine hotepinalekwimahi kcitawaafiiko mahkeeni hini honalescikanwa nihki pelesiiki chiine hini honalescika heletii hisiwe

And he charged them, saying, Take heed, beware of the leaven of the Pharisees and the leaven of Herod.

16. mecimi nihki memekiniteheemetiiki ksake mata kipoonaape takhwa hiwaki

And they reasoned one with another, saying, We have no bread.

17. chiine ciisisii homooleeleta hini koociwe kimemekiniteheepwa ksake mata kipoonaanaawa takhwa ha kiilawa mata keewaki kimoositeheepwa mata nohki kinenohseepwa ha neyehka siipfenwi kitehiwa hotelahi

And Jesus perceiving it saith unto them, Why reason ye, because ye have no bread? do ye not yet perceive, neither understand? have ye your heart hardened?

18. kipemi poonaanaawa hoskiiseko ha kitepinaapwa chiine kipemi poonaanaawa hotawakaawali ha mata kinootaakeepwa mecimi mata kimhkaweeletaanaawa

Having eyes, see ye not? and having ears, hear ye not? and do ye not remember?

19. hine yeh poskonama nili niyaalanwi weepskweeteewali heelekiina nihki niyaalane metahfene tepeewe kehfwi soosooniwali hokwaawi peekskinooteeki maayaalecihi kimamenaawa hotelahi metahfwi-kiteniiswi hotekohi

When I brake the five loaves among the five thousand, how many baskets full of broken pieces took ye up? They say unto him, Twelve.

20. chiine hine nili niiswahfwi heelekiina nihki niyeewene metahfene tepeewe kehfwi soosooni hokwaawi peekskinooteeki maayaalecihi kimamenaawa niiswahfwi hotekohi

And when the seven among the four thousand, how many basketfuls of broken pieces took ye up? And they say unto him, Seven.

21. chiine ha keewaki mata kinenohseepwa hotelahi

And he said unto them, Do ye not yet understand?

22. chiine pefseite si piyeeki chiine hopiyeetawaawaali kakeepiikweewi leniili mecimi hokcihkawaawaali wahsi pehsenaaci nili

And they come unto Bethsaida. And they bring to him a blind man, and beseech him to touch him.

23. mecimi hoteh fakileceenaali nili kakeepiikweewi leniili chiine hini hoteeweneefeki hoci lohfahaali nili chiine yeh mehci fekwaatamawaaci hoskiisekonilici mecimi hoskici si poonamawaaci holeciwali honatohtawaali ha kineeme wiyehi hotelaali

And he took hold of the blind man by the hand, and brought him out of the village; and when he had spit on his eyes, and laid his hands upon him, he asked him, Seest thou aught?

24. chiine hina maa laapi mecimi nineewaaki hileniiki ksake nitelaapamaaki paasi mhteko pemhfeeya hiwa hina

And he looked up, and said, I see men; for I behold them as trees, walking.

25. howe nohki hoskiisekonilici hoteh poonamawaali holeciwali mecimi hina mamiyeetaawaapi chiine petekishoofo mecimi hotepineeme caayahki wiyehi

Then again he laid his hands upon his eyes; and he looked stedfastly, and was restored, and saw all things clearly.

26. mecimi yeetaalici hoteleskawaali teki piicfaalo hini hoteewenehi hotelaali

And he sent him away to his home, saying, Do not even enter into the village.

27. chiine ciisisii hale weepfe mecimi hokakehkimaafhi nili heewa hoteeweneefa sisaliye filipaayi hoci yeelelhfeewaaci honatohtawahi hokakehkimaafhi neefawe hina nitaayekooki hileniiki niila hotelahi

And Jesus went forth, and his disciples, into the villages of Caesarea Philippi: and in the way he asked his disciples, saying unto them, Who do men say that I am?

28. mecimi howiitamaakohi caanii hina fafahkwiholelhiwena kotakaki hilaica weeka naaleta nekoti nihki hoci maamoosikiiskwecki hiwaki hotekohi

And they told him, saying, John the Baptist: and others, Elijah; but others, One of the prophets.

29. nohki honatohtawahi weeka neefawe kiteyopwa kiilawa hina niila piita haapafse chiine hiina hina klaistii kiila hotelaali

And he asked them, But who say ye that I am? Peter answereth and saith unto him, Thou art the Christ.

30. mecimi hotepinalekwimahi wahsi teki wiitamawaawaaci hileniili wiiya

And he charged them that they should tell no man of him.

31. chiine hotalemi kakehkimahi wahsi hina hokwihfali hileni kwiilahi hahkwinamoci meci wiyehi mecimi haalawinaakoci nihi kikilenihi chiine nihi hokimaawi mhkateewkolayehi chiine nihi yaayawikeelici mecimi

And he began to teach them, that the Son of man must suffer many things, and be rejected by the elders, and the

nhfeci chiine mayohkwaaci honhskaaci nohki nhfokonakike

chief priests, and the scribes, and be killed, and after three days rise again.

32. mecimi tawaaci kalawi hini hiyoowe chiine piita hoteh fookinaali mecimi hotalemi kwtelaali

And he spake the saying openly. And Peter took him, and began to rebuke him.

33. payeekwa maa si pemi kokiiwa hina honeewahi hokakehkimaafhi hokwtelaali piitali hotaanaaki niila haalo setenii ksake mata kimakofeeleta hini howiyehiimi maneto hini howiyehiimwa hileniiki weeka hotelaali

But he turning about, and seeing his disciples, rebuked Peter, and saith, Get thee behind me, Satan: for thou mindest not the things of God, but the things of men.

34. chiine hoteh wihkomahi nihi mehseelelici kileki hokakehkimaafhi chiine hotelahi kwehkwi wiyeefa hileni wiisa wiiteemite wiilaani wih kiyaateeleta wiiya mecimi wih mame hotaasitehfekiimi chiine nih neekalekwa

And he called unto him the multitude with his disciples, and said unto them, If any man would come after me, let him deny himself, and take up his cross, and follow me.

35. ksake kookwe-neefa-kaaci wiisa waapanesto hotelenaweewiiwe weh wanhto hini mecimi kookwe-neefa-kaaci weh wanhto hotelenaweewiiwe niila mecimi hini howesi piyeetaacimoowe hoci weh waapanesto hini

For whosoever would save his life shall lose it; and whosoever shall lose his life for my sake and the gospel's shall save it.

36. ksake nehiwe hini wi mhkahfo hileni katawihkake hini melhske yeelekokwahkamikiki mecimi wanhtoote hotelenaweewiiwe

For what doth it profit a man, to gain the whole world, and forfeit his life?

37. ksake nehiwe hileni wih miiliwe haasoonake hotelenaweewiiwe

For what should a man give in exchange for his life?

38. ksake kookwe-neefa-kaaci neh tekwehekwa mecimi nikalawiiwena heelekiina yooma weewaapasiphikeewefiiyaaki chiine meciilefiiyaaki skwiilenaweewiiwe niliini hina hokwihfali hileni weh tekwehaali hine piyaate hini hohfali howahfaacimekofiiweneki kileki nihi hofepi henhcalihi

For whosoever shall be ashamed of me and of my words in this adulterous and sinful generation, the Son of man also shall be ashamed of him, when he cometh in the glory of his Father with the holy angels.

Mark:9

1. chiine tepilo kitelepwa niila hapiiki hotasi naaleta neniipawicki maalaakwahi nihkiini mata wiyehi si weh kotataanaawa nepoowe paalohi weh neemenaawa hini hokimaawiiwe maneto weh piyeeya kileki waasikaki hotelahi

And he said unto them, Verily I say unto you, There be some here of them that stand by, which shall in no wise taste of death, till they see the kingdom of God come with power.

2. chiine nekotwahfokonakiki hahkowihi ciisisii hotaamwelahi piitali chiine ceemhsiili chiine caaniili mecimi hokkwiciwelahi spatenwi meekwahkiki naanhsihka wiilawa mecimi yeelahfamiilici nihi hale kotaki hitwa

And after six days Jesus taketh with him Peter, and James, and John, and bringeth them up into a high mountain apart by themselves: and he was transfigured before them:

3. mecimi hopiitenikana pemi wahfefiiya hanhhiweewi wahkanakiya weecikeenahi mata hoskitaamhkwe peekatenaka wiyehsimota hotah si katawi waapitoona nili

and his garments became glistering, exceeding white; so as no fuller on earth can whiten them.

4. chiine nitasi hotepinawaawaali hilaicali kileki moosisii chiine nihki peemi kiikaloolaawaaci ciisisiili

And there appeared unto them Elijah with Moses: and they were talking with Jesus.

5. chiine piita haapafse lepaayii howesa hini wahsi hotasi hapiyakwe ceh ne hostoope nhfwi haaciiwikamiko nekoti kiila chiine nekoti moosisii chiine nekoti hilaica hotelaali ciisisiili

And Peter answereth and saith to Jesus, Rabbi, it is good for us to be here: and let us make three tabernacles; one for thee, and one for Moses, and one for Elijah.

6. ksake mata howaakota hini wa haapafseeci holaami wiisaalepwaaki ksake

For he wist not what to answer; for they became sore afraid.

7. chiine paafkwahki nitasi piyeeya hotawikanhskaakonaawa chiine nitasi paafkwahkiiki hoci piyeeya kalaweewihsimoowe yoona yaama yeeahkweelemaka nikwihfa nootawehko hiyooya

And there came a cloud overshadowing them: and there came a voice out of the cloud, This is my beloved Son: hear ye him.

8. chiine kikamooci pemi kaayaawka laapiiki nihki mata wiyeefali honeewaawaali kiteeni weeciwephi ciisisiili pehi wiici wiilawa

And suddenly looking round about, they saw no one any more, save Jesus only with themselves.

9. chiine yeesi piyeci paalacsinowaaci hini meekwahkiki hoci hotepinalekwimahi nihi wahsi nihki pwaa wiitamawaawaaci hileniili hini wiyehi mayehci neemowaaci weeciwephi hine hina hokwihfali hileni wih mehci honhska nili nepelici hoci

And as they were coming down from the mountain, he charged them that they should tell no man what things they had seen, save when the Son of man should have risen again from the dead.

10. mecimi hokciitonaanaawa hini hiyoowe niinatohtwaatiiki heelekiina wiilawa nehiwe toke hini nohki honhskaawe hina nepeka hoci hiyopi

And they kept the saying, questioning among themselves what the rising again from the dead should mean.

11. chiine honatohtawaawaali nehiwe hini weeci nihki yaayawikeecki hiyowaaci wahsi hilaica kwiilahi nhhihta piyaaci hotelaawaali

And they asked him, saying, The scribes say that Elijah must first come.

12. sapkahi hilaica nhhihta piyeewa hotelahi mecimi hopetekfeto caayahki wiyehi chiine nehiwe hini lawikaafo hina hokwihfali hileni wahsi hahkwinaki hina meci wiyehi mecimi wahsi matawiyeefekisihoofoci

And he said unto them, Elijah indeed cometh first, and restoreth all things: and how is it written of the Son of man, that he should suffer many things and be set at nought?

13. payeekwa kitelepwa niila yeesi hilaica howe piyaaci mecimi nehfaapi neyehka nihki hotpenalaawaali nili kookwe-nehi-kaaci yeesiteheewaaci teetepilahi yeelawikaaloofolici hotelahi

But I say unto you, that Elijah is come, and they have also done unto him whatsoever they listed, even as it is written of him.

14. chiine ye hotfaawaaci nihi kakehkimaafhi honeewaawaali meci mehseelelici kaayaawka wiilawa chiine yaayawikeecki peemi natohtwaatiimaawaaci nihi

And when they came to the disciples, they saw a great multitude about them, and scribes questioning with them.

15. chiine weelena caayahki nihi mehseelelici yeh nookoci holaami cihsitehehi mecimi piyeeptohi hosilawaalekohi

And straightway all the multitude, when they saw him, were greatly amazed, and running to him saluted him.

16. chiine honatohtawahi nehiwe kinatohtwaatiimaawaaki nihki hotelahi

And he asked them, What question ye with them?

17. mecimi nekoti nihi mehseelelici hotaapaftaakooli keekehkimiwe kipiyeetoole nikwihfa peepoonaata keekeepitoneewi hilefiiwenali

And one of the multitude answered him, Master, I brought unto thee my son, which hath a dumb spirit;

18. kookwe-kaaci-tasi yeesiwelekoci nili sahkiki hota hpakilekooli mecimi paapihteewefi chiine hofaafookfetoona wiipitali mecimi paapemi saakweelemo chiine nikaloolaaki kikakehkimaafaki wahsi nihki lohfe pakilaawaaci nili mecimi haalwi katawefiiki hotekooli

and wheresoever it taketh him, it dasheth him down: and he foameth, and grindeth his teeth, and pineth away: and I spake to thy disciples that they should cast it out; and they were not able.

19. chiine haapafse mecimi o pwaayaa teepwehsaakanita skwiilenawe taaniwe laakwasi keh wiici hapiimelepwa kiilawa taaniwe laakwasi kiilawa keh wiisikitehehtoolepwa niila piyeetawiko hina hotelahi

And he answereth them and saith, O faithless generation, how long shall I be with you? how long shall I bear with you? bring him unto me.

20. mecimi nili hopiyeetaakohi nihi chiine yeh neewaaci nili weelena hina hilefiiwena homaatakoskahaali nili nanahpaacila chiine hini sahkiki si haakicfeeli mecimi kwakwaasakwiili pihteewefiili

And they brought him unto him: and when he saw him, straightway the spirit tare him grievously; and he fell on the ground, and wallowed foaming.

21. chiine honatohtawaali hina hohfali taaniwe laakwa hine hoci cihfena hotfeko yooma hotelaali nili ye hapelohfiwici hoci hiwa hina

And he asked his father, How long time is it since this hath come unto him? And he said, From a child.

22. chiine moosaki laakwa nili hota hpakilekooli hini skoteeki mecimi hini nepiki wahsi macilotaakoci wiiya payeekwa kiila katawi wiyehi silawiiyane poonamawinaake kiteminaakweeletiiwe mecimi naatamawinaake hotekooli

And oft-times it hath cast him both into the fire and into the waters, to destroy him: but if thou canst do anything, have compassion on us, and help us.

23. katawiilefiyane kiila caayahki wiyehi katawatwili hina teeteepwehseeta hotelaali ciisisii

And Jesus said unto him, If thou canst! All things are possible to him that believeth.

24. weelena nili hohfali hina hapelohfa wiyakahootamooli mecimi niteepwehse naatamaatano kiila nipwaateepwehseewe hiwali

Straightway the father of the child cried out, and said, I believe; help thou mine unbelief.

25. chiine yeh neewaaci ciisisii yeesi piyeci maawatwiptoolici hote kwtelaali nili wiyakilehfiili kiila keekeepitoneewi mecimi keekeepseewi hilefiiwena kitepimele hina hoci lohfaalo chiine teki kiteeni kipiicfaala hotelaali

And when Jesus saw that a multitude came running together, he rebuked the unclean spirit, saying unto him, Thou dumb and deaf spirit, I command thee, come out of him, and enter no more into him.

26. chiine yeesi mehci wiyakahootaki mecimi maatakoskahaaci nili piyeci lohfe hina chiine hina skilawehfiifa paasi wiyeefa nepeka hilefi weecikeenahi nihki halika tfwi nepwa hina hiwaki

And having cried out, and torn him much, he came out: and the child became as one dead; insomuch that the more part said, He is dead.

27. payeekwa ciisisii hoteh fakileceenaali chiine honhskaanaali mecimi hina honhska

But Jesus took him by the hand, and raised him up; and he arose.

28. chiine hini wiikiwaapeki yeh piicfaaci hokakehkimaafhi hokiimi natohtaakohi nehiwe hini nooci niilawe haalwi katawi lohfe pakilaape hina hotekohi

And when he was come into the house, his disciples asked him privately, saying, We could not cast it out.

29. matalaakwa wa hoci katawi piyeci lohfaaci yooma yeeteka weeciwephi mamaatomeewe hoci hotelahi

And he said unto them, This kind can come out by nothing, save by prayer.

30. chiine hini hoci weepfeeki saapwiiki keelelii mecimi mata hoteleeleta wiyeefali hileniili wih waakotamelici hini

And they went forth from thence, and passed through Galilee; and he would not that any man should know it.

31. ksake hokakehkimahi hokakehkimaafhi hina hokwihfali hileni howe nihki holeciwaaki hileniiki si miiletipi chiine we nhfaawaali nihki nili mecimi hine nhfekwite mehci nhfokonakike we honhska hina nohki hotelahi

For he taught his disciples, and said unto them, The Son of man is delivered up into the hands of men, and they shall kill him; and when he is killed, after three days he shall rise again.

32. payeekwa nihki mata honenohtaanaawa hini hiyoowe mecimi hokwtaanaawa wahsi natohtawaawaaci

But they understood not the saying, and were afraid to ask him.

33. chiine keepaaniamii si piyeeki chiine piitike hini wiikiwaapeki ye hapici honatohtawahi nehiwe kipiyeci memekineeletaanaawa heele miyeewiki hotelahi

And they came to Capernaum: and when he was in the house he asked them, What were ye reasoning in the way?

34. payeekwa mata wiye hiwaki nihki ksake pekihkaatiiki nihki hini heele miyeewiki nili wiyeefali kehci haliwi hilefilici

But they held their peace: for they had disputed one with another in the way, who was the greatest.

35. mecimi sahkiki si lematapiwa chiine hoteh wihkomahi nihi metahfwi-kite-niiswi kwehkwi wiyeefa hileni wiisa nhhihtaawite we hotaanaakiwi caayahki mecimi wi hotaloolaakaniiki nili caayahki hotelahi

And he sat down, and called the twelve; and he saith unto them, If any man would be first, he shall be last of all, and minister of all.

36. chiine hoteh mamaali caki hapelohfeefali chiine hoteh lemataphaali nili heelekiina nihi mecimi hote hotahpenaali honehkali

And he took a little child, and set him in the midst of them: and taking him in his arms, he said unto them,

37. kookwe-neefa-kaaci we hotahpenaali nekoti halayaama si caki hapelohfeefhi niwiifooweneki nootahpenekwa niila mecimi kookwe-neefa-kaaci nootahpenekwa niila mata niila nootahpenekwa weeka nili weewaawiinilici hotelahi

Whosoever shall receive one of such little children in my name, receiveth me: and whosoever receiveth me, receiveth not me, but him that sent me.

38. keekehkimiwe nineewaape nekoti peemi lohfe pakilaaci waninehfihi kiwiifooweneki mecimi teki nitelaape ksake mata kineekalekona hotelaali caanii

John said unto him, Master, we saw one casting out devils in thy name: and we forbade him, because he followed not us.

39. payeekwa hiwa ciisisii teki kikwtelaawa ksake matalaakwa hileni wah silawiita waasikaki pekatefiiwe niwiifooweneki mecimi yah teepiilefi wahsi weeweetepi mataamici

But Jesus said, Forbid him not: for there is no man which shall do a mighty work in my name, and be able quickly to speak evil of me.

40. ksake hina wiyeefa pwaayaa ppehtenelakwe kiwiiciimekona

For he that is not against us is for us.

41. ksake kookwe-neefa-kaaci keh miilekowa tephikaneki nepi wah meneyeekwe ksake klaistii wiila kiilawa tepilo kitelepwa niila mata hina wiyehisi hotah wanhto hotephofiiwe

For whosoever shall give you a cup of water to drink, because ye are Christ's, verily I say unto you, he shall in no wise lose his reward.

42. chiine kookwe-neefa-kaaci wahsi hotakikahsinelici we hpenalaali nekoti yohoma meciloofilici halika hina howesaali weekhi hokwekakaneki laapicitoofote mhsi poothaakanisiikonali mecimi hini mhsinepiki hipakiloofote

And whosoever shall cause one of these little ones that believe on me to stumble, it were better for him if a great millstone were hanged about his neck, and he were cast into the sea.

43. chiine kwehkwi kileci wahsi hotakikahsinani hpenalekoyane kwakwkotano hini howesa hini kiila wahsi piicfaayani lenaweewiiweeneki mamiyaalakifiyane noota kaaciika pemi poonamane niiswi kileciwali hahkwinamooweneki wa heeyaaki hini pwaayaa hahteewefiiyaaki skoteeki

And if thy hand cause thee to stumble, cut it off: it is good for thee to enter into life maimed, rather than having thy two hands to go into hell, into the unquenchable fire.

45. chiine kwehkwi kifici wahsi hotakikahsinani hpenalekoyane kwakwkotano hini howesa hini kiila wahsi piicfaayani lenaweewiiweneki kihkiicsinane noota kaaciika pemi poonamane niiswi kifitali hahkwinamooweneki wa hipakitooteeki

And if thy foot cause thee to stumble, cut it off: it is good for thee to enter into life halt, rather than having thy two feet to be cast into hell.

47. chiine kwehkwi kiskiisekwi wahsi hotakikahsinani hpenalekoyane lohfe pakitano hini howesa hini kiila wahsi piicfaayani hini hokimaawitaamhkomi maneto nekoti hoskiisekowiyane noota kaaciika pemi poonamane niiswi hoskiiseko hahkwinamooweneki wa hipakitooteeki

And if thine eye cause thee to stumble, cast it out: it is good for thee to enter into the kingdom of God with one eye, rather than having two eyes to be cast into hell;

48. yaatah pwaa nepelici homanetoolefemwahi mecimi hini skote tah pwaa-laakwa hahtehooteeki

where their worm dieth not, and the fire is not quenched.

49. ksake caakiwiyeefa we pskipefoofo skote

For every one shall be salted with fire.

50. howesa nepipemi payeekwa kwehkwi hini nepipemi mehci haseke hopskipefiiwe taaniwe ke hoci hipokwanwihtoonaawa hini kiilawa poonamoko nepipemi kiiyaawaaki mecimi howesi nhhalweeletiimetiko

Salt is good: but if the salt have lost its saltness, wherewith will ye season it? Have salt in yourselves, and be at peace one with another.

Mark:10

1. chiine hini hoci pafekwi mecimi hini skwaaya cotiye si piyeewa hini caatenii halika mecimi nohki hopiyeci maawatweelotaakohi mehseelelici chiine yaasilawiici keela nohki hokakehkimahi nihi

And he arose from thence, and cometh into the borders of Judaea and beyond Jordan: and multitudes come together unto him again; and, as he was wont, he taught them again.

2. chiine nitasi hotfekohi pelesihi mecimi honatohtaakohi ha mayaawatwi hini kwteletiiweneki hileni wahsi pakilaaci wiiwali hotekohi hokocihkaakohi

And there came unto him Pharisees, and asked him, Is it lawful for a man to put away his wife? tempting him.

3. chiine haapafse mecimi nehiwe kitepimekowa moosisii hotelahi

And he answered and said unto them, What did Moses command you?

4. moosisii wiilaani hoteleeleta wahsi hawikeeki pkehotiiwi heewikaateeki wahsi hina pakilaaci nili hiwaki nihki

And they said, Moses suffered to write a bill of divorcement, and to put her away.

5. payeekwa ciisisii ksake siipefiiya kitehiwe weeci hawikoolwaakwe yooma tepikeemoowe hotelahi

But Jesus said unto them, For your hardness of heart he wrote you this commandment.

6. weeka hine halemahkamikatwi hini weeskahkamikiki hoci hileni mecimi hkweewa hotesi mechahi hina

But from the beginning of the creation, Male and female made he them.

7. ksake yooma hoci hileni weh nakalaali hohfali mecimi hokeeli chiine weh si haayicsinwa wiiwali

For this cause shall a man leave his father and mother, and shall cleave to his wife;

8. mecimi nihki niiswi weh nekotiiyaali wiyawfi weecikeenahi nihki mata kiteeni niiswi nekoti wiyawfi weeka

and the twain shall become one flesh: so that they are no more twain, but one flesh.

9. kookweenehi weecikeenahi maneto mayehci takotooci teki wiilaani hileni wih poskona

What therefore God hath joined together, let not man put asunder.

10. chiine nihki kakehkimaafaki hini wiikiwaapeki nohki honatohtawaawaali yooma si wiyehi

And in the house the disciples asked him again of this matter.

11. mecimi kookwe-neefa-kaaci weh pakilaali wiiwali mecimi kotakali howiiwinaali homacilawihtawaali waapasiphikeewe nili

And he saith unto them, Whosoever shall put away his wife, and marry another, committeth adultery against her:

12. chiine kwehkwi wiila hina hkweewa weh pakilaali wehsici mecimi kotakali hosinaali macilawi hina waapasiphikeewe hotelahi

and if she herself shall put away her husband, and marry another, she committeth adultery.

13. chiine nihki hopemi piyeetawaawaali caki hapelohfeefhi wih pehsenaaci nihi mecimi nihki kakehkimaafaki hokwtelaawahi nihi

And they brought unto him little children, that he should touch them: and the disciples rebuked them.

14. payeekwa yeh neemeki hini ciisisii homaacilepwahekohi kisfetiiwe mecimi wiilaani nihki caki hapelohfeefaki nipiyeelotaakooki teki kinanakohwaawaaki ksake nihkiini yeetekiki wiilawa hini hokimaawitaamhkomi maneto

But when Jesus saw it, he was moved with indignation, and said unto them, Suffer the little children to come unto me; forbid them not: for of such is the kingdom of God.

15. tepilo kitelepwa niila kookwe-neefa-kaaci mata hotah si hotahpena hini hokimaawitaamhkomi maneto paasi caki hapelohfeefa mata yah wiyehisi piicfe nitasi hotelahi

Verily I say unto you, Whosoever shall not receive the kingdom of God as a little child, he shall in no wise enter therein.

16. chiine hoteh mamahi nihi honehkiki mecimi hokisaateelemekowhahi chiine hoteh poonamawahi holeciwali hoskici nihi

And he took them in his arms, and blessed them, laying his hands upon them.

17. chiine yeesi hale weepfeeci hini yehaaci nekoti nitasi piyeeptooli mecimi honatohtaakooli howesi keekehkimiwe nehiwe neh silawi wahsi menawahi laapitepeeletama pwaayaa ceeyehkwaaki lenaweewiiwe hotekooli

And as he was going forth into the way, there ran one to him, and kneeled to him, and asked him, Good Master, what shall I do that I may inherit eternal life?

18. chiine ciisisii koociwe kiila howesi kitesi mata wiyeefa holefi weeciwephi nekoti maneto hina hotelaali

And Jesus said unto him, Why callest thou me good? none is good save one, even God.

19. kiwaakotaana nili tepikeemoowena teki kinhsiwe teki kih macilawi waapasiphikeewe teki kih kimoote teki kih wiicitehaata miyaasi ciikinhkemoowe teki kih wanikeemo hotakeelemi kohfa mecimi kikiya hotelaali

Thou knowest the commandments, Do not kill, Do not commit adultery, Do not steal, Do not bear false witness, Do not defraud, Honour thy father and mother.

20. keekehkimiwe caayahki yooloma wiyehi neyehka nikcitawaafi yeh mayaanileniwiya hoci hotekooli

And he said unto him, Master, all these things have I observed from my youth.

21. hotelaapamaali ciisisii mecimi hotahkweelemaali nekoti wiyehi kinootkwiilefi nhhaalo miyeekilo kookwe-nehi-kaaci kipoona chiine miili hina kitemaafa mecimi keh poona paweewe piitike weefepahkamikiki mecimi piyaalo neekasilo hotelaali

And Jesus looking upon him loved him, and said unto him, One thing thou lackest: go, sell whatsoever thou hast, and give to the poor, and thou shalt have treasure in heaven: and come, follow me.

22. payeekwa hina kotaki laapeska hini hiyoowe hoci mecimi hale weepfe hokwaawefi macilepwaawe ksake hina nekoti peepoonaka mhsi nhhalwaafiiwena

But his countenance fell at the saying, and he went away sorrowful: for he was one that had great possessions.

23. chiine ciisisii kaayaawka laapi mecimi ceh fakaaki nihki peepoonakki pawaawena weh piicfeeki hini hokimaawitaamhkomi maneto hotelahi hokakehkimaafhi

And Jesus looked round about, and saith unto his disciples, How hardly shall they that have riches enter into the kingdom of God!

24. mecimi nihki kakehkimaafaki hokwakwehtaaneeletamawaawaali hokalawiiwena payeekwa nohki haapafse ciisisii hapelohfeti lakokwe kiisenaaci hini nihki wiisaala yeeleeletakki pawaawena wahsi piicfaawaaci hini hokimaawitaamhkomi maneto

And the disciples were amazed at his words. But Jesus answereth again, and saith unto them, Children, how hard is it for them that trust in riches to enter into the kingdom of God!

25. haliwi weecihi hini wahsi keemali saapwiici saaponika hoskiisekwi noota paweewi hileni wahsi piicfaaci hini hokimaawitaamhkomi maneto hotelahi

It is easier for a camel to go through a needle's eye, than for a rich man to enter into the kingdom of God.

26. mecimi nihki hanhhiweewi cihsiteheeki howe neefawe wih katawi waapaneshoofo hotekohi

And they were astonished exceedingly, saying unto him, Then who can be saved?

27. ciisisii homemekinaapamahi wiilawa hileniiki matayeeciwatwi hini weeka wiila maneto mata ksake wiila maneto caayahki wiyehi teepiwatwi hiwa

Jesus looking upon them saith, With men it is impossible, but not with God: for all things are possible with God.

28. piita hotalemi hilaali cih neyehka niilawe ninakataape caayahki mecimi neyehka kineekalelepe hotelaali

Peter began to say unto him, Lo, we have left all, and have followed thee.

29. tepilo kitelepwa niila hiwa ciisisii mata hileni hapiwa mayehci nakataka wiikiwa weelaa hoceeninaanhhi weelaa hotkwemimahi weelaa hokeeli weelaa hohfimaali weelaa hapelofhi weelaa hasiskiwali niila hoci mecimi hini howesi piyeetaacimoowe hoci

Jesus said, Verily I say unto you, There is no man that hath left house, or brethren, or sisters, or mother, or father, or children, or lands, for my sake, and for the gospel's sake,

30. weeka hina we hotfeko tepeewe yeetfweekifeki hinoki howe wiikiwaapali chiine hoceeninaanhhi chiine hotkwemimahi chiine hapelofhi chiine hasiskiwali kileki noochaaletiiwe mecimi pwaayaa ceeyehkwaaki lenaweewiiwe piitike hini weeskahkamikiki waasa piyeeyaaki

but he shall receive a hundredfold now in this time, houses, and brethren, and sisters, and mothers, and children, and lands, with persecutions; and in the world to come eternal life.

31. payeekwa meci nenhhihtaawicki we hotaanaakiwiiki mecimi nihki hotaanaaki nhhihta

But many that are first shall be last; and the last first.

32. chiine maa halemhfeeki hini yehaawaaci pemi colooseelemii si kkwicsinooki mecimi ciisisii hale niikaani nihi chiine kwakwehtaaniteheeki nihki mecimi nihki neeneekasiweecki kwpeneeki chiine nohki hotaamwelahi nihi metahfwi-kite-niiswi mecimi hotalemi wiitamawahi hini wiyehi waasa sinaki wiila

And they were in the way, going up to Jerusalem; and Jesus was going before them: and they were amazed; and they that followed were afraid. And he took again the twelve, and began to tell them the things that were to happen unto him,

33. waapatamoko colooseelemii kite kkwicsinepe chiine nili hokwihfali hileni weh miiloofooki nihki hokimaawi mhkateewkolayeeki chiine nihki yaayawikeecki mecimi nihki nepooweneki weh si matahkowaalaawaali nili chiine weh miilaawahi nihi nanahkawilenawehi nili

saying, Behold, we go up to Jerusalem; and the Son of man shall be delivered unto the chief priests and the scribes; and they shall condemn him to death, and shall deliver him unto the Gentiles:

34. mecimi nihki weh waapalaachaawaali chiine weh fiifekwaalaawaali chiine weh lihfiiwanhhwaawaali mecimi we nhfaawaali nili chiine mehci nhfokonakike hina we honhska nohki hiwa

and they shall mock him, and shall spit upon him, and shall scourge him, and shall kill him; and after three days he shall rise again.

35. chiine nitasi piyehi maalaakwahi ceemhsiili chiine caaniili nihi hokwifhi sepetii keekehkimiwe skata nitesiteheepe wahsi kiila hini hpenasiyaake kookwe-nehi-kaaci keh natotamoolepe hotekohi

And there come near unto him James and John, the sons of Zebedee, saying unto him, Master, we would that thou shouldest do for us whatsoever we shall ask of thee.

36. nehiwe kitesiteheepwa wa hpenalelako kiilawa hotelahi

And he said unto them, What would ye that I should do for you?

37. wiilaani leeletamawinaake wahsi menawahi niilawe lematapiyaake nekoti kimayaawiinhkiki mecimi nekoti kinamaciinhkiki hine kiwahfaacimekofiiweneki hotekohi

And they said unto him, Grant unto us that we may sit, one on thy right hand, and one on thy left hand, in thy glory.

38. payeekwa ciisisii mata kiwaakotaanaawa neetotameekwe ha kiteepiilefipwa kiilawa wahsi meneyeekwe hina tephika meneya niila weelaa wahsi fafahkwi holelhoofoyeekwe hini fafahkwiholelwiiwe weelelhoofoya hotelahi

But Jesus said unto them, Ye know not what ye ask. Are ye able to drink the cup that I drink? or to be baptized with the baptism that I am baptized with?

39. mecimi niteepiilefipe hotekohi hina tephika meemeneya keh menepwa yo chiine kileki hini fafahkwiholelwiiwe feefafahkwi holelhoofoya nehfaapi keh fafahkwi holelhekoopwa

And they said unto him, We are able. And Jesus said unto them, The cup that I drink ye shall drink; and with the baptism that I am baptized withal shall ye be baptized:

40. weeka wahsi lematapiyeekwe nimayaawiinhkiki weelaa ninamaciinhkiki mata niila hini wahsi miiliweeya weeka nihki wiilawa hini yeekawaacfetoofocki hotelahi ciisisii

but to sit on my right hand or on my left hand is not mine to give: but it is for them for whom it hath been prepared.

41. chiine nihki metahfwi yeh nootaakeewaaci hini halemi maaciteheeki kisfetiiwe nihiisi ceemhsiili chiine caaniili

And when the ten heard it, they began to be moved with indignation concerning James and John.

42. hoteh wihkomahi nihi ciisisii mecimi kiwaakomaawaaki nihki yeelakimoofocki wahsi mhsikilohtawaawaaci nihi nanahkawilenawehi yeesi hini teepeeletamhpenalaawaaci nihi mecimi wiilawa homhsiilefiimwahi homaamhsimekofihtaakowahi hotelahi

And Jesus called them to him, and saith unto them, Ye know that they which are accounted to rule over the Gentiles lord it over them; and their great ones exercise authority over them.

43. payeekwa mata hini hinwi heelekiina kiilawa weeka kookwe-neefa-kaaci wih wiisa mhsiilefi heelekiina kiilawa ke homiisamaakeemipwa

But it is not so among you: but whosoever would become great among you, shall be your minister:

44. chiine kookwe-neefa-kaaci wih wiisa nhhihtaawi heelekiina kiilawa ke hotaloolaakanipwa caayahki

and whosoever would be first among you, shall be servant of all.

45. ksake hina hokwihfali hileni nehfaapi piyeewa mata wahsi miisamaweci wahsi miisamaakeeci weeka mecimi wahsi miiliweeci hotelenaweewiiwe meci hotwenikani hini

For verily the Son of man came not to be ministered unto, but to minister, and to give his life a ransom for many.

46. chiine celekoo si piyeeki chiine yeesi celekoo hoci lohfaaci kileki hokakehkimaafhi mecimi meci mehseelelici hina hokwihfali taamiyasi paatamiias sifo kaakatoweeta kakeepiikwe lematapiwa pakackana

And they come to Jericho: and as he went out from Jericho, with his disciples and a great multitude, the son of Timaeus, Bartimaeus, a blind beggar, was sitting by the way side.

47. chiine hina yeh nootaakeeci yeesi ciisisiiwilici nili naaseliiniiwileniili halemahootamwa ciisisii kiila hokwihfali teepitii poonamawilo kiteminaakweeletiiwe hiwa

And when he heard that it was Jesus of Nazareth, he began to cry out, and say, Jesus, thou son of David, have mercy on me.

48. mecimi meci hokwtelaawaali wih nooleewilici payeekwa hina hini halika si holaamahootamwa kiila hokwihfali teepitii poonamawilo kiteminaakweeletiiwe

And many rebuked him, that he should hold his peace: but he cried out the more a great deal, Thou son of David, have mercy on me.

49. chiine ciisisii noole niipawi mecimi hotahpimehko hiwa chiine nihki hotahpimaawaali nili keekeepiikweelici hileniili howesilepwaawefilo pafekwiilo kootahpimekwa hotelaawaali

And Jesus stood still, and said, Call ye him. And they call the blind man, saying unto him, Be of good cheer: rise, he calleth thee.

50. mecimi hina hopemi maa hipakita hopiitenika pafekwicfe chiine ciisisiili si piyeewa

And he, casting away his garment, sprang up, and came to Jesus.

51. chiine hotaapaftawaali ciisisii nehiwe kitesitehe wi hpenalela niila hotelaali leponaayi wahsi menawahi niila hotfekoya nitepinamoowe hotelaali hina keekeepiikweeta hileni

And Jesus answered him, and said, What wilt thou that I should do unto thee? And the blind man said unto him, Rabboni, that I may receive my sight.

52. mecimi ciisisii weepfeelo yehaayani kiteepwehseewe kimehci mefefiheko hotelaali mecimi hina weelena hotfeko hotepinamoowe mecimi honeekalekooli yehaaci

And Jesus said unto him, Go thy way; thy faith hath made thee whole. And straightway he received his sight, and followed him in the way.

Mark:11

1. chiine maalaakwahi ye halemhfeewaaci pefeciiki chiine pefeneki hini halifiwi meekwahkiki tasi howaawiinahi niiswi hokakehkimaafhi

And when they draw nigh unto Jerusalem, unto Bethphage and Bethany, at the mount of Olives, he sendeth two of his disciples,

2. mecimi hini haakone hoteeweneefeki yeelahfamiiyeekwe yehteeki mecimi weelena yeesi hottameekwe hini ke mhkawaawa mahkootelefa kciipifo pwaayaa laakwa keewaki nayekoci hileni pelhhohko hina mecimi piyeelehko

and saith unto them, Go your way into the village that is over against you: and straightway as ye enter into it, ye shall find a colt tied, whereon no man ever yet sat; loose him, and bring him.

3. chiine wiyeefa koociwe yooma kitesilawiipwa hilelwaakwe hina teepeelemiweeta hotakaawaalaali hiyoko weelena hina peteki hotahfa weh leskawaali hotelahi

And if any one say unto you, Why do ye this? say ye, The Lord hath need of him; and straightway he will send him back hither.

4. mecimi nihki weepfeeki chiine homhkawaawaali mahkootelefali faakici skwaateeki kciipifooli hini tawaaci hoteewenimiyeeweneki chiine hopelhhwaawaali nili

And they went away, and found a colt tied at the door without in the open street; and they loose him.

5. mecimi naanekoti nihi nitasi neniipawilici nehiwe kitesilawiipwa kipemi pelhhwaawa hina makootelefa hotekowahi

And certain of them that stood there said unto them, What do ye, loosing the colt?

6. chiine howiitamawaawahi nihi teetepilahi mayehci yolici ciisisiili mecimi nihi wiilaani hoteleelemekowahi

And they said unto them even as Jesus had said: and they let them go.

7. chiine ciisisiili hopiyeetawaawaali nili mecimi hoskici nili hotipakitaanaawa hopiitenikanwa mecimi hina honayekooli nili

And they bring the colt unto Jesus, and cast on him their garments; and he sat upon him.

8. chiine meci hosekatenaanaawa hopiitenikanwa hoskici heele hini miyeeweniki mecimi naaleta mhsiske meemehci kiskotamowaaci nili ktikaana hoci

And many spread their garments upon the way; and others branches, which they had cut from the fields.

9. chiine nihki naakaaniicki mecimi nihki neeneekasiweecki hoosena cehi kisaateelemekofi hina peepiyaata howiifooweneki teepeelemiweeta

And they that went before, and they that followed, cried, Hosanna; Blessed is he that cometh in the name of the Lord:

10. kisaatetiwi cehi hini hokimaawitaamhkwe peepiyeeyaaki hini hokimaawitaamhkomi kohfena teepitii hoosena cehi hini wihkoci lhspi lahootamooki

Blessed is the kingdom that cometh, the kingdom of our father David: Hosanna in the highest.

11. chiine hotta colooseelemii piitike hini mamaatomeewikamikwi heewa chiine yeh mehci waapataki kaayaawka caayahki wiyehi howe hini holaakwiifi lohfe pefeneki heewa kileki nihi metahfwi-kite-niiswi

And he entered into Jerusalem, into the temple; and when he had looked round about upon all things, it being now eventide, he went out unto Bethany with the twelve.

12. chiine hini wayaapaki pefene ye hoci lohfaawaaci ceh skwaalawe

And on the morrow, when they were come out from Bethany, he hungered.

13. chiine pelowihi hoteh neeme kicimiisi mhsiskiwiiya nhheewa kwehkwi menawahke wi mhkaki wiyehi nitasi mecimi hini yeh piyeelotaki mata wiyehi homhka mhsiske pehi ksake mata hini laakwa yaatah teeki kicimi

And seeing a fig tree afar off having leaves, he came, if haply he might find anything thereon: and when he came to it, he found nothing but leaves; for it was not the season of figs.

14. mecimi hotaapafta mata hileni hotah miici mawifoowe kiila hoci yooci hinoki kookwelaakwasi hoteta hini mecimi hokakehkimaafhi honootaakohi hini

And he answered and said unto it, No man eat fruit from thee henceforward for ever. And his disciples heard it.

15. chiine colooseelemii si piyeeki mecimi hini mamaatomeewikamikwi si piicfe mecimi hotalemi lohfe pakilahi nihi waawiitkiilici chiine nihi taatepenikeelici piitike hini mamaatomeewikamikwi chiine hokolepi-pakitamawahi nili hoteepaliimilici nihi moni haasoonikehfihi mecimi nili hotpapiiwenilici nihi maamiyeekinelici miyaasipawiifhi

And they come to Jerusalem: and he entered into the temple, and began to cast out them that sold and them that bought in the temple, and overthrew the tables of the money-changers, and the seats of them that sold the doves;

16. chiine mata wiilaani sitehe wahsi wiyeefa hileni haamwetooci wiyehsi poonahfocika saapwi hini mamaatomeewikamikwi

and he would not suffer that any man should carry a vessel through the temple.

17. chiine kakehkimiwe ha mata hini yeelawikeeki niwiikiwaapimi homamaatomeewika hina caayahki tfweelena si lenawe weh sitoote weeka kiilawa neyehka ciikoniwehfiiki howaasaalakomwa kitestoonaawa hotelahi

And he taught, and said unto them, Is it not written, My house shall be called a house of prayer for all the nations? but ye have made it a den of robbers.

18. mecimi nihki hokimaawi mhkateewkolayeeki chiine nihki yaayawikeecki nootaakeeki hini mecimi natonehikeeki wahsi menawahke macilotawaawaaci nili ksake hokwfaawaali ksake caayahki nihki mehseelekki hocihfeeletamawaawaali nili hokakehkimiweewenilici

And the chief priests and the scribes heard it, and sought how they might destroy him: for they feared him, for all the multitude was astonished at his teaching.

19. chiine tfene weelaakwiifiki hini hoteewe wahoci lohfe

And every evening he went forth out of the city.

20. chiine yeesi pemhfeewaaci hini kwelahwaapaki nihki honeemenaawa hini kicimiisi caakisahte nili hoceepkahkato hoci

And as they passed by in the morning, they saw the fig tree withered away from the roots.

21. chiine piita hopemi mhkaweeleta lepaayii waapatano hini kicimiisi meemacikalootamani sahte hotelaali

And Peter calling to remembrance saith unto him, Rabbi, behold, the fig tree which thou cursedst is withered away.

22. mecimi haapafse ciisisii poonamoko teepwehseewe wiiyaaki maneto hotelahi

And Jesus answering saith unto them, Have faith in God.

23. tepilo kitelepwa niila kookwe-neefa-kaaci mamoofolo mecimi hini mhsinepiki hipakiloofolo we hita halayooma meekwahkiki mecimi mata we ppehci tehe hotehiki weeka weh teepwehta hini yeeyoci wahsi piyeemikaki hina weh poona hini

Verily I say unto you, Whosoever shall say unto this mountain, Be thou taken up and cast into the sea; and shall not doubt in his heart, but shall believe that what he saith cometh to pass; he shall have it.

24. weecikeenahi kitelepwa niila caayahki wiyehi kookwe-nehi-kaaci meemamaatomaayeekwe mecimi neetotamaakeeyeekwe teepwehseeko wahsi hotfekoyeekwe mecimi keh poonaanaawa nili

Therefore I say unto you, All things whatsoever ye pray and ask for, believe that ye have received them, and ye shall have them.

25. chiine kookwe-laakwa-kaaci kiniipawipwa kipemi mamaatomaapwa pakfeeletamawiweeko kwehkwi poonamaweekwe ppehci wiyehi wiyeefa wahsi kohfwa weefepahkamikiki yeepita nehfaapi menawahi pakfeeletamoolwaakwe kiilawa kithalhfwaacilawiiwenwa

And whensoever ye stand praying, forgive, if ye have aught against any one; that your Father also which is in heaven may forgive you your trespasses.

27. chiine nohki colooseelemii si piyeeki chiine yeesi paamhfeeci hini mamaatomeewikamikoki hotfekohi nitasi hokimaawi mhkateewkolayehi chiine nihi yaayawikeelici chiine nihi kikilenihi

And they come again to Jerusalem: and as he was walking in the temple, there come to him the chief priests, and the scribes, and the elders;

28. mecimi nihi taaniwe hoci mekofiiwe kiwahoci lawi kiila yooloma wiyehi weelaa neefawe kimiilekwa yooma simekofiiwe wahsi yooloma wiyehi silawiiyani hotekohi

and they said unto him, By what authority doest thou these things? or who gave thee this authority to do these things?

29. keh natohtoolepwa nekoti kalawiiwe mecimi haapaftawiko chiine keh wiitamoolepwa niila hini simekofiiwe wahoci lawiiya yooloma wiyehi

And Jesus said unto them, I will ask of you one question, and answer me, and I will tell you by what authority I do these things.

30. hini hofafahkwiholelhiweewe caanii ha weefepahkamikiki hoci hini weelaa toke hileniiki hoci haapaftawiko hotelahi ciisisii

The baptism of John, was it from heaven, or from men? answer me.

31. mecimi nihki memekini tehehtwaatiiki wiilawa chiine kwehkwi weefepahkamikiki hoci ke hiyope koociwe chiine mata kiteepwehtawaawa we hiwa hiwaki

And they reasoned with themselves, saying, If we shall say, From heaven; he will say, Why then did ye not believe him?

32. weeka hileniiki hoci hiyoyakwe hokwfaawahi nihi lenawehi nihki ksake caayahki tepilo maamoosikiiskweeta hotelakimaawaali caaniili

But should we say, From men—they feared the people: for all verily held John to be a prophet.

33. chiine hotaapaftawaawaali ciisisiili mata niwaakotaape hiwaki mecimi ciisisii mata nohki niila kitah wiitamoolepwa simekofiiwe wahoci yooloma wiyehi silawiiya hotelahi

And they answered Jesus and say, We know not. And Jesus saith unto them, Neither tell I you by what authority I do these things.

Mark:12

1. chiine hotalemi kaloolahi pemaatoweewena hileni hototo mhfaloomiktika mecimi howakha kaayaawka hini chiine waalhke waasaalakwi wah ta hahteeki waiiniiwi fiikiceepicika chiine hopatena mhkahkwika mecimi hotawhhahi ktikeewilenihi hini chiine payakila taamhkwe heewa

And he began to speak unto them in parables. A man planted a vineyard, and set a hedge about it, and digged a pit for the winepress, and built a tower, and let it out to husbandmen, and went into another country.

2. chiine tah kwena hini laakwaamhki hoteleskamawahi haloolaakaafali nihi ktikeewilenihi wahsi menawahke nihi ktikeewilenihi hoci hotfekoci nili mawifoowena hini mhfaloomiktika hoci

And at the season he sent to the husbandmen a servant, that he might receive from the husbandmen of the fruits of the vineyard.

3. mecimi nihki homesenaawaali nili chiine hoppaktehwaawaali chiine hotaameskawaawaali sesipaafiili

And they took him, and beat him, and sent him away empty.

4. chiine nohki hoteleskamawahi nihi kotakali haloolaakaafali mecimi nihki homamiyaalakhaawaali nili hini wiileki chiine howaapalaaci hpenalaawaali

And again he sent unto them another servant; and him they wounded in the head, and handled shamefully.

5. chiine hoteleskawaali nohki kotakali mecimi nili honhfaawaali nihki mecimi meci kotakhi hopemi ppaktehwaawahi naaleta chiine honhfaawahi naaleta

And he sent another; and him they killed: and many others; beating some, and killing some.

6. hina keewaki hahsi nekoti hopoonaali yahkweelemekofilici hokwihfimaali niliini hoteleskamawahi nihi ceeyehkwi we hotakeelemaawaali nikwihfali hiwapi

He had yet one, a beloved son: he sent him last unto them, saying, They will reverence my son.

7. payeekwa nehke ktikeewileniiki hitiiki heelekiina wiilawa hina yaama layaapitepeelecikeeta wiilaani nhfaataako mecimi hini laapitepeelecikeewe ke howiilaamipe

But those husbandmen said among themselves, This is the heir; come, let us kill him, and the inheritance shall be ours.

8. mecimi homesenaawaali nili chiine honhfaawaali chiine hini mhfaloomiktikaaneki hoci lohfe pakilaawaali

And they took him, and killed him, and cast him forth out of the vineyard.

9. nehiwe weecikeenhhi weh silawi hina teepeeletaka hini mhfaloomiktika weh piyeewa hina mecimi weh macilotawahi nihi ktikeewilenihi chiine kotakhi weh miilahi hini mhfaloomiktika

What therefore will the lord of the vineyard do? he will come and destroy the husbandmen, and will give the vineyard unto others.

10. ha mata kimeh laapaatotaanaawa halayooma teetepilahi tepilo heewikaateeki nili siikonali

Have ye not read even this scripture; The stone which the builders rejected, yeelawinawaawaaci nihki waakkaacki hina yaska mechoofo howiisiwi hini poocaaki

The same was made the head of the corner:

11. yaama hina teepeelemiweeta hociwi mecimi hina hina hanhhiweewi naakofi kiskiisekonaaki

This was from the Lord, And it is marvelous in our eyes?

12. chiine natonehikeeki nihki wahsi mesenaawaaci mecimi hokwfaawahi nihi mehseelelici ksake nihki moositeheeki yeesi hina kilekimaaci nihi hini pemaatoweeweneki chiine weepfeeki nihki mecimi honakalaawaali nili

And they sought to lay hold on him; and they feared the multitude; for they perceived that he spake the parable against them: and they left him, and went away.

13. chiine hoteleskawaawaali nihki naanekoti nihi pelesihi chiine nihi hoci heletiifhi wahsi nihi menawahke pethanekoci hokalawiiweneki

And they send unto him certain of the Pharisees and of the Herodians, that they might catch him in talk.

14. chiine yeh piyaawaaci nihki keekehkimiwe niwaakotaape kiila kimayaawiilefi mecimi mata wiyeh kiteleelema wiyeefa ksake mata wiyeh kiteleeletaana nili wiiyaawa hileniiki weeka teepweewe hoci kikakehkimiwe hini homiyeewi maneto ha mayaawatwi hini kwteletiiweneki wahsi miiloofoci teeksiiwi moni siisa weelaa toke mata hotekohi

And when they were come, they say unto him, Master, we know that thou art true, and carest not for any one: for thou regardest not the person of men, but of a truth teachest the way of God: Is it lawful to give tribute unto Caesar, or not?

15. ha neh miiliweepe weelaa teki neh miiliweepe payeekwa wiila hopemi waakotamawahi honelohcilawiiwenilici koociwe kikotahkowaasipwa piyeetawiko teneliyas wahsi neemeya hini hotelahi

Shall we give, or shall we not give? But he, knowing their hypocrisy, said unto them, Why tempt ye me? bring me a penny, that I may see it.

16. mecimi nihki hopiyeetoonaawa hini neefawe hokiishoowe yooma mecimi holhspawikaafoowe hotelahi mecimi siisa wiila hotekohi

And they brought it. And he saith unto them, Whose is this image and superscription? And they said unto him, Caesar's.

17. peteki miilehko siisa hini wiyehi siisa wiila mecimi maneto hini wiyehi maneto wiila hotelahi chiine holaami hokwakwehtaaneelemekohi nihi

And Jesus said unto them, Render unto Caesar the things that are Caesar's, and unto God the things that are God's. And they marveled greatly at him.

18. chiine nitasi hotfekohi setosihi nihki matalaakwa haapefiiwi-honhskaawe yaayocki chiine honatohtaakohi nihi

And there come unto him Sadducees, which say that there is no resurrection; and they asked him, saying,

19. keekehkimiwe moosisii nitawikaakona kwehkwi hileni hoceeninaali nepelite mecimi hotaanaaki nakalaate hina wiiwali chiine pwaa nakalaate hapelohfali wahsi hoceeninaali laapsinelici nili wiiwali mecimi hopatenamawaaci miinhka hoceeninaali

Master, Moses wrote unto us, If a man's brother die, and leave a wife behind him, and leave no child, that his brother should take his wife, and raise up seed unto his brother.

20. nitasi hapiiki niiswahfwi hoceeninaaki chiine hina weski hosiletamwa wiiwali mecimi nepoofi mata honakata miinhka

There were seven brethren: and the first took a wife, and dying left no seed;

21. chiine hina mawi-niiswi laapsinwa nili hkweeli mecimi nepwa mata nakatame miinhka hotaanaaki chiine hina mawi-nhfwi hini yaska

and the second took her, and died, leaving no seed behind him; and the third likewise:

22. mecimi hina niiswahfwi mata honakata miinhka ceeyehkwi nihki caayahki hina hkweewa nehfaapi nepwa

and the seven left no seed. Last of all the woman also died.

23. hini haapefiiwi-honhskaaweneki taanawe weh wiiwinaali nili nihki ksake nihki niiswahfwi homehci poonaawaali nili wahsi wiiwiwaaci hotekohi

In the resurrection whose wife shall she be of them? for the seven had her to wife.

24. ha mata yooni wahoci piimilawiiyeekwe ye pwaa kiilawa waakotameekwe nili tepilo heewikaateewali nohki hini howiisikatowiiwe maneto hotelahi ciisisii

Jesus said unto them, Is it not for this cause that ye err, that ye know not the scriptures, nor the power of God?

25. ksake hine we honhskaaki nihki nili nepelici hoci mata nihki weh wiichetiiki mata nohki wiichetiiweneki weh si miiletipi weeka paasi henhcaliiki piitike weefepahkamikiki

For when they shall rise from the dead, they neither marry, nor are given in marriage; but are as angels in heaven.

26. weeka yeesinamowaaci nihki neepekiki honhskaanoofooki nihki ha mata kimeh laapaatotaanaawa hini hoteewikaateemeki moosisii hini ta haatotooteeki hini piiwalwi yeesi kaloolekoci manetooli niiya niliini homanetoomali heplehemii chiine niliini homanetoomali haisiki chiine niliini homanetoomali ceekapii

But as touching the dead, that they are raised; have ye not read in the book of Moses, in the place concerning the Bush, how God spake unto him, saying, I am the God of Abraham, and the God of Isaac, and the God of Jacob?

27. mata niliini homanetoomali hina nepeka hina peemi lenaweewita weeka holaami kipaapiimi lawiipwa kiilawa

He is not the God of the dead, but of the living: ye do greatly err.

28. chiine nekoti nihki yaayawikeecki piyeewa mecimi honootawahi nihi pemi maawatwi natohsehi mecimi waakotamwa yeesi hina mehci howesi haapaftawaaci nihi honatohtawaali taaniwe tepikeemoowe hini nenhhihtaawiki caayahki hotelaali

And one of the scribes came, and heard them questioning together, and knowing that he had answered them well, asked him, What commandment is the first of all?

29. ciisisii haapafse hini nhhihtaawiki halayooma nootaakeelo o hiswiila hina teepeelemelakwe kimanetoomena hina hina teepeelemiweeta nekotiwi

Jesus answered, The first is, Hear, O Israel; The Lord our God, the Lord is one:

30. chiine hahkweelemi kiila hina teepeelemiweeta kimanetooma kileki caayahki kitehi chiine kileki caayahki kimayaawikiiya chiine kileki caayahki kimemekinitehaaka chiine kileki caayahki kiwiisikatowiiwe

and thou shalt love the Lord thy God with all thy heart, and with all thy soul, and with all thy mind, and with all thy strength.

31. hini mawi-niiswi halayooma hahkweelemi kiila kimaapiyeecikaaletiima paasi kiiya matalaakwa kotaki tepikeemoowe halika yeeki yooloma hotelaali

The second is this, Thou shalt love thy neighbour as thyself. There is none other commandment greater than these.

32. mecimi teepweewe keekehkimiwe koowesi mehtowe yeesi hina nekotiifici chiine matalaakwa kotaka hina pehi hotekooli nili yaayawikeelici

And the scribe said unto him, Of a truth, Master, thou hast well said that he is one; and there is none other but he:

33. mecimi wahsi hahkweelemoofoci kileki caayahki hini hotehi chiine kileki caayahki hini lepwaawe chiine kileki caayahki hini wiisikatowiiwe mecimi wahsi hahkweelemaaci maaopiyeecikaaletiimali paasi wiiya mhsi halika hinwi noota caayahki mefi fakfikeewipootefamaacikana chiine hapenaweewena hotekooli

and to love him with all the heart, and with all the understanding, and with all the strength, and to love his neighbour as himself, is much more than all whole burnt offerings and sacrifices.

34. chiine yeh neemeki ciisisii yeesi kcitawaafi haapafseeci mata pelowi kitapi hoci hini maneto hokimaawitaamhkomi hotelaali mecimi mata kiteeni hileni hine hoci wiisa natohtawaali wiyehsi natohseewe

And when Jesus saw that he answered discreetly, he said unto him, Thou art not far from the kingdom of God. And no man after that durst ask him any question.

35. chiine haapafse ciisisii yeesi kakehkimiweeci hini mamaatomeewikamikoki nehiwesi hiwaki nihki yaayawikeecki yeesi nili klaistiili hokwihfici teepitii

And Jesus answered and said, as he taught in the temple, How say the scribes that the Christ is the son of David?

36. teepitii nehalwaaka wiila hiwa piitike nili hofepi hocacaalahkwali hina teepeelemiweeta hotelaali niteepeelemiweemali lematapilo kiila nimayaawiinhkiki paalohi nineshaaki kimateeletiiwenaki hini hotpalhkiiwe kifitali

David himself said in the Holy Spirit, The Lord said unto my Lord, Sit thou on my right hand, Till I make thine enemies the footstool of thy feet.

37. teepitii nehalwaaka wiila teepeelemiweeta hotesinaali nehiwe hotesi hokwihfinaali nili hiwa mecimi nihi nehcipehi lenawehi homenwi nootaakohi

David himself calleth him Lord; and whence is he his son? And the common people heard him gladly.

38. chiine hopemikakehkimiweeweneki mahkeeni cehi nihki yaayawikeecki maamaatawi paamhfeecki kinwi pihtawipiitenikaneki chiine wahsi poonamowaaci hosilawaaletiiwena piitike nili yaatah wiiwiitkiiki

And in his teaching he said, Beware of the scribes, which desire to walk in long robes, and to have salutations in the marketplaces,

39. chiine haliwi yeeki hpapiiwena piitike nili mhsikamiko mecimi haliwi yeeki tah wiiwihfenhcikeeki

and chief seats in the synagogues, and chief places at feasts:

40. caacaakatamawaacki yeetaalici wiikiwaapali siikawi-ykwehi chiine nelohcilawiiwe howahoci hostoonaawa pihci mamaatomeewena yohkooni we hotfekonaawa haliwi yeeki matahkowaafoowe hiwa

they which devour widows' houses, and for a pretence make long prayers; these shall receive greater condemnation.

41. chiine yeelahfamhfeki hini monika si lematapi mecimi hotelaapata yaasi hini monikaaneki hipakitamowaaci moni nihki mehseelekki mecimi meci peepawaacki hotipakitaanaawa mecilekhi

And he sat down over against the treasury, and beheld how the multitude cast money into the treasury: and many that were rich cast in much.

42. chiine nitasi piyeewa nekoti kitema siikawi-ykwe mecimi hopiicfe pakitaana niiswi maackwaafi moni pahfi senhsi piyeeya nili

And there came a poor widow, and she cast in two mites, which make a farthing.

43. chiine hoteh wihkomahi hokakehkimaafhi mecimi tepilo kitelepwa niila yaama kitema siikawi-ykwe hopiicfe pakita halika tfwi noota caayahki nihki peemi hini si piicfe pakitakki monikaaneki

And he called unto him his disciples, and said unto them, Verily I say unto you, This poor widow cast in more

44. ksake caayahki nihki hotipakitaanaawa hotaamefiiwenwa weeka hina hotakaawaafiiwe hopiicfe pakita caayahki peepoonaki teetepilahi hini caayahki weeci lenaweewici hotelahi

than all they which are casting into the treasury:
for they all did cast in of their superfluity; but she of her want did cast in all that she had, even all her living.

Mark:13

1. chiine yeesi faakici si weepfeeci hini mamaatomeewikamikwi hoci nekoti nihi hokakehkimaafhi keekehkimiwe waapatano ceh lakokwe yeetowaaci siikonaki mecimi wiikiwaapali ceh lakokwe yeeki hotekooli

And as he went forth out of the temple, one of his disciples saith unto him, Master, behold, what manner of stones and what manner of buildings!

2. mecimi ha kineemena yooloma maki wiikiwaapali mata we ckonoofo hotasi nekoti siikona hoskici kotakali wah pwaa sahkiki hipakiloofota hotelaali ciisisii

And Jesus said unto him, Seest thou these great buildings? there shall not be left here one stone upon another, which shall not be thrown down.

3. chiine yeesi lematapici wehseteki hini halifiwi meekwahkiki yeelahfamhfeki hini mamaatomeewikamikwi piitali chiine ceemhsiili chiine caaniili mecimi heenhtlooli hokiimi natohtaakohi

And as he sat on the mount of Olives over against the temple, Peter and James and John and Andrew asked him privately,

4. wiitamawinaake taaniwe laakwa yooloma wiyehi we hahteewa chiine nehiwe we hinwi hini kikinooloowe hine nawito caayahki yooloma wiyehi weh mectaakwato hotekohi

Tell us, when shall these things be? and what shall be the sign when these things are all about to be accomplished?

5. mecimi ciisisii hotalemi hilahi kcitawaafiiko wahsi pwaa hileni piimiwelelwaakwe

And Jesus began to say unto them, Take heed that no man lead you astray.

6. meci weh piyeeki niwiifooweneki niiya hina we hiwaki mecimi meci weh piimiwelaawahi

Many shall come in my name, saying, I am he; and shall lead many astray.

7. chiine hine nootaakeeyeekwe noochetiiwena mecimi noochetiiwena laacimoowena teki peetfakiteheeyeekwe yooloma wiyehi kwiilahi paapiyeeci weh piyeemikato payeekwa hini ceeyehkwiiwe mata keewaki

And when ye shall hear of wars and rumours of wars, be not troubled: these things must needs come to pass; but the end is not yet.

8. ksake nekotweelena si lenawe weh pafekwicfatawaali nekotweelena si lenaweeli mecimi hokimaawiiwe hoppehtena hokimaawiiwe we hahteewa nitasi hasiskinoomeskaawena caceepi tasi we hahteewa nitasi seeskwaalaweewahkamikiki yoolooni wiyehi howe weeci halemahkamikiki hini hahkwilaasamamoowe

For nation shall rise against nation, and kingdom against kingdom: there shall be earthquakes in divers places; there shall be famines: these things are the beginning of travail.

9. payeekwa kiiyawaaki mameko kcitawaafiiwe ksake tepoweewena nihki keh si pakfenekowaaki chiine piitike mhsikamiko ke ppaktehokoopwa mecimi yeelahfamiiwaaci kapenaliiki chiine maki hokimaaki keh niipawipwa ksake niiya hoci wahsi nihki hoteepweemiwaaci

But take ye heed to yourselves: for they shall deliver you up to councils; and in synagogues shall ye be beaten; and before governors and kings shall ye stand for my sake, for a testimony unto them.

10. chiine hini howesi piyeetaacimoowe paapiyeeci nhhihta weh nanahimoofooki caayahki nihki tfweelena si lenaweeki

And the gospel must first be preached unto all the nations.

11. chiine tepoweeweneki siwelelwaakwe nihki mecimi mesenelwaakwe teki kih niikaani wiisaafiipwa wa hiyoyeekwe weeka kookwe-nehi-kaaci keh miilekoopwa hine hini yaatefaki yooni kalawiko kiilawa ksake mata hini kiilawa keekalawicki hina hofepi hocacaalahkwa weeka

And when they lead you to judgment, and deliver you up, be not anxious beforehand what ye shall speak: but whatsoever shall be given you in that hour, that speak ye: for it is not ye that speak, but the Holy Ghost.

12. chiine hoceeninaana nepooweneki weh si pakfenaali hoceeninaanaali chiine hina hohfima hotapelohfemali chiine hapelohfaki weh pafekwicfatawaawahi hokehkiyaamwahi mecimi wahsi nhfekwilici we hpenalaawahi nihi

And brother shall deliver up brother to death, and the father his child; and children shall rise up against parents, and cause them to be put to death.

13. chiine keh siikeelemekofiimekowaaki kiilawa caayahki hileniiki ksake niwiifoowe hoci payeekwa hina nahiika yehkwi wiisikiteheeta hiina hina weh waapaneshoofo

And ye shall be hated of all men for my name's sake: but he that endureth to the end, the same shall be saved.

14. payeekwa hine neeweekwe kiilawa hina lasiikaaci si-siikwahkamikifiiwena pemi niipawi wah tah pwaa silawiici hina leelaapaatotaka wiilaani wih nenohse hiine howe wiilaani nihki cotiyeeki yeepicki nili meekwahkiki wih lesimooki

But when ye see the abomination of desolation standing where he ought not (let him that readeth understand), then let them that are in Judaea flee unto the mountains:

15. chiine hina hini hakocikami wiikiwa yeepita wiilaani teki wih laasiwe weelaa teki wih piicfe wahsi lohfatooci wiyehi yeetaaci wiikiwa hoci

and let him that is on the housetop not go down, nor enter in, to take anything out of his house:

16. chiine wiilaani hina hini laa ktika yeepita teki peteki hotaanaaki wihsi naate hokootiimi

and let him that is in the field not return back to take his cloke.

17. weeka macilepwaaweniiki cehi nihki leelaamotaakocki hapelohfali chiine nihki neenoonhhiweecki nele kaasekiki

But woe unto them that are with child and to them that give suck in those days!

18. mecimi mamaatomeeko cehi kiilawa wahsi pwaa hini hahteeki kwena hini pepooki

And pray ye that it be not in the winter.

19. ksake nele kaasekiki we hahteewi kiisenaacinamoowe yeeki nitasi matalaakwa me hahteewi hini yeeki hine halemahkamikatwi hini mehteelemiweewe hoci mayehteeletaki maneto paalohi hinoki mecimi mata kiteeni we hteewi

For those days shall be tribulation, such as there hath not been the like from the beginning of the creation which God created until now, and never shall be.

20. chiine weeciwephi hina teepeelemiweeta neyehka hoceekinake nili kaasekiki hiyehki mata wiyawfi yah mehci waapanestoote weeka ksake hina hoci meemayaawhoofota meemamaaci hina hina hoceekinaana nili kaasekiki

And except the Lord had shortened the days, no flesh would have been saved: but for the elect's sake, whom he chose, he shortened the days.

21. chiine hine howe kwehkwi wiyeefa hileni sci halayaama hina klaistii weelaa sci nitasi ke hikowa teki teepwehtamoko hini

And then if any man shall say unto you, Lo, here is the Christ; or, Lo, there; believe it not:

22. ksake weh pafekwiiki nitasi miyaasi klaistiiki chiine miyaasi maamoosikiiskwecki mecimi weh waapatesiweeki kikinooloowena chiine lakokwehtaani wiyehi wahsi menawah piimiwesiweewaaci nihki kwehkwi katawi-ike nili meeyaawhoofolici

for there shall arise false Christs and false prophets, and shall shew signs and wonders, that they may lead astray, if possible, the elect.

23. payeekwa kcitawaafiiko kiilawa waapatamoko neyehka kimehci wiitamoolepwa caayahki wiyehi kaasa

But take ye heed: behold, I have told you all things beforehand.

24. hine nele kaasekiki hahkowihi hini kiisenaacinamoowe hina kiisekikiisfwa weh pepekichoofo mecimi hina tepehkikiisfwa mata weh miiliwe howahfeeyaami

But in those days, after that tribulation, the sun shall be darkened, and the moon shall not give her light,

25. chiine nihki halaakwaki weh pemi menhkwatwi hoci penhsinooki mecimi nili waasikaki piitike yehteeki nili menhkwato weh naanoomenoote

and the stars shall be falling from heaven, and the powers that are in the heavens shall be shaken.

26. mecimi hine howe nihki weh neewaawaali nili hokwihfali hileni pemi piyeeli paafkwahkiiki kileki mhsaawi waasikaki mecimi wahfaacimekofiiwe

And then shall they see the Son of man coming in clouds with great power and glory.

27. chiine howe hina weh waawiinahi nihi henhcalihi mecimi weh maawatwi maawatonaali homayaawefiimali nili niyeewi mehsikkaki hoci hini wihkoci lekhi hini hasiskitaamhkwe hoci paalohi hini wihkoci lekhi hini menhkwatwi

And then shall he send forth the angels, and shall gather together his elect from the four winds, from the uttermost part of the earth to the uttermost part of heaven.

28. howe hina kicimiisa hoci waakotefiko hopemaatoweewe hine hina hopkeeyahkofiiwe howe ye kokoskwaafiki mecimi paskahkweeya homhsiskeema kiwaakotaanaawa kiilawa yeesi maalaakwaamatoofiki hini peelaawiki

Now from the fig tree learn her parable: when her branch is now become tender, and putteth forth its leaves, ye know that the summer is nigh;

29. yooni teetepilahi nehfaapi kiilawa hine neemeyeekwe yooloma wiyehi pemi piyeemikato waakotamoko yeesi howe hina maalaakwaamefici teetepilahi nahiika nili skwaateewali

even so ye also, when ye see these things coming to pass, know ye that he is nigh, even at the doors.

30. tepilo kitelepwa niila yaama hinoki skwiiwena mata we hasenwa paalohi caayahki yooloma wiyehi weh mectaakwato

Verily I say unto you, This generation shall not pass away, until all these things be accomplished.

31. menhkwatwi mecimi hasiskitaamhkwe we haseno weeka nikalawiiwena mata we haseno

Heaven and earth shall pass away: but my words shall not pass away.

32. payeekwa hine hini kaasekiki weelaa hini yaatefaki mata wiyeefa howaakota mata wiikinaakwi nihki henhcaliiki piitike weefepahkamikiki mata nohki hina hokwihfima hina hohfima weeka

But of that day or that hour knoweth no one, not even the angels in heaven, neither the Son, but the Father.

33. kcitawaafiiko kiilawa kcitawaapiko mecimi mamaatomeeko ksake mata kiwaakotaanaawa hine hini laakwa

Take ye heed, watch and pray: for ye know not when the time is.

34. paasi hine hileni hinwi hini pemi haami kotaki hasiskiiki hopemi mehci nakata yeetaaci wiikiwa mecimi homehci miilahi simekofiiwe hotaloolaakanhhi moosa nekoti hopekatefiiwe nehfaapi hotepimaali nili skwaatekehcitawahtoolici wahsi kcitawaapilici

It is as when a man, sojourning in another country, having left his house, and given authority to his servants, to each one his work, commanded also the porter to watch.

35. kcitawaapiko weecikeenahi ksake mata kiwaakotaanaawa kiilawa hine hina teepeeletaka hini wiikiwa wah piyaaci kwehkwi toke holaakwiifike weelaa laawi tepehkike weelaa naapeeya kalhootake weelaa hini kolahwaapake

Watch therefore: for ye know not when the lord of the house cometh, whether at even, or at midnight, or at cockcrowing, or in the morning;

36. piilepeeke kikamooci pemi piyaate kimhkaakowa hina peemi nepaayeekwe

lest coming suddenly he find you sleeping.

37. chiine yeelelako kiilawa nitelaaki niila caayahki kcitawaapiko

And what I say unto you I say unto all, Watch.

Mark:14

1. howe yeesi mehci niisokonakiki hahteewi hini pemhfaasiweewi lemafkohkweewe mecimi hini pwaayaa honeteeki takhwa chiine nihki hokimaawi mhkateewkolayeeki mecimi nihki yaayawikeecki honatonehaanaawa wahsi menawahke mesenaawaaci nili nhhilawiiwe hoci mecimi nhfaawaaci nili

Now after two days was the feast of the passover and the unleavened bread: and the chief priests and the scribes sought how they might take him with subtilty, and kill him:

2. ksake nihki hiwaki teki hini laakwasi weewihfenhcikeeki piilepeeke kikamooci nitasi we hahteewi hotatawaanhkeewenwa nihki lenaweeki

for they said, Not during the feast, lest haply there shall be a tumult of the people.

3. chiine heeyehi pefeneki hapici hini wiikiwa yeetaaci saimanii hina weeskilhakeemekita yeesi lematapici tah wihfeniki nitasi piyeeli hkweeli hopemi niimeli heelepeestaawi wihfakakkoofeki lomhkoowe nehtawatwi naati lakokwe kisoweelemekwatwi mecimi hina hkweewa hopohkinaali nili wihfakakkoofali chiine wiileki hoteh fiikinamaakooli hini

And while he was in Bethany in the house of Simon the leper, as he sat at meat, there came a woman having an alabaster cruse of ointment of spikenard very costly; and she brake the cruse, and poured it over his head.

4. payeekwa naaleta hapiiki nitasi peepoonakki kisfetiiwe heelekiina wiilawa taaniwe hoci yooma waleskhotoote hini lomhkoowe

But there were some that had indignation among themselves, saying, To what purpose hath this waste of the ointment been made?

5. ksake yooma lomhkoowe menawahke neyehka nhfene tepeewe seleni halika wih si mehci miyeekipi mecimi miilekwi hina kitemaafa hiwaki mecimi nihki hopekihkawaawaali nili hkweeli

For this ointment might have been sold for above three hundred pence, and given to the poor. And they murmured against her.

6. payeekwa wiilaani koociwe kipetfakhaawa kiilawa nimehci hina pekatenamaakwa howesi pekatefiiwe niiyaaki hiwa ciisisii

But Jesus said, Let her alone; why trouble ye her? she hath wrought a good work on me.

7. kipoonaawaaki ksake nihki kitemaafaki moosatawi wiici kiilawa mecimi kookwe-laakwa-kaaci siteheeyeekwe kiilawa kih katawi howesi hpenalaawaaki nihki weeka niila mata moosatawi kipoonipwa

For ye have the poor always with you, and whensoever ye will ye can do them good: but me ye have not always.

8. mehci lawi hina wah katawiilefici homehci lomhkoonaali niiyaanali kaasa wahsi hini pemi lekonoofolici

She hath done what she could: she hath anointed my body aforehand for the burying.

9. chiine tepilo kitelepwa niila kookwe-tasi-kaaci hini howesi piyeetaacimoowe weh nanahimiweepi mefhiike hini yeelekokwahkamikiki hini nehfaapi yaama hkweewa mayehci lawiici we haatotoote wahsi homaamhkaweelemoofoowenici

And verily I say unto you, Wheresoever the gospel shall be preached throughout the whole world, that also which this woman hath done shall be spoken of for a memorial of her.

10. chiine cootasii hiskeeletii hina nekoti nihki metahfwi-kite-niiswi weepfe nihi hokimaawi mhkateewkolayehi heewa wahsi menawahke nihi si mestaawhaaci nili

And Judas Iscariot, he that was one of the twelve, went away unto the chief priests, that he might deliver him unto them.

11. chiine nihki yeh nootamowaaci hini howesilepwaaki mecimi homehcimaawaali wahsi miilaawaaci moni mecimi hina honatoneha wahsi menawahi nihi si laakeeci mestaawhaaci nili

And they, when they heard it, were glad, and promised to give him money. And he sought how he might conveniently deliver him unto them.

12. chiine hine weski kaasekiki weeci hahteeki pwaayaa honeteeki takhwa ye hapeneewaaci nihki hini pemhfaasiweewe hotekohi hokakehkimaafhi taaniwe tasi kitesitehe wi haayaake mecimi hosimecfetooyaake wahsi menawahke kiila miiciyani hini pemhfaasiweewe

And on the first day of unleavened bread, when they sacrificed the passover, his disciples say unto him, Where wilt thou that we go and make ready that thou mayest eat the passover?

13. mecimi howaawiinahi niiswi hokakehkimaafhi nhhaakone hini hoteeweneki mecimi nitasi keh nakskaakowa hileni hopemi niime hasiskiwakkoki nepi neekalehko

And he sendeth two of his disciples, and saith unto them, Go into the city, and there shall meet you a man bearing a pitcher of water: follow him;

14. chiine kookwe-kaaci-tasi hina weh piicfe hina keekehkimiwe taaniwe cehi ninawhetiiwika wah tah miiciya hini pemhfaasiweewe kileki nikakehkimaafaki hiwa hilehko hina hini wiikiwa hoci mestele hotelahi

and wheresoever he shall enter in, say to the goodman of the house, The Master saith, Where is my guest-chamber, where I shall eat the passover with my disciples?

15. mecimi hina nehalwaaka keh waapatelekowa hakocipokwanefo mhsaawi yaataaki teepfenwi hawoocika mecimi mecfenwi chiine hini tasi hosimecfetawinaake

And he will himself shew you a large upper room furnished and ready: and there make ready for us.

16. mecimi nihki kakehkimaafaki weepfeeki chiine hini hoteeweneki si piyeeki mecimi homhkaanaawa yeesi

And the disciples went forth, and came into the city, and found as he had mehcimekowaaci nili chiine homecfetoonaawa hini pemhfaasiweewe

said unto them: and they made ready the passover.

17. chiine ye holaakwiifiki piyeewa kileki nihi metahfwi-kite-niiswi

And when it was evening he cometh with the twelve.

18. chiine yeesi lematapiwaaci mecimi pemi wihfeniwaaci ciisisii tepilo kitelepwa niila nekoti kiilawa neh mestaawhekwa teetepilahi hina weewihpomita hiwa

And as they sat and were eating, Jesus said, Verily I say unto you, One of you shall betray me, even he that eateth with me.

19. nihki halemi hokwaawefiiki macilepwaawe mecimi maasa nekoti ha niila hina hotekohi

They began to be sorrowful, and to say unto him one by one, Is it I?

20. nekoti hina nihki metahfwi-kite-niiswi weewiici hina pemhkaamita hini holaakaneki

And he said unto them, It is one of the twelve, he that dippeth with me in the dish.

21. ksake hina hokwihfali hileni teetepilahi heewa hini yeelawikaaloofoci payeekwa macilepwaaweni cehi hina hileni weeci saapwi mestaawhoofoci hina hokwihfali hileni howesaali hini weekhi hina hileni pwaa neyehka mehci lenaweewite hotelahi

For the Son of man goeth, even as it is written of him: but woe unto that man through whom the Son of man is betrayed! good were it for that man if he had not been born.

22. chiine yeesi wihfeniwaaci hoteh mame takhwa chiine yeh mehci kisaacitooci hoposkona hini mecimi homiilahi nihi chiine hamoko niila niiyaana yooma hiwa

And as they were eating, he took bread, and when he had blessed, he brake it, and gave to them, and said, Take ye: this is my body.

23. chiine hoteh mamaali tephikanali chiine yeh mehci miiliweeci niyaawe homiilahi nihi mecimi caayahki nihki nili hoci menooki

And he took a cup, and when he had given thanks, he gave to them: and they all drank of it.

24. mecimi nimhskomi yooma hini mehtaacimoowe hoci feefiikinamawoofoci meci wiyeefa

And he said unto them, This is my blood of the covenant, which is shed for many.

25. tepilo kitelepwa niila mata kiteeni neh mene hini mawifoowe hini tetepahtekwi hoci paalohi hine kaasekiki meneya hini weskiki piitike hini hokimaawitaamhkomi maneto hotelahi

Verily I say unto you, I will no more drink of the fruit of the vine, until that day when I drink it new in the kingdom of God.

26. chiine yeh mehci nakamowaaci hofepekamoowe lohfeeki hini halifiwi meekwahkiki heeki

And when they had sung a hymn, they went out unto the mount of Olives.

27. chiine hotelahi ciisisii caayahki kiilawa keh kisfekoopwa ksake mehtawikeepi hini neh kicithwa hina kehcitawahaata meekiifhi mecimi nihki meekiifaki mefhiike weh si lhfwelhkoofooki

And Jesus saith unto them, All ye shall be offended: for it is written, I will smite the shepherd, and the sheep shall be scattered abroad.

28. payeekwa mehci honhskaanike niila keeleliiki keh si niikaanihelepwa hotelahi

Howbeit, after I am raised up, I will go before you into Galilee.

29. payeekwa piita wiikinaakwi caayahki weh kisfekwiiki mata weeka niila hotelaali

But Peter said unto him, Although all shall be offended, yet will not I.

30. tepilo kitele niila yeesi hinoki kiisekiki tepilahi hinoki tepehkike wihsi pwaa niisene kalhootaki hina naapeeya nhfene ke mehci kiyaacimi hotelaali ciisisii

And Jesus saith unto him, Verily I say unto thee, that thou today, even this night, before the cock crow twice, shalt deny me thrice.

31. payeekwa hina hanhhiweewi wiisikowe kwiilahiike wiici nepoomela mata kiila kitah kiyaacimele hiwa mecimi nehfaapi hini yaska yeeyowaaci nihki caayahki

But he spake exceeding vehemently, If I must die with thee, I will not deny thee. And in like manner also said they all.

32. chiine howe nahiika tasi piyeeki keefsemeni yeesitooteeki chiine maatasi lematapiko kiilawa yeheeyehi mamaatomeeya hotelahi hokakehkimaafhi

And they come unto a place which was named Gethsemane: and he saith unto his disciples, Sit ye here, while I pray.

33. mecimi hotaamwelahi piitali chiine ceemhsiili chiine caaniili mecimi holaami halemi kwakwehtaanitehe chiine hahkwi petfakitehe

And he taketh with him Peter and James and John, and began to be greatly amazed, and sore troubled.

34. mecimi nimayaawiniiya hanhhiweewi hokwaawefi macilepwaawe teetepilahi nepooweneki hotasi hapiko mecimi kcitawaapiko hotelahi nihi

And he saith unto them, My soul is exceeding sorrowful even unto death: abide ye here, and watch.

35. chiine hale weepfe tekawihi chiine hini hasiskiiki si haakicfe mecimi mamaatome wahsi kwehkwi katawi hinike hini yaatefaki menawahke pemhfaalekoci

And he went forward a little, and fell on the ground, and prayed that, if it were possible, the hour might pass away from him.

36. mecimi hapa hohfima caayahki wiyehi katawatwi kiiyaaki kiila niiyaaki hoci haateni yaama tephika payeekwa mata yeesi teheeya niila yeesiteheeyani kiila weeka hiwa

And he said, Abba, Father, all things are possible unto thee; remove this cup from me: howbeit not what I will, but what thou wilt.

37. chiine piyeewa mecimi homhkawahi peemi nepaalici nihi mecimi saimanii ha kinepa ha mata kikatawi kcitawaapi nekoti yaatefaki hotelaali piitali

And he cometh, and findeth them sleeping, and saith unto Peter, Simon, sleepest thou? couldest thou not watch one hour?

38. kcitawaapiko chiine mamaatomeeko wahsi pwaa hottameekwe miyaasi-ashetiiwe sapka hini hilefiiwe teepiteheeya payeekwa hini wiyawfi mekihkofiiya

Watch and pray, that ye enter not into temptation: the spirit indeed is willing, but the flesh is weak.

39. chiine nohki hale weepfe mecimi mamaatome niliini yaska kalawiiwena hiwa

And again he went away, and prayed, saying the same words.

40. chiine nohki piyeewa mecimi homhkawahi nihi peemi nepaalici ksake hoskiisekowa lakokwe kofekwanili nihki mecimi mata howaakotaanaawa wa haapaftawaawaaci nili

And again he came, and found them sleeping, for their eyes were very heavy; and they wist not what to answer him.

41. chiine hini mawi-nhfene laakwa piyeewa mecimi nepaako howe chiine mameko halwaakahsiiwe teepi howe hini hini yaatefaki howe piyeeya waapamehko hina hokwihfali hileni nili holeciwa meciilefiicki si mestaawhoofo hotelahi

And he cometh the third time, and saith unto them, Sleep on now, and take your rest: it is enough; the hour is come; behold, the Son of man is betrayed into the hands of sinners.

42. honhskaako weepfeetaako waapamehko hina waasa mestaawhita howe maalaakwahi

Arise, let us be going: behold, he that betrayeth me is at hand.

43. mecimi weelena yeheeyehi keewaki kalawici piyeewa cootasii nekoti nihki metahfwi-kite-niiswi mecimi wiici mehseelelici kiskhikanihi mecimi cifhikana nihi hokimaawi mhkateewkolayehi chiine nihi yaayawikeelici chiine nihi kikilenihi homooki nihki

And straightway, while he yet spake, cometh Judas, one of the twelve, and with him a multitude with swords and staves, from the chief priests and the scribes and the elders.

44. howe hina memestaawhaata nili homehci miilahi kikinooloowe nihi kookwe-neefa-kaaci neh packama hiina hina mesenehko mecimi haamwelehko waapanaaci hotelahi

Now he that betrayed him had given them a token, saying, Whomsoever I shall kiss, that is he; take him, and lead him away safely.

45. mecimi yeh piyaaci weelena hotfaali nili mecimi lepaayii hiwa chiine hopackamaali

And when he was come, straightway he came to him, and saith, Rabbi; and kissed him.

46. mecimi nihki homawinachaawaali holeciwa chiine homesenaawaali

And they laid hands on him, and took him.

47. payeekwa nekoti nihi maalaakwahi neniipawita holohfena hokiskhika mecimi hopkitehwaali nili hotaloolaakanali hina moospimekofiiwi mhkateewkolaye chiine hokiskehsethwaali

But a certain one of them that stood by drew his sword, and smote the servant of the high priest, and struck off his ear.

48. mecimi haapafse ciisisii ha kipiyeci lohfaapwa paasi kimawinehwaawa ciikoniwehfi kipiyeci kiskhikanipwa chiine cifhikana wahsi mawinachiyeekwe

And Jesus answered and said unto them, Are ye come out, as against a robber, with swords and staves to seize me?

49. tfene waapaki nitapi wiici kiilawa hini mamaatomeewikamikoki nipemi kakehkimiwe mata kimesenipwa payeekwa wahsi menawah nili tepilo heewikaateewali hokwaawfetooteeki hoci yooma silawiipi hotelahi

I was daily with you in the temple teaching, and ye took me not: but this is done that the scriptures might be fulfilled.

50. mecimi caayahki nihki hosimooki chiine honakalaawaali

And they all left him, and fled.

51. chiine naanekoti mayaanileniili howiici neekalekooli hopah niimeli mafaanimota hakhooli sahsaakitwiili mecimi nihki homesenaawaali nili

And a certain young man followed with him, having a linen cloth cast about him, over his naked body: and they lay hold on him;

52. payeekwa hina honakacita hini mafaanimota mecimi hosimo sahsaakitwi

but he left the linen cloth, and fled naked.

53. chiine nihki nili moospimekofiiwi mhkateewkolayeeli hotesiwelaawaali ciisisiili mecimi nitasi hopiyeci maawaskaamekohi hina nihi caayahki hokimaawi mhkateewkolayehi chiine nihi kikilenihi chiine nihi yaayawikeelici

And they led Jesus away to the high priest: and there come together with him all the chief priests and the elders and the scribes.

54. chiine piita neyehka pelowihi hoteh neekalaali tepilooke piitike hini yaatah tepoweelici nili moospimekofiiwi mhkateewkolayeeli mecimi peemi wiitapiimaaci nihi wiyehsimekofiiwenhhi chiine peemi hawafoci hini tah teepahkoleeki skote

And Peter had followed him afar off, even within, into the court of the high priest; and he was sitting with the officers, and warming himself in the light of the fire.

55. howe nihki hokimaawi mhkateewkolayeeki chiine hina caayahki teepoweeta honatonehamawaawaali ciisisiili teepweewe wahsi nepooweneki si poonaawaaci mecimi hokwiilaanaawa hini

Now the chief priests and the whole council sought witness against Jesus to put him to death; and found it not.

56. ksake meci miyaasi teepweewe hopahkinamawaawaali mecimi hini hoteepweewenwa mata maawatwi nekotwaacimooyaali

For many bare false witness against him, and their witness agreed not together.

57. chiine nitasi naanekoti pemi pafekwi mecimi miyaasi teepweewe hopahkinamawaali

And there stood up certain, and bare false witness against him, saying,

58. ninootawaape hina neh macilota yooma mamaatomeewikamikwi holeciwali weeci mectooteeki mecimi nhfoko ne hopatena kotaki pwaayaa holeciwali hoci mectooteeki hiwa hiwali

We heard him say, I will destroy this temple that is made with hands, and in three days I will build another made without hands.

59. chiine mata teetepilahi yooni si maawatwi nekotwaacimooyaali hoteepweewenwa

And not even so did their witness agree together.

60. chiine hina moospimekofiiwi mhkateewkolaye pafekwi hini heelekhi chiine honatohtawaali ciisisiili ha mata wiyehi kithaapafse nehiwe hini yohkoma kicahtawaacimekooki hotelaali

And the high priest stood up in the midst, and asked Jesus, saying, Answerest thou nothing? what is it which these witness against thee?

61. payeekwa hotaayitatena honooleewiiwe mecimi mata wiyehi haapafse nohki hina moospimekofiiwi mhkateewkolaye honatohtawaali ha kiiya hina klaistii nili hokwihfali hina kisaaciwefina hotelaali

But he held his peace, and answered nothing. Again the high priest asked him, and saith unto him, Art thou the Christ, the Son of the Blessed?

62. mecimi ciisisii niiya hina mecimi keh neewaawa kiilawa hina hokwihfali hileni pemi lematapite hini homayaawiinhkiki waasikaki chiine pemi piyeci wiiteetake nili paafkwahki menhkwatoki hoci hisiwe

And Jesus said, I am: and ye shall see the Son of man sitting at the right hand of power, and coming with the clouds of heaven.

63. mecimi hina moospimekofiiwi mhkateewkolaye holelhkinaana hopiitenikana chiine nehiwe keewaki ke hoci skata leelemaape teepweewenaki

And the high priest rent his clothes, and saith, What further need have we of witnesses?

64. kimehci nootaanaawa hini pahtaamoowe nehiwe kitesiteheepwa hisiwe mecimi caayahki nihki homatahkowaalaawaali wahsi nepoowefilici

Ye have heard the blasphemy: what think ye? And they all condemned him to be worthy of death.

65. mecimi naaleta hoalemi fiifekwaalaawaali chiine hokipiikweewhaawaali chiine hopiipkwilecwhaawaali chiine moosikiiskwaacimolo hotelaawaali chiine nihki wiyehsimekofiiwenaki hotahpenaawaali howiitatwhaawaali holeciwa

And some began to spit on him, and to cover his face, and to buffet him, and to say unto him, Prophesy: and the officers received him with blows of their hands.

66. chiine yeesi piita siipaaci hapici hini tah tepoweeki nitasi piyeeli nekoti nihi hotikwefemhhi hina moospimekofiiwi mhkateewkolaye

And as Peter was beneath in the court, there cometh one of the maids of the high priest;

67. mecimi hina honeewaali piitali peemi hawafolici homemekinaapamaali chiine kiila nehfaapi kiwiiciwi hina naaseliinileni ciisisii hiwali

and seeing Peter warming himself, she looked upon him, and saith, Thou also wast with the Nazarene, even Jesus.

68. payeekwa kiyaacimo mata niwaakota nohki mata ninenohta kiila yeeyoyani hisiwe chiine lohfe hini ta-spahkwikaaniki heewa mecimi hina naapeeya kalhootamwa

But he denied, saying, I neither know, nor understand what thou sayest: and he went out into the porch; and the cock crew.

69. chiine nili hkweefali honookooli mecimi yaama hina nekoti nihki hotalemi hilahi hina nihi neniipawilici maalaakwahi

And the maid saw him, and began again to say to them that stood by, This is one of them.

70. payeekwa nohki kiyaacimo hini chiine peloocihi nohki nihki neniipawicki maalaakwahi teepweewe kiila hina nekoti nihki ksake keeleliiwileni kiila hotekohi piita

But he again denied it. And after a little while again they that stood by said to Peter, Of a truth thou art one of them; for thou art a Galilaean.

71. payeekwa halemi maci kalawi mecimi mataamo mata niwaakoma yaama hileni yaacimeekwe hisiwe

But he began to curse, and to swear, I know not this man of whom ye speak.

72. mecimi weelena hini mawi-niisene hina naapeeya kalhootamwa chiine piita homhkaweeleta hini kalawiiwe wihsi pwaa hini niisene kalhootaki hina naapeeya nhfene keh kiyaacimi yeekoci ciisisiili mecimi yeh memekineeletaki hini wihfakwe

And straightway the second time the cock crew. And Peter called to mind the word, how that Jesus said unto him, Before the cock crow twice, thou shalt deny me thrice. And when he thought thereon, he wept.

Mark:15

1. chiine weelena hini wayaapaki nihki hokimaawi mhkateewkolayeeki kileki nihki kikileniiki chiine yaayawikeecki mecimi hina caayahki teepoweeta tepoweeki chiine hokiciipilaawaali ciisisiili mecimi hotaamwelaawaali chiine paalatiili hopakfenamawaawaali nili

And straightway in the morning the chief priests with the elders and scribes, and the whole council, held a consultation, and bound Jesus, and carried him away, and delivered him up to Pilate.

2. mecimi paalatii honatohtawaali ha kiila hina hokimaamwaali nihki coosaki hotelaali mecimi hina pemi haapafse kiila kiteyo hotelaali

And Pilate asked him, Art thou the King of the Jews? And he answering saith unto him, Thou sayest.

3. chiine nihki hokimaawi mhkateewkolayeeki hocahtawaacimaawaali meci wiyehi

And the chief priests accused him of many things.

4. chiine paalatii nohki honatohtawaali ha mata wiyehi kithaapafse waapatano meci wiyehi kicahtawaacimekooki nihki hotelaali

And Pilate again asked him, saying, Answerest thou nothing? behold how many things they accuse thee of.

5. payeekwa ciisisii mata kiteeni haapafse wiyehi weecikeenahi paalatii kwakwehtaanitehe

But Jesus no more answered anything; insomuch that Pilate marveled.

6. howe hini tah wihfenhcikeeki hopaapakfenamawahi nihi nekoti kiikeenikaafali nili neetotamaakoci nihi

Now at the feast he used to release unto them one prisoner, whom they asked of him.

7. mecimi nitasi hapiwa nekoti palepasii yaaloofo seksinwa kciipifo wiici nihi mayehci noochetiitamelici hokapenaliimwa hileniiki hini tah noochetiitamowaaci macilawiiki nhsiweewe

And there was one called Barabbas, lying bound with them that had made insurrection, men who in the insurrection had committed murder.

8. chiine nihki mehseelekki spemeki heeki mecimi hotalemi natotamawaawaali wahsi hini silawiilici yaasilawihtawaaci

And the multitude went up and began to ask him to do as he was wont to do unto them.

9. mecimi paalatii hotaapaftawahi ha kitesiteheepwa wahsi pakfenamoolako hina hokimaamwaali nihki coosaki hotelahi

And Pilate answered them, saying, Will ye that I release unto you the King of the Jews?

10. ksake homooleeleta yeesi hahpeeletiiwe nihki hokimaawi mhkateewkolayeeki hoci mehci pakfenamaakeeki nili

For he perceived that for envy the chief priests had delivered him up.

11. payeekwa nihki hokimaawi mhkateewkolayeeki hokicitaamaawahi nihi mehseelelici wahsi palepasiili kaaciika pelhamawaaci hina

But the chief priests stirred up the multitude, that he should rather release Barabbas unto them.

12. chiine paalatii nohki haapafse mecimi nehiwe howe ne hpenala hina hokimaamwaali nihki coosaki yeeleekwe hotelahi

And Pilate again answered and said unto them, What then shall I do unto him whom ye call the King of the Jews?

13. mecimi nihki haasitefhwi lahootamooki nohki

And they cried out again, Crucify him.

14. chiine paalatii koociwe nehiwesi mecaafiki silawi hotelahi payeekwa nihki hanhhiweewi wiyakahootamooki haasitefhwi lahootamooki

And Pilate said unto them, Why, what evil hath he done? But they cried out exceedingly, Crucify him.

15. mecimi paalatii wahsi teepeelemhaaci nihi mehseelelici pemi sitehe hopelhamawahi palepasiili chiine hoteh pakfenaali ciisisiili yeh mehci lihfiiwanhhwaaci wahsi haasitefhoofolici

And Pilate, wishing to content the multitude, released unto them Barabbas, and delivered Jesus, when he had scourged him, to be crucified.

16. chiine nihki samaakanaki hotesiwelaawaali piitike hini tah tepoweeki pletooliyami hini mecimi homaawatomaawahi melhske nekotweelena samaakanhhi

And the soldiers led him away within the court, which is the Praetorium; and they call together the whole band.

17. chiine nihki hopiitenikehaawaali meskwiskipakiyaaki mecimi hopemi hapkeenaanaawa kaawihi hoci hokimaawipetakhoowe hini hopetakhwaawaali nili

And they clothe him with purple, and plaiting a crown of thorns, they put it on him;

18. chiine hotalem hosilawaalaawaali hei hokimaamwaali nihki coosaki

and they began to salute him, Hail, King of the Jews!

19. chiine hopaapkitewhaawaali wiileki mhfaskwalwi chiine hofiifekwaalaawaali mecimi pemi waakiciikwaneskaaki hosasilawehaawaali

And they smote his head with a reed, and did spit upon him, and bowing their knees worshipped him.

20. chiine yeh mehci waapalaachaawaaci nihki holiikinaawaali hini meskwiskipakiyaaki chiine hopiitenikehaawaali wiila hopiitenikana

And when they had mocked him, they took off from him the purple, and put on him his garments. And they lead him out to crucify him.

21. chiine nihki homamiiloowihkawaawaali nekoti pemi pemhfeeli saimanii saailiinii hoci hini piileski homooli nili hohfwaali heeleksenhta chiine loofasi wahsi wiiteemekowaaci wahsi hina menawahke haamwetawaaci hotaasitehfekiimilici

And they compel one passing by, Simon of Cyrene, coming from the country, the father of Alexander and Rufus, to go with them, that he might bear his cross.

22. chiine nihki hoteh piyeelaawaali nili hini kalhkoofa tasi hini hokanaatepiki yaasi laapaatotoote hini

And they bring him unto the place Golgotha, which is, being interpreted, The place of a skull.

23. mecimi wiisa miilaawaali waiini kilekfetoote maa payeekwa hina mata hotahpena hini

And they offered him wine mingled with myrrh: but he received it not.

24. chiine hotaasitefhwaawaali nihki mecimi lelhskonamaatihi hopiitenikana heelekiina nihi kiskinikanitalwaatihi nili wah mameki moosa nekoti

And they crucify him, and part his garments among them, casting lots upon them, what each should take.

25. chiine hini hine mawi-nhfene yaatefaki chiine hotaasitefhwaawaali nili

And it was the third hour, and they crucified him.

26. chiine hini spawikeewe hocahtawaacimoofoowe hoci mehtawikaate spemeki niliini hokimaamwaali nihki coosaki lawikaate

And the superscription of his accusation was written over, THE KING OF THE JEWS.

27. chiine wiici nili nihki hotaasitefhwaawahi niiswi ciikoniwehfihi nekoti homayaawiinhkiki chiine nekoti honamaciinhkiki

And with him they crucify two robbers; one on his right hand, and one on his left.

29. chiine nihki nitasi peepemhfecki holhskimaawaali pemi papawkweskaaki chiine hei kiila mecilotaka hini mamaatomeewikamikwi mecimi nhfoko hini weepatenaka

And they that passed by railed on him, wagging their heads, and saying, Ha! thou that destroyest the temple, and buildest it in three days,

30. waapanestoolo kiiya mecimi hini yaasitehfeki hoci laasiweelo hotelaawaali

save thyself, and come down from the cross.

31. hiini yaska nehfaapi nihki hokimaawi mhkateewkolayeeki hopemi waapalaachaawaali heelekiina wiilawa kileki nihki yaayawikeecki howaapaneshahi kotakhi wiiya hotaalwi waapanesto

In like manner also the chief priests mocking him among themselves with the scribes said, He saved others; himself he cannot save.

32. wiilaani hina klaistii nili hokimaamali hiswiila howe kwasfaate hini yaasitehfeki hoci wahsi menawah neekeeyakwe mecimi teepwehseeyakwe hiwaki chiine nihi weewiici haasitefhoofolici homaci kaloolekohi

Let the Christ, the King of Israel, now come down from the cross, that we may see and believe. And they that were crucified with him reproached him.

33. chiine hine hini mawi-nekotwahfene yaatefaki yeh piyeeyaaki nitasi hahteewi peepekicaaki hini mefhiike hasiskiiki paalohi hini mawi-caakatfene yaatefaki

And when the sixth hour was come, there was darkness over the whole land until the ninth hour.

34. chiine ta hini caakatefene haatefaki ciisisii holaamahootamwa hiloi hiloi lema sepakfenai nimanetooma nimanetooma koociwe kiila kipakiteelemi yaasi laapaatotoote hini

And at the ninth hour Jesus cried with a loud voice, Eloi, Eloi, lama sabachthani? which is, being interpreted, My God, my God, why hast thou forsaken me?

35. chiine naaleta nihki maalaakwahi neniipawicki yeh nootamowaaci hini waapamehko howihkomaali hilaicali hiwaki

And some of them that stood by, when they heard it, said, Behold, he calleth Elijah.

36. chiine nekoti memekwi mecimi hopemi hokwikamhaali kcikamiiwihatowali hokwaawi pskipaapo mhfaskwalwiki hoteh poonaali nili chiine homiilaali

And one ran, and filling a sponge full of vinegar, put it on a reed, and gave him to drink, saying, Let be; let us see

wahsi menelici wiilaani waapamaataako kwehkwi hilaicali weh piyeeli wahsi laasiwenekoci hiwa

whether Elijah cometh to take him down.

37. chiine ciisisii holaamahootamwa mecimi hopakfenaali nili ciipali

And Jesus uttered a loud voice, and gave up the ghost.

38. mecimi hini laapicimota hini mamaatomeewikamikoki hoci niisweelena si pahfehka hini spemeki hoci paalohi hini sahkiki

And the veil of the temple was rent in twain from the top to the bottom.

39. chiine hina kaptiina maalaakwahi neniipawita yeelahfamiilici nili yeh neemeki yeesi yooni si pakfenaaci nili ciipali teepweewe yoolooni hokwihfali maneto hiwa

And when the centurion, which stood by over against him, saw that he so gave up the ghost, he said, Truly this man was the Son of God.

40. chiine nitasi nehfaapi hapiiki hkweeki hopemi hilaapamaawaali pelowihi hoci heelekiina nihi hapiiki neyiiswi melii mekiteliina chiine melii nili hokiwaali ceemhsii hina hotahpiifa chiine coosisi mecimi seloomi

And there were also women beholding from afar: among whom were both Mary Magdalene, and Mary the mother of James the less and of Joses, and Salome;

41. nihiini hine keeleliiki ye hapici honeekalekohi mecimi homiisamaakohi chiine meci kotakaki hkweeki peepiyeci wiitfeemekoci colooseelemiiki si

who, when he was in Galilee, followed him, and ministered unto him; and many other women which came up with him unto Jerusalem.

42. chiine ye holaakwiifiki howe ksake hini hahteewi hini nanahiwe hini keela hini waapake hini halwaakahsi kaasekiki

And when even was now come, because it was the Preparation, that is, the day before the sabbath,

43. nitasi piyeewa coosii haalimefiye hoci hileni taatepoweeta hotakeelemekwi nhhalwaafiiweni hiina nehfaapi netawaapataka hini hokimaawitaamhkomi maneto mecimi wiisikiteheewi nhheewa paalatiili chiine natotamaake nili wiiyaanali ciisisii

there came Joseph of Arimathaea, a councillor of honourable estate, who also himself was looking for the kingdom of God; and he boldly went in unto Pilate, and asked for the body of Jesus.

44. mecimi paalatii kwakwehtaanitehe kwehkwi toke neyehka hina nepwa mecimi hotahpimaali nili kaptiinali honatohtawaali kwehkwi toke hina neyehka maalaakwasi mehci nepwa

And Pilate marveled if he were already dead: and calling unto him the centurion, he asked him whether he had been any while dead.

45. chiine hini yeh waakotelekoci nili kaptiinali wiilaani hoteleeletamawaali coosiili nili nepoowenali

And when he learned it of the centurion, he granted the corpse to Joseph.

46. chiine hina hotepena mafaanimota mecimi hopemi penenaali nili hofepatenaali hini mafaanimotaaki mecimi hoteh seksimaali nepoowaalakoki mayehci siikoneki hoci waalhkwathooteeki chiine hoteh kolepenaali siikonali hini skwaateeki hini nepoowaalakwi

And he bought a linen cloth, and taking him down, wound him in the linen cloth, and laid him in a tomb which had been hewn out of a rock; and he rolled a stone against the door of the tomb.

47. mecimi melii mekiteliina chiine melii nili hokeeli coosisi hotelaapataanaawa tah seksimoofolici

And Mary Magdalene and Mary the mother of Joses beheld where he was laid.

152   MARK

Mark:16

1. chiine yeh pemhfeeyaaki hini halwaakahsi kaasekiki melii mekiteliina chiine melii nili hokeeli ceemhsii chiine seloomi hopiyeetoonaawa seekimiyaakoki wahsi nihki menawahke piyaawaaci mecimi sesonamawaawaaci nili

And when the sabbath was past, Mary Magdalene, and Mary the mother of James, and Salome, bought spices, that they might come and anoint him.

2. chiine kwelahwaapaki hini weski kaasekiki yeesi mehci hini manetoowi kiisekiki piyeeki nihki hini nepoowaalakoki ye hina kiisekikiisfwa piyeetahkofaki

And very early on the first day of the week, they come to the tomb when the sun was risen.

3. mecimi neefawe ke hoci kolepenamaakona nili siikonali hini skwaateeki hini nepoowaalakwi pemi hitiiki heelekiina wiilawa

And they were saying among themselves, Who shall roll us away the stone from the door of the tomb?

4. mecimi pemi maa laapiiki honeemenaawa yeesi nili siikonali hotaanaaki si kolepenoofolici teewa hina hanhhiweewi mhsikilwa

and looking up, they see that the stone is rolled back: for it was exceeding great.

5. chiine pemi piicfeeki hini nepoowaalakwi honeewaawaali mayaanileniili hoskici lematapiili hini mayaawi wayeetahkwe waapi pihtawipiitenikeeli mecimi kwakwehtaaniteheeki

And entering into the tomb, they saw a young man sitting on the right side, arrayed in a white robe; and they were amazed.

6. chiine hina teki kwakwehtaaniteheeko kinatonewhaawa ciisisii hina naaselefileni mayehci haasitefhoofota honhska mata hotasi hapiwa waapatamoko hini tah seksimaawaaci nihki hotelahi

And he saith unto them, Be not amazed: ye seek Jesus, the Nazarene, which hath been crucified: he is risen; he is not here: behold, the place where they laid him!

7. weeka nhhaakone wiitamawehko hokakehkimaafhi mecimi piita keeleliiki kiteh niikaanihekowa nitasi keh neewaawa yeelelwaakwe hina

But go, tell his disciples and Peter, He goeth before you into Galilee: there shall ye see him, as he said unto you.

8. chiine nihki lohfeeki mecimi hini nepoowaalakwi hotesimooki ksake neyehka papaweskaawe chiine kwakwehtaaniteheewe hotfekonaawa mecimi mata wiyehi hotelaawaali wiyeefali ksake kwpeneeki

And they went out, and fled from the tomb; for trembling and astonishment had come upon them: and they said nothing to any one; for they were afraid.

9. howe ye honhskaaci kwelahwaapaki hini weski kaasekiki yeesi mehci hini manetoowi kiisekiki honawtiimaali melii mekiteliinali nhhihta niliini hoci mehci lohfe pakitamawaali niiswahfwi waninehfihi

Now when he was risen early on the first day of the week, he appeared first to Mary Magdalene, from whom he had cast out seven devils.

10. hina weepfe mecimi howiitamawahi nihi mayehci pah wiitfeemaacki nili yeesi nihki maweewaaci mecimi wihfakweewaaci

She went and told them that had been with him, as they mourned and wept.

11. mecimi nihki yeh nootaakeewaaci yeesi nili lenaweewilici mecimi mehci neewaaci hina haanwehseeki

And they, when they heard that he was alive, and had been seen of her, disbelieved.

12. chiine hahkowihi hine yooloma wiyehi hina kotaki yeeki hotesi tepinawkofiimahi niiswi nihi yeesi nihki pemhfeewaaci yeele haawaaci hini piileski

And after these things he was manifested in another form unto two of them, as they walked, on their way into the country.

13. chiine nihki weepfeeki mecimi hini howiitamawaawahi nihi maisi naaleta mata nohki nihki hoteepwehtawaawahi nihi

And they went away and told it unto the rest: neither believed they them.

14. chiine hahkowihi hina hotepinawkofiimahi nihi metahfwi-kite-nekoti nhhalwaaka nihi yeelahkeepilici tah wihfenilici chiine hocihkawahi nihi hopwaateepwehseewenwa mecimi hosiipiteheewenwa ksake mata nihki hoteepwehtawaawahi nihi mayehci nookoci yeesi mehci honhskaaci

And afterward he was manifested unto the eleven themselves as they sat at meat; and he upbraided them with their unbelief and hardness of heart, because they believed not them which had seen him after he was risen.

15. mecimi nhhaakone kiilawa mefhiike hini yeelekokwahkamikiki chiine pemi nanahimiweeko hini howesi piyeetaacimoowe melhske hini mehteelemekofiiweneki hotelahi

And he said unto them, Go ye into all the world, and preach the gospel to the whole creation.

16. hina teeteepwehseeta mecimi fafahkwi holelhoofo weh waapaneshoofo weeka hina yaanwehseeta weh miyaalahkowaaloofo

He that believeth and is baptized shall be saved; but he that disbelieveth shall be condemned.

17. chiine halayooloma kikinooloowena weh wiiteemekonaawa nihki teeteepwehseecki niwiifooweneki weh lohfe pakilaawahi waninehfihi weh kalawiiki nihki weskiki wiilano

And these signs shall follow them that believe: in my name shall they cast out devils; they shall speak with new tongues;

18. weh mamaawahi manetohi nihki mecimi kwehkwi menowaate wiyehisi naanhsiweeyaaki mata hini weh wiyehisi hahkwinalekonaawa hoskici weh si pakfenamawaawahi holeciwa nihi yeekwilokeelici mecimi nihki weh waapanhsiiki

they shall take up serpents, and if they drink any deadly thing, it shall in no wise hurt them; they shall lay hands on the sick, and they shall recover.

19. weecikeenahi howe hina teepeelemiweeta ciisisii yeh mehci kaloolaaci nihi menhkwatoki si hotahpenoofo mecimi hini ta homayaawiinhkiki maneto si lematapiwa

So then the Lord Jesus, after he had spoken unto them, was received up into heaven, and sat down at the right hand of God.

20. chiine nihki weepfeeki mecimi pemi nanahimiweeki mefhiike tasi hina teepeelemiweeta hopemi wiici pekatefiimahi nihi chiine hopemi wiitootamawahi hini kalawiiwe nili hoci kikinooloowena nayeekasiweeyaaki heemen

And they went forth, and preached everywhere, the Lord working with them, and confirming the word by the signs that followed. Amen.

LUKE

Luke:1

1. ksake yeesi meci neyehka mamowaaci holecwaaki wahsi halemaapiyeenamowaaci haacimoowe nele si wiyehi mayehci hokwaawfeki heelekiina kiilawe

Forasmuch as many have taken in hand to draw up a narrative concerning those matters which have been fulfilled among us,

2. teetepilahi yeesi nihki pakfenamoolakwe nili nihkiini hine halemahkamikatwi hoci hoskiisekowi teepweeweniwiiki mecimi maamiisamaakeecki hini kalawiiwe

even as they delivered them unto us, which from the beginning were eyewitnesses and ministers of the word,

3. howesa sinaakwatwi hini wahsi niila nehfaapi teewahi nimehci mayaawi neekatona hini yeelaamiyehfeki caayahki wiyehi hine weski hoci wahsi hawikoola weelahkootiiyaaki kiila kici kisowileni fiaafilas

it seemed good to me also, having traced the course of all things accurately from the first, to write unto thee in order, most excellent Theophilus;

4. wahsi kiila menawahi waakotamani hini meeyaawhki yooni si nili kalawiiwena keekehkimoofoyani

that thou mightest know the certainty concerning the things wherein thou wast instructed.

5. hine tah kakiisekanemici heletii cotiyeewi hokima nitasi hapiwa nekoti mhkateewkolaye sekolaayes' sifo hini yeelaapiyehsiki hepaica hoci chiine hina hopoonaali wiiwali nihi hotaaneefhi helani hoci mecimi hilisipef si wiifooli

There was in the days of Herod, king of Judaea, a certain priest named Zacharias, of the course of Abijah: and he had a wife of the daughters of Aaron, and her name was Elisabeth.

6. chiine neyiiswi nihki mayaawiilefiiki yeelahfamiilici manetooli hopemi neekataanaawa caayahki nili tepikeemoowena mecimi hokotaacimiweewena hina teepeelemiweeta matalaakwa mataiini

And they were both righteous before God, walking in all the commandments and ordinances of the Lord blameless.

7. chiine mata hopoonaawaali hapelohfali ksake hina hilisipef mata hayackofi mecimi neyiiswi howe pelowi piyeeki hokakiisekanemwa

And they had no child, because that Elisabeth was barren, and they both were now well stricken in years.

8. howe hini piyeemikatwi yeheeyehi hina pekatenaki hini hotesimekofiiwe mhkateewkolaye yeelahfamiici maneto hini yeelahkootiiyaaki hotelaapiyehsinoowe

Now it came to pass, while he executed the priest's office before God in the order of his course,

9. yeesfeki hini yaasilawiiki hini mhkateewkolaye hotesimekofiiwe wahsi piicfaaci hinwili hini homamaatomeewikamikomi hina teepeelemiweeta mecimi fakfaki waakimiyaakoki

according to the custom of the priest's office, his lot was to enter into the temple of the Lord and burn incense.

10. chiine nihki caayahki mehseelekki lenaweeki peemi mamaatomeewaaci faakici hine yaatefaki tah fakfooteeki waakimiyaakoki

And the whole multitude of the people were praying without at the hour of incense.

11. chiine honawtiimekooli nitasi hotenhcaliimali hina teepeelemiweeta pemi niipawiili hini mayaawi wayeetahkwe hini waakimiyaakokiwi pootefamaacika

And there appeared unto him an angel of the Lord standing on the right side of the altar of incense.

12. mecimi sekolaayes' petfakitehe yeh neewaaci nili chiine kwpeneewe hotfeko

And Zacharias was troubled when he saw him, and fear fell upon him.

13. payeekwa hina henhcali teki kwpenelo sekolaayes' ksake hini kinanahpaacimoowe nootoote mecimi kiiwa hilisipef keh pah niimaakwa hokwihfimaali chiine kiila caanii keh sitamawa howiifoowe hotelaali

But the angel said unto him, Fear not, Zacharias: because thy supplication is heard, and thy wife Elisabeth shall bear thee a son, and thou shalt call his name John.

14. mecimi keh poona kiila hosasilepwaawe mecimi howesilepwaawe chiine meci we hosasilepwaawefiiki tah niikilici

And thou shalt have joy and gladness; and many shall rejoice at his birth.

15. ksake we mhsiilefi hina hini hotelaapiiweneki hina teepeelemiweeta mecimi teki hina weh menwa waiini weelaa teki waasikaki menoowe chiine nili hofepi hocacaalahkwali we hokwihsinooli teetepilahi hokeeli holaamotaakanilici hoci

For he shall be great in the sight of the Lord, and he shall drink no wine nor strong drink; and he shall be filled with the Holy Ghost, even from his mother's womb.

16. chiine hina meci nihi hotapelohfemhhi hiswiila nili teepeelemiweelici homanetoomwaali weh si kotekonahi nihi

And many of the children of Israel shall he turn unto the Lord their God.

17. mecimi yeelahfamiikwelici we heewa hini hilaica hotelefiiweneki mecimi howiisikatowiiweneki wahsi nihi hapelofhi si kotekonamawaaci nili hotehiwa nihki hofimaaki mecimi nili pwaayaa melonehseelici wahsi pemhfeelici hini holepwaaweneki hina teepasawiilefita wahsi hosimehcilotamawaaci nili teepeelemiweelici lenawehi homehcitehehtaakohi

And he shall go before his face in the spirit and power of Elijah, to turn the hearts of the fathers to the children, and the disobedient to walk in the wisdom of the just; to make ready for the Lord a people prepared for him.

18. mecimi sekolaayes' taaniwe ne hoci waakota yooma ksake pasitoofa hileni niila mecimi niiwa pelowi piyeewa hokakiisekanema hotelaali nili henhcaliili

And Zacharias said unto the angel, Whereby shall I know this? for I am an old man, and my wife well stricken in years.

19. mecimi hina henhcali pemi haapafse keepyeelii niila naaniipawita hini hotapiiweneki maneto chiine niwaawiinekoopi wahsi kaloolela kiila mecimi wahsi piyeetoola yooloma howesi piyeetaacimoowena

And the angel answering said unto him, I am Gabriel, that stand in the presence of God; and I was sent to speak unto thee, and to bring thee these good tidings.

20. chiine waapatano keh matalaakwa tasimoowefi kiila mecimi ke haalwi kalawi paalohi hine kaasekiki yooloma wiyehi weh piyeemikato ksake mata kiteepwehtaana nikalawiiwena we hokwaawfetoote nili hine yeelaakwaamefiiyaaki hotelaali

And behold, thou shalt be silent and not able to speak, until the day that these things shall come to pass, because thou believedst not my words, which shall be fulfilled in their season.

21. chiine nihki lenaweeki peemi hahkawaapamaawaaci sekolaayesiili mecimi kwakwehtaaniteheeki yeh neekaafiilici hini mamaatomeewikamikoki

And the people were waiting for Zacharias, and they marveled while he tarried in the temple.

22. mecimi hina yeh piyeci lohfaaci hotaalwi kaloolahi nihi chiine nihki moositeheeki yeesi hina mehci neemeki wiyehsi namoowe hini mamaatomeewikamikoki chiine yaska hina hokci pemi kakehkinootenamawahi nihi mecimi yaska mata kalawi

And when he came out, he could not speak unto them: and they perceived that he had seen a vision in the temple: and he continued making signs unto them, and remained dumb.

23. chiine hini piyeemikatwi hine laakwasi nili tfoko homiisamaakeewe ye hokwihfeki weepfe hini hoci yeetaaci wiikiwa heewa

And it came to pass, when the days of his ministration were fulfilled, he departed unto his house.

24. chiine hahkowihi hine yooloma kaasekiki wiiwali hilisipefiili hackooli mecimi hina hokkito wiiya niyaalanwi kiisahfo

And after these days Elisabeth his wife conceived; and she hid herself five months, saying,

25. halayini hina teepeelemiweeta yeesi mehci hpenasici hine kaasekiki tah waapamici wahsi pakfatenaki nimacimoofoowe heelekiina hileniiki hiwapi

Thus hath the Lord done unto me in the days wherein he looked upon me, to take away my reproach among men.

26. howe hini mawi-nekotwahfwi kiisfoki henhcali keepyeelii manetooli hoci keeleliiwi hoteewe si waawiinoofo naaselefi sitoote

Now in the sixth month the angel Gabriel was sent from God unto a city of Galilee, named Nazareth,

27. seskiikweefali leskoofo kaloosiwehoofooli hileniili coosii sifooli hini teepitiiwika hoci hina mecimi hina seskiikweefa melii sifo

to a virgin betrothed to a man whose name was Joseph, of the house of David; and the virgin's name was Mary.

28. mecimi hina hopiicfeemaali nili chiine hei kiila meemoospeelemoofota hina teepeelemiweeta wiiciwi kiila hotelaali

And he came in unto her, and said, Hail, thou that art highly favoured, the Lord is with thee.

29. payeekwa hina holaami hopetfakiteheeskaako hini hiyoowe mecimi memekinitehe nehiwe toke si hosilawaatiiwe menawahi yooma si tehe

But she was greatly troubled at the saying, and cast in her mind what manner of salutation this might be.

30. mecimi hina henhcali teki wiisaalepwaalo melii ksake kimehci mhka maneto hoci haliweelemoofoowe

And the angel said unto her, Fear not, Mary: for thou hast found favour with God.

31. mecimi waapatano kiila ke hacko kilaamotaakaneki chiine keh piyeela hokwihfima mecimi ciisisii keh sitamawa howiifoowe

And behold, thou shalt conceive in thy womb, and bring forth a son, and shalt call his name JESUS.

32. we mhsiilefi hina chiine nili hokwihfali hina kci moospi we haaloofo mecimi hina teepeelemiweeta maneto weh miilaali nili hini hokimaawi hotpapiiwenilici hohfali teepitiili

He shall be great, and shall be called the Son of the Most High: and the Lord God shall give unto him the throne of his father David:

33. chiine we hokimaawta hini ceekapii hotfwikamikifiiwe kookwelaakwasi mecimi hini hokimaawiiwe matalaakwa weh ceeyehkwatwi hotelaali

and he shall reign over the house of Jacob for ever; and of his kingdom there shall be no end.

34. mecimi melii nehiwe weh si hini hinwi yooma nipemi neeme mata niwaakoma hileni hotelaali nili henhcaliili

And Mary said unto the angel, How shall this be, seeing I know not a man?

35. chiine haapafse hina henhcali mecimi hina hofepi hocacaalahkwa weh piyeewa kiiyaaki mecimi hini howaasikakiimi hina kci moospi ke hawikanhskaako kiila yooni hoci nehfaapi hini hofepi wiyehi keekikatkwihtooteeki nili hokwihfali maneto weh sitoote

And the angel answered and said unto her, The Holy Ghost shall come upon thee, and the power of the Most High shall overshadow thee: wherefore also that which is to be born shall be called holy, the Son of God.

36. chiine waapami hilisipef kinhhalweeletiiwena hkweewa hina nehfaapi neyehka hacko hokwihfimaali homekipwehfiifiwiiweneki mecimi halayaama hina mawi-nekotwahfwi kiisfwa hoci hapiili hina pwaayaa hackota yaaloofota

And behold, Elisabeth thy kinswoman, she also hath conceived a son in her old age: and this is the sixth month with her that was called barren.

37. ksake maneto hoci kalawiiwe mata seskatwi waasikaki hotelaali

For no word from God shall be void of power.

38. mecimi melii waapami nili hotaloolaakaniikweefali hina teepeelemiweeta wiilaani hini hike niiyaaki yeesfeki kikalawiiwe hisiwe mecimi hina henhcali weepfe nili hoci

And Mary said, Behold, the handmaid of the Lord; be it unto me according to thy word. And the angel departed from her.

39. chiine melii pafekwi yooloone kaasekiki mecimi weeweetepi hini heele mamakwahkiki piileski heewa cotiyeewi hoteewe heewa

And Mary arose in these days and went into the hill country with haste, into a city of Judah;

40. chiine hini wiikiwa yeetaalici sekolaayesiili si piicfe mecimi hosilawaalaali hilisipefiili

and entered into the house of Zacharias and saluted Elisabeth.

41. chiine hini piyeemikatwi yeh nootaki hilisipef hini hosilawaatiiwe melii lemacfeeli nili hapelohfali holaamotaakaneki mecimi hokwihsinooli hilisipef nili hofepi hocacaalahkwali

And it came to pass, when Elisabeth heard the salutation of Mary, the babe leaped in her womb; and Elisabeth was filled with the Holy Ghost;

42. mecimi hopatena hokalaweewihsimoowe kileki holaami kalaweewihsimo kikisaacimekofi cehi kiila heelekiina hkweeki mecimi kisaacimekwatwi cehi hini mawifoowe kilaamotaakaneki hoci

and she lifted up her voice with a loud cry, and said, Blessed art thou among women, and blessed is the fruit of thy womb.

43. mecimi taaniwe hoci yooma niila wahsi nili hokeeli teepeelemita piyeci hotsici niila

And whence is this to me, that the mother of my Lord should come unto me?

44. ksake waapami hina hapelohfa lemacfe nilaamotaakaneki nitawakaawali yeh si piyeeyaaki hini kosilaweewihsimoowe ksake howesilepwa

For behold, when the voice of thy salutation came into mine ears, the babe leaped in my womb for joy.

45. mecimi kisaacimekofi cehi hina hkweewa teeteepwehseeta ksake nitasi we hahteeli hina hokwihsinoowe nili wiyehi hina teepeelemiweeta weeci mehci kalooloofoci hisiwe

And blessed is she that believed; for there shall be a fulfillment of the things which have been spoken to her from the Lord.

46. mecimi hisiwe melii mayaawiniiya tepilo homhsiilakimaali nili teepeelemiweelici

And Mary said, My soul doth magnify the Lord,

47. chiine nicacaalahkwa neyehka hosasilepwa manetooli niwaapanhsiimali

And my spirit hath rejoiced in God my Saviour.

48. ksake hina homehtaapata hini honanahpaaciilefiiwenilici hotaloolaakaniikweefali

For he hath looked upon the low estate of his handmaiden: For behold, from

ksake waapatano yooci hinoki caayahki
skwiilenaweeki kisaacimekofi ne haayekooki

henceforth all generations shall call me
blessed.

49. ksake hina waasikimekofita nimehcilotaakwa
mehsaaki wiyehi mecimi hofepiyaali cehi howiifoowe

For he that is mighty hath done to me
great things; And holy is his name.

50. chiine hokiteminaakweeletiiwe skwiilenawehi kite
skwiilenawehi sfenili nihi kwehfekoci

And his mercy is unto generations and
generations On them that fear him.

51. mehci waapatesiwe wiisikatowiiwe honehki hoci
homehci lhfwenahi nihi mehsiisiteheelici hini
hotehiwa hoci nanaacimemekiniteheeweneki

He hath shewed strength with his arm;
He hath scattered the proud in the
imagination of their heart.

52. homehci hokimaawi hotpapiiwenwa hoci penenahi
hokimaawoosaakanhhi mecimi homehci
moospeelemekwhahi nihi neenahpaaciilefilici

He hath put down princes from their
thrones, And hath exalted them of low
degree.

53. nihi sehkwaalawelici homehci teephoolahi howesi
wiyehi mecimi nihi peewaalici homehci
haameskawahi sesipaafihi

The hungry he hath filled with good
things; And the rich he hath sent empty
away.

54. homehci miilaali naatamaatiiwe hisfiilali
hotaloolaakanali wahsi hina menawahke
mhkaweeletaki kiteminaakweeletiiwe

He hath holpen Israel his servant, That he
might remember mercy

55. yeesi kaloolaaci hina kohfenahi heplehemiili
wayeeci mecimi homiinhkaanilici kookwelaakwasi

(As he spake unto our fathers) Toward
Abraham and his seed for ever.

56. mecimi melii howiicikeemaali nili nawito nhfwi
kiisahfo chiine peteki heewa yeetaaci wiikiwa

And Mary abode with her about three
months, and returned unto her house.

57. howe hilisipef nahiika piyeeyaali wahsi
niikiniweeci mecimi hopiyeelaali hokwihfimaali

Now Elisabeth's time was fulfilled that
she should be delivered; and she brought
forth a son.

58. chiine maapayecikaalekoci mecimi
nehalweelemaaci nootaakehi yeesi hina
teepeelemiweeta mehci mhsilotaki
hokiteminaakweeletiiwe nili wayeeci mecimi nihki
hosasilawaatiimaawaali nili

And her neighbours and her kinsfolk
heard that the Lord had magnified his
mercy towards her; and they rejoiced
with her.

59. chiine hini piyeemikatwi ta hini mawi-
nhfwaasikfokonakiki yeesi nihki piyaawaaci wahsi
kaawackolaawaaci nili hapelohfali mecimi nihki yehki
wih mehci sekolaayes' sinaawaali nili naawalwi hini
yeesifolici hohfali

And it came to pass on the eighth day,
that they came to circumcise the child;
and they would have called him
Zacharias, after the name of his father.

60. mecimi hokeeli haapafseeli mata hini weeka caanii
we haaloofo hiwali

And his mother answered and said, Not
so; but he shall be called John.

61. matalaakwa nehalweelemacki yaaloofota yooma
wiifoowe hotelaawaali nihki

And they said unto her, There is none of
thy kindred that is called by this name.

62. mecimi hoteh kakehkinootenamawaawaali hohfali
yeesiteheeci hina wah sinoofolici nili

And they made signs to his father, what
he would have him called.

63. chiine hina honatota wah ta hawikeeci mecimi
caanii si wiifooweni lawike mecimi nihki
kwakwehtaaniteheeki caayahki

And he asked for a writing tablet, and
wrote, saying, His name is John. And
they marveled all.

64. chiine hini hotooni tawenooteeli weelena chiine howiilani pelhskohkaali mecimi kalawi hopemi kisaacimekofihaali manetooli

And his mouth was opened immediately, and his tongue loosed, and he spake, blessing God.

65. chiine cihfefiiwe hotfekonaawa caayahki nihki kaayaawka peemi kaalaacki nihi mecimi caayahki yooloma hiyoowena pemi haatotoote saapoci mefhiike hini cotiyeewi mamakwahki piileski

And fear came on all that dwelt round about them: and all these sayings were noised abroad throughout all the hill country of Judaea.

66. chiine caayahki neenootakki nili hokicitaweeletaanaawa hotehiwaaki nehiwe howe weh lefi yaama hapelohfa ksake hini holeci hina teepeelemiweeta howiiciimeko hina hiwaki

And all that heard them laid them up in their heart, saying, What then shall this child be? For the hand of the Lord was with him.

67. chiine hohfali sekolaayesiili hokwihsinooli nili hofepi hocacaalahkwali mecimi moosikiiskwaacimooli

And his father Zacharias was filled with the Holy Ghost, and prophesied, saying,

68. kisaacimekofi cehi hina teepeelemiweeta nili homanetoomali hiswiila ksake hina mehci nawhiwe mecimi hopatenamawahi petekinoofoowe hotelenaweemhhi

Blessed be the Lord, the God of Israel; For he hath visited and wrought redemption for his people,

69. chiine kimehci kokwitenamaakona waapanhsiiwi wiiwiilali yeetaalici hini wiikiwaapeki hotaloolaakanali teepitiili

And hath raised up a horn of salvation for us In the house of his servant David

70. yeesi kalawici hini hotoonwa hoci hofepi homaamoosikiiskwemhhi mayehci hapilici sehkamika hoci

(As he spake by the mouth of his holy prophets which have been since the world began),

71. waapanhsiiwe kimateeletiiwenaaki hoci mecimi hini holeci caayahki saakeelemelakwe

Salvation from our enemies, and from the hand of all that hate us;

72. wahsi waapatesiweeci kiteminaakweeletiiwe kohfenahi wayeeci mecimi wahsi mhkaweeletaki hofepi homehtaacimoowe

To shew mercy towards our fathers, And to remember his holy covenant;

73. hini ciikinhkemoowe ceeciikinhkemaaci heplehemiili kohfenaali

The oath which he sware unto Abraham our father,

74. wahsi wiilaani leeletamoolakwe yeesi pemi kwakwatenoofoyakwe nili holeciwa hoci kimateeletiiwenaaki wih pekatenakwe hina teki kwsiweewe

To grant unto us that we being delivered out of the hand of our enemies Should serve him without fear,

75. hofepefiiweneki mecimi mayaawiilefiiweneki yeelahfamiici hina caayahki kikiisekanoomena

In holiness and righteousness before him all our days.

76. haanhka chiine kiila hapelohfa nili homaamoosikiiskwemali hina kci moospi ke haayekoopi ksake kiila hini yeelahfamiikweci hina teepeelemiweeta ke ha wahsi hosimecfetawaci homiyeewali

Yea and thou, child, shalt be called the prophet of the Most High: For thou shalt go before the face of the Lord to make ready his ways;

77. wahsi miilaci waapanhsiiwi lepwaawe hotelenaweemhhi hini homaciilefiiwenwa hoci pakfefiiweneki

To give knowledge of salvation unto his people In the remission of their sins,

78. ksake hini hokokoskwi kiteminaakweeletiiwe
kimanetoomena weeci spemeki hoci lemacfeeyaaki
hini meewaapaki keh nawhhekope

Because of the tender mercy of our God,
Whereby the dayspring from on high
shall visit us,

79. wahsi wahfehtawaaci nihi lematapilici laa
pepekica mecimi hini nepoowe si yeewikakiiki wahsi
hini kaamaaniilefiiwi miyeeweneki si
mayaawiwetooci kifitena hiwapi

To shine upon them that sit in darkness
and the shadow of death; To guide our
feet into the way of peace.

80. chiine hina hapelohfa skwiniiki mecimi halalika si
wiisikatowi lefiiweneki chiine hini laa papskwahki
hapiwa paalohi hini kaasekiki howaapamekofiiweneki
laa hiswiila

And the child grew, and waxed strong in
spirit, and was in the deserts till the day
of his shewing unto Israel.

Luke:2

1. howe hini piyeemikatwi nele kaasekiki nitasi
lohfeya kotaacimetiiwe siisa haakastas hoci wahsi hini
caayahki keekkehsilotooteeki hasiski hakimawikeeki

Now it came to pass in those days, there
went out a decree from Caesar Augustus,
that all the world should be enrolled.

2. hiini yooma weski hakimawikeewe mectoote hine
kwiliinias kapenaliiwi siliyeki

This was the first enrollment made when
Quirinius was governor of Syria.

3. chiine caayahki nhheeki wahsi hakimawikeewaaci
wiiyaawa caakiwiyeefa nehalwaaka hoteewenemi
heewa

And all went to enroll themselves, every
one to his own city.

4. mecimi coosii nehfaapi keeleliiki hoci kkwicsinwa
hini hoteewe naaselefi hoci cotiyeeki heewa hini
hoteewenemi teepitii peflihemi sitoote ksake hina nili
teepitiili hoci kamikifi mecimi si nhhalweeletamwa

And Joseph also went up from Galilee,
out of the city of Nazareth, into Judaea,
to the city of David, which is called
Bethlehem, because he was of the house
and family of David;

5. wahsi hakimawikeeci wiiya kileki meliili
keekaloosiwehoofolici wiiya peemi hina
mhsinaakofici hapelohfali

to enroll himself with Mary, who was
betrothed to him, being great with child.

6. chiine hini piyeemikatwi yeheeyehi nitasi hapiwaaci
nihki nili kaasekiki hokwaawfeno wahsi hina
niikinikeeci

And it came to pass, while they were
there, the days were fulfilled that she
should be delivered.

7. mecimi hopiyeelaali weski niikilici hokwihfali
mecimi hotetepahpilaali tetepapifoowena chiine hoteh
seksimaali mekinhhweeki yaata hsameci ksake mata
tawaali hini kkehsiiwikaaneki

And she brought forth her firstborn son;
and she wrapped him in swaddling
clothes, and laid him in a manger,
because there was no room for them in
the inn.

8. chiine nitasi kehcitawahaacki meekiifhi yaska hini
tasi piileski pemi hapiiki hini ktikaaneki mecimi
peemi kcitawahaawaaci homeekiifemwahi tepehki

And there were shepherds in the same
country abiding in the field, and keeping
watch by night over their flock.

9. mecimi hotenhcaliimali hina teepeelemiweeta
pakaci niipawiili nihi chiine hini
howahfaacimekofiiwe hina teepeelemiweeta
wahfefamooya kaayaawka nihi mecimi nihki holaami
wiisaalepwaaki

And an angel of the Lord stood by them,
and the glory of the Lord shone round
about them: and they were sore afraid.

10. chiine hina henhcali teki wiisaalepwaako ksake waapatamoko kipiyeetoolepwa howesi piyeetaacimoowena hoci mhsaawi hosasilepwaawe we hinwilici caayahki nihki lenaweeki

And the angel said unto them, Be not afraid; for behold, I bring you good tidings of great joy which shall be to all the people:

11. ksake nitasi lenaweewi kiilawa hinoki kaasekiki hini teepitii hototeeweneki waapanhsiiwena klaistii hina hina teepeelemiweeta

for there is born to you this day in the city of David a Saviour, which is Christ the Lord.

12. mecimi halayooma hini kikinoolooweniko ke mhkawaawa hapelohfeefa tetepahpifo tetepahpifoowena mecimi peemi seksiki mekinhhweeki yaata hsameci hotelahi

And this is the sign unto you; Ye shall find a babe wrapped in swaddling clothes, and lying in a manger.

13. mecimi kikamooci nitasi wiici nili henhcaliili mehseeleka hina menhkwatoowi mehseeleka hoci hopemi wiyawaacimekwhaali manetooli mecimi

And suddenly there was with the angel a multitude of the heavenly host praising God, and saying,

14. wahfaacimekofiiwe cehi maneto si hini wihkoci lhspi mecimi hoskitaamhkwe kaamaaniilefiiwe heelekiina hileniiki yohoma weeoweleelemaaci hina hiwapi

Glory to God in the highest, And on earth peace among men in whom he is well pleased.

15. chiine hini piyeemikatwi hine nihki henhcaliiki nihi hociweepfeeki menhkwatoki heeki nihki kehcitawahaacki meekiifhi wehi howe nhhaataako peflihemiki mecimi neemetaako yooma wiyehi peepiyeemikaki mayehci waakotelelakwe hina teepeelemiweeta hitiiki

And it came to pass, when the angels went away from them into heaven, the shepherds said one to another, Let us now go even unto Bethlehem, and see this thing that is come to pass, which the Lord hath made known unto us.

16. mecimi weeweetepi piyeeki mecimi homhkawaawahi neyiiswi meliili chiine coosiili chiine nili hapelohfeefali peemi seksinelici yaata hsameci mekinhhweeki

And they came with haste, and found both Mary and Joseph, and the babe lying in the manger.

17. chiine yeh neewaawaaci nili waakotesiweeki yeeki hini hiyoowe mayehci laatotamaweci yooloma hapelohfali

And when they saw it, they made known concerning the saying which was spoken to them about this child.

18. mecimi caayahki neenootakki hokwakwehtaaneeletaanaawa nili wiyehi mayehci hikowaaci nihi meekiifhi kehcitawahaacki

And all that heard it wondered at the things which were spoken unto them by the shepherds.

19. weeka melii hokciitonaana yooloma hiyoowena hopemi memekineeletaana nili hotehiki

But Mary kept all these sayings, pondering them in her heart.

20. chiine peteki heeki nihki kehcitawahaacki meekiifhi hopemi wahfaacimekhwaawaali mecimi howiyawaachaawaali manetooli ksake hini wiyehi caayahki mayehci nootamowaaci mecimi neemowaaci teetepila hinwili yeeloofowaaci

And the shepherds returned, glorifying and praising God for all the things that they had heard and seen, even as it was spoken unto them.

21. chiine nhfwaasikifoko ye hokwihfeki wahsi hina pemi kaawackofoci ciisisii sitoote howiifoowe yooni yeesitaki hina henhcali wihsi pwaa hina kikatkwiici hini laamotaakaneki

And when eight days were fulfilled for circumcising him, his name was called JESUS, which was so called by the angel before he was conceived in the womb.

22. chiine hine nili tfoko hofafahkweewenwa yeesfeki hini moosisii hokwteletiiwe ye hokwihfeki nihki colooseelemiiki hote kkwiciwelaawaali wahsi nili teepeelemiweelici si teephiweewaaci nili

And when the days of their purification according to the law of Moses were fulfilled, they brought him up to Jerusalem, to present him to the Lord

23. yeesi hini mehtawikaateeki hini hokwteletiiweneki hina teepeelemiweeta caaki skilawehfiwi hapelohfa teetawskaka hini laamotaaka nili teepeelemiweelici si hofepefi we haaloofo

(as it is written in the law of the Lord, Every male that openeth the womb shall be called holy to the Lord),

24. mecimi wahsi miiliweeki pakfenikeewe yeesfeki hini yeeyoki hokwteletiiweneki hina teepeelemiweeta niiswi miyaasipawiifaki weelaa niiswi pawiifaki

and to offer a sacrifice according to that which is said in the law of the Lord, A pair of turtledoves, or two young pigeons.

25. mecimi waapamehko nitasi hileni colooseelemiiki hapiwa saimanii si wiifooweni chiine mayaawiilefi yaama hileni mecimi mamaatomeewefi peemi natawaapataki hokaakilweewinamoowe hiswiila chiine nili hofepi hocacaalahkwali hoskici hina hapiili

And behold, there was a man in Jerusalem, whose name was Simeon; and this man was righteous and devout, looking for the consolation of Israel: and the Holy Spirit was upon him.

26. chiine hini homehci pahkinamaakooli nili hofepi hocacaalahkwali wahsi pwaa neemeki nepoowe wihsi pwaa mehci neewaaci hina teepeelemiweeta hoklaistiimali

And it had been revealed unto him by the Holy Spirit, that he should not see death, before he had seen the Lord's Christ.

27. chiine hina piyeewa hini hocacaalahkofiiweneki hini mamaatomeewikamikoki mecimi nihki kehkiyaaki yeh piyeelaawaaci nili hapelohfali ciisisiili wahsi menawahke hpenalaawaaci hini naawalwi yaasilawiiki hini kwteletiiweneki

And he came in the Spirit into the temple: and when the parents brought in the child Jesus, that they might do concerning him after the custom of the law,

28. hine hina hote hotahpenaali nili honehkiki chiine hokisaachaali manetooli mecimi

then he received him into his arms, and blessed God, and said,

29. howe wiilaani leelemi teepeelemiweeta kitaloolaaka weepfeete kaamaaniilefiiweneki yeesfeki hini kikalawiiwe

Now lettest thou thy servant depart, O Lord, According to thy word, in peace;

30. ksake niskiisekonaki homehci neemenaawa kiwaapanescika

For mine eyes have seen thy salvation,

31. mayehci nanahi mectooyani hini yeelahfamiikweewaaci caayahki lenaweeki

Which thou hast prepared before the face of all peoples;

32. wayahfeeyaaki wahsi tayeewahi sinamowaaci nihki nanahkawileniiki mecimi hini howahfaacimekofiiwe hina kitelenaweema hiswiila hiwapi

A light for revelation to the Gentiles, And the glory of thy people Israel.

33. chiine hina hapelohfa hohfali mecimi hokeeli pemi kwakwehtaaneeletamehi hini wiyehi yeelaacimoofoci

And his father and his mother were marveling at the things which were spoken concerning him;

34. mecimi saimanii hokisaachahi nihi mecimi waapami yooloma hapelohfali lemataptaakwi hina peemi haakicfaata mecimi hina peemi honhskaata

and Simeon blessed them, and said unto Mary his mother, Behold, this child is set for the falling and rising up of many in

meci laa hiswiila hoci mecimi kikinooloowe ksake peekicihkooteeki

Israel; and for a sign which is spoken against;

35. haanhka mecimi kiskhika weh saapoci pasiphoofo nehalwaaka kiiya wahsi menawahke pahkinooteeki memekiniteheewena meci hotehiwali hoci hotelaali meliili hokeeli hina hapelohfa

yea and a sword shall pierce through thine own soul; that thoughts out of many hearts may be revealed.

36. mecimi nitasi nekoti henna maamoosikiiskweewi hkwe nili hotaanehfali fenoel hini hesa hotfweeloowe hoci lenawe mekipwehfiifiwi homehci wiicikeemaali wehsici niiswahfwi kkato hoseskiikwefiwiiweneki hoci

And there was one Anna, a prophetess, the daughter of Phanuel, of the tribe of Asher (she was of a great age, having lived with a husband seven years from her virginity,

37. mecimi neyehka mehci siikawi-yhkweewi teetepilahi nhfwaasii-kite-niyeewi kkato matalaakwa hini mamaatomeewikamikwi hoci saawe hina pemi hosasilawe kileki hocikeewena mecimi nanahpaacimoowena tepehki chiine kiiseki

and she had been a widow even for fourscore and four years), which departed not from the temple, worshipping with fastings and supplications night and day.

38. mecimi pemi piyeewa hina spemeki kwena tepilo hini yaatefaki homiilaali manetooli niyaawena mecimi niliini hotaatotamawahi caayahki nihi peemi natawaapatamelici hini hopetekinoofoowe colooseelemii

And coming up at that very hour she gave thanks unto God, and spake of him to all them that were looking for the redemption of Jerusalem.

39. chiine nihki yeh mehcilotamowaaci caayahki wiyehi yeesfeki yehteeki hini hokwteletiiweneki hina teepeelemiweeta peteki keeleliiki heeki nehalwaaka hoteewenemwa naaselefi heeki

And when they had accomplished all things that were according to the law of the Lord, they returned into Galilee, to their own city Nazareth.

40. chiine hina hapelohfa skwiniiki mecimi halalika si wiisikatowi si hokwaawefi lepwaawe mecimi hini hokisaaciweefiiwe maneto hahteeli hoskici hina

And the child grew, and waxed strong, filled with wisdom: and the grace of God was upon him.

41. chiine nihi hokehkiyaamhhi colooseelemiiki yaahehi tfene nekoti kkato tah lemafkohkweki hini pemhfaasiweewe

And his parents went every year to Jerusalem at the feast of the passover.

42. chiine hina yeh metahfwi-kite-niiswi tfwi kkatoowici nihki kkwicsinooki naawalwi hini yaasilawiiki hini lemafkohkweewe hoci

And when he was twelve years old, they went up after the custom of the feast;

43. mecimi yeh mehci hokwaawfetoowaaci nili kaasekiki yeesi pemi peteki haawaaci hina skilawehfiifa ciisisii nakahsinwa hotaanaaki colooseelemiiki chiine hokehkiyaamhhi mata howaakotamehi hini

and when they had fulfilled the days, as they were returning, the boy Jesus tarried behind in Jerusalem; and his parents knew it not;

44. payeekwa laakwa hapiwa nihi weewiitfeemiweelici hopemi leelemekohi nihki nekoti kiiskwe laamiiki mecimi honatonehwaawaali heelekiina nehalweelemaawaaci mecimi howaakometiiwenwahi

but supposing him to be in the company, they went a day's journey; and they sought for him among their kinsfolk and acquaintance:

45. chiine yeh kwiilawaawaaci peteki colooseelemiiki heeki hopemi natonehwaawaali nili

and when they found him not, they returned to Jerusalem, seeking for him.

46. chiine hini piyeemikatwi mayehci nhfokonakiki homhkawaawaali piitike hini mamaatomeewikamikwi peemi lematapilici hini heelekhi nihi keekehkimiweelici peemi hahkawehtawaaci nihi mecimi peemi natohtawaaci natohtwaatiiwena

And it came to pass, after three days they found him in the temple, sitting in the midst of the doctors, both hearing them, and asking them questions:

47. chiine caayahki neenootawaacki nili hokwakwehtaaneeletamawaawaali honenohseewe mecimi hotaapafseewena

and all that heard him were amazed at his understanding and his answers.

48. chiine yeh neewaawaaci nihki cihfefiiki mecimi hokwihfima koociwe kimehci yooni hpenasipe waapatano kohfa mecimi niila kinatoneholepe nipemi macilepwaape hotekooli hokeeli

And when they saw him, they were astonished: and his mother said unto him, Son, why hast thou thus dealt with us? behold, thy father and I sought thee sorrowing.

49. mecimi nehiwe hini weeci natonehwiyeekwe ha mata kiwaakotaanaawa wahsi hapiya kwiilahi nohfa yeetaaci wiikiwaapeki hotelahi

And he said unto them, How is it that ye sought me? wist ye not that I must be in my Father's house?

50. chiine nihki mata honenohtaanaawa hini hiyoowe keekaloolaaci nihi

And they understood not the saying which he spake unto them.

51. chiine howiici paalacsinoomahi nihi mecimi naaselefi si piyeeki chiine homelonehtawahi mecimi hokeeli haayici poonameli yooloma hiyoowena hotehiki

And he went down with them, and came to Nazareth; and he was subject unto them: and his mother kept all these sayings in her heart.

52. chiine ciisisii skwiiwa lepwaaweneki mecimi spefiiweneki chiine maneto hoci haliweelemoofooweneki mecimi hileniiki

And Jesus advanced in wisdom and stature, and in favour with God and men.

Luke:3

1. howe hine mawi-metahfwi-kite-niyaalanwi tfwi kkatoowiiya hini hokimaawiiwe taapilias' siisa panhtas paalatii pemi kapenaliiwi cotiye chiine heletii pemi nekotehfepatiwi hokimaawi keelelii chiine hoceeninaali filapiili nekotehfepatiwi hokimaawiili hini hitolie tasi mecimi twekonaatis chiine laasenias nekotehfepatiwi hokimaawi hepeliini

Now in the fifteenth year of the reign of Tiberius Caesar, Pontius Pilate being governor of Judaea, and Herod being tetrarch of Galilee, and his brother Philip tetrarch of the region of Ituraea and Trachonitis, and Lysanias tetrarch of Abilene,

2. hine homoospimhkateewkolayeewimekofiiwenwaaki henas' chiine keeyeefesii hini hokalawiiwe maneto caaniili si piyeeya nili hokwihfali sekolaayes' hini piileski

in the high-priesthood of Annas and Caiaphas, the word of God came unto John the son of Zacharias in the wilderness.

3. chiine hina piyeewa hini mefhiike kaayaawka tasi hini caatenii pemi nanahimiwe hini fafahkwiholelwiiwe mataiini siteheewe hoci wahsi pakfefiiweniki maciilefiiwena

And he came into all the region round about Jordan, preaching the baptism of repentance unto remission of sins;

4. yeesi hini mehtawikeeki hini heewikaateekiiki nili hokalawiiwena haisaya hina maamoosikiiskweeta hina nekoti wiyeefa hini talahootamwa laa piileski mecfetooko hini homiyeewi hina teepeelemiweeta tepilahi stooko homiyeeweneefa

as it is written in the book of the words of Isaiah the prophet, The voice of one crying in the wilderness, Make ye ready the way of the Lord, Make his paths straight.

5. caaki wayaalhkwahkiki we hokwihfetoote chiine caaki meekwahkiki mecimi meekwahkiifiki weh maalespi waamekhoote mecimi nili wayaakiyaaki weh pesikwa mecimi nili kahsi miyeewali fefikwa

Every valley shall be filled, And every mountain and hill shall be brought low; And the crooked shall become straight, And the rough ways smooth;

6. chiine caayahki wiyawfima weh neeme hini howaapanhsiweewe maneto

And all flesh shall see the salvation of God.

7. weecikeenahi hina hotelahi nihi mehseelelici leelohfaalici wahsi fafahkwi holelhaaci neefawe kitalenekowa kiilawa leewaki hotoosaakanaki wahsi hositameekwe hini hahkwikiteewe wah piyeeyaaki

He said therefore to the multitudes that went out to be baptized of him, Ye offspring of vipers, who warned you to flee from the wrath to come?

8. niikitooko weecikeenahi mawifoowena nahiika yeyhkweelemekoki mataiini siteheewe mecimi teki halemi hiyoko piitike kiiyaawa nipoonaape heplehemii niyohfipe ksake kitelepwa niila yeesi maneto teepiilefici wahsi yohoma siikonhhi hoci honhskaanamawaaci heplehemiili hapelofhi

Bring forth therefore fruits worthy of repentance, and begin not to say within yourselves, We have Abraham to our father: for I say unto you, that God is able of these stones to raise up children unto Abraham.

9. chiine teetepilahi hinoki hini tekhaaka nehfaapi sekfenwi hini hoceepkahkatoki nili mhteko caaki mhtekwi weecikeenahi pwaayaa hini hoci niikiki howesi mawifoowe kawhoote mecimi hini skoteeki hipakitoote

And even now is the axe also laid unto the root of the trees: every tree therefore that bringeth not forth good fruit is hewn down, and cast into the fire.

10. chiine nihki mehseelekki honatohtawaawaali nehiwe kwiilahi howe neh silawiipe hotelaawaali

And the multitudes asked him, saying, What then must we do?

11. chiine hina haapafse mecimi hina peepoonaka niiswi kootiiwali wiilaani hina pakfenamawaate nili pwaayaa poonamelici mecimi hina peepoonaka wihfeniiwe wiilaani hina yaska hini silawiite hotelahi

And he answered and said unto them, He that hath two coats, let him impart to him that hath none; and he that hath food, let him do likewise.

12. chiine nitasi nehfaapi piyeeki teeksiiwi-maawatonikehfiiki wahsi fafahkwi holelhoofowaaci chiine nihki keekehkimiwe nehiwe niilawe kwiilahi nih silawiipe hotelaawaali

And there came also publicans to be baptized, and they said unto him, Master, what must we do?

13. teki kwakwatenamaakeeko halika lekhi noota yeesi mamoofoyeekwe hotelahi nihi

And he said unto them, Extort no more than that which is appointed you.

14. chiine samaakanaki nehfaapi honatohtawaawaali chiine niilawe nehiwe kwiilahi nih silawiipe hisiweeki chiine teki mamiiloowi kwakwtenamaakeeko hileni hoci teki nohki naanhhaacimoowi mestaawimehko wiyeefa mecimi teepi siteheeko kitephotiiwenwa hotelahi nihi

And soldiers also asked him, saying, And we, what must we do? And he said unto them, Do violence to no man, neither exact anything wrongfully; and be content with your wages.

15. chiine yeesi nihki lenaweeki hahkawaafiiwaaci
mecimi hileniiki caayaki memekineelemaawaaci
caaniili hotehiwaaki kwehkwi toke hina hina klaistii

And as the people were in expectation,
and all men reasoned in their hearts
concerning John, whether haply he were
the Christ;

16. caanii haapafse niila sapkahi kifafahkwi
holelhelepwa nepi payeekwa nitasi piyeewa hina
halika mehsiilefita noota niila homahkifena hoci hini
menihfepi ninootkwiilefi wahsi pelhama hiina keh
fafahkwi holelhekowa nili hofepi hocacaalahkwali
mecimi skoteeki

John answered, saying unto them all, I
indeed baptize you with water; but there
cometh he that is mightier than I, the
latchet of whose shoes I am not worthy to
unloose: he shall baptize you with the
Holy Ghost and with fire:

17. howeewefhoowe holeciki hahteeli tateekakwi
wahsi fafayaakilotaki pawaskwhaawi
hotepakofenoomi mecimi wahsi hini kawaskwi
hokawaskwikaaneki si maawatonaki weeka nili
wihsiikwaya weh caakatefaana hina pwaayaa katawi
hahtehooteeki skote we hawe hopemi hilahi nihi
caayahki

whose fan is in his hand, throughly to
cleanse his threshing-floor, and to gather
the wheat into his garner; but the chaff he
will burn up with unquenchable fire.

18. wiici meci kotakali kicitaamoowena weecikeenahi
honanahimahi howesi piyeetaacimoowena nihi
lenawehi

With many other exhortations therefore
preached he good tidings unto the people;

19. payeekwa heletii hina nekotehfepatiwi hokima
teewahi holhskimekooli nili ksake helootiasiili hoci
hoceeninaali wiiwali mecimi ksake nili hoci maci
wiyehi caayahki mayehci silawiici heletii

but Herod the tetrarch, being reproved by
him for Herodias his brother's wife, and
for all the evil things which Herod had
done,

20. koolotoote yooma nehfaapi nili si caayahki yeesi
hina kiphwaaci caaniili kiphotiiweneki

added yet this above all, that he shut up
John in prison.

21. howe hini piyeemikatwi yeh caayahki nihki
lenaweeki fafahkwi holelhoofowaaci yeesi nehfaapi
ciisisii pemi mehci fafahkwi holelhoofoci mecimi
pemi mamaatomeeci hini menhkwatwi tawenoote

Now it came to pass, when all the people
were baptized, that, Jesus also having
been baptized, and praying, the heaven
was opened,

22. chiine hina hofepi hocacaalahkwa hoskici nili si
laasiyofe wiyehliyeeweeweneki paasi miyaasipawiifa
mecimi kalaweewihsimoowe menhkwatwiki homooya
kiila hina yeeahkweelemaka nikwihfa kiiyaaki
nimenwilepwa hiyooya

and the Holy Ghost descended in a bodily
form, as a dove, upon him, and a voice
came out of heaven, Thou art my beloved
Son; in thee I am well pleased.

23. chiine ciisisii wiila ye halemi kakehkimiweeci
nawito nhfwaapitaki tfwi kkatoowi nili hokwihfali
toke yeesiteheeki coosii nili hokwihfali hiilaa

And Jesus himself, when he began to
teach, was about thirty years of age,
being the son (as was supposed) of
Joseph, the son of Heli,

24. nili hokwihfali metfete nili hokwihfali liifaai nili
hokwihfali melhkaaya nili hokwihfali cene nili
hokwihfali coosii

the son of Matthat, the son of Levi, the
son of Melchi, the son of Jannai, the son
of Joseph,

25. nili hokwihfali metefaaesi nili hokwihfali hemasi
nili hokwihfali nehami nili hokwihfali heslaa nili
hokwihfali nekeeya

the son of Mattathias, the son of Amos,
the son of Nahum, the son of Esli, the son
of Naggai,

26. nili hokwihfali meef nili hokwihfali metefaaesi nili hokwihfali semiyani nili hokwihfali cooseki nili hokwihfali coote

the son of Maath, the son of Mattathias, the son of Semein, the son of Josech, the son of Joda,

27. nili hokwihfali cooeneni nili hokwihfali liise nili hokwihfali silopeepalii nili hokwihfali sialhtiali nili hokwihfali niilaai

the son of Joanan, the son of Rhesa, the son of Zerubbabel, the son of Shealtiel, the son of Neri,

28. nili hokwihfali melhkaaya nili hokwihfali heta nili hokwihfali koosaami nili hokwihfali hilmetami nili hokwihfali yaami

the son of Melchi, the son of Addi, the son of Cosam, the son of Elmadam, the son of Er,

29. nili hokwihfali ciisisii nili hokwihfali hiliisa nili hokwihfali coolimi nili hokwihfali metfete nili hokwihfali liifaai

the son of Jesus, the son of Eliezer, the son of Jorim, the son of Matthat, the son of Levi,

30. nili hokwihfali simiyani nili hokwihfali cootasii nili hokwihfali coosii nili hokwihfali coonemi nili hokwihfali hilaikimii

the son of Symeon, the son of Judas, the son of Joseph, the son of Jonam, the son of Eliakim,

31. nili hokwihfali miilia nili hokwihfali mena nili hokwihfali metefa nili hokwihfali nefeni nili hokwihfali teepitii

the son of Melea, the son of Menna, the son of Mattatha, the son of Nathan, the son of David,

32. nili hokwihfali cesii nili hokwihfali hoopitii nili hokwihfali pooesii nili hokwihfali selmanii nili hokwihfali naasani

the son of Jesse, the son of Obed, the son of Boaz, the son of Salmon, the son of Nahshon,

33. nili hokwihfali hemeniteepi nili hokwihfali hena nili hokwihfali heslanii nili hokwihfali piilesii nili hokwihfali coota

the son of Amminadab, the son of Arni, the son of Hezron, the son of Perez, the son of Judah,

34. nili hokwihfali ceekapii nili hokwihfali haisiki nili hokwihfali heplehemii nili hokwihfali tiila nili hokwihfali neha

the son of Jacob, the son of Isaac, the son of Abraham, the son of Terah, the son of Nahor,

35. nili hokwihfali siilaki nili hokwihfali liiyoo nili hokwihfali piileki nili hokwihfali hipa nili hokwihfali siila

the son of Serug, the son of Reu, the son of Peleg, the son of Eber, the son of Shelah,

36. nili hokwihfali keeananii nili hokwihfali hefekseti nili hokwihfali sem nili hokwihfali nowa nili hokwihfali lemeki

the son of Cainan, the son of Arphaxad, the son of Shem, the son of Noah, the son of Lamech,

37. nili hokwihfali mefoosila nili hokwihfali hinaka nili hokwihfali ceelati nili hokwihfali mehaleli nili hokwihfali keeananii

the son of Methuselah, the son of Enoch, the son of Jared, the son of Mahalaleel, the son of Cainan,

38. nili hokwihfali hinasi nili hokwihfali sefi nili hokwihfali hetami nili hokwihfali maneto

the son of Enos, the son of Seth, the son of Adam, the son of God.

Luke:4

1. chiine ciisisii hokwihsinooli nili hofepi hocacaalahkwali hini caatenii hoci kotekwi mecimi hini piileski siwelekwi hini hocacaalahkofiiweneki

And Jesus, full of the Holy Spirit, returned from the Jordan, and was led by the Spirit in the wilderness

2. niyeewaapitaki tfoko laakwasi hopemi koci miyaasi-ashekooli nili macimanetooli mecimi mata

during forty days, being tempted of the devil. And he did eat nothing in those

wiyehi homiici nele kaasekiki ye hokwihfeki nili tfoko chiine skwaalawe days: and when they were completed, he hungered.

3. mecimi hina macimaneto kiila kwehkwi howiiyaawiyane nili hokwihfali maneto tepimi yaama siikona wahsi hina takhwaaniwici hotelaali

And the devil said unto him, If thou art the Son of God, command this stone that it become bread.

4. mecimi hotaapaftawaali ciisisii mehtawikeepi hini mata hileni takhwa naanhsihka we hoci lenaweewi hotelaali

And Jesus answered unto him, It is written, Man shall not live by bread alone.

5. chiine hina hokkwiciwelaali nili mecimi howaapatelaali caayahki nili hokimaawitaamhkweewali hini yeelekokwahkamikiki hini nekoti meniti laakwasi

And he led him up, and shewed him all the kingdoms of the world in a moment of time.

6. mecimi niila keh miilele caayahki yooma simekofiiwe mecimi hini nili si wahfaacimekofiiwe ksake hini neyehka nimehci pakfenamaakoopi mecimi kookwe-neefa-kaaci yeesiteheeya niila nimiila hini

And the devil said unto him, To thee will I give all this authority, and the glory of them: for it hath been delivered unto me; and to whomsoever I will I give it.

7. kwehkwi kiila weecikeenahi ke hosasilawe yeelahfamiiya niila ke howiilaami hini caayahki hotelaali hina macimaneto

If thou therefore wilt worship before me, it shall all be thine.

8. chiine ciisisii haapafse mecimi mehtawikeepi hini ke hosasilaweha kiila hina teepeelemiweeta kimanetooma mecimi hina pehi keh memekinilotawa hotelaali

And Jesus answered and said unto him, It is written, Thou shalt worship the Lord thy God, and him only shalt thou serve.

9. chiine hina colooseelemii hotesiwelaali mecimi hini hakocikami mamaatomeewikamikwi holemataphaali mecimi kwehkwi kiilaawiyane nili hokwihfali maneto yooci sahkiki hipakitano kiiya

And he led him to Jerusalem, and set him on the pinnacle of the temple, and said unto him, If thou art the Son of God, cast thyself down from hence:

10. ksake hini mehtawikeepi weh miilahi hina hotenhcaliimhhi tepimoofoowe kiila hisi wahsi kcitawahehki kiila

for it is written, He shall give his angels charge concerning thee, to guard thee:

11. chiine holeciwaaki nihki keh niimekooki piilepeeke ke pkitehfeto kifici siikoneki hotelaali

and, On their hands they shall bear thee up, Lest haply thou dash thy foot against a stone.

12. chiine ciisisii pemi haapafse teki kiila ke hosto hotepowaafoowe hina teepeelemiweeta kimanetooma hiyopi hini hotelaali

And Jesus answering said unto him, It is said, Thou shalt not tempt the Lord thy God.

13. chiine hina macimaneto yeh mehcilotaki caaki koci miyaasi-ashetiiwe saawe nili hoci maalaakwasi

And when the devil had completed every temptation, he departed from him for a season.

14. chiine ciisisii peteki hini howiisikatowiiweneki hina hocacaalahkwa heewa keeleliiki mecimi hotelaacimekofiiwe mefhiike si lohfeya saapwi hini kaayaawka tasi

And Jesus returned in the power of the Spirit into Galilee: and a fame went out concerning him through all the region round about.

15. chiine kakehkimiwe homhsikamikomwaaki hopemi wahfaacimekofihekohi caayahki

And he taught in their synagogues, being glorified of all.

16. chiine naaselefi si piyeewa tah mehci katenoofoci mecimi piicfe yeesi nakatefiiwenici hini mhsikamikwi ta hini halwaakahsi kiisekiki chiine pafekwi wahsi laapaatotaki heewikaateeki

And he came to Nazareth, where he had been brought up: and he entered, as his custom was, into the synagogue on the sabbath day, and stood up to read.

17. mecimi nitasi piyeci pakfenamaakwi hini hoteewikaateemi hina maamoosikiiskweeta haisaya chiine hopahkina hini heewikaateeki mecimi homhka hini tasi ta hini mehtawikeeki

And there was delivered unto him the book of the prophet Isaiah. And he opened the book, and found the place where it was written,

18. nili hocacaalahkomali hina teepeelemiweeta hapiili hoskici niila ksake hina nilomhkoonekwa wahsi nanahimaki howesi piyeetaacimoowena hina kitemaafa nimehci waawiinekwa wahsi lhfwaatotamawaki pelhoofoowe nihki kiikeenikaafaki mecimi pemi petekinamoowe hina keekeepiikweeta wahsi tepeeletamefiiwahkeephaki nihki keekishoofocki

The Spirit of the Lord is upon me, Because he anointed me to preach good tidings to the poor: He hath sent me to proclaim release to the captives, And recovering of sight to the blind, To set at liberty them that are bruised,

19. wahsi lhfwaatotama hini menwi hotahpenooteeki hokkatoomi hina teepeelemiweeta

To proclaim the acceptable year of the Lord.

20. chiine hokipooliikwena hini heewikaateeki mecimi hini peteki hoteh miilaali nili yeekawaafiilici chiine lematapiwa mecimi nili hoskiisekowa caayahki hini mhsikamikoki homamiyeetaawaapamaawaali nili

And he closed the book, and gave it back to the attendant, and sat down: and the eyes of all in the synagogue were fastened on him.

21. chiine hotalemi hilahi nihi hinoki kaasekiki yooma tepilo heewikaateeki mehci hokwaawfetoote kitawakaawaaki

And he began to say unto them, Today hath this scripture been fulfilled in your ears.

22. mecimi caayahki hopahkinamawaawaali teepweewe holakokweeletamawaawaali nili kisaaciilefiiwe hoci kalawiiwena weemooyaaki hotooneki chiine nihki ha mata yaama coosii hokwihfali hiwaki

And all bare him witness, and wondered at the words of grace which proceeded out of his mouth: and they said, Is not this Joseph's son?

23. chiine hina kwiilayini kiilawa yooma pemaatoweewe naanatawhcikeeta kiikehtoolo kiiya kookwe-nehi-kaaci mayehci nootamaake yeesilawiiki kehpaaniamiiki silawiilo nehfaapi hotasi nehalwaaka kitasiskiimeki ke hisipwa hotelahi

And he said unto them, Doubtless ye will say unto me this parable, Physician, heal thyself: whatsoever we have heard done at Capernaum, do also here in thine own country.

24. mecimi tepilo kitelepwa niila matalaakwa maamoosikiiskweeta menweelemoofo nehalwaaka hotasiskiimeki

And he said, Verily I say unto you, No prophet is acceptable in his own country.

25. payeekwa sapkahi teepeewe kitelepwa meci nitasi hapiiki siikawi-ykweeki laa hiswiila hine hokakiisekanemiki hilaica hine hini menhkwatwi kiphoote nhfwi kkato kite nekotwahfwi kiisahfo hine nitasi piyeeya mhsaawi seeskwaalaweeweniki mefhiike hini hasiskiiki

But of a truth I say unto you, There were many widows in Israel in the days of Elijah, when the heaven was shut up three years and six months, when there came a great famine over all the land;

26. mecimi mata wiyeefali nihi leskoofo hilaica weeka
selifeli pehi hini saataniiwi hasiskiiki hkweeli
sesiikawi-yhkweewilici

and unto none of them was Elijah sent,
but only to Zarephath, in the land of
Sidon, unto a woman that was a widow.

27. chiine meci nitasi hapiiki weeskilhakeemekicki laa
hiswiila hine hotelaakwaafiiweneki hilaica hina
maamoosikiiskweeta mecimi mata wiyeefa nihki
hofepilotoofo weeka neemani pehi hina siliyeewileni
hisiwe

And there were many lepers in Israel in
the time of Elisha the prophet; and none
of them was cleansed, but only Naaman
the Syrian.

28. mecimi caayahki nihki hini mhsikamikoki
hokwaawefiiki macikiteewe yeesi nootamowaaci
yooloma wiyehi

And they were all filled with wrath in the
synagogue, as they heard these things;

29. chiine pafekwiiki nihki mecimi hini hoteeweneki
hoci lohfelhkawaawaali nili chiine hini weeci
kiskahkiki hini meekwahkiifiki ta hopatenooteeki
hoteewenwa hotesiwelaawaali wahsi menawahke
wiileki hoci pakilaawaaci lwaameki hisi

and they rose up, and cast him forth out
of the city, and led him unto the brow of
the hill whereon their city was built, that
they might throw him down headlong.

30. payeekwa hina pemi saapwi pemhfe hini heelekhi
nihi weepfe yehaaci

But he passing through the midst of them
went his way.

31. chiine kehpaaniamii si piyeci paalacsinwa keelelii
hoci hoteewe mecimi peemi kakehkimaaci nihi ta
halwaakahsi kiisekiki

And he came down to Capernaum, a city
of Galilee. And he was teaching them on
the sabbath day:

32. chiine hocihfeeletamaakohi nihi
hokakehkimiweewe ksake kileki wiyehsimekofiiwe
hinwili hokalawiiwe

and they were astonished at his teaching;
for his word was with authority.

33. chiine nitasi mhsikamikoki hapiwa hileni
peepoonaata hocacaalahkomali wiyakiwaninehfi
mecimi hina wiyakahootamwa kalaweewihsimoowe

And in the synagogue there was a man,
which had a spirit of an unclean devil;
and he cried out with a loud voice,

34. haa nehiwe nipoonaape wa hpenalelaake kiila
ciisisii naaselefileni ha kipiya wahsi macilotawiyaake
kiwaakomele kiila weeciwiyani hina hofepi wiyeefa
maneto hoci hisiwe

Ah! what have we to do with thee, thou
Jesus of Nazareth? art thou come to
destroy us? I know thee who thou art, the
Holy One of God.

35. mecimi ciisisii hokwtelaali nili nooleewilo mecimi
hina hoci lohfaalo hotelaali mecimi hina waninehfi
yeh mehci sahkiki pakilaaci nili hini heelekhi piyeci
nili hoci lohfe mata hopemi kisinaali

And Jesus rebuked him, saying, Hold thy
peace, and come out of him. And when
the devil had thrown him down in the
midst, he came out of him, having done
him no hurt.

36. mecimi hotfekonaawa kwakwehtaaniteheewe
caayahki chiine maawatwi kalooletiiki nihki nehiwe
yooma kalawiiwe yeesi kileki wiyehsimekofiiwe
mecimi waasikaki hina tepimaaci nihi wiyakilehfihi
mecimi nihki piyeci lohfeeki hiwaki

And amazement came upon all, and they
spake together, one with another, saying,
What is this word? for with authority and
power he commandeth the unclean
spirits, and they come out.

37. chiine nitasi weepfeeya laacimoowe hina hisi caaki
tasi hini maalekhitaamhkwe kaayaawka heeya

And there went forth a rumour
concerning him into every place of the
region round about.

38. chiine hina hoci pafekwi hini mhsikamikoki mecimi hini wiikiwa si piicfe yeetaaci saimanii mecimi saimanii wiiwali hokeeli peemi fookinekoci mhsi kisifoowe mecimi nili hoci nanahpaacimekohi nihi

And he rose up from the synagogue, and entered into the house of Simon. And Simon's wife's mother was holden with a great fever; and they besought him for her.

39. chiine nili si niipawi hokoteta hini kisfoowe mecimi hina honakaleko hini chiine weelena honhska mecimi homiisamawahi nihi

And he stood over her, and rebuked the fever; and it left her: and immediately she rose up and ministered unto them.

40. chiine hina kiisekikiisfwa yeh paksimoci caayahki nihki peepoonaacki wiyeefhi yeekwilokeelici kwakwetaki silokeewena nili hopiyeetawaawaali nihi mecimi hina hoskici caaki wiyeefali nihi hoteh poonaana holeciwali mecimi hokiikehahi

And when the sun was setting, all they that had any sick with divers diseases brought them unto him; and he laid his hands on every one of them, and healed them.

41. chiine waninehfiiki nehfaapi meci nihi hoci piyeci lohfeeki wiyakahootamooki mecimi kiila hina nili hokwihfali maneto hisiweeki mecimi hopemi kwtelahi nihi mata wiilaani hoteleelemahi wahsi kalawilici ksake nihki howaakotaanaawa yeesi nili klaistiiwilici

And devils also came out from many, crying out, and saying, Thou art the Son of God. And rebuking them, he suffered them not to speak, because they knew that he was the Christ.

42. chiine hini yeh waapaki kaasekiki piyeci lohfe mecimi laa papskwahki tasi heewa chiine nihki mehseelekki hoteh natonehwaawaali nili mecimi hotfaawaali chiine homehci wiisa nakinaawaali nili wahsi pwaa hina nihi hoci weepfeeci

And when it was day, he came out and went into a desert place: and the multitudes sought after him, and came unto him, and would have stayed him, that he should not go from them.

43. payeekwa kwiilahi nili howesi piyeetaacimoowena hini maneto hokimaawitaamhkomi hoci nehfaapi neh nanahitaana nili kotakali hoteewena ksake hini weeci waawiiniki hotelahi

But he said unto them, I must preach the good tidings of the kingdom of God to the other cities also: for therefore was I sent.

44. mecimi pemi nanahimiwe piitike nili keeleliiwi mhsikamiko

And he was preaching in the synagogues of Galilee.

Luke:5

1. howe hini piyeemikatwi yeheeyehi hina mehseeleka fakikeeskawaaci nili mecimi nootaki hini hokalawiiwe maneto pcemi niipawici hina pakaci hini kinesoletiiwi mhskeekwi

Now it came to pass, while the multitude pressed upon him and heard the word of God, that he was standing by the lake of Gennesaret;

2. chiine niiswi holakeelali honeemena hina peemi niipawiiyaaki pakaci hini mhskeekwi payeekwa nihki namehfileniiki neyehka nili hoci lohfeeki mecimi peemi kifinamowaaci hotaakwaskwhaawenwa

and he saw two boats standing by the lake: but the fishermen had gone out of them, and were washing their nets.

3. chiine hina hini nekoti nili holakeelali lhkamwa hini saimanii wiila mecimi hokocimaali nili wahsi hini hasiski hoci maalhokwilici tekawihi chiine lematapiwa mecimi hokakehkimahi nihi mehseelelici hini holakeeleki hoci

And he entered into one of the boats, which was Simon's, and asked him to put out a little from the land. And he sat down and taught the multitudes out of the boat.

4. chiine yeh mehci tfwi kalawici halika lhokwilo hini tah tamakaki mecimi sahkiki latenano kitaakwaskwhaawena wahsi haakwaskwhaayani hotelaali saimaniili

And when he had left speaking, he said unto Simon, Put out into the deep, and let down your nets for a draught.

5. mecimi haapafse saimanii mestele nehkatepkwe nipekatefipe mecimi mata wiyehi nipethatoope payeekwa kikalawiiweneki ne hoci sahkiki latenaana nili haakwaskwhaawena hisiwe

And Simon answered and said, Master, we toiled all night, and took nothing: but at thy word I will let down the nets.

6. chiine yeh mehci yooma silawiiwaaci hopethanaawahi nihki meci mehseelelici namefhi mecimi nili hotaakwaskwhaawenwa peemi pkehkaalici

And when they had this done, they enclosed a great multitude of fishes; and their nets were breaking;

7. chiine piyaako hotelatenamawaawahi wihkaanwahi hini kotaki holakeeleki wahsi piyaawaaci nihki mecimi naatamawaawaaci nihi mecimi nihki piyeeki chiine hokwihfetoonaawa neyiiswi nili holakeelali weecikeenahi nili halemi kookhano

and they beckoned unto their partners in the other boat, that they should come and help them. And they came, and filled both the boats, so that they began to sink.

8. payeekwa saiman' piita yeh neemeki hini sahkiki sfe pakaci hociikwaniiwali ciisisii o teepeelemiweeta niila hoci saawelo ksake meciilefita hileni niila hisiwe

But Simon Peter, when he saw it, fell down at Jesus' knees, saying, Depart from me; for I am a sinful man, O Lord.

9. ksake kwakwehtaanitehe mecimi caayahki weewiiciimekoci hini ta haakwaskwahoofolici nihi namefhi mayehci nihki pethanaawaaci

For he was amazed, and all that were with him, at the draught of the fishes which they had taken;

10. mecimi yooni yeelefiwaaci nehfaapi ceemhsii chiine caanii hokwifhi sepetii weewihkaaninaacki saimaniili mecimi ciisisii teki kaawilaweko yooci hinoki hileniiki keh pethanaaki hotelaali saimaniili

and so were also James and John, sons of Zebedee, which were partners with Simon. And Jesus said unto Simon, Fear not; from henceforth thou shalt catch men.

11. chiine yeh mehci nihki hasiski si hakwahfetoowaaci holakeelemwa honakataanaawa caayahki mecimi honeekalaawaali nili

And when they had brought their boats to land, they left all, and followed him.

12. chiine hini piyeemikatwi yeheeyehi hapici nekoti nili hoteewena waapamehko hileni hokwaawefi hoskilhakeemekiiwe chiine hina yeh neewaaci ciisisiili holemhkwi paksinwa mecimi honanahpaacimaali teepeelemiweeta kwehkwi siteheeyane kih katawi fafayaakhi hisiwe

And it came to pass, while he was in one of the cities, behold, a man full of leprosy: and when he saw Jesus, he fell on his face, and besought him, saying, Lord, if thou wilt, thou canst make me clean.

13. mecimi maa si ciikileceska chiine hoteh pehsenaali nili mecimi hiini yeesiteheeya fafayaakhoofolo hotelaali mecimi weelena hini hoskilhakeemekiiwe hina hoci saaweyaali

And he stretched forth his hand, and touched him, saying, I will; be thou made clean. And straightway the leprosy departed from him.

14. mecimi hotepimaali nili wahsi pwaa hina wiitamawaaci hileniili weeka nhhaale wa haayani mecimi waapatesi kiiya hina mhkateewkolaye chiine kifafayaakhoofoowe hoci pakfenikeelo yeesfeki yeesi

And he charged him to tell no man: but go thy way, and shew thyself to the priest, and offer for thy cleansing,

tepikeemoci moosisii wa hoteepweeweniwaaci nihki hotelaali

according as Moses commanded, for a testimony unto them.

15. payeekwa paameci hini halika si weepfeeya hini laacimoowe hina si mecimi meci mehseelekki piyeci maawaskaaki wahsi nootaakeewaaci mecimi wahsi kiikehoofowaaci hotesilokeewenwa

But so much the more went abroad the report concerning him: and great multitudes came together to hear, and to be healed of their infirmities.

16. payeekwa hina hini laa papskwahki hotesiweto wiiya mecimi mamaatome

But he withdrew himself in the deserts, and prayed.

17. chiine hini piyeemikatwi nekoti tah nele kiisekiki yeesi pemi kakehkimiweeci chiine nitasi hapiiki pelesiiki chiine kwteletiiwi taakteliiki peemi pakaci lematapiwaaci caaki hoteewenehi keeleliiki hoci chiine cotiyeeki mecimi colooseelemiiki weeci piyeci lohfaacki mecimi hini howiisikatowiiwe hina teepeelemiweeta howiiciimeko hina wahsi kiikehiweeci

And it came to pass on one of those days, that he was teaching; and there were Pharisees and doctors of the law sitting by, which were come out of every village of Galilee and Judaea and Jerusalem: and the power of the Lord was with him to heal.

18. chiine waapamehko hileniiki hopiyeelaawaali tfaneki hileniili nenekifilici chiine nihki honatonehaanaawa wahsi piicfahaawaaci nili mecimi sekfetaakoci nili yeelahfamiici

And behold, men bring on a bed a man that was palsied: and they sought to bring him in, and to lay him before him.

19. mecimi nihki hopemi kwiilaanaawa hini wayeeci wa hoci menawahi piicfahaawaaci nili ksake hina mehseeleka hoci nihki spemeki hini hakocikami wiikiwa heeki mecimi hini heelekhi hoteh laasiweenaawaali nili saapwi nihi hapahkwehfiwakkohi kileki hotfani piitike yeelahfamiilici ciisisiili

And not finding by what way they might bring him in because of the multitude, they went up to the housetop, and let him down through the tiles with his couch into the midst before Jesus.

20. mecimi hina pemi neemawahi hoteepwehseewenwa nihki hileni kimaciilefiiwena kipakfeeletamaakoopi hotelaali

And seeing their faith, he said, Man, thy sins are forgiven thee.

21. mecimi nihki yaayawikeecki chiine nihki pelesiiki halemi memekiniteheeki neefawe yaama keekalawita pahtaamoowe neefawe katawi pakfeeletamawiwe maciilefiiwena maneto payeekwa naanhsihka hiwaki

And the scribes and the Pharisees began to reason, saying, Who is this that speaketh blasphemies? Who can forgive sins, but God alone?

22. payeekwa ciisisii hopemi mooleeletamawahi yeesiteheewenilici haapafse koociwe kimemekiniteheepwa kitehiwaaki hotelahi

But Jesus perceiving their reasonings, answered and said unto them, What reason ye in your hearts?

23. taaniwe halika weecihi wahsi hiyoki kimaciilefiiwena kipakfeeletamaakoopi weelaa toke honhskaalo mecimi pemhfeelo wahsi hiyoki

Whether is easier, to say, Thy sins are forgiven thee; or to say, Arise and walk?

24. weeka wahsi kiilawa menawahi waakotameekwe yeesi hina hokwihfali hileni poonaki simekofiiwe hoskitaamhkwe wahsi pakfeeletamawiweeci maciilefiiwena hoteh kaloolaali nili nenekifilici kitele

But that ye may know that the Son of man hath power on earth to forgive sins (he said unto him that was palsied), I say unto thee, Arise, and take up thy couch, and go unto thy house.

niila honhskaalo chiine mamelo kitfani mecimi
nhhaale wiikiwa yeetaayani hotelaali nili

25. mecimi weelena hina honhska yeelahfamiilici nihi
chiine hoteh mame hini tah seksiki mecimi nhheewa
wiikiwa yeetaaci hopemi wahfaacimekohwaali
manetooli

And immediately he rose up before them, and took up that whereon he lay, and departed to his house, glorifying God.

26. chiine kwakwehtaaniteheewe homesenekonaawa
caayahki mecimi howahfaacimekohwaawaali nihki
manetooli chiine hokwihfenwili kaawilaweewe
kimehci neemepe mayaci wiyehi hinoki kaasekiki
hiwaki

And amazement took hold on all, and they glorified God; and they were filled with fear, saying, We have seen strange things today.

27. chiine hahkowihi hine yooloma wiyehi hale
weepfe mecimi halika honeewaali teeksiiwi-
maawatonikehfiili liifaai sifooli peemi lematapilici
hini yaatah teekshiweeki chiine neekasilo hotelaali

And after these things he went forth, and beheld a publican, named Levi, sitting at the place of toll, and said unto him, Follow me.

28. mecimi hina honakata caayahki chiine pafekwi
mecimi honeekalaali nili

And he forsook all, and rose up and followed him.

29. chiine liifaai homectawaali nili mhsi
wihfenhcikeewe piitike yeetaaci wiikiwa mecimi
nitasi meci mehseelekki teeksiiwi-maawatonikehfiiki
chiine kotakhi peemi wiitapiimekowaaci tah wihfeniki

And Levi made him a great feast in his house: and there was a great multitude of publicans and of others that were sitting at meat with them.

30. chiine nihki pelesiiki mecimi hoteewikeemwahi
hopekihkawaawahi hokakehkimaafhi koociwe kiilawa
kiwihpomaawaaki mecimi kiwiitaapowemaawaaki
nihki teeksiiwi-maawatonikehfiiki mecimi
meciileficki hisiweeki

And the Pharisees and their scribes murmured against his disciples, saying, Why do ye eat and drink with the publicans and sinners?

31. mecimi pemi haapafse ciisisii nihki
weeowesilaasamamocki mata skata siteheeki
naanatawhcikeelici nihki weeka yeeakwilokeecki

And Jesus answering said unto them, They that are whole have no need of a physician; but they that are sick.

32. mata niila wahsi hotahpimaki nihki
meeyaawiileficki nooci piya meciileficki weeka wahsi
mataiini siteheeweniwaaci hotelahi

I am not come to call the righteous but sinners to repentance.

33. chiine hotelaawaali nihki nihi hokakehkimaafhi
caanii ktawilahi hocikeeki mecimi hostoonaawa
nanahpaacimoowena nehfaapi hini yaska nihi
hokakehkimaafwahi nihki pelesiiki weeka kiila
wihfeniiki mecimi menooki hotekohi

And they said unto him, The disciples of John fast often, and make supplications; likewise also the disciples of the Pharisees; but thine eat and drink.

34. mecimi ciisisii ha kih katawi hocikehaawaaki nihi
hokwifhi hina mayakinhhaakanehkweewika yeheeyehi
nili mayakinhhaakanali wiicikeemekowaaci

And Jesus said unto them, Can ye make the sons of the bride-chamber fast, while the bridegroom is with them?

35. weeka weh piyeeya kaasekiki mecimi hine nili
mayakinhhaakanali weh mamaakwiiki nihki hine
howe we hocikeeki hotelahi

But the days will come; and when the bridegroom shall be taken away from them, then will they fast in those days.

36. chiine pemaatoweewe nehfaapi hokaloolahi nihi
mata hileni weskiki piitenika hoci lelhkina maalekhi

And he spake also a parable unto them; No man rendeth a piece from a new

mecimi kehta piitenikaneki hoteh poona hini piilepe weh lelhkina hini weskiki mecimi hini maalekhi hini weskiki hoci nehfaapi mata we howesfenwi hini kehta

garment and putteth it upon an old garment; else he will rend the new, and also the piece from the new will not agree with the old.

37. chiine mata hileni hotah si poona weskiki waiini kehta pootaalaawahi piilepe hini weskiki weh pohkiceskaakonaawa nihki pootaalaawaaki mecimi hini weh fiikfenwi mecimi nihki pootaalaawaaki weh miyaalefiiki

And no man putteth new wine into old wineskins; else the new wine will burst the skins, and itself will be spilled, and the skins will perish.

38. weeka weskiki waiini kwiilahi mayaki waiiniiwi pootaalaawaaki si poonoote

But new wine must be put into fresh wineskins.

39. chiine mata hileni pemi mehci menwa kehta waiini skata sitehe weskiki ksake hini kehta howesa hiwa hina

And no man having drunk old wine desireth new: for he saith, The old is good.

Luke:6

1. howe hini piyeemikatwi ta halwaakahsiwiki yeesi hale saapwi haaci nili wiyehsi kawaskwiktikaana mecimi hokakehkimaafhi hale pkinamehi nili kikahkwimi mecimi miicilici pemi nenekonamehi nili holeciwaaki

Now it came to pass on a sabbath, that he was going through the cornfields; and his disciples plucked the ears of corn, and did eat, rubbing them in their hands.

2. payeekwa naanekoti nihki pelesiiki hoci koociwe kitesilawiipwa hini pwaayaa mayaawhki kwteletiiweneki wahsi lawiiki hini ta halwaakahsi kiisekiki hiwaki

But certain of the Pharisees said, Why do ye that which it is not lawful to do on the sabbath day?

3. mecimi hopemi haapaftawahi ciisisii ha mata kimeh laapaatotaanaawa teetepilahi yooma yeesilawiici teepitii ye skwaalaweeci wiila mecimi nihki weewiitfemaacki nili

And Jesus answering them said, Have ye not read even this, what David did, when he was an hungred, he, and they that were with him;

4. yeesi hina piicfaaci hini wiikiwa yeetaaci maneto chiine mameki mecimi miicici hini hofepi takhwa peepoonooteeki mecimi nehfaapi miilaaci nihi weewiitfemekoci peepwaa hini mayaawhki kwteletiiweneki wahsi miiciki weeciwephi nihki mhkateewkolayeeki pehi

how he entered into the house of God, and did take and eat the shewbread, and gave also to them that were with him; which it is not lawful to eat save for the priests alone?

5. chiine nili hokwihfali hileni hina teepeeletaka hini halwaakahsiiwe hotelahi

And he said unto them, The Son of man is lord of the sabbath.

6. chiine hini piyeemikatwi nohki kotaki ta halwaakahsiwiki yeesi piicfaaci hini mhsikamikwi mecimi kakehkimiweeci chiine nitasi hapiwa hileni mecimi homayaawiinhkiki holeci hahkapatwili

And it came to pass on another sabbath, that he entered into the synagogue and taught: and there was a man there, and his right hand was withered.

7. mecimi nihki yaayawikeecki chiine nihki pelesiiki hokcitawaapamaawaali nili kwehkwi toke hina wih kiikehiwe hini ta halwaakasiwiki wahsi menawahke mhkamowaaci wahsi mestaawimaawaaci nili

And the scribes and the Pharisees watched him, whether he would heal on the sabbath; that they might find how to accuse him.

8. payeekwa hina howaakotamawahi homemekiniteheeeweenilici mecimi pafekwiilo chiine hini heelekhi si niipawilo hotelaali nili hileniili peepoonamelici hahkapwileceewe mecimi hina pafekwi chiine pemi niipawi

But he knew their thoughts; and he said to the man that had his hand withered, Rise up, and stand forth in the midst. And he arose and stood forth.

9. chiine ciisisii kinatohtoolepwa ha mayaawatwi hini kwteletiiweneki wahsi weeowesaaki silawiiki hini ta halwaakahsiwiki weelaa wahsi miyaasi lawiiki wahsi waapanestooteeki lenaweewiiwe weelaa wahsi macilotooteeki hini hotelahi nihi

And Jesus said unto them, I ask you, Is it lawful on the sabbath to do good, or to do harm? to save a life, or to destroy it?

10. chiine hoteh waapamahi kaayaawka caayahki nihi mecimi maa si ciikileceelelo hotelaali nili mecimi yooni silawi hina mecimi petekistooteeli holeci

And he looked round about on them all, and said unto him, Stretch forth thy hand. And he did so: and his hand was restored.

11. payeekwa nihki hokwihfenili wiyakoweewe mecimi kiikalooletiiki menawahi wa hpenalaawaaci ciisisiili

But they were filled with madness; and communed one with another what they might do to Jesus.

12. chiine hini piyeemikatwi yoolooni kaasekiki yeesi hina hini meekwahkiki si lohfaaci wahsi mamaatomeeci mecimi yaska hina homamaatomaali manetooli nehkatepkwe

And it came to pass in these days, that he went out into the mountain to pray; and he continued all night in prayer to God.

13. chiine hini yeh waapaki kaasekiki hotahpimahi hokakehkimaafhi mecimi nihi hoci mekinahi metahfwi-kite-niiswi nihiiini nehfaapi hepastaliiki hotesi wiinahi

And when it was day, he called his disciples: and he chose from them twelve, whom also he named apostles;

14. saimaniili niliini nehfaapi piita hotesi wiinaali chiine heenhtlooli hoceeninaali chiine ceemhsiili mecimi caaniili chiine filapiili mecimi pafalamiyoli

Simon, whom he also named Peter, and Andrew his brother, and James and John, and Philip and Bartholomew,

15. chiine mefiyooli mecimi taamosiili chiine ceemhsiili nili hokwihfali halhfiyas chiine saimaniili hina siilat yaaleta

and Matthew and Thomas, and James the son of Alphaeus, and Simon which was called the Zealot,

16. chiine cootasiili nili hokwihfali ceemhsii chiine cootas' hiskeeletiili hina mayestaawhiweewita

and Judas the son of James, and Judas Iscariot, which was the traitor;

17. chiine howiici piyeci paalacsinoomahi nihi mecimi laa tepkiki niipawi chiine meci mehseelelici hokakehkimaafhi chiine meci tfwiiki nihki caayahki cotiye hoci lenaweeki mecimi colooseelemii chiine hini mhsinepi skwaapiye taayaa mecimi saatanii nihkiiini piyeeki wahsi nootawaawaaci nili mecimi wahsi kiikehoofowaaci hotesilokeewenwa

and he came down with them, and stood on a level place, and a great multitude of his disciples, and a great number of the people from all Judaea and Jerusalem, and the sea coast of Tyre and Sidon, which came to hear him, and to be healed of their diseases;

18. mecimi nihki peetfakhekocki wiyakilehfihi kiikehoofooki

and they that were troubled with unclean spirits were healed.

19. chiine caayahki nili mehseelelici natonehikeeli wahsi pehsenekoci ksake wiila homooya waasikaki mecimi hokiikehahi caayahki

And all the multitude sought to touch him: for power came forth from him, and healed them all.

20. chiine hoteh waapamahi hokakehkimaafhi mecimi hiwa kikisaateelemekofipwa cehi kiilawa kitemaafaki ksake kiilawa hini hokimaawitaamhkomi maneto

And he lifted up his eyes on his disciples, and said, Blessed are ye poor: for yours is the kingdom of God.

21. kikisaateelemekofipwa cehi kiilawa seeskwaalaweecki hinoki ksake keh teephoolopwa kiilawa kikisaateelemekofipwa cehi kiilawa weewihfakweecki hinoki ksake ke haayaayelipwa kiilawa

Blessed are ye that hunger now: for ye shall be filled. Blessed are ye that weep now: for ye shall laugh.

22. kikisaateelemekofipwa cehi kiilawa hine hileniiki keh siikeelemekowaaki mecimi nihki howihkaanwahi ke hoci nohpiyeenekowaaki mecimi lhskimelwaakwe chiine lohfe pakitamoolwaakwe kiwiifoowenwa paasi mecaafiki ksake nili hokwihfali hileni hoci

Blessed are ye, when men shall hate you, and when they shall separate you from their company, and reproach you, and cast out your name as evil, for the Son of man's sake.

23. hosasilepwaako hine hini kaasekiki mecimi lalemacfaako hosasilepwaawe hoci ksake waapatamoko mhsaawi kitephofiiwenwa piitike weefepahkamikiki ksake hofwahi hini yaska yeesilawihtawaawaaci nihki nihi maamoosikiiskwelici

Rejoice in that day, and leap for joy: for behold, your reward is great in heaven: for in the same manner did their fathers unto the prophets.

24. payeekwa macilepwaawe cehi kiilawa peepawaacki ksake neyehka kimehci hotfekonaawa kiwiikehoofoowenwa kiilawa

But woe unto you that are rich! for ye have received your consolation.

25. macilepwaawe cehi kiilawa kiilawa teeteephoolocki hinoki ksake ke skwaalaweepwa kiilawa macilepwaawe cehi kiilawa kiilawa yeeyaayelicki hinoki ksake keh mawepwa mecimi keh wihfakweepwa kiilawa

Woe unto you, ye that are full now! for ye shall hunger. Woe unto you, ye that laugh now! for ye shall mourn and weep.

26. macilepwaawe cehi kiilawa hine caayahki hileniiki ke howelaacimekowaaki kiilawa ksake hofwahi hini yaska yeesilawihtawaawaaci nihki nihi miyaasi maamoosikiiskwelici

Woe unto you, when all men shall speak well of you! for in the same manner did their fathers to the false prophets.

27. payeekwa kitelepwa niila kiilawa neenootaakeeyeekwe hahkweelemehko kimateeletiiwenwaaki howespenalehko nihki seesiikeelemelwaakwe

But I say unto you which hear, Love your enemies, do good to them that hate you,

28. kisaateelemehko nihki meemacikaloolelwaakwe mamaatomawehko nihki meemoyaleewilotoolwaakwe

bless them that curse you, pray for them that despitefully use you.

29. hina wiyeefa peepkitehohka hini kimayaawi-nowaaki nehfaapi miili hini hasowe kotaki chiine hina meemamawehka kipihtawipiitenika teki hina hahkweeletamawi hini kikootiimi nehfaapi

To him that smiteth thee on the one cheek offer also the other; and from him that taketh away thy cloke withhold not thy coat also.

30. miili caakiwiyeefa neetotamawehka mecimi hina meemamawehka kiwiyehiimi teki nili natotamawi nohki

Give to every one that asketh thee; and of him that taketh away thy goods ask them not again.

31. chiine yeesiteheeyeekwe wi hpenalelwaakwe hileniiki nehfaapi kiilawa yaska hini hpenalehko nihki

And as ye would that men should do to you, do ye also to them likewise.

32. chiine kwehkwi hahkweelemeekwe nihki yeeakweelemelwaakwe nehiwesi niyaawe kipoonaanaawa ksake teetepilahi meciileficki hotahkweelemaawahi yohoma yeeakweelemekowaaci

And if ye love them that love you, what thank have ye? for even sinners love those that love them.

33. chiine kwehkwi howespenaleekwe nihki weeowespenalelwaakwe nehiwesi niyaawe kipoonaanaawa ksake teetepilahi meciileficki yaska hini silawiiki

And if ye do good to them that do good to you, what thank have ye? for even sinners do the same.

34. chiine kwehkwi kiilawa hawhheekwe nihki nihkiini keela yeeleelemeekwe wa hotatenikeeyeekwe nehiwesi niyaawe kipoonaanaawa teetepilahi meciileficki hotawhhaawahi meciilefilici wahsi nohki hotefiwaaci hini lekhi

And if ye lend to them of whom ye hope to receive, what thank have ye? even sinners lend to sinners, to receive again as much.

35. payeekwa hahkweelemehko kimateeletiiwenwaaki mecimi howespenalehko chiine hawhiweeko teki laakwa pemi kwiilah siteheeko mecimi we mhsaawi kitephofiiwenwa chiine ke hokwihfinekowa hina kci moospi ksake howesitehe hina nihi wayeeci pwaayaa niyaawe hilefilici mecimi meciilefilici

But love your enemies, and do them good, and lend, never despairing; and your reward shall be great, and ye shall be sons of the Most High: for he is kind toward the unthankful and evil.

36. hokwaawefiko kiteminaakweeletiiwe teetepilahi yeesi kohfwa hokwaawefici kiteminaakweeletiiwe

Be ye merciful, even as your Father is merciful.

37. chiine teki wiyehileelemiweeko mecimi mata wiyehi ke hileelemekoopwa chiine teki matahkowaasiweeko mecimi mata keh matahkowaalekoopwa pakfeniweeko mecimi keh pakfenekoopwa

And judge not, and ye shall not be judged: and condemn not, and ye shall not be condemned: release, and ye shall be released:

38. miiliweeko mecimi keh miilekoopwa hini howesi tepacika fafakikinoote maawatwi naanoomenoote haamaamhfenwi keh si miilekowaaki nihki kipaleewaaki ksake kookweenehi si tepacika keh tepacikeepwa hini nohki keh tepacikaalekoopwa

give, and it shall be given unto you; good measure, pressed down, shaken together, running over, shall they give into your bosom. For with what measure ye mete it shall be measured to you again.

39. chiine pemaatoweewe nehfaapi hokaloolahi ha hina keekeepiikweeta wih katawi niikaaniwelaali nili keekeepiikweelici ha mata nihki neeyiiswi waasaalakoki weh si penhsinooki

And he spake also a parable unto them, Can the blind guide the blind? shall they not both fall into a pit?

40. hina kakehkimaafa mata haliwi lhspimekofi keekehkimekoci weeka caakiwiyeefa yeh mehcilotoofoci paasi keekehkimekoci we hilefi

The disciple is not above his master: but every one when he is perfected shall be as his master.

41. chiine koociwe kineeme hini pefenoowe kiceenina hoskiisekoki yehteeki payeekwa mata kiteh memekineeleta hini peemitakofeki nehalwaaka kiskiisekoki yehteeki

And why beholdest thou the mote that is in thy brother's eye, but considerest not the beam that is in thine own eye?

42. weelaa nehiwe keh si katawi hila kiceenina hoceeninaana wiilaani nih lohfe pakita hini pefenoowe kiskiisekoki yehteeki hine kiila mata kitelaapata hini

Or how canst thou say to thy brother, Brother, let me cast out the mote that is in thine eye, when thou thyself beholdest peemitakofeki nehalwaaka kiskiisekoki yehteeki kiila nelohcilawiwehfi nhhihta nehalwaaka kiskiisekoki hoci lohfe pakitano hini peemitakofeki mecimi hine howe ke tepinaakwi neeme wahsi lohfe pakitamani hini pefenoowe kiceenina hoskiisekoki yehteeki

not the beam that is in thine own eye? Thou hypocrite, cast out first the beam out of thine own eye, and then shalt thou see clearly to cast out the mote that is in thy brother's eye.

43. ksake matalaakwa howesi mhtekwi weeci niikiki wiyakaaci mawifoowe weelaa nohki wiyakaaci mhtekwi weeci niikiki howesi mawifoowe

For there is no good tree that bringeth forth corrupt fruit; nor again a corrupt tree that bringeth forth good fruit.

44. ksake caaki mhtekwi nehalwaaka homawifoowe hoci waakotoote ksake hileniiki mata kaawihi si mawifooki kicimi weelaa mata pesipehteemi miinikaawisehi si mawifooki nihki

For each tree is known by its own fruit. For of thorns men do not gather figs, nor of a bramble bush gather they grapes.

45. hina howesi hileni hini hotehi hoci howesi paweewe hoci piyeeto hini weeowesaaki mecimi hina maciilenihfefa hini maci paweewe hoci piyeeto mecaafiki ksake hini yaamhfeki hini hotehi hoci kalawiiya hotooni

The good man out of the good treasure of his heart bringeth forth that which is good; and the evil man out of the evil treasure bringeth forth that which is evil: for out of the abundance of the heart his mouth speaketh.

46. chiine koociwe teepeelemiweeta teepeelemiweeta kitesipwa chiine mata kitesilawiipwa nili wiyehi niila yeeyoya

And why call ye me, Lord, Lord, and do not the things which I say?

47. caakiwiyeefa peepiyeelotawita chiine honootaana nikalawiiwena mecimi hotesilawihtaana nili keh waapatelelepwa nili yeelawaaci hina

Every one that cometh unto me, and heareth my words, and doeth them, I will shew you to whom he is like:

48. paasi hileni hina hilefi peemi hopatenaki wiikiwa waalhke hina mecimi spaalakwi heewa chiine hoskici nili siikonali hotelahkehfeto laamatahkehfecika mecimi hine yaamikamiki pafekwiiya hini peemhtaki pkitehfenwi hini wiikiwaapeki mecimi haalwi noomeska hini ksake hini mehci haayictoote

he is like a man building a house, who digged and went deep, and laid a foundation upon the rock: and when a flood arose, the stream brake against that house, and could not shake it: because it had been well builded.

49. weeka hina neenootaakeeta mecimi mata wiyehi silawi paasi hileni hilefi hina weeopatenaka wiikiwa hini hoskitaamhkwe matalaakwa laamatahkehfecika yeepkitehfeki hini peemhtaki mecimi weelena hini haakicfeeya mecimi mhsaawi hini holiikatefiiwe hina wiikiwa

But he that heareth, and doeth not, is like a man that built a house upon the earth without a foundation; against which the stream brake, and straightway it fell in; and the ruin of that house was great.

Luke:7

1. yeh mehci ceeyehkwilotaki caayahki hoteyoowena nili hotawakaawaaki nihki lenaweeki hote hotta kehpaaniamii

After he had ended all his sayings in the ears of the people, he entered into Capernaum.

2. mecimi naanekoti kaptiina hotaloolaakanali niliini keesoweelemaaci hahkwilokeeli chiine howe nahiika hkwiilefiili hini nepoowe

And a certain centurion's servant, who was dear unto him, was sick and at the point of death.

3. mecimi hina yeh nootaakeeci ciisisiili hoteleskamawaali hokikileniimwahi nihki coosaki hopemi kocimaali nili wahsi piyaalici mecimi waapanestaakoci hotaloolaakanali

And when he heard concerning Jesus, he sent unto him elders of the Jews, asking him that he would come and save his servant.

4. chiine nihki ye hotfaawaaci ciisisiili holaami honanahpaacimaawaali nahiika hikweelemekofi hina wahsi kiila yooma hpenatawaci

And they, when they came to Jesus, besought him earnestly, saying, He is worthy that thou shouldest do this for him:

5. ksake hotahkweeleta hina kitfweeloowenena chiine wiila noopatenamaakona nimhsikamikomena hisiweeki nihki

for he loveth our nation, and himself built us our synagogue.

6. mecimi howiiteemahi ciisisii chiine hine howe mata pelowi piyeetfe hini wiikiwa hoci hina kaptiina hoteleskamawaali wihkaanhhi teepeelemiweeta teki petfakitoolo kiiya ksake ninootkweelemekofi wahsi kiila piyaayani siipaaci nitapahkwehfecika

And Jesus went with them. And when he was now not far from the house, the centurion sent friends to him, saying unto him, Lord, trouble not thyself: for I am not worthy that thou shouldest come under my roof:

7. yooni hoci mata nohki niteepileeleta niiya wahsi niila piyeelotoola weeka kalawilo hini kalawiiwe mecimi nitaloolaaka weh kiikehoofo hotelaali nili

wherefore neither thought I myself worthy to come unto thee: but say the word, and my servant shall be healed.

8. ksake nehfaapi niila hileni lematapiwa siipaaci wiisikatowiiwe peemi poonaki siipaaci niila samaakanaki mecimi nhhaale nitela yaama nekoti mecimi hina nhheewa chiine nohki kotaka piyaalo mecimi hina piyeewa chiine nitaloolaaka yooma silawiilo mecimi hini silawi hina hisiwe

For I also am a man set under authority, having under myself soldiers: and I say to this one, Go, and he goeth; and to another, Come, and he cometh; and to my servant, Do this, and he doeth it.

9. chiine yeh nootaakeeci ciisisii yooloma wiyehi hokwakwehtaaneelemaali nili chiine nihi si kokiiwa mehseelelici neekalekoci mecimi kitelepwa niila mata nime mhka yooni yeesi mhsaaki teepwehseewe mata matalaakwa laa hiswiileki hotelahi

And when Jesus heard these things, he marveled at him, and turned and said unto the multitude that followed him, I say unto you, I have not found so great faith, no, not in Israel.

10. mecimi nihki weewaawiinoofocki pemi peteki si kotekwiiki hini wiikiwa homhkawaawaali nili haloolaakanali mefefiili

And they that were sent, returning to the house, found the servant whole.

11. chiine hini piyeemikatwi peloocihi mayohkwaaci yeesi hoteeweneki haaci neini sitoote mecimi hokakehkimaafhi howiiteemekohi chiine meci mehseelelici

And it came to pass soon afterwards, that he went to a city called Nain; and his disciples went with him, and a great multitude.

12. howe maalaakwahi yeh piyeetfeci hini hoteeweni skwaate waapamehko nitasi piyeci lohfahoofo nekoti nepeka niliini pehi hokwihfali hokiifa mecimi hina siikawi-ykwe chiine meci hini hoteewe hoci lenaweeki wiici nili hkweeli

Now when he drew near to the gate of the city, behold, there was carried out one that was dead, the only son of his mother, and she was a widow: and much people of the city was with her.

13. mecimi hina teepeelemiweeta yeh neewaaci nili hkweeli hopoonamawaali kiteminaakweeletiiwe mecimi teki wihfakweelo hotelaali

And when the Lord saw her, he had compassion on her, and said unto her, Weep not.

14. chiine maalaakwahi heewa mecimi hoteh pehsena hini nepoowiyaamwecika chiine nihki yaamwelaacki noole niipawiiki mecimi mayaanileni kitele niila honhskaalo hiwa

And he came nigh and touched the bier: and the bearers stood still. And he said, Young man, I say unto thee, Arise.

15. mecimi hina nepeka lematapiwa chiine halemi kalawi mecimi ye hokilici si miiliwe nili

And he that was dead sat up, and began to speak. And he gave him to his mother.

16. mecimi kaawilaweewe homesenekonaawa caayahki chiine howahfaacimekohwaawaali nihki manetooli mhsi maamoosikiiskweeta pemi pafekwi heelekiina kiilawa chiine neyehka honawhhahi hotelenaweemhhi maneto hiwaki

And fear took hold on all: and they glorified God, saying, A great prophet is arisen among us: and, God hath visited his people.

17. chiine yooma laacimoowe hina hisi mefhiike hini cotiye si weepfeeya mecimi mefhiike hini kaayaawka tasi

And this report went forth concerning him in the whole of Judaea, and all the region round about.

18. chiine nihi hokakehkimaafhi caanii howiitamaakohi caayahki yooloma wiyehi

And the disciples of John told him of all these things.

19. mecimi hotahpimahi niiswi hokakehkimaafhi caanii nili teepeelemiweelici hoteh waawiinahi nihi ha kiila hina wah piyaata weelaa toke nih natawaapamaape kotaka hisiwe

And John calling unto him two of his disciples sent them to the Lord, saying, Art thou he that cometh, or look we for another?

20. chiine nihki hileniiki ye hotfaawaaci nili caanii hina fafahkwiholelhiwena niteh waawiinekona kiila ha kiila hina wah piyaata weelaa toke nih natawaapamaape kotaka hiwa hisiweeki nihki

And when the men were come unto him, they said, John the Baptist hath sent us unto thee, saying, Art thou he that cometh, or look we for another?

21. hine hini yaatefaki meci hokiikehahi silokeewena hoci mecimi hpeneewena chiine macilehfihi hoci chiine meci keekeepiikweelici hoteh poona tepinamoowe

In that hour he cured many of diseases and plagues and evil spirits; and on many that were blind he bestowed sight.

22. chiine haapafse mecimi nhhaakone mecimi wiitamawehko caanii nili wiyehi kiilawa mayehci nccmcycckwc mecimi nootamcckwc nihki keekeepiikweecki hotfekonaawa hotepinamoowenwa nihki meemiyaalakatowikaateecki pemhfeeki nihki weeskilhakeemekicki fafayaakhoofooki mecimi nihki keekeepseeki nootaakeeki nihki neepekiki honhskaanoofooki nihki kitemaafaki hopoonaanaawa howesi piyeetaacimoowena nanahimoofooki

And he answered and said unto them, Go your way, and tell John what things ye have seen and heard; the blind receive their sight, the lame walk, the lepers are cleansed, and the deaf hear, the dead are raised up, the poor have good tidings preached to them.

23. mecimi kisaateelemekofi cehi hina kookwe-neefa- kaaci mata we mhka wa hoci niiyaaki hotakikahsiki hotelahi nihi

And blessed is he, whosoever shall find none occasion of stumbling in me.

24. chiine hine nihi caanii homiisamaakeemhhi yeh weepfeelici hotalemi hilahi nihi mehseelelici caaniili

And when the messengers of John were departed, he began to say unto the

hisi nehiwe kiilawa kimawaapataanaawa weeci hini si multitudes concerning John, What went
lohfaayeekwe piileski ha mhfaskwalwi ye out into the wilderness to behold? a
naanoomilohanwi reed shaken with the wind?

25. weeka nehiwe kimawaapataanaawa weeci But what went ye out to see? a man
lohfaayeekwe ha hileni piitenike skanoofi piitenika clothed in soft raiment? Behold, they
waapamehko nihki weewaawesiwasecki mecimi which are gorgeously apparelled, and live
neenaaswi lenaweewicki hapiiki piitike mhsi-okimaaki delicately, are in kings' courts.
howakhoowikaanwa

26. payeekwa nehiwe kimawaapataanaawa weeci But what went ye out to see? a prophet?
lohfaayeekwe ha maamoosikiiskweeta haanhka Yea, I say unto you, and much more than
kitelepwa niila mecimi mhsi halika si a prophet.
maamoosikiiskweeta

27. hiina yaama mayehtawikeeki hini waapami This is he of whom it is written, Behold, I
niteleskawa nimiisaama yeelahfamiikweeyani hiina send my messenger before thy face, Who
weh nanahihfeto kimiyeewi yeelahfamiiyani shall prepare thy way before thee.

28. kitelepwa niila heelekiina nihki hkwehi I say unto you, Among them that are born
neeniikinekocki mata wiyeefa nitasi halika yeelefita of women there is none greater than
caaniili payeekwa hina meciloofita piitike hini John: yet he that is but little in the
hokimaawitaamhkomi maneto halika hilefi noota hina kingdom of God is greater than he.

29. chiine nihki caayahki lenaweeki mecimi nihki And all the people when they heard, and
teeksiiwi-maawatonikehfiiki yeh nootaakeewaaci the publicans, justified God, being
hotepasawhaawaali manetooli teewahi mehci fafahkwi baptized with the baptism of John.
holelhoofooki hini hofafahkwiholelhiweewe caanii

30. weeka nihki pelesiiki mecimi nihki layaki wiilawa But the Pharisees and the lawyers
si hotaalawinaanaawa hini hokakehkimoowe maneto rejected for themselves the counsel of
teewahi mata hofafahkwi holelhekowaali nili God, being not baptized of him.

31. taaniwe howe neh si hilawehaaki nihki yooma Whereunto then shall I liken the men of
hinoki skwiiwe hoci leniiki mecimi nehiwe nihki this generation, and to what are they like?
hotelaanaawa

32. paasi hapelohfaki hilefiiki nihki lematapicki hini They are like unto children that sit in the
yaatah wiitkiiki mecimi waawihkometiiki marketplace, and call one to another;
kipepikwehtoolepe chiine mata kimenyeelepwa which say, We piped unto you, and ye did
nimaweewahootaape mecimi mata kiwihfakweepwa not dance; we wailed, and ye did not
ya hitiiki weep.

33. ksake caanii hina fafahkwiholelhiwena piyeewa For John the Baptist is come eating no
mata hopemi miici takhwa mata pemi menwa waiini bread nor drinking wine; and ye say, He
mecimi kiilawa hopoonaali waninehfiili kiteyopwa hath a devil.

34. hina hokwihfali hileni piyeewa pemi wihfeni The Son of man is come eating and
mecimi pemi menwa mecimi kiilawa waapamehko drinking; and ye say, Behold, a
pkamefiwi-leni chiine maciweenefo teeksiiwi- gluttonous man, and a winebibber, a
maawatonikehfiiki mecimi meciileficki wihkaanwaali friend of publicans and sinners!
kiteyopwa

35. mecimi lepwaawe hotepasawhekohi caayahki And wisdom is justified of all her
hotapelohfemhhi children.

36. chiine nekoti nihki pelesiiki skata hoteleelemaali nili wahsi wiici-wihfeniimekoci mecimi nili pelesiili yeetaalici wiikiwa si piicfe hina chiine mesahke wahsi wihfenici

And one of the Pharisees desired him that he would eat with him. And he entered into the Pharisee's house, and sat down to meat.

37. mecimi waapamehko hkweewa hini hoteeweneki meciilefita chiine hina yeh waakotaki yeesi peemahkeepilici nili tah wihfeniki hina pelesi yeetaaci wiikiwaapeki hopiyeeto heelepeestaawi wihfakakkoofeki lomhkoowe

And behold, a woman which was in the city, a sinner; and when she knew that he was sitting at meat in the Pharisee's house, she brought an alabaster cruse of ointment,

38. chiine hotaanaaki niipawi nahiika hofitali ciisisii wihfakwe hofekikawiikweewena hoci halemi skahotaakooli hofitali chiine nili wiilehfa hoci kafhaana nili mecimi hopackataana hofitali ciisisii chiine hini lomhkoowe hoci lominaana nili

and standing behind at his feet, weeping, she began to wet his feet with her tears, and wiped them with the hair of her head, and kissed his feet, and anointed them with the ointment.

39. howe hina pelesi mayehci halanaata nili yeh neemeki hini kalawi laameki wiiya yaama hileni kwehkwi maamoosikiiskweewite neyehka wih mooleeleta si wiyeefali mecimi yeesiweefilici yooloma hkweeli peepehsenekoci meciilefita hina hiwapi

Now when the Pharisee which had bidden him saw it, he spake within himself, saying, This man, if he were a prophet, would have perceived who and what manner of woman this is which touched him, that she is a sinner.

40. chiine ciisisii pemi haapafse saimanii nipoona tekawi wa hilela kiila hotelaali mecimi kalawilo keekehkimiwe hotelaali hina

And Jesus answering said unto him, Simon, I have somewhat to say unto thee. And he saith, Master, say on.

41. naanekoti yaayawhiweeta hopoonahi niiswi moosinehikanhhi hina nekoti moosinehike niyaalane tepeewe seleni chiine hina kotaka niyaalanwaapitaki

A certain lender had two debtors: the one owed five hundred pence, and the other fifty.

42. yeh pwaa nihki poonamowaaci wa hoci tephikeewaaci hopakfeeletamawahi hina neyiiswi taaniliwe weecikeenahi we kci halika si hahkweelemekooli nihi

When they had not wherewith to pay, he forgave them both. Which of them therefore will love him most?

43. mecimi haapafse saimanii hina weenahkwi nili hini halika lekhi peepakfeeletamawaaci hisiwe neyehka kimayaawahkowaata hotelaali

Simon answered and said, He, I suppose, to whom he forgave the most. And he said unto him, Thou hast rightly judged.

44. mecimi nili hkweeli si pemi kokiiwa ha kineewa yaama hkweewa hotelaali saimaniili niyotta wiikiwa yeetaayani mata nifitali kitesi miili nepi weeka hina hofekikawiikweewena hoci mehci skahotoona nifitali mecimi wiilehfa hoci kafhaana nili

And turning to the woman, he said unto Simon, Seest thou this woman? I entered into thine house, thou gavest me no water for my feet: but she hath wetted my feet with her tears, and wiped them with her hair.

45. mata kimiili packametiiwe weeka hina hini yeelaakwa piicfaaya hoci mata home tfwihka wahsi packakataki nifitali

Thou gavest me no kiss: but she, since the time I came in, hath not ceased to kiss my feet.

46. niisi mata kilomhkoona lomhkoowe weeka hina lomhkoowe hoci mehci lominaana nifitali

My head with oil thou didst not anoint: but she hath anointed my feet with ointment.

47. hiini hoci kitele niila hina homaciilefiiwena meci
nili pakfeeletoote ksake hina hahkweelemiwe holaami
weeka maalecihi yeesi miiloofota hiina hina maalecihi
si hahkweelemiwe

Wherefore I say unto thee, Her sins, which are many, are forgiven; for she loved much: but to whom little is forgiven, the same loveth little.

48. mecimi nili hkweeli kimaciilefiiwena
pakfeeletoote hotelaali

And he said unto her, Thy sins are forgiven.

49. chiine nihki weewiitapiimekoci tah wihfeniki
neefawe yaama peepakfenaka wiikinaakwi
maciilefiiwena halemi hiwaki laameki wiilawa

And they that sat at meat with him began to say within themselves, Who is this that even forgiveth sins?

50. mecimi kiteepwehseewe kimehci waapanesheko
kaamaani si weepfeelo hotelaali nili hkweeli

And he said unto the woman, Thy faith hath saved thee; go in peace.

Luke:8

1. chiine hini piyeemikatwi peloocihi mayohkwaaci
yeesi saapwi paamhfeeci kaayaawka hoteewena
mecimi hoteeweneefa pemi nanahimiwe mecimi pemi
piyeetawiwe nili howesi piyeetaacimoowena hini
maneto hokimaawitaamhkomi hoci chiine wiici nili
nihki metahfwi-kite-niiswi

And it came to pass soon afterwards, that he went about through cities and villages, preaching and bringing the good tidings of the kingdom of God, and with him the twelve,

2. chiine naanekoti hkweeki mayehci kiikehoofocki
macilehfihi hoci mecimi katoneewena melii
mekiteliina yaaloofo niliini hoci mehci lohfeeki
niiswahfwi waninehfiiki

and certain women which had been healed of evil spirits and infirmities, Mary that was called Magdalene, from whom seven devils had gone out,

3. chiine cooena nili wiiwali kosaasi honoosaacikanali
heletii chiine soosiyena chiine meci kotakaki nihkiini
howiyehiimwa hoci kisaacihaawahi nihi

and Joanna the wife of Chuza Herod's steward, and Susanna, and many others, which ministered unto them of their substance.

4. chiine hine meci mehseelekki yeh tepetwi
piyaawaaci mecimi nihki caaki hoteewe hoci
hotootfaawaali nili kalawi hina pemaatoweewe hoci

And when a great multitude came together, and they of every city resorted unto him, he spake by a parable:

5. hina yeeahcikeeta hale weepfe wahsi hahtooci
homiinhka chiine yeesi hina hahtooci naaleta hini
pakacikana si penhfenwi mecimi hini kakeelhkoote
laameki hofici chiine nihki menhkwatwi hoci
wiskilohfaki hocaakataanaawa hini

The sower went forth to sow his seed: and as he sowed, some fell by the way side; and it was trodden under foot, and the birds of the heaven devoured it.

6. chiine naaleta hoskici nili siikonali si penhfenwi
mecimi yeesi kola hini faakiki hale sahte hini ksake
mata poonameya meelemawaaki

And other fell on the rock; and as soon as it grew, it withered away, because it had no moisture.

7. chiine naaleta heelekhi nihi kaawihi si penhfenwi
mecimi nihki kaawiiki wiici skwiniikiiki hini mecimi
honepwaskwehtoonaawa hini

And other fell amidst the thorns; and the thorns grew with it, and choked it.

8. chiine naaleta hini howesi hasiskiiki si penhfenwi
chiine skwiniikinwi mecimi hini niikinwi mawifoowe
tepeewe tfweekinwi hisiwe yeesi yooloma wiyehi yoci

And other fell into the good ground, and grew, and brought forth fruit a hundredfold. As he said these things, he holaamowe hina peepoonaka hotawakaawali wahsi nootaakeeci wiilaani hina nootaakeete hisiwe

cried, He that hath ears to hear, let him hear.

9. chiine honatohtaakohi hokakehkimaafhi yooma pemaatoweewe menawahi yeeki

And his disciples asked him what this parable might be.

10. mecimi hisiwe kiilawa si miiliweepi wahsi waakotameekwe nili kiyaaciilefiiwena hini maneto hokimaawitaamhkomi hoci weeka nihki maisi naaleta pemaatoweewena hisi wahsi nihki pemi neekeewaate menawahi pwaa neemowaaci mecimi pemi nootaakeewaate nihki menawahi pwaa nenohseewaaci

And he said, Unto you it is given to know the mysteries of the kingdom of God: but to the rest in parables; that seeing they may not see, and hearing they may not understand.

11. howe hini pemaatoweewe halayooma hinwi hini miinhka hokalawiiwe maneto hini

Now the parable is this: The seed is the word of God.

12. chiine nelene hini pakackana nihkiini nihki mayehci nootaakeecki hine howe piyeewa hina macimaneto mecimi homame hini kalawiiwe hotehiwaaki hoci wahsi nihki menawah pwaa teepwehseewaaci mecimi waapanhsiwaaci

And those by the way side are they that have heard; then cometh the devil, and taketh away the word from their heart, that they may not believe and be saved.

13. chiine nele hoskici nili siikonali nihkiini nihki yeh mehci nootaakeewaaci hotahpenaanaawa hini kalawiiwe wiici howesilepwaawe mecimi yohkooni mata hopoonaanaawa hoceepkahatwi nihki maalaakwasi teepwehseeki mecimi kolaa laakwa miyaasi-ashetiiweneki hale haakicfeeki

And those on the rock are they which, when they have heard, receive the word with joy; and these have no root, which for a while believe, and in time of temptation fall away.

14. chiine hini heelekiina nihi kaawihi yeesi penhfeki yohkooni nihki mayehci nootaakeecki mecimi yeelelhfeewaaci yehaawaaci hokihkitoneskaakonaawa hotamefiiwena chiine paweewena chiine wiiceekilawiiwena yooma lenaweewiiwe hoci mecimi mata hoteh piyeetoonaawa mawifoowe mefefiiweneki

And that which fell among the thorns, these are they that have heard, and as they go on their way they are choked with cares and riches and pleasures of this life, and bring no fruit to perfection.

15. chiine hini hini howesi hasiskiiki yohkooni yeeleficki paasi teepasawiki mecimi howesiteheeweneki hopemi mehci nootaanaawa hini kalawiiwe hotaayitatenaanaawa hini mecimi hopiyeetoonaawa mawifoowe wiici piisiteheewe

And that in the good ground, these are such as in an honest and good heart, having heard the word, hold it fast, and bring forth fruit with patience.

16. chiine mata hileni yeh mehci fakifwaaci niitawaakanali hopetakhwaali nili poonahfecika weelaa laamitahfa tfani hoteh poonaali nili weeka hoskici tah niipawilici hoteh poonaali nili wahsi nihki peepiicfaacki menawah neemowaaci hini wayahfeeyaaki

And no man, when he hath lighted a lamp, covereth it with a vessel, or putteth it under a bed; but putteth it on a stand, that they which enter in may see the light.

17. ksake mata wiyehi kikitoote weh pwaa ini tepinaakwifenwi weelaa mata wiyehi kiyaaciwi weh pwaa ini pemi waakotoote mecimi wayahfeeyaaki si piyeeya

For nothing is hid, that shall not be made manifest; nor anything secret, that shall not be known and come to light.

18. kcitawaafiiko weecikeenahi yeesi nootaakeeyeekwe ksake kookwe-neefa-kaaci hopoona hiina weh miiloofo mecimi kookwe-neefa-kaaci mata hopoona hiina we hoci mamoote teetepilahi hini hina nipoona yeesiteheeci

Take heed therefore how ye hear: for whosoever hath, to him shall be given; and whosoever hath not, from him shall be taken away even that which he thinketh he hath.

19. chiine nitasi hotfekohi hokeeli chiine hoceeninahi mecimi hotaalwi nahiika si piyeelotaakohi ksake hina yeefoskaata hoci

And there came to him his mother and brethren, and they could not come at him for the crowd.

20. mecimi hini wiitamaakwi kikiya mecimi kiceeninaaki faakici niipawiiki kipemi maatawi nookooki

And it was told him, Thy mother and thy brethren stand without, desiring to see thee.

21. payeekwa haapafse yohkoma nihki nikiya mecimi niceeninaaki neenootakki hini hokalawiiwe maneto mecimi hini silawiiki hotelahi nihi

But he answered and said unto them, My mother and my brethren are these which hear the word of God, and do it.

22. howe hini piyeemikatwi nele tah nekoti kaasekiki wahsi hini holakeeleki lhkaki wiila mecimi hokakehkimaafhi hini kaameki wayeetahkwe hini mhskeekwi haataako hotelahi nihi mecimi hini lhokwiiki nihki

Now it came to pass on one of those days, that he entered into a boat, himself and his disciples; and he said unto them, Let us go over unto the other side of the lake: and they launched forth.

23. payeekwa yeelelhokwiwaaci nepeewa wiila chiine nitasi piyeeya mhsaawi mehsikkaki hoskitepiye hini mhskeekwi mecimi nihki peemi hokwikamilici nepi chiine nanaskaci hilefiiki

But as they sailed he fell asleep: and there came down a storm of wind on the lake; and they were filling with water, and were in jeopardy.

24. chiine nihki hopiyeelotawaawaali nili mecimi hotamachaawaali mestele mestele kitikwiinamipe cehi hisiweeki mecimi hina hamamo chiine hokoteta hini mehsikkaki mecimi hini peemi kiteewafehkaaki hini nepi mecimi nakeeska nili chiine mhsi kaamehkawanwi nitasi

And they came to him, and awoke him, saying, Master, master, we perish. And he awoke, and rebuked the wind and the raging of the water: and they ceased, and there was a calm.

25. mecimi taaniwe kiteepwehseewenwa hotelahi chiine teewahi kaawilaweeki nihki kwakwehtaaniteheeki neefawe howe yaama yeesi tepaataki wiikinaakwi nili mehsikkaki mecimi hini nepi chiine homelonehtaakona nili pemi hitiiki nihki

And he said unto them, Where is your faith? And being afraid they marveled, saying one to another, Who then is this, that he commandeth even the winds and the water, and they obey him?

26. mecimi nahiika piyeethokwiiki hini hotasiskiimwa nihki kiyaalesiinaki kaameki hini keeleliiki

And they arrived at the country of the Gerasenes, which is over against Galilee.

27. chiine yeh piyeci hakwahsiki hini hasiskiiki hotfekooli nitasi naanekoti hini hoteeweneki hoci leniili peepoonaata waninehfihi mecimi sehkamika hoci hina mata piitenike piitenikana chiine mata wiikiwaapeki teewa piitike weeka nili nepoowaalako

And when he was come forth upon the land, there met him a certain man out of the city, who had devils; and for a long time he had worn no clothes, and abode not in any house, but in the tombs.

28. chiine hina yeh neewaaci ciisisiili wiyakahootamwa mecimi sahkiki sfe yeelahfamiilici chiine holaami kalaweewihsimo nehiwe nipoona wahsi lawiimela ciisisii kiila hokwihfali hina kci

And when he saw Jesus, he cried out, and fell down before him, and with a loud voice said, What have I to do with thee,

moospi maneto kinanahpaacimele teki
mamiyenaanhhilo hisiwe

29. ksake hina peemi tepimaaci nili wiyakilehfiili
wahsi nili hileniili hoci piyeci lohfaalici ksake hina
moosaki laakwa homaamawinachekooli nili chiine
kcitawahoofo mecimi kciipifo hokwaanhhi chiine
fakifiteepifoowena mecimi hopemi pkinaana nili
kciipifoowena hoteleskaakooli nili waninehfiili hini
laa papskwahki

30. chiine ciisisii honatohtawaali nehiwe kitesifo
mehseeleka hisiwe hina ksake meci waninehfihi
hotwaalekohi

31. mecimi nihiini honanahpaacimekohi wahsi pwaa
tepimaaci wahsi hini waasaalakwi pwaayaa hahteeki
yeekwaalakiki si saawelici

32. howe nitasi hapiiki nekotweelekiki meci koskooki
peemi wihfeniwaaci wehseteki hini meekwahkiki
mecimi honanahpaacimaawaali nihki wahsi wiilaani si
miilekowaaci wahsi hotfaalaawaaci nihi koskohi
mecimi homiilahi wiilaani

33. mecimi nihki waninehfiiki nili hileniili hoci piyeci
lohfeeki chiine hotfaawahi nihi koskohi mecimi hina
nekotweeleka hini sehpaalakiki hini mhskeekwi si
paalacipto mecimi nephokwiiki

34. chiine nihki yeesamaacki nihi yeh neemowaaci
hini mayehci piyeemikaki hosimooki chiine hini
hotaatotaanaawa hini hoteeweneki chiine hini piileski

35. chiine nihki lohfeeki homa waapataanaawa hini
mayehci piyeemikaki chiine hotfaawaali ciisisiili
mecimi homhkawaawaali nili hileniili nihki
waninehfiiki weeci lohfaawaaci peemi lematapilici
piitenikeeli mecimi homayaawi memekinitehaakaniili
nahiika hofitali ciisisii chiine kaawilaweeki caayahki

36. chiine nihki neeneemekki hini howiitamawaawahi
nihi yeesi hina peepoonaata waninehfihi
waapaneshoofoci

37. mecimi caayahki nihki lenaweeki hini
hotasiskiimwaaki nihki kiyaalesiinaki kaayaawka hoci
hokocimekohi wahsi nihi hoci saaweci ksake nihki
hopemi fookinekonaawa mhsi kaawilaweewe chiine
holakeeleki lhkamwa mecimi peteki heewa

38. weeka nili hileniili weeci lohfaawaaci nihki
waninehfiiki homamaatomekooli wahsi menawahke
wiiciimekoci payeekwa hotaameskawaali

Jesus, thou Son of the Most High God? I
beseech thee, torment me not.

For he commanded the unclean spirit to
come out from the man. For oftentimes it
had seized him: and he was kept under
guard, and bound with chains and fetters;
and breaking the bands asunder, he was
driven of the devil into the deserts.

And Jesus asked him, What is thy name?
And he said, Legion; for many devils
were entered into him.

And they entreated him that he would not
command them to depart into the abyss.

Now there was there a herd of many
swine feeding on the mountain: and they
entreated him that he would give them
leave to enter into them. And he gave
them leave.

And the devils came out from the man,
and entered into the swine: and the herd
rushed down the steep into the lake, and
were choked.

And when they that fed them saw what
had come to pass, they fled, and told it in
the city and in the country.

And they went out to see what had come
to pass; and they came to Jesus, and
found the man, from whom the devils
were gone out, sitting, clothed and in his
right mind, at the feet of Jesus: and they
were afraid.

And they that saw it told them how he
that was possessed with devils was made
whole.

And all the people of the country of the
Gerasenes round about asked him to
depart from them; for they were holden
with great fear: and he entered into a
boat, and returned.

But the man from whom the devils were
gone out prayed him that he might be
with him: but he sent him away, saying,

39. peteki haale yeetaayani wiikiwa mecimi lhfwaatotano yeesi hini mhsi wiyehi mehcilotoolehki maneto hotelaali mecimi hina weepfe yehaaci hopemi lhfwena hini saapwi hini mefhiike hoteewe yeesi mhsi wiyehi mehcilotaakoci ciisisiili

Return to thy house, and declare how great things God hath done for thee. And he went his way, publishing throughout the whole city how great things Jesus had done for him.

40. chiine yeesi peteki piyaaci ciisisii hosilawaalekohi nihi mehseelelici ksake caayahki nihki peemi hahkawaapamaawaaci nili

And as Jesus returned, the multitude welcomed him; for they were all waiting for him.

41. mecimi waapamehko nitasi piyeewa hileni ceeaalas' sifo mecimi teepeelecikeeta hina hini mhsikamikoki chiine sahkiki sfe nahiika hofitali ciisisii mecimi honanahpaacimaali nili wahsi piicfaalici yeetaaci wiikiwa

And behold, there came a man named Jairus, and he was a ruler of the synagogue: and he fell down at Jesus' feet, and besought him to come into his house;

42. ksake hopoonaali nekotiimehi hotaanehfali nawito metahfwi-kite-niiswi tfwi kkatoowiili mecimi hina peemi nepeki payeekwa yeesi hina nhhaaci nihi mehseelelici hokiposkaakohi

for he had an only daughter, about twelve years of age, and she lay a dying. But as he went the multitudes thronged him.

43. chiine hkweewa peemi poonaki mhskowilokeewe metahfwi-kite-niiswi kkato neyehka hina homehci caayahki pakite meemhfeeletaki naanatawhcikeelici si mecimi hotaalwi kiikehekooli wiyeefali

And a woman having an issue of blood twelve years, which had spent all her living upon physicians, and could not be healed of any,

44. piyeewa hotaanaaki nili chiine hoteh pehsena hini ta nhpenikwaateeki hopiitenikanilici mecimi weelena hini homhskowilokeewe nakikahtooteeli

came behind him, and touched the border of his garment: and immediately the issue of her blood stanched.

45. chiine ciisisii neefawe hina nipehsenekwa hisiwe mecimi yeh caayahki kiyaacimolici piita chiine nihi peepah wiitfeemekoci mestele ceh nihki mehseelekki kifakkehkaakooki mecimi kineposkaakooki hotelaali

And Jesus said, Who is it that touched me? And when all denied, Peter said, and they that were with him, Master, the multitudes press thee and crush thee.

46. payeekwa ciisisii wiyeefa sapkahi nipehsenekwa ksake nimoosto yeesi waasikaki mehci niiya hoci weepfeeyaaki hisiwe

But Jesus said, Some one did touch me: for I perceived that power had gone forth from me.

47. chiine hina hkweewa yeh neemeki yeesi pwaa kkifoci piyeewa pemi papaweska mecimi pemi sahkiki sfe yeelahfamiilici nili mohkaacimo hini yeelahfamiilici nihi caayahki lenawehi hini weeci pehsenaaci nili mecimi yeesi weelena kiikehoofoci

And when the woman saw that she was not hid, she came trembling, and falling down before him declared in the presence of all the people for what cause she touched him, and how she was healed immediately.

48. mecimi hotaanhfima kiteepwehseewe kimehci mefefiheko nhhaale kaamaaniilefiiweneki hotelaali nili

And he said unto her, Daughter, thy faith hath made thee whole; go in peace.

49. yeheeyehi keewaki kalawici nitasi piyeeli nekoti yeetaaci wiikiwa hoci hina teepeelecikeeta hini mhsikamikoki hina kitaanehfa howe hasenwa teki petfakhi hina keekehkimiwe hisiweeli

While he yet spake, there cometh one from the ruler of the synagogue's house, saying, Thy daughter is dead; trouble not the Master.

50. payeekwa ciisisii pemi nootaake hini hotaapaftawaali nili teki cihfefilo teepwehseelo pehi mecimi hina weh mefefihoofo

But Jesus hearing it, answered him, Fear not: only believe, and she shall be made whole.

51. mecimi hini wiikiwa yeh si piyaaci mata wiilaani sitehe wahsi nehcipe hileniili wiici piicfaamekoci weeciwephi piitali chiine caaniili chiine ceemhsiili chiine nili hohfali hina hkweefa mecimi hokeeli

And when he came to the house, he suffered not any man to enter in with him, save Peter, and John, and James, and the father of the maiden and her mother.

52. mecimi peemi wihfakweewaaci caayahki chiine peemi mawimaawaaci nili payeekwa teki wihfakweeko ksake mata hina nepwa nepeewa weeka hisiwe

And all were weeping, and bewailing her: but he said, Weep not; for she is not dead, but sleepeth.

53. mecimi howiyameskwi waapaleelemekohi nihi waakotamehi yeesi nepelici nili

And they laughed him to scorn, knowing that she was dead.

54. payeekwa wiila hoteh fakileceenaali nili wihkokeemo hkweefa honhskaalo hisiwe

But he, taking her by the hand, called, saying, Maiden, arise.

55. mecimi hina hocacaalahkwali peteki piyeeli chiine honhska weelena mecimi tepikeemo wahsi wiyehi wah miicilici miiloofolici nili

And her spirit returned, and she rose up immediately: and he commanded that something be given her to eat.

56. mecimi hina hkweefa hokehkiyaamhhi kwakwehtaanitehehi payeekwa ciisisii hotepimahi nihi wahsi teki wiitamawaawaaci hileniili hini mayehci silawiiki

And her parents were amazed: but he charged them to tell no man what had been done.

Luke:9

1. chiine homaawatwimahi nihi metahfwi-kite-niiswi chiine homiilahi waasikaki wahsi mekofihtawaawaaci caayahki waninehfihi mecimi wahsi kiikehtoolici hahkwilokeewena

And he called the twelve together, and gave them power and authority over all devils, and to cure diseases.

2. chiine howaawiineskawahi wahsi nanahimiweelici hini hokimaawitaamhkomi maneto mecimi wahsi kiikehaawaaci nihi yeeahkwilokeelici

And he sent them forth to preach the kingdom of God, and to heal the sick.

3. chiine mata wiyehi haamwetooko yeelaamiiyeekwe mata haapathoowe mata piitaaka mata takhwa mata moni mata nohki poonamoko niiswi kootiiwali

And he said unto them, Take nothing for your journey, neither staff, nor wallet, nor bread, nor money; neither have two coats.

4. mecimi kookwenehsi wiikiwa hottameekwe nitasi hapiko mecimi hini hoci weepfeeko

And into whatsoever house ye enter, there abide, and thence depart.

5. chiine yeetfwi pwaa hotahpenelwaakwe hine hini hoteewe hoci weepfeeyeekwe pawatenamoko hini pekwi kifitwaaki hoci wahsi teepweewenhheekwe nihki hotelahi

And as many as receive you not, when ye depart from that city, shake off the dust from your feet for a testimony against them.

6. chiine nihki saaweeki mecimi nili hoteeweneefa si saapwiiki pemi nanahimiweeki hini howesi

And they departed, and went throughout the villages, preaching the gospel, and healing everywhere.

piyeetaacimoowe chiine pemi kiikehiweeki mefhiike
tasi

7. howe heletii hina nekotehfepatiokima nootaake
caayahki yeesilawiiki mecimi holaami wanhfoneewefi
ksake hini yeeyowaaci naaleta yeesi caanii honhskaaci
nili nepelici hoci

Now Herod the tetrarch heard of all that
was done: and he was much perplexed,
because that it was said by some, that
John was risen from the dead;

8. mecimi naaleta yeesi hilaica mehci tepinawkofici
chiine kotakaki yeesi nekoti nihki pasitoowi
maamoosikiiskwecki honhskaaci nohki

and by some, that Elijah had appeared;
and by others, that one of the old
prophets was risen again.

9. chiine hiwa heletii caanii nikiskikwethwa payeekwa
neefawe yaama yeelaacimoofoci ninoota halayini si
wiyehi mecimi honatoneha wahsi neewaaci

And Herod said, John I beheaded: but
who is this, about whom I hear such
things? And he sought to see him.

10. chiine nihki hepastaliiki yeh piyaawaaci peteki
homohkaatotamawaawaali si wiyehi
mayehcilotamowaaci nihki mecimi hotaamwelahi nihi
chiine tepaane si saawe hoteewe pefseite sitoote

And the apostles, when they were
returned, declared unto him what things
they had done. And he took them, and
withdrew apart to a city called Bethsaida.

11. payeekwa nihki mehseelekki hopemi
mooleeletaanaawa hini honeekalaawaali mecimi
hosilawenahi nihi chiine hokaloolahi hini
hokimaawitaamhkomi maneto chiine nihi
yeekaawaatamelici kiikehetiiwe hokiikehahi

But the multitudes perceiving it followed
him: and he welcomed them, and spake
to them of the kingdom of God, and them
that had need of healing he healed.

12. chiine hini kaasekiki halemi holaakwiifi chiine
nihki metahfwi-kite-niiswi piyeeki mecimi
haameskawi nihki mehseelekki wahsi menawahke
nihki nili hoteeweneefa chiine kaayaawka piileski
haawaaci mecimi kkehsiwaaci chiine mamowaaci
wihfeniiwe ksake hotasi kitapipe tah papskwahkiki
hotelaawaali nihki

And the day began to wear away; and the
twelve came, and said unto him, Send the
multitude away, that they may go into the
villages and country round about, and
lodge, and get victuals: for we are here in
a desert place.

13. payeekwa miilehko wah miiciwaaci hotelahi
nipoonaape mata halika tfwi niyaalanwi
weepskweeteewali mecimi niiswi namehfaki
weeciwephi ni haayaake chiine tepenamawakite
wihfeniiwe caayahki yohkoma lenaweeki hiwaki nihki

But he said unto them, Give ye them to
eat. And they said, We have no more than
five loaves and two fishes; except we
should go and buy food for all this
people.

14. ksake nihki nawito niyaalane metahfene tepeewe
hileniiki mecimi lemataphehko wah tiitfweelowaaci
nawito maasa niyaalanwaapitaki hotelahi
hokakehkimaafhi

For they were about five thousand men.
And he said unto his disciples, Make
them sit down in companies, about fifty
each.

15. mecimi nihki yooni silawiiki chiine
holemataphaawahi caayahki nihi

And they did so, and made them all sit
down.

16. chiine hoteh mamena nili niyaalanwi
weepskweeteewali mecimi nihi niiswi namefhi chiine
spemeki menhkwatoki pemi laapi hokisaacilotaana nili
chiine hoposkonaana mecimi homiilahi nihi
kakehkimaafhi wahsi pakfenamelici yeelahfamiilici
nihi mehseelelici

And he took the five loaves and the two
fishes, and looking up to heaven, he
blessed them, and brake; and gave to the
disciples to set before the multitude.

17. chiine nihki wihfeniiki mecimi caayahki teephoolooki chiine nitasi maawatonamaakwiiki seskwatooteeki peekskahki metahfwi-kite-niiswi soosoone

And they did eat, and were all filled: and there was taken up that which remained over to them of broken pieces, twelve baskets.

18. chiine hini piyeemikatwi yeesi peemi mamaatomeeci tepaane nihi kakehkimaafhi wiici mecimi honatohtawahi neefawe hiwaki niiya nihki mehseelekki hisiwe

And it came to pass, as he was praying alone, the disciples were with him: and he asked them, saying, Who do the multitudes say that I am?

19. chiine pemi haapafseeki nihki ceh caanii hina fafahkwiholelhiwena weeka naaleta hilaica hiwaki chiine kotakaki yeesi hina nekoti nihki pasitoowi maamoosikiiskwecki pemi honhskaaci nohki hisiweeki

And they answering said, John the Baptist; but others say, Elijah; and others, that one of the old prophets is risen again.

20. weeka kiilawa neefawe kiteyopwa niila hotelahi mecimi piita pemi haapafse ce hina hoklaistiimali maneto hisiwe

And he said unto them, But who say ye that I am? And Peter answering said, The Christ of God.

21. payeekwa hotaayicimahi mecimi hotepimahi wahsi pwaa yooma wiitamawaawaaci hileniili

But he charged them, and commanded them to tell this to no man;

22. hina hokwihfali hileni kwiilahi we hahkwinamwa meci wiyehi mecimi we haalawinekohi nihi kikilenihi chiine hokimaawi mhkateewkolayehi chiine yaayawikeelici mecimi we nhfekwi chiine hini mawi-nhfokonakike we honhskaanoofo hisiwe

saying, The Son of man must suffer many things, and be rejected of the elders and chief priests and scribes, and be killed, and the third day be raised up.

23. chiine caayahki hotelahi kwehkwi wiyeefa hileni nih piyeci hahkookwa wiilaani hina kiyaateeletake wiiya chiine hokokwitena hotaasitehfekiimi tfene waapaki mecimi nineekalekwa

And he said unto all, If any man would come after me, let him deny himself, and take up his cross daily, and follow me.

24. ksake kookwe-neefa-kaaci wi waapanesto hotelenaweewiiwe weh wanhto hini weeka kookwe-neefa-kaaci weh wanhto hotelenaweewiiwe ksake niila hoci hiina we waapanesto hini

For whosoever would save his life shall lose it; but whosoever shall lose his life for my sake, the same shall save it.

25. ksake nehiwe hileni mhkahfo kwehkwi katawihkake hini melhske yeelekokwahkamikiki mecimi howanhto weelaa hopakitaana nehalwaaka wiiya

For what is a man profited, if he gain the whole world, and lose or forfeit his own self?

26. ksake kookwe-neefa-kaaci neh tekwehekwa mecimi nikalawiiwe niliini hina hokwihfali hileni weh tekwehaali hine piyaate nehalwaaka howahfaacimekofiiweneki mecimi hini howahfaacimekofiiwe hina hohfima chiine nihki hofepi henhcaliiki

For whosoever shall be ashamed of me and of my words, of him shall the Son of man be ashamed, when he cometh in his own glory, and the glory of the Father, and of the holy angels.

27. payeekwa teepweewe kitelepwa hapiiki nihki naaleta neniipawicki hotasi nihkiini mata weh wiyehisi kotataanaawa nepoowe paalohi honeemenaawa nihki hini hokimaawitaamhkomi maneto

But I tell you of a truth, There be some of them that stand here, which shall in no wise taste of death, till they see the kingdom of God.

28. chiine hini piyeemikatwi nawito nhfwaasikfoko mayohkwaaci yooloma hiyoowena hotaamwelahi piitali chiine caaniili chiine ceemhsiili mecimi piici hini meekwahkiki si kkwicsinwa wahsi mamaatomeeci

And it came to pass about eight days after these sayings, he took with him Peter and John and James, and went up into the mountain to pray.

29. chiine yeesi pemi mamaatomeeci hini yeeki hotelaapeewe kotaki hinwi chiine hopiitenika hale wahkanakiya mecimi pemi wahfiikwfoowatwi

And as he was praying, the fashion of his countenance was altered, and his raiment became white and dazzling.

30. chiine waapamehko nitasi hokiikaloolekohi niiswi hilenihi nihkiini moosisii chiine hilaica

And behold, there talked with him two men, which were Moses and Elijah;

31. nihki wahfaacimekofiiweneki nookofiiki mecimi hotaatotaanaawa hotesinamoowe waasa hina mehcilotaki colooseelemiiki

who appeared in glory, and spake of his decease which he was about to accomplish at Jerusalem.

32. howe piita chiine nihi peepah wiiciimekoci kofekofiiki katokwaamoowe payeekwa ye hokwaawi si hamamowaaci nihki honeemenaawa howahfaacimekofiiwenilici mecimi nihi niiswi hilenihi weewiici kaapawiimekoci hina

Now Peter and they that were with him were heavy with sleep: but when they were fully awake, they saw his glory, and the two men that stood with him.

33. chiine hini piyeemikatwi yeesi nili hoci pemi tepaane haawaaci nihki piita hotelaali ciisisiili mestele ce howesa hini hotasi hapiyakwe mecimi wiilaani ne hostoope nhfwi haaciiwikamiko nekoti kiila chiine moosisii wiila nekoti chiine hilaica wiila nekoti mata howaakota peemi yoci

And it came to pass, as they were parting from him, Peter said unto Jesus, Master, it is good for us to be here: and let us make three tabernacles; one for thee, and one for Moses, and one for Elijah: not knowing what he said.

34. chiine yeheeye howeci yooloma wiyehi nitasi piyeeya paafkwahki mecimi hotawikanhskaakonaawa chiine kwpeneeki yeesi hottamowaaci hini paafkwahki

And while he said these things, there came a cloud, and overshadowed them: and they feared as they entered into the cloud.

35. chiine hini paafkwahki hoci lohfeya kalawihsimoowe hiina yaama nikwihfa nimamaawena nootawehko kiilawa hiyooya

And a voice came out of the cloud, saying, This is my Son, my chosen: hear ye him.

36. chiine yeh piyeeyaaki hini kalawihsimoowe naanhsihka mhkoofo ciisisii mecimi nooleewiiki nihki chiine mata howiitamawaawaali hileniili hini hoci wiyehi mayehci neemowaaci nele kaasekiki

And when the voice came, Jesus was found alone. And they held their peace, and told no man in those days any of the things which they had seen.

37. chiine hini piyeemikatwi hini wayaapaki yeh piyeci paalacsinowaaci hini meekwahkiki hoci meci mehseelelici honakskaakohi

And it came to pass, on the next day, when they were come down from the mountain, a great multitude met him.

38. chiine waapamehko hileniili nihi mehseelelici hotahootamooli keekehkimiwe kinanahpaacimele wahsi waapamaci nikwihfa ksake hina pehi nitapelohfema

And behold, a man from the multitude cried, saying, Master, I beseech thee to look upon my son; for he is mine only child:

39. mecimi waapami wiye hilefiiwenali homesenekooli chiine kikamooci waawiyakoohootamwa chiine nili

and behold, a spirit taketh him, and he suddenly crieth out; and it teareth him

homaamaatakoskahekooli weecikeenahi paapihteewefi mecimi fakaaki wiiya wahoci saaweeli nili holaami hopemi kakissimekooli

that he foameth, and it hardly departeth from him, bruising him sorely.

40. mecimi ninanahpaacimaaki kikakehkimaafaki wahsi lohfe pakilaawaaci nili chiine haalwi katawefiiki hiwali

And I besought thy disciples to cast it out; and they could not.

41. chiine ciisisii haapafse mecimi o pwaayaa teepwehsaakanita mecimi mamiyaasimamiiloowefita skwiilenawe taaniwe laakwasi keh wiici hapiimelepwa kiilawa mecimi wiisikitehehtoolepwa piyeesi hotasi hina kikwihfa hisiwe

And Jesus answered and said, O faithless and perverse generation, how long shall I be with you, and bear with you? bring hither thy son.

42. chiine yeesi hina keewaki pemi piyaaci hina waninehfi sahkiki hotpakilaali nili mecimi hotahkwi maatakoskahaali payeekwa ciisisii hokwtelaali nili wiyakilehfiili mecimi hokiikehaali nili skilawehfiifali chiine peteki hohfali si miiliwe nili

And as he was yet a coming, the devil dashed him down, and tare him grievously. But Jesus rebuked the unclean spirit, and healed the boy, and gave him back to his father.

43. mecimi caayahki nihki hokwakwehtaaneeletaanaawa hini homakiiciweefiiwe maneto payeekwa yeheeyehi caayahki pemi kwakwehtaaneeletamowaaci hini caayahki wiyehi yeesilawiici hoteh kaloolahi hokakehkimaafhi

And they were all astonished at the majesty of God. But while all were marveling at all the things which he did, he said unto his disciples,

44. wiilaani yooloma kalawiiwena kitawakaawaaki si kofaapiyeeyaake ksake hina hokwihfali hileni nili holeciwa hileniiki weh si pakfenoofo hotelahi

Let these words sink into your ears: for the Son of man shall be delivered up into the hands of men.

45. payeekwa yooma hiyoowe mata honenohtaanaawa nihki chiine hini kkitaakwiiki wahsi pwaa mooleeletamowaaci hini mecimi hokwtaanaawa wahsi natohtawaawaaci nili yooma hiyoowe

But they understood not this saying, and it was concealed from them, that they should not perceive it: and they were afraid to ask him about this saying.

46. chiine nitasi pafekwiiya memekiniteheewe heelekiina nihki taanawe hina nihki halika mhsiilefi

And there arose a reasoning among them, which of them should be greatest.

47. payeekwa yeh neemeki ciisisii hini yeesi memekiniteheeyaaki hotehiwa hoteh mamaali caki hapelohfeefali mecimi pakaci wiila hoteh lemataphaali nili

But when Jesus saw the reasoning of their heart, he took a little child, and set him by his side,

48. chiine kookwe-neefa-kaaci we hotahpenaali yooloma caki hapelohfeefali niwiifooweneki nootahpenekwa niila mecimi kookwe-neefa-kaaci ne hotahpenekwa hotahpenaali nili weewaawiinilici ksake hina kci hotahpiifa heelekiina kiilawa caayahki hiina mhsiilefi hotelahi nihi

and said unto them, Whosoever shall receive this little child in my name receiveth me: and whosoever shall receive me receiveth him that sent me: for he that is least among you all, the same is great.

49. chiine caanii haapafse mecimi mestele nineewaape nekoti peemi lohfe pakilaaci waninehfihi kiwiifiiweneki chiine nikwtelaape hina ksake mata kiwiici neekalekona hina hisiwe

And John answered and said, Master, we saw one casting out devils in thy name; and we forbade him, because he followeth not with us.

50. payeekwa teki kwtelehko ksake hina pwaayaa ppehtenelwaakwe wiiciwi kiilawa hotelaali ciisisii

But Jesus said unto him, Forbid him not: for he that is not against you is for you.

51. chiine hini piyeemikatwi hine nili kaasekiki naanemi piyeeya wahsi spemeki si hotahpenoofoci kaakika wahsi colooseelemiiki haaci laapeska

And it came to pass, when the days were well-nigh come that he should be received up, he stedfastly set his face to go to Jerusalem,

52. mecimi yeelahfamiikweci hoteleskawahi weewaawiinaaci mecimi nihki weepfeeki chiine hottaanaawa nihki semeliaki hoteeweneefwa wahsi nanahi mecfetaakoci

and sent messengers before his face: and they went, and entered into a village of the Samaritans, to make ready for him.

53. mecimi nihki mata hotahpenaawaali nili ksake hotelaapeewe yeeki paasi weekhi wiisa colooseelemiiki heewa

And they did not receive him, because his face was as though he were going to Jerusalem.

54. chiine hokakehkimaafhi ceemhsiili chiine caaniili yeh neemelici yooma teepeelemiweeta ha kitesitehe wahsi hitamakwe skote wahsi menhkwatwi hoci sahkiki piyeeyaaki mecimi caakamekowaaci nihki hiwaki nihki

And when his disciples James and John saw this, they said, Lord, wilt thou that we bid fire to come down from heaven, and consume them?

55. payeekwa kokiiwa mecimi hokwtelahi nihi

But he turned, and rebuked them.

56. chiine kotaki hoteewenehi heeki

And they went to another village.

57. chiine yeele lhfeewaaci hini wayeeci naanekoti hileniili keh neekalele kookwekaaci wayeeci yehaayani hotekooli

And as they went in the way, a certain man said unto him, I will follow thee whithersoever thou goest.

58. mecimi ciisisii nihki waakocehfiiki hopoonaanaawa waasaalako chiine nihki menhkwatwi hoci wiskilohfaki hopoonaanaawa hofihfanwa weeka hina hokwihfali hileni mata hopoona wah tah sekfetooci wiisi hotelaali nili

And Jesus said unto him, The foxes have holes, and the birds of the heaven have nests; but the Son of man hath not where to lay his head.

59. chiine kotakali nohki neekasilo hotelaali payeekwa teepeelemiweeta wiilaani leelemilo wahsi nhhihta nhhaaya mecimi lekonaki nohfa hisiwe hina

And he said unto another, Follow me. But he said, Lord, suffer me first to go and bury my father.

60. payeekwa nakasi nihki neepekiki wahsi lekonaawaaci nehalwaaka honepoomwahi weeka kiila nhhaale mecimi lhfwaacimolo mefhiike hini hokimaawitaamhkomi maneto hotelaali nili

But he said unto him, Leave the dead to bury their own dead; but go thou and publish abroad the kingdom of God.

61. chiine nohki kotakali nehfaapi keh neekalele teepeelemiweeta payeekwa nhhihta wiilaani leelemilo wahsi hosilawaalaki nihki yeetaaya wiikiwa yeepicki hiwali

And another also said, I will follow thee, Lord; but first suffer me to bid farewell to them that are at my house.

62. payeekwa mata hileni hopemi mehci fookina ciikikeepicika mecimi hotaanaaki pemi laapi yah si howesisinwa hini hokimaawitaamhkomi maneto hotelaali ciisisii

But Jesus said unto him, No man, having put his hand to the plough, and looking back, is fit for the kingdom of God.

Luke:10

1. howe mayohkwaaci hine yooloma wiyehi hina teepeelemiweeta homamahi niiswaasi kotakhi chiine mefhiike tasi mecimi caaki hoteewe yeelahfamiikweci hoteh waawiineskawahi nihi maasa niiswi wayeeci waasa haaci wiila peloocihi

Now after these things the Lord appointed seventy others, and sent them two and two before his face into every city and place, whither he himself was about to come.

2. mecimi hotelahi hini kawaskwhaawe sapkahi maaletwi payeekwa nihki paapekateficki maatfwihi weecikeenahi mamaatomehko hina teepeeletaka hini kawaskwhaawe wahsi hina piyeelhkawaaci paapekatefilici hini hokawaskwhaaweneki

And he said unto them, The harvest is plenteous, but the labourers are few: pray ye therefore the Lord of the harvest, that he send forth labourers into his harvest.

3. nhhaakone yehaayeekwe waapatamoko kiteleskoolepwa paasi palasaanimekiifaki hini heelekiina mhhweewhi

Go your ways: behold, I send you forth as lambs in the midst of wolves.

4. teki haamwetooko monipiitaaka teki piitaaka teki mhkifena mecimi teki hosilawaalehko hileni hini yeele haayeekwe

Carry no purse, no wallet, no shoes: and salute no man on the way.

5. chiine kookwenehsi wiikiwa ke hottaanaawa nhhihta kaamaaniilefiiwe cehi yooma wiikiwaapeki hiyoko

And into whatsoever house ye shall enter, first say, Peace be to this house.

6. chiine kwehkwi kaamaaniilefiiwe hoci hokwihfima nitasi hapite hoskici hina we hahteeli kikaamaaniilefiiwenwa weeka kwehkwi mata peteki hini kiilawa we heeya nohki

And if a son of peace be there, your peace shall rest upon him: but if not, it shall turn to you again.

7. mecimi yaska hini wiikiwaapeki hapiko pemi miiciko mecimi meneko yeeki wiyehi yeesi nihki miiliweewaaci ksake hina peekatefita nahiika hikweelemekofi hotephoofoowe teki wiikiwa hoci hanhka wiikiwa haako

And in that same house remain, eating and drinking such things as they give: for the labourer is worthy of his hire. Go not from house to house.

8. chiine kookwenehsi hoteewe hottameekwe mecimi kootahpenekowaaki nihki miiciko yeeki wiyehi yeesi pakfenooteeki yeelahfamiiyeekwe

And into whatsoever city ye enter, and they receive you, eat such things as are set before you:

9. chiine kiikehehko nihki yeeakwilokeecki nitasi piitike yeepicki mecimi hini hokimaawitaamhkomi maneto howe kiilawa maalaakwahi piyeeya hilehko

and heal the sick that are therein, and say unto them, The kingdom of God is come nigh unto you.

10. weeka kookwenehsi hoteewe ke hottaanaawa mecimi mata nihki kootahpenekowaaki nili si lohfaako nitasi hoteewenimiyeewali mecimi

But into whatsoever city ye shall enter, and they receive you not, go out into the streets thereof and say,

11. wiikinaakwi hini koteewenwa hoci pekwi peefakofeki nifitenaaki kiiyaawa niteh kafhaape payeekwa waakotamoko yooma yeesi hini hokimaawitaamhkomi maneto piyeeyaaki maalaakwahi hiyoko

Even the dust from your city, that cleaveth to our feet, we do wipe off against you: howbeit know this, that the kingdom of God is come nigh.

12. kitelepwa niila hini we halika kaakilweewenwi saatanii halayine kaasekiki noota halayini hoteewe

I say unto you, It shall be more tolerable in that day for Sodom, than for that city.

13. macilepwaawe cehi kiila kolesin macilepwaawe cehi kiila pefseite ksake kwehkwi nili waasikaki pekatefiiwena neyehka mehci lawiike taayaaki chiine saataniiki mayehci lawiiki kiiyaawaaki neyehka nihki sehkamika wih mehci mataiini siteheeki wih pemi lematapiiki piitaakanimotaaki mecimi pekoki

Woe unto thee, Chorazin! woe unto thee, Bethsaida! for if the mighty works had been done in Tyre and Sidon, which were done in you, they would have repented long ago, sitting in sackcloth and ashes.

14. weeka hini we halika kaakilweewenwi taayaa chiine saatanii hini ceeyehkwahkoweeweneki noota kiilawa

Howbeit it shall be more tolerable for Tyre and Sidon in the judgment, than for you.

15. chiine kiila keepaaniam' ha menhkwatwi keh si speelemekofihekoopi sahkiki keh si piyeelekoopi kiila hahkwinamooweneki

And thou, Capernaum, shalt thou be exalted unto heaven? thou shalt be brought down unto Hades.

16. hina neenootoolwaakwe kiilawa ninootaakwa niila chiine hina yehaalawinelwaakwe kiilawa nitaalawinaakwa niila mecimi hina yaalawinawita hotaalawinawaali nili weewaawiinilici

He that heareth you heareth me; and he that rejecteth you rejecteth me; and he that rejecteth me rejecteth him that sent me.

17. chiine nihki niiswaasi peteki piyeeki piyeci howesilepwaaki teepeelemiweeta wiikinaakwi nihki waninehfiiki nootayipe kiwiifooweneki hisiweeki

And the seventy returned with joy, saying, Lord, even the devils are subject unto us in thy name.

18. mecimi nitelaapama setenii penhsinwa paasi peepaki menhkwatoki hoci hotelahi

And he said unto them, I beheld Satan fallen as lightning from heaven.

19. waapatamoko kimehci miilelepwa simekofiiwe wahsi kakeelhkaweekwe manetooki mecimi keekahkasaapileceecki chiine wah simekofihtamaweekwe caayahki hini howiisikatowiiwe hina mateeletiiwena mecimi mata wiyehi keh wiyehisi hahkwipenalekonaawa

Behold, I have given you authority to tread upon serpents and scorpions, and over all the power of the enemy: and nothing shall in any wise hurt you.

20. payeekwa teki yooma si hosasilepwaako yeesi nihki hilefiiwenaki hotayineekwe weeka hosasilepwaako yeesi kiwiifoowenwa mehtawikaateeki piitike weefepahkamikiki

Howbeit in this rejoice not, that the spirits are subject unto you; but rejoice that your names are written in heaven.

21. yaska hini yaatefaki hosasilepwa piici nili hofepi hocacaalahkwali mecimi honiyaawe kiila hohfima teepeeletaka weefepahkamikiki mecimi hasiskitaamhkwe yeesi sapkahi kiila kkitawaci yooloma wiyehi hina lepwaawefita mecimi nenohseewefita chiine sapkahi hapelohfeefaki kipahkinamawaaki nili hanhka hohfima ksake yooni hini yeesi menwilaasamamooweniki kitelaapiiweneki hiwapi

In that same hour he rejoiced in the Holy Spirit, and said, I thank thee, O Father, Lord of heaven and earth, that thou didst hide these things from the wise and understanding, and didst reveal them unto babes: yea, Father; for so it was well-pleasing in thy sight.

22. caayahki wiyehi nimehci piyeci pakfenamaakwa nohfa mecimi mata wiyeefa howaakomaali si wiyeefa hina hokwihfima weeciwephi hina hohfima mecimi si wiyeefa hina hohfima weeciwephi hina hokwihfima

All things have been delivered unto me of my Father: and no one knoweth who the Son is, save the Father; and who the Father is, save the Son, and he to

mecimi hina kookwe-neefali-kaaci hina hokwihfima sitehe wahsi pahkinamawaaci nili

whomsoever the Son willeth to reveal him.

23. mecimi nihi kakehkimaafhi si pemi kokiiwa hotelahi tepaane kisaaciwi cehi nili hoskiiseko weeci neemooteeki nili wiyehi kiilawa neeneemeyeekwe

And turning to the disciples, he said privately, Blessed are the eyes which see the things that ye see:

24. ksake kitelepwa niila yeesi meci maamoosikiiskwecki mecimi maki hokimaaki maatawiteheewaaci wahsi neemowaaci nili wiyehi neeneemeyeekwe kiilawa mecimi mata honeemenaawa chiine wahsi nootamowaaci nili wiyehi neenootameekwe mecimi mata honootaanaawa nili

for I say unto you, that many prophets and kings desired to see the things which ye see, and saw them not; and to hear the things which ye hear, and heard them not.

25. chiine waapamehko naanekoti layali pafekwiili mecimi hokotahkowaalekooli keekehkimiwe nehiwe neh silawi wahsi laapisina kookwelaakwasi lenaweewiiwe hotekooli

And behold, a certain lawyer stood up and tempted him, saying, Master, what shall I do to inherit eternal life?

26. mecimi nehiwe lawikeepi hini kwteletiiweneki nehiwe kitesi laapaatota hotelaali

And he said unto him, What is written in the law? how readest thou?

27. chiine hina pemi haapafse hahkweelemi kiila hina teepeelemiweeta kimanetooma kileki caayahki kitehi mecimi kileki caayahki kimayaawikiiya mecimi kileki caayahki kiwiisikatowiiwe mecimi kileki caayahki kimemekinitehaaka chiine kimaapiyeecikaaletiima paasi kiiya hisiwe

And he answering said, Thou shalt love the Lord thy God with all thy heart, and with all thy soul, and with all thy strength, and with all thy mind; and thy neighbour as thyself.

28. kimayaawi haapafse yooma silawiilo mecimi keh lenaweewi hotelaali

And he said unto him, Thou hast answered right: this do, and thou shalt live.

29. payeekwa hina peemi maatawi tepasaweelemekofihtooci wiiya mecimi neefawe nimaapiyeecikaaletiima hotelaali ciisisiili

But he, desiring to justify himself, said unto Jesus, And who is my neighbour?

30. ciisisii homecto hotaapafseewe chiine naanekoti hileni pemi paalacsinwa colooseelemii hoci celekoo heewa chiine heelekiina ciikoniwehfihi hina haakicfe nihi holiikinekohi mecimi hoppaktehokohi chiine saawehi honakalekohi pahfi nepwa

Jesus made answer and said, A certain man was going down from Jerusalem to Jericho; and he fell among robbers, which both stripped him and beat him, and departed, leaving him half dead.

31. chiine kwena naanekoti mhkateewkolaye pemi hini wayeeci si paalacsinwa chiine hina yeh neewaaci nili hini payakila wiyeetahkwe si pemhfe

And by chance a certain priest was going down that way: and when he saw him, he passed by on the other side.

32. chiine hini yaska liifaaiti nehfaapi yeh piyaaci nitasi mecimi yeh neewaaci nili hini payakila wiyeetahkwe si pemhfe

And in like manner a Levite also, when he came to the place, and saw him, passed by on the other side.

33. weeka naanekoti semelia yeesi paamaamiici piyeewa ta hapilici nili chiine yeh neewaaci hina maacilepwa kiteminaakwiteheewe

But a certain Samaritan, as he journeyed, came where he was: and when he saw him, he was moved with compassion,

34. mecimi hopiyeelotawaali nili chiine howiiwapilaali yeelilathoofolici hoteh fiikinamawaali pemi chiine waiini chiine hoteh lemataphaali hoskici hotayeli chiine hoteh piyeelaali yaata kkehsiki mecimi honoosaalaali

and came to him, and bound up his wounds, pouring on them oil and wine; and he set him on his own beast, and brought him to an inn, and took care of him.

35. chiine hini wayaapaki homamena niiswi seleni mecimi nili homiilaali nili keekehsilotawaaci chiine noosaasi hina mecimi kookwe-nehi-kaaci halika keh si pakitahfo niila hine nohki peteki piyaaya keh laapitephole hiwapi

And on the morrow he took out two pence, and gave them to the host, and said, Take care of him; and whatsoever thou spendest more, I, when I come back again, will repay thee.

36. taanawe hina kitesitehe kiila yohkoma nhfwi hoteepi maapayecikaasiweeta hpenalaali nili yaakicfaalici heelekiina nihi ciikoniwehfihi hotelaali

Which of these three, thinkest thou, proved neighbour unto him that fell among the robbers?

37. mecimi hina nili keela weewaapatelekoci hina kiteminaakweeletiiwe hisiwe chiine nhhaale mecimi hini silawiilo hotelaali ciisisii

And he said, He that shewed mercy on him. And Jesus said unto him, Go, and do thou likewise.

38. howe yeele lhfeewaaci nihki yehaawaaci hote hotta naanekoti hoteewenehi mecimi naanekoti hkweeli maafe sifooli hote hotahpenekooli yeetaalici wiikiwa

Now as they went on their way, he entered into a certain village: and a certain woman named Martha received him into her house.

39. chiine hina hkweewa hopoonaali hoceeninaali melii yaaloofooli nehfaapi hina lematapiwa maalaakwahi hina teepeelemiweeta hofitali mecimi honootamawaali hokalawiiwenilici

And she had a sister called Mary, which also sat at the Lord's feet, and heard his word.

40. payeekwa maafe kitelaakwi yeesi holaami kisaacilawiici mecimi hoteh piyeelotawaali nili teepeelemiweeta ha mata kimakofeeleta yeesi niceenina nakasici wahsi naanhsihka kisaachiweeya wiitamawi weecikeenahi wahsi naatamawici hotelaali

But Martha was cumbered about much serving; and she came up to him, and said, Lord, dost thou not care that my sister did leave me to serve alone? bid her therefore that she help me.

41. payeekwa hina teepeelemiweeta haapafse maafe maafe kiwiisaafi mecimi kipetfakheko meci wiyehi

But the Lord answered and said unto her, Martha, Martha, thou art anxious and troubled about many things:

42. payeekwa wiyehi hakaawaatetwi ksake melii homehci mame hini howesi wayeetahkwe hini mata hina we hoci mamaakwi hotelaali

but one thing is needful: for Mary hath chosen the good part, which shall not be taken away from her.

Luke:11

1. chiine hini piyeemikatwi yeesi pemi mamaatomeeci naanekoti tasi yeesi hine tfwilawiici nekoti hokakehkimaafhi teepeelemiweeta kakehkiminaake wahsi mamaatomeeyaake teetepilahi yeesi caanii nehfaapi kakehkimaaci hokakehkimaafhi hotekooli

And it came to pass, as he was praying in a certain place, that when he ceased, one of his disciples said unto him, Lord, teach us to pray, even as John also taught his disciples.

2. mecimi hine mamaatomaayeekwe hohfima kisaaciwi cehi kiwiifoowe kookimaawiiwe piyeeya

And he said unto them, When ye pray, say, Father, Hallowed be thy name. Thy kingdom come.

3. miilinaake tfene kaasekiki nitakhwaanemena tfene waapaki

Give us day by day our daily bread.

4. chiine pakfeeletamawinaake nimaciilefiiwenena ksake nehfaapi niilawe nipakfeeletamawaape caakiwiyeefa meemoosinehwiyameta chiine teki miyaasi-ashetiiweneki si piyeesinaake hiyoko hotelahi

And forgive us our sins; for we ourselves also forgive every one that is indebted to us. And bring us not into temptation.

5. chiine hotelahi nihi neefawe kiilawa weh poonaali wihkaanimaali mecimi nili we heewa laawi tepehkike chiine wihkaanima hawhhilo nhfwi weepskweeteewali

And he said unto them, Which of you shall have a friend, and shall go unto him at midnight, and say to him, Friend, lend me three loaves;

6. ksake paamaamiiwe nooci hotfekwa nihkaana mecimi mata wiyehi nipoona yeelahfamiici wahsi pakfenamawaki we hilaali

for a friend of mine is come to me from a journey, and I have nothing to set before him;

7. mecimi nili piitike we hoci haapafseeli teki petfakhilo hini skwaate howe kiphoote mecimi nitapelohfemaki tfaneki niwihpeemekooki matayeeciwi nita honhska mecimi miilele we hiwali

and he from within shall answer and say, Trouble me not: the door is now shut, and my children are with me in bed; I cannot rise and give thee?

8. kitelepwa niila weekhi hina mata we honhska mecimi miilaali nili ksake wihkaanali weeka we honhska hina ksake yeekcikaatiiwenilici hoci mecimi weh miilaali tfwi yeekaawaatamelici nili

I say unto you, Though he will not rise and give him, because he is his friend, yet because of his importunity he will arise and give him as many as he needeth.

9. chiine kitelepwa niila natotamoko mecimi keh miilekoopwa hini natonehikeeko mecimi ke mhkahfopwa tiitowathamoko mecimi keh tawenamaakoopwa hini

And I say unto you, Ask, and it shall be given you; seek, and ye shall find; knock, and it shall be opened unto you.

10. ksake caakiwiyeefa neetotaka hotatenike chiine hina neetonehaka mhkahfo mecimi hina teetowathaka weh tawenamaakwi hini

For every one that asketh receiveth; and he that seeketh findeth; and to him that knocketh it shall be opened.

11. chiine neefawe kiilawa weeofimaawita hokwihfali weh natotameli weepskweeteeki mecimi siikonali homiilaali nili weelaa namehfali mecimi manetooli honamehfiwi miilaali nili

And of which of you that is a father shall his son ask a loaf, and he give him a stone? or a fish, and he for a fish give him a serpent?

12. weelaa kwehkwi nili hoowaawi weh natotameli ha hina keekahkasaapileceelici weh miilaali nili

Or if he shall ask an egg, will he give him a scorpion?

13. kwehkwi kiilawa weecikeenahi weekhi kimaciilefipwa kiwaakotaanaawa wahsi miileekwe howesi teephetiiwena kitapelohfemwaaki taaniwe lekhi si halika hofepi kohfwa weh si miilahi nili hofepi hocacaalahkwali nihi neetotamaakoci

If ye then, being evil, know how to give good gifts unto your children, how much more shall your heavenly Father give the Holy Spirit to them that ask him?

14. chiine peemi lohfe pakilaaci waninehfiili keekeepitonelici mecimi hini piyeemikatwi yeh lohfaalici nili waninehfiili hina keekeepileni kalawi mecimi nihki mehseelekki kwakwehtaaniteheeki

And he was casting out a devil which was dumb. And it came to pass, when the devil was gone out, the dumb man spake; and the multitudes marveled.

15. payeekwa naaleta nihki piyeelhsipaliili nili hokimaawoosaakanwaali nihki waninehfiiki hoci katawi lohfe pakilahi waninehfihi hiwaki

But some of them said, By Beelzebub the prince of the devils casteth he out devils.

16. chiine kotakhi hopemi kocihekohi honatonemaakohi weefepahkamikiki hoci kikinooloowe

And others, tempting him, sought of him a sign from heaven.

17. payeekwa hina waakotamwa hotesiteheewenilici caaki hokimaawiiwe pahfenetiiya liikatahkamikifiiweneki si piyeetoote mecimi wiikiwa wiikiwaapeki si pahfehka haakicifeeya hotelahi nihi

But he, knowing their thoughts, said unto them, Every kingdom divided against itself is brought to desolation; and a house divided against a house falleth.

18. chiine kwehkwi setenii nehfaapi pahfenetite wiiya nehiwe weh si niipawiiya hokimaawiiwe ksake kiteyopwa kiilawa yeesi niila piyeelhsipalii hoci katawi lohfe pakilaki waninehfiiki

And if Satan also is divided against himself, how shall his kingdom stand? because ye say that I cast out devils by Beelzebub.

19. chiine kwehkwi niila piyeelhsipalii hoci katawi lohfe pakilake waninehfiiki neefaliwe kikwihfwaaki hoci katawi lohfe pakilaawahi nihi weecikeenahi nihkiini ke hoteepahkowemipwa

And if I by Beelzebub cast out devils, by whom do your sons cast them out? therefore shall they be your judges.

20. weeka kwehkwi niila nili holeceeli maneto hoci katawi lohfe pakilake waninehfiiki howe keela hini hokimaawitaamhkomi maneto hoskici kiilawa si piyeeya

But if I by the finger of God cast out devils, then is the kingdom of God come upon you.

21. hina wiisikileni ye hokwaawi si homhtekwaapici hokcitawahto nehalwaaka yeetasiweeci honawicika kaamaani hateeli

When the strong man fully armed guardeth his own court, his goods are in peace:

22. payeekwa hine halika waasikatowilici noota wiila weh piyeelotaakooli mecimi hotaliskaakooli homamaakooli nili melhske homhtekwaapiiwe meemhfeeletaki chiine papahfenameli hosiikwitahfoowe

but when a stronger than he shall come upon him, and overcome him, he taketh from him his whole armour wherein he trusted, and divideth his spoils.

23. hina peepwaa wiiciimita nippehtenekwa mecimi hina peepwaa wiici maawatonikeemita lhfwenike

He that is not with me is against me; and he that gathereth not with me scattereth.

24. hina wiyakilehfi ye hina lohfaaci nili hileniili hoci saapwi pemhfe tayah pwaa-laakwasi nepiwiki hopemi natoneha halwaakahsiiwe mecimi matalaakwa homhka peteki neh si kotekwi yeetaaya wiikiwa weeci lohfaaya yaa-iwapi

The unclean spirit when he is gone out of the man, passeth through waterless places, seeking rest; and finding none, he saith, I will turn back unto my house whence I came out.

25. chiine yeh piyaaci homhka hini ciikathoote mecimi waawesihtoote

And when he is come, he findeth it swept and garnished.

26. hine howe nhheewa hina mecimi homamahi wiiyaaki niiswahfwi kotakhi hilefiiwenhhi halika maciilefihi noota wiila chiine nihki piicfeeki mecimi nitasi teeki chiine hini ceeyehkwi hotelefiiwe hina hileni halika macaafi noota hini weski

Then goeth he, and taketh to him seven other spirits more evil than himself; and they enter in and dwell there: and the last state of that man becometh worse than the first.

27. chiine hini piyeemikatwi yeesi yoci yooloma wiyehi naanekoti hkweewa nili mehseelelici hoci hopahootamwa chiine kisaaciwi cehi hini laamataaka peepah kasenekoyani mecimi nihki holeniyeki neenooneyani hotekooli

And it came to pass, as he said these things, a certain woman out of the multitude lifted up her voice, and said unto him, Blessed is the womb that bare thee, and the breasts which thou didst suck.

28. payeekwa hanhka kaaciika kisaaciwiiki nihki neenootakki hini hokalawiiwe maneto mecimi hokciitonaanaawa hini hisiwe

But he said, Yea rather, blessed are they that hear the word of God, and keep it.

29. chiine nihi mehseelelici yeh pemi maawatoskaamekoci halemi hiwa yooma hinoki skwiiwe macaafi skwiilenaweewiiwe kikinooloowe si natonehikeeya chiine mata kikinooloowe hini weh si miiliweepi hini coona hokikinooloowe weeka

And when the multitudes were gathering together unto him, he began to say, This generation is an evil generation: it seeketh after a sign; and there shall no sign be given to it but the sign of Jonah.

30. ksake teetepilahi yeesi coona kikinooloowefihtawaaci nihi nenifahi yooni nehfaapi weh si hina hokwihfali hileni hilefihtaki hinoki yooma skwiilenaweewiiwe

For even as Jonah became a sign unto the Ninevites, so shall also the Son of man be to this generation.

31. hina hokimaawiyhkwe hini yeelaawahkweeki we hoci pafekwi hini ceeyehkwahkoweeweneki kileki nihi yooma hinoki skwiilenaweewiiwe hoci lenihi mecimi hina nihi weh miyaalahkowaalahi ksake hina hini yeekwahkamikiki hini hasiskitaamhkwe hoci piyeewa wahsi nootaki hini holepwaawe salamanii mecimi waapamehko halika mhsiilefi noota salamanii hotasi hapiwa

The queen of the south shall rise up in the judgment with the men of this generation, and shall condemn them: for she came from the ends of the earth to hear the wisdom of Solomon; and behold, a greater than Solomon is here.

32. nihki nenifa hoci leniiki weh pafekwiiki hini ceeyehkwahkoweeweneki kileki yooma hinoki skwiilenaweewiiwe mecimi weh miyaalahkowaataanaawa hini ksake nihki mataiini siteheeki hini tah pemi nanahimiweelici coonali chiine waapamehko halika mhsiilefi noota coona hotasi hapiwa

The men of Nineveh shall stand up in the judgment with this generation, and shall condemn it: for they repented at the preaching of Jonah; and behold, a greater than Jonah is here.

33. mata hileni yeh mehci fakfwaaci niitawaakanali laamahkikaaneki hotesi poonaali nili weelaa mata laameki hini posili hini hoskici tah niipawilici weeka wahsi nihki peepiicfaacki menawah neemowaaci hini wayahfeeyaaki

No man, when he hath lighted a lamp, putteth it in a cellar, neither under the bushel, but on the stand, that they which enter in may see the light.

34. honiitawaakani kiiya hini kiskiisekwi ye hofepiyaaki kiskiisekwi nehfaapi melhske kiiya hokwihfenwi wayahfeeyaaki weeka hini yeh macaafiki nehfaapi hokwihfenwi kiiya peepekicaaki

The lamp of thy body is thine eye: when thine eye is single, thy whole body also is full of light; but when it is evil, thy body also is full of darkness.

35. waapatano weecikeenahi kwehkwi toke hini wayahfeeyaaki kiiyaaki yehteeki mata peepekicaaki hinwi

Look therefore whether the light that is in thee be not darkness.

36. kwehkwi weecikeenahi melhske kiiya hokwihfeke wayahfeeyaaki pooname mata maalekhi pepekica hina weh mefhiike hokwihfenwi wayahfeeyaaki paasi hina niitawaaka hopemi wahfefikeewe miilehki kiila wayahfeeyaaki

If therefore thy whole body be full of light, having no part dark, it shall be wholly full of light, as when the lamp with its bright shining doth give thee light.

37. howe yeesi kalawici pelesiili hokocimekooli wahsi wihpomekoci chiine piicfe mecimi lematapi wahsi wihfenici

Now as he spake, a Pharisee asketh him to dine with him: and he went in, and sat down to meat.

38. chiine hina pelesi kwakwehtaanitehe yeh neemeki hini yeesi pwaa nhhihta nili mehci holelwiilici wihsi pwaa wihfenilici

And when the Pharisee saw it, he marveled that he had not first washed before dinner.

39. mecimi hina teepeelemiweeta howe kiilawa nihki pelesiiki kifafayaakhaawa hini faakici wiyeetahkwe hina tephika chiine hini seswilaaka weeka laameki lekhi kiilawa hokwihfenwi siikwitoowefiiwe mecimi wanaatefiiwe hotelaali nili

And the Lord said unto him, Now do ye Pharisees cleanse the outside of the cup and of the platter; but your inward part is full of extortion and wickedness.

40. kiilawa wanihsakaaki makha mata hina mayectoota hini faakici wiyeetahkwe nehfaapi hosto hini piitike wiyeetahkwe

Ye foolish ones, did not he that made the outside make the inside also?

41. weeka kiteminaakwi miiliweeko nele wiyehi piitike yehteeki mecimi waapatamoko caayahki wiyehi fafayaakiya kiilawa si

Howbeit give for alms those things which are within; and behold, all things are clean unto you.

42. payeekwa macilepwaawe cehi kiilawa pelesiiki ksake kiteekshaanaawa mhseeweewaskwi chiine lowaskwi mecimi caaki miinhkawaskwi chiine kitalwihkaataanaawa tepasawhki mecimi hini hotahkweelemiweewe maneto weeka yoolooni kwiilahi yo hinwi wahsi neyehka mehcilotameekwe mecimi teki nakatamoko hini kotaki mata mehcilotoote

But woe unto you Pharisees! for ye tithe mint and rue and every herb, and pass over judgment and the love of God: but these ought ye to have done, and not to leave the other undone.

43. macilepwaawe cehi kiilawa pelesiiki ksake kimenweeletaanaawa nili haliwiisi hpapiiwena piitike nili mhsikamiko mecimi nili hosilawaaletiiwena piitike nili yaatah wiiwiitkiiki

Woe unto you Pharisees! for ye love the chief seats in the synagogues, and the salutations in the marketplaces.

44. macilepwaawe cehi kiilawa ksake paasi nili nepoowaalako kiilawa yeelefiyeekwe mata tepinaakwato nili mecimi nihki hileniiki yeelwihkaatakki nili mata howaakotaanaawa hini

Woe unto you! for ye are as the tombs which appear not, and the men that walk over them know it not.

45. chiine nekoti nihki layaki pemi haapafse keekehkimiwe yooma peemi yoyani kimacimipe nehfaapi hotekooli

And one of the lawyers answering saith unto him, Master, in saying this thou reproachest us also.

46. mecimi macilepwaawe cehi kiilawa layaki nehfaapi ksake kiwiiwashaawaaki hileniiki wiiwasiiwena hahkwato wahsi nayooteeki mecimi

And he said, Woe unto you lawyers also! for ye lade men with burdens grievous to be borne, and ye yourselves touch not the burdens with one of your fingers.

kiilawa mata nehalwaaka nekoti kileceefwa kita hoci
pehsenaanaawa nili wiiwasiiwena hisiwe

47. macilepwaawe cehi kiilawa ksake kiilawa ki
hostawaawaaki nepoowaalako nihki
maamoosikiiskwecki mecimi kohfwaaki honhfaawahi
nihi

Woe unto you! for ye build the tombs of the prophets, and your fathers killed them.

48. caalayini kiilawa teepweewenaki mecimi
kinhkotaanaawa nili hopekatefiiwenwa kohfwaaki
ksake nihki honhfaawahi nihi mecimi kiilawa ki
hostawaawaaki honepoowaalakomwa

So ye are witnesses and consent unto the works of your fathers: for they killed them, and ye build their tombs.

49. weecikeenahi hiyooya nehfaapi hini holepwaawe
maneto nineh leskamawaaki maamoosikiiskwelici
mecimi hepastalihi chiine naaleta nihi we nhfaawahi
nihki mecimi weh naanohkaachaawahi

Therefore also said the wisdom of God, I will send unto them prophets and apostles; and some of them they shall kill and persecute;

50. wahsi hini homhskomwa caayahki nihki
maamoosikiiskwecki fefiikhooteeki hine
halemahkehfenwi hini yeelekokwahkamikiki hoci
menawah paapiyeeci leeletamaweci yaama hinoki
skwiilenawe

that the blood of all the prophets, which was shed from the foundation of the world, may be required of this generation;

51. hini homhskomi hepalii hoci paalohi hini
homhskomi sekolaaya yehkwineta lalakwi hini
pootefamaacika chiine hini hofepikamikwi hanhka
kitelepwa niila hini paapiyeeci weh leeletamaakwi
yaama hinoki skwiilenawe

from the blood of Abel unto the blood of Zachariah, who perished between the altar and the sanctuary: yea, I say unto you, it shall be required of this generation.

52. macilepwaawe cehi kiilawa layaki ksake
kitaamwetoonaawa lepwaaweewi tawenehika mata
kipiicfaapwa kiilawa mecimi kwtamhaawaaki nihki
peemi piicfaacki

Woe unto you lawyers! for ye took away the key of knowledge: ye entered not in yourselves, and them that were entering in ye hindered.

53. chiine hini ye hoci piyeci lohfaaci nihi
yaayawikeelici chiine nihi pelesihi hotalemi
wiyakoweewi fakkehkaakohi wiisa kisfekohi wahsi
meci wiyehi si kalawici

And when he was come out from thence, the scribes and the Pharisees began to press upon him vehemently, and to provoke him to speak of many things;

54. hopemi hahkonehokohi wahsi pethataakoci wiyehi
hotooneki hoci

laying wait for him, to catch something out of his mouth.

Luke:12

1. hini heelekhi laakwa hine hina meci tfene
metahfene tepeewe mehseeleka maawatoska
weecikeenahi kakeelhkaatiiki nihki hotalemi hilahi
hokakehkimaafhi nhhihta mahkeeni kiilawa hini
honalescikanwa nihki pelesiiki nelohcilawiiwe hini

In the mean time, when the many thousands of the multitude were gathered together, insomuch that they trode one upon another, he began to say unto his disciples first of all, Beware ye of the leaven of the Pharisees, which is hypocrisy.

2. payeekwa mata hahteewi wiyehi petakhoote yah pwaa hini pahkaseenoote mecimi kikitoote yah pwaa hini waakotoote

But there is nothing covered up, that shall not be revealed: and hid, that shall not be known.

3. yooni hoci kookwe-nehi-kaaci kiilawa kimehtowepwa hini laa pepekica weh nootoote hini laa wayahfeya chiine kookweenehi kiilawa hini hotawakaaki kimehci kalawipwa piitike nili piitikaana we lhfwaacimopi hoskici nili wiikiwaapi hakocikami

Wherefore whatsoever ye have said in the darkness shall be heard in the light; and what ye have spoken in the ear in the inner chambers shall be proclaimed upon the housetops.

4. chiine kitelepwa niila nihkaaneti teki kwfehko nihki naanhfaacki nili wiyawfi wiiyaanali mecimi mayohkwaaci mata kiteeni hopoonaanaawa wah katawi silawiiwaaci

And I say unto you my friends, Be not afraid of them which kill the body, and after that have no more that they can do.

5. weeka ke halenelepwa hina wiyeefa we kwfeekwe kwfehko hina hina yeh mehci nhsiweeci hopoona waasikaki wahsi hahkwinamooweneki hipakisiweeci hanhka kitelepwa niila kwfehko hina

But I will warn you whom ye shall fear: Fear him, which after he hath killed hath power to cast into hell; yea, I say unto you, Fear him.

6. makha mata niyaalanwi hoteeweniwiskilohfaki niyeewi senhsi yaasi miyeekipi mecimi mata nekoti wanihkaaloofo hini hotelaapiiweneki maneto

Are not five sparrows sold for two farthings? and not one of them is forgotten in the sight of God.

7. weeka tepilo nili kiilehfwa caayahki kikinootakite teki kwsiweeko haliwi kiteleelemekofipwa kiilawa noota meci hoteeweniwiskilohfaki

But the very hairs of your head are all numbered. Fear not: ye are of more value than many sparrows.

8. chiine kitelepwa niila caakiwiyeefa neh mohkaaci tepaaci haacimekwa yeelahfamiiwaaci hileniiki niliini hina hokwihfali hileni nehfaapi weh mohkaaci tepaaci haacimaali yeelahfamiilici nihi hotenhcaliimhhi maneto

And I say unto you, Every one who shall confess me before men, him shall the Son of man also confess before the angels of God:

9. weeka hina keekiyaacimita ta hapiwaaci hileniiki weh kiyaacimoofo hini ta hapilici nihi hotenhcaliimhhi maneto

but he that denieth me in the presence of men shall be denied in the presence of the angels of God.

10. chiine caakiwiyeefa we ppehcimaali kalawiiwe nili hokwihfali hileni hini weh pakfeeletamaakwi hina weeka hina peeppehci pahtaamaata nili hofepi hocacaalahkwali mata hini yah pakfeeletoote

And every one who shall speak a word against the Son of man, it shall be forgiven him: but unto him that blasphemeth against the Holy Spirit it shall not be forgiven.

11. chiine hine nihki yeelahfamiiyaaki nili mhsikamiko si piyeelelwaakwa chiine nihi teepeelecikehi chiine nihi wiyehisimekofiiwenhhi teki wiisaafiiko wah saiyeekwe weelaa wa haapafseeyeekwe weelaa wa hiyoyeekwe

And when they bring you before the synagogues, and the rulers, and the authorities, be not anxious how or what ye shall answer, or what ye shall say:

12. ksake hina hofepi hocacaalahkwa keh kakehkimekowa tepilo hini yaatefaki wa hiyoyeekwe

for the Holy Spirit shall teach you in that very hour what ye ought to say.

13. chiine nekoti wiyeefali nili mehseelelici hoci kaloolekooli keekehkimiwe wiitamawi niceenina nipahfenamaakwa hini siikwi wiyehi

And one out of the multitude said unto him, Master, bid my brother divide the inheritance with me.

14. payeekwa hileni neefawe teepasawateniweeta weelaa peepahfeniweeta wahsi simekofihtoolako niteshekwa hotelaali

But he said unto him, Man, who made me a judge or a divider over you?

15. mecimi kcitawaafiiko chiine caayahki hapeeletiiwe hoci kicitawi nohpiyeenamoko kiiyaawa ksake hileni hotelenaweewiiwe mata hini hotetwi maalefiiweneki hoci hini wiyehi peepoonaki hotelahi nihi

And he said unto them, Take heed, and keep yourselves from all covetousness: for a man's life consisteth not in the abundance of the things which he possesseth.

16. chiine pemaatoweewe hokaloolahi hini hotasiskiimi naanekoti paweewi hileni maali niikicikeeya hiwapi

And he spake a parable unto them, saying, The ground of a certain rich man brought forth plentifully:

17. mecimi memekinitehe hina wiiyaaki ceh nehiwe neh silawi ksake mata nipoona wah tah poonama nimawifoowena hiwapi

and he reasoned within himself, saying, What shall I do, because I have not where to bestow my fruits?

18. ceh yooma neh silawi neh liikatenaana nikawaskwikaana mecimi ne hopatena halika mehsaaki chiine nitasi neh poona caayahki nikawaskomi mecimi niwiyehiimi

And he said, This will I do: I will pull down my barns, and build greater; and there will I bestow all my corn and my goods.

19. mecimi ne hila niiya niiya kipoona meci wiyehi meci tfwi kkato si nhhaawaataakwate mamelo kikaamaanefiiwe wihfenilo menelo kilakifilo hiwapi

And I will say to my soul, Soul, thou hast much goods laid up for many years; take thine ease, eat, drink, be merry.

20. payeekwa manetooli kiila wanihsakaafa hinoki tepehkike paapiyeeci kiteleeletamaakoopi kiiya chiine hini wiyehi nenhhaawaacfetooyani neefawe we howiilaami hini hotekooli

But God said unto him, Thou foolish one, this night is thy soul required of thee; and the things which thou hast prepared, whose shall they be?

21. yooni yeeki hina peepoonahfotaka wiiya paweewe mecimi mata paweewa manetooli wiyeeci

So is he that layeth up treasure for himself, and is not rich toward God.

22. chiine weecikeenahi kitelepwa niila hotelahi hokakehkimaafhi teki kitelenaweewiiwenwa hoci wiisaafiiko wiyehi wah miiciyeekwe weelaa teki nohki kiiyaawa wiyehi wah laseyeekwe

And he said unto his disciples, Therefore I say unto you, Be not anxious for your life, what ye shall eat; nor yet for your body, what ye shall put on.

23. ksake hini lenaweewiiwe halika hinwi noota hini wihfeniiwe mecimi hina wiiyaana noota hini piitenika

For the life is more than the food, and the body than the raiment.

24. memekineelemehko nihki kaakalhhweeki yaasi pwaa nihki hahcikeewaaci nohki mata kawaskwhaaweki mata nihki hopoonaanaawa poonahfoowika weelaa kawaskwika mecimi maneto hotsamahi nihi kehfwi si halika kiteleelemekofipwa kiilawa nihki wiskilohfaki

Consider the ravens, that they sow not, neither reap; which have no store-chamber nor barn; and God feedeth them: of how much more value are ye than the birds!

25. chiine taanawe hina kiilawa pemi wiisaafiite we hoci katawi kooloto nekoti kiopit hini hotelenaweewiiwe si tepacikaneki

And which of you by being anxious can add a cubit unto his stature?

26. kwehkwi yo weecikeenahi kitaalwi silawiipwa mohci hini kehci maackwaafiki koociwe nili kiteh wiisaafiipwa maa si naaleta

If then ye are not able to do even that which is least, why are ye anxious concerning the rest?

27. memekineeletamoko nili wiisiwalakeemi yaasi nili skwiniikiki mata paapekatefiiya nili nohki mata paapiyeeminakweya payeekwa kitelepwa niila wiikinaakwi salaman' caayahki howahfaacimekofiiweneki mata paasi nekoti yooloma si waawesi

Consider the lilies, how they grow: they toil not, neither do they spin; yet I say unto you, Even Solomon in all his glory was not arrayed like one of these.

28. weeka kwehkwi maneto yooni lasehtoote nili mhskotehkwalo hini heele lhskahkiki yeeki hinoki kaasekiki mecimi waapake hini kisifikaneki hipakitoote taaniwe lekhi si halika keh lasekhokowa hina o kiilawa caki teepwehseefaki

But if God doth so clothe the grass in the field, which today is, and tomorrow is cast into the oven; how much more shall he clothe you, O ye of little faith?

29. chiine kiilawa teki natonehamoko wah miiciyeekwe mecimi wah meneyeekwe teki nohki niiswitehaakaniko

And seek not ye what ye shall eat, and what ye shall drink, neither be ye of doubtful mind.

30. ksake sapkahi nihki caakisi lenaweeki hini yeelekokwahkamikiki honatonehaanaawa caayahki yooloma wiyehi weeka kohfwa howaakota yeesi kiilawa mhfeeletameekwe yooloma wiyehi

For all these things do the nations of the world seek after: but your Father knoweth that ye have need of these things.

31. payeekwa natonehamoko kiilawa hokimaawitaamhkomi mecimi yooloma wiyehi keh koolotaakoopwa

Howbeit seek ye his kingdom, and these things shall be added unto you.

32. teki kwtamoko caki nekotweeloofaki ksake hini yeesi howesi menwiteheewenici kohfwa wahsi miilelwaakwe hini hokimaawitaamhkwe

Fear not, little flock; for it is your Father's good pleasure to give you the kingdom.

33. miyeekiko hini peepoonameekwe mecimi kisaaci si miiliweeko hostooko pesikwi kiilawa monipiitaakana pwaayaa halalika si kehteeyaaki paweewe piitike nili menhkwato pwaayaa nootkwahki yaatah pwaa maalaakwa haaci kaakimooteka mata nohki manetooleefa macilawiici

Sell that ye have, and give alms; make for yourselves purses which wax not old, a treasure in the heavens that faileth not, where no thief draweth near, neither moth destroyeth.

34. ksake tah teeki kipawaawe nehfaapi nitasi we hahteewi kitehi

For where your treasure is, there will your heart be also.

35. wiilaani kisehkiwa kitapifooyaake mecimi kiniitawaakanwaaki peemi fakifowaaci

Let your loins be girded about, and your lamps burning;

36. mecimi hilefiko kiilawa paasi hileniiki peemi hahkawaapamaacki teepeelemekowaaci laakwa nili peteki hini wiichetiiwi wihfenhcikeewe we hoci piyeeli wahsi hine piyaalite mecimi tiitowathikeelite menawahke weelena tawenamawaawaaci nili

and be ye yourselves like unto men looking for their lord, when he shall return from the marriage feast; that, when he cometh and knocketh, they may straightway open unto him.

37. kisaateelemekofiiki cehi nehke haloolaakanaki nihi hina teepeelemiweeta hine piyaate we mhkawahi peemi kcitawaapilici tepilo kitelepwa niila we kitapito wiiya hina chiine weh lemataphahi nihi wahsi wihfenilici mecimi weh piyeewa chiine weh kisaacilotawahi nihi

Blessed are those servants, whom the lord when he cometh shall find watching: verily I say unto you, that he shall gird himself, and make them sit down to meat, and shall come and serve them.

38. chiine kwehkwi hina weh piyeewa hini mawi-niisene ta kcitawahtooteeki laakwa mecimi kwehkwi hini mawi-nhfene mecimi yooni weh si mhkawaaci nihi kisaateelemekofiiki cehi nehke haloolaakanaki

And if he shall come in the second watch, and if in the third, and find them so, blessed are those servants.

39. payeekwa waakotamoko halayooma kwehkwi hina hini wiikiwa hoci mestele neyehka waakotake hini yaatefaki waasa piyaaci hina kaakimooteka neyehka wi kcitawaapi mecimi mata hotah neyehka nakata wiikiwa yeetaaci wahsi saapwi pokhooteelici

But know this, that if the master of the house had known in what hour the thief was coming, he would have watched, and not have left his house to be broken through.

40. nehfaapi kiilawa mehciweefiko ksake pwaayaa hini yaatefaki siteheeyeekwe hina hokwihfali hileni piyeewa

Be ye also ready: for in an hour that ye think not the Son of man cometh.

41. chiine teepeelemiweeta ha niilawe kikaloosipe yooma pemaatoweewe weelaa toke teetepilahi caayahki hisiwe piita

And Peter said, Lord, speakest thou this parable unto us, or even unto all?

42. neefawe chiine hina tepasawefi mecimi lepwaawefi noosaacikana wah talwahfekota teepeelemekoci yeetaalici wiyehi wahsi miilaaci lekhi wiilawa nihi howihfeniiwenilici kwenaani laakwa hisiwe hina teepeelemiweeta

And the Lord said, Who then is the faithful and wise steward, whom his lord shall set over his household, to give them their portion of food in due season?

43. kisaateelemekofi cehi hina haloolaaka hine piyaalite teepeelemekoci we mhkaakooli peemi yooni silawiici

Blessed is that servant, whom his lord when he cometh shall find so doing.

44. teepweewe kitelepwa niila nili weh talwahfwaali hina caayahki peepoonaki

Of a truth I say unto you, that he will set him over all that he hath.

45. weeka kwehkwi hina haloolaaka ce honaakahto hopiyaawe teepeelemita we hiwa hotehiki mecimi we halemi ppaktehwahi nihi haloolaakanilenihi chiine nihi haloolaakaniikwefhi mecimi wihfeni chiine menwa mecimi wahsi wanefoci

But if that servant shall say in his heart, My lord delayeth his coming; and shall begin to beat the menservants and the maidservants, and to eat and drink, and to be drunken;

46. nili teepeelemekoci hina haloolaaka weh piyeeli hine kaasekiki mata hopiyeeteeleta mecimi hine yaatefaki mata howaakota chiine we hahkwinalekooli nili wch si takwinamaakooli hini wiila nihi pwaayaa tepasawefilici

the lord of that servant shall come in a day when he expecteth not, and in an hour when he knoweth not, and shall cut him asunder, and appoint his portion with the unfaithful.

47. mecimi hina haloolaaka weewaakotaka yeesiteheewenilici teepeelemekoci chiine mata mehcilawiiwefi chiine mata nohki yeesiteheewenilici silawi we ppaktehoofo hina meci lihfiiwanhhotiiwawikaafoowena

And that servant, which knew his lord's will, and made not ready, nor did according to his will, shall be beaten with many stripes;

48. weeka hina peepwaa waakotaka mecimi wiyehi silawi nahiika hikwatwi lihfiiwanhhotiiwawikaafoowena we ppaktehoofo laakofwiimehi lihfiiwanhhotiiwawikaafoowena chiine kookwe-neefa-kaaci mecilekhi miiloofo mecilekhi we

but he that knew not, and did things worthy of stripes, shall be beaten with few stripes. And to whomsoever much is given, of him shall much be required: and

hina hoteeletamaakwi mecimi nili nihki mecilekhi teelwahfwaawaaci niliini weh natotamawaawaali hini halika lekhi

to whom they commit much, of him will they ask the more.

49. nipiya niila wahsi hini hoskitaamhkwe hipakitama skote mecimi nehiwe skata niteleeleta kwehkwi yo hini neyehka pkaleenoote

I came to cast fire upon the earth; and what will I, if it is already kindled?

50. payeekwa nipoona fafahkwiholelwiiwe wah fafahkwi holelwiiya mecimi nikiisenaacina paalohi hini mehcilotooteeke

But I have a baptism to be baptized with; and how am I straitened till it be accomplished!

51. ha kiilawa kitesiteheepwa yeesi piyaaya niila wahsi miiliweeya kaamaaniilefiiwe hini hoskitaamhkwe kitelepwa niila mata kaaciika pahfehkaawe weeka

Think ye that I am come to give peace in the earth? I tell you, Nay; but rather division:

52. ksake yooci hinoki we hapiiki niyaalanwi nekoti wiikiwaapeki pahfehkaaki nhfwi homawinahkaalaawahi niiswi chiine niiswi nihi nhfwi

for there shall be from henceforth five in one house divided, three against two, and two against three.

53. weh pahfehkaaki nihki hohfima homawinahkaalaali hokwihfimaali mecimi hokwihfima hofimaali hokeefa hotaanhfimaali mecimi hotaanhfima hokeefali hofemiyokiifa hofemiyeli mecimi hofemiya hofemiyokiifali

They shall be divided, father against son, and son against father; mother against daughter, and daughter against her mother; mother in law against her daughter in law, and daughter in law against her mother in law.

54. chiine nehfaapi hotelahi nihi mehseelelici hine yeh neemeyeekwe paafkwahki peemi pafekwiiyaaki hini yeepaksimoki halayini piyeeya keemowaaki kiteyopwa weelena mecimi niicaphi yooni hini yeesi piyeemikaki

And he said to the multitudes also, When ye see a cloud rising in the west, straightway ye say, There cometh a shower; and so it cometh to pass.

55. chiine yeh neemeyeekwe yeelaawahkweeki peemi hocikikaki weh kisiteewi kiiseki kiteyopwa mecimi hini piyeemikatwi

And when ye see a south wind blowing, ye say, There will be a scorching heat; and it cometh to pass.

56. kiilawa nelohcilawiwehfiiki kiwaakotaanaawa wahsi laapaatotameekwe hini yeelaapeskaaki hini hoskitaamhkwe mecimi hini menhkwatwi payeekwa nehiwe kitesi pwaa ini waakotaanaawa wahsi laapaatotameekwe yooma hinoki yeelhkamikiki

Ye hypocrites, ye know how to interpret the face of the earth and the heaven; but how is it that ye know not how to interpret this time?

57. chiine koociwe wiikinaakwi pesikwi kiilawa mata mayaawi kitelahkowaaletipwa

And why even of yourselves judge ye not what is right?

58. ksake yeesi kiila wiiteemaci kimateeletiiwena yeelahfamiici hina teepowaasiweeta kcitawaafiilo yeelelhfeeyani wahsi tfwihkawehki hina piilepe nili teepasawateniweelici keh si soskholekwa mecimi hina teepasawateniweeta nili wiyehsimekofiiwenali keh si pakfenekwa mecimi hina wiyehsimekofiiwena kiphotiiwikaaneki ke hpakilekwa

For as thou art going with thine adversary before the magistrate, on the way give diligence to be quit of him; lest haply he hale thee unto the judge, and the judge shall deliver thee to the officer, and the officer shall cast thee into prison.

59. kitele niila mata wiyehisi ke hini hoci lohfa paalohi hini tepilo ceeyehkwi maalecihi keh caaki mehci tepha

I say unto thee, Thou shalt by no means come out thence, till thou have paid the very last mite.

Luke:13

1. howe nitasi hapiiki naaleta wiyeefaki kwena hine laakwa hotaatotamawaawaali nihi keeleliiwi lenawehi nihiini homhskomilici paalatii hokilekfeto hotapeneewenilici

Now there were some present at that very season which told him of the Galilaeans, whose blood Pilate had mingled with their sacrifices.

2. mecimi haapafse ha kitesiteheepwa halika meciileficki yohkoma keeleliiwilenaweeki yeecsiwaaci caayahki nihki keeleliiwilenaweeki ksake mehci maciisinamooki yooma wiyehi hotelahi

And he answered and said unto them, Think ye that these Galilaeans were sinners above all the Galilaeans, because they have suffered these things?

3. kitelepwa niila mata weeka weeciwephi mataiini siteheeyeekwe yooni yaska weh si hkwineyeekwe caayahki kiilawa

I tell you, Nay: but, except ye repent, ye shall all in like manner perish.

4. weelaa nehke metahfwi-kite-nhfwaasikfwi nepolaakwicki hini taweeteewika sailoomiki haakicfeeya mecimi honhfekonaawa ha kitesiteheepwa halika keesfiweeficki nihki noota caayahki nihki hileniiki colooseelemiiki yeetaacki

Or those eighteen, upon whom the tower in Siloam fell, and killed them, think ye that they were offenders above all the men that dwell in Jerusalem?

5. kitelepwa niila mata weeka weeciwephi mataiini siteheeyeekwe yooni hofepi weh si hkwineyeekwe caayahki kiilawa hotelahi

I tell you, Nay: but, except ye repent, ye shall all likewise perish.

6. chiine yooma pemaatoweewe kalawi naanekoti hileni mehci hahtaakwi kicimiisi homhfaloomiktikaaneki chiine piyeewa peemi natonehaki mawifoowe nitasi mecimi mata homhka

And he spake this parable; A certain man had a fig tree planted in his vineyard; and he came seeking fruit thereon, and found none.

7. chiine waapamilo yooloma nhfwi kkato nipaapiya peemi natonehama mawifoowe yooma kicimiisiki mecimi mata nimhka kawhano hini koociwe nehfaapi hini hotamhskaaweya hini hasiskiiki hotelaali nili paapakickwahkotamelici

And he said unto the vinedresser, Behold, these three years I come seeking fruit on this fig tree, and find none: cut it down; why doth it also cumber the ground?

8. chiine hina pemi haapafse teepeelemiweeta wiilaani hini nehfaapi hinoki nekoti kkatwi pelahci neh lohkaamekhaawe kaayaawka hini mecimi neh mohto hini

And he answering saith unto him, Lord, let it alone this year also, till I shall dig about it, and dung it:

9. chiine kwehkwi niikike hini mawifoowe yooci hinoki howesa weeka kwehkwi mata keh kawha hini hotelaali hina

and if it bear fruit thenceforth, well; but if not, thou shalt cut it down.

10. chiine peemi kakehkimiweeci piitike nekoti nili mhsikamiko hini ta halwaakahsi kiisekiki

And he was teaching in one of the synagogues on the sabbath day.

11. mecimi waapamehko hkweewa peepoonaka katoneewi hilefiiwe metahfwi-kite-nhfwaasikfwi

And behold, a woman which had a spirit of infirmity eighteen years; and she was

kkato mecimi maatakoce chiine hotaalwi wiyehisi kokwitena wiiya

12. chiine yeh neewaaci ciisisii hotahpimaali mecimi hkweewa kikatoneewe kite hoci pelhskonekoopi hotelaali

13. mecimi hoskici nili hoteh poonaana holeciwali mecimi weelena hina pesikwahkocehoofo chiine howahfaacimekohwaali manetooli

14. chiine hina teepeelecikeeta hini mhsikamikoki teewahi maacitehe kisfekwiiwe ksake ciisisiili mehci kiikehiweeli hini ta halwaakahsi kiisekiki haapafse hahteewa nekotwahfwi kaasekiki wah ta hileniiki pekatefiwaaci hine nili weecikeenahi piyaako chiine kiikehoofoko mecimi teki ta hini kiisekiki hini halwaakahsiiwe hotelahi nihi mehseelelici

15. payeekwa hina teepeelemiweeta hotaapaftawaali mecimi kiilawa nelohcilawiwehfiiki ha mata maasa nekoti wiyeefa kiilawa hini tah wihfenilici hoci pelhhwaali hotaaksiniimali weelaa hoceekiifemali ta hini halwaakahsi kiisekiki mecimi hotale fakinaapiyaalaali nili wahsi menhhaaci

16. mecimi ha mata yaama hkweewa teewahi heplehemii hotaanehfali niliini homehtahpilaali setenii scih halaniliini metahfwi-kite-nhfwaasikfwi kkato ya hina mehci yooma haayitahpifoowe hoci pelhoofo hina ta hini kiisekiki hina halwaakahsiiwe hisiwe

17. chiine yeesi yooloma wiyehi yoci caayahki homateeletiiwenhhi wiyanaatihoofohi mecimi caayahki nihi mehseelelici hosasilawaatamehi caayahki nili wahfaaci wiyehi mayehci silawiilici nili

18. nehiwe hini hokimaawitaamhkomi maneto sinaakwatwi hiwa weecikeenhhi mecimi taaniwe neh si takwaatota hini

19. paasi hini nekoti pekwe mastatiiwi miinhka meemameki hileni mecimi wiila homemekinhcikaneki hotipakita chiine hini skwiniikinwi mecimi mhtekoniwi chiine nihki wiskilohfaki hini menhkwatwi hoci lwahsinooki nili pehkeeyakoki nitasi

20. chiine taaniwe neh si takwaatota hini hokimaawitaamhkomi maneto hiwa nohki

21. paasi hini honalescika meemameki hkweewa hote kkito nhfwi tepacikaneki lokhaana paalohi hini caayahki honete

---

bowed together, and could in no wise lift herself up.

And when Jesus saw her, he called her, and said to her, Woman, thou art loosed from thine infirmity.

And he laid his hands upon her: and immediately she was made straight, and glorified God.

And the ruler of the synagogue, being moved with indignation because Jesus had healed on the sabbath, answered and said to the multitude, There are six days in which men ought to work: in them therefore come and be healed, and not on the day of the sabbath.

But the Lord answered him, and said, Ye hypocrites, doth not each one of you on the sabbath loose his ox or his ass from the stall, and lead him away to watering?

And ought not this woman, being a daughter of Abraham, whom Satan had bound, lo, these eighteen years, to have been loosed from this bond on the day of the sabbath?

And as he said these things, all his adversaries were put to shame: and all the multitude rejoiced for all the glorious things that were done by him.

He said therefore, Unto what is the kingdom of God like? and whereunto shall I liken it?

It is like unto a grain of mustard seed, which a man took, and cast into his own garden; and it grew, and became a tree; and the birds of the heaven lodged in the branches thereof.

And again he said, Whereunto shall I liken the kingdom of God?

It is like unto leaven, which a woman took and hid in three measures of meal, till it was all leavened.

22. chiine weepfe yeele haaci saapwi hoteewena mecimi hoteeweneefa pemi kakehkimiwe mecimi colooseelemii pemi hale laami

And he went on his way through cities and villages, teaching, and journeying on unto Jerusalem.

23. chiine nekoti wiyeefali teepeelemiweeta ha maatfwihi nihki weewaapaneshoofocki hotekooli mecimi hotelahi

And one said unto him, Lord, are they few that be saved? And he said unto them,

24. wiisikihkamoko wahsi hoci piicfaayeekwe hini maackwaalakatoofi skwaate ksake meci kitelepwa niila weh natonehaanaawa wahsi piicfaawaaci mecimi we haalwi hilefiiki

Strive to enter in by the narrow door: for many, I say unto you, shall seek to enter in, and shall not be able.

25. hayenwi peeleko pafekwiite hina hini wiikiwaapeki hoci mestele mecimi mehci kiphake hini skwaateeki chiine kiilawa ke halemi niipawipwa faakici mecimi tiitowathaanaawa hini skwaate teepeelemiweeta tawenamawinaake ke hisiweepwa chiine hina we haapafse mata kiwaakomelepwa weeciwiyeekwe ke hikowa

When once the master of the house is risen up, and hath shut to the door, and ye begin to stand without, and to knock at the door, saying, Lord, open to us; and he shall answer and say to you, I know you not whence ye are;

26. hine howe kiilawa sapkahi niwihfenipe mecimi nimenepe kitapiiweneki chiine kiila sapkahi kikakehkimiwe noteewenimiyeewenenaaki ke halemi hiyopwa

then shall ye begin to say, We did eat and drink in thy presence, and thou didst teach in our streets;

27. mecimi hina kitelepwa mata niwaakota weeciwiyeekwe kiilawa niiyaaki hoci saaweko caayahki kiilawa peekatenakki maciilefiiwe we hiwa

and he shall say, I tell you, I know not whence ye are; depart from me, all ye workers of iniquity.

28. nitasi we hahteewi hini wihfakweewe mecimi hini weh talweewehfeki wiipitali hine keh neewaawaaki heplehemii chiine haisiki chiine ceekapii chiine caayahki nihki maamoosikiiskwecki piitike hini hokimaawitaamhkomi maneto mecimi kiilawa faakici kitipakilekoopwa

There shall be the weeping and gnashing of teeth, when ye shall see Abraham, and Isaac, and Jacob, and all the prophets, in the kingdom of God, and yourselves cast forth without.

29. chiine nihki hini weetahkofaki we hoci piyeeki mecimi yeepaksimoki chiine hini pepoonhkiiki mecimi yeelaawahkweeki hoci chiine piitike hini hokimaawitaamhkomi maneto weh lematapiiki

And they shall come from the east and west, and from the north and south, and shall sit down in the kingdom of God.

30. mecimi waapamehko hapiiki nitasi hotaanaakiwiiki nihkiini we nhhihtaawiiki mecimi hapiiki nitasi nhhihtaawiiki nihkiini we hotaanaakiwiiki

And behold, there are last which shall be first, and there are first which shall be last.

31. hine hofepi yaatefaki piyehi nitasi naanekoti pelesihi chiine lohfaalo mecimi yooci weepfeelo ksake heletii kimaatawi nhfekwa hotekohi

In that very hour there came certain Pharisees, saying to him, Get thee out, and go hence: for Herod would fain kill thee.

32. mecimi nhhaakone chiine hilehko hina waakocehfi waapatano nilohfe pakilaaki waninehfiiki mecimi nipekatenaana kiikehetiiwena hinoki kaasekiki mecimi

And he said unto them, Go and say to that fox, Behold, I cast out devils and

waapake chiine hini mawi-nhfwi kiisekike nimefefihekoopi hotelahi nihi

33. mata-ini-otahpi kwiilahi nine ha yehaaya hinoki kaasekiki mecimi waapake chiine hini hahkowi kaasekiki ksake mata yah katawi hinwi wahsi maamoosikiiskweeta colooseelemii hoci hkwineci

34. o colooseelem' colooseelem' naanhfaata nihi maamoosikiiskwelici chiine hosiikonhhwahi nihi peepiyeelhkamawoofoci taaniwe tfene neyehka nih mehci maawatonaaki kiniicaaneefaki teetepilahi paasi peleewa maawatonaaci nehalwaaka hopalasaanhhi laameki holekwana mecimi mata kitesiteheepwa

35. waapatamoko yeetaayeekwe wiikiwa kinakatamaakoopwa liikatahkamikatwi chiine kitelepwa niila mata kitah neewipwa paalohi kisaateelemekofi ce hina peepiyaata hini howiifooweneki hina teepeelemiweeta ke hiyopwa

perform cures today and tomorrow, and the third day I am perfected.

Howbeit I must go on my way today and tomorrow and the day following: for it cannot be that a prophet perish out of Jerusalem.

O Jerusalem, Jerusalem, which killeth the prophets, and stoneth them that are sent unto her! how often would I have gathered thy children together, even as a hen gathereth her own brood under her wings, and ye would not!

Behold, your house is left unto you desolate: and I say unto you, Ye shall not see me, until ye shall say, Blessed is he that cometh in the name of the Lord.

Luke:14

1. chiine hini piyeemikatwi hini yeh si piicfaaci wiikiwa yeetaaci nekoti nihki teepeelemaacki nihi pelesihi ta halwaakahsi kiisekiki wahsi miicici takhwa yeesi nihki peemi kcitawaapamaawaaci

And it came to pass, when he went into the house of one of the rulers of the Pharisees on a sabbath to eat bread, that they were watching him.

2. chiine waapamehko nitasi yeelahfamiici hapiili naanekoti hileniili peepoonamelici nepiwilokeewe

And behold, there was before him a certain man which had the dropsy.

3. chiine peemi haapafseeci ciisisii mecimi hokaloolahi nihi layahi chiine pelesihi ha mayaawatwi hini kwteletiiweneki wahsi kiikehiweeki hini ta halwaakahsi kiisekiki weelaa toke mata peemi yoci

And Jesus answering spake unto the lawyers and Pharisees, saying, Is it lawful to heal on the sabbath, or not?

4. payeekwa mata wiye hiwaki nihki chiine hotahpenaali nili mecimi hokiikehaali chiine hopakfenaali

But they held their peace. And he took him, and healed him, and let him go.

5. mecimi taanawe hina kiilawa weh poonaali ceekiifali weelaa haaksiniili tkikamiiwaalakoki si penhsinooli chiine mata weelena we kokwitapilaali nili ta halwaakahsi kiisekiki hotelahi nihi

And he said unto them, Which of you shall have an ass or an ox fallen into a well, and will not straightway draw him up on a sabbath day?

6. chiine nohki nihki hotaalwi haapaftaanaawa yooloma wiyehi

And they could not answer again unto these things.

7. chiine hokaloolahi pemaatoweewe nehe yeelenoofolici yeh kciyeesi nihi mekinamelici nili haliwi yeeki hpapiiwena peemi hilaaci nihi

And he spake a parable unto those which were bidden, when he marked how they chose out the chief seats; saying unto them,

8. hine kiila wiyeefa hileni wiichetiiwi wihfenhcikeewe si halenehke teki lematapilo hini

When thou art bidden of any man to a marriage feast, sit not down in the chief

haliwi yeeki hpapiiweneki piilepe kwena halika
hotakeelemekwi leniili noota kiila hotalenaali hina

seat; lest haply a more honourable man
than thou be bidden of him,

9. mecimi hina yeelenehka kiila chiine nili weh
piyeeki mecimi miili yaama hileni maatasi ke hikwa
chiine hine howe kiila ke halemi lawi kileki
wiyanaatiiwe wahsi mameyani hini kcimaalespihi tasi

and he that bade thee and him shall come
and say to thee, Give this man place; and
then thou shalt begin with shame to take
the lowest place.

10. weeka hine kiila halenoofoyane nhhaale mecimi
lematapilo hini kcimaalespihi tasi wahsi hine hina
mayehci halenehka piyaate wihkaanima halika lhspi
haale menawa hilehki hine howe kiila keh poona
wahfaacimekofiiwe hini hotapiiwenwaaki caayahki
weewiitapiimehka tah wihfeniki

But when thou art bidden, go and sit
down in the lowest place; that when he
that hath bidden thee cometh, he may say
to thee, Friend, go up higher: then shalt
thou have glory in the presence of all that
sit at meat with thee.

11. ksake caakiwiyeefa memoospeelemekwitoota
wiiya weh nanahpaacimekwhoofo mecimi hina
neenanahpaacimekwtoota wiiya weh
moospeelemekwhoofo

For every one that exalteth himself shall
be humbled; and he that humbleth
himself shall be exalted.

12. chiine hotelaali nili nehfaapi mayehci halenekoci
hine kiila hostooyane tenaliiwe weelaa sapaawe teki
hotahpimi kihkaanaki weelaa kiceeninaaki weelaa
kinhhalweelecikanileniiki weelaa paweewi
maapiyeecikaaletiiwenaki piilepe neeyoole nehfaapi
nihki kitalenekooki haasowe mecimi petekfetwaatiiwe
ke hostaakoopi

And he said to him also that had bidden
him, When thou makest a dinner or a
supper, call not thy friends, nor thy
brethren, nor thy kinsmen, nor rich
neighbours; lest haply they also bid thee
again, and a recompense be made thee.

13. weeka hine kiila hostooyane wihfenhcikeewe
haleni hina kitemaafa hina meemiyaalakatowita hina
mamiyaalakikaata hina keekeepiikweeta

But when thou makest a feast, bid the
poor, the maimed, the lame, the blind:

14. mecimi keh kisaateelemekofi kiila ksake nihki
mata hopoonaanaawa wa hoci ceeceesipetekfetawehki
kiila ksake keh petekfetaakoopi kiila hine hini
hotaapefiiwi-honhskaaweneki hina teepasawiilefita

and thou shalt be blessed; because they
have not wherewith to recompense thee:
for thou shalt be recompensed in the
resurrection of the just.

15. chiine hine nekoti nihi weewiitapiimekoci tah
wihfeniki honootaana yooloma wiyehi
kisaateelemekofi ce hina wah miicita takhwa piitike
hokimaawitaamhkomi maneto hotekooli nili

And when one of them that sat at meat
with him heard these things, he said unto
him, Blessed is he that shall eat bread in
the kingdom of God.

16. hotelaali payeekwa naanekoti hileni homecto mhsi
sapaawe chiine meci hotalenahi

But he said unto him, A certain man
made a great supper; and he bade many:

17. chiine hoteleskawaali hotaloolaakanali tah
sapaawiki laakwa wahsi piyaako ksake howe caayahki
wiyehi mecfenwi hilaaci nihi yeelenoofolici

and he sent forth his servant at supper
time to say to them that were bidden,
Come; for all things are now ready.

18. mecimi nihki caayahki nekotwesi hotalemi
hostoonaawa pakfenoofoowe nili nhhihta nimehci
tepena ktika mecimi nikwiilaalefi nine ha mecimi
neeme hini kimamaatomele neh pakfenekoopi
hotekooli

And they all with one consent began to
make excuse. The first said unto him, I
have bought a field, and I must needs go
out and see it: I pray thee have me
excused.

19. chiine nohki kotakali nimehci tepenaaki niyaalanwi fakikwehika haaksiniiki mecimi nine ha wahsi nakacilotawaki kimamaatomele neh pakfenekoopi hiwali

And another said, I have bought five yoke of oxen, and I go to prove them: I pray thee have me excused.

20. chiine nohki kotakali nimehci hosileta wiiwa mecimi weecikeenahi ne haalwi piyaa hiwali

And another said, I have married a wife, and therefore I cannot come.

21. chiine hina haloolaaka piyeewa mecimi howiitamawaali yooloma wiyehi teepeelemekoci hine howe hina hini wiikiwa hoci mestele teewahi wiyakowe nili si lohfaalo weeweetepi hoteewenimiyeewena mecimi miyeeweneefa hini hoteeweneki chiine hotahfa si piyeesi hina kitemaafa chiine meemiyaalakatowita chiine keekeepiikweeta chiine mamiyaalakikaata hotelaali hotaloolaakanali

And the servant came, and told his lord these things. Then the master of the house being angry said to his servant, Go out quickly into the streets and lanes of the city, and bring in hither the poor and maimed and blind and lame.

22. mecimi hina haloolaaka teepeelemiweeta mehcilotoote hini teepikeemoyani mecimi keewaki tawaawi nitasi hiwa

And the servant said, Lord, what thou didst command is done, and yet there is room.

23. chiine hina teepeelemiweeta nili si lohfaalo makimiyeewali mecimi hapasiwakhoowena chiine mamiiloowihkawi wahsi piyeci piicfaawaaci wahsi yeetaaya wiikiwa hokwihfetooteeki hotelaali nili haloolaakanali

And the lord said unto the servant, Go out into the highways and hedges, and constrain them to come in, that my house may be filled.

24. ksake kitelepwa niila mata nekoti nehke yeelenoofocki hileniiki weh pehsata nisapaawe

For I say unto you, that none of those men which were bidden shall taste of my supper.

25. howe nitasi howiiteemekohi meci mehseelelici chiine kokiiwa mecimi hotelahi nihi

Now there went with him great multitudes: and he turned, and said unto them,

26. kwehkwi wiyeefa hileni piyeelotawite mecimi mata hosiikeelemaali nehalwaaka hohfali chiine hokeeli chiine wiiwali chiine hotapelohfemhhi chiine hoceeninahi chiine hotikwemhhi hanhka mecimi nehalwaaka hotelenaweewiiwe nehfaapi matayeeciwi hina nita hokakehkimaafimi

If any man cometh unto me, and hateth not his own father, and mother, and wife, and children, and brethren, and sisters, yea, and his own life also, he cannot be my disciple.

27. kookwe-neefa-kaaci mata hopah niime nehalwaaka hotaasitehfekiimi mecimi nipiyeci neekalekwa matayeeciwi nita hokakehkimaafimi

Whosoever doth not bear his own cross, and come after me, cannot be my disciple.

28. ksake taanawe hina kiilawa peemi maatawi hopatenaki taweeteewika mata nhhihta ya lematapiwa mecimi hotakita hini yeeleelemekoki kwehkwitoke hopoona wa hoci mectooci hini

For which of you, desiring to build a tower, doth not first sit down and count the cost, whether he have wherewith to complete it?

29. piilepe neeyoole hine mehtahkehfetoote hahpanahkehfecika mecimi hotaalwi mehcilota caayahki yeelaapacikeecki hotalemi waapaleelemaawaali nili

Lest haply, when he hath laid a foundation, and is not able to finish, all that behold begin to mock him,

30. yaama hileni halemi hopatenike mecimi hotaalwi mehcilota hiwaki

saying, This man began to build, and was not able to finish.

31. weelaa taanawe mhsi-okima yeesi hina mawinehwaaci kotakali mhsi-okimaali noochetiiweneki ha mata nhhihta weh lematapi mecimi homame tepoweewe kwehkwitoke teepiilefi hina wiici metahfene metahfene tepeewe wahsi nakskaatiimaaci nili meewinehokoci kileki niiswaapitakitfene metahfene tepeewe

Or what king, as he goeth to encounter another king in war, will not sit down first and take counsel whether he is able with ten thousand to meet him that cometh against him with twenty thousand?

32. weelaake heeyehi keewaki pelowi hapilici hotesfato mecicikeemoowe mecimi natotamaake wa sfetoofoci kaamaaniilefiiwe

Or else, while the other is yet a great way off, he sendeth an ambassage, and asketh conditions of peace.

33. yooni yeeki weecikeenahi hina kookwe-neefa-kaaci hapiwa kiilawa pwaayaa pakiteeletaka caayahki hini peepoonaki matayeeciwi hina nita hokakehkimaafimi

So therefore whosoever he be of you that renounceth not all that he hath, he cannot be my disciple.

34. nepipemi weecikeenahi howesa payeekwa kwehkwi wiikinaakwi hini nepipemi haseke yeepokwaki taaniwe we hoci hini hipokwanwihtoote

Salt therefore is good: but if even the salt have lost its savour, wherewith shall it be seasoned?

35. mata hini hasiskiiki si howesa hini mata nohki hini yaakwateekimoowi hileniiki hopakitaanaawa hini hina peepoonaka hotawakaawali wahsi nootaakeeci wiilaani hina nootaakeete

It is fit neither for the land nor for the dunghill: men cast it out. He that hath ears to hear, let him hear.

Luke:15

1. howe nihki caayahki teeksiiwi-maawatonikehfiiki mecimi meciileficki peemi maalaakwahi haawaaci nili wahsi nootawaawaaci

Now all the publicans and sinners were drawing near unto him for to hear him.

2. chiine neyiisweelena nihki pelesiiki mecimi yaayawikeecki pekiskoweeki yaama hileni hotahpenahi meciilefilici mecimi howihpomahi peemi hiyowaaci

And both the Pharisees and the scribes murmured, saying, This man receiveth sinners, and eateth with them.

3. mecimi hoteh kaloolahi yooma pemaatoweewe

And he spake unto them this parable, saying,

4. taanawe kiilawa hoci hileni hopoonahi tepeewe meekiifhi chiine howanhhaali nekoti nihi ha mata hina honakalahi nihi caakakitecaakatwi hini piileski mecimi nhheewa honatonehwaali nili weewaaniilici paalohi homhkawaali hiwapi

What man of you, having a hundred sheep, and having lost one of them, doth not leave the ninety and nine in the wilderness, and go after that which is lost, until he find it?

5. mecimi yeh mehci mhkawaaci hina hoteliki hopoonaali nili hosasilepwa

And when he hath found it, he layeth it on his shoulders, rejoicing.

6. chiine yeetaaci yeh piyaaci homaawatomahi wihkaanhhi mecimi maaopiyeecikaaletiiwenhhi wiici hosasilawemiko nimehci mhkawa ksake nimeekiifema weewaaniita hotelahi nihi

And when he cometh home, he calleth together his friends and his neighbours, saying unto them, Rejoice with me, for I have found my sheep which was lost.

7. kitelepwa niila teetepilahi yooni weh si hahteeki howesilepwaawe nitasi weefepahkamikiki nekoti meciilefita mataiini cehi yeesiteheeta noota nihki caakakitecaakatwi meeyaawiileficki wiyeefaki pwaayaa skata leeletakki mataiini siteheewe

I say unto you, that even so there shall be joy in heaven over one sinner that repenteth, more than over ninety and nine righteous persons, which need no repentance.

8. weelaa taanawe hkweewa hopoonaana metahfwi peekskahki waapimoni kwehkwi wanhtoote nekoti maalekhi ha mata hofakfwaali niitawaakanali mecimi hociikatha hini wiikiwa chiine wiisiki natonehike paalohi hini homhka

Or what woman having ten pieces of silver, if she lose one piece, doth not light a lamp, and sweep the house, and seek diligently until she find it?

9. mecimi yeh mehci mhkaki hini homaawatomahi wihkaanhhi mecimi maaopiyeecikaaletiiwenhhi wiici hosasilawemiko nimehci mhka ksake hini maalekhi mayehci wanhtooya hisiwe

And when she hath found it, she calleth together her friends and neighbours, saying, Rejoice with me, for I have found the piece which I had lost.

10. teetepilahi yooni kitelepwa niila hahteewi nitasi howesilepwaawe hini hotapiiwenwaaki nihki hotenhcaliimhhi maneto yeesi nekoti meciilefita ceh mataiini siteheeci

Even so, I say unto you, there is joy in the presence of the angels of God over one sinner that repenteth.

11. chiine naanekoti hileni hopoonahi niiswi hokwihfimahi hiwa

And he said, A certain man had two sons:

12. chiine hina hofiimema nihki hotelaali hohfali hohfima miililo kiwiyehiimi hini lekhi niila wasfaaki mecimi hina hoteh pahfenamawahi nihi hini hopeemi-hoci-lenaweewiiwe

and the younger of them said to his father, Father, give me the portion of thy substance that falleth to me. And he divided unto them his living.

13. chiine mata meci tfoko hotahfa laakwa hina hofiimema hokwihfima caayahki takwi maawatonike mecimi pelowi taamhkwe laami chiine nitasi howaleskhoto howiyehiimi tatawaanhkeewi lenaweewiiweneki

And not many days after the younger son gathered all together, and took his journey into a far country; and there he wasted his substance with riotous living.

14. chiine yeh mehci pakitaki caayahki nitasi hini piici taamhkwe pafekwiiya mhsaawi sehkwaalaweeweniki mecimi halemi hakaawaaciilefi

And when he had spent all, there arose a mighty famine in that country; and he began to be in want.

15. chiine nhheewa mecimi hoteh takwifeto wiiya nekoti nihi sitasinihi hini hoci taamhkwe chiine nili hoteleskaakooli hoktikaanilici wahsi hahsamaaci koskohi

And he went and joined himself to one of the citizens of that country; and he sent him into his fields to feed swine.

16. mecimi wi howesilepwaawi mehci nili hoci hokwihfeto hopehkwata holhakaawali nihki koskooki meemiiciwaaci mecimi mata hileniili homiilekooli

And he would fain have been filled with the husks that the swine did eat: and no man gave unto him.

17. payeekwa ye hottaki wiiya kehfwi yeeloolaaci hotaloolaakanhhi nohfa hopoonaanaawa takhwa teepi mecimi wa skwihfenamowaaci mecimi niila skwaalaweewe nothpene hotasi hiwa

But when he came to himself he said, How many hired servants of my father's have bread enough and to spare, and I perish here with hunger!

18. neh pafekwi mecimi nohfeki ne ha mecimi ne hila hina hohfima nimehci maciisilota weefepahkamikiki mecimi kitelaapiiweneki

I will arise and go to my father, and will say unto him, Father, I have sinned against heaven, and in thy sight:

19. mata kiteeni niteleelemekofi wahsi kikwihfa siniki hoshilo paasi nekoti yeeloolata kitaloolaakanaki

I am no more worthy to be called thy son: make me as one of thy hired servants.

20. chiine pafekwi mecimi hopiyeelotawaali hohfali payeekwa yeheeyehi keewaki pelowihi hapici honookooli hohfali chiine maaciteheeli kiteminaakweeletiiwe mecimi memekwiili chiine hokwekakaneki sfeeli mecimi hopackamekooli

And he arose, and came to his father. But while he was yet afar off, his father saw him, and was moved with compassion, and ran, and fell on his neck, and kissed him.

21. chiine hina hokwihfima hotelaali nili hohfima nimehci maciisilota weefepahkamikiki mecimi kitelaapiiweneki mata kiteeni niteleelemekofi wahsi kikwihfa siniki hisiwe

And the son said unto him, Father, I have sinned against heaven, and in thy sight: I am no more worthy to be called thy son.

22. payeekwa hina hohfima piyeetooko weeweetepi hini kci haliwi yeeki pihtawikooti mecimi hini piitenikehehko chiine kkileceepifoowe holeciki si poonamoko chiine mhkifena hofiteki

But the father said to his servants, Bring forth quickly the best robe, and put it on him; and put a ring on his hand, and shoes on his feet:

23. mecimi piyeelehko hina weelakwheta mhfoofoofa chiine nhfehko hina mecimi wihfenitaako chiine kilakifiiwe hostootaako

and bring the fatted calf, and kill it, and let us eat, and make merry:

24. ksake nikwihfa yaama nepwa mecimi nohki lenaweewi waani mecimi mhkoofo hotelahi hotaloolaakanhhi mecimi nihki halemi kilakifiiki

for this my son was dead, and is alive again; he was lost, and is found. And they began to be merry.

25. howe hofeefemaali hokwihfali ktikaaneki hapiili chiine yeesi hina piyaaci mecimi maalaakwa' haaci hini wiikiwa honoota hina nakamoowe mecimi peemi menyeeleki

Now his elder son was in the field: and as he came and drew nigh to the house, he heard music and dancing.

26. mecimi hote hotahpimaali nekoti nihi haloolaakanhhi chiine natohse yeeki nehiwe toke yooma wiyehi

And he called to him one of the servants, and inquired what these things might be.

27. mecimi ceh kiceenina piyeewa chiine kohfa homehci nhfaali nili weelakwhelici mhfoofoofali ksake homehci hotahpenaali nili waapanhsiili mecimi howesilaasamamooli hotelaali hina

And he said unto him, Thy brother is come; and thy father hath killed the fatted calf, because he hath received him safe and sound.

28. payeekwa wiyakowe hina mecimi mata wiisa piicfe chiine hohfali piyeci lohfeeli mecimi honanahpaacimekooli

But he was angry, and would not go in: and his father came out, and entreated him.

29. payeekwa hina haapafse mecimi scih yooloma meci tfwi kkato kimemekinilotoole mecimi matalaakwa nitalhfwaacilota kiila kitepikeemoowe chiine keewaki matalaakwa kimiili palasaana macimiyaakwimekiifa wahsi niila menawa hostooya kilakifiiwe wiici nihkaanaki

But he answered and said to his father, Lo, these many years do I serve thee, and I never transgressed a commandment of thine: and yet thou never gavest me a kid, that I might make merry with my friends:

30. weeka hine yaama kikwihfa piyeewa mayehci caakataka kipeemi-hoci-lenaweewiiwe wiici naakawhkwehi kinhtamawa nili weelakwhelici mhfoofoofali hotelaali hohfali

but when this thy son came, which hath devoured thy living with harlots, thou killedst for him the fatted calf.

31. hokwihfima moosatawi kiwiici hapiimi kiila mecimi caayahki weewiilaamiya kiila hini

And he said unto him, Son, thou art ever with me, and all that is mine is thine.

32. payeekwa hini mayaawfenwi wahsi hostooyakwe kilakifiiwe mecimi howesilepwaafiiyakwe ksake yaama kiceenina nepwa mecimi nohki lenaweewi chiine waani mecimi mhkoofo hotelaali hina

But it was meet to make merry and be glad: for this thy brother was dead, and is alive again; and was lost, and is found.

Luke:16

1. chiine nehfaapi hotelahi nihi kakehkimaafhi naanekoti nitasi paweewi hileni peepoonaata noosaafiiwenali chiine niliini mataacimohtaakwi yeesi peemi nili waleskhotaakoci howiyehiima

And he said also unto the disciples, There was a certain rich man, which had a steward; and the same was accused unto him that he was wasting his goods.

2. chiine hotahpimaali nili mecimi nehiwe yooma yeesi nootaakeeya kiila si petekakitano hini kinoosaafiiwe ksake mata halika laakwasi kitah katawi noosaafiiwena hilefi hotelaali

And he called him, and said unto him, What is this that I hear of thee? render the account of thy stewardship; for thou canst be no longer steward.

3. chiine hina noosaafiiwena hiwapi laameki wiiya nehiwe neh silawi peemi neemeya wahsi teepeelemita mamawici hini noosaafiiwe mata nipoona wiisikatowiiwe wahsi waalhkeeya wahsi katoweya nitekwefi

And the steward said within himself, What shall I do, seeing that my lord taketh away the stewardship from me? I have not strength to dig; to beg I am ashamed.

4. nimehci tehe hini wah silawiiya hine hini noosaafiiwe hoci lohfelhkoofoya wahsi menawahi nihki yeetaawaaci wiikiwaapali si hotahpeniwaaci

I am resolved what to do, that, when I am put out of the stewardship, they may receive me into their houses.

5. mecimi hote hotahpimahi maasa nekoti teepeelemekoci homoosinehikanhhi taaniwe lekhi kimoosinehwa teepeelemita hotelaali nili nhhihta

And calling to him each one of his lord's debtors, he said to the first, How much owest thou unto my lord?

6. mecimi hina tepeewe tepacikana pemi hisiwe chiine mamelo kiteewikaateemi mecimi lematapilo weeweetepi chiine niyaalanwaapitaki lawikeelo hotelaali nili

And he said, A hundred measures of oil. And he said unto him, Take thy bond, and sit down quickly and write fifty.

7. howe kotakali chiine kiila taaniwe lekhi kimoosinehike hotelaali mecimi hina tepeewe tepacikana kawaskwi hisiwe chiine mamelo kiteewikaateemi mecimi niyeewi-niiswaapitaki lawikeelo hotelaali nili

Then said he to another, And how much owest thou? And he said, A hundred measures of wheat. He saith unto him, Take thy bond, and write fourscore.

8. chiine teepeelemekoci howiyawaacimekooli hina pwaayaa tepasawiilefita noosaafiiwena ksake hina mehci lepwaawi lawi nihi ksake hokwifhi yaama yeelekokwahkamikiki haliwi lepwaawefihi

And his lord commended the unrighteous steward because he had done wisely: for the sons of this world are for their own generation wiser than the sons of the light.

nehalwaaka hoskwiilenaweewiiwenwa si noota nihi hokwifhi hina wayahfeeyaaki

9. chiine kitelepwa niila pesikwi kiiyaawaaki si wihkaanetihkeeko hini maciilefiiwe hoci paweewe haweko wahsi hine weh matayeeciweefiiya hini menawahi nihki piitike si hotahpenelwaakwa nili kookwelaakwasi haaciiwikamiko

And I say unto you, Make to yourselves friends by means of the mammon of unrighteousness; that, when it shall fail, they may receive you into the eternal tabernacles.

10. hina meemayaawiilefita tepilo maalecihiki mayaawiilefi nehfaapi hini mecilekhiki

He that is faithful in a very little is faithful also in much: and he that is unrighteous in a very little is unrighteous also in much.

11. kwehkwi weecikeenahi mata neyehka kimehci mayaawiilefipwa hini pwaayaa tepasawhki paweeweneki neefawe keh talwahfekowa nili mayaawi paweewena

If therefore ye have not been faithful in the unrighteous mammon, who will commit to your trust the true riches?

12. chiine kwehkwi mata neyehka kimehci mayaawiilefipwa hini weewiilaamici kotaka wiyeefa neefawe keh miilekowa hini nehalwaaka weewiilaamiyeekwe

And if ye have not been faithful in that which is another's, who will give you that which is your own?

13. mata haloolaaka hotah katawi memekinilotawahi niiswi mestelehi ksake naanekoti weh siikeelemaali mecimi hotahkweelemaali nili kotakali weelaake we haayitatenaali nekoti mecimi homoyaleeweelemaali nili kotakali mata kitah katawi memekinilotawaawa maneto mecimi paweewe

No servant can serve two masters: for either he will hate the one, and love the other; or else he will hold to one, and despise the other. Ye cannot serve God and mammon.

14. mecimi nihki pelesiiki yahkweeletakki moni nootaakeeki caayahki yooloma wiyehi chiine howaapalaacimaawaali nili

And the Pharisees, who were lovers of money, heard all these things; and they scoffed at him.

15. mecimi hina hotelahi nihi nihkiini kiilawa pesikwi teepasawhtooci wiiyaawa hini hileniiki hotelaapiiwenwaaki payeekwa maneto howaakotaana kitehiwa ksake hini meemoospeelemekwitooteeki heelekiina hileniiki lasiikaaciweefiiwe hini hini hotelaapiiweneki maneto

And he said unto them, Ye are they that justify yourselves in the sight of men; but God knoweth your hearts: for that which is exalted among men is an abomination in the sight of God.

16. hahteewi hini kwteletiiwe mecimi nihki maamoosikiiskwecki hapiiki paalohi caanii hine laakwa hoci nanahimiweepi hini howesi piyeetaacimoowe yeeki hini hokimaawitaamhkomi maneto mecimi caaki hileni mamiiloowi hotta piicfe hini

The law and the prophets were until John: from that time the gospel of the kingdom of God is preached, and every man entereth violently into it.

17. payeekwa hini haliwi weecihi menhkwatwi mecimi hasiskitaamhkwe wahsi haseki noota wahsi hini kwteletiiwe hoci nekoti hanhhiweewi maalecihi penhfeki

But it is easier for heaven and earth to pass away, than for one tittle of the law to fall.

18. caakiwiyeefa peepkehwaata wiiwali mecimi kotakali howiiwinaali macilawi waapasiphikeewe chiine hina weewiiwinaata nekoti peepkehoofolici wehsici hoci macilawi waapasiphikeewe

Every one that putteth away his wife, and marrieth another, committeth adultery: and he that marrieth one that is put away from a husband committeth adultery.

19. howe nitasi hapiwa naanekoti paweewi hileni chiine hina mhkateewi mhskwaawi piitenike mecimi naaswi waapi mafaanimota peemi kisoweelemekwi waawesiwi lenaweewici tfene waapaki

Now there was a certain rich man, and he was clothed in purple and fine linen, faring sumptuously every day:

20. chiine naanekoti kaakatoweeta lesolesii sinoofo seksimoofooli hoskwaateemeki hokwaawefiili homekiiwena

and a certain beggar named Lazarus was laid at his gate, full of sores,

21. mecimi peemi skata siteheelici wahsi hahsamoofolici nili peekskinooteeki hina paweewi hileni yaatah wihfenici weeci penhfeki hanhka mohci nihki wihsiiki piyeeki mecimi honohkwaatamawaawaali homekiiwenilici

and desiring to be fed with the crumbs that fell from the rich man's table; yea, even the dogs came and licked his sores.

22. chiine hini piyeemikatwi yeesi hina kaakatoweeta nepeki mecimi yeesi hotakoniyeeweneki heplehemii siwelekoci hina nihi henhcalihi mecimi nehfaapi hina paweewi hileni nepwa chiine lekonoofo

And it came to pass, that the beggar died, and that he was carried away by the angels into Abraham's bosom: and the rich man also died, and was buried.

23. mecimi hahkwinamooweneki hale paskaapi peemi namoci hanhhiweewatkaawena mecimi pelowihi hoteh neewaali heplehemiili chiine lesolesiili hina hotakoniyeeweneki

And in Hades he lifted up his eyes, being in torments, and seeth Abraham afar off, and Lazarus in his bosom.

24. mecimi nhtalahootamwa hohfima heplehemii poonamawilo kiteminaakweeletiiwe mecimi waawiini lesolesii wahsi menawa hina nepiki si kookinaaci hini hanahkwi holeceeli mecimi tikihfetawici niilani ksake peemi hahkwinamoya niila piici yooma pehkaleki hiwapi

And he cried and said, Father Abraham, have mercy on me, and send Lazarus, that he may dip the tip of his finger in water, and cool my tongue; for I am in anguish in this flame.

25. payeekwa hiwa heplehemii hokwihfima mhkaweeletano yeesi kiila hotfekoyani koowesi wiyehiima mecimi nehfaapi lesolesii maci wiyehi payeekwa howe hina hotasi howesilepwahoofo mecimi kiila peemi hahkwinamoyani

But Abraham said, Son, remember that thou in thy lifetime receivedst thy good things, and Lazarus in like manner evil things: but now here he is comforted, and thou art in anguish.

26. chiine kooloci caayahki yooma nitasi hahteewi lalakwi niilawe chiine kiilawa mhsaawi kookwe laakwasi pemaalakwi wahsi nihki wah kiilawa si yooci hoci pemhfeecki menawa haalwi hilefiwaaci mecimi wahsi mata wiyeefa menawa hiini hoci niilawe si kaameki haaci hotelaali

And beside all this, between us and you there is a great gulf fixed, that they which would pass from hence to you may not be able, and that none may cross over from thence to us.

27. mecimi hina kimamaatomele weecikeenahi hohfima wahsi nohfa yeetaaci wiikiwa si waawiinaci hina

And he said, I pray thee therefore, father, that thou wouldest send him to my father's house;

28. ksake nipoonaaki niyaalanwi hoceeninaaki wahsi menawa hina tepaacimohtawaaci nihi piilepe nihki nehfaapi yooma hanhhiweewatkaaweneki tasi wih si piyeeki hisiwe

for I have five brethren; that he may testify unto them, lest they also come into this place of torment.

29. payeekwa heplehemii hopoonaawahi nihki moosisiili chiine nihi maamoosikiiskwelici wiilaani nihki pefetawaawaate nihi hiwa

But Abraham saith, They have Moses and the prophets; let them hear them.

30. chiine hina mata hohfima heplehemii weeka kwehkwi nekoti nihi haate nili nepelici hoci mataiini weh siteheeki nihki hiwa

And he said, Nay, father Abraham: but if one go to them from the dead, they will repent.

31. chiine kwehkwi nihki pwaa pefetawaawaate moosisiili chiine nihi maamoosikiiskwelici mata nohki nihki yah katawihkoofooki kwehkwi nekoti nili nepelici hoci honhskaalite hotelaali nili

And he said unto him, If they hear not Moses and the prophets, neither will they be persuaded, if one rise from the dead.

Luke:17

1. chiine hotelahi hokakehkimaafhi matayeeciwi hini kwiilaani wa hoci hotakikahsineki wih piyeeya payeekwa macilepwaawe cehi hina weeci saapwi piyeeyaaki nili

And he said unto his disciples, It is impossible but that occasions of stumbling should come: but woe unto him, through whom they come!

2. wi howesaali hina poothaakanisiikonali laapicinelite hohkweekakaneki mecimi hini mhsinepiki hipakiloofote noota kaaciika hina wahsi hotakikahsinelici hpenalaate nekoti yohoma meciloofilici

It were well for him if a millstone were hanged about his neck, and he were thrown into the sea, rather than that he should cause one of these little ones to stumble.

3. kcitawaafiiko kiiyaawa kwehkwi kiceenina maciisilawiite kwtesi mecimi kwehkwi mataiini siteheete pakfeeletamawi

Take heed to yourselves: if thy brother sin, rebuke him; and if he repent, forgive him.

4. chiine kwehkwi hina maciisilotawehke niiswahfene hini heele kaasekiki mecimi niiswahfene nohki piyeci kokihtawehke mataiini nitesitehe hiyote keh pakfeeletamawa

And if he sin against thee seven times in the day, and seven times turn again to thee, saying, I repent; thou shalt forgive him.

5. chiine nihki hepastaliiki skwiinamawinaake niteepwehseewenena hotelaawaali nili teepeelemiweelici

And the apostles said unto the Lord, Increase our faith.

6. mecimi hina teepeelemiweeta hisiwe kwehkwi neyehka poonameekwe teepwehseewe paasi nekoti pekwe mastatiiwi miinhka yaama kicimiiwimhtekwaapalwa pokwahkeeskaalo mecimi hini mhsinepiki si haacfolo ki hilaawa mecimi hina kih melonehtaakowa

And the Lord said, If ye have faith as a grain of mustard seed, ye would say unto this sycamine tree, Be thou rooted up, and be thou planted in the sea; and it would have obeyed you.

7. payeekwa neefawe kiilawa nitasi hapiwa peemi poonaaci haloolaakanali ciikikeepitaaweeli weelaa kciitoneeli meekiifhi hine hini ktikaaneki hoci

But who is there of you, having a servant plowing or keeping sheep, that will say unto him, when he is come in from the

piyaalite weelena piyaalo mecimi lematapilo wahsi wihfeniyani we hilaali nili

field, Come straightway and sit down to meat;

8. chiine ha mata kaaciika mecfetawilo wah menawa hoci sapaawiya mecimi kitapifolo chiine memekinilotawilo paalohi mehci wihfeniya mecimi meneya chiine mayohkwaaci kiila keh wihfeni mecimi mene we hilaali nili

and will not rather say unto him, Make ready wherewith I may sup, and gird thyself, and serve me, till I have eaten and drunken; and afterward thou shalt eat and drink?

9. ha nili haloolaakanali niyaawe hotelaali hina ksake nili silawiili nili wiyehi teepikeemoki

Doth he thank the servant because he did the things that were commanded?

10. yooni teetepilahi nehfaapi kiilawa hine keh mehcilotaanaawa caayahki nili wiyehi teepikeemoofoyeekwe matawiyeefekisiwi haloolaakanaki niilawe nimehcilotaape hini niilawe wayeecitaiki wah silawiiyaake hiyoko

Even so ye also, when ye shall have done all the things that are commanded you, say, We are unprofitable servants; we have done that which it was our duty to do.

11. chiine hini piyeemikatwi yeesi nihki hale haawaaci colooseelemiiki yeele nili hikwihfeki semelie chiine keeleliiwi taamhkweewali pemi pemhfe hina

And it came to pass, as they were on the way to Jerusalem, that he was passing through the midst of Samaria and Galilee.

12. chiine yeesi piicfataki naanekoti hoteewenehi nitasi honakskaakohi metahfwi hilenihi weeskilhakeemekilici pelowihi piyeci niipawihi nihi

And as he entered into a certain village, there met him ten men that were lepers, which stood afar off:

13. chiine nihki hopatenaanaawa hotasimoowenwa ciisisii mestele poonamawinaake kiteminaakweeletiiwe hisiweeki

and they lifted up their voices, saying, Jesus, Master, have mercy on us.

14. mecimi yeh neewaaci nihi nhhaakone mecimi waapatelehko kiiyaawa nihki mhkateewkolayeeki hotelahi nihi chiine hini piyeemikatwi yeesi nihki weepfeewaaci fafayaakhoofooki

And when he saw them, he said unto them, Go and shew yourselves unto the priests. And it came to pass, as they went, they were cleansed.

15. chiine nekoti nihki peteki heewa yeh neemeki yeesi kiikehoofoci kileki holaamihsimo howahfaacimekohwaali manetooli

And one of them, when he saw that he was healed, turned back, with a loud voice glorifying God;

16. mecimi maalaakwahi hofitali si holemhkwi paksinooli niyaawe homiilekooli chiine semeliyewilenawe hina

and he fell upon his face at his feet, giving him thanks: and he was a Samaritan.

17. chiine peemi haapafseeci ciisisii ha mata nihki metahfwi fafayaakhoofooki weeka taanihkiwe nihki caakatfwi

And Jesus answering said, Were not the ten cleansed? but where are the nine?

18. ha mata nekoti mhkoofo nihki kweetekwiita wahsi miilaaci wahfaacimekofiiwe manetooli weeciwephi yaama kookweeneefa hiwapi

Were there none found that returned to give glory to God, save this stranger?

19. chiine pafekwiilo mecimi nhhaale yehaayani kiteepwehseewe kimehci waapanesheko hotelaali nili

And he said unto him, Arise, and go thy way: thy faith hath made thee whole.

20. chiine peemi natohtaakoci nihi pelesihi laakwa hini hokimaawitaamhkomi maneto piyeeya hotaapaftawahi hini hokimaawitaamhkomi maneto piyeeya mata nawkofiiwatwi

And being asked by the Pharisees, when the kingdom of God cometh, he answered them and said, The kingdom of God cometh not with observation:

21. mata nohki nihki we hiwaki scih hotasi weelaa nitasi ksake scih hini hokimaawitaamhkomi maneto laameki hahteewi kiilawa hotelahi

neither shall they say, Lo, here! or, There! for lo, the kingdom of God is within you.

22. chiine hotelahi nihi kakehkimaafhi nili kaasekiki weh piyeeya hine kiilawa keh maatawi neemenaawa nekoti nili hokakiisekanema hina hokwihfali hileni mecimi mata keh neemenaawa hini

And he said unto the disciples, The days will come, when ye shall desire to see one of the days of the Son of man, and ye shall not see it.

23. mecimi nihki ke hikowaaki scih nitasi scih hotasi teki weepfeeko weelaa neekalehko nihki

And they shall say to you, Lo, there! Lo, here! go not away, nor follow after them:

24. ksake paasi hini peepaki ye hini nekotweelena hoci wahfeskaaki siipaaci hini menhkwatwi hini si wahfekeeya payakila siipaaci menhkwatwi yooni we hilefici hina hokwihfali hileni hokaasekikiimeki

for as the lightning, when it lighteneth out of the one part under the heaven, shineth unto the other part under heaven; so shall the Son of man be in his day.

25. payeekwa nhhihta hina kwiilahi we hahkwiisinamwa meci wiyehi mecimi we haalawineko yooma hinoki skwiilenaweewiiwe

But first must he suffer many things and be rejected of this generation.

26. chiine yeesi hini piyeemikaki hine ta hokakiisekanemici nowa yooni teetepilahi we hiki nehfaapi nili hokakiisekanema hina hokwihfali hileni

And as it came to pass in the days of Noah, even so shall it be also in the days of the Son of man.

27. nihki wihfeniiki menooki wiichetiiki wiichetiiweneki si miiletipi nihki paalohi hini kaasekiki yeesi nowa piicfataki hini mhsi-olakeesi chiine hini lekhokwiiwe piyeeya mecimi hotasenhhekonaawa nihki caayahki

They ate, they drank, they married, they were given in marriage, until the day that Noah entered into the ark, and the flood came, and destroyed them all.

28. hofepiini teetepilahi yeesi hini piyeemikaki hine ta hokakiisekanemici latii wihfeniiki nihki menooki tepenikeeki hahcikeeki wiikkaaki

Likewise even as it came to pass in the days of Lot; they ate, they drank, they bought, they sold, they planted, they builded;

29. payeekwa hini kaasekiki yeesi saatami hoci weepfeeci latii kimowaanwi skote mecimi piikone siikona

but in the day that Lot went out from Sodom it rained fire and brimstone from heaven, and destroyed them all:

30. hofepiini yaska we hiki hini kaasekiki ta hina hokwihfali hileni tepinawkhoofoci

after the same manner shall it be in the day that the Son of man is revealed.

31. hine kaasekiki hina wiyeefa hakocikami we hapiwa mecimi howiyehiima hini wiikiwaapeki wiilaani hina teki laasiweete wahsi haamwetooci nili chiine wiilaani hina hini laa ktika yeepita nehfaapi teki peteki haate

In that day, he which shall be on the housetop, and his goods in the house, let him not go down to take them away: and let him that is in the field likewise not return back.

32. mhkaweelemehko latii wiiwali

Remember Lot's wife.

33. kookwe-neefa-kaaci weh natoneha wahsi katawihkaki hotelenaweewiiwe weh wanhto hini weeka kookwe-neefa-kaaci weh wanhto hotelenaweewiiwe weh waapanesto hini

Whosoever shall seek to gain his life shall lose it: but whosoever shall lose his life shall preserve it.

34. kitelepwa niila hine tepehkiki niiswi hileniiki nitasi we hapiiki nekoti tfaneki nekoti hina weh mamoofo mecimi we ckonoofo hina kotaka

I say unto you, In that night there shall be two men on one bed; the one shall be taken, and the other shall be left.

35. niiswi hkweeki nitasi we hapiiki peemi takwhikeewaaci niisohkalaatiiki nekoti hina weh mamoofo mecimi we ckonoofo hina kotaka

There shall be two women grinding together; the one shall be taken, and the other shall be left.

37. mecimi pemi haapafsehi nihi teepeelemiweeta taaniwe tasi hotekohi mecimi laakwa ta hapici nepeka nehfaapi weh si maawatweelooki nihki kaakalhhweeki hotelahi

And they answering say unto him, Where, Lord? And he said unto them, Where the body is, thither will the eagles also be gathered together.

Luke:18

1. chiine hokaloolahi pemaatoweewe hini wayeeci wahsi kaakika yo mamaatomeelici mecimi wahsi teki saakweelemolici

And he spake a parable unto them to the end that they ought always to pray, and not to faint;

2. hapiwa nitasi hoteeweneki teepasawateniweeta pwaayaa kwfaata manetooli mecimi mata homakofeelemaali hileniili hiwapi

saying, There was in a city a judge, which feared not God, and regarded not man:

3. chiine hapiwa nitasi siikawi-ykwe hini hoteeweneki mecimi moosaki nili howaotfekooli halotamawilo nimateeletiiwena hotekooli

and there was a widow in that city; and she came oft unto him, saying, Avenge me of mine adversary.

4. mecimi hina mata sitehe maalaakasi payeekwa mayohkwaaci hiwapi laameki wiiya weekhi mata nikwfa maneto mata nohki nimakofeelema hileni

And he would not for a while: but afterward he said within himself, Though I fear not God, nor regard man;

5. payeekwa ksake nipetfakhekwa yaama siikawi-ykwe ne halotamawa hina piilepe homoosatawi piyaawe nooci lohkachekwa

yet because this widow troubleth me, I will avenge her, lest she wear me out by her continual coming.

6. chiine hiwa hina teepeelemiweeta nootamoko yeeyoci hina pwaayaa tepasawiilefita teepasawateniweeta

And the Lord said, Hear what the unrighteous judge saith.

7. mecimi maneto ha mata we halotamawaali homamaawenali meemawimekoci kiiseki mecimi tepehki mecimi keewaki hina peemi hahkwi pooneelemaaci nihi

And shall not God avenge his elect, which cry to him day and night, and he is longsuffering over them?

8. kitelepwa niila hina weh kwakwi halotawahi nihi payeekwa hine hina hokwihfali hileni piyaate ha we mhka teepwehseewe hini hoskitaamhkoki

I say unto you, that he will avenge them speedily. Howbeit when the Son of man cometh, shall he find faith on the earth?

9. chiine yooma pemaatoweewe nehfaapi hokaloolahi nihi naanekoti yeepeeletakki wiiyaawa yeesi tepasawiilefiwaaci nihki mecimi homatawiyeefekisihaawahi caayahki kotakhi

And he spake also this parable unto certain which trusted in themselves that they were righteous, and set all others at nought:

10. niiswi hileniiki spemeki heeki piicfeeki hini mamaatomeewikamikwi wahsi mamaatomeewaaci pelesi hina nekoti chiine teeksiiwi-maawatonikehfi hina kotaka

Two men went up into the temple to pray; the one a Pharisee, and the other a publican.

11. niipawi hina pelesi mecimi mamaatome halayini kileki wiiya maneto niyaawe kiila yeesi pwaa hilefiya niila paasi nihki maisi hileniiki sesiikwitooweficki pwaayaa tepasaweficki waapasiphikehfiiki weelaa teetepilahi paasi yaama teeksiiwi-maawatonikehfi

The Pharisee stood and prayed thus with himself, God, I thank thee, that I am not as the rest of men, extortioners, unjust, adulterers, or even as this publican.

12. noocike niisene hini peeleko menetoowikiisekiki mawi-metahfwi lekhi nimiiliwe caayahki keekatawihkama hiwapi

I fast twice in the week; I give tithes of all that I get.

13. weeka hina teeksiiwi-maawatonikehfi peemi niipawici pelowihi mata mohci spemeki menhkwatoki wih laapici hoskiiseko payeekwa hopkiteha hopalecika maneto kiteminaakwi hilefilo niila meciilefita hiwapi

But the publican, standing afar off, would not lift up so much as his eyes unto heaven, but smote his breast, saying, God, be merciful to me a sinner.

14. kitelepwa niila yaama hileni wiikiwa yeetaaci si paalacsinwa tepasawi tehe kaaciika noota hina kotaka ksake caakiwiyeefa memoospeelemekwitoota wiiya weh nanahpaacilotoofo weeka hina neenanahpaacilotaka wiiya weh moospeelemekwihoofo

I say unto you, This man went down to his house justified rather than the other: for every one that exalteth himself shall be humbled; but he that humbleth himself shall be exalted.

15. chiine nihki peemi piyeetawaawaaci nehfaapi hotapelohfemwahi wahsi hina pehsenaaci nihi payeekwa nihki kakehkimaafaki yeh neemowaaci hini hokwtelaawahi nihi

And they brought unto him also their babes, that he should touch them: but when the disciples saw it, they rebuked them.

16. payeekwa ciisisii hote hotahpimahi nihi wiilaani nihki hapelohfeefaki piyeelotawiwaate mecimi teki kwtelehko ksake nihkiin wiilawa hini hokimaawitaamhkomi maneto

But Jesus called them unto him, saying, Suffer the little children to come unto me, and forbid them not: for of such is the kingdom of God.

17. tepilo kitelepwa niila kookwe-neefa-kaaci mata paasi hapelohfeefa weh si hotahpena hini hokimaawitaamhkomi maneto mata hina weh wiyehisi piicfe nitasi hiwapi

Verily I say unto you, Whosoever shall not receive the kingdom of God as a little child, he shall in no wise enter therein.

18. chiine naanekoti teepeelecikeelici honatohtaakooli howesi keekehkimiwe nehiwe neh silawi wahsi laapsina kookwelaakwasi lenaweewiiwe hiwali

And a certain ruler asked him, saying, Good Master, what shall I do to inherit eternal life?

19. mecimi ciisisii koociwe kiila howesi kitesini matalaakwa howesi weeciwephi nekoti maneto hina

And Jesus said unto him, Why callest thou me good? none is good, save one, even God.

20. kiwaakotaana nili tepikeemoowena teki macilawiilo waapasiphikeewe teki nhsiweelo teki kimootelo teki pah niimiweelo miyaasi teepweewe hotakeelemi kohfa mecimi kikiya hotelaali

Thou knowest the commandments, Do not commit adultery, Do not kill, Do not steal, Do not bear false witness, Honour thy father and mother.

21. mecimi neyehka caayahki yooloma wiyehi nitakinaye nimayaanileniiweneki hoci hiwa hina

And he said, All these things have I observed from my youth up.

22. mecimi ciisisii yeh nootaakeeci hini nekoti wiyehi keewaki kinootkofi miyeekilo caayahki peepoonamani mecimi lelhskonamawi hina kitemaafa mecimi keh

And when Jesus heard it, he said unto him, One thing thou lackest yet: sell all that thou hast, and distribute unto the

poona pawaawe menhkwatoki chiine piyaalo
neekasilo hotelaali

poor, and thou shalt have treasure in
heaven: and come, follow me.

23. payeekwa yeh nootaakeeci hina yooloma wiyehi
hokwaawefi hanhhiweewi macilepwaawe ksake hina
holaami paweewa

But when he heard these things, he
became exceeding sorrowful; for he was
very rich.

24. mecimi ciisisii peemi haapamaaci lakokwe fakaaki
nihki peepoonakki pawaawena weh piicfataanaawa
hini hokimaawitaamhkomi maneto

And Jesus seeing him said, How hardly
shall they that have riches enter into the
kingdom of God!

25. ksake hini halika weecihi wahsi keemali piicfaaci
saapwi hoskiisekwi saaponika noota paweewi hileni
wahsi piicfataki hini hokimaawitaamhkomi maneto
hiwapi

For it is easier for a camel to enter in
through a needle's eye, than for a rich
man to enter into the kingdom of God.

26. chiine nihki neenootaakeecki hini neefawe howe
weh katawi waapaneshoofo hiwaki

And they that heard it said, Then who can
be saved?

27. payeekwa hina nili wiyehi meetayeeciweefiwaaci
hileniiki katawatwili maneto hiwapi

But he said, The things which are
impossible with men are possible with
God.

28. chiine piita scih neyehka ninakataape
ninhhalwaafiiwenena mecimi kineekalelepe hisiwe

And Peter said, Lo, we have left our own,
and followed thee.

29. mecimi hotelahi nihi tepilo kitelepwa niila mata
hileni hapiwa mayehci nakataka wiikiwa weelaa
wiiwali weelaa hoceeninaanhhi weelaa kehkiyaamhi
weelaa hapelofhi hini hokimaawitaamhkomi maneto
hoci

And he said unto them, Verily I say unto
you, There is no man that hath left house,
or wife, or brethren, or parents, or
children, for the kingdom of God's sake,

30. we hina pwaa hotfeko meci tfweekinwi haliwi
hinoki yeelaakweeweniki mecimi kookwelaakwasi
lenaweewiiwe hini wah piyeetahkamikiki

who shall not receive manifold more in
this time, and in the world to come
eternal life.

31. chiine homamahi nihi metahfwi-kite-niiswi
mecimi waapatamoko colooseelemiiki kite
kkwicsinepe mecimi nili caayahki wiyehi yeewikeeki
saapwi nihki maamoosikiiskwecki weh mecfetaakwi
hina hokwihfali hileni

And he took unto him the twelve, and
said unto them, Behold, we go up to
Jerusalem, and all the things that are
written by the prophets shall be
accomplished unto the Son of man.

32. ksake hina nihi nanahkawilenihi weh si
pakfenoofo chiine weh waapalaachoofo mecimi weh
tekwaacipenaloofo chiine weh fiifekwaaloofo

For he shall be delivered up unto the
Gentiles, and shall be mocked, and
shamefully entreated, and spit upon:

33. chiine weh lihfiiwanhhwaawaali nihki mecimi we
nhfaawaali chiine hini mawi-nhfokonakike hina we
honhska nohki hotelahi

and they shall scourge and kill him: and
the third day he shall rise again.

34. chiine nihki mata nekoti honenohtaanaawa
yooloma wiyehi mecimi yooma hiyoowe kkitaakwiiki
nihki chiine mata homooleeletaanaawa nili wiyehi
yeeyoki

And they understood none of these
things; and this saying was hid from
them, and they perceived not the things
that were said.

35. chiine hini piyeemikatwi yeesi maalaakwahi
piyaaci celekoo naanekoti kakeepiikwe hileni
lematapiwa hini pakackana peemi katoweci

And it came to pass, as he drew nigh unto
Jericho, a certain blind man sat by the
way side begging:

36. mecimi hopemi nootawahi mehseelelici pemhfehi maalaakwahi natohse hina nehiwe hoci yooma hinwi

and hearing a multitude going by, he inquired what this meant.

37. mecimi howiitamawaawaali nihki yeesi naaselefileni ciisisii pemhfeeci maalaakwahi

And they told him, that Jesus of Nazareth passeth by.

38. mecimi nhtalahootamwa hina ciisisii kiila hokwihfali teepitii poonamawilo kiteminaakweeletiiwe hisiwe

And he cried, saying, Jesus, thou son of David, have mercy on me.

39. mecimi nihki neniikaaniicki hokwtelaawaali nili wahsi nooleewilici payeekwa hina mhsi halika hini lahootamwa kiila hokwihfali teepitii poonamawilo kiteminaakweeletiiwe

And they that went before rebuked him, that he should hold his peace: but he cried out the more a great deal, Thou son of David, have mercy on me.

40. mecimi niipawi ciisisii chiine tepikeemo nili wahsi piyeetoofoci chiine yeh maalaakwahi piyaalici

And Jesus stood, and commanded him to be brought unto him: and when he was come near, he asked him,

41. honatohtawaali nehiwe kiteleeleta niila wahsi lawihtoola mecimi teepeelemiweeta wahsi niila menawa hotfekoya nitepinamoowe hisiwe hina

What wilt thou that I should do unto thee? And he said, Lord, that I may receive my sight.

42. mecimi ciisisii hotfekolo kitepinamoowe kiteepwehseewe kimehci waapanesheko hotelaali

And Jesus said unto him, Receive thy sight: thy faith hath made thee whole.

43. mecimi weelena hina hotfeko hotepinamoowe mecimi honeekalekooli howahfaacimekofihaali manetooli mecimi caayahki nihki lenaweeki yeh neemowaaci hini wiyawaacimoowe homiilaawaali manetooli

And immediately he received his sight, and followed him, glorifying God: and all the people, when they saw it, gave praise unto God.

Luke:19

1. chiine hotta mecimi peemi pemhfeeci saapwi celekoo

And he entered and was passing through Jericho.

2. chiine waapamehko hileni sekias yaasi wiinoofo mecimi hokimaawi teeksiiwi-maawatonikehfi hina chiine paweewa

And behold, a man called by name Zacchaeus; and he was a chief publican, and he was rich.

3. chiine hina honatoneha wahsi neewaaci ciisisiili si wiyeefa hina mecimi haalwi katawefi ksake hina yeefoskaata hoci ksake maaspefiifi hina

And he sought to see Jesus who he was; and could not for the crowd, because he was little of stature.

4. chiine niikaani si kwakwi mecimi hakoofiwe kiisoowahkwatooli wahsi neewaaci ksake hini wayeeci si pemhfeeli nili

And he ran on before, and climbed up into a sycomore tree to see him: for he was to pass that way.

5. chiine ciisisii yeh piyaaci hini tasi spemeki laapi mecimi sekias haapetefilo chiine laasiweelo ksake hinoki kaasekiki kwiilahi yeetaayani wiikiwaapeki ni hapi hotelaali

And when Jesus came to the place, he looked up, and said unto him, Zacchaeus, make haste, and come down; for today I must abide at thy house.

6. chiine hina haapetefi chiine laasiwe mecimi hosasilawaalaali nili

And he made haste, and came down, and received him joyfully.

7. chiine nihki yeh neemowaaci hini caayahki pekihkaaweeki nhheewa hina homawi kehsilotawaali hileniili meciilefilici hiwaki nihki

And when they saw it, they all murmured, saying, He is gone in to lodge with a man that is a sinner.

8. mecimi niipawi sekias chiine waapatano teepeelemiweeta hini pahfi niwiyehiima nimiila hina kitemaafa chiine kwehkwi wiyeefa hileni nimehci hofaami piimi mayaawilotawa wiyehi nipetekfeto niyeewekfenwi hotelaali nili teepeelemiweelici

And Zacchaeus stood, and said unto the Lord, Behold, Lord, the half of my goods I give to the poor; and if I have wrongfully exacted aught of any man, I restore fourfold.

9. mecimi ciisisii hinoki kaasekiki waapanhsiiwe yooma si piyeeya wiikiwaapeki ksake nehfaapi yo niliini hokwihfali heplehemii

And Jesus said unto him, Today is salvation come to this house, forasmuch as he also is a son of Abraham.

10. ksake hina hokwihfali hileni hopiyeci natoneha mecimi waapanesto hini weewanhtooteeki hotelaali nili

For the Son of man came to seek and to save that which was lost.

11. chiine yeesi nihi nootamelici yooloma wiyehi hokooloto mecimi kalawi pemaatoweewe ksake maalaakwahi colooseelemiiki hapiwa chiine ksake nihki toke siteheeki wahsi hini hokimaawitaamhkomi maneto weelena tepinawkwki

And as they heard these things, he added and spake a parable, because he was nigh to Jerusalem, and because they supposed that the kingdom of God was immediately to appear.

12. weecikeena hiwa hina naanekoti hotakeelemekwileni weepfe pelowi taamhkwe heewa wahsi wiila hotefici hokimaawitaamhkwe mecimi wahsi peteki piyaaci

He said therefore, A certain nobleman went into a far country, to receive for himself a kingdom, and to return.

13. chiine hotahpimahi metahfwi haloolaakanhhi wiila mecimi homiilahi metahfwi pawniiwali chiine yooma hoci wiitkiiko paalohi piyaaya hotelahi nihi

And he called ten servants of his, and gave them ten pounds, and said unto them, Trade ye herewith till I come.

14. payeekwa hosiikeelemekohi hositasiniimhhi mecimi honaawalwi sfataakohi mecicikeemoowe mata nitesiteheepe wahsi yaama hileni hokimaawtawiyamekici hiyooya

But his citizens hated him, and sent an ambassage after him, saying, We will not that this man reign over us.

15. chiine hini piyeemikatwi yeh peteki piyaaci nohki mehci hotefi hini hokimaawitaamhkwe tepikeemo wahsi yohoma haloolaakanhhi mayehci miilaaci hini moni wiila si hotahpimoofolici wahsi menawahke waakotaki mayehci katawihkamelici wiitkiiwe hoci

And it came to pass, when he was come back again, having received the kingdom, that he commanded these servants, unto whom he had given the money, to be called to him, that he might know what they had gained by trading.

16. mecimi piyeeli yeelahfamiici nili nhhihta teepeelemiweeta kipawniima homectoona metahfwi si halika pawniiwali hiwalipi

And the first came before him, saying, Lord, thy pound hath made ten pounds more.

17. mecimi koowesilawi kiila howesi haloolaaka ksake kiila kimhkaakoopi kitepasawefi tepilo caki wiyehi poonano wah simekofiyotamani metahfwi hoteewena hotelaali nili

And he said unto him, Well done, thou good servant: because thou wast found faithful in a very little, have thou authority over ten cities.

18. chiine nili piyeeli mawi-niiswi kipawniima teepeelemiweeta homectoona niyaalanwi pawniiwali hiwali nili

And the second came, saying, Thy pound, Lord, hath made five pounds.

19. chiine kiila nehfaapi hilefiyotano niyaalanwi hoteewena hotelaali nili nehfaapi

And he said unto him also, Be thou also over five cities.

20. chiine nohki kotaka piyeewa teepeelemiweeta waapatano halayooma kipawniimi kehcitawfetooya kahfilecehooweneki

And another came, saying, Lord, behold, here is thy pound, which I kept laid up in a napkin:

21. ksake kikwfele kikofekwaaci leniwi kiila ksake kikokwitena hini pwaayaa kiila sekfetooyani mecimi kikawaskwhaawe hini pwaayaa hahtooyani kiila hisiwe hina

for I feared thee, because thou art an austere man: thou takest up that thou layedst not down, and reapest that thou didst not sow.

22. nehalwaaka kiila kitooni ke hotahkowaalele kiila weenaatefita haloolaaka kiwaakota yeesi kofekwaaci leniwiya nikokwitena hini pwaayaa niila sekfetooya mecimi nikawaskwhaawe hini pwaayaa niila hahtooya

He saith unto him, Out of thine own mouth will I judge thee, thou wicked servant. Thou knewest that I am an austere man, taking up that I laid not down, and reaping that I did not sow;

23. howe koociwe mata kiteh miiliwe nimonemi hini monikaaneki mecimi tah piyaaya neyehka nih mayaawi hotahpena hini kileki tah nooseyaaki hotelaali nili

then wherefore gavest thou not my money into the bank, and I at my coming should have required it with interest?

24. mecimi mamawehko hini pawni chiine hini hina miilehko peepoonaka nili metahfwi pawniiwali hotelahi nihi neniipawilici maalaakwahi

And he said unto them that stood by, Take away from him the pound, and give it unto him that hath the ten pounds.

25. chiine nihi teepeelemiweeta hopoonaana hina metahfwi pawniiwali hotekohi

And they said unto him, Lord, he hath ten pounds.

26. kitelepwa niila ksake caakiwiyeefa peepoonaka weh miilekwi weeka hina hoci peepwaa poonaka wiikinaakwi hini peepoonaki weh mamaakwi hina

I say unto you, that unto every one that hath shall be given; but from him that hath not, even that which he hath shall be taken away from him.

27. weeka yohkoma nimateeeletiiwenaki mata yeesiteheecki wi hokimaawtawaki hotasi piyeelehko mecimi nhfehko yeelahfamiiya hisiweepi hotelahi

Howbeit these mine enemies, which would not that I should reign over them, bring hither, and slay them before me.

28. chiine yeh mehtoweci halayini hale weepfe niikaani colooseelemiiki heewa

And when he had thus spoken, he went on before, going up to Jerusalem.

29. chiine hini piyeemikatwi yeh maalaakwahi piyaaci pefeciiki chiine pefeneki maalaakwahi hini meekwahkiifiki halifiet sitoote hoteleskawahi niiswi nihi kakehkimaafhi

And it came to pass, when he drew nigh unto Bethphage and Bethany, at the mount that is called the mount of Olives, he sent two of the disciples,

30. nhhaakone hini hoteewenehi yehteeki yeelahfamiiyeekwe piitike hini yeesi hottameekwe ke mhkawaawa mahkootelefa kciipifo pwaayaa laakwa keewaki hileni nayekoci pelhhohko hina mecimi piyeelehko

saying, Go your way into the village over against you; in the which as ye enter ye shall find a colt tied, whereon no man ever yet sat: loose him, and bring him.

31. chiine wiyeefa natohtoolwaakwe koociwe kipelhhwaawa halayini hina teepeelemiweeta hotakaawaalaali ke hiyopwa hotelahi

And if any one ask you, Why do ye loose him? thus shall ye say, The Lord hath need of him.

32. mecimi nihki weewaawiineskoofocki weepfeeki chiine teetepilahi si mhkahfooki yeesi hina mehcimaaci nihi

And they that were sent went away, and found even as he had said unto them.

33. chiine yeesi nihki pelhhwaawaaci nili mahkootelefali nihi weeowiilaamilici nitasi koociwe kipelhhwaawa hina mahkootelefa hotekowahi

And as they were loosing the colt, the owners thereof said unto them, Why loose ye the colt?

34. mecimi nihki hina teepeelemiweeta hotakaawaalaali hisiweeki

And they said, The Lord hath need of him.

35. mecimi ciisisiili hopiyeetawaawaali nili chiine nihki hoskici nili mahkootelefali hotipakitaanaawa hopiitenikanwa mecimi holemataphaawaali ciisisiili nitasi hoskici

And they brought him to Jesus: and they threw their garments upon the colt, and set Jesus thereon.

36. mecimi yeesi hina weepfeeci nihki hosekatenaanaawa hopiitenikanwa hini yeele miyeewiki

And as he went, they spread their garments in the way.

37. chiine yeesi hina howe maalaakwahi piyeetfeci teetepilahi hini weeci lwaamahkiki hini halhfiwi meekwahkiifiki melhske hina mehseeleka kakehkimaafa halemi hosasilepwa mecimi holaami nhtalahootamwa howiyawahkaalaali manetooli nili hoci caayahki waasikaki pekatefiiwena mayehci neemowaaci nihki

And as he was now drawing nigh, even at the descent of the mount of Olives, the whole multitude of the disciples began to rejoice and praise God with a loud voice for all the mighty works which they had seen;

38. kisaateelemekofi ce hina hokima peepiyeeta hini howiifooweneki hina teepeelemiweeta kaamaaniilefiiwe cehi piitike weefepahkamikiki mecimi wahfaacimekofiiwe hini wihkoci lhspi hiwaki

saying, Blessed is the King that cometh in the name of the Lord: peace in heaven, and glory in the highest.

39. chiine naaleta nihki pelesiiki hina mehseeleka hoci keekehkimiwe kwtesi kikakehkimaafaki hotelaawaali

And some of the Pharisees from the multitude said unto him, Master, rebuke thy disciples.

40. mecimi haapafse chiine kitelepwa hini kwehkwi weh nooleewiiki yohkoma nihki siikonaki weh wiyakahootamooki hiwa hina

And he answered and said, I tell you that, if these shall hold their peace, the stones will cry out.

41. chiine yeh maalaakwahi piyaaci honeeme hini hoteewe mecimi homawita hini

And when he drew nigh, he saw the city and wept over it,

42. kwehkwi yehki o waakotamane hinoki kaasekiki wiikinaakwi kiila nili wiyehi kaamaaniilefiiweneki yeetakoki weeka howe nili kikitoote kiskiiseko wayeeci hoci

saying, If thou hadst known in this day, even thou, the things which belong unto peace! but now they are hid from thine eyes.

43. ksake nili kaasekiki nahiika weh piyeeya kiila hine kimateeletiiwenaki kaawaci kiila we hipakitaanaawa peemaamehkiki mecimi keh kaawaci kiposkaakooki

For the days shall come upon thee, when thine enemies shall cast up a bank about thee, and compass thee round, and keep thee in on every side,

kiila chiine ke kciitonekooki piitike caaki
wiyeetahkwe

44. mecimi hini hasiskiiki ke hpakilekooki mecimi
kitapelohfemaki piitike kiila chiine nihki mata we
ckonaawaali kiiyaaki nekoti siikonali hoskici kotakali
ksake mata kiwaakota hini laakwa halotaafoowe
hiwapi

and shall dash thee to the ground, and thy
children within thee; and they shall not
leave in thee one stone upon another;
because thou knewest not the time of thy
visitation.

45. chiine hopiicfata hini mamaatomeewikamikwi
mecimi hotalemi lohfe pakilahi nihi waawiitkiilici

And he entered into the temple, and
began to cast out them that sold,

46. mehtawikeepi hini mecimi yeetaaya wiikiwa
mamaatomeewika we hinwi weeka kiilawa
ciikoniwehfiiki howiikiwaalakomwa kitesi
mectoonaawa hini hotelahi nihi

saying unto them, It is written, And my
house shall be a house of prayer: but ye
have made it a den of robbers.

47. chiine kakehkimiwe tfene waapaki hini
mamaatomeewikamikoki payeekwa nihki hokimaawi
mhkateewkolayeeki chiine nihki yaayawikeecki chiine
nihi hokimaawileniimwahi nihki lenaweeki
honatonehaanaawa wahsi hkwinehaawaaci nili

And he was teaching daily in the temple.
But the chief priests and the scribes and
the principal men of the people sought to
destroy him:

48. mecimi hotaalwi mhkaanaawa nihki wah
menawahi silawiiwaaci ksake nihki lenaweeki
caayahki nili hotakoocinooki hahkawehseeki

and they could not find what they might
do; for the people all hung upon him,
listening.

Luke:20

1. chiine hini piyeemikatwi hine nekoti nili kaasekiki
yeesi pemi kakehkimaaci nihi lenawehi hini
mamaatomeewikamikoki mecimi hini howesi
piyeetaacimoowe peemi kakehkimiweeci nihi
hokimaawi mhkateewkolayehi chiine nihi
yaayawikeelici kileki nihi kikilenihi nitasi
hopiyeelotaakohi

And it came to pass, on one of the days,
as he was teaching the people in the
temple, and preaching the gospel, there
came upon him the chief priests and the
scribes with the elders;

2. mecimi nihki kalawiiki wiitamawinaake nehiwe
hoci mekofiiwe kooci lawi yooloma wiyehi weelaa
neefawe hina meemiilehka yooma simekofiiwe kiila
hotekohi

and they spake, saying unto him, Tell us:
By what authority doest thou these
things? or who is he that gave thee this
authority?

3. mecimi haapafse chiine nehfaapi niila keh
natohtoolepwa natohseewe mecimi wiitamawiko

And he answered and said unto them, I
also will ask you a question; and tell me:

4. hini hofafahkwiholelhiweewe caanii ha hini
weefepahkamikiki hoci weelaa toke hileniiki hoci
hotelahi

The baptism of John, was it from heaven,
or from men?

5. mecimi nihki natawaaci teheeki pesikwi wiilawa
kwehkwi weefepahkamikiki hoci ke hiyope koociwe
mata kiteepwehtawaawa we hiwa

And they reasoned with themselves,
saying, If we shall say, From heaven; he
will say, Why did ye not believe him?

6. weeka kwehkwi hileniiki hoci ke hiyope caayahki
nihki lenaweeki keh siikonhhokonaaki ksake

But if we shall say, From men; all the
people will stone us: for they be
persuaded that John was a prophet.

kolepkaamoofooki nihki yeesi caaniili
maamoosikiiskweewilici hiwaki

7. mecimi haapafseeki nihki yeesi pwaa
waakotamowaaci weeciwiki hini

And they answered, that they knew not
whence it was.

8. chiine ciisisii mata nohki niila kitah wiitamoolepwa
simekofiiwe wahoci lawiiya yooloma wiyehi hotelahi
nihi

And Jesus said unto them, Neither tell I
you by what authority I do these things.

9. mecimi hotalemi kaloolahi nihi lenawehi yooma
pemaatoweewe hileni ktike mhfaloomiktika chiine
hini ktikeewilenihi hotawhhahi mecimi weepfe kotaki
taamhkwe heewa pihci

And he began to speak unto the people
this parable: A man planted a vineyard,
and let it out to husbandmen, and went
into another country for a long time.

10. chiine hini nahiika laakwa nihi ktikeewilenihi
hoteleskawaali haloolaakanali wahsi nihki miilaawaaci
nili mawifoowe hini mhfaloomiktika hoci payeekwa
nihki ktikeewileniiki hoppaktehwaawaali nili mecimi
hotaameskawaawaali seskifiili

And at the season he sent unto the
husbandmen a servant, that they should
give him of the fruit of the vineyard: but
the husbandmen beat him, and sent him
away empty.

11. chiine hina nohki kotakali hoteleskawaali
haloolaakanali mecimi nehfaapi nili
hoppaktehwaawaali nihki mecimi
hotekwaacipenalaawaali chiine seskifiili
hotaameskawaawaali

And he sent yet another servant: and him
also they beat, and handled him
shamefully, and sent him away empty.

12. chiine hina nohki hoteleskawaali mawi-nhfwi
mecimi nehfaapi nili homamiyaalakhaawaali nihki
mecimi halika hotpakilaawaali nili

And he sent yet a third: and him also they
wounded, and cast him forth.

13. chiine nehiwe neh silawi hiwapi hina teepeeletaka
hini mhfaloomiktika nineh leskawa yeeahkweelemaka
nikwihfa menawahi nili we hofepeelemaawaali nihki

And the lord of the vineyard said, What
shall I do? I will send my beloved son: it
may be they will reverence him.

14. payeekwa nihki ktikeewileniiki yeh neewaawaaci
nili natawaaci tehehtwaatiiki hina yaama
layaapitepeelecikeeta wehi nhfaataako wahsi menawa
hini laapitepeelecikeewe howiilaamiyakwe hiwakipi

But when the husbandmen saw him, they
reasoned one with another, saying, This
is the heir: let us kill him, that the
inheritance may be ours.

15. chiine nihki hini mhfaloomiktikaaneki hoci lohfe
pakilaawaali nili mecimi honhfaawaali nehiwe
weecikeenahi we hpenalahi nihi hina teepeeletaka hini
mhfaloomiktika

And they cast him forth out of the
vineyard, and killed him. What therefore
will the lord of the vineyard do unto
them?

16. weh piyeewa hina chiine we hkwinehahi yohoma
ktikeewilenihi mecimi kotakhi weh miilahi hini
mhfaloomiktika mecimi nihki yeh nootamowaaci hini
teki hini wi hinwi hiwaki nihki

He will come and destroy these
husbandmen, and will give the vineyard
unto others. And when they heard it, they
said, God forbid.

17. payeekwa hoteh waapamahi mecimi hiwa nehiwe
howe yooma mayehtawikeeki nili siikonali
yeelawinawaawaaci nihki waakkaacki hina yaska
mechoofo howiisiwi hini poocaaki

But he looked upon them, and said, What
then is this that is written, The stone
which the builders rejected, The same
was made the head of the corner?

18. caakiwiyeefa nili siikonali yeesi haakicfaata weh poposkwihsinwa weeka kookweeneefali hina weh si penhsinwa we lhfweskawaali nili paasi pekwi

Every one that falleth on that stone shall be broken to pieces; but on whomsoever it shall fall, it will scatter him as dust.

19. chiine nihki yaayawikeecki mecimi nihki hokimaawi mhkateewkolayeeki honatonehaanaawa wahsi mesenaawaaci nili hine yaatefaki tepilo chiine hokwfaawahi nihi lenawehi ksake nihki moositeheeki yeesi hina kalawici yooma pemaatoweewe nihiini hilaaci

And the scribes and the chief priests sought to lay hands on him in that very hour; and they feared the people: for they perceived that he spake this parable against them.

20. chiine hokcitawaapamekohi mecimi hoteleskawaawahi kiimaapacikanhhi nayelohci tepasawefiiwi lawiilici wiiyaawa wahsi menawahi mesenaamaakoci hopekikalawiiwe wahsi weecikeenahi hini teepeelecikaneki mecimi hotesimekofiiweneki hina kapenali si pakfenekoci

And they watched him, and sent forth spies, which feigned themselves to be righteous, that they might take hold of his speech, so as to deliver him up to the rule and to the authority of the governor.

21. chiine honatohtaakohi keekehkimiwe niwaakotaape yeesi kiila mayaawi yoyani mecimi kakehkimiweeyani mecimi pwaa hotahpenaci hina wiyeefa kookweeneefa weeka teepweewe kikakehkimiwe hini homiyeewi maneto

And they asked him, saying, Master, we know that thou sayest and teachest rightly, and acceptest not the person of any, but of a truth teachest the way of God:

22. ha hini mayaawatwi kwteletiiweneki wahsi niilawe miilakici teekshoofoowe siisa weelaa toke mata hotekohi

Is it lawful for us to give tribute unto Caesar, or not?

23. payeekwa homooleeletamawahi honhhefiiwenilici mecimi

But he perceived their craftiness, and said unto them,

24. waapatesiko seleni neefawe hokiishoowe yooma mecimi holhspawikaafoowe poonoote nitasi hotelahi mecimi siisa hiwaki nihki

Shew me a penny. Whose image and superscription hath it? And they said, Caesar's.

25. mecimi weecikeenahi peteki miilehko siisa nili wiyehi weewiilaamici siisa mecimi maneto nili wiyehi weewiilaamici maneto hotelahi

And he said unto them, Then render unto Caesar the things that are Caesar's, and unto God the things that are God's.

26. mecimi nihki haalwi hilefiiki wahsi fookinamowaaci hini hiyoowe yeelahfamiilici nihi lcnawehi chiine hokwakwehtaaneeletamawaawaali hotaapafseewe mecimi nooleewiiki

And they were not able to take hold of the saying before the people: and they marveled at his answer, and held their peace.

27. chiine hotfekohi nitasi naanekoti nihi setosihi nihki yaayocki yeesi pwaa hateeki haapefiiwi-honhskaawe

And there came to him certain of the Sadducees, they which say that there is no resurrection; and they asked him, saying, Master, Moses wrote unto us, that

28. mecimi honatohtaakohi nihi keekehkimiwe moosisii nitawikaakona kwehkwi hileni hoceeninaali nepooli howiiwili mecimi mata hotapelohfemiili hina hoceenina wih mamaali nili siikawi-ykweeli mecimi wih miinhkawaali hoceeninaali

if a man's brother die, having a wife, and he be childless, his brother should take the wife, and raise up seed unto his brother.

29. hapiiki weecikeenahi niiswahfwi hoceeninaaki mecimi hina nhhihta homamaali wiiwali chiine nepwa mata hotapelohfemi

There were therefore seven brethren: and the first took a wife, and died childless;

30. mecimi hina mawi-niiswi

and the second;

31. chiine hina mawi-nhfwi homamaali nili siikawi-ykweeli chiine hina niiswahfwi hini yaska nehfaapi mata honakalaali hapelohfali mecimi nepwa

and the third took her; and likewise the seven also left no children, and died.

32. mayohkwaaci hina hkweewa nehfaapi nepwa

Afterward the woman also died.

33. hini haapefiiwi-honhskaaweneki weecikeenahi neefawe nihki wiiwali we hilefi hina ksake nihki niiswahfwi homehci poonaawaali wahsi howiiwiwaaci nili hotekohi

In the resurrection therefore whose wife of them shall she be? for the seven had her to wife.

34. mecimi ciisisii nihi hokwifhi yaama hinoki yeelahkamikiki wiichetiiki mecimi wiichetiiweneki si miiliweepi

And Jesus said unto them, The sons of this world marry, and are given in marriage:

35. weeka nihki nahiika hikweelemekofiiki yeelakimoofocki wahsi katawihtamowaaci halayine yeelahkamikiki mecimi hini haapefiiwi-honhskaawe hoci nihki neepekiki mata wiichetiiki mata nohki wiichetiiweneki si miiliweepi

but they that are accounted worthy to attain to that world, and the resurrection from the dead, neither marry, nor are given in marriage:

36. ksake mata nohki kiteeni yah katawi nepooki nihki ksake hoceecelefiimaawahi nihi henhcalihi mecimi maneto hokwifhi nihi teewa hokwifhi hina haapefiiwi-honhskaawe

for neither can they die any more: for they are equal unto the angels; and are sons of God, being sons of the resurrection.

37. weeka hini nihki neepekiki honhskaanoofooki teetepilahi yeesi waapatesiweeci moosisii hini piiwaloki tasi hine nili homanetoomali heplehemii chiine nili homanetoomali haisiki chiine nili homanetoomali ceekapii yeh sinaaci nili teepeelemiweelici

But that the dead are raised, even Moses shewed, in the place concerning the Bush, when he calleth the Lord the God of Abraham, and the God of Isaac, and the God of Jacob.

38. howe mata niliini homanetoomwaali nihki neepekiki nihki peemi lenaweewicki weeka ksake holenaweewihtawaawaali nili hotelahi

Now he is not the God of the dead, but of the living: for all live unto him.

39. chiine naanekoti nihki yaayawikeecki haapafse keekehkimiwe koowesi mehtowe hotelaali

And certain of the scribes answering said, Master, thou hast well said.

40. ksake nihi mata kiteeni wiisa natohtaakohi wiyehisi natohseewe

For they durst not any more ask him any question.

41. chiine nehiwe hiwaki nihki yeesi teepitii hokwihfici nili klaistiili hotelahi nihi

And he said unto them, How say they that the Christ is David's son?

42. ksake hiwa teepitii nehalwaaka wiila hini saamiiwekamooweneki pok hina teepeelemiweeta hotelaali niteepeelemiweemali lematapilo kiila nimayaawiinhkiki

For David himself saith in the book of Psalms, The Lord said unto my Lord, Sit thou on my right hand,

43. paalohi hini kifitali si hpalhkiiwe neshaaki kimateeletiiwenaki

Till I make thine enemies the footstool of thy feet.

44. teepitii weecikeenahi teepeelemiweeta hotesinaali nili mecimi nehiwesi na hokwihfali

David therefore calleth him Lord, and how is he his son?

45. chiine hotelahi hokakehkimaafhi hini honootaakeewenwaaki nihki caayahki lenaweeki

And in the hearing of all the people he said unto his disciples,

46. mahkeeni nihki yaayawikeecki maamaatawi paamhfeecki kinwi pihtawipiitenikaneki mecimi honaasweeletaanaawa hosilawaaletiiwena nili tah wiiwiitkiiki mecimi haliwi si hpapiiwena piitike nili mhsikamiko mecimi haliwi tasi tah wiiwihfenhcikeeki

Beware of the scribes, which desire to walk in long robes, and love salutations in the marketplaces, and chief seats in the synagogues, and chief places at feasts;

47. caacaakatakki siikawi-ykwehi yeetaalici wiikiwaapali mecimi nelohcilawiiwe hoci hostoonaawa keenwaaki mamaatomeewena yohkooni halika miyaalahkowaafoowe we hotfekonaawa

which devour widows' houses, and for a pretence make long prayers: these shall receive greater condemnation.

Luke:21

1. chiine spemeki laapi mecimi honeewahi nihi paweewi lenihi peemi hini monikaaneki si piicfe pakitamelici hoteephetiiwenwa

And he looked up, and saw the rich men that were casting their gifts into the treasury.

2. mecimi honeewaali naanekoti kitemaafali siikawi-ykweeli peemi nhpakitamelici niiswi maackwaafi moni

And he saw a certain poor widow casting in thither two mites.

3. mecimi teepweewe kitelepwa yaama kitemaafa siikawi-ykwe halika lekhi hoteh piicfe pakita noota nihki

And he said, Of a truth I say unto you, This poor widow cast in more than they all:

4. ksake yohkoma caayahki hotaamefiiwenwa hoteh piicfe pakitaanaawa nili teephetiiwena weeka hina hotakaawaafiiwe hopiicfe pakita caayahki hini weeci lenaweewici peepoonaki hiwa

for all these did of their superfluity cast in unto the gifts: but she of her want did cast in all the living that she had.

5. chiine yeesi naaleta haatotamowaaci hini mamaatomeewikamikwi yeesi hini waawesihkatooteeki howesi siikonhhi mecimi teephiweewe

And as some spake of the temple, how it was adorned with goodly stones and offerings, he said,

6. weeka halanili wiyehi neeneemeyeekwe nili kaasekiki weh piyeeya hine mata we ckonoofo hotasi nekoti siikona hoskici kotakali wah pwaa sahkiki hipakiloofota hisiwe

As for these things which ye behold, the days will come, in which there shall not be left here one stone upon another, that shall not be thrown down.

7. chiine honatohtaakohi nihi keekehkimiwe taaniwe laakwa weecikeenahi yooloma wiyehi we hahteewa mecimi nehiwe we hinwi hini kikinooloowe hine yooloma wiyehi howe wiisa piyeemikake hotekohi

And they asked him, saying, Master, when therefore shall these things be? and what shall be the sign when these things are about to come to pass?

8. mecimi kcitawaafiiko wahsi pwaa kiilawa piimiweloofoyeekwe ksake meci weh piyeeki niwiifooweneki niila hina mecimi hini laakwa howe naanemi piyeeya we hiwaki teki naawalwi haako nihki

And he said, Take heed that ye be not led astray: for many shall come in my name, saying, I am he; and, The time is at hand: go ye not after them.

9. mecimi hine keh nootaakeepwa noochetiiwena chiine tatawaafiiwena teki cihfefiko ksake yooloma wiyehi kwiilahi weecita piyeemikato nhhihta payeekwa hini ceeyehkwi mata weelenawakatwi hisiwe

And when ye shall hear of wars and tumults, be not terrified: for these things must needs come to pass first; but the end is not immediately.

10. howe hine nekotweelena si lenawe weh pafekwicfatawaali nekotweelena si lenaweeli mecimi hokimaawitaamhkwe homawinacto hokimaawitaamhkwe

Then said he unto them, Nation shall rise against nation, and kingdom against kingdom:

11. chiine nitasi we hahteewa maki hasiskinoomeskaawali chiine caceepi tasi skwaalawaafiiwena mecimi metenetiiwe-ipeneewena mecimi kwpeneewena we hahteewa chiine maki kikinooloowena weefepahkamikiki hoci

and there shall be great earthquakes, and in divers places famines and pestilences; and there shall be terrors and great signs from heaven.

12. payeekwa wihsi pwaa caayahki yooloma wiyehi hiki keh mesenekowaaki nihki mecimi keh naanohkaachekowaaki nili mhsikamiko chiine kiphotiiwikaana keh si pakfenekowaaki yeelahfamiilici maki hokimahi mecimi kapenalihi keh si piyeelekowaaki ksake niwiifoowe hoci

But before all these things, they shall lay their hands on you, and shall persecute you, delivering you up to the synagogues and prisons, bringing you before kings and governors for my name's sake.

13. kiilawa hini weh si kotekwi lohfeya wahsi teepweeweniyeekwe

It shall turn unto you for a testimony.

14. mecfetooko weecikeena hini kitehiwaaki wahsi pwaa kaasa memekiniteheeyeekwe wahsi haapafseeyeekwe

Settle it therefore in your hearts, not to meditate beforehand how to answer:

15. ksake keh miilelepwa hotooni mecimi lepwaawe wa haalwi hilefihtamowaaci caayahki kimateeletiiwenwaaki weelaa nanahkotamowaaci

for I will give you a mouth and wisdom, which all your adversaries shall not be able to withstand or to gainsay.

16. weeka keh mestaawhekowaaki wiikinaakwi kehkiyaamaki chiine hoceeninaaki chiine nhhalweeletiiwenaki chiine wihkaanimaaki mecimi naaleta nihi kiilawa wahsi nepooweneki si poonoofolici we hpenalaawahi nihki

But ye shall be delivered up even by parents, and brethren, and kinsfolk, and friends; and some of you shall they cause to be put to death.

17. chiine keh siikeelemekofipwa kiilawa yeecsiwaaci caayahki hileniiki ksake niwiifoowe hoci

And ye shall be hated of all men for my name's sake.

18. mecimi mata nekoti kiilehfwa we hkwineya

And not a hair of your head shall perish.

19. kipiisiteheewenwaaki ke hoci hanhhiweepwa kitelenaweewiiwenwa

In your patience ye shall win your souls.

20. payeekwa hine kiilawa neemeyeekwe colooseelemii kiposkamowaate samaakanaki hine howe waakotamoko yeesi hosiikwahkamikifiiwe naanemi piyeeyaaki

But when ye see Jerusalem compassed with armies, then know that her desolation is at hand.

21. howe hine wiilaani nihki cotiyeeki yeepicki nili meekwahkiki lesimowaate mecimi nihki hini heelekiina nili yeepicki wiilaani lohfaawaate mecimi

Then let them that are in Judaea flee unto the mountains; and let them that are in

nihki hini piileski taamhkwe yeepicki teki wiilaani piicfaawaate nitasi

the midst of her depart out; and let not them that are in the country enter therein.

22. ksake yooloma yo halotamoowe si kaasekiki wahsi caayahki wiyehi yeelawikeeki menawahi hokwaawfetooteeki

For these are days of vengeance, that all things which are written may be fulfilled.

23. macilepwaaweniiki cehi nihki leelaamotaakocki hapelohfeefali mecimi nihki neenoonhhiweecki nele kaasekiki ksake hini hoskitaamhkwe we hahteewi mhsi kwiilahsiteheewe mecimi kisfekwiiwe yaama lenawe si

Woe unto them that are with child and to them that give suck in those days! for there shall be great distress upon the land, and wrath unto this people.

24. chiine nihki hini weeci kaskweeki hini kiskhika we hoci haakicfeeki mecimi nihi caayahki tfweelena si lenawehi weh si kiikeenikani fakinaapiyaaloofooki nihki mecimi colooseelemii sahkiki weh si kakeelhkaanaawa nihki nanahkawileniiki paalohi hotelaakwaafiiwenwa nihki nanahkawileniiki we hokwaawfetoote

And they shall fall by the edge of the sword, and shall be led captive into all the nations: and Jerusalem shall be trodden down of the Gentiles, until the times of the Gentiles be fulfilled.

25. chiine nitasi we hahteewa kikinooloowena kiisekikiisfoki chiine tepehkikiisfoki mecimi halaakoki mecimi hini hoskitaamhkwe hokwiilahsiteheewenwa caakisi lenaweeki wanhfoneeewefi ksake hini peemi neenekwaanwiki hini mhsinepi mecimi nili meemakipookaki

And there shall be signs in sun and moon and stars; and upon the earth distress of nations, in perplexity for the roaring of the sea and the billows;

26. hileniiki pkonaapatamooki kwpeneewe ksake mecimi hahkawaafiiki nili wiyehi peemi piyeeyaaki hini yeelekokwahkamikiki ksake nili menhkwato hoci waasikaki weh noomenoote

men fainting for fear, and for expectation of the things which are coming on the world: for the powers of the heavens shall be shaken.

27. mecimi hine howe nihki weh neewaawaali nili hokwihfali hileni paafkwahkiiki pemi piyeeli kileki waasikaki mecimi mhsi wahfaacimekofiiwe

And then shall they see the Son of man coming in a cloud with power and great glory.

28. payeekwa hine yooloma wiyehi halemi piyeemikake lematkweleko mecimi spemeki laapiko ksake kipetekinoofoowenwa naanemi piyeeya hotelahi nihi

But when these things begin to come to pass, look up, and lift up your heads; because your redemption draweth nigh.

29. chiine hokaloolahi nihi pemaatoweewe waapatamoko hini kicimiisi mecimi caayahki nili mhteko

And he spake to them a parable: Behold the fig tree, and all the trees:

30. hine nili howe ye holowiki kineemenaawa hini mecimi kiwaakotaanaawa nehalwaaka kiilawa yeesi hini peelaawiki howe maalaakwaamefiiyaaki

when they now shoot forth, ye see it and know of your own selves that the summer is now nigh.

31. teetepilahi yooni nehfaapi kiilawa hine neemeyeekwe yooloma wiyehi pemi piyeemikake waakotamoko yeesi hini hokimaawitaamhkomi maneto howe maalaakwaamefiiyaaki

Even so ye also, when ye see these things coming to pass, know ye that the kingdom of God is nigh.

32. tepilo kitelepwa niila yaama hinoki skwiilenawe mata we hasenwa paalohi weh ceeyehkwi mectoote caayahki wiyehi

Verily I say unto you, This generation shall not pass away, till all things be accomplished.

33. menhkwato mecimi hasiski we haseno weeka nikalawiiwena mata we haseno

Heaven and earth shall pass away: but my words shall not pass away.

34. payeekwa kcitawaafiiko kiiyaawaaki piilepe kitehiwa hofaamilaakwiiya hofaamhkaakwiiwe chiine wanefoowe mecimi yooma lenaweewiiwe si hotamefiiwe mecimi kikamooci paasi nakwaaka kootfekonaawa halayine kaasekiki

But take heed to yourselves, lest haply your hearts be overcharged with surfeiting, and drunkenness, and cares of this life, and that day come on you suddenly as a snare:

35. ksake hini yooni weh si hotfekowaaci nihki caayahki hini hoskitaamhkwe yeetaacki mefhiike hini hasiski

for so shall it come upon all them that dwell on the face of all the earth.

36. weeka kcitawaapatamoko caaki peemi laakweeweniki hostooko nanahpaacikeemoowe wahsi menawahi kiilawa katawesitameekwe yooloma caayahki wiyehi wah piyeemikaki mecimi wahsi niipawiyeekwe yeelahfamiici hina hokwihfali hileni hiwapi

But watch ye at every season, making supplication, that ye may prevail to escape all these things that shall come to pass, and to stand before the Son of man.

37. chiine tfene kaasekiki pemi kakehkimiwe hini mamaatomeewikamikoki mecimi tfene tepehkiki laalohfe chiine hini yaasi kkehsi meekwahkiki halifiet sitoote

And every day he was teaching in the temple; and every night he went out, and lodged in the mount that is called the mount of Olives.

38. mecimi caayahki nihi lenawehi hini yeekolahwaapaki howaotfekohi hini mamaatomeewikamikoki wahsi nootaakoci

And all the people came early in the morning to him in the temple, to hear him.

Luke:22

1. howe hini pwaayaa hopskweeteeki takhwa si wihfenhcikeewe maalaakwahi piyeeya pemhfaasiweewi wihfenhcikeewe sitoote hini

Now the feast of unleavened bread drew nigh, which is called the Passover.

2. chiine nihki hokimaawi mhkateewkolayeeki mecimi nihki yaayawikeecki honatonehaanaawa wahsi menawahi nhfaawaaci nili hokwfaawahi ksake nihi lenawehi

And the chief priests and the scribes sought how they might put him to death; for they feared the people.

3. chiine seteniili hopiicfaamekooli cootasii hiskeeletii yaaloofota teewahi nihi si wiitakimekofi metahfwi-kite-niiswi

And Satan entered into Judas who was called Iscariot, being of the number of the twelve.

4. chiine hina weepfe mecimi hokiikalootiimahi nihi hokimaawi mhkateewkolayehi chiine kaptiinhhi wahsi menawahi nihi si mestaawhaaci nili

And he went away, and communed with the chief priests and captains, how he might deliver him unto them.

5. mecimi nihi howesilepwahi chiine mehtaacimohi wahsi miilekoci moni

And they were glad, and covenanted to give him money.

6. chiine nhkokeemo wiila mecimi honatoneha tawaafiiwe wahsi nihi si mestaawhaaci nili hini pwaa hapilite nihi mehseelelici

And he consented, and sought opportunity to deliver him unto them in the absence of the multitude.

7. mecimi hini pwaayaa hopskweeteeki takhwa si kaasekiki piyeeya wah ta hini pemhfaasiweewe kwiilahi hapenaweki

And the day of unleavened bread came, on which the passover must be sacrificed.

8. mecimi piitali chiine caaniili howaawiineskawahi nhhaakone mecimi mawi mecfetawinaake hini pemhfaasiweewe wahsi menawahi miiciyakwe hotelahi nihi

And he sent Peter and John, saying, Go and make ready for us the passover, that we may eat.

9. mecimi taaniwe tasi kitesitehe nih mecfetoope hotekohi nihi

And they said unto him, Where wilt thou that we make ready?

10. mecimi waapatamoko hine piicfatameekwe hini hoteewe nitasi keh nakskaakowa hileni hopah niime hasiskiwakkoki nepi hini wiikiwaapeki si neekalehko hina

And he said unto them, Behold, when ye are entered into the city, there shall meet you a man bearing a pitcher of water; follow him into the house whereinto he goeth.

11. mecimi hina hini wiikiwa hoci mestele hina keekehkimiwe taaniwe hini nawhetiiwika wah tah miiciya hini pemhfaasiweewe kileki nikakehkimaafaki kitekwa ke hilaawa

And ye shall say unto the goodman of the house, The Master saith unto thee, Where is the guest-chamber, where I shall eat the passover with my disciples?

12. mecimi hina keh waapatelekowa mhsaawi yaataaki hakocipokwanefo teepfenwi hawoocika nitasi mecfetooko hotelahi

And he will shew you a large upper room furnished: there make ready.

13. chiine nihki weepfeeki mecimi homhkaanaawa yeesi mehcimekowaaci nili mecimi homecfetoonaawa nihki hini pemhfaasiweewe

And they went, and found as he had said unto them: and they made ready the passover.

14. chiine hini yaatefaki yeh piyeeyaaki lematapiwa hina mecimi nihi hepastalihi wiici

And when the hour was come, he sat down, and the apostles with him.

15. mecimi kileki maatawiteheewe nooci mehci maatawitehe wahsi wihpomelako kiilawa yooma pemhfaasiweewe wihsi pwaa hahkwinamoya

And he said unto them, With desire I have desired to eat this passover with you before I suffer:

16. ksake kitelepwa niila mata neh miici hini paalohi hini hokwaawfetooteeke hini hokimaawitaamhkomeki maneto hotelahi nihi

for I say unto you, I will not eat it, until it be fulfilled in the kingdom of God.

17. mecimi hotahpenaali tephikanali chiine yeh mehci miiliweeci niyaawe menoko yooma mecimi papahfenamaatiko heelekiina kiilawa

And he received a cup, and when he had given thanks, he said, Take this, and divide it among yourselves:

18. ksake kitelepwa niila mata niila neh mene hini tetepahtekwi mawifoowe yooci hinoki paalohi hini hokimaawitaamhkomi maneto weh piyeeya hisiwe

for I say unto you, I will not drink from henceforth of the fruit of the vine, until the kingdom of God shall come.

19. chiine takhwa hoteh mame mecimi yeh mehci miiliweeci niyaawe hoposkona hini chiine hoteh miilahi nihi niiya yooma kiilawa meemiiloofoyeekwe

And he took bread, and when he had given thanks, he brake it, and gave to them, saying, This is my body which is

yooma silawiiko nimaamhkaweelemoofooweneki hisiwe

given for you: this do in remembrance of me.

20. chiine nili tephikanali nehfaapi yeh mehci holaakwiifiwihfenici yaama tephika hina hini mayaki mehtaacimoowe nimhskomeki teetepila hini feefiikinamawoofoyeekwe kiilawa

And the cup in like manner after supper, saying, This cup is the new covenant in my blood, even that which is poured out for you.

21. payeekwa waapatamoko hini holeci hina memestaawhita niwiiciimeko hoskici hini tah wihfeniki

But behold, the hand of him that betrayeth me is with me on the table.

22. ksake hina hokwihfali hileni sapkahi nhheewa yeesi hini mehci tehehtooteeki payeekwa macilepwaaweni cehi hina hileni weeci saapwi mestaawhoofoci hina hisiwe

For the Son of man indeed goeth, as it hath been determined: but woe unto that man through whom he is betrayed!

23. chiine nihki halemi niinatohseeki heelekiina wiilawa taanawe nihki hina hini wah silawiici yooma wiyehi

And they began to question among themselves, which of them it was that should do this thing.

24. chiine pafekwiiya pekihkaatiiwe nehfaapi nitasi heelekiina nihki taanawe nihki kcimhsiilakimoofo

And there arose also a contention among them, which of them is accounted to be greatest.

25. mecimi hotelahi nihi nihi maki hokimaamwahi nihki nanahkawileniiki hotepeelemekofitaakowahi nihki mecimi nihi weewiyehsimekofihtaakowaaci howespenalefiiwenaki yaaloofohi nihi

And he said unto them, The kings of the Gentiles have lordship over them; and they that have authority over them are called Benefactors.

26. payeekwa teki kiilawa yooni we hilefiyeekwe weeka hina haliwi yeelefita heelekiina kiilawa wiilaani hina paasi hina hofiimema hilefite mecimi hina weekimaawita mememekinilotawiweeta

But ye shall not be so: but he that is the greater among you, let him become as the younger; and he that is chief, as he that doth serve.

27. ksake taanawe haliwi hilefi ha hina lematapita tah wihfeniki weelaa toke hina mememekinilotawiweeta ha mata hina lematapita tah wihfeniki weeka niila peemi hilefiya hini heelekiina kiilawa paasi hina mememekinilotawiweeta

For whether is greater, he that sitteth at meat, or he that serveth? is not he that sitteth at meat? but I am in the midst of you as he that serveth.

28. payeekwa nihkiini kiilawa mayehci nekotenwi wiitefiimicki nipiimi-ashoofooweneki

But ye are they which have continued with me in my temptations;

29. mecimi kipiyeetatenamoolepwa hokimaawitaamhkwe teetepilahi yeesi nohfa piyeetatenamawici

and I appoint unto you a kingdom, even as my Father appointed unto me,

30. wahsi menawahi wihfeniyeekwe kiilawa mecimi meneyeekwe tah wihfeniya nookimaawitaamhkomeki mecimi kiilawa ke hpapinaawa hokimaawi hpapiiwena peemahkowaaleekwe nihki metahfwi-kite-niiswi hotfweeloowena hiswiila

that ye may eat and drink at my table in my kingdom; and ye shall sit on thrones judging the twelve tribes of Israel.

31. saiman' saiman' waapami setenii natohse wahsi howiilaaminehki wahsi menawah hina pawenehki paasi kawaskwi

Simon, Simon, behold, Satan asked to have you, that he might sift you as wheat:

32. payeekwa kimectoole nanahpaacikeemoowe wahsi pwaa kiteepwehseewe haalwi hilefiiyaaki mecimi silawiilo kiila hine peeleko nohki mehci kokiiyane haayicsimi kiceeninaaki

but I made supplication for thee, that thy faith fail not: and do thou, when once thou hast turned again, stablish thy brethren.

33. chiine hina nimehci tehe teepeelemiweeta wahsi neyiisweelena si wiiteemela kiphotiiweneki mecimi nepooweneki hotelaali

And he said unto him, Lord, with thee I am ready to go both to prison and to death.

34. chiine kiwiitamoole piita hina naapeeya mata weh kalhootamwa hinoki kaasekiki paalohi kiila ke nhfene kiyaacimo yeesi waakomiyani hotelaali

And he said, I tell thee, Peter, the cock shall not crow this day, until thou shalt thrice deny that thou knowest me.

35. chiine hine kiwaawiineskoolepwa matalaakwanwi monipiitaaka chiine piitaakanhfecika chiine mhkifena ha kitakaawaafiipwa wiyehi hotelahi nihi mata wiyehi hiwaki nihki

And he said unto them, When I sent you forth without purse, and wallet, and shoes, lacked ye any thing? And they said, Nothing.

36. chiine weeka hinoki howe hina peepoonaka monipiitaaka wiilaani hina mameke hini mecimi piitaakanhfecika nehfaapi chiine hina pwaayaa poonaka wiilaani miyeekite hopihtawikootiimi mecimi tepenake kiskhika

And he said unto them, But now, he that hath a purse, let him take it, and likewise a wallet: and he that hath none, let him sell his cloke, and buy a sword.

37. ksake kitelepwa niila wahsi yooma yeelawikeeki kwiilah hokwaawfetooteeki niiyaaki chiine hina wiitakimoofo lhfwaacilawiiwenhhi ksake hini niila si wiyehi hokwaawefiiweniwi hotelahi nihi

For I say unto you, that this which is written must be fulfilled in me, And he was reckoned with transgressors: for that which concerneth me hath fulfillment.

38. mecimi nihki waapatano teepeelemiweeta niiswi hotasi kiskhikana hiwaki mecimi teepi nili hotelahi

And they said, Lord, behold, here are two swords. And he said unto them, It is enough.

39. chiine piyeci lohfe mecimi weepfe yaasilawiici hini halifiwi meekwahkiki heewa chiine nihki kakehkimaafaki nehfaapi honeekalaawaali

And he came out, and went, as his custom was, unto the mount of Olives; and the disciples also followed him.

40. mecimi nahiika hini tasi ye hapici mamaatomeeko wahsi pwaa piicfatameekwe piimi-ashetiiwe hotelahi nihi

And when he was at the place, he said unto them, Pray that ye enter not into temptation.

41. mecimi nihi hoci pkeewa nawito siikona wa hikoskaaci laakwa chiine hociikwanahkeepi sahkiki mecimi mamaatome

And he was parted from them about a stone's cast; and he kneeled down and prayed,

42. hohfima siteheeyane kiila niiya hoci payaakilahi pooni yaama tephika payeekwa mata niila nitesiteheewe kiila weeka weh silawiipi hiwapi

saying, Father, if thou be willing, remove this cup from me: nevertheless not my will, but thine, be done.

43. chiine nitasi hotepinaakofihtaakooli menhkwatoki hoci henhcaliili howiisikinekooli

And there appeared unto him an angel from heaven, strengthening him.

44. mecimi peemi hahkwiteheewenici halika si menwi mamaatome mecimi howiisafoowe paasi keela hini meeki-pakikawiki mhskwi hinwili sahkiki hoskitaamhkwe sfeeyaali

And being in an agony he prayed more earnestly: and his sweat became as it were great drops of blood falling down upon the ground.

45. chiine homamaatomeeweneki ye hoci pafekwiici nihi kakehkimaafhi si piyeewa mecimi homhkawahi nihi peemekwaamelici macilepwaawe hoci

And when he rose up from his prayer, he came unto the disciples, and found them sleeping for sorrow,

46. mecimi koociwe kinepaapwa honhskaako mecimi mamaatomeeko wahsi pwaa piicfatameekwe piimi-ashetiiwe hotelahi

and said unto them, Why sleep ye? rise and pray, that ye enter not into temptation.

47. yeheeyehi keewaki kalawici waapamehko mehseeleka mecimi hina cootasii yaaloofota nekoti nihki metahfwi-kite-niiswi piyeci niikaani nihi mecimi maalaakwahi ciisisiili heewa wahsi nili pacikamaaci

While he yet spake, behold, a multitude, and he that was called Judas, one of the twelve, went before them; and he drew near unto Jesus to kiss him.

48. payeekwa ciisisii cootasii ha pacikamiweewe kooci mestaawha hina hokwihfali hileni hotelaali

But Jesus said unto him, Judas, betrayest thou the Son of man with a kiss?

49. mecimi hine nihi maalaakwahi wiila neniipawilici yeh neemelici wah neekasiweeyaaki teepeelemiweeta ha ne pkitehikeepe hini kiskhika hiwaki nihki

And when they that were about him saw what would follow, they said, Lord, shall we smite with the sword?

50. mecimi naanekoti nihki hopkitehwaali nili hotaloolaakanali hina moospimekofiiwi mhkateewkolaye mecimi hokiskehsethwaali nili homayaaotawakaaki

And a certain one of them smote the servant of the high priest, and struck off his right ear.

51. payeekwa ciisisii haapafse mecimi wiilaani leelemehko yooni hkwi hisiwe mecimi hoteh pehsena hotawakanilici mecimi hokiikehaali nili

But Jesus answered and said, Suffer ye thus far. And he touched his ear, and healed him.

52. chiine hotelahi ciisisii nihi hokimaawi mhkateewkolayehi chiine hini mamaatomeewikamikwi hoci kaptiinhhi mecimi kikilenihi peepiyeci mawinehokoci ha kipiyeci lohfaapwa paasi ciikoniwehfi kinoochaawa wiici kiskhikana mecimi cifhikana

And Jesus said unto the chief priests, and captains of the temple, and elders, which were come against him, Are ye come out, as against a robber, with swords and staves?

53. ye tfene waapaki niila wiitefiimelako hini mamaatomeewikamikoki mata kimawinachi lecehtawipwa payeekwa yooma yo kiilawa kitaatefamoomwa mecimi hini peepekicaawi waasikaki hotelahi

When I was daily with you in the temple, ye stretched not forth your hands against me: but this is your hour, and the power of darkness.

54. mecimi nihki homawinachaawaali nili chiine piitike hina moospimekofiiwi mhkateewkolaye yeetaaci wiikiwa hoteh piyeelaawaali nili weeka piita pelowihi si neekasiwe

And they seized him, and led him away, and brought him into the high priest's house. But Peter followed afar off.

55. chiine nihki yeh mehci pkaleenamowaaci skote hini heelekhi hini tepoweewakhoowe mecimi mehci maawatwahkeepiiki piita lematapiwa hini heelekhi nihi

And when they had kindled a fire in the midst of the court, and had sat down together, Peter sat in the midst of them.

56. chiine naanekoti hkweefa honeewaali nili yeesi lematapilici hini tah teepahkoleeki hini skote mecimi homamiyetaawaapamaali nili yaama hileni nehfaapi wiici nili hiwa

And a certain maid seeing him as he sat in the light of the fire, and looking stedfastly upon him, said, This man also was with him.

57. payeekwa kiyaacimo hina hkweewa mata niila hina niwaakoma hisiwe

But he denied, saying, Woman, I know him not.

58. chiine peloociisi hakowihi nohki kotaka honeewaali kiila nehfaapi nekoti nihki hotelaali payeekwa piita yeeleniwiyani mata niila hina hisiwe

And after a little while another saw him, and said, Thou also art one of them. But Peter said, Man, I am not.

59. chiine nawito peeleko yaatefaki laakwasi hahkowihi nohki kotaka piisikalawi teepweewe yaama hileni nehfaapi wiici nili ksake keeleliiwilenawe hina hisiwe

And after the space of about one hour another confidently affirmed, saying, Of a truth this man also was with him: for he is a Galilaean.

60. payeekwa piita yeeleniwiyani mata niwaakota yeeyoyani hisiwe mecimi weelena yehi keewaki kalawici hina naapeeya kalhootamwa

But Peter said, Man, I know not what thou sayest. And immediately, while he yet spake, the cock crew.

61. mecimi hina teepeelemiweeta kokiiwa chiine hoteh waapamaali piitali mecimi piita homhkaweeleta hini hokalawiiwe hina teepeelemiweeta yeesi wihsi pwaa hina naapeeya kalhootaki hinoki kaasekiki nhfene kiila keh kiyaacimi hikoci nili

And the Lord turned, and looked upon Peter. And Peter remembered the word of the Lord, how that he said unto him, Before the cock crow this day, thou shalt deny me thrice.

62. mecimi lohfe chiine wihfakwe hofaamilepwa

And he went out, and wept bitterly.

63. chiine nihki hileniiki fefookinaacki ciisisiili howaapalaachaawaali mecimi hoppaktehwaawaali nili

And the men that held Jesus mocked him, and beat him.

64. chiine hokipiikwepilaawaali mecimi honatohtawaawaali moosikiiskwaacimolo neefawe hina kipkitehokwa hotelaawaali

And they blindfolded him, and asked him, saying, Prophesy: who is he that struck thee?

65. chiine meci kotakali wiyehi hotesi ppehcimaawaali homataamaawaali

And many other things spake they against him, reviling him.

66. chiine yeesi kolaa hini kiisekiki hini homaawaskaawenwa tepetwi maawaskahi nihi hokikileniimwahi nihki lenaweeki neyiisweelena hokimaawi mhkateewkolayeeki chiine yaayawikeecki mecimi hotesiwelaawaali nili hotepoweewenwaaki

And as soon as it was day, the assembly of the elders of the people was gathered together, both chief priests and scribes; and they led him away into their council, saying,

67. kwehkwi kiiyaawiyane hina klaistii wiitamawinaake hotelaawaali payeekwa hina kwehkwi niila wiitamoolako mata kitah teepwehtawipwa kiilawa

If thou art the Christ, tell us. But he said unto them, If I tell you, ye will not believe:

68. mecimi niila natohtoolako mata kita haapafseepwa kiilawa

and if I ask you, ye will not answer.

69. payeekwa yooci hinoki hina hokwihfali hileni weh lematapi hini tah mayaawiinhkiki hini howiisikatowiiwe maneto hotelahi nihi

But from henceforth shall the Son of man be seated at the right hand of the power of God.

70. mecimi caayahki nihki ha howe kiiya nili hokwihfali maneto hiwaki kiteyopwa yeesi hinawiya hotelahi hina

And they all said, Art thou then the Son of God? And he said unto them, Ye say that I am.

71. mecimi nihki nehiwe keewaki kipoonaape wa hoci skata leelemakwe teepweewenaki ksake kimehci

And they said, What further need have we of witness? for we ourselves have heard from his own mouth.

nehalwaaka nootawaape kiilawe nehalwaaka
hotooneki hoci hiwaki nihki

Luke:23

1. mecimi hini yeetfweelowaaci mefi pafekwiiki nihki
chiine paalatiili yeelahfamiilici hoteh piyeelaawaali
nili

And the whole company of them rose up,
and brought him before Pilate.

2. mecimi hotalemi hahtelaawaali nimhkawaape
yaama hileni peemi piimilotaki nitfweeloowenena
mecimi peemi kotesiweeci wahsi siisa si miiliweeki
teekshoofoowe chiine hiwa hina yeesi wiila
klaistiiwici hokima hiwaki nihki

And they began to accuse him, saying,
We found this man perverting our nation,
and forbidding to give tribute to Caesar,
and saying that he himself is Christ a
king.

3. mecimi paalatii honatohtawaali nili ha kiiya hina
hokimaamwaali coosaki hotelaali mecimi hina
hotaapaftawaali kiila kiteyo hotelaali

And Pilate asked him, saying, Art thou
the King of the Jews? And he answered
him and said, Thou sayest.

4. mecimi mata nimhkamawa miyaalefiiwe yaama
hileni hotelahi paalatii nihi hokimaawi
mhkateewkolayehi mecimi nihi mehseelelici

And Pilate said unto the chief priests and
the multitudes, I find no fault in this man.

5. payeekwa nihki hini halika si kcihkaaweeki
howiisaafihahi hina nihi lenawehi pemi kakehkimiwe
saapwi mefhiike cotiye mecimi keeleliiki hoci halemi
lawi paalohi ke hotasi hiwaki

But they were the more urgent, saying,
He stirreth up the people, teaching
throughout all Judaea, and beginning
from Galilee even unto this place.

6. payeekwa paalatii yeh nootaakeeci hini natohse
kwehkwi toke keeleliiwilenaweli nili hileniili

But when Pilate heard it, he asked
whether the man were a Galilaean.

7. chiine yeh waakotaki yeesi heletii
hokoteletiiwitaamhkwe hocilici nili hoteleskamawaali
heletiili nili nehfaapi wiila hina colooseelemiiki
hapiwa yoolooni kaasekiki

And when he knew that he was of
Herod's jurisdiction, he sent him unto
Herod, who himself also was at
Jerusalem in these days.

8. howe heletii yeh neewaaci ciisisiili hanhhiweewi
howesilepwa ksake heesaye hoci maatawi neewaali
nili nootaake ksake nili chiine hopiyeeteeleta wahsi
neemeki wiyehsi makiicilawiiwe yeesilawiilici

Now when Herod saw Jesus, he was
exceeding glad: for he was of a long time
desirous to see him, because he had heard
concerning him; and he hoped to see
some miracle done by him.

9. mecimi meci kalawiiwena hotesi natohtawaali nili
payeekwa mata wiyehi hotaapaftaakooli

And he questioned him in many words;
but he answered him nothing.

10. chiine nihki mhkateewkolayeeki mecimi nihki
yaayawikeecki niipawiiki peemi holaami
hahtelaawaaci nili

And the chief priests and the scribes
stood, vehemently accusing him.

11. mecimi heletii kileki hosamaakanemhhi
homatawiyeefekisiwahkeephaali nili mecimi
howaapalaachaali chiine hopiitenikehaali naaswasahte
piitenika peteki paalatiiki hoteleskawaali nili

And Herod with his soldiers set him at
nought, and mocked him, and arraying
him in gorgeous apparel sent him back to
Pilate.

12. mecimi heletii chiine paalatii tepilo hine kaasekiki
howihkaanetiiki ksake nihki yehki mateeletiiki
wiilawa

And Herod and Pilate became friends
with each other that very day: for before
they were at enmity between themselves.

13. mecimi paalatii homaawatomahi nihi hokimaawi mhkateewkolayehi chiine nihi teepeelecikeelici chiine nihi lenawehi

And Pilate called together the chief priests and the rulers and the people,

14. mecimi nihi kiilawa kipiyeetawipwa yaama hileni paasi nekoti peepiimilotawaata nihi lenawehi mecimi waapatamoko niila peemi si mehci memekinisemaki hina yeelahfamiiyeekwe kiilawa mata nimhka wiiyaaki yaama hileni miyaalefiiwe nele wiyehi yeesi pesfeki weeci hahteleekwe kiilawa

and said unto them, Ye brought unto me this man, as one that perverteth the people: and behold, I, having examined him before you, found no fault in this man touching those things whereof ye accuse him:

15. mata mata nohki heletii ksake hina peteki kiteleskamaakona nili mecimi waapatamoko mata wiyehi nepoowe lelemekwatwi mayehci silawiici hina

no, nor yet Herod: for he sent him back unto us; and behold, nothing worthy of death hath been done by him.

16. niila weecikeenahi neh lihfiiwanhhwa hina chiine neh pakfena hotelahi

I will therefore chastise him, and release him.

18. payeekwa nihki caayahki tepetwahootamooki haamwesi yaama hileni mecimi pakfenamawinaake palepasii hiwaki

But they cried out all together, saying, Away with this man, and release unto us Barabbas:

19. nekoti hina wiyeefa naanekoti siisesiiwinoochiweewe homecto hini hoteeweneki mecimi nhsiweewe hoci kiphotiiweneki hipakiloofo

one who for a certain insurrection made in the city, and for murder, was cast into prison.

20. chiine paalatii nohki hokaloolahi nihi peemi maatawi pakfenaaci ciisisiili

And Pilate spake unto them again, desiring to release Jesus;

21. payeekwa nihki ciilweeki haasitefhwi haasitefhwi hina hisiweeki

but they shouted, saying, Crucify, crucify him.

22. mecimi hina hini mawi-nhfene koociwe nehiwe mecaafiki mehci hisilawi yaama hileni mata nime mhka wiiyaaki wa hoci nepeki weecikeenahi neh lihfiiwanhhwa mecimi neh pakfena hotelahi nihi

And he said unto them the third time, Why, what evil hath this man done? I have found no cause of death in him: I will therefore chastise him and release him.

23. payeekwa nihki wiisikoweki kileki wiyakahootamoowena natotamaakeeki wahsi menawahi nili haasitefhoofolici mecimi hotalahootamoowenwa kolepkaaweya

But they were instant with loud voices, asking that he might be crucified. And their voices prevailed.

24. mecimi paalatii miiliwe metaamoowe wahsi nihi neetotamelici silawiiki

And Pilate gave sentence that what they asked for should be done.

25. chiine hopakfenamawahi nili mayehci siisesiiwinoochiweewe mecimi nhsiweewe hoci kiphotiiweneki hipakiloofolici neetotamaakeewaaci nihki weeka yeesiteheelici nihi hotesi pakfenaali ciisisiili

And he released him that for insurrection and murder had been cast into prison, whom they asked for; but Jesus he delivered up to their will.

26. chiine hine ye hale haamwelaawaaci nili nihki homesenaawaali nekoti saailiinii hoci saimanii peemi hini piileski taamhkwe homelici mecimi nili howiiwashaawaali hini yaasitehfeki wahsi naawalwi ciisisiili siwetoolici hini

And when they led him away, they laid hold upon one Simon of Cyrene, coming from the country, and laid on him the cross, to bear it after Jesus.

27. mecimi nitasi honeekalaawaali meci nihki mehseelekki lenaweeki mecimi hkweeki meemawehtawaacki mecimi meewimaacki nili

And there followed him a great multitude of the people, and of women who bewailed and lamented him.

28. payeekwa ciisisii nihi si kokiiwa hotaaneefhi colooseelemii teki niila mawimiko weeka mawitamoko kiiyaawa mecimi kitapelohfemwaaki hiwa

But Jesus turning unto them said, Daughters of Jerusalem, weep not for me, but weep for yourselves, and for your children.

29. ksake waapatamoko nili kaasekiki wiisa piyeeya hine nihki kisaateelemekofiiki cehi nihki seskificki mecimi nili laamotaakana pwaayaa laakwa pahkaseeyaaki mecimi nihki holeniyeki pwaayaa laakwa miiliweecki noonoowe we hiwaki

For behold, the days are coming, in which they shall say, Blessed are the barren, and the wombs that never bare, and the breasts that never gave suck.

30. hine howe nihki we halemi hitaanaawa nili meekwahkiiwali hoskici si haakicfaako niilawe mecimi nili meekwahkiifa petawhinaake

Then shall they begin to say to the mountains, Fall on us; and to the hills, Cover us.

31. ksake kwehkwi nihki yooloma wiyehi silawiiwaate hini skipaki mhtekoki nehiwe weh silawiipi hini kayahkiteeki hisiwe

For if they do these things in the green tree, what shall be done in the dry?

32. chiine nitasi nehfaapi niiswi kotakaki piimilehfiiki wiiciweloofooki nili wahsi nhfekwiwaaci

And there were also two others, malefactors, led with him to be put to death.

33. chiine nihki nahiika yeh piyaawaaci hini tasi hini hokanaatepi yeesitooteeki nitasi nihki hotaasitefhwaawaali nili mecimi nihi piimilehfihi nekoti hini mayaawiinhkiki mecimi hina kotaka hini namaciinhkiki

And when they came unto the place which is called The skull, there they crucified him, and the malefactors, one on the right hand and the other on the left.

34. mecimi ciisisii hohfima pakfeeletamawi ksake nihki mata howaakotaanaawa yaasilawiiwaaci hiwa chiine peemi pahfenamaatilici hopiitenikana heelekiina nihi kiskinikanitalwaatiiki nihki

And Jesus said, Father, forgive them; for they know not what they do. And parting his garments among them, they cast lots.

35. chiine nihki lenaweeki niipawiiki peemaapacikeewaaci chiine nihki teepeelecikeecki nehfaapi howaapalaacimaawaali nili kotakhi howaapaneshahi wiilaani waapanestoote wiiya kwehkwi hinawite yaama nili hoklaistiimali maneto homamaawenali hiwaki

And the people stood beholding. And the rulers also scoffed at him, saying, He saved others; let him save himself, if this is the Christ of God, his chosen.

36. chiine nihki samaakanaki nehfaapi howaapalaachaawaali nili howaotfaawaali howaawiisa miilaawaali pskipaapo

And the soldiers also mocked him, coming to him, offering him vinegar,

37. mecimi kwehkwi kiiyaawiyane hina hokimaamwaali nihki coosaki waapanestoolo kiiya yaawaki

and saying, If thou art the King of the Jews, save thyself.

38. mecimi nitasi nehfaapi lhspawikeewe hahteewi spemeki hina yaama hina hokimaamwaali nihki coosaki lawikaate

And there was also a superscription over him, THIS IS THE KING OF THE JEWS.

39. chiine nekoti nihi piimilehfihi layaapicimoofolici howaapalaacimekooli ha mata hina klaistii kiila waapanestoolo kiiya mecimi niilawe hotekooli

And one of the malefactors which were hanged railed on him, saying, Art not thou the Christ? save thyself and us.

40. payeekwa hina kotaka haapafse mecimi hokwtelaali nili ha mata kikwfa wiikinaakwi maneto kineeme hini yaska si matahkowaafooweneki kitapi

But the other answered, and rebuking him said, Dost thou not even fear God, seeing thou art in the same condemnation?

41. chiine kiilawe sapkahi tepasawi ksake kootfekope hini nehalwaaka kitephofiiwenena kitesilawiiwenena hoci weeka yaama hileni mata wiyehi piimilawi hisiwe

And we indeed justly; for we receive the due reward of our deeds: but this man hath done nothing amiss.

42. chiine ciisisii mhkaweelemilo hine piyaayane kokimaawitaamhkomeki hisiwe

And he said, Jesus, remember me when thou comest in thy kingdom.

43. mecimi hina tepilo kitele niila hinoki kaasekiki keh wiici hapiimi tah menwi lenaweewiki hotelaali nili

And he said unto him, Verily I say unto thee, Today shalt thou be with me in Paradise.

44. chiine hini howe nawito hini mawi-nekotwahfwi yaatefaki mecimi peepekicaaki piyeeya hini mefhiike hasiskiiki paalohi hini mawi-caakatfwi yaatefaki

And it was now about the sixth hour, and a darkness came over the whole land until the ninth hour,

45. hini howahfeeyaami hina kiisekikiisfwa haalofiiya mecimi hini laapicimota hini mamaatomeewikamikoki lelhkehka hini heelekhi

the sun's light failing: and the veil of the temple was rent in the midst.

46. chiine ciisisii pemi holaami kalawi hohfima kileciwali niteh wiyawena nicacaalahkwa hiwa mecimi yeesi mehtoweeci hopakfenaali nili ciipali

And when Jesus had cried with a loud voice, he said, Father, into thy hands I commend my spirit: and having said this, he gave up the ghost.

47. chiine hina kaptiina yeh neemeki yeesilawiiki howahfaacimekofihaali manetooli sapkahi yaama tepasawi-leni hiwa

And when the centurion saw what was done, he glorified God, saying, Certainly this was a righteous man.

48. chiine caayahki nihki mehseelekki meemaawatwi piyeelotakki yooma waapakeewe yeh neemowaaci hini wiyehi yeesilawiiki peteki heeki hopemi pkitehaanaawa hopaleewa

And all the multitudes that came together to this sight, when they beheld the things that were done, returned smiting their breasts.

49. chiine caayahki howaakometiimhhi mecimi nihi hkwehi keeleliiki weeci neekalekoci niipawihi pelowihi peemi laapatamelici yooloma wiyehi

And all his acquaintance, and the women that followed with him from Galilee, stood afar off, seeing these things.

50. chiine waapamehko hileni coosii sinoofo taatepoweeta hina howesiilefi mecimi tepasawi-leni

And behold, a man named Joseph, who was a councillor, a good man and a righteous

51. mata hina homehci nhkotamawahi hotelahkoweewenilici mecimi hotesilawiiwenilici haalimefiye hoci hileni hoteewenwa nihki coosaki peemi hina natawaapataki hini hokimaawitaamhkomi maneto

(he had not consented to their counsel and deed), a man of Arimathaea, a city of the Jews, who was looking for the kingdom of God:

52. yaama hileni paalatiili heewa mecimi natotamaake nili howiiyaanali ciisisii

this man went to Pilate, and asked for the body of Jesus.

53. mecimi holaasiweenaali nili chiine hotetepahpilaali nili waapimafaanimotaaki chiine hoteh seksimaali nepoowaalakoki siikoneki yeelaalakehooteeki tah matalaakwa keewaki hileni meh seksiki

And he took it down, and wrapped it in a linen cloth, and laid him in a tomb that was hewn in stone, where never man had yet lain.

54. chiine hine hini nanahiiwe si kaasekiki hini mecimi hini halwaakahsi kaasekiki halemi mawaapanwi

And it was the day of the Preparation, and the sabbath drew on.

55. chiine nihki hkweeki mayehci piyeci wiitfeemaacki nili keelelii hoci neekasiweeki mecimi hotelaapataanaawa hini nepoowaalakwi chiine yeesisimoofolici howiiyaanali

And the women, which had come with him out of Galilee, followed after, and beheld the tomb, and how his body was laid.

56. mecimi nihki peteki heeki chiine honanahilotaanaawa waakimiyaakoki mecimi lominoowena chiine hini ta halwaakahsi kiisekiki halwaakahsiiki nihki yeesfeki hini tepikeemoowe

And they returned, and prepared spices and ointments. And on the sabbath they rested according to the commandment.

Luke:24

1. payeekwa hini ta nhhihta kiisekiki hini nekoti niiswahfwikiiskwe piyeeki nihki hini nepoowaalakoki tah kolahwaapaki hopiyeetoonaawa nili waakimiyaakoki mayehci nanahilotamowaaci

But on the first day of the week, at early dawn, they came unto the tomb, bringing the spices which they had prepared.

2. chiine nihki nili siikonali homhkawaawaali kolepenoofooli hini nepoowaalakoki hoci

And they found the stone rolled away from the tomb.

3. chiine piicfeeki nihki mecimi mata homhkawaawaali nili howiiyaanali ciisisii hina teepeelemiweeta

And they entered in, and found not the body of the Lord Jesus.

4. chiine hini piyeemikatwi yeheeyehi nihki wanhfoneewaaci hini maalektasi waapamehko niiswi hileniiki niipawiiki maalaakwahi nihi wahfiikwifoowaseki

And it came to pass, while they were perplexed thereabout, behold, two men stood by them in dazzling apparel:

5. chiine yeesi nihi cihfefilici mecimi sahkiki hini hasiskiiki laapeskaalici nihki koociwe kinatonehwaawa hina lenaweewita heelekiina nili nepelici

and as they were affrighted, and bowed down their faces to the earth, they said unto them, Why seek ye the living among the dead?

6. mata hina hotasi hapiwa honhska weeka mhkaweeletamoko yeesi kaloolelwaakwe hina hine keewaki keeleliiki ye hapici

He is not here, but is risen: remember how he spake unto you when he was yet in Galilee,

7. hiwa wahsi hina hokwihfali hileni nili holeciwa meciileficki hileniiki kwiilahi si pakfenoofoci mecimi haasitefhoofoci chiine hini mawi-nhfoko honhskaaci nohki hotelaawahi nihi

saying that the Son of man must be delivered up into the hands of sinful men, and be crucified, and the third day rise again.

8. chiine nihki homhkaweeletaanaawa hina hokalawiiwe

And they remembered his words,

9. mecimi hini nepoowaalakoki hoci peteki heeki chiine howiitamawaawahi nihi metahfwi-kite-nekoti caayahki yooloma wiyehi mecimi nihi maisi caayahki

and returned from the tomb, and told all these things to the eleven, and to all the rest.

10. howe nihkiini melii mekiteliina chiine coena chiine melii nili hokeeli ceemhsii chiine wiici nihi nihki kotakaki hkweeki howiitamawaawahi nihi hepastalihi yooloma wiyehi

Now they were Mary Magdalene, and Joanna, and Mary the mother of James: and the other women with them told these things unto the apostles.

11. mecimi yooloma kalawiiwena paasi nelohci pekikalawiiwe hoteleeletaanaawa nihki mecimi mata hoteepwehtawaawahi nihi hkwehi

And these words appeared in their sight as idle talk; and they disbelieved them.

12. payeekwa piita pafekwi mecimi hini nepoowaalakoki si kwakwi chiine waakiceelwa piitike laapi honeemena nili mafaanimotaawali naanhsihka hahteewa nili mecimi pakici yeetaaci heewa hopemi mayateeleta hini peepiyeemikaki

But Peter arose, and ran unto the tomb; and stooping and looking in, he seeth the linen cloths by themselves; and he departed to his home, wondering at that which was come to pass.

13. chiine waapamehko niiswi nihi hoci tepilo hine kaasekiki hoteeweneefeki peemi haalici hemeasi sitoote niiswahfwi-kite-pahfi maiili hahteewi hini colooseelemiiki hoci

And behold, two of them were going that very day to a village named Emmaus, which was threescore furlongs from Jerusalem.

14. mecimi nihki haacimohtaatiiki caayahki yooloma wiyehi mayehci hiki

And they communed with each other of all these things which had happened.

15. chiine hini piyeemikatwi yehi nihki haacimowaaci mecimi natohtwaatiwaaci maa wiila piyeetfe ciisisii mecimi howiiteemahi nihi

And it came to pass, while they communed and questioned together, that Jesus himself drew near, and went with them.

16. payeekwa hoskiisekowa fookinooteeli wahsi pwaa nihki waakomaawaaci nili

But their eyes were holden that they should not know him.

17. chiine hina nehiwesi kalawiiwena yooloma kitiiyaasoonikaatipwa yeesi pemhfeeyeekwe hotelahi nihi mecimi noole niipawiiki nihki macilepwaawi naakofiiki

And he said unto them, What communications are these that ye have one with another, as ye walk? And they stood still, looking sad.

18. mecimi nekoti nihi kliiapasi sifooli haapafseeli ha naanhsihka kiila kikaakkehsi colooseelemiiki mecimi mata kiwaakotaana nili wiyehi nitasi peepiyeemikaki yoolooni kaasekiki hotekooli

And one of them, named Cleopas, answering said unto him, Dost thou alone sojourn in Jerusalem and not know the things which are come to pass there in these days?

19. nehiwesi wiyehi hotelaali mecimi hotekohi nihi nili wiyehi yeesinaki ciisisii naaselefilenawe maamoosikiiskweeta wiisikatowi silawiiweneki mecimi kalawiiweneki yeelahfamiilici manetooli chiine caayahki nihi lenawehi

And he said unto them, What things? And they said unto him, The things concerning Jesus of Nazareth, which was a prophet mighty in deed and word before God and all the people:

20. mecimi yeesi nihki hokimaawi
mhkateewkolayeeki chiine kiteepeelecikeemenaaki
nisi pakfenaawaaci nili wahsi nepooweneki si
miyaalahkowaaloofolici chiine haasitefhoofolici

and how the chief priests and our rulers
delivered him up to be condemned to
death, and crucified him.

21. payeekwa menawahike hina wah petekitepenaata
hiswiilali nitesiteheepe hanhka mecimi kooloci
caayahki yooma hini howe niinhfoko yooloma wiyehi
piyeemikato

But we hoped that it was he which should
redeem Israel. Yea and beside all this, it
is now the third day since these things
came to pass.

22. chiine nohki naanekoti hkweeki yeetfweeleyaake
hoci nimayacilepwahekonaaki hini nepoowaalakoki
homooki kwelahwaapaki

Moreover certain women of our company
amazed us, having been early at the
tomb;

23. chiine hine yeh pwaa mhkawaawaaci hina
howiiyaanali piyeeki nihki yeesi mehci nehfaapi
neemowaaci hiwaki honookofiiwenwa henhcaliiki
yeeyocki yeesi hina lenaweewici

and when they found not his body, they
came, saying, that they had also seen a
vision of angels, which said that he was
alive.

24. chiine naanekoti nihki niilawe yeesi wiiciwicki
hini nepoowaalakoki heeki mecimi homhkaanaawa
hini teetepila hinwi yeesi nihki hkweeki
mehtoweewaaci payeekwa nili mata homhkawaawaali
nihki

And certain of them that were with us
went to the tomb, and found it even so as
the women had said: but him they saw
not.

25. mecimi wiila hoteh kaloolahi nihi o wanihsakaawi
leniiki mecimi maalohfefiiya hotehiwa wahsi
teepwehtamowaaci mayehci nihki
maamoosikiiskwecki kalawiwaaci

And he said unto them, O foolish men,
and slow of heart to believe in all that the
prophets have spoken!

26. ha mata kwiila howesfenwi hini wahsi hina klaistii
hahkwinamoci yooloma wiyehi mecimi wahsi hottaki
howahfaacimekofiiwe

Behoved it not the Christ to suffer these
things, and to enter into his glory?

27. mecimi moosisiili chiine caayahki nihi
maamoosikiiskwelici hoci halemi laapaatotamawahi
nihi caayahki nili tepilo heewikaateewali hini wiyehi
wiila yeesfeki

And beginning from Moses and from all
the prophets, he interpreted to them in all
the scriptures the things concerning
himself.

28. chiine maalaakwahi piyeetfeeki nihki hini
hoteewenehi peemi haawaaci chiine hina paasi halika
laakwa wi haaci hotesto

And they drew nigh unto the village,
whither they were going: and he made as
though he would go further.

29. mecimi nihi hokcihkaakohi wiici kkehsiiminaake
ksake hini howe weelaakwiifiki wayeeci mecimi hini
kaasekiki howe maateefi hotekohi mecimi piicfe wahsi
wiici kkehsiimaaci nihi

And they constrained him, saying, Abide
with us: for it is toward evening, and the
day is now far spent. And he went in to
abide with them.

30. chiine hini piyeemikatwi hine hina yeh
mehtahkeepiimaaci nihi wahsi wihfeniwaaci hoteh
mame hini takhwa mecimi hokisaacto chiine
hoposkona hini hoteh miilahi nihi

And it came to pass, when he had sat
down with them to meat, he took the
bread, and blessed it, and brake, and gave
to them.

31. chiine hoskiisekowa tawenooteeli mecimi
howaakomaawaali nili mecimi yeelaapiwaaci hoci
hasenooli nili

And their eyes were opened, and they
knew him; and he vanished out of their
sight.

32. mecimi nihki ha mata kitehina fakte laameki kiiyaana yeelaakwasi kaloolelakwe hina hini miyeeweneki yeelaakwasi hina tawenamoolakwe nili tepilo heewikaateewali hitiiki

And they said one to another, Was not our heart burning within us, while he spake to us in the way, while he opened to us the scriptures?

33. mecimi tepilo hini yaatefaki pafekwiiki nihki chiine colooseelemii heeki chiine homhkawaawahi tepetwi maawaskahi nihi metahfwi-kite-nekoti mecimi nihi weewiiciimaacki nihi

And they rose up that very hour, and returned to Jerusalem, and found the eleven gathered together, and them that were with them,

34. hina teepeelemiweeta honhska sapkahi mecimi homehci tepinawkofihtawaali saimaniili hisiweeki

saying, The Lord is risen indeed, and hath appeared to Simon.

35. mecimi laapoweeki nili wiyehi yeesinamowaaci hini miyeeweneki chiine yeesi waakomekoci hina nihi ye hini poskonaki hini takhwa

And they rehearsed the things that happened in the way, and how he was known of them in the breaking of the bread.

36. chiine yeesi nihki kalawiwaaci yooloma wiyehi nehalwaaka nili maa niipawiili hini heelekhi nihi kaamaaniilefiiwe cehi kiilawa si hotelahi nihi

And as they spake these things, he himself stood in the midst of them, and saith unto them, Peace be unto you.

37. payeekwa nihki cihfefiiki chiine wiisaalepwaaki chiine yeesi toke neewaawaaci hocacaalahkwali siteheeki nihki

But they were terrified and affrighted, and supposed that they beheld a spirit.

38. chiine hina koociwe kipetfakifipwa mecimi nehiwe hoci natohseewena pafekwiiya kitehiwaaki hotelahi

And he said unto them, Why are ye troubled? and wherefore do reasonings arise in your heart?

39. waapatamoko nileciwali mecimi nifitali yeesi hini niila wiiya kotateniko mecimi neemoko ksake hocacaalahkwa mata hopoona wiyawfi chiine hokanali yeesi neewiyeekwe niila poonama

See my hands and my feet, that it is I myself: handle me, and see; for a spirit hath not flesh and bones, as ye behold me having.

40. mecimi hine yeemehtoweci yooma howaapatelhi nihi holeciwali mecimi hofitali

And when he had said this, he shewed them his hands and his feet.

41. chiine yehi keewaki pwaa teepwehseelici howesilepwaawe hoci mecimi kwakwehtaanitehehi ha hotasi kipoonaanaawa nehcipehi wiyehi wah miiciki hotelahi

And while they still disbelieved for joy, and wondered, he said unto them, Have ye here anything to eat?

42. mecimi homiilaawaali nihki maalekhi namehfali fahfikaafooli

And they gave him a piece of a broiled fish.

43. chiine hina homamaali nili mecimi hotamwaali yeelahfamiilici nihi

And he took it, and did eat before them.

44. mecimi hina yooloma nikalawiiwena keekaloolelako niila yeheeyehi keewaki wiiciwiya kiilawa wahsi caayahki wiyehi kwiilahi weecita hokwaawfetooteeki mayehtawikeeki hini hokwteletiiweneki moosisii chiine nihki maamoosikiiskwecki chiine nili saamiiwekamoowena niila yeesfeki hotelahi

And he said unto them, These are my words which I spake unto you, while I was yet with you, how that all things must needs be fulfilled, which are written in the law of Moses, and the prophets, and the psalms, concerning me.

45. hine howe hotawenamawahi
homemekinitehaakanilici wahsi nihki menawahi
nenohtamowaaci nili tepilo heewikaateewali

Then opened he their mind, that they might understand the scriptures;

46. mecimi halayini hini mayehtawikeeki wahsi hina
klaistii weecita hahkwinaki mecimi nili nepelici hoci
honhskaaci hini mawi-nhfoko

and he said unto them, Thus it is written, that the Christ should suffer, and rise again from the dead the third day;

47. chiine hina howiifooweneki wahsi weecita
nanahimoofoci matayinisiteheewe mecimi
laawatenamaatiiwe maciilefiiwena caayahki si lenawe
yeetfweeleki colooseelemiiki we hoci halemiiya

and that repentance and remission of sins should be preached in his name unto all the nations, beginning from Jerusalem.

48. kiilawa nihkiini teepweewenaki yooloma wiyehi

Ye are witnesses of these things.

49. mecimi waapatamoko hoskici kiilawa nitesfato
hini hokisaacimiweewe nohfa payeekwa kiilawa
hapiko hini hoteeweneki paalohi
piitenikehoofoyeekwe waasikaki spemeki hoci
hotelahi nihi

And behold, I send forth the promise of my Father upon you: but tarry ye in the city, until ye be clothed with power from on high.

50. chiine holohfewelahi nihi paalohi hapiiki
maalaakwahi pefeneki chiine spemeki si ciikileceska
hokisaacilotawahi nihi

And he led them out until they were over against Bethany: and he lifted up his hands, and blessed them.

51. chiine hini piyeemikatwi yeheeyehi
kisaacilotawaaci hina nihi hoci pahfehka mecimi
spemeki menhkwatoki siweloofo

And it came to pass, while he blessed them, he parted from them, and was carried up into heaven.

52. mecimi nihki hosilawehaawaali nili chiine peteki
colooseelemii heeki wiitefiiki mhsi howesilepwaawe

And they worshipped him, and returned to Jerusalem with great joy:

53. mecimi kaakika hini mamaatomeewikamikoki
hapiiki hokisaacilotawaawaali manetooli

and were continually in the temple, blessing God.

JOHN

John:1

1. hine halemahkamikatwi hapiwa hina kalawiiwena chiine hina kalawiiwena wiici hapiwa manetooli mecimi maneto hina kalawiiwena

In the beginning was the Word, and the Word was with God, and the Word was God.

2. hina yaska wiici hapiwa manetooli hine halemahkamikatwi

The same was in the beginning with God.

3. caayahki wiyehi mectoote saapwi hina mecimi faakici hina mata wiyehi mectoote mayectooteeki

All things were made by him; and without him was not anything made that hath been made.

4. wiiyaaki hina hahteewi lenaweewiiwe mecimi hini lenaweewiiwe hini howahfeeyaamwa hileniiki

In him was life; and the life was the light of men.

5. chiine hini wayahfeeyaaki wahfekeeya hini laa pepekica mecimi hina laa pepekica hotaalwi nenohta hini

And the light shineth in the darkness; and the darkness apprehended it not.

6. nitasi piyeewa hileni manetooli hoci waawiineskoofo caanii si wiifooweni

There came a man, sent from God, whose name was John.

7. yaska hina teepweewena weeci piyaaci wahsi menawahi pah niimeki hini wayahfeeyaaki si teepweewe wahsi menawahi caayahki teepwehseewaaci saapwi nili

The same came for witness, that he might bear witness of the light, that all might believe through him.

8. mata hina hini wayahfeeyaaki weeka piyeewa wahsi menawahi pah niimeki hini wayahfeeyaaki si teepweewe

He was not the light, but came that he might bear witness of the light.

9. nitasi hahteewi hini mayaawi wayahfeeyaaki teetepilahi hini wayahfeeyaaki wayahfemekoci caaki hileni payeci piyaata hini yeelekokwahkamikiki

There was the true light, even the light which lighteth every man, coming into the world.

10. hina hini yeelekokwahkamikiki hapiwa mecimi hini yeelekokwahkamikiki mectoote saapwi hina chiine hini yeelekokwahkamikiki mata howaakomeko

He was in the world, and the world was made by him, and the world knew him not.

11. honhhalwaafiiwena si piyeewa mecimi nihi nehalwaafiici hotahpenekohi mata

He came unto his own, and they that were his own received him not.

12. payeekwa yeetfwi hotahpenekoci nihiini hina homiilahi hini mayaawefiiwe wahsi hotapelohfeminaaci maneto teetepilahi nihi teeteepwehtamelici howiifoowe

But as many as received him, to them gave he the right to become children of God, even to them that believe on his name:

13. nihkiini hoskilenaweewiiki mata mhskwi hoci matanohki hini yeesiteheeweniki hini wiyawfi hoci weelaa mata nohki hini hileni hotesiteheewe hoci maneto hoci weeka

which were born, not of blood, nor of the will of the flesh, nor of the will of man, but of God.

14. chiine hina kalawiiwena wiyawfiwi mecimi wiici teewa heelekiina kiilawe mecimi kitelaapataape howahfaacimekofiiwe paasi howahfaacimekofiiwe

And the Word became flesh, and dwelt among us (and we beheld his glory, glory

hina nekotoosaaka hina hohfima hoci hokwihfenwili
kisaaciwiiwe chiine teepweewe

as of the only begotten from the Father),
full of grace and truth.

15. caanii hopah niimawaali teepweewe nili mecimi
yeelahootaki yaama hina yoona yaacimaka hina
peepiyeci neekasita howe niikaani hapiwa ksake hina
nhhihta niila si hiwa

John beareth witness of him, and crieth,
saying, This was he of whom I said, He
that cometh after me is become before me:
for he was before me.

16. ksake hini hotkwaawefiiwe caayahki kotefipe
kiilawe mecimi kisaaciwiiwe hasowe kisaaciwiiwe

For of his fulness we all received, and
grace for grace.

17. ksake hini kwteletiiwe miiliweepi saapwi
moosisii kisaaciwiiwe mecimi teepweewe piyeeya
saapwi ciisisii klaistii

For the law was given by Moses; grace
and truth came by Jesus Christ.

18. mata hileni homeh neewaali manetooli laakwa
nehcipehi hina nekotoosaaka hokwihfima yeepita
hotakonikeeweneki hina hohfima hina homehci
mohkaacimaali nili

No man hath seen God at any time; the
only begotten Son, which is in the bosom
of the Father, he hath declared him.

19. mecimi halayooma hini hoteepweeweniwiiwe
caanii hine nihki coosaki colooseelemii hoci
piyeelhkamawaawaali mhkateewkolayehi chiine
liifaaihi wahsi neefawe kiila si natohtaakoci

And this is the witness of John, when the
Jews sent unto him from Jerusalem priests
and Levites to ask him, Who art thou?

20. mecimi tepasawaacimo chiine mata kihaacimo
mecimi mata niiya hina klaistii si tepasawaacimo

And he confessed, and denied not; and he
confessed, I am not the Christ.

21. mecimi nihki neefawe howe ha hilaica kiila hotesi
natohtawaawaali nili mecimi hina mata hina niila
hisiwe ha hina maamoosikiiskweeta kiila mecimi
hina mata si haapafse

And they asked him, What then? Art thou
Elijah? And he saith, I am not. Art thou
the prophet? And he answered, No.

22. nihki weecikeenahi neefawe kiila wahsi
menawahi miilakici hotaapafseewe nihki
weewaawiineskawiyamekicki nehiwe kiteta kiiya
hotelaawaali nili

They said therefore unto him, Who art
thou? that we may give an answer to them
that sent us. What sayest thou of thyself?

23. yoona niila hina nekoti wiyeefa hini
talahootamwa laa piileski tepilahi sfetooko hini
homiyeewi hina teepeelemiweeta yeeyoci hina
maamoosikiiskweeta haisaya hisiwe

He said, I am the voice of one crying in
the wilderness, Make straight the way of
the Lord, as said Isaiah the prophet.

24. chiine nihki nihi pelesihi hoci mehci
waawiineskoofooki

And they had been sent from the
Pharisees.

25. chiine nihki honatohtawaawaali nili mecimi
koociwe howe kifafahkwi holelhiwe kiila kwehkwi
yo mata hina klaistii kiila mata nohki hilaica nohki
mata hina maamoosikiiskweeta hotelaawaali

And they asked him, and said unto him,
Why then baptizest thou, if thou art not
the Christ, neither Elijah, neither the
prophet?

26. hotaapaftawahi caanii nepiki niila nitesi fafahkwi
holelhiwe heelekiina kiilawa niipawi nekoti mata
kiwaakomaawa hina

John answered them, saying, I baptize
with water: in the midst of you standeth
one whom ye know not,

27. teetepila hina peepiyeci neekasita nili
homenifepiye ninootkwiilefi wahsi pelhamawaki
hisiwe

even he that cometh after me, the latchet
of whose shoe I am not worthy to unloose.

28. pefeneki tasi lawiipi yooloma wiyehi halika wiyeeci hini caatenii tah peemi fafahkwi holelhiweeci caanii

These things were done in Bethany beyond Jordan, where John was baptizing.

29. wayaapaki honeewaali ciisisiili peemi hotfekoci waapamehko nili hopalasaanimeekiifemali maneto yaamiwetoolici hini homaciilefiiwe hina yeelekokwahkamikiki hiwa mecimi

On the morrow he seeth Jesus coming unto him, and saith, Behold, the Lamb of God, which taketh away the sin of the world!

30. hina yaama yaacimaka hahkowi niila hileni piyeewa yeelahfamiwemita ksake hina nhhihta hapiwa niila

This is he of whom I said, After me cometh a man which is become before me: for he was before me.

31. mecimi mata niwaakoma hina payeekwa wi hina tepinaakwi shoofoci laa hiswiila yooni ksake weeci piyaaya niila peemi fafahkwi holelhiweeya nepiki

And I knew him not; but that he should be made manifest to Israel, for this cause came I baptizing with water.

32. mecimi caanii hopahkaseena teepweewe nimehci hilaapama hina hocacaalahkwa peemi menhkwatoki hoci laasiwehsiki paasi miyaasipawiifa mecimi hina nili hoskici hapiwa hiwa

And John bare witness, saying, I have beheld the Spirit descending as a dove out of heaven; and it abode upon him.

33. chiine mata niwaakoma hina payeekwa hina weewaawiineskawita wahsi fafahkwi holelhiweeya nepiki hoskici kookwe-neefali-kaaci keh neewa hina hocacaalahkwa si laasiwehsinwa mecimi hapiwa hoskici nili hiina hina faafafahkwi holelhiweeta nili hofepi hocacaalahkwali nitekwa

And I knew him not: but he that sent me to baptize with water, he said unto me, Upon whomsoever thou shalt see the Spirit descending, and abiding upon him, the same is he that baptizeth with the Holy Spirit.

34. chiine nimehci neeme mecimi nimehci pah niime teepweewe yeesi yooloma niliini hokwihfici maneto

And I have seen, and have borne witness that this is the Son of God.

35. nohki hini wayaapaki peemi niipawici caanii chiine niiswi hokakehkimaafhi

Again on the morrow John was standing, and two of his disciples;

36. mecimi hoteh waapamaali ciisisiili yeesi hina pemhfeeci chiine waapamehko hopalasaanimeekiifemali maneto hiwa

and he looked upon Jesus as he walked, and saith, Behold, the Lamb of God!

37. chiine nihki niiswi kakehkimaafaki honootawaawaali kalawiili mecimi nihki honeekalaawaali ciisisiili

And the two disciples heard him speak, and they followed Jesus.

38. chiine maa si kokiiwa ciisisii mecimi hotelaapamahi nihi honeekalekohi nehiwe kinatonehaanaawa hotelahi mecimi lepaayii keekehkimiwe hiyoowe hini yeelaapaaci kalawiki taaniwe kiteta kiila hotekohi

And Jesus turned, and beheld them following, and saith unto them, What seek ye? And they said unto him, Rabbi (which is to say, being interpreted, Master), where abidest thou?

39. piyaako mecimi keh neemenaawa hotelahi nihi nihki piyeeki weecikeenahi mecimi honeemenaawa ta hapilici nili chiine honawhhaawaali hine kaasekiki nawito hini metahfene yaatefaki

He saith unto them, Come, and ye shall see. They came therefore and saw where he abode; and they abode with him that day: it was about the tenth hour.

40. nekoti nihki niiswi neenootawaacki caaniili kalawiili mecimi honeekalekooli heenhtlo hina saiman' piita hoceeninaali

One of the two that heard John speak, and followed him, was Andrew, Simon Peter's brother.

41. hina homhkawaali nhhihta nhhalwaaka hoceeninaali saimaniili mecimi nimhkawaape hina mesaaya neyehka hotelaali nili klaistii hiyoowe hini yeelaapaaci kalawiki

He findeth first his own brother Simon, and saith unto him, We have found the Messiah (which is, being interpreted, Christ).

42. hina ciisisiili hopiyeetawaali nili ciisisii howaapamaali nili saimanii kiila hina hokwihfali caanii siifasi ke haayekoopi hotelaali piita hiyoowe hini yeelaapaaci kalawiki

He brought him unto Jesus. Jesus looked upon him, and said, Thou art Simon the son of John: thou shalt be called Cephas (which is by interpretation, Peter).

43. hini wayaapaki keeleliiki wahsi haaci sitehe mecimi homhkawaali filapiili chiine neekasilo hotelaali ciisisii

On the morrow he was minded to go forth into Galilee, and he findeth Philip: and Jesus saith unto him, Follow me.

44. howe filapii pefseite hoci hini hoteewenwa heenhtlo chiine piita

Now Philip was from Bethsaida, of the city of Andrew and Peter.

45. filapii homhkawaali nefenialiili mecimi nimehci mhkawaape hina hini hokwteletiiweneki moosisii mecimi nihki maamoosikiiskwecki yeetalawikaalaawaaci ciisisii naaselefi hoci hokwihfali coosii hotelaali

Philip findeth Nathanael, and saith unto him, We have found him, of whom Moses in the law, and the prophets, did write, Jesus of Nazareth, the son of Joseph.

46. mecimi nefeniali kanhha wiyehsi howesi wiyehi katawi hoci lohfeya hini naaselefi hotelaali piyaalo mecimi neemelo hotelaali filapii

And Nathanael said unto him, Can any good thing come out of Nazareth? Philip saith unto him, Come and see.

47. ciisisii honeewaali nefenialiili peemi hotfekoci waapamehko sapkahi hiswiila si lenawe wiiyaaki matalaakwa nhhiwanimefiiwe hotelaali nili

Jesus saw Nathanael coming to him, and saith of him, Behold, an Israelite indeed, in whom is no guile!

48. taaniwe kooci waakomi hotelaali nefeniali ciisisii haapafse mecimi wihsi pwaa hotahpimehki filapii hine siipaaci hini kicimiisi kitapi kinoole hotelaali

Nathanael saith unto him, Whence knowest thou me? Jesus answered and said unto him, Before Philip called thee, when thou wast under the fig tree, I saw thee.

49. nefeniali hotaapaftawaali lepaayii nili maneto hokwihfali kiila hokimaamali hiswiila kiila hotelaali

Nathanael answered him, Rabbi, thou art the Son of God; thou art King of Israel.

50. ciisisii haapafse mecimi ksake kinoole siipaaci hini kicimiisi kitele ha kiteepwehse keh neemena kiila halika yeeki wiyehi noota yooloma hotelaali

Jesus answered and said unto him, Because I said unto thee, I saw thee underneath the fig tree, believest thou? thou shalt see greater things than these.

51. chiine tepilo tepilo kitele niila keh neemenaawa hini menhkwatwi weh taweska mecimi nihi hotenhcaliimhhi maneto peemi hakoofiweelici chiine peemi laasiweelici hoskici nili hokwihfali hileni hotelaali

And he saith unto him, Verily, verily, I say unto you, Ye shall see the heaven opened, and the angels of God ascending and descending upon the Son of man.

John:2

1. chiine hini mawi-nhfwi kaasekiki keena tasi wiichetipi piicitaamhkwe keelelii chiine nili hokeeli ciisisii nitasi hapiili

And the third day there was a marriage in Cana of Galilee; and the mother of Jesus was there:

2. mecimi ciisisii nehfaapi si halenoofo mecimi hokakehkimaafhi hini wiichetiiweneki

and Jesus also was bidden, and his disciples, to the marriage.

3. chiine hine hini waiini yeh nootkoskaaki nili hokeeli ciisisii mata nihki hopoonaanaawa waiini hotekooli

And when the wine failed, the mother of Jesus saith unto him, They have no wine.

4. mecimi ciisisii hkweewa nehiwe nipoona wahsi lawihtoola niila nitaatefamoowe mata keewaki meh piyeeya hotelaali

And Jesus saith unto her, Woman, what have I to do with thee? mine hour is not yet come.

5. kookwe-nehi-kaaci hina ke hikowa hini silawiiko hotelahi hina hokeeli nihi haloolaakaafhi

His mother saith unto the servants, Whatsoever he saith unto you, do it.

6. howe nitasi hapiiki nekotwahfwi siikoninepiwakokooki lematapiiki nitasi yaasi hini hofepi lawiiwaaci coosaki hoci nhfwaasikfwi weelaa metahfwi keelena si piskaafi nekoti

Now there were six waterpots of stone set there after the Jews' manner of purifying, containing two or three firkins apiece.

7. hokwikomhehko nihki nepiwakokooki nepi hotelahi nihi ciisisii mecimi nihki hotepacikamhhwaawahi nihi

Jesus saith unto them, Fill the waterpots with water. And they filled them up to the brim.

8. chiine hina howe fiikinamoko mecimi hina siwetooko noosaacikana hini wihfenhcikeewe hotelahi nihi mecimi nihki hotesiwetoonaawa hini

And he saith unto them, Draw out now, and bear unto the ruler of the feast. And they bare it.

9. mecimi hine hina noosaacikana hini wihfenhcikeewe hokotata hini nepi howe waiiniiwi chiine mata howaakota weeciwiki hini weeka nihki haloolaakaafaki mayehci fiikinakki hini nepi howaakotaanaawa hina noosaacikana hini wihfenhcikeewe hotahpimaali nili mayakinhhaakanali

And when the ruler of the feast tasted the water now become wine, and knew not whence it was (but the servants which had drawn the water knew), the ruler of the feast calleth the bridegroom,

10. mecimi caaki hileni nhhihta hotaasi pakfena hini howesi waiini mecimi hileniiki yeh mehci tepeeletami menowaaci hine howe hini halika mecaafiki kiila hini kinhhaawaata howesi waiini paalohi hinoki hotelaali nili

and saith unto him, Every man setteth on first the good wine; and when men have drunk freely, then that which is worse: thou hast kept the good wine until now.

11. yooni yooma weeci halemiki hokikinooloowena silawi ciisisii hini keena tasi piicitaamhkwe keelelii mecimi hotepinawkofeto howahfaacimekofiiwe mecimi hokakehkimaafhi hoteepwehtaakohi

This beginning of his signs did Jesus in Cana of Galilee, and manifested his glory; and his disciples believed on him.

12. hahkowihi yooma keepaaniamii si paalacisinwa hina mecimi hokeeli chiine hoceeninahi chiine hokakehkimaafhi chiine nitasi hapiiki mata meci tfoko

After this he went down to Capernaum, he, and his mother, and his brethren, and his disciples: and there they abode not many days.

13. chiine hini hopemhfaasiweewenwa nihki coosaki howe maalaakwahi piyeeya mecimi ciisisii colooseelemii si kkwicsinwa

And the passover of the Jews was at hand, and Jesus went up to Jerusalem.

14. chiine homhkawahi hini mamaatomeewikamikoki nehke maamiyeekinaacki haaksinihi chiine meekiifhi chiine miyaasipawiifhi mecimi nihki yaasoonakki moni peemi lematapilici

And he found in the temple those that sold oxen and sheep and doves, and the changers of money sitting:

15. mecimi hina pihsaakana hoci mecto lihfiiwanhhika chiine hini mamaatomeewikamikoki hoci lohfelhkawahi caayahki neyiisweelena nihi meekiifhi chiine nihi haaksinihi chiine hofiikina homonemwa nihki moni yaasoonakki mecimi hokolepenaana hoteepaliimilici

and he made a scourge of cords, and cast all out of the temple, both the sheep and the oxen; and he poured out the changers' money, and overthrew their tables;

16. chiine nihi maamiyeekinaacki nihi miyaasipawiifhi yooci haamwetooko yooloma wiyehi teki wiitkiiwika stooko howiikiwaapimi nohfa hotelahi

and to them that sold the doves he said, Take these things hence; make not my Father's house a house of merchandise.

17. hokakehkimaafhi mhkaweeletamehi kiwiikiwaapeki si kisiteenaweewe neh caakameko yeesi hini si mehtawikeeki

His disciples remembered that it was written, The zeal of thine house shall eat me up.

18. nihki coosaki weecikeenahi haapafseeki mecimi nehiwesi kikinooloowe kiwaapatesipe yeesi yooloma wiyehi silawiiyani hotelaawaali nili

The Jews therefore answered and said unto him, What sign shewest thou unto us, seeing that thou doest these things?

19. ciisisii haapafse mecimi liikatenamoko yooma mamaatomeewikamikwi mecimi nhfoko hini ne hopatena hotelahi

Jesus answered and said unto them, Destroy this temple, and in three days I will raise it up.

20. nihki coosaki weecikeenahi niyeewaapitaki kite nekotwahfwi kkato yooma mamaatomeewikamikwi hopatenoote ha kiila nhfoko ke hopatena hini hiwaki

The Jews therefore said, Forty and six years was this temple in building, and wilt thou raise it up in three days?

21. payeekwa hini wiiya si mamaatomeewikamikwi si kalawi hina

But he spake of the temple of his body.

22. hine weecikeenahi hina nili nepelici ye hoci honhskaanoofoci hokakehkimaafhi mhkaweeletamehi yeesi hina kalawici yooma mecimi nihki hoteepwehtaanaawa hini tepilo heewikaateeki chiine hini kalawiiwe mayehci hiyoci ciisisii

When therefore he was raised from the dead, his disciples remembered that he spake this; and they believed the scripture, and the word which Jesus had said.

23. howe hine hina colooseelemiiki hapiwa ta hini pemhfaasiweeweniki laakwasi hini wihfenhcikeewe meci teepwehtamehi howiifoowe peemi hilaapatamelici hokikinooloowena yeesilawiici

Now when he was in Jerusalem at the passover, during the feast, many believed on his name, beholding his signs which he did.

24. payeekwa mata nihi hotalwahfeeletamawahi wiiya ciisisii ksake howaakomahi caayahki hilenihi

But Jesus did not trust himself unto them, for that he knew all men,

25. mecimi ksake mata hotakaawaata nehcipeh nekoti wih pah niimawaaci hileniili teepweewe ksake howaakota yehteelici wiiyaaki hileni

and because he needed not that any one should bear witness concerning man; for he himself knew what was in man.

John:3

1. howe hileni nitasi hapiwa nihki pelesiiki hoci nekatiimasi sinoofo teepeelemaata nihi coosahi

Now there was a man of the Pharisees, named Nicodemus, a ruler of the Jews:

2. hina yaska hotfaali nili tepehki piyeewa mecimi lepaayii niwaakotaape yeesi maneto hoci piyaayani kiila keekehkimiweeta ksake mata wiyeefa yah katawi yooloma kikinooloowena silawi yaasilawiiyani weeciwephi manetooli wiiciimekote hotelaali

The same came unto him by night, and said to him, Rabbi, we know that thou art a teacher come from God: for no man can do these signs that thou doest, except God be with him.

3. ciisisii haapafse mecimi tepilo tepilo kitele niila weeciwephi wiyeefa mayaki hoskilenaweewite mata hina hotah katawi neeme hini hokimaawitaamhkomi maneto hotelaali

Jesus answered and said unto him, Verily, verily, I say unto thee, Except a man be born anew, he cannot see the kingdom of God.

4. nehiwe wih si katawi hoskilenaweewi hileni hine pasitoofiwite ha wih katawi mawi-niisene piicfatamawaali holaamataakanilici hokeeli mecimi wi hoskilenaweewi hotelaali nekatiimasi

Nicodemus saith unto him, How can a man be born when he is old? can he enter a second time into his mother's womb, and be born?

5. haapafse ciisisii tepilo tepilo kitele niila weeciwephi wiyeefa nepi mecimi nili hocacaalahkwali hoci hoskilenaweewite mata hina hotah katawi piicfata hini hokimaawitaamhkomi maneto

Jesus answered, Verily, verily, I say unto thee, Except a man be born of water and the Spirit, he cannot enter into the kingdom of God.

6. hina weeoskilenaweewita hini wiyawfi hoci wiyawfiwi chiine hina weeoskilenaweewita nili hocacaalahkwali hoci hocacaalahkowi

That which is born of the flesh is flesh; and that which is born of the Spirit is spirit.

7. teki kwakwehtaaniteheelo kwiila hoskilenaweewiko yeesi hilela

Marvel not that I said unto thee, Ye must be born anew.

8. hini mehsikkaki pootaacikeeya kookwe tasi yeesiteheeyaaki mecimi kiila kinoota yeesilweki nitasi payeekwa mata kiwaakota weemooyaaki hini mecimi yeheeyaaki hini yooni yeeki caakiwiyeefa weeoskilenaweewita nili hocacaalahkwali hoci hotelaali

The wind bloweth where it listeth, and thou hearest the voice thereof, but knowest not whence it cometh, and whither it goeth: so is every one that is born of the Spirit.

9. nekatiimasi haapafse mecimi nehiwe wih si katawi hino yooloma wiyehi hotelaali

Nicodemus answered and said unto him, How can these things be?

10. ciisisii haapafse mecimi ha kiila nili hokakehkimaamali hiswiila mecimi mata kinenohtaana yooloma wiyehi

Jesus answered and said unto him, Art thou the teacher of Israel, and understandest not these things?

11. tepilo tepilo kitele niila nikalawipe hini wayaakotamaake chiine nipah niimepe teepweewe hini mayehci neemeyaake mecimi kiilawa mata kootahpenaanaawa niteepweewenena

Verily, verily, I say unto thee, We speak that we do know, and bear witness of that we have seen; and ye receive not our witness.

12. kwehkwi wiitamoolako hasiski si wiyehi mecimi mata kiteepwehtaanaawa nehiwe keh si kiilawa teepwehtaanaawa wiitamoolako menhkwatoowi si wiyehi

If I told you earthly things, and ye believe not, how shall ye believe, if I tell you heavenly things?

13. chiine mata wiyeefa menhkwatoki meh laafiwe hina weeka menhkwatoki weeci laasiweeta teetepilahi nili hokwihfali hileni yeepita menhkwatoki

And no man hath ascended into heaven, but he that descended out of heaven, even the Son of man, which is in heaven.

14. chiine yeesi moosisii niimathwaaci nili manetooli hini laa piileski yooni teetepilahi kwiilahi hina hokwihfali hileni si niimathoofoci

And as Moses lifted up the serpent in the wilderness, even so must the Son of man be lifted up:

15. wahsi weecikeenahi kookwe-neefa-kaaci teepwehse menawahi poonaki howiiyaawilici kookwelaakwasi lenaweewiiwe

that whosoever believeth may in him have eternal life.

16. ksake yooni hotesi hahkweeleta maneto hini yeelekokwahkamikiki weecikeenahi miiliwe honekotoosaakanali hokwihfali wahsi kookwe-neefa-kaaci teepwehtawaate nili pwaa hkwineci weeka poonaki kookwelaakwasi lenaweewiiwe

For God so loved the world, that he gave his only begotten Son, that whosoever believeth on him should not perish, but have eternal life.

17. ksake maneto mata hoteh waawiineskawaali nili hokwihfimaali hini yeelekokwahkamikiki wahsi wiyeh-lahkowaatamelici hini yeelekokwahkamikiki weeka wi hini yeelekokwahkamikiki waapanestooteeki saapwi nili

For God sent not the Son into the world to judge the world; but that the world should be saved through him.

18. hina teeteepwehtawaata nili mata wiyehlahkowaafo hina pwaayaa teepwehseeta neyehka mehtahkowaafo ksake hina mata neyehka hoteepwehta hini howiifoowe hina nekotoosaaka hokwihfali maneto

He that believeth on him is not judged: he that believeth not hath been judged already, because he hath not believed on the name of the only begotten Son of God.

19. chiine halayooma hini lahkowaafoowe yeesi hini wayahfeeyaaki hini yeelekokwahkamikiki piyeeyaaki mecimi hileniiki hahkweeletamowaaci kaaciika hini peepekicaaki noota hini wayahfeeyaaki ksake hopekatefiiwenwa macaafi

And this is the judgment, that the light is come into the world, and men loved the darkness rather than the light; for their works were evil.

20. ksake caakiwiyeefa mecaafiki yeesilawiita hosiikeeleta hini wayahfeeyaaki mecimi mata hini wayahfeeyaaki yah si piyeewa piilepe hopekatefiiwena wih mataatotooteeli

For every one that doeth ill hateth the light, and cometh not to the light, lest his works should be reproved.

21. weeka hina hini teepweewe yeesilawiita hini wayahfeeyaaki si piyeewa wahsi hopekatefiiwena menawahi tepinawkwitooteeki yeesi nili mehci pekatenooteeki manetooki

But he that doeth the truth cometh to the light, that his works may be made manifest, that they have been wrought in God.

22. hahkowihi hine yooloma wiyehi hini cotiyeewi taamhkweki si piyeeki ciisisii mecimi hokakehkimaafhi mecimi nitasi honakahsinoomahi nihi chiine fafahkwi holelhiwe

After these things came Jesus and his disciples into the land of Judaea; and there he tarried with them, and baptized.

23. chiine caanii nehfaapi peemi fafahkwi holelhiweeci einaniiki maalaakwahi selimi ksake

And John also was baptizing in AEnon near to Salim, because there was much

nitasi memekanwi nepi mecimi nihki piyeeki chiine fafahkwi holelhoofooki

water there: and they came, and were baptized.

24. ksake mata caanii meh piicfe pakiloofo kiphotiiweneki

For John was not yet cast into prison.

25. weecikeenahi nitasi pafekwiiya natohtwaatiiwe hini wayeetahkwe hokakehkimaafhi caanii kileki coosali yeeki hofepilawiiwe

There arose therefore a questioning on the part of John's disciples with a Jew about purifying.

26. chiine nihki caaniili si piyeeki mecimi lepaayii hina weewiitafoomehka hini halika wiyeeci caatenii mayehci pah niimawata teepweewe waapami fafahkwi holelhiwe hina yaska mecimi caayahki hileniiki nili si piyeeki hotelaawaali

And they came unto John, and said to him, Rabbi, he that was with thee beyond Jordan, to whom thou hast borne witness, behold, the same baptizeth, and all men come to him.

27. haapafse caanii mecimi hileni katawi hotefi mata wiyehi weeciwephi menhkwatoki hoci mehci miilete hini

John answered and said, A man can receive nothing, except it have been given him from heaven.

28. kiilawa nehalwaaka kipah niimawipwa teepweewe mata niiya hina klaistii yeesi hiyoya weeka yeesi niila niikaaneskawaki hina

Ye yourselves bear me witness, that I said, I am not the Christ, but, that I am sent before him.

29. hina peepoonaata nili mayakinhhaakanehkweli mayakinhhaakana hina weeka nili wihkaanali hina mayakinhhaakana neniipawilici mecimi nootaakoci mhsi hosasilepwaali ksake hini mayakinhhaakana hotesihsimoowe yooni yooma weecikeenahi niila noosasilepwaawe hokwaawi stoote

He that hath the bride is the bridegroom: but the friend of the bridegroom, which standeth and heareth him, rejoiceth greatly because of the bridegroom's voice: this my joy therefore is fulfilled.

30. kwiila hina we skwiilefi weeka niila kwiilahi ne hoceekiilefi

He must increase, but I must decrease.

31. hina spemeki weemeka speelemekofi caayahki hina hini hasiskitaamhkwe weeciwita hini hasiskitaamhkwe hociwi mecimi hini hasiskitaamhkwe hotaatota hina menhkwatoki weemeka speelemekofi caayahki

He that cometh from above is above all: he that is of the earth is of the earth, and of the earth he speaketh: he that cometh from heaven is above all.

32. hini mayehci hina neemeki mecimi nootaki hopah niime hini si teepweewe mecimi mata hileni hotahpenamawaali hoteepweewenilici

What he hath seen and heard, of that he beareth witness; and no man receiveth his witness.

33. hina mayehci hotahpenamawaata hoteepweewenilici mehci peshalwe yooma yeesi maneto teepweewici

He that hath received his witness hath set his seal to this, that God is true.

34. ksake hina maneto mayehci waawiineskawaaci kalawi nili maneto hokalawiiwena ksake hina mata tepacika si miiliwe nili hocacaalahkwali

For he whom God hath sent speaketh the words of God: for he giveth not the Spirit by measure.

35. hina hohfima hotahkweelemaali nili hokwihfimaali mecimi holeciwilici si miiliwe caayahki wiyehi

The Father loveth the Son, and hath given all things into his hand.

36. hina teeteepwehseeta nili hokwihfimaali hopoona kookwelaakwasi lenaweewiiwe weeka hina pwaayaa

He that believeth on the Son hath eternal life; but he that obeyeth not the Son shall

melonehtawaata nili hokwihfimaali mata weh neeme lenaweewiiwe weeka hini hokiteewe maneto we hateeli wiiyaaki

not see life, but the wrath of God abideth on him.

John:4

1. hine weecikeenahi hina teepeelemiweeta yeh waakotaki yeesi nihi pelesihi mehci nootaakeelici yeesi ciisisii peemi hoshaaci mecimi fafahkwi holelhaaci halika tfwi kakehkimaafhi noota caanii

When therefore the Lord knew how that the Pharisees had heard that Jesus was making and baptizing more disciples than John

2. weekhi ciisisii mata wiila fafahkwi holelhiwe hokakehkimaafhi weeka

(although Jesus himself baptized not, but his disciples),

3. honakata hina cotiye mecimi nohki keeleliiki heewa

he left Judaea, and departed again into Galilee.

4. mecimi kwiilahi semeliyeki si saapwi pemhfe

And he must needs pass through Samaria.

5. weecikeenahi semeliyewi hoteewe si piyeewa saika sitoote maalaakwahi hini maalekhi hasiski ceekapii meemiilaaci hokwihfali coosiili

So he cometh to a city of Samaria, called Sychar, near to the parcel of ground that Jacob gave to his son Joseph:

6. mecimi ceekapii hotkikami hahteewi nitasi ciisisii weecikeenahi teewahi lohkatefi hopaamhfeewe hini yeelahkeepici pakaci hini tkikami nawito nekotwahfene yaatefaki hini

and Jacob's well was there. Jesus therefore, being wearied with his journey, sat thus by the well. It was about the sixth hour.

7. nitasi piyeewa semeliye hoci hkweewa wahsi piyeetapitooci nepi miililo wahsi meneya hotelaali ciisisii

There cometh a woman of Samaria to draw water: Jesus saith unto her, Give me to drink.

8. ksake hokakehkimaafhi hini hoteeweneki hehi wahsi tepenamelici wihfeniiwe

For his disciples were gone away into the city to buy food.

9. hina semeliyewiikwe weecikeenahi nehiwe hinwi hini yeesi kiila weekhi coosa natotamawiyani menoowe semeliyewiikwe niila hotelaali ksake coosaki mata howesi nhhalweeletiimaawahi semeliyewilenawehi

The Samaritan woman therefore saith unto him, How is it that thou, being a Jew, askest drink of me, which am a Samaritan woman? (For Jews have no dealings with Samaritans.)

10. haapafse ciisisii mecimi kwehkwi waakotamane hini hoteephetiiwe maneto mecimi hina wiyeefa miililo wahsi meneya yeelehka neyehka kih natotamawa hina mecimi neyehka hina kih miilekwa kiila lenaweewiiyaaki nepi hotelaali

Jesus answered and said unto her, If thou knewest the gift of God, and who it is that saith to thee, Give me to drink; thou wouldest have asked of him, and he would have given thee living water.

11. yeeleniwiyani mata wiyehi kipoona wah piyeetapicikeeyani mecimi hini tkikami spaalakatwi taaniwe howe kooci poona hini lenaweewiiyaaki nepi hotelaali hina hkweewa

The woman saith unto him, Sir, thou hast nothing to draw with, and the well is deep: from whence then hast thou that living water?

12. ha halika kitelefi kohfena ceekapii hina meemiilelakwe hini tkikami mecimi nhhalwaaka wiila nitasi hoci menwa chiine hokwifhi mecimi homhfoofoomhhi

Art thou greater than our father Jacob, which gave us the well, and drank thereof himself, and his sons, and his cattle?

13. ciisisii haapafse mecimi caakiwiyeefa meemeneka yooma nepi weh kahkalaamo nohki

Jesus answered and said unto her, Every one that drinketh of this water shall thirst again:

14. weeka kookwe-neefa-kaaci menwa hini nepi wah miilaki niila matalaakwa yah kahkalaamo weeka hini nepi wah miilaki niila we tkikamiiwili wiiyaaki nepi kookwelaakwasi lenaweewiiweneki si mokitanwili hotelaali nili

but whosoever drinketh of the water that I shall give him shall never thirst; but the water that I shall give him shall become in him a well of water springing up unto eternal life.

15. yeeleniwiyani miililo yooma nepi wahsi pwaa niila kahkalaamoya mata nohki yooni lhkahi si mawi hotahpapitooya hotelaali hina hkweewa

The woman saith unto him, Sir, give me this water, that I thirst not, neither come all the way hither to draw.

16. nhhaale hotahpimi wehsiyana mecimi hotahfa wi heewa hotelaali ciisisii

Jesus saith unto her, Go, call thy husband, and come hither.

17. haapafse hina hkweewa mecimi mata nipoona wehsiya hotelaali koowesi mata nipoona wehsiya hiyo

The woman answered and said unto him, I have no husband. Jesus saith unto her, Thou saidst well, I have no husband:

18. ksake neyehka kimehci poonaaki niyaalanwi wehsiyani chiine hina peepoonata hinoki mata wehsiyana yooma kimehci teepwe hotelaali ciisisii

for thou hast had five husbands; and he whom thou now hast is not thy husband: this hast thou said truly.

19. yeeleniwiyani nimooleeleta yeesi kiila maamoosikiiskweewiyani hotelaali hina hkweewa

The woman saith unto him, Sir, I perceive that thou art a prophet.

20. nohfenaaki waosasilaweeki yooma tah- makwahkiki chiine kiilawa kiteyopwa wahsi colooseelemiiki hini tasi paapiyeeci hosasilaweewaaci hileniiki hotelaali hina hkweewa

Our fathers worshipped in this mountain; and ye say, that in Jerusalem is the place where men ought to worship.

21. hkweewa teepwehtawilo hini yaatefaki piyeeya hine mata yooma meekwahkiki mata nohki colooseelemiiki ke hosasilawehaawa hina hohfima hotelaali ciisisii

Jesus saith unto her, Woman, believe me, the hour cometh, when neither in this mountain, nor in Jerusalem, shall ye worship the Father.

22. kiwaosasilawehaawa kiilawa hina pwaayaa waakomeekwe niilawe niwaosasilawehaape hina weewaakomakita ksake waapanhsiiwe nihki coosaki hociwiiya

Ye worship that which ye know not: we worship that which we know: for salvation is from the Jews.

23. payeekwa hini yaatefaki piyeeya mecimi hinoki howe hine nihki tepilo weesasilawecki we hosasilawehaawaali nili hohfimaali hocacaalahkoki mecimi teepweeweneki ksake yohooni hina hohfima honatonehwahi wahsi hosasilawemici

But the hour cometh, and now is, when the true worshippers shall worship the Father in spirit and truth: for such doth the Father seek to be his worshippers.

24. hocacaalahkowi maneto mecimi nihki weeosasilawehaacki nili kwiilahi hosasilawehaawaali hocacaalahkoki mecimi teepweeweneki

God is a Spirit: and they that worship him must worship in spirit and truth.

25. niwaakota wahsi piyaaci mesaaya hina klaistii yaaloofota hine hina piyaate keh mohkaatotamaakona caayahki wiyehi hotelaali hina hkweewa

The woman saith unto him, I know that Messiah cometh (which is called Christ): when he is come, he will declare unto us all things.

26. niila keekaloolela niiya hina hotelaali ciisisii

Jesus saith unto her, I that speak unto thee am he.

27. chiine yoone howe piyehi hokakehkimaafhi mecimi nihki kwakwehtaaniteheeki yeesi hina kiikaloolaaci hkweeli payeekwa mata hileni nehiwe kinatoneha weelaa koociwe kikaloola hina hiwa

And upon this came his disciples; and they marveled that he was speaking with a woman; yet no man said, What seekest thou? or, Why speakest thou with her?

28. weecikeena hina hkweewa honakalaali honepiwakokooli mecimi weepfe hini hoteeweneki heewa mecimi nihi lenawehi

So the woman left her waterpot, and went away into the city, and saith to the men,

29. piyaako waapamehko hileni weewiitamawita caayahki wiyehi payeci silawiiya kanhha yaama hina klaistii hotelahi

Come, see a man, which told me all things that ever I did: can this be the Christ?

30. nihki hini hoteeweneki hoci lohfeeki mecimi homawi hotfaawaali nili

They went out of the city, and were coming to him.

31. hini heelekiini laakwa nihki kakehkimaafaki honanahpaacimaawaali lepaayii wihfenilo hiwaki

In the mean while the disciples prayed him, saying, Rabbi, eat.

32. payeekwa hina nipoona wihfeniiwe wah miiciya pwaayaa waakotameekwe hotelahi

But he said unto them, I have meat to eat that ye know not.

33. weecikeenahi nihki kakehkimaafaki kanhha wiyeefa hileni neyehka hopiyeetawaali wiyehi wah miicilici hitiiki

The disciples therefore said one to another, Hath any man brought him aught to eat?

34. wahsi silawiiya hini hotesiteheewe hina weewaawiineskawita mecimi wahsi mehcilotamawaki hopekatefiiwe hiini niwihfeniiwe hotelahi ciisisii

Jesus saith unto them, My meat is to do the will of him that sent me, and to accomplish his work.

35. ha hahsi niyeewi kiisahfo keewaki hahteewi chiine howe piyeeya hini kawaskwhaaweewe teki hiyoko waapatamoko kitelepwa niila maa laapiko kiskiisekowa mecimi maa si waapatamoko nili ktikaana yeesi nili neyehka wahkanakiyaaki wahsi kawaskwhaaweki

Say not ye, There are yet four months, and then cometh the harvest? behold, I say unto you, Lift up your eyes, and look on the fields, that they are white already unto harvest.

36. hina keekawaskwhaaweta hotfeko tephotiiwe mecimi hotesi maawatona mawifoowe kookwelaakwasi lenaweewiiweneki wahsi hina yeecikeeta mecimi hina keekawaskwhaaweta menawahi takwi hosasilepwaawaaci

He that reapeth receiveth wages, and gathereth fruit unto life eternal; that he that soweth and he that reapeth may rejoice together.

37. ksake yooni tasi hini hiyoowe teepweeweni nekoti hahcike mecimi kotaka kawaskwhaawe

For herein is the saying true, One soweth, and another reapeth.

38. kiteh waawiineskoolepwa wahsi kawaskwhaaweyeekwe tah pwaa kiilawa mehci pekatefiyeekwe kotakaki mehci pekatefiiki mecimi kiilawa kiteh piicfahekoopwa hopekatefiiwenwaaki

I sent you to reap that whereon ye have not laboured: others have laboured, and ye are entered into their labour.

39. mecimi hini hoteewe hoci meci nihki semeliyewilenaweeki hoteepwehtawaawaali nili ksake hini hokalawiiwe hina hkweewa

And from that city many of the Samaritans believed on him because of the

niwiitamaakwa caayahki wiyehi payeci silawiiya yeelaacimota

40. weecikeenahi hine nihki semeliyewilenaweeki hotfaawaali nili hokcihkawaawaali wahsi hapiimekowaaci mecimi nitasi hapiwa niisoko

41. chiine meci keewaki teepwehseeki ksake hokalawiiwe hoci

42. chiine nihki howe niteepwehseepe mata kiila kikalawiiwe hoci ksake niilawe nehalwaaka nimehci nootaakeepe mecimi niwaakotaape yeesi yaama sapkahi hinawici nili howaapanhsiiwenali hina yeelekokwahkamikiki hotelaawaali nili hkweeli

43. chiine hahkowihi nili niiswi kiiskwe nhhoci weepfe keeleliiki heewa

44. ksake nehalwaaka ciisisii tepinalekowe yeesi maamoosikiiskweeta pwaa poonaki hotakeelemekofiiwe honhhalwaakitaamhkoki

45. weecikeenahi hine keeleliiki yeh si piyaaci nihki keeleliiwilenaweeki hotahpenaawaali nili mehci neemooki caayahki nili wiyehi yeesilawiici colooseelemiiki ta hini wihfenhcikeeki ksake nihki nehfaapi hini heeki wihfenhcikeeweneki

46. nohki weecikeenahi keena si piyeewa piici taamhkwe keelelii ta hini nepi wayinihtooci mecimi nitasi hapiwa naanekoti hotakeelemekwileni hokwihfali hahkwilokeeli keepaaniamiiki

47. hine hina yeh nootaakeeci yeesi cotiye hoci piyeci lohfaalici ciisisiili keeleliiki haalici hina nili heewa mecimi honanahpaacimaali wahsi piyeci paalacisinelici chiine kiikehtaakoci hokwihfali ksake hina howe hini hilefi wah nepeka

48. weecikeenahi ciisisii mata kitah teepwehse wiyehisi weeciwephi neemeyane kikinooloowena mecimi kweekwehtaanhki hotelaali

49. yeeleniwiyani piyeci paalacsinelo wihsi pwaa nepeki nitapelohfema hotelaali hina hotakeelemekwileni

50. yehaayani haale kikwihfa lenaweewi hotelaali ciisisii hina hileni teepwehse hini kalawiiwe keekaloolaaci ciisisii mecimi hina weepfe yehaaci

51. chiine yeesi hina howe peemi paalacsiki honakskaakohi hotaloolaakaafhi yeesi hokwihfali lenaweewilici hiwahi

word of the woman, who testified, He told me all things that ever I did.

So when the Samaritans came unto him, they besought him to abide with them: and he abode there two days.

And many more believed because of his word;

and they said to the woman, Now we believe, not because of thy speaking: for we have heard for ourselves, and know that this is indeed the Saviour of the world.

And after the two days he went forth from thence into Galilee.

For Jesus himself testified, that a prophet hath no honour in his own country.

So when he came into Galilee, the Galilaeans received him, having seen all the things that he did in Jerusalem at the feast: for they also went unto the feast.

He came therefore again unto Cana of Galilee, where he made the water wine. And there was a certain nobleman, whose son was sick at Capernaum.

When he heard that Jesus was come out of Judaea into Galilee, he went unto him, and besought him that he would come down, and heal his son; for he was at the point of death.

Jesus therefore said unto him, Except ye see signs and wonders, ye will in no wise believe.

The nobleman saith unto him, Sir, come down ere my child die.

Jesus saith unto him, Go thy way; thy son liveth. The man believed the word that Jesus spake unto him, and he went his way.

And as he was now going down, his servants met him, saying, that his son lived.

52. honatohtawahi weecikeenahi hini yaatefaki hine hina halemi kakilweewefi holaako ta hini mawi-niiswahfene haatefaki hini kisifoowe honakaleko hotelaawaali weecikeenahi nihki

So he inquired of them the hour when he began to amend. They said therefore unto him, Yesterday at the seventh hour the fever left him.

53. yooni hoci hina hohfima howaakota yeesi hine hini yaatefaki hina kikwihfa lenaweewi hikoci ciisisiili mecimi teepwehse chiine caayahki hotfwikamikifiiwe

So the father knew that it was at that hour in which Jesus said unto him, Thy son liveth: and himself believed, and his whole house.

54. yooma nohki hini mawi-niiswi kikinooloowe yeesilawiici ciisisii cotiyeeki hoci mehci lohfe keeleliiki heewa

This is again the second sign that Jesus did, having come out of Judaea into Galilee.

John:5

1. hahkowihi hine yooloma wiyehi nitasi hahteewi howihfenhcikeewenwa nihki coosaki mecimi ciisisii colooseelemiiki si kkwicsinwa

After these things there was a feast of the Jews; and Jesus went up to Jerusalem.

2. howe nitasi colooseelemiiki hahteewi pehkwaakamiki pakaci hini meekiifiwi skwaate pefeste sitoote hiiploowaatoweeweneki niyaalanweelena spahkwikaani

Now there is in Jerusalem by the sheep gate a pool, which is called in Hebrew Bethesda, having five porches.

3. piitike yooloma seksinooki mhseelooki yeekwilokeecki keekeepiikweecki nenekificki yaapweeweficki

In these lay a multitude of them that were sick, blind, halt, withered.

5. chiine naanekoti hileni nhfwaapitaki-kite-nhfwaasikfwi kkato hoci nitasi hapiwa hokatoneeweneki

And a certain man was there, which had been thirty and eight years in his infirmity.

6. ciisisii yeh neewaaci nili peemi seksinelici mecimi howaakota yeesi nili howe mehci heesaye hoci hini hilefilici ha kih mefefihekoopi kitesitehe hotelaali

When Jesus saw him lying, and knew that he had been now a long time in that case, he saith unto him, Wouldest thou be made whole?

7. hina hahkwilokeewileni hotaapatawaali nili yeeleniwiyani mata nipoona hileni hini pehkwaakamiki wah si poonita hine yeh pookamhtooteeki hini nepi weeka yeheeyehi nhhaaya kotaka wiyeefa yeelahfamiiya sahkiki yaalhkamwa hisiwe

The sick man answered him, Sir, I have no man, when the water is troubled, to put me into the pool: but while I am coming, another steppeth down before me.

8. honhskaalo mamelo kitfani mecimi pemhfeelo hotelaali ciisisii

Jesus saith unto him, Arise, take up thy bed, and walk.

9. chiine weelena hina hileni mefefihoofo mecimi homame hotfani mecimi pemhfe howe hini halwaakahsiwiiwe hine kaasekiki

And straightway the man was made whole, and took up his bed and walked. Now it was the sabbath on that day.

10. weecikeenahi nihki coosaki ce hini halwaakahsiwiiwe hini mecimi hini mata mayaawatwi kwteletiiweneki wahsi mameyani kitfani hotelaawaali nili keekiikehoofolici

So the Jews said unto him that was cured, It is the sabbath, and it is not lawful for thee to take up thy bed.

11. payeekwa hina hotaapaftawahi hina memefefihita mamelo kitfani mecimi pemhfeelo nitekwa hotelahi

But he answered them, He that made me whole, the same said unto me, Take up thy bed, and walk.

12. honatohtawaawaali nihki neefawe hina hileni mamelo kitfani mecimi pemhfeelo yeelehka

They asked him, Who is the man that said unto thee, Take up thy bed, and walk?

13. payeekwa hina keekiikehoofota mata howaakomaali si wiyefali nili ksake ciisisii payakila homehci siweto wiiya teewahi mehseeleka nitasi

But he that was healed wist not who it was: for Jesus had conveyed himself away, a multitude being in the place.

14. mayohkwaaci ciisisii homhkawaali nili hini mamaatomeewikamikoki mecimi waapatano kimefefihekoopi teki kiteeni maciisilawiilo piilepe halika si maci wiyehi ke hpene hotelaali

Afterward Jesus findeth him in the temple, and said unto him, Behold, thou art made whole: sin no more, lest a worse thing befall thee.

15. hina hileni weepfe mecimi howiitamawahi nihi coosahi yeesi hini ciisisiiwilici nili mayehci mefefihekoci

The man went away, and told the Jews that it was Jesus which had made him whole.

16. chiine yooma hoci nihki coosaki noochaalaawaali ciisisiili ksake hina yooloma wiyehi silawi ta halwaakahsiwiki

And for this cause did the Jews persecute Jesus, because he did these things on the sabbath.

17. payeekwa nihi hotaapaftawahi ciisisii nohfa pekatefi teetepilahi paalohi hinoki mecimi niila nipekatefi hotelahi

But Jesus answered them, My Father worketh even until now, and I work.

18. yooma hoci weecikeenahi nihki coosaki hini halika hotesi natonehaanaawa wahsi nhfaawaaci nili ksake hina mata hini halwaakahsiwiiwe pehi hoposkona weeka nehfaapi nohfa hotesinaali manetooli hoceeceesto wiiya manetooli

For this cause therefore the Jews sought the more to kill him, because he not only brake the sabbath, but also called God his own Father, making himself equal with God.

19. weecikeenahi ciisisii haapafse mecimi tepilo tepilo kitelepwa niila hina hokwihfima mata wiyehi yah katawi silawi pesikwi wiila weeka wiyehi neeneemeki hina nili hohfimaali peemi silawiilici ksake kookwe-nehi-kaaci si wiyehi hina silawi yoolooni nehfaapi hina hokwihfima silawi hofepi yaska hini

Jesus therefore answered and said unto them, Verily, verily, I say unto you, The Son can do nothing of himself, but what he seeth the Father doing: for what things soever he doeth, these the Son also doeth in like manner.

20. ksake hina hohfima hotahkweelemaali nili hokwihfimaali mecimi howaapatelaali nili caayahki wiyehi wiila yaasilawiici chiine halika si pekatefiiwena noota yooloma wiyehi we hina waapatelaali nili wahsi kiilawa menawahi kwakwehtaaniteheeyeekwe

For the Father loveth the Son, and sheweth him all things that himself doeth: and greater works than these will he shew him, that ye may marvel.

21. ksake yeesi hina hohfima honhskaanaaci nihi nepelici mecimi miilaaci nihi lenaweewiiwe teetepilahi yooni hina hokwihfima nehfaapi miilaaci lenaweewiiwe wiyefali yoona yeeleelemaaci

For as the Father raiseth the dead and quickeneth them, even so the Son also quickeneth whom he will.

22. ksake mata nohki hina hohfima wiyeh hotelahkowaalaali wiyehsi hileniili weeka hina neyehka homiilaali caayahki wiyeh lahkoweewe nili hokwihfimaali

For neither doth the Father judge any man, but he hath given all judgment unto the Son;

23. wahsi caayahki menawahi hotakeelemaawaaci nili hokwihfimaali teetepilahi yeesi nihki hotakeelemaawaaci nili hohfimaali hina peepwaa hotakeelemaata nili hokwihfimaali mata hotakeelemaali nili hohfimaali weewaawiineskawaata nili

that all may honour the Son, even as they honour the Father. He that honoureth not the Son honoureth not the Father which sent him.

24. tepilo tepilo kitelepwa niila hina peefetaka nikalawiiwe mecimi teepwehse nili weewaawiineskawilici hopoona kookwelaakwasi lenaweewiiwe mecimi mata mehtahkowaafooweneki si piyeewa weeka mehci lohfi-pemhfe nepoowe lenaweewiiweneki si

Verily, verily, I say unto you, He that heareth my word, and believeth him that sent me, hath eternal life, and cometh not into judgment, but hath passed out of death into life.

25. tepilo tepilo kitelepwa niila hini yaatefaki piyeeya mecimi hinoki howe hine nihki neepekiki weh nootaanaawa hini hotesihsimoowe hina hokwihfali maneto mecimi nihki neenootakki weh lenaweewiiki

Verily, verily, I say unto you, The hour cometh, and now is, when the dead shall hear the voice of the Son of God; and they that hear shall live.

26. ksake yeesi hina hohfima poonaki lenaweewiiwe wiiyaaki yooni teetepilahi hotesi miilaali nili hokwihfimaali nehfaapi wahsi poonamelici lenaweewiiwe howiiyaawilici

For as the Father hath life in himself, even so gave he to the Son also to have life in himself:

27. chiine homiilaali simekofiiwe wahsi kicitaskamelici mehtahkoweewe ksake hina hileni hokwihfali

and he gave him authority to execute judgment, because he is the Son of man.

28. teki kwakwehtaaneeeletamoko yooma ksake hini yaatefaki piyeeya hine caayahki yeepicki nili nepoowaalako weh nootaanaawa hotesihsimoowe

Marvel not at this: for the hour cometh, in which all that are in the tombs shall hear his voice,

29. mecimi weh piyeci lohfeeki nihki mayehci lawiici weewesaaki hini haapefiiwi-honhskaawi lenaweewiiweneki heeki mecimi nihki mayehci lawiicki mecaafiki hini haapefiiwi-honhskaawi mehtahkowaafooweneki heeki

And shall come forth; they that have done good, unto the resurrection of life; and they that have done ill, unto the resurrection of judgment.

30. mata wiyehi pesikwi nitah katawi silawi yeesi nootaakeeya nitelahkowe mecimi nitelahkoweewe tepasawatwi ksake mata niila nitesiteheewe ninatoneha weeka hina hotesiteheewe weewaawiineskawita

I can of myself do nothing: as I hear, I judge: and my judgment is righteous; because I seek not mine own will, but the will of him that sent me.

31. kwehkwi niila pah niimeya pesikwi niteepweeweniwiiwe niteepweeweniwiiwe mata mayaawatwi

If I bear witness of myself, my witness is not true.

32. kotaka hina peepah niimawita teepweeweniwiiwe mecimi niwaakota yeesi hini teepweeweniwiiwe teeteepweewenhhici mayaawhki

It is another that beareth witness of me; and I know that the witness which he witnesseth of me is true.

33. kiilawa kimehci caanii si waawiinhkeepwa mecimi hina homehci hini si pah niime teepweeweneki

Ye have sent unto John, and he hath borne witness unto the truth.

34. payeekwa hini teepweeweniwiiwe weeotfekoya mata hileni hociwiiya payeekwa niteyo yooloma wiyehi wahsi kiilawa menawahi waapaneshoofoyeekwe

But the witness which I receive is not from man: howbeit I say these things, that ye may be saved.

35. hiina hina niitawaaka feefakfota chiine wahfefike mecimi kimenwiteheepwa wahsi hosasilepwaayeekwe maalaakwasi howahfeeyaamiki

He was the lamp that burneth and shineth: and ye were willing to rejoice for a season in his light.

36. payeekwa hini teepweewe peepoonama halika hinwi yeenwilici caanii ksake nili pekatefiiwena mayehci miilici hina hohfima wahsi mehcilotama nili tepilo pekatefiiwena yaasilawiiya niteepweewenhhekona yeesi hina hohfima mehci waawiineskawici

But the witness which I have is greater than that of John: for the works which the Father hath given me to accomplish, the very works that I do, bear witness of me, that the Father hath sent me.

37. mecimi hina hohfima weewaawiineskawita nimehci teepweewenhhekwa hina kiilawa mata kimeh nootaanaawa hotesihsimoowe nehcipeh laakwa mata nohki kimeh neemenaawa yeeliyeeweci

And the Father which sent me, he hath borne witness of me. Ye have neither heard his voice at any time, nor seen his form.

38. chiine mata kipoonaanaawa hokalawiiwe kiiyaawaaki ksake nili weewaawiineskawaaci mata kiteepwehtamawaawa nili

And ye have not his word abiding in you: for whom he sent, him ye believe not.

39. nili kiteh natonehikeepwa tepilo heewikaateewali ksake kitesiteheepwa kiilawa yeesi nili piitike poonameekwe kookwelaakwasi lenaweewiiwe mecimi yoolooni nili peepah niimekoya teepweeweniwiiwe

Ye search the scriptures, because ye think that in them ye have eternal life; and these are they which bear witness of me;

40. mecimi kiilawa mata kiisa piyeelotawipwa wahsi menawahi poonameekwe lenaweewiiwe

and ye will not come to me, that ye may have life.

41. mata hileni nooci hotfeko hini wahfaacimekofiiwe

I receive not glory from men.

42. payeekwa kiwaakomelepwa kiilawa yeesi pwaa poonameekwe kiiyaawaaki hini hotahkweeletiiwe maneto

But I know you, that ye have not the love of God in yourselves.

43. nohfa howiifooweneki nipiya niila mecimi mata kootahpenipwa kwehkwi kotaka weh piyeewa nehalwaaka howiifooweneki kiilawa hina ke hotahpenaawa

I am come in my Father's name, and ye receive me not: if another shall come in his own name, him ye will receive.

44. nehiwe kiilawa keh si katawi teepwehseepwa yohkoma pesikwi weetahpenamaaticki wahfaacimekofiiwe chiine hini wahfaacimekofiiwe

How can ye believe, which receive glory one of another, and the glory that cometh from the only God ye seek not?

hina maneto pehi weemooyaaki mata
kinatonehaanaawa

45. wahsi hina hohfima si mestaawimelako teki
siteheeko nitasi hapiwa nekoti
memestaawimelwaakwe teetepilahi moosisii hoskici
hina kimehci si poonaanaawa kinanaaciteheewenwa

Think not that I will accuse you to the
Father: there is one that accuseth you,
even Moses, on whom ye have set your
hope.

46. ksake kwehkwi kiilawa teepwehtaweekwe
moosisii kih teepwehtawipwa niila ksake hina
nitalawikaalekwa niila

For if ye believed Moses, ye would
believe me; for he wrote of me.

47. weeka kwehkwi kiilawa pwaa teepwehtameekwe
yeelawikeeci nehiwe keh si teepwehtaanaawa
nikalawiiwe hotelahi

But if ye believe not his writings, how
shall ye believe my words?

John:6

1. hahkowihi hine yooloma wiyehi ciisisii weepfe
hini kaameki hini keeleliiwi mhsinepi heewa
taapiliasiiwi mhsinepi hini

After these things Jesus went away to the
other side of the sea of Galilee, which is
the sea of Tiberias.

2. chiine meci mehseelekki honeekalaawaali nili
ksake nihki hotelaapataanaawa nili kikinooloowena
ye hpenalaaci hina nihi yeekwilokeelici

And a great multitude followed him,
because they beheld the signs which he
did on them that were sick.

3. chiine hini meekwahkiki si kkwicsinwa ciisisii
mecimi nitasi lematapi wiici hokakehkimaafhi

And Jesus went up into the mountain, and
there he sat with his disciples.

4. howe hini pemhfaasiweewe hini
howihfenhcikeewenwa nihki coosaki howe nahiika
piyeeya

Now the passover, the feast of the Jews,
was at hand.

5. weecikeenahi ciisisii maa laapi hoskiiseko mecimi
neeke yeesi meci mehseelelici hotfekoci taaniwe ke
hoci tepenaape takhwa wahsi yohkoma menawahi
miiciwaaci hotelaali filapiili

Jesus therefore lifting up his eyes, and
seeing that a great multitude cometh unto
him, saith unto Philip, Whence are we to
buy bread, that these may eat?

6. mecimi weecita yooma hotelaali wahsi
kocihkawaaci ksake wiila howaakota wah silawiici

And this he said to prove him: for he
himself knew what he would do.

7. hotaapaftawaali filapii niisene tepeewe seleni
yeeleelemekoki takhwa mata yah teepatwi nihki
wahsi caaki nekoti menawahi mameki maalecihi
hisiwe

Philip answered him, Two hundred
pennyworth of bread is not sufficient for
them, that every one may take a little.

8. nekoti hokakehkimaafhi heenhtlo saiman' piita
hoceeninaali hotelaali nili

One of his disciples, Andrew, Simon
Peter's brother, saith unto him,

9. hotasi hapiwa mayaanileniifa peepoonaka
niyaalanwi paaleewikawaskwi weepskweeteewali
mecimi niiswi namefhi payeekwa nehiwe yooloma
heelekiini yooni si meci

There is a lad here, which hath five barley
loaves, and two fishes: but what are these
among so many?

10. lemataphehko nihki lenaweeki hisiwe ciisisii
howe mhskotehkwalwihki holaami hini tasi
weecikeenahi nihki hileniiki sahkiki si lematapiiki
yeetfwiwaaci nawito niyaalane metahfene tepeewe

Jesus said, Make the people sit down.
Now there was much grass in the place.
So the men sat down, in number about
five thousand.

11. weecikeenahi ciisisii hoteh mamena nili weepskweeteewali mecimi yeesi mehci miiliweeci niyaawe holelhskonamawahi nihi lematapilici sahkiki hini yaska nehfaapi nihi namefhi lekhi yeeleeletamowaaci nihki

Jesus therefore took the loaves; and having given thanks, he distributed to them that were set down; likewise also of the fishes as much as they would.

12. chiine hine nihki yeh teephoolowaaci maawatonamoko nili peekskahki seskwatooteeki wahsi mata wiyehi wanhtooteeki hotelahi hokakehkimaafhi

And when they were filled, he saith unto his disciples, Gather up the broken pieces which remain over, that nothing be lost.

13. weecikeenahi nihki homaawatonaanaawa nili mecimi hokwihfetoonaawa metahfwi-kite-niiswi soosooniwali peekskahki hoci nili niyaalanwi kawaskwi weepskweeteewali mayehci skwatamelici nihi mayehci wihfenilici

So they gathered them up, and filled twelve baskets with broken pieces from the five barley loaves, which remained over unto them that had eaten.

14. yeh neemowaaci nihki lenaweeki weecikeenahi hini kikinooloowe yeesilawiici hina teepweewe yaama hina maamoosikiiskweeta hini yeelekokwahkamikiki peepiyaata hiwaki nihki

When therefore the people saw the sign which he did, they said, This is of a truth the prophet that cometh into the world.

15. weecikeenahi ciisisii peemi moositeheeci yeesi nawito nihki piyaawaaci mecimi mamiiloowi mamaawaaci wahsi hokimaawhaawaaci nili nohki hini meekwahkiki si saawe naanhsihka wiila

Jesus therefore perceiving that they were about to come and take him by force, to make him king, withdrew again into the mountain himself alone.

16. chiine yeh piyeeyaaki weelaakwiifiki hokakehkimaafhi hini mhsinepiki si paalacsinohi

And when evening came, his disciples went down unto the sea;

17. chiine nihki holakeeleki lhkamooki mecimi keepaaniamiiki kaameki hini mhsinepi wiisa heeki chiine howe hini pepekica mecimi ciisisii mata keewaki home hotfahi nihi

and they entered into a boat, and were going over the sea unto Capernaum. And it was now dark, and Jesus had not yet come to them.

18. chiine hini mhsinepi peemi skwikamiki ye mhsaaki mehsikkaki hoci pootaacikeeya

And the sea was rising by reason of a great wind that blew.

19. hine nihki weecikeenahi nawito niiswi-kite-pahfi weelaa toke nhfwi-kite-nhfwehfepati maiili yeh si mehci coomeewaaci hotelaapamaawaali ciisisiili pemhfeeli hoskici hini mhsinepi mecimi peemi maalaakwahi piyaalici hini holakeesi chiine kaawilaweeki nihki

When therefore they had rowed about five and twenty or thirty furlongs, they behold Jesus walking on the sea, and drawing nigh unto the boat: and they were afraid.

20. payeekwa hina niila teki kaawilaweko hotelahi nihi

But he saith unto them, It is I; be not afraid.

21. nihki weecikeenahi homenwi hini holakeeleki si hotahpenaawaali nili mecimi weelena hini holakeesi nahiika hini hasiski yehaawaaci nihki

They were willing therefore to receive him into the boat: and straightway the boat was at the land whither they were going.

22. hini wayaapaki nihki mehseelekki neniipawicki hini hasowe kaameki hini mhsinepi honeemenaawa yeesi pwaa hahteeki kotaki holakeesi nitasi

On the morrow the multitude which stood on the other side of the sea saw that there was none other boat there, save one, and

weeciwephi nekoti mecimi yeesi pwaa ciisisii wiici hokakehkimaafhi hini holakeeleki lhkaki yeesi weeka hokakehkimaafhi weepfeelici naanhsihka

that Jesus entered not with his disciples into the boat, but that his disciples went away alone

23. weeka nitasi piyeeya holakeelali taapiliasii hoci maalaakwahi hini tasi tah nihki miiciwaaci hini takhwa yeesi hina teepeelemiweeta mehci miiliweeci niyaawe

(howbeit there came boats from Tiberias nigh unto the place where they ate the bread after the Lord had given thanks):

24. hine weecikeenahi nihki mehseelekki yeh neemowaaci yeesi pwaa ciisisiili nitasi hapilici mata nohki hokakehkimaafhi wiilawa nihki nili lhkamooki holakeelali mecimi keepaaniamii si piyeeki honatonehwaawaali ciisisiili

when the multitude therefore saw that Jesus was not there, neither his disciples, they themselves got into the boats, and came to Capernaum, seeking Jesus.

25. chiine yeh mhkawaawaaci hini hasowe kaameki hini mhsinepi lepaayii taaniwe laakwa kipiya hotasi hotelaawaali

And when they found him on the other side of the sea, they said unto him, Rabbi, when camest thou hither?

26. hotaapaftawahi ciisisii mecimi tepilo tepilo kitelepwa niila kinatonehwipwa mata yeeneemeyeekwe ksake kikinooloowena hoci weeka ksake kimiicinaawa nili weepskweeteewali mecimi kiteephoolopwa

Jesus answered them and said, Verily, verily, I say unto you, Ye seek me, not because ye saw signs, but because ye ate of the loaves, and were filled.

27. teki pekatefihtamoko hini wihfeniiwe yeeyaseki hini weeka wihfeniiwe yehteeki kookwelaakwasi lenaweewiiweneki si hini hina hokwihfali hileni wah miilelwaakwe ksake niliini hina hohfima teetepilahi maneto homehci peshalwemaali hisiwe

Work not for the meat which perisheth, but for the meat which abideth unto eternal life, which the Son of man shall give unto you: for him the Father, even God, hath sealed.

28. nehiwe kwiilahi neh silawiipe wahsi menawahi pekatefiyaake nili hopekatefiiwena maneto hotelaawaali weecikeenahi nihki

They said therefore unto him, What must we do, that we may work the works of God?

29. haapafse ciisisii mecimi halayooma hini hopekatefiiwe maneto wahsi kiilawa teepwehtamaweekwe nili mayehci hina waawiineskawaaci hotelahi

Jesus answered and said unto them, This is the work of God, that ye believe on him whom he hath sent.

30. weecikeenahi nihki nehiwe howe keh silawi kiila kikinooloowe wahsi menawahi niilawe neemeyaake mecimi teepwehtoolaake nehiwe kiila kipekatena

They said therefore unto him, What then doest thou for a sign, that we may see, and believe thee? what workest thou?

31. kohfenaaki homiicinaawa hini mena hini piileski hina weefepahkamikiki hoci miilahi takhwa wah miicilici yeelawikeeki hini hotelaawaali

Our fathers ate the manna in the wilderness; as it is written, He gave them bread out of heaven to eat.

32. weecikeenahi ciisisii tepilo tepilo kitelepwa niila mata hina moosisii weefepahkamikiki weeci miilelwaakwe hini takhwa weeka nohfa kooci weefepahkamikiki miilekowa hini mayaawi takhwa

Jesus therefore said unto them, Verily, verily, I say unto you, It was not Moses that gave you the bread out of heaven; but my Father giveth you the true bread out of heaven.

33. ksake hini hotakhwaanemi maneto sahkiki hini yeesi piyeeyaaki weefepahkamikiki hoci lohfeya mecimi hini yeelekokwahkamikiki si miiliweeya lenaweewiiwe hotelahi

For the bread of God is that which cometh down out of heaven, and giveth life unto the world.

34. nihki weecikeenahi teepeelemiweeta miilinaake yooma kookwelaakwasi takhwa hotelaawaali

They said therefore unto him, Lord, evermore give us this bread.

35. niiya hini lenaweewiiwe si takhwa hina peepiyeelotawita mata we skwaalawe mecimi hina teeteepwehseeta niiya mata laakwasi weh kahkalaamo hotelahi ciisisii

Jesus said unto them, I am the bread of life: he that cometh to me shall not hunger, and he that believeth on me shall never thirst.

36. payeekwa kitelepwa niila yeesi kiilawa mehci neewiyeekwe mecimi mata keewaki kiteepwehseepwa

But I said unto you, that ye have seen me, and yet believe not.

37. caayahki nihi meemiilici hina hohfima ne hotfekooki mecimi hina peepiyeelotawita mata neh wiyehisi lohfe pakila

All that which the Father giveth me shall come unto me; and him that cometh to me I will in no wise cast out.

38. ksake niila weefepahkamikiki nooci sahkiki piya mata wahsi niila yeesiteheeya silawiiya hini hotesiteheewe weeka hina weewaawiineskawita

For I am come down from heaven, not to do mine own will, but the will of him that sent me.

39. chiine halayooma hini hotesiteheewe hina weewaawiineskawita wahsi caayahki hini hina mayehci miilici hoci teki wanhtooya wiyehi weeka wi honhskaanama hini hine tah ceeyehkwi kiisekiki

And this is the will of him that sent me, that of all that which he hath given me I should lose nothing, but should raise it up at the last day.

40. ksake yooma hini hotesiteheewe nohfa wahsi caakiwiyeefa yeelaapamaata nili hokwihfimaali mecimi teepwehse nili wih poonaki kookwelaakwasi lenaweewiiwe mecimi niila ne honhskaana hina ta hini ceeyehkwi kiisekiki

For this is the will of my Father, that every one that beholdeth the Son, and believeth on him, should have eternal life; and I will raise him up at the last day.

41. nihki coosaki weecikeenahi nili hoci petfakoweeki ksake hina niiya hini takhwa sahkiki yeesi piyeeyaaki weefepahkamikiki hoci lohfeya hiwa

The Jews therefore murmured concerning him, because he said, I am the bread which came down out of heaven.

42. chiine ha mata ciisisii yaama hokwihfali coosii hohfali mecimi hokeeli kiwaakomaape nehiwesi hinoki weefepahkamikiki nooci sahkiki si lohfa hiwa hiwaki nihki

And they said, Is not this Jesus, the son of Joseph, whose father and mother we know? how doth he now say, I am come down out of heaven?

43. ciisisii haapafse mecimi teki petfakoweko heelekiina kiilawa hotelahi

Jesus answered and said unto them, Murmur not among yourselves.

44. mata hileni nitah katawi piyeelotaakwa weeciwephi nili hohfimaali weewaawiineskawilici piyeetenekote chiine ne honhskaana hina ta hini ceeyehkwi kiisekiki

No man can come to me, except the Father which sent me draw him: and I will raise him up in the last day.

45. chiine nihki weh caayahki kakehkimekowaali manetooli lawikeepi hini laa maamoosikiiskwecki caakiwiyeefa mayehci nili hohfimaali hoci

It is written in the prophets, And they shall all be taught of God. Every one that hath

nootaakeeta mecimi mehci waakotefi
nipiyeelotaakwa

heard from the Father, and hath learned, cometh unto me.

46. mata yo wiyesi hileni homeh neewaali nili
hohfimaali weeciwephi hina manetooli weeciwita
hiina homehci neewaali nili hohfimaali

Not that any man hath seen the Father, save he which is from God, he hath seen the Father.

47. tepilo tepilo kitelepwa niila hina teeteepwehseeta
hopoona kookwelaakwasi lenaweewiiwe

Verily, verily, I say unto you, He that believeth hath eternal life.

48. niiya hini lenaweewiiwe si takhwa

I am the bread of life.

49. kohfenaaki homiicinaawa hini mena hini piileski
mecimi nihki nepooki

Your fathers did eat the manna in the wilderness, and they died.

50. halayooma hini takhwa peepiyeeyaaki sahkiki
weefepahkamikiki hoci lohfeya wahsi menawa hileni
hini miicici mecimi pwaa nepeki

This is the bread which cometh down out of heaven, that a man may eat thereof, and not die.

51. niiya hini leelenaweewiiyaaki takhwa
peepiyeeyaaki sahkiki weefepahkamikiki hoci
lohfeya kwehkwi wiyesi hileni miicite yooma takhwa
weh lenaweewi kookwelaakwasi hanhka mecimi hini
takhwa wah miiliweeya niila niwiyawfemi hini wahsi
hotelenaweewici hina yeelekokwahkamikiki hotelahi

I am the living bread which came down out of heaven: if any man eat of this bread, he shall live for ever: yea and the bread which I will give is my flesh, for the life of the world.

52. nihki coosaki weecikeenahi mawinahkaaletiiki
nehiwe keh si katawi miilekona yaama hileni
howiyawfemi wahsi miiciyakwe hiwaki

The Jews therefore strove one with another, saying, How can this man give us his flesh to eat?

53. weecikeenahi ciisisii tepilo tepilo kitelepwa niila
weeciwephi miiciyeekwe hini howiyawfemi hina
hokwihfali hileni mecimi meneyeekwe homhskomi
mata kipoonaanaawa lenaweewiiwe kiiyaawaaki
hotelahi

Jesus therefore said unto them, Verily, verily, I say unto you, Except ye eat the flesh of the Son of man and drink his blood, ye have not life in yourselves.

54. hina meemiicita niwiyawfemi mecimi meneka
nimhskomi hopoona kookwelaakwasi lenaweewiiwe
mecimi hina ne honhskaana ta hini ceeyehkwi
kiisekiki

He that eateth my flesh and drinketh my blood hath eternal life; and I will raise him up at the last day.

55. ksake niwiyawfemi wihfeniiwe sapkahi mecimi
nimhskomi menoowe sapkahi

For my flesh is meat indeed, and my blood is drink indeed.

56. hina meemiicita niwiyawfemi mecimi meneka
nimhskomi hapiwa niiyaaki mecimi niila wiiyaaki

He that eateth my flesh and drinketh my blood abideth in me, and I in him.

57. yeesi hina hohfima lenaweewita waawiineskawici
mecimi lenaweewiya ksake hina hohfima hoci yooni
yaska hina yemwita nehfaapi hina weh lenaweewi
ksake niiya hoci

As the living Father sent me, and I live because of the Father; so he that eateth me, he also shall live because of me.

58. hiini yooma takhwa peepiyeeyaaki sahkiki
weefepahkamikiki hoci lohfeya mata yeesi nihki
hohfimaaki miiciwaaci mecimi nepowaaci hina
meemiicita yooma takhwa weh lenaweewi
kookwelaakwasi

This is the bread which came down out of heaven: not as the fathers did eat, and died: he that eateth this bread shall live for ever.

59. piitike hini mhsikamikwi hiwa yooloma wiyehi yeesi kakehkimiweeci keepaaniamiiki

These things said he in the synagogue, as he taught in Capernaum.

60. meci weecikeenahi hokakehkimaafhi hine nihki yeh nootamowaaci yooma kiisenaatoweewe yooma neefawe weh katawi noota hini hiwaki

Many therefore of his disciples, when they heard this, said, This is a hard saying; who can hear it?

61. payeekwa peemi waakotaki ciisisii wiiyaaki yeesi hokakehkimaafhi pekihkaatamelici yooma ha ksake yooma kitpenalekonaawa wahsi hotakikahsineyeekwe hotelahi

But Jesus knowing in himself that his disciples murmured at this, said unto them, Doth this cause you to stumble?

62. nehiwe howe kwehkwi kiilawa ki hilaapamaawa hina hokwihfali hileni pemi spemeki haate ta hapici hiyehki

What then if ye should behold the Son of man ascending where he was before?

63. hocacaalahkwa hina maamiiliweeta lenaweewiiwe hini wiyawfi hotefihiweya mata wiyehi nili kalawiiwena mayehci kaloolelako hocacaalahkowiiya mecimi lenaweewiiweno

It is the spirit that quickeneth; the flesh profiteth nothing: the words that I have spoken unto you are spirit, and are life.

64. payeekwa hapiiki nitasi naaleta kiilawa peepwaa teepwehseecki hotelahi ksake ciisisii howaakomahi hine weski hoci siwiyeefhi nihi peepwaa teepwehseelici mecimi siwiyeefali wah mestaawhekoci

But there are some of you that believe not. For Jesus knew from the beginning who they were that believed not, and who it was that should betray him.

65. mecimi hiwa ksake yooma hoci kooci mehci hilelepwa wahsi hileni mata katawi piyeelotawici weecip hini miilete nili hohfimaali hoci

And he said, For this cause have I said unto you, that no man can come unto me, except it be given unto him of the Father.

66. yoone howe yooma meci hokakehkimaafhi kiiwehi mecimi mata kiteeni howiitfeemekohi

Upon this many of his disciples went back, and walked no more with him.

67. weecikeenahi ciisisii ha nehfaapi kiilawa keh weepfeepwa hotelahi nihi metahfwi-kite-niiswi

Jesus said therefore unto the twelve, Would ye also go away?

68. saiman' piita hotaapaftawaali teepeelemiweeta taanawe hina ne haape kiila kipoonaana nili kookwelaakwasi lenaweewiiwe si kalawiiwena

Simon Peter answered him, Lord, to whom shall we go? thou hast the words of eternal life.

69. chiine nimehci teepwehseepe mecimi niwaakotaape yeesi kiilaawiyani hina weefepefita nekoti maneto hoci hotelaali

And we have believed and know that thou art the Holy One of God.

70. hotaapaftawahi ciisisii ha mata niila kimamelepwa kiilawa nihki metahfwi-kite-niiswi mecimi nekoti kiilawa macimanetoowi hotelahi

Jesus answered them, Did not I choose you the twelve, and one of you is a devil?

71. howe coosali hotaacimaali hina nili hokwihfali saiman' hiskeeletii ksake yoona hina wah mestaawhaata nili nekoti nihki metahfwi-kite-niiswi

Now he spake of Judas the son of Simon Iscariot, for he it was that should betray him, being one of the twelve.

John:7

1. chiine hahkowihi hine yooloma wiyehi ciisisii paamhfe keeleliiki ksake mata sitehe wih paamhfeeci

And after these things Jesus walked in Galilee: for he would not walk in Judaea, because the Jews sought to kill him.

cotiyeeki ksake nihki coosaki honatonehaanaawa
wahsi nhfaawaaci nili

2. howe hini howihfenhcikeewenwa nihki coosaki
hini haaciiwikamiko si wihfenhcikeewe naanemi
nahiika

Now the feast of the Jews, the feast of
tabernacles, was at hand.

3. hoceeninahi weecikeenahi yooci weepfeelo mecimi
cotiyeeki haalo wahsi kikakehkimaafaki nehfaapi
menawa hilaapatamowaaci kipekatefiiwena
yaasilawiiyani hotekohi

His brethren therefore said unto him,
Depart hence, and go into Judaea, that thy
disciples also may behold thy works
which thou doest.

4. ksake mata hileni wiyehi kaakiimi lawi mecimi
pesikwi wiila honatoneha wahsi tawaaci
waakomekofici kwehkwi yooloma yaasilawiiyani
kiila hini yeelekokwahkamikiki si tepinawkotoolo
kiiya hotekohi

For no man doeth anything in secret, and
himself seeketh to be known openly. If
thou doest these things, manifest thyself to
the world.

5. ksake wiikinaakwi hoceeninahi mata
hoteepwehtaakohi

For even his brethren did not believe on
him.

6. weecikeenahi ciisisii nitelaakwaami mata keewaki
piyeeya weeka kitelaakwaamwa kiilawa moosatawi
mecfenwi

Jesus therefore saith unto them, My time
is not yet come; but your time is alway
ready.

7. hini yeelekokwahkamikiki mata kitah katawi
siikeelemekonaawa weeka hini nisiikeelemeko niila
ksake nitepinawkwaatota hini yeesi
hopekatefiiweniki macaafi

The world cannot hate you; but me it
hateth, because I testify of it, that its
works are evil.

8. kiilawa hini wihfenhcikeeweneki si kkwicsineko
mata niila yooma wihfenhcikeeweneki nih si
kkwicsine ksake nitelaakwaami mata keewaki
hokwaawfetoote hotelahi

Go ye up unto the feast: I go not up yet
unto this feast; because my time is not yet
fulfilled.

9. chiine yeesi mehci yooloma wiyehi hilaaci nihi
yaska keeleliiki hapiwa

And having said these things unto them,
he abode still in Galilee.

10. payeekwa hine hoceeninahi hini
wihfenhcikeeweneki si kkwicsinohi howe nehfaapi
kkwicsinwa mata tawaaci weeka paasi hini kiimefi

But when his brethren were gone up unto
the feast, then went he also up, not
publicly, but as it were in secret.

11. nihki coosaki weecikeenahi honatonehwaawaali
ta hini wihfenhcikeeki mecimi taanawe hina hiwaki

The Jews therefore sought him at the
feast, and said, Where is he?

12. mecimi meci petfakoweewe nitasi heelekiina
nihki mehseelekki nili hoci naaleta howesi hileni hina
hiwaki kotakaki mata weeka howaaniwelahi nihi
mehseelelici hiwaki

And there was much murmuring among
the multitudes concerning him: some said,
He is a good man; others said, Not so, but
he leadeth the multitude astray.

13. payeekwa mata hileni hotawaaci haacimaali nili
ksake nihki coosaki kwfoofooki

Howbeit no man spake openly of him for
fear of the Jews.

14. payeekwa hine howe heelekhi hini
wihfenhcikeewe ciisisii spemeki heewa hini
mamaatomeewikamikoki chiine kakehkimiwe

But when it was now the midst of the feast
Jesus went up into the temple, and taught.

15. kwakwehtaaniteheeki weecikeenahi nihki coosaki nehiwe hotesi waakotaana heewikaateewali yaama hileni matalaakwa meh waakotefi hiwaki

The Jews therefore marveled, saying, How knoweth this man letters, having never learned?

16. ciisisii hotaapaftawahi weecikeenahi mecimi nikakehkimiweewe mata niila weeka weewaawiineskawita wiila

Jesus therefore answered them, and said, My teaching is not mine, but his that sent me.

17. kwehkwi hileni siteheete wahsi hotesiteheewenilici silawiici we hina waakota hini kakehkimiweewe kwehkwi toke hini maneto hoci weelaa toke nikalawi pesikwi niila hoci

If any man willeth to do his will, he shall know of the teaching, whether it be of God, or whether I speak from myself.

18. hina keekalawita pesikwi wiila hoci honatoneha nehalwaaka wiila howahfaacimekofiiwe weeka hina neetonehaka hini howahfaacimekofiiwenilici nili weewaawiineskaakoci yoona hina mayaawefi mecimi wiiyaaki matalaakwa pwaatepasawiilefiiwe

He that speaketh from himself seeketh his own glory: but he that seeketh the glory of him that sent him, the same is true, and no unrighteousness is in him.

19. ha mata moosisii kimiilekowa hini kwteletiiwe mecimi keewaki mata nekoti kiilawa hini kwteletiiwe silawi koociwe kinatonehaanaawa wahsi nhsiyeekwe kiilawa hiwa

Did not Moses give you the law, and yet none of you doeth the law? Why seek ye to kill me?

20. haapafseeki nihki mehseelekki waninehfi kipoona kiila neefawe honatoneha wahsi nhfehki

The multitude answered, Thou hast a devil: who seeketh to kill thee?

21. ciisisii haapafse mecimi nekoti pekatefiiwe nitesilawi chiine caayahki kiilawa kikwakwehtaaniteheepwa ksake hini hoci

Jesus answered and said unto them, I did one work, and ye all marvel.

22. moosisii kimehci miilekowa kaawatkofoowe mata weekhi moosisii hoci hini weeka nihki hohfimaaki hoci chiine hini ta halwaakahsiweeki kikaawatkolaawa hileni

For this cause hath Moses given you circumcision (not that it is of Moses, but of the fathers); and on the sabbath ye circumcise a man.

23. kwehkwi hileni hotahpenake kaawatkofoowe hini ta halwaakahsiweeki wahsi menawa hini moosisii hokwteletiiwe pwaa poskonooteeki ha kooci wiyakowehtawipwa ksake nimefefiha hileni ta hini halwaakahsiweeki

If a man receiveth circumcision on the sabbath, that the law of Moses may not be broken; are ye wroth with me, because I made a man every whit whole on the sabbath?

24. teki yeesi nawiweeyeekwe lahkoweko weeka lahkoweko tepasawakoweewe hotelahi

Judge not according to appearance, but judge righteous judgment.

25. naaleta weecikeenahi nihki colooseelemii hoci ha mata hina yaama nili nihki neetonehwaawaaci wahsi nhfaawaaci

Some therefore of them of Jerusalem said, Is not this he whom they seek to kill?

26. chiine scih tawaaci kalawi hina mecimi mata wiyehi hotelwaali nihki kanhha hini yeeki yeesi nihki mehsikilohtawiweecki waakotamowaaci yeesi yaama klaistiiwici

And lo, he speaketh openly, and they say nothing unto him. Can it be that the rulers indeed know that this is the Christ?

27. payeekwa kiwaakotaape kiilawe yaama hileni weeciwici weeka hine hina klaistii piyaate mata wiyeefa howaakota weeciwilici nili hiwaki

Howbeit we know this man whence he is: but when the Christ cometh, no one knoweth whence he is.

28. weecikeenahi ciisisii hini
mamaatomeewikamikoki talahootamwa peemi
kakehkimiweeci mecimi peemi hiyoci neyiisweelena
kiwaakomipwa niila mecimi kiwaakotaanaawa
weeciwiya niila chiine mata pesikwi niila nipiya
payeekwa hina weewaawiineskawita mayaawefi
peepwaa waakomeekwe

Jesus therefore cried in the temple, teaching and saying, Ye both know me, and know whence I am; and I am not come of myself, but he that sent me is true, whom ye know not.

29. niwaakoma niila ksake hina hoci niila mecimi
hina niwaawiineskaakwa hiwa

I know him; because I am from him, and he sent me.

30. nihki honatonehaanaawa weecikeenahi wahsi
mesenaawaaci nili mecimi mata hileni holeciki
homesenaali nili ksake hotaatefamoowe mata
keewaki piyeeya

They sought therefore to take him: and no man laid his hand on him, because his hour was not yet come.

31. payeekwa nihki mehseelekki hoci meci
teepwehseeki nili chiine nihki hine hina klaistii
piyaate kanhha halika tfwi kikinooloowena weh
silawi noota yooloma yaama hileni mayehci silawiici
hiwaki

But of the multitude many believed on him; and they said, When the Christ shall come, will he do more signs than those which this man hath done?

32. nihki pelesiiki honootawaawahi nihi mehseelelici
peemi pekihkamelici yooma wiyehi nili si chiine
nihki hokimaawi mhkateewkolayeeki mecimi nihki
pelesiiki hoteleskawaawahi wiyehsimekofiiwenhhi
wahsi mesenaawaaci nili

The Pharisees heard the multitude murmuring these things concerning him; and the chief priests and the Pharisees sent officers to take him.

33. weecikeenahi ciisisii keewaki faapiimehi niwiici
hapi kiilawa mecimi hina nita weewaawiineskawita

Jesus therefore said, Yet a little while am I with you, and I go unto him that sent me.

34. keh natonehwipwa kiilawa mecimi mata ke
mhkawipwa chiine ta hapiya niila ke haalwi si
piyaapwa hiwa

Ye shall seek me, and shall not find me: and where I am, ye cannot come.

35. nihki coosaki weecikeena hiwaki heelekiina
wiilawa taaniwe we heewa yaama hileni wahsi pwaa
kiilawe mhkawakwe ha hini we heewa lhfweeweneki
heelekiina nihki kwiikiiwi lenaweeki mecimi
kakehkimahi nihi kwiikihi

The Jews therefore said among themselves, Whither will this man go that we shall not find him? will he go unto the Dispersion among the Greeks, and teach the Greeks?

36. nehiwe yooma kalawiiwe yeeyoci hina keh
natonehwipwa kiilawa mecimi mata ke mhkawipwa
chiine ta hapiya niila ke haalwi si piyaapwa

What is this word that he said, Ye shall seek me, and shall not find me: and where I am, ye cannot come?

37. howe ta hini ceeyehkwi kiisekiki hini
wihfenhcikeewesi mhsi kaasekiki ciisisii niipawi
mecimi nitasimo kwehkwi wiyehsi hileni
kahkalaamote wiilaani hina piyeelotawite mecimi
meneke

Now on the last day, the great day of the feast, Jesus stood and cried, saying, If any man thirst, let him come unto me, and drink.

38. hina teeteepwehtawita yeesi hini tepilo
heewikaateeki mehtoweyaaki wiiyaaki hina we
hocitano fiipiiwali lenaweewiiya nepi hiwa

He that believeth on me, as the scripture hath said, out of his belly shall flow rivers of living water.

39. payeekwa yooma nili hocacaalahkwali hina hotaacimaali niliini we hotfekowaali nihki teeteepwehtawaacki nili ksake hina hocacaalahkwa mata keewaki miiliweepi ksake ciisisii keewaki mata wahfaacimekofihoofo

But this spake he of the Spirit, which they that believed on him were to receive: for the Spirit was not yet given; because Jesus was not yet glorified.

40. naaleta nihki mehseelekki hoci weecikeenahi yeh nootamowaaci yooloma kalawiiwena teepweewenwi yaama hina maamoosikiiskweeta hiwaki

Some of the multitude therefore, when they heard these words, said, This is of a truth the prophet.

41. kotakaki yaama hina klaistii hiwaki payeekwa naaleta nehiwe ha hina klaistii keeleliiki hoci lohfe hiwaki

Others said, This is the Christ. But some said, What, doth the Christ come out of Galilee?

42. ha mata hini tepilo heewikaateeki mehtoweya wahsi hina klaistii homeki hini homiinhka teepitii mecimi peflihemi hoci hini hoteewenehi ta hapici teepitii hiwaki

Hath not the scripture said that the Christ cometh of the seed of David, and from Bethlehem, the village where David was?

43. weecikeenahi nitasi pafekwiiya pahfehkaawe nihki laa mehseelekki ksake nili hoci

So there arose a division in the multitude because of him.

44. mecimi naaleta nihki wih mehci mesenaawaali nili payeekwa mata hileni homesenaali

And some of them would have taken him; but no man laid hands on him.

45. weecikeenahi nihki wiyehsimekofiiwenaki nihi si piyeeki hokimaawi mhkateewkolayehi chiine pelesihi mecimi koociwe mata kipiyeelaawa hina hotekowahi nihi

The officers therefore came to the chief priests and Pharisees; and they said unto them, Why did ye not bring him?

46. nihki wiyehsimekofiiwenaki haapafseeki matalaakwa hileni yooni si kalawi hiwaki

The officers answered, Never man so spake.

47. weecikeenahi nihki pelesiiki hotaapaftawaawahi nihi ha nehfaapi kiilawa kiwaaniwelekoopwa

The Pharisees therefore answered them, Are ye also led astray?

48. ha wiyeefa nihki mehsikilohtawiweecki mehci teepwehse nili weelaa nihki hoci pelesiiki

Hath any of the rulers believed on him, or of the Pharisees?

49. weeka yohkoma mehseelekki peepwaa waakotakki hini kwteletiiwe pahtaafiiki hiwaki

But this multitude which knoweth not the law are accursed.

50. nekatiimasi hina peepiyeelotawaata nili nhhihta hisi teewahi nekoti hina nihi

Nicodemus saith unto them (he that came to him before, being one of them),

51. makha kikwteletiiwenena homehtahkowaaleko hileni weeciwep hini nhhihta honootaako nehalwaaka wiila mecimi howaakotamaako yeesilawiici hina hotelahi nihi

Doth our law judge a man, except it first hear from himself and know what he doeth?

52. haapafseeki nihki mecimi ha nehfaapi kiila keelelii hoci natonehikeelo mecimi waapatano wahsi mata keelelii hoci pafekwiici maamoosikiiskweeta hotelaawaali

They answered and said unto him, Art thou also of Galilee? Search, and see that out of Galilee ariseth no prophet.

53. chiine nihki weepfeeki caaki hileni nehalwaaka yeetaaci wiikiwa heewa

And they went every man unto his own house:

John:8

1. weeka ciisisii hini halifiwi meekwahkiki heewa

but Jesus went unto the mount of Olives.

2. chiine hini kwelahwaapaki piyeewa nohki hini mamaatomeewikamikoki chiine caayahki nihki lenaweeki hopiyeelotawaawaali nili mecimi lematapiwa chiine hokakehkimahi nihi

And early in the morning he came again into the temple, and all the people came unto him; and he sat down, and taught them.

3. chiine nihki yaayawikeecki mecimi nihki pelesiiki hopiyeelaawaali hkweeli mesenoofooli waapasiphikeeweneki mecimi yeesi mehtahkeephaawaaci nili

And the scribes and the Pharisees bring a woman taken in adultery; and having set her in the midst,

4. keekehkimiwe yaama hkweewa mehci mesenoofo waapasiphikeeweneki tepilo hini silawiiweneki

they say unto him, Master, this woman hath been taken in adultery, in the very act.

5. howe hini kwteletiiweneki moosisii nitepimekona wahsi siikonhhwakici yooni yeeteka nehiwe howe ke hila kiila hotelaawaali nili

Now in the law Moses commanded us to stone such: what then sayest thou of her?

6. mecimi weecita nihki yooma hiwaki hokochaawaali nili wahsi menawahi poonamowaaci wa hoci cahtawaacimaawaaci nili payeekwa ciisisii sahkiki si waaki mecimi holeceeli hoci hawike hini hasiskiiki

And this they said, tempting him, that they might have whereof to accuse him. But Jesus stooped down, and with his finger wrote on the ground.

7. payeekwa yeh nekotenwi nihki natohtawaawaaci nili hina soskiiwa mecimi hina peepwaa hahteelita maciilefiwilawiiwe heelekiina kiilawa wiilaani hina nhhihta siikonhhwaate nili hotelahi

But when they continued asking him, he lifted up himself, and said unto them, He that is without sin among you, let him first cast a stone at her.

8. chiine hina nohki sahkiki si waaki mecimi holeceeli hoci hawike hini hasiskiiki

And again he stooped down, and with his finger wrote on the ground.

9. mecimi nihki yeh nootamowaaci hini lohfeeki maasa nekoti hina kcikikileni hoci weski paalohi hina ceeyehkwi mecimi ciisisii naanhsihka nakaloofo chiine hina hkweewa ta hapici hini heelekhi

And they, when they heard it, went out one by one, beginning from the eldest, even unto the last: and Jesus was left alone, and the woman, where she was, in the midst.

10. mecimi ciisisii soskiiwa chiine hkweewa taanihkiwe nihki ha mata hileni kimiyaalahkowaalekwa hotelaali nili

And Jesus lifted up himself, and said unto her, Woman, where are they? did no man condemn thee?

11. mecimi hina teepeelemiweeta mata hileni hisiwe chiine mata nohki niila kimiyaalahkowaalele nhhaalo yehaayani yooci teki kiteeni maciisilawiilo hotelaali ciisisii

And she said, No man, Lord. And Jesus said, Neither do I condemn thee: go thy way; from henceforth sin no more.

12. nohki weecikeenahi ciisisii hokaloolahi nihi niiya hini wayahfeeyaaki hini yeelekokwahkamikiki hina neeneekasita mata yah paamhfe hini laa pepekica weeka weh poona hini wayahfeeyaaki lenaweewiiwe hiwa

Again therefore Jesus spake unto them, saying, I am the light of the world: he that followeth me shall not walk in the darkness, but shall have the light of life.

13. weecikeenahi nihki pelesiiki pesikwi kipah niime kiila si teepweewe mata mayaawatwi kiteepweewe hotelaawaali

The Pharisees therefore said unto him, Thou bearest witness of thyself; thy witness is not true.

14. haapafse ciisisii mecimi wiikinaakwi kwehkwi pesikwi pah niimeya niila si teepweewe niteepweewe mayaawatwi ksake niwaakota weemeya mecimi yehaaya weeka kiilawa mata kiwaakotaanaawa weemeya weelaa yehaaya

Jesus answered and said unto them, Even if I bear witness of myself, my witness is true; for I know whence I came, and whither I go; but ye know not whence I come, or whither I go.

15. nawaci hini wiyawfi yeeki kitelahkowepwa mata niila nitepowaala hileni

Ye judge after the flesh; I judge no man.

16. hanhka mecimi kwehkwi tepowaasiweeya niila nitepowaasiweewe mayaawatwi ksake mata naanhsihka niila weeka niila mecimi hina hohfima weewaawiineskawita

Yea and if I judge, my judgment is true; for I am not alone, but I and the Father that sent me.

17. hanhka mecimi hini kikwteletiiwenwaaki mehtawikaate hini yeesi hoteepweewenwa niiswi hileniiki mayaawhki

Yea and in your law it is written, that the witness of two men is true.

18. niila hina peepah niimeka pesikwi niiya si teepweewe mecimi hina hohfima weewaawiineskawita nipah niimaakwa teepweewe hotelahi

I am he that beareth witness of myself, and the Father that sent me beareth witness of me.

19. weecikeenahi nihki taanawe kohfa hotelaawaali ciisisii haapafse mata kiwaakomipwa niila mata nohki nohfa waakomiyeekwe kiilawa nehfaapi kih waakomaawa nohfa hotelahi

They said therefore unto him, Where is thy Father? Jesus answered, Ye know neither me, nor my Father: if ye knew me, ye would know my Father also.

20. hini moni poonahfoowikaaneki kalawi yooloma kalawiiwena yeesi kakehkimiweeci hini mamaatomeewikamikoki mecimi mata hileni homesenaali ksake hotaatefamoowe keewaki mata piyeeya

These words spake he in the treasury, as he taught in the temple: and no man took him; because his hour was not yet come.

21. weecikeenahi nohki hotelahi nihi neh weepfe mecimi keh natonehwipwa chiine keh nepepwa kimaciisilawiiwenwaaki yehaaya ke haalwi katawi si piyaapwa

He said therefore again unto them, I go away, and ye shall seek me, and shall die in your sin: whither I go, ye cannot come.

22. nihki coosaki weecikeenahi kanhha we nhto wiiya weeci hiyoci hina yehaaya ke haalwi katawi si piyaapwa hiwaki

The Jews therefore said, Will he kill himself, that he saith, Whither I go, ye cannot come?

23. chiine kiilawa siipaaci koociwipwa niila spemeki noociwi kiilawa yooma yeelekokwahkamikiki hoci mata niila yeelekokwahkamikiki hoci hotelahi nihi

And he said unto them, Ye are from beneath; I am from above: ye are of this world; I am not of this world.

24. weecikeenahi kitelepwa niila wahsi kiilawa nepeyeekwe kimaciisilawiiwenwaaki ksake weeciwephi kiilawa teepwehseeyeekwe yeesi niiyaawiya hina keh nepepwa kimaciisilawiiwenwaaki

I said therefore unto you, that ye shall die in your sins: for except ye believe that I am he, ye shall die in your sins.

25. nihki weecikeenahi neefawe kiila hotelaawaali teetepila hini mayehci nehfaapi kaloolelako hine weski hoci

They said therefore unto him, Who art thou? Jesus said unto them, Even that which I have also spoken unto you from the beginning.

26. meci wiyehi nipoona wahsi kalawiya mecimi wahsi mehtahkoweya kiilawa si payeekwa hina weewaawiineskawita mayaawefi chiine nili wiyehi mayehci hina hoci nootama niliini hini yeelekokwahkamikiki niteh kalawi hotelahi ciisisii

I have many things to speak and to judge concerning you: howbeit he that sent me is true; and the things which I heard from him, these speak I unto the world.

27. mata nihki homooleeletaanaawa yeesi hina nili hohfimaali haatotamawaaci nihi

They perceived not that he spake to them of the Father.

28. weecikeenahi ciisisii hine kiilawa mehci kokwiteneekwe hina hokwihfali hileni howe keh waakotaanaawa yeesi niiyaawiya hina mecimi yeesi mata wiyehi silawiiya pesikwi niila weeka yeesi hina hohfima kakehkimici nikalawi yooloma wiyehi

Jesus therefore said, When ye have lifted up the Son of man, then shall ye know that I am he, and that I do nothing of myself, but as the Father taught me, I speak these things.

29. chiine hina weewaawiineskawita niwiiciimekwa mata naanhsihka niila nimeh nakalekwa ksake nili wiyehi menwi lepwaskaakoci hina moosatawi nitesilawi hiwa

And he that sent me is with me; he hath not left me alone; for I do always the things that are pleasing to him.

30. yeesi hina kalawici yooloma wiyehi meci hoteepwehtawaawaali nili

As he spake these things, many believed on him.

31. weecikeenahi ciisisii kwehkwi nikalawiiweneki hapiyeekwe howe keela tepilo nikakehkimaafaki kiilawa

Jesus therefore said to those Jews which had believed him, If ye abide in my word, then are ye truly my disciples;

32. chiine keh waakotaanaawa hini teepweewe mecimi hini teepweewe keh miilekonaawa tepeeletamoowefiiwe hotelahi yohoma coosahi mayehci teepwehtaakoci

and ye shall know the truth, and the truth shall make you free.

33. hotaapaftaakohi nihi heplehemii homiinhka niilawe mecimi matalaakwa keewaki nimeh kiikeenikaninekona hileni nehiwe kiila kooci keh miilekonaawa tepeeletamoowefiiwe hiyo

They answered unto him, We be Abraham's seed, and have never yet been in bondage to any man: how sayest thou, Ye shall be made free?

34. hotaapaftawahi ciisisii tepilo tepilo kitelepwa niila caakiwiyeefa meemacilawiita maciisilawiiwe maciisilawiiwe hokiikeenikanali nili

Jesus answered them, Verily, verily, I say unto you, Every one that committeth sin is the bondservant of sin.

35. mecimi hina kiikeenikaafa mata kookwelaakwasi hapiwa hini wiikiwaapeki hina hokwihfima hapiwa kookwelaakwasi

And the bondservant abideth not in the house for ever: the son abideth for ever.

36. kwehkwi weecikeena hina hokwihfima miilelwaakwe tepeeletamoowefiiwe sapkahi keh tepeeletamoowefipwa kiilawa

If therefore the Son shall make you free, ye shall be free indeed.

37. kiwaakomelepwa yeesi heplehemii homiinhkaanici kiilawa payeekwa kinatonehaanaawa

I know that ye are Abraham's seed; yet ye seek to kill me, because my word hath not free course in you.

wahsi nhsiyeekwe ksake nikalawiiwe mata meh
tepeeletamhfeya kiiyaawaaki

38. nikalawi nili wiyehi mayehci neemeya wiici
nohfa mecimi kiilawa nehfaapi nili wiyehi
kitesilawiipwa mayehci kohfwa hoci nootameekwe

I speak the things which I have seen with
my Father: and ye also do the things
which ye heard from your father.

39. haapafseeki nihki mecimi niilawe heplehemii
nohfena hotelaawaali kwehkwi heplehemii
hotapelohfemite kiilawa nili hopekatefiiwena
heplehemii kih silawiipwa kiilawa hotelahi ciisisii

They answered and said unto him, Our
father is Abraham. Jesus saith unto them,
If ye were Abraham's children, ye would
do the works of Abraham.

40. weeka howe kinatonehaanaawa wahsi
nhsiyeekwe hileni mayehci wiitamoolwaakwe hini
teepweewe maneto weeci nootama mata heplehemii
yooma silawi

But now ye seek to kill me, a man that
hath told you the truth, which I heard from
God: this did not Abraham.

41. kitesilawiipwa kiilawa nili hopekatefiiwena
kohfwa nihki mata niilawe weepeeletiiwhetiiweneki
nooci niikipe nipoonaape nekoti hohfima teetepilahi
maneto hotelaawaali

Ye do the works of your father. They said
unto him, We were not born of
fornication; we have one Father, even
God.

42. kwehkwi maneto hohfiyeekwe ki
hahkweelemipwa ksake nipiyeci lohfa niila mecimi
maneto noome ksake mata nohki nimehci pesikwi
piya weeka hina niwaawiineskaakwa hotelahi ciisisii

Jesus said unto them, If God were your
Father, ye would love me: for I came forth
and am come from God; for neither have I
come of myself, but he sent me.

43. koociwe mata kinenohtaanaawa nipekikalawiiwe
ksake teetepilahi nikalawiiwe kitaalwi katawi
nootaanaawa

Why do ye not understand my speech?
Even because ye cannot hear my word.

44. hina macimaneto kohfwa koociwipwa kiilawa
mecimi nili holasiikaaci hakaawaatameewena kohfwa
hini kitesiteheewenwa wah silawiiyeekwe
naanhsiweeta hina hine halemahkamikatwi hoci
mecimi mata hini teepweeweneki niipawi
matalaakwa ksake teepweewe wiiyaaki yeh kalawici
naanhhaacimoowe hina honhhalwaafiiwe hoci kalawi
ksake hina naanaanhhaacimota mecimi hina hohfima
nitasi

Ye are of your father the devil, and the
lusts of your father it is your will to do.
He was a murderer from the beginning,
and stood not in the truth, because there is
no truth in him. When he speaketh a lie,
he speaketh of his own: for he is a liar,
and the father thereof.

45. weeka ksake hini teepweewe niteyo mata
kiteepwehtawipwa kiilawa

But because I say the truth, ye believe me
not.

46. taanawe kiilawa niteepimekwa maciisilawiiwe
kwehkwi teepweewe ni hiyo koociwe kiilawa mata
kiteepwehtawipwa

Which of you convicteth me of sin? If I
say truth, why do ye not believe me?

47. hina manetooli weeciwita honootaana nili
hokalawiiwena maneto ksake halayooma weeci mata
nootameekwe nili ksake mata maneto koociwipwa
kiilawa

He that is of God heareth the words of
God: for this cause ye hear them not,
because ye are not of God.

48. haapafseeki nihki coosaki mecimi ha mata
noowesi hiyope yeesi kiila semeliyewiyani mecimi
poonaci waninehfi hotelaawaali

The Jews answered and said unto him,
Say we not well that thou art a Samaritan,
and hast a devil?

49. ciisisii haapafse mata nipoona waninehfi weeka nootakeelema nohfa chiine kiilawa kimiyaasimekofihipwa

Jesus answered, I have not a devil; but I honour my Father, and ye dishonour me.

50. payeekwa mata ninatoneha niwahfaacimekofiiwe hapiwa nekoti neetonehikeeta mecimi teepowaasiweeta

But I seek not mine own glory: there is one that seeketh and judgeth.

51. tepilo tepilo kitelepwa niila kwehkwi hileni kciitonake nikalawiiwe hina matalaakwa weh neeme hkwinamoowe

Verily, verily, I say unto you, If a man keep my word, he shall never see death.

52. nihki coosaki howe niwaakotaape yeesi poonaci waninehfi heplehemii nepwa chiine nihki maamoosikiiskwecki mecimi kwehkwi hileni kciitonake nikalawiiwe hina matalaakwa weh kotata hkwinamoowe kiteyo kiila

The Jews said unto him, Now we know that thou hast a devil. Abraham is dead, and the prophets; and thou sayest, If a man keep my word, he shall never taste of death.

53. ha halika kitelefi nohfena heplehemii nepeka mecimi nihki maamoosikiiskwecki nepooki neefawe kitesto kiiya kiila hotelaawaali

Art thou greater than our father Abraham, which is dead? and the prophets are dead: whom makest thou thyself?

54. ciisisii haapafse kwehkwi wahfaacimekofihtooya niiya niwahfaacimekofiiwe matalaakwa wiyehi nohfa hina weewahfaacimekofihita yaacimeekwe yeesi hina homanetoomiyeekwe

Jesus answered, If I glorify myself, my glory is nothing: it is my Father that glorifieth me; of whom ye say, that he is your God;

55. chiine mata hina kimeh waakomaawa weeka niwaakoma niila chiine kwehkwi mata niwaakoma ni hiyo paasi kiilawa neh lefi naanaanhhaacimota payeekwa niwaakoma hina mecimi nikciitona hokalawiiwe

and ye have not known him: but I know him; and if I should say, I know him not, I shall be like unto you, a liar: but I know him, and keep his word.

56. kohfwa heplehemii hosasilepwa wahsi neemeki nikaasekiki chiine hini honeeme hina mecimi howesilepwa hotelahi

Your father Abraham rejoiced to see my day; and he saw it, and was glad.

57. weecikeenahi nihki coosaki mata keewaki niyaalanwaapitaki kime tfwi kkatoowi chiine kiila ha kimehci neewa heplehemii hotelaawaali

The Jews therefore said unto him, Thou art not yet fifty years old, and hast thou seen Abraham?

58. tepilo tepilo kitelepwa niila wihsi pwaa niikici heplehemii nitapi niila hotelahi ciisisii

Jesus said unto them, Verily, verily, I say unto you, Before Abraham was, I am.

59. nihki homamaawahi siikonhhi weecikeenahi wahsi pkitehwaawaaci nili payeekwa ciisisii hokkito wiiya mecimi lohfe hini mamaatomeewikamikwi

They took up stones therefore to cast at him: but Jesus hid himself, and went out of the temple.

John:9

1. chiine yeesi hina pemhfeeci honeewaali hileniili weecita kakeepiikweeli ta hoskilenaweewilici hoci

And as he passed by, he saw a man blind from his birth.

2. chiine hokakehkimaafhi honatohtaakohi lepaayii neefawe maciisilawi ha yaama hileni weelaa toke hokehkiyaamhhi weeci kakeepiikweewi hoskilenaweewici hotekohi

And his disciples asked him, saying, Rabbi, who did sin, this man, or his parents, that he should be born blind?

3. ciisisii haapafse mata yaama hileni maciisilawi nohki mata hokehkiyaamhhi weeka wahsi nili hopekatefiiwena maneto tepinawkwitooteeki wiiyaaki hina

Jesus answered, Neither did this man sin, nor his parents: but that the works of God should be made manifest in him.

4. kwiilahi pekatenaataako nili hopekatefiiwena hina weewaawiineskawita yeheeye hini kiisekiki hini tepehkiki piyeeya hine hileni mata katawi pekatefi

We must work the works of him that sent me, while it is day: the night cometh, when no man can work.

5. ye hapiya hini yeelekokwahkamikiki niiya hini wayahfeeyaaki hini yeelekokwahkamikiki hiwa

When I am in the world, I am the light of the world.

6. yeh mehtoweci hina hini hasiskiiki si fekwiwa mecimi hini fekoowe hoci hosto peefakwaakiasiski mecimi hosesonamawaali hoskiisekowilici hini peefakwaakiasiski

When he had thus spoken, he spat on the ground, and made clay of the spittle, and anointed his eyes with the clay,

7. chiine nhhaalo kifinolo hini pehkwaakamiki sailoomi hotelaali nili hini yeh laapaacimoki waawiineskoofo weecikeena hina weepfe chiine kifino mecimi piyeci tepinamwa

and said unto him, Go, wash in the pool of Siloam (which is by interpretation, Sent). He went away therefore, and washed, and came seeing.

8. nihki maapayecikaalaacki weecikeenahi chiine nihki neeneewaacki nhhihta laakwa nili yeesi katoweewilici ha mata hina yaama lematapita mecimi katowe hiwaki

The neighbours therefore, and they which saw him aforetime, that he was a beggar, said, Is not this he that sat and begged?

9. kotakaki hina hiwaki kotakaki mata weeka hina si naakofi hiwaki niiya hina hisiwe hina

Others said, It is he: others said, No, but he is like him. He said, I am he.

10. nihki weecikeenahi nehiwe howe si tawenoote kiskiiseko hotelaawaali nili

They said therefore unto him, How then were thine eyes opened?

11. hina haapafse hina hileni ciisisii yaaloofota hosto peefakwaakiasiski mecimi nisesonamaakwa niskiisekoki chiine nhhaalo sailoomiki mecimi kifinolo nitekwa weecikeenahi niweepfe chiine nikifino mecimi nootfeko tepinamoowe hisiwe

He answered, The man that is called Jesus made clay, and anointed mine eyes, and said unto me, Go to Siloam, and wash: so I went away and washed, and I received sight.

12. mecimi nihki taanawe hina hotelaawaali nili kookwe hotelahi hina

And they said unto him, Where is he? He saith, I know not.

13. nihki nihi pelesihi hoteh piyeelaawaali nili yehki keekeepiikweelici

They bring to the Pharisees him that aforetime was blind.

14. howe hini halwaakahsiweewe ta hini si kiisekiki hine ciisisii hosto hini peefakwaakiasiski mecimi hotawenamawaali nili hoskiisekowilici

Now it was the sabbath on the day when Jesus made the clay, and opened his eyes.

15. nohki weecikeenahi nihki pelesiiki nehfaapi honatohtawaawaali nili yeesi hina hotfekoci hotepinamoowe chiine hina peefakwaakiasiski niskiiseko hoteh poona chiine nikifino mecimi nitepina hotelahi nihi

Again therefore the Pharisees also asked him how he received his sight. And he said unto them, He put clay upon mine eyes, and I washed, and do see.

16. naaleta weecikeenahi nihki pelesiiki mata yaama hileni maneto hoci ksake mata hokcitaweeleta hini halwaakahsiweewe hiwaki weeka kotakaki nehiwe

Some therefore of the Pharisees said, This man is not from God, because he keepeth not the sabbath. But others said, How can

wih si katawi hileni meciisilawiita silawi yooloma
yeeki kikinooloowena hiwaki mecimi nitasi hahteewi
pahfehkaawe heelekiina nihki

17. nihki weecikeenahi nohki nehiwe kitelaacima
yeesi hina tawenamawehki kiskiiseko hotelaawaali
nili keekeepiikweewi leniili mecimi hina
maamoosikiiskweeta hina hisiwe

18. nihki coosaki weecikeenahi mata nili si
teepwehseeki yeesi hina hiyehki kakeepiikweeci
mecimi mehci hotfekoci tepinamoowe paalohi nihki
hotahpimaawahi nihi hokehkiyaamhhi hina mayehci
hotfekota hotepinamoowe

19. mecimi honatohtawaawahi nihi ha yaama
kikwihfwa weecita kakeepiikweewi niiki yeeleekwe
nehiwe howe hina si nohki tepinamwa hotelaawahi

20. hokehkiyaamhhi haapafsehi mecimi
niwaakotaape yeesi yaama hokwihfiyaake mecimi
yeesi hina kakeepiikweewi niikici

21. payeekwa yeesi hina hinoki tepinaki mata
niwaakotaape weelaa si wiyeefa teetawenamawaata
hoskiisekowilici mata niwaakomaape natohtawehko
katemo yo pesikwi we haatota wiiya hisiwehi

22. yooloma wiyehi hiwahi hokehkiyaamhhi ksake
nihki hokwfaawahi nihi coosahi ksake nihki coosaki
mehtaacimooki neyehka wahsi kwehkwi wiyehsi
hileni tepasawaacimaate nili yeesi klaistiiwilici hina
wih lohfelhkoofo hini mhsikamikwi hoci

23. weecikeenahi katemo yo natohtawehko hiwahi
hokehkiyaamhhi

24. yooni mawi-niisene nihki hotahpimaawaali nili
hileniili yehki keekakeepiikweelici chiine miili
wahfaacimekofiiwe maneto niwaakotaape yeesi
yaama hileni maciilefici hotelaawaali nili

25. weecikeena hina haapafse kwehkwi toke hina
meciisilawiita mata niwaakota nekoti wiyehi
niwaakota yeesi yehki kakeepiikweeya hinoki
nitepina

26. nihki weecikeenahi nehiwe kitpenalekwa hina
nehiwe kitesi tawenamaakwa kiskiiseko hotelaawaali

27. hotaapaftawahi hina kiwiitamoolepwa teetepila
hinoki mecimi mata kinootaakeepwa nehiwe hoci ha
kih nootaanaawa hini nohki ha nehfaapi kiilawa kih
kakehkimaafiimekowa

a man that is a sinner do such signs? And
there was a division among them.

They say therefore unto the blind man
again, What sayest thou of him, in that he
opened thine eyes? And he said, He is a
prophet.

The Jews therefore did not believe
concerning him, that he had been blind,
and had received his sight, until they
called the parents of him that had received
his sight,

and asked them, saying, Is this your son,
who ye say was born blind? how then doth
he now see?

His parents answered and said, We know
that this is our son, and that he was born
blind:

but how he now seeth, we know not; or
who opened his eyes, we know not: ask
him; he is of age; he shall speak for
himself.

These things said his parents, because
they feared the Jews: for the Jews had
agreed already, that if any man should
confess him to be Christ, he should be put
out of the synagogue.

Therefore said his parents, He is of age;
ask him.

So they called a second time the man that
was blind, and said unto him, Give glory
to God: we know that this man is a sinner.

He therefore answered, Whether he be a
sinner, I know not: one thing I know, that,
whereas I was blind, now I see.

They said therefore unto him, What did he
to thee? how opened he thine eyes?

He answered them, I told you even now,
and ye did not hear: wherefore would ye
hear it again? would ye also become his
disciples?

28. mecimi nihki holhskimaawaali nili chiine ha hokakehkimaafali kiila weeka niilawe moosisii hokakehkimaafhi hiwaki

And they reviled him, and said, Thou art his disciple; but we are disciples of Moses.

29. niwaakotaape yeesi mehci kaloolaaci moosisiili maneto weeka yaama hileni mata niwaakotaape weeciwici hiwaki

We know that God hath spoken unto Moses: but as for this man, we know not whence he is.

30. hina hileni haapafse mecimi koociwe yooni hini kwakwehtaani yeesi kiilawa mata waakotameekwe hina weeciwici chiine weekhi hina nitawenamaakwa niskiiseko

The man answered and said unto them, Why, herein is the marvel, that ye know not whence he is, and yet he opened mine eyes.

31. kiwaakotaape yeesi maneto mata nootawaaci meciisilawiilici payeekwa nehcipe hileni we hosasilawehaata manetooli hilefite mecimi hotesiteheewenilici silawiite niliini hina honootawaali

We know that God heareth not sinners: but if any man be a worshipper of God, and do his will, him he heareth.

32. yeelaakwa hini yeelekokwahkamikiki halemiki matalaakwa hini nootoote yeesi wiyeefa nekoti tawenamawaaci nili hoskiiseko hileni kakeepiikweewi niiki

Since the world began it was never heard that any one opened the eyes of a man born blind.

33. kwehkwi yaama hileni mata maneto hociwite mata wiyehi yah katawi silawi hina hotelahi nihi

If this man were not from God, he could do nothing.

34. haapafseeki nihki mecimi melhske maciisilawiiweneki kiniiki kiila mecimi ha kikakehkimipe hotelaawaali nili mecimi nili holohfe pakilaawaali nihki

They answered and said unto him, Thou wast altogether born in sins, and dost thou teach us? And they cast him out.

35. nootaake ciisisii yeesi nihki mehci lohfe pakilaawaaci nili mecimi nili homhkawaali ha kiteepwehse nili hokwihfali maneto hotelaali

Jesus heard that they had cast him out; and finding him, he said, Dost thou believe on the Son of God?

36. hina haapafse mecimi hiwa chiine teepeelemiweeta neefawe hina wahsi menawahi niila teepwehseeya hina

He answered and said, And who is he, Lord, that I may believe on him?

37. kimehci neewa hina mecimi hina hina keekiikalooletiimehka hotelaali ciisisii

Jesus said unto him, Thou hast both seen him, and he it is that speaketh with thee.

38. mecimi hina teepeelemiweeta niteepwehse hisiwe mecimi hina hosasilawehaali nili

And he said, Lord, I believe. And he worshipped him.

39. mecimi ksake mehtahkowaaletiiwe nooci yooma yeelekokwahkamikiki si piya wahsi nihki peepwaa tepinakiki menawahi tepinamowaaci chiine nihki teetepinakiki wahsi menawahi kakeepiikweewaaci hiwa ciisisii

And Jesus said, For judgment came I into this world, that they which see not may see; and that they which see may become blind.

40. yohkoma nihki pelesiiki hoci weewiici hapicki nili nootaakeeki yoolooma wiyehi mecimi ha nehfaapi niilawe nikakeepiikweepe hotelaawaali

Those of the Pharisees which were with him heard these things, and said unto him, Are we also blind?

41. kwehkwi kakeepiikweeyeekwe kiilawa mata kih poonaanaawa maciisilawiiwe weeka nitepinaape

Jesus said unto them, If ye were blind, ye would have no sin: but now ye say, We see: your sin remaineth.

kiteyopwa kimaciisilawiiwenwa yaska hahteewi
hotelahi ciisisii

John:10

1. tepilo tepilo kitelepwa niila hina mata hini skwaate
weeci piicfaata hini howakhoowenwa nihki
meekiifaki weeka payakila laakwa hotaafiwe yoona
kaakimooteka hina mecimi ciikoniwehfi

Verily, verily, I say unto you, He that entereth not by the door into the fold of the sheep, but climbeth up some other way, the same is a thief and a robber.

2. weeka hina hini skwaate weeci piicfaata
kehcitawahaata nihi meekiifhi hina

But he that entereth in by the door is the shepherd of the sheep.

3. niliini hina kehcitawahtoota hini skwaate
hotawenamawaali mecimi nihki meekiifaki
honootamawaaawaali hotesihsimoowenilici chiine
hina honehalwaaka meekiifhi yeesifolici hotesi
wihkomahi nihi mecimi holohfewelahi

To him the porter openeth; and the sheep hear his voice: and he calleth his own sheep by name, and leadeth them out.

4. ye hina mehci faakiciwelaaci caayahki
honhhalwaafiiwenhhi nihi yeelahfamiilici heewa
mecimi nihki meekiifaki honeekalaawaali nili ksake
howaakotaanaawa nihki hotesihsimoowenilici

When he hath put forth all his own, he goeth before them, and the sheep follow him: for they know his voice.

5. chiine kotakisi-kookwe-neefali mata weh
neekalaawaali nihki weeka nili we hoci hosimooki
ksake mata nihki howaakotaanaawa hini
hotesihsimoowenilici kotakisi-kookwe-neefhi

And a stranger will they not follow, but will flee from him: for they know not the voice of strangers.

6. yooma pemaatoweewe hokaloolahi ciisisii
payeekwa nihki mata honenohtaanaawa hini si wiyehi
keekaloolaaci

This parable spake Jesus unto them: but they understood not what things they were which he spake unto them.

7. ciisisii weecikeenahi hotelahi nohki tepilo tepilo
kitelepwa niila niiya hini hoskwaateemwa nihki
meekiifaki

Jesus therefore said unto them again, Verily, verily, I say unto you, I am the door of the sheep.

8. caayahki yeelahfamiiya peepiyaacki
kaakimootekiki chiine ciikoniwehfiiki payeekwa
nihki meekiifaki mata honootawaawahi nihi

All that came before me are thieves and robbers: but the sheep did not hear them.

9. niiya hini skwaate kwehkwi wiyeefa hileni niila
hoci piicfaate weh waapaneshoofo hina chiine weh
piicfe mecimi lohfe mecimi we mhka wah tah pah
wihfenici

I am the door: by me if any man enter in, he shall be saved, and shall go in and go out, and shall find pasture.

10. hina kaakimooteka mata piyeewa weeka wahsi
menawahi kimooteki mecimi nhsiweeci mecimi
macilotwaakeeci nipiya wahsi menawahi nihki
poonamowaaci lenaweewiiwe mecimi menawahi
maali poonamowaaci hini

The thief cometh not, but that he may steal, and kill, and destroy: I came that they may have life, and may have it abundantly.

11. niiya hina howesi kehcitawahaata meekiifhi hina
howesi kehcitawahaata hosekifetawahi
hotelenaweewiiwe nihi meekiifhi

I am the good shepherd: the good shepherd layeth down his life for the sheep.

12. hina yeelooleta mecimi mata kehcitawahaata mata nihi meekiifhi nhhalwaafiiweni hotelaapamaali nili mhhweewali piyeeli chiine honakalahi nihi meekiifhi mecimi hosimo mecimi hina mhhweewa homamhpwahi nihi chiine holhfwelhkawahi nihi

He that is a hireling, and not a shepherd, whose own the sheep are not, beholdeth the wolf coming, and leaveth the sheep, and fleeth, and the wolf snatcheth them, and scattereth them:

13. hosimo hina ksake yeelooleta mecimi mata homakofeelemahi nihi meekiifhi

he fleeth because he is a hireling, and careth not for the sheep.

14. niiya hina howesi kehcitawahaata meekiifhi chiine niwaakomaaki ninhhalwaafiiwenaki mecimi ninhhalwaafiiwenaki niwaakomekooki

I am the good shepherd; and I know mine own, and mine own know me,

15. teetepilahi yeesi hina hohfima waakomici mecimi niwaakoma hina hohfima chiine nisekifetawaaki nitelenaweewiiwe nihki meekiifaki

even as the Father knoweth me, and I know the Father; and I lay down my life for the sheep.

16. chiine kotakaki meekiifaki nipoonaaki mata yooma weeciwicki kwiilahi nehfaapi nihki neh piyeelaaki mecimi nihki weh nootaanaawa nitesihsimoowe chiine weh nekotiifiiki nekoti kehcitawahaata

And other sheep I have, which are not of this fold: them also I must bring, and they shall hear my voice; and they shall become one flock, one shepherd.

17. weecikeenahi hina hohfima sapkahi nitahkweelemekwa ksake nisekifeto nitelenaweewiiwe wahsi menawa hini mameya nohki

Therefore doth the Father love me, because I lay down my life, that I may take it again.

18. mata wiyeefa nimamaakwa hini weeka pesikwi niila hini nisekifeto nipoona waasikaki wahsi sekifetooya hini mecimi nipoona waasikaki wahsi mameya hini nohki yooma tepikeemoowe nohfa nootatena

No one taketh it away from me, but I lay it down of myself. I have power to lay it down, and I have power to take it again. This commandment received I from my Father.

19. nitasi nohki pafekwiiya pahfehkaawe heelekiina nihki coosaki ksake yooloma kalawiiwena hoci

There arose a division again among the Jews because of these words.

20. chiine meci nihki hopoonaali hina waninehfiili mecimi weepefi koociwe kinootawaawa kiilawa hiwaki

And many of them said, He hath a devil, and is mad; why hear ye him?

21. kotakaki mata yooloma nili hoteyoowena wiyeefa peepoonahfoomekota waninehfiili ha wih katawi waninehfi tawenamawaali nili hoskiiseko hina keekakeepiikweeta hiwaki

Others said, These are not the sayings of one possessed with a devil. Can a devil open the eyes of the blind?

22. chiine kwena hini hahteewi hini hofepaacilawiiwe si wihfenhcikeewe colooseelemii tasi

And it was the feast of the dedication at Jerusalem: it was winter;

23. pepoonwi hini chiine ciisisii paamhfe hini mamaatomeewikamikoki salamanii hotawikanefoowikaaneki

and Jesus was walking in the temple in Solomon's porch.

24. nihki coosaki weecikeenahi piyeeki kaayaawka nili mecimi taaniwe laakwasi kiila kitkawaaci fookinipe kwehkwi kiiyawiyane hina klaistii tepinalekwi wiitamawinaake hotelaawaali

The Jews therefore came round about him, and said unto him, How long dost thou hold us in suspense? If thou art the Christ, tell us plainly.

25. hotaapaftawahi ciisisii kiwiitamoolepwa mecimi mata kiteepwehseepwa kiilawa nili pekatefiiwena yaasilawiiya howiifooweneki nohfa niliini peepah niimaakoya teepweewe

Jesus answered them, I told you, and ye believe not: the works that I do in my Father's name, these bear witness of me.

26. payeekwa mata kiteepwehseepwa ksake mata nimeekiifemaki koociwipwa kiilawa

But ye believe not, because ye are not of my sheep.

27. nimeekiifemaki honootaanaawa nitesihsimoowe chiine niwaakomaaki mecimi nineekalekooki nihki

My sheep hear my voice, and I know them, and they follow me:

28. chiine nimiilaaki kookwelaakwasi lenaweewiiwe chiine matalaakwasi ya hkwinamooki mecimi mata wiyeefa weh nileciki hoci kwakwatenahi nihi

and I give unto them eternal life; and they shall never perish, and no one shall snatch them out of my hand.

29. nohfa mayehci miilita nihi halika mhsiilefi noota caayahki mecimi mata wiyeefa katawiilefi wahsi hina hohfima holeciki hoci kwakwatenaaci nihi

My Father, which hath given them unto me, is greater than all; and no one is able to snatch them out of the Father's hand.

30. niila chiine hina hohfima ninekotwiipe

I and the Father are one.

31. nihki coosaki homamaawahi siikonhhi nohki wahsi siikonhhwaawaaci nili

The Jews took up stones again to stone him.

32. hotaapatawahi ciisisii meci howesi pekatefiiwena kimehci hina hohfima hoci waapatelelepwa taaniwe nele pekatefiiwena kooci siikonhhwipwa hotelahi

Jesus answered them, Many good works have I shewed you from the Father; for which of those works do ye stone me?

33. hotaapatawaawaali nihki coosaki howesi pekatefiiwe mata kooci siikonhholepe weeka pahtaamoowe hoci mecimi yeesi ksake kiila kateski hileni maneto stooyani kiiya hotelaawaali

The Jews answered him, For a good work we stone thee not, but for blasphemy; and because that thou, being a man, makest thyself God.

34. hotaapaftawahi ciisisii ha mata kikwteletiiwenwaaki niila niteyo manetooki kiilawa si mehtawikaate

Jesus answered them, Is it not written in your law, I said, Ye are gods?

35. kwehkwi hina manetooki sinaate nihi weeotfekolici hini hokalawiiwe maneto mecimi hini tepilo heewikaateeki mata ya katawi poskonoote

If he called them gods, unto whom the word of God came (and the scripture cannot be broken),

36. ha kipahtaamo kiila kitelaawa hina nili hina hohfima yeeyaaphaaci mecimi hini yeelekokwahkamikiki yeewaawiineskawaaci ha ksake niiya hina hokwihfali maneto niteyo

say ye of him, whom the Father sanctified and sent into the world, Thou blasphemest; because I said, I am the Son of God'?

37. kwehkwi niila silawiiya mata nili hopekatefiiwena nohfa teki teepwehtawiko

If I do not the works of my Father, believe me not.

38. weeka kwehkwi nili silawiiya niila weekhi mata niila kiteepwehtawipwa teepwehtamoko nili pekatefiiwena wahsi kiilawa menawahi waakotameekwe mecimi nenohtameekwe yeesi hina hohfima hapici niiyaaki mecimi howiiyaaki hina hohfima niila

But if I do them, though ye believe not me, believe the works: that ye may know and understand that the Father is in me, and I in the Father.

39. nihki nohki natonehikeeki wahsi nhfaawaaci nili mecimi nili weepfeeli hososkwatenaawaali

They sought again to take him: and he went forth out of their hand.

40. chiine hina weepfe nohki halika hini caatenii tasi ta hapici caanii ta hine nhhihta fafahkwi holelhiweeki mecimi nitasi hapiwa

And he went away again beyond Jordan into the place where John was at the first baptizing; and there he abode.

41. chiine meci hopiyeelotaakohi hina chiine nihki caanii sapkahi mata kikinooloowe silawi payeekwa caayahki wiyehi kookwe-nehi-kaaci caanii yeelaacimaaci yooloma hileniili teepweewenwi hiwaki

And many came unto him; and they said, John indeed did no sign: but all things whatsoever John spake of this man were true.

42. chiine meci nitasi hoteepwehtawaawaali nili

And many believed on him there.

John:11

1. howe naanekoti hileni hahkwiloke lesolesii pefene hoci hini hotooteewenehi melii mecimi hoceeninaali maafeli

Now a certain man was sick, Lazarus of Bethany, of the village of Mary and her sister Martha.

2. chiine hina melii hina leelomhkoonaata nili teepeelemiweelici lomhkoowe mecimi hokafhamawaali hoficiwilici wiilehfa hiina hoskiimali lesolesiili hahkwilokeeli

And it was that Mary which anointed the Lord with ointment, and wiped his feet with her hair, whose brother Lazarus was sick.

3. nihki weeceeninaaticki hkweeki weecikeenahi nili si waawiinhkeeki teepeelemiweeta waapami hina yehahkweelemata hahkwiloke hisiweeki

The sisters therefore sent unto him, saying, Lord, behold, he whom thou lovest is sick.

4. payeekwa yeh nootaki hini ciisisii mata yooma hahkwilokeewe hkwinamooweneki hikwatwi weeka maneto wi hini howahfaacimekofiiwenici hoci wahsi hini hoci hokwihfali maneto wahfaacimekofiheci hiwa

But when Jesus heard it, he said, This sickness is not unto death, but for the glory of God, that the Son of God may be glorified thereby.

5. howe ciisisii hotahkweelemaali maafeli mecimi hoceeninaali maafe chiine lesolesiili

Now Jesus loved Martha, and her sister, and Lazarus.

6. hine weecikeenahi yeh nootaakeeci yeesi nili hahkwilokeelici hine laakwa niisoko hapiwa hini ta hapilici nili

When therefore he heard that he was sick, he abode at that time two days in the place where he was.

7. hine howe hahkowihi yooma nohki cotiyeeki haataako hotelahi nihi kakehkimaafhi

Then after this he saith to the disciples, Let us go into Judaea again.

8. lepaayii nihki coosaki payeekwa howe peemi natonehikeewaaci wahsi siikonhhohki mecimi ha nohki kiisa nhha hotelaawaali nihki kakehkimaafaki

The disciples say unto him, Rabbi, the Jews were but now seeking to stone thee; and goest thou thither again?

9. haapafse ciisisii ha mata hahteewi metahfwi-kite-niiswi yaatefaki hini nekoti kiiskwe kwehkwi hileni paamhfeete hini kiiseki mata hotakikahsinwa hina ksake hina honeeme hini yooma hoci wayahfaayaaki yeelekokwahkamikiki

Jesus answered, Are there not twelve hours in the day? If a man walk in the day, he stumbleth not, because he seeth the light of this world.

10. weeka kwehkwi hileni paamhfe hini tepehki hotakikahsinwa hina ksake hini wayahfeeyaaki matalaakwa howiiyaaki

But if a man walk in the night, he stumbleth, because the light is not in him.

11. yooni wiyehi kalawi hina mecimi hahkowihi yooma kihkaanena lesolesii kiipekwaamwa payeekwa nine ha wahsi menawahi nepaawe hoci hamachaki hotelahi nihi

These things spake he: and after this he saith unto them, Our friend Lazarus is fallen asleep; but I go, that I may awake him out of sleep.

12. nihki kakehkimaafaki weecikeenhhi teepeelemiweeta kwehkwi hina kiipekwaameke weh peteki howesilaasamamo hotelaawaali nili

The disciples therefore said unto him, Lord, if he is fallen asleep, he will recover.

13. howe hotkwinamoowenilici hotaatota ciisisii weeka yeesi halwaakahsiwi nepaalici hina hotaatota siteheeki nihki

Now Jesus had spoken of his death: but they thought that he spake of taking rest in sleep.

14. hine howe ciisisii hotepinalekwimahi nihi weecikeenhhi nepwa lesolesii

Then Jesus therefore said unto them plainly, Lazarus is dead.

15. mecimi ni howesilepwa yeesi pwaa nitasi hapiya kiilawa hoci wahsi hiniki menawahi kiilawa teepwehseeyeekwe payeekwa nhhaataako hina hotelahi

And I am glad for your sakes that I was not there, to the intent ye may believe; nevertheless let us go unto him.

16. weecikeenahi taamosii titimas yaaloofota nhhaataako nehfaapi wahsi menawahi wiitpenemakwe hotelahi howiici kakehkimaafhi

Thomas therefore, who is called Didymus, said unto his fellow-disciples, Let us also go, that we may die with him.

17. weecikeenahi hine yeh piyaaci ciisisii homhka yeesi neyehka niyeeko hapilici nili hini nepoowaalakoki

So when Jesus came, he found that he had been in the tomb four days already.

18. howe pefene maalaakwahi hahteewi colooseelemii si nawito niiswi maiili laakwa

Now Bethany was nigh unto Jerusalem, about fifteen furlongs off;

19. chiine meci nihki coosaki neyehka hotfaawahi maafeli chiine meliili wahsi kilakakawaawaaci nihi hoskiimwaali si

and many of the Jews had come to Martha and Mary, to console them concerning their brother.

20. maafe weecikeenahi yeh nootaakeeci yeesi peemi piyaalici ciisisiili weepfe mecimi honakskawaali nili weeka melii yaska lematapiwa piitike hini wiikiwa

Martha therefore, when she heard that Jesus was coming, went and met him: but Mary still sat in the house.

21. maafe weecikeenahi teepeelemiweeta kwehkwi kiila neyehka hotasi hapiyane nooskiima mata neyehka yah nepwa

Martha therefore said unto Jesus, Lord, if thou hadst been here, my brother had not died.

22. mecimi wiikinaakwi hinoki niwaakota hini kookwe-nehi-kaaci keh natotamawa maneto keh miilekwa maneto hotelaali ciisisiili

And even now I know that, whatsoever thou shalt ask of God, God will give thee.

23. kooskiima we honhska nohki hotelaali ciisisii

Jesus saith unto her, Thy brother shall rise again.

24. niwaakota wahsi hina nohki honhskaaci hini haapefiiwi-honhskaaweneki ta hini ceeyehkwi kiisekiki hotelaali maafe

Martha saith unto him, I know that he shall rise again in the resurrection at the last day.

25. niiya hini haapefiiwi-honhskaawe mecimi hini lenaweewiiwe hina teeteepwehseeta niiya weekhi hina nepwa keewaki weh lenaweewi hina

Jesus said unto her, I am the resurrection, and the life: he that believeth on me, though he die, yet shall he live:

26. chiine kookwe-neefa-kaaci lenaweewi mecimi teepwehse niiya matalaakwasi weh nepwa ha kiteepwehse yooma hotelaali ciisisii

and whosoever liveth and believeth on me shall never die. Believest thou this?

27. hanhka teepeelemiweeta neyehka niteepwehse yeesi kiiyawiyani hina klaistii nili hokwihfali maneto teetepilahi hina peepiyaata hini yeelekokwahkamikiki hotelaali maafe

She saith unto him, Yea, Lord: I have believed that thou art the Christ, the Son of God, even he that cometh into the world.

28. chiine yeh mehtoweci yooma hale weepfe mecimi hokiimi wihkomaali hoceeninaali hina keekehkimiwe hapiwa hotasi mecimi kinatomekwa hisiwe

And when she had said this, she went away, and called Mary her sister secretly, saying, The Master is here, and calleth thee.

29. mecimi hina yeh nootaki hini kwakwi pafekwi chiine weepfe nili heewa

And she, when she heard it, arose quickly, and went unto him.

30. howe ciisisii mata keewaki hini hoteeweneefeki si piyeewa weeka yaska hini tasi hapiwa maafe tah nakskawaaci nili

(Now Jesus was not yet come into the village, but was still in the place where Martha met him.

31. nihki coosaki hine weewiici hapicki nili piitike hini wiikiwa mecimi peemi kilakikawaacki nili yeh neewaawaaci meliili yeesi hina kwakwi pafekwiici mecimi lohfaaci honeekalaawaali nili yeesi keela toke hini nepoowaalakoki haalici mawi nitasi wihfakweelici siteheeki nihki

The Jews then which were with her in the house, and were comforting her, when they saw Mary, that she rose up quickly and went out, followed her, supposing that she was going unto the tomb to weep there.

32. melii weecikeenahi yeh piyaaci ta hapilici ciisisiili mecimi honeewaali nili sahkiki maalaakwahi yehoficiwilici si haakicife teepeelemiweeta kwehkwi kiila neyehka hotasi hapiyane nooskiima mata neyehka yah nepwa hotelaali nili

Mary therefore, when she came where Jesus was, and saw him, fell down at his feet, saying unto him, Lord, if thou hadst been here, my brother had not died.

33. hine weecikeenahi ciisisii honeewaali nili peemi wihfakweelici mecimi nihki coosaki nehfaapi peemi wihfakweewaaci peepiyeci wiitfeemaacki nili mamiyaatweewitehe hina hini hocacaalahkoki chiine petfakifi

When Jesus therefore saw her weeping, and the Jews also weeping which came with her, he groaned in the spirit, and was troubled,

34. mecimi taaniwe tasi kimehci sekisimaawa hina hisiwe teepeelemiweeta piyaalo mecimi neemelo hotelaawaali nihki

and said, Where have ye laid him? They say unto him, Lord, come and see.

35. wihfakwe ciisisii

Jesus wept.

36. nihki coosaki weecikeenahi waapamehko yeesi hina hahkweelemaaci nili hiwaki

The Jews therefore said, Behold how he loved him!

37. payeekwa naaleta nihki kanhha mata yaama hileni teetawenamawaata nili hoskiiseko hina keekakeepiikweeta homehci hpenato wahsi nehfaapi pwaa nepeki yaama hileni hiwaki

But some of them said, Could not this man, which opened the eyes of him that was blind, have caused that this man also should not die?

38. ciisisii weecikeenahi nohki peemi mamiyaatweewiteheeci wiiyaaki hini nepoowaalakwi

Jesus therefore again groaning in himself cometh to the tomb. Now it was a cave, and a stone lay against it.

si piyeewa howe pesikwi waasaalakwi hini mecimi
siikona hoskici hapiwa hini

39. halika siwelehko hina siikona hisiwe ciisisii mefe
nili hotikwemali hina nepeka teepeelemiweeta
laakwasi yooma howe hina wiiyaana wiskalelwa
ksake hina neyehka niiniyeeko hasenwa hotelaali nili

Jesus saith, Take ye away the stone. Martha, the sister of him that was dead, saith unto him, Lord, by this time he stinketh: for he hath been dead four days.

40. ha mata kitele niila wahsi kwehkwi kiila
teepwehseeyane neemeyani hini
howahfaacimekofiiwe maneto hotelaali ciisisii

Jesus saith unto her, Said I not unto thee, that, if thou believedst, thou shouldest see the glory of God?

41. weecikeenahi nihki halika hotesiwelaawaali nili
siikonali mecimi ciisisii spemeki laapi hoskiiseko
chiine hohfima niyaawe yeesi kiila nootawiyani

So they took away the stone. And Jesus lifted up his eyes, and said, Father, I thank thee that thou heardest me.

42. mecimi niwaakota yeesi kiila nootawiyani
moosatawi payeekwa ksake hina mehseeleka
neniipawita kaayaawka niteyo hini wahsi menawahi
nihki teepwehseewaaci yeesi kiila sapkahi
waawiineskawiyani hiwa

And I knew that thou hearest me always: but because of the multitude which standeth around I said it, that they may believe that thou didst send me.

43. chiine yeh mehci halayini si kalawici
holaamihsimo lesolesii piyeci lohfaalo

And when he had thus spoken, he cried with a loud voice, Lazarus, come forth.

44. piyeci lohfe hina nepeka kciipifo nepoowi
piitenikana holeciki mecimi hofiteki chiine
tetepiikwepifo pfiiwenehi pelhskonehko chiine
pakfenehko hotelahi ciisisii

He that was dead came forth, bound hand and foot with grave-clothes; and his face was bound about with a napkin. Jesus saith unto them, Loose him, and let him go.

45. meci weecikeenahi nihki coosaki
peepiyeelotawaacki meliili mecimi yeelaapatakki hini
yeesilawiici hina hoteepwehtawaawaali nili

Many therefore of the Jews, which came to Mary and beheld that which he did, believed on him.

46. payeekwa naaleta nihki weepfeeki nihi pelesihi
heeki mecimi howiitamawaawahi nihi nili wiyehi
ciisisii mayehci silawiici

But some of them went away to the Pharisees, and told them the things which Jesus had done.

47. nihki hokimaawi mhkateewkolayeeki
weecikeenahi chiine nihki pelesiiki
homaawatonaanaawa maawaskaawe mecimi nehiwe
silawiitaako ksake yaama hileni meci
kikinooloowena silawi

The chief priests therefore and the Pharisees gathered a council, and said, What do we? for this man doeth many signs.

48. kwehkwi halayini si wiilaani leelemakwe
caayahki hileniiki weh teepwehseeki nili chiine nihki
loomeniiki weh piyeeki mecimi keh mamaakonaaki
ta hapiyakwe chiine kitfweeloowenena hiwaki

If we let him thus alone, all men will believe on him: and the Romans will come and take away both our place and our nation.

49. payeekwa naanekoti nihki peemi
moospimekofiiwi mhkateewkolayeewici hini peemi
kkahki mata wiyehi kiwiyehisi waakotaanaawa
kiilawa

But a certain one of them, Caiaphas, being high priest that year, said unto them, Ye know nothing at all,

50. mata nohki hini kiteh memekineeletaanaawa
yeesi hini howesfeki kiilawa si wahsi nekoti hileni

nor do ye take account that it is expedient for you that one man should die for the

hotwaaci si nepeki nihi lenawehi mecimi wahsi hini melhske tfweeloowe pwaa haseki hotelahi

51. howe yooma hiwa hina mata pesikwi wiila hoci weeka peemi moospimekofiiwi mhkateewkolayeewici hini peemi kkahki homoosikiiskwaatota wahsi ciisisii hini tfweeloowe si hotwaaci nepeki

52. chiine mata hini tfweeloowe pehisi weeka wahsi hina menawahi nehfaapi maawatonaaci nekotweelena hisi nihi hotapelohfemhhi maneto lelhfweskaalici mefhiike

53. weecikeenahi hine kaasekiki hoci nihki homamenaawa tepoweewe wahsi menawahi hkwinamooweneki si poonaawaaci nili

54. ciisisii weecikeenahi mata kiteeni tawaaci paamhfe heelekiina nihi coosahi weeka hini hoci saawe hini piileski taamhkwe maalaakwahi hini peepskwahki hoteewe hiflami sitoote heewa mecimi nitasi nakahsinwa wiici nihi kakehkimaafhi

55. howe hini hopemhfaasiweewenwa nihki coosaki maalaakwahi hahteewi chiine meci colooseelemii si kkwicsinooki hini piileski taamhkwe homooki wihsi pwaa hini pemhfaasiweewiki wahsi hofepilotamowaaci wiiyaawa

56. nihki weecikeenahi honatonehwaawaali ciisisiili mecimi kiikalooletiiki yeesi niipawiwaaci hini mamaatomeewikamikoki nehiwe kitesiteheepwa ha mata hina weh piyeewa hini wihfenhcikeeweneki

57. howe nihki hokimaawi mhkateewkolayeeki chiine nihki pelesiiki mehci miiliweeki tepikeemoowe wahsi wiyeefa hileni waakotake ta hapilici nili wi hini waakotesiwe hina wahsi nihki menawahi mesenaawaaci nili

John:12

1. ciisisii weecikeenahi nekotwahfoko hisi wihsi pwaa hini pemhfaasiweewiki pefene si piyeewa ta hapici lesolesii nili nepelici weeci honhskaanaaci ciisisii

2. weecikeenahi nihki nitasi hoostawaawaali sapa mecimi maafe miisamaake weeka lesolesii nekoti nihki lematapicki tah wihfeniki wiici nili

3. melii weecikeenahi homame nekoti pawni hofepiya naatiiwi lomhkoowe kisoweelemekwatwi holaami chiine holominamawaali nili hofitali ciisisii

people, and that the whole nation perish not.

Now this he said not of himself: but being high priest that year, he prophesied that Jesus should die for the nation;

and not for the nation only, but that he might also gather together into one the children of God that are scattered abroad.

So from that day forth they took counsel that they might put him to death.

Jesus therefore walked no more openly among the Jews, but departed thence into the country near to the wilderness, into a city called Ephraim; and there he tarried with the disciples.

Now the passover of the Jews was at hand: and many went up to Jerusalem out of the country before the passover, to purify themselves.

They sought therefore for Jesus, and spake one with another, as they stood in the temple, What think ye? That he will not come to the feast?

Now the chief priests and the Pharisees had given commandment, that, if any man knew where he was, he should shew it, that they might take him.

Jesus therefore six days before the passover came to Bethany, where Lazarus was, whom Jesus raised from the dead.

So they made him a supper there: and Martha served; but Lazarus was one of them that sat at meat with him.

Mary therefore took a pound of ointment of spikenard, very precious, and anointed the feet of Jesus, and wiped his feet with

mecimi wiilehfa hotawena hokafhamawaali hoficiwilici mecimi hini wiikiwa hokwihfenwi hini yeesimiyaakoki hini lomhkoowe

her hair: and the house was filled with the odour of the ointment.

4. payeekwa cootas' hiskeeletii nekoti hokakehkimaafhi wah mestaawhaata nili

But Judas Iscariot, one of his disciples, which should betray him, saith,

5. koociwe mata yooma lomhkoowe nhfene tepeewe seleni si miyeekipi mecimi miilekwi hina kitemaafa hisiwe

Why was not this ointment sold for three hundred pence, and given to the poor?

6. howe yooma hiwa hina mata ksake homakofeelemaali nili kitemaafali weeka hina kaakimooteka mecimi hopah niime hini piitaaka homame hini yeepoonooteeki wiyehi

Now this he said, not because he cared for the poor; but because he was a thief, and having the bag took away what was put therein.

7. weecikeenahi ciisisii wiilaani hina hkweewa hini si kciitonake hini nilekonoofoowe si kaasekiki

Jesus therefore said, Suffer her to keep it against the day of my burying.

8. ksake hina kitemaafa moosatawi kipoonaawa wiici kiilawa weeka niila mata moosatawi kipoonipwa hisiwe

For the poor ye have always with you; but me ye have not always.

9. nihki coosaki hoci nehcipehi lenaweeki weecikeenahi waakotefiiki yeesi hina nitasi hapici mecimi nihki piyeeki mata ciisisiili pe hoci weeka wahsi menawahi nehfaapi neewaawaaci lesolesiili mayehci hina nili nepelici hoci honhskaanaaci

The common people therefore of the Jews learned that he was there: and they came, not for Jesus' sake only, but that they might see Lazarus also, whom he had raised from the dead.

10. payeekwa nihki hokimaawi mhkateewkolayeeki homamenaawa tepoweewe wahsi menawahi nehfaapi lesolesiili hkwinamooweneki si poonaawaaci

But the chief priests took counsel that they might put Lazarus also to death;

11. ksake niliini hoci meci nihki coosaki weepfeeki mecimi teepwehseeki ciisisiili

because that by reason of him many of the Jews went away, and believed on Jesus.

12. hini waayaapaki mhseelwa mehseeleka mayehci piyaata hini wihfenhcikeeweneki yeh nootaakeewaaci nihki yeesi ciisisiili wiisa colooseelemii si piyaalici

On the morrow a great multitude that had come to the feast, when they heard that Jesus was coming to Jerusalem,

13. homamenaawa nili pawiifalanimiise hoci nili pahkeeyakoki chiine weepfeeki homawi nakskawaawaali nili mecimi hoosena kisaateelemekofi hina peepiyaata hini howiifooweneki hina teepeelemiweeta teetepilahi nili hokimaamali hiswiila lahootamooki

took the branches of the palm trees, and went forth to meet him, and cried out, Hosanna: Blessed is he that cometh in the name of the Lord, even the King of Israel.

14. chiine ciisisii nakaye homehci mhkawaali mayaani ceekiifali hoskici nili lematapiwa yeesi hini mehtawikeeki

And Jesus, having found a young ass, sat thereon; as it is written,

15. teki kwpenelo hotaanehfali saayan' waapami kookimaama peemi piyaaci peemi hoskici lematapici ceekiifa homahkootelefemali

Fear not, daughter of Zion: behold, thy King cometh, sitting on an ass's colt.

16. yooloma wiyehi mata nenohsehi hokakehkimaafhi hini weski payeekwa hine ciisisii wahfaacimekofihoofo hine howe

These things understood not his disciples at the first: but when Jesus was glorified, then remembered they that these things

homhkaweeletaanaawa nihki yeesi nili si
mehtawikeeki yooloma wiyehi mecimi yeesi nihki
yooloma wiyehi mehcilotamowaaci nili si

were written of him, and that they had
done these things unto him.

17. hina mehseeleka weecikeenahi peepah
wiitfeemaata nili hine lesolesiili hini nepoowaalakwi
hoteh wihkomaali hina mecimi nili nepelici hoci
honhskaanaali nili hopahkina teepweewe

The multitude therefore that was with him
when he called Lazarus out of the tomb,
and raised him from the dead, bare
witness.

18. ksake yooma hini weeci nehfaapi weepfeewaaci
nihki mehseelekki mecimi nakskawaawaaci nili
ksake yeesi nootaakeewaaci nihki yeesi hina mehci
yooma silawiici kikinooloowe

For this cause also the multitude went and
met him, for that they heard that he had
done this sign.

19. nihki pelesiiki weecikeena hitiiki heelekiina
wiilawa waapatamoko yeesi kiilawa kolepkameekwe
mata wiyehi scih hini yeelekokwahkamikiki
honeekaleko hina

The Pharisees therefore said among
themselves, Behold how ye prevail
nothing: lo, the world is gone after him.

20. howe nitasi naanekoti kwiikiiwilenaweeki hapiiki
heelekiina yohoma hini tah wihfenhcikeeki yeesi
kkwicsinelici wahsi hosasilawaalici

Now there were certain Greeks among
those that went up to worship at the feast:

21. yohkooni weecikeenahi hopiyeelotawaawaali
filapiili pefseite hoci hina keelelii hoci taamhkwe
mecimi honatohtawaawaali yeeleniwiyani nih
neewaape ciisisii hisiweeki

these therefore came to Philip, which was
of Bethsaida of Galilee, and asked him,
saying, Sir, we would see Jesus.

22. filapii piyeewa mecimi howiitamawaali
heenhtlooli heenhtlo piyeewa chiine filapii mecimi
nihki howiitamawaawaali ciisisiili

Philip cometh and telleth Andrew:
Andrew cometh, and Philip, and they tell
Jesus.

23. chiine hotaapaftawahi ciisisii hini yaatefaki
piyeeya wi hina hokwihfali hileni
wahfaacimekofihoofoci

And Jesus answereth them, saying, The
hour is come, that the Son of man should
be glorified.

24. tepilo tepilo kitelepwa niila weeciwephi nekoti
pekwe kawaskwi hini hasiskiiki si penhfeke mecimi
nepooyaake hini naanhsihka pehi hapiiya weeka
kwehkwi hini nepooya meci mawifoowe hini hoci
niikinwi

Verily, verily, I say unto you, Except a
grain of wheat fall into the earth and die, it
abideth by itself alone; but if it die, it
beareth much fruit.

25. hina yahkweeletaka hotelenaweewiiwe howanhto
hini mecimi hina sesiikeeletaka hotelenaweewiiwe
yooma yeelekokwahkamikiki tasi weh nahiika hkwi
kciitona kookwelaakwasi lenaweewiiweneki

He that loveth his life loseth it; and he that
hateth his life in this world shall keep it
unto life eternal.

26. kwehkwi wiyeefa hileni miisamawite wiilaani
hina neekasite mecimi niila ta hapiya nehfaapi nitasi
we hapiwa nimiisamaakeema kwehkwi wiyeefa
hileni miisamawite niliini hina hohfima we
hotakeelemaali

If any man serve me, let him follow me;
and where I am, there shall also my
servant be: if any man serve me, him will
the Father honour.

27. howe nimayaawiniiya petfakatwi mecimi nehiwe
ne hiyo hohfima yooma hoci yaatefaki waapaneshilo

Now is my soul troubled; and what shall I
say? Father, save me from this hour. But
for this cause came I unto this hour.

payeekwa yooma yo ksake weeci yooma yaatefaki si
piyaaya

28. hohfima wahfaacimekwitoolo kiwiifoowe hiwa
nitasi weecikeenahi menhkwatoki hoci piyeeya
kalaweewihsimoowe nimehci neyiisweelena
wahfaacimekwito mecimi neh wahfaacimekwito hini
nohki hiyooya

Father, glorify thy name. There came
therefore a voice out of heaven, saying, I
have both glorified it, and will glorify it
again.

29. nihki mehseelekki weecikeenahi neniipawicki
maalaakwahi mecimi honootaanaawa hini yeesi
mehci nenemhkiwaki hini hiwaki kotakaki henhcaliili
homehci kaloolekooli hina hiwaki

The multitude therefore, that stood by, and
heard it, said that it had thundered: others
said, An angel hath spoken to him.

30. ciisisii haapafse mecimi yooma
kalaweewihsimoowe mata niila si kiteminaakwi hoci
piyeeya kiilawa weeka

Jesus answered and said, This voice hath
not come for my sake, but for your sakes.

31. howe hini hahteewi hotelahkowaafoowe yaama
yeelekokwahkamikiki howe hina yooma
yeelekokwahkamikiki hoci hokima hotoosaaka weh
lohfe pakiloofo

Now is the judgment of this world: now
shall the prince of this world be cast out.

32. chiine niila kwehkwi hini hasiskitaamhkwe hoci
kokwitenike niiyaaki neh si piyeetenaaki caayahki
hileniiki hiwa

And I, if I be lifted up from the earth, will
draw all men unto myself.

33. payeekwa yooma hiwa hina kikinootaacimo wa
hiki hotkwinamoowe wah nepeki

But this he said, signifying by what
manner of death he should die.

34. hina mehseeleka weecikeenahi hotaapaftawaali
nili nimehci hini kwteletiiwe hoci nootaape wahsi
hina klaistii hapici kookwelaakwasi mecimi nehiwe
kitesi hiyo kiila hina hokwihfali hileni kwiilahi we
kokwitenoofo neefawe yaama hokwihfali hileni

The multitude therefore answered him, We
have heard out of the law that the Christ
abideth for ever: and how sayest thou, The
Son of man must be lifted up? who is this
Son of man?

35. weecikeenahi ciisisii keewaki faapiimehi
hahteewi hini wayahfeeyaaki heelekiina kiilawa
hotelahi nihi paamhfeeki yeheeyehi kiilawa
poonameekwe hini wayahfeeyaaki wahsi mata hini
peepekicaaki matalekoyeekwe chiine hina
peepaamhfeeta hini laa pepekica mata howaakota
yehaaci

Jesus therefore said unto them, Yet a little
while is the light among you. Walk while
ye have the light, that darkness overtake
you not: and he that walketh in the
darkness knoweth not whither he goeth.

36. yeheeyehi kiilawa poonameekwe hini
wayahfeeyaaki teepwehseeko hini wayahfeeyaaki
wahsi menawahi kiilawa hokwihfinekoyeekwe
wayahfeeyaaki yooloma wiyehi kalawi ciisisii chiine
hina saawe mecimi hokkito wiiya nihi hoci

While ye have the light, believe on the
light, that ye may become sons of light.
These things spake Jesus, and he departed
and hid himself from them.

37. payeekwa weekhi holaami meci kikinooloowena
mehci silawi yeelahfamiilici nihi keewaki nihki mata
teepwehseeki nili

But though he had done so many signs
before them, yet they believed not on him:

38. wahsi hini hokalawiiwe haisaya hina
maamoosikiiskweeta menawahi hokwaawfeki hini

that the word of Isaiah the prophet might
be fulfilled, which he spake, Lord, who

hina yeeyoci teepeelemiweeta neefawe homehci
teepwehta nitelaacimoowenena mecimi neefawe
mehci pahkinamaakwi hini honehki hina
teepeelemiweeta

hath believed our report? And to whom
hath the arm of the Lord been revealed?

39. ksake yooma hoci haalwi teepwehseeki nihki
ksake yeesi haisaya nohki hiyoci

For this cause they could not believe, for
that Isaiah said again,

40. homehci kipwiliikwenahi hina mecimi
hosiipenamawahi hotehiwilici piilepe hoskiisekowa
nihki wi hoci neekeeki mecimi hotehiwa hoci
moositeheeki chiine wih kotekwiiki mecimi nih
kiikehaaki nihki

He hath blinded their eyes, and he
hardened their heart; Lest they should see
with their eyes, and perceive with their
heart, And should turn, And I should heal
them.

41. yooloma wiye hiwa haisaya ksake honeeme hina
howahfaacimekofiiwenilici mecimi hina hotaacimaali
nili

These things said Isaiah, because he saw
his glory; and he spake of him.

42. miiloowi nihki wiikinaakwi teepeelecikeecki hoci
meci hoteepwehtawaawaali nili payeekwa ksake
nihki pelesiiki hoci pwaa nihki tepaacimooki hini
piilepe nihki hini mhsikamikwi wi hoci
lohfelhkoofooki

Nevertheless even of the rulers many
believed on him; but because of the
Pharisees they did not confess it, lest they
should be put out of the synagogue:

43. ksake nihki halika honaasweeletaanaawa hini
wahfaacimekofiiwe hileniiki weeciwiki noota hini
wahfaacimekofiiwe maneto weeciwiki

for they loved the glory of men more than
the glory of God.

44. chiine nitasimo ciisisii mecimi hina
teeteepwehseeta niila mata teepwehse niila weeka nili
weewaawiineskawilici

And Jesus cried and said, He that
believeth on me, believeth not on me, but
on him that sent me.

45. chiine hina yeelaapamita niila hotelaapamaali nili
weewaawiineskawilici

And he that beholdeth me beholdeth him
that sent me.

46. nipiya wayahfeeyaaki hini yeelekokwahkamikiki
wahsi kookwe-neefa-kaaci teepwehse niila menawahi
mata hapici hini laa pepekicaaki

I am come a light into the world, that
whosoever believeth on me may not abide
in the darkness.

47. chiine kwehkwi wiyeefa hileni honootaana
niteyoowena mecimi mata hokciitonaana nili mata
nitepowaala hina ksake nipiya mata wahsi
tepowaatama hini yeelekokwahkamikiki weeka wahsi
hini yeelekokwahkamikiki waapanestooya

And if any man hear my sayings, and keep
them not, I judge him not: for I came not
to judge the world, but to save the world.

48. hina yehaalawinita mecimi mata hotahpenaana
niteyoowena hopoonaali nekoti wah tepowaalekoci
hini kalawiiwe keekalawiya hini yaska weh
tepowaaleko hina hine ceeyehkwi kaasekiki

He that rejecteth me, and receiveth not my
sayings, hath one that judgeth him: the
word that I spake, the same shall judge
him in the last day.

49. ksake mata niiya nooci kalawi weeka hina
hohfima weewaawiineskawita hina nimehci miilekwa
tepikeemoowe wa hiyoya mecimi wa haatotama

For I spake not from myself; but the
Father which sent me, he hath given me a
commandment, what I should say, and
what I should speak.

50. mecimi niwaakota yeesi hotepikeemoowe
lenaweewiiweniki nili wiyehi weecikeenahi

And I know that his commandment is life
eternal: the things therefore which I speak,

keekalawiya teetepilahi yeesi hina hohfima
mehcimici yooni nikalawi

even as the Father hath said unto me, so I
speak.

John:13

1. howe wihsi pwaa hini wihfenhcikeeki hini
pemhfaasiweewe ciisisii waakotefi yeesi hini
hotaatefamoowe piyeeyaaki wahsi hina yooma
yeelekokwahkamikiki hoci saaweci nili hohfimaali
haaci peemi hahkweelemaaci honhhalwaafiiwenhhi
yeepilici hini yeelekokwahkamikiki nihi hina
hotahkweelemahi hini ceeyehkwi si

Now before the feast of the passover,
Jesus knowing that his hour was come that
he should depart out of this world unto the
Father, having loved his own which were
in the world, he loved them unto the end.

2. chiine laakwasi sesapaawiki nili macimanetooli
neyehka teewa hini hotehiki cootasii hiskeeletii
saimanii hokwihfali hoteh poonamaakooli wahsi
mestaawhaaci nili

And during supper, the devil having
already put into the heart of Judas Iscariot,
Simon's son, to betray him,

3. ciisisii teewa howaakota yeesi nili hohfimaali
holeciwali si mehci miiliweelici caayahki wiyehi
chiine manetooli homeki hina mecimi manetooli
haaci

Jesus, knowing that the Father had given
all things into his hands, and that he came
forth from God, and goeth unto God,

4. pafekwi sapaaki hoci mecimi payakila hoteh
pakfenaana hopiitenikana chiine hoteh mame
kahfiikwehoowe mecimi hokitapito wiiya

riseth from supper, and layeth aside his
garments; and he took a towel, and girded
himself.

5. hine howe hoteh fiikina hini holaakaneki nepi
mecimi hotalemi kifalhfiteenahi nihi kakehkimaafhi
mecimi nili hina hokafhaana hini kahfiikwehoowe
kehtapifoci hotawe

Then he poureth water into the bason, and
began to wash the disciples' feet, and to
wipe them with the towel wherewith he
was girded.

6. weecikeena hina saiman' piitali si piyeewa
teepeelemiweeta ha kih kifinaana nifitali hotelaali
hina

So he cometh to Simon Peter. He saith
unto him, Lord, dost thou wash my feet?

7. ciisisii haapafse mecimi hini yeesilawiiya mata
kiwaakota kiila hinoki payeekwa keh nenohse
mayohkwaaci laakwa hotelaali

Jesus answered and said unto him, What I
do thou knowest not now; but thou shalt
understand hereafter.

8. mata laakwasi keh kifinaana nifitali hotelaali piita
hotaapaftawaali ciisisii kwehkwi niila pwaa kifinela
mata maalekhi kiweciimi kiila

Peter saith unto him, Thou shalt never
wash my feet. Jesus answered him, If I
wash thee not, thou hast no part with me.

9. teepeelemiweeta mata nifitali pehi weeka
nileciwali nehfaapi mecimi niisi hotelaali saiman'
piita

Simon Peter saith unto him, Lord, not my
feet only, but also my hands and my head.

10. hina weelelwiita mata hakaawaafi wahsi kifinaki
hofitali weeka peesekwi fafayaakifi chiine kiilawa
kifafayaakifipwa payeekwa mata caayahki hotelaali
ciisisii

Jesus saith to him, He that is bathed
needeth not save to wash his feet, but is
clean every whit: and ye are clean, but not
all.

11. ksake hina howaakomaali nili wah
mestaawhekoci weecikeenahi mata caayahki
kifafayaakifipwa hiwa hina

For he knew him that should betray him;
therefore said he, Ye are not all clean.

12. yooni hine hina yeh mehci kifalhfiteenaaci mecimi mameki hopiitenikana mecimi nohki lematapici ha kiwaakotaanaawa mayehci hpenalelako hotelahi

So when he had washed their feet, and taken his garments, and sat down again, he said unto them, Know ye what I have done to you?

13. keekehkimiwe chiine teepeelemiweeta kitaasipwa mecimi koowesi hiyopwa ksake yoona niiya

Ye call me, Master, and, Lord: and ye say well; for so I am.

14. kwehkwi niila howe hina teepeelemiweeta mecimi hina keekehkimiwe kimehci kifalhfiteenelepwa nehfaapi keela kiilawa kifalhfiteenetiko

If I then, the Lord and the Master, have washed your feet, ye also ought to wash one another's feet.

15. ksake kimehci miilelepwa yeeki wahsi kiilawa nehfaapi silawiiyeekwe yeesi mehci hpenalelako

For I have given you an example, that ye also should do as I have done to you.

16. tepilo tepilo kitelepwa niila haloolaaka mata halika hilefi teepeelemekoci mata nohki wiyeefa weewaawiineskaweta halika hilefi nili weewaawiineskaakoci

Verily, verily, I say unto you, A servant is not greater than his lord; neither one that is sent greater than he that sent him.

17. kwehkwi kiilawa waakotameekwe yooloma wiyehi kikisaateelemekofipwa kwehkwi kiilawa nili silawiiyeekwe

If ye know these things, blessed are ye if ye do them.

18. mata caayahki kiilawa nitesi kalawi niwaakoma hina mayehci mamaka payeekwa wahsi hini tepilo heewikaateeki menawahi hokwaawfeki hina meemiicita nitakhwaanemi niiyaaki hotekokwitena hokwani

I speak not of you all: I know whom I have chosen: but that the scripture may be fulfilled, He that eateth my bread lifted up his heel against me.

19. yooci hinoki kiwiitamoolepwa niila wihsi pwaa hini piyeemikaki wahsi hine hini piyeemikake menawahi teepwehseeyeekwe kiilawa yeesi niila hinawiya

From henceforth I tell you before it come to pass, that, when it is come to pass, ye may believe that I am he.

20. tepilo tepilo kitelepwa niila hina wiyeefa weetahpenaata kookwe-neefali-kaaci weewaawiineskawaka nootahpenekwa niila mecimi hina weetahpenita hotahpenaali nili weewaawiineskawilici

Verily, verily, I say unto you, He that receiveth whomsoever I send receiveth me; and he that receiveth me receiveth him that sent me.

21. hine ciisisii yeh mehtoweci halayini petfakifi hini hocacaalahkoki chiine tepinalekowe mecimi tepilo tepilo kitelepwa niila wahsi nekoti kiilawa mestaawhici hiwa

When Jesus had thus said, he was troubled in the spirit, and testified, and said, Verily, verily, I say unto you, that one of you shall betray me.

22. nihki kakehkimaafaki nanekoti si waapametiiki haanwehseeki yaacimaaci hina

The disciples looked one on another, doubting of whom he spake.

23. nitasi hini tah wihfeniki nekoti hokakehkimaafhi ciisisii hopaleeki peemi si haapacsinelici yeeahkweelemaaci ciisisii

There was at the table reclining in Jesus' bosom one of his disciples, whom Jesus loved.

24. saiman' piita weecikeenahi hoteh kakehkinootenamawaali nili wiitamawinaake neefaliwe nili yaacimaaci hina hotelaali

Simon Peter therefore beckoneth to him, and saith unto him, Tell us who it is of whom he speaketh.

25. hina peemi hattawassi hapacsiki yeesisiki hopaleeki ciisisii teepeelemiweeta neefawe hina hotelaali nili

He leaning back, as he was, on Jesus' breast saith unto him, Lord, who is it?

26. weecikeenahi ciisisii haapafse hina hina wah kookinamawaka pemhkaawe mecimi nimiila hini hotelaali yoone hine yeh mehci kookinaki hini pemhkaawe homame mecimi hini hoteh miilaali cootasiili nili hokwihfali saimanii hiskeeletii

Jesus therefore answereth, He it is, for whom I shall dip the sop, and give it him. So when he had dipped the sop, he taketh and giveth it to Judas, the son of Simon Iscariot.

27. chiine hahkowihi hini pemhkaawe hine howe hopiicfaamaali nili setenii weecikeenahi ciisisii waasa-silawiiyani silawiilo weeweetepi hotelaali nili

And after the sop, then entered Satan into him. Jesus therefore saith unto him, That thou doest, do quickly.

28. howe mata hileni hini tah wihfeniki howaakota weeci hina yooma si kaloolaaci nili

Now no man at the table knew for what intent he spake this unto him.

29. ksake naaleta siteheeki ksake yo cootasii hopah niime hini piitaaka tepenano wiyehi yeekaawaatamakwe hini tah wihfeniki weelaa wahsi hina miilaaci wiyehi nili kitemaafali ciisisii yeesi hilaaci nili

For some thought, because Judas had the bag, that Jesus said unto him, Buy what things we have need of for the feast; or, that he should give something to the poor.

30. hina howe homehcike hotahpena hini pemhkaawe lohfe weelena chiine hini howe tepehki

He then having received the sop went out straightway: and it was night.

31. hine weecikeena hina yeh lohfaaci ciisisii howe hina hokwihfali hileni wahfaacimekofihoofo mecimi maneto wahfaacimekofihoofo howiiyaawilici nili hiwa

When therefore he was gone out, Jesus saith, Now is the Son of man glorified, and God is glorified in him;

32. chiine maneto weh wahfaacimekofihaali nili mecimi hina weelena weh wahfaacimekofihaali

and God shall glorify him in himself, and straightway shall he glorify him.

33. hapelohfeefeti keewaki faapiimehi kiwiici hapiimelepwa keh natonehwipwa kiilawa chiine yeelaki nihki coosaki yehaaya ke haalwi piyaapwa yooni hinoki yeelelako kiilawa

Little children, yet a little while I am with you. Ye shall seek me: and as I said unto the Jews, Whither I go, ye cannot come; so now I say unto you.

34. mayaki tepikeemoowe kimiilelepwa wahsi kiilawa hahkweeletiyeekwe teetepilahi yeesi neyehka hahkweelemelako kiilawa wahsi nehfaapi si hahkweeletiyeekwe

A new commandment I give unto you, that ye love one another; even as I have loved you, that ye also love one another.

35. yooma we hoci waakotaanaawa caayahki hileniiki yeesi kiilawa hokakehkimaafimelako kwehkwi poonamaatiyeekwe hahkweeletiiwe

By this shall all men know that ye are my disciples, if ye have love one to another.

36. teepeelemiweeta taaniwe ki ha hotelaali saiman' piita haapafse ciisisii yehaaya ke haalwi neekasi hinoki weeka keh neekasi kiila mayohkwaaci

Simon Peter saith unto him, Lord, whither goest thou? Jesus answered, Whither I go, thou canst not follow me now; but thou shalt follow afterwards.

37. teepeelemiweeta koociwe mata kih katawi neekalele teetepilahi hinoki keh sekfetoole nitelenaweewiiwe kiila hotelaali piita

Peter saith unto him, Lord, why cannot I follow thee even now? I will lay down my life for thee.

38. ciisisii haapafse ha keh sekfetawi kitelenaweewiiwe tepilo tepilo kitele niila mata hina naapeeya weh kalhootamwa paalohi nhfene keh mehci kiyaacimi hotelaali

Jesus answereth, Wilt thou lay down thy life for me? Verily, verily, I say unto thee, The cock shall not crow, till thou hast denied me thrice.

John:14

1. teki wiilaani kitehiwa wih petfakifiiya teepwehseeko maneto teepwehseeko nehfaapi niila

Let not your heart be troubled: ye believe in God, believe also in me.

2. piitike howiikiwaapeki nohfa hahteewa meci yaataaki kwehkwi pwaa yooni hike hini neyehka kih wiitamoolepwa ksake ninita kimawi tasi nanahilotamoolepwa kiilawa

In my Father's house are many mansions; if it were not so, I would have told you; for I go to prepare a place for you.

3. mecimi kwehkwi nhhaaya chiine nanahilotamoolako tasi neh piya nohki mecimi niila keh si hotahpenelepwa wahsi ta hapiya niila nitasi menawa hapiyeekwe nehfaapi

And if I go and prepare a place for you, I come again, and will receive you unto myself; that where I am, there ye may be also.

4. chiine yehaaya kiwaakotaanaawa kiilawa hini wayeeci

And whither I go, ye know the way.

5. teepeelemiweeta mata niwaakotaape yehaayani nehiwe nitesi waakotaape hini wayeeci hotelaali taamosii

Thomas saith unto him, Lord, we know not whither thou goest; how know we the way?

6. niiya hini wayeeci chiine hini teepweewe mecimi hini lenaweewiiwe mata wiyeefa nili hohfimaali si piyeewa weeka saapwi niila hotelaali ciisisii

Jesus saith unto him, I am the way, and the truth, and the life: no one cometh unto the Father, but by me.

7. kwehkwi kiilawa neyehka waakomiyeekwe niila neyehka kih waakomaawa nohfa nehfaapi yooci hinoki kiwaakomaawa hina mecimi kimehci neewaawa

If ye had known me, ye would have known my Father also: from henceforth ye know him, and have seen him.

8. teepeelemiweeta waapatesinaake hina hohfima mecimi hini neh teepeelemope hotelaali filapii

Philip saith unto him, Lord, shew us the Father, and it sufficeth us.

9. ha yooni si sehkamika kimehci wiici hapiimelepwa chiine ha mata kiwaakomi filapii hina mayehci neewita homehci neewaali nili hohfimaali nehiwe kitesi waapatesinaake hina hohfima hiyo hotelaali ciisisii

Jesus saith unto him, Have I been so long time with you, and dost thou not know me, Philip? he that hath seen me hath seen the Father; how sayest thou, Shew us the Father?

10. ha mata kiila kiteepwehse yeesi hina hohfima wiiyaaki hapiya mecimi hina hohfima niiyaaki nili kalawiiwena yeelelako kiilawa mata nikalawi niiya hoci weeka hina hohfima peemi hapici niiyaaki hopekatefiiwena silawi

Believest thou not that I am in the Father, and the Father in me? the words that I say unto you I speak not from myself: but the Father abiding in me doeth his works.

11. teepwehtawilo yeesi niila hina hohfima wiiyaaki hapiya mecimi hina hohfima niiyaaki weelaa ke teepwehtawilo kapehi mohci nili tepilo pekatefiiwena hoci

Believe me that I am in the Father, and the Father in me: or else believe me for the very works' sake.

12. tepilo tepilo kitelepwa niila hina teeteepwehseeta niila nili pekatefiiwena yeesilawiiya weh silawi nehfaapi mecimi halika si pekatefiiwena noota yooloma weh silawi ksake niila hina hohfima nita

Verily, verily, I say unto you, He that believeth on me, the works that I do shall he do also; and greater works than these shall he do; because I go unto the Father.

13. chiine kookwe-nehi-kaaci keh natotaanaawa niwiifooweneki hini weh silawiiya wahsi hina hohfima menawahi wahfaacimekofihoofoci wiiyaaki hina hokwihfima

And whatsoever ye shall ask in my name, that will I do, that the Father may be glorified in the Son.

14. kwehkwi kiilawa keh natotaanaawa wiyehi niwiifooweneki hini weh silawiiya

If ye shall ask me anything in my name, that will I do.

15. kwehkwi kiilawa hahkweelemiyeekwe ke kciitonaanaawa nitepikeemoowena

If ye love me, ye will keep my commandments.

16. chiine neh kocima hina hohfima mecimi hina keh miilekowa nohki nekoti menwiteheetiiwenali wahsi menawa hina wiici hapiimelwaakwe kookwelaakwasi

And I will pray the Father, and he shall give you another Comforter, that he may be with you for ever,

17. teetepila hina teepweewe si hocacaalahkwa yaalwi hotahpenaaci hina yeelekokwahkamikiki ksake mata hina howaakomaali kiilawa kiwaakomaawa hina ksake hina kiwiici hapiimekowa kiilawa mecimi we hapiwa kiiyaawaaki

even the Spirit of truth: whom the world cannot receive; for it beholdeth him not, neither knoweth him: ye know him; for he abideth with you, and shall be in you.

18. mata nanhtaaki keh si nakalelepwa keh piyeelotoolepwa niila

I will not leave you desolate: I come unto you.

19. keewaki faapiimehi mecimi hina yeelekokwahkamikiki nitelaapamekwa mata kiteeni kiilawa weeka kitelaapamipwa ksake nitelenaweewi mecimi nehfaapi kiilawa keh lenaweewipwa

Yet a little while, and the world beholdeth me no more; but ye behold me: because I live, ye shall live also.

20. hine hini kaasekiki keh waakotaanaawa yeesi niila wiiyaaki nohfa hapiya mecimi kiilawa niiyaaki chiine niila kiiyaawaaki

In that day ye shall know that I am in my Father, and ye in me, and I in you.

21. hina peepoonaka nitepikeemoowena mecimi hokciitonaana nili hina hina yehahkweelemita chiine hina yehahkweelemita we hahkweelemekooli nohfali mecimi niila ne hahkweelema hina mecimi neh tepinawkofetawa niiya hina

He that hath my commandments, and keepeth them, he it is that loveth me: and he that loveth me shall be loved of my Father, and I will love him, and will manifest myself unto him.

22. teepeelemiweeta nehiwe piyeemikatwi wahsi kiiya tepinawkofetawiyaake niilawe chiine mata hina yeelekokwahkamikiki hotelaali cootasii mata hiskeeletii

Judas (not Iscariot) saith unto him, Lord, what is come to pass that thou wilt manifest thyself unto us, and not unto the world?

23. haapafse ciisisii mecimi kwehkwi hileni hahkweelemite we kciitona nikalawiiwe mecimi nohfa we hahkweelemaali nili chiine niilawe neh piyeelotawaape hina mecimi ne hostoope yeetaayaake kileki hina

Jesus answered and said unto him, If a man love me, he will keep my word: and my Father will love him, and we will come unto him, and make our abode with him.

24. hina peepwaa hahkweelemita mata hokciitonaana
nikalawiiwena chiine hini kalawiiwe
neenootameekwe kiilawa mata niila hini weeka hina
hohfima wiila weewaawiineskawita hotelaali

He that loveth me not keepeth not my
words: and the word which ye hear is not
mine, but the Father's who sent me.

25. kimehci kaloolelepwa yooloma wiyehi yeheeyehi
keewaki wiiciwiya kiilawa

These things have I spoken unto you,
while yet abiding with you.

26. weeka hina menwiteheetiiwena teetepila hina
hofepi hocacaalahkwa niliini hina hohfima weh
waawiineskawaali niwiifooweneki keh
kakehkimekowa hina caayahki wiyehi mecimi
kimhkawesiteheewenwaki keh si piyeetaakowa
caayahki yeelelako niila

But the Comforter, even the Holy Spirit,
whom the Father will send in my name, he
shall teach you all things, and bring to
your remembrance all that I said unto you.

27. kaamaaniilefiiwe kinakatamoolepwa
nikaamaaniilefiiwe kimiilelepwa mata hina
yeelekokwahkamikiki yeesi miiliweeci kitesi
miilelepwa teki wiilaani kitehiwa wih petfakifiiya
teki nohki wiilaani hini kwpeneya

Peace I leave with you; my peace I give
unto you: not as the world giveth, give I
unto you. Let not your heart be troubled,
neither let it be fearful.

28. kinootaanaawa yeelelako nih weepfe mecimi keh
piyeelotoolepwa kwehkwi hahkweelemiyeekwe
neyehka ki hosasilepwaapwa ksake hina hohfima nita
ksake hina hohfima halika hilefi noota niila

Ye heard how I said to you, I go away, and
I come unto you. If ye loved me, ye would
have rejoiced, because I go unto the
Father: for the Father is greater than I.

29. chiine howe kimehci wiitamoolepwa wihsi pwaa
hini piyeemikaki wahsi hine hini piyeemikake
menawahi kiilawa teepwehseeyeekwe

And now I have told you before it come to
pass, that, when it is come to pass, ye may
believe.

30. mata kiteeni mecilekhi keh si kaloolelepwa ksake
hina hini yeelekokwahkamikiki hokima hotoosaaka
piyeewa mecimi hina mata wiyehi hopoona niiyaaki

I will no more speak much with you, for
the prince of the world cometh: and he
hath nothing in me;

31. weeka wahsi hina yeelekokwahkamikiki
menawahi waakotaki yeesi niila hahkweelemaki hina
hohfima mecimi yeesi hina hohfima miilici
tepikeemoowe teetepilahi yooni nitesilawi
pafekwiitaako wiilaani yooci weepfeetaako

but that the world may know that I love
the Father, and as the Father gave me
commandment, even so I do. Arise, let us
go hence.

John:15

1. niiya hini mayaawi tetepahtekwi mecimi nohfa
hina ktikeewileni

I am the true vine, and my Father is the
husbandman.

2. caaki pehkeeyakoki niiyaaki weeci pwaa niikiki
mawifoowe hina homame hini halika hotesiweto
chiine caaki pehkeeyakoki weeci niikiki mawifoowe
hina hofafayaakilota hini wahsi menawa hini hoci
halika si niikiki mawifoowe

Every branch in me that beareth not fruit,
he taketh it away: and every branch that
beareth fruit, he cleanseth it, that it may
bear more fruit.

3. neyehka kiilawa kifafayaakifipwa ksake hini
kalawiiwe hoci mayehci niila kaloolelako

Already ye are clean because of the word
which I have spoken unto you.

4. hapiko niiyaaki mecimi niila kiiyaawaaki yeesi
hini pehkeeyakoki hini pesikwi hoci haalwi katawi

Abide in me, and I in you. As the branch
cannot bear fruit of itself, except it abide

niikiki mawifoowe weeciwep hini si takwi
lenaweewiiyaake hini tetepahtekwiki yooni hoci mata
katawi nohki kiilawa weeciwephi kiilawa niiyaaki
hapiyeekwe

in the vine; so neither can ye, except ye abide in me.

5. niiya hini tetepahtekwi kiiyaawa nili pehkeeyakoki hine yeepita niiyaaki mecimi niila wiiyaaki hina hina homaali niikito mawifoowe ksake niiya hoci tepaane kikatawi silawiipwa mata wiyehi

I am the vine, ye are the branches: He that abideth in me, and I in him, the same beareth much fruit: for apart from me ye can do nothing.

6. kwehkwi hileni hapite mata niiyaaki hina halika hipakiloofo paasi pehkeeyakoki mecimi sahfo chiine nihki homaawatonaanaawa nili chiine hini skoteeki hotipakitaanaawa nili mecimi nili fakte

If a man abide not in me, he is cast forth as a branch, and is withered; and they gather them, and cast them into the fire, and they are burned.

7. kwehkwi kiilawa niiyaaki hapiyeekwe mecimi nikalawiiwena hahteeke kiiyaawaaki natohseeko kookwe-nehi-kaaci yeesiteheeyeekwe mecimi hini ke hpenalekoopwa kiilawa

If ye abide in me, and my words abide in you, ask whatsoever ye will, and it shall be done unto you.

8. yooni tasi wahfaacimekofihoofo nohfa wahsi kiilawa maali niikitooyeekwe mawifoowe mecimi yooni keh si kakehkimaafiimelepwa

Herein is my Father glorified, that ye bear much fruit; and so shall ye be my disciples.

9. teetepilahi yeesi hina hohfima neyehka hahkweelemici nehfaapi niila kitesi hahkweelemelepwa hapiko nitahkweeletiiweneki

Even as the Father hath loved me, I also have loved you: abide ye in my love.

10. kwehkwi kciitonameekwe nitepikeemoowena ke hapipwa nitahkweeletiiweneki kiilawa teetepilahi yeesi neyehka kciitonama hotepikeemoowena nohfa mecimi hapiya hotahkweeletiiweneki

If ye keep my commandments, ye shall abide in my love; even as I have kept my Father's commandments, and abide in his love.

11. yooloma wiyehi kimehci kaloolelepwa wahsi noowesilepwaawe menawahi kiiyaawaaki hahteeki mecimi wahsi kiilawa koowesilepwaawenwa menawahi hokwaawi stooteeki

These things have I spoken unto you, that my joy may be in you, and that your joy may be fulfilled.

12. halayooma nitepikeemoowe wahsi kiilawa hahkweeletiyeekwe teetepilahi yeesi niila neyehka hahkweelemelako

This is my commandment, that ye love one another, even as I have loved you.

13. mata hileni hopoona halika yeeki hahkweeletiiwe yooma yeesi hileni sekfetawaaci hotelenaweewiiwe wihkaanhhi

Greater love hath no man than this, that a man lay down his life for his friends.

14. nihkaanaki kiilawa nili wiyehi silawiiyeekwe teetepimelako

Ye are my friends, if ye do the things which I command you.

15. mata kiteeni haloolaakaafaki kitelepwa ksake hina haloolaakaafa mata howaakota yeesilawiilici teepeelemekoci weeka neyehka niila wihkaanimaaki kitesinelepwa ksake caayahki wiyehi nohfa weeci nootama kimehci waakotestoolepwa

No longer do I call you servants; for the servant knoweth not what his lord doeth: but I have called you friends; for all things that I heard from my Father I have made known unto you.

16. mata kiilawa kimamipwa weeka niila kimamelepwa mecimi kimayaawsimelepwa wahsi

Ye did not choose me, but I chose you, and appointed you, that ye should go and

kiilawa haayeekwe mecimi niikitooyeekwe
mawifoowe chiine wahsi kimawifoowenwa hahteeki
wahsi kookwe-nehi-kaaci kiilawa keh
natotamawaawa hina hohfima niwiifooweneki
menawa hina miilelwaakwe hini

bear fruit, and that your fruit should abide:
that whatsoever ye shall ask of the Father
in my name, he may give it you.

17. yooloma wiyehi kitepimelepwa wahsi menawahi
kiilawa hahkweeletiyeekwe

These things I command you, that ye may
love one another.

18. kwehkwi hina yeelekokwahkamikiki
siikeelemelwaakwe kiwaakotaanaawa yeesi hina
neyehka siikeelemici niila wihsi pwaa hina
siikeelemelwaakwe kiilawa

If the world hateth you, ye know that it
hath hated me before it hated you.

19. kwehkwi hina yeelekokwahkamikiki
hociwiyeekwe hina yeelekokwahkamikiki wi
hahkweelemaali honhhalwaafiiwenali weeka ksake
kiilawa mata hina yeelekokwahkamikiki koociwipwa
payeekwa hina yeelekokwahkamikiki kooci
mekinelepwa weecikeena hina yeelekokwahkamikiki
kisiikeelemekowa

If ye were of the world, the world would
love its own: but because ye are not of the
world, but I chose you out of the world,
therefore the world hateth you.

20. kcitaweeletamoko hini kalawiiwe yeelelako
haloolaakaafa mata halika hilefi teepeelemekoci
kwehkwi nihki naanohkaachiwaate nehfaapi nihki
keh naanohkaachekowaaki kiilawa kwehkwi nihki
kciitonamowaate nikalawiiwe nehfaapi nihki ke
kciitonamaakowaaki kiilawa

Remember the word that I said unto you,
A servant is not greater than his lord. If
they persecuted me, they will also
persecute you; if they kept my word, they
will keep yours also.

21. weeka caayahki yooloma wiyehi ke
hpenalekowaaki nihki ksake niwiifoowe hoci ksake
nihki mata howaakomaaawaali nili
weewaawiineskawilici

But all these things will they do unto you
for my name's sake, because they know
not him that sent me.

22. kwehkwi nih pwaa mehci piya mecimi kaloolaaki
nihki mata hotah meh poonaanaawa maciisilawiiwe
weeka howe mata hopoonaanaawa
homaciisilawiiwenwa hoci hotwenika

If I had not come and spoken unto them,
they had not had sin: but now they have
no excuse for their sin.

23. hina seesiikeelemita nehfaapi hosiikeelemaali
nohfali

He that hateth me hateth my Father also.

24. kwehkwi nih pwaa neyehka silawi heelekiina
nihki nili pekatefiiwena pwaayaa kotaka wiyeefa
silawiici mata nihki hotah meh poonaanaawa
maciisilawiiwe weeka howe nihki nimehci nookooki
mecimi siikeelemekooki neyiiswi niila chiine nohfali

If I had not done among them the works
which none other did, they had not had
sin: but now have they both seen and
hated both me and my Father.

25. payeekwa piyeemikatwi yooma wahsi hini
kalawiiwe menawahi hokwaawfeki yeelawikeeki
hokwteletiiwenwaaki nisiikeelemekooki nihki
nelohci

But this cometh to pass, that the word may
be fulfilled that is written in their law,
They hated me without a cause.

26. payeekwa hine hina menwiteheetiiwena piyaate
kiilawa wah leskawaka hina hohfima hoci teetepila

But when the Comforter is come, whom I
will send unto you from the Father, even

hina teepweewe si hocacaalahkwa nili hohfimaali
weeotaamiita hina neh pah niimaakwa teepweewe

the Spirit of truth, which proceedeth from
the Father, he shall bear witness of me:

27. chiine nehfaapi kiilawa kipah niimenaawa
teepweewe ksake kimehci pah wiitfeemelepwa hine
hini weski hoci

and ye also bear witness, because ye have
been with me from the beginning.

John:16

1. yooloma wiyehi kimehci kaloolelepwa wih pwaa
kiilawa hpenaloofoyeekwe wahsi
hotakikahsineyeekwe

These things have I spoken unto you, that
ye should not be made to stumble.

2. nihki nili mhsikamiko ke hoci lohfe pakilekowaaki
hanhka hini yaatefaki piyeeya wahsi kookwe-neefa-
kaaci nhfelwaakwe weh sitehe yeesi hina
kisaacilotawaaci manetooli

They shall put you out of the synagogues:
yea, the hour cometh, that whosoever
killeth you shall think that he offereth
service unto God.

3. chiine yooloma wiyehi nihki weh silawiiki ksake
mata homeh waakomaawaali nili hohfimaali weelaa
niila mata

And these things will they do, because
they have not known the Father, nor me.

4. payeekwa yooloma wiyehi kimehci kaloolelepwa
wahsi hine hotaatefamoowenwa piyeeyaake
menawahi kiilawa mhkaweeletameekwe nili yeesi
wiitamoolako chiine hine weski hoci mata yooloma
wiyehi kitelepwa ksake kipah wiitfeemelepwa

But these things have I spoken unto you,
that when their hour is come, ye may
remember them, how that I told you. And
these things I said not unto you from the
beginning, because I was with you.

5. payeekwa howe hina nita weewaawiineskawita
mecimi mata nekoti kiilawa ninatohtaakwa taaniwe
kita

But now I go unto him that sent me; and
none of you asketh me, Whither goest
thou?

6. payeekwa ksake kimehci kaloolelepwa yooloma
wiyehi macilepwaawe hokwihfenwi kitehiwa

But because I have spoken these things
unto you, sorrow hath filled your heart.

7. payeekwa hini teepweewe kitelepwa howesfenwi
hini kiilawa si wahsi niila weepfeeya ksake kwehkwi
pwaa weepfeeya niila mata hina menwiteheetiiwena
keh piyeelotaakowa weeka kwehkwi niila nhhaaya
kiilawa neh leskawa hina

Nevertheless I tell you the truth; It is
expedient for you that I go away: for if I
go not away, the Comforter will not come
unto you; but if I go, I will send him unto
you.

8. chiine hina hine piyaate maciisilawiiweneki we
hoci haliskaita hini yeelekokwahkamikiki chiine
tepasawiilefiiweneki hoci mecimi
mehtahkoweeweneki hoci

And he, when he is come, will convict the
world in respect of sin, and of
righteousness, and of judgment:

9. maciisilawiiweneki hoci ksake mata nihki
teepwehseeki niila

of sin, because they believe not on me;

10. tepasawiilefiiweneki hoci ksake niila hina
hohfima nita mecimi kiilawa kitelaapamipwa mata
kiteeni

of righteousness, because I go to the
Father, and ye behold me no more;

11. mehtahkoweeweneki hoci ksake hina yooma
yeelekokwahkamikiki hokima hotoosaaka neyehka
mehtahkowaafo

of judgment, because the prince of this
world hath been judged.

12. keewaki nipoona meci wiyehi wa hilelako payeekwa kitaalwatenaanaawa kiilawa hinoki

I have yet many things to say unto you, but ye cannot bear them now.

13. payeekwa hine hina howe piyaate hina teepweewe si hocacaalahkwa hina keh si mayaawiwelekowa caayahki hini teepweewe ksake hina mata pesikwi wiila we hoci kalawi weeka kookwe-nehi-kaaci si wiyehi hina weh nootaake niliini hina weh kalawi mecimi keh mohkaatotamaakowa hina nili wiyehi waasa piyeeyaaki

Howbeit when he, the Spirit of truth, is come, he shall guide you into all the truth: for he shall not speak from himself; but what things soever he shall hear, these shall he speak: and he shall declare unto you the things that are to come.

14. neh wahfaacimekofihekwa hina ksake noowiilaamiiwe we hoci mame hina mecimi keh mohkaatotamaakowa hini

He shall glorify me: for he shall take of mine, and shall declare it unto you.

15. caayahki wiyehi kookwe-nehi-kaaci hopoona hina hohfima noowiilaami weecikeenahi niteyo wahsi hina mameki noowiilaamiiwe mecimi keh mohkaatotamaakowa hini kiilawa

All things whatsoever the Father hath are mine: therefore said I, that he taketh of mine, and shall declare it unto you.

16. faapiimehi chiine kiilawa kitelaapamipwa mata kiteeni mecimi nohki faapiimehi chiine keh neewipwa

A little while, and ye behold me no more; and again a little while, and ye shall see me.

17. naaleta hokakehkimaafhi weecikeenahi nehiwe yooma yeelelakwe hina faapiimehi chiine kiilawa mata kitelaapamipwa mecimi nohki faapiimehi chiine keh neewipwa chiine ksake hina hohfima nita hitiiki

Some of his disciples therefore said one to another, What is this that he saith unto us, A little while, and ye behold me not; and again a little while, and ye shall see me: and, Because I go to the Father?

18. nehiwe yooma yeeyoci hina faapiimehi mata kiwaakotaape yeeyoci hina hiwaki

They said therefore, What is this that he saith, A little while? We know not what he saith.

19. ciisisii homooleeleta yeesi nihki maatawi natohtawaawaaci nili mecimi hina ha kiniinatohtwaatipwa heelekiina kiilawa yooma si yeeyoya faapiimehi chiine kiilawa mata kitelaapamipwa mecimi nohki faapiimehi chiine keh neewipwa hotelahi

Jesus perceived that they were desirous to ask him, and he said unto them, Do ye inquire among yourselves concerning this, that I said, A little while, and ye behold me not, and again a little while, and ye shall see me?

20. tepilo tepilo kitelepwa niila keh wihfakweepwa mecimi keh mawepwa weeka hina yeelekokwahkamikiki we hosasilepwa kiilawa keh macilepwaawefipwa payeekwa kimacilepwaawenwa hosasilepwaaweneki weh si kotekonoote

Verily, verily, I say unto you, that ye shall weep and lament, but the world shall rejoice: ye shall be sorrowful, but your sorrow shall be turned into joy.

21. hkweewa hine hina hahkwiloowenecki ye hapici hopoona macilepwaawe ksake hotaatefamoowe howe piyeeya payeekwa hine hina yeh niikinaaci nili hapelohfali mata kiteeni homhkaweeleta hini hahkwatkaawe ksake hini hosasilepwaawe yeesi hileni si niikici hini yeelekokwahkamikiki

A woman when she is in travail hath sorrow, because her hour is come: but when she is delivered of the child, she remembereth no more the anguish, for the joy that a man is born into the world.

22. chiine kiilawa weecikeena hinoki kipoonaanaawa macilepwaawe payeekwa keh noolepwa nohki mecimi we hosasilepwaaya kitehiwa chiine koosasilepwaawenwa mata wiyeefa kitah mamaakowa

And ye therefore now have sorrow: but I will see you again, and your heart shall rejoice, and your joy no one taketh away from you.

23. chiine hine kaasekiki keh natohtawipwa mata wiyehi tepilo tepilo kitelepwa niila kwehkwi kiilawa keh natotamawaawa wiyehsi wiyehi hina hohfima hina keh miilekowa hini niwiifooweneki

And in that day ye shall ask me nothing. Verily, verily, I say unto you, If ye shall ask anything of the Father, he will give it you in my name.

24. yooni laakwasi mata wiyehi kimeh natotaanaawa niwiifooweneki natotamoko mecimi ke hotefipwa wahsi koosasilepwaawenwa menaw hokwaawi stooteeki

Hitherto have ye asked nothing in my name: ask, and ye shall receive, that your joy may be fulfilled.

25. yooloma wiyehi kimehci kaloolelepwa pepekici hiyooweneki hini haatefaki piyeeya hine mata kiteeni keh kaloolelepwa pepekici hiyooweneki weeka keh tepiwiitamoolepwa hina hohfima

These things have I spoken unto you in proverbs: the hour cometh, when I shall no more speak unto you in proverbs, but shall tell you plainly of the Father.

26. hine kaasekiki keh natohtamepwa niwiifooweneki mecimi mata wahsi keh kocitamoolepwa hina hohfima kitelepwa

In that day ye shall ask in my name: and I say not unto you, that I will pray the Father for you;

27. ksake hina hohfima kitahkweelemekowa wiila ksake kimehci kiilawa hahkweelemipwa mecimi kimehci teepwehseepwa yeesi hina hohfima hoci piyaaya

for the Father himself loveth you, because ye have loved me, and have believed that I came forth from the Father.

28. hina hohfima nooci piyeci lohfa mecimi hini yeelekokwahkamikiki niteh piya nohki ninakata hini yeelekokwahkamikiki mecimi hina hohfima nita

I came out from the Father, and am come into the world: again, I leave the world, and go unto the Father.

29. hokakehkimaafhi hiyohi scih howe tepinalekwi kalawilo kiila mecimi teki kalawilo pepekici hiyoowe

His disciples say, Lo, now speakest thou plainly, and speakest no proverb.

30. niwaakotaape howe yeesi kiila waakotamani caayahki wiyehi mecimi pwaa hakaawaatamani wahsi wiyeefa hileni natohtawehki yooma hoci niteepwehseepe yeesi kiila maneto hoci piyaayani

Now know we that thou knowest all things, and needest not that any man should ask thee: by this we believe that thou camest forth from God.

31. ciisisii hotaapaftawahi nihi ha howe kiteepwehseepwa

Jesus answered them, Do ye now believe?

32. waapatamoko hini yaatefaki piyeeya hanhka piyeeya howe wahsi kiilawa lhfweskaayeekwe caaki hileni honhhalwaafiiwe heewa mecimi neh nakalekoopi naanhsihka chiine mata weekhi ninaanhsikaawi ksake hina hohfima wiici niila

Behold, the hour cometh, yea, is come, that ye shall be scattered, every man to his own, and shall leave me alone: and yet I am not alone, because the Father is with me.

33. yooloma wiyehi kimehci kaloolelepwa wahsi niiyaaki menawahi kiilawa poonameekwe kaamaaniilefiiwe hini yeelekokwahkamikiki kiilawa kipoonaanaawa kiisenaacinamoowe payeekwa

These things have I spoken unto you, that in me ye may have peace. In the world ye have tribulation: but be of good cheer; I have overcome the world.

kilakiteheewefiko nimehci haliska hini
yeelekokwahkamikiki

John:17

1. yooloma wiyehi kalawi ciisisii mecimi spemeki
laapi hoskiiseko menhkwatoki chiine hohfima hini
yaatefaki piyeeya wahfaacimekofiiwhi kikwihfa
wahsi hina hokwihfima menawahi
wahfaacimekofihehki kiila

These things spake Jesus; and lifting up
his eyes to heaven, he said, Father, the
hour is come; glorify thy Son, that the Son
may glorify thee:

2. teetepilahi yeesi hina miilaci kiila simekofiiwe
wahsi mekofihtaki caayahki wiyawfi wahsi caayahki
nihi mayehci miilaci miilaaci kookwelaakwasi
lenaweewiiwe

even as thou gavest him authority over all
flesh, that whatsoever thou hast given
him, to them he should give eternal life.

3. chiine halayooma hini lenaweewiiwe
kookwelaakwasi wahsi nihki waakomehki kiila hina
pehi mayaawi maneto mecimi nili kiila sapkahi
weewaawiineskawata teetepilahi ciisis' klaistii

And this is life eternal, that they should
know thee the only true God, and him
whom thou didst send, even Jesus Christ.

4. kiwahfaacimekofihele kiila hini hoskitaamhkwe
nimehci lawi hini pekatefiiwe mayehci kiila miiliyani
wah silawiiya

I glorified thee on the earth, having
accomplished the work which thou hast
given me to do.

5. chiine howe hohfima wahfaacimekofihilo
nhhalwaaka kiiya kileki hini wahfaacimekofiiwe
peepoonama wiici kiila wihsi pwaa hahteeki hini
yeelekokwahkamikiki

And now, O Father, glorify thou me with
thine own self with the glory which I had
with thee before the world was.

6. nitepinawkofetawaaki kiwiifoowe nihki hileniiki
mayehci kiila hini yeelekokwahkamikiki hoci
miiliyani kiila yo nihki mecimi nihki kiila yo kimiili
chiine neyehka hokciitonaanaawa kikalawiiwe

I manifested thy name unto the men
whom thou gavest me out of the world:
thine they were, and thou gavest them to
me; and they have kept thy word.

7. howe howaakotaanaawa nihki caayahki wiyehi
kookwe-nehi-kaaci kimehci miili yeesi kiila hociwiki

Now they know that all things whatsoever
thou hast given me are from thee:

8. ksake nili kalawiiwena meemiiliyani nimehci
miilaaki nihki mecimi hotahpenaanaawa nili chiine
howaakotaanaawa teepweeweni yeesi niila kiiya hoci
piyaaya chiine teepwehseeki yeesi kiila sapkahi
waawiineskawiyani

for the words which thou gavest me I have
given unto them; and they received them,
and knew of a truth that I came forth from
thee, and they believed that thou didst
send me.

9. nihki nikocimawaaki mata nikocimawa hina
yeelekokwahkamikiki weeka nehke kiila mayehci
miiliyani ksake nihkiini kiila

I pray for them: I pray not for the world,
but for those whom thou hast given me;
for they are thine:

10. chiine caayahki wiyehi weewiilaamiya
koowiilaami mecimi nili kiila niila nili chiine
niwahfaacimekofihekoopi saapwi nili

and all things that are mine are thine, and
thine are mine: and I am glorified in them.

11. chiine mata kiteeni hini yeelekokwahkamikiki
nitapi chiine yohkoma hapiiki hini
yeelekokwahkamikiki mecimi kipiyeelotoole niila
hofepi hohfima kciitoni nihki kiwiifooweneki

And I am no more in the world, and these
are in the world, and I come to thee. Holy
Father, keep them in thy name which thou

mayehci kiila miiliyani wahsi menawahi nihki nekotiifiwaaci teetepilahi yeesi wiyakwe kiilawe

hast given me, that they may be one, even as we are.

12. yeheeyehi wiiciwiya nihki nikciitonaaki kiwiifooweneki kiila mayehci miiliyani mecimi nikcitawahaaki nihki chiine mata nekoti nihki hkwinamwa hina weeka hokwihfali miyaasinamoowe wahsi hini tepilo heewikaateeki menawahi hokwaawfeki

While I was with them, I kept them in thy name which thou hast given me: and I guarded them, and not one of them perished, but the son of perdition; that the scripture might be fulfilled.

13. payeekwa howe kipiyeelotoole mecimi yooloma wiyehi nikalawi hini yeelekokwahkamikiki wahsi menawahi nihki poonamowaaci noosasilepwaawe hokwaawi stoote howiiyaawaaki

But now I come to thee; and these things I speak in the world, that they may have my joy fulfilled in themselves.

14. nimehci miilaaki kikalawiiwe mecimi hina yeelekokwahkamikiki hosiikeelemahi nihi ksake nihki mata hina yeelekokwahkamikiki hociwiiki teetepilahi yeesi pwaa niila hina yeelekokwahkamikiki hociwiya

I have given them thy word; and the world hated them, because they are not of the world, even as I am not of the world.

15. mata nikocikeemo wahsi hini yeelekokwahkamikiki hoci lohfenaci nihki weeka wahsi nili maci wiyefali hoci tepaane si kciitonaci nihki

I pray not that thou shouldest take them from the world, but that thou shouldest keep them from the evil one.

16. mata nihki hina yeelekokwahkamikiki hociwiiki teetepilahi yeesi pwaa niila hina yeelekokwahkamikiki hociwiya

They are not of the world, even as I am not of the world.

17. fafayaakhi nihki hini teepweeweneki kikalawiiwe teepweewe

Sanctify them in the truth: thy word is truth.

18. yeesi kiila sapka hini yeelekokwahkamikiki si waawiineskawiyani teetepilahi yooni hini yeelekokwahkamikiki nitesi waawiineskawaaki nihki

As thou didst send me into the world, even so sent I them into the world.

19. chiine nihkiini hoci nifafayaakto niiya wahsi menawahi nihki nehfaapi fafayaakhoofowaaci teepweeweneki

And for their sakes I sanctify myself, that they themselves also may be sanctified in truth.

20. mata nohki yohkoma pehi nikocikeemawaaki weeka nehfaapi nihi teeteepwehseelici niila saapwi hokalawiiwenwa yohkoma

Neither for these only do I pray, but for them also that believe on me through their word;

21. wahsi menawahi nihki caayahki nekotiifiwaaci teetepilahi yeesi kiila hohfima hapiyani niiyaaki mecimi niila kiiyaaki wahsi nihki nehfaapi menawahi hapiwaaci kiiyaanenaaki wahsi menawa hina yeelekokwahkamikiki teepwehseeci yeesi kiila sapkahi waawiineskawiyani

that they may all be one; even as thou, Father, art in me, and I in thee, that they also may be in us: that the world may believe that thou didst send me.

22. chiine hini wahfaacimekofiiwe mayehci kiila miiliyani nimehci miilaaki nihki wahsi menawahi nekotiifiwaaci teetepilahi yeesi kiilawe nekotiifiyakwe

And the glory which thou hast given me I have given unto them; that they may be one, even as we are one;

23. niila wiiyaawaaki mecimi kiila niiyaaki wahsi
menawahi nihki nekoti si mefefihoofowaaci wahsi
hina yeelekokwahkamikiki waakotaki yeesi kiila
sapkahi waawiineskawiyani mecimi hahkweelemaci
nihki teetepilahi yeesi kiila hahkweelemiyani

24. hohfima nihki mayehci miiliyani kiila skata
nitesitehe wahsi ta hapiya nihki nehfaapi menawahi
wiici hapimiwaaci wahsi nihki menawa
hilaapatamowaaci niwahfaacimekofiiwe mayehci
kiila miiliyani ksake kitahkweelemi wihsi pwaa hini
hoskahkamikiki hini yeelekokwahkamikiki

25. hotepasawi hohfima mata kiwaakomekwa hina
yeelekokwahkamikiki weeka kiwaakomele niila
mecimi yohkoma howaakotaanaawa yeesi sapkahi
kiila waawiineskawiyani

26. mecimi niwaakotefihaaki kiwiifoowe mecimi weh
waakotefihiweeki hini wahsi hini hahkweeletiiwe
weeci kiila hahkweelemiyani menawahi hahteeki
wiiyaawaaki nihki mecimi niila wiiyaawaaki hiwa

I in them, and thou in me, that they may
be perfected into one; that the world may
know that thou didst send me, and lovedst
them, even as thou lovedst me.

Father, that which thou hast given me, I
will that, where I am, they also may be
with me; that they may behold my glory,
which thou hast given me: for thou
lovedst me before the foundation of the
world.

O righteous Father, the world knew thee
not, but I knew thee; and these knew that
thou didst send me;

and I made known unto them thy name,
and will make it known; that the love
wherewith thou lovedst me may be in
them, and I in them.

John:18

1. hine ciisisii mehtowe yooloma kalawiiwena
weepfe kileki hokakehkimaafhi kaameki hini
meftekonehi kitlani ta hahteeki memekinhcika piicfe
hini wiila mecimi hokakehkimaafhi

When Jesus had spoken these words, he
went forth with his disciples over the
brook Kidron, where was a garden, into
the which he entered, himself and his
disciples.

2. howe cootasii nehfaapi nili mayestaawhekoci hina
howaakota hini tasi ksake moosaki ciisisii hini
yaayeewa kileki hokakehkimaafhi

Now Judas also, which betrayed him,
knew the place: for Jesus oft-times
resorted thither with his disciples.

3. cootasii hine howe neyehka nakaye hini kamhpeni
samaakanhhi hotahpenahi mecimi nihi hokimaawi
mhkateewkolayehi hocimekofiiwenhhi chiine nihi
pelesihi piyeewa nitasi kileki tepehkiniitawaakanhhi
chiine looloosenikanhhi chiine hahkwi-hawoocikana

Judas then, having received the band of
soldiers, and officers from the chief priests
and the Pharisees, cometh thither with
lanterns and torches and weapons.

4. weecikeenahi ciisisii peemi waakotaki caayahki
nili wiyehi peemi hotfekoci nhheewa mecimi
neefawe kinatonehwaawa hotelahi nihi

Jesus therefore, knowing all the things
that were coming upon him, went forth,
and saith unto them, Whom seek ye?

5. hotaapaftawaawaali nihki ciisisii naaselefi hoci
hotelaawaali niiya hina hotelahi ciisisii chiine
cootasii nehfaapi mayestaawhekoci hina peemi wiici
kaapawiimaaci nihi

They answered him, Jesus of Nazareth.
Jesus saith unto them, I am he. And Judas
also, which betrayed him, was standing
with them.

6. hine weecikeenahi niiya hina yeelaaci nihi nihki
hasahkicehfeeki mecimi hini hasiskiiki si haakicfeeki

When therefore he said unto them, I am
he, they went backward, and fell to the
ground.

7. nohki weecikeenahi honatohtawahi nihi neefawe kinatonehwaawa chiine ciisisii naaselefi hoci hiwaki nihki

Again therefore he asked them, Whom seek ye? And they said, Jesus of Nazareth.

8. haapafse ciisisii kiwiitamoolepwa yeesi niiyaawiya hina kwehkwi weecikeenahi kiilawa natonehwiyeekwe niila wiilaani yohkoma nhhaawaate yehaawaaci

Jesus answered, I told you that I am he: if therefore ye seek me, let these go their way:

9. wahsi hini kalawiiwe menawahi hokwaawfeki keekalawici hina nehke mayehci miiliyani mata nekoti niwanhha

that the word might be fulfilled which he spake, Of those whom thou hast given me I lost not one.

10. saiman' piita weecikeenahi nakaye hopoona kiskhika holohfena hini mecimi hopkitehwaali nili hotaloolaakanali moospimekofiiwi mhkateewkolaye chiine hokiskehsethwaali homayaaotawaka howe hina haloolaakaafa melhkasi si howiifooweni

Simon Peter therefore having a sword drew it, and struck the high priest's servant, and cut off his right ear. Now the servant's name was Malchus.

11. ciisisii weecikeena hini piitaakaneki si poonano hini kiskhika ha mata neh mene hina tephika hina hohfima mayehci miilici hotelaali piitali

Jesus therefore said unto Peter, Put up the sword into the sheath: the cup which the Father hath given me, shall I not drink it?

12. weecikeenahi nihki kamhpeni chiine hina hokimaawi kaptiina mecimi nihki hocimekofiiwenaki nihki coosaki homawinachaawaali ciisisiili mecimi hokciipilaawaali nili

So the band and the chief captain, and the officers of the Jews, seized Jesus and bound him,

13. chiine henasiili nhhihta hotesiwelaawaali nili ksake niliini weesilemaaci hina keeyeefesii memoospimekofiiwi mhkateewkolayeewita hine peemi kkahki

and led him to Annas first; for he was father in law to Caiaphas, which was high priest that year.

14. howe keeyeefesii hina nenahimaata nihi coosahi yeesi hini howesfeki wahsi nekoti hileni hotwaaci nepeki nihi si lenawehi

Now Caiaphas was he which gave counsel to the Jews, that it was expedient that one man should die for the people.

15. chiine saiman' piita honeekalaali ciisisiili chiine nehfaapi kotaka nohki kakehkimaafa howe hina kakehkimaafa howaakomekooli nili moospimekofiiwi mhkateewkolayeeli mecimi hini hotepoweewiwakhoowe hina moospimekofiiwi mhkateewkolaye si piicfe kileki ciisisii

And Simon Peter followed Jesus, and so did another disciple. Now that disciple was known unto the high priest, and entered in with Jesus into the court of the high priest;

16. weeka piita peemi niipawici faakici hini skwaateeki weecikeena hina kotaka kakehkimaafa weewaakomaaci hina moospimekofiiwi mhkateewkolaye lohfe chiine hokaloolaali hkweefali kehcitawahtoolici hini skwaate mecimi hopiicfahaali piitali

but Peter was standing at the door without. So the other disciple, which was known unto the high priest, went out and spake unto her that kept the door, and brought in Peter.

17. weecikeena hina hkweefa kehcitawahtoota hini skwaate ha nehfaapi kiila nekoti hokakehkimaafhi yaama hileni hotelaali piitali mata niila hisiwe hina

The maid therefore that kept the door saith unto Peter, Art thou also one of this man's disciples? He saith, I am not.

18. howe nihki haloolaakaafaki chiine nihki
wiyehsimekofiiwenaki peemi nitasi niipawiwaaci
mehci pkaleenamooki mhkateewalo ksake hini weepi
chiine nihki peemi hawafowaaci mecimi piita
nehfaapi wiici nihi peemi niipawici mecimi hawafo

Now the servants and the officers were standing there, having made a fire of coals; for it was cold; and they were warming themselves: and Peter also was with them, standing and warming himself.

19. hina moospimekofiiwi mhkateewkolaye
weecikeenahi honatohtawaali ciisisiili
hokakehkimaafhi chiine hokakehkimiweewe

The high priest therefore asked Jesus of his disciples, and of his teaching.

20. hotaapaftawaali ciisisii nimehci tawaaci si kaloola
hina yeelekokwahkamikiki moosatawi
nikakehkimiwe mhsikamikoki chiine hini
mamaatomeewikamikoki yaatah caayahki nihki
coosaki maawatwi piyaawaaci mecimi mata wiyehi
nikiimi kalawi

Jesus answered him, I have spoken openly to the world; I ever taught in synagogues, and in the temple, where all the Jews come together; and in secret spake I nothing.

21. koociwe niila kinatohtawi natohtawi nihki
mayehci nootawicki hini yeelaki waapami yohkoma
howaakotaanaawa nili wiyehi yeeyoya hisiwe

Why askest thou me? ask them that have heard me, what I spake unto them: behold, these know the things which I said.

22. chiine yeh mehtoweci yooma nekoti nihki
wiyehsimekofiiwenaki peemi maalaakwahi niipawici
hopkitehwaali ciisisiili holeci ha yooni kitesi
haapaftawa hina moospimekofiiwi mhkateewkolaye
hotelaali

And when he had said this, one of the officers standing by struck Jesus with his hand, saying, Answerest thou the high priest so?

23. hotaapaftawaali ciisisii kwehkwi nimehci kalawi
mecaafiki teepweeminekolo hini mecaafiki weeka
kwehkwi howesa koociwe kipkitehwi hotelaali

Jesus answered him, If I have spoken evil, bear witness of the evil: but if well, why smitest thou me?

24. henasi weecikeenahi keeyefesiili hina
moospimekofiiwi mhkateewkolaye hoteleskamawaali
nili kciipifooli

Annas therefore sent him bound unto Caiaphas the high priest.

25. howe saiman' piita peemi niipawici mecimi
hawafo nihki weecikeena ha nehfaapi nekoti kiila
hokakehkimaafhi hotelaawaali kiyaacimo hina
mecimi mata niila hina hisiwe

Now Simon Peter was standing and warming himself. They said therefore unto him, Art thou also one of his disciples? He denied, and said, I am not.

26. nekoti nihi hotaloolaakaafhi hina
moospimekofiiwi mhkateewkolaye teewahi
nehalweelemaaci hina piita keekiskehsethwaaci ha
mata kinoole hini memekinhcikaneki wiici hina
hotelaali

One of the servants of the high priest, being a kinsman of him whose ear Peter cut off, saith, Did not I see thee in the garden with him?

27. weecikeenahi nohki piita kiyaacimo mecimi
weelena hina naapeeya kalhootamwa

Peter therefore denied again: and straightway the cock crew.

28. nihki weecikeenahi keeyefesiili hoci
fakinaapiyaalaawaali ciisisiili hini pletooliamiiki
heeki chiine hini kolahwaapanwi chiine mata nihki
wiilawa piicfeeki hini pletooliami wahsi menawahi
pwaa miyaashoofowaaci weeka menawahi
miiciwaaci hini pemhfaasiweewe

They lead Jesus therefore from Caiaphas into the palace: and it was early; and they themselves entered not into the palace, that they might not be defiled, but might eat the passover.

29. weecikeenahi paalatii nihi si lohfe mecimi nehiwesi mestaamoowe kipiyeetawaawa yaama hileni hiwa

Pilate therefore went out unto them, and saith, What accusation bring ye against this man?

30. haapafseeki nihki mecimi kwehkwi yaama hileni mata meemaciisilawiita wi hilefi mata neyehka kitah si pakfenamoolepe kiila hotelaawaali

They answered and said unto him, If this man were not an evil-doer, we should not have delivered him up unto thee.

31. weecikeenahi paalatii haamwelehko kiilawa mecimi tepowaalehko yeesfeki kikwteletiiwenwa hotelahi mata mayaawatwi kwteletiiweneki wahsi niilawe hileni hkwinamooweneki si poonakici hotelaawaali nihki coosaki

Pilate therefore said unto them, Take him yourselves, and judge him according to your law. The Jews said unto him, It is not lawful for us to put any man to death:

32. wahsi hini hokalawiiwe ciisisii menawahi hokwaawfeki keekalawici kikinootowe yeeki hkwinamoowe wa hocineeci

that the word of Jesus might be fulfilled, which he spake, signifying by what manner of death he should die.

33. paalatii nohki weecikeena hini pletooliami si piicfe mecimi hotahpimaali ciisisiili chiine ha kiila nili hokimaamwaali nihki coosaki hotelaali

Pilate therefore entered again into the palace, and called Jesus, and said unto him, Art thou the King of the Jews?

34. haapafse ha pesikwi kiila kiteyo yooma weelaa toke kotakaki kiwiitamaakooki niila si hotelaali

Jesus answered, Sayest thou this of thyself, or did others tell it thee concerning me?

35. haapafse paalatii ha niila coosa kinehalwaaka tfweeloowe mecimi nihki hokimaawi mhkateewkolayeeki niila kiteh pakfenekooki nehiwe kimehci silawi

Pilate answered, Am I a Jew? Thine own nation and the chief priests delivered thee unto me: what hast thou done?

36. haapafse ciisisii nookimaawiiwe mata yooma yeelekokwahkamikiki hociwi kwehkwi nookimaawiiwe yooma yeelekokwahkamikiki hociwike hine wih noochiweeki nitaloolaakanaki wahsi pwaa niila nihki coosaki si pakfeniki weeka howe mata yoociwiiya nookimaawiiwe hotelahi

Jesus answered, My kingdom is not of this world: if my kingdom were of this world, then would my servants fight, that I should not be delivered to the Jews: but now is my kingdom not from hence.

37. weecikeenahi ha howe hokima kiila hotelaali paalatii ciisisii haapafse kiteyo kiila yeesi hokimaawiya niila yooma nooci mehci niiki mecimi yooma nooci piya hini yeelekokwahkamikiki wahsi teepweeminekoya hini teepweewe caakiwiyeefa hini teepweewe weeciwita honoota nitesihsimoowe

Pilate therefore said unto him, Art thou a king then? Jesus answered, Thou sayest that I am a king. To this end have I been born, and to this end am I come into the world, that I should bear witness unto the truth. Every one that is of the truth heareth my voice.

38. nehiwe teepweewe hotelaali paalatii chiine hina yeh mehtoweci yooma nohki nihi coosahi si lohfe mecimi mata nimhka macilawiiwe wiiyaaki hina

Pilate saith unto him, What is truth? And when he had said this, he went out again unto the Jews, and saith unto them, I find no crime in him.

39. payeekwa kipoonaanaawa yaasilawiiki wahsi niila pakfenamoolako nekoti wiyeefa hini tah pemhfaasiweeki ha weecikeena hina hokimaamwaali

But ye have a custom, that I should release unto you one at the passover: will ye therefore that I release unto you the King of the Jews?

nihki coosaki wahsi pakfenamoolako kitesiteheepwa hotelahi nihi

40. weecikeenahi nihki wiyakahootamooki nohki mata yaama hileni palepasii weeka hiwaki howe ciikoniwehfi hina palepasii

They cried out therefore again, saying, Not this man, but Barabbas. Now Barabbas was a robber.

John:19

1. hine weecikeenahi hotahpenaali ciisisiili chiine holihfiiwanhhwaali

Then Pilate therefore took Jesus, and scourged him.

2. mecimi nihki samaakanaki kaawihi hoci hapkeenaanaawa hokimaawi petakhoowe chiine wiileki hina hoteh poonamawaawaali hini mecimi sehkipakimhskwaaki piitenika hotelasekhwaawaali

And the soldiers plaited a crown of thorns, and put it on his head, and arrayed him in a purple garment;

3. chiine nihki hopiyeelotawaawaali nili mecimi hei hokimaamwaali nihki coosaki hiwaki mecimi nihki hopkitehwaawaali holeciwa

and they came unto him, and said, Hail, King of the Jews! and they struck him with their hands.

4. chiine paalatii lohfe nohki mecimi waapamehko kipiyeci lohfatoolepwa hina wahsi kiilawa menawahi waakotameekwe yeesi pwaa niila mhkama wiiyaaki macilawiiwe hotelahi nihi

And Pilate went out again, and saith unto them, Behold, I bring him out to you, that ye may know that I find no crime in him.

5. ciisisii weecikeenahi piyeci lohfe hini hokimaawi petakhoowe hotawoota kaawihi mecimi hini sehkipakimhskwaaki piitenika chiine paalatii waapamehko hina hileni hotelahi

Jesus therefore came out, wearing the crown of thorns and the purple garment. And Pilate saith unto them, Behold, the man!

6. hine weecikeenahi nihki hokimaawi mhkateewkolayeeki chiine nihki wiyehsimekofiiwenaki yeh neewaawaaci nili wiyakahootamooki haasitefhohko haasitefhohko hiwaki pesikwi kiilawa mamehko hina mecimi haasitefhohko ksake mata nimhka niila wiiyaaki macilawiiwe hotelahi paalatii

When therefore the chief priests and the officers saw him, they cried out, saying, Crucify him, crucify him. Pilate saith unto them, Take him yourselves, and crucify him: for I find no crime in him.

7. hotaapaftawaawaali nihki coosaki nipoonaape kwteletiiwe mecimi hini kwteletiiwe kwiilahi wi hoci nepwa hina ksake hina nili hokwihfali maneto hotesto wiiya

The Jews answered him, We have a law, and by that law he ought to die, because he made himself the Son of God.

8. hine paalatii yeh nootaki yooma hiyoowe halalika hini si wiisaalepwa

When Pilate therefore heard this saying, he was the more afraid;

9. mecimi nohki hini pletooliami si piicfe chiine hina taaniwe hoci kiila hotelaali ciisisiili payeekwa ciisisii mata homiilaali hotaapafseewe

and he entered into the palace again, and saith unto Jesus, Whence art thou? But Jesus gave him no answer.

10. weecikeenahi paalatii ha mata kikaloosi kiila ha mata kiwaakota yeesi poonama waasikaki wahsi pelhhola kiila mecimi poonama waasikaki wahsi haasitefhola hotelaali

Pilate therefore saith unto him, Speakest thou not unto me? knowest thou not that I have power to release thee, and have power to crucify thee?

11. hotaapaftawaali ciisisii mata kippehci poonamawi waasikaki weeciwephi spemeki hoci miiloofoyane hini weecikeena hina kiila yeesi pakfenita hopoona halika mhsaawi maciisilawiiwe

Jesus answered him, Thou wouldest have no power against me, except it were given thee from above: therefore he that delivered me unto thee hath greater sin.

12. yoone howe yooma paalatii honatoneha wahsi pelhhwaaci nili payeekwa nihki coosaki wiyakahootamooki kwehkwi kiila pelhhwate yaama hileni mata siisa wihkaanali kiila caakiwiyeefa pesikwi wiila hokima yeestoota wiiya hoppehci kaloolaali siisali hiwaki

Upon this Pilate sought to release him: but the Jews cried out, saying, If thou release this man, thou art not Caesar's friend: every one that maketh himself a king speaketh against Caesar.

13. weecikeenahi paalatii yeh nootaki yooloma kalawiiwena hopiyeci lohfahaali ciisisiili mecimi lematapiwa hini tepoweewi hpapiiweneki hini tepakofeneki sitoote tasi weeka laa hiiploo keepaifa

When Pilate therefore heard these words, he brought Jesus out, and sat down on the judgment-seat at a place called The Pavement, but in Hebrew, Gabbatha.

14. howe hini pemhfaasiweewe hoci nanahiiwe hahteewi nawito hini nekotwahfene yaatefaki mecimi waapamehko kookimaamwa hotelahi nihi coosahi

Now it was the Preparation of the passover: it was about the sixth hour. And he saith unto the Jews, Behold, your King!

15. nihki weecikeenahi halika siwelehko halika siwelehko haasitefhohko lahootamooki ha ne haasitefhwa kookimaamwa hotelahi paalatii nihki hokimaawi mhkateewkolayeeki haapafseeki mata nipoonaape hokima siisa payeekwa

They therefore cried out, Away with him, away with him, crucify him. Pilate saith unto them, Shall I crucify your King? The chief priests answered, We have no king but Caesar.

16. hine howe weecikeenahi hoteh pakfenamawahi nili wahsi haasitefhoofolici

Then therefore he delivered him unto them to be crucified.

17. nihki weecikeena homamaawaali ciisisiili chiine hina lohfe pesikwi hotaamwetaa wiiya hini yaasitehfeki paalohi hini hohkanaatepiki sitoote kalhkoofe yeesitooteeki laa hiiploo

They took Jesus therefore: and he went out, bearing the cross for himself, unto the place called The place of a skull, which is called in Hebrew Golgotha:

18. tah nihki haasitefhwaawaaci nili chiine wiici nili kotakhi niiswi heeyiita wayeetahkwe nekoti mecimi ciisisii hini heelekhi

where they crucified him, and with him two others, on either side one, and Jesus in the midst.

19. chiine paalatii hawike hini sinetiiwe nehfaapi mecimi hini yaasitehfekiiki hoteh poona hini chiine nhtalawikaate ciisisii naaselefi hoci nili hokimaamwaali nihki coosaki

And Pilate wrote a title also, and put it on the cross. And there was written, JESUS OF NAZARETH, THE KING OF THE JEWS.

20. yooma sinetiiwe weecikeena holaapaatotaanaawa meci nihki coosaki hoci ksake hini tasi maalaakwa' hini hoteewe ta haasitefhoofoci ciisisii chiine hini hiiploowawikaate chiine letine chiine kwiiki

This title therefore read many of the Jews: for the place where Jesus was crucified was nigh to the city: and it was written in Hebrew, and in Latin, and in Greek.

21. nihki coosaki hoci nihki hokimaawi mhkateewkolayeeki weecikeenahi teki hawikeelo nili hokimaamwaali nihki coosaki weeka yeesi hina niila hokimaamwaali nihki coosaki hiyoci hotelaawaali paalatiili

The chief priests of the Jews therefore said to Pilate, Write not, The King of the Jews; but, that he said, I am King of the Jews.

22. haapafse paalatii mayehci lawikeeya nimehtawike Pilate answered, What I have written I have written.

23. nihki samaakanaki weecikeenahi yeh mehci haasitefhwaawaaci ciisisiili homamenaawa hina hopiitenikana mecimi honiyeeweelena latenaanaawa caaki nekoti samaakana maalekhi mecimi hini kooti nehfaapi howe hini kooti mata hahteewi tah takwikwaateeki hapkeenimota stoote spemeki hoci saapwi mefhiike

The soldiers therefore, when they had crucified Jesus, took his garments, and made four parts, to every soldier a part; and also the coat: now the coat was without seam, woven from the top throughout.

24. nihki weecikeenahi teki hini lelhkinaataako weeka hini kiskinikanitalwaatitaako wa howiilaamita hini hitiiki wahsi menawa hini tepilo heewikaateeki hokwaawfeki yeeyooyaaki nihki hopahfenaanaawa nipiitenikana heelekiina nihki mecimi nitelaseewe kiskinikanitalwaatiiki nihki nihki samaakanaki weecikeenahi sapkahi yooloma wiyehi silawiiki

They said therefore one to another, Let us not rend it, but cast lots for it, whose it shall be: that the scripture might be fulfilled, which saith, They parted my garments among them, And upon my vesture did they cast lots. These things therefore the soldiers did.

25. weeka nitasi peemi niipawiwaaci maalaakwa' hini hotaasitehfekiimi ciisisii hokeeli chiine hokeeli hoceeninaawilici melii nili wiiwali kloopasi chiine melii mekiteliina

But there were standing by the cross of Jesus his mother, and his mother's sister, Mary the wife of Clopas, and Mary Magdalene.

26. weecikeena hine ciisisii yeh neewaaci hokeeli mecimi nili kakehkimaafali peemi kaapawilici yeeahkweelemaaci hkweewa waapami kikwihfa hotelaali hokeeli

When Jesus therefore saw his mother, and the disciple standing by, whom he loved, he saith unto his mother, Woman, behold, thy son!

27. howe nili kakehkimaafali waapami kikiya hotelaali mecimi hine yaatefaki hoci hina kakehkimaafa nehalwaaka yeetaaci hotesiwelaali nili

Then saith he to the disciple, Behold, thy mother! And from that hour the disciple took her unto his own home.

28. hahkowihi yooma ciisisii waakotamwa yeesi caayahki wiyehi howe mectooteeki wahsi menawah hini tepilo heewikaateeki mehcilotooteeki nikahkalaamo hiwa

After this Jesus, knowing that all things are now finished, that the scripture might be accomplished, saith, I thirst.

29. nitasi lematapiwa poonahfoowakokwa hokwikami pskipaapo weecikeenahi nihki skipwaawiki hoteh poonaawaali kicikamiwiyatowali hokwikami hini pskipaapo mecimi hotooniwilici hoteh piyeetathamawaawaali nili

There was set there a vessel full of vinegar: so they put a sponge full of the vinegar upon hyssop, and brought it to his mouth.

30. hine ciisisii weecikeenahi yeh mehci hotefici hini pskipaapo hini mecfetoote hiwa hina chiine waakicikweska mecimi hina hopakfenaali hocacaalahkwali

When Jesus therefore had received the vinegar, he said, It is finished: and he bowed his head, and gave up his spirit.

31. nihki coosaki weecikeenahi ksake hahteewi hini nanahiiwe wahsi pwaa nihi wiiyaanahi hapilici hini haasitehfekiiki hini ta halwaakahsiwiki ksake hini kaasekiki hine halwaakahsiweewe speelemekwatwi kaasekiki hokocimaawaali paalatiili wahsi menawahi

The Jews therefore, because it was the Preparation, that the bodies should not remain on the cross upon the sabbath (for the day of that sabbath was a high day), asked of Pilate that their legs might be

poskwikaathoofolici mecimi wahsi menawa haamweleci

broken, and that they might be taken away.

32. nihki samaakanaki weecikeenahi piyeeki mecimi hoposkwikaathwaawaali nili weski chiine nili kotakali weewiici haasitefhoofoomekoci hina

The soldiers therefore came, and brake the legs of the first, and of the other which was crucified with him:

33. payeekwa hine nihki ciisisiili si piyeeki mecimi honeemenaawa yeesi hina neyehka nepeki mata nihki hoposkwikaathwaawaali nili

but when they came to Jesus, and saw that he was dead already, they brake not his legs:

34. weeka nekoti nihki samaakanaki hociipathwaali cifhika hosehkiwilici mecimi weelena nitasi piyeci lohfehtanwi mhskwi chiine nepi

howbeit one of the soldiers with a spear pierced his side, and straightway there came out blood and water.

35. chiine hina mayehci neemeka neyehka hopah niime teepweewe chiine teepweewenwi hoteepweewe chiine hina howaakota teepweewenwi yeeyoci wahsi menawahi kiilawa nehfaapi teepwehseeyeekwe

And he that hath seen hath borne witness, and his witness is true: and he knoweth that he saith true, that ye also may believe.

36. ksake yooloma wiyehi piyeemikato wahsi hini tepilo heewikaateeki menawahi hokwaawfetooteeki hokanemi hina mata weh poskhoote

For these things came to pass, that the scripture might be fulfilled, A bone of him shall not be broken.

37. chiine nohki kotaki tepilo heewikaateeki nihki weh waapamaawaali nili ceeciipathwaawaaci nihki hiyooya

And again another scripture saith, They shall look on him whom they pierced.

38. chiine hahkowihi yooloma wiyehi coosii haalimefiye hoci nakaye hokakehkimaafali ciisisii payeekwa kiimi ksake nihki coosaki si kwfetiiwe hokocimaali paalatiili wahsi menawa haamwelaaci nili howiiyaanali ciisisii mecimi paalatii homiilaali nili wiilaanisiweewe weecikeena hina piyeewa mecimi hotaamwelaali hina howiiyaanali

And after these things Joseph of Arimathaea, being a disciple of Jesus, but secretly for fear of the Jews, asked of Pilate that he might take away the body of Jesus: and Pilate gave him leave. He came therefore, and took away his body.

39. chiine nitasi piyeewa nehfaapi nekatiimasi hina hine weski peepiyeelotawaata nili tepehki hopiyeeto weewaawiyaakacfeki maa chiine haloosi nawito tepeewe pawni

And there came also Nicodemus, he who at the first came to him by night, bringing a mixture of myrrh and aloes, about a hundred pounds weight.

40. homamaawaali nili howiiyaanali ciisisii paasi hini hotasilawiiwenwa nihki coosaki wahsi lekoniweewaaci

So they took the body of Jesus, and bound it in linen cloths with the spices, as the custom of the Jews is to bury.

41. howe hini ta hina haasitefhoofoci tasi hahteewi memekinhcika mecimi hini memekinhcikaneki mayaki nepoowaalakwi tah pwaa laakwa keewaki hileni seksimoofoci

Now in the place where he was crucified there was a garden; and in the garden a new tomb wherein was never man yet laid.

42. nitasi hine howe ksake hini honanahiiwenwa nihki coosaki teewa hini nepoowaalakwi maalaakwahi hahteewi nihki hoseksimaawaali ciisisiili

There then because of the Jews' Preparation (for the tomb was nigh at hand) they laid Jesus.

John:20

1. howe hine weski kaasekiki hini peeleko tah manetoowi kiisekiki piyeewa melii mekiteliina hini nepoowaalakoki kwelahwaapaki yeheeye hini keewaki pepekicaaki mecimi honeewaali nili siikonali hini nepoowaalakoki hoci payakila latenoofooli

Now on the first day of the week cometh Mary Magdalene early, while it was yet dark, unto the tomb, and seeth the stone taken away from the tomb.

2. memekwi weecikeena hina chiine saiman' piitali si piyeewa mecimi nili kotakali kakehkimaafali ciisisii yeeahkweelemaaci mecimi neyehka nihki hini nepoowaalakoki hoci lohfahaawaali nili teepeelemiweelici mecimi mata niwaakota tah seksimaawaaci neyehka nili hotelahi nihi

She runneth therefore, and cometh to Simon Peter, and to the other disciple, whom Jesus loved, and saith unto them, They have taken away the Lord out of the tomb, and we know not where they have laid him.

3. weecikeenahi piita nhheewa chiine hina kotaka kakehkimaafa mecimi nihki hini nepoowaalakwi wayeeci heeki

Peter therefore went forth, and the other disciple, and they went toward the tomb.

4. chiine niiswipitooki nihki mecimi hina kotaka kakehkimaafa honawafwaali piitali chiine nhhihta hini nepoowaalakwi si piyeewa

And they ran both together: and the other disciple outran Peter, and came first to the tomb;

5. chiine maa si waaki mecimi piitike laapi hina honeemena nili waapi motaawali sekfeno payeekwa mata hina piicfe

and stooping and looking in, he seeth the linen cloths lying; yet entered he not in.

6. saiman' piita weecikeenahi nehfaapi piyeewa hopiyeci neekalaali nili mecimi hina hini si piicfe nepoowaalakwi chiine hotelaapataana nili waapi motaawali sekfeno

Simon Peter therefore also cometh, following him, and entered into the tomb; and he beholdeth the linen cloths lying,

7. mecimi hini pfiiwenehi yehteeki hina wiileki mata kilekfenwi nili waapi motaawali weeka tetepeceenoote tepaane tasi

and the napkin, that was upon his head, not lying with the linen cloths, but rolled up in a place by itself.

8. hine howe weecikeena hina kotaka kakehkimaafa nehfaapi piicfe peepiyaata nhhihta hini nepoowaalakoki chiine hina neeke mecimi teepwehse

Then entered in therefore the other disciple also, which came first to the tomb, and he saw, and believed.

9. ksake yeesi keewaki nihki mata waakotamowaaci hini tepilo heewikaateeki wahsi kwiila hina nili nepelici hoci honhskaaci

For as yet they knew not the scripture, that he must rise again from the dead.

10. weecikeenahi nihki kakehkimaafaki nohki weepfeeki nehalwaaka yeetaawaaci heeki

So the disciples went away again unto their own home.

11. weeka melii peemi kaapawici faakici hini nepoowaalakwi wihfakwe weecikeena hina yeesi wihfakweeci waaki chiine hini piitike nepoowaalakwi laapi

But Mary was standing without at the tomb weeping: so, as she wept, she stooped and looked into the tomb;

12. mecimi hotelaapamahi niiswi henhcalihi peemahkeepilici nekoti wiileki chiine nekoti hofiteki ta hina seksimoofoci howiiyaanali ciisisii

and she beholdeth two angels in white sitting, one at the head, and one at the feet, where the body of Jesus had lain.

13. chiine hkweewa koociwe kiila kiwihfakwe hotelaawaali nihki ksake nihki neyehka

And they say unto her, Woman, why weepest thou? She saith unto them,

hotaamwelaawaali niteepeelemiweemali mecimi
mata niwaakota tah mehci seksimaawaaci nihki
hotelahi hina

Because they have taken away my Lord,
and I know not where they have laid him.

14. halayini yeh si mehtoweci hina hotaanaaki si
kokiiwa mecimi hotelaapamaali ciisisiili peemi
kaapawilici chiine mata howaakota yeesi hini
ciisisiiwilici

When she had thus said, she turned herself
back, and beholdeth Jesus standing, and
knew not that it was Jesus.

15. hkweewa koociwe kiila kiwihfakwe neefawe
kinatonehwa hotelaali ciisisii hina toke
memekinhcikaafa hoteleelemaali nili yeeleniwiyani
kwehkwi kiila mehci yooci hoci haamweleta hina
wiitamawilo tah mehci seksimaci mecimi ne
haamwela hina hotelaali nili

Jesus saith unto her, Woman, why weepest
thou? whom seekest thou? She, supposing
him to be the gardener, saith unto him, Sir,
if thou hast borne him hence, tell me
where thou hast laid him, and I will take
him away.

16. melii hotelaali ciisisii hina kokiiwa mecimi
leponaayi hotelaali hina hiiplooki keekehkimiwe wa
hiyoki hini

Jesus saith unto her, Mary. She turneth
herself, and saith unto him in Hebrew,
Rabboni; which is to say, Master.

17. teki pehsenilo ksake niila mata keewaki hina
hohfima nitekkwicfe weeka niceeninaaki haalo
mecimi niila nohfa nitekkwicfe mecimi kiilawa
kohfwa chiine niila nimanetooma mecimi kiilawa
kimanetoomwa hisi nihki hotelaali ciisisii

Jesus saith to her, Touch me not; for I am
not yet ascended unto the Father: but go
unto my brethren, and say to them, I
ascend unto my Father and your Father,
and my God and your God.

18. piyeewa melii mekiteliina mecimi howiitamawahi
nihi kakehkimaafhi nimehci neewa hina
teepeelemiweeta mecimi yeesi mehci nili hilaaci hina
yooloma wiyehi

Mary Magdalene cometh and telleth the
disciples, I have seen the Lord; and how
that he had said these things unto her.

19. hine weecikeena hini holaakwiifi hine kaasekiki
hini weski kiiseki hini peeleko menetoowikiisekiki
mecimi hine nili skwaateewali kiphoote ta hapiwaaci
nihki kakehkimaafaki ksake nihki coosaki hoci
kwfetiiwe ciisisii piyeewa chiine hini heelekhi
niipawi mecimi kaamaaniilefiiwe hotwefiko hotelahi
nihi

When therefore it was evening, on that
day, the first day of the week, and when
the doors were shut where the disciples
were, for fear of the Jews, Jesus came and
stood in the midst, and saith unto them,
Peace be unto you.

20. chiine hina yeh mehtoweci yooma howaapatelahi
nihi holeciwali chiine hini hosehki weecikeena
howesilepwaaki nihki kakehkimaafaki yeh
neewaawaaci nili teepeelemiweelici

And when he had said this, he shewed
unto them his hands and his side. The
disciples therefore were glad, when they
saw the Lord.

21. weecikeenahi nohki ciisisii kaamaaniilefiiwe
hotwefiko kiilawa yeesi hina hohfima mehci
waawiineskawici teetepilahi yooni kiilawa kitesi
waawiineskoolepwa hotelahi

Jesus therefore said to them again, Peace
be unto you: as the Father hath sent me,
even so send I you.

22. chiine hina yeh mehtoweci yooma hoteh
lehfehtawahi nihi mecimi hotefiko kiilawa hina
hofepi hocacaalahkwa

And when he had said this, he breathed on
them, and saith unto them, Receive ye the
Holy Ghost:

23. kookwe-neefaki-kaaci homaciisilawiiwenwa kipakfeeletaanaawa nili pakfeeletamaakwiiki nihki kookwe-neefaki-kaaci homaciisilawiiwenwa kifookinaanaawa fookinoote nili hotelahi

whose soever sins ye forgive, they are forgiven unto them; whose soever sins ye retain, they are retained.

24. payeekwa taamosii nekoti nihki metahfwi-kite-niiswi titimas yaaloofo mata wiici nihi hine ciisisii piyeewa

But Thomas, one of the twelve, called Didymus, was not with them when Jesus came.

25. nihki kakehkimaafaki weecikeenahi nimehci neewaape hina teepeelemiweeta hotelaawaali nili payeekwa hina weeciwephi neh neeme hini holeciwali tasi yeesfaawaaci nihki fakhikanaki chiine nileca hini yeesfaawaaci nihki fakhikanaki si poonake mecimi nileci hosehkiki si poonama mata nitah teepwehse hotelahi hina

The other disciples therefore said unto him, We have seen the Lord. But he said unto them, Except I shall see in his hands the print of the nails, and put my finger into the print of the nails, and put my hand into his side, I will not believe.

26. chiine nhfwaasikfoko si hahkowihi hokakehkimaafhi nohki hapihi piitike mecimi taamosii wiici nihi piyeewa ciisisii nili skwaateewali nakaye kiphoote chiine hini heelekhi niipawi mecimi kaamaaniilefiiwe hotwefiko kiilawa hiwa

And after eight days again his disciples were within, and Thomas with them. Jesus cometh, the doors being shut, and stood in the midst, and said, Peace be unto you.

27. hine howe hina hotahfa lateni kileca mecimi neemelo nileciwali chiine hotahfa latenano kileci mecimi hini nisehkiki si piinhhano mecimi teki haanwehseewilo weeka teepwehseewilo hotelaali taamosiili

Then saith he to Thomas, Reach hither thy finger, and see my hands; and reach hither thy hand, and put it into my side: and be not faithless, but believing.

28. taamosii haapafse mecimi niteepeelemiweema chiine nimanetooma hotelaali hina

Thomas answered and said unto him, My Lord and my God.

29. ksake kimehci neewi kiila weeci mehci teepwehseeyani kisaateelemekofiiki nihki peepwaa mehci neekeecki mecimi miiloowi mehci teepwehseeki nihki hotelaali ciisisii

Jesus saith unto him, Because thou hast seen me, thou hast believed: blessed are they that have not seen, and yet have believed.

30. meci kotakali kikinooloowena silawi ciisisii weecikeena hini yeelahfamiiwaaci nihki kakehkimaafaki pwaayaa yooma heewikaateekiiki talawikeeki

Many other signs therefore did Jesus in the presence of the disciples, which are not written in this book:

31. weeka yooloma hawikeepi wahsi kiilawa menawahi teepwehseeyeekwe yeesi ciisisii hina klaistiiwici nili hokwihfali maneto mecimi wahsi teepwehseewiyeekwe menawahi kiilawa poonameekwe lenaweewiiwe howiifooweneki

but these are written, that ye may believe that Jesus is the Christ, the Son of God; and that believing ye may have life in his name.

John:21

1. hahkowihi hine yooloma wiyehi ciisisii nohki hotepinawkofetawahi wiiya nihi kakehkimaafhi maalaakwa' hini taapiliasiwi mhsinepi mecimi halayooma yeesi tepinawkofetooci wiiya

After these things Jesus manifested himself again to the disciples at the sea of Tiberias; and he manifested himself on this wise.

2. nitasi maawatwaapiiki saiman' piita chiine taamosii titimas yaaloofo chiine nefeniali keena hoci keeleliiwi taamhkwe chiine nihi hokwifhi sepetii chiine niiswi kotakhi hokakehkimaafhi

There were together Simon Peter, and Thomas called Didymus, and Nathanael of Cana in Galilee, and the sons of Zebedee, and two other of his disciples.

3. saiman' piita nih pah namefke hotelahi nihi nehfaapi kiwiiteemelepe hotelaawaali nihki nhheeki nihki mecimi hini holakeeleki lhkamooki chiine hine tepehki mata wiyehi hopethatoonaawa

Simon Peter saith unto them, I go a fishing. They say unto him, We also come with thee. They went forth, and entered into the boat; and that night they took nothing.

4. payeekwa howe hini kwelahwaapaki ciisisii niipawi hini skwaapiyeeki keewaki mata nihki kakehkimaafaki howaakotaanaawa hini yeesi ciisisiiwilici nili

But when day was now breaking, Jesus stood on the beach: howbeit the disciples knew not that it was Jesus.

5. weecikeenahi ciisisii hapelohfeti ha mata wiyehi kipoonaanaawa wah miiciki hotelahi nihi nihki hotaapatawaawaali mata

Jesus therefore saith unto them, Children, have ye aught to eat? They answered him, No.

6. chiine hina hini mayaawi wayeetahkwe hini holakeesi hipakitamoko hini haakwaskwhaaka mecimi ke mhkahfopwa hotelahi nihi weecikeenahi nihki hotipakitaanaawa mecimi howe haalwi hilefiiki nihki wahsi hotahpenamowaaci hini ksake hini homhseloowenwa nihki namehfaki

And he said unto them, Cast the net on the right side of the boat, and ye shall find. They cast therefore, and now they were not able to draw it for the multitude of fishes.

7. hina kakehkimaafa weecikeenahi yeeahkweelemaaci ciisisii teepeelemiweeta hina hotelaali piitali saiman' piita weecikeenahi yeh nootaakeeci hini yeesi hina teepeelemiweewici kitapifo hokootiimi ksake hina sahsaakitwi mecimi hini mhsinepiki hotipakita wiiya

That disciple therefore whom Jesus loved saith unto Peter, It is the Lord. So when Simon Peter heard that it was the Lord, he girt his coat about him (for he was naked), and cast himself into the sea.

8. weeka nihki kotakaki kakehkimaafaki hini caki holakeefeki piyeeki ksake nihki mata pelowi hini hasiski hoci weeka nawito niisene tepeewe kiopit laakwa soskwaafiiki hini haakwaskwhaaka hokwihsinohi namefhi

But the other disciples came in the little boat (for they were not far from the land, but about two hundred cubits off), dragging the net full of fishes.

9. hine weecikeenahi nihki ye hakwahsinowaaci hini hoskitaamhkwe honeemenaawa skote mhkateewalo nitasi mecimi namehfa seksinwa hoskici nitasi chiine takhwa

So when they got out upon the land, they see a fire of coals there, and fish laid thereon, and bread.

10. piyeelehko hina namehfa mayehci howe pethaneekwe hotelahi ciisisii

Jesus saith unto them, Bring of the fish which ye have now taken.

11. saiman' piita weecikeenahi spemeki heewa chiine hasiskiiki hotehakwahfeto hini haakwaskwhaaka hokwihsinooki maki namehfaki tepeewe kite niyaalanwaapitaki kite nhfwi mecimi caayahki weekhi hapiiki yooni si meci hini haakwaskwhaaka mata lelhkehka

Simon Peter therefore went up, and drew the net to land, full of great fishes, a hundred and fifty and three: and for all there were so many, the net was not rent.

12. piyaako mecimi poskonamoko koocikeewenwa hotelahi ciisisii mecimi mata nekoti teepitehe nihki kakehkimaafaki wahsi neefawe kiila si natohtawaaci nili waakotamooki hini yeesi teepeelemweewilici nili

Jesus saith unto them, Come and break your fast. And none of the disciples durst inquire of him, Who art thou? knowing that it was the Lord.

13. ciisisii piyeewa mecimi hoteh mame hini takhwa chiine hoteh miilahi nihi mecimi nehfaapi nili namehfali

Jesus cometh, and taketh the bread, and giveth them, and the fish likewise.

14. yooma howe hini mawi-nhfene yeesi ciisisiili tepinawkofetoofowaaci nihki kakehkimaafaki hahkowihi yeesi hina nili nepelici hoci honhskaanoofoci

This is now the third time that Jesus was manifested to the disciples, after that he was risen from the dead.

15. yooni hine nihki yeh mehci poskonamowaaci hocikeewenwa saimanii hokwihfali caanii ha halika kitahkweelemi noota yooloma hotelaali saiman' piitali ciisisii hina hanhka teepeelemiweeta kiwaakota kiila yeesi hahkweelemela hotelaali hahsami nipalasaanimeekiifaki hotelaali hina

So when they had broken their fast, Jesus saith to Simon Peter, Simon, son of John, lovest thou me more than these? He saith unto him, Yea, Lord; thou knowest that I love thee. He saith unto him, Feed my lambs.

16. nohki hina mawi-niisene saimanii hokwihfali caanii ha kitahkweelemi hotelaali hina hanhka teepeelemiweeta kiwaakota kiila yeesi hahkweelemela hotelaali kcitaweelemi nimeekiifaki hotelaali hina

He saith to him again a second time, Simon, son of John, lovest thou me? He saith unto him, Yea, Lord; thou knowest that I love thee. He saith unto him, Tend my sheep.

17. hina hini mawi-nhfene saimanii hokwihfali caanii ha kitahkweelemi hotelaali piita hahkwitehe ksake hina hini mawi-nhfene ha kitahkweelemi hotelaali nili mecimi hina teepeelemiweeta kiwaakota kiila caayahki wiyehi kiwaakota yeesi hahkweelemela hotelaali hahsami nimeekiifaki hotelaali ciisisii

He saith unto him the third time, Simon, son of John, lovest thou me? Peter was grieved because he said unto him the third time, Lovest thou me? And he said unto him, Lord, thou knowest all things; thou knowest that I love thee. Jesus saith unto him, Feed my sheep.

18. tepilo tepilo kitele niila hine yeh mayaanefiyani kiila kikaakitapito kiiya mecimi laakwa kitesi paamhfe yeesiteheeyani kiila payeekwa hine pasitoofiwiyane maa keh si ciikinhkeele kileciwali mecimi kotaka ke ktapilekwa mecimi laakwa keh siwelekwa pwaayaa kiila siteheeyani

Verily, verily, I say unto thee, When thou wast young, thou girdedst thyself, and walkedst whither thou wouldest: but when thou shalt be old, thou shalt stretch forth thy hands, and another shall gird thee, and carry thee whither thou wouldest not.

19. howe yooma hina kalawi kikinootaacimo wa hiki hkwinamoowe wih wahfaacimekofihaaci manetooli mecimi hine hina yeh mehci kalawici yooma neekasilo hotelaali nili

Now this he spake, signifying by what manner of death he should glorify God. And when he had spoken this, he saith unto him, Follow me.

20. piita maa si kolepi honeewaali nili kakehkimaafali yeeahkweelemaaci ciisisii neekasiweeli niliini nehfaapi hattawassi hapacsinooli hopaleeki hini tah sapaawiki mecimi teepeelemiweeta neefawe hina wah mestaahehka hiyoli

Peter, turning about, seeth the disciple whom Jesus loved following; which also leaned back on his breast at the supper, and said, Lord, who is he that betrayeth thee?

21. piita weecikeena honeewaali nili mecimi teepeelemiweeta chiine nehiwe yaama hileni weh silawi hotelaali ciisisiili

Peter therefore seeing him saith to Jesus, Lord, and what shall this man do?

22. kwehkwi niila siteheeya wahsi hina nakahsiki paalohi piyaaya nehiwe hini kiila si neekasilo kiila hotelaali ciisisii

Jesus saith unto him, If I will that he tarry till I come, what is that to thee? follow thou me.

23. yooma hiyoowe weecikeenahi weepfeeya heelekiina nihki hoceeninaanaki wahsi hina kakehkimaafa teki nepeki weekhi ciisisii mata hotelaali nili wahsi teki nepelici weeka kwehkwi niila siteheeya wahsi hina nakahsiki paalohi piyaaya nehiwe hini kiila si hotelaali

This saying therefore went forth among the brethren, that that disciple should not die: yet Jesus said not unto him, that he should not die; but, If I will that he tarry till I come, what is that to thee?

24. yaama hina kakehkimaafa peepah niimeka yooloma wiyehi si teepweewe mecimi hawike yooloma wiyehi chiine kiwaakotaape yeesi hoteepweewe teepweeweniki

This is the disciple which beareth witness of these things, and wrote these things: and we know that his witness is true.

25. chiine hahteewa nehfaapi meci kotakali wiyehi ciisisii yeesilawiici niliini kwehkwi wi hawikeepi caaki nekoti toke nitesitehe wiikinaakwi hini yeelekokwahkamikiki mata yah katawi teepfeno nili heewikaateewali wa hawikeeki

And there are also many other things which Jesus did, the which if they should be written every one, I suppose that even the world itself would not contain the books that should be written.

GLOSSARY

-eh *[future]* PV
    ke *PV*
    keh *PV*
    ne *PV*
    neh *PV*
    nine *PV*
    nineh *PV*
    we *PV*
    weh *PV*
-ih *[irrealis]* PV
    ki *PV*
    kih *PV*
    ni *PV*
    nih *PV*
    wi *PV*
    wih *PV*
-tehee *[thinking, thoughtful, feeling]* AI
    tehe *AI,ind,3s ; AI,ind,1s*
    teheeki *AI,ind,3p*
    teheeya *AI,conj,1s*
caakakitecaakatfwi *ninety-nine*
    caakakitecaakatfwi
    caakakitecaakatwi
caakam *consume TA*
    caakameko *TA,ind,0s,1s*
    caakamekowaaci *TA,conj,0,3p*
caakat *consume TI_1*
    caacaakatakki *TI,part,3p,0*
    caakataka *TI,part,3s,0*
    hocaakataanaawa *TI,ind,3p,0*
caakatamaw *devour TA*
    caacaakatamawaacki *TA,part,3p,4*
caakatef *burn up TI_1*
    caakatefaana *TI,ind,3s,0p*
caakatfwi *nine*
    caakatefene
    caakatfwi
caaki *all, every, completely PM*
    caaki *PM*
caakilot *consume TI_1*
    caakilotaki *TI,conj,3s,0*

caakisahte *withered, wilted*
    caakisahte
caakisi *all kinds of*
    caakisi
caakiwiyeefa *everyone PR*
    caakiwiyeefa *PR*
caakiwiyehi *everything PR*
    caakiwiyehi *PR*
caalayini *so, therefore*
    caalayini
caanii *John NA*
    caanii *NA,3s*
    caaniili *NA,4s*
caatenii *Jordan NI*
    caatenii *NI,s*
    caateniiki *NI/LOC*
caateniiwi *Jordan PM*
    caateniiwi *PM*
caayahki *all*
    caayahki
    caayaki
    hocaayahki
caceepi *several, various*
    caceepi
cacinal *hit TA*
    hocacinalaawaali *TA,ind,3p,4s*
cahtawaacim *witness against, accuse TA*
    cahtawaacimaawaaci *TA,conj,3p,4*
    cahtawaacimehki *TA,conj,3,2s*
    cahtawaacimekoci *TA,conj,4,3s*
    ceecahtawaacimehki *TA/IC,conj,3,2s*
    hocahtawaacimaawaali *TA,ind,3p,4s*
    kicahtawaacimekooki *TA,ind,3p,2s*
cahtawaacimo *witness AI*
    kicahtawaacimopwa *AI,ind,2p*
cahtawaacimoofoowe *accusation NI*
    hocahtawaacimoofoowe *NI/POSS,3s,s*
cahtokwaat *mend, fill TI_1*
    hocahtokwaataanaawa *TI,ind,3p,0*
cahtokwe *mend, fill II*
    ceecahtokweki *II/IC,conj,0*

cahtokwen *mend, fill TI_1*
    cahtokwenamowaaci *TI,conj,3p,0*
caki *little, small PM*
    caki *PM*
ceealasii *Jairus NA*
    ceeaalas' *NA,3s*
    ceealasii *NA,3s*
ceeceesipetekfetaw *recompense TA*
    ceeceesipetekfetawehki *TA,conj,3,2s*
ceeceest *make equal TI_2*
    hoceeceesto *TI,ind,2s,0s*
ceecelefiim *be equal to TA*
    hoceecelefiimaawahi *TA,ind,3p,4p*
ceeceshaaki *make equal TA*
    kiceeceshaaki *TA,ind,2s,3p*
ceekapii *Jacob NA*
    ceekap' *NA,3s*
    ceekapii *NA,3s*
    ceekapiili *NA,4s*
ceekiifa *ass NA*
    ceekiifa *NA,3s*
    ceekiifali *NA,4s*
    hoceekiifemali *NA/POSS,3s,4s*
ceelati *Jared NA*
    ceelati *NA,3s*
ceemhsi *James NA*
    ceemhsii *NA,3s*
    ceemhsiili *NA,4s*
ceetfwi *in a group*
    ceetfwi
ceeyehkofiiwe *end NI*
    ceeyehkofiiwe *NI,s*
ceeyehkwaa *be the end, be last II*
    ceeyehkwaake *II,subj,0*
    ceeyehkwaaki *II,conj,0*
ceeyehkwahkoweewe *judgment NI*
    ceeyehkwahkoweeweneki *NI/LOC*
ceeyehkwahkoweewi *judgment PM*
    ceeyehkwahkoweewi *PM*
ceeyehkwat *be the end, be the last II*
    ceeyehkwatwi *II,ind,0s*
ceeyehkwi *end, last PM*
    ceeyehkwi *PM*
ceeyehkwiifa *last one NA*
    ceeyehkwiifaki *NA,3p*
ceeyehkwiiwe *end NI*

ceeyehkwiiwe *NI,s*
ceeyehkwilot *bring to an end TI_1*
    ceeyehkwilotaki *TI,conj,3s,0*
ceeyekwahkamikat *end II*
    ceeyehkwahkamikike *II,subj,0*
    ceeyekwahkamikike *II,subj,0*
ceh *[interjection: calling attention]*
    ce
    ceh
    ci
    cih
cehi *to, unto*
    cehi
celekoo *Jericho NI*
    celekoo *NI,s*
celemaaya *Jeremiah NA*
    celemaaya *NA,3s*
    celimaaya *NA,3s*
cene *Jannai NA*
    cene *NA,3s*
cesii *Jesse NA*
    cesii *NA,3s*
    cesiili *NA,4s*
chiine *and, then CJN*
    chiine *CJN*
cifhika *spear, staff NI*
    cifhika *NI,s*
    cifhikana *NI,p*
cihfeeletamaw *marvel at TA*
    hocihfeeletamaakohi *TA,ind,4p,3s*
    hocihfeeletamaawaawaali *TA,ind,3p,4s*
    hocihfeeletamawaawaali *TA,ind,3p,4s*
cihfefi *afraid AI*
    cihfefiiki *AI,ind,3p*
    cihfefiko *AI,imp,2p*
    cihfefilici *AI,conj,4*
    cihfefilo *AI,imp,2s*
cihfefiiwe *fear, astonishment NI*
    cihfefiiwe *NI,s*
cihfena *time when; then*
    cihfena
cihkaw *rebuke TA*
    hocihkawahi *TA,ind,3s,4p*
cihoosifetii *Jehoshaphat NA*
    cihoosifetii *NA,3s*
    cihoosifetiili *NA,4s*

cihsitehee *be astonished* AI
    cihsiteheeki *AI,ind,3p*
    cihsitehehi *AI,ind,4p*
ciikath *sweep TI_1*
    hociikatha *TI,ind,3s,0s*
ciikathoote *be swept II*
    ciikathoote *II,ind,0*
ciikikeepicika *plow NI*
    ciikikeepicika *NI,s*
ciikikeepitaawe *plow AI*
    ciikikeepitaaweeli *AI,ind,4s*
ciikileceskaa *stretch out the hand AI*
    ciikileceska *AI,ind,3s*
    ciikileceskaalo *AI,imp,2s*
ciikinhkeel *stretch out the hand AI*
    ciikileceelelo *AI,imp,2s*
    ciikinhkeele *AI,ind,2s*
    ciikinhkeelwa *AI,ind,3s*
ciikinhkeeskaa *stretch out the hand AI*
    ciikinhkeeska *AI,ind,3s*
ciikinhkem *swear TA*
    ceeciikinhkemaaci *TA/IC,conj,3s,4*
ciikinhkemo *swear AI*
    ciikinhkemo *AI,ind,2s ; AI,ind,3s*
    ciikinhkemoko *AI,imp,2p*
    ciikinhkemota *AI,part,3s*
ciikinhkemoom *swear TA*
    hociikinhkemoomaali *TA,ind,3s,4s*
ciikinhkemoowe *oath NI*
    ciikinhkemoowe *NI,s*
    ciikinhkemoowena *NI,p*
    hociikinhkemoowena *NI/POSS,3s,p*
    kiciikinhkemoowena *NI/POSS,2s,p*
ciikinhkemot *swear TI_1*
    ciikinhkemota *TI,ind,2s,0s*
ciikoniwehfi *thief NA*
    ciikoniwehfi *NA,3s*
    ciikoniwehfihi *NA,4p*
    ciikoniwehfiiki *NA,3p*
ciilwe *shout AI*
    ciilweeki *AI,ind,3p*
ciipa *ghost, spirit NA*
    ciipa *NA,3s*
    ciipali *NA,4s*
ciipathw *pierce TA*
    ceeciipathwaawaaci *TA/IC,conj,3p,4*

hociipathwaali *TA,ind,3s,4s*
ciisisii *Jesus NA*
    ciisis' *NA,3s*
    ciisisii *NA,3s*
    ciisisiili *NA,4s*
ciisisiiwi *be Jesus AI*
    ciisisiiwilici *AI,conj,4*
cikonaaya *Jechoniah NA*
    cikonaaya *NA,3s*
    cikonaayali *NA,4s*
ckon *leave (in place) TA*
    ckonaawaali *TA,ind,3p,4s*
ckonoofo *be kept, be left AI*
    ckonoofo *AI,ind,3s*
coena *Joanna NA*
    coena *NA,3s*
colooseelemii *Jerusalem NI*
    colooseelem' *NI,s*
    colooseelemii *NI,s*
    colooseelemiiki *NI/LOC*
cooena *Joanna NA*
    cooena *NA,3s*
cooeneni *Joanan NA*
    cooeneni *NA,3s*
coofemii *Jotham NA*
    coofemii *NA,3s*
    coofemiili *NA,4s*
coolemii *Joram NA*
    coolemii *NA,3s*
    coolemiili *NA,4s*
coolimi *Jorim NA*
    coolimi *NA,3s*
coome *row AI*
    coomeelici *AI,conj,4*
    coomeewaaci *AI,conj,3p*
coona *Jonah NA*
    coona *NA,3s*
    coonali *NA,4s*
coonemi *Jonam NA*
    coonemi *NA,3s*
coosa *Jew NA*
    coosa *NA,3s*
    coosahi *NA,4p*
    coosaki *NA,3p*
    coosali *NA,4s*
coosaya *Josiah NA*

coosaya *NA,3s*
coosayali *NA,4s*
cooseki *Josech NA*
coaseki *NA,3s*
coosii *Joseph NA*
coosii *NA,3s*
coosiili *NA,4s*
coosisi *Joses NA*
coosisi *NA,3s*
coota *Judah NA*
coota *NA,3s*
cootali *NA,4s*
cootasii *Judas NA*
cootas' *NA,3s*
cootasii *NA,3s*
cootasiili *NA,4s*
coote *Joda NA*
coote *NA,3s*
cotiye *Judaea NI*
cotiye *NI,s*
cotiyeeki *NI/LOC*
cotiyeewi *Judaea PM*
cotiyeewi *PM*
einani *Aenon NI*
einaniiki *NI/LOC*
elaacim *report TA*
kitelaacima *TA,ind,2s,3s*
yeelaacimaaci *TA/IC,conj,3s,4*
elaacimekofiiwe *report NI*
hotelaacimekofiiwe *NI/POSS,3s,s*
elaacimo *report AI*
talaacimopi *AI,ind,3*
yeelaacimota *AI/IC,part,3s*
elaacimoofo *be spoken about AI*
yeelaacimoofoci *AI/IC,conj,3s*
yeelaacimoofolici *AI/IC,conj,4*
elaacimoowe *report NI*
laacimoowe *NI,s*
laacimoowena *NI,p*
nitelaacimoowenena *NI/POSS,1x*
elaakoom *have a relation TA*
laakooma *TA,ind,2s,3s*
elaakwaafiiwe *time, era NI*
hotelaakwaafiiweneki *NI/POSS/LOC,3s*
hotelaakwaafiiwenwa *NI/POSS,3p*
elaakwaam *time, season NI*

kitelaakwaamwa *NI/POSS,2p*
laakwaamhki *NI/LOC*
nitelaakwaami *NI/POSS,1s,s*
elaapam *look at TA*
hilaapamaawa *TA,ind,2p,3s*
hilaapamaawaali *TA,ind,3p,4s*
hotelaapamaali *TA,ind,3s,4s*
hotelaapamaawaali *TA,ind,3p,4s*
hotelaapamahi *TA,ind,3s,4p*
kitelaapamipwa *TA,ind,2p,1*
nitelaapama *TA,ind,1s,3s*
nitelaapamaaki *TA,ind,1s,3p*
nitelaapamekwa *TA,ind,3s,1s*
yeelaapamaata *TA/IC,part,3s,4*
yeelaapamaawaaci *TA,conj,3p,4*
yeelaapamita *TA/IC,part,3s,1s*
elaapame *oversee AI*
yeelaapameta *AI/IC,part,3s*
elaapat *see, look at TI_1*
hilaapama *TI,ind,1s,0s*
hilaapatamelici *TI,conj,4,0*
hilaapatamowaaci *TI,conj,3p,0*
hotelaapata *TI,ind,3s,0s*
hotelaapataana *TI,ind,3s,0p*
hotelaapataanaawa *TI,ind,3p,0*
kitelaapata *TI,ind,2s,0s*
kitelaapataape *TI,ind,1i,0*
laapatamelici *TI,conj,4,0*
yeelaapatakki *TI/IC,part,3p,0*
elaapatamaw *see, look at TA*
hotelaapatamaakohi *TA,ind,4p,3s*
elaapiyehsin *be in succession II*
yeelaapiyehsiki *II/IC,conj,0*
elaapiyehsinoowe *group (in a succession) NI*
hotelaapiyehsinoowe *NI/POSS,3s,s*
elahkowaafo *be judged AI*
lahkowaafoyeekwe *AI,conj,2p*
wiyehlahkowaafo *AI,ind,3s*
elahkowaafoowe *judgment NI*
hotelahkowaafoowe *NI/POSS,3s,s*
lahkowaafoowe *NI,s*
elahkowaal *judge TA*
hotelahkowaalaali *TA,ind,3s,4s*
peemahkowaaleekwe *TA/IC,part,2p,3*
pemahkowaalaawaaki *TA,ind,2p,3p*
elahkowaaleti *judge [reciprocal] AI*

kitelahkowaaletipwa *AI,ind,2p*
elahkowaasiwee *judge AI*
   lahkowaasiweeko *AI,imp,2p*
   lahkowaasiweeyeekwe *AI,conj,2p*
elahkowaasiweewe *judgment NI*
   lahkowaasiweewe *NI,s*
elahkowaat *judge TI*
   wiyeh-lahkowaatamelici *TI,conj,4,0*
elahkowe *judge AI*
   kitelahkowepwa *AI,ind,2p*
   lahkoweko *AI,imp,2p*
   nitelahkowe *AI,ind,1s*
elahkoweewe *counsel NI*
   hotelahkoweewenilici *NI/POSS,4*
   lahkoweewe *NI,s*
   nitelahkoweewe *NI/POSS,1s,s*
elakim *consider, account as, value TA*
   hotelakimaawaali *TA,ind,3p,4s*
   yeelakimaawaaci *TA/IC,conj,3p,4*
elakimoofo *be valued, be considered AI*
   yeelakimoofocki *AI/IC,part,3p*
   yeelakimoofota *AI/IC,part,3s*
elas *clothe TA*
   laseci *TA,conj,,3*
elas *clothe TI_3*
   laseyeekwe *TI/IC,conj,2p,0*
elaseewe *clothing NI*
   nitelaseewe *NI/POSS,1s,s*
elasekhw *clothe TA*
   hotelasekhwaawaali *TA,ind,3p,4s*
   lasekhokowa *TA,ind,3s,2s*
eleelem *intend for, consider as TA*
   hoteleelemaali *TA,ind,3s,4s*
   hoteleelemaawaali *TA,ind,3p,4s*
   hoteleelemahi *TA,ind,3s,4p*
   hoteleelemekowahi *TA,ind,4p,3p*
   kiteleelema *TA,ind,2s,3s*
   kiteleelemaawa *TA,ind,2p,3s*
   kiteleelemaawaaki *TA,ind,2p,3p*
   kiteleelemekowa *TA,ind,3s,2p*
   leelemaape *TA,ind,1i,3*
   leelemaate *TA,subj,3s,4*
   leelemakwe *TA,conj,1i,3 ; TA,subj,1i,3*
   leelemehko *TA,imp,2p,3*
   leelemekohi *TA,ind,4p,3s*
   leelemi *TA,ind,2s,1s*

leelemilo *TA,imp,2s,1s*
   yeeleelemaaci *TA/IC,conj,3s,4*
   yeeleelemeekwe *TA/IC,part,2p,3*
eleelemekofi *be valued, be worthy AI*
   kiteleelemekofipwa *AI,ind,2p*
   leelemekofi *AI,ind,3s*
   niteleelemekofi *AI,ind,1s*
   yeeleelemekofici *AI/IC,conj,3s*
eleelemekofiiyaa *worthy II*
   leelemekofiiyaake *II,subj,0*
eleelemekwat *be valued II*
   lelemekwatwi *II,ind,0s*
   yeeleelemekoki *II/IC,conj,0*
eleelet *intend TI_1*
   hoteleeleta *TI,ind,3s,0s*
   hoteleeletaanaawa *TI,ind,3p,0*
   kiteleeleta *TI,ind,2s,0s*
   kiteleeletaana *TI,ind,2s,0p*
   leeleta *TI,ind,3s,0s*
   leeletakki *TI/IC,part,3p,0*
   leeletano *TI,imp,2s,0*
   niteleeleta *TI,ind,1s,0s*
   yeeleeletakki *TI/IC,part,3p,0*
   yeeleeletamowaaci *TI/IC,conj,3p,0*
eleeletamaw *intend TA*
   hoteleeletamawaali *TA,ind,3s,4s*
   kiteleeletamaakoopi *TA,ind,3,2s*
   leeletamaakwi *TA,ind,,3s*
   leeletamaweci *TA,conj,,3*
   leeletamawinaake *TA,imp,2,1x*
   leeletamoolakwe *TA,conj,3,1i*
eleskamaw *send TA*
   hoteleskamawaali *TA,ind,3s,4s*
   hoteleskamawaawaali *TA,ind,3p,4s*
   hoteleskamawahi *TA,ind,3s,4p*
   kiteleskamaakona *TA,ind,3s,1i*
   kiteleskamoolepwa *TA,ind,1s,2p*
   leskamaakwa *TA,ind,3s,1s*
   leskamawaaki *TA,ind,1s,3p*
eleskaw *send TA*
   hoteleskaakooli *TA,ind,4s,3s*
   hoteleskawaali *TA,ind,3s,4s*
   hoteleskawaawaali *TA,ind,3p,4s*
   hoteleskawaawahi *TA,ind,3p,4p*
   hoteleskawahi *TA,ind,3s,4p*
   kiteleskoolepwa *TA,ind,1s,2p*

leskawa *TA,ind,1s,3s*
leskawaaci *TA,conj,3s,4*
leskawaaki *TA,ind,1s,3p*
leskawaali *TA,ind,3s,4s*
leskawahi *TA,ind,3s,4p*
leskawaka *TA/IC,part,1s,3s*
leskawake *TA,subj,1s,3*
leskawi *TA,imp,2s,3*
leskawinaake *TA,imp,2,1x*
nikiteleskoolepwa *TA,ind,1s,2p*
niteleskawa *TA,ind,1s,3s*
eleskoofo *be sent AI*
  leskoofo *AI,ind,3s*
esfaa *? enter ? II*
  yeesfaaki *II/IC,conj,0*
esfat *send TI_2*
  fatooya *TI,conj,1s,0*
  hotesfato *TI,ind,3s,0s*
  nitesfato *TI,ind,1s,0s*
  sfatooya *TI,conj,1s,0*
esfataw *send TA*
  hotesfatawaali *TA,ind,3s,4s*
  sfahahi *TA,ind,3s,4p*
  sfataakohi *TA,ind,4p,3s*
esfatoote *be sent II*
  sfatoote *II,ind,0*
esfee, esfaa *fall AI*
  sfaayane *AI,subj,2s*
  sfe *AI,ind,3s*
  sfeeki *AI,ind,3p*
  sfeeli *AI,ind,4s*
  yaasfe *AI,ind,3s*
  yeesfaawaaci *AI/IC,conj,3p*
esfeeyaa *fall II*
  sfccyaali *II,ind,4*
esfen *such manner, way II*
  sfenili *II,ind,4*
esfet *make, arrange TI_2*
  hosfetoonaawa *TI,ind,3p,0*
  sfetooko *TI,imp,2p,0*
esh *make, cause to become TA*
  hoshaaci *TA,conj,3s,4*
  hosheekwe *TA,conj,2p,3*
  hoshehko *TA,imp,2p,3*
  hoshilo *TA,imp,2s,1s*
  hoteshaali *TA,ind,3s,4s*

hoteshahi *TA,ind,3s,4p*
kitaashaawa *TA,ind,2p,3s*
neshaaki *TA,ind,1s,3p*
nineshaaki *TA,ind,1s,3p*
niteshekwa *TA,ind,3s,1s*
shaaci *TA,conj,3s,4*
shelepwa *TA,ind,1s,2p*
eshoofo *be made AI*
  shoofoci *AI,conj,3s*
esifo *be called, be named AI*
  kitesifo *AI,ind,2s*
  nitesifo *AI,ind,1s*
  sifo *AI,ind,3s*
  sifooli *AI,ind,4s*
  yeesifolici *AI/IC,conj,4*
esihsimoowe *voice NI*
  hotasimoowenwa *NI/POSS,3p*
  hotesihsimoowe *NI/POSS,3s,s*
  hotesihsimoowenilici *NI/POSS,4*
  nitesihsimoowe *NI/POSS,1s,s*
esilawiht *do to something TI_1*
  hotesilawihtaana *TI,ind,3s,0p*
esilawihtaw *do something to someone TA*
  lawihtoola *TA,conj,1s,2s*
  silawihtaakonaaki *TA,ind,3p,1x*
  silawihtawaaci *TA,conj,3s,4*
  silawihtawehko *TA,imp,2p,3*
  yaasilawihtawaaci *TA,conj,3s,4*
  yeesilawihtawaawaaci *TA/IC,conj,3p,4*
esilawii *do AI*
  hisilawi *AI,ind,3s*
  hisilawiipi *AI,ind,3*
  kitesilawiipwa *AI,ind,2p*
  lawiiki *AI,conj,3*
  lawiipi *AI,ind,3*
  nitesilawi *AI,ind,1s*
  silawi *AI,ind,3s ; AI,ind,1s ; AI,ind,2s*
  silawihi *AI,ind,4p*
  silawiici *AI,conj,3s*
  silawiiki *AI,ind,3p ; AI,conj,3*
  silawiiko *AI,imp,2p*
  silawiili *AI,ind,4s*
  silawiilici *AI,conj,4*
  silawiilo *AI,imp,2s*
  silawiipe *AI,ind,1x*
  silawiipi *AI,ind,3*

silawiipwa *AI,ind,2p*
silawiita *AI/IC,part,3s*
silawiitaako *AI,imp,1i*
silawiite *AI,subj,3s*
silawiiwaaci *AI,conj,3p*
silawiiwaate *AI,subj,3p*
silawiiya *AI,conj,1s ; AI,subj,1s*
silawiiyaake *AI,conj,1x*
silawiiyane *AI,subj,2s*
silawiiyani *AI,conj,2s*
silawiiyeekwe *AI,conj,2p ; AI,subj,2p*
waasa-silawiiyani *AI,conj,2s*
yaasilawiici *AI,conj,3s*
yaasilawiiki *AI,conj,3*
yaasilawiiwaaci *AI,conj,3p*
yaasilawiiya *AI,conj,1s*
yaasilawiiyani *AI,conj,2s*
yeesilawiici *AI/IC,conj,3s*
yeesilawiiki *AI/IC,conj,3*
yeesilawiilici *AI/IC,conj,4*
yeesilawiita *AI/IC,part,3s*
yeesilawiiwaaci *AI/IC,conj,3p*
yeesilawiiya *AI/IC,conj,1s*
esilawiiwe *deed NI*
hotasilawiiwenwa *NI/POSS,3p*
hotesilawiiwenilici *NI/POSS,4*
kitesilawiiwenena *NI/POSS,1i*
silawiiweneki *NI/LOC*
yeesilawiiwenilici *NI/POSS,4*
esilokeewe *sickness NI*
hotesilokeewenwa *NI/POSS,3p*
kitesilokeewenena *NI/POSS,1i*
silokeewena *NI,p*
esilwe *make such a sound II*
yeesilweki *II/IC,conj,0*
esimekofiiwe *authority NI*
hotesimekofiiwe *NI/POSS,3s,s*
hotesimekofiiweneki *NI/POSS/LOC,3s*
mekofiiwe *NI,s*
simekofiiwe *NI,s*
esin *call, name TA*
hotesinaali *TA,ind,3s,4s*
kitesinelepwa *TA,ind,1s,2p*
kitesini *TA,ind,2s,1s*
sinaaci *TA,conj,3s,4*
sinaate *TA,subj,3s,4*

sinaawaali *TA,ind,3p,4s*
sinaawaate *TA,subj,3p,4*
wiinaali *TA,ind,3s,4s*
wiinahi *TA,ind,3s,4p*
esinaakofiiwe *appearance NI*
hotesinaakofiiwe *NI/POSS,3s,s*
esinam *undergo AI*
sinaki *TI,conj,3s,0*
sinamowaaci *AI,conj,3p*
yeesinaki *TI/IC,conj,3s,0*
yeesinamelici *AI/IC,conj,4*
yeesinamowaaci *AI/IC,conj,3p*
esinamo *undergo AI*
namoci *AI,conj,3s*
esinamoowe *death, decrease NI*
hotesinamoowe *NI/POSS,3s,s*
esit *call, name TI_1*
sita *TI,ind,2s,0s*
sitaanaawa *TI,ind,3p,0*
yeesita *TI/IC,part,3s,0*
yeesitaki *TI/IC,conj,3s,0*
esitehee *think, wish AI*
kitesitehe *AI,ind,2s*
kitesiteheepwa *AI,ind,2p*
nitesitehe *AI,ind,1s*
nitesiteheepe *AI,ind,1x*
sitehe *AI,ind,3s*
siteheeci *AI,conj,3s*
siteheeki *AI,ind,3p*
siteheeko *AI,imp,2p*
siteheelici *AI,conj,4*
siteheete *AI,subj,3s*
siteheeya *AI,conj,1s ; AI,subj,1s*
siteheeyane *AI,subj,2s*
siteheeyani *AI,conj,2s*
siteheeyeekwe *AI,subj,2p ; AI,conj,2p*
yeesiteheeci *AI/IC,conj,3s*
yeesiteheecki *AI/IC,part,3p*
yeesiteheeki *AI/IC,conj,3*
yeesiteheelici *AI/IC,conj,4*
yeesiteheeta *AI/IC,part,3s*
yeesiteheewaaci *AI/IC,conj,3p*
yeesiteheeya *AI/IC,conj,1s*
yeesiteheeyani *AI/IC,conj,2s*
yeesiteheeyeekwe *AI/IC,conj,2p*
esiteheewe *will, wish, thought NI*

hotesiteheewe *NI/POSS,3s,s*
hotesiteheeweneki *NI/POSS/LOC,3s*
hotesiteheewenilici *NI/POSS,4*
kitesiteheewe *NI/POSS,2s,s*
kitesiteheewenwa *NI/POSS,2p*
nitesiteheewe *NI/POSS,1s,s*
siteheewe *NI,s*
siteheeweneki *NI/LOC*
yeesiteheewenilici *NI/POSS,4*
esiteheeyaa *wish, want [inanimate subject]*
II
    yeesiteheeyaaki *II/IC,conj,0*
esiwel *lead, take TA*
    hotesiwelaali *TA,ind,3s,4s*
    hotesiwelaawaali *TA,ind,3p,4s*
    hotesiwelekooli *TA,ind,4s,3s*
    siwelaali *TA,ind,3s,4s*
    siwelehko *TA,imp,2p,3*
    siwelekoci *TA,conj,4,3s*
    siwelekwa *TA,ind,3s,2s*
    siwelekwi *TA,ind,,3s*
    siwelelwaakwe *TA,conj,3,2p*
    yeesiwelekoci *TA/IC,conj,4,3s*
esiweletiiwe *carrying away NI*
    siweletiiwe *NI,s*
esiwet *take, carry TI_2*
    hotesiweto *TI,ind,3s,0s*
    hotesiwetoonaawa *TI,ind,3p,0*
    siweto *TI,ind,3s,0s*
    siwetooko *TI,imp,2p,0*
    siwetoolici *TI,conj,4,0*
esiwetaw *carry TA*
    hotesiwetawahi *TA,ind,3s,4p*
est *make TI_2*
    hosto *TI,ind,2s,0s ; TI,ind,3s,0s*
    hostooko *TI,imp,2p,0*
    hostoona *TI,ind,1s,0p*
    hostoonaawa *TI,ind,3p,0*
    hostoope *TI,ind,1x,0*
    hostootaako *TI,imp,1i,0*
    hostooya *TI,conj,1s,0*
    hostooyakwe *TI,conj,1i,0*
    hostooyane *TI,subj,2s,0*
    hotesto *TI,ind,3s,0s*
    howestooko *TI,imp,2p,0*
    kitesto *TI,ind,2s,0s*
    kitestoonaawa *TI,ind,2p,0*

    miyaastooko *TI,imp,2p,0*
    stooko *TI,imp,2p,0*
    stooyani *TI,conj,2s,0*
    weeostoocki *TI/IC,part,3p,0*
    yeestoota *TI/IC,part,3s,0*
estan *flow II*
    staki *II,conj,0*
faafihkaan *strain out, sift out TA*
    faafihkaanaacki *TA,part,3p,4*
faafookfet *grind TI_2*
    hofaafookfetoona *TI,ind,3s,0p*
faakici *outside*
    faakici
faakiciwel *let out, put out TA*
    faakiciwelaaci *TA,conj,3s,4*
faakin *grow, spring up II*
    faakiki *II,conj,0*
    faakino *II,ind,0p*
    faakinwi *II,ind,0s*
faakipakin *sprout II*
    faakipakiki *II,conj,0*
faapiimehi *a little while*
    faapiimehi
fafahkweewe *purification NI*
    hofafahkweewenwa *NI/POSS,3p*
fafahkwi *pure PM*
    faafafahkwi *PM*
    fafahkwi *PM*
    feefafahkwi *PM/IC*
    hofafahkwi *PM*
    kifafahkwi *PM*
fafahkwi-hocikee *fast, go without food AI*
    nifafahkwi-hocikeepe *AI,ind,1x*
fafahkwiholelhiweewe *baptism NI*
    fafahkwiholelhiweewe *NI,s*
    hofafahkwiholelhiweewe *NI/POSS,3s,s*
fafahkwiholelhiweewena *baptizer NA*
    fafahkwiholelhiweewena *NA,3s*
fafahkwiholelhiwena *baptizer NA*
    fafahkwiholelhiwena *NA,3s*
fafahkwiholelwiiwe *baptism NI*
    fafahkwiholelwiiwe *NI,s*
fafakikinoote *be pressed II*
    fafakikinoote *II,ind,0*
fafayaa *clean II*
    fafayaaki *II,conj,0*

fafayaakh *clean TA*
    fafayaakhehko *TA,imp,2p,3*
    fafayaakhi *TA,ind,2s,1s ; TA,imp,2s,3*
    kifaafafayaakhaawa *TA,ind,2p,3s*
    kifafayaakhaawa *TA,ind,2p,3s*
fafayaakhoofo *be made clean AI*
    fafayaakhoofo *AI,ind,3s*
    fafayaakhoofolo *AI,imp,2s*
    fafayaakhoofooki *AI,ind,3p*
    fafayaakhoofowaaci *AI,conj,3p*
    fafayaakhoofoyani *AI,conj,2s*
fafayaakhoofoowe *cleansing NI*
    kifafayaakhoofoowe *NI/POSS,2s,s*
fafayaakifi *clean AI*
    fafayaakifi *AI,ind,3s*
    kifafayaakifipwa *AI,ind,2p*
    nifafayaakifi *AI,ind,1s*
fafayaakilot *make clean TI_1*
    fafayaakilota *TI,ind,3s,0s*
    fafayaakilotaki *TI,conj,3s,0*
    hofafayaakilota *TI,ind,3s,0s*
fafayaakitoote *be made clean II*
    fafayaakitooteeli *II,ind,4*
fafayaakiyaa *be clean II*
    fafayaakiya *II,ind,0*
    fafayaakiyaaki *II,conj,0*
fafayaakt *clean TI_2*
    fafayaakto *TI,ind,3s,0s*
    nifafayaakto *TI,ind,1s,0s*
fahfikaafo *be broiled AI*
    fahfikaafooli *AI,ind,4s*
fakaaki *with difficulty*
    fakaaki
fakf *burn TI_1*
    fakfaki *TI,conj,3s,0*
    fakfameekwe *TI,conj,2p,0*
fakfamaw *burn TA*
    hofakfamawahi *TA,ind,3s,4p*
fakfikeewipootefamaacika *burnt offering NI*
    fakfikeewipootefamaacikana *NI,p*
fakfo *burn AI*
    fakifowaaci *AI,conj,3p*
    feefakfota *AI/IC,part,3s*
fakfoote *be burned II*
    fakfooteeki *II,conj,0*
fakfw *burn, ignite TA*

fakfwaaci *TA,conj,3s,4*
    fakifwaaci *TA,conj,3s,4*
    hofaafakfwaawaali *TA,ind,3p,4s*
    hofakfwaali *TA,ind,3s,4s*
fakhikana *nail NA*
    fakhikanaki *NA,3p*
fakifiteepifoowe *fetter NI*
    fakifiteepifoowena *NI,p*
fakikaapifoowe *fetter NI*
    fakikaapifoowena *NI,p*
fakikeeskaw *press TA*
    fakikeeskawaaci *TA,conj,3s,4*
fakikwehika *yoke NI*
    fakikwehika *NI,s*
fakikwehoowe *yoke NI*
    nifakikwehoowe *NI/POSS,1s,s*
fakileceen *take by the hand TA*
    fakileceenaali *TA,ind,3s,4s*
fakinaapiyaal *lead away TA*
    fakinaapiyaalaali *TA,ind,3s,4s*
    fakinaapiyaalaawaali *TA,ind,3p,4s*
fakinaapiyaaloofo *be led away AI*
    fakinaapiyaaloofooki *AI,ind,3p*
fakkehkaw *press, crowd TA*
    fakkehkaakohi *TA,ind,4p,3s*
    fakkehkaakooki *TA,ind,3p,2s*
    hofakkehkaakohi *TA,ind,4p,3s*
    kifakkehkaakooki *TA,ind,3p,2s*
faktee *burn II*
    fakte *II,ind,0*
fanoel *phaneul NA*
    fenoel *NA,3s*
fapa *supposedly*
    fapa
fatiyasii *Thaddaeus NA*
    fatiyasii *NA,3s*
fayaakitehee *pure in heart AI*
    feefayaakiteheecki *AI/IC,part,3p*
fayookin *get hold of TA*
    fayookinekocki *TA,part,0,3p*
feefa *older brother NA*
    hofeefemaali *NA/POSS,3s,4s*
fefikwi *smooth II*
    fefikwa *II,ind,0p*
fekikawiikweewe *tear NI*
    hofekikawiikweewena *NI/POSS,3s,p*

fekoowe *spittle* NI
  fekoowe *NI,s*
fekwaatamaw *spit on* TA
  fekwaatamawaaci *TA,conj,3s,4*
fekwiwa *spit* AI
  fekwiwa *AI,ind,3s*
fiaafilas *Theophilus* NA
  fiaafilas *NA,3s*
fiifekwaal *spit on* TA
  fiifekwaalaawaali *TA,ind,3p,4s*
  hofiifekwaalaawaali *TA,ind,3p,4s*
fiifekwaaloofo *be spit upon* AI
  fiifekwaaloofo *AI,ind,3s*
fiikehka *spill* II
  fiikehka *II,ind,0s*
fiikfen *be spilled* II
  fiikfenwi *II,ind,0s*
fiikhoote *be shed* II
  fefiikhooteeki *II/IC,conj,0*
fiikiceepicika *press (for making wine)* NI
  fiikiceepicika *NI,s*
fiikin *pour, spill* TI_1
  fiikina *TI,ind,3s,0s*
  fiikinakki *TI,part,3p,0*
  fiikinamoko *TI,imp,2p,0*
  hofiikina *TI,ind,3s,0s*
fiikinamaw *pour on* TA
  fiikinamaakooli *TA,ind,4s,3s*
  fiikinamawaali *TA,ind,3s,4s*
fiikinamawoofo *be poured out (for)* AI
  feefiikinamawoofoci *AI/IC,conj,3s*
  feefiikinamawoofoyeekwe *AI/IC,conj,2p*
fiime *younger sibling* NA
  hofiimema *NA,3s*
fiipii *river* NI
  fiipiiki *NI/LOC*
  fiipiiwali *NI,p*
filapii *Philip* NA
  filapii *NA,3s*
  filapiili *NA,4s*
filipaayi *Philippi* NI
  filipaayi *NI,s*
fookin *hold* TA
  fefookinaacki *TA/IC,part,3p,4*
  fookinaali *TA,ind,3s,4s*
  fookinamaakohi *TA,ind,4p,3s*

fookinekoci *TA,conj,0,3s*
fookinekohi *TA,ind,4p,3s*
fookinekonaawa *TA,ind,0,3p*
fookinipe *TA,ind,2s,1x*
fookin *hold* TI_1
  fookina *TI,ind,3s,0s*
  fookinaanaawa *TI,ind,3p,0*
  fookinamowaaci *TI,conj,3p,0*
  kifookinaanaawa *TI,ind,2p,0*
fookinoote *be held* II
  fookinoote *II,ind,0*
  fookinooteeli *II,ind,4*
ha *[interrogative]*
  ha
haa *ah [interjection]*
  haa
haacfo *plant* AI
  haacfolo *AI,imp,2s*
haaciiwikamikwi *tabernacle* NI
  haaciiwikamiko *NI,p*
haacim *speak about* TA
  haacima *TA,ind,1s,3s*
  haacimaaci *TA,conj,3s,4*
  haacimaali *TA,ind,3s,4s*
  haacimekwa *TA,ind,3s,1s*
  hotaacimaali *TA,ind,3s,4s*
  yaacimaaci *TA/IC,conj,3s,4*
  yaacimaka *TA/IC,part,1s,3s*
  yaacimeekwe *TA/IC,part,2p,3*
  yaacimeta *TA/IC,part,,3s*
haacimo *speak about* AI
  haacimooki *AI,ind,3p*
  haacimowaaci *AI,conj,3p*
haacimohtaati *say to [reciprocal]* AI
  haacimohtaatiiki *AI,ind,3p*
haacimohtaw *tell* TA
  hotaacimohtawaawahi *TA,ind,3p,4p*
haacimoowe *narrative* NI
  haacimoowe *NI,s*
haakastas *Augustus* NA
  haakastas *NA,3s*
haakicfaawe *fall* NI
  haakicfaawe *NI,s*
haakicfee, haakicfaa *fall* AI
  haakicfaacki *AI,part,3p*
  haakicfaako *AI,imp,2p*

haakicfaata *AI,part,3s*
haakicfe *AI,ind,3s*
haakicfeeki *AI,ind,3p*
haakicfeeli *AI,ind,4s*
haakicfehi *AI,ind,4p*
haakicife *AI,ind,3s*
yaakicfaalici *AI/IC,conj,4*
haakicfeeyaa *fall II*
haakicfeeya *II,ind,0*
haakicifeeya *II,ind,0*
haaksini *ox NA*
haaksinihi *NA,4p*
haaksiniiki *NA,3p*
haaksiniili *NA,4s*
hotaaksiniimali *NA/POSS,3s,4s*
nitaaksiniimaki *NA/POSS,1s,3p*
haakwaskwahoofo *be caught in a net AI*
haakwaskwahoofolici *AI,conj,4*
haakwaskwhaa *draw, gather in a net AI*
haakwaskwhaayani *AI,conj,2s*
haakwaskwhaaka *net NI*
haakwaskwhaaka *NI,s*
haakwaskwhaakana *NI,p*
hotaakwskwhaakanwa *NI/POSS,3p*
haakwaskwhaawe *net NI*
haakwaskwhaawena *NI,p*
hotaakwaskwhaawenwa *NI/POSS,3p*
kitaakwaskwhaawena *NI/POSS,2s,p*
haalakh *cut out TI_1*
hotaalakhaki *TI/IC,conj,3s,0*
haalawin *refuse TI_1*
haalawinake *TI,subj,3s,0*
haalawin *reject TI_1*
halawinaanaawa *TI,ind,2p,0*
hotaalawinaanaawa *TI,ind,3p,0*
haalawin *reject TA*
haalawineko *TA,ind,0s,3s*
haalawinekohi *TA,ind,4p,3s*
yehaalawinelwaakwe *TA/IC,part,3,2p*
yehaalawinita *TA/IC,part,3s,1s*
haalawinaw *reject TA*
haalawinaakoci *TA,conj,4,3s*
hotaalawinawaali *TA,ind,3s,4s*
nitaalawinaakwa *TA,ind,3s,1s*
yaalawinawita *TA/IC,part,3s,1s*
yeelawinawaawaaci *TA/IC,conj,3p,4*

haalhofiiweni *disappear II*
haalhofiiweniki *II,conj,0*
haalimefiye *Arimathaea NI*
haalimefiye *NI,s*
haalofiiyaa *fail II*
haalofiiya *II,ind,0*
haaloofo *be said AI*
haaloofo *AI,ind,3s*
haaloofooki *AI,ind,3p*
yaaloofo *AI,ind,3s*
yaaloofohi *AI,ind,4p*
yaaloofolici *AI/IC,conj,4*
yaaloofooli *AI,ind,4s*
yaaloofota *AI/IC,part,3s*
haalwaten *cannot bear TI_1*
kitaalwatenaanaawa *TI,ind,2p,0*
haalwi *[fail, not be able] PV*
haalwi *PV*
hotaalwi *PV*
kitaalwi *PV*
nitaalwi *PV*
yaalwi *PV/IC*
haamaamhfen *spill over II*
haamaamhfenwi *II,ind,0s*
haameskaw *send away TA*
haameskawaaci *TA,conj,3s,4*
haameskawahi *TA,ind,3s,4p*
haameskawi *TA,imp,2s,3*
hotaameskawaali *TA,ind,3s,4s*
hotaameskawaawaali *TA,ind,3p,4s*
hotaameskawahi *TA,ind,3s,4p*
haami *be away AI*
haami *AI,ind,3s*
haamwel *take away, carry away TA*
haamwela *TA,ind,1s,3s*
haamwelaaci *TA,conj,3s,4*
haamwelaawaaci *TA,conj,3p,4*
haamweleci *TA,conj,,3*
haamwelehko *TA,imp,2p,3*
haamweleta *TA,part,3s,*
haamwesi *TA,imp,2s,3*
hotaamwelaali *TA,ind,3s,4s*
hotaamwelaawaali *TA,ind,3p,4s*
hotaamwelahi *TA,ind,3s,4p*
hotaamwelekohi *TA,ind,4p,3s*
hotaamwelekonaawa *TA,ind,0,3p*

yaamwelaacki *TA/IC,part,3p,4*
haamwet *take away, carry away TI_2*
  haamwetooci *TI,conj,3s,0*
  haamwetooko *TI,imp,2p,0*
  haamwetoolici *TI,conj,4,0*
  hotaamwetaa *TI,ind,3s,0s*
  hotaamwetoonaawa *TI,ind,3p,0*
  kitaamwetoonaawa *TI,ind,2p,0*
  yaamiwetoolici *TI,conj,4,0*
haamwetaw *carry (for) TA*
  haamwetawaaci *TA,conj,3s,4*
haanhka *yea [interjection]*
  haanhka
haanwehsee *doubt AI*
  haanwehse *AI,ind,2s*
  haanwehseeki *AI,ind,3p*
  haanwehseeko *AI,imp,2p*
  yaanwehseeta *AI/IC,part,3s*
haanwehseew *doubt TA*
  haanwehseewilo *TA,imp,2s,1s*
haapafataw *answer TA*
  hotehaapafatawaali *TA,ind,3s,4s*
haapafsee *answer AI*
  haapafse *AI,ind,3s ; AI,ind,2s*
  haapafseeci *AI,conj,3s*
  haapafseeki *AI,ind,3p*
  haapafseeli *AI,ind,4s*
  haapafseepwa *AI,ind,2p*
  haapafseeyeekwe *AI,conj,2p*
  haapafsehi *AI,ind,4p*
  kithaapafse *AI,ind,2s*
haapafseewe *anwer NI*
  hotaapafseewe *NI/POSS,3s,s*
  hotaapafseewena *NI/POSS,3s,p*
haapaft *answer TI_1*
  haapaftaanaawa *TI,ind,3p,0*
  hotaapafta *TI,ind,3s,0s*
  kitaapafta *TI,ind,2s,0s*
haapaftaw *answer TA*
  haapaftawa *TA,ind,2s,3s*
  haapaftawaaci *TA,conj,3s,4*
  haapaftawaawaaci *TA,conj,3p,4*
  haapaftawaawaali *TA,ind,3p,4s*
  haapaftawahi *TA,ind,3s,4p*
  haapaftawiko *TA,imp,2p,1s*
  hotaapaftaakohi *TA,ind,4p,3s*

hotaapaftaakooli *TA,ind,4s,3s*
hotaapaftawaali *TA,ind,3s,4s*
hotaapaftawaawaali *TA,ind,3p,4s*
hotaapaftawaawahi *TA,ind,3p,4p*
hotaapaftawahi *TA,ind,3s,4p*
haapam *see TA*
  haapamaaci *TA,conj,3s,4*
haapataw *answer TA*
  hotaapatawaali *TA,ind,3s,4s*
  hotaapatawaawaali *TA,ind,3p,4s*
  hotaapatawahi *TA,ind,3s,4p*
haapathoowe *staff NI*
  haapathoowe *NI,s*
haapefiiwe *resurrection NI*
  haapefiiweneki *NI/LOC*
  hotaapefiiwe *NI/POSS,3s,s*
haapefiiwi-honhskaawe *resurrection NI*
  haapefiiwi-honhskaawe *NI,s*
  haapefiiwi-honhskaaweneki *NI/LOC*
  hotaapefiiwi-honhskaaweneki
NI/POSS/LOC,3s
haapefiiwi-honhskaaweni *have a
resurrection AI*
  haapefiiwi-honhskaawenici *AI,conj,3s*
haapefiiwi-honhskaawi *resurrection PM*
  haapefiiwi-honhskaawi *PM*
haapetefi *hurry AI*
  haapetefi *AI,ind,3s*
  haapetefilo *AI,imp,2s*
haaph *cause to regain life TA*
  yeeyaaphaaci *TA/IC,conj,3s,4*
haasitefhoofo *be crucified AI*
  haasitefhifolici *AI,conj,4*
  haasitefhoofo *AI,ind,3s*
  haasitefhoofoci *AI,conj,3s*
  haasitefhoofocki *AI,part,3p*
  haasitefhoofolici *AI,conj,4*
  haasitefhoofooki *AI,ind,3p*
  haasitefhoofota *AI,part,3s*
haasitefhoofoom *be crucified with TA*
  haasitefhoofoomekoci *TA,conj,4,3s*
haasitefhw *crucify TA*
  haasitefhohko *TA,imp,2p,3*
  haasitefhola *TA,conj,1s,2s*
  haasitefhwa *TA,ind,1s,3s*
  haasitefhwaawaaci *TA,conj,3p,4*
  haasitefhwaawaaki *TA,ind,2p,3p*

haasitefhwi *TA,imp,2s,3*
  hotaasitefhwaawaali *TA,ind,3p,4s*
  hotaasitefhwaawahi *TA,ind,3p,4p*
haasitehfeki *cross NI*
  haasitehfekiiki *NI/LOC*
  hotaasitehfekiimi *NI/POSS,3s,s*
  hotaasitehfekiimilici *NI/POSS,4*
  yaasitehfeki *NI,s*
  yaasitehfekiiki *NI/LOC*
haasoon *exchange TI_1*
  haasoonake *TI,subj,3s,0*
  yaasoonakki *TI/IC,part,3p,0*
haasoonikaati *exchange AI*
  kitiiyaasoonikaatipwa *AI,ind,2p*
haasoonike *exchange AI*
  haasoonike *AI,ind,3s*
haasoonikehfi *one who exchanges NA*
  haasoonikehfihi *NA,4p*
  haasoonikehfiiki *NA,3p*
haatefaki *hour NI*
  haatefaki *NI,s*
  yaatefaki *NI,s*
haatefamoowe *hour NI*
  hotaatefamoowe *NI,s*
  hotaatefamoowenwa *NI/POSS,3p*
  kitaatefamoomwa *NI/POSS,2p*
  nitaatefamoowe *NI/POSS,1s,s*
haaten *remove TA*
  haateni *TA,imp,2s,3*
haatot *speak about TI_1*
  haatota *TI,ind,1s,0s ; TI,ind,3s,0s*
  haatotama *TI,conj,1s,0*
  haatotamowaaci *TI,conj,3p,0*
  haatotano *TI,imp,2s,0*
  hotaatota *TI,ind,3s,0s*
  hotaatotaanaawa *TI,ind,3p,0*
haatotamaw *tell, speak about TA*
  haatotamaakowaaci *TA,conj,4,3p*
  haatotamawaaci *TA,conj,3s,4*
  haatotamoolako *TA,conj,1s,2p*
  hotaatotamawaawaali *TA,ind,3p,4s*
  hotaatotamawahi *TA,ind,3s,4p*
haatotoote *be spoken about II*
  haatotoote *II,ind,0*
  haatotooteeki *II,conj,0*
  yaatotooteeki *II/IC,conj,0*

haayaayeli *laugh AI*
  haayaayelipwa *AI,ind,2p*
  yeeyaayelicki *AI/IC,part,3p*
haayicfe *be secured, be bound II*
  haayicfeki *II,conj,0*
  yeeyicfeki *II/IC,conj,0*
haayici *secure PV*
  haayici *PV*
haayicifet *make secure TI_2*
  hotaayiicifetoonaawa *TI,ind,3p,0*
haayicit *make secure TI*
  haayicitooko *TI,imp,2p,0*
haayicsim *make secure TA*
  haayicsimi *TA,imp,2s,3*
  hotaayicimahi *TA,ind,3s,4p*
  hotaayicsimaawaali *TA,ind,3p,4s*
haayicsin *cling to AI*
  haayicsinwa *AI,ind,3s*
haayictoote *be made secure II*
  haayictoote *II,ind,0*
haayitahpifoowe *bond, constraint NI*
  haayitahpifoowe *NI,s*
haayitaten *cling to TA*
  haayitatenaali *TA,ind,3s,4s*
haayitaten *hold, cling to TI*
  hotaayitatena *TI,ind,3s,0s*
  hotaayitatenaanaawa *TI,ind,3p,0*
  kitaayiitatenaanaawa *TI,ind,2p,0*
haayiteelem *cling to TA*
  haayiteelemaali *TA,ind,3s,4s*
hacko *conceive AI*
  hacko *AI,ind,2s ; AI,ind,3s*
  hackooli *AI,ind,4s*
  hackota *AI,part,3s*
hacsi *being compared AI*
  yeecsiwaaci *AI/IC,conj,3p*
hafipit *bundle TI_2*
  hafipitooko *TI,imp,2p,0*
hahcika *plant NI*
  hahcika *NI,s*
hahcikee *sow, plant AI*
  hacikeeci *AI,conj,3s*
  hahcike *AI,ind,3s*
  hahcikeeci *AI,conj,3s*
  hahcikeeki *AI,ind,3p*
  hahcikeewaaci *AI,conj,3p*

hahcikeeya *AI,conj,1s*
hahcikeeyani *AI,conj,2s*
yeeahcikeeki *AI/IC,conj,3*
yeeahcikeeta *AI/IC,part,3s*
yeecikeeta *AI/IC,part,3s*
hahfawikaanasko *thistle NA*
hahfawikaanaskohi *NA,4p*
hahfo *extinguish, go out AI*
hahfooki *AI,ind,3p*
hahkapat *withered II*
hahkapatwili *II,ind,4*
hahkapwileceewe *withered hand NI*
hahkapwileceewe *NI,s*
hahkaw *wait for, anticipate TA*
hahkookwa *TA,ind,3s,1s*
hahkawaafi *expect, be in expectation AI*
hahkawaafiiki *AI,ind,3p*
hahkawaafiiwaaci *AI,conj,3p*
hahkawaapam *wait for TA*
hahkawaapamaacki *TA,part,3p,4*
hahkawaapamaawaaci *TA,conj,3p,4*
hahkawaapamekoci *TA,conj,0,3s*
hahkawehsee *listen AI*
hahkawehseeki *AI,ind,3p*
hahkawehseeko *AI,imp,2p*
hahkaweht *listen TI_1*
hahkawehtaki *TI,conj,3s,0*
hahkawehtaw *listen TA*
hahkawehtaakowaaki *TA,ind,3p,2p*
hahkawehtawaaci *TA,conj,3s,4*
hahkawehtawehke *TA,subj,3s,2s*
hahkom *cry to TA*
kitahkomekona *TA,ind,3s,1i*
hahkonehaw *wait for TA*
hahkonehokohi *TA,ind,4p,3s*
hahkow *follow TA*
hahkowiko *TA,imp,2p,1s*
hahkowaal *judge TA*
hotahkowaalele *TA,ind,1s,2s*
hahkowihi *after, later*
hahkowi
hahkowihi
hahkwat *emotionally heavy II*
hahkwato *II,ind,0p*
hahkwatkaawe *anguish NI*
hahkwatkaawe *NI,s*

hahkweelem *love TA*
hahkweelema *TA,ind,2s,3s ; TA,ind,1s,3s*
hahkweelemaaci *TA,conj,3s,4*
hahkweelemaali *TA,ind,3s,4s*
hahkweelemaci *TA,conj,2s,3*
hahkweelemaki *TA,conj,1s,3*
hahkweelemeekwe *TA,subj,2p,3*
hahkweelemehko *TA,imp,2p,3*
hahkweelemekooli *TA,ind,4s,3s*
hahkweelemela *TA,conj,1s,2s*
hahkweelemelako *TA,conj,1s,2p*
hahkweelemelepwa *TA,ind,1s,2p*
hahkweelemi *TA,imp,2s,3*
hahkweelemici *TA,conj,3s,1s*
hahkweelemipwa *TA,ind,2p,1 ; TA,ind,2p,1s*
hahkweelemita *TA,part,3s,1s*
hahkweelemite *TA,subj,3s,1s*
hahkweelemiyani *TA,conj,2s,1s*
hahkweelemiyeekwe *TA,subj,2p,1s*
hotahkweelemaali *TA,ind,3s,4s*
hotahkweelemaawahi *TA,ind,3p,4p*
hotahkweelemahi *TA,ind,3s,4p*
kitahkweelemekowa *TA,ind,3s,2p*
kitahkweelemi *TA,ind,2s,1s*
nitahkweelemekwa *TA,ind,3s,1s*
yeeahkweelemaaci *TA/IC,conj,3s,4*
yeeahkweelemaata *TA/IC,part,3s,4*
yeeahkweelemaka *TA/IC,part,1s,3s*
yeeahkweelemelwaakwe *TA/IC,part,3,2p*
yeeakweelemekowaaci *TA/IC,conj,4,3p*
yeeakweelemelwaakwe *TA/IC,part,3,2p*
yehahkweelemata *TA/IC,part,2s,3s*
yehahkweelemita *TA/IC,part,3s,1s*
hahkweelemekofi *beloved AI*
yahkweelemekofilici *AI/IC,conj,4*
hahkweelemiwee *love AI*
hahkweelemiwe *AI,ind,3s*
hahkweelemiweewe *love NI*
hotahkweelemiweewe *NI/POSS,3s,s*
hahkweelemoofo *be loved AI*
hahkweelemoofoci *AI,conj,3s*
hahkweelet *want TI_1*
hahkweeleta *TI,ind,3s,0s*
hahkweeletamowaaci *TI,conj,3p,0*
hotahkweeleta *TI,ind,3s,0s*
hotahkweeletaanaawa *TI,ind,3p,0*

yahkweeletaka *TI/IC,part,3s,0*
yahkweeletakki *TI/IC,part,3p,0*
hahkweeletamaw *want, desire* TA
  hahkweeletamawi *TA,imp,2s,3*
hahkweeleti *love [reciprocal]* AI
  hahkweeletiyeekwe *AI,conj,2p*
hahkweeletii *beloved* NA
  nitahkweeletiima *NA/POSS,1s,3s*
hahkweeletiiwe *love* NI
  hahkweeletiiwe *NI,s*
  hotahkweeletiiwe *NI/POSS,3s,s*
  hotahkweeletiiweneki *NI/POSS/LOC,3s*
  hotahkweeletiiwenwa *NI/POSS,3p*
  nitahkweeletiiweneki *NI/POSS/LOC,1s*
hahkwi *bad, suffering* PM
  hahkwi *PM*
hahkwi *serious, extreme* PV
  hotahkwi *PV*
hahkwi-hawoocika *weapon* NI
  hahkwi-hawoocikana *NI,p*
hahkwiisin *suffer, undergo* TI-O
  hahkwiisinamwa *TI,ind,3s,0*
hahkwikiteewe *anger, wrath* NI
  hahkwikiteewe *NI,s*
hahkwilaasamamoowe *travail* NI
  hahkwilaasamamoowe *NI,s*
hahkwiloke *sick* AI
  hahkwiloke *AI,ind,3s*
  hahkwilokeeli *AI,ind,4s*
  hahkwilokeelici *AI,conj,4*
  kitahkwiloke *AI,ind,2s*
  nitahkwiloke *AI,ind,1s*
  yee-hahkwilokeelici *AI/IC,conj,4*
  yeeahkwilokeelici *AI/IC,conj,4*
  yeeakwilokeecki *AI/IC,part,3p*
  yeekwilokeecki *AI/IC,part,3p*
  yeekwilokeelici *AI/IC,conj,4*
  yeekwilokeeta *AI/IC,part,3s*
hahkwilokeewe *sickness* NI
  hahkwilokeewe *NI,s*
  hahkwilokeewena *NI,p*
  hahkwilooweneki *NI/LOC*
  hotahkwilokeewe *NI/POSS,3s,s*
  kithahkwilokeewe *NI/POSS,2s,s*
hahkwilokeewileni *sick man* NA
  hahkwilokeewileni *NA,3s*

hahkwimawinahkaa *suffer* AI
  hahkwimawinahkaate *AI,subj,3s*
hahkwinal *hurt, harm* TA
  hahkwinalekonaawa *TA,ind,0,3p*
  hahkwinalekooli *TA,ind,4s,3s*
hahkwinamo *suffer* AI
  hahkwinamoci *AI,conj,3s*
  hahkwinamoya *AI,conj,1s*
  hahkwinamoyani *AI,conj,2s*
hahkwinamoowe *torment, hell* NI
  hahkwinamoowe *NI,s*
  hahkwinamooweneki *NI/LOC*
hahkwinamoowi *of hell* PM
  hahkwinamoowi *PM*
hahkwipenal *harm* TA
  hahkwipenalekonaawa *TA,ind,0,2p*
hahkwitehee *grieve* AI
  hahkwitehe *AI,ind,3s*
hahkwiteheeweni *have pain* AI
  hahkwiteheewenici *AI,conj,3s*
hahpanahkehfecika *foundation* NI
  hahpanahkehfecika *NI,s*
hahpeelemekwan *hallowed* II
  hahpeelemekwanwi *II,ind,0s*
hahpeeletiiwe *envy, covetousness*
  hahpeeletiiwe *NI,s*
  hahpeeletiiwena *NI,p*
  hapeeletiiwe *NI,s*
hahpoweewe *dream* NI
  hahpoweeweneki *NI/LOC*
hahsi *in addition, more*
  hahsi
haht *sow, plant* TI_2
  hahtooci *TI,conj,3s,0*
  hahtooya *TI,conj,1s,0*
  hahtooyani *TI,conj,2s,0*
  hotito *TI,ind,3s,0s*
  hototo *TI,ind,3s,0s*
  kitito *TI,ind,2s,0s*
  yeeahtoota *TI/IC,part,3s,0*
  yeetoota *TI/IC,part,3s,0*
  yehahtoota *TI/IC,part,3s,0*
hahtaw *sow* TA
  hahtaakwi *TA,ind,,3s*
  hotitaakooli *TA,ind,4s,3s*
hahteewefiiyaa *be quenched* II

hahteewefiiyaaki *II,conj,0*
hahteewi *exist, be located II*
  hahteeke *II,subj,0*
  hahteeki *II,conj,0*
  hahteeli *II,ind,4*
  hahteelita *II,conj,4*
  hahteewa *II,ind,0p*
  hahteewi *II,ind,0s*
  hateeki *II,conj,0*
  hateeli *II,ind,4*
  hateewa *II,ind,0p*
  hateewi *II,ind,0s*
  hatiteeki *II,conj,0*
  hteewi *II,ind,0s*
  teeki *II,conj,0*
  yehteeki *II/IC,conj,0*
  yehteelici *II/IC,conj,4*
hahtehoote *be extinguished II*
  hahtehooteeki *II,conj,0*
  yaalwi-ahtehooteeki *II/IC,conj,0*
hahtehw *extinguish TA*
  hahtehwaali *TA,ind,3s,4s*
hahtel *accuse, reproach TA*
  hahtelaawaaci *TA,conj,3p,4*
  hahtelaawaali *TA,ind,3p,4s*
  hahteleekwe *TA,part,2p,3*
  hahtelelwaakwe *TA,conj,3,2p*
hahtoocim *request solemnly, adjure TA*
  hahtoocimele *TA,ind,1s,2s*
hahtoofo *be sown AI*
  yeetoofocki *AI/IC,part,3p*
hahtoote *be sown II*
  hahtooteelici *II,conj,4*
  hatoote *II,ind,0*
  hatooteeki *II,conj,0*
  yeetooteeki *II/IC,conj,0*
haisaya *Isaiah NA*
  haisaya *NA,3s*
haisiki *Isaac NA*
  haisik' *NA,3s*
  haisiki *NA,3s*
  haisikiili *NA,4s*
haitoomiye *Iudmaea NI*
  haitoomiye *NI,s*
hakaaw *need TA*
  hotakaawaalaali *TA,ind,3s,4s*

hotakaawaalaawaali *TA,ind,3p,4s*
hakaawaaciilefi *need AI*
  hakaawaaciilefi *AI,ind,3s*
hakaawaafi *need AI*
  hakaawaafi *AI,ind,3s*
  hakaawaafiici *AI,conj,3s*
  kitakaawaafiipwa *AI,ind,2p*
  nitakaawaafi *AI,ind,1s*
hakaawaafiiwe *need, lack NI*
  hotakaawaafiiwe *NI/POSS,3s,s*
hakaawaat *need TI_1*
  hakaawaatamani *TI,conj,2s,0*
  hekaawaatameekwe *TI,conj,2p,0*
  hotakaawaata *TI,ind,3s,0s*
  yeekaawaatamakwe *TI/IC,conj,1i,0*
  yeekaawaatameekwe *TI/IC,conj,2p,0*
  yeekaawaatamelici *TI/IC,conj,4,0*
hakaawaatameewe *need NI*
  hakaawaatameewena *NI/POSS,3s,p*
hakaawaatet *be needed II*
  hakaawaatetwi *II,ind,0s*
hakhwi *be on, be over II*
  hakhooli *II,ind,4*
hakimawikee *enroll AI*
  hakimawikeeci *AI,conj,3s*
  hakimawikeeki *AI,conj,3*
  hakimawikeewaaci *AI,conj,3p*
hakimawikeewe *enrollment NI*
  hakimawikeewe *NI,s*
hakinaye *observe, adhere to AI*
  hakinaye *AI,ind,3s*
  nitakinaye *AI,ind,1s*
hakit *count TI_1*
  hotakita *TI,ind,3s,0s*
hakitahfo *settle accounts AI*
  hakitahfoci *AI,conj,3s*
hakitahfoom *settle accounts TA*
  hakitahfoomahi *TA,ind,3s,4p*
hakocikami *roof NI*
  hakocikami *NI,s*
hakocipokwanefo *upper, above*
  hakocipokwanefo
hakoofiwee *ascend AI*
  hakoofiwe *AI,ind,3s*
  hakoofiweelici *AI,conj,4*
hakowihi *in addition*

hakowihi
hakwahfet *bring to land TI_2*
    hakwahfetoowaaci *TI,conj,3p,0*
    hotehakwahfeto *TI,ind,3s,0s*
hakwahsin *come up to land AI*
    hakwahsiki *AI,conj,3s*
    hakwahsinowaaci *AI,conj,3p*
halaakwa *star NA*
    halaakoki *NA/LOC,3*
    halaakwa *NA,3s*
    halaakwaki *NA,3p*
    halaakwali *NA,4s*
    hotalaakomali *NA/POSS,3s,4s*
halaane *yonder*
    halaane
halah *[interrogative]*
    halah
halahootamoowe *voice, crying out NI*
    hotalahootamoowenwa *NI/POSS,3p*
halalika *increasingly*
    halalika
halanoofo *be invited AI*
    halanoofolici *AI,conj,4*
    yeelanoofocki *AI/IC,part,3p*
    yeelanoofolici *AI/IC,conj,4*
halayine *that, yonder, further*
    halayine
hale *[inchoative] PV*
    hale *PV*
    halemi *PV*
    hoalemi *PV*
    hotalem *PV*
    hotalemi *PV*
halemaapiyeen *compose TI_1*
    halemaapiyeenamowaaci *TI,conj,3p,0*
halemahkamikat *begin II*
    halemahkamikatwi *II,ind,0s*
    halemahkamikiki *II,conj,0*
halemahkehfen *be begun II*
    halemahkehfenwi *II,ind,0s*
halemahoot *cry out TI-O*
    halemahootamwa *TI,ind,3s,0*
halemhfee *approach AI*
    halemhfeeki *AI,ind,3p*
    halemhfeewaaci *AI,conj,3p*
halemiiyaa *begin II*

halemiiya *II,ind,0*
halemiki *II,conj,0*
halen *bid, ask; warn TA*
    halanaata *TA,part,3s,4*
    halanehko *TA,imp,2p,3*
    halenehka *TA,part,3,2s*
    halenehke *TA,subj,3s,2s*
    halenekoci *TA,conj,4,3s*
    halenelepwa *TA,ind,1s,2p*
    haleni *TA,imp,2s,3*
    hotalenaali *TA,ind,3s,4s*
    hotalenahi *TA,ind,3s,4p*
    hotalenekooli *TA,ind,4s,3s*
    hotalenekowaali *TA,ind,4s,3p*
    kitalenekooki *TA,ind,3p,2s*
    kitalenekowa *TA,ind,3s,2p*
    yeelenehka *TA/IC,part,3,2s*
halenoofo *be invited, be bidden AI*
    halenoofo *AI,ind,3s*
    halenoofoyane *AI,subj,2s*
    yeelenoofocki *AI/IC,part,3p*
    yeelenoofolici *AI/IC,conj,4*
halhfiyas *Alphaeus NA*
    halhfiyas *NA,3s*
    helhfiasi *NA,3s*
halhfwaacilawiiwe *transgression NI*
    hotalhfwaacilawiiwenwa *NI/POSS,3p*
    kitalhfwaacilawiiwenwa *NI/POSS,2p*
    kithalhfwaacilawiiwenwa *NI/POSS,2p*
halhfwaacilot *transgress TI_1*
    nitalhfwaacilota *TI,ind,1s,0s*
halifiet *Olive NI*
    halifiet *NI,s*
halifiwi *olive PM*
    halhfiwi *PM*
    halifiwi *PM*
halika *more*
    halika
halikaamehi *further*
    halikaamehi
halisk *overcome TI_1*
    haliska *TI,ind,1s,0s*
haliskait *convict TI_1*
    haliskaita *TI,ind,3s,0s*
haliskaw *overcome TA*
    hotaliskaakooli *TA,ind,4s,3s*

haliweelemoofoowe *favor NI*
   haliweelemoofoowe *NI,s*
   haliweelemoofooweneki *NI/LOC*
haliwi *above, greater*
   haliwi
   haliwiisi
halool *hire TA*
   haloolekona *TA,ind,3s,1x*
   yeeloolaaci *TA/IC,conj,3s,4*
   yeeloolata *TA/IC,part,2s,3s*
   yeelooleta *TA/IC,part,,3s*
haloola *laborer NA*
   haloolahi *NA,4p*
haloolaaka *servant NA*
   haloolaaka *NA,3s*
   haloolaakanaki *NA,3p*
   haloolaakanali *NA,4s*
   haloolaakanhhi *NA,4p*
   hotaloolaakanali *NA/POSS,3s,4s*
   hotaloolaakanhhi *NA/POSS,3s,4p*
   kitaloolaaka *NA/POSS,2s,3s*
   kitaloolaakanaki *NA/POSS,2s,3p*
   nitaloolaaka *NA/POSS,1s,3s*
   nitaloolaakanaki *NA/POSS,1s,3p*
haloolaakaafa *servant NA*
   haloolaakaafa *NA,3s*
   haloolaakaafaki *NA,3p*
   haloolaakaafali *NA,4s*
   haloolaakaafhi *NA,4p*
   hotaloolaakaafhi *NA/POSS,3s,4p*
haloolaakaniikweefa *handmaid NA*
   haloolaakaniikwefhi *NA,4p*
   hotaloolaakaniikweefali *NA/POSS,3s,4s*
haloolaakanileni *servant NA*
   haloolaakanilcnihi *NA,4p*
haloosi *aloes NI*
   haloosi *NI,s*
halotaafiiwe *punishment NI*
   halotaafiiweneki *NI/LOC*
halotaafoowe *punishment, vengeance NI*
   halotaafoowe *NI,s*
halotamaw *avenge TA*
   halotamawa *TA,ind,1s,3s*
   halotamawaali *TA,ind,3s,4s*
   halotamawilo *TA,imp,2s,1s*
halotamoowe *vengeance NI*

halotamoowe *NI,s*
halotaw *avenge TA*
   halotawahi *TA,ind,3s,4p*
halwaakahsi *in rest, at rest PV*
   halwaakahsi *PV*
halwaakahsi *rest AI*
   halwaakahsiiki *AI,ind,3p*
   halwaakahsiko *AI,imp,2p*
halwaakahsiiwe *rest NI*
   halwaakahsiiwe *NI,s*
   kitalwaakahsiiwenwa *NI/POSS,2p*
halwaakahsiwee *observe the sabbath AI*
   halwaakahsiweeki *AI,conj,3*
halwaakahsiweewe *sabbath NI*
   halwaakahsiweewe *NI,s*
halwaakahsiwi *be the sabbath II*
   halwaakahsiwiki *II,conj,0*
   halwaakasiwiki *II,conj,0*
halwaakahsiwi *in rest, at rest PV*
   halwaakahsiwi *PV*
halwaakahsiwiiwe *sabbath NI*
   halwaakahsiwiiwe *NI,s*
halwihkaat *walk past TI_1*
   kitalwihkaataanaawa *TI,ind,2p,0*
   yeelwihkaatakki *TI/IC,part,3p,0*
ham *eat (implied animate object) TI-O*
   hamoko *AI,imp,2p*
hamach *wake up TA*
   hamachaki *TA,conj,1s,3*
   hotamachaawaali *TA,ind,3p,4s*
   hotamacihaawaali *TA,ind,3p,4s*
hamamo *awake, wake up AI*
   hamamo *AI,ind,3s*
   hamamowaaci *AI,conj,3p*
hamw *consume, eat TA*
   hotamwaali *TA,ind,3s,4s*
   hotamwahi *TA,ind,3s,4p*
   yemwita *TA/IC,part,3s,1s*
hanahka *cushion NA*
   hanahkanali *NA,4s*
hanahkwaski *top, pinnacle NI*
   hanahkwaski *NI,s*
hanahkwi *tip NI*
   hanahkwi *NI,s*
hanhhiwee *win AI*
   hanhhiweepwa *AI,ind,2p*

hanhhiweewahoot *cry out exceedingly TI-O*
    hanhhiweewahootamooki *TI,ind,3p,0*
hanhhiweewatkaawe *great torment NI*
    hanhhiweewatkaawena *NI,p*
    hanhhiweewatkaaweneki *NI/LOC*
hanhhiweewi *very PV*
    hanhhiweewe *PV*
    hanhhiweewi *PV*
hanhka *in some future*
    hanhka
hanhkawi *interlaced; as a chain PV*
    hanhkawi *PV*
    hotananhkawi *PV*
hanhtaw *surpass TA*
    hanhtaweekwe *TA,subj,2p,3*
hapa *Abba NA*
    hapa *NA,3s*
hapacsin *lean AI*
    haapacsinelici *AI/IC,conj,4*
    hapacsiki *AI,conj,3*
    hapacsinooli *AI,ind,4s*
hapahkweewe *roof NI*
    nitapahkweewe *NI/POSS,1s,s*
hapahkwehfecika *roof NI*
    hapahkwehfecika *NI,s*
    nitapahkwehfecika *NI/POSS,1s,s*
hapahkwehfiwakkwa *roof tile NA*
    hapahkwehfiwakkohi *NA,4p*
hapaica *Abijah NA*
    hapaica *NA,3s*
    hapaicali *NA,4s*
hapakileceewi *with the palm of the hand PV*
    hotapakileceewi *PV*
hapasiwakhoowe *hedge NI*
    hapasiwakhoowena *NI,p*
hapelohfa *child NA*
    hapelofhi *NA,4p*
    hapelohfa *NA,3s*
    hapelohfaki *NA,3p*
    hapelohfali *NA,4s*
    hapelohfeefa *NA/DIM,3s*
    hapelohfeefaki *NA/DIM,3p*
    hapelohfeefali *NA/DIM,4s*
    hapelohfeefeti *NA/DIM,2p*
    hapelohfeefhi *NA/DIM,4p*
    hapelohfeti *NA,2p*

hotapelohfemali *NA/POSS,3s,4s*
hotapelohfemhhi *NA/POSS,3s,4p*
hotapelohfemwahi *NA/POSS,3p,4p*
kitapelohfemaki *NA/POSS,2s,3p*
kitapelohfemwaaki *NA/POSS,2p,3p*
nitapelohfema *NA/POSS,1s,3s*
nitapelohfemaki *NA/POSS,1s,3p*
nitapelohfemenaaki *NA/POSS,1x,3p*
hapelohfiwi *be a child AI*
    hapelohfiwici *AI,conj,3s*
hapen *sacrifice TI_3*
    hapeneewaaci *TI,conj,3p,0*
hapenawe *sacrifice NI*
    hapenaweewe *NI,s*
    hapenaweewena *NI,p*
    hotapeneewenilici *NI/POSS,4*
hapenawe *sacrifice AI*
    hapenaweki *AI,conj,3*
hapi *exist, be located AI*
    hapi *AI,ind,1s*
    hapici *AI,conj,3s*
    hapicki *AI,part,3p*
    hapihi *AI,ind,4p*
    hapiiki *AI,ind,3p*
    hapiili *AI,ind,4s*
    hapiko *AI,imp,2p*
    hapilici *AI,conj,4*
    hapilite *AI,subj,4s*
    hapilo *AI,imp,2s*
    hapipe *AI,ind,1x*
    hapipwa *AI,ind,2p*
    hapite *AI,subj,3s*
    hapiwa *AI,ind,3s*
    hapiwaaci *AI,conj,3p*
    hapiya *AI,conj,1s*
    hapiyakwe *AI,conj,1i*
    hapiyane *AI,subj,2s*
    hapiyani *AI,conj,2s*
    hapiyeekwe *AI,conj,2p ; AI,subj,2p*
    kitapi *AI,ind,2s*
    kitapipe *AI,ind,1i*
    nitapi *AI,ind,1s*
    yeepicki *AI/IC,part,3p*
    yeepilici *AI/IC,conj,4*
    yeepita *AI/IC,part,3s*
    yeepiyani *AI/IC,conj,2s*

hapiim *be with TA*
    hapiimaaci *TA,conj,3s,4*
    hapiimahi *TA,ind,3s,4p*
    hapiimekooki *TA,ind,3p,1s*
    hapiimekowa *TA,ind,3s,2p*
    hapiimekowaaci *TA,conj,4,3p*
    hapiimekowaali *TA,ind,4s,3p*
    hapiimelepwa *TA,ind,1s,2p*
    hapiimelwaakwe *TA,conj,3,2p*
    hapiimi *TA,ind,2s,1s*
    yeepiimekowaaci *TA/IC,conj,4,3p*
hapiiwe *presence NI*
    hotapiiweneki *NI/POSS/LOC,3s*
    hotapiiwenwaaki *NI/POSS/LOC,3p*
hapiiyaa *exist, be located II*
    hapiiya *II,ind,0*
hapim *be with TA*
    hapimiwaaci *TA,conj,3p,1s*
hapiwe *presence NI*
    kitapiiweneki *NI/POSS/LOC,2s*
hapkawh *lay flat on TA*
    hotapkawhaawahi *TA,ind,3p,4p*
hapkeen *weave, plait TI_1*
    hapkeenaanaawa *TI,ind,3p,0*
    hapkeenimota *TI,part,3s,0*
    hotapkeenaanaawa *TI,ind,3p,0*
hasahkicehfe *go backward AI*
    hasahkicehfeeki *AI,ind,3p*
hasen *pass, go away II*
    haseke *II,subj,0*
    haseki *II,conj,0*
    haseno *II,ind,0p*
    hasenwi *II,ind,0s*
    yeeyaseki *II/IC,conj,0*
hasen *pass, go away AI*
    hasenelici *AI,conj,4*
    hasenooli *AI,ind,4s*
    hasenwa *AI,ind,3s*
hasenh *destroy TA*
    hotasenhhekonaawa *TA,ind,0,3p*
hasiski *earth NI*
    hasiski *NI,s*
    hasiskiiki *NI/LOC*
    hasiskiwali *NI,p*
    hotasiskiiki *NI/POSS/LOC,3s*
    hotasiskiimeki *NI/POSS/LOC,3s*

hotasiskiimi *NI/POSS,3s,s*
    hotasiskiimwa *NI/POSS,3p*
    hotasiskiimwaaki *NI/POSS/LOC,3p*
    kitasiskiimeki *NI/POSS/LOC,2s*
hasiskinoomeskaawe *earthquake NI*
    hasiskinoomeskaawali *NI,p*
    hasiskinoomeskaawe *NI,s*
    hasiskinoomeskaawena *NI,p*
hasiskiwakkwa *earthenware vessel NI*
    hasiskiwakkoki *NI/LOC*
hasowe *in exchange; across*
    haasowe
    hasowe
hatooci *solemnly PV*
    hatooci *PV*
    yeeatooci *PV/IC*
hattawassi *being on one's back*
    hattawassi
hattee *ripe II*
    hatteelici *II,conj,4*
    yeetteeki *II/IC,conj,0*
haw *use TI_3*
    hawe *TI,ind,3s,0s*
    haweko *TI,imp,2p,0*
    hawelo *TI,imp,2s,0*
    hotawe *TI,ind,3s,0s*
    hotawena *TI,ind,3s,0p*
hawafo *warm oneself AI*
    hawafo *AI,ind,3s*
    hawafoci *AI,conj,3s*
    hawafolici *AI,conj,4*
    hawafowaaci *AI,conj,3p*
hawhh *lend to TA*
    hawhhahi *TA,ind,3s,4p*
    hawhheekwe *TA,subj,2p,3*
    hawhhilo *TA,imp,2s,1s*
    hotawhhaawahi *TA,ind,3p,4p*
    hotawhhahi *TA,ind,3s,4p*
hawhiwee *lend AI*
    hawhiweeko *AI,imp,2p*
    yaayawhiweeta *AI/IC,part,3s*
hawikanefoowika *porch NI*
    hawikanefoowikaaneki *NI/LOC*
    hotawikanefoowikaaneki *NI/POSS/LOC,3s*
hawikanhskaw *overshadow TA*
    hawikanhskaako *TA,ind,0s,2s*

hotawikanhskaakonaawa *TA,ind,0,3p*
hawikaw *write to, write for TA*
   hawikoola *TA,conj,1s,2s*
   hawikoolwaakwe *TA,conj,3,2p*
   nitawikaakona *TA,ind,3s,1i*
hawikee *write AI*
   hawike *AI,ind,3s*
   hawikeeci *AI,conj,3s*
   hawikeeki *AI,conj,3*
   hawikeelo *AI,imp,2s*
   hawikeepi *AI,ind,3*
   yaayawikeecki *AI/IC,part,3p*
   yaayawikeelici *AI/IC,conj,4*
   yaayawikeeta *AI/IC,part,3s*
   yeewikeeki *AI/IC,part,3p*
hawoocika *equipment, furnishing NI*
   hawoocika *NI,s*
hawoot *use, wear TI_1*
   hotawoota *TI,ind,3s,0s*
haya *pet, domesticated animal NA*
   hotayeli *NA/POSS,3s,4s*
hayackofi *conceive AI*
   hayackofi *AI,ind,3s*
hayen *? when, if ?*
   hayenwi
hee, haa *go AI*
   ha *AI,ind,2s ; AI,ind,1s*
   haaci *AI,conj,3s*
   haaki *AI,conj,3*
   haako *AI,imp,2p*
   haakone *AI,imp,2p*
   haale *AI,imp,2s*
   haalici *AI,conj,4*
   haalo *AI,imp,2s*
   haape *AI,ind,1x*
   haataako *AI,imp,1i*
   haate *AI,subj,3s*
   haawaaci *AI,conj,3p*
   haaya *AI,conj,1s*
   haayaake *AI,conj,1x ; AI,subj,1x*
   haayani *AI,conj,2s*
   haayeekwe *AI,conj,2p*
   heeki *AI,ind,3p*
   heewa *AI,ind,3s*
   hehi *AI,ind,4p*
   kita *AI,ind,2s*

nhha *AI,ind,2s*
nhhaaci *AI,conj,3s*
nhhaako *AI,imp,2p*
nhhaakone *AI,imp,2p*
nhhaale *AI,imp,2s*
nhhaalici *AI,conj,4*
nhhaalo *AI,imp,2s*
nhhaataako *AI,imp,1i*
nhhaawaaci *AI,conj,3p*
nhhaawaate *AI,subj,3p*
nhhaaya *AI,conj,1s ; AI,subj,1s*
nhheeki *AI,ind,3p*
nhheewa *AI,ind,3s*
ninita *AI,ind,1s*
nita *AI,ind,1s*
yaahehi *AI,ind,4p*
yaayeewa *AI,ind,3s*
yehaaci *AI/IC,conj,3s*
yehaawaaci *AI/IC,conj,3p*
yehaaya *AI/IC,conj,1s*
yehaayani *AI/IC,conj,2s*
yehaayeekwe *AI/IC,conj,2p*
heele *in, along*
   heele
heelekiina *among*
   heelekiina
   heelekiini
heeleksenhta *Alexander NA*
   heeleksenhta *NA,3s*
heelepeestaawi *alabaster PM*
   heelepeestaawi *PM*
heemen *amen*
   heemen
heenhtlo *Andrew NA*
   heenhtlo *NA,3s*
   heenhtlooli *NA,4s*
heepayeefa *Abiathar NA*
   heepayeefa *NA,3s*
heesaye *long time, long ago*
   heesaye
heewikaate *bond, debt, bill NI*
   kiteewikaateemi *NI/POSS,2s,s*
heewikaateeki *book, piece of writing NI*
   heewikaateeki *NI,s*
   heewikaateekiiki *NI/LOC*
   heewikaateewali *NI,p*

hoteewikaateemeki *NI/POSS/LOC,3s*
    hoteewikaateemi *NI/POSS,3s,s*
    hoteewikaateemwa *NI/POSS,3p*
heewikaki *shadow NI*
    heewikaki *NI,s*
    yeewikaki *NI,s*
    yeewikakiiki *NI/LOC*
heewike *scribe NA*
    hoteewikeemwahi *NA/POSS,3p,4p*
heeyaa *go II*
    heeya *II,ind,0*
    heeyaaki *II,conj,0*
    heeyaali *II,ind,4*
    heeyaalici *II,conj,4*
    nhheeya *II,ind,0*
    yeheeyaaki *II/IC,conj,0*
heeyiita *on both sides*
    heeyiita
hefekseti *Arphaxad NA*
    hefekseti *NA,3s*
hehesii *Ahaz NA*
    hehesii *NA,3s*
    hehesiili *NA,4s*
hei *hail [interjection]*
    hei
hekeeleasi *Archelaus NA*
    hekeeleasi *NA,3s*
hekimi *Achim NA*
    hekimii *NA,3s*
    hekimiili *NA,4s*
hel *say to TA*
    haayekooki *TA,ind,3p,1s*
    haayekoopi *TA,ind,3,2s*
    hikoci *TA,conj,4,3s*
    hikona *TA,ind,3s,1i*
    hikooki *TA,ind,3p,1s*
    hikoopwa *TA,ind,3,2p*
    hikowa *TA,ind,3s,2s*
    hikowaaci *TA,conj,4,3p*
    hikowaaki *TA,ind,3p,2p*
    hikwa *TA,ind,3s,2s*
    hila *TA,ind,2s,3s ; TA,ind,1s,3s*
    hilaaci *TA,conj,3s,4*
    hilaaki *TA,ind,1s,3p*
    hilaali *TA,ind,3s,4s*
    hilaate *TA,subj,3s,4*

    hilaawa *TA,ind,2p,3s*
    hilaawaaci *TA,conj,3p,4*
    hilaawaali *TA,ind,3p,4s*
    hilahi *TA,ind,3s,4p*
    hilehki *TA,conj,3,2s*
    hilehko *TA,imp,2p,3*
    hilela *TA,conj,1s,2s*
    hilelako *TA,conj,1s,2p*
    hilelepwa *TA,ind,1s,2p*
    hilelwaakwe *TA,subj,3,2p ; TA,conj,3,2p*
    hisilo *TA,imp,2s,1s*
    hisipwa *TA,ind,2p,1s*
    hotekohi *TA,ind,4p,3s*
    hotekooli *TA,ind,4s,3s*
    hotekowahi *TA,ind,4p,3p*
    hotelaali *TA,ind,3s,4s*
    hotelaawaali *TA,ind,3p,4s*
    hotelaawahi *TA,ind,3p,4p*
    hotelahi *TA,ind,3s,4p*
    hotelwaali *TA,ind,3s,4s*
    kitaasipwa *TA,ind,2p,1*
    kitekwa *TA,ind,3s,2s*
    kitelaawa *TA,ind,2p,3s*
    kitele *TA,ind,1s,2s*
    kitelepwa *TA,ind,1s,2p*
    kitesi *TA,ind,2s,1s*
    kitesipwa *TA,ind,2p,1*
    nitaayekooki *TA,ind,3p,1s*
    nitekwa *TA,ind,3s,1s*
    nitela *TA,ind,1s,3s*
    nitelaaki *TA,ind,1s,3p*
    nitelaape *TA,ind,1x,3*
    yaaleta *TA/IC,part,,3s*
    yeekoci *TA/IC,conj,4,3s*
    yeelaaci *TA/IC,conj,3s,4*
    yeelaawaaci *TA/IC,conj,3p,4*
    yeelaki *TA/IC,conj,1s,3*
    yeeleekwe *TA/IC,part,2p,3*
    yeelehka *TA/IC,part,3,2s*
    yeelelako *TA/IC,conj,1s,2p*
    yeelelakwe *TA/IC,conj,3,1i*
    yeelelwaakwe *TA/IC,part,3,2p*
hel *compare to TI_1*
    hotelaanaawa *TI,ind,3p,0*
helani *Aaron NA*
    helani *NA,3s*

helekhi *midst* NI
    heelekhi *NI,s*
helepeestawakokoofa *alabaster vessel* NI
    helepeestawakokoofeki *NI/LOC*
heletii *Herod* NA
    heletii *NA,3s*
    heletiili *NA,4s*
    hiiletiili *NA,4s*
heletiifa *Herodian* NA
    heletiifaki *NA,3p*
    heletiifhi *NA,4p*
helootiasii *Herodias* NA
    helootiasii *NA,3s*
    helootiasiili *NA,4s*
hemani *Amon* NA
    hemanii *NA,3s*
    hemaniili *NA,4s*
hemasi *Amos* NA
    hemasi *NA,3s*
hemeasi *Emmaus* NI
    hemeasi *NI,s*
heminitepii *Amminadab* NA
    hemeniteepi *NA,3s*
    heminitepii *NA,3s*
    heminitepiili *NA,4s*
hemoowimelaasi *honey* NI
    hemoowimelaasi *NI,s*
hena *Arni* NA
    hena *NA,3s*
henasi *Annas* NA
    henas' *NA,3s*
    henasi *NA,3s*
    henasiili *NA,4s*
henhcali *angel* NA
    henhcali *NA,3s*
    henhcalihi *NA,4p*
    henhcaliiki *NA,3p*
    henhcaliili *NA,4s*
    hotenhcaliimali *NA/POSS,3s,4s*
    hotenhcaliimhhi *NA/POSS,3s,4p*
    hotenhcaliimwahi *NA/POSS,3p,4p*
henna *Anna* NA
    henna *NA,3s*
hepaica *Abijah* NA
    hepaica *NA,3s*
hepaitii *Abiud* NA

hepaitii *NA,3s*
    hepaitiili *NA,4s*
hepalii *Abel* NA
    hepalii *NA,3s*
hepastali *apostle* NA
    heepastaliiki *NA,3p*
    hepastalihi *NA,4p*
    hepastaliiki *NA,3p*
hepeliini *Abilene* NI
    hepeliini *NI,s*
heplehemii *Abraham* NA
    heplehem' *NA,3s*
    heplehemii *NA,3s*
    heplehemiili *NA,4s*
hesa *Asher* NA
    hesa *NA,3s*
hesii *Asa* NA
    hesii *NA,3s*
    hesiili *NA,4s*
hesikaaya *Hezekiah* NA
    hesikaaya *NA,3s*
    hesikaayali *NA,4s*
heslaa *Esli* NA
    heslaa *NA,3s*
heslanii *Hezron* NA
    heslanii *NA,3s*
    heslaniili *NA,4s*
heso *Azor* NA
    heso *NA,3s*
    hesooli *NA,4s*
het *say* TI
    hoteta *TI,ind,3s,0s*
    kiteta *TI,ind,2s,0s*
heta *Addi* NA
    heta *NA,3s*
hetami *Adam* NA
    hetami *NA,3s*
heyo *say* AI
    hiwa *AI,ind,3s*
    hiwahi *AI,ind,4p*
    hiwaki *AI,ind,3p*
    hiwakipi *AI,ind,3*
    hiwali *AI,ind,4s*
    hiwalipi *AI,ind,4s*
    hiwapi *AI,ind,3*
    hiyo *AI,ind,2s ; AI,ind,1s*

hiyoci *AI,conj,3s*
hiyohi *AI,ind,4p*
hiyoki *AI,conj,3*
hiyoko *AI,imp,2p*
hiyoli *AI,ind,4s*
hiyolo *AI,imp,2s*
hiyope *AI,ind,1i*
hiyopi *AI,ind,3*
hiyopwa *AI,ind,2p*
hiyote *AI,subj,3s*
hiyowaaci *AI,conj,3p*
hiyoya *AI,conj,1s*
hiyoyakwe *AI,conj,1i*
hiyoyeekwe *AI,conj,2p*
kitaayopwa *AI,ind,2p*
kiteyo *AI,ind,2s*
kiteyopwa *AI,ind,2p*
niteyo *AI,ind,1s*
yaa-iwapi *AI,ind,3*
yaawaki *AI,ind,3p*
yaayocki *AI/IC,part,3p*
yeeyoci *AI/IC,conj,3s*
yeeyocki *AI/IC,part,3p*
yeeyoki *AI/IC,conj,3*
yeeyolici *AI/IC,conj,4*
yeeyowaaci *AI/IC,conj,3p*
yeeyoya *AI/IC,conj,1s*
yeeyoyani *AI/IC,conj,2s*
yoci *AI,conj,3s*
yolici *AI/IC,conj,4*
yoyani *AI,conj,2s*
hiceptii *Egypt NI*
   hiceptii *NI,s*
   hiceptiiki *NI/LOC*
hiflami *Ephraim NI*
   hiflami *NI,s*
hiilaa *heli NA*
   hiilaa *NA,3s*
hiiploo *Hebrew NI*
   hiiploo *NI,s*
   hiiplooki *NI/LOC*
hiiploowaatoweewe *Hebrew NI*
   hiiploowaatoweeweneki *NI/LOC*
hiiploowawikaate *written in Hebrew II*
   hiiploowawikaate *II,ind,0*
hikwakit *throw away, cast TI_1*

hikwakitano *TI,imp,2s,0*
hikwat *worthy of, fated for II*
   hikwatwi *II,ind,0s*
hikwefa *maid NA*
   hotikwefemhhi *NA/POSS,3s,4p*
hikwihfeki *? middle ?*
   hikwihfeki
hilai *Eli NA*
   hilai *NA,3s*
hilaica *Elijah NA*
   hilaica *NA,3s*
   hilaicali *NA,4s*
hilaikamii *Eliakim NA*
   hilaikamii *NA,3s*
   hilaikamiili *NA,4s*
   hilaikimii *NA,3s*
hilawaatot *compare TI_1*
   hilawaatota *TI,ind,1s,0s*
hilaweh *compare TA*
   hilawehaaki *TA,ind,1s,3p*
   yeelawaaci *TA/IC,conj,3s,4*
hileelem *judge TA*
   hileelemekoopwa *TA,ind,3,2p*
hilefi *be thus AI*
   hilefi *AI,ind,3s ; AI,ind,2s*
   hilefici *AI,conj,3s*
   hilefihi *AI,ind,4p*
   hilefiiki *AI,ind,3p*
   hilefiko *AI,imp,2p*
   hilefilici *AI,conj,4*
   hilefilo *AI,imp,2s*
   hilefipe *AI,ind,1x*
   hilefipwa *AI,ind,2p*
   hilefita *AI,part,3s*
   hilefitc *AI,subj,3s*
   hilefiwaaci *AI,conj,3p*
   hilefiya *AI,conj,1s*
   hilefiyani *AI,conj,2s*
   hilefiyeekwe *AI,subj,2p ; AI,conj,2p*
   lefi *AI,ind,3s ; AI,ind,1s*
   lefici *AI,conj,3s*
   yeeleficki *AI/IC,part,3p*
   yeelefita *AI/IC,part,3s*
   yeelefiwaaci *AI/IC,conj,3p*
   yeelefiyeekwe *AI/IC,conj,2p*
hilefiht *withstand TI_1*

hilefihtaki *TI,conj,3s,0*
   hilefihtamowaaci *TI,conj,3p,0*
hilefiim *be thus (with) TA*
   lefiimaate *TA,subj,3s,4*
hilefiiwe *spirit NI*
   hilefiiwe *NI,s*
   lefiiweneki *NI/LOC*
hilefiiwen *character, spirit NA*
   hilefiiwena *NA,3s*
   hilefiiwenaki *NA,3p*
   hilefiiwenali *NA,4s*
   hilefiiwenhhi *NA,4p*
hilefiiyaa *be thus II*
   hilefiiya *II,ind,0*
   hilefiiyaaki *II,conj,0*
hilefiyot *be over, be in charge of TI_1*
   hilefiyotano *TI,imp,2s,0*
hileni *man NA*
   hileni *NA,3s*
   hilenihi *NA,4p*
   hileniiki *NA,3p*
   hileniili *NA,4s*
   lenihi *NA,4p*
   leniiki *NA,3p*
   leniili *NA,4s*
hiliatii *Eliud NA*
   hiliatii *NA,3s*
   hiliatiili *NA,4s*
hiliisa *Eliezer NA*
   hiliisa *NA,3s*
hilisipef *Elizabeth NA*
   hilisipef *NA,3s*
   hilisipefiili *NA,4s*
hiliyeesa *Eleazar NA*
   hiliyeesa *NA,3s*
   hiliyeesali *NA,4s*
hilmetami *Elmadam NA*
   hilmetami *NA,3s*
hiloi *eloi [Aramaic word]*
   hiloi
hiloofo *be told AI*
   hiloofo *AI,ind,3s*
   hiloofoci *AI,conj,3s*
   hiloofowaaci *AI,conj,3p*
   yeeloofowaaci *AI/IC,conj,3p*
himenoel *Emmanual NA*

himenoel *NA,3s*
hin *be so, happen so II*
   hike *II,subj,0*
   hiki *II,conj,0*
   hinike *II,subj,0*
   hiniki *II,conj,0*
   hino *II,ind,0p*
   hinwi *II,ind,0s*
   hinwili *II,ind,4*
   hinwilici *II,conj,4*
   ke *II,subj,0*
   yeeki *II/IC,conj,0*
   yeenwilici *II/IC,conj,4*
hinaka *Enoch NA*
   hinaka *NA,3s*
hinasi *Enos NA*
   hinasi *NA,3s*
hinawi *be (this person) AI*
   hiinawiyane *AI,subj,2s*
   hinawici *AI,conj,3s*
   hinawite *AI,subj,3s*
   hinawiya *AI,conj,1s*
   howiiyaawiyane *AI,subj,2s*
   kiilaawiyane *AI,subj,2s*
   kiilaawiyani *AI,conj,2s*
   kiiyaawiyane *AI,subj,2s*
   kiiyawiyane *AI,subj,2s*
   kiiyawiyani *AI,conj,2s*
   niiyaawiya *AI,conj,1s*
hine *then, at that time*
   hine
hinisi *there*
   hinisi
   nisi
hinoki *now, at this time*
   hinoki
hipa *Eber NA*
   hipa *NA,3s*
hisi *about, for, toward*
   hisi
   nihiisi
   nihisi
hisiwee *say AI*
   hisiwe *AI,ind,3s*
   hisiweeki *AI,ind,3p*
   hisiweeko *AI,imp,2p*

hisiweeli *AI,ind,4s*
hisiweepi *AI,ind,3*
hisiweepwa *AI,ind,2p*
hisiwehi *AI,ind,4p*
saiyeekwe *AI,conj,2p*
hiskeeletii *Iscariot NA*
hiskeeletii *NA,3s*
hiskeeletiili *NA,4s*
hiswiila *people of Israel NA*
hisfiilali *NA,4s*
hiswiila *NA,3s*
hiswiilahi *NA,4p*
hiswiilali *NA,4s*
hiswiileki *NA/LOC,3*
hit *say TI_1*
hita *TI,ind,3s,0s*
hitaanaawa *TI,ind,2p,0 ; TI,ind,3p,0*
hitamakwe *TI,conj,1i,0*
hitameyeekwe *TI,conj,2p,0*
hiti *say [reciprocal] AI*
hitiiki *AI,ind,3p*
hitolie *Ituraea NI*
hitolie *NI,s*
hitwa *be such AI*
hitwa *AI,ind,3s*
yeetekiki *AI/IC,part,3p*
yeetowaaci *AI/IC,conj,3p*
hiyoowe *saying NI*
hiyoowe *NI,s*
hiyoowena *NI,p*
hiyooweneki *NI/LOC*
hoteyoowena *NI/POSS,3s,p*
niteyoowena *NI/POSS,1s,p*
hiyooyaa *say, mean II*
hiyooya *II,ind,0*
yeeyooyaaki *II/IC,conj,0*
hkawaaci *waiting for, anticipating PV*
kitkawaaci *PV*
hkofi *at the extreme AI*
hikofi *AI,ind,3s*
hkoskaa *at the limit AI*
hikoskaaci *AI,conj,3s*
hkwaawefiiwe *fullness NI*
hotkwaawefiiwe *NI/POSS,3s,s*
hkweewa *woman NA*
hkwe *NA,3s*

hkweefa *NA/DIM,3s*
hkweefali *NA/DIM,4s*
hkweeki *NA,3p*
hkweeli *NA,4s*
hkweewa *NA,3s*
hkwehi *NA,4p*
hkwi *[to such extent] PV*
hkwi *PV*
yehkwi *PV/IC*
hkwiilefi *be as far as; die AI*
hkwiilefi *AI,ind,3s*
hkwiilefiili *AI,ind,4s*
nitkwiilefi *AI,ind,1s*
nitkwiilefipe *AI,ind,1x*
hkwiinami *perish AI*
kitikwiinamipe *AI,ind,1i*
hkwin *suffer TI-O*
hahkwina *TI,ind,1s,0s*
hahkwinaki *TI,conj,3s,0*
hahkwinamwa *TI,ind,3s,0*
hkwinamooki *AI,ind,3p*
hkwinamwa *AI,ind,3s*
hkwinamo *perish AI*
hkwinamooyakwe *AI,conj,1i*
hkwinamoowe *death, destruction NI*
hkwinamoowe *NI,s*
hkwinamooweneki *NI/LOC*
hotkwinamoowe *NI/POSS,3s,s*
hotkwinamoowenilici *NI/POSS,4*
hkwine *perish AI*
hkwineci *AI,conj,3s*
hkwineyeekwe *AI,conj,2p*
yehkwineta *AI/IC,part,3s*
hkwineh *destroy, cause to perish TA*
hkwinchaawaaci *TA,conj,3p,4*
hkwinehahi *TA,ind,3s,4p*
hkwineyaa *perish II*
hkwineya *II,ind,0*
hocacaalahkofiiwe *spirit NI*
hocacaalahkofiiweneki *NI/LOC*
hocacaalahkowi *spirit NI*
hocacaalahkoki *NI/LOC*
hocacaalahkowi *NI,s*
hocacaalahkowiiyaa *be spirit II*
hocacaalahkowiiya *II,ind,0*
hocacaalahkwa *spirit NA*

hocacaalahkomali *NA/POSS,3s,4s*
hocacaalahkwa *NA,3s*
hocacaalahkwali *NA,4s*
nicacaalahkwa *NA/POSS,1s,3s*
hoceekiilefi *decrease AI*
    hoceekiilefi *AI,ind,1s*
hoceekin *shorten TI_1*
    hoceekinaana *TI,ind,3s,0p*
    hoceekinake *TI,subj,3s,0*
hoceekinoote *be shortened II*
    hoceekinoote *II,ind,0*
    hoceekinooteeke *II,subj,0*
hoceeninaali *brother, same-sex sibling NA*
    hoceenina *NA,3s*
    hoceeninaaki *NA,3p*
    hoceeninaali *NA/POSS,3s,4s*
    hoceeninaana *NA,3s*
    hoceeninaanaali *NA,4s*
    hoceeninaanahi *NA,4p*
    hoceeninaanaki *NA,3p*
    hoceeninaanali *NA,4s*
    hoceeninaanhhi *NA,4p*
    hoceeninaawilici *NA/POSS,4s,4s*
    hoceeninahi *NA/POSS,3s,4p*
    kiceenina *NA/POSS,2s,3s*
    kiceeninaaki *NA/POSS,2s,3p*
    kiceeninaawaaki *NA/POSS,2p,3p*
    niceenina *NA/POSS,1s,3s*
    niceeninaaki *NA/POSS,1s,3p*
hoceepkahkatwi *root NI*
    hoceepkahatwi *NI,s*
    hoceepkahkato *NI,p*
    hoceepkahkatoki *NI/LOC*
    hoceepkahkatowi *NI,s*
    hoceepkahkatowiki *NI/LOC*
    hoceepkahkatwi *NI,s*
hoci *from, because of; from there PP*
    hoci *PP*
    nhhoci *PP*
hoci *[reason] PV*
    hoci *PV*
    howahoci *PV*
    kiwahoci *PV*
    kooci *PV*
    nooci *PV*
    wahoci *PV*
    wayahoci *PV/IC*
    weeci *PV/IC*
    wehoci *PV/IC*
hocifeyaa *be from, come from II*
    hocifeya *II,ind,0*
    weecifaaki *II/IC,conj,0*
hocih *act for the sake of TA*
    hocihaali *TA,ind,3s,4s*
hociikin *put forth TI_1*
    hociikina *TI,ind,3s,0s*
hociikwanah-keeptaw *kneel to TA*
    hociikwanah-keeptaakooli *TA,ind,4s,3s*
hociikwanahkeepi *kneel AI*
    hociikwanahkeepi *AI,ind,3s*
    hociikwanahkeepiiki *AI,ind,3p*
    hociikwanahkeepiili *AI,ind,4s*
hociikwanii *knee NI*
    hociikwaniiwali *NI/POSS,3s,p*
hocikee *fast AI*
    hocikeeci *AI,conj,3s*
    hocikeeki *AI,ind,3p*
    hocikeewaaci *AI,conj,3p*
    hocikeeyane *AI,subj,2s*
    hocikeeyani *AI,conj,2s*
    hocikeeyeekwe *AI,conj,2p*
    noocike *AI,ind,1s*
hocikeewe *fasting NI*
    hocikeewena *NI,p*
    hocikeewenwa *NI/POSS,3p*
    koocikeewenwa *NI/POSS,2p*
hocikeh *cause to fast TA*
    hocikehaawaaki *TA,ind,2p,3p*
hocikikat *blow (from) II*
    hocikikaki *II,conj,0*
hocimekofiiwena *authority NA*
    hocimekofiiwenaki *NA,3p*
    hocimekofiiwenhhi *NA,4p*
hocinee *die of, die from AI*
    hocineeci *AI,conj,3s*
    hocineeki *AI,ind,3p*
hociwi *be from II*
    hociwi *II,ind,0s*
    hociwike *II,subj,0*
    weeciwiki *II/IC,conj,0*
hociwi *be from AI*
    hocilici *AI,conj,4*

hociwiiki *AI,ind,3p*
hociwite *AI,subj,3s*
hociwiya *AI,conj,1s*
hociwiyeekwe *AI,subj,2p*
koociwipwa *AI,ind,2p*
noociwi *AI,ind,1s*
weeciwici *AI/IC,conj,3s*
weeciwicki *AI/IC,part,3p*
weeciwilici *AI/IC,conj,4*
weeciwita *AI/IC,part,3s*
weeciwiya *AI/IC,conj,1s*
weeciwiyani *AI/IC,conj,2s*
weeciwiyeekwe *AI/IC,conj,2p*
hociwiiyaa *be from II*
    hociwiiya *II,ind,0*
    hociwiki *II,conj,0*
    yoociwiiya *II,ind,0*
hoctan *flow from II*
    hocitano *II,ind,0p*
    weectaki *II/IC,conj,0*
hofaamh *abuse TA*
    hofaamhelwaakwe *TA,conj,3,2p*
hofaamhkaakwiiwe *overindulging NI*
    hofaamhkaakwiiwe *NI,s*
hofaami *too much PM*
    hofaami *PM*
hofaamilaakwiiyaa *be overcome II*
    hofaamilaakwiiya *II,ind,0*
hofaamilawiiwe *excess NI*
    hofaamilawiiwe *NI,s*
hofaamilepwaa *feeling excessively AI*
    hofaamilepwa *AI,ind,3s*
hofaawakokwa *brass vessel; brass NA*
    hofaawakokooki *NA,3p*
    hofaawakokwa *NA,3s*
hofaawimoni *gold coin NI*
    hofaawimoni *NI,s*
hofemiya *daughter-in-law NA*
    hofemiya *NA,3s*
    hofemiyeli *NA,4s*
    hohfemima *NA,3s*
hofemiyokiifa *mother-in-law NA*
    hofemiyokiifa *NA,3s*
    hofemiyokiifali *NA,4s*
hofepaacilawiiwe *dedication NI*
    hofepaacilawiiwe *NI,s*

hofepahkamikat *heaven II*
    weefepahkamikiki *II/IC,conj,0*
hofepaten *wrap TA*
    hofepatenaali *TA,ind,3s,4s*
hofepeelem *reverence, give respect to TA*
    hofepeelemaawaali *TA,ind,3p,4s*
hofepefi *holy AI*
    hofepefi *AI,ind,3s*
    weefepeficki *AI,ind,3p*
    weefepefita *AI/IC,part,3s*
hofepefiiwe *holiness NI*
    hofepefiiweneki *NI/LOC*
hofepekamoowe *hymn NI*
    hofepekamoowe *NI,s*
hofepi *holy PM*
    hofepi *PM*
    koofepi *PM*
hofepiini *likewise*
    hofepiini
hofepikamikwi *sanctuary NI*
    hofepikamikwi *NI,s*
hofepilawiiwe *purifying, making holy NI*
    hofepilawiiwe *NI,s*
hofepilot *purify, make holy TI_1*
    hofepilotamowaaci *TI,conj,3p,0*
hofepilotoofo *be cleansed AI*
    hofepilotoofo *AI,ind,3s*
hofepiyaa *holy II*
    hofepiya *II,ind,0s*
    hofepiyaaki *II,conj,0*
    hofepiyaali *II,ind,4*
    weefepiyaaki *II/IC,conj,0*
hofepsim *(fold up and) bury TA*
    hofepsimaawaali *TA,ind,3p,4s*
hofici *foot NI*
    hofici *NI,s*
    hofeciwa *NI/POSS,3p*
    hoficiwilici *NI/POSS,4*
    hofitali *NI/POSS,3s,p*
    hofiteki *NI/POSS/LOC,3s*
    hofitwa *NI/POSS,3p*
    kifici *NI/POSS,2s,s*
    kifitali *NI/POSS,2s,p*
    kifitena *NI/POSS,1i*
    kifitwaaki *NI/POSS/LOC,2p*
    nifitali *NI/POSS,1s,p*

nifitenaaki *NI/POSS/LOC,1x*
yehoficiwilici *NI/POSS,4*
hofihfa *nest NI*
  hofihfana *NI,p*
  hofihfanwa *NI/POSS,3p*
hofimaawi *be a father AI*
  weeofimaawita *AI/IC,part,3s*
hohfali *father NA*
  hofimaaki *NA,3p*
  hofimaali *NA,4s*
  hofwaali *NA/POSS,3p,4s*
  hofwahi *NA/POSS,3p,4p*
  hohfali *NA/POSS,3s,4s*
  hohfima *NA,3s*
  hohfimaaki *NA,3p*
  hohfimaali *NA,4s*
  hohfwaali *NA/POSS,3p,4s*
  kohfa *NA/POSS,2s,3s*
  kohfena *NA/POSS,1i,3s*
  kohfenaaki *NA/POSS,1i,3p*
  kohfenaali *NA/POSS,1i,4s*
  kohfenahi *NA/POSS,1i,4p*
  kohfwa *NA/POSS,2p,3s*
  kohfwaaki *NA/POSS,2p,3p*
  nohfa *NA/POSS,1s,3s*
  nohfali *NA/POSS,1s,4s*
  nohfehi *NA/POSS,1s,2s*
  nohfeki *NA/POSS/LOC,1s,3s*
  nohfena *NA/POSS,1x,3s*
  nohfenaaki *NA/POSS,1x,3p*
hohfi *have as father AI*
  hohfiyeekwe *AI,subj,2p*
  niyohfipe *AI,ind,1x*
hohkani *bone NI*
  hokanali *NI,p*
  hokanemi *NI/POSS,3s,s*
  hokanemwa *NI/POSS,3p*
hohsihoofo *be betrothed AI*
  hohsihoofolici *AI,conj,4*
hokaaciwakokwa *pot NA*
  hokaaciwakokooki *NA,3p*
hokakehkimaafim *have as disciple TA*
  hokakehkimaafimelako *TA,conj,1s,2p*
hokakehkimaafimi *have as disciple AI*
  hokakehkimaafimi *AI,ind,1s*
hokakiisekanemi *have the day (live in the*

time of) AI
  hokakiisekanemici *AI,conj,3s*
  hokakiisekanemiki *AI,conj,3*
  kakiisekanemici *AI,conj,3s*
  kakiisekanemiwaaci *AI,conj,3p*
hokanaatepi *skull NI*
  hohkanaatepiki *NI/LOC*
  hokanaatepi *NI,s*
  hokanaatepiki *NI/LOC*
hoki *mother NA*
  hokeefa *NA/DIM,3s*
  hokeefali *NA/DIM/POSS,3s,4s*
  hokeeli *NA/POSS,3s,4s*
  hokiifa *NA/DIM,3s*
  hokilici *NA/POSS,4s,4s*
  hokiwaali *NA/POSS,3p,4s*
  hokiwahi *NA/POSS,3p,4p*
  kikiya *NA/POSS,2s,3s*
  nikiya *NA/POSS,1s,3s*
hokima *chief NA*
  hokima *NA,3s*
  hokimaaki *NA,3p*
  hokimaali *NA,4s*
  hokimaamali *NA/POSS,3s,4s*
  hokimaamwaali *NA/POSS,3p,4s*
  hokimaamwahi *NA/POSS,3p,4p*
  hokimahi *NA,4p*
  kookimaama *NA/POSS,2s,3s*
  kookimaamwa *NA/POSS,2p,3s*
hokimaawh *make (someone) king TA*
  hokimaawhaawaaci *TA,conj,3p,4*
hokimaawi *chief; of a king PM*
  hokimaawi *PM*
hokimaawi *be chief, king, in charge AI*
  hokimaawi *AI,ind,3s*
  hokimaawiili *AI,ind,4s*
  hokimaawiya *AI,conj,1s*
  weekimaawita *AI/IC,part,3s*
hokimaawiiwe *kingdom [as rule, reign?] NI*
  hokimaawiiwe *NI,s*
  hokimaawiiweneki *NI/LOC*
  hokimaawiiwenilici *NI/POSS,4*
  hookimaawiiwe *NI/POSS,3s,s*
  kookimaawiiwe *NI/POSS,2s,s*
  kookimaawiiweneki *NI/POSS/LOC,2s*
  nookimaawiiwe *NI/POSS,1s,s*

hokimaawikaa *house of a king* NI
  hokimaawikaana *NI/POSS,3p*
hokimaawilenii *chief person* NA
  hokimaawileniimwahi *NA/POSS,3p,4p*
hokimaawipetakhoowe *crown* NI
  hokimaawipetakhoowe *NI,s*
hokimaawitaamhkwe *kingdom [as region?]* NI
  hokimaawihotaamhkomi *NI/POSS,3s,s*
  hokimaawitaamhkomeki *NI/POSS/LOC,3s*
  hokimaawitaamhkomi *NI/POSS,3s,s*
  hokimaawitaamhkwe *NI,s*
  hokimaawitaamhkweewali *NI,p*
  hokimaawitaamhkwemi *NI/POSS,3s,s*
  kokimaawitaamhkomeki *NI/POSS/LOC,2s*
  nookimaawitaamhkomeki *NI/POSS/LOC,1s*
hokimaawiyhkwe *queen* NA
  hokimaawiyhkwe *NA,3s*
hokimaawoosaaka *prince* NA
  hokimaawoosaakanhhi *NA/POSS,3s,4p*
  hokimaawoosaakanwaali *NA/POSS,3p,4s*
hokimaawt *rule, reign over* TI
  hokimaawta *TI,ind,3s,0s*
  hokimaawtaki *TI,conj,3s,0*
hokimaawtaw *rule, reign over* TA
  hokimaawtawaki *TA,conj,1s,3*
  hokimaawtawiyamekici *TA,conj,3,1x*
hokokoskwi *tender* II
  hokokoskwi *II,ind,0s*
hokwaan *chain* NA
  hokwaanhhi *NA,4p*
hokwaawefi *full, fill with* AI
  hokwaawefi *AI,ind,3s*
  hokwaawefici *AI,conj,3s*
  hokwaawefiiki *AI,ind,3p*
  hokwaawefiili *AI,ind,4s*
  hokwaawefiko *AI,imp,2p*
hokwaawefiiweniwi *have fulfillment* II
  hokwaawefiiweniwi *II,ind,0s*
hokwaawfen *fill* II
  hokwaawfeki *II,conj,0*
  hokwaawfeno *II,ind,0p*
  hokwaawfenwi *II,ind,0s*
hokwaawfet *fill, fulfill* TI_2
  hokwaawfetoowaaci *TI,conj,3p,0*
  hokwaawfetooyakwe *TI,conj,1i,0*
hokwaawfetoote *be filled, be fulfilled* II

hokwaawfetoote *II,ind,0*
  hokwaawfetooteeke *II,subj,0*
  hokwaawfetooteeki *II,conj,0*
hokwaawi *fully* PV
  hokwaawi *PV*
hokwaawilawi *fulfill* AI
  hokwaawilawiiya *AI,conj,1s*
hokwakwehtaaneeletamaw *marvel at* TA
  hokwakwehtaaneeletamawaawaali *TA,ind,3p,4s*
  hokwakwehtaaneeletamawahi *TA,ind,3s,4p*
hokwani *heel* NI
  hokwani *NI,s*
hokweekaka *neck* NI
  hohkweekakaneki *NI/POSS/LOC,3s*
  hokwekakaneki *NI/POSS/LOC,3s*
hokwihfali *son* NA
  hokwifhi *NA/POSS,3s,4p*
  hokwihfali *NA/POSS,3s,4s*
  hokwihfima *NA,3s*
  hokwihfimaaki *NA,3p*
  hokwihfimaali *NA,4s*
  hokwihfimahi *NA,4p*
  hokwihfwahi *NA/POSS,3p,4p*
  kikwihfa *NA/POSS,2s,3s*
  kikwihfwa *NA/POSS,2p,3s*
  kikwihfwaaki *NA/POSS,2p,3p*
  nikwihfa *NA/POSS,1s,3s*
  nikwihfaki *NA/POSS,1s,3p*
  nikwihfali *NA/POSS,1s,4s*
hokwihfen *fill* II
  hohkwihfeki *II,conj,0*
  hokwihfeke *II,subj,0*
  hokwihfeki *II,conj,0*
  hokwihfenili *II,ind,4*
  hokwihfeno *II,ind,0p*
  hokwihfenwi *II,ind,0s*
  hokwihfenwili *II,ind,4*
hokwihfet *fill* TI_2
  hokwihfeto *TI,ind,3s,0s*
  hokwihfetooko *TI,imp,2p,0*
  hokwihfetoonaawa *TI,ind,3p,0*
hokwihfetoote *be filled* II
  hokwihfetoote *II,ind,0*
  hokwihfetooteeki *II,conj,0*
hokwihfi *have as son* AI
  hokwihfici *AI,conj,3s*

hokwihfiyaake *AI,conj,1x*
hokwihfin *have as son TA*
    hokwihfinaali *TA,ind,3s,4s*
    hokwihfinekowa *TA,ind,3s,2p*
    hokwihfinekoyeekwe *TA,conj,3,2p*
    hokwihfinelwaakwe *TA,conj,3,2p*
hokwihsino *fill AI*
    hokwihsinohi *AI,ind,4p*
    hokwihsinooki *AI,ind,3p*
    hokwihsinooli *AI,ind,4s*
    yeeikwihsinowaaci *AI/IC,conj,3p*
hokwihsinoowe *fulfillment NI*
    hokwihsinoowe *NI,s*
hokwikamh *fill TA*
    hokwikamhaali *TA,ind,3s,4s*
hokwikami *fill up II*
    hokwikami *II,ind,0*
hokwikami *fill up AI*
    hokwikamilici *AI,conj,4*
hokwikomh *fill TA*
    hokwikomhehko *TA,imp,2p,3*
holaaka *dish NI*
    holaakaneki *NI/LOC*
holaako *be over, be past, after*
    holaako
holaakosi *be over, be past, over*
    holaakosi
holaakwiifi *be over, be past, after II*
    holaakwiifi *II,ind,0s*
    holaakwiifike *II,subj,0*
    holaakwiifiki *II,conj,0*
    weelaakwiifiki *II/IC,conj,0*
holaakwiifiwihfeni *eat the evening meal AI*
    holaakwiifiwihfenici *AI,conj,3s*
holaamahoot *cry out TI-O*
    holaamahootamwa *TI,ind,3s,0*
holaami *greatly, strongly*
    holaami
holaamihsimo *cry out, use a loud voice AI*
    holaamihsimo *AI,ind,3s*
holaamowe *cry out AI*
    holaamowe *AI,ind,3s*
holaaya *Uriah NA*
    holaaya *NA,3s*
holakeelho *go by boat AI*
    holakeelho *AI,ind,3s*

holakeesi *boat NI*
    holakeefeki *NI/DIM/LOC,s*
    holakeelali *NI,p*
    holakeeleki *NI/LOC*
    holakeelemwa *NI/POSS,3p*
    holakeesi *NI,s*
    holakeesihi *NI/DIM,s*
holakwhe *fat AI*
    weelakwhelici *AI/IC,conj,4*
    weelakwheta *AI/IC,part,3s*
holeceeli *finger NA*
    holeceeli *NA/POSS,3s,4s*
    holecehi *NA/POSS,3s,4p*
    holeciwaali *NA/POSS,3p,4s*
    kileca *NA/POSS,2s,3s*
    kileceefwa *NA/DIM/POSS,2p,3s*
    nileca *NA/POSS,1s,3s*
holeci *hand NI*
    holeci *NI/POSS,3s,s*
    holeciki *NI/POSS/LOC,3s*
    holeciwa *NI/POSS,3p*
    holeciwaaki *NI/POSS/LOC,3p*
    holeciwali *NI/POSS,3s,p*
    holeciwilici *NI/POSS,4*
    holecwaaki *NI/POSS/LOC,3p*
    kileci *NI/POSS,2s,s*
    kileciwali *NI/POSS,2s,p*
    nileci *NI/POSS,1s,s*
    nileciki *NI/POSS/LOC,1s*
    nileciwali *NI/POSS,1s,p*
holefi *good AI*
    holefi *AI,ind,3s*
    weelefilici *AI/IC,conj,4*
    weelefita *AI/IC,part,3s*
holekwa *wing NI*
    holekwana *NI/POSS,3s,p*
holelh *bathe TA*
    holelhaaci *TA,conj,3s,4*
    holelhehko *TA,imp,2p,3*
    holelhekoci *TA,conj,4,3s*
    holelhekooli *TA,ind,4s,3s*
    holelhekoopwa *TA,ind,3,2p*
    holelhekowa *TA,ind,3s,2p*
    holelhekowaali *TA,ind,4s,3p*
    holelhelepwa *TA,ind,1s,2p*
    holelhiyani *TA,conj,2s,1s*

holelhiwee *wash AI*
    holelhiwe *AI,ind,3s ; AI,ind,1s ; AI,ind,2s*
    holelhiweeci *AI,conj,3s*
    holelhiweeki *AI,conj,3*
    holelhiweeta *AI/IC,part,3s*
    holelhiweeya *AI,conj,1s*
holelhoofo *be washed AI*
    holelhoofo *AI,ind,3s*
    holelhoofoci *AI,conj,3s*
    holelhoofooki *AI,ind,3p*
    holelhoofowaaci *AI,conj,3p*
    holelhoofoya *AI/IC,conj,1s*
    holelhoofoyeekwe *AI,conj,2p*
    weelelhoofoya *AI/IC,conj,1s*
holelwii *wash, swim AI*
    holelwiilici *AI,conj,4*
    holelwiiwaate *AI,subj,3p*
    holelwiiya *AI,conj,1s*
    weelelwiita *AI/IC,part,3s*
holemhkwi *underside, ventral PV*
    holemhkwi *PV*
holeniye *beast NI*
    holeniyeki *NI,p*
holhaka *husk NI*
    holhakaawali *NI,p*
holowi *? put out branches, leaves ? II*
    holowiki *II,conj,0*
holweht *sound TI_2*
    holwehtoolo *TI,imp,2s,0*
hom *come from AI*
    homeki *AI,conj,3s*
    homelici *AI,conj,4*
    homooki *AI,ind,3p*
    homooli *AI,ind,4s*
    homowaaci *AI,conj,3p*
    homwa *AI,ind,3s*
    noome *AI,ind,1s*
    weemeka *AI/IC,part,3s*
    weemelici *AI/IC,conj,4*
    weemeya *AI/IC,conj,1s*
homaamhkaweelemoofooweni *have as memorial AI*
    homaamhkaweelemoofoowenici *AI,conj,3s*
homanetoom *have as god TA*
    homanetoomiyeekwe *TA,conj,2p,3*
homayaaotawaka *right ear NI*

homayaaotawaka *NI/POSS,3s,s*
    homayaaotawakaaki *NI/POSS/LOC,3s*
homekiiwe *sore NI*
    homekiiwena *NI,p*
    homekiiwenilici *NI/POSS,4*
homhtekwaapi *have armor AI*
    homhtekwaapici *AI,conj,3s*
homiinhkaan *seed*
    homiinhkaanici
    homiinhkaanilici
homiisamaakeemi *have as minister AI*
    homiisamaakeemipwa *AI,ind,2p*
homooyaa *come from, come out of II*
    homooya *II,ind,0*
    homooyaaki *II,conj,0*
    weemooyaaki *II/IC,conj,0*
honalescika *leaven NI*
    honalescika *NI,s ; NI/POSS,3s,s*
    honalescikanwa *NI/POSS,3p*
honamehfiwi *have as a fish AI*
    honamehfiwi *AI,ind,3s*
honete *be leavened II*
    honete *II,ind,0*
    honeteeki *II,conj,0*
honhhalwaakitaamhkwe *own country NI*
    honhhalwaakitaamhkoki *NI/POSS/LOC,3s*
honhskaa *rise AI*
    honhska *AI,ind,3s ; AI,ind,1s*
    honhskaaci *AI,conj,3s*
    honhskaaki *AI,ind,3p*
    honhskaako *AI,imp,2p*
    honhskaalite *AI,subj,4s*
    honhskaalo *AI,imp,2s*
    honhskaata *AI,part,3s*
    honhskaatc *AI,subj,3s*
honhskaan *raise TA*
    honhskaana *TA,ind,1s,3s*
    honhskaanaaci *TA,conj,3s,4*
    honhskaanaali *TA,ind,3s,4s*
    honhskaanehko *TA,imp,2p,3*
    honhskaanike *TA,subj,,1s*
honhskaan *raise TI_1*
    honhskaanama *TI,conj,1s,0*
honhskaanamaw *raise TA*
    honhskaanamawaaci *TA,conj,3s,4*
    honhskaanamawaali *TA,ind,3s,4s*

honhskaanoofo *be raised AI*
    honhskaanoofo *AI,ind,3s*
    honhskaanoofoci *AI,conj,3s*
    honhskaanoofohi *AI,ind,4p*
    honhskaanoofooki *AI,ind,3p*
    honhskaanoofoya *AI,conj,1s*
honhskaawe *rising NI*
    honhskaawe *NI,s*
honiyeeweelena *four in number PV*
    honiyeeweelena *PV*
hoopitii *Obed NA*
    hoopitii *NA,3s*
    hoopitiili *NA,4s*
hoosena *hosanna*
    hoosena
hoowaawi *egg NI*
    hoowaawi *NI,s*
hopahoot *cry out TI-O*
    hopahootamwa *TI,ind,3s,0*
hopaten *build, raise up TI_1*
    hopatena *TI,ind,1s,0s ; TI,ind,3s,0s ; TI,ind,2s,0s*
    hopatenaanaawa *TI,ind,3p,0*
    hopatenaka *TI,part,3s,0*
    hopatenaki *TI,conj,3s,0*
    hopatenama *TI,conj,1s,0*
    hopatenike *TI,subj,3s,0*
    weeopatenaka *TI/IC,part,3s,0*
    weepatenaka *TI/IC,part,3s,0*
hopatenamaw *build, raise up TA*
    hopatenamawaaci *TA,conj,3s,4*
    hopatenamawahi *TA,ind,3s,4p*
    koopatenamawaawaaki *TA,ind,2p,3p*
    noopatenamaakona *TA,ind,3s,1x*
hopatenoote *be built II*
    hopatenoote *II,ind,0*
    hopatenooteeki *II,conj,0*
hopehkwata *belly NI*
    hopehkwata *NI/POSS,3s,s*
    hopehkwataaki *NI/POSS/LOC,3s*
hopekatefiiweni *have work (verb of possession) AI*
    hopekatefiiweniki *AI,conj,3*
hopskweete *be leavened II*
    hopskweeteeki *II,conj,0*
    weepskweeteeki *II/IC,conj,0*
hosaaya *Uzziah NA*

hosaaya *NA,3s*
    hosaayali *NA,4s*
hosasilaw *worship at TI*
    hosasilawaalici *TI,conj,4,0*
hosasilawaal *receive joyfully TA*
    hosasilawaalaali *TA,ind,3s,4s*
hosasilawaat *rejoice TI-O*
    hosasilawaatamehi *TI,ind,4p,0*
hosasilawaatiim *rejoice with TA*
    hosasilawaatiimaawaali *TA,ind,3p,4s*
hosasilawe *worship AI*
    hosasilawe *AI,ind,3s ; AI,ind,2s*
    hosasilaweewaaci *AI,conj,3p*
    waosasilaweeki *AI,ind,3p*
    weesasilawecki *AI/IC,part,3p*
hosasilaweh *worship TA*
    hosasilaweha *TA,ind,2s,3s*
    hosasilawehaali *TA,ind,3s,4s*
    hosasilawehaata *TA,part,3s,4*
    hosasilawehaawa *TA,ind,2p,3s*
    hosasilawehaawaali *TA,ind,3p,4s*
    hosasilawehaki *TA,conj,1s,3*
    hosasilawehakici *TA,conj,1x,3*
    hosasilawehekohi *TA,ind,4p,3s*
    hosasilawehekooli *TA,ind,4s,3s*
    hosasilawehiyane *TA,subj,2s,1s*
    hosilawehaawaali *TA,ind,3p,4s*
    kiwaosasilawehaawa *TA,ind,2p,3s*
    niwaaosasilawehekooki *TA,ind,3p,1s*
    niwaosasilawehaape *TA,ind,1x,3*
    weeosasilawehaacki *TA/IC,part,3p,4*
hosasilawem *rejoice TA*
    hosasilawemiko *TA,imp,2p,1s*
hosasilawemi *have as worshipper AI*
    hosasilawemici *AI,conj,3s*
hosasilepwaa *rejoice AI*
    hosasilepwa *AI,ind,3s*
    hosasilepwaaki *AI,ind,3p*
    hosasilepwaako *AI,imp,2p*
    hosasilepwaali *AI,ind,4s*
    hosasilepwaapwa *AI,ind,2p*
    hosasilepwaawaaci *AI,conj,3p*
    hosasilepwaayeekwe *AI,conj,2p*
hosasilepwaawe *joy NI*
    hosasilepwaawe *NI,s*
    hosasilepwaaweneki *NI/LOC*

koosasilepwaawenwa *NI/POSS,2p*
noosasilepwaawe *NI/POSS,1s,s*
hosasilepwaawefi *rejoice AI*
　　hosasilepwaawefiiki *AI,ind,3p*
hosasilepwaayaa *rejoice II*
　　hosasilepwaaya *II,ind,0*
hosehki *side NI*
　　hosehki *NI/POSS,3s,s*
　　hosehkiki *NI/POSS/LOC,3s*
　　hosehkiwilici *NI/POSS,4*
　　kisehkiwa *NI/POSS,2s,p*
　　nisehkiki *NI/POSS/LOC,1s*
hosilawaal *salute TA*
　　hosilawaalaali *TA,ind,3s,4s*
　　hosilawaalaawaali *TA,ind,3p,4s*
　　hosilawaalaki *TA,conj,1s,3*
　　hosilawaaleekwe *TA,subj,2p,3*
　　hosilawaalehko *TA,imp,2p,3*
　　hosilawaalekohi *TA,ind,4p,3s*
hosilawaaletiiwe *salutation NI*
　　hosilawaaletiiwena *NI,p*
hosilawaat *salute TI_1*
　　hosilawaatamoko *TI,imp,2p,0*
hosilawaatiiwe *salutation NI*
　　hosilawaatiiwe *NI,s*
　　hosilawaatiiwena *NI,p*
hosilaweewihsimoowe *voice of greeting NI*
　　kosilaweewihsimoowe *NI/POSS,2s,s*
hosilem *marry TA*
　　weesilemaaci *TA/IC,conj,3s,4*
hosilet *be married TI-O*
　　hosiletamwa *TI,ind,3s,0*
hosilet *marry TA*
　　hosileta *TA,ind,1s,3s*
hosimecfet *prepare TI_2*
　　hosimecfetooyaake *TI,conj,1x,0*
hosimecfetaw *prepare TA*
　　hosimecfetawaci *TA,conj,2s,3*
　　hosimecfetawinaake *TA,imp,2,1x*
hosimehcilotamaw *prepare TA*
　　hosimehcilotamawaaci *TA,conj,3s,4*
hosimo *flee AI*
　　hosimo *AI,ind,3s*
　　hosimooki *AI,ind,3p*
hosimoowe *flight NI*
　　koosimoowenwa *NI/POSS,2p*

hosit *flee from TI_1*
　　hositameekwe *TI,conj,2p,0*
hoskahkamiki *creation II*
　　hoskahkamikiki *II,conj,0*
　　weeskahkamikiki *II/IC,conj,0*
hoskahkehfen *be created II*
　　hoskahkehfenwi *II,ind,0s*
hoski *first*
　　hoski
　　weski
　　weskiki
　　weskilici
hoskici *upon*
　　hoskici
hoskiima *brother [of a sister] NA*
　　hoskiimali *NA/POSS,3s,4s*
　　hoskiimwaali *NA/POSS,3p,4s*
　　kooskiima *NA/POSS,2s,3s*
　　nooskiima *NA/POSS,1s,3s*
hoskiisekowi *have an eye AI*
　　hoskiisekowiyane *AI,subj,2s*
hoskiisekowi *eye PM*
　　hoskiisekowi *PM*
hoskiisekwi *eye NI*
　　hoskiiseko *NI/POSS,3s,p*
　　hoskiisekoki *NI/POSS/LOC,3s*
　　hoskiisekonilici *NI/POSS,4*
　　hoskiisekowa *NI/POSS,3p*
　　hoskiisekowiki *NI/POSS/LOC,3s*
　　hoskiisekowilici *NI/POSS,4*
　　hoskiisekwi *NI/POSS,3s,s*
　　kiskiiseko *NI/POSS,2s,p*
　　kiskiisekoki *NI/POSS/LOC,2s*
　　kiskiisekonaaki *NI/POSS/LOC,1i*
　　kiskiisekowa *NI/POSS,2p*
　　kiskiisekwi *NI/POSS,2s,s*
　　niskiiseko *NI/POSS,1s,p*
　　niskiisekoki *NI/POSS/LOC,1s*
　　niskiisekona *NI/POSS,1x*
　　niskiisekonaki *NI/POSS,1s,p*
hoskilenaweewi *be born AI*
　　hoskilenaweewi *AI,ind,3s*
　　hoskilenaweewici *AI,conj,3s*
　　hoskilenaweewiiki *AI,ind,3p*
　　hoskilenaweewiko *AI,imp,2p*
　　hoskilenaweewilici *AI,conj,4*

hoskilenaweewite *AI,subj,3s*
　weeoskilenaweewita *AI/IC,part,3s*
hoskilenaweewiiwe *birth NI*
　hoskilenaweewiiwe *NI,s*
hoskilhakeeme *have leprosy AI*
　weeskilhakeemekicki *AI/IC,part,3p*
　weeskilhakeemekilici *AI/IC,conj,4*
　weeskilhakeemekita *AI/IC,part,3s*
hoskilhakeemekiiwe *leprosy NI*
　hoskilhakeemekiiwe *NI,s*
hoskilhaki-mekiiwe *leprosy NI*
　hoskilhaki-mekiiwe *NI,s*
hoskimota *cloth NI*
　hoskimota *NI,s*
hoskin *new II*
　hoskinwi *II,ind,0s*
hoskini *new AI*
　hoskiniiki *AI,conj,3s*
hoskiniikiiwi *birth PM*
　honiikiiwi *PM*
　hooskiniikiiwi *PM*
hoskisa *lip NI*
　hoskisaawa *NI/POSS,3p*
hoskitaamhkwe *earth NI*
　hasiskitaamhkwe *NI,s*
　hoskitaamhkoki *NI/LOC*
　hoskitaamhkwe *NI,s*
hoskitepiye *upon*
　hoskitepiye
hostaw *make TA*
　hoostawaawaali *TA,ind,3p,4s*
　hostaakoopi *TA,ind,3,2s*
　hostaakwi *TA,ind,,3s*
　hostawaawaaki *TA,ind,2p,3p*
hotaafiwee *climb AI*
　hotaafiwe *AI,ind,3s*
hotaamefiiwe *over-abundance NI*
　hotaamefiiwenwa *NI/POSS,3p*
hotaami *bring forth, produce AI*
　weeotaamiita *AI/IC,part,3s*
hotaanaaki *behind, past*
　hotaanaaki
hotaanaakifi *behind, last AI*
　hotaanaakifiiki *AI,ind,3p*
hotaanaakiifa *last person NA*
　hotaanaakiifa *NA,3s*

hotaanaakiwi *be last AI*
　hotaanaakiwi *AI,ind,3s*
　hotaanaakiwiiki *AI,ind,3p*
hotaanehfa *daughter NA*
　hotaaneefhi *NA/POSS,3s,4p*
　hotaanehfali *NA/POSS,3s,4s*
　hotaanehfefali *NA/DIM/POSS,3s,4s*
　hotaanhfima *NA,3s*
　hotaanhfimaali *NA,4s*
　hotanhfima *NA,3s*
　kitaanehfa *NA/POSS,2s,3s*
　kitaanehfali *NA/POSS,2s,4s*
　nitaanehfa *NA/POSS,1s,3s*
　nitaanehfefa *NA/DIM/POSS,1s,3s*
hotaape *look AI*
　weetaapeeci *AI,conj,3s*
hotahfa *here, hither*
　hotahfa
hotahkofat *[the sun] rise; in the east II*
　weetahkofaki *II/IC,conj,0*
hotahkowaafo *judge AI*
　hotahkowaafopwa *AI,ind,2p*
hotahkwilokeemi *have disease AI*
　hotahkwilokeemilici *AI,conj,4*
hotahoot *cry out TI-O*
　hotahootamooli *TI,ind,4s,0*
hotahpapit *receive TI_2*
　hotahpapitooya *TI,conj,1s,0*
hotahpen *receive TA*
　hotahpenaaci *TA,conj,3s,4*
　hotahpenaali *TA,ind,3s,4s*
　hotahpenaata *TA,part,3s,4*
　hotahpenaawa *TA,ind,2p,3s*
　hotahpenaawaali *TA,ind,3p,4s*
　hotahpenaci *TA,conj,2s,3*
　hotahpenahi *TA,ind,3s,4p*
　hotahpenekoci *TA,conj,4,3s*
　hotahpenekohi *TA,ind,4p,3s*
　hotahpenekooli *TA,ind,4s,3s*
　hotahpenekoopwa *TA,ind,3,2p*
　hotahpenekowa *TA,ind,3s,2p*
　hotahpenekwa *TA,ind,3s,1s*
　hotahpenelepwa *TA,ind,1s,2p*
　hotahpenelwaakwa *TA,conj,3,2p*
　hotahpenelwaakwe *TA,part,3,2p*
　hotahpenita *TA,part,3s,1s*

hotahpeniwaaci *TA,conj,3p,1s*
kootahpenekowaaki *TA,ind,3p,2p*
kootahpenipwa *TA,ind,2p,1s*
nootahpenekwa *TA,ind,3s,1s*
weetahpenaata *TA/IC,part,3s,4*
weetahpenita *TA/IC,part,3s,1s*
hotahpen *receive TI_1*
    hotahpena *TI,ind,3s,0s ; TI,ind,1s,0s*
    hotahpenaana *TI,ind,3s,0p*
    hotahpenaanaawa *TI,ind,3p,0*
    hotahpenake *TI,subj,3s,0*
    hotahpenaki *TI,conj,3s,0*
    hotahpenakki *TI,part,3p,0*
    hotahpenameekwe *TI,conj,2p,0*
    hotahpenamowaaci *TI,conj,3p,0*
    kootahpenaanaawa *TI,ind,2p,0*
    weetahpenaka *TI/IC,part,3s,0*
hotahpenamaati *receive [reciprocal] AI*
    weetahpenamaaticki *AI/IC,part,3p*
hotahpenamaw *receive something from someone TA*
    hotahpenamawaali *TA,ind,3s,4s*
    hotahpenamawaata *TA,part,3s,4*
hotahpenoofo *be received AI*
    hotahpenoofo *AI,ind,3s*
    hotahpenoofoci *AI,conj,3s*
hotahpenoote *be received II*
    hotahpenooteeki *II,conj,0*
hotahpi *less*
    hotahpi
hotahpicike *moor AI*
    hotahpicikeeki *AI,ind,3p*
hotahpiifa *young, less AI*
    hotahpiifa *AI,ind,3s*
hotahpim *call, summon TA*
    hotahpimaali *TA,ind,3s,4s*
    hotahpimaawaaci *TA,conj,3p,4*
    hotahpimaawaali *TA,ind,3p,4s*
    hotahpimaawahi *TA,ind,3p,4p*
    hotahpimahi *TA,ind,3s,4p*
    hotahpimaki *TA,conj,1s,3*
    hotahpimehki *TA,conj,3,2s*
    hotahpimehko *TA,imp,2p,3*
    hotahpimekooli *TA,ind,4s,3s*
    hotahpimi *TA,imp,2s,3*
    kootahpimekwa *TA,ind,3s,2s*

hotahpimoofo *be called, be summoned AI*
    hotahpimoofolici *AI,conj,4*
hotakeelem *respect TA*
    hotakeelemaali *TA,ind,3s,4s*
    hotakeelemaata *TA,part,3s,4*
    hotakeelemaawaaci *TA,conj,3p,4*
    hotakeelemaawaali *TA,ind,3p,4s*
    hotakeelemekwi *TA,ind,,3s*
    hotakeelemi *TA,imp,2s,3*
    nootakeelema *TA,ind,1s,3s*
hotakeelemekofiiwe *honor NI*
    hotakeelemekofiiwe *NI,s*
hotakeelemekwileni *nobleman NA*
    hotakeelemekwileni *NA,3s*
hotakikahsin *stumble AI*
    hotakikahsiki *AI,conj,3s*
    hotakikahsinani *AI,conj,2s*
    hotakikahsinelici *AI,conj,4*
    hotakikahsineyeekwe *AI,conj,2p*
    hotakikahsinooki *AI,ind,3p*
    hotakikahsinowaaci *AI,conj,3p*
    hotakikahsinwa *AI,ind,3s*
hotakikahsin *stumble II*
    hotakikahsineki *II,conj,0*
hotakikahsinoowe *stumbling NI*
    hotakikahsinoowe *NI,s*
hotakonikeewe *bosom, chest NI*
    hotakonikeeweneki *NI/POSS/LOC,3s*
hotakoniyeewe *bosom, chest NI*
    hotakoniyeeweneki *NI/POSS/LOC,3s*
hotakoocino *be in suspense AI*
    hotakoocinooki *AI,ind,3p*
hotaloolaakani *have as servant AI*
    hotaloolaakaniiki *AI,ind,3p*
    hotaloolaakanipwa *AI,ind,2p*
hotamefiiwe *care, concern NI*
    hotamefiiwe *NI,s*
    hotamefiiwena *NI,p*
hotamh *bother TA*
    weetamhekoci *TA/IC,conj,0,3s*
hotamhskaaweyaa *occupy, take up II*
    hotamhskaaweya *II,ind,0*
hotapelohfemi *have as a child AI*
    hotapelohfemi *AI,ind,3s*
    hotapelohfemiili *AI,ind,4s*
    hotapelohfemite *AI,subj,3s*

hotapelohfeminaa *have as a child* AI
    hotapelohfeminaaci *AI,conj,3s*
hotaten *get, obtain* TI_1
    hotatenaanaawa *TI,ind,3p,0*
hotaten *receive from* TA
    nootatena *TA,ind,1s,3s*
hotatenikee *receive* AI
    hotatenike *AI,ind,3s*
    hotatenikeeyeekwe *AI,conj,2p*
hotawaka *ear* NI
    hotawakaaki *NI/LOC*
    hotawakaawa *NI/POSS,3p*
    hotawakaawaaki *NI/POSS/LOC,3p*
    hotawakaawali *NI,p*
    hotawakanilici *NI/POSS,4*
    kitawakaawa *NI/POSS,2p*
    kitawakaawaaki *NI/POSS/LOC,2p*
    nitawakaawali *NI/POSS,1s,p*
hotayi *have authority over* AI
    nootayipe *AI,ind,1x*
hotayin *have authority over* TA
    hotayineekwe *TA,conj,2p,3*
hoteepahkowemi *have as judge* AI
    hoteepahkowemipwa *AI,ind,2p*
hoteepweemi *have as testimony* AI
    hoteepweemiwaaci *AI,conj,3p*
hoteepweeweni *have as testimony* AI
    hoteepweeweniwaaci *AI,conj,3p*
    teepweeweniwaaci *AI,conj,3p*
    teepweeweniyeekwe *AI,conj,2p*
hoteewe *city, town, village* NI
    hoteewe *NI,s*
    hoteewena *NI,p*
    hoteeweneefa *NI/DIM,p*
    hoteeweneefeki *NI/DIM/LOC,s*
    hoteeweneefwa *NI/DIM/POSS,3p*
    hoteewenehi *NI/DIM,s*
    hoteeweneki *NI/LOC*
    hoteewenemi *NI/POSS,3s,s*
    hoteewenemwa *NI/POSS,3p*
    hoteewenilici *NI/POSS,4*
    hoteewenwa *NI/POSS,3p*
    hoteewenwaaki *NI/POSS/LOC,3p*
    hotooteewenehi *NI/DIM/POSS,4*
    hototeewe *NI/POSS,3s,s*
    hototeewena *NI/POSS,3s,p*

    hototeeweneki *NI/POSS/LOC,3s*
    hototeewenwa *NI/POSS,3p*
    koteewenwa *NI/POSS,2p*
hoteeweni *city* PM
    hoteeweni *PM*
hoteewenimiyeewe *street* NI
    hoteewenimiyeewena *NI,p*
    hoteewenimiyeeweneki *NI/LOC*
    noteewenimiyeewenenaaki
NI/POSS/LOC,1x
hoteewenimiyeewi *street* NI
    hoteewenimiyeewali *NI,p*
hoteeweniwiskilohfa *sparrow* NA
    hoteeweniwiskilohfaki *NA,3p*
hotefi *receive* AI
    hotefi *AI,ind,3s*
    hotefici *AI,conj,3s*
    hotefiko *AI,imp,2p*
    hotefipwa *AI,ind,2p*
    hotefiwaaci *AI,conj,3p*
    kotefipe *AI,ind,1i*
hotefihiweyaa *profit* II
    hotefihiweya *II,ind,0*
hoteliya *shoulder* NI
    hoteliki *NI/POSS/LOC,3s*
    hoteliwa *NI/POSS,3p*
hotepasawahkowemi *have as judge* AI
    hotepasawahkowemipwa *AI,ind,2p*
hotesimo *flee (from somewhere)* AI
    hotesimooki *AI,ind,3p*
hotet *exist in, consist of* II
    hotetwi *II,ind,0s*
hotf *appear, come to* TA
    hotfaali *TA,ind,3s,4s*
    hotfaawaaci *TA,conj,3p,4*
    hotfaawaali *TA,ind,3p,4s*
    hotfaawahi *TA,ind,3p,4p*
    hotfahi *TA,ind,3s,4p*
    hotfeko *TA,ind,0s,3s*
    hotfekoci *TA,conj,0,3s*
    hotfekohi *TA,ind,4p,3s*
    hotfekolo *TA,imp,0,2s*
    hotfekonaawa *TA,ind,0,3p ; TA,ind,0,2p*
    hotfekooki *TA,ind,0p,1s*
    hotfekooli *TA,ind,4s,3s*
    hotfekope *TA,ind,0,1x*
    hotfekota *TA,part,0,3s*

hotfekowaaci *TA,conj,0,3p*
hotfekowaali *TA,ind,4s,3p*
hotfekoya *TA,conj,0,1s*
hotfekoyani *TA,conj,3,2s*
hotfekoyeekwe *TA,conj,3,2p*
hotfekwa *TA,ind,3s,1s*
hotootfaawaali *TA,ind,3p,4s*
hotsici *TA,conj,3s,1s*
howaotfaawaali *TA,ind,3p,4s*
howaotfekohi *TA,ind,4p,3s*
howaotfekooli *TA,ind,4s,3s*
kootfekonaawa *TA,ind,0,2p*
kootfekope *TA,ind,0,1i*
kootfekowa *TA,ind,3s,2p*
kootfekwa *TA,ind,3s,2s*
nootfeko *TA,ind,0s,1s*
weeotfekolici *TA/IC,conj,0,4*
weeotfekoya *TA/IC,conj,0,1s*
hotfaal *enter TA*
hotfaalaawaaci *TA,conj,3p,4*
hotfeti *come together [reciprocal) AI*
hotfetiwaaci *AI,conj,3p*
hotikwema *sister NA*
hotikwemali *NA/POSS,3s,4s*
hotikwemhhi *NA/POSS,3s,4p*
hotikwemimahi *NA,4p*
hotkwemimahi *NA,4p*
nitikweema *NA/POSS,1s,3s*
hotkwipekatefiiwileni *carpenter NA*
hotkwipekatefiiwileni *NA,3s*
hotoon *mouth NI*
hotooneki *NI/POSS/LOC,3s*
hotooni *NI/POSS,3s,s ; NI,s*
hotooniki *NI/LOC*
hotooniwilici *NI/POSS/LOC,4*
hotoonwa *NI/POSS,3p*
kitooni *NI/POSS,2s,s*
nitooni *NI/POSS,1s,s*
hotoosaaka *offspring NA*
hotoosaaka *NA,3s*
hotoosaakanaki *NA,3p*
hott *enter TI_1*
hotta *TI,ind,3s,0s*
hottaanaawa *TI,ind,2p,0 ; TI,ind,3p,0*
hottaki *TI,conj,3s,0*
hottakki *TI,part,3p,0*

hottameekwe *TI,conj,2p,0*
hottamowaaci *TI,conj,3p,0*
hottano *TI,imp,2s,0*
niyotta *TI,ind,1s,0s*
hottamaw *enter TA*
hottamawehko *TA,imp,2p,3*
hotwaaci *to benefit PV*
hotwaaci *PV*
hotwaaf *profit from TA*
hotwaafiiyani *TA,conj,2s,1s*
hotwaal *enter TA*
hotwaalekohi *TA,ind,4p,3s*
hotwefi *receive AI*
hotwefiko *AI,imp,2p*
hotwen *deliver TA*
hotweninaake *TA,imp,2,1x*
hotwenika *recompense, excuse NI*
hotwenika *NI,s*
hotwenikani *recompense AI*
hotwenikani *AI,ind,3s*
hotwenikanici *AI,conj,3s*
howaapalaaci *shamefully PV*
howaapalaaci *PV*
howahfaacimekofiiweni *have glory AI*
howahfaacimekofiiwenici *AI,conj,3s*
howe *now, then*
howe
howe *say AI*
howeci *AI,conj,3s*
howelaacim *speak well of TA*
howelaacimekowaaki *TA,ind,3p,2p*
howelaacimoom *agree with TA*
howelaacimoomi *TA,imp,2s,3*
howelaakoom *treat well TA*
howelaakoomi *TA,imp,2s,3*
howeleelem *find pleasing TA*
weeoweleelemaaci *TA/IC,conj,3s,4*
howesaa *good II*
howesa *II,ind,0s*
howesaali *II,ind,4*
weewesaaki *II/IC,conj,0*
howesat *good II*
weeowesaaki *II/IC,conj,0*
howesfen *expedient, necessary, appropriate II*
howesfenwi *II,ind,0s*
howesfen *good; well done II*

howesfeki *II,conj,0*

howesi *good PM*

    howesi *PM*

    koowesi *PM*

    noowesi *PM*

howesiilefi *good AI*

    howesiilefi *AI,ind,3s*

    noowesiilefi *AI,ind,1s*

    weeowesiilefilici *AI/IC,conj,4*

howesilaasamamo *feel well AI*

    howesilaasamamo *AI,ind,3s*

    howesilaasamamooli *AI,ind,4s*

    weeowesilaasamamocki *AI/IC,part,3p*

howesilaasamamoowe *happiness NI*

    howesilaasamamoowe *NI,s*

howesilawi *do well AI*

    koowesilawi *AI,ind,2s*

howesilepwaa *feel good, be glad AI*

    howesilepwa *AI,ind,3s ; AI,ind,1s*

    howesilepwaafiiyakwe *AI,conj,1i*

    howesilepwaaki *AI,ind,3p*

    howesilepwaako *AI,imp,2p*

    howesilepwaalo *AI,imp,2s*

    howesilepwahi *AI,ind,4p*

howesilepwaafi *happy AI*

    howesilepwaafiiko *AI,imp,2p*

howesilepwaawe *good feeling NI*

    howesilepwaawe *NI,s*

    howesilepwaaweneki *NI/POSS/LOC,3s*

    howesilepwaaweni *NI/POSS,3s,s*

    koowesilepwaawenwa *NI/POSS,2p*

    noowesilepwaawe *NI/POSS,1s,s*

howesilepwaawefi *happy AI*

    howesilepwaawefilo *AI,imp,2s*

howesilepwaawi *gladly PV*

    howesilepwaawi *PV*

howesilepwahoofo *be comforted AI*

    howesilepwahoofo *AI,ind,3s*

howesinaakwat *beautiful II*

    howesinaakwato *II,ind,0p*

howesisin *be suitable AI*

    howesisinwa *AI,ind,3s*

howesitehee *kind AI*

    howesitehe *AI,ind,3s*

howesiteheewe *kind heart NI*

    howesiteheeweneki *NI/LOC*

howespenal *treat well TA*

    howespenaleekwe *TA,subj,2p,3*

    howespenalehko *TA,imp,2p,3*

    weeowespenalelwaakwe *TA/IC,part,3,2p*

howespenalefiiwena *benefactor NA*

    howespenalefiiwenaki *NA,3p*

howiifooweni *have the name AI*

    howiifooweni *AI,ind,3s*

    wiifooweni *AI,ind,3s*

howiilaami *own AI*

    howiilaami *AI,ind,2s ; AI,ind,3s*

    howiilaamiiki *AI,ind,3p*

    howiilaamiko *AI,imp,2p*

    howiilaamipe *AI,ind,1i*

    howiilaamita *AI,part,3s*

    howiilaamiyakwe *AI,conj,1i*

    koowiilaami *AI,ind,2s*

    noowiilaami *AI,ind,1s*

    weeowiilaamilici *AI/IC,conj,4*

    weewiilaamici *AI/IC,conj,3s*

    weewiilaamiya *AI/IC,conj,1s*

    weewiilaamiyani *AI/IC,conj,2s*

    weewiilaamiyeekwe *AI/IC,conj,2p*

howiilaamiiwe *possession NI*

    noowiilaamiiwe *NI/POSS,1s,s*

howiilaamin *own TA*

    howiilaaminehki *TA,conj,3,2s*

howiiwi *have as wife, marry AI*

    howiiwi *AI,ind,3s*

    howiiwili *AI,ind,4s*

    howiiwiwaaci *AI,conj,3p*

    wiiwili *AI,ind,4s*

    wiiwiwaaci *AI,conj,3p*

hpakil *throw TA*

    hotpakilaali *TA,ind,3s,4s*

    hotpakilaawaali *TA,ind,3p,4s*

    hotpakilaawahi *TA,ind,3p,4p*

    hpakilekooki *TA,ind,3p,2s*

    hpakilekooli *TA,ind,4s,3s*

    hpakilekoopi *TA,ind,3,2s*

    hpakilekwa *TA,ind,3s,2s*

    kitipakilekoopwa *TA,ind,3,2p*

    pakila *TA,ind,1s,3s*

    pakilaaci *TA,conj,3s,4*

    pakilaaki *TA,ind,1s,3p*

    pakilaali *TA,ind,3s,4s*

pakilaape *TA,ind,1x,3*
pakilaate *TA,subj,3s,4*
pakilaawaaci *TA,conj,3p,4*
pakilaawaali *TA,ind,3p,4s*
pakilaawahi *TA,ind,3p,4p*
pakilahi *TA,ind,3s,4p*
pakilake *TA,subj,1s,3*
pakilaki *TA,conj,1s,3*
pakilehko *TA,imp,2p,3*
pakilekowaaki *TA,ind,3p,2p*
pakisiyaake *TA,subj,2,1x*
hpalhkiiwe *footstool NI*
hotpalhkiiwe *NI/POSS,3s,s*
hpalhkiiwe *NI,s*
hpalhkiiwenili *NI/POSS,4s*
hpap *sit on TI_3*
hpapi *TI,ind,3s,0s*
hpapinaawa *TI,ind,2p,0*
hpapiiwe *seat NI*
hotpapiiwe *NI/POSS,3s,s*
hotpapiiwenilici *NI/POSS,4*
hotpapiiwenwa *NI/POSS,3p*
hpapiiwe *NI,s*
hpapiiwena *NI,p*
hpapiiweneki *NI/LOC*
hpenal *treat, do to TA*
hotpenalaawaali *TA,ind,3p,4s*
hotpenalaawahi *TA,ind,3p,4p*
hpenala *TA,ind,1s,3s*
hpenalaaci *TA,conj,3s,4*
hpenalaali *TA,ind,3s,4s*
hpenalaape *TA,ind,1i,3*
hpenalaate *TA,subj,3s,4*
hpenalaawaaci *TA,conj,3p,4*
hpenalaawaaki *TA,ind,2p,3p*
hpenalaawaali *TA,ind,3p,4s*
hpenalaawahi *TA,ind,3p,4p*
hpenalaci *TA,conj,2s,3*
hpenalahi *TA,ind,3s,4p*
hpenaleekwe *TA,conj,2p,3*
hpenalehki *TA,conj,3,2s*
hpenalehko *TA,imp,2p,3*
hpenalekoci *TA,conj,4,3s*
hpenalekoopwa *TA,ind,3,2p*
hpenalekowaaki *TA,ind,3p,2p*
hpenalekoyane *TA,subj,0,2s*
hpenalela *TA,conj,1s,2s*
hpenalelaake *TA,conj,1x,2*
hpenalelako *TA,conj,1s,2p*
hpenalelwaakwe *TA,conj,3,2p*
hpenasici *TA,conj,3s,1s*
hpenasipe *TA,ind,2s,1x*
hpenasiyaake *TA,conj,2,1x*
kitpenalekonaawa *TA,ind,0,2p*
kitpenalekwa *TA,ind,3s,2s*
kitpenasipwa *TA,ind,2p,1*
yehpenalaawaaci *TA/IC,conj,3p,4*
hpenaloofo *be caused, be done unto AI*
hpenaloofoci *AI,conj,3s*
hpenaloofoko *AI,imp,2p*
hpenaloofolo *AI,imp,2s*
hpenaloofoyeekwe *AI,conj,2p*
hpenat *do with, do to TI_2*
hpenato *TI,ind,3s,0s*
hpenatooya *TI,conj,1s,0*
hpenataw *do to/for TA*
hpenatawaaci *TA,conj,3s,4*
hpenatawaci *TA,conj,2s,3*
hpenatoote *be done II*
hpenatoote *II,ind,0*
yehpenatooteeki *II/IC,conj,0*
hpene *have happen to AI*
hpene *AI,ind,2s*
nothpene *AI,ind,1s*
hpeneewe *plague, disease NI*
hpeneewena *NI,p*
hpokwanwiht *season TI_2*
hipokwanwihtoonaawa *TI,ind,2p,0*
hpokwanwihtoote *be seasoned II*
hipokwanwihtoote *II,ind,0*
hsam *feed TA*
hahsamaaci *TA,conj,3s,4*
hahsami *TA,imp,2s,3*
hotsamahi *TA,ind,3s,4p*
hsameci *TA,conj,,3*
kitsamelepe *TA,ind,1x,2*
yeesamaacki *TA/IC,part,3p,4*
hsamoofo *be fed AI*
hahsamoofolici *AI,conj,4*
hskwaalawee *hungry AI*
kiskwaalawe *AI,ind,2s*
niskwaalawe *AI,ind,1s*

seeskwaalaweecki *AI/IC,part,3p*
skwaalawe *AI,ind,3s*
skwaalaweeci *AI,conj,3s*
skwaalaweepwa *AI,ind,2p*
skwaalaweewaate *AI,subj,3p*
skwaalawehi *AI,ind,4p*
hteeletamaw *want, require TA*
hoteeletamaakwi *TA,ind,,3s*
iffafa *ephphatha [Aramaic]*
iffafa
ihpakiloofo *be thrown AI*
hipakiloofo *AI,ind,3s*
hipakiloofolici *AI,conj,4*
hipakiloofolo *AI,imp,2s*
hipakiloofota *AI,part,s*
hipakiloofote *AI,subj,3s*
pakiloofo *AI,ind,3s*
pakiloofolici *AI,conj,4*
pakiloofooki *AI,ind,3p*
ihpakisiwee *throw AI*
hipakisiweeci *AI,conj,3s*
ihpakit *throw TI_1*
hipakita *TI,ind,3s,0s*
hipakitaanaawa *TI,ind,3p,0*
hipakitama *TI,conj,1s,0*
hipakitamelici *TI,conj,4,0*
hipakitamoko *TI,imp,2p,0*
hipakitamowaaci *TI,conj,3p,0*
hipakitano *TI,imp,2s,0*
hotipakita *TI,ind,3s,0s*
hotipakitaanaawa *TI,ind,3p,0*
nhpakitamelici *TI,conj,4,0*
nhpakitano *TI,imp,2s,0*
ihpakitamaw *throw TA*
hipakitamawaaki *TA,ind,1s,3p*
hipakitamaweci *TA,conj,,3*
hotpakitamawaawaali *TA,ind,3p,4s*
pakitamawaali *TA,ind,3s,4s*
pakitamoole *TA,ind,1s,2s*
pakitamoolwaakwe *TA,conj,3,2p*
ihpakiteelem *forsake*
kipakiteelemi *TA,ind,2s,1s*
ihpakiteelet *renounce TI_1*
pakiteeletaka *TI/IC,part,3s,0*
ihpakitoote *be thrown II*
hipakitoote *II,ind,0*

hipakitooteeki *II,conj,0*
pakitooteeki *II,conj,0*
kaaciika *now*
kaaciika
kaakalhhwe *raven NA*
kaakalhhweeki *NA,3p*
kaakika *continually*
kaakika
kaakilweewefiiyaa *be tolerable II*
kaakilweewefiiya *II,ind,0*
kaakilweewen *be tolerable II*
kaakilweewenwi *II,ind,0s*
kaakilweewinamoowe *consolation NI*
hokaakilweewinamoowe *NI/POSS,3s,s*
kaakkehsi *stay AI*
kikaakkehsi *AI,ind,2s*
kaal *live near TA*
kaalaacki *TA,part,3p,4*
kaamaani *peace PV*
kaamaani *PV*
kaamaaniilefiiwe *peace NI*
kaamaaniilefiiwe *NI,s*
kaamaaniilefiiweneki *NI/LOC*
kikaamaaniilefiiwenwa *NI/POSS,2p*
nikaamaaniilefiiwe *NI/POSS,1s,s*
kaamaaniilefiiwi *peace PM*
kaamaaniilefiiwi *PM*
kaamehkan *calm II*
kaamehkawaki *II,conj,0*
kaamehkawanwi *II,ind,0s*
kaamehkawefiiwe *calm NI*
kaamehkawefiiwe *NI,s*
kaameki *across, other side*
kaameki
kaapawi *stand AI*
kaapawici *AI,conj,3s*
kaapawilici *AI,conj,4*
kaapawiim *stand TA*
kaapawiimaaci *TA,conj,3s,4*
kaapawiimekoci *TA,conj,4,3s*
kaapeni *korban [Aramaic]*
kaapeni
kaasa *beforehand*
kaasa
kaawaci *around*
kaawaci

kaawaci *around, in a circle* PV
    kaawaci *PV*
kaawackofo *be circumcised* AI
    kaawackofoci *AI,conj,3s*
kaawatkofoowe *circumcision* NI
    kaawatkofoowe *NI,s*
kaawatkol *circumcise* TA
    kaawackolaawaaci *TA,conj,3p,4*
    kikaawatkolaawa *TA,ind,2p,3s*
kaawi *thorn* NA
    kaawihi *NA,4p*
    kaawiiki *NA,3p*
kaawiise *thorn* NA
    kaawiisehi *NA,3p*
    kaawiiseki *NA,3p*
kaawilawe *afraid* AI
    kaawilawe *AI,ind,3s*
    kaawilaweeki *AI,ind,3p*
    kaawilaweko *AI,imp,2p*
    kaawilawepwa *AI,ind,2p*
kaawilaweewe *fear* NI
    kaawilaweewe *NI,s*
kaayaawka *around, about*
    kaayaawka
kaayaawkitaamhkwe *surrounding region* NI
    kaayaawkitaamhkwe *NI,s*
kaayaawkwi *surrounding* PM
    kaayaawkwi *PM*
kafh *wipe* TI_1
    hokafhaana *TI,ind,3s,0p*
    kafhaana *TI,ind,3s,0p*
    kafhaape *TI,ind,1x,0*
kafhamaw *wipe* TA
    hokafhamawaali *TA,ind,3s,4s*
kahfiikwehoowe *towel* NI
    kahfiikwehoowe *NI,s*
kahfilecehoowe *napkin* NI
    kahfilecehooweneki *NI/LOC*
kahkalaamo *thirsty* AI
    kahkalaamo *AI,ind,3s*
    kahkalaamocki *AI,part,3p*
    kahkalaamote *AI,subj,3s*
    kahkalaamoya *AI,conj,1s*
    kikahkalaamo *AI,ind,2s*
    nikahkalaamo *AI,ind,1s*
kahkasaapilece *scorpion* AI

keekahkasaapileceecki *AI/IC,part,3p*
    keekahkasaapileceelici *AI/IC,conj,4*
kahkite *dry up* II
    kahkiteeli *II,ind,4*
    kayahkiteeki *II/IC,conj,0*
kahsi *rough*
    kahsi
kakeelhk *trample, tread on* TI_1
    kakeelhkaanaawa *TI,ind,3p,0*
kakeelhkaati *trample, tread [reciprocal]* AI
    kakeelhkaatiiki *AI,ind,3p*
kakeelhkaw *trample, tread on* TA
    hokakeelhkawaawahi *TA,ind,3p,4p*
    kakeelhkaweekwe *TA,conj,2p,3*
kakeelhkoote *be trampled, be tread upon* II
    kakeelhkoote *II,ind,0*
    kakeelhkooteeki *II,conj,0*
kakeepiikwa *blind person* NA
    kakeepiikwaki *NA,3p*
kakeepiikwee *blind* AI
    kakeepiikwe *AI,ind,3s*
    kakeepiikweeci *AI,conj,3s*
    kakeepiikweeli *AI,ind,4s*
    kakeepiikweewaaci *AI,conj,3p*
    kakeepiikweeya *AI,conj,1s*
    kakeepiikweeyeekwe *AI,subj,2p*
    keekakeepiikweelici *AI/IC,conj,4*
    keekakeepiikweeta *AI/IC,part,3s*
    keekeepiikweecki *AI/IC,part,3p*
    keekeepiikweelici *AI/IC,conj,4*
    keekeepiikweeta *AI/IC,part,3s*
    nikakeepiikweepe *AI,ind,1x*
kakeepiikweewi *blind* PM
    kakeepiikweewi *PM*
    keekeepiikwccwi *PM*
kakehkim *teach* TA
    hokakehkimahi *TA,ind,3s,4p*
    kakehkimaaci *TA,conj,3s,4*
    kakehkimahi *TA,ind,3s,4p*
    kakehkimehko *TA,imp,2p,3*
    kakehkimekowa *TA,ind,3s,2p*
    kakehkimekowaali *TA,ind,4s,3p*
    kakehkimici *TA,conj,3s,1s*
    kakehkiminaake *TA,imp,2,1x*
    keekehkimekoci *TA/IC,conj,4,3s*
    kikakehkimipe *TA,ind,2,1x*

kakehkima *teacher, master NA*
  hokakehkimaamali *NA/POSS,3s,4s*
  kikakehkimaamwa *NA/POSS,2p,3s*
kakehkimaafa *disciple NA*
  hokakehkimaafali *NA/POSS,3s,4s*
  hokakehkimaafemwahi *NA/POSS,3p,4p*
  hokakehkimaafhi *NA/POSS,3s,4p*
  hokakehkimaafwahi *NA/POSS,3p,4p*
  kakehkimaafa *NA,3s*
  kakehkimaafaki *NA,3p*
  kakehkimaafali *NA,4s*
  kakehkimaafhi *NA,4p*
  kakehkmaafhi *NA,4p*
  kikakehkimaafaki *NA/POSS,2s,3p*
  nikakehkimaafaki *NA/POSS,1s,3p*
kakehkimaafihoofo *be made a disciple AI*
  kakehkimaafihoofota *AI,part,3s*
kakehkimaafiim *make a disciple of TA*
  kakehkimaafiimekowa *TA,ind,3s,2p*
  kakehkimaafiimelepwa *TA,ind,1s,2p*
kakehkimiwe *teacher NA*
  keekehkimiwe *NA,3s*
  kikakehkimiwemwa *NA/POSS,2p,3s*
kakehkimiwee *teach AI*
  kakehkimiwe *AI,ind,3s ; AI,ind,1s*
  kakehkimiweeci *AI,conj,3s*
  kakehkimiweeki *AI,ind,3p*
  kakehkimiweeyani *AI,conj,2s*
  keekehkimiweelici *AI/IC,conj,4*
  keekehkimiweeta *AI/IC,part,3s*
  kiikehkimiweewaaci *AI,conj,3p*
  kikakehkimiwe *AI,ind,2s*
  nikakehkimiwe *AI,ind,1s*
kakehkimiweewe *teaching NI*
  hokakehkimiweewe *NI/POSS,3s,s*
  hokakehkimiweewenilici *NI/POSS,4*
  hokakehkimiweewenwa *NI/POSS,3p*
  hopemikakehkimiweeweneki
NI/POSS/LOC,3s
  kakehkimiweewe *NI,s*
  nikakehkimiweewe *NI/POSS,1s,s*
kakehkimoofo *be taught AI*
  kakehkimoofowaaci *AI,conj,3p*
  keekehkimoofoyani *AI/IC,conj,2s*
kakehkimoowe *teaching, counsel NI*
  hokakehkimoowe *NI/POSS,3s,s*
kakehkinootenamaw *motion to, make signs*

TA
  kakehkinootenamawaali *TA,ind,3s,4s*
  kakehkinootenamawaawaali *TA,ind,3p,4s*
  kakehkinootenamawahi *TA,ind,3s,4p*
kakilweewefi *improve AI*
  kakilweewefi *AI,ind,3s*
kakissim *bruise TA*
  kakissimekooli *TA,ind,4s,3s*
kalaweewihsimo *speak loudly AI*
  kalaweewihsimo *AI,ind,3s*
kalaweewihsimoowe *voice NI*
  hokalaweewihsimoowe *NI/POSS,3s,s*
  kalaweewihsimoowe *NI,s*
kalawi *speak AI*
  kalawi *AI,ind,3s ; AI,ind,2s ; AI,ind,1s*
  kalawici *AI,conj,3s*
  kalawihi *AI,ind,4p*
  kalawiiki *AI,ind,3p*
  kalawiili *AI,ind,4s*
  kalawiki *AI,conj,3*
  kalawiko *AI,imp,2p*
  kalawilici *AI,conj,4*
  kalawilo *AI,imp,2s*
  kalawipwa *AI,ind,2p*
  kalawiwaaci *AI,conj,3p*
  kalawiya *AI,conj,1s*
  kalawiyeekwe *AI,conj,2p*
  keekalawici *AI/IC,conj,3s*
  keekalawicki *AI/IC,part,3p*
  keekalawiki *AI/IC,conj,3*
  keekalawita *AI/IC,part,3s*
  keekalawiwaaci *AI/IC,conj,3p*
  keekalawiya *AI/IC,conj,1s*
  kikalawipwa *AI,ind,2p*
  nikalawi *AI,ind,1s*
  nikalawipe *AI,ind,1x*
kalawihsimoowe *voice NI*
  hokalawihsimoowe *NI/POSS,3s,s*
  kalawihsimoowe *NI,s*
kalawiiwe *word, speech NI*
  hokalawiiwe *NI/POSS,3s,s*
  hokalawiiwena *NI/POSS,3s,p*
  hokalawiiweneki *NI/POSS/LOC,3s*
  hokalawiiwenilici *NI/POSS,4*
  hokalawiiwenwa *NI/POSS,3p*
  kalawiiwe *NI,s*
  kalawiiwena *NI,p*

kalawiiweneki *NI/LOC*
kikalawiiwe *NI/POSS,2s,s*
kikalawiiwena *NI/POSS,2s,p*
kikalawiiweneki *NI/POSS/LOC,2s*
kikalawiiwenwa *NI/POSS,2p*
nikalawiiwe *NI/POSS,1s,s*
nikalawiiwena *NI/POSS,1s,p*
nikalawiiweneki *NI/POSS/LOC,1s*
kalawiiwena *Word NA*
kalawiiwena *NA,3s*
kalawiiyaa *speak II*
kalawiiya *II,ind,0*
kalhkoofa *Golgotha NI*
kalhkoofa *NI,s*
kalhkoofe *NI,s*
kalhoot *crow TI-O*
kalhootake *TI,subj,3s,0*
kalhootaki *TI,conj,3s,0*
kalhootamwa *TI,ind,3s,0*
kalool *speak TA*
hokaloolaali *TA,ind,3s,4s*
hokaloolahi *TA,ind,3s,4p*
hokiikaloolekohi *TA,ind,4p,3s*
kaloola *TA,ind,1s,3s*
kaloolaaci *TA,conj,3s,4*
kaloolaaki *TA,ind,1s,3p*
kaloolaali *TA,ind,3s,4s*
kaloolahi *TA,ind,3s,4p*
kaloolehki *TA,conj,3,2s*
kaloolekoci *TA,conj,4,3s*
kaloolekohi *TA,ind,4p,3s*
kaloolekooli *TA,ind,4s,3s*
kaloolela *TA,conj,1s,2s*
kaloolelako *TA,conj,1s,2p*
kaloolelakwe *TA,conj,3,1i*
kaloolelepwa *TA,ind,1s,2p*
kaloolelwaakwe *TA,conj,3,2p*
keekaloolaaci *TA/IC,conj,3s,4*
keekaloolela *TA/IC,conj,1s,2s*
keekaloolelako *TA/IC,conj,1s,2p*
kiikaloolaaci *TA,conj,3s,4*
kiikaloolaawaaci *TA,conj,3p,4*
kikaloola *TA,ind,2s,3s*
kikaloolaaki *TA,ind,2s,3p*
kikaloosi *TA,ind,2s,1s*
kikaloosipe *TA,ind,2,1x*

nikaloolaaki *TA,ind,1s,3p*
kalooleti *speak AI*
kalooletiiki *AI,ind,3p*
kiikalooletiiki *AI,ind,3p*
kalooletiim *speak with TA*
hokalooletiimahi *TA,ind,3s,4p*
hokiikalootiimahi *TA,ind,3s,4p*
keekiikalooletiimehka *TA/IC,part,3,2s*
kalooloofo *be spoken to AI*
kalooloofoci *AI,conj,3s*
kaloosiwehoofo *be betrothed AI*
kaloosiwehoofooli *AI,ind,4s*
keekaloosiwehoofolici *AI/IC,conj,4*
kamhpeni *company, band NI*
kamhpeni *NI,s*
kamiki *house, clan NI*
kamiki *NI,s*
kamikifi *NI/DIM,s*
kaminiwaskwi *cumin NI*
kaminiwaskwi *NI,s*
kamooci *perhaps, suddenly, soon*
kikamooci
kanhha *is it the case, could it be*
kanhha
kapaa *cross AI*
kapaaci *AI,conj,3s*
kapaawaaci *AI,conj,3p*
kapehi *? otherwise ?*
kapehi
kapenali *governor NA*
kapenali *NA,3s*
kapenalihi *NA,4p*
kapenaliiki *NA,3p*
kapenaliili *NA,4s*
kapenali *government NI*
hokapenaliimwa *NI/POSS,3p*
kapenaliiwi *be governor AI*
kapenaliiwi *AI,ind,3s*
kaptiina *centurion, captain NA*
kaptiina *NA,3s*
kaptiinali *NA,4s*
kaptiinhhi *NA,4p*
kasen *bear TA*
kasenekoyani *TA,conj,0,2s*
kashkwe *sharp II*
kaskweeki *II,conj,0*

katawahkonoote *be overcome* II
  katawahkonoote *II,ind,0*
katawat *be possible* II
  katawatwi *II,ind,0*
  katawatwili *II,ind,4*
katawefi *be able* AI
  katawefi *AI,ind,3s*
  katawefiiki *AI,ind,3p*
katawesit *be able to flee* TI_1
  katawesitaanaawa *TI,ind,2p,0*
  katawesitameekwe *TI,conj,2p,0*
katawi *[can, be able]* MDL
  hokatawi *MDL*
  katawi *MDL*
  keekatawi *MDL/IC*
  kikatawi *MDL*
katawi *can, be able* AI
  katawi *AI,ind,2s*
katawi *be possible* II
  katawi-ike *II,subj,0*
katawihk *get, obtain* TI_1
  hokatawihkaana *TI,ind,3s,0p*
  katawihkaanaawa *TI,ind,3p,0*
  katawihkake *TI,subj,3s,0*
  katawihkaki *TI,conj,3s,0*
  katawihkamelici *TI,conj,4,0*
  katawihtamowaaci *TI,conj,3p,0*
  keekatawihkama *TI/IC,conj,1s,0*
  nikatawihkaana *TI,ind,1s,0p*
katawihkaw *obtain* TA
  katawihkawa *TA,ind,2s,3s*
katawihkoofo *be persuaded* AI
  katawihkoofooki *AI,ind,3p*
katawiilefi *can* AI
  katawiilefi *AI,ind,3s*
  katawiilefici *AI,conj,3s*
  katawiilefiwaaci *AI,conj,3p*
  katawiilefiyane *AI,subj,2s*
  katawiilefiyeekwe *AI,conj,2p*
katawiilefiiwe *ability* NI
  hokatawiilefiiwena *NI/POSS,3s,p*
katemo *grown, mature* AI
  katemo *AI,ind,3s*
katemooyaa *grown, mature* II
  katemooyaaki *II,conj,0*
katenoofo *be reared* AI

katenoofoci *AI,conj,3s*
kateski *just, only*
  kateski
katokwaamo *slumber, sleep* AI
  katokwaamooki *AI,ind,3p*
katokwaamoowe *sleep* NI
  katokwaamoowe *NI,s*
katoneewe *infirmity* NI
  hokatoneeweneki *NI/POSS/LOC,3s*
  katoneewe *NI,s*
  katoneewena *NI,p*
  kikatoneewe *NI/POSS,2s,s*
  kikatoneewenena *NI/POSS,1i*
katoneewi *infirmity* PM
  katoneewi *PM*
katowam *beseech* TA
  hokatowamaawaali *TA,ind,3p,4s*
katowe *beg* AI
  kaakatoweeta *AI/IC,part,3s*
  katowe *AI,ind,3s*
  katoweci *AI,conj,3s*
  katoweya *AI,conj,1s*
katoweewi *beg* AI
  katoweewilici *AI,conj,4*
kawaacfetoofo *be prepared* AI
  yeekawaacfetoofocki *AI/IC,part,3p*
kawaafi *attend to* AI
  yeekawaafiilici *AI/IC,conj,4*
kawaskwhaawe *reap* AI
  kawaskwhaawaaci *AI,conj,3p*
  kawaskwhaawe *AI,ind,2s ; AI,ind,3s*
  kawaskwhaaweke *AI,subj,3*
  kawaskwhaaweki *AI,conj,3*
  kawaskwhaaweya *AI,conj,1s*
  kawaskwhaaweyeekwe *AI,conj,2p*
  keekawaskwhaawecki *AI/IC,part,3p*
  keekawaskwhaaweta *AI/IC,part,3s*
  kikawaskwhaawe *AI,ind,2s*
  nikawaskwhaawe *AI,ind,1s*
kawaskwhaawe *harvest* NI
  kawaskwhaawe *NI,s*
kawaskwhaaweewe *harvest* NI
  hokawaskwhaaweneki *NI/POSS/LOC,3s*
  kawaskwhaaweewe *NI,s*
kawaskwi *wheat* NI
  hokawaskomi *NI/POSS,3s,s*

kawaskwi *NI,s*
nikawaskomi *NI/POSS,1s,s*
kawaskwika *barn NI*
hokawaskwikaaneki *NI/POSS/LOC,3s*
kawaskwika *NI,s*
kawaskwikaana *NI,p*
nikawaskwikaana *NI/POSS,1s,p*
nikawaskwikaaneki *NI/POSS/LOC,1s*
kawaskwikitika *cornfield NI*
kawaskwikitikaana *NI,p*
kawaskwiktikaana *NI,p*
kawh *cut down TI*
kawha *TI,ind,2s,0s*
kawhano *TI,imp,2s,0*
kawhoote *be cut down II*
kawhoote *II,ind,0*
kci *big, superlative PM*
hokci *PM*
kci *PM*
kehci *PM*
kici *PM*
kcihkaaawe *urge, be urgent AI*
kcihkaaweeki *AI,ind,3p*
kcihkaw *persuade, ask for TA*
hokcihkaakohi *TA,ind,4p,3s*
hokcihkawaawaali *TA,ind,3p,4s*
kcihkawaawaali *TA,ind,3p,4s*
kciipifo *be bound AI*
kciipifo *AI,ind,3s*
kciipifooli *AI,ind,4s*
kciipifoowe *band NI*
kciipifoowena *NI,p*
kciipil *bind TA*
hokciipilaali *TA,ind,3s,4s*
hokciipilaawaali *TA,ind,3p,4s*
hokciipilekohi *TA,ind,4p,3s*
hokiciipilaali *TA,ind,3s,4s*
hokiciipilaawaali *TA,ind,3p,4s*
kciipilaali *TA,ind,3s,4s*
kciipilaate *TA,subj,3s,4*
kciipilehko *TA,imp,2p,3*
kciipil *bind, tie TI_3*
hokaakciipilenaawa *TI,ind,3p,0*
kciipile *TI,ind,2s,0s*
kciipilenaawa *TI,ind,2p,0*
kciipite *be bound II*

kciipite *II,ind,0*
kciitawefi *keep, observe AI*
kciitawefilo *AI,imp,2s*
nikciitawefi *AI,ind,1s*
kciiton *keep, observe TI_1*
hokciitonaana *TI,ind,3s,0p*
hokciitonaanaawa *TI,ind,3p,0*
kciitona *TI,ind,3s,0s*
kciitonaanaawa *TI,ind,2p,0*
kciitonake *TI,subj,3s,0*
kciitonama *TI,conj,1s,0*
kciitonameekwe *TI,conj,2p,0 ; TI,subj,2p,0*
kciitonamowaate *TI,subj,3p,0*
nikciitona *TI,ind,1s,0s*
kciiton *keep, observe TA*
kciitonaci *TA,conj,2s,3*
kciitonekooki *TA,ind,3p,2s*
kciitoni *TA,imp,2s,3*
nikciitonaaki *TA,ind,1s,3p*
kciitonamaw *keep, observe TA*
kciitonamaakowaaki *TA,ind,3p,2p*
kciitone *keep, observe AI*
kciitoneeli *AI,ind,4s*
kcikaatiiwe *insistence NI*
yeekcikaatiiwenilici *NI/POSS,4*
kcikamiiwatowa *sponge NA*
kcikamiiwatowali *NA,4s*
kcikamiiwihatowali *NA,4s*
kicikamiwiyatowali *NA,4s*
kcikikileni *eldest person NA*
kcikikileni *NA,3s*
kcimaalespihi *lowest*
kcimaalespihi
kcimeciloofi *least AI*
kcimecilooficki *AI,part,3p*
kehcimecilooficki *AI/IC,part,3p*
kcimeckwaafin *least II*
kcimeckwaafiki *II,conj,0*
kcimhsiilakimoofo *be thought the greatest AI*
kcimhsiilakimoofo *AI,ind,3s*
kcipto *run AI*
kciptooki *AI,ind,3p*
kcitawaafi *take care, watch out for AI*
kcitawaafi *AI,ind,3s*
kcitawaafiiki *AI,conj,3*
kcitawaafiiko *AI,imp,2p*

kcitawaafiilo *AI,imp,2s*
    nikcitawaafi *AI,ind,3s*
kcitawaafiim *keep watch with TA*
    kcitawaafiimiko *TA,imp,2p,1s*
    kcitawaafiimipwa *TA,ind,2p,1s*
kcitawaafiiwe *heed NI*
    kcitawaafiiwe *NI,s*
kcitawaapam *watch TA*
    hokcitawaapamaawaali *TA,ind,3p,4s*
    hokcitawaapamekohi *TA,ind,4p,3s*
    kcitawaapamaacki *TA,part,3p,4*
    kcitawaapamaawaaci *TA,conj,3p,4*
kcitawaapat *keep watch on TI_1*
    kcitawaapatamoko *TI,imp,2p,0*
kcitawaapi *keep watch AI*
    kcitawaapi *AI,ind,3s ; AI,ind,2s*
    kcitawaapiko *AI,imp,2p*
    kcitawaapilici *AI,conj,4*
    kehcitawaapicki *AI/IC,part,3p*
kcitawah *guard, keep safe TA*
    hokcitawahaali *TA,ind,3s,4s*
    kcitawahaawaaci *TA,conj,3p,4*
    kcitawahehki *TA,conj,3,2s*
    kehcitawahaacki *TA/IC,part,3p,4*
    kehcitawahaata *TA/IC,part,3s,4*
    kehcitawahekoci *TA/IC,conj,4,3s*
    kehcitawahekowaaci *TA/IC,conj,4,3p*
    kicitawi *TA,ind,2s,1s*
    nikcitawahaaki *TA,ind,1s,3p*
kcitawahoofo *be kept under guard AI*
    kcitawahoofo *AI,ind,3s*
kcitawaht *guard, take heed, watch TI_2*
    hokcitawahto *TI,ind,3s,0s*
    kaakcitawahtoota *TI/IC,part,3s,0*
    kehcitawahtoocki *TI/IC,part,3p,0*
    kehcitawahtoolici *TI/IC,conj,4,0*
    kehcitawahtoota *TI/IC,part,3s,0*
kcitawahtoote *be guarded II*
    kcitawahtooteeki *II,conj,0*
kcitaweelem *keep in mind TA*
    kcitaweelemi *TA,imp,2s,3*
kcitaweelet *keep in mind TI_1*
    hokcitaweeleta *TI,ind,3s,0*
    hokicitaweeletaanaawa *TI,ind,3p,0*
    kcitaweeletamoko *TI,imp,2p,0*
kcitawfet *guard, keep safe TI_2*

kehcitawfetooya *TI/IC,conj,1s,0*
kciyeesi *? being observed ? PV*
    kciyeesi *PV*
keeananii *Cainan NA*
    keeananii *NA,3s*
keefsemeni *Gethsemane NI*
    keefsemeni *NI,s*
keekeepilenii *dumb person NA*
    keekeepileni *NA,3s*
    keekeepileniili *NA,4s*
keekeepitoneewi *dumb PM*
    keekeepitoneewi *PM*
keekeepse *deaf person NA*
    keekeepseeki *NA,3p*
keekeepse *deaf AI*
    keekeepehseelici *AI,conj,4*
    keekeepseelici *AI,conj,4*
keekeepseewi *deaf PM*
    keekeepseewi *PM*
keekiskaapkahki *steep place NI*
    keekiskaapkahki *NI,s*
keela *? that is to say ?*
    keela
keelelii *Galilee NI*
    hokeeleliimwa *NI/POSS,3p*
    keelelii *NI,s*
    keeleliiki *NI/LOC*
keeleliiwi *Galilee PM*
    keeleliiwi *PM*
keeleliiwilenawe *Galilean NA*
    keeleliiwilenawe *NA,3s*
    keeleliiwilenaweeki *NA,3p*
    keeleliiwilenaweli *NA,4s*
keeleliiwileni *Galilaean NA*
    keeleliiwileni *NA,3s*
keeleni *gallon NI*
    keelena *NI,p*
keelo *long (time), late*
    keelo
keemali *camel NA*
    keemali *NA,3s*
    keemaliili *NA,4s*
keemaliiwi *camel PM*
    keemaliiwi *PM*
keemowaaki *rain NI*
    keemowaaki *NI,s*

keena *Cana* NI
    keena *NI,s*
keenaniiwiikweewa *Canaanite woman* NA
    keenaniiwiikweewa *NA,3s*
keenaniiwileni *Cananaean* NA
    keenaniiwileni *NA,3s*
keepaaniamii *Capernaum* NI
    keepaaniam' *NI,s*
    keepaaniamii *NI,s*
    keepaaniamiiki *NI/LOC*
    kehpaaniamii *NI,s*
    kehpaaniamiiki *NI/LOC*
keepaifa *Gabbatha* NI
    keepaifa *NI,s*
keepiyeelii *Gabriel* NA
    keepyeelii *NA,3s*
keesite *heat, furnace* NI
    keesiteeki *NI/LOC*
keesoweelem *be valuable to* TA
    keesoweelemaaci *TA,conj,3s,4*
keesoweelemekofi *valuable* AI
    keesoweelemekofilici *AI,conj,4*
keeteliina *Gadarene* NA
    keeteliinaki *NA,3p*
keetemaasilepwaskaa *poor in spirit* AI
    keetemaasilepwaskaacki *AI,part,3p*
keewaki *more, still, yet*
    keewaki
keeyefesii *Caiaphas* NA
    keeyeefesii *NA,3s*
    keeyefesiili *NA,4s*
kehfwi *how many*
    kehfwi
kehkiyaama *parent* NA
    hokehkiyaamhhi *NA/POSS,3s,4p*
    hokehkiyaamwahi *NA/POSS,3p,4p*
    kehkiyaaki *NA,3p*
    kehkiyaamaki *NA,3p*
    kehkiyaamhi *NA,4p*
kehsilotaw *live with, lodge with* TA
    keekehsilotawaaci *TA/IC,conj,3s,4*
    kehsilotawaali *TA,ind,3s,4s*
kehta *old*
    kehta
kehtaacimoowe *tradition* NI
    hokehtaacimoowenwa *NI/POSS,3p*

kikehtaacimoowenwa *NI/POSS,2p*
kehteeyaa *old* II
    kehteeyaaki *II,conj,0*
kicima *fig* NI
    kicimi *NI,p*
kicimiisa *fig tree [personified]* NA
    kicimiisa *NA,3s*
kicimiisi *fig tree* NI
    kicimiisi *NI,s*
    kicimiisiki *NI/LOC*
kicimiiwimhtekwaapalwa *sycamore fig* NA
    kicimiiwimhtekwaapalwa *NA,3s*
kicitaam *stir up, exhort* TA
    hokicitaamaawahi *TA,ind,3p,4p*
kicitaamoowe *exhortation* NI
    kicitaamoowena *NI,p*
kicitask *execute, carry out* TI_1
    kicitaskamelici *TI,conj,4,0*
kicithw *strike; kill* TA
    kicithwa *TA,ind,1s,3s*
kifalhfiteen *wash the feet* TA
    kifalhfiteenaaci *TA,conj,3s,4*
    kifalhfiteenahi *TA,ind,3s,4p*
    kifalhfiteenelepwa *TA,ind,1s,2p*
kifalhfiteeneti *wash the feet [reciprocal]* AI
    kifalhfiteenetiko *AI,imp,2p*
kifiikwa *wash* AI
    kifiikwaalo *AI,imp,2s*
kifilecaa *wash one's hands* AI
    kaakifilecaaki *AI,ind,3p*
    kifileca *AI,ind,3s*
    kifilecaaki *AI,ind,3p*
    kifilecaate *AI,subj,3s*
    kifilecaawaate *AI,subj,3p*
kifin *wash* TI_1
    kifinaana *TI,ind,2s,0p*
    kifinaki *TI,conj,3s,0*
    kifinamowaaci *TI,conj,3p,0*
kifin *wash* TA
    kifinela *TA,subj,1s,2s*
kifinikeewe *washing* NI
    kifinikeewena *NI,p*
kifino *wash* AI
    kifino *AI,ind,3s*
    kifinolo *AI,imp,2s*
    nikifino *AI,ind,1s*

kifoofo *be hidden from* AI
    kikifooya *AI/IC,conj,1s*
kifoskaatiiyaa *be preserved II*
    kifoskaatiiya *II,ind,0*
kihaacimo *deny AI*
    kihaacimo *AI,ind,3s*
kihfehwaacihk *endure, stand for TA*
    kihfehwaacihkoolepwa *TA,ind,1s,2p*
kihkiicsin *lame AI*
    kihkiicsinane *AI,subj,2s*
kihkitonen *choke TA*
    hokihkitonenaali *TA,ind,3s,4s*
kihkitoneskaw *choke TA*
    hokihkitoneskaakonaawa *TA,ind,0,3p*
kiikee *recover, get better AI*
    kiikeelo *AI,imp,2s*
kiikeen *be a shepherd to TA*
    kiikeenaata *TA,part,3s,4*
kiikeenikaafa *captive, bondservant, prisoner NA*
    kiikeenikaafa *NA,3s*
    kiikeenikaafaki *NA,3p*
    kiikeenikaafali *NA,4s*
kiikeenikana *captive, bond servant NA*
    hokiikeenikanali *NA/POSS,3s,4s*
kiikeenikani *in capture PV*
    kiikeenikani *PV*
kiikeenikanin *capture, hold in bond TA*
    kiikeenikaninekona *TA,ind,3s,1x*
kiikeh *heal TA*
    hokiikehaali *TA,ind,3s,4s*
    hokiikehaawahi *TA,ind,3p,4p*
    hokiikehahi *TA,ind,3s,4p*
    kiikeha *TA,ind,1s,3s*
    kiikehaaki *TA,ind,1s,3p*
    kiikehaali *TA,ind,3s,4s*
    kiikehaawaaci *TA,conj,3p,4*
    kiikehaawaali *TA,ind,3p,4s*
    kiikehahi *TA,ind,3s,4p*
    kiikehehko *TA,imp,2p,3*
    kiikehekooli *TA,ind,4s,3s*
kiikehetiiwe *healing, cure NI*
    kiikehetiiwe *NI,s*
    kiikehetiiwena *NI,p*
kiikehiwee *heal AI*
    kiikehiwe *AI,ind,3s*
    kiikehiweeci *AI,conj,3s*

kiikehiweeki *AI,conj,3*
kiikehiweeki *AI,ind,3p ; AI,conj,3*
kiikehiweeli *AI,ind,4s*
kiikehiweewaaci *AI,conj,3p*
kiikehoofo *be healed AI*
    keekiikehoofolici *AI/IC,conj,4*
    keekiikehoofota *AI/IC,part,3s*
    kiikehoofo *AI,ind,3s*
    kiikehoofoci *AI,conj,3s*
    kiikehoofocki *AI,part,3p*
    kiikehoofoko *AI,imp,2p*
    kiikehoofooki *AI,ind,3p*
    kiikehoofooli *AI,ind,4s*
    kiikehoofowaaci *AI,conj,3p*
kiikeht *heal TI_2*
    kiikehtoolici *TI,conj,4,0*
    kiikehtoolo *TI,imp,2s,0*
kiikehtaw *heal TA*
    hokiikehtawahi *TA,ind,3s,4p*
    kiikehtaakoci *TA,conj,4,3s*
kiimaapacika *spy NA*
    kiimaapacikanhhi *NA,3p*
kiimefi *secret AI*
    kiimefi *AI,ind,3s*
kiimi *privately, secretly PV*
    hokiimi *PV*
    kaakiimi *PV*
    kiimi *PV*
    nikiimi *PV*
kiiminhhefiiwe *subtilty NI*
    kiiminhhefiiwe *NI,s*
kiimiwel *take away in secret TA*
    hokiimiwelaawaali *TA,ind,3p,4s*
    kiimiwelaawaaci *TA,conj,3p,4*
kiipekwaam *fall asleep AI*
    kiipekwaameke *AI,subj,3*
    kiipekwaamwa *AI,ind,3s*
kiisafwi *month NI*
    kiisahfo *NI,p*
kiiseka *day NI*
    hokaasekikiimeki *NI/POSS/LOC,3s*
    hokakiisekanema *NI/POSS,3s,p*
    hokakiisekanemwa *NI/POSS,3p*
    hokiisekanema *NI/POSS,3s,p*
    kakiisekanemi *NI/POSS,3s,s*
    kikiisekanoomena *NI/POSS,1i*

nikaasekiki *NI/POSS/IC,1s,s*
kiiseki *be day II*
    kaasekiki *II/IC,conj,0*
    kiisekike *II,subj,0*
    kiisekiki *II,conj,0*
kiiseki *sun NI*
    kiiseki *NI,s*
kiisekikiisfwa *sun NA*
    hokiisekikiisfoomali *NA/POSS,3s,4s*
    kiisekikiisfoki *NA/LOC,3*
    kiisekikiisfwa *NA,3s*
    kiisekikiisfwi *NA,3s*
kiisenaaci *with difficulty PV*
    kiisenaaci *PV*
kiisenaacileniwi *be a strict person AI*
    kiisenaacileniwiyani *AI,conj,2s*
kiisenaacin *be in difficulty TI-O*
    nikiisenaacina *TI,ind,1s,0s*
kiisenaacinamoowe *tribulation NI*
    kiisenaacinamoowe *NI,s*
    kiisenaacinamooweneki *NI/LOC*
kiisenaatet *difficult II*
    kiisenaatetwi *II,ind,0s*
kiisenaatoweewe *difficult saying NI*
    kiisenaatoweewe *NI,s*
kiisfwa *luminary, month NA*
    kiisfoki *NA/LOC,3*
    kiisfwa *NA,3s*
kiishoowe *image NI*
    hokiishoowe *NI/POSS,3s,s*
kiiskwe *day NI*
    kiiskwe *NI,s*
kiiskwe *? awake ? AI*
    kiiskweeli *AI,ind,4s*
kiisoowahkwatwa *sycamore tree NA*
    kiisoowahkwatooli *NA,4s*
kiiwee *go back AI*
    kiiwehi *AI,ind,4p*
kikaamaanefiiwe *rest, peace NI*
    kikaamaanefiiwe *NI/POSS,2s,s*
kikahkwimi *kernel and cob of corn NI*
    kikahkwimi *NI,p*
kikatkwi *be conceived AI*
    kikatkwiici *AI,conj,3s*
kikatkwihtoote *be conceived II*
    keekikatkwihtooteeki *II/IC,conj,0*

kikeemohkaa *profess, prescribe II*
    kikeemohkaaki *II,conj,0*
kikeemoowe *doctrine NI*
    hokikeemoowenwa *NI/POSS,3p*
kikileni *elder, old person NA*
    hokikileniimwahi *NA/POSS,3p,4p*
    kikilenihi *NA,4p*
    kikileniiki *NA,3p*
kikin *follow, imitate, observe TI_1*
    kikinamoko *TI,imp,2p,0*
    kikinamowaaci *TI,conj,3p,0*
kikinoocipiitenika *phylactery NI*
    hokikinoocipiitenikanwa *NI/POSS,3p*
kikinooloowe *sign, miracle NI*
    hokikinooloowe *NI/POSS,3s,s*
    hokikinooloowena *NI/POSS,3s,p*
    kikinooloowe *NI,s*
    kikinooloowena *NI,p*
kikinooloowefihtaw *be a sign (for someone) TA*
    kikinooloowefihtawaaci *TA,conj,3s,4*
kikinoolooweni *have as a sign AI*
    kikinoolooweniko *AI,imp,2p*
kikinoolooweniwi *be a sign, be a miracle II*
    kikinoolooweniwi *II,ind,0s*
kikinootaacimo *signify AI*
    kikinootaacimo *AI,ind,3s*
kikinootakite *significant II*
    kikinootakite *II,ind,0*
kikinooteelemekofi *notable AI*
    kikinooteelemekofiili *AI,ind,4s*
kikinootowe *signify AI*
    kikinootowe *AI,ind,3s*
kikitoote *be hidden II*
    kikitoote *II,ind,0*
kilakakaw *console TA*
    kilakakawaawaaci *TA,conj,3p,4*
kilakifi *merry AI*
    kilakifiiki *AI,ind,3p*
    kilakifilo *AI,imp,2s*
kilakifiiwe *merriness NI*
    kilakifiiwe *NI,s*
kilakikaw *comfort TA*
    kilakikawaacki *TA,part,3p,4*
kilakiteheewefi *rejoice AI*
    kilakiteheewefiko *AI,imp,2p*
kilekfen *mix with II*

kilekfenwi *II,ind,0s*
kilekfet *mix with TI_2*
    hokilekfeto *TI,ind,3s,0s*
kilekfetoote *be mixed with II*
    kilekfetoote *II,ind,0*
kileki *also; with, accompanied by*
    kileki
kileki *with, accompanied by PV*
    hokileki *PV*
kilekim *speak against TA*
    kilekimaaci *TA,conj,3s,4*
kilekin *have with TI_1*
    hokilekina *TI,ind,3s,0s*
kilekin *have with, have in company TA*
    kilekinaawahi *TA,ind,3p,4p*
kilhamaat *rebuke TI_1*
    hokilhamaata *TI,ind,3s,0s*
kilhamaw *rebuke TA*
    hokilhamawaawahi *TA,ind,3p,4p*
    kilhamawaali *TA,ind,3s,4s*
kimoot *steal AI*
    kaakimooteka *AI/IC,part,3s*
    kaakimootekiki *AI/IC,part,3p*
    kimoote *AI,ind,2s*
    kimooteki *AI,conj,3*
    kimootelo *AI,imp,2s*
    kimootowaaci *AI,conj,3p*
kimootoowe *theft NI*
    kimootoowena *NI,p*
kimowaan *rain II*
    kimowaanwi *II,ind,0s*
kin *long II*
    keenwaaki *II/IC,conj,0*
    kinwi *II,ind,0s*
kinesoletiiwi *Gennesaret NI*
    kinesoletiiwi *NI,s*
kiopit *cubit NI*
    kiopit *NI,s*
kipakokwat *thick II*
    kipakokwatwi *II,ind,0s*
kiph *shut TI_1*
    kiphake *TI,subj,3s,0*
    kiphamane *TI,subj,2s,0*
kiphamaw *shut TA*
    kikiphamawaawaaki *TA,ind,2p,3p*
kipho *be imprisoned AI*

kikipho *AI,ind,2s*
nikipho *AI,ind,1s*
kiphoote *be shut II*
    kiphoote *II,ind,0*
kiphotiiwe *prison NI*
    kiphotiiweneki *NI/LOC*
kiphotiiwikaana *prison NI*
    kiphotiiwikaana *NI,p*
    kiphotiiwikaaneki *NI/LOC*
kiphw *lock up TA*
    kiphwaaci *TA,conj,3s,4*
kipiikweewh *cover the face TA*
    hokipiikweewhaawaali *TA,ind,3p,4s*
kipiikwepil *cover the face, blindfold TA*
    hokipiikwepilaawaali *TA,ind,3p,4s*
kipiton *dumb AI*
    keekeepitonelici *AI/IC,conj,4*
    kipitonwa *AI,ind,3s*
kipitoneewilenii *dumb person NA*
    kipitoneewileni *NA,3s*
kipokwaat *sew TI_1*
    kipokwaata *TI,ind,3s,0s*
kipooliikwen *close TI_1*
    hokipooliikwena *TI,ind,3s,0s*
kiposkaamo *encircle AI*
    kiposkamowaate *AI,subj,3p*
kiposkaw *encircle, throng TA*
    hokiposkaakohi *TA,ind,4p,3s*
    kiposkaakohi *TA,ind,4p,3s*
    kiposkaakooki *TA,ind,3p,2s*
kipwiliikwen *make blind TA*
    kipwiliikwenahi *TA,ind,3s,4p*
kisaach *bless TA*
    hokisaachaali *TA,ind,3s,4s*
    hokisaachahi *TA,ind,3s,4p*
    kikisaachekoopwa *TA,ind,3,2p*
kisaachiwee *serve AI*
    kisaachiweeya *AI,conj,1s*
kisaaci *freely PV*
    kisaaci *PV*
kisaacih *minister to TA*
    kisaacihaawahi *TA,ind,3p,4p*
kisaaciilefiiwe *grace, blessing NI*
    kisaaciilefiiwe *NI,s*
kisaacike *bless AI*
    kisaacike *AI,ind,3s*

kisaacikeewe *alms NI*
    kikisaacikeewe *NI/POSS,2s,s*
    kisaacikeewe *NI,s*
kisaacilawi *bless AI*
    kisaacilawi *AI,ind,3s*
    kisaacilawiici *AI,conj,3s*
kisaacilot *bless TI_1*
    hokisaacilotaana *TI,ind,3s,0p*
kisaacilotaw *bless TA*
    hokisaacilotawaawaali *TA,ind,3p,4s*
    hokisaacilotawahi *TA,ind,3s,4p*
    kisaacilotawaaci *TA,conj,3s,4*
    kisaacilotawahi *TA,ind,3s,4p*
kisaacimekofi *be blessed AI*
    kikisaacimekofi *AI,ind,2s*
    kisaacimekofi *AI,ind,3s*
kisaacimekofih *bless TA*
    kisaacimekofihaali *TA,ind,3s,4s*
kisaacimekwat *be blessed II*
    kisaacimekwatwi *II,ind,0s*
kisaacimiweewe *promise NI*
    hokisaacimiweewe *NI/POSS,3s,s*
kisaacipenal *minister to TA*
    kikisaacipenalelepe *TA,ind,1x,2*
kisaacit *bless TI_2*
    hokisaacto *TI,ind,3s,0s*
    kisaacitooci *TI,conj,3s,0*
kisaaciweefiiwe *grace, blessing NI*
    hokisaaciweefiiwe *NI/POSS,3s,s*
kisaaciwefina *blessed one NA*
    kisaaciwefina *NA,3s*
kisaaciwi *blessed PM*
    kisaaciwi *PM*
kisaaciwi *be blessed AI*
    kisaaciwiiki *AI,ind,3p*
kisaaciwiiwe *grace, blessing NI*
    kisaaciwiiwe *NI,s*
kisaateelem *bless TA*
    keekisaateelemaaci *TA/IC,conj,3s,4*
    kisaateelemehko *TA,imp,2p,3*
kisaateelemekofi *be blessed AI*
    kikisaateelemekofipwa *AI,ind,2p*
    kisaateelemekofi *AI,ind,3s ; AI,ind,2s*
    kisaateelemekofiiki *AI,ind,3p*
kisaateelemekowh *bless TA*
    hokisaateelemekowhahi *TA,ind,3s,4p*

kisaateelemekwat *be blessed II*
    kisaateelemekwato *II,ind,0p*
kisaatefi *bless AI*
    kikisaatefi *AI,ind,2s*
    kisaatefi *AI,ind,3s*
kisaatetiwi *blessed II*
    kisaatetiwi *II,ind,0s*
kisf *offend, provoke TA*
    hokisfekowaali *TA,ind,4s,3p*
    kisfaaki *TA,ind,2s,3p*
    kisfekohi *TA,ind,4p,3s*
    kisfekoopi *TA,ind,3,1s*
    kisfekoopwa *TA,ind,3,2p*
    kisfekwiiki *TA,ind,,3p*
    kisfelepwa *TA,ind,1s,2p*
kisfekwiiwe *anger NI*
    kisfekwiiwe *NI,s*
kisfetiiwe *indignation NI*
    kisfetiiwe *NI,s*
kisfi *with anger PV*
    kisfi *PV*
kisfiweefi *offend AI*
    keesfiweeficki *AI/IC,part,3p*
kisfoofo *be made angry AI*
    kisfoofowaaci *AI,conj,3p*
kisfoowe *fever NI*
    kisfoowe *NI,s*
kishoofo *be bruised AI*
    keekishoofocki *AI/IC,part,3p*
kisifikan *oven NI*
    kisifikaneki *NI/LOC*
kisifoowe *fever NI*
    kisifoowe *NI,s*
kisin *hurt TA*
    kisinaali *TA,ind,3s,4s*
kisiteenaweewe *zeal NI*
    kisiteenaweewe *NI,s*
kisiteewi *be hot II*
    kisiteewi *II,ind,0s*
kiskahkiki *edge NI*
    kiskahkiki *NI,s*
kiskathika *sickle NI*
    kiskathika *NI,s*
kiskehsethw *cut off TA*
    hokiskehsethwaali *TA,ind,3s,4s*
    keekiskehsethwaaci *TA/IC,conj,3s,4*

kiskhika *sword* NI
    hokiskhika *NI/POSS,3s,s*
    kikiskhika *NI/POSS,2s,s*
    kiskhika *NI,s*
    kiskhikana *NI,p*
kiskhikani *have a sword* AI
    hokiskhikaniiki *AI,ind,3p*
    kikiskhikanipwa *AI,ind,2p*
    kiskhikanihi *AI,ind,4p*
    kiskhikanipwa *AI,ind,2p*
kiskhw *cut up, cut apart* TA
    kiskhokooli *TA,ind,4s,3s*
kiskikwen *pluck* TI_1
    kiskikwenaanaawa *TI,ind,3p,0*
    kiskikwenamehi *TI,ind,4p,0*
kiskikwethw *behead* TA
    hokiskikwethwaali *TA,ind,3s,4s*
    keekiskikwethwaka *TA/IC,part,1s,3s*
    nikiskikwethwa *TA,ind,1s,3s*
kiskinikanitalwaati *cast lots* AI
    kiskinikanitalwaatihi *AI,ind,4p*
    kiskinikanitalwaatiiki *AI,ind,3p*
    kiskinikanitalwaatitaako *AI,imp,1i*
kiskipiyeeth *cut from* TI_1
    hokiskipiyeethaanaawa *TI,ind,3p,0*
kiskot *cut* TI_1
    kakiskotaa *TI,ind,3s,0s*
    kiskotamowaaci *TI,conj,3p,0*
kisoweelemekwat *precious, costly* II
    kisoweelemekwatwi *II,ind,0s*
kisoweelemekwi *precious, costly* PV
    kisoweelemekwi *PV*
kisowi *worth much* PV
    kisowi *PV*
kisowileni *worthy person* NA
    kisowileni *NA,3s*
kitapifo *be girded* AI
    kehtapifoci *AI,conj,3s*
    kitapifo *AI,ind,3s*
    kitapifolo *AI,imp,2s*
kitapifoowe *belt* NI
    kitapifoowe *NI,s*
kitapifooyaa *be girded* II
    kitapifooyaake *II,subj,0*
kitapit *gird* TI_2
    hokitapito *TI,ind,3s,0s*

kikaakitapito *TI,ind,2s,0s*
    kitapito *TI,ind,3s,0s*
kitawilahi *often*
    kitawilahi
    ktawilahi
kite *and, in addition, plus*
    kite
kiteeni *any more*
    kiteeni
kiteewafehkaa *rage* II
    kiteewafehkaaki *II,conj,0*
kiteewe *anger, wrath* NI
    hokiteewe *NI/POSS,3s,s*
kitel *keep busy* TA
    kitelaakwi *TA,ind,,3s*
kitema *poor; [in prayer] have pity on*
    kitema
kitemaafa *poor person* NA
    kitemaafa *NA,3s*
    kitemaafaki *NA,3p*
    kitemaafali *NA,4s*
kiteminaakweelem *pity* TA
    hokiteminaakweelemahi *TA,ind,3s,4p*
    kiteminaakweelemaaci *TA,conj,3s,4*
    kiteminaakweelemekoci *TA,conj,4,3s*
    nikiteminaakweelemaaki *TA,ind,1s,3p*
kiteminaakweelemefi *merciful* AI
    keeteminaakweelemeficki *AI/IC,part,3p*
kiteminaakweelemefiiwe *mercy* NI
    kiteminaakweelemefiiwe *NI,s*
kiteminaakweeletiiwe *sympathy* NI
    hokiteminaakweeletiiwe *NI/POSS,3s,s*
    kiteminaakweeletiiwe *NI,s*
kiteminaakwi *altruistic, in compassion* PV
    kiteminaakwi *PV*
kiteminaakwiteheewe *compassion* NI
    kiteminaakwiteheewe *NI,s*
kiteniiswi *plus two*
    kiteniiswi
kitlani *Kidron* NI
    kitlani *NI,s*
kiyaacfe *secret* II
    kiyaacfeki *II,conj,0*
kiyaaci *secretly* PV
    keekiyaaci *PV/IC*
kiyaaciilefiiwe *secret, mystery* NI

kiyaaciilefiiwena *NI,p*
kiyaacim *deny* *TA*
    keekiyaacimita *TA/IC,part,3s,1s*
    kiyaacima *TA,ind,1s,3s*
    kiyaacimekwa *TA,ind,3s,1s*
    kiyaacimele *TA,ind,1s,2s*
    kiyaacimi *TA,ind,2s,1s*
kiyaacimo *deny* *AI*
    kiyaacimo *AI,ind,3s ; AI,ind,2s*
    kiyaacimolici *AI,conj,4*
kiyaacimoofo *be denied* *AI*
    kiyaacimoofo *AI,ind,3s*
kiyaacitoote *be made a secret* *II*
    kiyaacitoote *II,ind,0*
kiyaaciwi *secret* *II*
    kiyaaciwi *II,ind,0s*
kiyaacsi *secret* *AI*
    keekiyaacsika *AI/IC,part,3s*
kiyaalesiina *Gerasene* *NA*
    kiyaalesiinaki *NA,3p*
kiyaateelet *deny, conceal* *TI_1*
    kiyaateeleta *TI,ind,3s,0s*
    kiyaateeletake *TI,subj,3s,0*
kkahki *be the year* *II*
    kkahki *II,conj,0*
kkatoowi *have/be so many years* *AI*
    kkatoowi *AI,ind,3s ; AI,ind,2s*
    kkatoowici *AI,conj,3s*
    kkatoowiili *AI,ind,4s*
    kkatoowilici *AI,conj,4*
kkatoowiiyaa *be so many years* *II*
    kkatoowiiya *II,ind,0*
kkatwi *year* *NI*
    hokkatoomi *NI/POSS,3s,s*
    kkato *NI,p*
    kkatwi *NI,s*
kkehsi *dwell, lodge, camp* *AI*
    kkehsi *AI,ind,3s*
    kkehsiki *AI,conj,3*
    kkehsiwaaci *AI,conj,3p*
kkehsiim *stay with* *TA*
    kkehsiimaaci *TA,conj,3s,4*
    kkehsiiminaake *TA,imp,2,1x*
kkehsilotoote *be inhabited* *II*
    keekkehsilotooteeki *II/IC,conj,0*
kkehsiwiika *inn* *NI*

kkehsiiwikaaneki *NI/LOC*
kkifo *be hidden* *AI*
    kkifo *AI,ind,3s*
    kkifoci *AI,conj,3s*
kkileceepifoowe *ring* *NI*
    kkileceepifoowe *NI,s*
kkit *hide* *TI_2*
    hokkito *TI,ind,3s,0s*
    kkito *TI,ind,3s,0s*
    nikkito *TI,ind,1s,0s*
kkitaw *hide* *TA*
    kkitaakwiiki *TA,ind,,3p*
    kkitawaci *TA,conj,2s,3*
kkwicfe *ascend* *AI*
    nitekkwicfe *AI,ind,1s*
kkwiciwel *lead up* *TA*
    hokkwiciwelaali *TA,ind,3s,4s*
    hokkwiciwelahi *TA,ind,3s,4p*
    hotekkwiciwelahi *TA,ind,3s,4p*
    kkwiciwelaawaali *TA,ind,3p,4s*
kkwicsin *go up* *AI*
    kkwicsine *AI,ind,1s*
    kkwicsineko *AI,imp,2p*
    kkwicsinelici *AI,conj,4*
    kkwicsinepe *AI,ind,1i*
    kkwicsinohi *AI,ind,4p*
    kkwicsinooki *AI,ind,3p*
    kkwicsinowaaci *AI,conj,3p*
    kkwicsinwa *AI,ind,3s*
klaisti *be the Christ* *AI*
    klaistiiwici *AI,conj,3s*
    klaistiiwilici *AI,conj,4*
klaistii *Christ* *NA*
    hoklaistiimali *NA/POSS,3s,4s*
    klaistii *NA,3s*
    klaistiiki *NA,3p*
    klaistiili *NA,4s*
kliiapasi *Cleopas* *NA*
    kliiapasi *NA,3s*
kloopasi *Clopas* *NA*
    kloopasi *NA,3s*
koch *tempt* *TA*
    hokochaawaali *TA,ind,3p,4s*
    kocihekohi *TA,ind,4p,3s*
koci *try* *PM*
    koci *PM*

kocihkaw *tempt TA*
   hokocihkaakohi *TA,ind,4p,3s*
   kocihkawaaci *TA,conj,3s,4*
kocikeemaw *pray TA*
   nikocikeemawaaki *TA,ind,1s,3p*
kocikeemo *pray AI*
   nikocikeemo *AI,ind,1s*
kocilehfi *tempter NA*
   kocilehfi *NA,3s*
kocim *ask, pray TA*
   hokocimaali *TA,ind,3s,4s*
   hokocimaawaali *TA,ind,3p,4s*
   hokocimekohi *TA,ind,4p,3s*
   hokocimekooli *TA,ind,4s,3s*
   kocima *TA,ind,1s,3s*
   kocimaali *TA,ind,3s,4s*
kocimaw *pray TA*
   nikocimawa *TA,ind,1s,3s*
   nikocimawaaki *TA,ind,1s,3p*
kocitamaw *pray TA*
   kocitamoolepwa *TA,ind,1s,2p*
kofaapiyeeyaa *sink II*
   kofaapiyeeyaake *II,subj,0*
kofekofi *heavy AI*
   kofekofiiki *AI,ind,3p*
kofekolaakwi *be burdened AI*
   kweekofekolaakwicki *AI/IC,part,3p*
kofekwaa *austere AI*
   kofekwaaci *AI,conj,3s*
kofekwaaci *austere PV*
   kikofekwaaci *PV*
kofekwan *heavy II*
   kofekwanili *II,ind,4*
   kofekwanwi *II,ind,0s*
   kwefekwaki *II/IC,conj,0*
kofekwi *heavy PM*
   kofekwi *PM*
kokaati *hook NI*
   kokaati *NI,s*
kokihtaw *turn to TA*
   kokihtawehke *TA,subj,3s,2s*
kokiikwehtaw *turn to TA*
   kokiikwehtawi *TA,imp,2s,3*
kokiiwa *turn AI*
   kokiiki *AI,ind,3p*
   kokiiwa *AI,ind,3s*

kokiiyane *AI,subj,2s*
kokoskwaafi *tender II*
   kokoskwaafi *II,ind,0s*
   kokoskwaafiki *II,conj,0*
kokwitapil *pull out, pull up TA*
   hokokwitapilaali *TA,ind,3s,4s*
   kokwitapilaali *TA,ind,3s,4s*
kokwiten *lift up, raise TI_1*
   hokokwitena *TI,ind,3s,0s*
   hotekokwitena *TI,ind,3s,0s*
   kikokwitena *TI,ind,2s,0s*
   kokwitena *TI,ind,3s,0s*
   nikokwitena *TI,ind,1s,0s*
kokwiten *lift up, raise TA*
   kokwiteneekwe *TA,part,2p,3*
   kokwitenike *TA,subj,,1s*
kokwitenamaw *lift up, raise TA*
   kokwitenamaakona *TA,ind,3s,1i*
kokwitenoofo *be lifted up AI*
   kokwitenoofo *AI,ind,3s*
kola *soon*
   kola
   kolaa
kolahwaapan *be dawn, be morning II*
   kolahwaapake *II,subj,0*
   kolahwaapaki *II,conj,0*
   kolahwaapanwi *II,ind,0s*
   kwelahwaapaki *II/IC,conj,0*
   yeekolahwaapaki *II/IC,conj,0*
kolepen *roll TA*
   kolepenaali *TA,ind,3s,4s*
   kolepenamaakona *TA,ind,3s,1i*
kolepen *overturn TI_1*
   hokolepenaana *TI,ind,3s,0p*
kolepenoofo *be rolled back AI*
   kolepenoofolici *AI,conj,4*
   kolepenoofooli *AI,ind,4s*
kolepi *turn AI*
   kolepi *AI,ind,3s*
kolepi-pakitamaw *overturn TA*
   hokolepi-pakitamawahi *TA,ind,3s,4p*
kolepk *prevail over TI_1*
   kolepkameekwe *TI,conj,2p,0*
kolepkaam *persuade, prevail TA*
   hokolepkaamaawahi *TA,ind,3p,4p*
   kolepkaamaape *TA,ind,1x,3*

kolepkaamoofo *be persuaded* AI
kolepkaamoofooki *AI,ind,3p*
kolepkaaweewe *victory* NI
kolepkaaweeweneki *NI/LOC*
kolepkaaweyaa *prevail* II
kolepkaaweya *II,ind,0*
kolesinii *Chorazin* NI
kolesin *NI,s*
kolesinii *NI,s*
komaalawi *Gomorrah* PM
komaalawi *PM*
komai *cumi [Aramaic]*
komai
koociwe *why*
koociwe
kookhan *sink* II
kookhano *II,ind,0p*
kooki *sink* AI
kooki *AI,ind,3s*
kookin *dip* TA
kookinaaci *TA,conj,3s,4*
kookin *dip* TI_1
kookinaki *TI,conj,3s,0*
kookinamaw *dip (on behalf of someone)* TA
kookinamawaka *TA,part,1s,3s*
kookinoofo *be dipped, be sunk* AI
kookinoofo *AI,ind,3s*
kookwe *[indefinite]*
kookwe
kookwe-kaaci-laakwa *whenever*
kookwe-kaaci-laakwa
kookwe-kaaci-tasi *wherever* PR
kookwe-kaaci-tasi *PR*
kookwe-laakwa-kaaci *wherever, whenever*
kookwe-laakwa-kaaci
kookwe-neefa-kaaci *whoever* PR
kookwe-neefa-kaaci *NA,3s*
kookwe-neefaki-kaaci *NA,3p*
kookwe-neefali-kaaci *NA,4s*
kookwe-nehi-kaaci *whatever* PR
kookwe-nehi-kaaci *PR*
kookwe-nehi-si *whatever [premodifier]* PR
kookwe-neh-si *PR*
kookwe-nehi-si *PR*
kookwe-tasi-kaaci *wherever* PR
kookwe-tasi-kaaci *PR*

kookweneefa *whoever, stranger* NA
kookweneefa *NA,3s*
kookweneefali *NA,4s*
kookweneefhi *NA,4p*
kookweneefiwi *be a stranger* AI
kikookweneefiwi *AI,ind,2s*
nikookweneefiwi *AI,ind,1s*
kookweenehi *whatever; it is unknown*
kookweenehi
kookwekaaci *ever [indefinite]*
kookwekaaci
kookwelaakwa *indef. time, forever*
kookwelaakwa
kookwelaakwasi *forever*
kookwelaakwasi
kookwenehsi *whichever*
kookwenehsi
kooli *gold* NI
kooli *NI,s*
kooloci *in addition to*
kooloci
koolot *add to* TI_2
hokooloto *TI,ind,3s,0s*
kooloto *TI,ind,3s,0s*
koolotaw *add to* TA
koolotaakoopwa *TA,ind,3,2p*
koolotoote *be added* II
koolotoote *II,ind,0*
koona *snow* NA
koona *NA,3s*
koosaami *Cosam* NA
koosaami *NA,3s*
kootii *coat, cloak* NI
hokootiimi *NI/POSS,3s,s*
kikootiimi *NI/POSS,2s,s*
kooti *NI,s*
kootiiwali *NI,p*
kosaasi *Chuza* NA
kosaasi *NA,3s*
kosko *pig, swine* NA
kosko *NA,3s*
koskohi *NA,4p*
koskooki *NA,3p*
kotaacimetiiwe *decree* NI
kotaacimetiiwe *NI,s*
kotaacimiweewe *ordinance* NI

hokotaacimiweewena *NI/POSS,3s,p*
kotahkowaafoowe *temptation NI*
   hokotahkowaafoowe *NI/POSS,3s,s*
kotahkowaal *tempt TA*
   hokotahkowaalekooli *TA,ind,4s,3s*
   kikotahkowaasipwa *TA,ind,2p,1*
   kotahkowaalaali *TA,ind,3s,4s*
   kotahkowaalaawaali *TA,ind,3p,4s*
   kotahkowaalekohi *TA,ind,4p,3s*
kotaka *other, another [anim] PR*
   kotaka *PR*
   kotakaki *PR*
   kotakali *PR*
   kotakhi *PR*
kotaki *other, another*
   kotaki
kotakisi-kookwe-neefa *stranger NA*
   kotakisi-kookwe-neefali *NA,4s*
   kotakisi-kookwe-neefhi *NA,4p*
kotakoocitaw *? weigh ? TA*
   hokotakoocitawaawaali *TA,ind,3p,4s*
kotat *taste TI_1*
   hokotata *TI,ind,3s,0s*
   kotata *TI,ind,3s,0s*
   kotataanaawa *TI,ind,3p,0*
   kotataki *TI,conj,3s,0*
kotaten *handle TA*
   kotateniko *TA,imp,2p,1s*
kotekon *turn TA*
   hokotekoneko *TA,ind,0s,3s*
   kotekonahi *TA,ind,3s,4p*
kotekon *turn TI_1*
   kotekonamawaaci *TI,conj,3p,0*
kotekonoote *be turned II*
   kotekonoote *II,ind,0*
kotekwi *turn, return AI*
   kotekwi *AI,ind,3s ; AI,ind,1s*
   kotekwiiki *AI,ind,3p*
   kotekwiilo *AI,imp,2s*
   kotekwiiyeekwe *AI,subj,2p*
   kweetekwiita *AI/IC,part,3s*
kotekwi *becoming, turning into PV*
   kotekwi *PV*
koteletiiwitaamhkwe *jurisdiction NI*
   hokoteletiiwitaamhkwe *NI/POSS,3s,s*
kotesiwee *forbid AI*

kotesiweeci *AI,conj,3s*
kotet *rebuke TI_1*
   hokoteta *TI,ind,3s,0s*
ksake *for, because CJN*
   ksake *CJN*
ktapilekwa *gird, bind with a belt TA*
   ktapilekwa *TA,ind,3s,2s*
ktik *plant TI_3*
   ktike *TI,ind,3s,0s*
ktika *field NI*
   hoktika *NI/POSS,3s,s*
   hoktikaaneki *NI/POSS/LOC,3s*
   hoktikaanilici *NI/POSS,4*
   kiktikaaneki *NI/POSS/LOC,2s*
   ktika *NI,s*
   ktikaana *NI,p*
   ktikaaneki *NI/LOC*
ktikeewilenii *farmer NA*
   ktikeewileni *NA,3s*
   ktikeewilenihi *NA,4p*
   ktikeewileniiki *NA,3p*
ktohfee *walk AI*
   ktohfe *AI,ind,3s*
   ktohfeeki *AI,ind,3p*
   ktohfeeli *AI,ind,4s*
kwaakon *swallow TA*
   kwaakonaacki *TA,part,3p,4*
kwaalakat *empty II*
   yeekwaalakiki *II/IC,conj,0*
kwahkamikat *end II*
   yeekwahkamikiki *II/IC,conj,0*
kwakwaasakwi *wallow AI*
   kwakwaasakwiili *AI,ind,4s*
kwakwaten *snatch, pluck TI*
   kwakwatenano *TI,imp,2s,0*
kwakwaten *snatch, pluck TA*
   kwakwatenaaci *TA,conj,3s,4*
   kwakwatenahi *TA,ind,3s,4p*
kwakwatenamaake *snatch, pluck AI*
   kwakwatenamaakeeko *AI,imp,2p*
   kwakwtenamaakeeko *AI,imp,2p*
kwakwatenamaw *snatch, pluck TA*
   hokwakwatenamaakooli *TA,ind,4s,3s*
kwakwatenoofo *be snatched, be plucked AI*
   kwakwatenoofoyakwe *AI,conj,1i*
kwakwecihkaw *tempt TA*

hokwakwecihkaakooli *TA,ind,4s,3s*
kwakwehtaaneelem *marvel at TA*
    hokwakwehtaaneelemaali *TA,ind,3s,4s*
    hokwakwehtaaneelemekohi *TA,ind,4p,3s*
kwakwehtaaneelet *marvel at TI-O*
    hokwakwehtaaneeletaanaawa *TI,ind,3p,0*
    kwakwehtaaneeletamehi *TI,ind,4p,0*
    kwakwehtaaneeletamoko *TI,imp,2p,0*
    kwakwehtaaneeletamowaaci *TI,conj,3p,0*
kwakwehtaani *something great NI*
    kwakwehtaani *NI,s*
    kweekwehtaanhki *NI,p*
    kweekwehtaaniki *NI,p*
kwakwehtaanitehee *marvel AI*
    kikwakwehtaaniteheepwa *AI,ind,2p*
    kwakwehtaanitehe *AI,ind,3s*
    kwakwehtaaniteheeki *AI,ind,3p*
    kwakwehtaaniteheeko *AI,imp,2p*
    kwakwehtaaniteheelo *AI,imp,2s*
    kwakwehtaaniteheeyeekwe *AI,conj,2p*
    kwakwehtaanitehehi *AI,ind,4p*
kwakwehtaaniteheewe *amazement NI*
    kwakwehtaaniteheewe *NI,s*
kwakwetaki *various*
    kwakwetaki
kwakwi *run AI*
    kwakwiiki *AI,ind,3p*
kwakwi *[quickly] PV*
    kwakwi *PV*
kwakwkot *cut off TI_1*
    kwakwkotano *TI,imp,2s,0*
kwasfaa *come down, descend AI*
    kwasfaalo *AI,imp,2s*
    kwasfaate *AI,subj,3s*
kweeyehkwi *immediately*
    kweeyehkwi
kwehf *fear TA*
    kwehfekoci *TA,conj,4,3s*
kwehkwi *if CJN*
    kwehkwi *CJN*
    kwehkwike *CJN*
    kwekkwi *CJN*
kwehkwitoke *whether*
    kwehkwitoke
kwelepkoofo *be converted AI*
    kwelepkoofota *AI,part,3s*

kwena *at the time, on the occasion; by chance*
    kwena
kwenaani *due PM*
    kwenaani *PM*
kwf *fear TA*
    hokwfaali *TA,ind,3s,4s*
    hokwfaawaali *TA,ind,3p,4s*
    hokwfaawahi *TA,ind,3p,4p*
    hokwfahi *TA,ind,3s,4p*
    kikwfa *TA,ind,2s,3s*
    kikwfaape *TA,ind,1i,3*
    kikwfele *TA,ind,1s,2s*
    kwfaata *TA,part,3s,4*
    kwfeekwe *TA,part,2p,3*
    kwfehko *TA,imp,2p,3*
    nikwfa *TA,ind,1s,3s*
kwfetiiwe *fear NI*
    kwfetiiwe *NI,s*
kwfoofo *be feared AI*
    kwfoofooki *AI,ind,3p*
kwiiki *Greek NA*
    kwiikihi *NA,4p*
kwiiki *Greek (language) NI*
    kwiiki *NI,s*
kwiikiiwi *Greek PM*
    kwiikiiwi *PM*
kwiikiiwiikwe *Greek woman NA*
    kwiikiiwiikwe *NA,3s*
kwiikiiwilenawe *Greek person NA*
    kwiikiiwilenaweeki *NA,3p*
kwiil *lack, miss, not find TI_1*
    hokwiila *TI,ind,3s,0s*
    hokwiilaanaawa *TI,ind,3p,0*
    kwiilaanaawa *TI,ind,3p,0*
kwiilaalefi *lack, miss, not find AI*
    nikwiilaalefi *AI,ind,1s*
kwiilaani *lack, miss, not find*
    kwiilaani
    kwiilayini
kwiilahi *fail to, need to MDL*
    kwiila *MDL*
    kwiilah *MDL*
    kwiilahi *MDL*
    kwiilahiike *MDL*
kwiilahsilepwah *distress TA*

hokwiilahsilepwahekonaawa *TA,ind,0,3p*
kwiilahsitehee *be in distress AI*
  kwiilahsiteheeki *AI,ind,3p*
  kwiilahsitehehi *AI,ind,4p*
kwiilahsiteheewe *distress NI*
  hokwiilahsiteheewenwa *NI/POSS,3p*
  kwiilahsiteheewe *NI,s*
kwiilaw *miss, not find TA*
  kwiilawaawaaci *TA,conj,3p,4*
kwiliinias *Quirinius NA*
  kwiliinias *NA,3s*
kwpene *fear AI*
  kwpeneeki *AI,ind,3p*
  kwpeneko *AI,imp,2p*
  kwpenelo *AI,imp,2s*
  nikwpene *AI,ind,1s*
kwpeneewe *fear NI*
  kwpeneewe *NI,s*
  kwpeneewena *NI,p*
kwpeneyaa *fear II*
  kwpeneya *II,ind,0*
kwsiwee *fear AI*
  kwsiweeko *AI,imp,2p*
kwsiweewe *fear NI*
  kwsiweewe *NI,s*
kwt *fear TI_1*
  hokwta *TI,ind,3s,0s*
  hokwtaanaawa *TI,ind,3p,0*
  kwtamoko *TI,imp,2p,0*
  kwtano *TI,imp,2s,0*
kwtamh *hinder TA*
  kwtamhaawaaki *TA,ind,2p,3p*
kwtel *advise TA*
  hokwtelaali *TA,ind,3s,4s*
  hokwtelaawaali *TA,ind,3p,4s*
  hokwtelaawahi *TA,ind,3p,4p*
  hokwtelahi *TA,ind,3s,4p*
  kikwtelaawa *TA,ind,2p,3s*
  kwtelaali *TA,ind,3s,4s*
  kwtelahi *TA,ind,3s,4p*
  kwtelehko *TA,imp,2p,3*
  kwtesi *TA,imp,2s,3*
  nikwtelaape *TA,ind,1x,3*
kwteletiiwe *law NI*
  hokwteletiiwe *NI/POSS,3s,s*
  hokwteletiiweneki *NI/POSS/LOC,3s*

hokwteletiiwenwaaki *NI/POSS/LOC,3p*
kikwteletiiwenena *NI/POSS,1i*
kikwteletiiwenwa *NI/POSS,2p*
kikwteletiiwenwaaki *NI/POSS/LOC,2p*
kwteletiiwe *NI,s*
kwteletiiweneki *NI/LOC*
kwteletiiwi *law PM*
  kwteletiiwi *PM*
laa *in, there*
  laa
laafiwe *ascend AI*
  laafiwe *AI,ind,3s*
laakanoofi *light (not heavy) II*
  laakanoofi *II,ind,0*
laakeeci *at any time PV*
  laakeeci *PV*
laakeeletawt *make light of TI_2*
  holaakeeletawtoonaawa *TI,ind,3p,0*
laakofw *few*
  laakofwi
  laakofwihi
  laakofwiimehi
laakwa *time, place*
  laakwa
  laakwaanike
laakwaamefiiwe *time, season NI*
  laakwaamefiiwe *NI,s*
  nitelaakwaamefiiwe *NI/POSS,1s,s*
laakwaamefiiyaa *be the season II*
  yeelaakwaamefiiyaaki *II/IC,conj,0*
laakwahkamikat *be the time II*
  laakwahkamikiki *II,conj,0*
laakwasi *lenth of time*
  laakwasi
laakweeweni *be the time II*
  laakweeweniki *II,conj,0*
  yeelaakweeweniki *II/IC,conj,0*
laakwfoko *several days*
  laakofoko
laalakehoote *be hollowed out II*
  yeelaalakehooteeki *II/IC,conj,0*
laalhfwaacilot *transgress TI_1*
  holaalhfwaacilotaanaawa *TI,ind,3p,0*
  kilaalhfwaacilotaanaawa *TI,ind,2p,0*
laamahkika *cellar NI*
  laamahkikaaneki *NI/LOC*

laamataaka *womb* NI
  holaamataakanilici *NI/POSS,4*
  laamataaka *NI,s*
laamatahkehfecika *foundation* NI
  laamatahkehfecika *NI,s*
laameki *within, under*
  laameki
laami *journey* AI
  laami *AI,ind,3s*
  laamiiki *AI,ind,3p*
  yeelaamiici *AI/IC,conj,3s*
  yeelaamiilici *AI/IC,conj,4*
  yeelaamiiyeekwe *AI/IC,conj,2p*
laamitahfa *under*
  laamitahfa
laamiyehfe *move in a direction, follow a course II*
  yeelaamiyehfeki *II/IC,conj,0*
laamotaaka *womb* NI
  holaamotaakaneki *NI/POSS/LOC,3s*
  holaamotaakanilici *NI/POSS,4*
  kilaamotaakaneki *NI/POSS/LOC,2s*
  laamotaaka *NI,s*
  laamotaakana *NI,p*
  laamotaakaneki *NI/LOC*
  nilaamotaakaneki *NI/POSS/LOC,1s*
laamotaw *be carried by [pregnancy] TA*
  leelaamotaakocki *TA/IC,part,4,3p*
laapaacimo *read, interpret AI*
  laapaacimoki *AI,conj,3*
laapaatot *interpret, repeat TI_1*
  holaapaatotaanaawa *TI,ind,3p,0*
  kilaapaatotaanaawa *TI,ind,2p,0*
  laapaatota *TI,ind,2s,0s*
  laapaatotaanaawa *TI,ind,2p,0*
  laapaatotaki *TI,conj,3s,0*
  laapaatotameekwe *TI,conj,2p,0*
  leelaapaatotaka *TI/IC,part,3s,0*
laapaatotamaw *interpret, repeat TA*
  laapaatotamawahi *TA,ind,3s,4p*
laapaatotoote *be interpreted II*
  laapaatotoote *II,ind,0*
  yeelaapaatotooteeki *II/IC,conj,0*
laapacikee *look AI*
  yeelaapacikeecki *AI/IC,part,3p*
laapamoofo *be seen AI*

yeelaapamoofota *AI/IC,part,3s*
laape *face toward AI*
  yeelaapeelici *AI/IC,conj,4*
laapeewe *face NI*
  hotelaapeewe *NI/POSS,3s,s*
  hotelaapeewenwa *NI/POSS,3p*
laapeeyaa *face toward II*
  yeelaapeeyaaki *II/IC,conj,0*
laapeskaa *face AI*
  laapeska *AI,ind,3s*
  laapeskaalici *AI,conj,4*
laapeskaa *face II*
  yeelaapeskaaki *II/IC,conj,0*
laapi *inherited PM*
  laapi *PM*
laapi *look AI*
  laapi *AI,ind,3s*
  laapici *AI,conj,3s*
  laapiiki *AI,ind,3p*
  laapiko *AI,imp,2p*
  yeelaapiwaaci *AI/IC,conj,3p*
laapicimoofo *have hung around AI*
  laapicimoofolici *AI,conj,4*
  layaapicimoofolici *AI/IC,conj,4*
laapicimota *veil NI*
  laapicimota *NI,s*
laapicin *be hung around AI*
  laapicinelite *AI,subj,4s*
laapicit *hang, suspend TI_2*
  holaapicito *TI,ind,3s,0s*
laapicitoofo *have hanging around AI*
  laapicitoofote *AI,subj,3s*
laapiiwe *sight NI*
  hotelaapiiweneki *NI/POSS/LOC,3s*
  hotelaapiiwenwaaki *NI/POSS/LOC,3p*
  kitelaapiiweneki *NI/POSS/LOC,2s*
laapilenaweewiiwe *regeneration NI*
  laapilenaweewiiweneki *NI/LOC*
laapiten *hang II*
  laapiteki *II,conj,0*
laapitepeelecikee *inherit AI*
  layaapitepeelecikeeta *AI/IC,part,3s*
laapitepeelecikeewe *inheritance NI*
  laapitepeelecikeewe *NI,s*
laapitepeelet *inherit TI_1*
  laapitepeeletama *TI,conj,1s,0*

layaapitepeeletaka *TI/IC,part,3s,0*
laapitephaw *repay TA*
    laapitephole *TA,ind,1s,2s*
laapowe *rehearse, go over again AI*
    laapoweeki *AI,ind,3p*
laapsin *inherit AI*
    laapisina *AI,conj,1s*
    laapsina *AI,conj,1s*
    laapsinelici *AI,conj,4*
    laapsinwa *AI,ind,3s*
laasenias *Lysanias NA*
    laasenias *NA,3s*
laasiwee *get down AI*
    laasiwe *AI,ind,3s*
    laasiweelici *AI,conj,4*
    laasiweelo *AI,imp,2s*
    laasiweeta *AI,part,3s*
    laasiweete *AI,subj,3s*
laasiween *let down, take down TA*
    holaasiweenaali *TA,ind,3s,4s*
    laasiweenaawaali *TA,ind,3p,4s*
    laasiwenekoci *TA,conj,4,3s*
laasiwehfen *descend II*
    laasiwehfenwi *II,ind,0s*
laasiwehsin *descend AI*
    laasiwehsiki *AI,conj,3s*
    laasiwehsinooli *AI,ind,4s*
    laasiwehsinwa *AI,ind,3s*
laasiwen *let down, take down TI_1*
    laasiwenaanaawa *TI,ind,3p,0*
laasiyofe *descend AI*
    laasiyofe *AI,ind,3s*
    laasiyofeeli *AI,ind,4s*
    laasiyofelici *AI,conj,4*
laatotamaw *speak of TA*
    laatotamaweci *TA,conj,,3*
laatotoote *be rumored II*
    yeelaatotooteeki *II/IC,conj,0*
laawatenamaatiiwe *remission NI*
    laawatenamaatiiwe *NI,s*
laawi *among, in the middle of PV*
    laawi *PV*
laawitaamhkwe *region NI*
    laawitaamhkwe *NI,s*
laawtekwe *in midst of*
    laawtekwe

lahkeeph *set, place TA*
    lahkeephaki *TA,conj,1s,3*
lahkeepi *sit AI*
    yeelahkeepici *AI/IC,conj,3s*
    yeelahkeepilici *AI/IC,conj,4*
lahkehfen *be built on II*
    lahkehfenwi *II,ind,0s*
lahkehfet *present, set forth TI_2*
    hotelahkehfeto *TI,ind,3s,0s*
    lahkehfetoope *TI,ind,1i,0*
lahkootiiyaa *in order, according to II*
    weelahkootiiyaaki *II/IC,conj,0*
    yeelahkootiiyaaki *II/IC,conj,0*
lahoot *cry out TI-O*
    lahootamelici *TI,conj,4,0*
    lahootamooki *TI,ind,3p,0*
    lahootamwa *TI,ind,3s,0*
    yeelahootaki *TI/IC,conj,3s,0*
lahootamo *cry out AI*
    lahootamohi *AI,ind,4p*
lakokwe *very*
    lakokwe
lakokweeletamaw *wonder at TA*
    holakokweeletamawaawaali *TA,ind,3p,4s*
lakokwehtaani *wonderful PM*
    lakokwehtaani *PM*
lalakwi *between*
    lalakwi
lalemacfaa *leap AI*
    lalemacfaako *AI,imp,2p*
lasehto *clothe AI*
    lasehtoote *AI,subj,3s*
lasiikaaci *abominable PM*
    holasiikaaci *PM*
    lasiikaaci *PM*
lasiikaaciweefiiwe *abomination NI*
    lasiikaaciweefiiwe *NI,s*
    lasiikaaciwefiiwe *NI,s*
laten *move TI_1*
    latenaana *TI,ind,1s,0p*
    latenaanaawa *TI,ind,3p,0*
    latenano *TI,imp,2s,0*
laten *move TA*
    lateni *TA,imp,2s,3*
latenamaw *move, guide TA*
    hotelatenamawaawahi *TA,ind,3p,4p*

latenoofo *be moved AI*
    latenoofooli *AI,ind,4s*
latii *Lot NA*
    latii *NA,3s*
lawi *do AI*
    lawi *AI,ind,3s ; AI,ind,2s ; AI,ind,1s*
    lawiici *AI,conj,3s*
    lawiicki *AI,part,3p*
    lawiike *AI,subj,3*
    lawiilici *AI,conj,4*
    lawiilo *AI,imp,2s*
    lawiipe *AI,ind,1x*
    lawiipwa *AI,ind,2p*
    lawiiwaaci *AI,conj,3p*
    lawiiya *AI,conj,1s*
lawikaafo *be written about AI*
    lawikaafo *AI,ind,3s*
lawikaaloofo *be written about AI*
    yeelawikaaloofoci *AI/IC,conj,3s*
    yeelawikaaloofolici *AI/IC,conj,4*
lawikaate *be written II*
    lawikaate *II,ind,0*
lawikee *write AI*
    lawike *AI,ind,3s*
    lawikeelo *AI,imp,2s*
    lawikeepi *AI,ind,3*
    lawikeeya *AI,conj,1s*
    yeelawikeeci *AI/IC,conj,3s*
    yeelawikeeki *AI/IC,conj,3*
laya *lawyer NA*
    laya *NA,3s*
    layahi *NA,4p*
    layaki *NA,3p*
    layali *NA,4s*
lccali *Rachel NA*
    lecali *NA,3s*
lecehtaw *use hands on TA*
    lecehtawipwa *TA,ind,2p,1s*
leceskaa *stretch out the hand AI*
    leceska *AI,ind,3s*
leekawi *sand NI*
    leekawi *NI,s*
leewa *viper NA*
    leewaaki *NA,3p*
    leewaki *NA,3p*
lehapi *Rahab NA*

lehapiili *NA,4s*
lehfe *breathe AI*
    lehfe *AI,ind,3s*
lehfehtaw *breathe on TA*
    lehfehtawahi *TA,ind,3s,4p*
lehfi *spirit NA*
    lehfihi *NA,4p*
lekhi *length of time*
    lekhi
lekhokwiiwe *flood NI*
    lekhokwiiwe *NI,s*
lekokwa *? than ?*
    lekokwa
lekokwaape *face AI*
    yeelekokwaapeeci *AI/IC,conj,3s*
lekon *bury TA*
    holekonaawaali *TA,ind,3p,4s*
    lekonaawaaci *TA,conj,3p,4*
    lekonaki *TA,conj,1s,3*
lekoniwee *bury AI*
    lekoniweewaaci *AI,conj,3p*
lekonoofo *be buried AI*
    lekonoofo *AI,ind,3s*
    lekonoofolici *AI,conj,4*
lekonoofoowe *burial, being buried NI*
    nilekonoofoowe *NI/POSS,1s,s*
lekoskaw *possess TA*
    holekoskaakooli *TA,ind,4s,3s*
    lekoskaakocki *TA,part,4,3p*
    lekoskaakolici *TA,conj,0,4*
    lekoskaakota *TA,part,4,3s*
lekowhaske *cliff NI*
    lekowhaske *NI,s*
lelhfeeyaa *continue II*
    ycclhfccyaaki *II/IC,conj,0*
lelhkam *tear TA*
    kilelhkamekowaaki *TA,ind,3p,2p*
lelhkehkaa *tear II*
    lelhkehka *II,ind,0*
    lelhkehkaaki *II,conj,0*
lelhkin *tear TI*
    holelhkinaana *TI,ind,3s,0p*
    holiilelhkinaana *TI,ind,3s,0p*
    lelhkina *TI,ind,3s,0s*
    lelhkinaataako *TI,imp,1i,0*
lelhskonamaati *distribute AI*

lelhskonamaatihi *AI,ind,4p*
lelhskonamaw *distribute* TA
　holelhskonamawahi *TA,ind,3s,4p*
　lelhskonamawi *TA,imp,2s,3*
lema *Ramah* NI
　lema *NI,s*
lema *lama [Aramaic word]*
　laama
　lema
lemacfe *leap* AI
　lemacfe *AI,ind,3s*
　lemacfeeli *AI,ind,4s*
lemacfeeyaa *leap* II
　lemacfeeyaaki *II,conj,0*
lemafkohkwe *be the feast* II
　lemafkohkweki *II,conj,0*
lemafkohkweewe *feast* NI
　lemafkohkweewe *NI,s*
lemataph *set, place* TA
　holemataphaali *TA,ind,3s,4s*
　holemataphaawaali *TA,ind,3p,4s*
　holemataphaawahi *TA,ind,3p,4p*
　lemataphaali *TA,ind,3s,4s*
　lemataphahi *TA,ind,3s,4p*
　lemataphehko *TA,imp,2p,3*
　lemataptaakwi *TA,ind,,3s*
lematapi *sit* AI
　lematapi *AI,ind,3s*
　lematapici *AI,conj,3s*
　lematapicki *AI,part,3p*
　lematapiiki *AI,ind,3p*
　lematapiili *AI,ind,4s*
　lematapiko *AI,imp,2p*
　lematapilici *AI,conj,4*
　lematapilo *AI,imp,2s*
　lematapita *AI,part,3s*
　lematapite *AI,subj,3s*
　lematapiwa *AI,ind,3s*
　lematapiwaaci *AI,conj,3p*
　lematapiyaake *AI,conj,1x*
　lematapiyeekwe *AI,conj,2p*
　nilematapi *AI,ind,1s*
lematkwele *look up* AI
　lematkweleko *AI,imp,2p*
lemeki *Lamech* NA
　lemeki *NA,3s*

lemii *Ram* NA
　lemii *NA,3s*
　lemiili *NA,4s*
lenawe *Indian, person* NA
　hotelenaweemhhi *NA/POSS,3s,4p*
　kitelenaweema *NA/POSS,2s,3s*
　lenawe *NA,3s*
　lenaweeki *NA,3p*
　lenaweeli *NA,4s*
　lenawehi *NA,4p*
　nitelenaweemhi *NA/POSS,1s,4p*
lenaweewi *live* AI
　hotelenaweewici *AI,conj,3s*
　lenaweewi *AI,ind,3s ; AI,ind,2s*
　lenaweewici *AI,conj,3s*
　lenaweewicki *AI,part,3p*
　lenaweewiiki *AI,ind,3p*
　lenaweewilici *AI,conj,4*
　lenaweewipwa *AI,ind,2p*
　lenaweewita *AI,part,3s*
　lenaweewite *AI,subj,3s*
　lenaweewiya *AI,conj,1s*
　nitelenaweewi *AI,ind,1s*
lenaweewi *be life* II
　lenaweewiki *II,conj,0*
lenaweewihtaw *live for* TA
　holenaweewihtawaawaali *TA,ind,3p,4s*
lenaweewiiwe *life; way of living, custom* NI
　hotelenaweewiiwe *NI/POSS,3s,s*
　kitelenaweewiiwe *NI/POSS,2s,s*
　kitelenaweewiiwenwa *NI/POSS,2p*
　lenaweewiiwe *NI,s*
　lenaweewiiweeneki *NI/LOC*
　lenaweewiiweneki *NI/LOC*
　nitelenaweewiiwe *NI/POSS,1s,s*
lenaweewiiwen *be life* II
　lenaweewiiweno *II,ind,0p*
lenaweewiiweni *be life* II
　lenaweewiiweniki *II,conj,0*
lenaweewiiyaa *live* II
　leelenaweewiiyaaki *II/IC,conj,0*
　lenaweewiiya *II,ind,0*
　lenaweewiiyaake *II,subj,0*
　lenaweewiiyaaki *II,conj,0*
leniwi *be (that sort of) a man* AI
　leniwi *AI,ind,3s*

leniwiya *AI,conj,1s*
  yeeleniwiyani *AI/IC,conj,2s*
lepaayii *Rabbi NA*
  lepaayii *NA,3s*
leponaayi *Rabboni NA*
  leponaayi *NA,3s*
lepwaa *wise AI*
  lepwaacki *AI,part,3p*
  lepwaalici *AI,conj,4*
lepwaawe *intelligence NI*
  holepwaawe *NI/POSS,3s,s*
  holepwaaweneki *NI/POSS/LOC,3p*
  lepwaawe *NI,s*
  lepwaaweneki *NI/LOC*
lepwaaweewi *wise, wisdom PM*
  lepwaaweewi *PM*
lepwaawefi *wise AI*
  lepwaawefi *AI,ind,3s*
  lepwaawefihi *AI,ind,4p*
  lepwaawefiiki *AI,ind,3p*
  lepwaawefiko *AI,imp,2p*
  lepwaawefita *AI,part,3s*
lepwaaweleni *person of wisdom NA*
  lepwaawelenihi *NA,4p*
lepwaawi *wise PV*
  lepwaawi *PV*
lepwaawileni *wise person NA*
  lepwaawilenihi *NA,4p*
  lepwaawileniiki *NA,3p*
lepwah *make feel TA*
  lepwahekooli *TA,ind,4s,3s*
lepwaskaw *make feel TA*
  lepwaskaakoci *TA,conj,4,3s*
  lepwaskawaali *TA,ind,3s,4s*
lesimo *flee (to somewhere) AI*
  lesimoko *AI,imp,2p*
  lesimolo *AI,imp,2s*
  lesimooki *AI,ind,3p*
  lesimowaate *AI,subj,3p*
lesolesii *Lazarus NA*
  lesolesii *NA,3s*
  lesolesiili *NA,4s*
letine *Latin NI*
  letine *NI,s*
lhfee *go AI*
  lhfeelici *AI,conj,4*

lhfeewaaci *AI,conj,3p*
  yaalhfeeki *AI,ind,3p*
  yeelelhfeewaaci *AI/IC,conj,3p*
  yeelelhfeeyani *AI/IC,conj,2s*
lhfwaacilawiiwe *transgressor NA*
  lhfwaacilawiiwenhhi *NA,4p*
lhfwaacimo *proclaim AI*
  lhfwaacimolo *AI,imp,2s*
  lhfwaacimopi *AI,ind,3*
lhfwaatot *proclaim TI_1*
  holhfwaatotaanaawa *TI,ind,3p,0*
  lhfwaatota *TI,ind,3s,0s*
  lhfwaatotama *TI,conj,1s,0*
  lhfwaatotamoko *TI,imp,2p,0*
  lhfwaatotamowaaci *TI,conj,3p,0*
  lhfwaatotano *TI,imp,2s,0*
lhfwaatotamaw *proclaim TA*
  lhfwaatotamawaki *TA,conj,1s,3*
lhfweewe *dispersion NI*
  lhfweeweneki *NI/LOC*
lhfwelhkaw *scatter TA*
  holhfwelhkawahi *TA,ind,3s,4p*
lhfwelhkoofo *be scattered AI*
  lhfwelhkoofo *AI,ind,3s*
  lhfwelhkoofooki *AI,ind,3p*
lhfwen *spread around TI_1*
  holhfwena *TI,ind,3s,0s*
  lhfwena *TI,ind,3s,0s*
lhfwen *scatter, disperse TA*
  lhfwenahi *TA,ind,3s,4p*
lhfweni *scatter, disperse AI*
  lhfwenike *AI,subj,3*
lhfwenoote *be spread II*
  lhfwenoote *II,ind,0*
lhfwepakitaawe *scatter AI*
  lhfwepakitaaweya *AI,conj,1s*
  lhfwepakitaaweyani *AI,conj,2s*
lhfwesk *scatter TA*
  lhfweskawaali *TA,ind,3s,4s*
lhfweskaa *be scattered AI*
  lelhfweskaalici *AI/IC,conj,4*
  lhfweskaaki *AI,ind,3p*
  lhfweskaayeekwe *AI,conj,2p*
lhk *get in (a boat) TI-O*
  lhkaki *TI,conj,3s,0*
  lhkamelici *TI,conj,4,0*

lhkamooki *TI,ind,3p,0*
lhkamwa *TI,ind,3s,0*
yaalhkamwa *TI,ind,3s,0*
lhkahi *instant, length of time PV*
lhkahi *PV*
lhokwi *launch AI*
lhokwiiki *AI,ind,3p*
lhokwilo *AI,imp,2s*
yeelelhokwiwaaci *AI/IC,conj,3p*
lhskahki *field NI*
lhskahki *NI,s*
lhskahkiki *NI/LOC*
lhskim *revile TA*
holhskimaawaali *TA,ind,3p,4s*
lhskim *reproach TA*
holhskimekooli *TA,ind,4s,3s*
lhskimelwaakwe *TA,conj,3,2p*
lhskimetiiwe *reviling NI*
lhskimetiiwe *NI,s*
lhskimetiiwena *NI,p*
lhskit *reproach TI_1*
lhskitaana *TI,ind,3s,0p*
lhspawikaafoowe *superscription NI*
holhspawikaafoowe *NI/POSS,3s,s*
lhspawikeewe *superscription NI*
lhspawikeewe *NI,s*
spawikeewe *NI,s*
lhspi *high*
lhspi
lhspimekofi *be made higher, be placed above AI*
lhspimekofi *AI,ind,3s*
lihfiiwanhhika *scourge NI*
lihfiiwanhhika *NI,s*
lihfiiwanhhotiiwawikaafoowe *lash, stripe NI*
lihfiiwanhhotiiwawikaafoowena *NI,p*
lihfiiwanhhw *scourge TA*
holihfiiwanhhwaali *TA,ind,3s,4s*
lihfiiwanhhokowaaki *TA,ind,3p,2p*
lihfiiwanhhwa *TA,ind,1s,3s*
lihfiiwanhhwaaci *TA,conj,3s,4*
lihfiiwanhhwaawaaci *TA,conj,3p,4*
lihfiiwanhhwaawaaki *TA,ind,2p,3p*
lihfiiwanhhwaawaali *TA,ind,3p,4s*
lihoopoemii *Rehoboam NA*
lihoopoemii *NA,3s*

lihoopoemiili *NA,4s*
liifaaiti *Levite NA*
liifaaihi *NA,4p*
liifaaiti *NA,3s*
liifaayi *Levi NA*
liifaai *NA,3s*
liifaayiili *NA,4s*
liikatahkamikat *dismantled II*
liikatahkamikatwi *II,ind,0s*
liikatahkamikifiiwe *desolation NI*
liikatahkamikifiiweneki *NI/LOC*
liikatefiiwe *ruin, destruction NI*
holiikatefiiwe *NI/POSS,3s,s*
liikaten *destroy TI_1*
liikatenaana *TI,ind,1s,0p*
liikatenaka *TI,part,3s,0*
liikatenama *TI,conj,1s,0*
liikatenamoko *TI,imp,2p,0*
liikin *take off clothing TA*
holiikinaawaali *TA,ind,3p,4s*
holiikinekohi *TA,ind,4p,3s*
liise *Rhesa NA*
liise *NA,3s*
liiwafikee *smoke AI*
liiwafikeelici *AI,conj,4*
liiyoo *Reu NA*
liiyoo *NA,3s*
lilathoofo *be wounded AI*
yeelilathoofolici *AI/IC,conj,4*
liyeewe *have (such an) appearance AI*
yeeliyeeweci *AI/IC,conj,3s*
lohfah *bring out, remove TA*
lohfahaali *TA,ind,3s,4s*
lohfahaawaali *TA,ind,3p,4s*
lohfahoofo *be brought out AI*
lohfahoofo *AI,ind,3s*
lohfaleti *make each other go out [reciprocal] AI*
lohfaleti *AI,ind,3*
lohfat *bring out TI_2*
lohfato *TI,ind,3s,0s*
lohfatooci *TI,conj,3s,0*
lohfataw *bring out someone for someone TA*
lohfatoolepwa *TA,ind,1s,2p*
lohfe *[out, out of] PV*
holohfe *PV*

lohfe *PV*
nilohfe *PV*
lohfee, lohfaa *go out AI*
    kilohfaapwa *AI,ind,2p*
    laalohfe *AI,ind,3s*
    leelohfaalici *AI/IC,conj,4*
    lohfa *AI,ind,2s ; AI,ind,1s*
    lohfaaci *AI,conj,3s*
    lohfaacki *AI,part,3p*
    lohfaako *AI,imp,2p*
    lohfaalici *AI,conj,4*
    lohfaalo *AI,imp,2s*
    lohfaapwa *AI,ind,2p*
    lohfaawaaci *AI,conj,3p*
    lohfaawaate *AI,subj,3p*
    lohfaaya *AI,conj,1s*
    lohfaayeekwe *AI,conj,2p*
    lohfe *AI,ind,3s*
    lohfeeki *AI,ind,3p*
    lohfeeli *AI,ind,4s*
    lohfehi *AI,ind,4p*
lohfehtan *flow out II*
    lohfehtanwi *II,ind,0s*
lohfelhkaw *put out TA*
    lohfelhkawaaci *TA,conj,3s,4*
    lohfelhkawaawaali *TA,ind,3p,4s*
    lohfelhkawahi *TA,ind,3s,4p*
lohfelhkoofo *be put out AI*
    lohfelhkoofo *AI,ind,3s*
    lohfelhkoofooki *AI,ind,3p*
    lohfelhkoofowaaci *AI,conj,3p*
    lohfelhkoofoya *AI,conj,1s*
lohfen *remove from, take out TI_1*
    holohfena *TI,ind,3s,0s*
    lohfenaanaawa *TI,ind,3p,0*
lohfen *remove from, take out TA*
    lohfenaci *TA,conj,2s,3*
lohfeskaa *go out II*
    lohfeska *II,ind,0s*
    lohfeskaaki *II,conj,0*
lohfewel *lead out TA*
    holohfewelahi *TA,ind,3s,4p*
lohfeyaa *go out II*
    lohfeya *II,ind,0*
lohkaamekhaawe *dig, till the ground AI*
    lohkaamekhaawe *AI,ind,1s*

lohkach *tire, make tired TA*
    lohkachekwa *TA,ind,3s,1s*
lohkatefi *tired AI*
    lohkatefi *AI,ind,3s*
lokhaana *flour NI*
    lokhaana *NI,s*
lomhkoon *anoint TA*
    holomhkoonaawahi *TA,ind,3p,4p*
    kilomhkoona *TA,ind,2s,3s*
    leelomhkoonaata *TA/IC,part,3s,4*
    lomhkoonaali *TA,ind,3s,4s*
    nilomhkoonekwa *TA,ind,3s,1s*
lomhkoowe *ointment NI*
    lomhkoowe *NI,s*
lomhkwi *anoint AI*
    lomhkwiilo *AI,imp,2s*
lomin *anoint TI_1*
    lominaana *TI,ind,3s,0p*
lominamaw *anoint TA*
    holominamawaali *TA,ind,3s,4s*
lominoowe *ointment NI*
    lominoowena *NI,p*
loofasi *Rufus NA*
    loofasi *NA,3s*
loofii *Ruth NA*
    loofiili *NA,4s*
looloofo *be hired AI*
    yeelooloofocki *AI/IC,part,3p*
looloosenikana *torch NA*
    looloosenikanhhi *NA,4p*
loomeni *Roman NA*
    loomeniiki *NA,3p*
lowaskwi *rue [herb] NI*
    lowaskwi *NI,s*
lwaamat *descend II*
    lwaamahkiki *II,conj,0*
lwaami *down, bottom NI*
    lwaameki *NI/LOC*
lwahsin *lodge AI*
    lwahsinooki *AI,ind,3p*
lwe *make a sound II*
    lweki *II,conj,0*
maa *myrrh NI*
    maa *NI,s*
maa *[indefinite remote]*
    maa

maacilepwaa *feel moved* AI
    maacilepwa *AI,ind,3s*
maacilepwah *move, instill feeling* TA
    homaacilepwahekohi *TA,ind,4p,3s*
maaciloofi *small* AI
    kcimaaciloofi *AI,ind,2s ; AI,ind,3s*
    maaciloofihi *AI,ind,4p*
maacitehee *feel moved* AI
    maacitehe *AI,ind,3s*
    maaciteheeki *AI,ind,3p*
    maaciteheeli *AI,ind,4s*
maackwaafi *little* II
    maackwaafi *II,ind,0s*
    maackwaafiki *II,conj,0*
maackwaalakatoofi *narrow* II
    maackwaalakatoofi *II,ind,0 ; II,ind,0s*
maafe *Martha* NA
    maafe *NA,3s*
    maafeli *NA,4s*
    mefe *NA,3s*
maalaakasi *a while*
    maalaakasi
maalaakwaamatoofi *near* II
    maalaakwaamatoofiki *II,conj,0*
maalaakwaamefi *near* AI
    maalaakwaamefici *AI,conj,3s*
maalaakwaamefiiyaa *near* II
    maalaakwaamefiiyaaki *II,conj,0*
maalaakwahi *nearby*
    maalaakwa
    maalaakwa'
    maalaakwahi
maalaakwahi *near* II
    maalaakwahiki *II,conj,0*
maalaakwahiwi *near* AI
    maalaakwahiwici *AI,conj,3s*
maalaakwasihi *period of time, a while*
    maalaakwasi
    maalaakwasihi
maalecihi *little, small amount* NI
    kcimaalecihi *NI,s*
    maalecihi *NI,s*
    maalecihiki *NI/LOC*
maalefiiwe *abundance* NI
    maalefiiwe *NI,s*
    maalefiiweneki *NI/LOC*

maalekhi *piece; little bit* NI
    maalekhi *NI,s*
    maayaalecihi *NI,p*
    maayaalekhi *NI,p*
maalekhitaamhkwe *region* NI
    maalekhitaamhkwe *NI,s*
maalektasi *in that area, around there*
    maalektasi
maalespi *low*
    maalespi
maalet *abundant* II
    maaletwi *II,ind,0s*
maalhokwi *launch (out)* AI
    maalhokwilici *AI,conj,4*
maali *much, many, greatly* PM
    homaali *PM*
    maali *PM*
maalohfefiiyaa *slow* II
    maalohfefiiya *II,ind,0*
maamaatakoskaa *epileptic* AI
    maamaatakoska *AI,ind,3s*
maamamiyeenaanhhiwee *torment* AI
    maamamiyeenaanhhiweelici *AI,conj,4*
maamawaapam *turn to* TA
    homaamawaapamaawaali *TA,ind,3p,4s*
maamhfaapiyeht *broaden* TI_2
    homaamhfaapiyehtoonaawa *TI,ind,3p,0*
maamhkaweelemoofoowe *remembrance* NI
    nimaamhkaweelemoofooweneki
NI/POSS/LOC,1s
maamhsiht *enlarge* TI_2
    homaamhsihtoonaawa *TI,ind,3p,0*
maamhsimekofihtaw *exercise authority over*
TA
    homaamhsimekofihtaakowahi
TA,ind,4p,3p
maamoosikiiskwe *prophet* NA
    homaamoosikiiskwemali *NA/POSS,3s,4s*
    homaamoosikiiskwemhhi *NA/POSS,3s,4p*
maamoosikiiskweewi *prophet* PM
    maamoosikiiskweewi *PM*
maamoosikiiskweewi *be a prophet* AI
    maamoosikiiskweewilici *AI,conj,4*
    maamoosikiiskweewite *AI,subj,3s*
    maamoosikiiskweewiyani *AI,conj,2s*
maapayecikaasiwee *be a neighbor* AI
    maapayecikaasiweeta *AI,part,3s*

maapayeecikaal *be a neighbor to* TA
    maapayecikaalaacki *TA,part,3p,4*
    maapayecikaalekoci *TA,conj,4,3s*
    maapayeecikaalehka *TA,part,3,2s*
maapiyeecikaaletiima *neighbor* NA
    kimaapiyeecikaaletiima *NA/POSS,2s,3s*
    maaopiyeecikaaletiimali *NA/POSS,3s,4s*
    nimaapiyeecikaaletiima *NA/POSS,1s,3s*
maapiyeecikaaletiiwe *neighbor* NA
    maaopiyeecikaaletiiwenhhi *NA/POSS,3s,4p*
    maapiyeecikaaletiiwenaki *NA,3p*
maasa *in number of*
    maasa
maaspefiifi *of short stature* AI
    maaspefiifi *AI,ind,3s*
maatakoce *bent, doubled up* AI
    maatakoce *AI,ind,3s*
maatakoskaa *epileptic* AI
    maamaatakoskaacki *AI,part,3p*
maatakoskah *tear* TA
    homaamaatakoskahekooli *TA,ind,4s,3s*
    homaatakoskahaali *TA,ind,3s,4s*
    maatakoskahaaci *TA,conj,3s,4*
    maatakoskahaali *TA,ind,3s,4s*
maatasi *here*
    maatasi
maatawi *[desiring]* PV
    kimaatawi *PV*
    maamaatawi *PV*
    maatawi *PV*
maatawitehee *desire* AI
    maatawitehe *AI,ind,1s*
    maatawiteheewaaci *AI,conj,3p*
maatawiteheewe *desire* NI
    maatawiteheewe *NI,s*
maateefi *over, at an end*
    maateefi
maaten *move* TI_1
    maatenaanaawa *TI,ind,3p,0*
maatfwihi *few*
    maatfwihi
maatwiimehi *few*
    maatwiimehi
maawaskaa *gather* AI
    maawaskaaki *AI,ind,3p*
    maawaskaawaaci *AI,conj,3p*

maawaskahi *AI,ind,4p*
maawaskaam *gather* TA
    homaawaskaamaawaali *TA,ind,3p,4s*
    maawaskaamekohi *TA,ind,4p,3s*
maawaskaawe *gathering, assembly* NI
    homaawaskaawenwa *NI/POSS,3p*
    maawaskaawe *NI,s*
maawaskotaw *gather* TA
    homaawaskotawaawaali *TA,ind,3p,4s*
maawatom/maawatwim *call together* TA
    homaawatomaawahi *TA,ind,3p,4p*
    homaawatomahi *TA,ind,3s,4p*
    homaawatwimahi *TA,ind,3s,4p*
maawaton *gather* TA
    homaawatonaawahi *TA,ind,3p,4p*
    maawatonaaci *TA,conj,3s,4*
    maawatonaaki *TA,ind,1s,3p*
    maawatonaali *TA,ind,3s,4s*
    maawatonaawahi *TA,ind,3p,4p*
    maawatonahi *TA,ind,3s,4p*
maawaton *collect, gather* TI_1
    homaawatonaanaawa *TI,ind,3p,0*
    maawatona *TI,ind,3s,0s*
    maawatonaki *TI,conj,3s,0*
    maawatonamaake *TI,conj,1x,0*
    maawatonameekwe *TI,conj,2p,0*
    maawatonamoko *TI,imp,2p,0*
maawatonamaw *gather* TA
    maawatonamaakwiiki *TA,ind,,3p*
maawatonikee *gather with* AI
    maawatonike *AI,ind,2s ; AI,ind,3s*
    maawatonnikeeya *AI,conj,1s*
    mawatonikeewaaci *AI,conj,3p*
maawatonikeem *gather (something) along with (someone)* TA
    maawatonikeemita *TA,part,3s,1s*
maawatonikeeyaa *gather* II
    maawatonikeeya *II,ind,0*
maawatonikehfii *tax collector* NA
    maawatonikehfi *NA,3s*
    maawatonikehfihi *NA,4p*
    maawatonikehfiiki *NA,3p*
maawatonoote *be gathered* II
    maawatonooteeki *II,conj,0*
maawatoskaa *gather* AI
    maawatoska *AI,ind,3s*

maawatoskaaki *AI,ind,3p*

maawatoskaalici *AI,conj,4*

maawatoskahi *AI,ind,4p*

maawatoskaam *gather around (someone)* TA

homaawatoskaamekohi *TA,ind,4p,3s*

maawatoskaamekoci *TA,conj,4,3s*

maawatwaapi *be together* AI

maawatwaapiiki *AI,ind,3p*

maawatwahkeepi *sit together* AI

maawatwahkeepiiki *AI,ind,3p*

maawatweel *be gathered* AI

maawatweelooki *AI,ind,3p*

maawatweelotaw *gather around (someone)* TA

homaawatweelotaakohi *TA,ind,4p,3s*

homaawatweelotaakooli *TA,ind,4s,3s*

homaawatweelotawaawaali *TA,ind,3p,4s*

maawatweelotaakohi *TA,ind,4p,3s*

maawatwi *[together]* PV

maawatwi *PV*

meemaawatwi *PV/IC*

maawatwipto *run together* AI

maawatwiptoolici *AI,conj,4*

macaafi *evil* II

macaafi *II,ind,0*

macaafike *II,subj,0*

macaafiki *II,conj,0*

maci *bad, evil* PM

homaci *PM*

maci *PM*

maci-ash *tempt* TA

maci-ashekoci *TA,conj,4,3s*

maciilefi *evil* AI

kimaciilefipwa *AI,ind,2p*

maciilefi *AI,ind,3s*

maciilefici *AI,conj,3s*

maciilefihi *AI,ind,4p*

meciileficki *AI/IC,part,3p*

meciilefilici *AI/IC,conj,4*

meciilefita *AI/IC,part,3s*

meciilefiyeekwe *AI/IC,conj,2p*

maciilefiiwe *evil, sin* NI

homaciilefiiwe *NI/POSS,3s,s*

homaciilefiiwena *NI/POSS,3s,p*

homaciilefiiwenwa *NI/POSS,3p*

kimaciilefiiwena *NI/POSS,2s,p*

maciilefiiwe *NI,s*

maciilefiiwena *NI,p*

nimaciilefiiwenena *NI/POSS,1x*

maciilefiwilawiiwe *sin* NI

maciilefiwilawiiwe *NI,s*

maciileni *evil person* NA

maciilenihfefa *NA/DIM,3s*

maciisilawi *sin, do wrong* AI

maciisilawi *AI,ind,3s*

maciisilawiilo *AI,imp,2s*

maciisilawiite *AI,subj,3s*

meciisilawiilici *AI/IC,conj,4*

meciisilawiita *AI/IC,part,3s*

meemaciisilawiita *AI/IC,part,3s*

maciisilawiiwe *sin* NI

homaciisilawiiwenilici *NI/POSS,4*

homaciisilawiiwenwa *NI/POSS,3p*

kimaciisilawiiwenwa *NI/POSS,2p*

kimaciisilawiiwenwaaki *NI/POSS/LOC,2p*

maciisilawiiwe *NI,s*

maciisilawiiweneki *NI/LOC*

maciisilot *sin against* TI_1

maciisilota *TI,ind,1s,0s*

maciisilotaw *sin against* TA

maciisilotawehke *TA,subj,3s,2s*

maciisin *suffer, ungergo* TI-O

maciisinamooki *TI,ind,3p,0*

macikalawi *curse, swear* AI

macikalawi *AI,ind,3s*

macikalawiiwe *oath* NI

macikalawiiwe *NI,s*

macikalool *curse, speak evil of* TA

meemacikaloolaata *TA/IC,part,3s,4*

meemacikaloolelwaakwe *TA/IC,part,3,2p*

macikaloot *curse, speak evil of* TI_1

meemacikalootamani *TI/IC,conj,2s,0*

macikiiseki *bad day, bad weather* II

macikiiseki *II,ind,0s*

macikiteewe *anger, wrath* NI

macikiteewe *NI,s*

macilawi *do wrong, commit* AI

macilawi *AI,ind,2s ; AI,ind,3s*

macilawiici *AI,conj,3s*

macilawiicki *AI,part,3p*

macilawiiki *AI,ind,3p ; AI,conj,3*

macilawiilo *AI,imp,2s*

macilawiiya *AI,conj,1s*

meemacilawiita *AI/IC,part,3s*
nimacilawi *AI,ind,1s*
macilawihtaw *do wrong to someone TA*
 homacilawihtawaali *TA,ind,3s,4s*
 macilawihtawaaci *TA,conj,3s,4*
macilawiiwe *crime NI*
 macilawiiwe *NI,s*
macilehfi *evil spirit NA*
 macilehfihi *NA,4p*
macilepwaa *feel bad, be sorrowful AI*
 macilepwa *AI,ind,3s*
 macilepwaaki *AI,ind,3p*
 macilepwaape *AI,ind,1x*
 macilepwahi *AI,ind,4p*
macilepwaapeskaa *look sorrowful AI*
 macilepwaapeskaaki *AI,ind,3p*
macilepwaawe *sorrow, bad feeling NI*
 kimacilepwaawenwa *NI/POSS,2p*
 macilepwaawe *NI,s*
macilepwaawefi *be sorry AI*
 macilepwaawefipwa *AI,ind,2p*
macilepwaaweni *have sorrow AI*
 kimacilepwaawenipwa *AI,ind,2p*
 macilepwaaweni *AI,ind,3s*
 macilepwaaweniiki *AI,ind,3p*
macilepwaawi *sad PV*
 macilepwaawi *PV*
macilepwaskaw *grieve TA*
 homacilepwaskaako *TA,ind,0s,3s*
maciliikweewe *evil eye NI*
 maciliikweewe *NI,s*
macilot *destroy TI_1*
 macilota *TI,ind,1s,0s*
 macilotama *TI,conj,1s,0*
 mccilotaka *TI/IC,part,3s,0*
macilotamaw *destroy, spoil TA*
 macilotamawaali *TA,ind,3s,4s*
macilotaw *ruin, destroy TA*
 macilotaakoci *TA,conj,4,3s*
 macilotawaaci *TA,conj,3s,4*
 macilotawaawaaci *TA,conj,3p,4*
 macilotawahi *TA,ind,3s,4p*
 macilotawiyaake *TA,conj,2,1x*
macilotoote *be destroyed II*
 macilotooteeki *II,conj,0*
macilotwaake *destroy AI*

macilotwaakeeci *AI,conj,3*
macim *reproach TA*
 kimacimipe *TA,ind,2,1x*
macimaneto *devil NA*
 macimaneto *NA,3s*
 macimanetooli *NA,4s*
macimanetoowi *be a devil AI*
 macimanetoowi *AI,ind,3s*
macimiyaakwimekiifa *goat NA*
 macimiyaakwimekiifa *NA,3s*
macimoofoowe *reproach NI*
 nimacimoofoowe *NI/POSS,1s,s*
macipenal *sin against TA*
 macipenaleekwe *TA,conj,2p,3*
 macipenalehke *TA,subj,3s,2s*
maciskata *lust NI*
 maciskata *NI,s*
maciweenefwi *wine drinker NA*
 maciweenefo *NA,3p*
maciwiyeefa *evil one NA*
 maciwiyeefa *NA,3s*
mafaana *flax NA*
 mafaanali *NA,4s*
mafaanimota *linen cloth NI*
 mafaanimota *NI,s*
 mafaanimotaaki *NI/LOC*
 mafaanimotaawali *NI,p*
mahkeen *beware of TA*
 mahkeeni *TA,imp,2s,3*
mahkootelefa *colt NA*
 homahkootelefemali *NA/POSS,3s,4s*
 mahkootelefa *NA,3s*
 mahkootelefali *NA,4s*
maiili *mile NI*
 maiili *NI*
maisi *remaining ones, rest, others*
 maisi
makamaki *big PV*
 makamaki *PV*
makha *[interrogative]*
 makha
maki *great, large, a lot PM*
 maki *PM*
makiici *mighty PM*
 makiici *PM*
makiicilawiiwe *miracle NI*

makiicilawiiwe *NI,s*
makiiciweefiiwe *majesty NI*
   homakiiciweefiiwe *NI/POSS,3s,s*
makimiyeewi *highway NI*
   makimiyeewali *NI,p*
makipookat *wave II*
   meemakipookaki *II/IC,conj,0*
makofeelem *care for, regard TA*
   homakofeelemaali *TA,ind,3s,4s*
   homakofeelemahi *TA,ind,3s,4p*
   makofeelemaci *TA,conj,2s,3*
   nimakofeelema *TA,ind,1s,3s*
makofeelet *heed, take care TI-O*
   kimakofeeleta *TI,ind,2s,0s*
   makofeeletamwa *TI,ind,3s,0*
makootakooti *robe NI*
   makootakooti *NI,s*
makootelefa *colt NA*
   makootelefa *NA,3s*
maloomiktika *vineyard NI*
   maloomikitika *NI,s*
mam *take TA*
   homamaali *TA,ind,3s,4s*
   homamaawaali *TA,ind,3p,4s*
   homamaawahi *TA,ind,3p,4p*
   homamahi *TA,ind,3s,4p*
   kimamelepwa *TA,ind,1s,2p*
   kimamipwa *TA,ind,2p,1*
   mamaali *TA,ind,3s,4s*
   mamaawaaci *TA,conj,3p,4*
   mamaawahi *TA,ind,3p,4p*
   mamaci *TA,conj,2s,3*
   mamahi *TA,ind,3s,4p*
   mamaka *TA,part,1s,3s*
   mamawehko *TA,imp,2p,3*
   mamawici *TA,conj,3s,1s*
   mamehko *TA,imp,2p,3*
   mami *TA,imp,2s,3*
   meemaacki *TA/IC,part,3p,4*
   meemamaaci *TA/IC,conj,3s,4*
mam *take TI_3*
   homame *TI,ind,3s,0s*
   homamena *TI,ind,3s,0p*
   homamenaawa *TI,ind,3p,0*
   kimamenaawa *TI,ind,2p,0*
   kimamepe *TI,ind,1i,0*

mame *TI,ind,3s,0s*
mameka *TI,part,3s,0*
mameke *TI,subj,3s,0*
mameki *TI,conj,3s,0*
mameko *TI,imp,2p,0*
mamelo *TI,imp,2s,0*
mamena *TI,ind,3s,0p*
mametaako *TI,imp,1i,0*
mameya *TI,conj,1s,0*
mameyani *TI,conj,2s,0*
mamowaaci *TI,conj,3p,0*
meemameki *TI/IC,conj,3s,0*
meemamekki *TI/IC,part,3p,0*
mamaakeeyaa *take II*
   mamaakeeya *II,ind,0*
mamaatom *pray to TA*
   homamaatomaali *TA,ind,3s,4s*
   homamaatomekooli *TA,ind,4s,3s*
   kimamaatomele *TA,ind,1s,2s*
   mamaatomehko *TA,imp,2p,3*
   mamaatomi *TA,imp,2s,3*
mamaatomaa *pray AI*
   mamaatomaako *AI,imp,2p*
   mamaatomaapwa *AI,ind,2p*
   mamaatomaawaaci *AI,conj,3p*
   mamaatomaayeekwe *AI,conj,2p*
   meemamaatomaayeekwe *AI/IC,conj,2p*
mamaatomaw *pray for TA*
   mamaatomawehko *TA,imp,2p,3*
mamaatomee *pray AI*
   mamaatome *AI,ind,3s*
   mamaatomeeci *AI,conj,3s*
   mamaatomeeko *AI,imp,2p*
   mamaatomeelici *AI,conj,4*
   mamaatomeewaaci *AI,conj,3p*
   mamaatomeeya *AI,conj,1s*
   mamaatomeeyaake *AI,conj,1x*
   mamaatomeeyane *AI,subj,2s*
   mamaatomeeyeekwe *AI,conj,2p*
mamaatomeewe *prayer NI*
   homamaatomeeweneki *NI/POSS/LOC,3s*
   mamaatomeewe *NI,s*
   mamaatomeewena *NI,p*
   mamaatomeeweneki *NI/LOC*
mamaatomeewefi *prayerful, devout AI*
   mamaatomeewefi *AI,ind,3s*

mamaatomeewika *prayer house NI*
  homamaatomeewika *NI/POSS,3s,s*
  mamaatomeewika *NI,s*
  nimamaatomeewika *NI/POSS,1s,s*
mamaatomeewikamikwi *temple NI*
  homamaatomeewikamikomi *NI/POSS,3s,s*
  homamaatomeewikamikwi *NI/POSS,3s,s*
  mamaatomeewikamikoki *NI/LOC*
  mamaatomeewikamikwi *NI,s*
mamaatomeewimaawatweloowe *church NI*
  mamaatomeewimaawatweloowe *NI,s*
  mamaatomeewimaawatwelooweneki
NI/LOC
mamaawena *elect, selected NA*
  homamaawenali *NA/POSS,3s,4s*
  homamaawenhhi *NA/POSS,3s,4p*
  nimamaawena *NA/POSS,1s,3s*
mamaw *take TA*
  homamaakooli *TA,ind,4s,3s*
  kimamaakwa *TA,ind,3s,2s*
  mamaakonaaki *TA,ind,3p,1i*
  mamaakoopwa *TA,ind,3,2p*
  mamaakowa *TA,ind,3s,2p*
  mamaakwi *TA,ind,,3s*
  mamaakwiiki *TA,ind,,3p*
  meemamawehka *TA/IC,part,3,2s*
  nimamaakwa *TA,ind,3s,1s*
mamawiweyaa *take II*
  mamawiweya *II,ind,0*
mameteelemo *hunger AI*
  meemameteelemocki *AI/IC,part,3p*
mamhpw *snatch TA*
  homamhpwahi *TA,ind,3s,4p*
mamiiloowi *by force PV*
  mamiiloowi *PV*
mamiiloowih *compel TA*
  mamiiloowihekwa *TA,ind,3s,2s*
mamiiloowihkaw *compel TA*
  homamiiloowihkawaawaali *TA,ind,3p,4s*
  homamiiloowihkawahi *TA,ind,3s,4p*
  mamiiloowihkawi *TA,imp,2s,3*
mamiiloowilawiiwe *extortion NI*
  mamiiloowilawiiwe *NI,s*
mamiiloowilot *compel TI_1*
  homamiiloowilotaanaawa *TI,ind,3p,0*
mamiyaalakatowi *maimed AI*
  mamiyaalakatowiyane *AI,subj,2s*

meemiyaalakatowilici *AI/IC,conj,4*
  meemiyaalakatowita *AI/IC,part,3s*
mamiyaalakatowikaate *lame AI*
  meemiyaalakatowikaateecki *AI/IC,part,3p*
mamiyaalakh *wound TA*
  homamiyaalakhaawaali *TA,ind,3p,4s*
mamiyaalakifi *maimed AI*
  mamiyaalakifiyane *AI,subj,2s*
mamiyaalakika *lame AI*
  mamiyaalakikaata *AI,part,3s*
  meemiyaalakikaateelici *AI/IC,conj,4*
mamiyaatweewahoot *wail TI-O*
  mamiyaatweewahootamooki *TI,ind,3p,0*
mamiyaatweewitehee *groan AI*
  mamiyaatweewitehe *AI,ind,3s*
  mamiyaatweewiteheeci *AI,conj,3s*
mamiyeenaanh *torment TA*
  mamiyeenaanhhilo *TA,imp,2s,1s*
  mamiyeenaanhhiyaake *TA,conj,2,1x*
  mamiyenaanhhilo *TA,imp,2s,1s*
mamiyeenaani *grievous PM*
  mamiyeenaani *PM*
mamiyeenila *in torment, grievously*
  mamiyeenenila
mamiyeetaakwi *miserably PV*
  mamiyeetaakwi *PV*
mamiyeetaawaapi *fix one's gaze AI*
  mamiyeetaawaapi *AI,ind,3s*
mamiyeetaawat *grievous II*
  mamiyeetaawato *II,ind,0p*
mamiyeetahkweyi *miserable PM*
  mamiyeetahkweyi *PM*
mamiyetaawaapam *fix one's gaze on TA*
  homamiyeetaawaapamaawaali
TA,ind,3p,4s
  homamiyetaawaapamaali *TA,ind,3s,4s*
mamoofo *be taken, be chosen AI*
  mamoofo *AI,ind,3s*
  mamoofolo *AI,imp,2s*
  mamoofooki *AI,ind,3p*
  mamoofoyeekwe *AI,conj,2p*
  memoofolici *AI/IC,conj,4*
  memoofota *AI/IC,part,3s*
mamoote *be taken II*
  mamoote *II,ind,0*
  mamooteeki *II,conj,0*
maneto *spirit; snake NA*

homanetoomali *NA/POSS,3s,4s*
homanetoomwaali *NA/POSS,3p,4s*
kimanetooma *NA/POSS,2s,3s*
kimanetoomena *NA/POSS,1i,3s*
kimanetoomwa *NA/POSS,2p,3s*
maneto *NA,3s*
manetohi *NA,4p*
manetooki *NA,3p*
manetooki *NA/LOC,3 ; NA,3p*
manetooli *NA,4s*
manetooli *NA,4s*
nimanetooma *NA/POSS,1s,3s*
manetoolefa *worm NA*
homanetoolefemwahi *NA/POSS,3p,4p*
manetooleefa *NA,3s*
manetoowi *sacredly, powerful PM*
manetoowi *PM*
mastatiiwi *mustard PM*
mastatiiwi *PM*
mata *[negative]*
mata
mata-ini-otahpi *nevertheless*
mata-ini-otahpi
mataacimohtaw *accuse TA*
mataacimohtaakwi *TA,ind,,3s*
mataam *condemn, speak evil of TA*
homataamaawaali *TA,ind,3p,4s*
mataamaali *TA,ind,3s,4s*
mataamaawaali *TA,ind,3p,4s*
mataamici *TA,conj,3s,1s*
meemataamaata *TA/IC,part,3s,4*
mataametiiwe *reproach NI*
mataametiiwe *NI,s*
mataamo *swear AI*
mataamo *AI,ind,3s*
mataatotoote *be reproved II*
mataatotooteeli *II,ind,4*
matahkowaafoowe *condemnation NI*
matahkowaafoowe *NI,s*
matahkowaafooweneki *NI/LOC*
matahkowaal *condemn, sentence TA*
homatahkowaalaawaali *TA,ind,3p,4s*
matahkowaalaawaali *TA,ind,3p,4s*
matahkowaalekoopi *TA,ind,3,2s*
matahkowaalekoopwa *TA,ind,3,2p*
matahkowaasiwee *condemn AI*

matahkowaasiweeko *AI,imp,2p*
mataiini *blame*
mataiini
matal *come upon, overtake TA*
kimatalekonaawa *TA,ind,0,2p*
matalekoyeekwe *TA,conj,0,2p*
matalaakwa *never*
matalaakwa
matalaakwan *without*
matalaakwanwi
matalaakwasi *never*
matalaakwasi
matanohki *neither*
matanohki
matawiyeefekisi *worthless II*
matawiyeefekisi *II,ind,0s*
matawiyeefekisih *treat as nothing TA*
homatawiyeefekisihaawahi *TA,ind,3p,4p*
matawiyeefekisihoofo *be considered worhless AI*
matawiyeefekisihoofoci *AI,conj,3s*
matawiyeefekisiht *treat as nothing TI_2*
kimatawiyeefekisihtoonaawa *TI,ind,2p,0*
matawiyeefekisihtoonaawa *TI,ind,2p,0*
matawiyeefekisiwahkeeph *treat as nothing TA*
homatawiyeefekisiwahkeephaali *TA,ind,3s,4s*
matawiyeefekisiwi *as nothing, worthless PM*
matawiyeefekisiwi *PM*
matayeeci *impossible II*
matayeeciwi *II,ind,0s*
matayeeciwat *impossible II*
matayeeciwatwi *II,ind,0s*
matayeeciweefi *fail AI*
meetayeeciweefiwaaci *AI/IC,conj,3p*
matayeeciweefiiyaa *fail II*
matayeeciweefiiya *II,ind,0*
matayinisiteheewe *repentence NI*
matayinisiteheewe *NI,s*
mateelem *oppose TA*
homateelemaali *TA,ind,3s,4s*
mateeleti *oppose [reciprocal] AI*
mateeletiiki *AI,ind,3p*
mateeletiiwena *adversary, enemy NA*
homateeletiiwenali *NA/POSS,3s,4s*
homateeletiiwenhhi *NA/POSS,3s,4p*

kimateeletiiwena *NA/POSS,2s,3s*
kimateeletiiwenaaki *NA/POSS,1i,3p*
kimateeletiiwenaki *NA/POSS,2s,3p*
kimateeletiiwenwaaki *NA/POSS,2p,3p*
mateeletiiwena *NA,3s*
nimateeletiiwena *NA/POSS,1s,3s*
nimateeletiiwenaki *NA/POSS,1s,3p*
matefiifi *evil AI*
matefiifi *AI,ind,3s*
mawaapan *be near (dance or ceremony) II*
mawaapanwi *II,ind,0s*
mawaapat *look at (over there) TI_1*
homawaapataanaawa *TI,ind,3p,0*
kimawaapataanaawa *TI,ind,2p,0*
mawe *mourn AI*
kimawepwa *AI,ind,2p*
mawe *AI,ind,3s*
maweeki *AI,conj,3 ; AI,ind,3p*
maweewaaci *AI,conj,3p*
mawepwa *AI,ind,2p*
meemaweecki *AI/IC,part,3p*
maweewahoot *wail TI-O*
nimaweewahootaape *TI,ind,1x,0*
mawehtaw *mourn for TA*
meemawehtawaacki *TA/IC,part,3p,4*
mawi *going there PV*
homa *PV*
homawi *PV*
kimah *PV*
kimawi *PV*
mawi *PV*
mawi-caakatfwi *ninth*
mawi-caakatfene
mawi-caakatfwi
mawi-metahfwi *tenth*
mawi-metahfwi
mawi-metahfwi-kite-niyaalan *fifteenth*
mawi-metahfwi-kite-niyaalanwi
mawi-nekotwahfwi *sixth*
mawi-nekotwahfene
mawi-nekotwahfwi
mawi-nhfoko *thrid day*
mawi-nhfoko
mawi-nhfokonaki *be the third day II*
mawi-nhfokonakike *II,subj,0*
meewinhfokonakiki *II/IC,conj,0*

mawi-nhfwaasikfokonakiki *eighth day*
mawi-nhfwaasikfokonakiki
mawi-nhfwi *third*
mawi-nhfene
mawi-nhfwi
mawi-niiswahfwi *seventh*
mawi-niiswahfene
mawi-niiswahfwi
mawi-niiswi *second*
mawi-niisene
mawi-niiswi
mawi-niyeewene *fourth*
mawi-niyeewene
mawifo *gather fruit AI*
mawifooki *AI,ind,3p*
mawifoowe *fruit NI*
homawifoowe *NI/POSS,3s,s*
homawifoowenwa *NI/POSS,3p*
kimawifoowenwa *NI/POSS,2p*
mawifoowe *NI,s*
mawifoowena *NI,p*
nimawifoowena *NI/POSS,1s,p*
mawifooweniwi *fruitful II*
mawifooweniwi *II,ind,0s*
mawim *cry, weep TA*
mawimaaci *TA,conj,3s,4*
mawimaawaaci *TA,conj,3p,4*
mawimiko *TA,imp,2p,1s*
meemawimekoci *TA/IC,conj,4,3s*
mawinach *seize*
homaamawinachekooli *TA,ind,4s,3s*
homawinachaali *TA,ind,3s,4s*
homawinachaawaali *TA,ind,3p,4s*
homawinactaakohi *TA,ind,4p,3s*
mawinachiyeekwe *TA,conj,2p,1s*
mawinachi *seizing PV*
kimawinachi *PV*
mawinact *seize TI_2*
homawinacto *TI,ind,3s,0s*
mawinahk *oppose, struggle*
homawinahkaalaali *TA,ind,3s,4s*
homawinahkaalaawahi *TA,ind,3p,4p*
mawinahkaaletiiki
mawinahke
mawinahkeewi
mawinehw *go against TA*

kimawinehwaawa *TA,ind,2p,3s*
mawinehokoci *TA,conj,4,3s*
mawinehwaaci *TA,conj,3s,4*
mawit *weep for, mourn TI_1*
   homawita *TI,ind,3s,0s*
   mawitamoko *TI,imp,2p,0*
mayaanefi *young AI*
   mayaanefiyani *AI,conj,2s*
mayaani *young PM*
   mayaani *PM*
mayaanileni *young man NA*
   mayaanileni *NA,3s*
   mayaanileniifa *NA/DIM,3s*
   mayaanileniili *NA,4s*
mayaanileniiwe *youth NI*
   nimayaanileniiweneki *NI/POSS/LOC,1s*
mayaaoskiisekwi *right eye NI*
   kimayaaoskiisekwi *NI/POSS,2s,s*
mayaawahkowaat *judge correctly TI_1*
   kimayaawahkowaata *TI,ind,2s,0s*
mayaawat *lawful, correct II*
   mayaawatwi *II,ind,0s*
   mayaawhki *II,conj,0*
   meeyaawhki *II/IC,conj,0*
mayaawefi *true AI*
   mayaawefi *AI,ind,3s*
mayaawefiima *elect, selected person NA*
   homayaawefiimali *NA/POSS,3s,4s*
mayaawefiiwe *right, privilege NI*
   mayaawefiiwe *NI,s*
mayaawfen *true, right, correct II*
   mayaawfenwi *II,ind,0s*
mayaawhoofo *be chosen, be elect AI*
   meemayaawhoofota *AI/IC,part,3s*
   meeyaawhoofolici *AI/IC,conj,4*
mayaawi *true, right, correct PM*
   mayaawi *PM*
mayaawi *truly, rightly, correctly PV*
   homayaawi *PV*
   kimayaawi *PV*
   mayaawi *PV*
mayaawi[nkw]iiya *soul (true self) NA*
   kimayaawikiiya *NA/POSS,2s,3s*
   mayaawikiiya *NA/POSS,2s,3s*
   mayaawikiiyaanwaaki *NA/POSS,2p,3p*
   mayaawiniiya *NA/POSS,1s,3s*

mayaawiniiyaana *NA/POSS,1s,3s*
mayaawiwiiyaanali *NA,4s*
nimayaawiniiya *NA/POSS,1s,3s*
mayaawiilefi *righteous, faithful AI*
   kimayaawiilefi *AI,ind,2s*
   mayaawiilefi *AI,ind,3s*
   mayaawiilefiiki *AI,ind,3p*
   mayaawiilefilici *AI,conj,4*
   mayaawiilefipwa *AI,ind,2p*
   meemayaawiilefita *AI/IC,part,3s*
   meeyaawiileficki *AI/IC,part,3p*
   meeyaawiilefilici *AI/IC,conj,4*
   meeyaawiilefita *AI/IC,part,3s*
mayaawiilefiiwe *righteousness NI*
   mayaawiilefiiwe *NI,s*
   mayaawiilefiiweneki *NI/LOC*
mayaawiilefiiwi *as righteous PV*
   kimayaawiilefiiwi *PV*
mayaawiilefiiwi *righteous II*
   mayaawiilefiiwi *II,ind,0s*
mayaawiinhki *right side NI*
   homayaawiinhkiki *NI/POSS/LOC,3s*
   kimayaawiinhki *NI/POSS,2s,s*
   kimayaawiinhkiki *NI/POSS/LOC,2s*
   mayaawiinhkiki *NI/LOC*
   nimayaawiinhkiki *NI/POSS/LOC,1s*
mayaawilotaw *take from TA*
   mayaawilotawa *TA,ind,1s,3s*
mayaawim *instruct, command TA*
   homayaawimaali *TA,ind,3s,4s*
   homayaawimahi *TA,ind,3s,4p*
mayaawiwel *guide (correctly) TA*
   mayaawiwelekowa *TA,ind,3s,2p*
mayaawiwet *guide TI_2*
   mayaawiwetooci *TI,conj,3s,0*
mayaawsim *appoint TA*
   kimayaawsimelepwa *TA,ind,1s,2p*
mayaci *strange PM*
   mayaci *PM*
mayacilepwah *amaze TA*
   nimayacilepwahekonaaki *TA,ind,3p,1x*
mayacitehee *marvel AI*
   mayacitehe *AI,ind,3s*
   mayaciteheeki *AI,ind,3p*
mayaki *new PM*
   mayaki *PM*

mayakinhhaakana *bridegroom* NA
   mayakinhhaakana *NA,3s*
   mayakinhhaakanali *NA,4s*
mayakinhhaakanehkwe *bride* NA
   mayakinhhaakanehkweli *NA,4s*
mayakinhhaakanehkweewika *bride-chamber*
NI
   mayakinhhaakanehkweewika *NI,s*
   mayakinhhaakanehkweewikaaneki
NI/LOC
   mayakinhhaakaneykweewika *NI,s*
mayat *be a mystery* II
   meemayatki *II/IC,conj,0*
   meeyatki *II/IC,conj,0*
mayateelet *wonder at* TI_1
   mayateeleta *TI,ind,3s,0s*
mayectoote *be made* II
   mayectooteeki *II,conj,0*
mayeelawaatefi *lazy, slothful* AI
   mayeelawaatefi *AI,ind,3s*
mayohkwaaci *afterward, later*
   mayohkwaaci
mecaafiki *evil* NI
   mecaafiki *NI,s*
mecfen *ready* II
   mecfenwi *II,ind,0s*
mecfet *prepare* TI_2
   homecfetoonaawa *TI,ind,3p,0*
   mecfetooko *TI,imp,2p,0*
   mecfetoope *TI,ind,1x,0*
   nimecfeto *TI,ind,1s,0s*
mecfetaw *prepare* TA
   mayecfetawaata *TA/IC,part,3s,4*
   mecfetaakoci *TA,conj,4,3s*
   mecfetaakwi *TA,ind,,3s*
   mecfetawilo *TA,imp,2s,1s*
   mecfetawinaake *TA,imp,2,1x*
mecfetoofo *have prepared for* AI
   mayecfetoofoci *AI/IC,conj,3s*
   mayecfetoofoyeekwe *AI/IC,conj,2p*
mecfetoote *be prepared, be finished* II
   mecfetoote *II,ind,0*
mech *make (as, to be)* TA
   mechahi *TA,ind,3s,4p*
   memechaata *TA/IC,part,3s,4*
mechoofo *be made into* AI
   mechoofo *AI,ind,3s*

meci *many, much*
   meci
mecicikeemoowe *representative* NI
   mecicikeemoowe *NI,s*
mecicim *send* TA
   mecicimahi *TA,ind,3s,4p*
meciilefiiyaa *evil* II
   meciilefiiyaaki *II,conj,0*
mecilekhi *much, large amount* NI
   mecilekhi *NI,s*
   mecilekhiki *NI/LOC*
meciloofi *little* AI
   mecilooficki *AI,part,3p*
   meciloofilici *AI,conj,4*
   meciloofita *AI,part,3s*
mecimi *and* CJN
   mecimi *CJN*
meckwaalakatoofin *narrow* II
   meckwaalakatoofiki *II,conj,0*
mect *make* TI_2
   homecto *TI,ind,3s,0s*
   homectoona *TI,ind,3s,0p*
   mayectoota *TI/IC,part,3s,0*
   mecto *TI,ind,3s,0s*
   mectooci *TI,conj,3s,0*
   mectoonaawa *TI,ind,2p,0*
   mectooyani *TI,conj,2s,0*
mectaakwat *be accomplished* II
   mectaakwato *II,ind,0p*
mectaw *make* TA
   homectawaali *TA,ind,3s,4s*
   homectawahi *TA,ind,3s,4p*
   kimectoole *TA,ind,1s,2s*
mectoote *be made* II
   mectoote *II,ind,0*
   mectooteeki *II,conj,0*
meef *Maath* NA
   meef *NA,3s*
meeki-pakikawiki *? large drop ?*
   meeki-pakikawiki
meekiif *goat, sheep* NA
   homeekiifemwahi *NA/POSS,3p,4p*
   meekiifa *NA,3s*
   meekiifaki *NA,3p*
   meekiifali *NA,4s*
   meekiifhi *NA,4p*

nimeekiifaki *NA/POSS,1s,3p*
nimeekiifema *NA/POSS,1s,3s*
nimeekiifemaki *NA/POSS,1s,3p*
meekiifiwi *goat, sheep PM*
   meekiifiwi *PM*
meekwahkii *mountain NI*
   mamakwahki *NI,s*
   mamakwahkiki *NI/LOC*
   meekwahkiifa *NI/DIM,p*
   meekwahkiifiki *NI/DIM/LOC,s*
   meekwahkiiwali *NI,p*
   meekwahkiki *NI/LOC*
   tah-makwahkiki *NI/LOC*
meelawaaci *unwillingly PV*
   homeelawaaci *PV*
   meelawaaci *PV*
meelemawaaki *moisture NI*
   meelemawaaki *NI,s*
meewaapaki *dawn NI*
   meewaapaki *NI,s*
meewim *lament TA*
   meewimaacki *TA,part,3p,4*
meewineh *come against TA*
   meewinehokoci *TA,conj,4,3s*
mefahkwimi *ear (of corn) NI*
   mefahkwimi *NI,s*
   mefahkwimiki *NI/LOC*
mefefi *whole AI*
   mefefici *AI,conj,3s*
   mefefihi *AI,ind,4p*
   mefefiili *AI,ind,4s*
   mefefipwa *AI,ind,2p*
   mefefiyane *AI,subj,2s*
mefefih *make whole TA*
   kimefefiheko *TA,ind,0s,2s*
   kimefefihekoopi *TA,ind,3,2s*
   mefefiheko *TA,ind,0s,2s*
   mefefihekoci *TA,conj,4,3s*
   mefefihekoopi *TA,ind,3,2s*
   memefefihita *TA/IC,part,3s,1s*
   nimefefiha *TA,ind,1s,3s*
   nimefefihekoopi *TA,ind,3,1s*
mefefihoofo *be made whole AI*
   mefefihoofo *AI,ind,3s*
   mefefihoofoci *AI,conj,3s*
   mefefihoofooki *AI,ind,3p*

   mefefihoofowaaci *AI,conj,3p*
mefefiiwe *wholeness NI*
   mefefiiweneki *NI/LOC*
mefhiike *all around*
   mefhiike
mefi *whole*
   mefi
mefikwahfoowe *sandal NI*
   mefikwahfoowena *NI,p*
mefiyoo *Matthew NA*
   mefiyoo *NA,3s*
   mefiyooli *NA,4s*
mefoosila *Methuselah NA*
   mefoosila *NA,3s*
meftekonehi *brook NI*
   meftekonehi *NI,s*
meftoote *be made whole II*
   meftoote *II,ind,0*
   meftooteeli *II,ind,4*
meh *[prioritive] PV*
   home *PV*
   homeh *PV*
   kime *PV*
   kimeh *PV*
   me *PV*
   meh *PV*
   nime *PV*
   nimeh *PV*
meh-tapiim *come together with TA*
   meh-tapiimaawaaci *TA,conj,3p,4*
mehaleli *Mahalaleel NA*
   mehaleli *NA,3s*
mehci *[perfective] PV*
   homehci *PV*
   homehcike *PV*
   kimehci *PV*
   mayehci *PV/IC*
   meemehci *PV*
   mehci *PV*
   nimehci *PV*
mehciilefi *ready AI*
   mehciilefiko *AI,imp,2p*
mehcilawiiwefi *make ready AI*
   mehcilawiiwefi *AI,ind,3s*
mehcilot *accomplish TI_1*
   mayehcilotamowaaci *TI/IC,conj,3p,0*

mehcilota *TI,ind,3s,0s*
mehcilotaanaawa *TI,ind,2p,0*
mehcilotaki *TI,conj,3s,0*
mehcilotama *TI,conj,1s,0*
mehcilotameekwe *TI,conj,2p,0*
mehcilotamowaaci *TI,conj,3p,0*
nimehcilotaape *TI,ind,1x,0*
mehcilotamaw *accomplish TA*
mehcilotamawaki *TA,conj,1s,3*
mehcilotaw *do something for someone TA*
mehcilotaakoci *TA,conj,4,3s*
mehcilotoolehki *TA,conj,3,2s*
nimehcilotaakwa *TA,ind,3s,1s*
mehcilotoofo *be perfected AI*
mehcilotoofoci *AI,conj,3s*
mehcilotoote *be accomplished II*
mehcilotoote *II,ind,0*
mehcilotooteeke *II,subj,0*
mehcilotooteeki *II,conj,0*
mehcim *have said to, promise TA*
homehcimaawaali *TA,ind,3p,4s*
mehcimaaci *TA,conj,3s,4*
mehcimekowaaci *TA,conj,4,3p*
mehcimici *TA,conj,3s,1s*
mehcimiwee *promise AI*
mehcimiwe *AI,ind,3s*
mehcitehehtaw *prepare TA*
homehcitehehtaakohi *TA,ind,4p,3s*
mehciweefi *ready AI*
mehciweefiko *AI,imp,2p*
mehsaaki *great PM*
mehsaaki *PM*
mehseel *be many; assemble AI*
mayehseelelici *AI/IC,conj,4*
mchscclcka *AI/IC,part,3s*
mehseelekki *AI/IC,part,3p*
mehseelelici *AI/IC,conj,4*
mehsi *great*
mehsi
mehsiilefi *great AI*
mehsiilefi *AI,ind,3s*
mehsiilefita *AI,part,3s*
mehsiisitehee *proud AI*
mehsiisiteheelici *AI,conj,4*
mehsikkaki *wind, approaching storm NI*
mehsikkaki *NI,p*

mehtaacimo *agree AI*
mehtaacimohi *AI,ind,4p*
mehtaacimooki *AI,ind,3p*
mehtaacimoom *agree TA*
mehtaacimoomaaci *TA,conj,3s,4*
mehtaacimoomi *TA,ind,2s,1s*
mehtaacimoowe *agreement, covenant NI*
homehtaacimoowe *NI/POSS,3s,s*
mehtaacimoowe *NI,s*
mehtaapat *see, look at [perfective] TI_1*
homehtaapata *TI,ind,3s,0s*
mehtahkeeph *puin the midst of TA*
mehtahkeephaawaaci *TA,conj,3p,4*
mehtahkeepi *be seated AI*
mehtahkeepici *AI,conj,3s*
mehtahkeepiim *be seated with TA*
mehtahkeepiimaaci *TA,conj,3s,4*
mehtahkehfen *be prepared II*
mehtahkehfenwi *II,ind,0s*
mehtahkehfetoote *be prepared II*
mehtahkehfetoote *II,ind,0*
mehtahkowaafo *be judged AI*
mehtahkowaafo *AI,ind,3s*
mehtahkowaafoowe *judgment NI*
mehtahkowaafoowe *NI,s*
mehtahkowaafooweneki *NI/LOC*
mehtahkowaal *judge TA*
homehtahkowaaleko *TA,ind,0s,3s*
mehtahkowaaletiiwe *judgment NI*
mehtahkowaaletiiwe *NI,s*
mehtahkowe *judge AI*
mehtahkoweya *AI,conj,1s*
mehtahkoweewe *judgment NI*
mehtahkoweewe *NI,s*
mehtahkoweeweneki *NI/LOC*
mehtahpil *bind [perfective] TA*
homehtahpilaali *TA,ind,3s,4s*
mehtawikaate *be written II*
mehtawikaate *II,ind,0*
mehtawikaateeki *II,conj,0*
mehtawikee *write [perfective] AI*
mayehtawikeeki *AI,conj,3*
mehtawikeeci *AI,conj,3s*
mehtawikeeki *AI,conj,3*
mehtawikeepi *AI,ind,3*
nimehtawike *AI,ind,1s*

mehteelemekofiiwe *creation NI*
  mehteelemekofiiweneki *NI/LOC*
mehteelemiweewe *creation NI*
  mehteelemiweewe *NI,s*
mehteelet *create TI_1*
  mayehteeletaki *TI/IC,conj,3s,0*
mehtek *sing TI*
  mehtekamowaaci *TI,conj,3p,0*
mehtowe *say, speak [perfective] AI*
  kimehtowe *AI,ind,2s*
  kimehtowepwa *AI,ind,2p*
  mehtowe *AI,ind,3s ; AI,ind,2s*
  mehtoweci *AI,conj,3s*
  mehtoweeci *AI,conj,3s*
  mehtoweewaaci *AI,conj,3p*
  yeemehtoweci *AI/IC,conj,3s*
mehtoweyaa *say, state II*
  mehtoweya *II,ind,0*
  mehtoweyaaki *II,conj,0*
mekeeteni *Magadan NI*
  mekeeteni *NI,s*
mekihkofi *weak AI*
  mekihkofiiki *AI,ind,3p*
mekihkofiiyaa *be weak, faint II*
  mekihkofiiya *II,ind,0*
mekin *pick, choose TI_1*
  homekinaanaawa *TI,ind,3p,0*
  mekinamelici *TI,conj,4,0*
mekin *pick, choose TA*
  mekinahi *TA,ind,3s,4p*
  mekinelepwa *TA,ind,1s,2p*
mekinhhwe *animal NA*
  mekinhhweeki *NA,3p*
  mekinhhwehi *NA,4p*
mekini *picking PV*
  memekini *PV*
mekipwehfiifiwi *old, aged AI*
  mekipwehfiifiwi *AI,ind,3s*
mekipwehfiifiwiiwe *old age NI*
  homekipwehfiifiwiiweneki
NI/POSS/LOC,3s
mekiteliina *Magdalene NA*
  mekiteliina *NA,3s*
  mekiteliinali *NA,4s*
mekofiht *exercise authority over TI_1*
  mekofihtaki *TI,conj,3s,0*
mekofihtaw *have authority over TA*

mekofihtaakowaaci *TA,conj,4,3p*
mekofihtawaawaaci *TA,conj,3p,4*
simekofihtoolako *TA,conj,1s,2p*
weewiyehsimekofihtaakowaaci
TA/IC,conj,4,3p
melhkaaya *Melchi NA*
  melhkaaya *NA,3s*
melhkasi *Malchus NA*
  melhkasi *NA,3s*
melhske *whole, completely*
  melhske
melii *Mary NA*
  melii *NA,3s*
  meliili *NA,4s*
melonehse *obey AI*
  melonehseelici *AI,conj,4*
melonehtaw *obey, be subject to TA*
  homelonehtaakona *TA,ind,0p,3s*
  homelonehtawahi *TA,ind,3s,4p*
  melonehtaakowa *TA,ind,3s,2p*
  melonehtawaata *TA,part,3s,4*
memekan *plentiful II*
  memekanwi *II,ind,0s*
memekinaapam *look at TA*
  homemekinaapamaali *TA,ind,3s,4s*
  homemekinaapamahi *TA,ind,3s,4p*
memekinaapat *look at TI_1*
  memekinaapatamoko *TI,imp,2p,0*
  memekinaapatano *TI,imp,2s,0*
memekinaskwi *herb NI*
  memekinasko *NI,p*
memekineelem *consider TA*
  memekineelemaawaaci *TA,conj,3p,4*
  memekineelemehko *TA,imp,2p,3*
memekineelet *think about, remember TI_1*
  kimemekineeleta *TI,ind,2s,0s*
  kimemekineeletaana *TI,ind,2s,0p*
  kimemekineeletaanaawa *TI,ind,2p,0*
  memekineeleta *TI,ind,2s,0s*
  memekineeletaana *TI,ind,3s,0p*
  memekineeletaanaawa *TI,ind,2p,0*
  memekineeletaki *TI,conj,3s,0*
  memekineeletamoko *TI,imp,2p,0*
memekinhcika *garden NI*
  homemekinhcikaneki *NI/POSS/LOC,3s*
  memekinhcika *NI,s*
  memekinhcikaneki *NI/LOC*

memekinhcikaafa *gardener NA*
    memekinhcikaafa *NA,3s*
memekinilotaw *serve TA*
    kimemekinilotoole *TA,ind,1s,2s*
    memekinilotawa *TA,ind,2s,3s*
    memekinilotawaawa *TA,ind,2p,3s*
    memekinilotawahi *TA,ind,3s,4p*
    memekinilotawilo *TA,imp,2s,1s*
memekinilotawiwee *serve AI*
    mememekinilotawiweeta *AI,part,3s*
memekinisem *question, examine TA*
    memekinisemaki *TA,conj,1s,3*
memekinitehaaka *mind NI*
    homemekinitehaakanilici *NI/POSS,4*
    kimemekinitehaaka *NI/POSS,2s,s*
memekinitehaakani *have a mind, use the mind AI*
    memekinitehaakaniili *AI,ind,4s*
memekinitehee *think, reason AI*
    kimemekiniteheepwa *AI,ind,2p*
    memekinitehe *AI,ind,3s*
    memekiniteheeki *AI,ind,3p*
    memekiniteheelici *AI,conj,4*
    memekiniteheeyeekwe *AI,conj,2p*
memekiniteheemeti *reason, think [reciprocal] AI*
    memekiniteheemetiiki *AI,ind,3p*
memekiniteheewe *thinking, mind NI*
    homemekiniteheewenilici *NI/POSS,4*
    memekiniteheewe *NI,s*
    memekiniteheewena *NI,p*
memekiniteheeyaa *think, reason II*
    memekiniteheeyaaki *II,conj,0*
memekwii *run AI*
    memekwi *AI,ind,3s*
    memekwiiki *AI,ind,3p*
    memekwiili *AI,ind,4s*
memoospeelemekwitoote *be exhalted II*
    meemoospeelemekwitooteeki *II/IC,conj,0*
men *drink AI*
    meemeneka *AI/IC,part,3s*
    meemeneya *AI/IC,conj,1s*
    mene *AI,ind,1s ; AI,ind,2s*
    meneka *AI,part,3s*
    meneke *AI,subj,3*
    meneko *AI,imp,2p*

menelici *AI,conj,4*
    menelo *AI,imp,2s*
    menepe *AI,ind,1i*
    menepwa *AI,ind,2p*
    meneya *AI,conj,1s ; AI,subj,1s*
    meneyeekwe *AI,conj,2p ; AI,subj,2p*
    menoko *AI,imp,2p*
    menooki *AI,ind,3p*
    menowaaci *AI,conj,3p*
    menowaate *AI,subj,3p*
    menwa *AI,ind,3s*
    nimenepe *AI,ind,1x*
men *[willing, pleasing] PV*
    homenwi *PV*
    menwi *PV*
mena *Menna NA*
    mena *NA,3s*
menawahi *may, might MDL*
    menaw *MDL*
    menawa *MDL*
    menawah *MDL*
    menawahi *MDL*
menawahke *it might be*
    menawahike
    menawahke
menesa *Manasseh NA*
    menesa *NA,3s*
    menesali *NA,4s*
menetoowikiiseki *week NI*
    menetoowikiisekiki *NI/LOC*
menhh *cause one to drink TA*
    menhhaaci *TA,conj,3s,4*
menhkwatoowi *heavenly PM*
    menhkwatoowi *PM*
menhkwatwi *heaven NI*
    menhkwato *NI,p*
    menhkwatoki *NI/LOC*
    menhkwatwi *NI,s*
    menhkwatwiki *NI/LOC*
menihfepi *fastening NI*
    homenifepiye *NI/POSS,3s,s*
    menihfepi *NI,s*
meniti *moment [? minute ?]*
    meniti
menoowe *drink NI*
    menoowe *NI,s*

menweelem *please TA*
    menweelemaaci *TA,conj,3s,4*
menweelemoofo *be accepted AI*
    menweelemoofo *AI,ind,3s*
menweelet *find pleasing TI_1*
    homenwiiletaanaawa *TI,ind,3p,0*
    kimenweeletaanaawa *TI,ind,2p,0*
menwilaasamamooweni *be pleasing II*
    menwilaasamamooweniki *II,conj,0*
menwilepwaa *be pleased AI*
    nimenwilepwa *AI,ind,1s*
menwitehee *be pleased AI*
    kimenwiteheepwa *AI,ind,2p*
    nimenwitehe *AI,ind,1s*
menwiteheeskoofo *be comforted AI*
    menwiteheeskoofo *AI,ind,3s*
    menwiteheeskoofooki *AI,ind,3p*
menwiteheetiiwena *comforter NA*
    menwiteheetiiwena *NA,3s*
    menwiteheetiiwenali *NA,4s*
menwiteheeweni *be pleased AI*
    menwiteheewenici *AI,conj,3s*
menyeel *dance AI*
    kimenyeelepwa *AI,ind,2p*
    menyeeleki *AI,conj,3*
    menyeelooli *AI,ind,4s*
mesaaya *messiah NA*
    mesaaya *NA,3s*
mesahke *sit down AI*
    mesahke *AI,ind,3s*
mesen *take hold TA*
    homesenaali *TA,ind,3s,4s*
    homesenaawaali *TA,ind,3p,4s*
    homesenaawahi *TA,ind,3p,4p*
    homesenekonaawa *TA,ind,0,3p*
    homesenekooli *TA,ind,4s,3s*
    kimesenipwa *TA,ind,2p,1*
    mesenaacki *TA,part,3p,4*
    mesenaali *TA,ind,3s,4s*
    mesenaamaakoci *TA,conj,4,3s*
    mesenaawaaci *TA,conj,3p,4*
    mesenaawaali *TA,ind,3p,4s*
    mesenehko *TA,imp,2p,3*
    mesenekowaaki *TA,ind,3p,2p*
    mesenelwaakwe *TA,conj,3,2p*
    meseniyeekwe *TA,conj,2p,1s*

mesenoofo *be taken hold of AI*
    mesenoofo *AI,ind,3s*
    mesenoofolici *AI,conj,4*
    mesenoofooli *AI,ind,4s*
meskwahteeki *leather PM*
    meskwahteeki *PM*
meskwiskipakiyaa *purple II*
    meskwiskipakiyaaki *II,conj,0*
mestaamoowe *accusation NI*
    mestaamoowe *NI,s*
mestaawh *betray TA*
    mayehtaawhita *TA/IC,part,3s,1s*
    mayestaawhaata *TA/IC,part,3s,4*
    mayestaawhekoci *TA/IC,conj,4,3s*
    memestaawhaata *TA/IC,part,3s,4*
    memestaawhekoci *TA,conj,4,3s*
    memestaawhita *TA/IC,part,3s,1s*
    mestaahehka *TA,part,3,2s*
    mestaawha *TA,ind,2s,3s*
    mestaawhaaci *TA,conj,3s,4*
    mestaawhaata *TA,part,3s,4*
    mestaawhekoci *TA,conj,4,3s*
    mestaawhekowaaki *TA,ind,3p,2p*
    mestaawhekwa *TA,ind,3s,1s*
    mestaawhici *TA,conj,3s,1s*
    mestaawhita *TA,part,3s,1s*
mestaawheti *betray, deliver [reciprocal] AI*
    mestaawhetiiki *AI,ind,3p*
mestaawhiweewi *betray AI*
    mayestaawhiweewita *AI/IC,part,3s*
mestaawhoofo *be betrayed AI*
    mestaawhoofo *AI,ind,3s*
    mestaawhoofoci *AI,conj,3s*
mestaawim *accuse, deliver, betray TA*
    memestaawimekoci *TA/IC,conj,4,3s*
    memestaawimelwaakwe *TA/IC,part,3,2p*
    mestaawimaawaaci *TA,conj,3p,4*
    mestaawimehko *TA,imp,2p,3*
    mestaawimelako *TA,conj,1s,2p*
mestaawt *betray TI_2*
    mestaawtooya *TI,conj,1s,0*
mestele *master NA*
    homestelemwahi *NA/POSS,3p,4p*
    kimestelemwa *NA/POSS,2p,3s*
    mestele *NA,3s*
    mestelehi *NA,4p*

mesteleki *NA,3p*
mesteleli *NA,4s*
metaamoowe *decision, judgement NI*
metaamoowe *NI,s*
metahfwi *ten*
metahfene
metahfwi
metahfwi-kite-nekoti *eleven*
metahfwi-kite-nekoti
metahfwi-kite-nhfwaasikfwi *eighteen*
metahfwi-kite-nhfwaasikfwi
metahfwi-kite-niiswi *twelve*
metahfwi-kite-niiswi
metahfwi-kite-niyeewi *fourteen*
metahfwi-kite-niyeewi
metefa *Mattatha NA*
metefa *NA,3s*
metefaaesi *Mattathias NA*
metefaaesi *NA,3s*
metefiifi *bad, not usable AI*
metefiifilici *AI,conj,4*
metemiye *follow the path AI*
metemiye *AI,ind,3s*
metenetiiwe-ipeneewe *pestilence NI*
metenetiiwe-ipeneewena *NI,p*
metfenii *Matthan NA*
metfenii *NA,3s*
metfeniili *NA,4s*
metfete *Matthat NA*
metfete *NA,3s*
meyale *[translation of Aramaic raca]*
meyale
mhfaalakat *wide II*
mhfaalakatwi *II,ind,0s*
mhfaapiyccyaa *wide II*
mhfaapiyeeya *II,ind,0s*
mhfaloomi *grape*
mhfaloomi
mhfaloomiktika *vineyard NI*
homhfaloomiktikaaneki *NI/POSS/LOC,3s*
mhfaloomiktika *NI,s*
mhfaloomiktikaaneki *NI/LOC*
mhfaskwalwi *reed NI*
mhfaskwaloki *NI/LOC*
mhfaskwalwi *NI,s*
mhfaskwalwiki *NI/LOC*

mhfe *abundant II*
yaamhfeki *II/IC,conj,0*
mhfeelem *benefit from, rely on TA*
homhfeelemaali *TA,ind,3s,4s*
mhfeelet *need, rely on TI_1*
meemhfeeletaki *TI/IC,conj,3s,0*
mhfeeletameekwe *TI,conj,2p,0*
mhfoofoofa *calf NA*
homhfoofoomhhi *NA/POSS,3s,4p*
mhfoofoofa *NA,3s*
mhfoofoofali *NA,4s*
mhhweewa *wolf NA*
mhhweewa *NA,3s*
mhhweewaki *NA,3p*
mhhweewali *NA,4s*
mhhweewhi *NA,4p*
mhk *find TI_1*
homhka *TI,ind,3s,0s*
homhkaanaawa *TI,ind,3p,0*
meemhkaka *TI/IC,part,3s,0*
meemhkaki *TI/IC,conj,3s,0*
meemhkakki *TI/IC,part,3p,0*
mhka *TI,ind,3s,0s ; TI,ind,2s,0s ; TI,ind,1s,0s*
mhkaanaawa *TI,ind,2p,0 ; TI,ind,3p,0*
mhkaki *TI,conj,3s,0*
mhkama *TI,conj,1s,0*
mhkamowaaci *TI,conj,3p,0*
nimeemhka *TI,ind,1s,0s*
nimhka *TI,ind,1s,0s*
mhkahfo *find AI*
mhkahfo *AI,ind,3s*
mhkahfooki *AI,ind,3p*
mhkahfopwa *AI,ind,2p*
mhkahfoowefi *profitable AI*
mhkahfoowefita *AI,part,3s*
mhkahfooweni *profitable II*
mhkafooweni *II,ind,0s*
mhkahfooweni *II,ind,0s*
mhkahkwika *tower NI*
mhkahkwika *NI,s*
mhkamaw *find TA*
nimhkamawa *TA,ind,1s,3s*
mhkateewalwi *coal NI*
mhkateewalo *NI,p*
mhkateewi *black PM*
mhkateewi *PM*

mhkateewkolaye *priest NA*
    mhkateewkolaye *NA,3s*
    mhkateewkolayeeki *NA,3p*
    mhkateewkolayeeli *NA,4s*
    mhkateewkolayeemwahi *NA/POSS,3p,4p*
    mhkateewkolayehi *NA,4p*
mhkateewt *make black TI_2*
    mhkateewto *TI,ind,2s,0s*
mhkateokolayeewi *be a priest AI*
    mhkateewkolayeewici *AI,conj,3s*
    mhkateewkolayeewita *AI,part,3s*
mhkaw *find TA*
    homhkawaali *TA,ind,3s,4s*
    homhkawaawaali *TA,ind,3p,4s*
    homhkawaawahi *TA,ind,3p,4p*
    homhkawahi *TA,ind,3s,4p*
    kimhkaakoopi *TA,ind,3,2s*
    kimhkaakowa *TA,ind,3s,2p*
    mhkaakooli *TA,ind,4s,3s*
    mhkawa *TA,ind,1s,3s*
    mhkawaaci *TA,conj,3s,4*
    mhkawaali *TA,ind,3s,4s*
    mhkawaape *TA,ind,1x,3*
    mhkawaawa *TA,ind,2p,3s*
    mhkawaawaaci *TA,conj,3p,4*
    mhkawaawaaki *TA,ind,2p,3p*
    mhkawahi *TA,ind,3s,4p*
    mhkawakwe *TA,conj,1i,3*
    mhkaweekwe *TA,conj,2p,3*
    mhkawipwa *TA,ind,2p,1s*
    nimhkawaape *TA,ind,1x,3*
mhkaweelem *remember TA*
    mhkaweelemehko *TA,imp,2p,3*
    mhkaweelemilo *TA,imp,2s,1s*
mhkaweelemoofo *be remembered AI*
    maamhkaweelemoofoci *AI,conj,3s*
mhkaweelet *remember TI_1*
    homhkaweeleta *TI,ind,3s,0s*
    homhkaweeletaanaawa *TI,ind,3p,0*
    kimhkaweeletaanaawa *TI,ind,2p,0*
    mhkaweeleta *TI,ind,3s,0s*
    mhkaweeletaki *TI,conj,3s,0*
    mhkaweeletamane *TI,subj,2s,0*
    mhkaweeletameekwe *TI,conj,2p,0*
    mhkaweeletamehi *TI,ind,4p,0*
    mhkaweeletamoko *TI,imp,2p,0*

    mhkaweeletano *TI,imp,2s,0*
    nimhkaweeletaape *TI,ind,1x,0*
mhkawesiteheewe *recollection NI*
    kimhkawesiteheewenwaki
NI/POSS/LOC,2p
mhkife *shoe NI*
    homahkifena *NI/POSS,3s,p*
    mhkifena *NI,p*
mhkoofo *be found AI*
    mhkoofo *AI,ind,3s*
mhsaawi *big, great II*
    mhsaaki *II,conj,0*
    mhsaawi *II,ind,0s*
mhseelwa *large group NA*
    mhseelooki *NA,3p*
    mhseelwa *NA,3s*
mhseeweewaskwi *mint NI*
    mhseeweewaskwi *NI,s*
mhseloowe *large group, multitude NI*
    homhseloowenwa *NI/POSS,3p*
mhsi *much, a lot PM*
    mhsi *PM*
mhsi-okima *great chief, great king NA*
    mhsi-okima *NA,3s*
    mhsi-okimaaki *NA,3p*
    mhsi-okimaali *NA,4s*
mhsi-olakeesi *big boat NI*
    mhsi-olakeeleki *NI/LOC*
    mhsi-olakeesi *NI,s*
mhsiilakim *magnify TA*
    homhsiilakimaali *TA,ind,3s,4s*
mhsiilefi *big, great AI*
    mhsiilefi *AI,ind,3s*
    mhsiilefiwi *AI,ind,3s*
mhsiilefi *great one NA*
    homhsiilefiimwahi *NA/POSS,3p,4p*
mhsikamikwi *synagogue NI*
    homhsikamikomwaaki *NI/POSS/LOC,3p*
    kimhsikamikomwaaki *NI/POSS/LOC,2p*
    mhsikamiko *NI,p*
    mhsikamikoki *NI/LOC*
    mhsikamikwi *NI,s*
    nimhsikamikomena *NI/POSS,1x*
mhsikil *big, great AI*
    mhsikilwa *AI,ind,3s*
mhsikilo *great one NA*
    homhsikiloomwahi *NA/POSS,3p,4p*

mhsikilohtaw *rule TA*
    mhsikilohtawaawaaci *TA,conj,3p,4*
mhsikilohtawiwee *rule AI*
    mehsikilohtawiweecki *AI/IC,part,3p*
mhsilot *magnify TI_1*
    mhsilotaki *TI,conj,3s,0*
mhsinaakofi *appear large AI*
    mhsinaakofici *AI,conj,3s*
mhsinepi *sea NI*
    mhsinepi *NI,s*
    mhsinepiki *NI/LOC*
mhsiski *leaf, branch NI*
    homhsiskeema *NI/POSS,3s,p*
    mhsiske *NI,p*
    mhsiski *NI,s*
mhsiskiwiiyaa *be in leaf II*
    mhsiskiwiiya *II,ind,0*
mhskeekwi *lake NI*
    mhskeekwi *NI,s*
mhskotehkwalwi *grass NI*
    mhskotehkwalo *NI,p*
mhskotehkwalwihki *grassy II*
    mhskotehkwalwihki *II,ind,0s*
mhskowilokeewe *blood disease NI*
    homhskowilokeewe *NI/POSS,3s,s*
    mhskowilokeewe *NI,s*
mhskwaawi *red*
    mhskwaawi
mhskwakokwe *farthing NI*
    mhskwakkwe *NI,s*
    mhskwakokwe *NI,s*
mhskwi *blood NI*
    homhskomi *NI/POSS,3s,s*
    homhskomilici *NI/POSS,4*
    homhskomwa *NI/POSS,3p*
    mhskwi *NI,s*
    nimhskomeki *NI/POSS/LOC,1s*
    nimhskomi *NI/POSS,1s,s*
mhtekoniwi *become a tree II*
    mhtekoniwi *II,ind,0s*
mhtekwaapiiwe *armor NI*
    homhtekwaapiiwe *NI/POSS,3s,s*
mhtekwi *tree NI*
    mhteko *NI,p*
    mhtekoki *NI/LOC*
    mhtekwi *NI,s*

miic *eat TI_3*
    homiici *TI,ind,3s,0s*
    homiicinaawa *TI,ind,3p,0*
    kimiicinaawa *TI,ind,2p,0*
    meemiicicki *TI/IC,part,3p,0*
    meemiicita *TI/IC,part,3s,0*
    meemiiciwaaci *TI/IC,conj,3p,0*
    miici *TI,ind,3s,0s ; TI,ind,1s,0s*
    miicici *TI,conj,3s,0*
    miiciki *TI,conj,3,0*
    miiciko *TI,imp,2p,0*
    miicilici *TI,conj,4,0*
    miicinaawa *TI,ind,3p,0*
    miicipe *TI,ind,1x,0*
    miicita *TI,part,3s,0*
    miicite *TI,subj,3s,0*
    miiciwaaci *TI,conj,3p,0*
    miiciya *TI,conj,1s,0*
    miiciyakwe *TI,conj,1i,0*
    miiciyani *TI,conj,2s,0*
    miiciyeekwe *TI,conj,2p,0 ; TI,subj,2p,0*
miikeefa *pearl NA*
    miikeefali *NA,4s*
    miikeefhi *NA,4p*
miikehfa *pearl NA*
    kimiikehfemwaaki *NA/POSS,2p,3p*
miil *give TA*
    homiilaali *TA,ind,3s,4s*
    homiilaawaali *TA,ind,3p,4s*
    homiilaawahi *TA,ind,3p,4p*
    homiilahi *TA,ind,3s,4p*
    homiilekooli *TA,ind,4s,3s*
    kimiilekowa *TA,ind,3s,2p*
    kimiilekwa *TA,ind,3s,2s*
    kimiilelepe *TA,ind,1x,2*
    kimiilelepwa *TA,ind,1s,2p*
    kimiili *TA,ind,2s,1s*
    kimiilipwa *TA,ind,2p,1*
    meemiilaaci *TA/IC,conj,3s,4*
    meemiilehka *TA/IC,part,3,2s*
    meemiilelakwe *TA/IC,part,3,1i*
    meemiilici *TA/IC,conj,3s,1s*
    meemiiliyani *TA/IC,conj,2s,1s*
    miilaaci *TA,conj,3s,4*
    miilaaki *TA,ind,1s,3p*
    miilaali *TA,ind,3s,4s*

miilaape *TA,ind,1x,3*
miilaata *TA,part,3s,4*
miilaawa *TA,ind,2p,3s*
miilaawaaci *TA,conj,3p,4*
miilaawaali *TA,ind,3p,4s*
miilaawahi *TA,ind,3p,4p*
miilaci *TA,conj,2s,3*
miilahi *TA,ind,3s,4p*
miilaki *TA,conj,1s,3*
miilakici *TA,conj,1x,3*
miileekwe *TA,conj,2p,3*
miilehki *TA,conj,3,2s*
miilehko *TA,imp,2p,3*
miilekoci *TA,conj,4,3s*
miilekona *TA,ind,3s,1i*
miilekonaawa *TA,ind,0,2p*
miilekoopi *TA,ind,3,1s*
miilekoopwa *TA,ind,3,2p*
miilekowa *TA,ind,3s,2p*
miilekowaaci *TA,conj,4,3p*
miilekowaaki *TA,ind,3p,2p*
miilekwa *TA,ind,3s,2s ; TA,ind,3s,1s*
miilekwi *TA,ind,,3s*
miilele *TA,ind,1s,2s*
miilelepwa *TA,ind,1s,2p*
miilelwaakwe *TA,conj,3,2p ; TA,subj,3,2p*
miilete *TA,subj,,3*
miili *TA,imp,2s,3 ; TA,ind,2s,1s*
miilici *TA,conj,3s,1s*
miiliko *TA,imp,2p,1s*
miililo *TA,imp,2s,1s*
miilinaake *TA,imp,2,1x*
miilipwa *TA,ind,2p,1s*
miilita *TA,part,3s,1s*
miiliyani *TA,conj,2s,1s*
nimiila *TA,ind,1s,3*
nimiilaaki *TA,ind,1s,3p*
miileti *give [reciprocal] AI*
miiletipi *AI,ind,3*
miilia *Melea NA*
miilia *NA,3s*
miiliwee *give AI*
maamiiliweeta *AI/IC,part,3s*
miiliwe *AI,ind,3s ; AI,ind,2s*
miiliweeci *AI,conj,3s*
miiliweecki *AI,part,3p*

miiliweeki *AI,ind,3p ; AI,conj,3*
miiliweeko *AI,imp,2p*
miiliweelici *AI,conj,4*
miiliweepe *AI,ind,1x*
miiliweepi *AI,ind,3*
miiliweewaaci *AI,conj,3p*
miiliweeya *AI,conj,1s*
nimiiliwe *AI,ind,1s*
miiliweewe *gift NI*
miiliweewe *NI,s*
miiloofo *be given AI*
meemiiloofoci *AI/IC,conj,3s*
meemiiloofocki *AI/IC,part,3p*
meemiiloofoyeekwe *AI/IC,conj,2p*
miiloofo *AI,ind,3s*
miiloofoci *AI,conj,3s*
miiloofolici *AI,conj,4*
miiloofooki *AI,ind,3p*
miiloofota *AI,part,3s*
miiloofoyane *AI,subj,2s*
miiloowi *nevertheless, yet*
miiloowi
miinhka *seed NI*
homiinhka *NI/POSS,3s,s*
miinhka *NI,s*
miinhkaana *NI,s*
miinhkaw *raise up seed TA*
miinhkawaali *TA,ind,3s,4s*
miinhkawaskwi *herb NI*
miinhkawaskwi *NI,s*
miinikaawise *bramble bush NA*
miinikaawisehi *NA,4p*
miisaama *messenger NA*
nimiisaama *NA/POSS,1s,3s*
miisamaakee *serve, minister AI*
maamiisamaakeecki *AI/IC,part,3p*
miisamaake *AI,ind,3s*
miisamaakeeci *AI,conj,3s*
miisamaakeema *servant, messenger*
homiisamaakeemhhi *NA/POSS,3s,4p*
nimiisamaakeema *NA/POSS,1s,3s*
miisamaakeewe *ministering, ministration NI*
homiisamaakeewe *NI/POSS,3s,s*
miisamaw *serve, minister to TA*
homiisamaakohi *TA,ind,4p,3s*
homiisamawaali *TA,ind,3s,4s*

homiisamawaawaali *TA,ind,3p,4s*
homiisamawahi *TA,ind,3s,4p*
miisamaakohi *TA,ind,4p,3s*
miisamaweci *TA,conj,,3*
miisamawite *TA,subj,3s,1s*
miyaalahkowaafo *be condemned AI*
miyaalahkowaafolici *AI,conj,4*
miyaalahkowaafoowe *condemnation NI*
miyaalahkowaafoowe *NI,s*
miyaalahkowaal *condemn TA*
kimiyaalahkowaalekwa *TA,ind,3s,2s*
kimiyaalahkowaalele *TA,ind,1s,2s*
miyaalahkowaalahi *TA,ind,3s,4p*
miyaalahkowaaloofo *be condemned, be sentenced AI*
miyaalahkowaaloofo *AI,ind,3s*
miyaalahkowaaloofolici *AI,ind,3s*
miyaalahkowaat *condemn TI*
miyaalahkowaataanaawa *TI,ind,3p,0*
miyaalefii *fail AI*
miyaalefiiki *AI,ind,3p*
miyaalefiiwe *failure, fault NI*
miyaalefiiwe *NI,s*
miyaalefiiyaa *fail II*
miyaalefiiya *II,ind,0*
miyaalet *corrupt II*
miyaaletwi *II,ind,0s*
miyaanileniwi *be a young person AI*
mayaanileniwiya *AI/IC,conj,1s*
miyaash *affect, injure TA*
homaamiyaasheko *TA,ind,0s,3s*
homaamiyaashekona *TA,ind,0p,3s*
homiyaasheko *TA,ind,0s,3s*
homiyaashekona *TA,ind,0p,3s*
maamiyaashekoci *TA/IC,conj,0,3s*
miyaasheko *TA,ind,0s,3s*
miyaashoofo *be defiled AI*
miyaashoofowaaci *AI,conj,3p*
miyaasi *false PM*
miyaasi *PM*
miyaasi-ash *tempt TA*
miyaasi-ashekooli *TA,ind,4s,3s*
miyaasi-ashetiiwe *temptation NI*
miyaasi-ashetiiwe *NI,s*
miyaasi-ashetiiweneki *NI/LOC*
miyaasimamiiloowefi *perverse AI*

mamiyaasimamiiloowefita *AI/IC,part,3s*
miyaasimeekiifa *goat NA*
miyaasimeekiifhi *NA,4p*
miyaasimekofih *dishonor TA*
kimiyaasimekofihipwa *TA,ind,2p,1*
miyaasinamoowe *perdition NI*
miyaasinamoowe *NI,s*
miyaasipawiifa *dove NA*
miyaasipawiifa *NA,3s*
miyaasipawiifaki *NA,3p*
miyaasipawiifhi *NA,4p*
miyaasiwaskwi *weed NI*
miyaasiwasko *NI,p*
miyaast *ruin, defile TI_2*
miyaastoowaaci *TI,conj,3p,0*
miyeek *sell TI_3*
homiyeeke *TI,subj,3s,0*
miyeeki *sell AI*
miyeekicki *AI,part,3p*
miyeekiko *AI,imp,2p*
miyeekilo *AI,imp,2s*
miyeekipi *AI,ind,3*
miyeekite *AI,subj,3s*
miyeekin *sell TA*
maamiyeekinaacki *TA/IC,part,3p,4*
miyeekine *sell AI*
maamiyeekinelici *AI/IC,conj,4*
miyeekinoofo *be sold AI*
miyeekinoofoci *AI,conj,3s*
miyeewe *way, path NI*
homiyeeweneefa *NI/DIM/POSS,3s,p*
miyeeweneefa *NI/DIM,p*
miyeeweneki *NI/LOC*
miyeeweniki *NI/LOC*
miyeewi *way, path NI*
homiyeewali *NI/POSS,3s,p*
homiyeewi *NI/POSS,3s,s*
kimiyeewi *NI/POSS,2s,s*
miyeewali *NI,p*
miyeewi *NI,s*
miyeewiki *NI/LOC*
mohci *even, even so*
mohci
mohkaaci *[as declaration] PV*
mohkaaci *PV*
mohkaacimo *declare AI*

mohkaacimo *AI,ind,3s*
mohkaatotamaw *declare TA*
   homohkaatotamawaawaali *TA,ind,3p,4s*
   mohkaacimaali *TA,ind,3s,4s*
   mohkaatotamaakona *TA,ind,3s,1i*
   mohkaatotamaakowa *TA,ind,3s,2p*
   mohkaatotamawahi *TA,ind,3s,4p*
mohkeeska *appearing suddenly PV*
   mohkeeska *PV*
moht *put dung on TI_2*
   mohto *TI,ind,1s,0s*
mokitan *spring up II*
   mokitanwili *II,ind,4*
moni *money [loanword] NI*
   homonemilici *NI/POSS,4*
   homonemwa *NI/POSS,3p*
   moni *NI,s*
   nimonemi *NI/POSS,1s,s*
monika *treasury NI*
   monika *NI,s*
   monikaaneki *NI/LOC*
monikaafa *banker NA*
   monikaafaki *NA,3p*
monipiitaaka *purse NI*
   homoni-piitaakanwaaki *NI/POSS/LOC,3p*
   kimonipiitaakanwaaki *NI/POSS/LOC,2p*
   monipiitaaka *NI,s*
   monipiitaakana *NI,p*
mookwatekwa *moth NA*
   mookwatekwa *NA,3s*
mooleelet *perceive TI_1*
   homooleeleta *TI,ind,3s,0s*
   homooleeletaanaawa *TI,ind,3p,0*
   mooleeleta *TI,ind,3s,0s*
   mooleeletaanaawa *TI,ind,2p,0 ; TI,ind,3p,0*
   mooleeletamowaaci *TI,conj,3p,0*
   nimooleeleta *TI,ind,1s,0s*
mooleeletamaw *perceive TA*
   homooleeletamawahi *TA,ind,3s,4p*
   mooleeletamawahi *TA,ind,3s,4p*
moosa *each*
   moosa
moosaki *often*
   moosaki
moosatawi *always PV*
   homoosatawi *PV*

moosatawi *PV*
nimoosatawi *PV*
moosikiiskwaacim *prophesy TA*
   moosikiiskwaacimekowa *TA,ind,3s,2p*
moosikiiskwaacimo *prophesy AI*
   moosikiiskwaacimolo *AI,imp,2s*
   moosikiiskwaacimooki *AI,ind,3p*
   moosikiiskwaacimooli *AI,ind,4s*
   nimoosikiiskwaacimope *AI,ind,1x*
moosikiiskwaacimohtaw *prophesy TA*
   moosikiiskwaacimohtawinaake
TA,imp,2,1x
moosikiiskwaatot *prophesy TI_1*
   homoosikiiskwaatota *TI,ind,3s,0s*
moosikiiskwe *prophesy AI*
   maamoosikiiskwecki *AI/IC,part,3p*
   maamoosikiiskweeta *AI/IC,part,3s*
   maamoosikiiskwelici *AI/IC,conj,4*
moosikiiskweewe *prophecy NI*
   homoosikiiskweewe *NI/POSS,3s,s*
moosinehikan *debt NI*
   moosinehika *NI,s*
   nimoosinehikanena *NI/POSS,1x*
moosinehikan *debtor NA*
   homoosinehikanhhi *NA/POSS,3s,4p*
   moosinehikanhhi *NA,4p*
moosinehikee *owe AI*
   kimoosinehike *AI,ind,2s*
   memoosinehikeeta *AI/IC,part,3s*
   memoosinehikeeyani *AI/IC,conj,2s*
   moosinehike *AI,ind,3s*
moosinehw *owe to TA*
   kimoosinehwa *TA,ind,2s,3s*
   meemoosinehokoci *TA/IC,conj,4,3s*
   meemoosinehwiyamekicki
TA/IC,part,3p,1x
   meemoosinehwiyameta *TA/IC,part,3s,1x*
moosisii *Moses NA*
   moosisii *NA,3s*
   moosisiili *NA,4s*
moositehee *perceive AI*
   kimoositeheepwa *AI,ind,2p*
   moositehe *AI,ind,3s*
   moositeheeci *AI,conj,3s*
   moositeheeki *AI,ind,3p*
   moositeheewaaci *AI,conj,3p*
moospaten *high PM*

moospatenwi *PM*
moospeelemehoofo *be exhalted AI*
   moospeelemehoofo *AI,ind,3s*
moospeelemekofih *exhalt TA*
   moospeelemekofihekoopi *TA,ind,3,2s*
moospeelemekofiht *exhalt TI_2*
   moospeelemekofihto *TI,ind,3s,0s*
moospeelemekwh *exhalt TA*
   moospeelemekwhahi *TA,ind,3s,4p*
moospeelemekwhoofo *be exalted AI*
   moospeelemekwhoofo *AI,ind,3s*
   moospeelemekwihoofo *AI,ind,3s*
moospeelemekwit *exhalt TI_2*
   memoospeelemekwitoota *TI/IC,part,3s,0*
moospeelemoofo *be highly esteemed AI*
   meemoospeelemoofota *AI/IC,part,3s*
moospi *high*
   moospi
moospimekofiiwi *high PM*
   memoospimekofiiwi *PM*
   moospimekofiiwi *PM*
moospimhkateewkolayeewimekofiiwe *high-priesthood NI*
   homoospimhkateewkolayeewimekofiiwe
nwaaki *NI/POSS/LOC,3p*
moost *have a premonition about TI_2*
   homoosto *TI,ind,3s,0s*
   moosto *TI,ind,3s,0s*
   nimoosto *TI,ind,1s,0s*
moskifaa *come to the surface AI*
   memoskifaata *AI/IC,part,3s*
moskofe *come to the surface AI*
   moskofe *AI,ind,3s*
   moskwife *AI,ind,3s*
mota *cloth NI*
   motaawali *NI,p*
moyaleeweelem *despise TA*
   homoyaleeweelemaali *TA,ind,3s,4s*
moyaleewilotaw *wrong TA*
   meemoyaleewilotoolwaakwe *TA/IC,part,3,2p*
naakaafi *stay, tarry AI*
   naakaafi *AI,ind,3s*
   naakaafiilici *AI,conj,4*
   neekaafiilici *AI/IC,conj,4*
naakaani *guide, lead AI*
   naakaaniicki *AI,part,3p*

naakahoowefiiwe *lasciviousness NI*
   naakahoowefiiwe *NI,s*
naakahoowiikweka *harlot NA*
   naakahoowiikweki *NA,3p*
naakaht *delay TI_2*
   honaakahto *TI,ind,3s,0s*
naakawhkwe *harlot NA*
   naakawhkwehi *NA,4p*
naakofi *appear, look like AI*
   naakofi *AI,ind,3s*
   naakofiiki *AI,ind,3p*
   naakofiyeekwe *AI,conj,2p*
naaleta *some*
   naaleta
naanaanhhaacimo *lie AI*
   naanaanhhaacimota *AI,part,3s*
naanatawhcikee *heal, be a physician AI*
   naanatawhcikeelici *AI,conj,4*
   naanatawhcikeeta *AI,part,3s*
naanemi *near*
   naanemi
naanhhaaci *falsely PV*
   naanhhaaci *PV*
naanhhaacim *lie TA*
   naanhhaacimelwaakwe *TA,conj,3,2p*
naanhhaacimoowe *lie NI*
   naanhhaacimoowe *NI,s*
naanhhaacimoowi *falsely PV*
   naanhhaacimoowi *PV*
naanhsihka *alone*
   naanhsihka
naanhsikaawi *alone AI*
   ninaanhsikaawi *AI,ind,1s*
naanohkaach *abuse TA*
   naanohkaachaawaaci *TA,conj,3p,4*
   naanohkaachaawaaki *TA,ind,2p,3p*
   naanohkaachaawahi *TA,ind,3p,4p*
   naanohkaachekowaaki *TA,ind,3p,2p*
   naanohkaachelwaakwe *TA,conj,3,2p*
   naanohkaachiwaate *TA,subj,3p,1s*
   neenaanohkaachelwaakwe *TA/IC,part,3,2p*
naanohkaachetiiwe *persecution NI*
   naanohkaachetiiwe *NI,s*
naanohkaachoofo *be persecuted AI*
   naanohkaachoofocki *AI,part,3p*
naanoomilohan *shake in the wind II*

naanoomilohanwi *II,ind,0s*

naapeeya *cock, rooster*
naapeeya *NA,3s*

naapehfemh *make into a eunuch TA*
nenaapehfemhaawaaci *TA/IC,conj,3p,4*

naapehfemht *make into a eunuch TI*
nenaapehfemhtoocki *TI/IC,part,3p,0*

naapehfemo *eunuch*
naapehfemooki *NA,3p*

naasani *Nahshon NA*
naasani *NA,3s*
naasoniili *NA,4s*

naaselefi *Nazareth NI*
naaselefi *NI,s*

naaselefilenawe *Nazarene NA*
naaselefilenawe *NA,3s*

naaselefileni *Nazarene NA*
naaselefileni *NA,3s*

naaseliini *Nazarene NA*
naaseliini *NA,3s*

naaseliiniiwileni *Nazarene NA*
naaseliiniiwileniili *NA,4s*

naaseliinileni *Nazarene NA*
naaseliinileni *NA,3s*

naasonii *Nashon NA*
naasonii *NA,3s*

naaswasahte *beautiful II*
naaswasahte *II,ind,0s*

naasweelet *like, love TI_1*
honaasweeletaanaawa *TI,ind,3p,0*

naaswi *fine, delicate PM*
naaswi *PM*
neenaaswi *PM/IC*

naaswihtaw *make beautiful, decorate TA*
kinaaswihtawaawaaki *TA,ind,2p,3p*

naatamaat *help TI_1*
naatamaatano *TI,imp,2s,0*

naatamaatiiwe *help NI*
naatamaatiiwe *NI,s*

naatamaw *help TA*
naatamawaawaaci *TA,conj,3p,4*
naatamawici *TA,conj,3s,1s*
naatamawilo *TA,imp,2s,1s*
naatamawinaake *TA,imp,2,1x*

naate *go after, recover AI*
naate *AI,ind,3s*

naateke *AI,subj,3*

naati *nard [loanword] NI*
naati *NI,s*

naatiiwi *nard PM*
naatiiwi *PM*

naawaloskaw *follow TA*
naawaloskawiko *TA,imp,2p,1s*

naawalwi *according to, after PV*
honaawalwi *PV*
naawalwi *PV*
ninaawalwi *PV*

nahalweelem *have as kin TA*
nehalweelemaaci *TA/IC,conj,3s,4*
nehalweelemaawaaci *TA/IC,conj,3p,4*
nehalweelemacki *TA/IC,part,2s,3p*

nahiika *up there, near, up to, ready*
nahiika

nakacilotaw *try out TA*
nakacilotawaki *TA,conj,1s,3*

nakacit *leave TI_1*
honakacita *TI,ind,3s,0s*

nakahsin *stay, tarry AI*
nakahsiki *AI,conj,3s*
nakahsinwa *AI,ind,3s*

nakahsinoom *stay with, tarry with TA*
honakahsinoomahi *TA,ind,3s,4p*

nakal *leave TA*
honakalaali *TA,ind,3s,4s*
honakalaawaali *TA,ind,3p,4s*
honakalaawahi *TA,ind,3p,4p*
honakalahi *TA,ind,3s,4p*
honakaleko *TA,ind,0s,3s*
honakalekohi *TA,ind,4p,3s*
nakalaali *TA,ind,3s,4s*
nakalaate *TA,subj,3s,4*
nakalahi *TA,ind,3s,4p*
nakalekoci *TA,conj,4,3s*
nakalekoopi *TA,ind,3,1s*
nakalekwa *TA,ind,3s,1s*
nakalelepwa *TA,ind,1s,2p*
nakasi *TA,imp,2s,3*
nakasici *TA,conj,3s,1s*

nakaloofo *be left AI*
nakaloofo *AI,ind,3s*

nakamo *sing AI*
nakamowaaci *AI,conj,3p*

nakamoowe *music NI*
   nakamoowe *NI,s*
nakat *leave TI_1*
   honakata *TI,ind,3s,0s*
   honakataanaawa *TI,ind,3p,0*
   kinakataanaawa *TI,ind,2p,0*
   nakata *TI,ind,3s,0s*
   nakataka *TI,part,3s,0*
   nakatamoko *TI,imp,2p,0*
   nakatano *TI,imp,2s,0*
   ninakata *TI,ind,1s,0s*
   ninakataape *TI,ind,1x,0*
nakatamaw *leave TA*
   honakatamawaali *TA,ind,3s,4s*
   kinakatamaakoopwa *TA,ind,3,2p*
   kinakatamoolepwa *TA,ind,1s,2p*
nakatame *leave AI*
   nakatame *AI,ind,3s*
nakatefiiweni *have as a custom AI*
   nakatefiiwenici *AI,conj,3s*
nakaye *? since; it being the case that ?*
   nakaye
nakeeskaa *cease II*
   nakeeska *II,ind,0*
nakikahtoote *be stopped II*
   nakikahtooteeli *II,ind,4*
nakin *hinder TA*
   nakinaali *TA,ind,3s,4s*
   nakinaawaali *TA,ind,3p,4s*
naksk *meet, go against TI_1*
   honakskaanaawa *TI,ind,3p,0*
nakskaatiim *meet with TA*
   nakskaatiimaaci *TA,conj,3s,4*
nakskaw *meet TA*
   honakskaakohi *TA,ind,4p,3s*
   honakskaakooli *TA,ind,4s,3s*
   honakskawaali *TA,ind,3s,4s*
   honakskawahi *TA,ind,3s,4p*
   nakskaakowa *TA,ind,3s,2p*
   nakskawaaci *TA,conj,3s,4*
   nakskawaawaaci *TA,conj,3p,4*
   nakskawaawaali *TA,ind,3p,4s*
   nakskawehko *TA,imp,2p,3*
nakwaaka *trap NI*
   nakwaaka *NI,s*
nal *go after TA*

nalaawaaci *TA,conj,3p,4*
   nalaawaali *TA,ind,3p,4s*
namaciinhki *left side NI*
   honamaciinhkiki *NI/POSS/LOC,3s*
   kinamaciinhki *NI/POSS,2s,s*
   kinamaciinhkiki *NI/POSS/LOC,2s*
   namaciinhkiki *NI/LOC*
   ninamaciinhkiki *NI/POSS/LOC,1s*
namefkaal *fish for TA*
   naanamefkaalaacki *TA/IC,part,3p,4*
   neenamefkaalaacki *TA/IC,part,3p,4*
namefkee *fish AI*
   naanamefkeecki *AI/IC,part,3p*
   namefke *AI,ind,1s*
namehfa *fish NA*
   namefhi *NA,4p*
   namehfa *NA,3s*
   namehfaki *NA,3p*
   namehfali *NA,4s*
   namehfiifaki *NA/DIM,3p*
namehfilehfi *whale NA*
   namehfilehfi *NA,3s*
namehfileni *fisherman NA*
   namehfileniiki *NA,3p*
namoowe *vision, happening NI*
   namoowe *NI,s*
   namooweneki *NI/LOC*
nanaacimemekiniteheewe *imagination NI*
   nanaacimemekiniteheeweneki *NI/LOC*
nanaacitehee *hope AI*
   nanaaciteheeki *AI,ind,3p*
nanaaciteheewe *hope NI*
   kinanaaciteheewenwa *NI/POSS,2p*
nanahi *ready, prepared PV*
   nanahi *PV*
nanahihfet *prepare TI_2*
   nanahihfeto *TI,ind,3s,0s*
nanahii *prepare AI*
   nanahiicki *AI,part,3p*
nanahiiwe *preparation NI*
   honanahiiwenwa *NI/POSS,3p*
   nanahiiwe *NI,s*
   nanahiwe *NI,s*
nanahilot *prepare TI_1*
   honanahilotaanaawa *TI,ind,3p,0*
   nanahilotamowaaci *TI,conj,3p,0*

nanahilotamaw *prepare* TA
    nanahilotamawici *TA,conj,3s,1s*
    nanahilotamoolako *TA,conj,1s,2p*
    nanahilotamoolepwa *TA,ind,1s,2p*
nanahim *preach* TA
    honanahimahi *TA,ind,3s,4p*
    nanahimaki *TA,conj,1s,3*
    nenahimaata *TA/IC,part,3s,4*
nanahimiwee *preach* AI
    honanahimiweewilici *AI,conj,4*
    nanahimiwe *AI,ind,3s*
    nanahimiweeci *AI,conj,3s*
    nanahimiweeki *AI,ind,3p*
    nanahimiweeko *AI,imp,2p*
    nanahimiweelici *AI,conj,4*
    nanahimiweepi *AI,ind,3*
    nanahimiweeya *AI,conj,1s*
nanahimoofo *be preached to* AI
    nanahimoofoci *AI,conj,3s*
    nanahimoofooki *AI,ind,3p*
nanahit *preach* TI_1
    nanahitaana *TI,ind,1s,0p*
nanahkawi *Gentile* NA
    nanahkawilenawehi *NA,4p*
    nanahkawileni *NA,3s*
    nanahkawilenihi *NA,4p*
    nanahkawileniiki *NA,3p*
    nanahkawiyeeniiki *NA,3p*
nanahkot *contradict* TI_1
    nanahkotamowaaci *TI,conj,3p,0*
nanahpaachoofo *be humbled* AI
    nanahpaachoofo *AI,ind,3s*
nanahpaaciilefi *humble* AI
    nanahpaaciilefi *AI,ind,3s*
    nanahpaaciilefiko *AI,imp,2p*
    neenahpaaciilefilici *AI/IC,conj,4*
    ninanahpaaciilefi *AI,ind,1s*
nanahpaaciilefiiwe *lowliness* NI
    honanahpaaciilefiiwenilici *NI/POSS,4*
nanahpaacikeemoowe *begging* NI
    nanahpaacikeemoowe *NI,s*
nanahpaacila *[humble]*
    nanahpaacila
nanahpaacilefa *humble person* NA
    nanahpaacilefaki *NA,3p*
nanahpaacilot *humble* TI_1

nanahpaacilotaa *TI,ind,3s,0s*
    neenanahpaacilotaka *TI/IC,part,3s,0*
nanahpaacilotoofo *be humbled* AI
    nanahpaacilotoofo *AI,ind,3s*
nanahpaacim *beg, pray, beseech* TA
    honanahpaacimaali *TA,ind,3s,4s*
    honanahpaacimaawaali *TA,ind,3p,4s*
    honanahpaacimekohi *TA,ind,4p,3s*
    honanahpaacimekooli *TA,ind,4s,3s*
    kinanahpaacimele *TA,ind,1s,2s*
    kinanahpaacimi *TA,ind,2s,1s*
    nanahpaacimaki *TA,conj,1s,3*
    nanahpaacimekohi *TA,ind,4p,3s*
    nanahpaacimekooli *TA,ind,4s,3s*
    ninanahpaacimaaki *TA,ind,1s,3p*
nanahpaacimekwhoofo *be humbled* AI
    nanahpaacimekwhoofo *AI,ind,3s*
nanahpaacimekwt *humble* TI_2
    neenanahpaacimekwtoota *TI/IC,part,3s,0*
nanahpaacimoowe *begging* NI
    kinanahpaacimoowe *NI/POSS,2s,s*
    nanahpaacimoowena *NI,p*
nanahpaaciteheeweni *humble, lowly in heart* AI
    ninanahpaaciteheeweni *AI,ind,3s*
nanahpaact *humble* TI_2
    nanahpaacto *TI,ind,3s,0s*
nanakohw *forbid* TA
    kinanakohwaawaaki *TA,ind,2p,3p*
nanasfetaw *prepare* TA
    nanasfetawaaci *TA,conj,3s,4*
nanaskaci *endangered* PV
    nanaskaci *PV*
nanawacitehee *doubt* AI
    nanawaciteheeki *AI,ind,3p*
nanhtaaki *alone*
    nanhtaaki
naphtalii *Naphtali* NI
    niftelii *NI,s*
natawaaci *inquiring* PV
    natawaaci *PV*
natawaapam *look for* TA
    natawaapamaape *TA,ind,1x,3*
natawaapat *look for* TI_1
    natawaapataki *TI,conj,3s,0*
    natawaapatamelici *TI,conj,4,0*
    netawaapataka *TI/IC,part,3s,0*

natawaapi *look around* AI
   natawaapi *AI,ind,3s*
natohsee *ask* AI
   natohse *AI,ind,3s*
   natohseeko *AI,imp,2p*
   natohsehi *AI,ind,4p*
   niinatohseeki *AI,ind,3p*
natohseewe *question* NI
   natohseewe *NI,s*
   natohseewena *NI,p*
natohtame *ask* AI
   natohtamepwa *AI,ind,2p*
natohtaw *ask* TA
   honatohtaakohi *TA,ind,4p,3s*
   honatohtaakooli *TA,ind,4s,3s*
   honatohtawaali *TA,ind,3s,4s*
   honatohtawaawaali *TA,ind,3p,4s*
   honatohtawaawahi *TA,ind,3p,4p*
   honatohtawahi *TA,ind,3s,4p*
   kinatohtawi *TA,ind,2s,1s*
   kinatohtoolepwa *TA,ind,1s,2p*
   natohtaakoci *TA,conj,4,3s*
   natohtaakohi *TA,ind,4p,3s*
   natohtawaaci *TA,conj,3s,4*
   natohtawaali *TA,ind,3s,4s*
   natohtawaawaaci *TA,conj,3p,4*
   natohtawaawaali *TA,ind,3p,4s*
   natohtawehki *TA,conj,3,2s*
   natohtawehko *TA,imp,2p,3*
   natohtawi *TA,imp,2s,3*
   natohtawipwa *TA,ind,2p,1s*
   natohtoolako *TA,conj,1s,2p*
   natohtoolepwa *TA,ind,1s,2p*
   natohtoolwaakwe *TA,conj,3,2p*
   ninatohtaakwa *TA,ind,3s,1s*
natohtwaati *question, discuss [reciprocal]* AI
   kiniinatohtwaatipwa *AI,ind,2p*
   natohtwaatiwaaci *AI,conj,3p*
   niinatohtwaatiiki *AI,ind,3p*
natohtwaatiim *ask questions of, discuss with* TA
   kinatohtwaatiimaawaaki *TA,ind,2p,3p*
   natohtwaatiimaawaaci *TA,conj,3p,4*
natohtwaatiiwe *question* NI
   natohtwaatiiwe *NI,s*
   natohtwaatiiwena *NI,p*
natom *call for, ask for* TA

honatomaali *TA,ind,3s,4s*
kinatomekwa *TA,ind,3s,2s*
natomaali *TA,ind,3s,4s*
natomaawaaci *TA,conj,3p,4*
natomaki *TA,conj,1s,3*
ninatoma *TA,ind,1s,3s*
natoneh *seek* TI_1
   honatoneha *TI,ind,3s,0s*
   honatonehaanaawa *TI,ind,3p,0*
   kinatoneha *TI,ind,2s,0s*
   kinatonehaanaawa *TI,ind,2p,0*
   natoneha *TI,ind,3s,0s*
   natonehaanaawa *TI,ind,3p,0*
   natonehaki *TI,conj,3s,0*
   natonehama *TI,conj,1s,0*
   natonehamelici *TI,conj,4,0*
   natonehamoko *TI,imp,2p,0*
   natonehamowaaci *TI,conj,3p,0*
   neetonehaka *TI/IC,part,3s,0*
   neetonehakki *TI/IC,part,3p,0*
   ninatoneha *TI,ind,1s,0s*
natonehamaw *seek* TA
   honatonehamawaawaali *TA,ind,3p,4s*
   natonehamawaawaali *TA,ind,3p,4s*
natonehikee *seek* AI
   natonehike *AI,ind,3s*
   natonehikeeki *AI,ind,3p*
   natonehikeeko *AI,imp,2p*
   natonehikeeli *AI,ind,4s*
   natonehikeelo *AI,imp,2s*
   natonehikeepwa *AI,ind,2p*
   natonehikeewaaci *AI,conj,3p*
   neetonehikeeta *AI/IC,part,3s*
natonehikeeyaa *seek* II
   natonehikeeya *II,ind,0*
natonehw *seek* TA
   honatonehwaali *TA,ind,3s,4s*
   honatonehwaawaali *TA,ind,3p,4s*
   honatonehwahi *TA,ind,3s,4p*
   kinatonehokooki *TA,ind,3p,2s*
   kinatoneholepe *TA,ind,1x,2*
   kinatonehwa *TA,ind,2s,3s*
   kinatonehwaawa *TA,ind,2p,3s*
   kinatonehwipwa *TA,ind,2p,1*
   kinatonewhaawa *TA,ind,2p,3s*
   natonehohko *TA,imp,2p,3*

natonehokooki *TA,ind,3p,2s*
natonehwaali *TA,ind,3s,4s*
natonehwaawaali *TA,ind,3p,4s*
natonehwahi *TA,ind,3s,4p*
natonehweekwe *TA,conj,2p,3*
natonehwipwa *TA,ind,2p,1s*
natonehwiyeekwe *TA,conj,2p,1s ; TA,subj,2p,1s*
neetonehwaawaaci *TA/IC,conj,3p,4*
natonemaw *seek TA*
honatonemaakohi *TA,ind,4p,3s*
natot *ask for, seek TI_1*
honatota *TI,ind,3s,0s*
natota *TI,ind,3s,0s ; TI,ind,1s,0s*
natotaanaawa *TI,ind,2p,0*
natotameli *TI,ind,4s,0*
natotamoko *TI,imp,2p,0*
natotamowaaci *TI,conj,3p,0*
neetotaka *TI/IC,part,3s,0*
neetotameekwe *TI/IC,conj,2p,0*
neetotamelici *TI/IC,conj,4,0*
natotamaake *ask for AI*
natotamaake *AI,ind,3s*
natotamaakeeki *AI,ind,3p*
natotamaakeeko *AI,imp,2p*
neetotamaakeeta *AI/IC,part,3s*
neetotamaakeewaaci *AI/IC,conj,3p*
neetotamaakeeyeekwe *AI/IC,conj,2p*
natotamaw *ask TA*
honatotamaakooli *TA,ind,4s,3s*
natotamaakooli *TA,ind,4s,3s*
natotamawa *TA,ind,2s,3s*
natotamawaawa *TA,ind,2p,3s*
natotamawaawaali *TA,ind,3p,4s*
natotamaweekwe *TA,conj,2p,3*
natotamawi *TA,ind,2s,1s ; TA,imp,2s,3*
natotamawilo *TA,imp,2s,1s*
natotamawiyani *TA,conj,2s,1s*
natotamoolepe *TA,ind,1x,2*
neenatotamaakoci *TA/IC,conj,4,3s*
neetotamaakoci *TA,conj,4,3s*
neetotamawehka *TA/IC,part,3,2s*
nawaci *in passing; according to PV*
nawaci *PV*
nawafw *outrun TA*
honawafwaali *TA,ind,3s,4s*
honawafwaawahi *TA,ind,3p,4p*

nawhetiiwika *guest room NI*
nawhetiiwika *NI,s*
ninawhetiiwika *NI/POSS,1s,s*
nawhh *visit TA*
honawhhaawaali *TA,ind,3p,4s*
honawhhahi *TA,ind,3s,4p*
kinawhhelepe *TA,ind,1x,2*
kinawhhipwa *TA,ind,2p,1*
nawhhekope *TA,ind,0,1i*
nawhiwee *visit AI*
nawhiwe *AI,ind,3s*
nawicika *possessions NI*
honawicika *NI/POSS,3s,s*
nawito *about, approximately*
nawito
nawiwee *appear, seem AI*
nawiweeyeekwe *AI,conj,2p*
nawkofiiwat *be observed II*
nawkofiiwatwi *II,ind,0s*
nawoote *be carried, be borne II*
nawooteeki *II,conj,0*
nawtiim *appear to TA*
honawtiimaali *TA,ind,3s,4s*
honawtiimekooli *TA,ind,4s,3s*
nay *sit on, ride TA*
honayekohi *TA,ind,4p,3s*
honayekooli *TA,ind,4s,3s*
nayekoci *TA,conj,4,3s*
nayekooli *TA,ind,4s,3s*
nayehfaawi *? healthy, whole ? II*
nayehfaawike *II,subj,0*
nayelohci *pretending PV*
nayelohci *PV*
nayoote *be carried II*
nayooteeki *II,conj,0*
neefawe *who PR*
neefakiwe *PR*
neefaliwe *PR*
neefawe *PR*
neefhiwe *PR*
neekal *follow TA*
honeekalaali *TA,ind,3s,4s*
honeekalaawaali *TA,ind,3p,4s*
honeekaleko *TA,ind,0s,3s*
honeekalekohi *TA,ind,4p,3s*
honeekalekooli *TA,ind,4s,3s*

kineekalekona *TA,ind,3s,1i*
kineekalelepe *TA,ind,1x,2*
neekalaali *TA,ind,3s,4s*
neekalaawaali *TA,ind,3p,4s*
neekalehko *TA,imp,2p,3*
neekalekoci *TA,conj,4,3s*
neekalekona *TA,ind,3s,1i*
neekalekooli *TA,ind,4s,3s*
neekalekwa *TA,ind,3s,1s*
neekalele *TA,ind,1s,2s*
neekasi *TA,ind,2s,1s*
neekasilo *TA,imp,2s,1s*
neekasita *TA,part,3s,1s*
neekasite *TA,subj,3s,1s*
neeneekalekoci *TA/IC,conj,4,3s*
neeneekasita *TA/IC,part,3s,1s*
nineekalekooki *TA,ind,3p,1s*
nineekalekwa *TA,ind,3s,1s*
neekasiwee *follow AI*
    neekasiwe *AI,ind,3s*
    neekasiweeki *AI,ind,3p*
    neekasiweeli *AI,ind,4s*
    neeneekasiweecki *AI/IC,part,3p*
    neeneekasiyeekwe *AI/IC,conj,2p*
neekasiweeyaa *follow, come after II*
    nayeekasiweeyaaki *II/IC,conj,0*
    neekasiweeyaaki *II,conj,0*
neekat *follow TI_2*
    neekatona *TI,ind,1s,0s*
neekat *follow TI_1*
    neekataanaawa *TI,ind,3p,0*
neekee *see AI*
    neeke *AI,ind,3s*
    neekeeci *AI,conj,3s*
    neekeecki *AI,part,3p*
    neekeeki *AI,ind,3p*
    neekeepwa *AI,ind,2p*
    neekeewaate *AI,subj,3p*
    neekeeyakwe *AI,conj,1i*
neelohcilawi *be a hypocrite AI*
    nayeelohcilawiicki *AI/IC,part,3p*
neem *see TI_3*
    honeeme *TI,ind,3s,0s*
    honeemena *TI,ind,3s,0p*
    honeemenaawa *TI,ind,3p,0*
    kineeme *TI,ind,2s,0s*

kineemena *TI,ind,2s,0s*
kineemenaawa *TI,ind,2p,0*
kineemepe *TI,ind,1i,0*
neeme *TI,ind,2s,0s ; TI,ind,3s,0s ; TI,ind,1s,0s*
neemeka *TI,part,3s,0*
neemeki *TI,conj,3s,0*
neemelici *TI,conj,4,0*
neemelo *TI,imp,2s,0*
neemena *TI,ind,2s,0s*
neemenaawa *TI,ind,3p,0 ; TI,ind,2p,0*
neemepe *TI,ind,1x,0 ; TI,ind,1i,0*
neemetaako *TI,imp,1i,0*
neemeya *TI,conj,1s,0*
neemeyaake *TI,conj,1x,0*
neemeyane *TI,subj,2s,0*
neemeyani *TI,conj,2s,0*
neemeyeekwe *TI,conj,2p,0*
neemoko *TI,imp,2p,0*
neemooki *TI,conj,3s,0*
neemowaaci *TI,conj,3p,0*
neeneemeki *TI/IC,conj,3s,0*
neeneemekki *TI/IC,part,3p,0*
neeneemeyeekwe *TI/IC,conj,2p,0*
yeeneemeyeekwe *TI/IC,conj,2p,0*
neemani *Naaman NA*
    neemani *NA,3s*
neemaw *see TA*
    honeemawahi *TA,ind,3s,4p*
    neemawahi *TA,ind,3s,4p*
neemoote *be seen II*
    neemoote *II,ind,0*
    neemooteeki *II,conj,0*
neew *see TA*
    honeewaali *TA,ind,3s,4s*
    honeewaawaali *TA,ind,3p,4s*
    honeewaawahi *TA,ind,3p,4p*
    honeewahi *TA,ind,3s,4p*
    honookohi *TA,ind,4p,3s*
    honookooli *TA,ind,4s,3s*
    kineewa *TA,ind,2s,3s*
    kineewaaki *TA,ind,2s,3p*
    kinoole *TA,ind,1s,2s*
    kinoolepe *TA,ind,1x,2*
    naakowaaki *TA,ind,3p,2p*
    neeneewaacki *TA/IC,part,3p,4*
    neewa *TA,ind,2s,3s ; TA,ind,1s,3s*

neewaaci *TA,conj,3s,4*
neewaali *TA,ind,3s,4s*
neewaape *TA,ind,1x,3*
neewaawa *TA,ind,2p,3s*
neewaawaaci *TA,conj,3p,4*
neewaawaaki *TA,ind,2p,3p*
neewaawaali *TA,ind,3p,4s*
neewahi *TA,ind,3s,4p*
neeweekwe *TA,conj,2p,3*
neewi *TA,ind,2s,1s*
neewipwa *TA,ind,2p,1*
neewita *TA,part,3s,1s*
neewiyeekwe *TA,conj,2p,1s*
neewohki *TA,conj,3,2s*
nineewaaki *TA,ind,1s,3p*
nineewaape *TA,ind,1x,3*
nookoci *TA,conj,4,3s*
nookooki *TA,ind,3p,1s ; TA,ind,3p,2s*
nookowaaci *TA,conj,4,3p*
noolepwa *TA,ind,1s,2p*
noolwaakwe *TA,conj,3,2p*
yeeneewaawaaci *TA/IC,conj,3p,4*
neewiwee *perceive AI*
neewiweeki *AI,ind,3p*
neewiweepwa *AI,ind,2p*
neeyiiswi *both*
neeyiiswi
neeyoole *maybe*
neeyoole
nefeni *Nathan NA*
nefeni *NA,3s*
nefeniali *Nathanael NA*
nefeniali *NA,3s*
nefenialiili *NA,4s*
neha *Nahor NA*
neha *NA,3s*
nehalwaafi *related, own AI*
nehalwaafiici *AI,conj,3s*
nehalwaaka *own, belonging to oneself*
honehalwaaka
kinehalwaaka
nehalwaaka
nehami *Nahum NA*
nehami *NA,3s*
nehcipe *any*
nehcipe

nehcipehi *any PR*
nehcipeh *PR*
nehcipehi *PR*
nehfaapi *also*
nehfaapi
nehiwe *what, who PR*
nehiwe *PR*
nehiwesi *PR*
nehkatepkwe *throughout the night*
nehkatepkwe
nehki *arm NI*
honehkali *NI/POSS,3s,p*
honehki *NI/POSS,3s,s*
honehkiki *NI/POSS/LOC,3s*
nehkiiskwe *throughout the day*
nehkiiskwe
nehtawatwi *unique PM*
nehtawatwi *PM*
neini *Nain NI*
neini *NI,s*
nekatiimasi *Nicodemus NA*
nekatiimasi *NA,3s*
nekeewe *seeing NI*
nekeewe *NI,s*
nekeeya *Naggai NA*
nekeeya *NA,3s*
nekotehfepatiokima *tetrarch NA*
nekotehfepati-hokima *NA,3s*
nekotehfepatiokima *NA,3s*
nekotehfepatiwi *tetrarch PM*
nekotehfepatiwi *PM*
nekoten *[continuous] PV*
nekotenwi *PV*
nekoti *one PR*
naanekoti *PR*
nanekoti *PR*
nekoti *PR*
nekotihi *PR*
nekotiifen *be one II*
nekotiifenili *II,ind,4*
nekotiifi *be one AI*
nekotiifici *AI,conj,3s*
nekotiifiiki *AI,ind,3p*
nekotiifiwaaci *AI,conj,3p*
nekotiifiyakwe *AI,conj,1i*
nekotiimehi *one, single PM*

nekotiimehi *PM*
nekotiiyaa *become one II*
   nekotiiyaali *II,ind,4*
nekotiwi *be one AI*
   nekotiwi *AI,ind,3s*
   ninekotwiipe *AI,ind,1x*
nekotoosaaka *single offspring NA*
   honekotoosaakanali *NA/POSS,3s,4s*
   nekotoosaaka *NA,3s*
nekotoskaawe *crowd NI*
   nekotoskaaweneki *NI/LOC*
nekotwaacimooyaa *agree, be consistent II*
   nekotwaacimooyaali *II,ind,4*
nekotwaasi *sixty*
   nekotwaasi
nekotwahfoko *six days*
   nekotwahfoko
nekotwahfokonakat *three days II*
   nekotwahfokonakiki *II,conj,0*
nekotwahfwi *six*
   nekotwahfene
   nekotwahfwi
nekotweel *group AI*
   nekotweeleka *AI,part,3s*
   nekotweelekiki *AI,part,3p*
nekotweelena *one (from a group); nation NA*
   nekotweelena *NA,3s*
nekotweeloofa *flock NA*
   nekotweeloofaki *NA/DIM,3p*
nekotweloowe *crowd NI*
   nekotwelooweneki *NI/LOC*
nekotwesi *in a group*
   nekotwesi
nekwaan *roar II*
   neenekwaanwiki *II/IC,conj,0*
nelohci *vain, in vain PM*
   nelohci *PM*
nelohcilawiiwe *pretense, hypocrisy NI*
   honelohcilawiiwenilici *NI/POSS,4*
   nelohcilawiiwe *NI,s*
nelohcilawiwehfi *hypocrite NA*
   nelohcilawiwehfi *NA,3s*
   nelohcilawiwehfihi *NA,4p*
   nelohcilawiwehfiiki *NA,3p*
nenaan *perceive TI-O*
   kinenaanaawa *TI,ind,2p,0*

nenekifi *palsied AI*
   nenekificki *AI,part,3p*
   nenekifilici *AI,conj,4*
nenekifiiwe *palsy NI*
   nenekifiiwe *NI,s*
nenekonam *rub loose TI_3*
   nenekonamehi *TI,ind,4p,0*
nenemhki *thunder NI*
   nenemhki *NI,s*
nenemhkiwa *thunder II*
   nenemhkiwaki *II,conj,0*
nenhhihtaawi *first AI*
   nenhhihtaawicki *AI,part,3p*
nenifa *Nineveh NI*
   nenifa *NI,s*
nenifa *Ninevite NA*
   nenifahi *NA,4p*
nenofi *discern AI*
   nenofipwa *AI,ind,2p*
   nenofiyeekwe *AI,conj,2p*
nenohsee *understand AI*
   kinenohseepwa *AI,ind,2p*
   nenohsaakaniyeekwe *AI,conj,2p*
   nenohse *AI,ind,3s ; AI,ind,2s*
   nenohseeki *AI,ind,3p*
   nenohseeko *AI,imp,2p*
   nenohseepwa *AI,ind,2p*
   nenohseete *AI,subj,3s*
   nenohseewaaci *AI,conj,3p*
   nenohsehi *AI,ind,4p*
nenohseewe *understanding NI*
   honenohseewe *NI/POSS,3s,s*
   nenohseewe *NI,s*
nenohseewefi *understand AI*
   nenohseewefita *AI,part,3s*
nenoht *understand TI_1*
   honenohtaanaawa *TI,ind,3p,0*
   kinenohtaana *TI,ind,2s,0p*
   kinenohtaanaawa *TI,ind,2p,0*
   nenohta *TI,ind,3s,0s*
   nenohtameekwe *TI,conj,2p,0*
   nenohtamowaaci *TI,conj,3p,0*
   ninenohta *TI,ind,1s,0s*
nep *die, be dead AI*
   neepekiki *AI/IC,part,3p*
   nepeka *AI,part,3s*

nepeke *AI,subj,3*
nepeki *AI,conj,3s*
nepelici *AI,conj,4*
nepelite *AI,subj,4s*
nepepwa *AI,ind,2p*
nepeyeekwe *AI,conj,2p*
nepoofi *AI,ind,3s*
nepooki *AI,ind,3p*
nepooli *AI,ind,4s*
nepowaaci *AI,conj,3p*
nepwa *AI,ind,3s*
nepaaawe *sleep NI*
   honepaaawe *NI/POSS,3s,s*
   nepaaawe *NI,s*
nepee, nepaa *sleep AI*
   kinepa *AI,ind,2s*
   kinepaapwa *AI,ind,2p*
   nepaako *AI,imp,2p*
   nepaalici *AI,conj,4*
   nepaayaake *AI,conj,1x*
   nepaayeekwe *AI,conj,2p*
   nepeeki *AI,ind,3p*
   nepeewa *AI,ind,3s*
nephokwi *drown AI*
   nephokwiiki *AI,ind,3p*
nepi *water NI*
   nepi *NI,s*
   nepiki *NI/LOC*
nepipemi *salt NI*
   nepipemi *NI,s*
nepiwakokwa *water jug NA*
   honepiwakokooli *NA/POSS,3s,4s*
   nepiwakokooki *NA,3p*
nepiwi *be water II*
   nepiwiki *II,conj,0*
nepiwilokeewe *dropsy NI*
   nepiwilokeewe *NI,s*
nepolaw *kill TA*
   nepolaakwicki *TA,part,0,3p*
nepoo *dead person NA*
   honepoomwahi *NA/POSS,3p,4p*
nepoom *die together with TA*
   nepoomela *TA,conj,1s,2s*
   nepoomele *TA,ind,1s,2s*
nepoowaalakwi *tomb NI*
   honepoowaalakomwa *NI/POSS,3p*

nepoowaalako *NI,p*
nepoowaalakoki *NI/LOC*
nepoowaalakwi *NI,s*
nepoowe *death, grave, sepulchre NI*
   honepoowe *NI/POSS,3s,s*
   honepoowenwa *NI/POSS,3p*
   nepoowe *NI,s*
   nepoowena *NI,p*
   nepooweneki *NI/LOC*
nepoowefi *die AI*
   nepoowefi *AI,ind,3s*
   nepoowefilici *AI,conj,4*
nepoowena *corpse NA*
   honepoowenwaali *NA/POSS,3p,4s*
   nepoowenali *NA,4s*
nepoowi *of death PM*
   nepoowi *PM*
nepoowiyaamwecika *bier NI*
   nepoowiyaamwecika *NI,s*
nepooyaa *die II*
   nepooya *II,ind,0*
   nepooyaake *II,subj,0*
neposkaw *crush TA*
   kineposkaakooki *TA,ind,3p,2s*
nepote *die, wither II*
   nepote *II,ind,0*
nepwaskweht *choke TI_2*
   honepwaskwehtoonaawa *TI,ind,3p,0*
nepwaskwehtoote *be choked II*
   nepwaskwehtoote *II,ind,0*
nepwaskweyaa *choke II*
   nepwaskweyaali *II,ind,4*
neyehka *already*
   neyehka
neyiisweelena *both*
   neyiisweelena
neyiiswi *both*
   neyiiswi
nhf *kill TA*
   honhfaawaali *TA,ind,3p,4s*
   honhfaawahi *TA,ind,3p,4p*
   honhfahi *TA,ind,3s,4p*
   honhfekonaawa *TA,ind,0,3p*
   naanhfaacki *TA/IC,part,3p,4*
   naanhfaata *TA/IC,part,3s,4*
   nenhfaacki *TA/IC,part,3p,4*

nenhfeekwe *TA/IC,part,2p,3*
nhfaaci *TA,conj,3s,4*
nhfaali *TA,ind,3s,4s*
nhfaataako *TA,imp,1i,3*
nhfaawaaci *TA,conj,3p,4*
nhfaawaaki *TA,ind,2p,3p*
nhfaawaali *TA,ind,3p,4s*
nhfaawahi *TA,ind,3p,4p*
nhfahi *TA,ind,3s,4p*
nhfeci *TA,conj,,3*
nhfehki *TA,conj,3,2s*
nhfehko *TA,imp,2p,3*
nhfekowaaki *TA,ind,3p,2p*
nhfekwa *TA,ind,3s,2s*
nhfekwi *TA,ind,,3s*
nhfelwaakwe *TA,conj,3,2p*
nhsiyeekwe *TA,conj,2p,1s*
nhfekwi *dead, be killed AI*
  nhfekwici *AI,conj,3s*
  nhfekwiiki *AI,ind,3p*
  nhfekwilici *AI,conj,4*
  nhfekwite *AI,subj,3s*
  nhfekwiwaaci *AI,conj,3p*
nhfetiiwe *murder NI*
  nhfetiiwena *NI,p*
nhfoko *three days*
  nhfoko
nhfokonakat *three days II*
  nhfokonakike *II,subj,0*
  nhfokonakiki *II,conj,0*
nhfwaapitaki *thirty*
  nhfwaapitaki
nhfwaapitaki-kite-nhfwaasikfwi *thirty-eight*
  nhfwaapitaki-kite-nhfwaasikfwi
nhfwaasii-kite-niyeewi *eighty-four*
  nhfwaasii-kite-niyeewi
nhfwaasikfoko *eight days*
  nhfwaasikfoko
  nhfwaasikifoko
nhfwaasikfwi *eight*
  nhfwaasikfwi
nhfwi *three*
  nhfene
  nhfwi
nhfwi-kite-nhfwehfepati *three and three-quarters*

nhfwi-kite-nhfwehfepati
nhhaawaacfet *prepare TI_2*
  nenhhaawaacfetooyani *TI/IC,conj,2s,0*
nhhaawaat *store up, keep TI_1*
  kinhhaawaata *TI,ind,2s,0s*
nhhaawaataw *store up TA*
  nhhaawaataakwate *TA,subj,,2s*
nhhalwaafiiwe *related person or thing NI*
  honhhalwaafiiwe *NI/POSS,3s,s*
  honhhalwaafiiwena *NI/POSS,3s,p*
  honhhalwaafiiwenali *NA/POSS,3s,4s*
  honhhalwaafiiwenhhi *NA/POSS,3s,4p*
  nhhalwaafiiwena *NI,p*
  ninhhalwaafiiwenaki *NA/POSS,1s,3p*
  ninhhalwaafiiwenena *NA/POSS,1x,3p*
nhhalwaafiiweni *be as one's own AI*
  nhhalwaafiiweni *AI,ind,3s*
nhhalwaaka *own self PR*
  nhhalwaaka *PR*
nhhalweelet *be of the family TI-O*
  nhhalweeletamwa *TI,ind,3s,0*
nhhalweeletiim *have dealings with TA*
  nhhalweeletiimaawahi *TA,ind,3p,4p*
nhhalweeletiimeti *deal with one another AI*
  nhhalweeletiimetiko *AI,imp,2p*
nhhalweeletiiwen *kin NA*
  kinhhalweeletiiwena *NA/POSS,2s,3s*
  nhhalweeletiiwe *NA,3s*
  nhhalweeletiiwenaki *NA,3p*
nhhalwelecikanileni *kin NA*
  kinhhalweelecikanileniiki *NA/POSS,2s,3p*
nhhawaaci *saving (for the future) PV*
  nhhawaaci *PV*
nhhefiiwe *craftiness, subtility NI*
  honhhefiiwenilici *NI/POSS,4*
nhhekol *trim TA*
  honhhekolaawahi *TA,ind,3p,4p*
nhhihta *first*
  nhhihta
nhhihtaafa *first*
  nhhihtaafa
nhhihtaawefi *be first AI*
  nhhihtaawefi *AI,ind,3s*
nhhihtaawi *be first AI*
  nhhihtaawi *AI,ind,3s*
  nhhihtaawiiki *AI,ind,3p*

nhhihtaawite *AI,subj,3s*
nhhihtaawi *be first II*
    nenhhihtaawiki *II/IC,conj,0*
    nhhihtaawiki *II,conj,0*
nhhihtawat *first II*
    nhhihtawatwi *II,ind,0s*
nhhilawiiwe *subtilty, cleverness NI*
    nhhilawiiwe *NI,s*
nhhiwanimefiiwe *deceit NI*
    nhhiwanimefiiwe *NI,s*
nhkokeemo *consent AI*
    nhkokeemo *AI,ind,3s*
nhkom *answer, assent TA*
    nhkomaali *TA,ind,3s,4s*
nhkot *consent to TI_1*
    kinhkotaanaawa *TI,ind,2p,0*
nhkotamaw *consent to TA*
    nhkotamawahi *TA,ind,3s,4p*
nhpenikwaate *border II*
    nhpenikwaateeki *II,conj,0*
    nhpenikwaateelici *II,conj,4*
    nipenikwaateeki *II,conj,0*
nhsiwee *kill AI*
    kinhsiwe *AI,ind,2s*
    naanhsiweelici *AI/IC,conj,4*
    naanhsiweeta *AI/IC,part,3s*
    nhsiwe *AI,ind,2s ; AI,ind,3s*
    nhsiweeci *AI,conj,3s*
    nhsiweeki *AI,conj,3*
    nhsiweelo *AI,imp,2s*
nhsiweewe *murder NI*
    nhsiweewe *NI,s*
nhsiweeyaa *deadly II*
    naanhsiweeyaaki *II/IC,conj,0*
nht *kill TI_2*
    nhto *TI,ind,3s,0s*
nhtalawikaate *be written (there) II*
    nhtalawikaate *II,ind,0*
nhtamaw *kill TA*
    kinhtamawa *TA,ind,2s,3s*
nifteliiwi *Naphtali PM*
    nifteliiwi *PM*
niicaana *offspring NA*
    honiicaanali *NA/POSS,3s,4s*
niicaaneefa *offspring NA*
    kiniicaaneefaki *NA/POSS,2s,3p*

niicaanin *beget*
    honiicaaninaali *TA,ind,3s,4s*
niicaphi *that's so, thus*
    niicaphi
niikaaneskaw *precede TA*
    niikaaneskawaki *TA,conj,1s,3*
niikaani *go ahead, go before AI*
    neniikaaniicki *AI/IC,part,3p*
    niikaaniilici *AI,conj,4*
niikaani *before, in front of*
    niikaani
niikaanih *precede TA*
    niikaanihekowa *TA,ind,3s,2p*
    niikaanihelepwa *TA,ind,1s,2p*
niikaaniwel *lead astray TA*
    niikaaniwelaali *TA,ind,3s,4s*
    niikaaniwelaate *TA,subj,3s,4*
niiki *be born AI*
    kiniiki *AI,ind,2s*
    niiki *AI,ind,3s ; AI,ind,1s*
    niikici *AI,conj,3s*
    niikicki *AI,part,3p*
    niikilici *AI,conj,4*
    niikipe *AI,ind,1x*
    niikita *AI,part,3s*
niikicikeeyaa *bring forth, bear II*
    niikicikeeya *II,ind,0*
niikin *bear, bring forth TA*
    neeniikinekocki *TA/IC,part,4,3p*
    neniikinaata *TA/IC,part,3s,4*
    niikinaaci *TA,conj,3s,4*
    niikinaali *TA,ind,3s,4s*
niikin *come from II*
    niikike *II,subj,0*
    niikiki *II,conj,0*
    niikinwi *II,ind,0s*
niikinikee *give birth AI*
    niikinikeeci *AI,conj,3s*
niikiniwee *give birth AI*
    niikiniweeci *AI,conj,3s*
niikit *bear, bring forth TI_2*
    honiikito *TI,ind,3s,0s*
    honiikto *TI,ind,3s,0s*
    honiiktoonaawa *TI,ind,3p,0*
    niikito *TI,ind,3s,0s*
    niikitooko *TI,imp,2p,0*

niikitooyeekwe *TI,conj,2p,0*
niila/kiila/wiila *[emphatic pronoun] PR*
    kiila *PR*
    kiilama *PR*
    kiilawa *PR*
    kiilawe *PR*
    kiiyaanenaaki *PR*
    niila *PR*
    niilawa *PR*
    niilawe *PR*
    wiila *PR*
    wiilawa *PR*
niilaai *Neri NA*
    niilaai *NA,3s*
niim *carry, bear TI_3*
    niime *TI,ind,3s,0s ; TI,ind,1s,0s ; TI,ind,2s,0s*
    niimeka *TI,part,3s,0*
    niimeki *TI,conj,3s,0*
    niimeli *TI,ind,4s,0*
    niimenaawa *TI,ind,2p,0*
    niimepe *TI,ind,1x,0*
    niimeya *TI,conj,1s,0 ; TI,subj,1s,0*
    niimiweelo *TI,imp,2s,0*
niimathoofo *be lifted up AI*
    niimathoofoci *AI,conj,3s*
niimathw *lift up TA*
    niimathwaaci *TA,conj,3s,4*
niimaw *carry, bear TA*
    honiimaawaali *TA,ind,3p,4s*
    niimaakoya *TA,conj,0,1s*
    niimaakwa *TA,ind,3s,2s ; TA,ind,3s,1s*
    niimawaaci *TA,conj,3s,4*
    niimawaali *TA,ind,3s,4s*
    niimawata *TA,part,2s,3s*
    niimawipwa *TA,ind,2p,1*
    niimawita *TA,part,3s,1s*
    niimekooki *TA,ind,3p,2s*
    niimekoya *TA,part,3,1s*
niinhfoko *third day*
    niinhfoko
niinhkaw *? put forward, encourage ? TA*
    niinhkaakooli *TA,ind,4s,3s*
niipawi *stand AI*
    kiniipawipwa *AI,ind,2p*
    naaniipawita *AI/IC,part,3s*
    neniipawicki *AI/IC,part,3p*

neniipawilici *AI/IC,conj,4*
neniipawita *AI/IC,part,3s*
niipawi *AI,ind,3s*
niipawici *AI,conj,3s*
niipawihi *AI,ind,4p*
niipawiiki *AI,ind,3p*
niipawiili *AI,ind,4s*
niipawilici *AI,conj,4*
niipawilo *AI,imp,2s*
niipawipwa *AI,ind,2p*
niipawiwaaci *AI,conj,3p*
niipawiyeekwe *AI,conj,2p*
niipawiiyaa *stand II*
    niipawiiya *II,ind,0*
    niipawiiyaaki *II,conj,0*
    niipawiiyaali *II,ind,4*
niipen *bear fruit, mature II*
    niipeki *II,conj,0*
niisohkalaatiiki *two together AI*
    niisohkalaatiiki *AI,ind,3p*
niisoko *two days*
    niisoko
niisokonakat *two days II*
    niisokonakike *II,subj,0*
    niisokonakiki *II,conj,0*
niiswaapitakitfene *twenty times*
    niiswaapitakitfene
niiswaasi *seventy*
    niiswaasi
    niiswahfene
niiswaasiitfene *seventy times*
    niiswaasiitfene
niiswahfwi *seven*
    niiswahfwi
niiswahfwi-kite-pahfi *seven and one-half*
    niiswahfwi-kite-pahfi
niiswahfwikiiskwe *week NI*
    niiswahfwikiiskwe *NI,s*
niisweelena *two in number PV*
    niisweelena *PV*
niiswi *two*
    niisene
    niiswi
niiswi *be two AI*
    niiswiwaaci *AI,conj,3p*
niiswi-kite-pahfi *two and one-half*

niiswi-kite-pahfi
niiswipito *run together (as a pair)* AI
    niiswipitooki *AI,ind,3p*
niiswitehaakani *be of two minds, doubt* AI
    niiswitehaakaniko *AI,imp,2p*
niitaw *shine upon* TA
    honiitawaalekowaali *TA,ind,4s,3p*
niitaw *shine* TI_3
    niitaweyeekwe *TI,conj,2p,0*
niitawaaka *lamp* NA
    honiitawaakani *NA/POSS,3s,3s*
    honiitawaakanwahi *NA/POSS,3p,4p*
    kiniitawaakanwaaki *NA/POSS,2p,3p*
    niitawaaka *NA,3s*
    niitawaakanali *NA,4s*
    niniitawaakanenaaki *NA/POSS,1x,3p*
niiya/kiiya/wiiya *[object pronoun]* PR
    howiiyaaki *PR*
    kiiya *PR*
    kiiyaaki *PR*
    niiya *PR*
    niiyaaki *PR*
    wiiya *PR*
    wiiyaaki *PR*
niiyaana/kiiyaana/wiiyaana *self, body* PR
    howiiyaanali *PR*
    howiiyaanwahi *PR*
    kiiyaana *PR*
    kiiyaanwa *PR*
    niiyaana *PR*
    niiyaanali *PR*
    wiiyaana *PR*
    wiiyaanahi *PR*
    wiiyaanali *PR*
niiyaawa/kiiyaawa/wiiyaawa *self* PR
    howiiyaawaaki *PR*
    howiiyaawilici *PR*
    kiiyaawa *PR*
    kiiyaawaaki *PR*
    wiiyaawa *PR*
    wiiyaawaaki *PR*
niwi *bear* AI
    niwi *AI,ind,3s*
niyaalan *five*
    niyaalane
    niyaalanwi

niyaalanwaapitaki *fifty*
    niyaalanwaapitaki
niyaalanweelena *five in number*
    niyaalanweelena
niyaawe *thanks* NI
    honiyaawe *NI/POSS,3s,s*
    niyaawe *NI,s*
    niyaawena *NI,p*
niyeeko *four days*
    niiniyeeko
    niyeeko
niyeewaapitaki *forty*
    niyeewaapitaki
niyeewekfen *fourfold* II
    niyeewekfenwi *II,ind,0s*
niyeewene *fourth, four times*
    niyeewene
niyeewi *four*
    niyeewi
niyeewi-niiswaapitaki *fourscore*
    niyeewi-niiswaapitaki
nohki *again*
    nohki
nohkwaatamaw *lick* TA
    honohkwaatamawaawaali *TA,ind,3p,4s*
nohpiyeen *separate* TA
    nohpiyeenaaci *TA,conj,3s,4*
    nohpiyeenahi *TA,ind,3s,4p*
    nohpiyeenekowaaki *TA,ind,3p,2p*
nohpiyeen *separate* TI_1
    nohpiyeenamoko *TI,imp,2p,0*
nooch *fight* TA
    kinoochaawa *TA,ind,2p,3s*
noochaal *persecute* TA
    noochaalaawaali *TA,ind,3p,4s*
noochaaletiiwe *persecution* NI
    noochaaletiiwe *NI,s*
noochetiit *fight* TI-O
    noochetiitamelici *TI,conj,4,0*
    noochetiitamowaaci *TI,conj,3p,0*
noochetiiwe *war* NI
    noochetiiwena *NI,p*
    noochetiiweneki *NI/LOC*
noochiwee *fight* AI
    noochiweeki *AI,ind,3p*
nookofi *appear* AI

nookofiiki *AI,ind,3p*
nookofiiwe *vision NI*
    honookofiiwenwa *NI/POSS,3p*
nookwat *appear II*
    nookwato *II,ind,0p*
noole *quiet, still*
    noole
nooleewi *quiet, still AI*
    nooleewi *AI,ind,3s*
    nooleewiiki *AI,ind,3p*
    nooleewilici *AI,conj,4*
    nooleewilo *AI,imp,2s*
nooleewiiwe *peace, stillness, quiet NI*
    honooleewiiwe *NI/POSS,3s,s*
noomenoote *be shaken II*
    naanoomenoote *II,ind,0*
    noomenoote *II,ind,0*
noomeskwa *shake II*
    noomeska *II,ind,0s*
noon *suck TI_3*
    neenooneyani *TI/IC,conj,2s,0*
noonhhiwee *suckle AI*
    neenoonhhiweecki *AI/IC,part,3p*
noonoofi *be suckled AI*
    neenoonooficki *AI/IC,part,3p*
noonoowe *nursing, suckling NI*
    noonoowe *NI,s*
noosaacikana *steward, servant NA*
    honoosaacikanali *NA/POSS,3s,4s*
    noosaacikana *NA,3s*
noosaafiiwe *stewardship NI*
    kinoosaafiiwe *NI/POSS,2s,s*
    noosaafiiwe *NI,s*
noosaafiiwena *steward NA*
    noosaafiiwena *NA,3s*
    noosaafiiwenali *NA,4s*
noosaal *take care of TA*
    honoosaalaali *TA,ind,3s,4s*
    noosaasi *TA,imp,2s,3*
nooseyaa *produce interest II*
    nooseyaaki *II,conj,0*
noot *hear TI_1*
    honoota *TI,ind,3s,0s*
    honootaana *TI,ind,3s,0p*
    honootaanaawa *TI,ind,3p,0*
    kinoota *TI,ind,2s,0s*

kinootaanaawa *TI,ind,2p,0*
neenootaka *TI/IC,part,3s,0*
neenootakki *TI/IC,part,3p,0*
neenootameekwe *TI/IC,conj,2p,0*
neenootameekwe *TI/IC,conj,2p,0*
ninoota *TI,ind,1s,0s*
noota *TI,ind,3s,0s*
nootaanaawa *TI,ind,2p,0 ; TI,ind,3p,0*
nootaape *TI,ind,1x,0*
nootaki *TI,conj,3s,0*
nootakki *TI,part,3p,0*
nootama *TI,conj,1s,0*
nootamaake *TI,conj,1x,0*
nootameekwe *TI,conj,2p,0*
nootamelici *TI,conj,4,0*
nootamoko *TI,imp,2p,0*
nootamowaaci *TI,conj,3p,0*
noota *than; less*
    noota
nootaakee *hear something [indefinite object] said AI*
    kinootaakeepwa *AI,ind,2p*
    neenootaakeecki *AI/IC,part,p*
    neenootaakeeta *AI/IC,part,s*
    neenootaakeeyeekwe *AI/IC,conj,2p*
    nootaake *AI,ind,3s*
    nootaakeeci *AI,conj,3s*
    nootaakeecki *AI,part,p*
    nootaakeeki *AI,ind,3p*
    nootaakeeko *AI,imp,2p*
    nootaakeelici *AI,conj,4*
    nootaakeelo *AI,imp,2s*
    nootaakeepe *AI,ind,1x*
    nootaakeepwa *AI,ind,2p*
    nootaakeeta *AI,part,s*
    nootaakeete *AI,subj,3s*
    nootaakeewaaci *AI,conj,3p*
    nootaakeewaate *AI,subj,3p*
    nootaakeeya *AI,conj,1s*
    nootaakeeyeekwe *AI,conj,2p*
    nootaakehi *AI,ind,4p*
nootaakeewe *hearing NI*
    honootaakeewenwaaki *NI/POSS/LOC,3p*
    nootaakeewe *NI,s*
nootaakwat *be heard II*
    nootaakwatwi *II,ind,0s*

nootakeelem *honor TA*
   nootakeelemekwa *TA,ind,3s,1s*
nootamaw *hear (it) [of animate object] TA*
   honootamawaali *TA,ind,3s,4s*
   honootamawaawaali *TA,ind,3p,4s*
   nootamawaali *TA,ind,3s,4s*
   nootamawaawaaci *TA,conj,3p,4*
nootamawoofo *be heard AI*
   nootamawoofowaaci *AI,conj,3p*
nootaw *hear TA*
   honootaako *TA,ind,0s,3s*
   honootaakohi *TA,ind,4p,3s*
   honootawaali *TA,ind,3s,4s*
   honootawaawaali *TA,ind,3p,4s*
   honootawaawahi *TA,ind,3p,4p*
   honootawahi *TA,ind,3s,4p*
   kinootawaaki *TA,ind,2s,3p*
   kinootawaawa *TA,ind,2p,3s*
   neenootawaacki *TA/IC,part,3p,4*
   neenootoolwaakwe *TA/IC,part,3,2p*
   ninootaakwa *TA,ind,1s,3s*
   ninootawaape *TA,ind,1x,3*
   nootaakoci *TA,conj,4,3s*
   nootaakohi *TA,ind,4p,3s*
   nootawaaci *TA,conj,3s,4*
   nootawaali *TA,ind,3s,4s*
   nootawaape *TA,ind,1i,3*
   nootawaawaaci *TA,conj,3p,4*
   nootawahi *TA,ind,3s,4p*
   nootawehko *TA,imp,2p,3*
   nootawicki *TA,part,3p,1s*
   nootawiko *TA,imp,2p,1s*
   nootawiyani *TA,conj,2s,1s*
nootkofi *lack AI*
   kinootkofi *AI,ind,2s*
   kinootkofipwa *AI,ind,2p*
   ninootkofi *AI,ind,1s*
nootkoskaa *lack AI*
   nootkoskaaki *AI,conj,3*
nootkwat *fail II*
   nootkwahki *II,conj,0*
nootkweelemekofi *worthy AI*
   ninootkweelemekofi *AI,ind,1s*
   nootkweelemekofi *AI,ind,3s*
   nootkweelemekofiiki *AI,ind,3p*
nootkwiilefi *lack AI*

kinootkwiilefi *AI,ind,2s*
   ninootkwiilefi *AI,ind,1s*
nootoote *be heard II*
   nootoote *II,ind,0*
notakeelem *honor TA*
   notakeelemekwa *TA,ind,3s,1s*
nowa *cheek NI*
   kimayaawi-nowaaki *NI/POSS/LOC,2s*
nowa *Noah NA*
   nowa *NA,3s*
o *oh [exclamation]*
   o
paacoona *Bar-Jonah NA*
   paacoona *NA,3s*
paafkwahki *cloud NI*
   paafkwahki *NI*
   paafkwahkiiki *NI/LOC*
   paafkwaki *NI*
paalacipt *rush down II*
   paalacipto *II,ind,0p*
paalacsin *down AI*
   paalacisinelici *AI,conj,4*
   paalacisinwa *AI,ind,3s*
   paalacsiki *AI,conj,3s*
   paalacsikiki *AI,part,3p*
   paalacsinelo *AI,imp,2s*
   paalacsinohi *AI,ind,4p*
   paalacsinowaaci *AI,conj,3p*
   paalacsinwa *AI,ind,3s*
paalacsinoom *go down with TA*
   paalacsinoomahi *TA,ind,3s,4p*
paalatii *Pilate NA*
   paalatii *NA,3s*
   paalatiiki *NA/LOC,3*
   paalatiili *NA,4s*
paaleewikawaskwi *barley NI*
   paaleewikawaskwi *NI,s*
paalohi *until, as far as, finally*
   paalohi
   paalohinoki
paamaami *journey AI*
   paamaamiici *AI,conj,3s*
paamaamiiwe *journey NI*
   paamaamiiwe *NI,s*
paameci *nevertheless, all the more PV*
   paameci *PV*

paamhfee *walk AI*
    paamhfe *AI,ind,3s ; AI,ind,2s*
    paamhfeeci *AI,conj,3s*
    paamhfeecki *AI,part,3p*
    paamhfeeki *AI,ind,3p*
    paamhfeete *AI,subj,3s*
    peepaamhfeeta *AI/IC,part,s*
paamhfeewe *journey NI*
    hopaamhfeewe *NI/POSS,3s,s*
paamwel *carry around TA*
    paamwelaawahi *TA,ind,3p,4p*
paapaakehfiifa *gnat NA*
    paapaakehfiifali *NA,4s*
paapemesit *go around, encompass TI_2*
    kipaapemesitoonaawa *TI,ind,2p,0*
paapiyeeci *necessarily, obligatorily*
    paapiyeeci
paapiyeeminakweyaa *spin [thread] II*
    paapiyeeminakweya *II,ind,0*
paasi *it seems*
    paasi
paatamiias *Bartimaeus NA*
    paatamiias *NA,3s*
pacikam *kiss TA*
    hopacikamaali *TA,ind,3s,4s*
    hopackamaali *TA,ind,3s,4s*
    hopackamekooli *TA,ind,4s,3s*
    pacikama *TA,ind,1s,3s*
    pacikamaaci *TA,conj,3s,4*
    packama *TA,ind,1s,3s*
pacikamiweewe *kiss NI*
    pacikamiweewe *NI,s*
packametiiwe *kiss NI*
    packametiiwe *NI,s*
packat *kiss TI_1*
    hopackataana *TI,ind,3s,0p*
    packakataki *TI,conj,3s,0*
pafalamiyo *Bartholomew NA*
    pafalamiyo *NA,3s*
    pafalamiyoli *NA,4s*
pafekwicfat *rise up against TI*
    pafekwicfatake *TI,subj,3s,0*
pafekwicfataw *rise up against TA*
    pafekwicfatawaali *TA,ind,3s,4s*
    pafekwicfatawaawahi *TA,ind,3p,4p*
pafekwicfe *jump up AI*

pafekwicfe *AI,ind,3s*
pafekwii *rise, stand AI*
    pafekwi *AI,ind,3s ; AI,ind,1s*
    pafekwiici *AI,conj,3s*
    pafekwiiki *AI,ind,3p*
    pafekwiiko *AI,imp,2p*
    pafekwiili *AI,ind,4s*
    pafekwiilo *AI,imp,2s*
    pafekwiitaako *AI,imp,1i*
    pafekwiite *AI,subj,3s*
pafekwiiyaa *arise II*
    pafekwiiya *II,ind,0*
    pafekwiiyaaki *II,conj,0*
    pafekwiiyaalici *II,conj,4*
pah *[andative] PV*
    hopa *PV*
    hopah *PV*
    kipah *PV*
    nipah *PV*
    pah *PV*
    peepah *PV/IC*
pahfehka *divided II*
    pahfehka *II,ind,0*
pahfehkaa *separate, be divided AI*
    pahfehka *AI,ind,3s*
    pahfehkaaki *AI,ind,3p*
    papahfehkaaki *AI,ind,3p*
pahfehkaati *separate, divide [reciprocal] AI*
    pahfehkaati *AI,ind,3*
pahfehkaatiiyaa *divided II*
    pahfehkaatiiya *II,ind,0*
pahfehkaawe *division NI*
    pahfehkaawe *NI,s*
pahfen *divide TI_1*
    hopahfenaanaawa *TI,ind,3p,0*
    papahfenameli *TI,ind,4s,0*
pahfenamaati *divide [reciprocal] AI*
    pahfenamaatilici *AI,conj,4*
    papahfenamaatiiki *AI,ind,3p*
    papahfenamaatiko *AI,imp,2p*
pahfenamaw *divide TA*
    hopahfenamawahi *TA,ind,3s,4p*
    nipahfenamaakwa *TA,ind,3s,1s*
    pahfenamawahi *TA,ind,3s,4p*
pahfeneti *divide [reciprocal] AI*
    pahfenetite *AI,subj,3s*

pahfenetiiyaa *divided II*
    pahfenetiiya *II,ind,0*
    pahfenetiiyaake *II,subj,0*
pahfeniwee *divide AI*
    peepahfeniweeta *AI/IC,part,3s*
pahfi *half*
    pahfi
pahfisekali *half-shekel NI*
    pahfisekali *NI,s*
pahkaseen *reveal TI_1*
    hopahkaseena *TI,ind,3s,0s*
pahkaseenoote *be revealed II*
    pahkaseenoote *II,ind,0*
pahkaseeyaa *open II*
    pahkaseeyaaki *II,conj,0*
pahkin *open, reveal TI_1*
    hopahkina *TI,ind,3s,0s*
    hopahkinaanaawa *TI,ind,3p,0*
pahkinamaw *open, reveal, bear [witness] TA*
    hopahkinamawaali *TA,ind,3s,4s*
    hopahkinamawaawaali *TA,ind,3p,4s*
    kipahkinamawaaki *TA,ind,2s,3p*
    pahkinamaako *TA,ind,0s,2s*
    pahkinamaakooli *TA,ind,4s,3s*
    pahkinamaakwi *TA,ind,,3s*
    pahkinamawaaci *TA,conj,3s,4*
pahkinoote *be revealed II*
    pahkinooteeki *II,conj,0*
pahtaafi *accursed AI*
    pahtaafiiki *AI,ind,3p*
pahtaam *blaspheme TA*
    pahtaamaali *TA,ind,3s,4s*
    pahtaamaata *TA,part,3s,4*
pahtaamo *blaspheme AI*
    kipahtaamo *AI,ind,2s*
    pahtaamo *AI,ind,3s*
    pahtaamooki *AI,ind,3p*
pahtaamoofoowe *blasphemy NI*
    hopahtaamoofoowe *NI,s*
pahtaamoowe *blasphemy NI*
    hopahtaamoowenwa *NI/POSS,3p*
    pahtaamoowe *NI,s*
pahtahkaafa *one cursed NA*
    pahtahkaafaki *NA,3p*
pakaci *near, by*
    pakaci

pakacikana *along the path, by the wayside*
    pakacikana
    pakackana
pakfaten *take away TI_1*
    pakfatenaki *TI,conj,3s,0*
pakfeelet *forgive TI_1*
    kipakfeeletaanaawa *TI,ind,2p,0*
    pakfeeletaana *TI,ind,3s,0p*
    pakfeeletaki *TI,conj,3s,0*
pakfeeletamaw *release, forgive, deliver TA*
    hopakfeeletamaakooli *TA,ind,4s,3s*
    hopakfeeletamawahi *TA,ind,3s,4p*
    kipakfeeletamaakoopi *TA,ind,3,2s*
    kipakfeeletamoole *TA,ind,1s,2s*
    kipakfenamawi *TA,ind,2s,1s*
    nipakfeeletamawaape *TA,ind,1x,3*
    pakfeeletamaakowa *TA,ind,3s,2p*
    pakfeeletamaakwi *TA,ind,,3s*
    pakfeeletamaakwihi *TA,ind,,4p*
    pakfeeletamaakwiiki *TA,ind,,3p*
    pakfeeletamawa *TA,ind,1s,3s ; TA,ind,2s,3s*
    pakfeeletamawakici *TA,conj,1x,3*
    pakfeeletamaweekwe *TA,subj,2p,3 ;*
TA,conj,2p,3
    pakfeeletamawi *TA,imp,2s,3*
    pakfeeletamawinaake *TA,imp,2,1x*
    pakfeeletamoolwaakwe *TA,conj,3,2p*
    peepakfeeletamawaaci *TA/IC,conj,3s,4*
pakfeeletamawiwee *forgive AI*
    pakfeeletamawiwe *AI,ind,3s*
    pakfeeletamawiweeci *AI,conj,3s*
    pakfeeletamawiweeko *AI,imp,2p*
pakfeeletamawoofo *be forgiven AI*
    pakfeeletamawoofooki *AI,ind,3p*
pakfeeletamawoofoowe *forgiveness NI*
    pakfeeletamawoofoowe *NI,s*
pakfeeletoote *be forgiven II*
    pakfeeletoote *II,ind,0*
pakfefiiwe *release, forgiveness NI*
    pakfefiiweneki *NI/LOC*
pakfefiiweni *have forgiveness AI*
    pakfefiiweniki *AI,conj,3*
pakfemaw *release, forgive, deliver TA*
    pakfemoolepwa *TA,ind,1s,2p*
pakfen *let loose, deliver TI_1*
    pakfena *TI,ind,3s,0s*
    pakfenaana *TI,ind,3s,0p*

pakfenaanaawa *TI,ind,3p,0*
pakfenameekwe *TI,conj,2p,0*
pakfenamelici *TI,conj,4,0*
pakfenano *TI,imp,2s,0*
peepakfenaka *TI/IC,part,3s,0*
pakfen *deliver, release TA*
  hopakfenaali *TA,ind,3s,4s*
  hopakfenekooli *TA,ind,4s,3s*
  pakfena *TA,ind,1s,3s*
  pakfenaaci *TA,conj,3s,4*
  pakfenaali *TA,ind,3s,4s*
  pakfenaawaaci *TA,conj,3p,4*
  pakfenaawaali *TA,ind,3p,4s*
  pakfenaawahi *TA,ind,3p,4p*
  pakfenehko *TA,imp,2p,3*
  pakfenekoci *TA,conj,4,3s*
  pakfenekohi *TA,ind,4p,3s*
  pakfenekooki *TA,ind,3p,2s*
  pakfenekooli *TA,ind,4s,3s*
  pakfenekoopi *TA,ind,3,1s*
  pakfenekoopwa *TA,ind,3,2p*
  pakfenekote *TA,subj,4,3s*
  pakfenekowaaki *TA,ind,3p,2p*
  pakfenekwa *TA,ind,3s,2s*
  pakfenelepe *TA,ind,1x,2*
  pakfeniki *TA,conj,3,1s*
  pakfenita *TA,part,3s,1s*
pakfenamaake *deliver AI*
  pakfenamaake *AI,ind,3s*
  pakfenamaakeeki *AI,conj,3*
pakfenamaw *deliver, hand over TA*
  hopaapakfenamawahi *TA,ind,3s,4p*
  hopakfenamawaawaali *TA,ind,3p,4s*
  hopakfenamawahi *TA,ind,3s,4p*
  pakfenamaakoopi *TA,ind,3,2s*
  pakfenamaakwa *TA,ind,3s,1s*
  pakfenamaakwi *TA,ind,,3s*
  pakfenamawaaci *TA,conj,3s,4*
  pakfenamawaate *TA,subj,3p,4*
  pakfenamawaawahi *TA,ind,3p,4p*
  pakfenamawahi *TA,ind,3s,4p*
  pakfenamawaki *TA,conj,1s,3*
  pakfenamawinaake *TA,imp,2,1x*
  pakfenamoolako *TA,conj,1s,2p*
  pakfenamoolakwe *TA,conj,3,1i*
  pakfenamoolepe *TA,ind,1x,2*

pakfenikee *offer AI*
  pakfenikeelo *AI,imp,2s*
  pakfenikeeyane *AI,subj,2s*
pakfenikeewe *offering, gift NI*
  pakfenikeewe *NI,s*
pakfeniwee *release, deliver AI*
  pakfeniweeko *AI,imp,2p*
pakfenoofo *be delivered, be placed AI*
  pakfenoofo *AI,ind,3s*
  pakfenoofoci *AI,conj,3s*
  pakfenoofolici *AI,conj,4*
pakfenoofoowe *excuse NI*
  pakfenoofoowe *NI,s*
pakfenoote *be delivered, be handed over II*
  pakfenooteeki *II,conj,0*
pakici *going home PV*
  pakici *PV*
pakicihkaatiim *oppose TA*
  pakicihkaatiimaaci *TA,conj,3s,4*
pakicihkoote *be spoken against II*
  peekicihkooteeki *II/IC,conj,0*
pakickwahkot *tend a vineyard TI-O*
  paapakickwahkotamelici *TI/IC,conj,4,0*
pakit *throw, spend, put away from TI_1*
  hopakitaana *TI,ind,3s,0p*
  hopakitaanaawa *TI,ind,3p,0*
  pakita *TI,ind,3s,0s ; TI,ind,1s,0s*
  pakitaana *TI,ind,3s,0p*
  pakitaanaawa *TI,ind,3p,0*
  pakitaki *TI,conj,3s,0*
  pakitakki *TI,part,3p,0*
  pakitamani *TI,conj,2s,0*
  pakitamelici *TI,conj,4,0*
  pakitano *TI,imp,2s,0*
  pakite *TI,ind,3s,0s*
  pakiteenake *TI,subj,3s,0*
pakitaam *condemn TA*
  pakitaamaawaaki *TA,ind,2p,3p*
pakitahfo *spend AI*
  pakitahfo *AI,ind,2s*
pakiteht *leave as a crumb TI_1*
  peekitehtamowaaci *TI/IC,conj,3p,0*
pakitehtoote *be left as a crumb II*
  peekitehtooteeki *II/IC,conj,0*
paksim *go down; be in the west II*
  yeepaksimoki *II/IC,conj,0*

paksimo *go down* AI
    paksimoci *AI,conj,3s*
paksin *fall* AI
    paksinooli *AI,ind,4s*
    paksinwa *AI,ind,3s*
pakwaci *wild* PM
    pakwaci *PM*
pakwatahki *land, ground* NI
    pakwatahki *NI,s*
palasaana *offspring of an animal* NA
    hopalasaanhhi *NA/POSS,3s,4p*
    palasaana *NA,3s*
palasaanimeekiife *lamb* NA
    hopalasaanimeekiifemali *NA/POSS,3s,4s*
    nipalasaanimeekiifaki *NA/POSS,1s,4p*
palasaanimekiifa *lamb* NA
    palasaanimekiifaki *NA,3p*
paleecika *chest bone* NI
    hopalecika *NI/POSS,3s,s*
paleewa *chest* NI
    hopaleeki *NI/POSS/LOC,3s*
    hopaleewa *NI/POSS,3p*
    kipaleewaaki *NI/POSS/LOC,2s*
palepasii *Barabbas* NA
    palepasii *NA,3s*
    palepasiili *NA,4s*
panhtas *Pontius* NA
    panhtas *NA,3s*
papaweskaa *tremble* AI
    papaeskaaki *AI,ind,3p*
    papaweska *AI,ind,3s*
papaweskaaawe *trembling* NI
    papaweskaaawe *NI,s*
papawkwehtaw *wag one's head at* TA
    papawkwehtawaawaali *TA,ind,3p,4s*
papawkweskaa *wag the head* AI
    papawkweskaaki *AI,ind,3p*
papskwahkwat *be desert* II
    papskwahkiki *II,conj,0*
    peepskwahki *II/IC,conj,0*
papskwat *be desert* II
    papskwahki *II,conj,0*
pasiphoofo *be pierced* AI
    pasiphoofo *AI,ind,3s*
pasito *husband, old man* NA
    pasitoofa *NA,3s*

pasitoofiwi *old* AI
    pasitoofiwite *AI,subj,3s*
    pasitoofiwiyane *AI,subj,2s*
pasitoowi *old* PM
    pasitoowi *PM*
paskaapi *open the eyes, look up* AI
    paskaapi *AI,ind,3s*
paskahkweeyaa *emerge* II
    paskahkweeya *II,ind,0*
pawaawe *treasure, riches* NI
    hopawaawe *NI/POSS,3s,s*
    hopawaawenwa *NI/POSS,3p*
    kipawaawe *NI/POSS,2s,s*
    pawaawe *NI,s*
    pawaawena *NI,p*
pawaawilehfi *richness personified, mammon* NA
    pawaawilehfi *NA,3s*
pawaskwhaawi *threshing* PM
    hopawaskwhaawi *PM*
    pawaskwhaawi *PM*
pawaten *shake off*
    papawatenamoko *TI,imp,2p,0*
    pawatenamoko *TI,imp,2p,0*
pawee, pawaa *rich* AI
    paweewa *AI,ind,3s*
    peepawaacki *AI/IC,part,p*
    peewaalici *AI/IC,conj,4*
paweewe *treasure, riches* NI
    hopaweeweneki *NI/POSS/LOC,3s*
    kipaweewe *NI/POSS,2s,s*
    paweewe *NI,s*
    paweewena *NI,p*
    paweeweneki *NI/LOC*
paweewi *rich* PM
    paweewi *PM*
pawen *sift* TA
    pawenehki *TA,conj,3,2s*
pawiifa *pigeon* NA
    pawiifaki *NA,3p*
pawiifalanimiise *palm tree*
    pawiifalanimiise
pawnii *pound (unit of money)* NI
    kipawniima *NI/POSS,2s,s*
    kipawniimi *NI/POSS,2s,s*
    pawni *NI,s*
    pawniiwali *NI,p*

payaakilahi *away PV*
   payaakilahi *PV*
   payakila *PV*
   peepayakila *PV/IC*
payeci *ever PV*
   payeci *PV*
payeekwa *but CJN*
   payeekwa *CJN*
peefakofe *adhere II*
   peefakofeki *II,conj,0*
peefakwaakiasiski *clay NI*
   peefakwaakiasiski *NI,s*
peekskehka *piece NI*
   peekskahki *NI,p*
   peekskehkaaki *NI,p*
peelaawiki *summer NI*
   peelaawiki *NI,s*
peelekaaya *Barachiah NA*
   peelekaaya *NA,3s*
peeleko *at the time, once*
   peeleko
peelet *trust TI_1*
   yeepeeletakki *TI/IC,part,3p,0*
peeliyeesii *Perez NA*
   peeliyeesii *NA,3s*
   peeliyeesiili *NA,4s*
   piilesii *NA,3s*
peemaamehkiki *embankment NI*
   peemaamehkiki *NI,s*
peemaapacikee *be looking AI*
   peemaapacikeewaaci *AI,conj,3p*
peemahkeepi *be sitting AI*
   peemahkeepilici *AI,conj,4*
peemakofeki *beam NI*
   peemakofeki *NI,s*
peemekwaam *be sleeping AI*
   peemekwaamelici *AI,conj,4*
peemhtaki *stream NI*
   peemhtaki *NI,s*
peemi-hoci-lenaweewiiwe *that from which
one lives NI*
   hopeemi-hoci-lenaweewiiwe *NI/POSS,3s,s*
   kipeemi-hoci-lenaweewiiwe *NI/POSS,2s,s*
peemitakofeki *beam NI*
   peemitakofeki *NI,s*
peepaki *lightning NI*

peepaki *NI,s*
peepekicaawi *dark PM*
   peepekicaawi *PM*
peesekwi *completely PV*
   peesekwi *PV*
pefakokwiin *close AI*
   pefakokwiinooki *AI,ind,3p*
pefeci *Bethphage NI*
   pefeci *NI,s*
pefeciiki *Bethpage NI*
   pefeciiki *NI,s*
pefene *Bethany NI*
   pefene *NI,s*
   pefeneki *NI/LOC*
pefenoowe *speck NI*
   pefenoowe *NI,s*
pefeste *Bethesda NI*
   pefeste *NI,s*
pefet *pay attention to TI_1*
   hopefetaana *TI,ind,3s,0p*
   peefetaka *TI/IC,part,3s,0*
pefetaw *obey, pay attention to TA*
   hopefetaakohi *TA,ind,4p,3s*
   pefetaakoci *TA,conj,4,3s*
   pefetawaawaate *TA,subj,3p,4*
peflihemi *Bethlehem NI*
   peflihemi *NI,s*
   peflihemiki *NI/LOC*
pefseite *Bethesaida NI*
   pefseite *NI,s*
pehi *only, alone*
   pe
   pehi
   pehisi
pehkali *flame NI*
   pehkaleki *NI/LOC*
pehkeeyakoki *branch NI*
   pahkeeyakoki *NI,p*
   peepkeeyakoki *NI,p*
   pehkeeyakoki *NI,p*
pehkwaakamiki *pool NI*
   pehkwaakamiki *NI,s*
pehsat *taste TI_1*
   pehsata *TI,ind,3s,0s*
pehsen *touch TA*
   hopehsenaali *TA,ind,3s,4s*

nipehsenekwa *TA,ind,3s,1s*
peepehsenekoci *TA/IC,conj,4,3s*
pehsekoci *TA,conj,4,3s*
pehsenaaci *TA,conj,3s,4*
pehsenaali *TA,ind,3s,4s*
pehsenahi *TA,ind,3s,4p*
pehsenekoci *TA,conj,4,3s*
pehsenilo *TA,imp,2s,1s*
pehsen *touch TI_1*
    pehsena *TI,ind,3s,0s*
    pehsenaanaawa *TI,ind,2p,0*
pehsenamaw *touch TA*
    hopehsenaamawaali *TA,ind,3s,4s*
    nipehsenamaakwa *TA,ind,3s,1s*
    pehsenamaakoci *TA,conj,4,3s*
    pehsenamaawaali *TA,ind,3p,4s*
    pehsenamawaali *TA,ind,3s,4s*
    pehsenamawaawaaci *TA,conj,3p,4*
    pehsenamawahi *TA,ind,3s,4p*
    pehsenamawake *TA,subj,1s,3*
    pehsenamowaaci *TA,conj,3s,4*
pehsileceen *touch the hand TA*
    pehsileceenaali *TA,ind,3s,4s*
pekatefi *work AI*
    nipekatefi *AI,ind,1s*
    nipekatefipe *AI,ind,1x*
    paapekateficki *AI/IC,part,3p*
    paapekatefilici *AI/IC,conj,4*
    peekateficki *AI/IC,part,3p*
    peekatefita *AI/IC,part,3s*
    pekatefi *AI,ind,3s*
    pekatefiiki *AI,ind,3p*
    pekatefilici *AI,conj,4*
    pekatefilo *AI,imp,2s*
    pekatefiwaaci *AI,conj,3p*
    pekatefiyaake *AI,conj,1x*
    pekatefiyeekwe *AI,conj,2p*
pekatefiht *work for something TI_1*
    pekatefihtamoko *TI,imp,2p,0*
pekatefiim *work with TA*
    pekatefiimahi *TA,ind,3s,4p*
pekatefiiwe *work NI*
    hopekatefiiwe *NI/POSS,3s,s*
    hopekatefiiwena *NI/POSS,3s,p*
    hopekatefiiwenwa *NI/POSS,3p*
    hopekatefiiwenwaaki *NI/POSS/LOC,3p*

kipekatefiiwena *NI/POSS,2s,p*
pekatefiiwe *NI,s*
pekatefiiwena *NI,p*
pekatefiiwenwa *NI/POSS,2p*
pekatefiiyaa *work, be in effect II*
    paapekatefiiya *II,ind,0*
    pekatefiiyaali *II,ind,4*
    pekatefiiyaalici *II,conj,4*
pekaten *perform TI_1*
    kipekatena *TI,ind,2s,0s*
    nipekatenaana *TI,ind,1s,0p*
    peekatenaka *TI/IC,part,3s,0*
    peekatenakki *TI/IC,part,3p,0*
    pekatenaana *TI,ind,3s,0p*
    pekatenaataako *TI,imp,1i,0*
    pekatenaki *TI,conj,3s,0*
pekaten *serve TA*
    pekatenakwe *TA,conj,1i,3*
pekatenamaw *do something for someone TA*
    pekatenamaakwa *TA,ind,3s,1s*
    pekatenamawa *TA,ind,2s,3s*
pekatenoote *be performed II*
    pekatenooteeki *II,conj,0*
pekihk *mumur TI_1*
    pekihkamelici *TI,conj,4,0*
pekihkaat *mumur TI_1*
    pekihkaatamelici *TI,conj,4,0*
pekihkaati *dispute [reciprocal] AI*
    pekihkaatiiki *AI,ind,3p*
pekihkaatiiwe *contention NI*
    pekihkaatiiwe *NI,s*
pekihkaawe *mumur AI*
    pekihkaaweeki *AI,ind,3p*
pekihkaw *mumur TA*
    hopekihkawaawaali *TA,ind,3p,4s*
    hopekihkawaawahi *TA,ind,3p,4p*
pekikalawiiwe *troublesome speech NI*
    hopekikalawiiwe *NI/POSS,3s,s*
    nipekikalawiiwe *NI/POSS,1s,s*
    pekikalawiiwe *NI,s*
    pekikalawiiwenwa *NI/POSS,3p*
pekilot *do in a troublesome way TI_1*
    pekilotameekwe *TI,conj,2p,0*
pekiskim *revile TA*
    hopekiskimaawaali *TA,ind,3p,4s*
pekiskowe *murmur (against) AI*

pekiskoweeki *AI,ind,3p*
pekskin *break into pieces TI_1*
   hopekskinaana *TI,ind,3s,0p*
pekskinoote *be broken into pieces II*
   peekskinooteeki *II/IC,conj,0*
pekwe *grain, bit NI*
   pekwe *NI,s*
pekwi *dust, ash NI*
   pekoki *NI/LOC*
   pekwi *NI,s*
pelahci *first, before*
   pelahci
peleef *chick NA*
   hopelefemhhi *NA/POSS,3s,4p*
peleewa *turkey NA*
   peleewa *NA,3s*
pelesi *Pharisee NA*
   pelesi *NA,3s*
   pelesihi *NA,4p*
   pelesiiki *NA,3p*
   pelesiili *NA,4s*
pelh *unbind TI_1*
   pelha *TI,ind,2s,0s*
   pelhaanaawa *TI,ind,2p,0*
   pelhama *TI,conj,1s,0*
pelhamaw *release to someone TA*
   hopelhamawahi *TA,ind,3s,4p*
   pelhamawaaci *TA,conj,3s,4*
   pelhamawaki *TA,conj,1s,3*
pelhhw *unbind TA*
   hopelhhwaawaali *TA,ind,3p,4s*
   kipelhhwaawa *TA,ind,2p,3s*
   pelhhohko *TA,imp,2p,3*
   pelhhola *TA,conj,1s,2s*
   pelhhwaaci *TA,conj,3s,4*
   pelhhwaali *TA,ind,3s,4s*
   pelhhwaawa *TA,ind,2p,3s*
   pelhhwaawaaci *TA,conj,3p,4*
   pelhhwate *TA,subj,2s,3*
pelhoofo *be released AI*
   pelhoofo *AI,ind,3s*
pelhoofoowe *release NI*
   pelhoofoowe *NI,s*
pelhoote *be unbound II*
   pelhoote *II,ind,0*
pelhskohkaa *become loose II*

pelhskohkaali *II,ind,4*
pelhskon *release TA*
   pelhskonehko *TA,imp,2p,3*
   pelhskonekoopi *TA,ind,3,2s*
peloocihi *afterwards, soon*
   peloocih
   peloocihi
   peloociisi
pelowaamat *far II*
   pelowaamatwi *II,ind,0s*
pelowi *far*
   pelowi
   pelowihi
pemaalakwi *? hole ? NI*
   pemaalakwi *NI,s*
pemaatowaafoowe *parable NI*
   hopemaatowaafoowe *NI/POSS,3s,s*
pemaatoweewe *parable NI*
   hopemaatoweewe *NI/POSS,3s,s*
   pemaatoweewe *NI,s*
   pemaatoweewena *NI,p*
   pemaatoweeweneki *NI/LOC*
pemapiwa *be sitting AI*
   pemapiiki *AI,ind,3p*
pemhfaal *pass (someone) TA*
   pemhfaalahi *TA,ind,3s,4p*
   pemhfaalekoci *TA,conj,0,3s*
pemhfaasiweewe *passover NI*
   hopemhfaasiweewenwa *NI/POSS,3p*
   pemhfaasiweewe *NI,s*
pemhfaasiweeweni *be the passover II*
   pemhfaasiweeweniki *II,conj,0*
pemhfaasiweewi *be the passover II*
   pemhfaasiweeki *II,conj,0*
   pemhfaasiweewi *II,ind,0s*
   pemhfaasiweewiki *II,conj,0*
pemhfee *go, pass, walk AI*
   lohfi-pemhfe *AI,ind,3s*
   peepemhfecki *AI/IC,part,p*
   pemhfe *AI,ind,3s*
   pemhfeeci *AI,conj,3s*
   pemhfeecki *AI,part,3p*
   pemhfeeki *AI,ind,3p*
   pemhfeeli *AI,ind,4s*
   pemhfeelici *AI,conj,4*
   pemhfeelo *AI,imp,2s*

pemhfeete *AI,subj,3s*
pemhfeewaaci *AI,conj,3p*
pemhfeeyeekwe *AI,conj,2p*
pemhfehi *AI,ind,4p*
pemhfeeyaa *pass II*
pemhfeeya *II,ind,0*
pemhfeeyaake *II,subj,0*
pemhfeeyaaki *II,conj,0*
pemhkaam *? dip ? TA*
pemhkaamita *TA,part,3s,1s*
pemhkaawe *piece of bread, sop NI*
pemhkaawe *NI,s*
pemi *[progressive] PV*
hopemi *PV*
kipemi *PV*
nipemi *PV*
paapemi *PV*
peemi *PV*
pemi *PV*
pemi *oil, grease NI*
kipemimwa *NI/POSS,2p*
pemi *NI,s*
pemoote *walk AI*
pemooteeki *AI,ind,3p*
penen *take down TA*
penenaali *TA,ind,3s,4s*
penenahi *TA,ind,3s,4p*
penenoofo *be thrown down AI*
penenoofota *AI,part,3s*
penhfen *fall II*
penhfeke *II,subj,0*
penhfeki *II,conj,0*
penhfeno *II,ind,0p*
penhfenwi *II,ind,0s*
penhsin *fall AI*
penhsika *AI,part,3s*
penhsinooki *AI,ind,3p*
penhsinooli *AI,ind,4s*
penhsinwa *AI,ind,3s*
pepekicaa *dark II*
peepekicaaki *II/IC,conj,0*
pepekica *II,ind,0*
pepekicaake *II,subj,0*
pepekicaaki *II,conj,0*
pepekichoofo *be darkened AI*
pepekichoofo *AI,ind,3s*

pepekici *dark PM*
pepekici *PM*
pepelooni *Babylon PM*
pepelooni *PM*
pepikwa *trumpet NI*
pepikwa *NI,s*
pepikwe *play the flute AI*
peepikwelici *AI/IC,conj,4*
pepikwehtaw *play the flute TA*
kipepikwehtoolepe *TA,ind,1x,2*
pepoon *winter, north II*
pepooki *II/IC,conj,0*
pepoonhkiiki *II,conj,0*
pepoonwi *II,ind,0s*
pesfen *touch on, concern II*
pesfeki *II,conj,0*
peshalwe *certify AI*
peshalwe *AI,ind,3s*
peshalwem *certify TA*
peshalwemaali *TA,ind,3s,4s*
pesikwahkocehoofo *be made straight AI*
pesikwahkocehoofo *AI,ind,3s*
pesikwi *alone, oneself*
pesikwi
pesikwi *straight II*
pesikwa *II,ind,0p*
pesipehteemi *? grape ? NI*
pesipehteemi *NI,p*
petakhoote *be covered II*
petakhoote *II,ind,0*
petakhoowe *covering NI*
petakhoowe *NI,s*
petakhooyaa *cover II*
petakhooya *II,ind,0*
petakhw *cover TA*
hopetakhwaali *TA,ind,3s,4s*
hopetakhwaawaali *TA,ind,3p,4s*
petakwfen *be covered II*
petakwfenwi *II,ind,0s*
petawh *cover TA*
petawhinaake *TA,imp,2,1x*
petekakit *restore, redeem TI_1*
petekakitano *TI,imp,2s,0*
petekfet *restore, redeem TI_2*
hopetekfeto *TI,ind,3s,0s*
nipetekfeto *TI,ind,2s,0s*

petekfeto *TI,ind,3s,0s*
petekfetaw *redeem, restore (to) TA*
    petekfetaakoopi *TA,ind,3,2s*
    petekfetaakwa *TA,ind,3s,2s*
petekfetwaatiiwe *recompense NI*
    petekfetwaatiiwe *NI,s*
peteki *back (to)*
    peteki
petekinamoowe *recovery NI*
    petekinamoowe *NI,s*
petekinoofoowe *redemption NI*
    hopetekinoofoowe *NI/POSS,3s,s*
    kipetekinoofoowenwa *NI/POSS,2p*
    petekinoofoowe *NI,s*
petekishoofo *be restored AI*
    petekishoofo *AI,ind,3s*
petekistoote *be restored II*
    petekistooteeli *II,ind,4*
petekitepen *redeem TA*
    petekitepenaata *TA,part,3s,4*
petfakat *be troubled II*
    petfakatwi *II,ind,0s*
petfakh *trouble, vex TA*
    kipetfakhaawa *TA,ind,2p,3s*
    kipetfakheko *TA,ind,0s,2s*
    nipetfakhekwa *TA,ind,3s,1s*
    peetfakhekocki *TA/IC,part,4,3p*
    petfakha *TA,ind,2s,3s*
    petfakhekooli *TA,ind,4s,3s*
    petfakhi *TA,imp,2s,3*
    petfakhilo *TA,imp,2s,1s*
petfakifi *be troubled AI*
    kipetfakifipwa *AI,ind,2p*
    petfakifi *AI,ind,3s*
    petfakifiyeekwe *AI,conj,2p*
petfakifiiyaa *be troubled II*
    petfakifiiya *II,ind,0*
petfakit *trouble TI_2*
    petfakitoolo *TI,imp,2s,0*
petfakitehee *be troubled AI*
    peetfakiteheeyeekwe *AI,conj,2p*
    petfakitehe *AI,ind,3s*
    petfakiteheeki *AI,ind,3p*
petfakiteheesk *trouble, vex TA*
    hopetfakiteheeskaako *TA,ind,0s,3s*
petfakiteheewe *care, trouble NI*

petfakiteheewe *NI,s*
petfakowe *murmur AI*
    petfakoweeki *AI,ind,3p*
    petfakoweko *AI,imp,2p*
petfakoweewe *murmur NI*
    petfakoweewe *NI,s*
pethan *catch TA*
    hopethanaawahi *TA,ind,3p,4p*
    pethanaaki *TA,ind,2s,3p*
    pethanaawaaci *TA,conj,3p,4*
    pethaneekwe *TA,part,2p,3*
    pethanekoci *TA,conj,4,3s*
pethatat *catch TI_2*
    hopethatoonaawa *TI,ind,3p,0*
    nipethatoope *TI,ind,1x,0*
pethataw *catch TA*
    pethataakoci *TA,conj,4,3s*
pfekho *? wear ? AI*
    pfekhohi *AI,ind,4p*
pfiiwe *piece of cloth, handkerchief NI*
    pfiiwenehi *NI,s*
pihci *long, long time*
    pihci
pihsaaka *cloth; cord; harness NI*
    pihsaakana *NI,p*
pihtawi *joined PM*
    pihtawi *PM*
pihtawikooti *coat, cloak NI*
    hopihtawikootiimi *NI/POSS,3s,s*
    pihtawikooti *NI,s*
pihtawiniisene *twice, two-fold*
    pihtawiniisene
pihtawipiitenika *coat, cloak NI*
    kipihtawipiitenika *NI/POSS,2s,s*
    pihtawipiitenikaneki *NI/LOC*
pihtawipiitenikee *wear a robe AI*
    pihtawipiitenikeeli *AI,ind,4s*
pihteewefi *foam AI*
    paapihteewefi *AI,ind,3s*
    pihteewefiili *AI,ind,4s*
pihtowe *repetition NI*
    pihtoweewena *NI,p*
piicfaal *enter into TA*
    kipiicfaala *TA,ind,2s,3s*
piicfaam *enter into TA*
    hopiicfaamaali *TA,ind,3s,4s*

hopiicfaamekooli *TA,ind,4s,3s*

piicfaamakici *TA,conj,1x,3*

piicfaamekoci *TA,conj,4,3s*

piicfah *cause to enter, bring in TA*

hopiicfahaali *TA,ind,3s,4s*

piicfahaawaaci *TA,conj,3p,4*

piicfahekoopwa *TA,ind,3,2p*

piicfat *enter TI_1*

hopiicfata *TI,ind,3s,0s*

piicfata *TI,ind,3s,0s*

piicfataanaawa *TI,ind,3p,0*

piicfataki *TI,conj,3s,0*

piicfatameekwe *TI,conj,2p,0*

piicfatamaw *enter TA*

piicfatamawaali *TA,ind,3s,4s*

piicfe *[in, into] PV*

hopiicfe *PV*

piicfe *PV*

piicfee, piicfaa *enter AI*

kipiicfaapwa *AI,ind,2p*

peepiicfaacki *AI/IC,part,3p*

piicfa *AI,ind,2s*

piicfaaci *AI,conj,3s*

piicfaacki *AI,part,3p*

piicfaako *AI,imp,2p*

piicfaalici *AI,conj,4*

piicfaalo *AI,imp,2s*

piicfaapwa *AI,ind,2p*

piicfaata *AI,part,3s*

piicfaate *AI,subj,3s*

piicfaawaaci *AI,conj,3p*

piicfaawaate *AI,subj,3p*

piicfaaya *AI,conj,1s*

piicfaayane *AI,subj,2s*

piicfaayani *AI,conj,2s*

piicfaayeekwe *AI,conj,2p*

piicfe *AI,ind,3s*

piicfeeki *AI,ind,3p*

piicfeeli *AI,ind,4s*

piicfeem *enter (to where someone is) TA*

hopiicfeemaali *TA,ind,3s,4s*

piicfeeyaa *enter II*

piicfeeya *II,ind,0*

piicfehfen *be thrown in II*

piicfehfeno *II,ind,0p*

piici *inside*

piici

piicika *inner room NI*

piicikaana *NI,p*

piictaamhkwe *country, region NI*

piicitaamhkwe *NI,s*

piictaamhkwe *NI,s*

piikone *? sulphur [with siikona] ? PM*

piikone *PM*

piikwehsin *fall AI*

piikwehsinooki *AI,ind,3p*

piileki *Peleg NA*

piileki *NA,3s*

piilepe *lest*

piilepe

piilepeeke *lest*

piilepeeke

piileski *wilderness NI*

piileski *NI,s*

piimeelem *think bad of TA*

piimeelemehki *TA,conj,3,2s*

piimi *wrongly PV*

kipaapiimi *PV*

piimi *PV*

piimi-ashetiiwe *temptation NI*

piimi-ashetiiwe *NI,s*

piimi-ashoofoowe *temptation NI*

nipiimi-ashoofooweneki *NI/POSS/LOC,1s*

piimilawi *do wrong AI*

piimilawi *AI,ind,3s*

piimilawiiyeekwe *AI,conj,2p*

piimilawiiwe *error NI*

hopiimilawiiwe *NI/POSS,3s,s*

piimilawiiwe *NI,s*

piimilehfi *malefactor NA*

piimilehfihi *NA,4p*

piimilehfiiki *NA,3p*

piimilot *pervert, mislead TI_1*

piimilotaki *TI,conj,3s,0*

piimilotaw *wrong TA*

kipiimilotoole *TA,ind,1s,2s*

peepiimilotawaata *TA/IC,part,3s,4*

piimiwel *lead astray TA*

piimiwelaawahi *TA,ind,3p,4p*

piimiwelelwaakwe *TA,conj,3,2p*

piimiweloofo *be led astray AI*

piimiweloofoyeekwe *AI,conj,2p*

piimiwesiwee *lead astray* AI
    piimiwesiweewaaci *AI,conj,3p*
piimotaw *conceive in* TA
    peepiimotaakoci *TA/IC,conj,4,3s*
piinh *put in* TI
    piinhhano *TI,imp,2s,0*
piipkeeweni *be apart* II
    piipkeeweniki *II,conj,0*
piipkwilecwh *beat* TA
    hopiipkwilecwhaawaali *TA,ind,3p,4s*
piipokwilecwh *hit* TA
    hopiipokwilecwhaawaali *TA,ind,3p,4s*
piisikalawi *affirm* AI
    piisikalawi *AI,ind,3s*
piisiteheewe *patience* NI
    kipiisiteheewenwaaki *NI/POSS/LOC,2p*
    piisiteheewe *NI,s*
piita *Peter* NA
    piita *NA,3s*
    piitali *NA,4s*
piitaaka *wallet* NI
    piitaaka *NI,s*
    piitaakaneki *NI/LOC*
piitaakanhfecika *wallet* NI
    piitaakanhfecika *NI,s*
piitaakaniko *wallet* NI
    piitaakaniko *NI,s*
piitaakanimota *sackcloth* NI
    piitaakanimotaaki *NI/LOC*
piitaalakehseen *touch inside the ear* TA
    hopiitaalakehseenaali *TA,ind,3s,4s*
piitawi *be Peter* AI
    piitawiyani *AI,conj,2s*
piiten *wear* TI_1
    paapiitenakki *TI/IC,part,3p,0*
    piitenameekwe *TI,conj,2p,0*
piitenika *clothing* NI
    hopiitenika *NI/POSS,3s,s*
    hopiitenikana *NI/POSS,3s,p*
    hopiitenikani *NI/POSS,3s,s*
    hopiitenikanilici *NI/POSS,4*
    hopiitenikanwa *NI/POSS,3p*
    nipiitenikana *NI/POSS,1s,p*
    piitenika *NI,s*
    piitenikana *NI,p*
    piitenikaneki *NI/LOC*

piitenikee *wear, dress* AI
    piitenike *AI,ind,3s*
    piitenikeeli *AI,ind,4s*
    piitenikeelici *AI,conj,4*
    piitenikeepe *AI,ind,1i*
    piitenikeepwa *AI,ind,2p*
piitenikeh *clothe* TA
    hopiitenikehaali *TA,ind,3s,4s*
    hopiitenikehaawaali *TA,ind,3p,4s*
    kipiitenikehelepe *TA,ind,1x,2*
    kipiitenikehipwa *TA,ind,2p,1*
    piitenikehehko *TA,imp,2p,3*
piitenikehoofo *be clothed* AI
    piitenikehoofoyeekwe *AI,conj,2p*
piitika *inside room* NI
    piitikaana *NI,p*
piitike *in, within*
    piitike
piitikeen *take in, house*
    kipiitikeenelepe *TA,ind,1x,2*
    kipiitikeenipwa *TA,ind,2p,1*
piiwalwi *bush* NI
    piiwaloki *NI/LOC*
    piiwalwi *NI,s*
pikee *stray* AI
    peepikeelici *AI/IC,conj,4*
    pikeeli *AI,ind,4s*
    pikeelici *AI,conj,4*
pikeewh *put away, set aside* TA
    pikeewhaaci *TA,conj,3s,4*
piyaawe *coming* NI
    hopiyaawe *NI/POSS,3s,s*
    kipiyaawe *NI/POSS,2s,s*
    piyaawe *NI,s*
piyeci *[come]* PV
    hopiyeci *PV*
    kipiyeci *PV*
    nipiyeci *PV*
    peepiyeci *PV/IC*
    piyeci *PV*
piyee, piyaa *come* AI
    kipiya *AI,ind,2s*
    nipaapiya *AI,ind,1s*
    nipiya *AI,ind,1s*
    nipiyaape *AI,ind,1x*
    peepiyaacki *AI/IC,part,3p*

peepiyaata *AI/IC,part,s*
peepiyeeta *AI/IC,part,s*
piya *AI,ind,1s*
piyaa *AI,ind,1s*
piyaaci *AI,conj,3s*
piyaako *AI,imp,2p*
piyaalici *AI,conj,4*
piyaalite *AI,subj,4s*
piyaalo *AI,imp,2s*
piyaapwa *AI,ind,2p*
piyaata *AI,part,s*
piyaate *AI,subj,3s*
piyaawaaci *AI,conj,3p*
piyaaya *AI,conj,1s*
piyaayane *AI,subj,2s*
piyaayani *AI,conj,2s*
piyeeki *AI,ind,3p*
piyeeli *AI,ind,4s*
piyeewa *AI,ind,3s*
piyehi *AI,ind,4p*
yeepiyaaci *AI/IC,conj,3s*
piyeel *bring TA*
hopiyeelaali *TA,ind,3s,4s*
hopiyeelaawaali *TA,ind,3p,4s*
kipiyeelaawa *TA,ind,2p,3s*
piyeela *TA,ind,2s,3s*
piyeelaaki *TA,ind,1s,3p*
piyeelaali *TA,ind,3s,4s*
piyeelaawaaci *TA,conj,3p,4*
piyeelaawaali *TA,ind,3p,4s*
piyeelehko *TA,imp,2p,3*
piyeelekoopi *TA,ind,3,2s*
piyeelekoopwa *TA,ind,3,2p*
piyeelekowaaki *TA,ind,3p,2p*
piyeelelwaakwa *TA,conj,3,2p*
piyeesi *TA,imp,2s,3*
piyeesinaake *TA,imp,2,1x*
piyeelaakwaam *the time comes II*
piyeelaakwaamhki *II,conj,0*
piyeelhkamaw *send TA*
peepiyeelhkamaweci *TA/IC,conj,,3*
piyeelhkamawaawaali *TA,ind,3p,4s*
piyeelhkamawoofo *be sent AI*
peepiyeelhkamawoofoci *AI/IC,conj,3s*
piyeelhkaw *send TA*
piyeelhkawaaci *TA,conj,3s,4*

piyeelhsipalii *Beelzebub NA*
piyeelhsipalii *NA,3s*
piyeelhsipaliili *NA,4s*
piyeeloofo *be brought out AI*
piyeeloofo *AI,ind,3s*
piyeelot *come to TI_1*
piyeelotaki *TI,conj,3s,0*
piyeelotakki *TI,part,3p,0*
piyeelotamaw *come TA*
piyeelotamaakoci *TA,conj,4,3s*
piyeelotaw *bring to TA*
hopiyeelotaakohi *TA,ind,4p,3s*
hopiyeelotaakooli *TA,ind,4s,3s*
hopiyeelotawaali *TA,ind,3s,4s*
hopiyeelotawaawaali *TA,ind,3p,4s*
kipiyeelotawi *TA,ind,2s,1s*
kipiyeelotawipwa *TA,ind,2p,1*
kipiyeelotoole *TA,ind,1s,2s*
nipiyeelotaakooki *TA,ind,3p,1s*
nipiyeelotaakwa *TA,ind,1s,3s*
peepiyeelotawaacki *TA/IC,part,3p,4*
peepiyeelotawaata *TA/IC,part,3s,4*
peepiyeelotawita *TA/IC,part,3s,1s*
peepiyeelotoolwaakwe *TA/IC,conj,3,2p*
piyeelotaakohi *TA,ind,4p,3s*
piyeelotaakooli *TA,ind,4s,3s*
piyeelotaakowa *TA,ind,3s,2p*
piyeelotaakwa *TA,ind,3s,1s*
piyeelotawaali *TA,ind,3s,4s*
piyeelotawaape *TA,ind,1x,3*
piyeelotawici *TA,conj,3s,1s*
piyeelotawiko *TA,imp,2p,1s*
piyeelotawipwa *TA,ind,2p,1s*
piyeelotawite *TA,subj,3s,1s*
piyeelotawiwaaci *TA,conj,3p,1s*
piyeelotawiwaate *TA,subj,3p,1s*
piyeelotoola *TA,conj,1s,2s*
piyeelotoolepwa *TA,ind,1s,2p*
piyeemikat *happen II*
peepiyeemikaki *II/IC,conj,0*
piyeemikake *II,subj,0*
piyeemikaki *II,conj,0*
piyeemikato *II,ind,0p*
piyeemikatwi *II,ind,0s*
piyeepto *run to someone AI*
piyeeptohi *AI,ind,4p*

piyeeptooli *AI,ind,4s*
piyeet *bring TI_2*
    hopiyeeto *TI,ind,3s,0s*
    hopiyeetoona *TI,ind,3s,0p*
    hopiyeetoonaawa *TI,ind,3p,0*
    piyeeto *TI,ind,3s,0s*
    piyeetooko *TI,imp,2p,0*
    piyeetoonaawa *TI,ind,3p,0*
    piyeetoota *TI,part,3s,0*
piyeetaacimoowe *news NI*
    hopiyeetaacimoowe *NI/POSS,3s,s*
    piyeetaacimoowe *NI,s*
    piyeetaacimoowena *NI,p*
piyeetahkamikat *come to be II*
    piyeetahkamikiki *II,conj,0*
piyeetahkofa *rise AI*
    piyeetahkofaki *AI,conj,3s*
piyeetahkofamaw *rise for TA*
    piyeetahkofamawaaci *TA,conj,3s,4*
piyeetapicikee *draw (water) AI*
    piyeetapicikeeyani *AI,conj,2s*
piyeetapit *draw, fetch TI_2*
    piyeetapitooci *TI,conj,3s,0*
piyeetathamaw *bring, present TA*
    kipiyeetatenamoolepwa *TA,ind,1s,2p*
    piyeetatenamawici *TA,conj,3s,1s*
    piyeetathamawaawaali *TA,ind,3p,4s*
piyeetaw *bring TA*
    hopiyeetaakohi *TA,ind,4p,3s*
    hopiyeetawaali *TA,ind,3s,4s*
    hopiyeetawaawaali *TA,ind,3p,4s*
    kipiyeetawaawa *TA,ind,2p,3s*
    kipiyeetawipwa *TA,ind,2p,1*
    kipiyeetoole *TA,ind,1s,2s*
    kipiyeetoolepwa *TA,ind,1s,2p*
    nipiyeetawaaki *TA,ind,1s,3p*
    piyeetaakoci *TA,conj,4,3s*
    piyeetaakowa *TA,ind,3s,2p*
    piyeetaakwi *TA,ind,,3s*
    piyeetawaawaaci *TA,conj,3p,4*
    piyeetawaawaali *TA,ind,3p,4s*
    piyeetawiko *TA,imp,2p,1s*
    piyeetawilo *TA,imp,2s,1s*
    piyeetoola *TA,conj,1s,2s*
piyeetawiwee *bring AI*
    piyeetawiwe *AI,ind,3s*

piyeeteelet *expect TI_1*
    hopiyeeteeleta *TI,ind,3s,0s*
piyeeten *bring to TA*
    piyeetenaaki *TA,ind,1s,3p*
    piyeetenekote *TA,subj,4,3s*
piyeetfe *come near AI*
    piyeetfe *AI,ind,3s*
    piyeetfeci *AI,conj,3s*
    piyeetfeeki *AI,ind,3p*
piyeethan *get to, arrive at II*
    piyeethanwi *II,ind,0s*
piyeethw *bring to TA*
    piyeethokwiiki *TA,ind,,3p*
piyeetoofo *be brought AI*
    piyeetoofoci *AI,conj,3s*
piyeetoote *be brought II*
    piyeetoote *II,ind,0*
    piyeetooteeki *II,conj,0*
piyeeyaa *come II*
    peepiyeeyaaki *II/IC,conj,0*
    piyeeya *II,ind,0*
    piyeeyaake *II,subj,0*
    piyeeyaaki *II,conj,0*
    piyeeyaali *II,ind,4*
    piyeeyaalite *II,subj,4*
    yeepiyeeyaaki *II/IC,conj,0*
pkaleen *light, kindle TI-O*
    pkaleenamooki *TI,ind,3p,0*
    pkaleenamowaaci *TI,conj,3p,0*
pkaleenoote *be lit, be kindled II*
    pkaleenoote *II,ind,0*
pkameewi *gluttonous, ravenous PM*
    pkameewi *PM*
pkamefiwi-leni *gluttonous person NA*
    pkamefiwi-leni *NA,3s*
pkee, pkaa *apart from AI*
    pkeewa *AI,ind,3s*
pkeewh *put apart TA*
    pkeewheekwe *TA,conj,2p,3*
pkeeyahkofiiwe *branch NI*
    hopkeeyahkofiiwe *NI/POSS,3s,s*
pkeeyahkwat *put forth branches II*
    pkeeyahkwatwi *II,ind,0s*
pkehkaa *come apart, break II*
    pkehkaalici *II,ind,4*
pkehoofo *be set apart AI*

peepkehoofolici *AI/IC,conj,4*

pkehoofoci *AI,conj,3s*

pkehoofolici *AI,conj,4*

pkehotiiwi *separating PV*

pkehotiiwi *PV*

pkehw *set apart TA*

peepkehwaata *TA/IC,part,3s,4*

pkehwaaci *TA,conj,3s,4*

pkehwaali *TA,ind,3s,4s*

pkin *tear, separate TA*

pkinaawahi *TA,ind,3p,4p*

pkinahi *TA,ind,3s,4p*

pkin *tear, separate, pluck TI_1*

pikina *TI,ind,3s,0s*

pkinaana *TI,ind,3s,0p*

pkinamehi *TI,ind,4p,0*

pkiteh *hit TI_1*

hopkiteha *TI,ind,3s,0s*

pkitehaanaawa *TI,ind,3p,0*

pkitehfen *be hit II*

pkitehfeno *II,ind,0p*

pkitehfenwi *II,ind,0s*

yeepkitehfeki *II/IC,conj,0*

pkitehfet *hit TI_2*

pkitehfeto *TI,ind,2s,0s*

pkitehikee *hit AI*

pkitehikeepe *AI,ind,1x*

pkitehw *hit TA*

hopaapkitewhaawaali *TA,ind,3p,4s*

hopkitehwaali *TA,ind,3s,4s*

hopkitehwaawaali *TA,ind,3p,4s*

kipkitehokwa *TA,ind,3s,2s*

kipkitehwi *TA,ind,2s,1s*

peepkitehohka *TA/IC,part,3,2s*

pkitehwaawaaci *TA,conj,3p,4*

pkitewhaawaali *TA,ind,3p,4s*

pkonaapat *faint TI-O*

pkonaapatamooki *TI,ind,3p,0*

pletooliyami *Praetorium NI*

pletooliam' *NI,s*

pletooliami *NI,s*

pletooliamiiki *NI/LOC*

pletooliyami *NI,s*

pohkiceskaa *break, burst AI*

pohkiceskaaki *AI,ind,3p*

pohkiceskaw *burst TA*

pohkiceskaakonaawa *TA,ind,0,3p*

pohkin *break TA*

hopohkinaali *TA,ind,3s,4s*

pohkwahkeen *root up, tear out TI_1*

pohkwahkeenanaawa *TI,ind,2p,0*

pok *book NI*

pok *NI,s*

pokh *break TI_1*

pokhamowaaci *TI,conj,3p,0*

pokhoote *be broken into II*

pokhooteelici *II,conj,4*

pokwahkeesk *uproot TI*

pokwahkeeskaalo *TI,imp,2s,0*

pokwan *taste II*

yeepokwaki *II/IC,conj,0*

poocaaki *corner NI*

poocaaki *NI,s*

pooceeyaa *make a corner II*

piipooceeyaaki *II,conj,0*

pooenaciis *Boanerges NA*

pooenaciis *NA,3s*

pooesii *Boaz NA*

pooesii *NA,3s*

pooesiili *NA,4s*

poofi *perhaps*

poofi

pookamhtoote *be disturbed II*

pookamhtooteeki *II,conj,0*

pookat *wave II*

peepookaki *II/IC,conj,0*

poon *have, put TA*

hopoonaali *TA,ind,3s,4s*

hopoonaawaali *TA,ind,3p,4s*

hopoonaawahi *TA,ind,3p,4p*

hopoonahi *TA,ind,3s,4p*

kipoona *TA,ind,2s,3s*

kipoonaape *TA,ind,1i,3*

kipoonaawa *TA,ind,2p,3s*

kipoonaawaaki *TA,ind,2p,3p*

kipoonipwa *TA,ind,2p,1*

nipoona *TA,ind,1s,3s*

nipoonaaki *TA,ind,1s,3p*

nipoonaape *TA,ind,1x,3*

peepoonaacki *TA/IC,part,3p,4*

peepoonaata *TA/IC,part,3s,4*

peepoonaawaaci *TA/IC,conj,3p,4*

peepoonata *TA/IC,part,2s,3s*
poona *TA,ind,1s,3s*
poonaaci *TA,conj,2s,3*
poonaacki *TA,part,3p,4*
poonaaki *TA,ind,2s,3p*
poonaali *TA,ind,3s,4s*
poonaata *TA,part,3s,4*
poonaate *TA,subj,3s,4*
poonaawaaci *TA,conj,3p,4*
poonaawaali *TA,ind,3p,4s*
poonaci *TA,conj,2s,3*
poonake *TA,subj,1s,3*
poonakici *TA,conj,1x,3*
poonekoci *TA,conj,4,3s*
poonekwa *TA,ind,3s,2s*
pooni *TA,imp,2s,3*
poonita *TA,part,3s,1s*

poon *have, put TI_1*
hopoona *TI,ind,3s,0s*
hopoonaana *TI,ind,3s,0p*
hopoonaanaawa *TI,ind,3p,0*
hopoonameli *TI,ind,4s,0*
kipoona *TI,ind,2s,0s*
kipoonaana *TI,ind,2s,0p*
kipoonaanaawa *TI,ind,2p,0*
kipoonaape *TI,ind,1i,0*
nipoona *TI,ind,1s,0s*
nipoonaape *TI,ind,1x,0*
peepoonaka *TI/IC,part,3s,0*
peepoonaki *TI/IC,conj,3s,0*
peepoonakki *TI/IC,part,3p,0*
peepoonama *TI/IC,conj,1s,0*
peepoonamani *TI/IC,conj,2s,0*
peepoonameekwe *TI/IC,conj,2p,0*
peepoonamelici *TI/IC,conj,4,0*
poona *TI,ind,3s,0s ; TI,ind,2s,0s ; TI,ind,1s,0s*
poonaana *TI,ind,3s,0p*
poonaanaawa *TI,ind,3p,0 ; TI,ind,2p,0*
poonaape *TI,ind,1i,0*
poonaka *TI,part,3s,0*
poonake *TI,subj,3s,0*
poonaki *TI,conj,3s,0*
poonama *TI,conj,1s,0*
poonamaatiyeekwe *TI,subj,2p,0*
poonamane *TI,subj,2s,0*
poonamani *TI,conj,2s,0*

poonameekwe *TI,conj,2p,0 ; TI,subj,2p,0*
poonameli *TI,ind,4s,0*
poonamelici *TI,conj,4,0*
poonamoko *TI,imp,2p,0*
poonamowaaci *TI,conj,3p,0*
poonanaana *TI,ind,3s,0p*
poonano *TI,imp,2s,0*

poonahfat *store away TI_1*
peepoonahfotaka *TI/IC,part,3s,0*
poonahfatamoko *TI,imp,2p,0*

poonahfocika *container NI*
poonahfecika *NI,s*
poonahfocika *NI,s*
poonahfocikana *NI,p*

poonahfoom *possess TA*
peepoonahfoomekota *TA/IC,part,4,3s*

poonahfoowakokwa *container NI*
hopoonahfowakokonwaaki *NI/POSS/LOC,3p*
poonahfoowakokwa *NI,s*

poonahfoowika *storage place NI*
poonahfoowika *NI,s*
poonahfoowikaaneki *NI/LOC*

poonamaw *put TA*
hopoonamawaali *TA,ind,3s,4s*
nipoonamawaaki *TA,ind,1s,3p*
poonamaakooli *TA,ind,4s,3s*
poonamawa *TA,ind,2s,3s*
poonamawaaci *TA,conj,3s,4*
poonamawaali *TA,ind,3s,4s*
poonamawaawaali *TA,ind,3p,4s*
poonamawahi *TA,ind,3s,4p*
poonamawanaake *TA,imp,2,1x*
poonamaweekwe *TA,subj,2p,3*
poonamawi *TA,imp,2s,3 ; TA,ind,2s,1s*
poonamawilo *TA,imp,2s,1s*
poonamawinaake *TA,imp,2,1x*
poonamoola *TA,conj,1s,2s*
poonamoolehki *TA,conj,3,2s*

poonameyaa *have II*
pooname *II,subj,0*
poonameya *II,ind,0*

pooneelem *have in mind TA*
pooneelemaaci *TA,conj,3s,4*

poonoofo *be had, be put AI*
poonoofoci *AI,conj,3s*
poonoofolici *AI,conj,4*

poonoofooli *AI,ind,4s*
poonoote *be put* II
  peepoonooteeki *II/IC,conj,0*
  poonoote *II,ind,0*
  poonooteeki *II,conj,0*
  yeepoonooteeki *II/IC,conj,0*
pootaacikeeyaa *blow* II
  pootaacikeeya *II,ind,0*
pootaalaawaa *(skin) sack* NA
  pootaalaawaaki *NA,3p*
  pootaalaawahi *NA,4p*
pootefamaacika *altar* NI
  nipootefamaacika *NI,s*
  pootefamaacika *NI,s*
  pootefamaacikaneki *NI/LOC*
pootefamaacikani *altar* PM
  pootefamaacikani *PM*
poothaaka *mill* NI
  poothaakaneki *NI/LOC*
  poothaakani *NI,s*
poothaakanisiikona *millstone* NA
  poothaakanisiikonali *NA,4s*
poposkwihsin *be broken* AI
  pohposkwihsinwa *AI,ind,3s*
  poposkwihsinwa *AI,ind,3s*
posili *bushel* NI
  posili *NI,s*
  posiliiki *NI/LOC*
posk *break* TI_1
  poska *TI,ind,3s,0s*
poskhoote *be broken* II
  poskhoote *II,ind,0*
poskon *break* TI_1
  hoposkona *TI,ind,3s,0s*
  hoposkonaana *TI,ind,3s,0p*
  poskona *TI,ind,3s,0s*
  poskonaki *TI,conj,3s,0*
  poskonama *TI,conj,1s,0*
  poskonamoko *TI,imp,2p,0*
  poskonamowaaci *TI,conj,3p,0*
poskonoote *be broken* II
  poskonoote *II,ind,0*
  poskonooteeki *II,conj,0*
poskwikaathoofo *have the leg broken* AI
  poskwikaathoofolici *AI,conj,4*
poskwikaathw *break the leg* TA

hoposkwikaathwaawaali *TA,ind,3p,4s*
ppaktehoofo *be beaten* AI
  ppaktehoofo *AI,ind,3s*
ppaktehw *beat* TA
  hoppaktehokohi *TA,ind,4p,3s*
  hoppaktehwaawaali *TA,ind,3p,4s*
  ppaktehokoopwa *TA,ind,3,2p*
  ppaktehwaawahi *TA,ind,3p,4p*
  ppaktehwahi *TA,ind,3s,4p*
ppehci *[in opposition]* PV
  hoppehci *PV*
  kippehci *PV*
  peeppehci *PV*
  ppehci *PV*
ppehcim *speak against* TA
  ppehcimaali *TA,ind,3s,4s*
  ppehcimaawaali *TA,ind,3p,4s*
ppehten *resist, oppose* TA
  nippehtenekwa *TA,ind,3s,1s*
  ppehtenehko *TA,imp,2p,3*
  ppehtenelakwe *TA,part,3,1i*
  ppehtenelwaakwe *TA,part,3,2p*
ppehten *oppose* TI_1
  hoppehtena *TI,ind,3s,0s*
pskipaapo *vinegar* NI
  pskipaapo *NI,s*
pskipefiiwe *taste* NI
  hopskipefiiwe *NI/POSS,3s,s*
pskipefoofo *be seasoned* AI
  pskipefoofo *AI,ind,3s*
pskipetee *be seasoned, salted* II
  pskipete *II,ind,0*
pwaa *[negative]* PV
  paapwaa *PV*
  peepwaa *PV/IC*
  pwaa *PV*
  pwaayaa *PV*
pwaa-laakwasi *never*
  pwaa-laakwa
  pwaa-laakwasi
pwaateepwehseewe *unbelief* NI
  hopwaateepwehseewenilici *NI/POSS,4*
  hopwaateepwehseewenwa *NI/POSS,3p*
  nipwaateepwehseewe *NI/POSS,1s,s*
pwaatepasawiilefiiwe *unrighteousness* NI
  pwaatepasawiilefiiwe *NI,s*

saailiinii *Cyrene* NI
    saailiinii *NI,s*
saakweelemo *faint, pine away* AI
    saakweelemo *AI,ind,3s*
    saakweelemolici *AI,conj,4*
saamiiwekamoowe *psalm* NI
    saamiiwekamoowena *NI,p*
    saamiiwekamooweneki *NI/LOC*
saapoci *through* PV
    saapoci *PV*
saaponika *needle* NI
    saaponika *NI,s*
saapwi *through*
    saapwi
saapwi *through, go through* AI
    saapwiici *AI,conj,3s*
    saapwiiki *AI,ind,3p*
    saapwiipwa *AI,ind,2p*
    saapwiiwaaci *AI,conj,3p*
saatami *Sodom* NI
    saatami *NI,s*
    saatamiiki *NI/LOC*
saatamiiwi *Sodom* PM
    saatamiiwi *PM*
saatanii *Sidon* NI
    saatanii *NI,s*
    saataniiki *NI/LOC*
    saatenii *NI,s*
saataniiwi *Sidon* PM
    saataniiwi *PM*
saawe *withdraw, depart* AI
    saawe *AI,ind,3s*
    saaweci *AI,conj,3s*
    saaweeki *AI,ind,3s*
    saaweeli *AI,ind,4s*
    saaweewaaci *AI,conj,3p*
    saawehi *AI,ind,4p*
    saaweko *AI,imp,2p*
    saawelici *AI,conj,4*
    saawelo *AI,imp,2s*
saaweyaa *leave, depart* II
    saaweya *II,ind,0*
    saaweyaali *II,ind,4*
saayan *Zion* NI
    saayan' *NI,s*
    saayani *NI,s*

sahfo *wither* AI
    sahfo *AI,ind,3s*
sahkiki *down*
    sahkiki
sahsaakitoon *make naked* TA
    hosahsaakitoonaawaali *TA,ind,3p,4s*
sahsaakitwi *naked* AI
    kisahsaakitwi *AI,ind,2s*
    nisahsaakitwi *AI,ind,1s*
    sahsaakitwi *AI,ind,3s*
    sahsaakitwiili *AI,ind,4s*
sahte *scorched,, withered*
    sahte
saika *Sychar* NI
    saika *NI,s*
sailoomi *Siloam* NI
    sailoomi *NI,s*
    sailoomiki *NI/LOC*
saimanii *Simon* NA
    saiman' *NA,3s*
    saimanii *NA,3s*
    saimaniili *NA,4s*
salamanii *Solomon* NA
    salaman' *NA,3s*
    salamanii *NA,3s*
    salamaniili *NA,4s*
samaakana *soldier* NA
    hosamaakanemhhi *NA/POSS,3s,4p*
    samaakana *NA,3s*
    samaakanaki *NA,3p*
    samaakanali *NA,4s*
    samaakanhhi *NA,4p*
sapa *supper* NI
    sapa *NI,s*
sapaa *dine* AI
    sapaawiki *AI,conj,3*
    sapaawiya *AI,conj,1s*
    sesapaawiki *AI,conj,3*
sapaawe *supper* NI
    nisapaawe *NI/POSS,1s,s*
    sapaaki *NI/LOC*
    sapaawe *NI,s*
sapkahi *indeed*
    sapka
    sapkahi
sci *lo [interjection]*

sci
scih *lo [exclamation]*
    scih
seekimiyaakwa *spice NI*
    seekimiyaakoki *NI,p*
seekwa *aroma NI*
    sekwa *NI,s*
seekwan *dull II*
    sekwano *II,ind,0p*
sefi *Seth NA*
    sefi *NA,3s*
sehkamika *long time, long time ago*
    sehkamika
sehkipakimhskwaa *purple II*
    sehkipakimhskwaaki *II,conj,0*
sehkwaalawe *hungry AI*
    sehkwaalawelici *AI,conj,4*
sehkwaalaweeweni *exist hunger II*
    sehkwaalaweeweniki *II,conj,0*
sehpaalakiki *steep hill NI*
    sehpaalakiki *NI,s*
sehpaamehki *steep II*
    sehpaamehkiki *II,conj,0*
sehpateki *high*
    sehpateki
sekalaaya *Zachariah NA*
    sekalaaya *NA,3s*
    sekolaaya *NA,3s*
sekali *shekel NI*
    sekali *NI,s*
sekaten *spread TI_1*
    hosekatenaanaawa *TI,ind,3p,0*
sekfen *be laid on, lie II*
    sekfeno *II,ind,0p*
    sekfenwi *II,ind,0s*
sekfet *lay TI_2*
    sekfetooci *TI,conj,3s,0*
    sekfetooya *TI,conj,1s,0*
    sekfetooyani *TI,conj,2s,0*
sekfetaw *lay TA*
    sekfetaakoci *TA,conj,4,3s*
    sekfetawaaci *TA,conj,3s,4*
    sekfetawi *TA,ind,2s,1s*
    sekfetoole *TA,ind,1s,2s*
sekias *Zacchaeus NA*
    sekias *NA,3s*

sekifet *lay down TI_2*
    nisekifeto *TI,ind,1s,0s*
    sekifetooya *TI,conj,1s,0*
sekifetaw *lay down TA*
    hosekifetawahi *TA,ind,3s,4p*
    nisekifetawaaki *TA,ind,1s,3p*
sekisim *lay TA*
    sekisimaawa *TA,ind,2p,3s*
sekolaayes' *Zacharias NA*
    sekolaayes' *NA,3s*
    sekolaayesiili *NA,4s*
seksim *lay TA*
    hoseksimaawaali *TA,ind,3p,4s*
    hoseksimaawahi *TA,ind,3p,4p*
    seksimaali *TA,ind,3s,4s*
    seksimaawaaci *TA,conj,3p,4*
    seksimaci *TA,conj,2s,3*
seksimoofo *be laid AI*
    seksimoofoci *AI,conj,3s*
    seksimoofolici *AI,conj,4*
    seksimoofooli *AI,ind,4s*
seksin *lie, recline AI*
    seksiki *AI,conj,3s*
    seksinelici *AI,conj,4*
    seksinooki *AI,ind,3p*
    seksinooli *AI,ind,4s*
    seksinwa *AI,ind,3s*
sekwafkoote *be bruised II*
    sesekwafkooteeki *II/IC,conj,0*
sele *Zerah NA*
    seleli *NA,4s*
seleni *penny NI*
    seleni *NI*
selhtiye *Shealtiel NA*
    selhtiye *NA,3s*
    selhtiyeeli *NA,4s*
    sialhtiali *NA,3s*
selife *Zarephath NA*
    selifeli *NA,4s*
selimi *Salim NI*
    selimi *NI,s*
selmanii *Salmon NA*
    selmanii *NA,3s*
    selmaniili *NA,4s*
seloomi *Salome NA*
    seloomi *NA,3s*

sem *Shem* NA
    sem *NA,3s*
semelia *Samaritan* NA
    semelia *NA,3s*
    semeliaki *NA,3p*
semelie *Samaria* NI
    semelie *NI,s*
    semeliye *NI,s*
    semeliyeki *NI/LOC*
semeliyewi *Samaritan* PM
    semeliyewi *PM*
semeliyewiikwe *Samaritan woman*
    semeliyewiikwe *NA,3s*
semeliyewilenawe *Samaritan* NA
    semeliyewilenawe *NA,3s*
    semeliyewilenaweeki *NA,3p*
    semeliyewilenawehi *NA,4p*
semeliyewiyani *be from Samaria* AI
    semeliyewiyani *AI,conj,2s*
semiyani *Semein* NA
    semiyani *NA,3s*
senhsi *farthing* NI
    senhsi *NI,s ; NI,p*
sepakfenai *sabachthani [Aramaic word]*
    sepakfenai
sepetii *Zebedee* NA
    sepetii *NA,3s*
    sepetiili *NA,4s*
sesipaafi *empty* AI
    sesipaafihi *AI,ind,4p*
    sesipaafiili *AI,ind,4s*
sesipaayaa *empty* II
    sesipaaya *II,ind,0*
seskifi *empty-handed; barren* AI
    seskificki *AI,part,3p*
    seskifiili *AI,ind,4s*
seskihkwe *virgin* NA
    seskihkwe *NA,3s*
seskiikweefa *virgin* NA
    seskiikweefa *NA,3s*
    seskiikweefaki *NA,3p*
    seskiikweefali *NA,4s*
seskiikwefiwiiwe *virginity* NI
    hoseskiikwefiwiiweneki *NI/POSS/LOC,3s*
seskwat *? be devoid of ?* II
    seskatwi *II,ind,0s*

sesonamaw *anoint* TA
    hosesonamawaali *TA,ind,3s,4s*
    nisesonamaakwa *TA,ind,1s,3s*
    sesonamawaawaaci *TA,conj,3p,4*
seswilaaka *plate* NI
    seswilaaka *NI,s*
    seswilaakaneki *NI/LOC*
setaka *Sadoc* NA
    setaka *NA,3s*
    setakali *NA,4s*
setenii *Satan* NA
    setenii *NA,3s*
    seteniili *NA,4s*
setosii *Sadducee* NA
    setosihi *NA,4p*
    setosiiki *NA,3p*
sfetaw *order; prepare* TA
    hosfetoolaake *TA,conj,1x,2*
    yeesfetaakowaaci *TA/IC,conj,4,3p*
    yeesfetawaaci *TA/IC,conj,3s,4*
sfetoofo *be prepared* AI
    sfetoofoci *AI,conj,3s*
si *[manner]* PV
    hotaasi *PV*
    hotesi *PV*
    kitesi *PV*
    nitesi *PV*
    si *PV*
    yaasi *PV/IC*
    yeesi *PV/IC*
si *kind of* PM
    si *PM*
si-siikwahkamikifiiwena *desolation (personified)* NA
    si-siikwahkamikifiiwena *NA,3s*
siifasi *Cephas* NA
    siifasi *NA,3s*
siikawi-yhkweewi *be a widow* AI
    sesiikawi-yhkweewilici *AI/IC,conj,4*
    siikawi-yhkweewi *AI,ind,3s*
siikawi-ykwe *widow* NA
    siikawi-ykwe *NA,3s*
    siikawi-ykweeki *NA,3p*
    siikawi-ykweeli *NA,4s*
    siikawi-ykwehi *NA,4p*
siikeelem *hate* TA

holasiikaateelemaali *TA,ind,3s,4s*
hosiikeelemaali *TA,ind,3s,4s*
hosiikeelemahi *TA,ind,3s,4p*
hosiikeelemekohi *TA,ind,4p,3s*
kisiikeelemekowa *TA,ind,3s,2p*
nisiikeelemeko *TA,ind,0s,1s*
nisiikeelemekooki *TA,ind,3p,1s*
saakeelemelakwe *TA/IC,part,3,1i*
seesiikeelemelwaakwe *TA/IC,part,3,2p*
seesiikeelemita *TA/IC,part,3s,1s*
siikeelemaali *TA,ind,3s,4s*
siikeelemeekwe *TA,conj,2p,3*
siikeelemekonaawa *TA,ind,0,2p*
siikeelemekooki *TA,ind,3p,1s*
siikeelemekowaaki *TA,ind,3p,2p*
siikeelemelwaakwe *TA,subj,3,2p ;*
TA,conj,3,2p
  siikeelemi *TA,imp,2s,3*
  siikeelemici *TA,conj,3s,1s*
siikeelemekofi *be hated AI*
  siikeelemekofipwa *AI,ind,2p*
siikeelemekofiim *cause to be hated TA*
  siikeelemekofiimekowaaki *TA,ind,3p,2p*
siikeelet *hate TI_1*
  hosiikeeleta *TI,ind,3s,0s*
  sesiikeeletaka *TI/IC,part,3s,0*
siikeeleti *hate [reciprocal] AI*
  siikeeletiiki *AI,ind,3p*
siikona *stone NA*
  siikona *NA,3s*
  siikonaki *NA,3p*
  siikonali *NA,4s*
  siikoneki *NA/LOC,3*
  siikonhhi *NA,4p*
siikonahkat *rocky II*
  siikonahkiki *II,conj,0*
siikonakat *rocky II*
  siikonakiki *II,conj,0*
siikonhhw *stone TA*
  hosiikonhhwaawaali *TA,ind,3p,4s*
  hosiikonhhwahi *TA,ind,3s,4p*
  saasiikonhhwaata *TA/IC,part,3s,4*
  siikonhhohki *TA,conj,3,2s*
  siikonhhokonaaki *TA,ind,3p,1x*
  siikonhholepe *TA,ind,1x,2*
  siikonhhwaate *TA,subj,3s,4*
  siikonhhwaawaaci *TA,conj,3p,4*

siikonhhwakici *TA,conj,1x,3*
siikonhhwipwa *TA,ind,2p,1s*
siikoninepiwakokwa *stone water jug NA*
  siikoninepiwakokooki *NA,3p*
siikwahkamikifiiwe *desolation NI*
  hosiikwahkamikifiiwe *NI/POSS,3s,s*
  siikwahkamikifiiwe *NI,s*
siikwi *left over [after death] PM*
  siikwi *PM*
siikwitahfoowe *goods obtained by force NI*
  hosiikwitahfoowe *NI/POSS,3s,s*
siikwitoowefi *extort AI*
  sesiikwitooweficki *AI/IC,part,3p*
siikwitoowefiiwe *extortion NI*
  siikwitoowefiiwe *NI,s*
siila *Shelah NA*
  siila *NA,3s*
siilaki *Serug NA*
  siilaki *NA,3s*
siilat *Zealot NA*
  siilat *NA,3s*
siipaaci *under, beneath*
  siipaaci
siipefiiyaa *harden II*
  siipefiiya *II,ind,0*
siipenamaw *harden TA*
  hosiipenamawahi *TA,ind,3s,4p*
siipfen *become hard II*
  siipenilici *II,conj,4*
  siipfenwi *II,ind,0s*
  siipfenwili *II,ind,4*
siipiteheewe *hardness of heart NI*
  hosiipiteheewenwa *NI/POSS,3p*
siisa *Caesar NA*
  siisa *NA,3s*
  siisali *NA,4s*
siisesiiwinoochiweewe *insurrection NI*
  siisesiiwinoochiweewe *NI,s*
silawen *welcome TA*
  hosilawenahi *TA,ind,3s,4p*
silawiim *do with, concern onself with TA*
  lawiimela *TA,conj,1s,2s*
silawiiyaa *do II*
  yeesilawiiyaaki *II/IC,conj,0*
siliye *Syria NI*
  siliye *NI,s*

siliyeki *NI/LOC*
siliyeewifeniisiyeewi *Syro-Phoenician PM*
    siliyeewifeniisiyeewi *PM*
siliyeewileni *Syrian NA*
    siliyeewileni *NA,3s*
simekofihtamaw *have authority over TA*
    simekofihtamaweekwe *TA,conj,2p,3*
simekofiyot *have authority over TI_1*
    simekofiyotamani *TI,conj,2s,0*
simiyaakwi *have an odor II*
    yeesimiyaakoki *II/IC,conj,0*
simiyani *Symeon NA*
    simiyani *NA,3s*
sin *marry TA*
    hosinaali *TA,ind,3s,4s*
sinaakwat *seem, be like II*
    sinaakwatwi *II,ind,0s*
sinamoowe *vision NI*
    sinamoowe *NI,s*
sinetiiwe *title NI*
    sinetiiwe *NI,s*
sini *call, name AI*
    siniki *AI,conj,3*
sinoofo *be called AI*
    sinoofo *AI,ind,3s*
    sinoofoci *AI,conj,3s*
    sinoofolici *AI,conj,4*
    wiinoofo *AI,ind,3s*
sipolanii *Zebulun NA*
    sipolani *NA,3s*
sipolaniiwi *Zebulun PM*
    sipolaniiwi *PM*
sisaliye *Caesarea NI*
    sisaliye *NI,s*
sisimoofo *be laid AI*
    yeesisimoofolici *AI/IC,conj,4*
sisin *be thus AI*
    yeesisiki *AI/IC,conj,3*
siskiwakkonhke *make earthenware pots AI*
    yeesiskiwakkonhkeeta *AI/IC,part,3s*
sitamaw *call, name TA*
    sitamawa *TA,ind,2s,3s*
sitasini *citizen NA*
    hositasiniimhhi *NA/POSS,3s,4p*
    sitasinihi *NA,4p*
siteheeweni *have a wish, have a feeling AI*

siteheeweniwaaci *AI,conj,3p*
sitoote *be called, be named II*
    sitoote *II,ind,0*
    yeesitooteeki *II/IC,conj,0*
siweloofo *be led, be taken AI*
    siweloofo *AI,ind,3s*
skahot *make wet TI_2*
    skahotoona *TI,ind,3s,0p*
skahotaw *make wet TA*
    skahotaakooli *TA,ind,4s,3s*
skanoofi *soft II*
    skanoofi *II,ind,0*
skata *it is to be desired*
    skata
skilawehfiifa *boy NA*
    skilawehfiifa *NA,3s*
    skilawehfiifali *NA,4s*
skilawehfiwi *male PM*
    skilawehfiwi *PM*
skipaki *green, blue*
    skipaki
skipakskahki *green grass NI*
    skipakskahki *NI,s*
skipwaawi *green plant NI*
    skipwaawiki *NI/LOC*
skonoofo *be left AI*
    skonoofo *AI,ind,3s*
skote *fire NI*
    skote *NI,s*
    skoteeki *NI/LOC*
skwaalawaafiiwe *famine NI*
    skwaalawaafiiwena *NI,p*
skwaalaweewahkamikat *famine II*
    seeskwaalaweewahkamikiki *II/IC,conj,0*
skwaalaweewe *hunger NI*
    skwaalaweewe *NI,s*
skwaalaweeweni *famine II*
    seeskwaalaweeweniki *II/IC,conj,0*
skwaapiye *edge, coast NI*
    skwaapiye *NI,s*
    skwaapiyeeki *NI/LOC*
    skwaapiyeekiisi *NI/LOC*
skwaate *gate, door NI*
    hoskwaateemeki *NI/POSS/LOC,3s*
    hoskwaateemwa *NI/POSS,3p*
    kiskwaateemi *NI/POSS,2s,s*

skwaate *NI,s*
skwaateeki *NI/LOC*
skwaateewali *NI,p*
skwaatekehcitawaht *guard a gate TI_2*
skwaatekehcitawahtoolici *TI,conj,4,0*
skwaaya *border NI*
hoskwaayaamwaaki *NI/POSS/LOC,3p*
skwaaya *NI,s*
skwat *have left over TI-O*
skwatamelici *TI,conj,4,0*
skwatoote *be left over, be excess II*
seskwatooteeki *II/IC,conj,0*
skwihfen *spare, have left over TI_1*
skwihfenamowaaci *TI,conj,3p,0*
skwiilefi *increase, become larger AI*
skwiilefi *AI,ind,3s*
skwiilenawe *generation NA*
skwiilenawe *NA,3s*
skwiilenaweeki *NA,3p*
skwiilenawehi *NA,4p*
skwiilenaweewiiwe *generation NI*
hoskwiilenaweewiiwenwa *NI/POSS,3p*
skwiilenaweewiiwe *NI,s*
skwiinamaw *increase TA*
skwiinamawinaake *TA,imp,2,1x*
skwiiwa *grow, increase AI*
skwiiwa *AI,ind,3s*
skwiiwe *generation NI*
skwiiwe *NI,s*
skwiiwena *generation NA*
skwiiwena *NA,3s*
skwiiwenali *NA,4s*
skwiiyaa *increase II*
skwiiya *II,ind,0*
skwiiyaaki *II,conj,0*
skwikami *rise II*
skwikamiki *II,conj,0*
skwiniiki *grow AI*
skwiniiki *AI,conj,3s*
skwiniikiiki *AI,ind,3p*
skwiniikin *grow II*
skwiniikiki *II,conj,0*
skwiniikino *II,ind,0p*
skwiniikinwi *II,ind,0s*
solopeepalii *Zerubbabel NA*
silopeepalii *NA,3s*

solopeepalii *NA,3s*
solopeepaliili *NA,4s*
soosiyena *Susanna NA*
soosiyena *NA,3s*
soosooni *basket NI*
soosoona *NI,s*
soosoone *NI,s*
soosooni *NI,s*
soosooniwali *NI,p*
soskhol *summon TA*
soskholekwa *TA,ind,3s,2s*
soskiiwa *get up AI*
soskiiwa *AI,ind,3s*
soskwaafi *drag AI*
soskwaafiiki *AI,ind,3p*
soskwaten *let get away (fail to keep) TA*
hososkwatenaawaali *TA,ind,3p,4s*
spaalakat *deep II*
spaalakatwi *II,ind,0s*
spaalakwi *deep PV*
spaalakwi *PV*
spahkwikaani *porch NI*
spahkwikaani *NI,s*
ta-spahkwikaaniki *NI/LOC*
spaten *high PM*
spatenwi *PM*
speelemekofi *be above AI*
speelemekofi *AI,ind,3s*
speelemekofih *exhalt TA*
speelemekofihekoopi *TA,ind,3,2s*
speelemekwat *important II*
speelemekwatwi *II,ind,0s*
spefiiwe *stature, height NI*
spefiiweneki *NI/LOC*
spemefeki *above*
spemefeki
spemeki *above, up*
spemeki
spihfen *deep II*
spihfenwi *II,ind,0s*
spitemi *deep II*
yeespitemiki *II/IC,conj,0*
stoote *be made II*
stoote *II,ind,0*
stooteeki *II,conj,0*
stooteeli *II,ind,4*

taakteli *doctor [loanword]* NA
    taakteliiki *NA,3p*
taamhkwe *country, region* NI
    hotaamhkomwaaki *NI/POSS/LOC,3p*
    taamhkwe *NI,s*
    taamhkweewali *NI,p*
    taamhkweki *NI/LOC*
taamiyasi *Timaeus* NA
    taamiyasi *NA,3s*
taamosii *Thomas* NA
    taamosii *NA,3s*
    taamosiili *NA,4s*
taanihkiwe *where*
    taanihkiwe
taaniwe *which, what; where* PR
    taanawe *PR*
    taaniliwe *PR*
    taaniwe *PR*
taapiliasii *Tiberius* NA
    taapilias' *NA,3s*
taapiliasii *Tiberias* NI
    taapiliasii *NI,s*
taapiliasiiwi *Tiberias* PM
    taapiliasiiwi *PM*
    taapiliasiwi *PM*
taawalon *open the mouth* TA
    taawalonate *TA,subj,2s,3*
taayaa *Tyre* NI
    taayaa *NI,s*
    taayaaki *NI/LOC*
tah *[locational]* PV
    ta *PV/IC*
    tah *PV/IC*
    tayah *PV/IC*
    yaata *PV/IC*
    yaatah *PV/IC*
tah *there*
    ta
    tah
takhwa *bread* NI
    hotakhwaanemi *NI/POSS,3s,s*
    hotakhwaanemwa *NI/POSS,3p*
    nitakhwaanemena *NI/POSS,1x*
    nitakhwaanemi *NI/POSS,1s,s*
    nitakhwaanena *NI/POSS,1x*
    takhwa *NI,s*

takhwaani *bread* PM
    takhwaani *PM*
takhwaaniwi *be bread* AI
    takhwaaniwici *AI,conj,3s*
    takhwaaniwiwaaci *AI,conj,3p*
takot *join together* TI_2
    takotooci *TI,conj,3s,0*
takwaacimo *agree* AI
    takwaacimooki *AI,ind,3p*
takwaatot *compare, liken* TI_1
    takwaatota *TI,ind,1s,0s*
takweelemekofi *be compared to, be likened to* AI
    takweelemekofi *AI,ind,3s*
takweelemekwat *be compared to, be likened to* II
    takweelemekwatwi *II,ind,0s*
takweelet *compare to, liken* TI_1
    takweeletaape *TI,ind,1i,0*
takwhikee *grind* AI
    takwhikeeki *AI,ind,3p*
    takwhikeewaaci *AI,conj,3p*
takwi *together* PV
    takwi *PV*
takwi *belong to, be part of* II
    yeetakoki *II/IC,conj,0*
takwifet *join to* TI_2
    takwifeto *TI,ind,3s,0s*
takwikwaate *be joined* II
    takwikwaateeki *II,conj,0*
takwin *join together* TI_1
    takwinaki *TI,conj,3s,0*
takwinamaaw *assign a thing to someone* TA
    takwinamaakooli *TA,ind,4s,3s*
talahoot *cry out* TI-O
    nhtalahootamwa *TI,ind,3s,0*
    talahootaki *TI,conj,3s,0*
    talahootamwa *TI,ind,3s,0*
talatefo *be burdened (burden oneself)* AI
    yeetalatefoyaake *AI/IC,conj,1x*
talatelaakwi *be burdened* AI
    yeetalatelaakwiyaake *AI/IC,conj,1x*
talawikaal *write about* TA
    nitalawikaalekwa *TA,ind,3s,1s*
    yeetalawikaalaawaaci *TA/IC,conj,3p,4*
talawike *write about* AI

talawikeeki *AI,conj,3*
  tale *away from PV*
  hotale *PV*
talife *talitha [Aramaic]*
  talife
talmanoofa *Dalmanutha NI*
  talmanoofa *NI,s*
talwahfeeletamaw *entrust to TA*
  hotalwahfeeletamawahi *TA,ind,3s,4p*
talwahfw *put in charge TA*
  talwahfekota *TA,part,4,3s*
  talwahfekowa *TA,ind,3s,2p*
  talwahfele *TA,ind,1s,2s*
  talwahfwaali *TA,ind,3s,4s*
  teelwahfwaawaaci *TA/IC,conj,3p,4*
talwe *make sound II*
  yeetalweki *II/IC,conj,0*
talweewehfen *fall making noise II*
  talweewehfeki *II,conj,0*
  talweewehfeno *II,ind,0p*
  yeetalweewehfeki *II/IC,conj,0*
tamaka *? deep ? II*
  tamakaki *II,conj,0*
tasi *location, place*
  hotasi
  nitasi
  tasi
tasimo *cry out*
  nitasimo *AI,ind,3s*
  nitasimopi *AI,ind,3*
  tasimooki *AI,ind,3p*
tasimoowefi *use the voice, speak AI*
  tasimoowefi *AI,ind,2s*
tasiwee *? be somewhere ? AI*
  yeetasiweeci *AI/IC,conj,3s*
tatawaafiiwe *tumult NI*
  tatawaafiiwena *NI,p*
tatawaan *noisy II*
  tatawaanwi *II,ind,0s*
tatawaanhkee *make noise AI*
  kitatawaanhkeepwa *AI,ind,2p*
  tatawaanhkehi *AI,ind,4p*
tatawaanhkeewe *tumult NI*
  hotatawaanhkeewenwa *NI/POSS,3p*
  tatawaanhkeewe *NI,s*
tatawaanhkeewi *noisy, riotous PM*

tatawaanhkeewi *PM*
tateekakwi *thoroughly PV*
  tateekakwi *PV*
tawaaci *openly PV*
  hotawaaci *PV*
  tawaaci *PV*
tawaafiiwe *opportunity NI*
  tawaafiiwe *NI,s*
tawaawi *open II*
  tawaali *II,ind,4*
  tawaawi *II,ind,0s*
  teetawaaki *II/IC,conj,0*
  teewaaki *II/IC,conj,0*
tawaawiinamiiwe *free time, leisure NI*
  tawaawiinamiiwe *NI,s*
taweeteewika *tower NI*
  taweeteewika *NI,s*
  taweteewika *NI,s*
tawen *open TI_1*
  hotawena *TI,ind,3s,0s*
  hotawenaanaawa *TI,ind,3p,0*
  tawena *TI,ind,1s,0s*
tawenamaw *open TA*
  hotawenamawaali *TA,ind,3s,4s*
  hotawenamawahi *TA,ind,3s,4p*
  nitawenamaakwa *TA,ind,3s,1s*
  tawenamaakoopwa *TA,ind,3,2p*
  tawenamaakwa *TA,ind,3s,2s*
  tawenamaakwi *TA,ind,,3s*
  tawenamawaaci *TA,conj,3s,4*
  tawenamawaali *TA,ind,3s,4s*
  tawenamawaawaaci *TA,conj,3p,4*
  tawenamawehki *TA,conj,3,2s*
  tawenamawinaake *TA,imp,2,1x*
  tawenamoolakwe *TA,conj,3,1i*
  teetawenamawaata *TA/IC,part,3s,4*
tawenehika *key NI*
  tawenehika *NI,s*
  tawenehikana *NI,p*
tawenoofo *be opened AI*
  tawenoofolo *AI,imp,2s*
tawenoote *be opened II*
  tawenoote *II,ind,0*
  tawenooteeki *II,conj,0*
  tawenooteeli *II,ind,4*
taweskaa *open II*

taweska *II,ind,0s*
tawsk *open TI_1*
    teetawskaka *TI/IC,part,3s,0*
tayeewahi *opening, openly PV*
    tayeewahi *PV*
tee, taa *live, reside AI*
    teewa *AI,ind,3s*
    yeetaaci *AI/IC,conj,3s*
    yeetaacki *AI/IC,part,3p*
    yeetaalici *AI/IC,conj,4*
    yeetaawaaci *AI/IC,conj,3p*
    yeetaaya *AI/IC,conj,1s*
    yeetaayaake *AI/IC,conj,1x*
    yeetaayani *AI/IC,conj,2s*
    yeetaayeekwe *AI/IC,conj,2p*
teeksh *tithe, tax TI_1*
    kitaateekshaanaawa *TI,ind,2p,0*
    kiteekshaanaawa *TI,ind,2p,0*
teekshiwee *tax, collect tolls AI*
    teekshiweeki *AI,conj,3*
teekshoofoowe *tribute NI*
    teekshoofoowe *NI,s*
teekshotiiwe *tribute NI*
    teekshotiiwe *NI,s*
teeksiiwi *tax PM*
    teeksiiwi *PM*
teeksiiwi-maawatonikehfii *tax collector NA*
    teeksiiwi-maawatonikehfi *NA,3s*
    teeksiiwi-maawatonikehfihi *NA,4p*
    teeksiiwi-maawatonikehfiiki *NA,3p*
    teeksiiwi-maawatonikehfiili *NA,4s*
teemaa *Tamar NA*
    teemaali *NA,4s*
teenial *Daniel NA*
    teenial' *NA,3s*
teepahkole *give light thus far II*
    teepahkoleeki *II,conj,0*
teepali *table NI*
    hoteepaliimilici *NI/POSS,4*
    hoteepaliimwa *NI/POSS,3p*
teepasawahkoniwe *judge NA*
    teepasawahkoniwe *NA,3s*
    teepasawahkoniweeli *NA,4s*
teepasawateniwee *judge AI*
    teepasawateniweelici *AI,conj,4*
    teepasawateniweeta *AI,part,3s*

teepasawht *justify TI_2*
    teepasawhtooci *TI,conj,3s,0*
teepasawi *honest AI*
    teepasawiki *AI,ind,3p*
teepasawiilefi *just AI*
    teepasawiilefita *AI,part,3s*
    tepasawiilefita *AI,part,3s*
    tepasawiilefiwaaci *AI,conj,3p*
teepat *be enough II*
    teepatwi *II,ind,0s*
teepeelecikan *rule NI*
    teepeelecikaneki *NI/LOC*
teepeelecike *ruler, lord NA*
    hoteepeelecikeemhhi *NA/POSS/IC,3s,4p*
    kiteepeelecikeemenaaki *NA/POSS/IC,1i,3p*
    teepeelecikehi *NA/IC,4p*
teepeelecikee *rule, be lord over AI*
    teepeelecikeecki *AI/IC,part,3p*
    teepeelecikeelici *AI/IC,conj,4*
    teepeelecikeeta *AI/IC,part,3s*
teepeelem *rule TA*
    teepeelemaacki *TA/IC,part,3p,4*
    teepeelemaata *TA/IC,part,3s,4*
    teepeelemehka *TA/IC,part,3,2s*
    teepeelemekoci *TA/IC,conj,4,3s*
    teepeelemekowaaci *TA/IC,conj,4,3p*
    teepeelemelakwe *TA,part,3,1i*
    teepeelemelwaakwe *TA/IC,part,3,2p*
    teepeelemita *TA/IC,part,3s,1s*
teepeelemh *fill, satisfy TA*
    teepeelemhaaci *TA,conj,3s,4*
teepeelemiwee *rule, be lord AI*
    teepeelemiweelici *AI/IC,conj,4*
    teepeelemiweeta *AI/IC,part,3s*
teepeelemiwen *ruler, lord NA*
    niteepeelemiweema *NA/POSS,1s,3s*
    niteepeelemiweemali *NA/POSS,1s,4s*
teepeelemo *be satisfied, be content AI*
    teepeelemooki *AI,ind,3p*
    teepeelemope *AI,ind,1x*
teepeelemweewi *be the lord AI*
    teepeelemiweewici *AI,conj,3s*
    teepeelemweewilici *AI,conj,4*
teepeelet *rule, control TI_1*
    teepeeletaka *TI,part,3s,0*
    teepeeletamelici *TI/IC,conj,4,0*

teepeeletamhpenal *lord over* TA
    teepeeletamhpenalaawaaci *TA,conj,3p,4*
    teepeeletamhpenalekowaaci *TA,conj,4,3p*
teepfen *enough* II
    teepfeke *II,subj,0*
    teepfeno *II,ind,0p*
    teepfenwi *II,ind,0s*
teephetiiwe *gift* NI
    hoteephetiiwe *NI/POSS,3s,s*
    hoteephetiiwenwa *NI/POSS,3p*
    kiteephetiiwe *NI/POSS,2s,s*
    teephetiiwena *NI,p*
teephiwee *offer, present* AI
    teephiweewaaci *AI,conj,3p*
teephiweewe *offering* NI
    teephiweewe *NI,s*
teephool *fill* TA
    teephoolaaci *TA,conj,3s,4*
    teephoolahi *TA,ind,3s,4p*
    teephoolakwe *TA,conj,1i,3*
teephoolo *be filled* AI
    kiteephoolopwa *AI,ind,2p*
    teephoolooki *AI,ind,3p*
    teephoolopwa *AI,ind,2p*
    teephoolowaaci *AI,conj,3p*
    teeteephoolocki *AI/IC,part,3p*
teepi *enough* PM
    hoteepi *PM*
    teepi *PM*
    teeteepi *PM/IC*
teepiilefi *able, worthy, enough* AI
    kiteepiilefipwa *AI,ind,2p*
    niteepiilefi *AI,ind,1s*
    niteepiilefipe *AI,ind,1x*
    teepiilefi *AI,ind,3s*
    teepiilefici *AI,conj,3s*
    teepiilefiya *AI,conj,1s*
teepileelet *consider worthy* TI_1
    niteepileeleta *TI,ind,1s,0s*
teepim *convict* TA
    niteepimekwa *TA,ind,3s,1s*
    teepimaaci *TA,conj,3s,4*
teepinaakofi *appear* AI
    teepinaakofici *AI,conj,3s*
teepitehee *dare, be willing* AI
    teepitehe *AI,ind,3s*

teepiteheeyaa *willing* II
    teepiteheeya *II,ind,0*
teepitii *David* NA
    teepitii *NA,3s*
    teepitiili *NA,4s*
teepitiiwika *house of David* NI
    teepitiiwika *NI,s*
teepiwat *possible* II
    teepiwatwi *II,ind,0s*
teepowaasiwee *adjudicate* AI
    teepowaasiweeta *AI,part,3s*
teepowe *counsel* AI
    teepoweeta *AI,part,3s*
teepwe *true* AI
    teepwe *AI,ind,2s*
    teepweewici *AI,conj,3s*
teepweemineko *bear witness* AI
    teepweeminekolo *AI,imp,2s*
    teepweeminekoya *AI,conj,1s*
teepweewe *truth* NI
    hoteepweewe *NI/POSS,3s,s*
    hoteepweewenilici *NI/POSS,4*
    hoteepweewenwa *NI/POSS,3p*
    kiteepweewe *NI/POSS,2s,s*
    niteepweewe *NI/POSS,1s,s*
    niteepweewenena *NI/POSS,1x*
    teepeewe *NI,s*
    teepweewe *NI,s*
    teepweeweneki *NI/LOC*
teepweewen *truly* PV
    teepweewenwi *PV*
teepweewena *witness* NA
    teepweewena *NA,3s*
    teepweewenaki *NA,3p*
    teepweeweniwiiki *NA,3p*
teepweewenh *testify* TA
    niteepweewenhhekona *TA,ind,0p,1s*
    teepweewenhheekwe *TA,conj,2p,3*
    teepweewenhhekwa *TA,ind,3s,1s*
    teeteepweewenhhici *TA/IC,conj,3s,1s*
teepweewenhkaa *make testimony* AI
    teepweewenhkaawaaci *AI,conj,3p*
teepweeweni *have truth, be true* II
    teepweeweni *II,ind,0s*
    teepweeweniki *II,conj,0*
teepweeweniwiiwe *witnessing* NI

hoteepweeweniwiiwe *NI/POSS,3s,s*
niteepweeweniwiiwe *NI/POSS,1s,s*
teepweeweniwiiwe *NI,s*
teepwehsaakani *have faith AI*
   teepwehsaakanita *AI,part,3s*
teepwehsee *believe AI*
   kiteepwehse *AI,ind,2s*
   kiteepwehseepwa *AI,ind,2p*
   niteepwehse *AI,ind,1s*
   niteepwehseepe *AI,ind,1x*
   teepwehse *AI,ind,3s ; AI,ind,2s ; AI,ind,1s*
   teepwehseeci *AI,conj,3s*
   teepwehseecki *AI,part,3p*
   teepwehseeki *AI,ind,3p*
   teepwehseeko *AI,imp,2p*
   teepwehseelici *AI,conj,4*
   teepwehseelo *AI,imp,2s*
   teepwehseepe *AI,ind,1x*
   teepwehseepwa *AI,ind,2p*
   teepwehseeta *AI,part,3s*
   teepwehseewaaci *AI,conj,3p*
   teepwehseeya *AI,conj,1s*
   teepwehseeyakwe *AI,conj,1i*
   teepwehseeyane *AI,subj,2s*
   teepwehseeyani *AI,conj,2s*
   teepwehseeyeekwe *AI,conj,2p ; AI,subj,2p*
   teeteepwehseecki *AI/IC,part,3p*
   teeteepwehseelici *AI/IC,conj,4*
   teeteepwehseeta *AI/IC,part,3s*
teepwehseefa *believer [dimunitive] NA*
   teepwehseefa *NA,3s*
   teepwehseefaki *NA,3p*
teepwehseewe *belief, faith NI*
   hoteepwehseewenilici *NI/POSS,4*
   hoteepwehseewenwa *NI/POSS,3p*
   kiteepwehseewe *NI/POSS,2s,s*
   kiteepwehseewenwa *NI/POSS,2p*
   niteepwehseewenena *NI/POSS,1x*
   teepwehseewe *NI,s*
teepwehseeweni *have faith AI*
   teepwehseeweni *AI,ind,3s*
   teepwehseewenihi *AI,ind,4p*
teepwehseewi *believe AI*
   teepwehseewilo *AI,imp,2s*
   teepwehseewiyeekwe *AI,conj,2p*
teepweht *believe TI_1*

hoteepwehta *TI,ind,3s,0s*
hoteepwehtaanaawa *TI,ind,3p,0*
kiteepwehtaana *TI,ind,2s,0p*
kiteepwehtaanaawa *TI,ind,2p,0*
teepwehta *TI,ind,3s,0s*
teepwehtaanaawa *TI,ind,2p,0*
teepwehtameekwe *TI,subj,2p,0*
teepwehtamehi *TI,ind,4p,0*
teepwehtamoko *TI,imp,2p,0*
teepwehtamowaaci *TI,conj,3p,0*
teeteepwehtamelici *TI/IC,conj,4,0*
teepwehtamaw *believe TA*
   kiteepwehtamawaawa *TA,ind,2p,3s*
   teepwehtamaweekwe *TA,conj,2p,3*
teepwehtaw *believe TA*
   hoteepwehtaakohi *TA,ind,4p,3s*
   hoteepwehtawaawaali *TA,ind,3p,4s*
   hoteepwehtawaawahi *TA,ind,3p,4p*
   kiteepwehtawaawa *TA,ind,2p,3s*
   kiteepwehtawipwa *TA,ind,2p,1*
   teepwehtaakoci *TA,conj,4,3s*
   teepwehtawaape *TA,ind,1i,3*
   teepwehtawaate *TA,subj,3s,4*
   teepwehtaweekwe *TA,conj,2p,3 ; TA,subj,2p,3*
   teepwehtawiko *TA,imp,2p,1s*
   teepwehtawilo *TA,imp,2s,1s*
   teepwehtawipwa *TA,ind,2p,1*
   teepwehtoolaake *TA,conj,1x,2*
   teeteepwehtawaacki *TA/IC,part,3p,4*
   teeteepwehtawaata *TA/IC,part,3s,4*
   teeteepwehtawita *TA/IC,part,3s,1s*
teetahkwa *eagle NA*
   teetahkwaki *NA,3p*
teewahi *for, because*
   teewa
   teewahi
teh *[teh] PV*
   hote *PV*
   hoteh *PV*
   kite *PV*
   kiteh *PV*
   niteh *PV*
tehehtoote *be determined II*
   tehehtooteeki *II,conj,0*
tehehtwaati *think, wish [reciprocal] AI*
   tehehtwaatiiki *AI,ind,3p*

tehi *heart* NI
    hotehi *NI/POSS,3s,s*
    hotehiki *NI/POSS/LOC,3s*
    hotehiwa *NI/POSS,3p*
    hotehiwaaki *NI/POSS/LOC,3p*
    hotehiwali *NI,p*
    hotehiwilici *NI/POSS,4*
    kitehi *NI/POSS,2s,s*
    kitehina *NI/POSS,1i*
    kitehiwa *NI/POSS,2p*
    kitehiwaaki *NI/POSS/LOC,2p*
    kitehiwe *NI/POSS,2p*
tehka *cold* II
    tehkaki *II,conj,0*
tekawihi *a little, somewhat*
    tekawi
    tekawihi
tekhaaka *axe* NI
    tekhaaka *NI,s*
teki *[prohibitive]*
    teki
tekwaacipenal *treat shamefully* TA
    hotekwaacipenalaawaali *TA,ind,3p,4s*
tekwaacipenaloofo *be treated shamefully* AI
    tekwaacipenaloofo *AI,ind,3s*
tekweewhpenal *treat badly* TA
    hotekweewpenalaawahi *TA,ind,3p,4p*
tekwefi *be ashamed* AI
    nitekwefi *AI,ind,1s*
tekweh *be ashamed of* TA
    tekwehaali *TA,ind,3s,4s*
    tekwehekwa *TA,ind,3s,1s*
telef *befit, be in a state*
    hotelefiiwe
    hotelefiiweneki
    kitelefi
    kitelefipe *AI,ind,1i*
telenht-moni *talent [monetary unit]* NI
    telenht-moni *NI,s*
teleni *talent [monetary unit]* NI
    kitelenimi *NI/POSS,2s,s*
    teleni *NI,s*
    teleniwali *NI,p*
tenaliiwe *dinner* NI
    nitenaliiwe *NI/POSS,1s,s*
    tenaliiwe *NI,s*

teneliyas *denarius, penny* NI
    teneliyas *NI,s*
tepaaci *[as testimony]* PV
    tepaaci *PV*
tepaacimo *confess, testify* AI
    tepaacimooki *AI,ind,3p*
tepaacimohtaw *confess, testify* TA
    tepaacimohtawaaci *TA,conj,3s,4*
    tepaacimohtawaaki *TA,ind,1s,3p*
tepaane *apart, separate*
    tepaane
tepaani *separately* PV
    hotepaani *PV*
tepaatan *command* TI_1
    tepaataki *TI,conj,3s,0*
tepacikaal *measure* TA
    tepacikaalekoopwa *TA,ind,3,2p*
tepacikamhhw *fill up* TA
    hotepacikamhhwaawahi *TA,ind,3p,4p*
tepacikan *measure* NI
    hotepacikanwa *NI/POSS,3p*
    tepacika *NI,s*
    tepacikana *NI,p*
    tepacikaneki *NI/LOC*
tepacikee *measure* AI
    teepacikeeyeekwe *AI/IC,conj,2p*
    tepacikeepwa *AI,ind,2p*
tepakofen *floor*
    hotepakofenoomi *NI/POSS,3s,s*
    tepakofeneki *NI/LOC*
tepakofenoowe *floor* NI
    tepakofenoowe *NI/POSS,3s,s*
tepal *measure* TA
    tepalekoopwa *TA,ind,3,2p*
tepasawaacim *confess* TA
    tepasawaacimaate *TA,subj,3s,4*
tepasawaacimo *confess* AI
    tepasawaacimo *AI,ind,3s*
tepasawaacimoowe *account* NI
    tepasawaacimoowe *NI,s*
tepasawakoweewe *righteous judgment* NI
    tepasawakoweewe *NI,s*
tepasawat *righteous* II
    tepasawatwi *II,ind,0s*
    tepasawhki *II,conj,0*
tepasaweelemekofiht *justify* TI_2

tepasaweelemekofihtooci *TI,conj,3s,0*
tepasawefi *faithful, just AI*
    kitepasawefi *AI,ind,2s*
    pwaayaatepasawefilici *AI,conj,4*
    teepasawefilici *AI,conj,4*
    tepasawefi *AI,ind,3s ; AI,ind,2s*
    tepasaweficki *AI,part,3p*
    tepasawefilici *AI,conj,4*
tepasawefiiwi *[righteously] PV*
    tepasawefiiwi *PV*
tepasawh *judge TA*
    hotepasawhaawaali *TA,ind,3p,4s*
    hotepasawhekohi *TA,ind,4p,3s*
    hotepasawhekona *TA,ind,0p,3s*
    tepasawhekoopi *TA,ind,3,2s*
tepasawhpenaletiiwe *judgment NI*
    tepasawhpenaletiiwe *NI,s*
tepasawi *true, just PM*
    hotepasawi *PM*
    tepasawi *PM*
tepasawi-lenii *righteous person NA*
    tepasawi-leni *NA,3s*
    tepasawi-leniiki *NA,3p*
    tepasawi-leniili *NA,4s*
tepasawiilefiiwe *righteousness NI*
    hotepasawiilefiiwe *NI/POSS,3s,s*
    hotepasawiilefiiwenwa *NI/POSS,3p*
    kitepasawiilefiiwenwa *NI/POSS,2p*
    tepasawiilefiiwe *NI,s*
    tepasawiilefiiweneki *NI/LOC*
tepeelemekofitaw *have lordship over TA*
    hotepeelemekofitaakowahi *TA,ind,4p,3p*
tepeeletamefi *free AI*
    tepeeletamefiiki *AI,ind,3p*
tepeeletamefiiwahkeeph *make free TA*
    tepeeletamefiiwahkeephaki *TA,conj,1s,3*
tepeeletamhfeyaa *free II*
    tepeeletamhfeya *II,ind,0s*
tepeeletami *freely PV*
    tepeeletami *PV*
tepeeletamoowefi *free AI*
    tepeeletamoowefipwa *AI,ind,2p*
tepeeletamoowefiiwe *freedom NI*
    tepeeletamoowefiiwe *NI,s*
tepeewe *hundred*
    tepeewe

tepehki *night, at night NI*
    tepehki *NI,s*
    tepokwe *NI,p*
tepehki *be night II*
    tepehkike *II,subj,0*
    tepehkiki *II,conj,0*
tepehkikiisfwa *moon NA*
    tepehkikiisfoki *NA/LOC,3*
    tepehkikiisfwa *NA,3s*
tepehkiniitawaaka *lantern NA*
    tepehkiniitawaakanhhi *NA,4p*
tepehse *hear AI*
    tepehseeki *AI,ind,3s*
    tepehseelici *AI,conj,4*
tepen *buy TI_1*
    hotepena *TI,ind,3s,0s*
    tepena *TI,ind,1s,0s*
    tepenaanaawa *TI,ind,3p,0*
    tepenaape *TI,ind,1x,0 ; TI,ind,1i,0*
    tepenake *TI,subj,3s,0*
    tepenamelici *TI,conj,4,0*
    tepenamoko *TI,imp,2p,0*
    tepenamowaaci *TI,conj,3p,0*
    tepenano *TI,imp,2s,0*
tepen *buy TA*
    hotepenaali *TA,ind,3s,4s*
    tepenaaki *TA,ind,1s,3p*
tepenamaw *buy TA*
    tepenamawakite *TA,subj,1x,3*
tepenikee *buy AI*
    taatepenikeelici *AI/IC,conj,4*
    teepenikeelici *AI/IC,conj,4*
    tepenikeeki *AI,ind,3p*
    tepenikeewaaci *AI,conj,3p*
tepetwahoot *cry out together TI-O*
    tepetwahootamooki *TI,ind,3p,0*
tepetwi *together PV*
    hotepetwi *PV*
    tepetwi *PV*
teph *pay TI_1*
    tepha *TI,ind,3s,0s ; TI,ind,2s,0s*
    tephamelite *TI,subj,4s,0*
tephaw *pay TA*
    tephole *TA,ind,1s,2s*
tephika *cup NA*
    nitephika *NA/POSS,1s,3s*

tephika *NA,3s*
tephikanaki *NA,3p*
tephikanali *NA,4s*
tephikaneki *NA/LOC,3*
tephikee *pay AI*
    taatephike *AI,ind,3s*
    tephike *AI,ind,2s*
    tephikeeci *AI,conj,3s*
    tephikeelo *AI,imp,2s*
    tephikeewaaci *AI,conj,3p*
tephikeewe *payment NI*
    tephikeewe *NI,s*
tephofiiwe *reward NI*
    hotephofiiwe *NI/POSS,3s,s*
    hotephofiiwenwa *NI/POSS,3p*
    kitephofiiwenena *NI/POSS,1i*
    kitephofiiwenwa *NI/POSS,2p*
    tephofiiwe *NI,s*
tephoofoowe *wage NI*
    hotephoofoowe *NI/POSS,3s,s*
tephotiiwe *wage NI*
    hotephotiiwenwa *NI/POSS,3p*
    kitephotiiwenwa *NI/POSS,2p*
    tephotiiwe *NI,s*
tepikeem *give commandment to TA*
    tepikeemahi *TA,ind,3s,4p*
tepikeemo *command AI*
    teepikeemoci *AI,conj,3s*
    teepikeemoki *AI,conj,3*
    teepikeemoyani *AI/IC,conj,2s*
    tepikeemo *AI,ind,3s*
    tepikeemoci *AI,conj,3s*
    tepikeemolo *AI,imp,2s*
    tepikeemooli *AI,ind,4s*
tepikeemoofo *be commanded AI*
    teepikeemoofoyeekwe *AI,conj,2p*
tepikeemoowe *commandment NI*
    hotepikeemoowe *NI/POSS,3s,s*
    hotepikeemoowena *NI/POSS,3s,p*
    kitepikeemoowe *NI/POSS,2s,s*
    nitepikeemoowe *NI/POSS,1s,s*
    nitepikeemoowena *NI/POSS,1s,p*
    tepikeemoowe *NI,s*
    tepikeemoowena *NI,p*
tepilahi *even, just, precisely PM*
    teetepila *PM*

teetepilahi *PM*
tepila *PM*
tepilahi *PM*
tepilo *truly, exact*
    tepilo
    tepilooke
tepim *command TA*
    hotepimaali *TA,ind,3s,4s*
    hotepimahi *TA,ind,3s,4p*
    kitepimekowa *TA,ind,3s,2p*
    kitepimele *TA,ind,1s,2s*
    kitepimelepwa *TA,ind,1s,2p*
    nitepimekona *TA,ind,3s,1x*
    teetepimelako *TA/IC,conj,1s,2p*
    tepimaaci *TA,conj,3s,4*
    tepimahi *TA,ind,3s,4p*
    tepimekoci *TA,conj,4,3s*
    tepimi *TA,imp,2s,3*
tepimetiiwe *charge, command NI*
    tepimetiiwe *NI,s*
tepimoofoowe *charge, command NI*
    tepimoofoowe *NI,s*
tepin *see TI-O*
    kitepinaapwa *TI,ind,2p,0*
    nitepina *TI,ind,1s,0*
    nitepinaape *TI,ind,1x,0*
    teetepinakiki *TI/IC,part,3p,0*
    tepinaka *TI,part,3s,0*
    tepinaki *TI,conj,3s,0*
    tepinakiki *TI,part,3p,0*
    tepinamohi *AI,ind,4p*
    tepinamooki *TI,ind,3p,0*
    tepinamowaaci *TI,conj,3p,0*
    tepinamwa *TI,ind,3s,0*
tepinaakofihtaw *appear to TA*
    hotepinaakofihtaakooli *TA,ind,4s,3s*
    hotepinaakofihtawaawahi *TA,ind,3p,4p*
tepinaakwat *appear II*
    tepinaakwato *II,ind,0p*
    tepinaakwatwi *II,ind,0s*
tepinaakwi *open, apparent, plain PV*
    hotepinaakwi *PV*
    tepinaakwi *PV*
tepinaakwifen *be made clear II*
    tepinaakwifenwi *II,ind,0s*
tepinalekowe *pronounce, testify AI*

tepinalekowe *AI,ind,3s*
tepinalekwi *by testifying PV*
   tepinalekwi *PV*
tepinalekwim *pronounce, instruct, command TA*
   hotepinalekwimahi *TA,ind,3s,4p*
   tepinalekwimaaci *TA,conj,3s,4*
tepinamoowe *sight NI*
   hotepinamoowe *NI/POSS,3s,s*
   hotepinamoowenwa *NI/POSS,3p*
   kitepinamoowe *NI/POSS,2s,s*
   nitepinamoowe *NI/POSS,1s,s*
   tepinamoowe *NI,s*
tepinamooyaa *see II*
   tepinamooya *II,ind,0*
tepinaw *see TA*
   hotepinawaawaali *TA,ind,3p,4s*
tepinawkfetoofo *be manifested AI*
   tepinawkofetoofowaaci *AI,conj,3p*
tepinawkhoofo *be revealed AI*
   tepinawkhoofoci *AI,conj,3s*
tepinawkofet *show, manifest TI_2*
   hotepinawkofeto *TI,ind,3s,0s*
   tepinawkofetooci *TI,conj,3s,0*
tepinawkofetaw *show to, manifest to TA*
   hotepinawkofetawahi *TA,ind,3s,4p*
   nitepinawkofetawaaki *TA,ind,1s,3p*
   tepinawkofetawa *TA,ind,1s,3s*
   tepinawkofetawiyaake *TA,conj,2,1x*
tepinawkofetoote *be shown II*
   tepinawkofetooteeki *II,conj,0*
   tepinawkwitooteeki *II,conj,0*
tepinawkofi *appear AI*
   tepinawkofici *AI,conj,3s*
tepinawkofihtaw *appear to TA*
   tepinawkofihtawaali *TA,ind,3s,4s*
tepinawkofiim *be manifested to TA*
   hotepinawkofiimahi *TA,ind,3s,4p*
   tepinawkofiimahi *TA,ind,3s,4p*
tepinawkot *make apparent, manifest TI_2*
   tepinawkotoolo *TI,imp,2s,0*
tepinawkwaatot *testify about TI_1*
   nitepinawkwaatota *TI,ind,1s,0s*
tepinawkwi *appear II*
   tepinawkwki *II,conj,0*
tepineem *see clearly TI_3*
   hotepineeme *TI,ind,3s,0s*

tepiskwi *openly PV*
   tepiskwi *PV*
tepiwiitamaw *tell, explain TA*
   tepiwiitamawahi *TA,ind,3s,4p*
   tepiwiitamawinaake *TA,imp,2,1x*
   tepiwiitamoolepwa *TA,ind,1s,2p*
tepki *level ground NI*
   tepkiki *NI/LOC*
tepow *counsel TA*
   tepoweci *TA,conj,,3*
tepowaafoowe *test, trial, temptation NI*
   hotepowaafoowe *NI/POSS,3s,s*
tepowaal *conspire against, judge TA*
   hotepowaalaawaali *TA,ind,3p,4s*
   hotepowaalekohi *TA,ind,4p,3s*
   nitepowaala *TA,ind,1s,3s*
   tepowaalehko *TA,imp,2p,3*
   tepowaaleko *TA,ind,0s,3s*
   tepowaalekoci *TA,conj,4,3s*
tepowaasiwee *judge AI*
   tepowaasiweeya *AI,subj,1s*
tepowaasiweewe *judgment NI*
   nitepowaasiweewe *NI/POSS,1s,s*
tepowaat *judge TI_1*
   tepowaatama *TI,conj,1s,0*
tepowee *council AI*
   taatepoweeta *AI/IC,part,3s*
   tepoweeki *AI,ind,3p ; AI,conj,3*
   tepoweelici *AI/IC,conj,4*
tepoweewakhoowe *courtyard NI*
   tepoweewakhoowe *NI,s*
tepoweewe *council, counsel NI*
   hotepoweewenwaaki *NI/POSS/LOC,3p*
   tepoweewe *NI,s*
   tepoweewena *NI,p*
   tepoweeweneki *NI/LOC*
tepoweewi *judgment PM*
   tepoweewi *PM*
tepoweewiwakhoowe *courtyard NI*
   hotepoweewiwakhoowe *NI/POSS,3s,s*
tepoweewiyahpapiiwe *judgment seat NI*
   tepoweewiyahpapiiweneki *NI/LOC*
tepwh *pay TA*
   tepwhi *TA,imp,2s,3*
tetaa *abide, stay AI*
   kiteta *AI,ind,2s*

tetepahpifo *be wrapped AI*
    tetepahpifo *AI,ind,3s*
tetepahpifoowe *band NI*
    tetepahpifoowena *NI,p*
tetepahpil *wrap TA*
    hotetepahpilaali *TA,ind,3s,4s*
tetepahtekwi *vine NI*
    tetepahtekwi *NI,s*
    tetepahtekwiki *NI/LOC*
tetepapifoowe *swaddling clothing NI*
    tetepapifoowena *NI,p*
tetepeceenoote *be rolled up II*
    tetepeceenoote *II,ind,0*
tetepen *roll TA*
    tetepenaali *TA,ind,3s,4s*
tetepiikwepifo *have the face covered AI*
    tetepiikwepifo *AI,ind,3s*
tfani *bed NI*
    hotfanemwaaki *NI/POSS/LOC,3p*
    hotfani *NI/POSS,3s,s*
    kitfani *NI/POSS,2s,s*
    tfaneki *NI/LOC*
    tfani *NI,s*
tfen *be so much II*
    tfeki *II,conj,0*
    tfenwi *II,ind,0s*
tfene *every, quantity, amount PM*
    tfene *PM*
tfokwi *day NI*
    tfoko *NI,p*
tfwahoot *quit crying out TI-O*
    tfwahootamowaaci *TI,conj,3p,0*
tfweekfen *times as much, -fold II*
    tfweekfenwi *II,ind,0s*
    yeetfweekifeki *II/IC,conj,0*
tfweekin *times as much, -fold II*
    tfweekinwi *II,ind,0s*
tfweel *number among, make up a group AI*
    tiitfweelowaaci *AI,conj,3p*
    yeetfweeleki *AI/IC,conj,3*
    yeetfweeleyaake *AI/IC,conj,1x*
    yeetfweelowaaci *AI/IC,conj,3p*
tfweelena *group, kind*
    tfweelena
tfweelenawa *number among AI*
    yeetfweelenawakiki *AI/IC,conj,3*

tfweelenawakifi *be in a group, be in order AI*
    yeetiitfweelenawakifiwaaci *AI/IC,conj,3p*
tfweeloowe *group NI*
    hotfweeloowe *NI/POSS,3s,s*
    hotfweeloowena *NI/POSS,3s,p*
    hotfweeloowenhhi *NA/POSS,3s,4p*
    kitfweeloowenena *NI/POSS,1i*
    nitfweeloowenena *NI/POSS,1x*
    tfweeloowe *NI,s*
tfwi *as many as PM*
    tfwi *PM*
    yeetfwi *PM/IC*
tfwi *as many as AI*
    tfwiiki *AI,ind,3p*
    yeetfwici *AI/IC,conj,3s*
    yeetfwilici *AI/IC,conj,4*
    yeetfwiwaaci *AI/IC,conj,3p*
tfwihk *stop TI_1*
    tfwihka *TI,ind,3s,0s*
tfwihkaw *stop TA*
    tfwihkawehki *TA,conj,3,2s*
tfwikamikifiiwe *membership of clan NI*
    hotfwikamikifiiwe *NI/POSS,3s,s*
tfwikee *be a group AI*
    yeetfwikeeci *AI/IC,conj,3s*
tfwilawi *stop AI*
    tfwilawiici *AI,conj,3s*
tiikeepolasi *Decapolis NI*
    tiikeepolasiiki *NI/LOC*
    tikeepolasi *NI,s*
tiila *Terah NA*
    tiila *NA,3s*
tikihfetaw *cool TA*
    tikihfetawici *TA,conj,3s,1s*
tikiniikin *become cold II*
    tikiniikinili *II,ind,4*
tiliwaskwi *anise NI*
    tiliwaskwi *NI,s*
titimas *Didymus NA*
    titimas *NA,3s*
tkikamii *spring NI*
    hotkikami *NI/POSS,3s,s*
    tkikami *NI,s*
tkikamiiwaalakwi *well NI*
    tkikamiiwaalakoki *NI/LOC*
tkikamiiwi *be a well II*

tkikamiiwili *II,ind,4*

toke *perhaps, it may be; whether, else*
    toke

towath *knock TI_1*
    teetowathaka *TI/IC,part,3s,0*
    tiitowathaanaawa *TI,ind,2p,0*
    tiitowathamoko *TI,imp,2p,0*

towathikee *knock AI*
    teetowathikeeta *AI/IC,part,3s*
    tiitowathikeelite *AI,subj,4s*
    towathikeeko *AI,imp,2p*

twekonaatis *Trachonitis NI*
    twekonaatis *NI,s*

waakeefa *locust NA*
    waakeefhi *NA,4p*

waaki *stoop, bend AI*
    waaki *AI,ind,3s*
    waakiiya *AI,conj,1s*

waakiceel *stoop AI*
    waakiceelwa *AI,ind,3s*

waakiciikwaneskaa *kneel AI*
    waakiciikwaneskaaki *AI,ind,3p*

waakicikweskaa *bow the head AI*
    waakicikweska *AI,ind,3s*

waakimiyaakokiwi *spice, incense PM*
    waakimiyaakokiwi *PM*

waakimiyaakwa *spice, incense NI*
    waakimiyaakoki *NI,p*

waakocehfi *fox NA*
    waakocehfi *NA,3s*
    waakocehfiiki *NA,3p*

waakom *know TA*
    howaakomaali *TA,ind,3s,4s*
    howaakomaawaali *TA,ind,3p,4s*
    howaakomaawahi *TA,ind,3p,4p*
    howaakomahi *TA,ind,3s,4p*
    howaakomeko *TA,ind,0s,3s*
    howaakomekooli *TA,ind,4s,3s*
    kiwaakomaape *TA,ind,1i,3*
    kiwaakomaawa *TA,ind,2p,3s*
    kiwaakomaawaaki *TA,ind,2p,3p*
    kiwaakomekwa *TA,ind,3s,2s*
    kiwaakomele *TA,ind,1s,2s*
    kiwaakomelepwa *TA,ind,1s,2p*
    kiwaakomi *TA,ind,2s,1s*
    kiwaakomipwa *TA,ind,2p,1*

niwaakoma *TA,ind,1s,3s*
niwaakomaaki *TA,ind,1s,3p*
niwaakomaape *TA,ind,1x,3*
niwaakomekooki *TA,ind,3p,1s*
waakomaawa *TA,ind,2p,3s*
waakomaawaaci *TA,conj,3p,4*
waakomaawaaki *TA,ind,2s,3p*
waakomaawaali *TA,ind,3p,4s*
waakomeekwe *TA,part,2p,3*
waakomehki *TA,conj,3,2s*
waakomekoci *TA,conj,4,3s*
waakomi *TA,ind,2s,1s*
waakomici *TA,conj,3s,1s*
waakomiyani *TA,conj,2s,1s*
waakomiyeekwe *TA,conj,2p,3 ; TA,subj,2p,3*
weewaakomaaci *TA/IC,conj,3s,4*
weewaakomakita *TA/IC,part,1x,3s*

waakomekofi *be known AI*
    waakomekofici *AI,conj,3s*
    waakomekofilici *AI,conj,4*

waakomekofih *make known TA*
    kiwaakomekofiheko *TA,ind,0s,2s*
    waakomekofihaawaaci *TA,conj,3p,4*
    waakomekofihekoci *TA,conj,4,3s*

waakometiim *acquaintance NA*
    howaakometiimhhi *NA/POSS,3s,4p*

waakometiiwen *acquaintance NA*
    howaakometiiwenwahi *NA/POSS,3p,4p*

waakot *know TI-O*
    howaakota *TI,ind,3s,0s*
    howaakotaana *TI,ind,3s,0p*
    howaakotaanaawa *TI,ind,3p,0*
    howaakotamehi *TI,ind,4p,0*
    kiwaakota *TI,ind,2s,0s*
    kiwaakotaana *TI,ind,2s,0p*
    kiwaakotaanaawa *TI,ind,2p,0*
    kiwaakotaape *TI,ind,1i,0*
    niwaakota *TI,ind,1s,0s*
    niwaakotaape *TI,ind,1x,0*
    waakota *TI,ind,3s,0s ; TI,ind,1s,0s*
    waakotaana *TI,ind,3s,0p*
    waakotaanaawa *TI,ind,2p,0 ; TI,ind,3p,0*
    waakotaape *TI,ind,1x,0*
    waakotaka *TI,part,3s,0*
    waakotake *TI,subj,3s,0*
    waakotaki *TI,conj,3s,0*

waakotakki *TI,part,3p,0*
waakotamane *TI,subj,2s,0*
waakotamani *TI,conj,2s,0*
waakotameekwe *TI,subj,2p,0 ; TI,conj,2p,0*
waakotamehi *TI,ind,4p,0*
waakotamelici *TI,conj,4,0*
waakotamoko *TI,imp,2p,0*
waakotamooki *TI,ind,3p,0*
waakotamowaaci *TI,conj,3p,0*
waakotamwa *TI,ind,3s,0*
wayaakotamaake *TI/IC,conj,1x,0*
weewaakotaka *TI/IC,part,3s,0*
waakotamaw *know TA*
   howaakotamaako *TA,ind,0s,3s*
   howaakotamawahi *TA,ind,3s,4p*
   waakotamawahi *TA,ind,3s,4p*
waakotefi *learn AI*
   waakotefi *AI,ind,3s*
   waakotefici *AI,conj,3s*
   waakotefiiki *AI,ind,3p*
   waakotefiiko *AI,imp,2p*
waakotefih *make known TA*
   niwaakotefihaaki *TA,ind,1s,3p*
waakotefihiwee *make known AI*
   waakotefihiweeki *AI,ind,3p*
waakotefiiyaa *know II*
   waakotefiiyaake *II,subj,0*
waakotel *notify TA*
   waakotelekoci *TA,conj,4,3s*
   waakotelelakwe *TA,conj,3,1i*
   waakotestoolepwa *TA,ind,1s,2p*
waakotesiwee *make known AI*
   waakotesiwe *AI,ind,3s*
   waakotesiweeki *AI,ind,3p*
waakotoote *be known II*
   waakotoote *II,ind,0*
waalhke *dig AI*
   waalhke *AI,ind,3s*
   waalhkeeya *AI,conj,1s*
waalhkwat *valley II*
   wayaalhkwahkiki *II/IC,conj,0*
waalhkwathoote *be cut, be hewn II*
   waalhkwathooteeki *II,conj,0*
waamekhoote *be caused to become II*
   waamekhoote *II,ind,0*
waani *be lost AI*

waani *AI,ind,3s*
   weewaaniilici *AI/IC,conj,4*
   weewaaniita *AI/IC,part,3s*
waaniiwi *lost PM*
   waaniiwi *PM*
waaniwel *lead astray TA*
   howaaniwelahi *TA,ind,3s,4p*
   kiwaaniwelekoopwa *TA,ind,3,2p*
waapakeewe *sight NI*
   waapakeewe *NI,s*
waapaki *daily, every day*
   waapaki
waapalaach *deceive TA*
   howaapalaachaali *TA,ind,3s,4s*
   howaapalaachaawaali *TA,ind,3p,4s*
   waapalaachaawaaci *TA,conj,3p,4*
   waapalaachaawaali *TA,ind,3p,4s*
   waapalaacihekoci *TA,conj,4,3s*
waapalaachoofo *be mocked AI*
   waapalaachoofo *AI,ind,3s*
waapalaacim *insult, mock TA*
   howaapalaacimaawaali *TA,ind,3p,4s*
   howaapalaacimekooli *TA,ind,4s,3s*
   waapalaacimaawaali *TA,ind,3p,4s*
waapaleelem *mock TA*
   howaapaleelemaawaali *TA,ind,3p,4s*
   waapaleelemaawaali *TA,ind,3p,4s*
   waapaleelemekohi *TA,ind,4p,3s*
waapam *look at TA*
   howaapamaali *TA,ind,3s,4s*
   waapamaaci *TA,conj,3s,4*
   waapamaali *TA,ind,3s,4s*
   waapamaataako *TA,imp,1i,3*
   waapamaawaali *TA,ind,3p,4s*
   waapamaci *TA,conj,2s,3*
   waapamahi *TA,ind,3s,4p*
   waapamehko *TA,imp,2p,3*
   waapami *TA,imp,2s,3*
   waapamici *TA,conj,3s,1s*
   waapamilo *TA,imp,2s,1s*
waapamekofiiwe *showing NI*
   howaapamekofiiweneki *NI/POSS/LOC,3s*
waapameti *look at [reciprocal] AI*
   waapametiiki *AI,ind,3p*
waapan *morning, day II*
   waapake *II,subj,0*

waapaki *II,conj,0*
waayaapaki *II,conj,0*
wayaapaki *II/IC,conj,0*
waapanaaci *safely PV*
    waapanaaci *PV*
waapanescika *salvation NI*
    kiwaapanescika *NI/POSS,2s,s*
waapanesh *save, make whole TA*
    howaapaneshahi *TA,ind,3s,4p*
    waapaneshaaci *TA,conj,3s,4*
    waapaneshahi *TA,ind,3s,4p*
    waapanesheko *TA,ind,0s,2s*
    waapaneshilo *TA,imp,2s,1s*
waapaneshiwee *save AI*
    waapaneshiweelo *AI,imp,2s*
waapaneshoofo *be saved AI*
    waapaneshoofo *AI,ind,3s*
    waapaneshoofoci *AI,conj,3s*
    waapaneshoofoyeekwe *AI,conj,2p*
    weewaapaneshoofocki *AI/IC,part,3p*
waapanest *save, make whole TI_2*
    waapanesto *TI,ind,3s,0s*
    waapanestoolo *TI,imp,2s,0*
    waapanestooya *TI,conj,1s,0*
waapanestaw *save TA*
    waapanestaakoci *TA,conj,4,3s*
waapanestoote *be saved, be made whole II*
    waapanestoote *II,ind,0*
    waapanestooteeki *II,conj,0*
waapanhsi *recover, be saved AI*
    waapanhsiiki *AI,ind,3p*
    waapanhsiili *AI,ind,4s*
    waapanhsiwaaci *AI,conj,3p*
waapanhsii *savior NA*
    niwaapanhsiimali *NA/POSS,1s,4s*
waapanhsiiwe *salvation NI*
    waapanhsiiwe *NI,s*
waapanhsiiwena *savior NA*
    howaapanhsiiwenali *NA/POSS,3s,4s*
    waapanhsiiwena *NA,3s*
waapanhsiiwi *salvation PM*
    waapanhsiiwi *PM*
waapanhsiweewe *salvation NI*
    howaapanhsiweewe *NI/POSS,3s,s*
waapasiphikeewe *adultery NI*
    waapasiphikeewe *NI,s*

waapasiphikeewena *NI,p*
    waapasiphikeeweneki *NI/LOC*
waapasiphikeewefi *adulterous AI*
    waapasiphikeewefi *AI,ind,3s*
waapasiphikeewefiiyaa *adulterous II*
    weewaapasiphikeewefiiyaaki *II/IC,conj,0*
waapasiphikeewiikwe *adulteress NA*
    waapasiphikeewiikweli *NA,4s*
waapasiphikehfi *adulterer NA*
    waapasiphikehfiiki *NA,3p*
waapat *look at TI_1*
    waapataanaawa *TI,ind,2p,0*
    waapataki *TI,conj,3s,0*
    waapatamoko *TI,imp,2p,0*
    waapatano *TI,imp,2s,0*
waapatel *show TA*
    howaapatelaali *TA,ind,3s,4s*
    howaapatelahi *TA,ind,3s,4p*
    howaapatelhi *TA,ind,3s,4p*
    kiwaapatesipe *TA,ind,2,1x*
    waapatelaali *TA,ind,3s,4s*
    waapatelahi *TA,ind,3s,4p*
    waapatelehko *TA,imp,2p,3*
    waapatelekoci *TA,conj,4,3s*
    waapatelekowa *TA,ind,3s,2p*
    waapatelekowaaci *TA,conj,4,3p*
    waapatelelepwa *TA,ind,1s,2p*
    waapatesi *TA,imp,2s,3*
    waapatesiko *TA,imp,2p,1s*
    waapatesinaake *TA,imp,2,1x*
    weewaapatelekoci *TA/IC,conj,4,3s*
waapatesiwee *show AI*
    waapatesiwe *AI,ind,3s*
    waapatesiweeci *AI,conj,3s*
    waapatesiweeki *AI,ind,3p*
waapi *white PM*
    waapi *PM*
waapimafaanimota *linen cloth NI*
    waapimafaanimotaaki *NI/LOC*
waapimoni *silver coin NI*
    waapimoni *NI,s*
waapit *make white TI_2*
    waapito *TI,ind,2s,0s*
    waapitoona *TI,ind,3s,0p*
waaptoote *be whitened II*
    weewaaptooteeki *II/IC,conj,0*

waasaalakwi *den, hole NI*
  howaasaalakomwa *NI/POSS,3p*
  waasaalako *NI,p*
  waasaalakoki *NI/LOC*
  waasaalakwi *NI,s*
waasikaki *power NI*
  howaasikakiimi *NI/POSS,3s,s*
  waasikaki *NI,s*
waaawesi *be dressed, be decorated AI*
  waaawesi *AI,ind,3s*
  weewaaawesiwasecki *AI/IC,part,3p*
waaawesihkate *decorated II*
  waaawesihkate *II,ind,0*
waaawesihkatoote *be decorated II*
  waaawesihkatooteeki *II,conj,0*
  waaawesihtoote *II,ind,0*
waaawesiwi *decorative, sumptious PV*
  waaawesiwi *PV*
waaawiin *send TA*
  howaawiinahi *TA,ind,3s,4p*
  niwaawiinekoopi *TA,ind,3,1s*
  waawiinaci *TA,conj,2s,3*
  waawiinahi *TA,ind,3s,4p*
  waawiinekona *TA,ind,3s,1x*
  waawiinekoopi *TA,ind,3,1s*
  waawiinekwa *TA,ind,3s,1s*
  waawiini *TA,imp,2s,3*
  waawiiniki *TA,conj,3,1s*
  weewaawiinaaci *TA/IC,conj,3s,4*
  weewaawiinilici *TA/IC,conj,4,1s*
waaawiinekofiiwe *fame NI*
  howaawiinekofiiwe *NI/POSS,3s,s*
  waawiinekofiiwe *NI,s*
waaawiineskaw *send TA*
  howaawiineskawaali *TA,ind,3s,4s*
  howaawiineskawahi *TA,ind,3s,4p*
  kiwaawiineskoolepwa *TA,ind,1s,2p*
  niwaawiineskaakwa *TA,ind,3s,1s*
  waawiineskawaaci *TA,conj,3s,4*
  waawiineskawaaki *TA,ind,1s,3p*
  waawiineskawaali *TA,ind,3s,4s*
  waawiineskawahi *TA,ind,3s,4p*
  waawiineskawici *TA,conj,3s,1s*
  waawiineskawiyani *TA,conj,2s,1s*
  waawiineskoolepwa *TA,ind,1s,2p*
  weewaawiineskaakoci *TA/IC,conj,4,3s*

weewaawiineskawaaci *TA/IC,conj,3s,4*
weewaawiineskawaata *TA/IC,part,3s,4*
weewaawiineskawaka *TA/IC,part,1s,3s*
weewaawiineskawata *TA/IC,part,2s,3s*
weewaawiineskaweta *TA/IC,part,,3s*
weewaawiineskawilici *TA/IC,conj,4,1s*
weewaawiineskawita *TA/IC,part,3s,1s*
weewaawiineskawiyamekicki
TA/IC,part,3p,1x
  yeewaawiineskawaaci *TA/IC,conj,3s,4*
waaawiineskoofo *be sent AI*
  waawiineskoofo *AI,ind,3s*
  waawiineskoofooki *AI,ind,3p*
  weewaawiineskoofocki *AI/IC,part,3p*
waaawiinhkee *send to AI*
  waawiinhke *AI,ind,3s*
  waawiinhkeeki *AI,ind,3p*
  waawiinhkeeli *AI,ind,4s*
  waawiinhkeepwa *AI,ind,2p*
waaawiinoofo *be sent AI*
  waawiinoofo *AI,ind,3s*
  weewaawiinoofocki *AI/IC,part,3p*
waaawiyaakacfen *be mixed II*
  weewaawiyaakacfeki *II/IC,conj,0*
waciwahki *mountain NI*
  waciwahki *NI,s*
wah *[dependent future] PV*
  wa *PV/IC*
  wah *PV/IC*
wahataam *borrow TA*
  wahataamehka *TA,part,3,2s*
wahfaaci *glorious PM*
  wahfaaci *PM*
wahfaacimekofih *glorify TA*
  howahfaacimekofihaali *TA,ind,3s,4s*
  kiwahfaacimekofihele *TA,ind,1s,2s*
  niwahfaacimekofihekoopi *TA,ind,3,1s*
  wahfaacimekofihaaci *TA,conj,3s,4*
  wahfaacimekofihaali *TA,ind,3s,4s*
  wahfaacimekofiheci *TA,conj,,3*
  wahfaacimekofiheekwe *TA,conj,2p,3*
  wahfaacimekofihehki *TA,conj,3,2s*
  wahfaacimekofihekohi *TA,ind,4p,3s*
  wahfaacimekofihekwa *TA,ind,3s,1s*
  wahfaacimekofihilo *TA,imp,2s,1s*
  weewahfaacimekofihita *TA/IC,part,3s,1s*
wahfaacimekofihoofo *be glorified AI*

wahfaacimekofihoofo *AI,ind,3s*
wahfaacimekofihoofoci *AI,conj,3s*
wahfaacimekofiht *glorify TI_2*
wahfaacimekofihtooya *TI,subj,1s,0*
wahfaacimekofiiwe *glory NI*
howahfaacimekofiiwe *NI/POSS,3s,s*
howahfaacimekofiiweneki
NI/POSS/LOC,3s
howahfaacimekofiiwenilici *NI/POSS,4*
howahfaacimekofiiwenwa *NI/POSS,3p*
kiwahfaacimekofiiweneki *NI/POSS/LOC,2s*
niwahfaacimekofiiwe *NI/POSS,1s,s*
wahfaacimekofiiwe *NI,s*
wahfaacimekofiiweneki *NI/POSS/LOC,3s ; NI/LOC*
wahfaacimekofiiwh *glorify TA*
wahfaacimekofiiwhi *TA,imp,2s,3*
wahfaacimekohw *glorify TA*
howahfaacimekohwaali *TA,ind,3s,4s*
howahfaacimekohwaawaali *TA,ind,3p,4s*
howahfaacimekowhaawaali *TA,ind,3p,4s*
wahfaacimekhwaawaali *TA,ind,3p,4s*
wahfaacimekohwaali *TA,ind,3s,4s*
wahfaacimekwit *glorify TI_2*
wahfaacimekwito *TI,ind,1s,0s*
wahfaacimekwitoolo *TI,imp,2s,0*
wahfeeya *light NI*
howahfaayaami *NI/POSS,3s,s*
howahfeeyaami *NI/POSS,3s,s*
howahfeeyaamiki *NI/POSS/LOC,3s*
howahfeeyaamwa *NI/POSS,3p*
kiwahfeeyaamwa *NI/POSS,2p*
wahfef *shine TI-O*
wahfefamooki *TI,ind,3p,0*
wahfefamooyaa *shine II*
wahfefamooya *II,ind,0*
wahfefiiyaa *shine II*
wahfefiiya *II,ind,0*
wahfefikee *shine AI*
wahfefike *AI,ind,3s*
wahfefikeewe *shining NI*
wahfefikeewe *NI,s*
wahfehtaw *shine upon TA*
wahfehtawaaci *TA,conj,3s,4*
wahfekeeyaa *shine II*
wahfekeeya *II,ind,0*
wahfeskaa *appear (as light), flash II*

wahfeskaaki *II,conj,0*
wahfete *bright II*
wahfete *II,ind,0*
wahfiikwfoowat *dazzle II*
wahfiikwfoowatwi *II,ind,0s*
wahfiikwifoowasi *shining clothing NI*
wahfiikwifoowaseki *NI/LOC*
wahkanaki *white II*
wahkanakiya *II,ind,0*
wahkanakiyaaki *II,conj,0*
waiini *wine NI*
waiini *NI,s*
waiiniiwi *wine PM*
waiiniiwi *PM*
wakh *fence in TI_1*
howakha *TI,ind,3s,0s*
wakhoowe *fence, enclosure NI*
howakhoowenwa *NI/POSS,3p*
wakhoowika *court NI*
howakhoowikaanwa *NI/POSS,3p*
waleskhot *waste TI_2*
howaleskhoto *TI,ind,3s,0s*
waleskhotaw *waste TA*
waleskhotaakoci *TA,conj,4,3s*
waleskhotoote *be wasted II*
waleskhotoote *II,ind,0*
wanaatefiiwe *wickedness NI*
howanaatefiiwenilici *NI/POSS,4*
wanaatefiiwe *NI,s*
wanefo *drunk AI*
wanefoci *AI,conj,3s*
weenefolici *AI/IC,conj,4*
wanefoowe *drunkness NI*
wanefoowe *NI,s*
wanh *lose TA*
howanhhaali *TA,ind,3s,4s*
niwanhha *TA,ind,1s,3s*
wanhfoneewefi *be perplexed AI*
wanhfoneewaaci *AI,conj,3p*
wanhfoneewefi *AI,ind,3s*
wanht *lose TI_2*
howanhto *TI,ind,3s,0s*
wanhto *TI,ind,3s,0s*
wanhtooya *TI,conj,1s,0*
weewanhtoota *TI/IC,part,3s,0*
wanhtoote *be lost II*

wanhtoote *II,ind,0*
　　wanhtooteeki *II,conj,0*
　　weewanhtooteeki *II/IC,conj,0*
wanihkaaloofo *be forgotten AI*
　　wanihkaaloofo *AI,ind,3s*
wanihkaat *forget TI_1*
　　howanihkaataanaawa *TI,ind,3p,0*
wanihsakaa *fool NA*
　　wanihsaka *NA,3s*
　　wanihsakaafa *NA/DIM,3s*
　　wanihsakaaki *NA,3p*
wanihsakaawefi *foolish AI*
　　wanihsakaawefiiki *AI,ind,3p*
wanihsakaawi *foolish PM*
　　wanihsakaawi *PM*
wanihsakaawiiwe *foolishness NI*
　　wanihsakaawiiwe *NI,s*
wanikeemo *deceive AI*
　　wanikeemo *AI,ind,2s*
wanimefiiwe *deceit NI*
　　wanimefiiwe *NI,s*
wanimetiiwe *deceit NI*
　　wanimetiiwe *NI,s*
waninehfi *devil*
　　waninehfi *NA,3s*
　　waninehfihi *NA,3p*
　　waninehfiiki *NA,3p*
　　waninehfiili *NA,4s*
wasfaa *be part of II*
　　wasfaaki *II,conj,0*
wayaakiyaa *crooked II*
　　wayaakiyaaki *II,conj,0*
wayahfem *cast light on TA*
　　wayahfemekoci *TA,conj,0,3s*
wayahfeyaa *light II*
　　wayahfaayaaki *II/IC,conj,0*
　　wayahfeeyaaki *II/IC,conj,0*
　　wayahfeya *II/IC,ind,0*
wayeeci *towards, direction, side PP*
　　wayeeci *PP*
wayeetahkwe *side NI*
　　wayeetahkwe *NI,s*
　　wiyeetahkwe *NI,s*
wayiniht *make into wine TI_2*
　　wayinihtooci *TI,conj,3s,0*
weecameh *tame TA*

weecamehaaci *TA,conj,3s,4*
weeceeninaati *be a sibling AI*
　　weeceeninaaticki *AI,part,3p*
　　weeceeninaatihi *AI,ind,4p*
weecihi *easy*
　　weecihi
weecihiwat *easy II*
　　weecihiwatwi *II,ind,0s*
weecikeenahi *therefore CJN*
　　weecikeena *CJN*
　　weecikeenahi *CJN*
　　weecikeenhhi *CJN*
weecita *naturally*
　　weecita
weecitayaa *necessary II*
　　wayeecitaiki *II/IC,conj,0*
weeciwephi *except for, unless CJN*
　　weecip *CJN*
　　weeciwe *CJN*
　　weeciwep *CJN*
　　weeciwephi *CJN*
weeka *but CJN*
　　weeka *CJN*
weekhi *though*
　　weekhi
weelaa *or CJN*
　　weelaa *CJN*
weelaake *or else*
　　weelaake
weelakwiima *fatling NA*
　　niweelakwiimaki *NA/POSS,1s,3p*
weelena *immediately*
　　weelena
weelenawakat *immediate II*
　　weelenawakatwi *II,ind,0s*
weenaatefi *wicked AI*
　　weenaatefi *AI,ind,3s*
　　weenaatefilici *AI,conj,4*
　　weenaatefita *AI,part,3s*
weenahkwi *? presumably ?*
　　weenahkwi
weenefo *drunk NA*
　　weenefo *NA,3s*
weenikeemo *deceiver NA*
　　weenikeemo *NA,3s*
weepeelem *fornicate TA*

weepeelemaaci *TA,conj,3s,4*
weepeeletiiwe *fornication NI*
  weepeeletiiwe *NI,s*
  weepeeletiiwena *NI,p*
weepeeletiiwhetiiwe *fornication NI*
  weepeeletiiwhetiiweneki *NI/LOC*
weepefi *mad, insane AI*
  weepefi *AI,ind,3s*
weepfee *go AI*
  hociweepfeeki *AI,ind,3p*
  niweepfe *AI,ind,1s*
  weepfe *AI,ind,3s ; AI,ind,1s*
  weepfeeci *AI,conj,3s*
  weepfeeki *AI,ind,3p*
  weepfeeko *AI,imp,2p*
  weepfeeli *AI,ind,4s*
  weepfeelici *AI,conj,4*
  weepfeelo *AI,imp,2s*
  weepfeepwa *AI,ind,2p*
  weepfeetaako *AI,imp,1i*
  weepfeete *AI,subj,3s*
  weepfeewaaci *AI,conj,3p*
  weepfeeya *AI,conj,1s ; AI,subj,1s*
  weepfeeyeekwe *AI,conj,2p*
  weepfehi *AI,ind,4p*
weepfeeyaa *go II*
  weepfeeya *II,ind,0*
  weepfeeyaaki *II,conj,0*
  weepfeeyaali *II,ind,4*
weepi *cold II*
  weepi *II,ind,0s*
weepikisifoowe *fever NI*
  weepikisifoowe *NI,s*
weepokwahkiceephoote *be uprooted II*
  weepokwahkiceephoote *II,ind,0*
weepskweete *loaf NI*
  howeepskweteemwa *NI/POSS,3p*
  weepskweeteewali *NI,p*
weeweetepi *quickly*
  weeweetepi
weewefhoowe *fan NI*
  howeewefhoowe *NI/POSS,3s,s*
weeya *person, appearance NI*
  howeeyaanwa *NI/POSS,3p*
weeyahka *depth, goodness NI*
  weeyahka *NI,s*

wehi *[suggestion] PV*
  wehi *PV*
wehseteki *high*
  wehseteki
wehsiya *husband NA*
  wehsici *NA/POSS,3s,4s*
  wehsiya *NA,3s*
  wehsiyana *NA/POSS,2s,3s*
  wehsiyani *NA,3p*
weyahkaawi *get better (health) AI*
  weyahkaawi *AI,ind,3s*
weyakaacaaki *uncleanness NI*
  weyakaacaaki *NI,s*
wihfakakkoofa *jar NA*
  wihfakakkoofali *NA,4s*
  wihfakakkoofeki *NA/LOC,3*
wihfakwee *cry, weep AI*
  kiwihfakwe *AI,ind,2s*
  kiwihfakweepwa *AI,ind,2p*
  weewihfakweecki *AI/IC,part,3p*
  wihfakwe *AI,ind,3s*
  wihfakweeci *AI,conj,3s*
  wihfakweeki *AI,conj,3*
  wihfakweeko *AI,imp,2p*
  wihfakweelici *AI,conj,4*
  wihfakweelo *AI,imp,2s*
  wihfakweepwa *AI,ind,2p*
  wihfakweewaaci *AI,conj,3p*
wihfakweewe *crying, weeping NI*
  wihfakweewe *NI,s*
wihfakweeweni *there is crying, weeping II*
  wihfakweeweni *II,ind,0*
wihfaya *hair NI*
  wihfaya *NI,s*
wihfenhcikee *cause eating, hold a feast AI*
  weewihfenhcikeeki *AI/IC,conj,3*
  wihfenhcikeeki *AI,conj,3*
  wiiwihfenhcikeeki *AI,conj,3*
wihfenhcikeewe *feast NI*
  howihfenhcikeewenwa *NI/POSS,3p*
  wihfenhcikeewe *NI,s*
  wihfenhcikeeweneki *NI/LOC*
  wihfenhcikeewesi *NI,s*
wihfeni *eat AI*
  niwihfenipe *AI,ind,1x*
  waawihfeniiki *AI,ind,3p*

weewihfenicki *AI/IC,part,3p*
wihfeni *AI,ind,3s ; AI,ind,2s*
wihfenici *AI,conj,3s*
wihfeniiki *AI,ind,3p*
wihfeniki *AI,conj,3*
wihfenilici *AI,conj,4*
wihfenilo *AI,imp,2s*
wihfenitaako *AI,imp,1i*
wihfeniwaaci *AI,conj,3p*
wihfeniya *AI,conj,1s*
wihfeniyani *AI,conj,2s*
wihfeniyeekwe *AI,conj,2p*
wihfeniiwe *food NI*
   howihfeniiwe *NI/POSS,3s,s*
   howihfeniiweni *NI/POSS,3s,s*
   howihfeniiwenilici *NI/POSS,4*
   niwihfeniiwe *NI/POSS,1s,s*
   wihfeniiwe *NI,s*
wihkaana *friend, companion NA*
   howihkaanwahi *NA/POSS,3p,4p*
   kihkaanaki *NA/POSS,2s,3p*
   kihkaanena *NA/POSS,1i,3s*
   nihkaana *NA/POSS,1s,3s*
   nihkaanaki *NA/POSS,1s,3p*
   nihkaaneti *NA/POSS,1s,2p*
   wihkaanali *NA/POSS,3s,4s*
   wihkaanhhi *NA/POSS,3s,4p*
   wihkaanima *NA,3s*
   wihkaanimaaki *NA,3p*
   wihkaanimaali *NA,4s*
   wihkaanwaali *NA/POSS,3p,4s*
   wihkaanwahi *NA/POSS,3p,4p*
wihkaaneti *be friends [reciprocal] AI*
   howihkaanetiiki *AI,ind,3p*
wihkaanetihke *make friends with AI*
   wihkaanetihkeeko *AI,imp,2p*
wihkaanin *be a partner of TA*
   weewihkaaninaacki *TA/IC,part,3p,4*
wihkoci *most, extremely*
   wihkoci
wihkokeemo *call AI*
   wihkokeemo *AI,ind,3s*
wihkom *call TA*
   howaawihkomaawahi *TA,ind,3p,4p*
   howihkomaali *TA,ind,3s,4s*
   howihkomahi *TA,ind,3s,4p*

wihkomaali *TA,ind,3s,4s*
wihkomahi *TA,ind,3s,4p*
wihkomi *TA,imp,2s,3*
wihkometi *call to [reciprocal] AI*
   waawihkometiiki *AI,ind,3p*
wihkomoofo *be called AI*
   wihkomoofooki *AI,ind,3p*
wihkwihkaw *compel TA*
   howihkwihkawahi *TA,ind,3s,4p*
wihpeem *be with TA*
   niwihpeemekooki *TA,ind,3p,1s*
wihpom *eat with TA*
   howihpomahi *TA,ind,3s,4p*
   kiwihpomaawaaki *TA,ind,2p,3p*
   weewihpomita *TA/IC,part,3s,1s*
   wihpomaaci *TA,conj,3s,4*
   wihpomaacki *TA,part,3p,4*
   wihpomahi *TA,ind,3s,4p*
   wihpomekoci *TA,conj,4,3s*
   wihpomelako *TA,conj,1s,2p*
wihsi *[purposive] PV*
   wahsi *PV/IC*
   wihsi *PV*
wihsi *dog NA*
   wihsiiki *NA,3p*
wihsiikwaya *chaff NI*
   wihsiikwaya *NI,s*
wiiceekilawiiwe *pleasure NI*
   wiiceekilawiiwena *NI,p*
wiicheti *marry [reciprocal] AI*
   waawiichetiiki *AI,ind,3p*
   wiichetiiki *AI,ind,3p*
   wiichetiki *AI,conj,3*
   wiichetipi *AI,ind,3*
wiichetiiwe *marriage, wedding NI*
   wiichetiiwe *NI,s*
   wiichetiiweneki *NI/LOC*
wiichetiiwi *marriage PM*
   wiichetiiwi *PM*
wiichetiiwipiitenika *wedding garment NI*
   wiichetiiwipiitenika *NI,s*
wiici *together with*
   wiici
wiici *with, in the company of PV*
   howiici *PV*
   kiwiici *PV*

niwiici *PV*
weewiici *PV/IC*
wiici *PV*
wiici-aloolaakaafa *fellow-servant NA*
   howiici-aloolaakaafali *NA/POSS,3s,4s*
   howiici-aloolaakaafhi *NA/POSS,3s,4p*
   howiici-aloolaakanhhi *NA/POSS,3s,4p*
   kiwiici-aloolaaka *NA/POSS,2s,3s*
wiici-wihfeniim *eat in the company of TA*
   wiici-wihfeniimekoci *TA,conj,4,3s*
wiiciim *be with, accompany TA*
   howiiciimeko *TA,ind,0s,3s*
   kiweciimi *TA,ind,2s,1s*
   kiwiiciimekona *TA,ind,3s,1i*
   niwiiciimeko *TA,ind,0s,1s*
   niwiiciimekooki *TA,ind,3p,1s*
   niwiiciimekwa *TA,ind,3s,1s*
   weewiiciimaacki *TA/IC,part,3p,4*
   weewiiciimekoci *TA/IC,conj,4,3s*
   wiiciimaci *TA,conj,2s,3*
   wiiciimekoci *TA,conj,4,3s*
   wiiciimekote *TA,subj,4,3s*
   wiiciimita *TA,part,3s,1s*
wiicikeem *live with TA*
   howiicikeemaali *TA,ind,3s,4s*
   wiicikeemaali *TA,ind,3s,4s*
   wiicikeemekowaaci *TA,conj,4,3p*
wiicikwakwileni *companion*
   howiicikwakwileniimwahi *NA/POSS,3p,4p*
wiicitehaat *participate in TI_1*
   wiicitehaata *TI,ind,2s,0s*
wiiciwefi *accompanied by, having AI*
   wiiciwefi *AI,ind,3s*
wiiciweloofo *be led with AI*
   wiiciweloofooki *AI,ind,3p*
wiiciwi *be with AI*
   kiwiiciwi *AI,ind,2s*
   wiiciwi *AI,ind,3s*
   wiiciwicki *AI,part,3p*
   wiiciwiya *AI,conj,1s*
wiifo *be named AI*
   wiifooli *AI,ind,4s*
wiifoowe *name NI*
   howiifoowe *NI/POSS,3s,s*
   howiifooweneki *NI/POSS/LOC,3s*
   howiifoowenilici *NI/POSS,4*

howiifoowenwa *NI/POSS,3p*
kiwiifiiweneki *NI/POSS/LOC,2s*
kiwiifoowe *NI/POSS,2s,s*
kiwiifooweneki *NI/POSS/LOC,2s*
kiwiifoowenwa *NI/POSS,2p*
niwiifoowe *NI/POSS,1s,s*
niwiifooweneki *NI/POSS/LOC,1s*
wiifoowe *NI,s*
wiifwi *gall NI*
   wiifwi *NI,s*
wiikehoofoowe *consolation NI*
   kiwiikehoofoowenwa *NI/POSS,2p*
wiikinaakwi *even, even if*
   wiikinaakwi
wiikiwa *house NI*
   howiikiwaapeki *NI/POSS/LOC,3s*
   howiikiwaapimi *NI/POSS,3s,s*
   kiwiikiwaapeki *NI/POSS/LOC,2s*
   niwiikiwaapimi *NI/POSS,1s,s*
   wiikiwa *NI,s*
   wiikiwaapali *NI,p*
   wiikiwaapeki *NI/LOC*
   wiikiwe *NI,s*
wiikiwaalakwi *den NI*
   howiikiwaalakomwa *NI/POSS,3p*
wiikiwaapi *house PM*
   wiikiwaapi *PM*
wiikkaa *build AI*
   waakkaacki *AI/IC,part,3p*
   wiikkaaki *AI,ind,3p*
wiilaani *let, allow; let it be*
   wiilaani
wiilaanisiweewe *permission NI*
   wiilaanisiweewe *NI,s*
wiilan *tongue NI*
   howiilani *NI/POSS,3s,s*
   howiilanilici *NI/POSS,4*
   niilani *NI/POSS,1s,s*
   wiilano *NI,p*
wiilehfi *hair NI*
   kiilehfwa *NI/POSS,2s,p*
   wiilehfa *NI/POSS,3s,s*
   wiilehfi *NI,s*
wiipici *tooth NI*
   wiipici *NI,s*
   wiipitali *NI,p*

wiisa *[volitional]* PV
    howaawiisa *PV*
    kiisa *PV*
    niisa *PV*
    waasa *PV/IC*
    wiisa *PV*
    yeewiisa *PV/IC*
wiisaacitehee *be fearful* AI
    wiisaaciteheeko *AI,imp,2p*
    yeewiisaaciteheeci *AI/IC,conj,3s*
wiisaafi *fear* AI
    kiwiisaafi *AI,ind,2s*
    wiisaafiiko *AI,imp,2p*
    wiisaafiipwa *AI,ind,2p*
    wiisaafiite *AI,subj,3s*
wiisaafih *stir up, arouse* TA
    howiisaafihahi *TA,ind,3s,4p*
wiisaafiiyaa *fear* II
    wiisaafiiya *II,ind,0*
wiisaala *let it be that; even if*
    wiisaala
wiisaalepwaa *fear* AI
    kiwiisaalepwaapwa *AI,ind,2p*
    wiisaalepwa *AI,ind,3s*
    wiisaalepwaaki *AI,ind,3p*
    wiisaalepwaako *AI,imp,2p*
    wiisaalepwaalo *AI,imp,2s*
wiisafoowe *sweat* NI
    howiisafoowe *NI,s*
wiiseyaa *constricted* II
    wiiseya *II,ind,0*
wiisi *head* NI
    howiisi *NI/POSS,3s,s*
    howiisiwi *NI,s*
    howiisiwilici *NI/POSS,4*
    kiisi *NI/POSS,2s,s*
    niisi *NI/POSS,1s,s*
    wiileki *NI/POSS/LOC,3s*
    wiisi *NI/POSS,3s,s*
wiisikatowi *strong* AI
    waasikatowicki *AI/IC,part,3p*
    waasikatowilici *AI/IC,conj,4*
    weewiisikatowicki *AI/IC,part,3p*
    wiisikatowi *AI,ind,3s*
wiisikatowiiwe *strength, power* NI
    howiisikatowiiwe *NI/POSS,3s,s*

howiisikatowiiweneki *NI/POSS/LOC,3s*
    kiwiisikatowiiwe *NI/POSS,2s,s*
    wiisikatowiiwe *NI,s*
wiisiki *endure* AI
    wiisikifi *AI,ind,3s*
    wiisikifiiki *AI,ind,3p*
    wiisikifita *AI,part,3s*
wiisiki *strongly, diligently* PV
    wiisiki *PV*
wiisikihk *strive* TI_1
    wiisikihkamoko *TI,imp,2p,0*
wiisikileni *strong man* NA
    wiisikileni *NA,3s*
    wiisikileniili *NA,4s*
wiisikimekofi *mighty* AI
    waasikimekofita *AI/IC,part,3s*
wiisikin *strengthen* TA
    howiisikinekooli *TA,ind,4s,3s*
wiisikitehee *endure, bear up* AI
    wiisikiteheeta *AI,part,3s*
wiisikiteheewi *boldly* PV
    wiisikiteheewi *PV*
wiisikitehehtaw *bear up with, stand for* TA
    wiisikitehehtoolepwa *TA,ind,1s,2p*
wiisikowe *be loud* AI
    wiisikowe *AI,ind,3s*
    wiisikoweki *AI,ind,3p*
wiisiwalakeema *lily* NI
    wiisiwalakeemi *NI,p*
wiitaapowem *drink with* TA
    kiwiitaapowemaawaaki *TA,ind,2p,3p*
    wiitaapoweemahi *TA,ind,3s,4p*
    wiitaapowemaaci *TA,conj,3s,4*
wiitafoom *be with* TA
    weewiitafoomehka *TA/IC,part,3,2s*
wiitakimekofi *associate with* AI
    wiitakimekofi *AI,ind,3s*
wiitakimoofo *be associated with* AI
    wiitakimoofo *AI,ind,3s*
wiitamaw *tell* TA
    howiitamaakohi *TA,ind,4p,3s*
    howiitamawaali *TA,ind,3s,4s*
    howiitamawaawaali *TA,ind,3p,4s*
    howiitamawaawahi *TA,ind,3p,4p*
    howiitamawahi *TA,ind,3s,4p*
    kiwiitamaakooki *TA,ind,3p,2s*

kiwiitamoole *TA,ind,1s,2s*
kiwiitamoolepwa *TA,ind,1s,2p*
niwiitamaakwa *TA,ind,3s,1s*
weewiitamaakoci *TA/IC,conj,4,3s*
weewiitamawita *TA/IC,part,3s,1s*
weewiitamoolako *TA/IC,conj,1s,2p*
wiitamaakwi *TA,ind,,3s*
wiitamawaaci *TA,conj,3s,4*
wiitamawaawaaci *TA,conj,3p,4*
wiitamawahi *TA,ind,3s,4p*
wiitamawehko *TA,imp,2p,3*
wiitamawi *TA,imp,2s,3*
wiitamawiko *TA,imp,2p,1s*
wiitamawilo *TA,imp,2s,1s*
wiitamawinaake *TA,imp,2,1x*
wiitamawiyaake *TA,conj,2,1x*
wiitamawiyeekwe *TA,subj,2p,1s*
wiitamoola *TA,conj,1s,2s*
wiitamoolako *TA,subj,1s,2p ; TA,conj,1s,2p*
wiitamoolepwa *TA,ind,1s,2p*
wiitamoolwaakwe *TA,conj,3,2p*
yeewiitamawaaci *TA/IC,conj,3s,4*
wiitapiim *sit with TA*
   howiitapiimaawaali *TA,ind,3p,4s*
   weewiitapiimehka *TA/IC,part,3,2s*
   weewiitapiimekoci *TA/IC,conj,4,3s*
   wiitapiimaaci *TA,conj,3s,4*
   wiitapiimaawaali *TA,ind,3p,4s*
   wiitapiimekowaaci *TA,conj,4,3p*
wiitatwh *hit TA*
   howiitatwhaawaali *TA,ind,3p,4s*
wiiteem *go with TA*
   howiiteemaali *TA,ind,3s,4s*
   howiiteemahi *TA,ind,3s,4p*
   howiiteemekohi *TA,ind,4p,3s*
   howiiteemekona *TA,ind,0p,3s*
   kiwiiteemelepe *TA,ind,1x,2*
   wiiteemaawaali *TA,ind,3p,4s*
   wiiteemaci *TA,conj,2s,3*
   wiiteemekonaawa *TA,ind,0,3p*
   wiiteemekowaaci *TA,conj,4,3p*
   wiiteemela *TA,conj,1s,2s*
   wiiteemi *TA,imp,2s,3*
   wiiteemite *TA,subj,3s,1s*
wiiteet *go with TI_1*
   wiiteetake *TI,subj,3s,0*

wiitefi *go with II*
   wiitefiiki *II,conj,0*
wiitefiim *be with TA*
   wiitefiimelako *TA,conj,1s,2p*
   wiitefiimicki *TA,part,3p,1s*
wiitfeem *be with TA*
   howiitfeemekohi *TA,ind,4p,3s*
   weewiitfemaacki *TA/IC,part,3p,4*
   weewiitfemekoci *TA/IC,conj,4,3s*
   wiitfeemaacki *TA,part,3p,4*
   wiitfeemaata *TA,part,3s,4*
   wiitfeemekoci *TA,conj,4,3s*
   wiitfeemelepwa *TA,ind,1s,2p*
wiitfeemiwee *be in company AI*
   weewiitfeemiweelici *AI/IC,conj,4*
wiitki *trade, buy and sell AI*
   waatkiita *AI/IC,part,3s*
   waawiitkiilici *AI/IC,conj,4*
   weewiitkiilici *AI/IC,conj,4*
   wiitkiiki *AI,conj,3*
   wiitkiiko *AI,imp,2p*
   wiiwiitkiiki *AI,conj,3*
wiitkiiwe *trading NI*
   howiitkiiweneki *NI/POSS/LOC,3s*
   wiitkiiwe *NI,s*
wiitkiiwika *store NI*
   wiitkiiwika *NI,s*
wiitootamaw *tell, confirm TA*
   wiitootamawahi *TA,ind,3s,4p*
wiitpenem *die with TA*
   wiitpenemakwe *TA,conj,1i,3*
wiiwa *wife NA*
   kiiwa *NA/POSS,2s,3s*
   kiiwaaki *NA/POSS,2p,3p*
   niiwa *NA/POSS,1s,3s*
   wiiwa *NA,3s*
   wiiwali *NA/POSS,3s,4s*
wiiwapil *bind, cover TA*
   howiiwapilaali *TA,ind,3s,4s*
wiiwash *load, place a burden on TA*
   howiiwashaawaali *TA,ind,3p,4s*
   kiwiiwashaawaaki *TA,ind,2p,3p*
wiiwasi *bear AI*
   wiiwasi *AI,ind,3s*
wiiwasiiwe *burden NI*
   niwiiwasiiwe *NI/POSS,1s,s*

wiiwasiiwena *NI,p*
wiiwiilali *horn NI*
 wiiwiilali *NI,s*
wiiwin *marry TA*
 howiiwinaali *TA,ind,3s,4s*
 weewiiwinaata *TA/IC,part,3s,4*
 wiiwinaali *TA,ind,3s,4s*
wiskalel *stink AI*
 wiskalelwa *AI,ind,3s*
wiskalet *rot II*
 waskalhki *II/IC,conj,0*
wiskilohfaka *bird*
 wiskilohfaki *NA,3p*
wiyakaaci *corrupt*
 wiyakaaci
wiyakaacit *distort TI_2*
 howiyakaacitoonaawa *TI,ind,3p,0*
wiyakahoot *cry out TI-O*
 waawiyakoohootamwa *TI,ind,3s,0*
 wiyakahootaki *TI,conj,3s,0*
 wiyakahootamooki *TI,ind,3p,0*
 wiyakahootamwa *TI,ind,3s,0*
wiyakahootamo *cry out AI*
 wiyakahootamohi *AI,ind,4p*
 wiyakahootamooli *AI,ind,4s*
wiyakahootamoowe *outcry NI*
 wiyakahootamoowena *NI,p*
wiyakileci *dirty hand NI*
 wiyakileceeki *NI,p*
wiyakilehfi *unclean spirit NA*
 wiyakilehfi *NA,3s*
 wiyakilehfihi *NA,4p*
 wiyakilehfiili *NA,4s*
 wiyakilehfiiwi *NA,3p*
wiyakiwaninehfi *unclean spirit, devil NA*
 wiyakiwaninehfi *NA,3s*
wiyakowe *angry AI*
 wiyakowe *AI,ind,3s*
 wiyakoweeli *AI,ind,4s*
 wiyakowehi *AI,ind,4p*
wiyakoweewe *anger NI*
 wiyakoweewe *NI,s*
wiyakoweewi *angrily, fiercely PM*
 wiyakoweewi *PM*
wiyakowehtaw *be angry at TA*
 weewiyakowehtawaata *TA/IC,part,3s,4*

wiyakowehtawipwa *TA,ind,2p,1s*
wiyakwe *we are AI*
 wiyakwe *AI,conj,1i*
wiyameskwi *? PV*
 howiyameskwi *PV*
wiyanaatihoofo *be shamed AI*
 wiyanaatihoofohi *AI,ind,4p*
wiyanaatiiwe *shame NI*
 wiyanaatiiwe *NI,s*
wiyawaach *praise TA*
 howiyawaachaawaali *TA,ind,3p,4s*
wiyawaacim *praise TA*
 howiyawaacimekooli *TA,ind,4s,3s*
wiyawaacimekwh *praise TA*
 wiyawaacimekwhaali *TA,ind,3s,4s*
wiyawaacimetiiwe *praise NI*
 wiyawaacimetiiwe *NI,s*
wiyawaacimoowe *praise NI*
 wiyawaacimoowe *NI,s*
wiyawahkaal *praise TA*
 howiyawahkaalaali *TA,ind,3s,4s*
wiyawen *? surrender, commend to ? TA*
 wiyawena *TA,ind,1s,3s*
wiyawfi *flesh, meat NI*
 howiyawfemi *NI/POSS,3s,s*
 niwiyawfemi *NI/POSS,1s,s*
 wiyawfi *NI,s*
wiyawfima *flesh NA*
 wiyawfima *NA,3s*
wiyawfiwi *be flesh II*
 wiyawfiwi *II,ind,0s*
wiyawfiwiiyaana *body NA*
 wiyawfiwiiyaanali *NA,4s*
wiyeeci *in the direction of, toward*
 wiyeeci
wiyeefa *someone PR*
 siwiyeefali *PR*
 siwiyeefhi *PR*
 wiyeefa *PR*
 wiyeefaki *PR*
 wiyeefali *PR*
 wiyeefhi *PR*
 wiyefali *PR*
 wiyeh *PR*
wiyehi *something PR*
 wiye *PR*

wiyehi *PR*
wiyehi *things, goods NI*
   howiyehiima *NI/POSS,3s,p*
   howiyehiimi *NI/POSS,3s,s*
   howiyehiimilici *NI/POSS,4*
   howiyehiimwa *NI/POSS,3p*
   kiwiyehiimi *NI/POSS,2s,s*
   niwiyehiima *NI/POSS,1s,p*
   niwiyehiimi *NI/POSS,1s,s*
   wiyehiima *NI,p*
wiyehileelemiwee *judge AI*
   wiyehileelemiweeko *AI,imp,2p*
wiyehisi *means, manner PV*
   kiwiyehisi *PV*
   wiyehisi *PV*
wiyehliyeeweewe *bodily form NI*
   wiyehliyeeweeweneki *NI/LOC*
wiyehsi *any*
   wiyehsi
wiyehsimekofiiwe *authority NI*
   wiyehsimekofiiwe *NI,s*
wiyehsimekofiiwena *authority, power NA*
   wiyehisimekofiiwenhhi *NA,4p*
   wiyehsimekofiiwena *NA,3s*
   wiyehsimekofiiwenaki *NA,3p*
   wiyehsimekofiiwenali *NA,4s*
   wiyehsimekofiiwenhhi *NA,4p*
wiyehsimota *cloth, textile NI*
   wiyehsimota *NI,s*
wiyehsiwa *skin NA*
   wiyehsiwaaki *NA,3p*
wiyesi *any PR*
   wiyesi *PR*
yaakwateekimoowi *dunghill NI*
   yaakwateekimoowi *NI,s*
yaami *Er NA*
   yaami *NA,3s*
yaamikami *flood NI*
   yaamikamiki *NI,p*
yaapweewefi *withered AI*
   yaapweeweficki *AI,part,3p*
yaataaki *room NI*
   yaataaki *NI,s ; NI,p*
yah *[indef. time, place] PV*
   hota *PV*
   hotah *PV*

kita *PV*
kitah *PV*
nita *PV*
nitah *PV*
ya *PV*
yah *PV*
yaska *all the same, still*
   yaska
yeefoskaa *crowd AI*
   yeefoskaacki *AI/IC,part,3p*
   yeefoskaalici *AI/IC,conj,4*
   yeefoskaata *AI/IC,part,3s*
yeekwaaki *end NI*
   yeekwaaki *NI,s*
yeekwaakwalhki *rust NI*
   yeekwaakwalhki *NI,s*
yeekwihfe *end NI*
   yeeikwihkwihfeki *NI/LOC*
   yeekwihfeki *NI/LOC*
yeelaakwa *since the time*
   yeelaakwa
yeelaakwasi *while*
   yeelaakwasi
yeelaapaaci *by interpretation PV*
   yeelaapaaci *PV*
yeelaawahkweeki *south NI*
   yeelaawahkweeki *NI,s*
yeelahfamefite *in front of, opposite AI*
   yeelahfamefiteelici *AI,conj,4*
yeelahfamhfen *in front of, opposite II*
   yeelahfamhfeki *II,conj,0*
yeelahfami *in front of, opposite AI*
   yeelahfamiici *AI/IC,conj,3s*
   yeelahfamiilici *AI/IC,conj,4*
   yeelahfamiiwaaci *AI/IC,conj,3p*
   yeelahfamiiya *AI/IC,conj,1s*
   yeelahfamiiyani *AI/IC,conj,2s*
   yeelahfamiiyeekwe *AI/IC,conj,2p*
yeelahfamiikwe *in front of, opposite AI*
   yeelahfamiikweci *AI/IC,conj,3s*
   yeelahfamiikweewaaci *AI/IC,conj,3p*
   yeelahfamiikweeyani *AI/IC,conj,2s*
   yeelahfamiikwelici *AI/IC,conj,4*
yeelahfamiiyaa *in front of, opposite II*
   yeelahfamiiyaaki *II,conj,0*
yeelahfamiwem *in front of, opposite TA*

yeelahfamiwemita *TA,part,3s,1s*

yeelahkamikiki *era, temporal stage*
yeelahkamikiki
yeelhkamikiki

yeele *[as something was happening, in the process of] PV*
yeele *PV/IC*

yeelekokwahkamikiki *world NI*
yeelekokwahkamikiki *NI,s*

yeepfateki *side*
yeepfateki

yeesfeki *according to, following*
yeesfeki

yeesim *say (so) to TA*
yeesimekowaaci *TA,conj,4,3p*

yeesiteheeweni *will, wish II*
yeesiteheeweniki *II,conj,0*

yeesiweefi *be thus AI*
yeesiweefilici *AI,conj,4*

yeeteka *kind, sort, such*
yeeteka

yeh *[when] PV*
ye *PV/IC*
yeh *PV/IC*

yeheeyehi *while CJN*
heeyehi *CJN*
yeheeye *CJN*
yeheeyehi *CJN*
yehi *CJN*

yehki *deceased, earlier, in the past*
hiyehki
yehki

yhkweelemekofi *worthy AI*
hikweelemekofi *AI,ind,3s*
hikweelemekofiiki *AI,ind,3p*

yhkweelemekwat *worthy II*
yeyhkweelemekoki *II/IC,conj,0*

yo *? [indeed] ?*
yo

yoo/ni/hi *[this, that] PR*
halanili *PR*
halaniliini *PR*
halayaama *PR*
halayini *PR*
halayooloma *PR*
halayooma *PR*
hiina *PR*
hiine *PR*
hiini *PR*
hina *PR*
hini *PR*
ini *PR*
na *PR*
nehe *PR*
nehke *PR*
nele *PR*
nelene *PR*
nihi *PR*
nihiini *PR*
nihki *PR*
nihkiin *PR*
nihkiini *PR*
nili *PR*
niliini *PR*
yaama *PR*
yohkoma *PR*
yohkooni *PR*
yohoma *PR*
yohooni *PR*
yooloma *PR*
yooloone *PR*
yoolooni *PR*
yooma *PR*
yoona *PR*
yoone *PR*
yooni *PR*
yooniisi *PR*

yooci *hence, henceforth*
yooci